W9-ADG-428

The American Fishing Schooners 1825–1935

Books by

HOWARD I. CHAPELLE

THE AMERICAN FISHING SCHOONERS 1825–1935

THE HISTORY OF AMERICAN SAILING SHIPS

YACHT DESIGNING AND PLANNING

BOATBUILDING

THE HISTORY OF THE AMERICAN SAILING NAVY

AMERICAN SMALL SAILING CRAFT

THE BALTIMORE CLIPPER

AMERICAN SAILING CRAFT

REPORT TO THE TURKISH GOVERNMENT ON FISHING BOATS

THE NATIONAL WATERCRAFT COLLECTION

THE BARK CANOES AND SKIN BOATS OF NORTH AMERICA

THE *Constellation* STORY

SEARCH FOR SPEED UNDER SAIL

The American Fishing Schooners 1825–1935

by

Howard I. Chapelle

W · W · NORTON & COMPANY · INC ·

New York

First Edition

Library of Congress Cataloging in Publication Data

Chapelle, Howard Irving.
The American fishing schooners, 1825–1935.

Includes bibliographical references.
1. Fishing boats—History. 2. Schooners—History.
I. Title
VM431.C47 387.2'2 72-3983
ISBN 0-393-03123-3

Published simultaneously in Canada
by George J. McLeod Limited, Toronto

PRINTED IN THE UNITED STATES OF AMERICA

1 2 3 4 5 6 7 8 9 0

Contents

Plates

Illustrations

Between pages 158 and 159

Acknowledgments

In the research that is represented here, I must acknowledge the great aid that I received from the following friends and associates.

The late:

David Foster Taylor	surveys, notes on details
Lewis H. Story	ship carpenter, joiner: surveys, testimony, notes on details, history, half-model take-offs, etc.
Charles McLean	master shipwright: Canadian testimony
Alden Burnham	shipwright: historical matters
Frank Adams	master shipwright: plans, half-models
Arthur D. Story	master shipwright: historical data
John Prince Story	master shipwright: historical data
Everett James	master shipwright: half-models
George Roberts	rigger: plans, testimony
Harry Christiansen	rigger: plans, testimony
William Walters	ship smith: testimony
Charles A. Andrews	sparmaker: testimony
E. H. Oxner	master shipwright: testimony
Edward Perkins	ship carpenter (joiner): testimony, plans
Frank Paine	naval architect: plans
Starling Burgess	naval architect: plans
Thomas McManus	naval architect: plans
Charlton L. Smith	author, yachting historian

John McKay	master shipwright (Canadian): plans
W. J. Roué	naval architect (Canadian): plans
William McLean	shipyard operator (Canadian)
William A. Baker	naval architect: plans
James Hardy	master shipwright (Canadian)
Edward Sohier Bosley	Schooner *Columbia* researcher
Lawrence Jenkins	Director, Peabody Marine Museum: Archer B. Poland plans, from mould loft at Essex, Massachusetts

Gordon W. Thomas	historian
Frank Taylor	Smithsonian Institution
Charles F. Sayle	historian

Also, I must express my obligation to those who helped in the preparation of plans and drawings: Robert Maffett, Jarvis Appleton, Lt. Robert F. Cairo, USN, and Howard Hoffman.

I wish further to offer my thanks for the courtesies extended to me by The Peabody Marine Museum of Salem, Salem, Massachusetts; The Cape Ann Historical Society, Gloucester, Massachusetts; The Museum of History and Technology, Smithsonian Institution, Washington, D.C.; and the Maine Historical Society, Portland, Maine.

In the preface to sketches and notes of the details of fittings, rigging, and gear, I have acknowledged the generous aid I received from friends who had collected detail measurements, notes, photographs, and sketches that were most valuable in supplementing my notes and sketches.

Space will not permit acknowledgments to the numerous collectors who gave me access to half-models, take-offs, plans, photographs, and the results of their research, but to these I wish to express my gratitude.

Introduction

The American fishing schooners have now gone out of existence, except for one or two vessels preserved as museum exhibits. During the last sixty years of their evolution, as sail-driven commercial craft, they were admired at home and abroad for their sailing qualities, seaworthiness, and beauty. While much has been written about these fine schooners and their crews, their development has been described in only a fragmentary fashion, with but a small number of examples shown. This has led to a very limited knowledge of the developments in design of these schooners during any period of their existence.

With the passing of time, the characteristics of the fishing schooners are becoming forgotten, and the builders' half-models and plans are being lost or destroyed at an increasing rate. It is therefore desirable as a matter of technical history to record the range of design developed in each stage of evolution of the American fishing schooner in plans and descriptions, at least as far as is now possible.

Since the fishing schooner's evolution began in the first quarter of the eighteenth century and ended about 1935 there is a difficulty in tracing the origins of its development. The available technical evidence of its evolution is limited to the years after about 1830, for the plans or half-models of fishing schooners built earlier have not been found, with but a single known exception. It is therefore necessary to resort to extensive reconstruction to show the probable characteristics of the New England fishing vessels of the first quarter of the nineteenth century, even though a good deal is known about them, as will be seen.

The fact remains, though, that there is no possibility of tracing the complete history of the fishing schooner types during the first hundred years of their existence. The best known of the American fishing schooner types was the New England North Atlantic fishermen. These had the longest, most intensive evolution. After 1849 they were often described as the finest fishing vessels in the world and were the pride of their owners and of the northeastern fishing ports from which they hailed.

The objective here will be to illustrate in plans and to describe in detail the typical vessels of each period of development, so far as available information permits. Outstanding schooners will be representative of some periods—vessels whose designs influenced that of contemporary schooners, or were good examples of the result of such influence in hull and rig. The changes in hull design and in rig were usually accompanied by changes in deck arrangement, deck furniture, deck fittings, and in hardware on deck and aloft. Because of the rather rigid requirements in the deck arrangement of a fishing schooner, however, the general deck layout in any period, say of about twenty-year duration, was remarkably standardized.

Research with this objective in view was carried on at Essex, Gloucester, Salem, and Boston, Massachusetts, beginning in the spring of 1933. After 1935 much research was done in Maine, and also in the model collection at the Smithsonian Institution, Washington, D.C. Essex and Gloucester proved to be most productive areas, as would be expected since these towns built most of the North Atlantic fishing vessels—Essex built about 3500 registered vessels according to United States Custom House records.

In 1933 there were two shipyards still in operation in Essex and the men who had manned them could be interviewed. Many were aged, with memories extending back to the late 1860s or 1870s. In Essex I was fortunate enough to become friendly with the late Lewis H. Story, a highly intelligent inboard-joiner and ship carpenter, much interested in the history of Essex shipbuilding and in the design of fishing schooners. Through Lew Story's help and interest, I had access to many half-models preserved in Essex, Gloucester, and vicinity and we were able to take off the lines of these. The relationship with Lew Story also led to the discovery of a large number of plans in the late Archer B. Poland's mould loft in Essex. These plans dated back to the late 1870s. With the cooperation of the Director of the Peabody Marine Museum of Salem, Mr. Lawrence Jenkins, the Poland plans were copied and preserved and it was also made possible for me to obtain take-offs of the fishing schooner half-models in this museum. Half-models and plans were also found in vessel managers' offices in Gloucester and Boston. During the early 1930s the fishing schooner half-models in the National Watercraft Collection were taken off through the courtesy of the then curator, Mr. Frank A. Taylor. Here we found half-models not only of New England fishing schooners but also of oyster schooners of the Chesapeake and of New Jersey, and fishing schooners of the Gulf Coast and Florida, and also of the Pacific Coast.

After World War II some research was carried on in Nova Scotia, to obtain lines and other details of Canadian fishing schooners. Mr. William McLean of Mahone Bay, Nova Scotia, shipbuilder, was most helpful in making the models and plans in the John McLean and Sons shipyard available. Mr. John McKay of Shelburne, Nova Scotia, also made his shipyard files available as did the Shelbourne Shipbuilding Company, through the kindness of Mr. James Hardy.

In 1934 I became acquainted with the late D. Foster Taylor of Wollaston, Massachusetts, who had started to build a rigged, scale model fishing schooner on ⅜″ = 1′-0″ scale. He had obtained lines and sail plan of an unidentified fishing schooner of approximately 1906, designed by Mr. Thomas McManus, the noted Boston fishing schooner designer. No deck arrangement or construction details were shown in the plans, as was universal in fishing schooner designs by naval architects. Due to the friendship that had developed with Foster Taylor, I obtained a most competent aide in my research, particularly in recording exact details of deck gear, hatch, companionways, trunks, bitts, fife rails, rigging, hull structure, as well as deck and spar ironwork. With the model under construction, we had a guide in determining what was necessary in recording details. As Foster was a meticulous craftsman, the research had to produce accurate, well-detailed information to be acceptable to him and this standard was applied to all details whether or not they were to be used by him.

So far as detailed information was concerned, the availability of rigged fishing schooners for taking measurements and making sketches insured reasonably complete information on vessels built after, say 1900. The problem of obtaining details of earlier schooners now had to be solved. Questioning of the riggers, retired blacksmiths, shipwrights, sparmakers, vessel managers, joiners, painters, and the shipbuilders—the late A. D. Story and the late Everett James—produced a mass of information, extending back to the late 1860s, relating to design, construction, fitting, and to vessel history.

There was another source of information, scale models. Vessel owners had scale models built of favorite schooners to adorn their offices, and the international fishery exhibitions, held during the last quarter of the nineteenth century, caused exhibit models to be constructed by some shipbuilders, not only of contemporary vessels but also of some much older craft. In general, these models were carefully built from half-models, plans, and measurements, though ironwork was often "faked" by painted twine, paper, or lead. Such models were particularly useful in giving deck layouts and cutwater details, and made up most of the collections of fishing schooners in the National

Watercraft Collection, Cape Ann Historical Society, and some private collections.

The early models, built for exhibition purposes, usually had proper deck arrangements, but the hulls were constructed with excessively full ends and barrel-shaped midsections in representing early schooners, pinkies, and Chebacco boats or dogbodies. These models are probably much too burdensome and primitive. None of the early models can be proven to be contemporary with the vessels they supposedly represent.

A few plans by builders and naval architects were found. These were dated after 1886 and were found in shipyards, in Poland's loft, and in collections of individuals. Half-models, however, greatly outnumbered plans, even in the late period of sailing fishing schooners.

Documents, such as contracts for building were rarely preserved and when found gave little information other than cost-per-ton. Specifications were also rarely found and, like contracts, gave little useful information. It was obvious that most schooners were built on honor, to a general standard of scantlings.

Caution must be used in accepting the rigged-models as correct in rigging details, for many had suffered damage in movements to and from the museums and exhibitions. Repairs were obviously incorrect in some instances. The overly full ends mentioned earlier on the Chebacco, dogbody, pinky, and colonial schooner models seem to have been due to a nineteenth-century maritime history concept that vessels built earlier than the contemporary craft were necessarily crude, slow-sailing tubs of a primitive age.

It was found that half-models were misidentified in some instances, particularly in the National Watercraft Collection. These errors seem to have originated with the donors, whose memories had failed in identifying a model. Many plans and half-models could not be identified as they had no markings of any kind, on model, backboard, or on the plans.

One failure in research could not be corrected. The demand for scrap iron in the 1930s for Japanese armament led to the destruction of collections of old and obsolete marine hardware in the hands of vessel owners or managers, blacksmiths, and ship chandlers. Hence measured drawings of some old hardware could not be obtained.

Photographs of fishing schooners were numerous, a few dating back to the 1880s. They furnished much useful information. Collections of such photographs existed in the Peabody Marine Museum of Salem, Massachusetts; Society for the Preservation of New England Antiquities, Boston, Massachusetts; Smithsonian Institution, Washington, D.C.; and the Mariners' Museum (Barnes Collection), Newport News, Virginia. There are also some private collections containing useful material of this kind.

The riggers' plans, obtained from riggers' lofts in Gloucester, were useful as they show standing rigging and location and length of masts, lengths of topmasts, mainboom, and also the stive of the bowsprit. The head stays were set up so that the masts and topmasts actually curved forward, though stepped with more or less rake aft, which is shown in some riggers' plans. Likewise, sailmakers' plans show sail dimensions, usually as measured from the spars of the actual vessel. These plans were found in great number and show spar lengths, mast positions, and peak of gaffs as well as the cut of sails.

In a few instances the deck-framing plans of schooners were found. These were sometimes drawn on a plank, but usually on paper. Construction drawings and rigging detail drawings were not found except in two instances.

Fishing schooners were built from hawk's-nest models, or very commonly, from plans, from about 1740 to 1830.* Then lift-models came into use and were employed in the design of fishing vessels until after the end of the period of sail. Plans were used to some extent after about 1800, generally when a designer or model maker did not build a vessel himself but designed the schooner for the builder or owner. In such cases the designer usually retained either the half-model or a copy of the plan. With one exception, no plan of a fishing schooner built before the appearance of the lift-model has been found. The fragile hawk's-nest schooner models seem to have disappeared, though models of this type for merchant vessels made before 1805 have been preserved. Small fishing craft of the Chebacco types were probably built "by eye" and patterns. Half-models of the lift type were apparently introduced into New England first, about 1800, at New York about 1820, and on the Chesapeake about 1840. The half-model was introduced on the Great Lakes and on the Pacific Coast in the 1830–1850 period.

The most useful publications available were the work of Joseph William Collins of the U.S. Fish Commission, of George Brown Goode of the Smithsonian Institution, and of Henry Hall, agent of the U.S. Census Office. Goode's publication and Hall's were published in the 1884–1887 period. Collins published between 1880 and 1898. These publications give very extensive information about contemporary schooners but are not wholly reliable when dealing with older craft.

The limitations imposed upon this study of the American fishing schooners have been established and the kinds of evidence to be utilized have been de-

* Derby Papers, Vol. 30, 1786, 24 Nov. 1786, Essex Institute Collection, Salem Massachusetts.—An agreement between Retire Parker and Nathaniel Balch of Bradford, Massachusetts, and Elias Hasket Derby of Salem, to build two fishing schooners not to exceed 42 tons each, agreeable to a plan given them by Mr. Wm. Swett of Salisbury, to be planked with good white oak, to have long quarterdecks. Delivery date—April 1, 1787. \$10 per ton (3£) 45£ cash, good and iron at 28£ per ton. Derby paid for ironwork, oakum, joiner work, and pitch.

scribed. Rather than attempting to draw conclusions on the basis of limited and inadequate available documents, description of the vessels themselves—given in text, plans, and pictures—will provide the only evidence of the evolution in the design of hull, rigging, and fittings. Only by showing a number of plans of schooners of each period can the evolution of the types be traced.

The American Fishing Schooners 1825–1935

Chapter One

Colonial Period and The Pinkies

The development of the American fishing schooner apparently began about 1720. Earlier than this the characteristics of the colonial fishing craft have not been established with certainty. It is known from colonial records that craft called "shallops" were used in the shore fisheries, and "barks" and "catches" in the offshore fisheries, after the makeshift fishing boats of the early years of colonization had ceased to serve the needs of the colonists.

There is no contemporary information available by which the hull forms and rigs of the shallops, barks, and catches of the seventeenth and early eighteenth century can be described with technical precision. This field of inquiry, colonial vessels of the seventeenth century, has been thoroughly explored by competent authority, William A. Baker, naval architect, who has published his conclusions.* There is, then, no need to re-explore this area, nor to speculate further with the evidence available. All that need be stated here is that in the early eighteenth century the shallop classification seems to have included a type called a two-mast boat, with two gaffsails and a raised-deck cuddy forward. Some of these had square sterns, but others had "pink" sterns, which will be described later. The barks and catches were succeeded by the schooner, and a special type, the Marblehead schooner, gradually developed for use in the offshore fisheries. Also, in this period, the pinky schooner came into being; these were commonly smaller vessels than the Marblehead schooners. It is not possible to date their first appearance in the fisheries.

Long before the American Revolution, the Marblehead fishing schooners

* For Mr. Baker's conclusions on colonial vessels see *Colonial Vessels, Some Seventeenth-Century Ship Designs* (Barre, Mass.: Barre Publishing Company, 1962); and *Sloops and Shallops* (Barre, Mass.: Barre Publishing Company, 1966).

acquired a reputation for sailing well. After 1745 the American fishing fleet was a convenient target for French cruisers. A number of notices to mariners in colonial newspapers mention that Marblehead fishing schooners that had been taken were being used by the French as raiders. During the Revolution this type of schooner was used by Canadian-based privateers to attack American vessels. Colonial fishing schooners offered for sale were occasionally described as "prime sailers." As late as August 5, 1799, President John Adams wrote the secretary of the navy that ". . . we must have Bermuda Sloops, Virginia Pilot Boats or Marblehead Schooners . . ." for light cruisers against the French.

The single plan of a vessel identified as a "Marble Head Scooner" was found in the Admiralty Collection of Draughts, in the National Maritime Museum at Greenwich, England. This plan was used to build two schooners for the Royal Navy in 1767, at New York. These were named *Sir Edward Hawke* and *Earl of Egmont;* they were employed in the West Indies. As redrawings of this plan have been published twice * there is no need to reproduce it here.

The plan shows a fine-lined schooner, designed to sail fast, having some of the hull characteristics of the contemporary fast Chesapeake Bay vessels. There is no way of determining whether or not the Admiralty plan was typical of the Marblehead type. The design may well represent the model built only during wartime and therefore sharper and faster than the schooners built in peacetime. In any case, the Marblehead schooners were probably built on many models. It is possible that there were degrees of sharpness in this type, ranging from rather full carriers to the sharp-lined schooner shown in the Admiralty plan.

The fishing schooners need not have been of extremely large capacity for their dimensions. The full carrier in the fisheries would be most profitable only when the fishing grounds were a great distance from the home ports. Before the Revolution the New England fishermen did not need to fish the eastern Grand Banks and most of the colonial offshore fishing was on the banks in the Gulf of Maine, or on the banks between Cape Cod and the Bay of Fundy, relatively close to home.

It is also true that rather large carriers, for their dimensions, could be designed so as to be prime sailers. This was always difficult, but recent research has shown that eighteenth-century ship designers were capable of producing such vessels in both merchant and naval craft.

The Marblehead schooners were called heeltappers because of their imagined likeness to a shoe in appearance, according to government publications

* Howard I. Chapelle, *The Search for Speed Under Sail, 1700–1855* (New York: W. W. Norton & Co., 1967) and *The National Watercraft Collection,* U.S. Government Printing Office, Washington, D.C., 1960 (U.S. National Museum Bulletin 219).

in the late nineteenth century. This claim has not yet been verified in the very limited contemporary documentation now available. The type went through a normal refinement, and in the period 1825–1830 still had a raised, short quarterdeck, by then at the height of the main rail rather than above, as in the original type, with solid, rather high quarterdeck bulwarks. It is possible that the name heeltapper was applied to the schooners of 1825–1830, rather than to the earlier type. The recollections of heeltappers, described by old fishermen and shipyard hands, living in, say, 1880, and recorded by the authors of government publications, could hardly reach back to the eighteenth century. It seems likely, therefore, that the name heeltapper was applied locally to the 1825–1830 schooners rather than to the earlier type, if used at all.

After the War of 1812, there was little need for fast-sailing fishing vessels. Hence, full-modeled craft were usually built, though some were evidently good sailers, the pinky schooners in particular.

The craft used on the inshore banks, during the last half of the eighteenth century, were usually two-masted boats, fitted with the foremast stepped in the eyes of the craft and the mainmast placed just abaft midlength—the foremast the shorter of the two. No bowsprit or headsail was employed. The fore and main sails were gaffsails; the mainsail with a boom; the foresail sometimes boomed, but might be loose-footed, with its clew slightly overlapping the main. These boats seem to have been 24 to 38 feet long. The larger boats, by 1800, were decked, usually with three hatches. Two of these were cockpits or "standing rooms," in which the fishermen stood to fish. The middle hatch was to give access to the fishhold. The after hatch doubled as the helmsman's cockpit. Forward there was a low raised deck, under which were spartan accommodations for the crew. As the boats grew in size, a fireplace and chimney were fitted to make the cuddy more comfortable and to give greater range of operation. The crew of a large boat was commonly two fishermen and a boy. The smaller boats had a short raised deck forward for the cuddy, with the washboards from the break aft for rails. The long cockpit probably was divided by bin-boards, to form a standing room and a fish bin. These small craft were employed in the inshore fishery and were not intended for more than a two-day operation; the crew was usually a man and a boy.

The hulls of these boats were generally rather sharp-ended, but with the entrance fuller than the run. As a result, many of them apparently sailed well, in spite of a rig restricted to two gaffsails. The freeboard was rather low and the draft moderate. Sometime before the Revolution the two-sail boats were improved by adding low log bulwarks running from the break in the deck to the stern with chock rails on the raised deck. Some of these boats, the dogbodies, were built with square sterns, having lower, middle, and upper transoms, so as to allow the rudder stock to pass through the middle transom. The lower transom raked with the rabbet of the sternpost, the upper transom was abaft the rudder stock and raked more. Boats were also built with pink sterns, the log rail being carried to the tombstone transome abaft the rudder head, with the top of the log rail swept up sharply aft to permit the tombstone's top to be high enough to form a boom rest. The boats grew in size during the late eighteenth century and the large craft were fitted with log windlasses, placed afore or abaft the foremast.

The Revolution practically destroyed the colonial fishing fleet and capital was lacking to build schooner replacements. As a result, the low-cost two-masted boats became very popular and were built in large numbers, particularly at Essex, then part of Ipswich, Massachusetts, and called Chebacco Parish. As a result the two-masted boats become known as Chebacco Boats, or Jebacco Boats if pink-sterned; Chebacco Dogbodies or Dogbodies if square-sterned. The origin of this name is unknown. Another name for these boats was Ram's-head Boats; some had their high stemposts raked aft above deck or rail level in profile, which suggested some slight resemblance to the horns of a ram.

As substitutes for schooners and pinkies, the dogbody and Chebacco Boats continued to grow in dimensions. The common size in 1790–1800 seems to have been 22 to 23 tons register, or about 36 to 38 feet on deck, 11 to 12 feet beam, and 5 to 5½ feet depth in hold. By 1810 the common size had apparently grown to about 30 tons register, or about 38 to 40 feet on deck, 11½ to 12½ feet beam, and 5½ to 6 feet depth in hold. By 1814 a few boats, at least, were built having a length of 40 to 48 feet on deck. A British naval officer,* serving on the British blockade of the American coast in 1814, wrote of a "beautiful sebacque [Chebacco] boat, schooner, called the Rambler" cut out and fitted as a naval tender, and armed with one 12-pdr cannon. She seems to have been a satisfactory tender, large enough to carry a rather heavy gun and fast enough for that service. A mention of a Nantucket Chebacco voyaging "from Virginia" is also made; all of which suggests Chebacco Boats well over 40 feet on deck and sharp enough to sail fast. These large Chebaccos had bulwarks instead of low log rails, but the bulwarks were sometimes cut down to deck level on each side of the high stemhead, and a wooden chock fitted there as a hawse for the anchor cable. These boats would have windlasses; the high stemhead was commonly employed as a mooring bitt.

Local tradition in Essex has it that the first Chebacco Boat was built there, in the attic of a house. In view of the weight and the known dimensions of a Chebacco, this is obviously false. There can be no doubt, how-

* *New England Blockaded in 1814, The Journal of Henry Edward Napier, Lieutenant in H. M. S. Nymphe*, ed. Walter Muir Whitehill (Salem, Mass.: Peabody Museum, 1939), pp. 26, 62, etc.

ever, that the Chebacco owed much of its popularity to the skill of the Essex shipbuilders.

The Gloucester Custom House registers began in 1789. The data available from this source is generally unsatisfactory since schooners, pinkies, Chebacco Boats, and dogbodies are all registered as "schooners." However, pink-sterned craft and square-sterned vessels can be identified by the register descriptions. Nevertheless, without additional evidence it is impossible to reach a conclusion as to which type the register of vessel represents: a pinky schooner or a Chebacco Boat, in one case, perhaps, or a small square-stern schooner, or a dogbody in another. In the early registers before 1800 it is probable that the Chebacco and dogbody are those vessels under 40 feet Custom House register length. However this probability becomes an uncertainty in the later registrations, particularly after 1810, when boats up to about 50 feet register length may have been in use.

Fast-sailing Chebaccos and dogbodies certainly existed, but these types were handicapped in some degree by their rig, which had no provision for any light sails. Some small boats were fitted with an overlapping foresail in order to obtain increased sail area. Only in a hull of relatively light displacement would fast sailing be possible with such a rig. These clipper-built craft would be of small capacity for their dimensions, and in hull lines would be somewhat similar to a small pilot-boat schooner in lines and proportions.

The Chebacco Boats and dogbodies continued to be employed in some of the smaller New England fishing ports and many were built during the business depression that followed the War of 1812. Boats of these types were in use as late as the 1850s in Maine, New Brunswick, and Nova Scotia, and in the more isolated fishing ports. On the other hand, they disappeared rapidly in the large fishing ports, replaced by pinkies or small square-stern schooners in the inshore fisheries. The last boats of the Chebacco type in the fisheries seem to have been the Gaspé boats on the Gulf of St. Lawrence.

Chebacco Boats and dogbodies were sometimes moored in coves that gave only moderate protection from heavy weather, as at Pigeon Cove on Cape Ann, for example. An effective mooring gear was required; on Cape Ann this consisted of a large rectangular block of local granite, 3 or 4 tons in weight, with a hole in its center of about 8 inches in diameter. In this hole an oak pole 14 to 18 feet long, was inserted and secured under the stone block by a fid driven through a hole in the butt of the pole. The block and pole were placed in the desired location, which allowed the top of the pole to stand 3 or 4 feet above normal high tide. A block of timber, 18 to 24 inches long, in which a hole large enough to fit loosely over the head of the long pole was bored, was then fitted, held in place by a fid through the head of the pole. The short block, or "crab," could then revolve on the pole, floating on the surface of the water. A piece of heavily tarred hemp cable, about 2 inches in diameter, was made fast to one end of the floating block, passing through a hole bored in the block for this purpose. This cable was usually 4 to 5 fathoms long, with a large eye spliced in the free end, which was buoyed by a brightly painted wooden buoy. The Chebacco would pick up the buoy and haul up the cable so that the eye could be dropped over the high stemhead. This mooring was sufficiently flexible to avoid sudden shocks and great strain on the cable and, if the stone were heavy enough, the gear would hold the vessel securely in extremely heavy weather.

The pinkies apparently went through a parallel growth in size to become a very popular type of fishing vessel in New England and eastern Canada. The expansion of American fishing activities into the Gulf of St. Lawrence, after the War of 1812, produced a need for a larger vessel than the Chebaccos and dogbodies and an equally seaworthy type. The pinky met the requirements of this need. Differences over fishing treaties, between the United States and Great Britain led to American poaching on Canadian fishing grounds and this brought about a demand for fast-sailing pinkies. However the pinkies do not seem to have been built above 55 feet, Custom House register length, for the fisheries. A three-masted pinky named *Spy* was built at Essex in 1823, described as being 70′ Custom House length, 17′ beam, 8′-6″ depth in hold, 91-61/95 tons register, pink-stern, three-masts, no galleries, no head, in her register. Her dimensions show that she was a long, rather narrow vessel, probably with moderate deadrise. However she does not appear to have been employed in the fisheries; rather she went into the East Indian trade. The *Spy* is the largest pinky yet found in the records and the only three-masted pinky known to have been built.

The historical background and state of evolution of the New England fishing schooner types immediately prior to the period in which detailed, technical information is available, has been described. An attempt can now be made to illustrate these types of fishing vessels by means of reconstructed scale drawings based on old models and a few sketches believed to be contemporary, or nearly so. Such reconstructions will not represent any individual vessel; rather the drawings might be said to show the general features of the three types; offshore banks schooners, Chebaccos, and dogbodies of the periods stated in their descriptions.

In the Hall of American Merchant Shipping, Museum of History and Technology, Smithsonian Institution, Washington, D.C., there is a small rigged-model of a Chebacco boat named *Lion*. This appears to be a fisherman's "jacknife" model of great age. Unfortunately the history of the model before museum accession is unknown, but the model was assumed to represent a boat of about 1790. Using probable standing room width as a guide, it was possible to arrive at tentative length, beam, and depth estimates: about 38′ on deck, 11′-4″ beam, and 5′-6″ depth in hold (Plate 1). In the Glou-

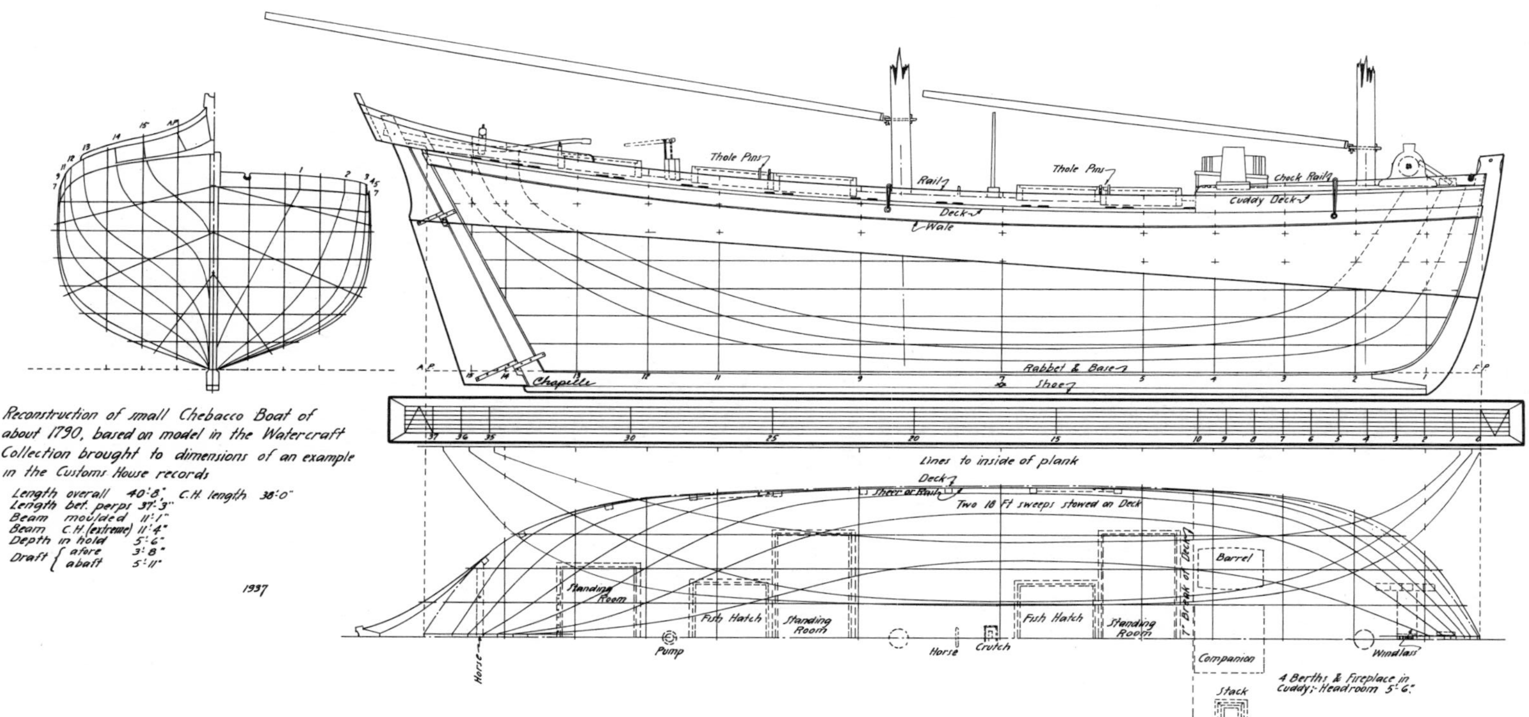
Reconstruction of small Chebacco Boat of about 1790, based on model in the Watercraft Collection brought to dimensions of an example in the Customs House records
Length overall 40'8", C.H. length 38'0"
Length bet. perps 37'3"
Beam moulded 11'1"
Beam C.H.(extreme) 11'4"
Depth in hold 5'6"
Draft { afore 3'8"
abaft 5'11"
1937
Thole Pins
Thole Pins
Rail
Check Rails
Cuddy Deck
Deck
Wale
Rabbet & Base
Shoe
Chapelle
Lines to inside of plank
Deck
Sheer or Rail
Two 18 Ft sweeps stowed on Deck
Barrel
Standing Room
Fish Hatch
Standing Room
Fish Hatch
Standing Room
Break of Deck
Horse
Pump
Horse
Crutch
Companion
Windlass
Stack
4 Berths & Fireplace in Cuddy; Headroom 5'6"

PLATE 1. *Lion*, Chebacco boat, 1804, reconstruction

cester Custom House registers a Chebacco named *Lion* was found, built in 1804 at Essex (then Ipswich): 37′-9″ on deck, 11′-2″ beam, 5′-10″ depth of hold, 22-47/95 tons register. This close similarity in dimensions verified the tentative estimates of scale. The lines were developed to show the degree of fullness found in latter pinky half-models and with the same characteristics in level lines and buttocks. So far as judgment can be trusted, the result seemed to be reasonable and would produce a very seaworthy boat with a fair turn of speed.

The deck arrangement, as interpreted from the rigged-model, showed the low, raised deck forward, under which was the cuddy, containing two berths and on deck a hearth of brick with a chimney generally of wood plastered on the inside. This usually could be unshipped, leaving a small scuttle that could be closed by a hatch cover. There was a small wooden, handspike windlass well forward, close to the foreside of the foremast. The entrance to the cuddy at the end of the raised deck was through a small hatch with a hinged cover—the hinges were usually of raw hide. A water keg was carried alongside this hatch, to port, in a cradle. The raised deck had a chock rail, or log rail, carried to the high stemhead, in which a cross-fid was driven near its top. Abaft the break there was a low log rail carried aft to the tombstone transom of the pink-stern.

The main deck layout, abaft the break, showed a standing room about 30 inches long, fore and aft, and about 7 feet 6 inches wide athwartships. Abaft this, and alongside, was a fish hatch opening into the fish bins, and hold below deck. Next was a foreboom crotch, then the foresheet horse, then the mainmast with a sheet cleat on its foreside. Abaft the mainmast was a second standing room with fish hatch alongside, then a wooden pump and, finally the helmsman's standing room. A wooden horse for the mainsheet gave support for the bulwarks where they left the main deck to form the pink-stern. The model seems to be finished to represent tarred bottom and topside, probably a narrow color band, say of red, would run along the top of the wales.

Tholepins were located in the log rail so that the boat could be rowed with sweeps. Instead of chain plates a link was used, with a single bolt in the wales. This served also in lieu of a lower deadeye or heart for the lanyards. There was a single shroud on each side at fore and main masts. No stays were employed.

No description has been found of the running rigging of these boats. However it is probable that the foresail sheet had an iron horse or a pair of deck blocks. The topping lift led from the end of the foreboom, if one was employed, to a block at the foremast head with the fall belayed in the shrouds. Peak and throat halyards would be employed, belayed to mast cleats in the large boats, but some of the smaller boats may have employed single

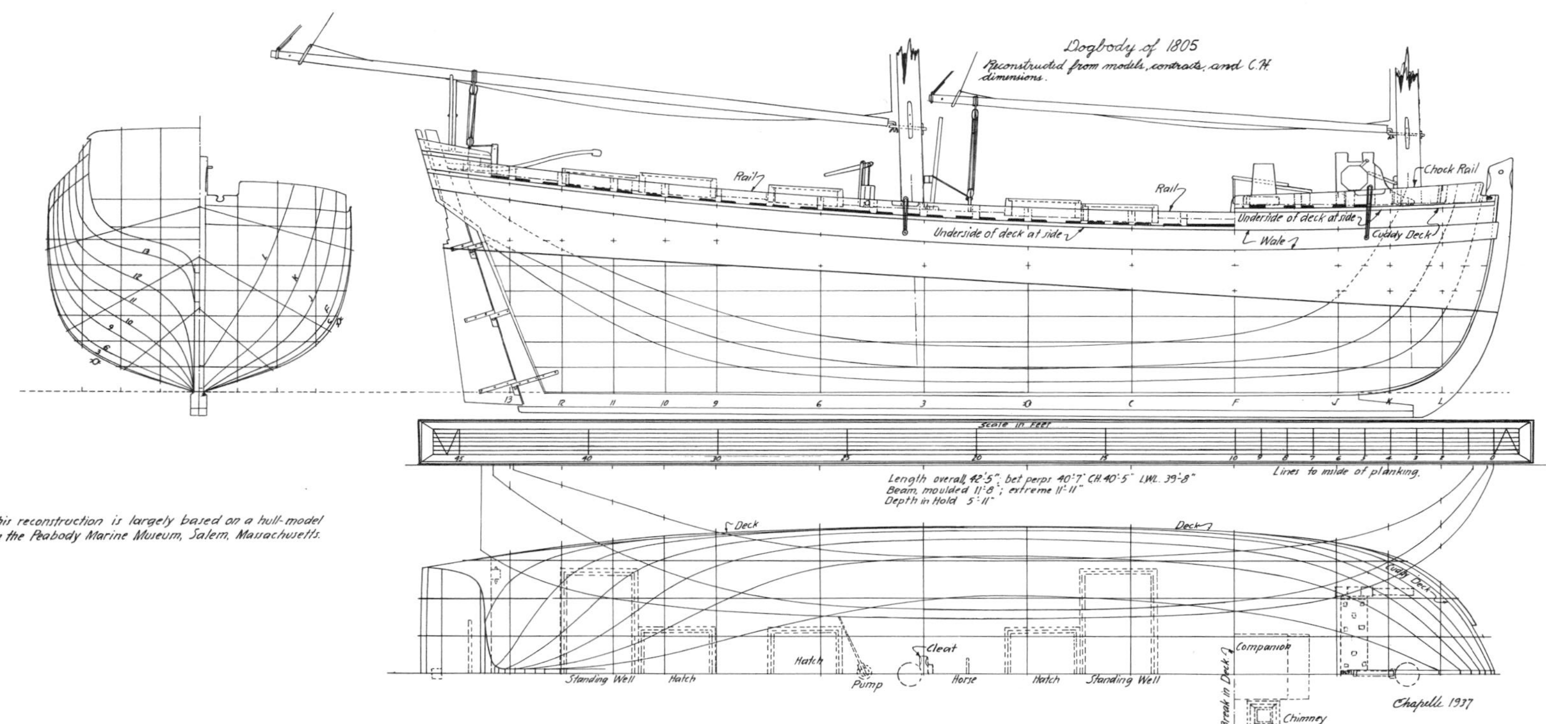
Dogbody of 1805
Reconstructed from models, contracts, and C.H. dimensions.
Chock Rail
Rail
Rail
Underside of deck at side
Underside of deck at side
Cuddy Deck
Wale
Scale in Feet
Length overall 42'5"; bet perps 40'7" CH. 40'5" LWL. 39'-8"
Beam, moulded 11'8"; extreme 11'-11"
Depth in Hold 5'-11"
Lines to inside of planking.
Deck
Deck
Cuddy Deck
Companion
Cleat
Hatch
Standing Well
Hatch
Pump
Horse
Hatch
Standing Well
Break in Deck
Chimney
Chapelle 1937
This reconstruction is largely based on a hull-model in the Peabody Marine Museum, Salem, Massachusetts.

PLATE 2. Dogbody, Chebacco Boat, 1805, reconstruction

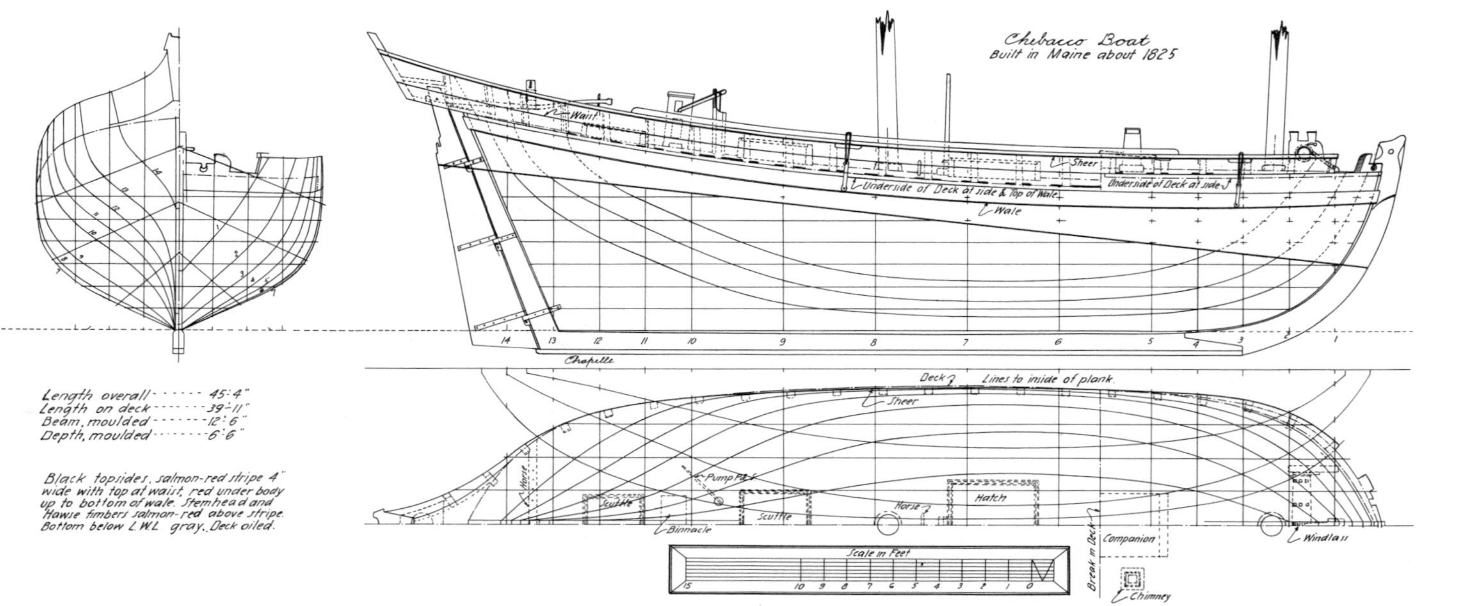
Chebacco Boat
Built in Maine about 1825
Waist
Sheer
Underside of Deck at side & Top of Wale
Underside of Deck at side
Wale
Chapelle
Deck
Lines to inside of plank.
Sheer
Horse
Pump
Scuttle
Binnacle
Scuttle
Horse
Hatch
Break in Deck
Companion
Windlass
Chimney
Scale in Feet
Length overall 45' 4"
Length on deck 39' 11"
Beam, moulded 12' 6"
Depth, moulded 6' 6"
Black topsides, salmon-red stripe 4" wide with top at waist, red under body up to bottom of wale. Stemhead and Hawse timbers salmon-red above stripe. Bottom below L.W.L. gray. Deck oiled.
Drawn from rigged model at East Boothbay, 1936

PLATE 3. Chebacco, 1825, reconstruction

halyards on their gaffs. The main-topping lift would be the same as the foreboom lift; the main and fore sheets were probably guntackle purchases; the mainsheet led to the wooden horse in the pink-stern or to an iron horse in the dogbodies, or there may have been double sheets in a dogbody. No model in which the rigging has not been "repaired" has been found, therefore the foregoing description may not be wholly correct.

The rigged-model of a dogbody in the National Collection appears to have been built at a much later date than the Chebacco shown in Plate 1. This dogbody model does not show clearly the upper and lower transoms of the assigned date, about 1800, furthermore, the deck layout shows standing rooms too narrow athwartships to be practical. Instead of using this, a jacknife hull model, in the Peabody Marine Museum, Salem, Massachusetts, was chosen. This model not only shows useful deck details but also characteristics that seem to show knowledge of some specific boat. It was picked up at sea in the last century; otherwise nothing is known of its history. No other model of a dogbody that has any evidence of being old has yet been found.

Employing the same methods of reconstructing the dimensions of this boat that were used in Plate 1, the model shown in Plate 2 would measure about 40′-5″ Custom House length, 11′-11″ beam, 5′-11″ depth in hold. *Mercatore*, built at Essex in 1805, measured 40′ Custom House length, 11′-4″ beam, 5′-10½″ depth in hold, 23-25/95 tons register. Hence, the estimated dimensions are again very close to the proportions of an actual vessel of the type. This model has many of the features of the Chebacco in deck arrangement. There was the short, raised deck forward, with chock rails, the main deck with low log rails, but there were only two standing rooms instead of three, and one of the two was for the helmsman. The small log windlass was abaft the foremast in this boat; one would judge that this was the best location for it, for there was then sufficient room to work it effectively in handling ground tackle. This seems to have been the most common position for a windlass for it appears in this position in the drafts of American merchant ships of the Revolutionary period in the Admiralty Collection of Draughts, National Maritime Museum, Greenwich, London, England. Whether or not the fore and main sail sheets had iron horses and travelers might be questioned, for double sheets led through deck blocks were commonly used in American schooners before and after 1800. This was not so much a matter of economy as one of custom and practice. Ironwork was readily obtainable, even in rather isolated building sites, in the period between 1785 and 1830. The use of a wooden or iron main horse in pink-sterned boats and schooners should also be considered, for this indicates that a foresheet horse of iron or wood would not be an innovation.

Plate 3 shows an attempt at reconstruction of a large Chebacco of about

1825, based upon a model once owned by an East Boothbay, Maine, shipyard owner. This model is thought to have been made by the shipbuilder's father who as a boy had earned his first dollar by building the plastered chimney of a local Chebacco. The boat was said to have been old at that time, reputedly having been built in 1825. The model seems to represent a rather sharp, large Chebacco, having a deck arrangement very like that of a contemporary pinky and of the class of the *Rambler* mentioned by the British naval officer. The East Boothbay model also showed close similarity to some drawings in a schoolboy's copy book preserved in the Cape Ann Historical Society, Gloucester, Massachusetts. The boat represented in the model was of a seagoing type and of pinky model, rather sharp and fine-ended. The model has disappeared, probably destroyed by a fire in the Goudy and Stevens shipyard before World War II. In drawing the lines, the deadrise was not changed from that of the model.

Using the dimensions of the companionway as a guide, the measurements of the boat represented in the model are estimated to have been about 40′-9″ Custom House length, 12′-9″ beam, 5′-10″ depth of hold, and 45′-4″ over-all length. In so large a boat, standing rooms could be dispensed with, though a small standing room for the helmsman was shown. The cutdown bulwarks and hawse chock mentioned earlier were prominent in the model.

Another model of a Chebacco Boat, named *Washington* is in the Mystic Seaport Museum. This model, when I first saw it, was in a New London bank. It represented a large, seagoing Chebacco with bulwarks very much on the pinky model, but with less deadrise than shown in Plate 3, and without the cutdown bulwarks at the stem. There is no explanation yet found as to why such large Chebacco Boats were built, for the hulls could have carried the full schooner rig, as some did in their later years.

Plate 4 is a scale drawing of a reconstruction of a banks schooner of about 1785–1790, based upon rigged-models in the Smithsonian Institution and in the Peabody Museum at Salem. This drawing is intended to represent as well as is now possible, a schooner of rather large burden, yet one that was a fair sailer at least. In model the reconstruction was based on half-models of full banks schooners of the 1830s so far as the fullness of the ends were concerned. Admittedly this is not sound reasoning but it does produce what I think may be an approximate representation of the hull form of a vessel of this type and date, though the rigged-models available do not seem to be contemporary with the actual vessels they are supposed to represent, as has been noted. There might be some question as to the amount of deadrise shown, but later banks schooner half-models show a marked variation in rise of floor. And reference can be made to the Admiralty draft of a "Marble Head Scooner" of 1767, mentioned earlier, which shows much more deadrise than Plate 4. At any rate, the reconstruction produces a schooner 60′–8″

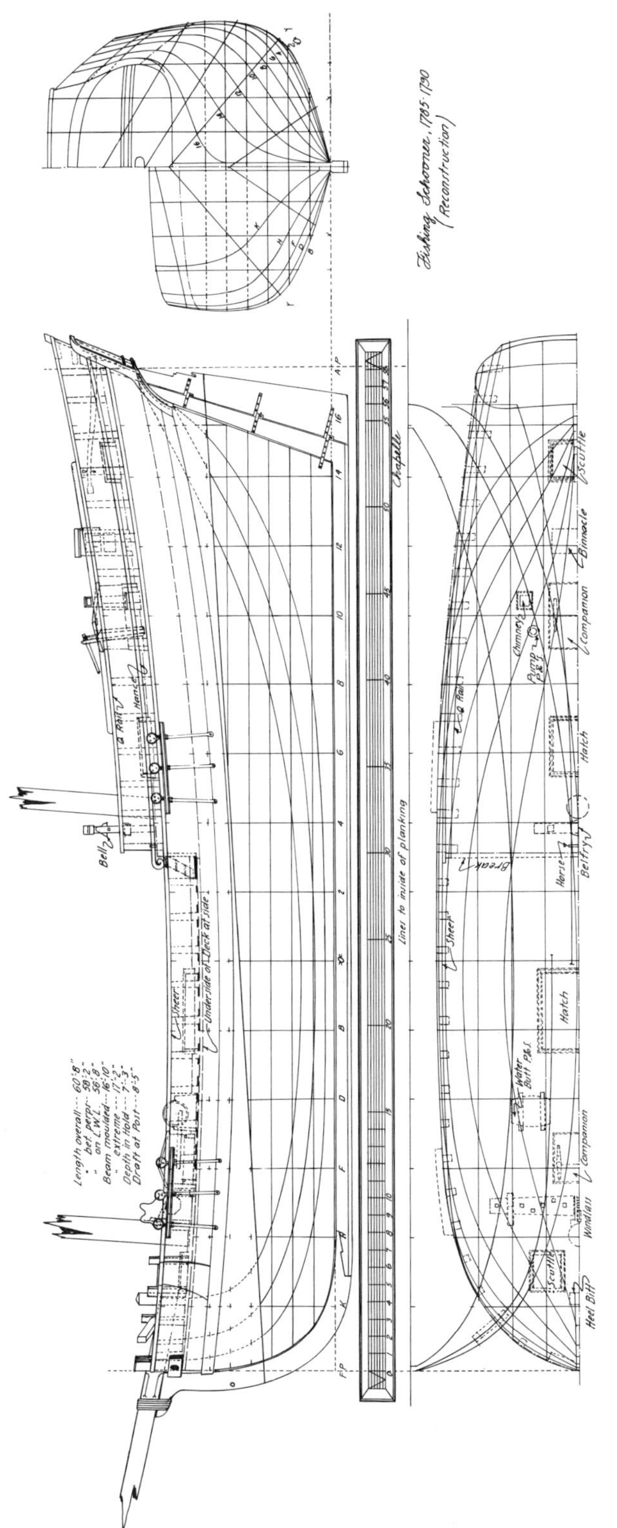

Fishing Schooner, 1785-1790
(Reconstruction)
Length overall 60'8"
" bet. perpr. 58'2"
" on L.W.L. 56'8"
Beam moulded 16'10"
" extreme 17'2"
Depth in Hold 7'3"
Draft at Post 8'5"
Bell
Rail
Hance
Sheer
Underside of Deck at side
Lines to inside of planking
Chapelle
Heel Bitt
Scuttle
Windlass
Companion
Water Butt P&S
Hatch
Sheer
Break
Horse
Belfry
Hatch
Rail
Pump P&S
Chimney
Companion
Binnacle
Scuttle

PLATE 4. Fishing schooner, 1785, reconstruction

overall, 58′-2″ length between perpendiculars, 17′-2″ extreme beam, 7′-3″ depth in hold. Custom House length works out to be about 59′-3″. The schooner *Friendship*, built at Essex in 1789, measured 60′ Custom House length, 18′-8″ beam, 7′-10″ depth of hold, 75-5/95 tons register. *Primrose*, built at Ipswich in 1792, was 58′ registered length, 17′-2″ beam, 7′-2″ depth in hold, 61-74/95 tons. These examples serve to show that the reconstruction is close, in hull proportions at least, to some fishing schooners of the period under discussion.

The deck arrangements of these early fishing schooner rigged-models varied a good deal. There are indications that the crews of some of the Marblehead schooners lived aft, under the quarterdeck, in colonial times and even as late as the 1820s. The forecastle would then be used for gear, stores, and other stowage.

The period in which extensive reconstruction is required in this study now ends. Beginning in the 1820s or 1830s the recording of pinky-type characteristics is possible chiefly because of the introduction of the lift half-model in designing fishing vessels. Up to the time this type of model came into use the hawk's-nest model was employed. The hawk's-nest model was fragile and probably for this reason, only a few such models survived. Lift-models, as first made, showed the hull to the level of the main deck only, but later they were made with a lift representing the bulwarks. The lift-models were made of planks fastened together to form a solid block but which could be taken apart to obtain the shape of the hull. These models were therefore strong enough to survive much abuse, so many models have survived in New England and in the Maritime Provinces. Also, the pinky was a popular type, remaining in use for a long time—almost two centuries. A pink schooner is mentioned in Massachusetts records in 1727, and a photograph in the U.S. Museum of History and Technology, Smithsonian Institution, shows a large pinky fishing off the Isle of Shoals about 1885. Pinkies were employed as late as 1910 in eastern Maine and in the Canadian Maritime Provinces, hence their hull forms and other characteristics remained known. Even though these went through some "modernization" during the long life of the type, the changes were relatively small and consisted mostly of minor improvements in deck furniture, windlasses, steering gear, and the like.

The leading reasons for the survival of the pinky were her weatherliness and seaworthiness; and many could sail quite fast, particularly going to windward. These characteristics made the pinky suitable for the offshore mackerel fisheries, for these fish generally moved to windward in large schools, often rather rapidly. This fishery, after 1820 or thereabouts, was carried on with the use of fishing gear called a mackerel jig. As a result, pinkies were sometimes called jiggers, according to Collins and others.

While the pinkies of the 1820s were often fast sailers on the wind, few were modeled for all-around speed. In the American North Atlantic fisheries windward ability was prized in a vessel because of geographic conditions and prevailing winds. These combined to make it usually necessary for a fishing vessel to come home against the westerlies, often very strong and accompanied by a very heavy sea, particularly in the winter months. But even on the New England coast in summer, weatherliness was desirable, for a fisherman bound to Gloucester or Boston from the Gulf of Maine fishing banks would usually have a dead beat against a fresh sou'westerly for the whole distance.

"Clipper" pinkies were built in New England when quarrels over the fishery treaties with Great Britain led to American poaching on the Canadian fishing banks. During the 1820s the pinkies were built larger in size than before so as to be suitable for working farther from home in the Gulf of St. Lawrence and the Labrador cod, halibut, and mackerel fisheries. The natural development took place, a refining of the lines to fit the pinky for illegal fishing. Because of this, the sharp pinky became well known in eastern Canada, and this may be the reason that surviving Canadian half-models of pinkies are almost all of the clipper or semi-clipper type. These combined nearly all the good qualities of the full-ended pinky with those of a fast schooner, producing craft that were profitable and desirable well into the twentieth century.

Due to the very distinctive characteristics of the pinky, its limited development was almost independent of that of the North Atlantic fishing schooner. It is proper, therefore, to discuss the type to the end of its existence rather than to include its later modifications in an examination of the other types of North Atlantic fishing vessels.

Plate 5 is a plan of a pinky taken from a half-model once in the possession of the U.S. Fish Commission but now lost. From these lines, a rigged-model was built and later exhibited in the Smithsonian Collection as the *Tiger*. Recently this model was brought into question, both as to identification and because the lines were not closely followed. This resulted in a new exhibition model, built according to the plan. As far as can now be determined, Plate 5 may represent the pinky *Essex*, built at Essex in 1821. As shown in Plate 5, the vessel measured 48′-9″ Custom House length, 14′-1½″ moulded beam, and about 6′-7″ depth in hold. *Essex* was 48′-10″ Custom House length, 14′-3″ beam (extreme), 6′-10″ depth in hold, 41-29/95 tons register.

The lines plan shows an attractive pinky of the older, deeper, and rather narrow model. It was believed at that time that narrow, deep pinkies sailed to windward better than wide models. But in the 1830s, the builders were slowly becoming satisfied that wider pinkies could be designed which were as weatherly as the old narrow models. The wider pinkies could carry full

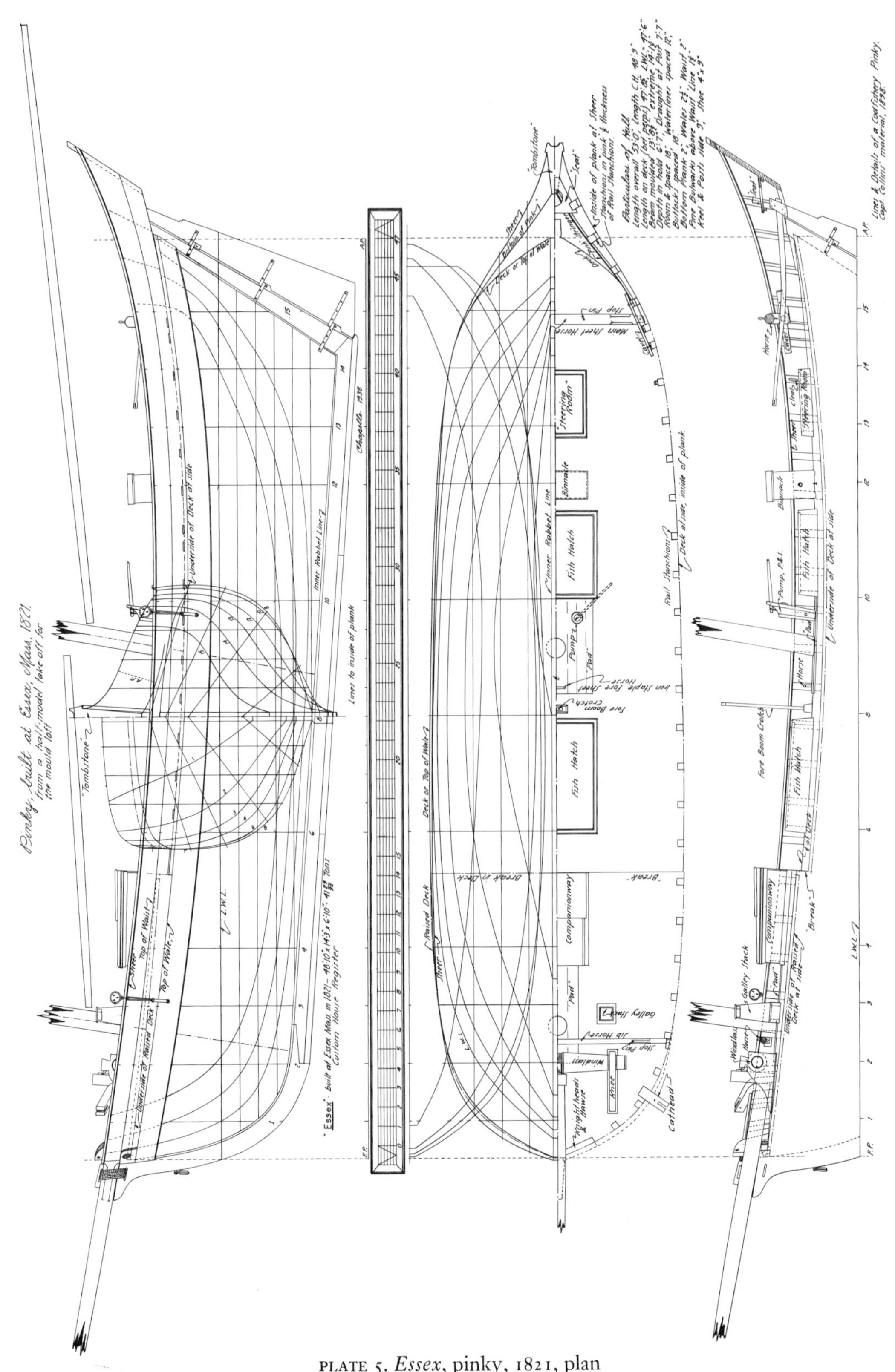
Pinky, built at Essex, Mass. 1821.
from a half-model take off for the mould loft
"Essex" built at Essex Mass. in 1821 – 48'10" x 14'3" x 6'10" – 41 89/95 Tons Custom House Register
Chapelle 1938
Lines to inside of plank
Inner Rabbet Line
Underside of Deck at side
Top of Waist
Underside of Raised Deck
"Tombstone"
L.W.L.
Raised Deck
Sheer
Deck or Top of Waist
Break in Deck
Companionway
Fish Hatch
Binnacle
"Steering Room"
Pump
Windlass
Knee
Catheads
Rail Stanchions
Deck at side, inside of plank
Inside of plank at Sheer
Stanchions in pink, & thickness of Rail Stanchions.
Particulars of Hull
Galley Stack
Fore Boom Crotch
Lines & Details of a Codfishery Pinky.
Capt. Collins' material, 1898.

PLATE 5. *Essex*, pinky, 1821, plan

sail longer in blowing weather and so make faster passages to the banks—or home—than could the narrow model. The increase in beam also increased the hold capacity of a pinky, which was desirable because they worked farther and farther from home. This made designers seek an effective fast-carrier model of the pinky.

Rigs of pinkies are shown in Figures 1, 2 and 3. These are simple schooners carrying three lowers—jib, fore-gaffsail, and gaff-mainsails. The only light-weather sails they had were a main-topmast staysail and, occasionally, a main-gaff topsail. A few employed an overlapping loose-footed, gaff-foresail instead of the boom-foresail shown in the sail plans. It was not until the clipper pinkies appeared after 1850 that the full schooner rig, with fore-topmast, jibboom, fore-gaff topsail, and jib topsail appeared in a few of the large pinkies, but the change did not become popular for it destroyed the simplicity of the pinky rig.

In the 1820s and 1830s some of the large Chebacco Boats were fitted with bowsprits, jib, main-topmasts and main-topmast staysails; a change easily made. It was said that such conversions were easily identified by the position of the foremast close to the bows and the large mainsails they required to balance properly.

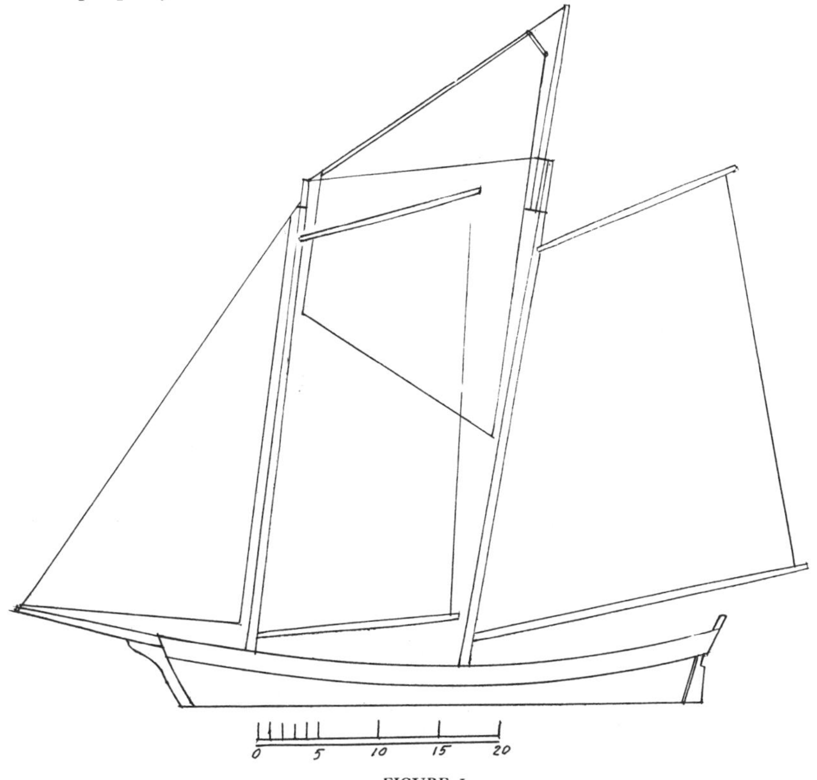
0
5
10
15
20

FIGURE 1

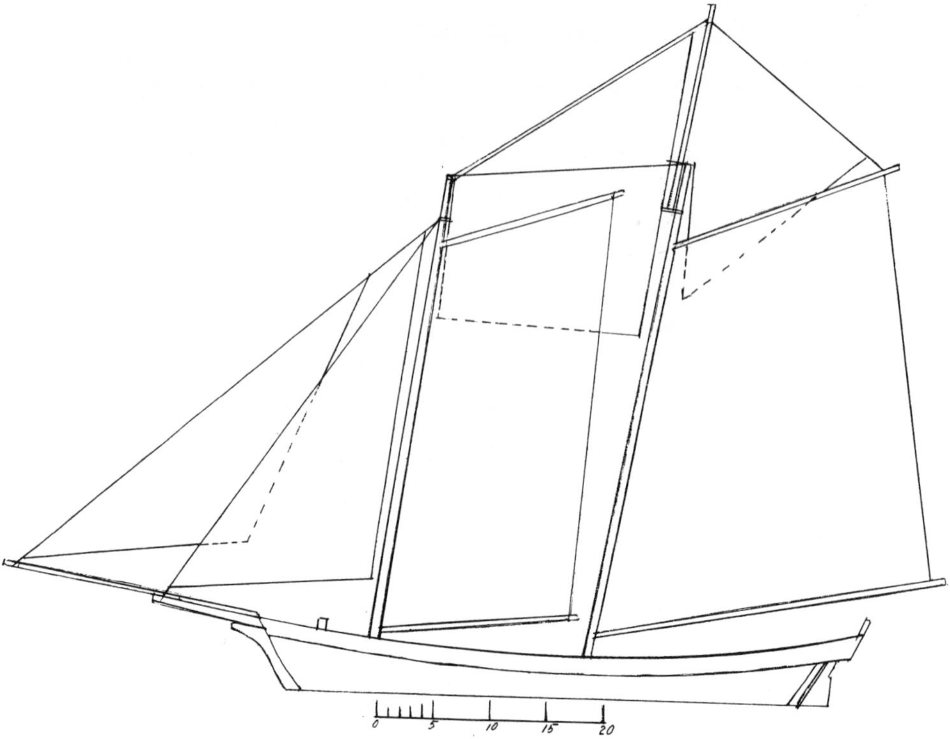

0
5
10
15
20

FIGURE 2

FIGURE 3

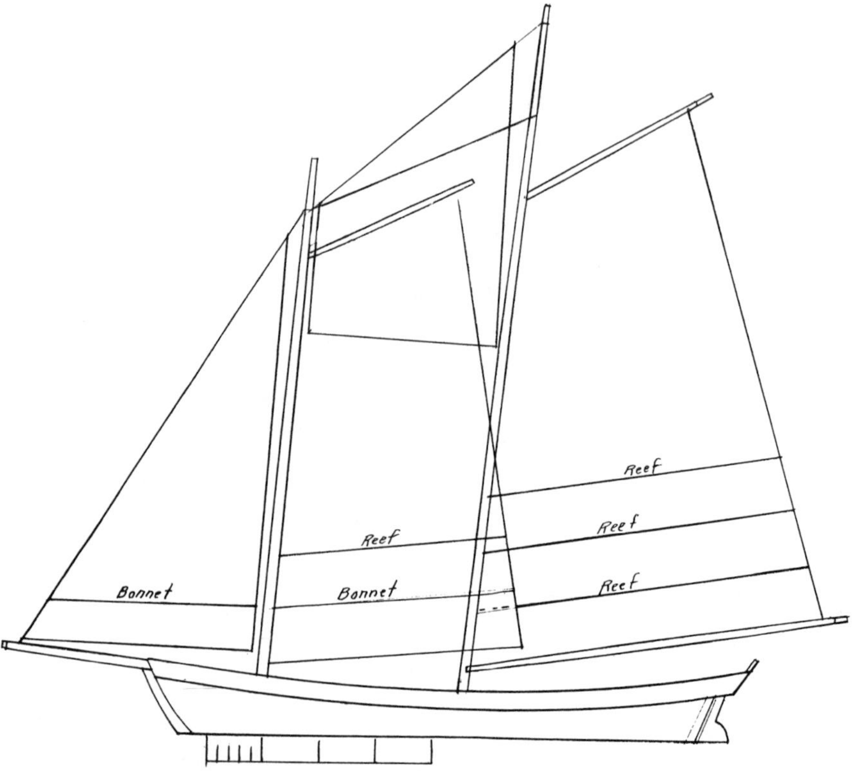

Reef
Reef
Reef
Reef
Bonnet
Bonnet

Plate 6 shows the lines of a pinky half-model found in East Boothbay, Maine, in 1937, in the possession of the late Frank Adams. Mr. Adams believed the model had been made prior to 1840. It was a lift-model on a scale of ½ inch to the foot. The model had many markings showing it had been built to a number of times. A pinky on this model would measure 39′-7½″ on deck, 40′-9″ Custom House length, 11′-9¼″ moulded beam, 12′-¾″ extreme beam, 4′-9″ depth in hold.

The deck layout marked on the model was the usual one with low, raised deck forward. A wooden chimney that could be unshipped is shown in the plan, but by 1840 the pinkies were being fitted with iron hearths or stoves and iron stacks. Wooden pump barrels were retained and the old wooden handspike-windlass continued in use into the 1850s. Simple wooden binnacle stands, with dry compasses (card on needle), and candle lanterns remained in use also until about the mid-1850s, and later in Maine and in the Maritime Provinces.

Though it is traditional on Cape Ann and to the eastward that pinkies were roughly built and crudely fitted, there seems to be no contemporary evidence of this. It is traditional also on Cape Ann that some of Chebaccos were roughly fitted and had no proper hearth and stack; the cooking fire was on loose bricks with the smoke escaping through the cabin hatch. This also implies that the boats were without all but the most primitive forecastle accommodations; but this does not seem true of the pinkies. Like the better class of Chebaccos, the pinkies were built of white oak, copper, and treenail fastened below the load line; wrought iron nailed above. Deck and deck furniture were of white pine and oak, with a proper hearth and stack forward. Suitable accommodations must have existed to enable manning for the Gulf of St. Lawrence and other distant fisheries. It is also apparent, judging by the last survivors, that the vessels were generally well built, finished, and fitted. American fishermen in the days of sail took pride in their vessels and lavished care and paint on their craft, whether a sailing skiff or a schooner. They also demanded some bodily comforts, and in the 1820s these and better food became possible, as the fisheries became more profitable.

In Plate 6 the hull is somewhat shallower and wider, in proportion, than in the *Essex*. Like her, however, there were full ends at deck level with fine lines below, the run was often very fine, giving easy bow and buttock lines. There was generally a slight flattening of the buttocks near the intersections with the load line aft. This shows in most pinky half-models, sometimes so slightly as to be hardly noticeable. But in some clipper pinky half-models this characteristic was often quite apparent. Symmetry in the curves of the bow line and buttock line, in profile, are rarely seen in these half-models. The hull having such symmetry would pitch constantly; the

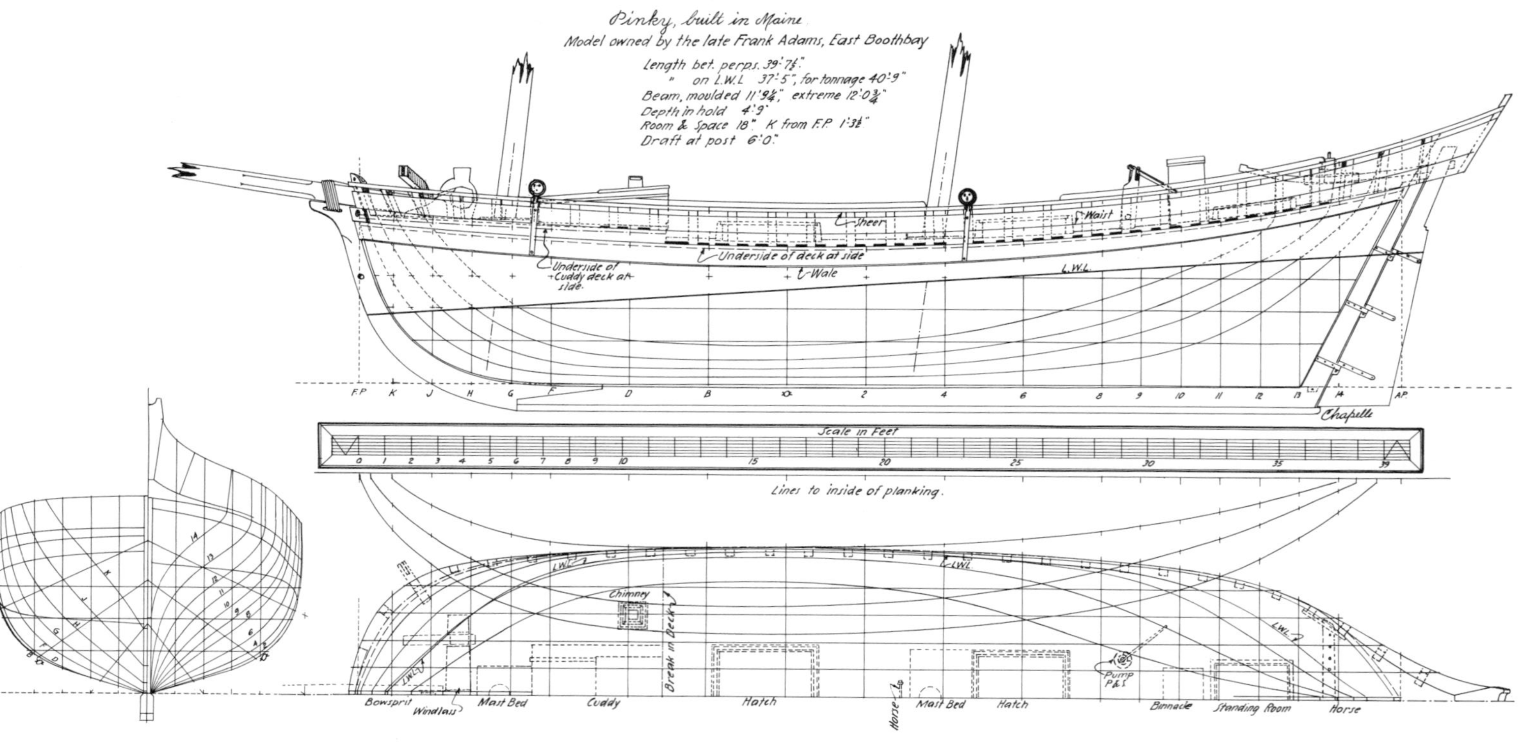
Pinky, built in Maine
Model owned by the late Frank Adams, East Boothbay
Length bet. perps. 39'7½"
" on L.W.L. 37'5", for tonnage 40'9"
Beam, moulded 11'9¼", extreme 12'0¾"
Depth in hold 4'9"
Room & Space 18". K from F.P. 1'3½"
Draft at post 6'0"
Sheer
Waist
Underside of deck at side
Underside of Cuddy deck at side.
Wale
L.W.L.
Chapelle
Scale in Feet
Lines to inside of planking.
Chimney
Break in Deck
Pump P&S
Bowsprit
Windlass
Mast Bed
Cuddy
Hatch
Horse
Binnacle
Standing Room

PLATE 6. Pinky, Maine, 1840, half-model

"rocking-horse" motion that often mars the designs of deep-draft sailing double-enders, so far as comfort aboard is concerned.

Pinkies carried their anchor cables coiled on deck. A pinky of the size we are discussing usually carried seven men, including skipper and cook; the latter after about 1840. Earlier a boy served as cook and extra hand. Water was carried in a barrel chocked alongside the forecastle companionway, on the opposite side from the galley stack. In some pinkies the hearth and stack were on the center line just abaft the foremast and forward of the companionway. The timber mainsheet horse had an iron rod let into its underside so the ring, or traveler, would not chafe the timber.

The use of the steersman's standing room was usually confined to small pinkies. In large pinkies a small scuttle was located under the tiller which gave access to the lazerette. Here supplies of water, in barrels, and gear were stowed. As will be seen, some pinkies did not have their bulwarks closed in, they were open for about two inches above the deck or plank-sheer and some were open for a few inches below the main rail cap as well. Open bulwarks of this construction seem to have been often used in the pinkies employed in the Labrador fisheries.

Plate 7 illustrates the lines of a half-model in the Smithsonian Collection from which four pinkies were built between 1832 and 1835. These were easy-lined vessels of the wide model; the run was unusually fine. The deck layout shows what seems to be a plan of a small trunk on the raised deck forward, about which Lew Story had doubts; otherwise the details of deck arrangement require no comment.

The plan shows a pinky 51′-3″ Custom House length, 50′-4″ on deck, 15′-6″ moulded beam, 15′-10″ extreme beam, and 6′-7″ depth in hold.

The four vessels supposed to have been built on this model were *Splendid*, built at Essex in 1832 (53′-10″ x 15′-9½″ x 6′-7″, 48-82/95 tons register). She had a billet head by 1849. *Meridian*, built at Essex in 1834 (53′-3″ x 15′-6″ x 6′-11″, 50-2/95 tons register). *Planet*, built in Essex in 1835 (51′-10″ x 16′-4″ x 6′-10″, 47-5/95 tons register), and *July*, built at Essex, also in 1835 (55′-9″ x 15′-8″ x 7′-1″, 54-8/95 tons register). It is impossible to account for the variations in dimensions. The Custom House dimensions in this instance show the difficulties in using them for an identification of a half-model or plan when no other means are available.

The plan (Plate 7) shows a model intended to be a fast carrier, with very moderate rise of floor, easy bilge with slightly flaring topside amidships. The entrance is not very full. The run is long and fine. It seems probable that the *Splendid* proved such a good sailer and carrier that her model was used in building the other pinkies. *July* was registered as late as 1889, owned at Blue Hill, Maine. She was built by Parker Burnham, Jr., in one month, for which she was named.

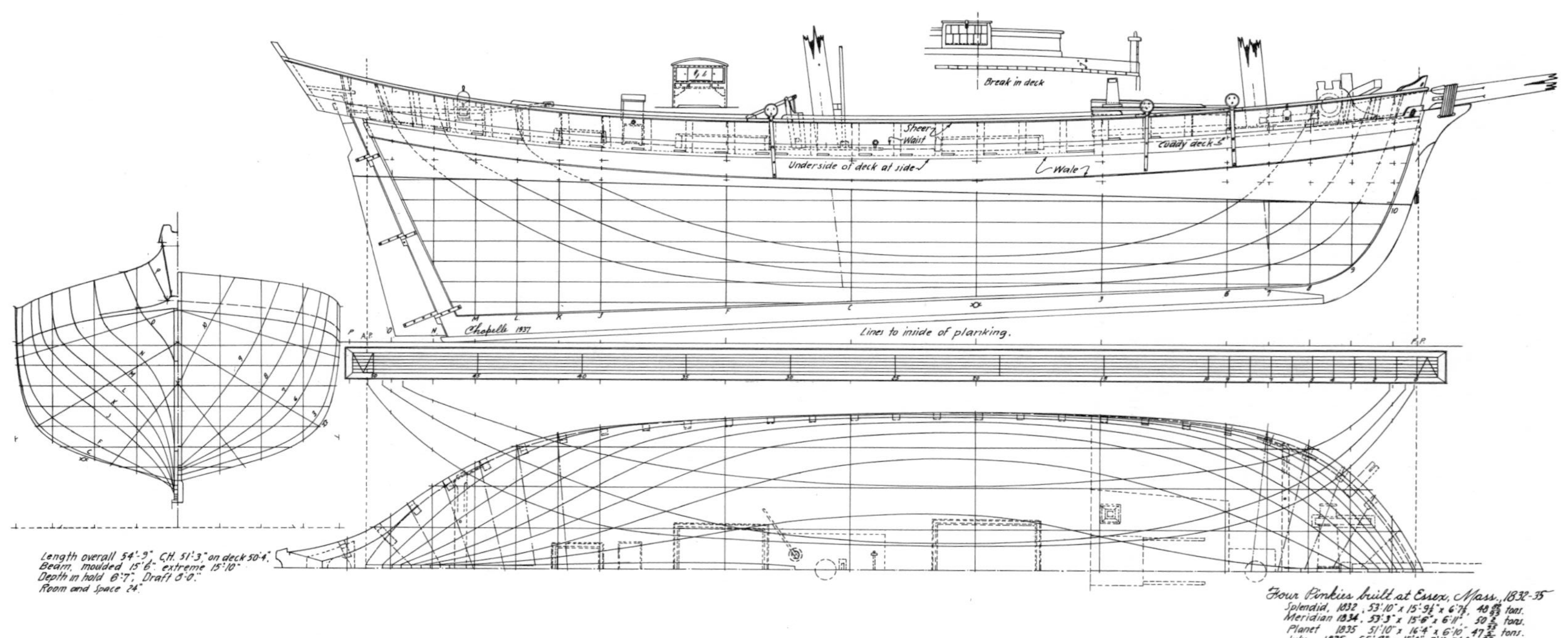
Break in deck
Sheer
Waist
Underside of deck at side
Wale
Cuddy deck
Chapelle 1937
Lines to inside of planking.
Length overall 54'-9". C.H. 51'-3." on deck 50'-4".
Beam, moulded 15'6". extreme 15'-10"
Depth in hold 6'-7", Draft 8'-0."
Room and Space 24".
Four Pinkies built at Essex, Mass., 1832-35
Splendid, 1832, 53'-10" x 15'-9½" x 6'-7½", 48 67/95 tons.
Meridian 1834, 53'-3" x 15'-6" x 6'-11", 50 2/95 tons.
Planet 1835 51'-10" x 16'-4" x 6'-10" 47 5/95 tons.
July 1835 55'-9" x 15'-8" x 7'-1" 54 8/95 tons

PLATE 7. Pinkies: *July*, *Splendid*, *Planet*, *Meridan*, 1832, half-model

Pinkies usually had a simple gammon knee on the stem; the gammoning was hemp rope until the late 1840s when an iron strap gammoning became standard. No carving was employed as a rule, but in 1834 the first pinky in the Gloucester register to have a billet head was the *Metamore* (*Metamora*). She was built at Gloucester and her Custom House dimensions were 54′-10″ x 17′ x 7′-2″. She had a schooner's cutwater. Some pinkies had a plain curved stem with an iron gammoning, pilot-boat fashion.

The building of large pinkies, over 55 feet Custom House length, appears to have begun in the 1820s: *Enterprise*, built at Essex in 1829 (55′-4″ x 15′-10″ x 7′-1″); *Nautilus*, built in 1829, with a gammon knee head (58′-6″ x 14′-9″ x 6′-8″), had a figurehead when re-measured in 1851; *Ida*, built at Alna, Maine, in 1829 (58′-8″ x 16′-10″ x 7′-7″) are examples.

Newbury built large pinkies in the 1830s as well as Essex. The Newbury pinkies were *Palm*, built in 1832 (55′ x 15′-2½″ x 6′-7″); *Margaret*, built in 1837 (59′-11″ x 16′-3″ x 6′-8″); *Equater*, built in 1837 (62′-11″ x 16′-5″ x 6′-11″).

Large pinkies were built in Maine in the 1830s and 1840s: *Leader*, built at Ellsworth in 1843 (56′-2″½ x 16′-2½″ x 7′-1½″, 66-43/95 tons register) and *Porpoise*, built at Deer Isle in 1838, had a billet head (56′-9″ x 16′-1″ x 7′-9″, 61-74/95 tons register), are examples.

The pinky *Tiger*, noted as a poacher during the Canadian troubles, was built at Essex in 1830 (53′-6″ x 16′ x 7′, 51-73/95 tons register). The *Atlantic*, launched at Essex in 1834 (55′-6″ x 16′-1″ x 7′-1½″, 55-27/95 tons register), was also a poacher.

The beam dimensions given show that the old narrow model went slowly out of fashion in the 1820s—later in Newburyport and in Maine. However the differences in beam-length ratios were relatively small.

The peak in the registration of pinkies at Gloucester Custom House was in 1829, when sixty-four were registered in the district—Gloucester–Essex–Manchester–Newbury–Ipswich–Amesbury–Wells–Newburyport. The decline in the number of pinkies registered in the district was very rapid after that year and only eleven were registered in 1847, five in 1859, and two in 1868.

Plate 8 shows the lines of a pinky half-model that the private owner had obtained in eastern Maine. This half-model was made to deck level, the bulwarks were reconstructed from penciled dimensions on the model. No date or other identification marks could be seen on the model. The drawing shows a full-model pinky, having small deadrise amidships. The model was evidently on ½ inch to the foot scale and would produce a pinky 44′-9″ length on deck, 14′-4″ moulded beam, and 6′-3″ depth in hold. Such pinkies as this seem to have been popular in the Gulf of Maine cod fisheries. The date of the half-model can only be guessed, but the form and appearance of the

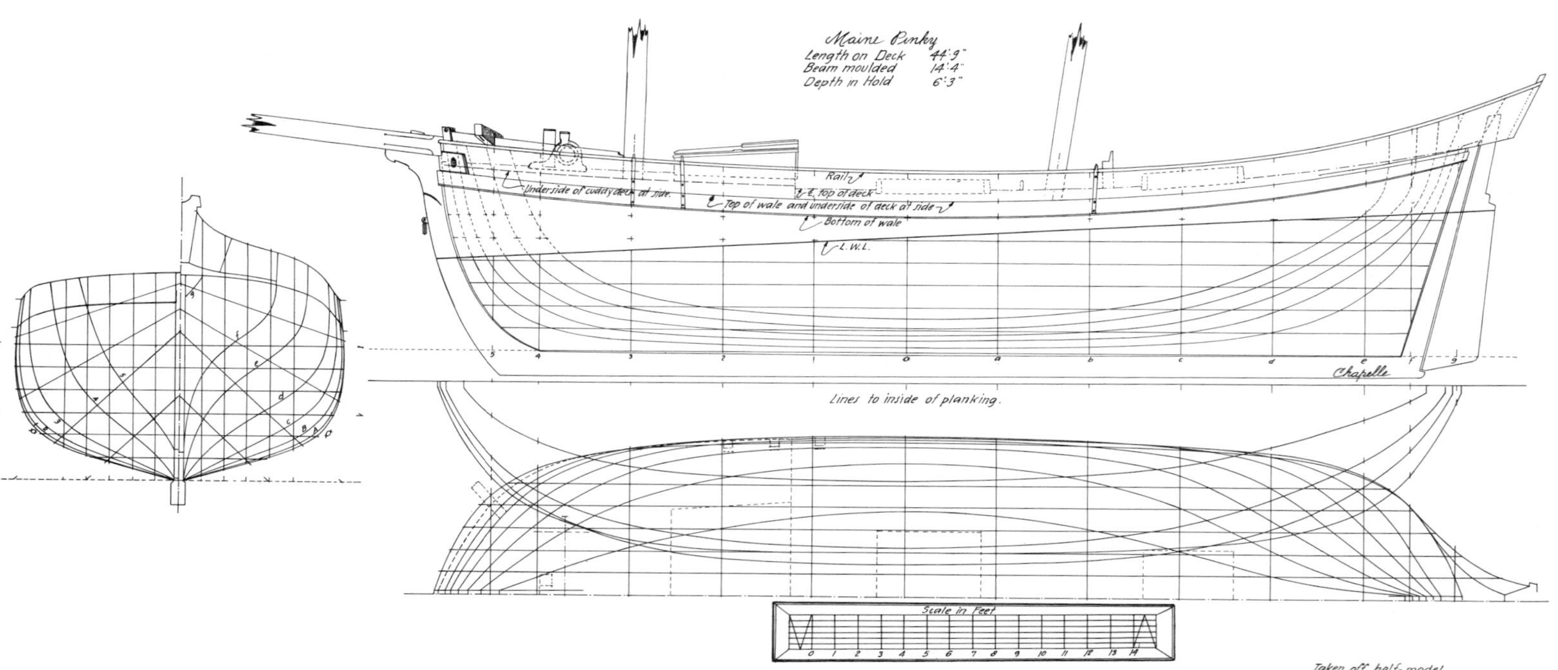
Maine Pinky
Length on Deck 44'9"
Beam moulded 14'4"
Depth in Hold 6'3"
Rail
℄ top of deck
Underside of cuddy deck at side
Top of wale and underside of deck at side
Bottom of wale
L.W.L.
Chapelle
Lines to inside of planking.
Scale in Feet
0 1 2 3 4 5 6 7 8 9 10 11 12 13 14
Taken off half-model

PLATE 8. Pinky, Maine, 1830s, half-model

half-model suggest a date somewhere in the 1830s. The model was well made and in good condition.

Plate 9 shows the pinky *Trenton,* built at Trenton, Maine, sometime about 1840. The half-model of this pinky is in the Smithsonian Collection and was donated by Gillman Hodgkins, Lamoine, Maine. The *Trenton* was built for the Gulf of Maine codfishery. The model is on a scale of ½ inch to the foot; it is a lift-model to the deck but with bulwarks added. The model was made to produce a pinky 48′-6″ long, Custom House measurement, 47′-7″ on deck, 13′7″ moulded beam, 14′ extreme beam, 6′-8″ depth of hold. The Custom House register of the *Trenton* has not been found.

This pinky was of the fast-carrier type, with a rather full entrance and a very fine run. She belonged to the old narrow, deep model with rather marked deadrise amidships. The deck layout shown is reconstructed from descriptions of pinkies in U.S. Fish Commission papers and markings on the half-model, formerly visible but now obliterated by well-intended refinishing and painting. It is a typical pinky deck arrangement, having a handspike windlass forward, with wood catheads fitted inside the bulwarks as in larger vessels. The hawse holes are in the prominent knightheads and hawse timbers which are shown in the model. A small trunk cabin was fitted at the break, extending forward to within a foot of the foremast; Lew Story believed such trunks were not employed in Essex pinkies but may have been used in Maine by 1840. On the starboard side, abreast the middle of the cabin trunk, is the wooden stack of the fire hearth which was plastered on the inside and fitted over a small scuttle. The stack could be unshipped and stowed below deck; the scuttle could be closed with a cover and a canvas coat, lashed down to make a watertight closing. A slide hatch is shown on the trunk—this type of companionway hatch seems to have been coming into rather general use in the 1840s, but the two-leaf, hinged, folding hatches of early times did not entirely disappear until well into the 1850s.

The fish hatches, main and after, were often small on fishing vessels. However, if the owners of a pinky intended to do a little freighting, larger hatches would be constructed. Pinkies owned in small ports in Maine were often required to carry freight, as were fishing schooners, even until coastal steamers came into service.

The use of horses on pinkies was sometimes confined to fore and main sheets—the jib would then have double sheets. However some pinkies had a wooden horse for the jib sheet, as in the square-stern schooners. In any case, a wooden horse was employed for the mainsheet which, as mentioned before, had an iron rod secured to its underside to take care of the wear and chafe caused by the traveler ring. Belaying pins were placed in holes in wooden horses, to serve as stops, controlling the length of travel of the lower sheet block. The jib horse was of similar description. The foresail

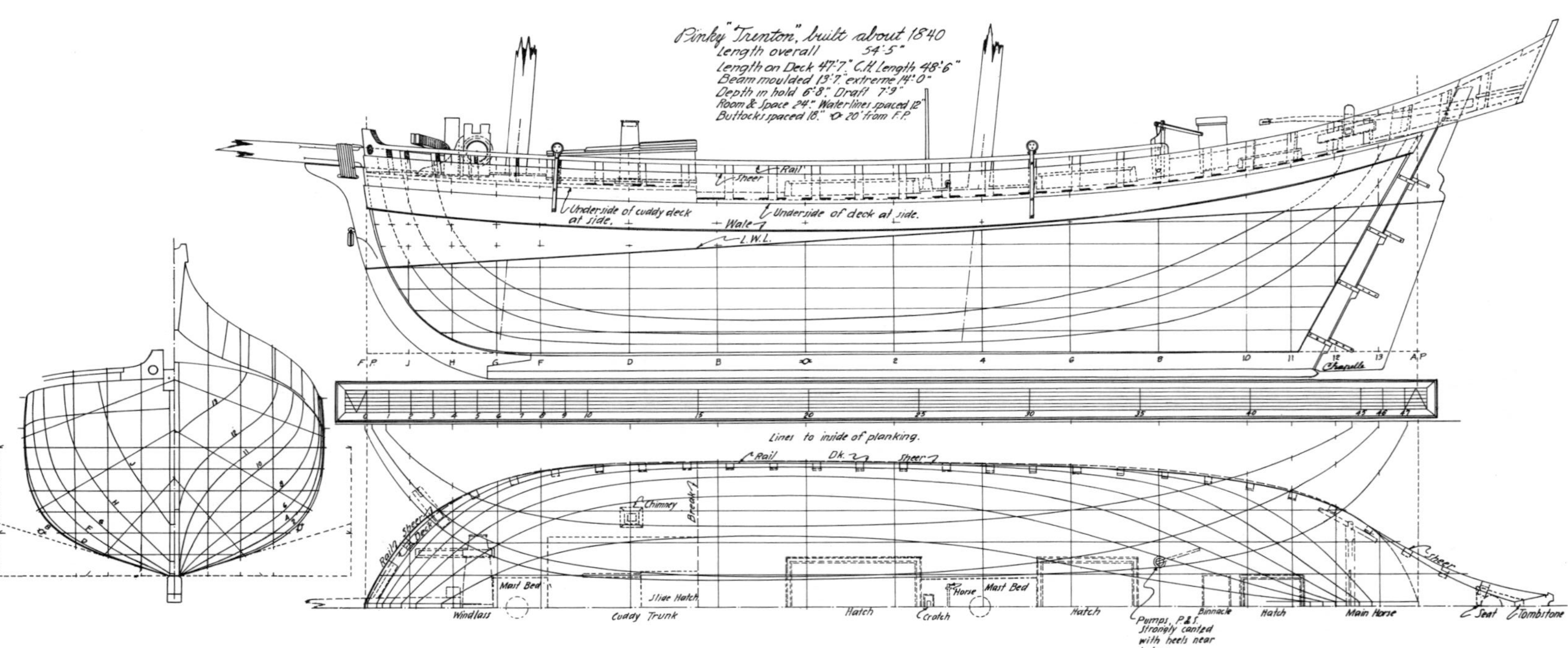
Pinky "Trenton," built about 1840
Length overall 54'5"
Length on Deck 47'7" C.H. Length 48'6"
Beam moulded 13'7" extreme 14'0"
Depth in hold 6'8" Draft 7'9"
Room & Space 24" Waterlines spaced 12"
Buttocks spaced 18" 20' from F.P.
Rail
Sheer
Underside of cuddy deck at side.
Wale
Underside of deck at side.
L.W.L.
F.P.
A.P.
Chapelle
Lines to inside of planking.
Rail
Dk.
Sheer
Chimney
Break
Mast Bed
Slide Hatch
Horse
Mast Bed
Binnacle
Windlass
Cuddy Trunk
Hatch
Crotch
Hatch
Pumps, P.& S. Strongly canted with heels near kelson.
Hatch
Main Horse
Seat
Tombstone

PLATE 9. *Trenton*, Maine pinky, 1840, half-model

horse, however, seems to have been commonly made of two shouldered eye-bolts driven through deck and a beam, with a long bolt or rod through the eyes athwartships, with ends upset or keyed.

The wooden pump barrels were either just abaft the mainmast, or just abaft the after fish hatch, the heels of the pumps close to the keelson, and raking outboard so that the pumpheads were sometimes well apart. Wooden pump barrels, like wooden windlasses, were retained until almost the end of the nineteenth century. The reason for this seems to have been that these wooden fittings would not be affected by freezing. Attempts to introduce iron windlasses failed, old fishermen claimed, because these windlasses broke when they were pounded with mallets to free them of ice prior to getting up anchors on the banks. New England fishing schooners retained the wooden windlass until the end of their construction.

In the *Trenton* the lazerette hatch or scuttle was under the tiller and could serve as the helmsman's standing room, wtih the binnacle just forward of it and the mainsheet horse abaft it. Though the *Trenton* was large for the retention of a standing room, it would be useful in winter as a footwell.

The pink-stern varied in width; some pinkies had very narrow tombstones, others had wide ones. The framing was sawn timber, with planking thin enough to allow the bending of the bulwark plank that this type of stern required. Sometimes the pink-stern was fitted to serve as a "head," or toilet seat having a seat and cover. The top of the tombstone also served as a mainboom crotch as well as a convenient place to dry nets or other fishing gear. The pink-stern seems to have been retained chiefly because it gave protection to the helmsman when running in a heavy sea. The original reason for the stern—to protect the rudder in crowded slips—was no longer valid when wharves and slips became more numerous as the fishing ports expanded and overcrowding became rare.

Plate 10 is a composite drawing, made by using the lines of a pinky lift-model in the possession of the Maine Historical Society, Portland, Maine, and the details of the pinky *Maine* photographed and measured by the late Albert Cook Church at Gloucester in 1910. The date and identity of the half-model are not recorded but it was probably made between 1830 and 1840. It was for a vessel 48′-5″ registered length, 13′-3½″ moulded beam, 13′-7″, 6′-1″ depth in hold, and 7′-6″ draft at post. The *Maine* was built at Essex in 1845; her register dimensions were 46.4′ x 13.7′ x 6.6′, 24.51 gross tons, new measurement.

It will be seen that the "modernization" of a pinky would readily be very limited, with most changes confined to improved fittings. Plate 10 serves as an illustration of this. Most of the large New England pinkies, over 40 feet register length, were no longer regularly employed in the fisheries by 1880. Instead the old pinkies were engaged in short-haul coastal freighting

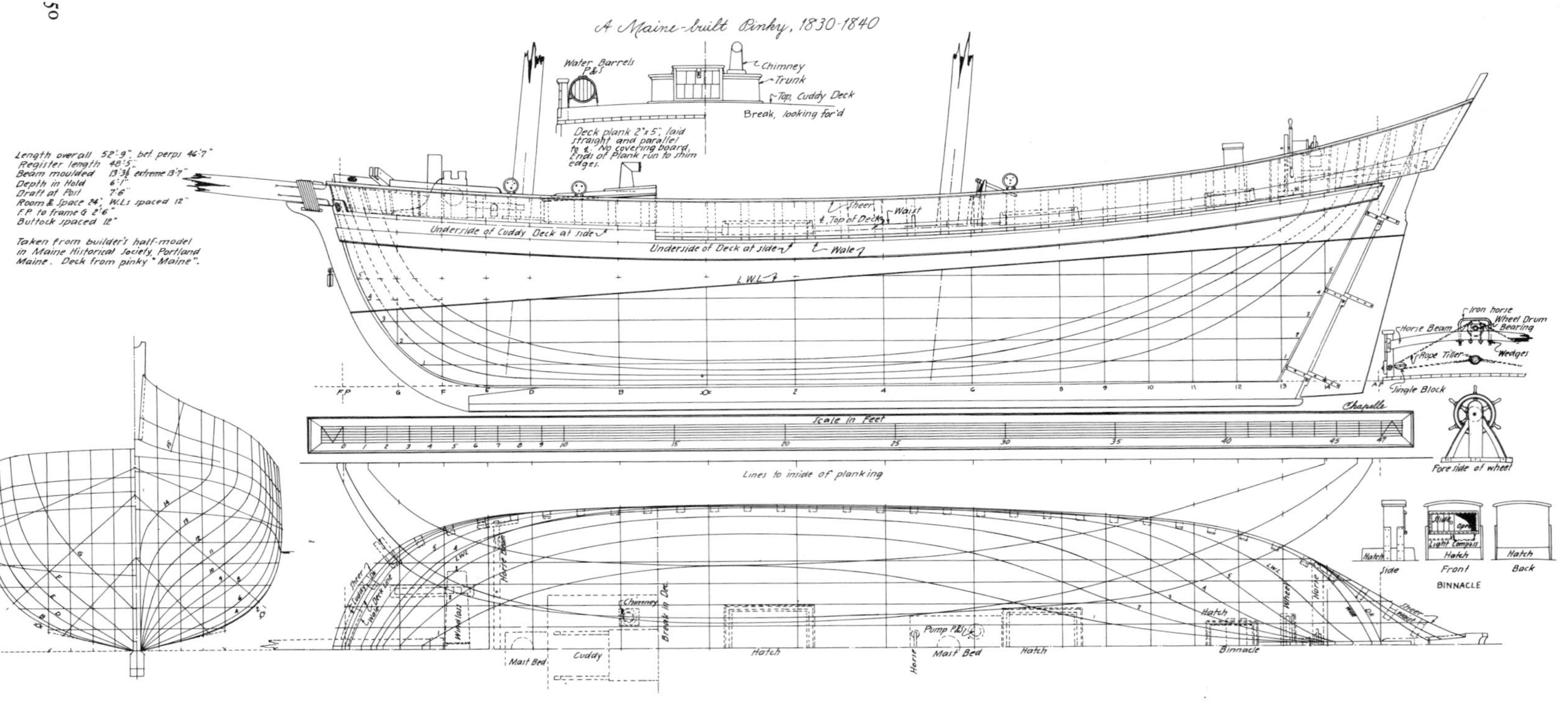
A Maine-built Pinky, 1830-1840
Length overall 52'-9", bet. perps 46'-7"
Register length 48'-5"
Beam moulded 13'-3½" extreme 13'-7"
Depth in Hold 6'-1"
Draft at Post 7'-6"
Room & Space 24", W.Ls spaced 12"
F.P. to frame G 2'-6"
Buttock spaced 12"
Taken from builder's half-model in Maine Historical Society, Portland Maine. Deck from pinky "Maine".
Water Barrels P&S
Chimney
Trunk
Top, Cuddy Deck
Break, looking for'd
Deck plank 2"x5", laid straight and parallel to ℄. No covering board, Ends of Plank run to shim edges.
Sheer
℄ Top of Deck
Waist
Underside of Cuddy Deck at side
Underside of Deck at side
Wale
L.W.L.
Horse Beam
Iron horse
Wheel Drum Bearing
Rope Tiller
Wedges
Single Block
Chapelle
Scale in Feet
Fore side of wheel
Lines to inside of planking
Hatch
Side
Front
Back
BINNACLE
Chimney
Break in Dec.
Windlass
Mast Bed
Cuddy
Hatch
Horse
Pump P&S
Mast Bed
Hatch
Binnacle
Wheel
Horse

PLATE 10. Pinky, Maine, 1830–1840, half-model

and most of the modifications were related to their new employment.

The modifications usually included the conversion or replacement of the old wooden handspike windlass with the pump-brake (or "Armstrong Patent" of coastal sailors) windlass so that fewer hands were required to handle the ground tackle. In many pinkies the construction of a cabin trunk on the raised deck made the forecastle more comfortable. The use of a slide on the companionway hatch of the trunk developed in the 1840s in fishing schooners, but both trunk and slide had been used as early as about 1785 in some American vessels. The old folding top and hinged companionway hatch had "cupboard doors" and these were retained with sliding covers until about 1880. Double drop-doors then replaced them, being less liable to damage and more watertight.

Plate 11 shows the lines of a clipper pinky half-model from which at least three pinkies were built at Port Maitland, Nova Scotia, by Samuel Perry, sometime between 1850 and 1860. Two of the pinkies built on this half-model can be identified—*Flash* and *Orno*. The lines show a wide pinky, 38′-7″ long on deck (moulded), 12′-8″ moulded beam, and 5′-3¾″ depth in hold. In form, the model has a short, moderately sharp, convex entrance and a long, fine run, with rather marked deadrise amidships and a slight hollow in the floor. For her dimensions and type she had less displacement than usual. Such a vessel had great power to carry sail, a necessary characteristic in the waters for which the model was intended—the Bay of Fundy, with its strong tidal currents. These pinkies were first employed around Wedgeport and Yarmouth, Nova Scotia, in the local fisheries, but after the sardine canneries became established some of the type became carriers between the traps and the packing houses.

Plate 12 shows the lines of a half-model of a larger Canadian pinky, also built at Port Maitland, or Maitland as it was later known, in 1875 by Josiah Ellis. This pinky was designed as a sardine carrier but because of her good sailing qualities she was employed as a packet, sailing between Boston, Massachusetts, and St. John, New Brunswick, for a few years. The half-model was the property of the late Dr. C. K. Stillman and now is in the Mystic Marine Museum. This model was of the hawk's-nest type and in good condition.

The pinky built on this model was the *Maitland* and she measured 55′-2″ moulded length on deck, 18′-4″ moulded beam, and 6′-7½″ moulded depth, rabbet to underside of deck at side.

In model this pinky was a fast carrier, having a full midsection with slight rise of floor, rather sharp, but short, convex entrance with marked hollow in the level lines just abaft the stem rabbet, below the load line. The run was long and fine, with marked hollow in the level lines forward of the stern-

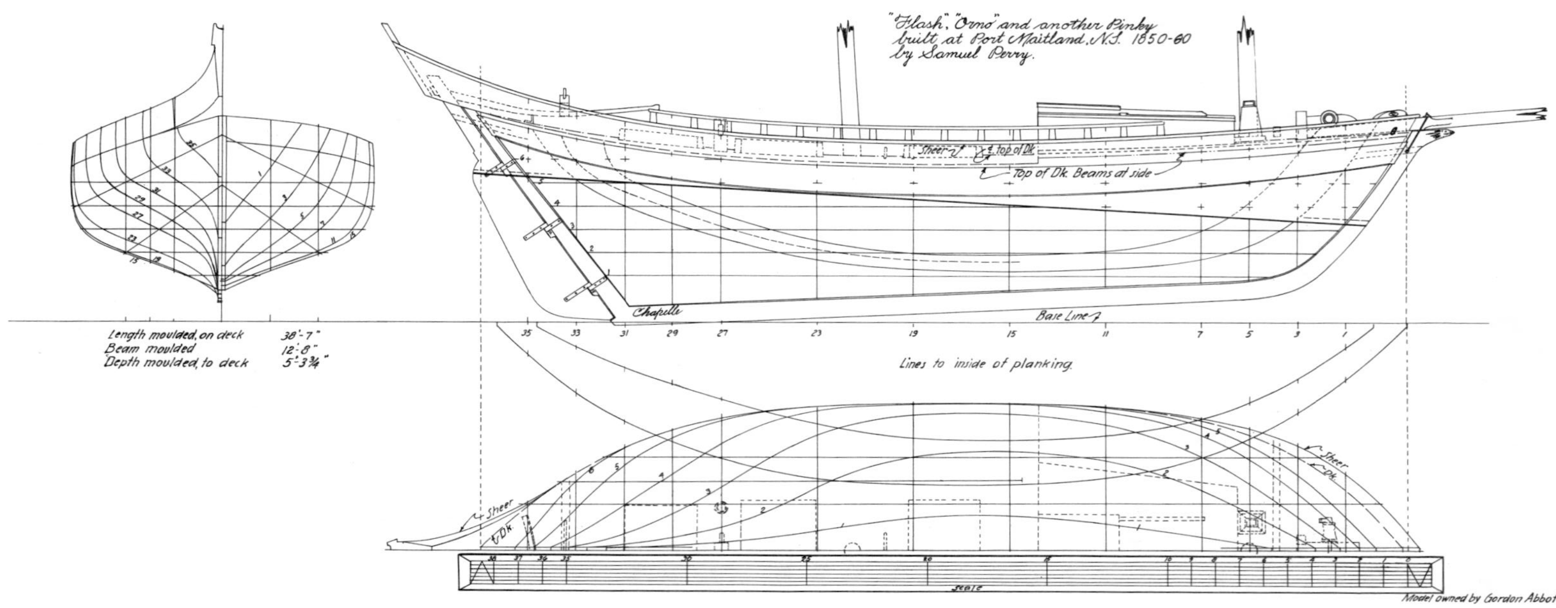
"Flash", "Orno" and another Pinky
built at Port Maitland, N.S. 1850-60
by Samuel Perry.
Sheer
top of Dk.
Top of Dk. Beams at side
Base Line
Chapelle
Length moulded, on deck 38'-7"
Beam moulded 12'-8"
Depth moulded, to deck 5'-3¾"
Lines to inside of planking.
Sheer
Dk.
scale
Model owned by Gordon Abbot.

PLATE 11. Pinky, Nova Scotia, 1850–1860, half-model

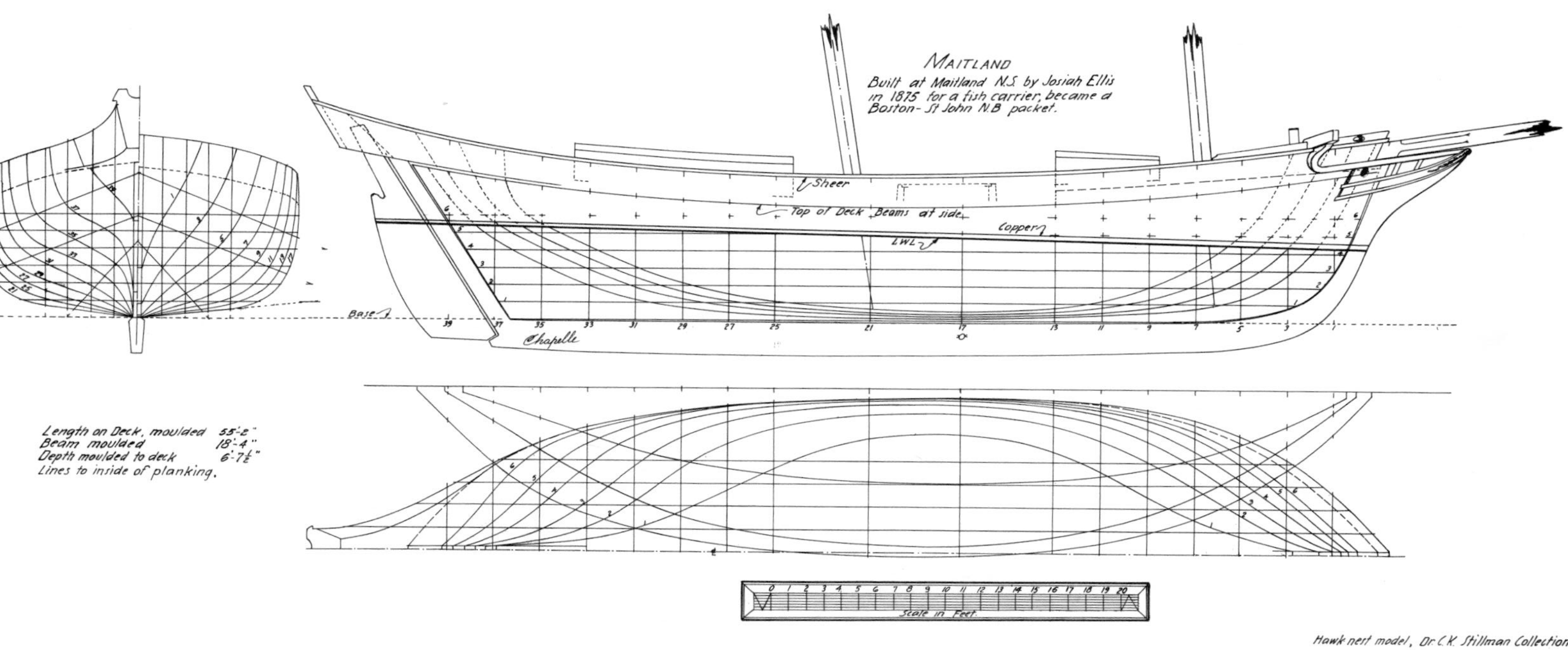

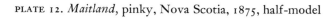

MAITLAND
Built at Maitland N.S. by Josiah Ellis in 1875 for a fish carrier, became a Boston-St John N.B. packet.
Sheer
Top of Deck Beams at side
Copper
LWL
Base
Chapelle
Length on Deck, moulded 55'-2"
Beam moulded 18'-4"
Depth moulded to deck 6'-7½"
Lines to inside of planking.
Scale in Feet
Hawk-nest model, Dr. C.K. Stillman Collection

PLATE 12. *Maitland*, pinky, Nova Scotia, 1875, half-model

post. The *Maitland* was said to have sailed very fast, particularly so to windward and reaching.

Port Maitland, at the head of Minas Basin, Bay of Fundy, was once a very active shipbuilding center. This town was on the eastern side near the head, of Minas Basin. It became a deserted village after shipbuilding ended.

Plates 13, 14, and 15 are the plans of the pinky *Dove*, built at the now extinct village of Preaux, on the west side of Minas Basin, by Sylvester S. Baltzer in 1875. Modeled for fishing, this pinky was employed as a pilot boat at Eastport and was noted for her sailing qualities. The plans were drawn from the builder's lift half-model and the construction and sail plans owned by his son, an accomplished boat builder who intended to build a duplicate of the *Dove* but died before he could begin construction.

The *Dove* measured 42′-11″, moulded length, on deck, 13′ moulded beam, 6′-¼″ moulded depth, rabbet to underside of deck at side, and drew 6′-3″ at post. She carried about 1100 square feet of sail in her three lowers.

This pinky had much rake in stem and stern posts and marked drag to the keel. Her entrance was long, convex, and moderately sharp. The run was also long and easy, with no straight in the quarterbeam buttock, yet with a small angle at its intersection with the load line. Her midsection showed very rising floor with much hollow just above the keel rabbet. The bilge was marked, and topside slightly flaring. In this model the midsection is raking so that each lift line has its greatest beam abaft that of the one below it in the half-breadth plan. This allowed the maximum effective length of entrance and run, and was common in fast schooners built after the 1850s.

The *Dove* was unusually yacht-like for a working pinky. A number of pinkies were built at Eastport and Lubec, Maine, in the 1870s. These had much deadrise, rake in the ends, and drag to the keel. They were soon replaced by double-ended sloops having nearly the same model of hull.

The technical evolution of the pinky has been traced, so far as available information permits, and the evolution of the North Atlantic fishing schooners can now be considered.

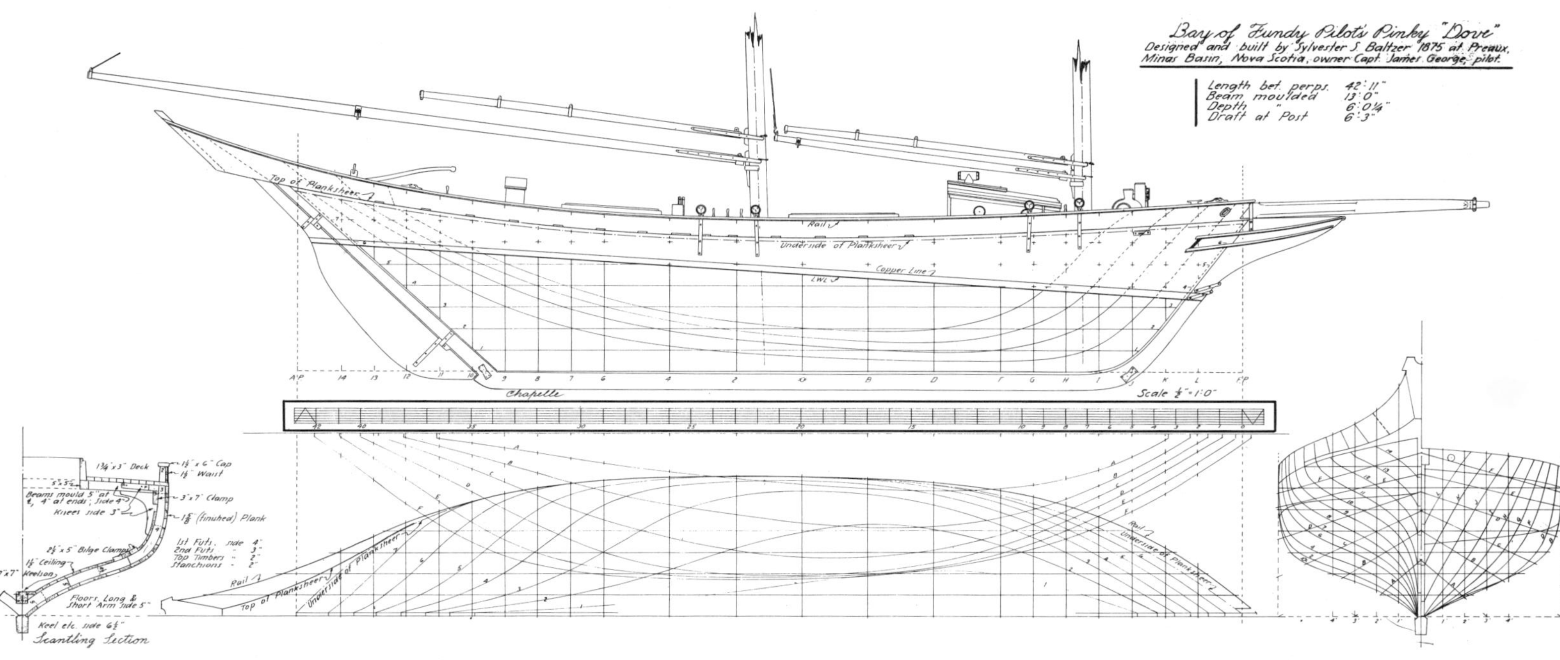
Bay of Fundy Pilot's Pinky "Dove"
Designed and built by Sylvester S Baltzer 1875 at Preaux, Minas Basin, Nova Scotia, owner Capt. James George, pilot.
Length bet. perps. 42' 11"
Beam moulded 13' 0"
Depth " 6' 0¼"
Draft at Post 6' 3"
Top of Planksheer
Rail
Underside of Planksheer
Copper Line
LWL
Chapelle
Scale ½" = 1' 0"
Underside of Planksheer
Top of Planksheer
Rail
1¾" x 3" Deck
1½" x 6" Cap
1½" Waist
5" x 5½"
Beams mould 5" at ℄, 4" at ends; side 4"
3" x 7" Clamp
Knees side 3"
1⅝" (finished) Plank
1st Futs. side 4"
2nd Futs " 3"
Top Timbers " 2"
Stanchions " 2"
2½" x 5" Bilge Clamps
1½" Ceiling
7" x 7" Keelson
Floors, Long & Short Arm side 5"
Keel etc. side 6½"
Scantling Section

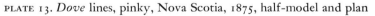

PLATE 13. *Dove* lines, pinky, Nova Scotia, 1875, half-model and plan

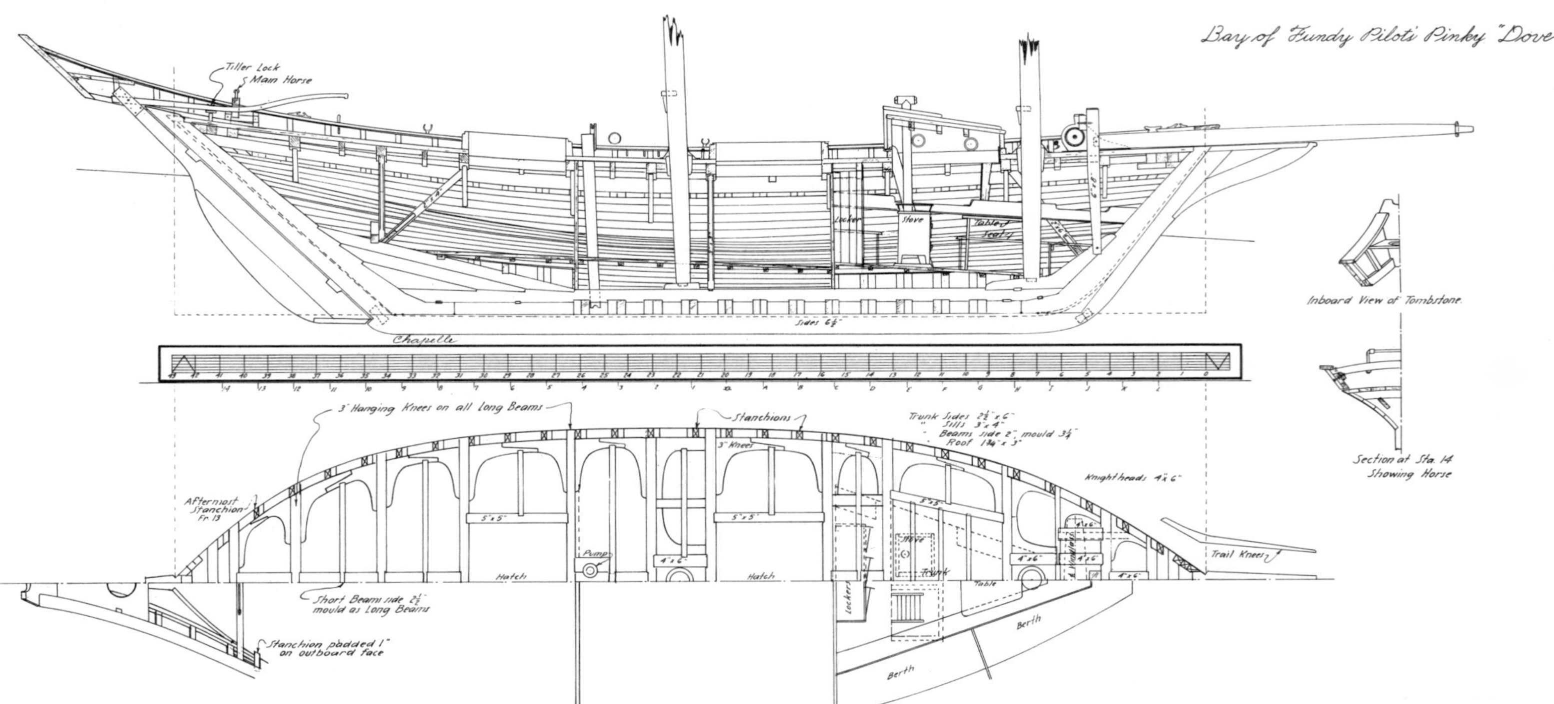
Bay of Fundy Pilots' Pinky "Dove"
Tiller Lock
Main Horse
Locker
Stove
Table & Seat
Sides 6½"
Chapelle
Inboard View of Tombstone
Section at Sta. 14 Showing Horse
3" Hanging Knees on all Long Beams
Stanchions
3" Knees
Trunk Sides 2½" x 6"
" Sills 3" x 4"
" Beams side 2", mould 3¼"
" Roof 1¾" x 3"
Knightheads 4" x 6"
Aftermost Stanchion Fr. 13
5" x 5"
Pump
Hatch
Trunk
Table
Lockers
Berth
Trail Knees
Short Beams side 2½" mould as Long Beams
Stanchion padded 1" on outboard face

PLATE 14. *Dove* construction, Nova Scotia, 1875, builder's plan

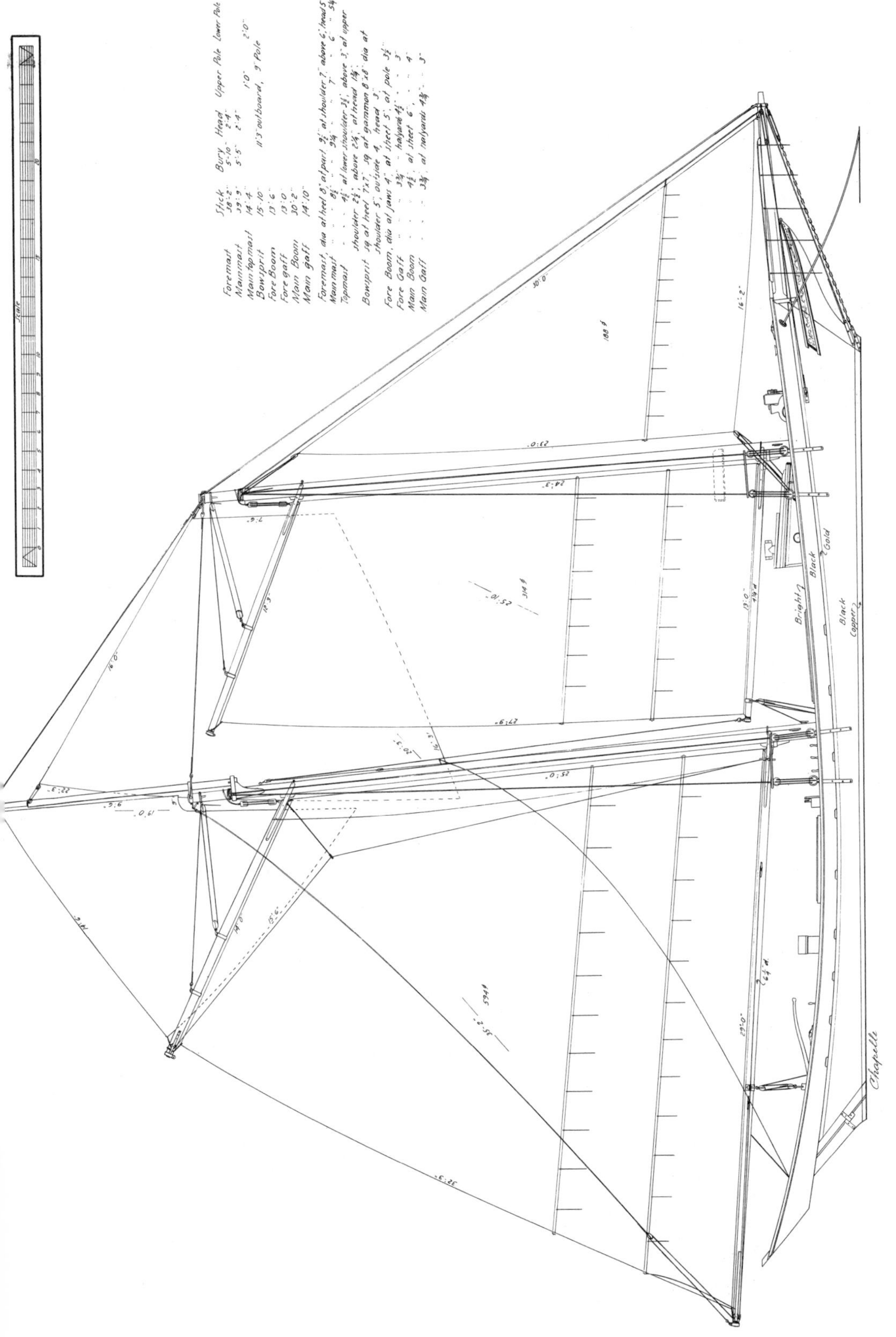
Scale
Stick Bury Head Upper Pole Lower Pole
Foremast 38'-2" 5-10" 2'4"
Mainmast 39'9" 5'5" 2'4"
Main top mast 14'4" 1'0" 2'0"
Bowsprit 15-10" 11'3" outboard, 9" Pole
Fore Boom 13'6"
Fore gaff 13'0"
Main Boom 30'2"
Main gaff 14'10"
Foremast, dia at heel 8", at part 9½" at shoulder 7" above 6", head 5
Main mast " " " 8½" " " 9¼" " " 7" " 6" " 5¼
Topmast " " " 4½" at lower shoulder 3½", above 3", at upper shoulder 2½", above 2¼", at head 1¾".
Bowsprit sq at heel 7"x7", sq at gammon 8"x8" dia at shoulder 5", outside 4, head 3".
Fore Boom, dia at jaws 4", at sheet 5", at pole 3½"
Fore Gaff " " " 3¾" " halyards 4½" " " 3"
Main Boom " " " 4½", at sheet 6", " " 4"
Main Gaff " " " 3¾", at halyards 4¾" " " 3"
Bright
Black
Gold
Black
Copper
Chapelle

PLATE 15. *Dove* sail plan, Nova Scotia, 1875, builder's plan

Chapter Two

1830–1850

The 1830s was a period of great expansion in the New England fisheries. Though the West Indian salt-fish market had been lost to the Canadian fishermen, as had the European trade in dried, pickled, and smoked fish, the home consumption of these products was increasing by leaps and bounds. The opening of the Erie Canal and the rapid construction of railroads from New England to the West and South during the 1830s and '40s, opened vast areas inland for the marketing of dried, salt, and smoked fish. Also, the growth of towns and cities along the coast was gradually developing profitable markets for fresh fish which, in the 1840s, received great impetus when the icing of fish in transit became possible.

This steadily increasing demand for fish led to a sharp increase in the building of fishing vessels. Early in the 1830s the demand for fresh fish increased to a level that could not be met by the existing small-boat inshore fisheries. Large vessels then entered the fresh fisheries; these were called "market fishermen," and they ranged far to sea. This lengthened the "trip," of course, and the preservation of fresh fish in transit became an immediate problem.

To meet this problem, the shipbuilders introduced the "smack," or "well boat." The smack had been used in the small-boat shore fisheries since colonial times but now schooner smacks 50 to 60 feet in length were built, having large wells, about 16 feet long, 12 feet wide, and 4′-6″ deep, in a 60′-0″ schooner. Such vessels were considered to be of adequate capacity for trips to Georges Bank in the 1830s. The most numerous vessels on Georges Bank were those making salt-fish trips, however.

Fishing began on Georges Bank in 1831. In the first two or three years vessels did not anchor on the Georges for fear of the vessel being drawn under by the fast-moving tides. The vessels drifted, using handlines. This belief did not last long and soon numerous vessels were anchoring on Georges and fishing there; quite a few of these were smacks. There appears to be no way in which all the schooner smacks can be identified, but from various sources the dimensions of five smacks can be established, and the names and dimensions of five others given.

These smacks were all built in Essex:

One, 58′-4″ x 16′-8″ x 6′-9″	builder's name not legible, built in 1831
One, 55′-6″ x 16′-8″ x 7′	built by Moses Burnham in 1832
One, 54′ x 16′-7″ x 7′	built by Eli F. Burnham in 1832
One, 60′-3″ x 16′-7″ x 6′-4½″	built by Eli F. Burnham in 1832
One, 56′ x 16′-3″ x 6′-8½″	built by Daniel A. Burnham in 1837
Glide, 59′-8″ x 17′-2″ x 7′-2″	built by Willard R. Burnham in 1836
Virgin, 57′ x 16′-11″ x 7′-4½″	built by Aaron Burnham II in 1837
Enchantress, 57′-4″ x 16′-9″ x 71′-1″	built by Aaron Burnham II in 1837
Eli, 55′-4″ x 16′-8″ x 6′-10″	built by Eli F. Burnham in 1837
Blooming Youth, 60′-4″ x 16′-10″ x 6′-11″	built by Aaron Burnham II in 1839

The *Glide* was one of the earliest vessels built at Essex from a lift half-model. Prior to about 1835 fishing schooners were built from a hawk's-nest half-model, but plans were used before 1800 apparently, in the vicinity of Cape Ann, but had been replaced by hawk's-nest models.

The *Glide* is shown in Plate 16. The dimensions just listed were register, the plan shows those scaled from the half-models that was given to the U.S. Fish Commission by the son of the builder.

This schooner was full-ended, the entrance short and convex, and the run short and full. The keel was straight with some drag, the stem rabbet was curved and slightly raking, and the sternpost had small rake; the stern was round tuck, upper-and-lower transoms, square stern. There was marked dead flat. The midsection was formed with slightly rising short straight floor, full-rounded slack bilge, and slightly flaring straight topside.

The well-room was between fore and main masts. It was rectangular in plan and profile, up to the load waterline. Above this it was in the form of a truncate, four-sided pyramid reaching up to the underside of the main hatch carlin. The hatch was fitted only with gratings. Inside the lower well there was no ceiling plank, 1½ inch diameter holes were bored in the bottom planking, closely spaced, between the floors and futtocks. Because of the displacement of the well, a smack needed little more than some trim ballast; stone or iron ore stowed under the floor or sole of the after holds.

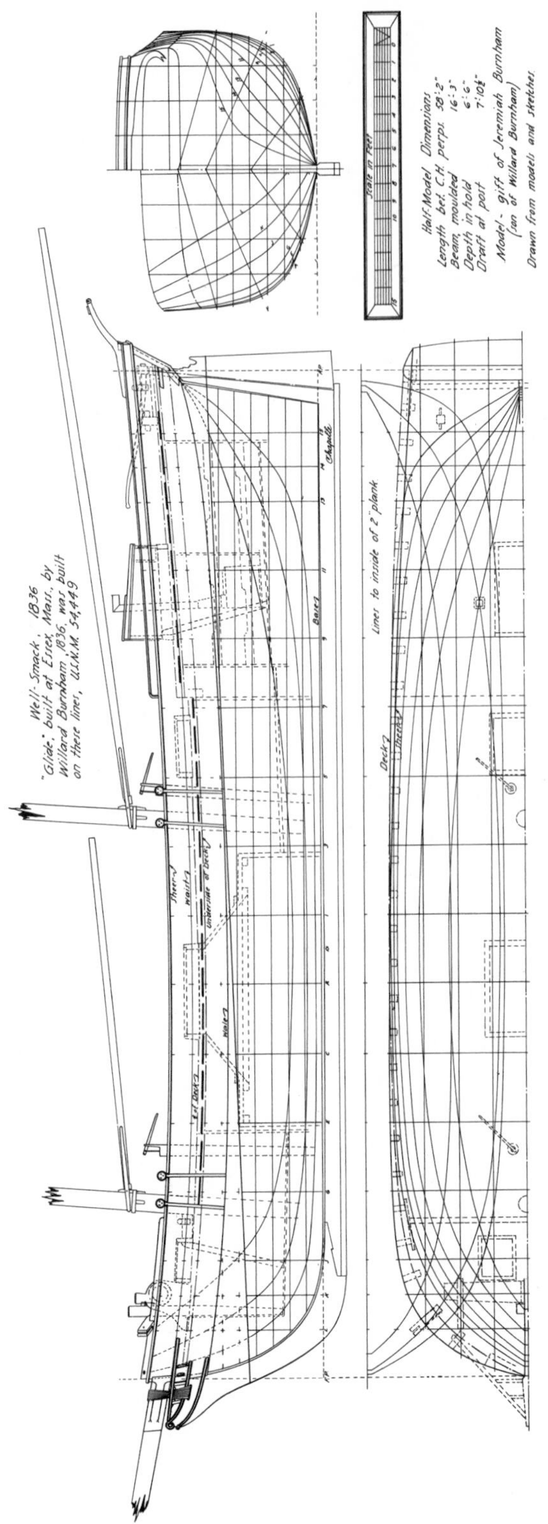
Well-Smack, 1836
"Glide", built at Essex, Mass., by Willard Burnham, 1836, was built on these lines, U.S.N.M. 54,449
Half-Model Dimensions
Length bet. C.H. perps. 58'-2"
Beam, moulded 16'-3"
Depth in hold 6'-6"
Draft at post 7'-10⅜"
Model - gift of Jeremiah Burnham (son of Willard Burnham)
Drawn from models and sketches.
Scale in Feet
Lines to inside of 2" plank
Chapelle

PLATE 16. *Glide*, smack, 1836, half-model

Forward of the well, cut off from it by a bulkhead, was a small forecastle berthing four men when fitted. The forecastle was entered through a small hatch on deck, just abaft the windlass, to starboard of the hull center line. No hearth or stove was fitted in the forecastle, according to the drawings in Goode.* Between the well and foremast there were a pair of wooden pumps. Abaft the well was the mainmast, a pair of wooden pumps were next, then came the after hold with a rather small hatch to enter it. The break in the deck was abaft this hatch, rising to a low quarterdeck 9 to 12 inches high. On the quarterdeck was a large companionway opening into the cabin below. The cabin berthed eight men. There was no cabin trunk. There was a bulkhead between after hold and cabin.

The smacks had the same rig as the pinkies, a large jib, gaff-and-boom foresail, gaff-and-boom mainsail; the rig was rather small for the size of the hull.

The smacks carried a yawl boat on wooden stern davits; this was for general service and not utilized in a fishing operation. These yawls were usually about 15 feet long, 5′-6″ beam, and 2′-3″ deep amidships.

The most numerous type of fishing schooners were those built for the salt fisheries, known as "bankers." These were commonly employed on the North Atlantic fishing grounds, that is to say Georges, Browns, LaHave, Sable, and Banquereau, also on Orphan, Bradelle, and Magdalen. Having salt on board, these vessels proceeded to the selected bank and anchored, cleaning and salting as the catch was brought aboard. The fish were caught on handlines and the vessels remained on the banks until filled.

Plate 17 shows a banker of the 1830s. It will be immediately seen that the model of this banker was very much like that of the *Glide* in both form and proportions, and of approximately the same range in size. The half-model of this banker is now in the U.S. Museum of History and Technology, Smithsonian Institution, USNM 54427, the gift of Captain Joseph W. Collins to the U.S. Fish Commission.

The model showed a vessel having a straight keel of moderate drag, a slightly raking sternpost, a round tuck, upper-and-lower transoms giving a wide square stern, the stem rabbet curved and of moderate rake, fitted with a short, heavy-appearing cutwater and head. The midsection was formed with short, straight rising floor, a full, round, rather slack bilge, with some tumble home in the topside. The entrance was short, full, and convex, the run was short and quite full. The body was carried well fore-and-aft. In the model the deck lift showed bulwarks 32 inches high, an unusual height.

* George Brown Goode, *The Fisheries and Fishery Industries of the United States.* Prepared through the cooperation of the commissioner of fisheries and the superintendent of the tenth census, Washington, D.C. Government Printing Office, 1884–1887, 2 vols. and atlas.

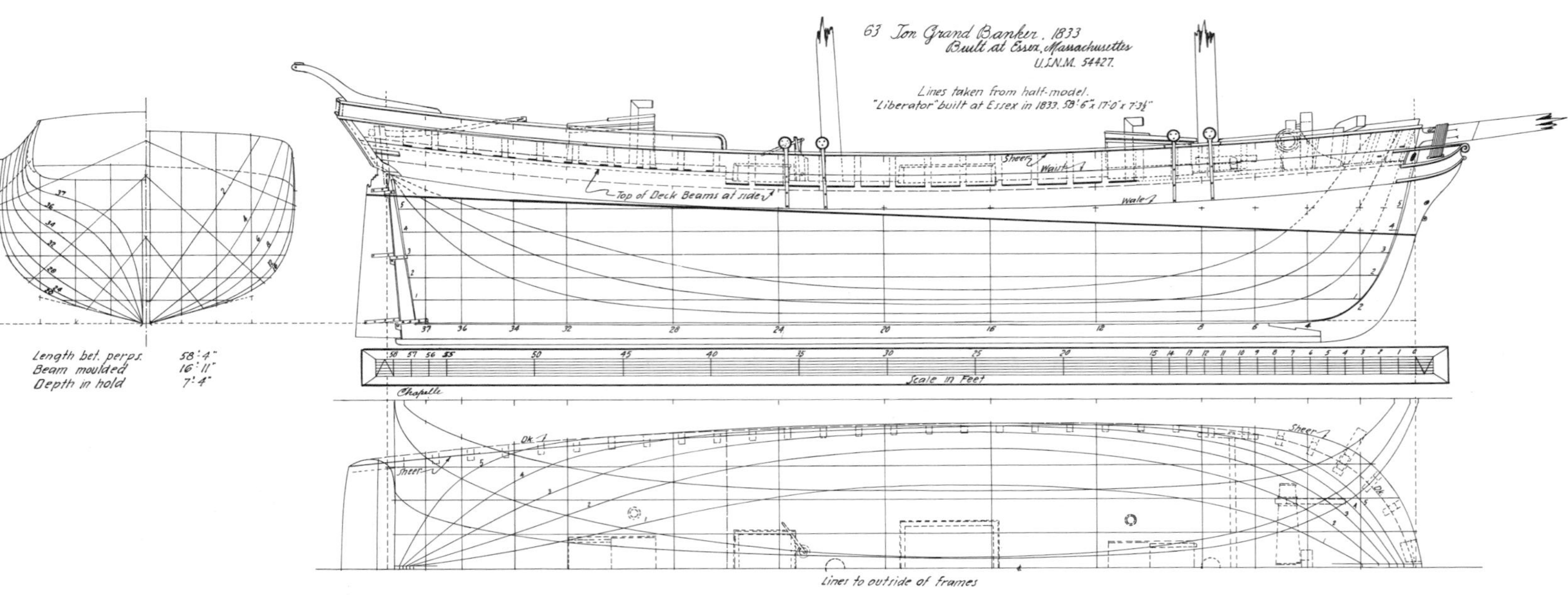
63 Ton Grand Banker, 1833
Built at Essex, Massachusetts
U.S.N.M. 54427.
Lines taken from half-model.
"Liberator" built at Essex in 1833. 58'6" x 17'0" x 7'3½"
Top of Deck Beams at side
Sheer
Waist
Wale
Scale in Feet
Chapelle
Length bet. perps. 58'4"
Beam moulded 16'11"
Depth in hold 7'4"
Lines to outside of frames

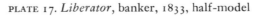

PLATE 17. *Liberator*, banker, 1833, half-model

This would produce a shallow hold. Markings on the model seem to indicate the deck had been raised so that the bulwarks, as built, were 24 inches high. Her register dimensions, scaled from the model and plan, were 58′-4″ x 16′-11″ x 7′-4″. The half-model has been identified as the *Liberator*, built at Essex in 1833, register dimensions 58′-6″ x 17′-0″ x 7′-3½″.

These vessels were built of white oak and white pine, in a very substantial manner. When no longer considered suitable for the fisheries many of these schooners were placed in the Down East coasting trade. With much of their structure impregnated with the salt brine of their fish cargoes many of the bankers had very long lives in spite of considerable neglect in their later years.

The deck arrangement shown was nearly standard: log windlass forward, with the wooden jib sheet horse just forward of the foremast. Abaft this was the forecastle companionway, with iron chimney on the starboard side of it, as a rule. Amidships was the main hatch, next abaft was the mainmast with two wooden pumps just aft of it. Next was the after hatch, then a 9- to 10-inch break in the deck up to quarterdeck, on which there was a cabin companionway with chimney of the cabin stove to port (or starboard). Fishing schooners of the 1830s steered with a long oak tiller. Some of the companionways to the cabin faced forward, others aft. In the former case, the binnacle was in the after end of the companionway, in the latter case the binnacle was portable, lashed to ringbolts on deck just forward of the fore end of the tiller.

An examination of the Gloucester Custom House registers showed that the *Glide* and *Liberator* were in the common range of size and that little variation in size took place in the 1830s. There seems to have been no economic reason for building many vessels for the fisheries of over 65 feet in length during this period.

The limited number of half-models of fishing schooners that can be dated earlier than 1840—four, in the Museum of History and Technology, Smithsonial Institution—would be insufficient to allow technical comment were it not for the fact that all four are of the same general model and basic design and also that some other models that can be dated a little later carry the family resemblance along for nearly five years, or until the changes in model began to appear, that will be described.

The reasons for the introduction of improved models are very difficult to assess because of the lack of adequate documentary or other evidence. Hence there must be an aura of speculation in any discussion of these matters. One reason may have been that the periods of prosperity caused by rapidly growing markets made it possible to build more expensive vessels. There were also changes in methods of handling fish that not only increased production but also produced obsolescence in both the model and the size of some fishing schooners.

Captain Joseph W. Collins, writing in the Gloucester *Advertiser*, April 14, 1882, and in government publications, made invidious comments on the old bankers and smacks of the 1830s and early '40s. He stated, in effect, that these schooners were very slow sailers—more suited to drifting than sailing—and not weatherly. In addition, their lack of depth and, in fact, their general form, made them liable to being knocked down and swamped in a gale. Collins compared them very unfavorably with the deep-draft pinkies. Nevertheless the old bankers and some smacks remained in the fisheries well into the 1840s.

The inability of the 1830 bankers to work to windward in heavy weather was the cause of many losses of vessels and lives. If they went adrift when anchored on the windward side of the Georges, for example, or were embayed in Chaleur Bay on the north shore of Prince Edward Island, for another example, many could not work clear in a gale and were soon in breaking seas on the shoals. Here they were out of control and were soon knocked down and swamped, or grounding, they broke up.

While all of these were practical objections to the type, none of them were really valid reasons for discarding the old model, for the safety of fishermen and vessel property were not always prime considerations in the improvement of vessels, the brutal facts being that the men lost cost the shipowner nothing, and insurance could take care of the loss of vessel property. What then, was the most effective influence in the creation of improved vessels in the fisheries in the 1840s? The answer was the use of ice!

The use of ice for preservation of food on a commercial basis had been well established in New England by Frederic Tudor, the "Ice King," and his associates, in the 1820s. It was not until another fifteen or more years had passed that attention was given to the use of ice to preserve fish caught and cleaned aboard vessels on the fishing grounds. By this time icehouses had been built in Boston and Gloucester and the possibilities of fresh fish, preserved in transit, then became recognized.

Though a few smacks were built between 1840 and 1845, their day had passed. By 1850 vessels were building intended for the use of the iced catch. No longer were slow-sailing schooners desirable in any of the fisheries, except for the distant banks, such as the Gulf of St. Lawrence and Labrador or the Grand Banks of Newfoundland. Even here speed was no handicap in a fishing schooner, but a lack of capacity was in a banker. Hence this class of fishing schooner began to be built larger as the mid-century passed. With the appearance of iced fish the demand for it soon began to absorb much of the fisheries catch formerly used for the salt-, smoked, or dried-fish markets.

This condition led to an increase in construction of fishing schooners intended for the fresh-fish market.

The generally accepted history of the development of the fishing schooner types in this period may be compressed into the following outline.

The first sharp schooner built for the New England fisheries reputedly was the *Romp*,* built at Essex in the winter of 1846–1847 by Andrew Story. Introducing the "sharpshooter," or "file bottom," *Romp* was 65′-3″ x 19′-9″ x 7′-1″ register. No half-model or plan of this schooner appears to exist, but she was described as having a straight keel of marked drag, moderately raking sternpost, with round tuck, upper-and-lower transoms, square stern, raking stem rabbet with a rather long, pointed cutwater fitted with headrails and billet. The sheer was moderate; in some models of sharp schooners the sheer was rather straight. The entrance was rather short, convex, and moderately full; the run long and fine. The midsection was formed with sharply rising, long straight floors, high, hard turn of bilge, and some tumble home in the topside. The model was supposed to have some slight resemblance in lines to the Chesapeake Bay keel schooners, but wider and more powerful.

It was traditional that, when fitting out in her homeport, Gloucester, for her first trip, the crew of the *Romp* refused to sail in her, considering her so sharp as to be unseaworthy.

It was also believed that the *Romp* went to California in the "Gold Rush," after a short career in the fisheries. It has been accepted, also, that the sharpshooter quickly developed into the shoal "clipper" type, said to have first appeared about 1852.

The primary statements above were largely extracted from the extensive articles and notes written by Captain Joseph W. Collins.† He joined the U.S. Fish Commission in 1880 and was an experienced fishing schooner master, particularly prominent at Gloucester as a mackerel fisherman. Between 1882 and 1886 he wrote articles and reports on fishing gear and on the history of fishing schooners, making proposals for their improvement.

This history of the development of the fishing schooners now needs some revisions and also some comment. The *Romp* may have been the first sharpshooter built but she could hardly be much of a novelty to the Gloucester and Boston fishermen in the 1840s, for fishermen must have been well acquainted with the Boston pilot boats and they also must have known how seaworthy and fast these vessels were. It is therefore difficult to believe that the New England fishermen would refuse to sail on a sharp schooner of this period because of fear that she lacked seaworthiness.

* *Romp* was built for Samuel and George F. Wonson and Samuel Giles of Gloucester.

† Howard I. Chapelle, *American Sailing Craft* (New York: Kennedy Bros. Inc., 1936; Crown, 1939) and *The National Watercraft Collection*, Smithsonian Institution, Washington, D.C., 1960, U.S. National Museum Bulletin 219.

How sharp were the sharpshooters? Existing half-models made between 1848 and 1855 show that these were much less sharp than the contemporary Boston pilot schooners, a number of which, dated between the 1840s and 1855, exist in model or plan. The lack of extremely sharp schooners of the sharpshooter class will be apparent when the schooners of the late 1840s and early '50s are described.

The statement that the *Romp* carried gold-seekers to California during the "Gold Rush" is incorrect. She was still on the Gloucester register in 1866. The schooner named *Romp* that went to California was a Salem-built vessel.

The alleged development of schooners from sharpshooter to clipper will be examined in some detail when schooners of the 1840s and '50s are illustrated.

The connection thought to exist between the Chesapeake-built schooners and the sharpshooters is very difficult to establish. While at least ten Chesapeake-built schooners were sold to Gloucester and Cape Cod owners between 1848 and 1854, some of these were bought for the Cape oyster fisheries and the registers show that most of them were rather shoal-bodied; in fact some were centerboarders. The southern schooners can be identified in the Gloucester registers, where their register dimensions can be seen. It has not yet been established that any of the southern schooners were at Gloucester prior to 1847, when *Romp* was launched, so it is doubtful that these schooners could have had any influence on the sharpshooter model. It should be noticed that Chesapeake schooners of the 1850s, of the keel model (pungy), whose half-models are preserved, do not show the extreme rise of floor at midsection that was characteristic of the older "Baltimore Clipper" schooners.

One southern schooner bought for the Gloucester fisheries in 1855–1856, the *Iowa,* built in Dorchester County, Maryland in 1854, was converted to a Boston-Newburyport packet after a short service as a fishing schooner. About 1860 her lines were taken off to build the packet schooner *Charmer.* The register dimensions of *Iowa* were 76′-9″ x 23′ x 6′-7″, while *Charmer*'s half-model, made from the take-off, scaled 77′-0½″ x 22′-6″ x 7′-8″. This comparison of dimensions suggests that the *Charmer* was made 1′-0″ deeper in the hold than *Iowa.* The importance of this reference is that the half-model of *Charmer,* shown in a lines drawing, can be seen in the catalog * of the U.S. Museum of History and Technology Collection, Smithsonian Institution. It will be seen from this that the southern schooners, registered at Gloucester, may not have resembled the early sharpshooters that will be illustrated later.

Accepting *Romp* as the prototype of the sharpshooter, it is surprising to

* Howard I. Chapelle, *The National Watercraft Collection,* Smithsonian Institution, Washington, D.C., 1960, U.S. National Museum Bulletin 219, p. 78.

see how rapidly the new, improved models appeared—and how completely their half-models have now disappeared. Within four years the sharpshooter was very well known in Nova Scotia as well as in New England. But today only a very small number of their builders' models can be found. Of six half-models dated between 1848 and 1850 that have survived, four have been selected as illustrations of the improved types of the 1840s.

These are two half-models in the Museum of History and Technology: USNM 54450 and USNM 54455. Both were Essex models. The other two were models found and taken off at Essex. One of these last models was identified by the names of two schooners built from it, written on the half-model.

Plate 18 shows a model dated 1848–1849, representing a vessel built for the mackerel fishery on a form more related to the clipper than to the sharpshooter, which raises a question to be dealt with later. This vessel had a straight keel having moderate drag, slight rake to sternpost, with upper-and-lower transoms. Instead of the then-common round tuck this schooner had a vestigial counter, the tuck of which was carried far enough abaft the outer rudderpost to allow construction of the rudder trunk. The stem rabbet had a very moderate rake, fitted with a short cutwater having trails, headrails, and billet. The entrance was convex, rather long, and slightly sharp. The run was long and fine. The midsection showed rising, straight floor carried well out, of small deadrise, a hard turn of the bilge, and vertical topside. A model intended to produce a fast carrier, it might be described as a half-clipper due to the form of the midsection shown. This half-model had a multicolored stripe along its waistline, and shows a short, low quarterdeck having the outlines of a cabin trunk in pencil lines on it. A schooner built to this model would measure 61′–10½″ x 18′-0″ x 6′-4″; the moulded depth of side, rabbet to plank-sheer, measured 7′-1½″.

A schooner of much the same type is shown in Plate 19. This half-model was incorrectly cataloged in the National Watercraft Collection. It was a model obtained by the U.S. Fish Commission dated 1849. On it the name *Elisha Holmes* had been painted, with the caption "an early sharpshooter." It has been recently found that the model, when received by the U.S. Fish Commission, had been captioned "A Georges Bank schooner, 1848, built at Essex."

It will be seen that the schooner built from this model would have somewhat low, easy bilges amidships, with slight tumble home. The rise of straight floor was somewhat greater than in the previous example; it was also shorter. The schooner would have moderate sheer. The straight keel had an easy drag and there was slight rake to the sternpost. As in the previous schooner, there was a vestigial counter, in this case carried aft in the tuck to the foreside of the rudderpost where there was a cross seam and raking

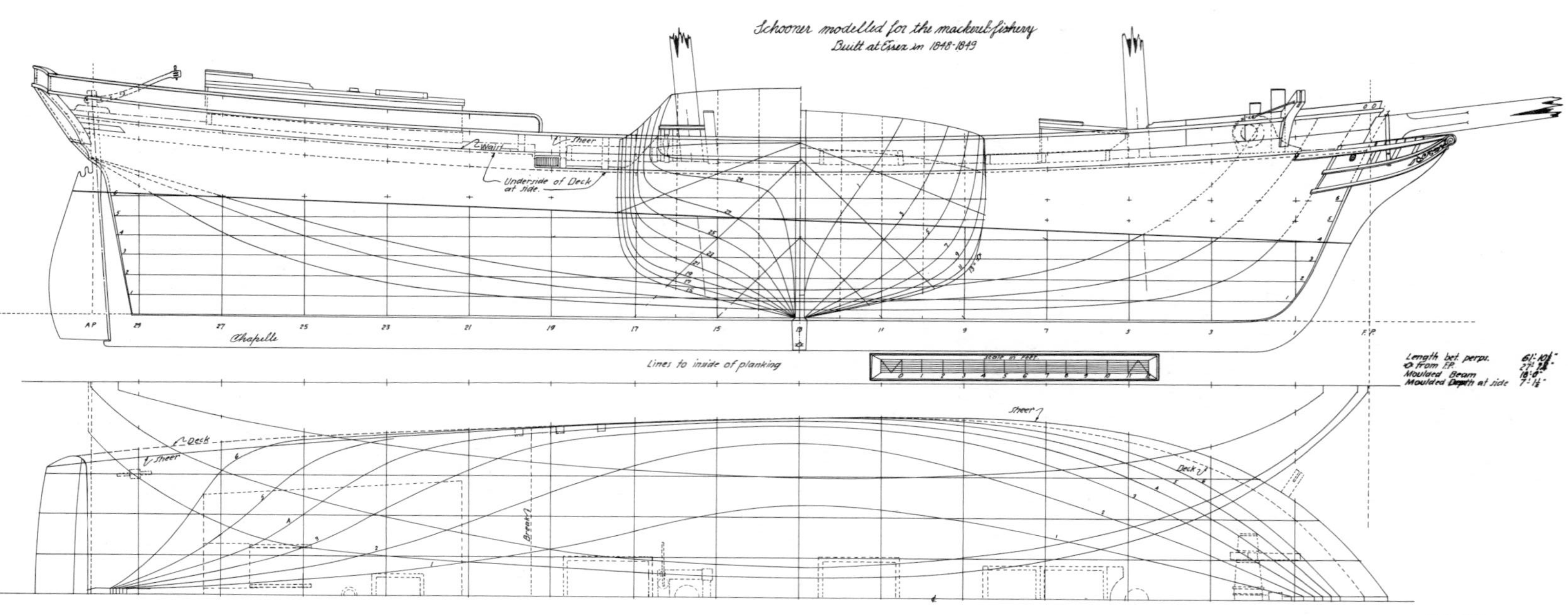
Schooner modelled for the mackerel fishery
Built at Essex in 1848-1849
Sheer
Wale
Underside of Deck at side.
Lines to inside of planking
Chapelle
A.P.
F.P.
Scale in feet
Length bet. perps.
from F.P.
Moulded Beam 18'-0"
Moulded Depth at side 7'-1½"
Deck
Sheer
Breadth
USNM 54.455

PLATE 18. Sharpshooter or clipper, 1848–1849, half-model

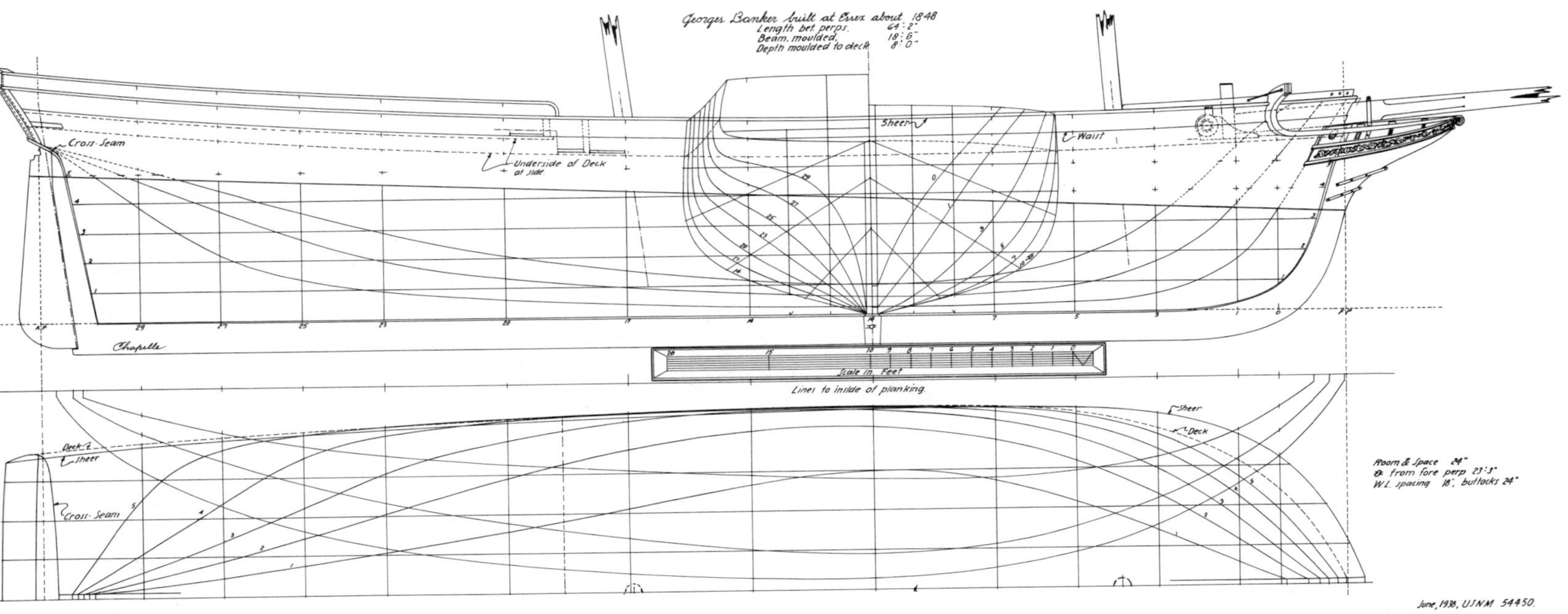

Georges Banker built at Essex about 1848
Length bet. perps. 64' 2"
Beam. moulded, 18' 6"
Depth moulded to deck 8' 0"
Sheer
Waist
Cross-Seam
Underside of Deck at side
Chapelle
Scale in Feet
Lines to inside of planking.
Sheer
Deck
Deck
Sheer
Cross-Seam
Room & Space 24"
⊗ from fore perp 23' 3"
W.L. spacing 18", buttocks 24"
June, 1938, USNM 54450.

PLATE 19. Georges Bank schooner, early clipper, 1848, half-model upper-and-lower transoms. The rudder stock came through the lower transom. The fore rake was round on the rabbet, raking forward a little at the top. The entrance was rather short, convex, and quite full. The run was long and fine. The model scaled to the following register dimensions: 64′-2″ x 18′-6″ x 6′-9″; the moulded depth from rabbet to plank-sheer was 8′-0″. This schooner should be classed as an early clipper in my opinion, and was not a sharpshooter in model. Thus far the existence of the clipper type, so close to the date of the *Romp*, seems to prove that the two types existed in the same period, in their early development.

For a model that complied with the accepted description of a sharpshooter, Plate 20 will serve. This half-model was found in Essex and dated 1849 in pencil on its top. The schooner built on this model was, for her period, an average-sized market schooner, having an easy sheer, straight keel with much drag, slightly raking post, round tuck with upper-and-lower transoms but with the lower transom much rounded on the bottom. The stem rabbet raking moderately, straight from just below the load line to the main rail. The cutwater was rather long, having trails and headrails. The entrance was rather short, convex, and somewhat sharp. The run was long and quite fine. The quarterdeck came forward almost to the pumps abaft the mainmast.

This schooner was about the size of most of her type that was market fishing in 1860–1865. She was of the following scaled register dimension: 59′-6″ x 17′-8″ x 5′-2″, 6′-0½″ moulded depth from rabbet to plank-sheer.

The midsection shows long, straight floors, rising sharply; the bilge high and hard, only an extremely slight tumble home. The model appeared wide and rather shallow in comparison with length; a stiff, fast sailer no doubt, but it is questionable that a vessel on this model was fully self-righting if knocked down.

The schooners shown in Plate 21, *Grace Darling* and *Sophronia*, were built at Essex in 1849 and 1850. Their half-model was found and taken off by L. H. Story. This model has a different beam-length ratio than the previous example of a sharpshooter.

The two vessels were built by Oliver Burnham, the register dimensions of *Sophronia* were 65′-3″ x 18′-3″ x 7′-2″, those of *Grace Darling* were 64′ x 18′-4″ x 7″; the *Darling* was built in 1850.

The model of these schooners showed a rather straight sheer, straight keel with much drag, raking sternpost with round tuck, upper-and-lower transoms, square stern. The stem rabbet had a slight fore rake, flaring at rail. The cutwater was a longhead, complete with trails and headrails. The entrance was rather short, sharp, and convex; the run very long and fine. The midsection was formed with long, rising straight floors, high, rather hard bilge,

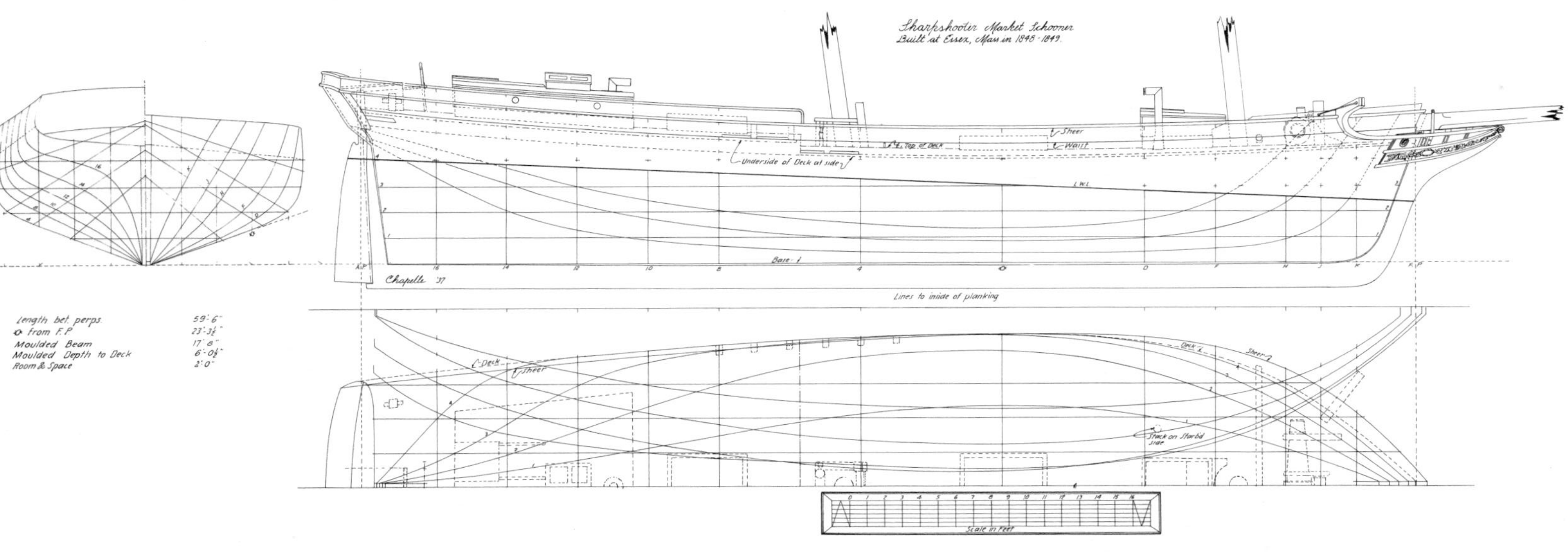
Sharpshooter Market Schooner
Built at Essex, Mass in 1848-1849.
Sheer
Wale
Top of Deck
Underside of Deck at side
LWL
Base-1
Chapelle '37
Lines to inside of planking
Length bet. perps. 59'-6"
⊕ from F.P 23'-3½"
Moulded Beam 17'-8"
Moulded Depth to Deck 6'-0½"
Room & Space 2'-0"
Deck
Sheer
Stack on Starb'd side
Scale in Feet

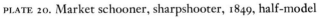

PLATE 20. Market schooner, sharpshooter, 1849, half-model

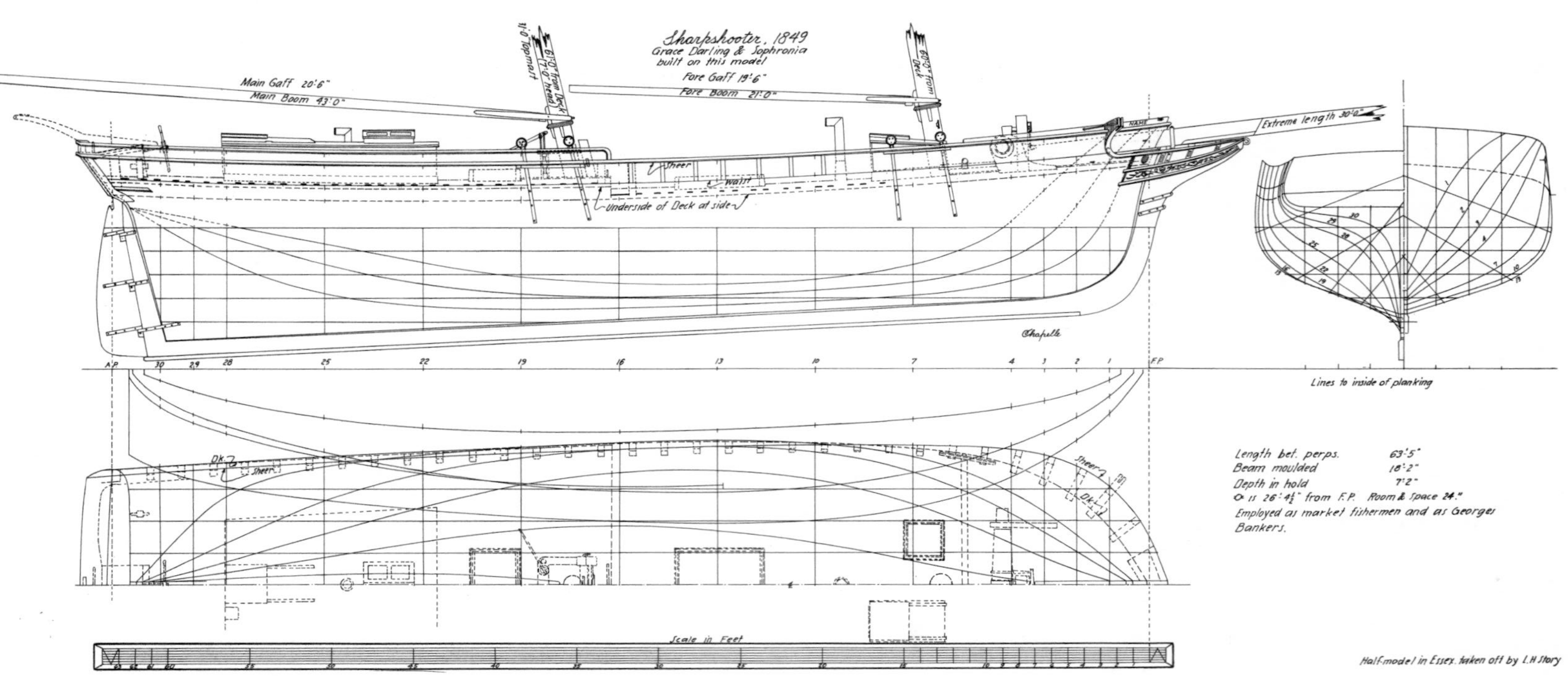

Sharpshooter, 1849
Grace Darling & Sophronia
built on this model
Fore Gaff 19'6"
Fore Boom 21'0"
Main Gaff 20'6"
Main Boom 43'0"
61'0" from Deck
(7'0" head)
31'0" Topmast
60'0" from Deck
Extreme length 30'0"
Sheer
Waist
Underside of Deck at side
Chapelle
Lines to inside of planking
Length bet. perps. 63'5"
Beam moulded 18'2"
Depth in hold 7'2"
⊗ is 26'4½" from F.P. Room & Space 24."
Employed as market fishermen and as Georges Bankers.
Scale in Feet
Half-model in Essex, taken off by L.H. Story

PLATE 21. *Grace Darling* and *Sophronia*, sharpshooters, 1849–1850, half-model and marked tumble home. The model's scaled dimensions (register) were 63′-5″ x 18′-2″ x 7′-2″.

The schooners built on this half-model were employed in market fishing off the New England coast and they also fished on Georges Bank. It seems probable that the two schooners were "extreme" designs in the minds of their owners when they were launched. While they were seaworthy and strongly built, their wide, flat sterns, having the bottom of the lower transom very close to the water, must have been the cause of much discomfort and, occasionally, damage in heavy weather, due to the pounding such sterns would receive. The schooners in Plate 21 were probably of sufficient depth to be self-righting, or almost so, if knocked down.

All of these schooners of the 1840s employed ice for the preservation of their catches; these were the schooners of the improved type of the era. They were designed to meet completely the supposed requirements of their occupations. However, it is not surprising to find that there were not only wide variations in models, dimensions, and proportions of sharpshooters but that there were some requirements that this type would not meet properly. Hence another form of fast-sailing fishermen was sought, the clipper. These could be developed in step with the earliest sharpshooters, the evolution of the two types overlapping.

By 1850 Essex had become the shipbuilding center for the New England fisheries. Located close to Gloucester, fishermen having schooners built in Essex could easily get there to keep close watch on their new vessels—and on those building for other fishermen. If some improvement or departure from the norm in design was seen on a new vessel, it was immediately the subject of examination, argument, and, if thought to be desirable, of adaption or of copying. The evolution of fishing schooner types, in such a theater, was continuous and at times very rapid. This is apparently the only explanation of the sudden appearance of very numerous schooners of the new designs within four or five years. It will be seen, in the reference that follows, that there is good reason to believe that as early as 1851 the improved Essex types were common enough to have become well known in the fisheries of the Canadian Maritime Provinces.

The speedy sharpshooters would naturally be considered for the distant fisheries, though the small size of the early schooners was a handicap. This could be solved by building large sharpshooters, producing a modified clipper that became popular in the Gulf of St. Lawrence fisheries where they soon achieved a dubious reputation. The report of Paul Crowell, *Journals of the Assembly*,* stated that

* Report of Paul Crowell, *Journals of the Assembly, Nova Scotia,* 1852, Appendixes Nos. 25 and 13, cited by Harold A. Innis, The Cod Fisheries, The History of an International Economy (New Haven: Yale University Press) p. 332.

> The American vessels which fit out for the hook fisheries are of a superior class from those in Nova Scotia. Their tonnage is generally from 60 to 130 tons, very sharp built, well fitted in every respect; those they term sharpshooters are very superior sailing vessels. . . . Those vessels are likewise well manned, varying from 12 to 24 men. They offer great opposition—a common threat among them is to run the Nova Scotia vessels down—they are usually prepared for this, their bowsprits are fitted large and strong, and the end well ironed; they have double chained (sic) bobstays, and shrouds well bolted and geared (sic). A number of them came armed for opposition. . . . These vessels with Nova Scotia masters, called white washed Yankees are generally the worst.

There seems to be sufficient evidence to conclude that the sharpshooter and clipper developed together, based on a common need for speed but with each type having special use requirements. In the early stages of development the sharpshooter and the clipper resembled one another, differing chiefly in proportions. However, the description of the clipper type will clarify the relation of the two.

The clipper was generally longer and shoaler than the sharpshooter. As shown in the two early examples (Plates 18 and 19), the midsection of the clipper was formed with slight or very moderate rise of straight floor, usually carried well outboard, a low and commonly hard bilge, and upright or slightly tumble home topside. The sheer was usually moderate, the keel straight and with some drag. The sternpost raked slightly, the square stern was wide with the bottom of the transom close to the load line. The stem rabbet usually had very moderate rake, often flaring somewhat at the rail. The cutwater was usually long, supported by headrails and trails. The clipper in the late '50s and later, had a long, hollow entrance with the midsection abaft midlength. The run was very fine and sometimes rather short, but usually with long, straight buttocks. The clippers sat low in the water and were often handsome vessels. In the early stages of development the clipper had a short, convex, slightly sharp entrance, with midsection noticeably forward of midlength, as shown in the plans of the 1840 schooners. The clippers were usually larger than the sharpshooters. By 1855 the clipper fisherman had not only developed to its final form but was also the most numerous of the two types.

There are various reasons for the clipper's becoming the most numerous type of fishing schooner in New England. First, the clipper was very fast and, in the larger sizes, of good capacity and working space on deck for its dimensions. It should be noted here that after the mid-'50s, the clipper type competed with the sharpshooters for the market fisheries, employing models having extremely sharp ends and rather deep keels outside the rabbet. Another class was the "Georgesmen," larger and less sharp than the market boats. Next were the "clipper bankers" which were less sharp than the Georgesman. The class in which the clipper was the particular favorite was the mackerel schooners. The mackerel fishery always attracted the fastest models of schooners, including some of the most extreme designs. This distinction of vessels lasted into the 1880s, then the "all-around fishing schooner" developed, leaving size-of-vessel and length-of-trip the sole controls of the choice of schooner for a specific fishery.

Another reason for the long existence of the clipper schooner was the limitations of Gloucester Harbor, where the North Atlantic fisheries were gradually centering. Slips in this port were shoal, limiting berths to schooners not exceeding 12 feet draft, many slips were not over 10 feet deep. These could be used by clippers of about 70 to 85 feet on deck. As the shores of Gloucester Harbor were made up of granite ledges it was expensive to attempt the deepening of the slips. This eventually became a distinction between Boston- and Gloucester-owned vessels—the average Boston fishing schooner was deeper than the average Gloucester fishing schooner in the same class. This important matter will be referred to again.

The establishment of the sharpshooter and of the early clippers came at a time when the North Atlantic fisheries were expanding rapidly and the demand for new vessels was mounting.

Chapter Three

1850–1870

The early 1850s were years of active shipbuilding; many fishing schooners were laid down in Boston, Gloucester, Essex, Ipswich, Newburyport, and along the coast of Maine. Essex, by 1845, was the leading town in fishing schooner construction and between November 1, 1850 and November 1, 1853, 170 schooners were launched there. One builder, Andrew Story (builder and modeler of the *Romp* in 1847), launched 32 vessels, and another builder, Aaron Burnham, launched 26 schooners in this same period.

Though a small town located on a narrow, winding, shoal, tidal river (requiring new vessels to await high tides before any attempt could be made to get them to sea), Essex had fifteen yards in operation in the early 1850s. Until steam tugs came into use in New England, the fishing schooners built at Essex—and elsewhere to the eastward—were sparred, rigged, and ballasted at or near the building site so that they could be sailed to their port-of-hail for final fitting out. After 1850 it became the custom to track or tow new vessels out of Essex river—sparring, rigging, and fitting-out being done at Gloucester, Boston, or at the port-of-hail. The spars were usually made at the building site and were stowed on the deck of a new schooner when she was ready to be towed out.

The number of shipyards in Essex varied; those in operation in any one year, before 1930, were from two to seventeen. The same plot of ground might be used over and over again by successive builders. Some of these might build only one or two vessels before closing down, or they might build thirty or more. Some builders operated yards at Boston or Gloucester, as well as at Essex, but normally they utilized only one yard at a time.

By 1850 timber had become an increasingly difficult problem for the Essex and Gloucester shipbuilders. In colonial times and up until about

1845, timber could be brought from nearby stands by oxen and carts, or by water, to the shipyards in logs or in sawn timber. Tidal and river sawmills were employed. These had been established in early times, the first sawmill in Ipswich was in the township which then included Chebacco Parish, now Essex. In the early 1800s, and for some time afterward, timber could be hauled from a nearby stand to one of the mills, and then in plank or squared timber, or as flitch, it could be hauled to the shipyards by means of timber carts, or sledges, and in winter by sleds drawn by oxen or draft-horses. But by 1850 the stands of timber near the mills and shipyards had been cut and available stands were too distant for the old methods of transportation. However, the construction of railways in New England, running south, west, and northwest, opened up new sources of fine timber. Timber was also brought to the shipbuilding towns by water, either in schooners or by barges on inland waters. At one time there was a narrow canal, running from the Merrimac and Essex rivers through the Ipswich marshes, by which timber was taken to Essex.

By these means timber was brought from Georgia, Virginia, and Maryland—the white oak and longleaf yellow pine. Spruce and white pine came from Maine and New Hampshire. Rock maple and white oak had been used for keels and white oak for stems and sternposts. Birch, maple, and elm, with white oak, were used for frames and stanchions. Top timbers, and planking were white oak and yellow pine. Ceiling was usually oak or maple but spruce, white and yellow pine might also be used. Masts and spars were of white pine or spruce. Decking, cabin trunks, hatch coamings were white pine. White oak was made into bitts, pinrails, and turned stanchions, rail caps, chock rails, etc. Rigging fittings, rope, anchors, pumps, windlasses, and ironwork were made in Essex until the '60s, but after that only pumps, windlasses, and spar ironwork continued to be made in the town.

The quality of construction at Essex was highly praised; after 1845 the vessels were almost yacht-like in finish and many were built on honor, of superb construction. The peculiar employment conditions that grew up in Essex made for specialization by the workmen and this required that the individual workman had to establish a personal reputation for good workmanship. This became an important factor in the relationship between the builder and his workmen. Most shipyard laborers on Cape Ann did not work for any one builder as a regular employee but hired out wherever there was work in his specialty. In some instances, three or more men would work as a gang ("framing gang," "planking gang," etc.). The result was that the relationship between the skilled yard labor and the builder was more that of prime- and sub-contractors, though the men were paid on an hourly rate. Also, the men were very jealous of their reputations for quality workmanship. This not only gave quality control but also lightened the load of builders' supervision, allowing one-man control of a shipyard. These labor practices were employed to the eastward, into Nova Scotia, with exchanges in labor across the border.

Until the Civil War began, labor cost was low and material relatively cheap in New England. The labor worked from "sunrise to sunset" in the shipyards, as was then the practice elsewhere. In the '50s vessels were cheap, costing about $35 per register ton. The builders were slow in utilizing steam power saws; they employed pit saws and the broadax and adze. The shipyards were no more than waterfront lots with, perhaps a single small building serving as a stable for a pair of horses or oxen, a toolhouse and an office and sometimes a joiner shop. The yard itself represented a very small capital investment. Yet, with hand tools, Essex builders could build vessels rapidly. One builder, in 1856–1857, built twenty-two vessels in twenty-two months. As mentioned, the pinky *July* was built in that month, in 1837, by Parker Burnham. Andrew Story built thirteen vessels in one year.

While no formal apprentice system seems to have existed in Essex, boys became skilled by working with skilled men, becoming infused with the idea that a reputation for good workmanship was a prime objective. Working with a "gang" for example, a young Essex carpenter might work in Boston for a few months, thus coming under the influence of shipwrights trained in the naval dockyards at Boston and Portsmouth. The gang leader would see to it that young members of his crew would learn their trade well enough to maintain the standards of workmanship and production that marked his gang.

The design of the schooners was commonly done by means of the lift builders' half-model. The lifts were made of planks, temporarily fastened to form the bread-and-butter wooden block which was shaped to the desired hull form. This type of half-model had replaced the old hawk's-nest model of colonial times with the profile of the hull formed by the backboard and plank cross sections made to represent the mould frames. The hawk's-nest model went out of favor at Essex and Gloucester in the 1830s.

The lift half-model, carefully made and faired, was easier to form than the hawk's-nest model and gave a good representation of the desired hull form, as well as a quick and easy way to learn how to judge hull form without long technical training. It was the lift half-model that enabled young carpenters, master builders, owners, and even fishermen to learn how to design schooners. At Essex, Gloucester, and Rockport on Cape Ann, and in neighboring villages, there were men who had become well known as successful makers of builders' models. Usually, however, in the 1840s and '50s, the half-models were made in the building yard by the master builder or by a carpenter.

In the 1850s the half-models were usually made on half inch to the foot scale, with lifts one inch in thickness, or two feet thick to scale. The tops of the lifts, representing level lines, were often too widely spaced to give good control for the mould loft fairing. This became a troublesome matter in lofting of the extreme clipper-type schooners with their sudden changes in hull form. The loftsman sometimes took off sections with a soft lead bar, about one quarter of an inch square, to supplement the lift offsets. The hull forms found in half-models of clipper-type schooners that have survived are very difficult to fair, and two loftsmen, moulding clipper schooners from the same half-model could readily produce vessels of somewhat different form.

By the late 1850s models produced by the more skillful model makers were made with one-half or three-eights inch lifts and this led the mould loft to become more precise in reproducing the design intended in the half-model.

The half-models of fishing schooners were usually made of white pine, but a few had walnut lifts alternating with white pine lifts. The layout of the deck beams, showing the size and place of cabin trunk, hatches, masts, and windlass was sometimes drawn on top of the half-model. The lifts of a half-model were sometimes traced on the backboard. Commonly they were traced on a smooth pine board or on a piece of paper in the mould loft, before measuring the offsets. The frame spacing was usually shown on the loft drawings, for taking offsets, and occasionally the frame spacing and rake of masts were marked on the back of the half-model as well.

Details of deck arrangement varied a little in the 1850s. The length and height of the quarterdeck changed gradually; the short, high deck of 1800–1825, at main rail cap height, had been replaced by quarterdecks 9 to 12 inches above the main deck by 1840, with the break in the deck placed a little forward of the fore end of the cabin trunk. The day of the cabin under the quarterdeck had passed, the cabin trunk had become standard in New England and Nova Scotia fishing schooners.

Later, the break in the deck was shifted to a little forward of the hatch of the after hold; then, in the late 1840s, the break was placed in its final position, 3 to 5 feet forward of the mainmast. The changes in length of the quarterdeck overlapped—short quarterdecks were placed on new vessels after the long quarterdeck had come into popularity.

During the late 1840s and through the 1850s the form of the counter of Essex-built fishing schooners underwent many changes. The old round tuck and upper-and-lower transoms seen in schooners built before 1850 were first modified by setting the bottom of the lower transom a little abaft the rudder stock, supported at the center line by a pair of cheek timbers on each side of the after deadwood and sternpost, with fillers afore and abaft the rudder case. The bottom of the lower transom gradually moved farther aft, and a single large and raking transom replaced the upper-and-lower transoms (see plates). By 1855 the short-overhang counter with sharply raking transom had become popular. However, half-models show that the old upper-and-lower transoms stern were favored as late at 1850–1855 by some builders and owners. Once an innovation appeared, it seems to have taken about a decade before it was widely accepted, for owners and builders were conservative in such matters.

Plate 22 shows the Georges Banker *Annah*, built in Essex in 1851. It will be seen that this schooner shows no innovation compared to schooners built in the late 1840s. She complies with the description of the Georgesmen that have been given. The *Annah* had the full midsection and small rise of straight floor, combined with sharp ends that marked her type. Her register dimensions, scaled from her half-model, were 62′-8″ x 18′-6″ x 7′-1″. She had moderate sheer, straight keel with modest drag, raking sternpost, round tuck, upper-and-lower transoms, square stern, and raking, straight stem rabbet. She had a long head fitted with headrails, trails, and a billet. Her entrance was rather long for her time, with the midsection a little forward of midlength. The entrance was convex and moderately sharp. Her run was very fine with straight buttocks.

This vessel was considered a fast sailer and an excellent seaboat. She was one of the early schooners built at Essex with a long quarterdeck and a cabin trunk.

A number of whaling vessels were built in Essex between 1830 and 1860. The majority of these were schooners, with only a few brigs and brigantines being built. One of these whalers was the fore-and-aft schooner *Agate*, shown in Plate 23, built in 1853. She was a burdensome vessel but her ends were not very full. Most of the whalers built in New England in the 1850s were of the clipper model, as represented in the ship *Reindeer*, whose lines are shown in *The National Watercraft Collection.**

Some of the banks schooners, built later than *Agate*, were converted into whalers in their old age. Some of these built in Essex were relatively sharp-ended.

The *Agate* was of the following register dimensions: 74′-10½″ x 20′-1″ x 8′-6″. This schooner, especially built for whaling, had small sheer, straight keel with slight drag, raking sternpost, short counter, square stern with strongly raking transom. The stem rabbet was curved, raking and flaring, fitted with a short, deep, heavy cutwater, with headrails, trails, and billet. She had a short poop at main rail level and a short top gallant forecastle deck at the same level. The bulwarks were high, 3 feet 8 inches above the main deck. The entrance was moderately full with the midsection well forward of the midlength. This was required in schooner whalers, to bear the weight of the heavy tryworks carried well forward. The run was somewhat fine, but short, so the buttocks were rather steep. The *Agate* was built of

* Chapelle, *The National Watercraft Collection*, pp. 245–246.

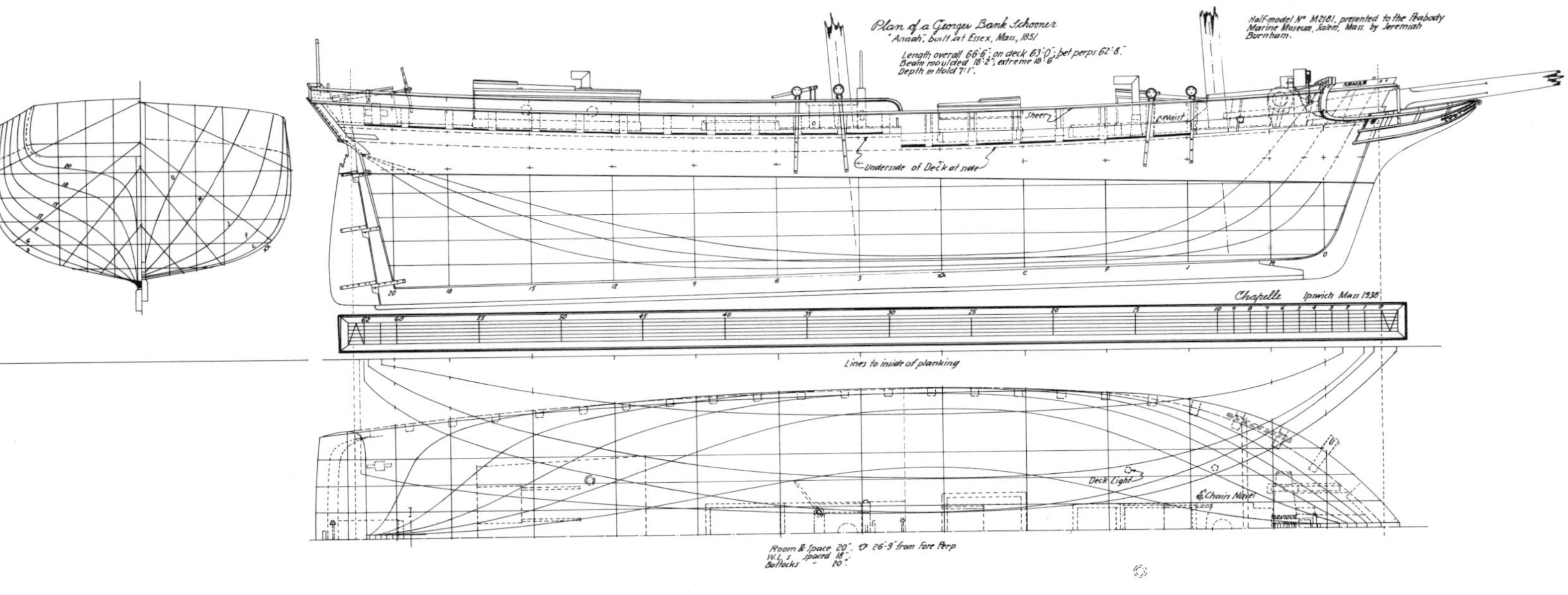
Plan of a Georges Bank Schooner
"Annah", built at Essex, Mass., 1851
Length overall 66'6"; on deck 63'0"; bet perps 62'8."
Beam moulded 18'2"; extreme 18'6"
Depth in Hold 7'1".
Half-model Nº M2181, presented to the Peabody Marine Museum, Salem, Mass. by Jeremiah Burnham.
Sheer
Waist
Underside of Deck at side
Chapelle Ipswich Mass 1938
Lines to inside of planking
Deck Light
Chain Navel
Room & Space 20". ⊕ 26'-9" from Fore Perp.
W.L.s spaced 18".
Buttocks " 20".

PLATE 22. *Annah*, Georges Banker clipper, 1851, half-model

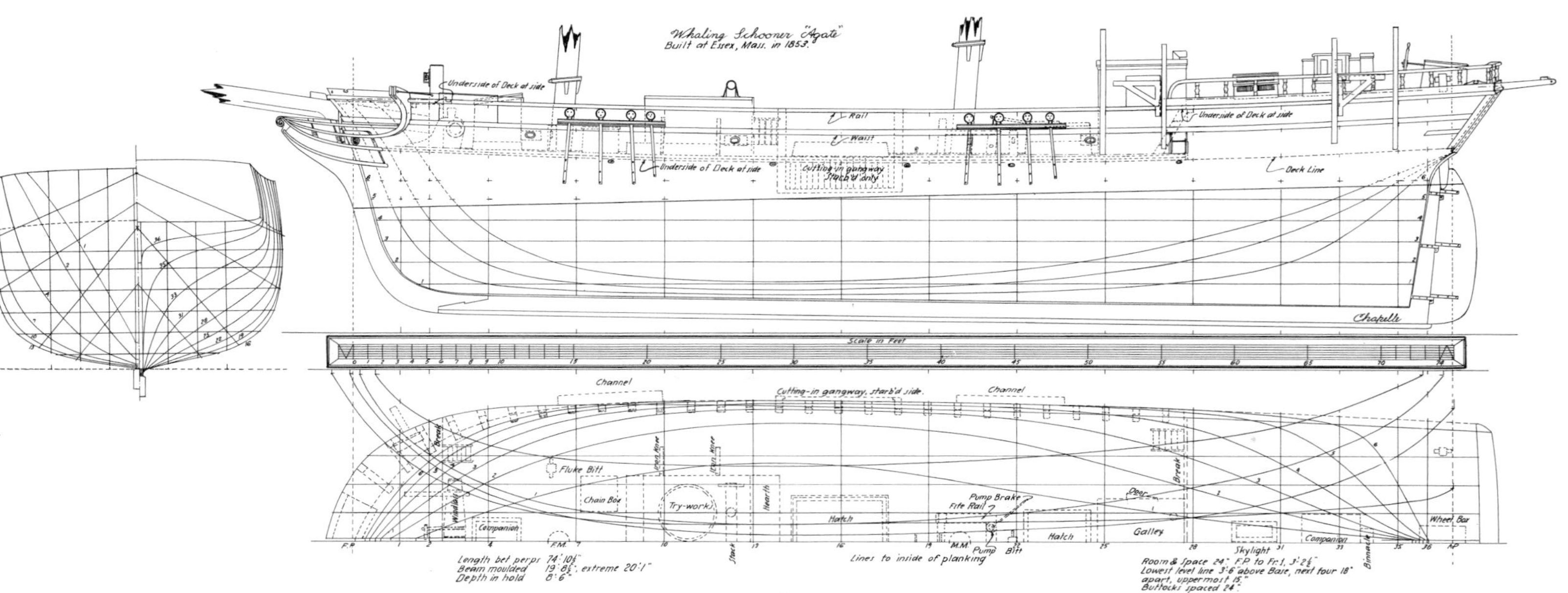

Whaling Schooner "Agate"
Built at Essex, Mass. in 1853.
Underside of Deck at side
Rail
Waist
Cutting-in gangway Starb'd only
Underside of Deck at side
Deck Line
Chapelle
Scale in Feet
Channel
Cutting-in gangway, starb'd side.
Channel
Fluke Bitt
Chain Box
Try-works
Hearth
Hatch
Pump Brake
Fife Rail
Hatch
Galley
Break
Companion
Wheel Box
Windlass
Companion
Stack
Pump
Bitt
Skylight
Binnacle
Length bet perps 74' 10½"
Beam moulded 19' 8½", extreme 20' 1"
Depth in hold 8' 6"
Lines to inside of planking
Room & Space 24". F.P. to Fr. 1, 3' 2½"
Lowest level line 3' 6" above Base, next four 18" apart, uppermost 15".
Buttocks spaced 24".

PLATE 23. *Agate*, whaler, 1853, half-model

Massachusetts white oak and New Hampshire white pine; traditionally she was the last vessel of large size entirely built of New England timber at Essex.

Plate 24 is the lines of an unidentified schooner whose half-model is in the Peabody Marine Museum of Salem, No. M2180. The model dates from about 1850–1855. It was described as a sharpshooter, however the proportions of this model are nearly those of the clipper type. In this period of development, combinations of sharpshooter and clipper design such as this model were tried.

The register dimensions of this schooner were about 67′-9″ x 19′-11″ x 6′-″, scaled from the model. She had moderate sheer, straight keel with small drag, raking sternpost, round tuck, upper-and-lower transoms, square stern, strongly raking, flaring stem rabbet with long cutwater, fitted with trails, headrails, and billet. Midship section was a little forward of midlength, giving a fairly long, sharp, convex entrance. The run was long and very fine. This schooner was built with a long quarterdeck and a cabin trunk. She was probably intended for the summer mackerel fishery, for which many schooners were built in the early 1850s. The vessel could also have served as a market fisherman.

Some of the early clipper schooners were built for the Cape Cod oyster fisheries centering around Wellfleet. These were all keel schooners of rather small size and light draft. In the 1850s a number of Chesapeake Bay schooners were purchased for this fishery. Some were large, compared to New England-built schooners in the business, and were fitted with centerboards. No example of an early New England oyster schooner of this period has been found, but half-models of Bay schooners exist. Plate 25 shows one of these schooners, built at Baltimore in 1855 by William Skinner and Sons for the Chesapeake oyster business. This schooner was named the *Sunny South*, her register dimensions were 71′-0″ x 22′-4″ x 5′-3″. The draft of this schooner would be about 6′-3″. Vessels of her size were usually "buy boats," purchasing oysters from the dredging and tonging sloops, canoes, and small schooners that then made up the oyster fishing fleet on the Bay. The *Sunny South* was a very fast sailer. She had a small sheer, straight keel with small drag, moderate rake of sternpost, round tuck, upper-and-lower transom square stern, the stem curved, raking and flaring on the rabbet. She had the "long head" cutwater extending well outboard, fitted with trails, headrails, and billet. Her mainmast was to port of her keel center line, the center board case to starboard, to allow the centerboard to be placed in the best position. Her midsection was slightly forward of midlength, allowing her to have quite a long, fine, convex entrance. Her run was long and very fine. She had a long, low quarterdeck with cabin trunk. The half-model of this

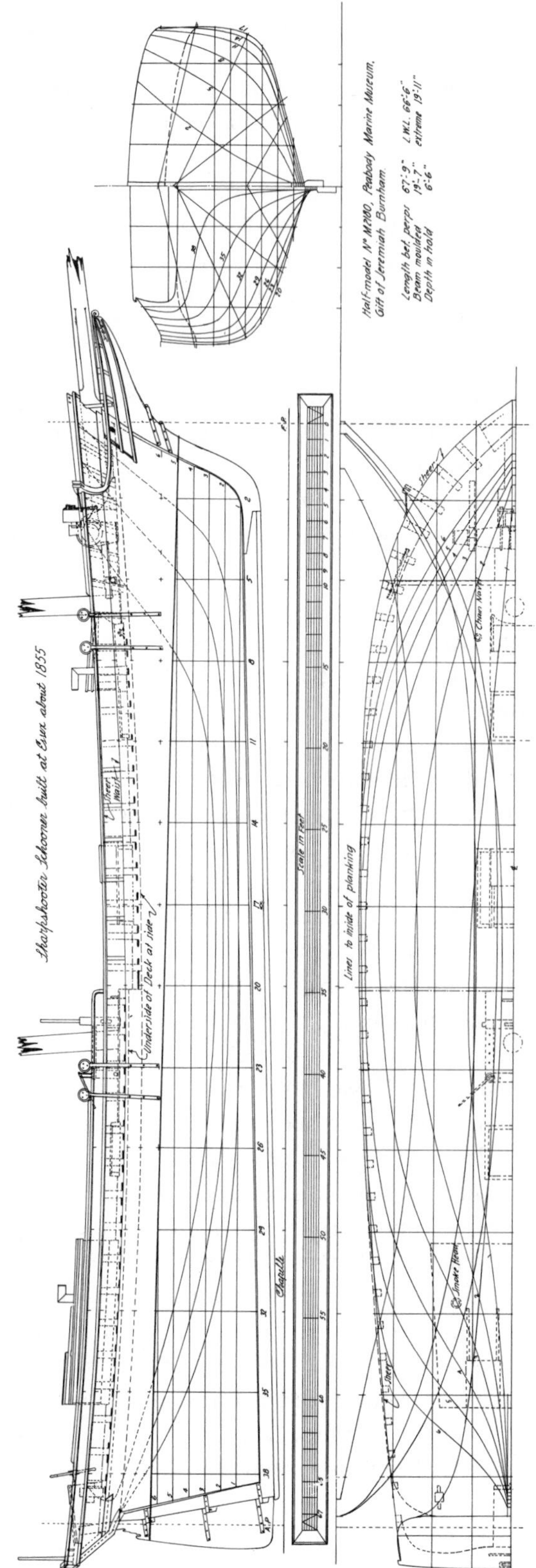

Sharpshooter Schooner built at Essex about 1855
Half-model Nº M2180, Peabody Marine Museum,
Gift of Jeremiah Burnham
Length bet. perps 67'-9" L.W.L. 66'-6"
Beam moulded 19'-7" extreme 19'-11"
Depth in hold 6'-6"
Underside of Deck at side
Scale in Feet
Liner to inside of planking
Chapelle

PLATE 24. Unidentified clipper, sharpshooter, 1850–1855, half-model

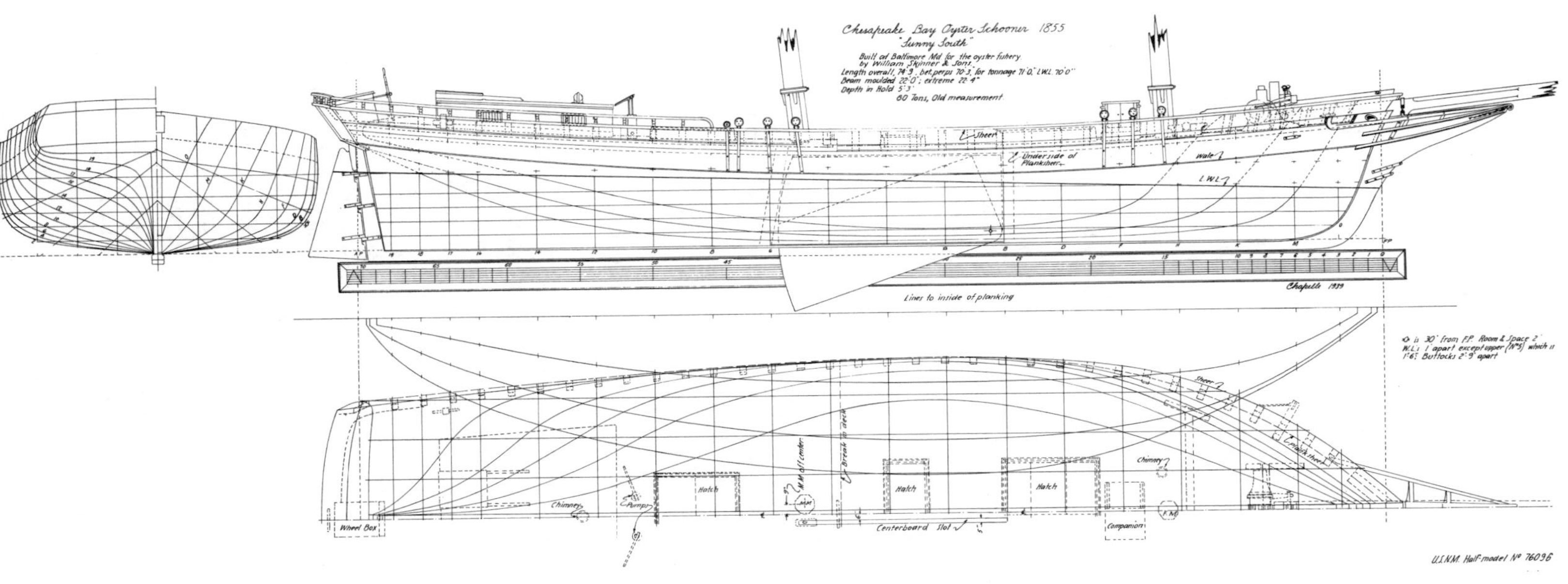
Chesapeake Bay Oyster Schooner 1855
"Sunny South"
Built at Baltimore Md for the oyster fishery
by William Skinner & Sons.
Length overall, 74'9", bet.perps 70'3", for tonnage 71'0", L.W.L. 70'0"
Beam moulded 22'0"; extreme 22'4"
Depth in Hold 5'3"
60 Tons, Old measurement
Sheer
Underside of Planksheer
Wale
L.W.L.
Chapelle 1939
Lines to inside of planking
is 30' from F.P. Room & Space 2'
W.L.'s 1' apart except upper (Nº5) which is
1'6": Buttocks 2'9" apart
Sheer
Clamp & shelf
Chimney
Break in deck
M.M. off center
Hatch
Hatch
Hatch
Chimney
Pumps
Wheel Box
Centerboard Slot
Companion
F.M.
U.S.N.M. Half-model Nº 76096

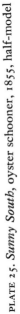

PLATE 25. *Sunny South*, oyster schooner, 1855, half-model

schooner is in the Museum of History and Technology, Smithsonian Institution, No. 76096.

This type of schooner had developed from about 1830–1835 and had proven well suited to her business and to conditions on the Bay. It was remarkable that, with such a short period of evolution, so satisfactory a type appeared. As a result, the Bay schooners did not change much in the last period of their commercial life, say from 1855–1920. Similar schooners were used in the oyster fisheries in New Jersey and along the Gulf Coast, also in the New England oyster business after the Civil War. Like the oyster sloops, these oyster schooners became almost a stock type, though varying somewhat in detail.

Plate 26 shows the lines of a clipper schooner, the *William H. Thorndike*, built at Essex in 1856, by Benjamin Courtney, a very competent builder who designed many fine schooners. He retired to Dorchester, Massachusetts in 1859. The register dimensions, scaled from the half-model, were 83′-2″ x 22′-10″ x 7′-3″. This schooner was another compromise, a clipper sharpshooter having a graceful sheer, straight keel with little drag, slightly raking sternpost, short counter, raking transom curved athwartships. The stem rabbet raked rather markedly, with a slight flare. A long cutwater was fitted, having trails, headrails, and billet. The midsection was abaft midlength, a long entrance was the result, sharp but slightly convex. The run was long, fine, and straight in the quarter-beam buttocks. The midsection was formed with rising straight floor carried well out, rather hard bilges, slight tumble home, increasing toward the transom. This vessel's career cannot be traced. It is obvious, however, that this schooner would be a good sailer and sea boat. Her lines show that at least one builder of the 1850s was progressing toward a deeper model and away from the very shallow clippers that were then becoming numerous. However, Lewis Story thought the *Thorndike* was probably owned at Boston or in some nearby port, were draft was less a problem in the slips than it was at Gloucester. This schooner may have been designed for a Georgesman, mackerel fishing in season.

The market schooners were slowly being refined; by 1856 these vessels were on a well-developed sharpshooter model, with maximum beam slightly forward of midlength, permitting long, reasonably fine entrances and runs. An example is shown in Plate 27. The half-model of this schooner was given to the U.S. Fish Commission by Joseph Story in 1882. It was first identified as the *Ripple*, built by the donor in 1856, and the first schooner built at Essex with an oval or elliptical transom. The register dimensions of *Ripple* were 61′-0″ x 18′-8″ x 6′-7″. The model and drawing show a schooner measuring only 54′-2″ x 18′-0″ x 6′-0″ bringing the former identification into question, to which no answer has yet been found.

The schooner built from this model would have a graceful, lively sheer,

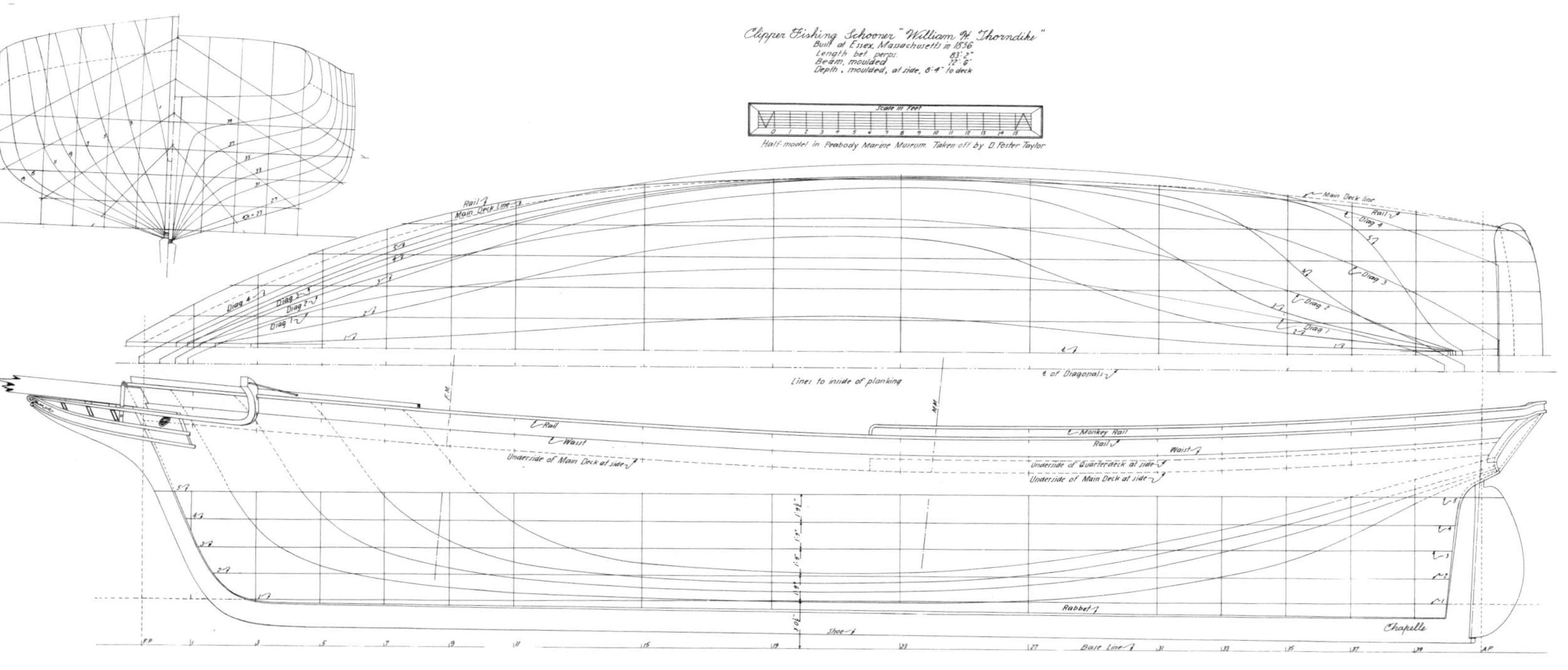
Clipper Fishing Schooner "William H. Thorndike"
Built at Essex, Massachusetts in 1856
Length bet. perps. 83' 2"
Beam, moulded 22' 6"
Depth, moulded, at side, 8' 4" to deck
Scale in Feet
0 1 2 3 4 5 6 7 8 9 10 11 12 13 14 15
Half-model in Peabody Marine Museum. Taken off by D. Foster Taylor
Rail
Main Deck Line
Main Deck line
Diag 4
Diag 3
Diag 2
Diag 1
℄ of Diagonals
Lines to inside of planking
Rail
Waist
Underside of Main Deck at side
Monkey Rail
Rail
Waist
Underside of Quarterdeck at side
Underside of Main Deck at side
Rabbet
Shoe
Base Line
Chapelle
FP
AP

PLATE 26. *William H. Thorndike*, clipper, 1856, half-model

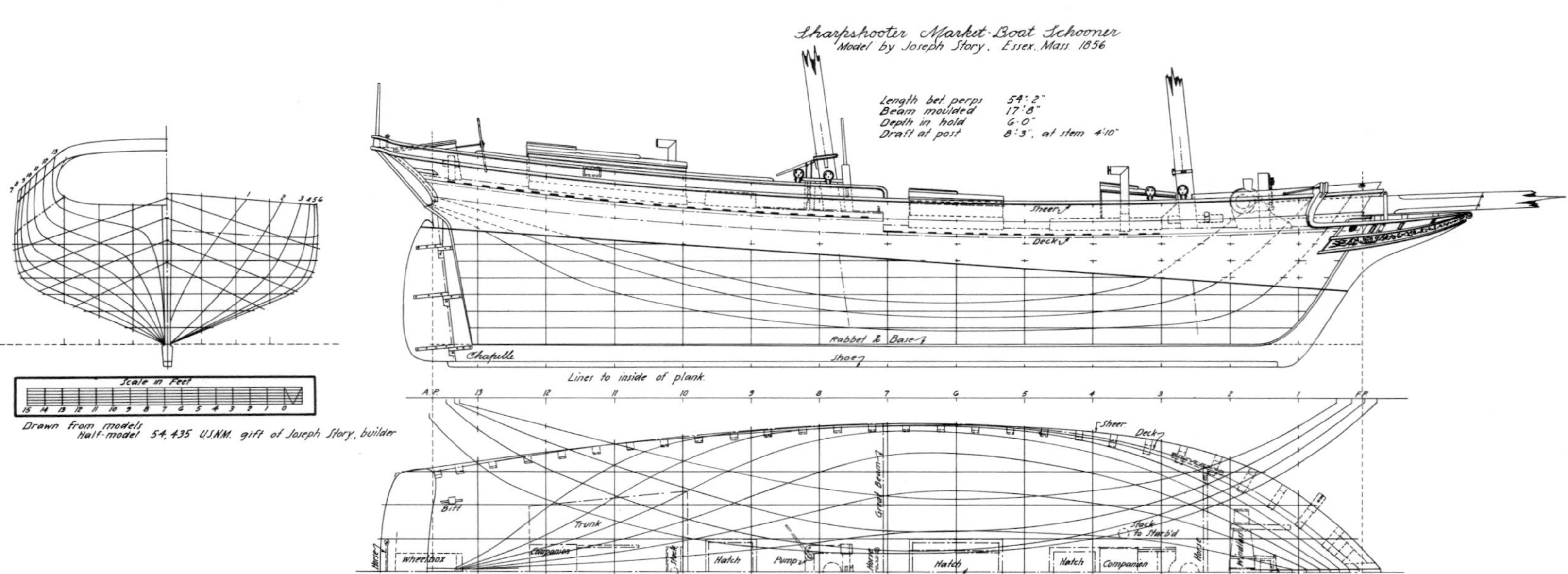
Sharpshooter Market Boat Schooner
Model by Joseph Story. Essex, Mass. 1856
Length bet. perps 54'-2"
Beam moulded 17'-8"
Depth in hold 6'-0"
Draft at post 8'-3", at stem 4'-10"
Sheer
Deck
Rabbet & Base
Shoe
Chapelle
Lines to inside of plank.
Scale in Feet
Drawn from models
Half-model 54,435 U.S.N.M. gift of Joseph Story, builder
Great Beam
Bitt
Trunk
Companion
Wheelbox
Horse
Stack
Hatch
Pump
Stack to Starb'd
Windlass

PLATE 27. Market schooner, sharpshooter, 1856, half-model

straight keel with strong drag, moderate rake of post, short counter, elliptical transom sharply raked, straight, strongly raking bow rabbet, long standard cutwater fitted with billet, trails, and headrails. Draft would be 8′-3″ at post, and 4′-10″ forward, when ready for sea.

The midsection was formed with a sharply rising straight floor, carried far out, with high, hard bilge and very slight tumble home in topside. The midsection was very slightly forward of midlength; the entrance was convex, moderately sharp, the run long and very fine.

The Chesapeake Bay keel schooner, usually called a "pungy," was commonly fitted with low log rails, if intended to be employed on the Bay. However these schooners were also employed in the West Indian pineapple trade. In the 1850s a few schooners, built with bulwarks, were brought to New England for the Cape Cod oyster fishery and some of these were also used in the mackerel fishery. The appearance of the Bay schooners in the New England fisheries has been mentioned earlier.

Plate 28 is an example of a seagoing pungy schooner built at Baltimore in 1857–1858 by William Skinner and Sons for New England owners who have not been identified. Hence the schooner's name cannot be determined and no means of identification are now available.

This schooner had moderate sheer, straight keel, modest drag, almost vertical sternpost, round tuck, upper-and-lower transom, square stern, with lower transom excessively raked so that rudder stock passes through it well abaft the cross-seam. The stem rabbet was curved at forefoot and flaring at rail, fitted with the long, pointed cutwater that had begun to mark the Maryland-built sloops and schooners in the 1850s. These often had a small figurehead, sometimes a grotesque monster's head. The midsection was nearly at midlength, giving a long, slightly convex sharp entrance and a long, very fine run. The midsection had long, rising straight floor, a well-rounded, rather high bilge with small tumble home topside. It is interesting to compare the Skinner model with that by Joseph Story. The register dimensions of the Skinner half-model are 57′-9½″ x 18′-6″ x 6′-6″. This schooner was flush decked with trunk cabin, and had a low turned stanchion rail abaft the mainmast. By New England standards the Bay schooners were lightly ironed aloft and lightly built. However, built of good material, they were quite strong and lasted well.

Some of the Bay schooners transferred to Gloucester registry that have been identified were the *Mary Niles*, built at Baltimore in 1851, 63′-6″ x 18′-3″ x 6′-11″, billet, square stern, registered at Gloucester in 1851. *John*, built in Dorchester County, Maryland in 1847, 73′-9″ x 22′-6″ x 6′-6″, billet, square stern, registered at Gloucester in 1851. *Mary Jones*, built in Baltimore in 1851, 64′-4″ x 21′ x 5′-8″, billet, square stern, registered at Baltimore about 1853. *Susan Chase*, built at Baltimore in 1843, rebuilt at Greenport, New

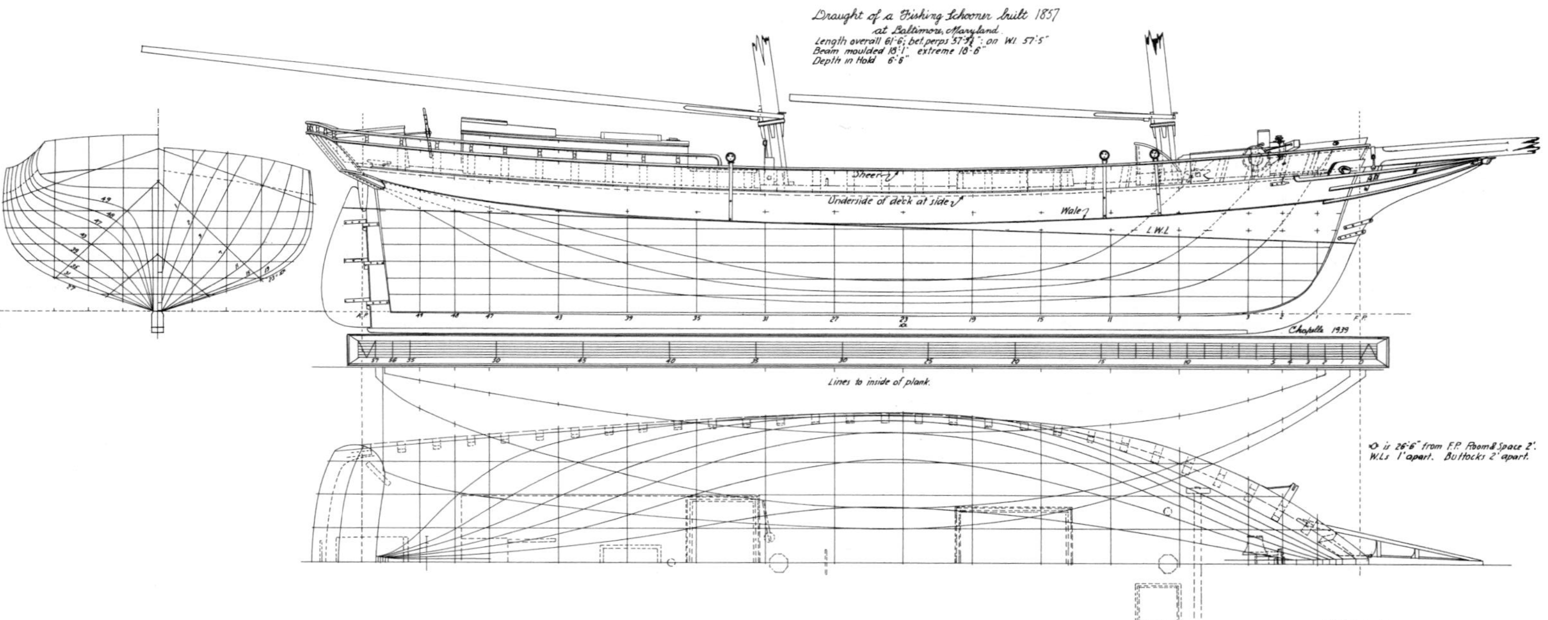
Draught of a Fishing Schooner built 1857
at Baltimore, Maryland.
Length overall 61'-6"; bet. perps 57'-9¼"; on Wl. 57'-5"
Beam moulded 18'-1" extreme 18'-6"
Depth in Hold 6'-6"
Sheer
Underside of deck at side
Wale
L.W.L.
A.P.
F.P.
Chapelle 1939
Lines to inside of plank.
⊕ is 26'-6" from F.P. Room & Space 2'.
W.Ls 1' apart. Buttocks 2' apart.
U.S.N.M. half-model No. 76101

PLATE 28. Pungy schooner, 1857–1858, half-model

York, 1849, 64′-6″ x 20′ x 5′-9″, figurehead, square stern, registered at Gloucester after 1850. *Bloomfield,* built in Talbot County, Maryland, 1850, 75′-4″ x 20′-7″ x 5′-1″, billet, square stern, register date at Gloucester not known. *Leading Star,* built at Baltimore in 1851, 69′-11″ x 20′-0″ x 6′, billet, square stern, registered at Gloucester, June 1851. *Garland* built at Baltimore in 1850, 82′-0″ x 21′-4″ x 7′-3″, billet, square stern, register date at Gloucester not known. The centerboard schooner *C. Chase,* launched at Baltimore about 1846, 60′-7″ x 19′-6″ x 5′-0″, billet head, square stern, is stated to have been built by William Skinner and Son for Wellfleet owners, but no registration can be found for her, neither on Cape Cod nor at Boston or Gloucester. Her lines are shown in *The National Watercraft Collection,* page 189.

The fashion of naming fishing schooners after individual men and women becomes noticeable in the 1830s. In the 1850s many schooners were given poetical, romantic names like those of the clipper ships of the period. Such names and those of some of the romantic type that were found in the Gloucester registers include: *Flying Cloud, Wild Pigeon, Shooting Star, Express, Witch of the Wave, Ocean Star, Flying Arrow, Golden Eagle, Challenge, Telegraph, Gazelle, Snow Squall, Winged Racer, Fearless, Sparkling Wave, Reporter, Ringleader, Typhoon, Boston Light, Eclipse, Flying Eagle, Grapeshot, Queen of Clippers, Racer, Light of Home, Weather Gage, Lookout, Island Home, Queen of the Cape, Sunny Side, Flag of Truce, Cock of the Walk, Harvest Home, Reaper, Blue Sea, Dawning Day, Flying Fish, Empire,* and *Rising Sun.*

Some of the names of pinkies were unusual to say the least, *Thinks-I-to-Myself,* or *The Reverend Salvation John Murray,* or *Wart.* During and after the War of 1812, *Enterprise, Wasp, Boxer, Java, United States, Essex, Constitution* are in the registers. From the 1850s on, the names of persons became predominant in the Gloucester Custom House registers, as will be seen.

The practice of building a number of vessels of one model or design was undoubtedly of long standing at Essex. This was the case with some pinkies in the 1830s and '40s, and may have occurred with the *Romp,* if she was as successful and original as claimed. However, one of the first models to have a large number of schooners built from it was that of the *Lookout,* built in 1857 (Plate 29). It was claimed for Joseph Story of Essex, modeler and builder of the *Lookout,* that over twenty vessels were built on her model or moulds by 1868. In donating the model to the U.S. Fish Commission this was stated by Charles O. Story, and the claim was apparently known to Captain Collins. However, only four vessels were named in the donation, as listed on the plan.

The practice of building sister ships had one factor to be remembered, however. The sister ships might vary a good deal in register dimensions. A

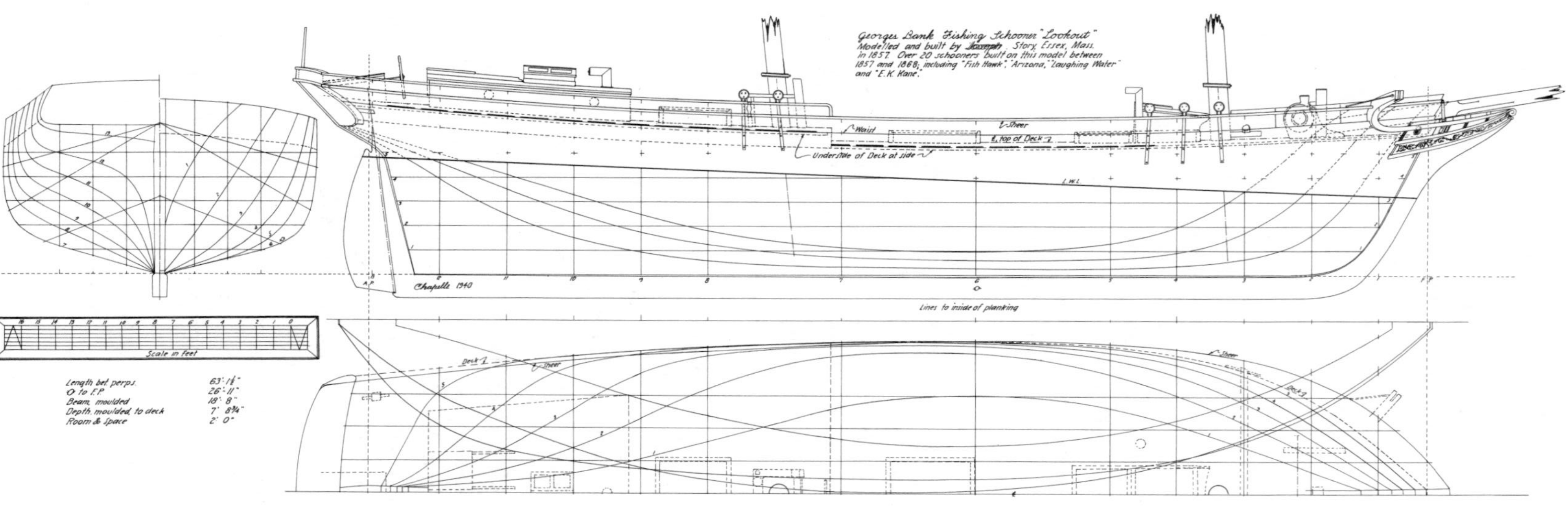
Georges Bank Fishing Schooner "Lookout"
Modelled and built by Story, Essex, Mass.
in 1857. Over 20 schooners built on this model between
1857 and 1868; including "Fish Hawk", "Arizona," "Laughing Water"
and "E.K. Kane".
Sheer
Waist
top of Deck 2
Underside of Deck at side
L.W.L.
Chapelle 1940
Lines to inside of planking
Deck 1
Deck 2
Scale in feet
Length bet. perps. 63'-1½"
O to F.P. 26'-11"
Beam, moulded 18'-8"
Depth, moulded, to deck 7' 8¾"
Room & Space 2' 0"

PLATE 29. *Lookout*, Georgesman, 1857, half-model

model of a schooner 68′-0″ registered length might have produced a very handy, fast, seaworthy schooner. Another owner wanted the same vessel, "but 4 feet longer." Frame spacing was 24 inches in the original. The additional length would be obtained by inserting one frame at midship section giving two additional frame spaces and thus adding 4′-0″ to the length of the sister ship. If this were all that had to be done, it would be a simple undertaking. However, in a straight keel hull, having drag and, often, having waterlines whose greatest widths are not all on the midsection (the "raking midsection" that can be seen on many lines plans here), it is necessary to start some distance either way from the midsection, or ⊕ frame, and refair the lines so that sides and sheer of the hull will be fair. This usually led to tracing the old moulds on the loft floor, divided to place the extra frame for the increased hull length. In refairing, the whole middle third or fourth might have to be refaired. In the process not only was the length increased to meet the owner's demands but beam and depth were usually altered—the degree depending upon what had to be done in the lofting. Generally those vessels having length added—or subtracted, as was the case in some instances—were quite different schooners, in appearance as well as in performance, from the original.

Another mode of lengthening sometimes employed was to change the bow by placing the stempost farther forward and then beginning some distance abaft the position of the original stempost, to refair the forebody into the new stem, which often produced quite a different profile from that of the original. Lengthening by the stern seems to have been the least drastic change. In this the original counter was struck off and a new one built in its place. This change took place when the model had a short counter or V-stern that had gone out of fashion and a long counter was desired in the new vessel under construction.

It was impractical for any such basic hull changes to be made to a schooner already built. These design changes had to be done first in the loft or on the drawing board, usually in the loft. Such alterations in a design necessitated new mast positions, of course.

There were numerous cases where the spaces between all the frames were increased to obtain a longer hull. This could be done without re-lofting if the keel were straight, but if curved it was usually partly lofted to get an accurate profile. The change in frame spacing was small, often the frame spaces were altered only a fraction of an inch.

There were instances where only the deck was raised as an alteration of an existing model. This could be done after the frames were raised in building and offered no serious problem. The purpose was to increase capacity, of course.

One of the difficulties in trying to connect the identification of a half-model with a given schooner or to verify a supposed sister ship is that the Custom House dimensions were never very precise, compared with lofting dimensions. Hence other supporting evidence is required before identification is possible. It is this that forbids trying to identify the sister ships of the *Lookout* by use of registry dimensions or any other available means, and also brings into doubt the true identity of the *Lookout* model.

The *Lookout* was built at Essex in 1857 as a Georgesman. Her builder-designer, Joseph Story, was one of the outstanding shipwrights of Essex in this period. The vessel's register dimensions were, by model, 63′-1½″ x 19′-0″ x 6′-4″. This does not agree with Custom House dimensions, which were 67′ x 19′-6″ x 7′-3″. However, the model is marked with names, etc. that support the identity of the model in the Museum of History and Technology (USNM 160251).

This schooner had a very moderate sheer, straight keel with some drag, raking sternpost, short counter, strongly raking transom curved athwartships, strongly raking stem rabbet, easy curve at forefoot, and slight flare carried to rail. Midsection was a little before midlength; entrance long, convex, not very sharp; run long and fine. The midship section shows straight, long floor with very modest rise, full, round bilge, and very slight tumble home in the topside.

The schooner *Flying Fish*, shown in Plate 30, was built in Essex by Jeremiah Burnham in 1857 for a mackerel fisherman. After being engaged in this fishery, out of Gloucester, for some years, she was sold to New London, out of which port she engaged in the Antarctic seal and sea elephant fisheries. Owing to her sharp lines and a large rig, she was a very fast sailer. She was a fair example of the relatively shallow-bodied clipper fisherman of the 1850s, depending to some extent on a rather deep keel and shoe outside the keel rabbet to make her weatherly. Vessels of this type and size usually had 15 to 24 inch depth of keel outside of the keel rabbet.

This clipper schooner had moderate sheer, straight keel with very modest drag, slight rake in sternpost, short counter, strong rake to transom, which was much curved athwartship. The stem rabbet raked a little, with very slight flare at rail cap. The midsection was forward of midlength. The entrance was moderately long, convex but sharp and slightly hollow about the forefoot. The run was long and very fine. The *Flying Fish* had a low raised quarterdeck and an after cabin trunk. The midsection was formed with a small rise of long, straight floor, a moderately hard turn of bilge and slight tumble home in the topside. This form of midsection had come to mark many of the clipper-type hulls, varying a little in the amount of rise of floor, hardness of the bilge, and a very small variation in tumble home. The schooners of the 1840s and '50s were all wide across the transom in proportion to thier maximum beam, with moulded hull depth to deck as little as

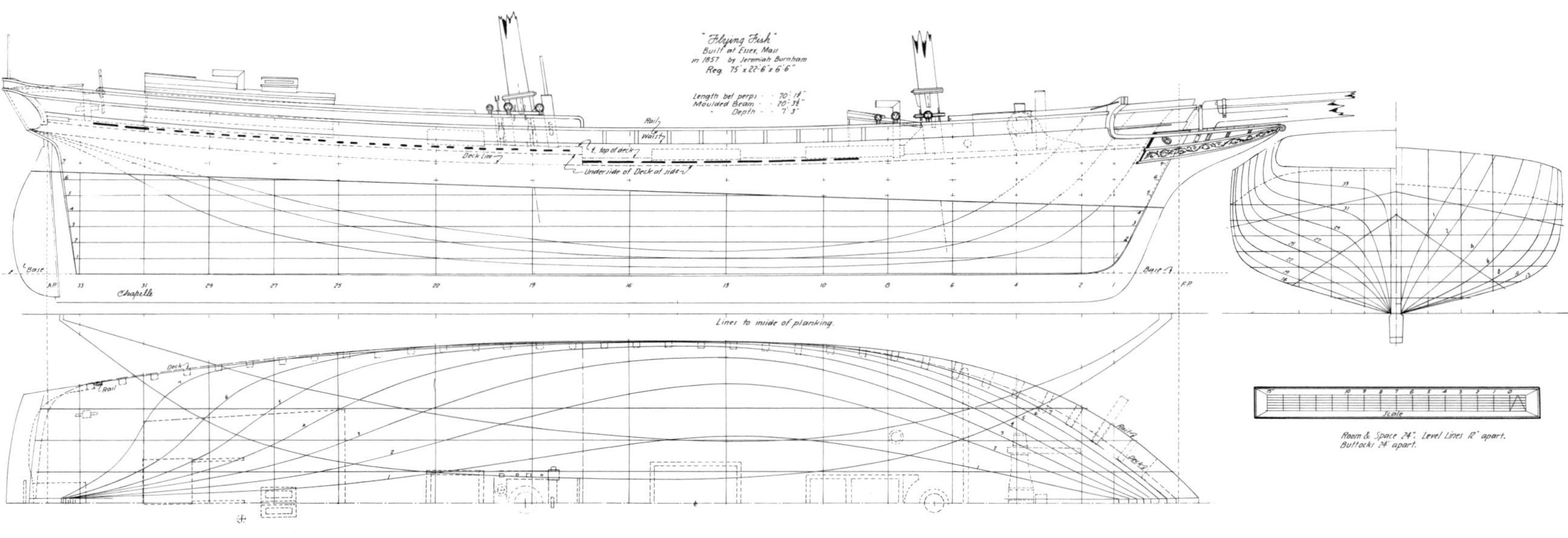
"Flying Fish"
Built at Essex, Mass
in 1857 by Jeremiah Burnham
Reg. 75' x 22'6" x 6'6"
Length bet perps - - 70' 1¼"
Moulded Beam - - 20' 3½"
" Depth - - 7' 3"
Rail
Waist
℄ top of deck
Deck Line
Underside of Deck at side
Base
AP
FP
Chapelle
Lines to inside of planking.
Deck
Rail
Scale
Room & Space 24". Level Lines 12" apart.
Buttocks 24" apart.

PLATE 30. *Flying Fish*, 1857, half- and rigged-models

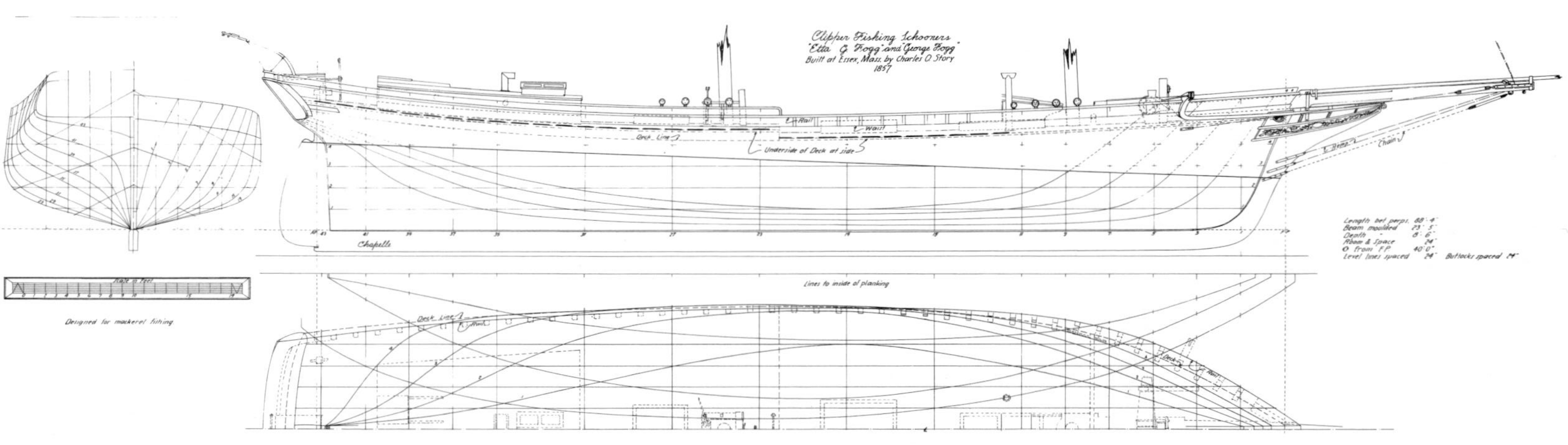
Clipper Fishing Schooners
"Etta G. Fogg" and "George Fogg"
Built at Essex, Mass. by Charles O. Story
1857
Rail
Waist
Deck Line
Underside of Deck at side
Chain
Chapelle
Length bet. perps. 88' 4"
Beam moulded 23' 5"
Depth 8' 6"
Room & Space 24"
O from F.P. 40' 0"
Level lines spaced 24"
Buttocks spaced 24"
Lines to inside of planking
Deck Line
Rail
Scale in Feet
Designed for mackerel fishing

PLATE 31. *Etta G. Fogg*, *George Fogg*, clippers, 1857 half- and rigged-models one third the moulded beam, producing a hull having a small range of safe heel; that is, a heel from which a schooner could right herself and not capsize.

Plate 31 illustrates another example of a clipper fishing schooner of the 1850s. The half-model was used to build the sister ships *Etta G. Fogg* and *George Fogg* at Essex in 1857. The designer-builder was Charles D. Story, who gave the model to the U.S. Fish Commission. These schooners were extreme clippers built for Wellfleet owners and used in the summer mackerel fishery; in winter they were used to freight oysters from Chesapeake Bay to Wellfleet. Fast sailers were required, so these schooners were heavily canvassed. The vessels were nearly identical sister ships, having register dimensions 88′-4″ x 23′-9″ x 7′-9″, by scale from the model; and the Custom House dimensions of the *Etta G. Fogg* were 88.7′ x 24.7′ x 8.3′, new measurement.

The half-model had a rather straight sheer, a straight keel with a good deal of drag for a clipper; the sternpost nearly vertical, a short rather deep counter, an elliptical transom with marked rounding athwartships. The stem rabbet was rounded at the forefoot, raking forward, flaring moderately, to rail, fitted with a long cutwater having billet, trails, and headrails. The entrance was long, sharp, and slightly concave below the load line. The run was long and easy but a little steeper than in *Flying Fish*. The midsection was formed with small rise of straight floor, carried well outboard, giving a low, rather hard turn of the bilge, with somewhat marked tumble home in the topside. These schooners were handsome, having the "long, low look of the clipper" as one newspaper reporter wrote about a later schooner of this type.

The rigged-model in the National Watercraft Collection had the following spar dimensions: bowsprit, total length 36′, jibboom outside cap 17′, foremast cap above deck 64′, fore-topmast, total length 36′-6″, foreboom, 30′, fore gaff 29′, mainboom, 58′, main gaff 33′, mainmast, above deck 71′-6″, main-topmast, total length, 37′, mainmast head, 7′-9″, and foremast head 7′-6″.

The deep, outside keel shows prominently in Plate 31. The curving profile of the rudder became common in the 1850s, that shown on the *Foggs* seems to have become more or less standard for a while at Essex. The rig of the clippers was, in summer, gaff mainsail, gaff foresail, jumbo, fore and main gaff topsails, fisherman staysail, jib and jib topsail; in winter the jibboom and fore topmast were struck; the jib topsail, fisherman staysail, fore-gaff topsail, and jib were left ashore.

In 1858 a schooner named *We're Here* was built on the lines shown in Plate 32 by Willard R. and Daniel A. Burnham, having the Custom House register dimensions of 69′ x 21′-2″ x 7′-6″. Intended for the mackerel fishery, in which she was employed during the summer, she was also used in the

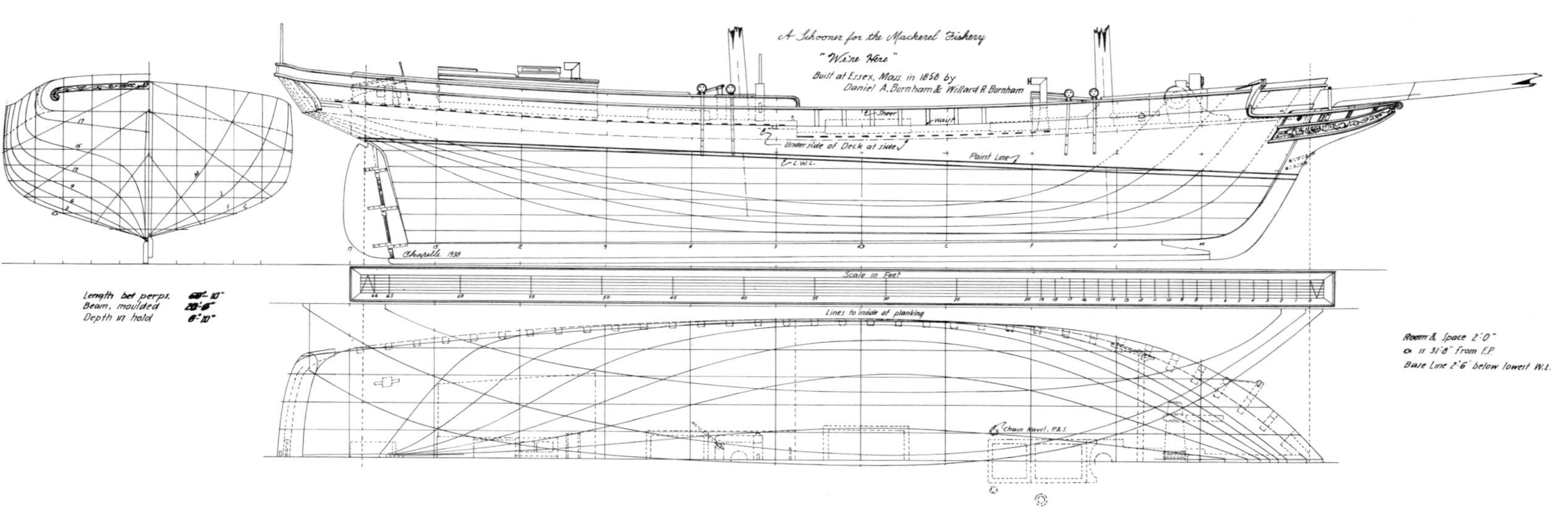
A Schooner for the Mackerel Fishery
"We're Here"
Built at Essex, Mass. in 1858 by
Daniel A. Burnham & Willard R. Burnham
Sheer
Waist
Underside of Deck at side
Paint Line
L.W.L.
Chapelle 1938
Scale in Feet
Lines to inside of planking
Chain Navel, P&S.
Length bet perps.
Beam, moulded
Depth in hold
Room & Space 2'0"
⊗ 11 31'8" from F.P.
Base Line 2'6" below lowest W.L.
Half-model USNM 54471

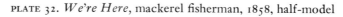

PLATE 32. *We're Here*, mackerel fisherman, 1858, half-model

winter fruit trade to the Gulf of Mexico. She was seized by the Confederates at the outbreak of the Civil War and is supposed to have become a blockade runner; her end is unknown.

The name of this vessel was appropriated by Kipling for *Captains Courageous*, but the schooner of this name had disappeared from the New England fisheries long before the novel was written.

The *We're Here* was a sharpshooter schooner having moderate sheer, straight keel with marked drag, raking sternpost, a longer and shallower counter than has been shown earlier, elliptical transom, heavily curved athwartships. The stem rabbet curved a good deal at forefoot and raked forward to rail line. The midsection was a little forward of midlength; the entrance was convex, somewhat sharp and long. The run was very fine and fairly long. The midsection showed a straight rising floor carried well outboard, with a high, rather hard bilge and with some tumble home in the topside. The register dimensions by scale are 66′-10″ x 20′-10″ x 6′-10″. The half-model of this schooner was painted in what are supposed to be the original colors: dark green (forest) with a multicolored stripe along the underside of the waist of white, yellow, red, white and with the trailboard and billet carvings gilded and painted. The bottom was a dull red but showed evidence of repainting. At any rate, Wattersteds' copper-bearing paint appeared in some parts of the United States in 1851 and Tarr and Wonson came on the market at Gloucester in 1863 and became the standard brand at Gloucester. (See "Paint" in Appendix.)

Plate 33 is the lines of a small Georges Banker whose model, marked "1859, scale ⅜ inches," was found in Essex. It cannot be otherwise identified. A handsome, able-appearing schooner, she was a good example of a fast carrier, for she shows a well-distributed displacement. Her model would produce register dimensions 65′-1″ x 18′-5″x 7′-6″. The model showed a lively sheer, much drag to the straight keel, moderate rake of sternpost, short counter, an elliptical transom set at a very sharp rake, moderate rake and small flare to stem rabbet, rather short cutwater fitted with trails and headrails. The midsection was nearly at midlength, permitting a rather long, sharp entrance with some hollow at forefoot and a moderately long and fine run. She had a long, low quarterdeck.

The midsection had very little rise to the straight floor, which is unusually short for this period; a rather slack turn of the bilge with very slight tumble home in the topside. This schooner was obviously a departure from the clipper model and shows that some of the bankers were not built to the popular proportions but rather to a deeper and somewhat safer pattern.

The "salt bankers" of the 1840s and early 1850s appear to have included some fast carriers of more conservative design. Plate 34 shows the lines of a half-model from which two bankers were built at Wells, Maine, in 1850 or

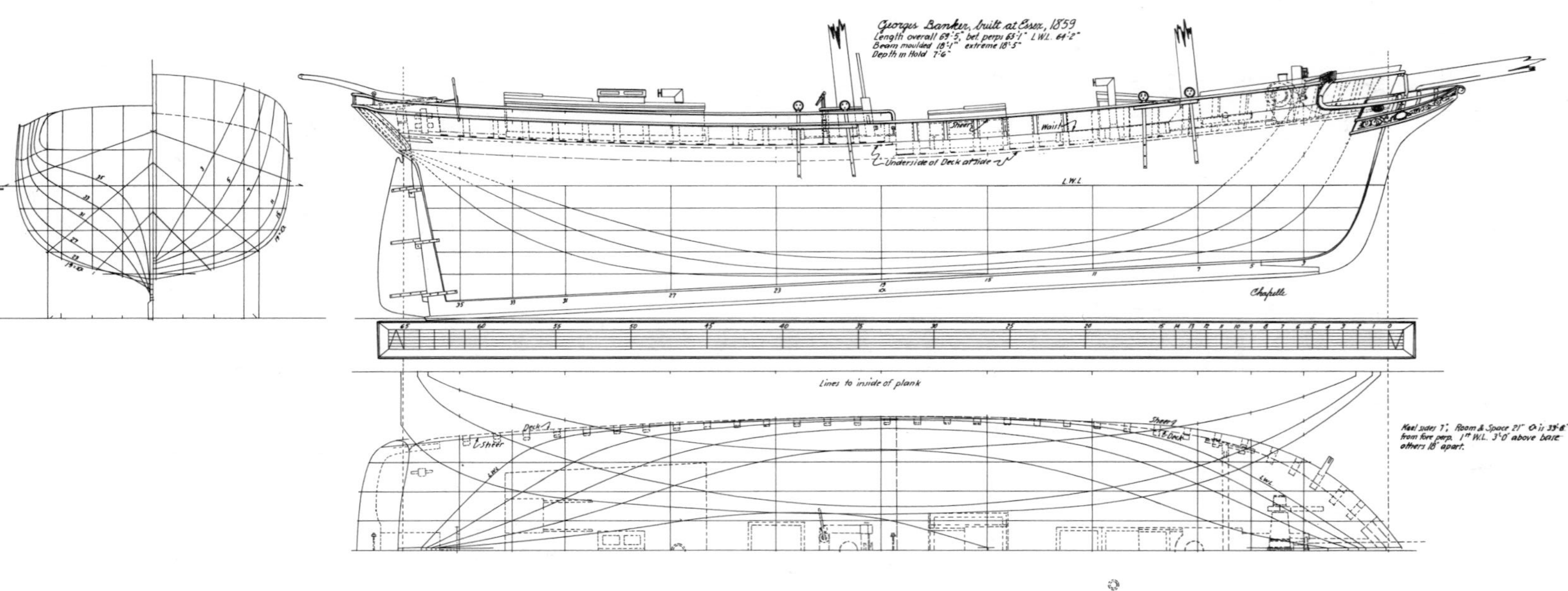
Georges Banker, built at Essex, 1859
Length overall 69'-5", bet. perps 65'-1" L.W.L. 64'-2"
Beam moulded 18'-1" extreme 18'-5"
Depth in Hold 7'-6"
Sheer
Waist
Underside of Deck at side
L.W.L.
Chapelle
Lines to inside of plank
Deck
Sheer
Keel sides 7", Room & Space 21" ⊙ is 33'-6" from fore perp. 1st W.L. 3'-0" above base others 18" apart.
Essex model found by L.H.S.

PLATE 33. Unidentified Georges Banker, 1859, half-model

1851. For a banker this was a sharp model, but in stern and head, as well as in other details, the sisters were bankers of their date. This model represents a banker of about average size for her time: 73′-6″ on the main rail, 68′ between perpendiculars, 19′-6″ moulded beam, 19′-11″ extreme beam and 7′-6″ depth in hold, showing a straight keel of moderate drag, a rather straight sheer, slightly raking sternpost, curved and flaring stem rabbet of moderate rake. Her entrance was short, full, and convex. The run was long, fine, and straight in the buttocks. The greatest beam was a little forward of midlength. The midsection was formed with much rise in the long, straight floor, a well-rounded bilge with slight tumble home in the rail close to the rail cap. The cutwater was short and heavy in the old fashion, and her stern was formed with upper-and-lower transoms, popular earlier.

This schooner had a much finer run and more rise of floor than was usual in her type; a fast-carrier design, perhaps, intended for two or more employments. So much effort to design fast carriers marks the evolution of the bankers from the 1850s to the 1890s that there was nothing unusual in finding the bankers, after 1855, no longer the heavy-sailing vessels traditional for those of the type in the 1830s and early '40s. Rather, they became half-clippers, or sharp-lined vessels of relatively great size and speed, suitable for multiple employment.

A second banker of the fast-carrier type is shown in Plate 35. This schooner was built in 1852, at Newburyport for the cod fishery in the Gulf of St. Lawrence. She was more carrier than fast, compared to the Maine-built schooners shown in Plate 34, but her well-formed run suggests that she may have a good turn of speed, under favorable conditions. This model showed a straight keel of moderate drag, slight sheer, some rake to the sternpost, upper-and-lower transoms formed with a flat lower transom, the upper transom curved athwartship. The effect was that of a transition toward the short counter-and-transom. The stem rabbet flared moderately, with little fore rake. The entrance was short, full, and convex. The cutwater was short and heavy in the old fashion. The run was quite fine of moderate length.

The vessel on this model would measure 79′-5″ on the rail, 74′-4″ between perpendiculars, 20′-10″ moulded beam, 21′-3″ extreme beam, and 8′-10″ depth of hold. The midsection was a little forward of midlength and had a slightly rising, long straight floor, low, firm turn of bilge, and slight tumble home in the topside. The short, heavy cutwater, shown in the last two plates, was rapidly going out of fashion when these models were made.

The early 1860s were not years in which there was much construction of fishing craft, but up until the outbreak of the Civil War there was some activity. An interesting occurrence during the late 1850s and early 1860s was the building of four fishing schooners in the shipyard of Donald McKay, the great Massachusetts clipper ship builder. These were the *R. R. Higgins,*

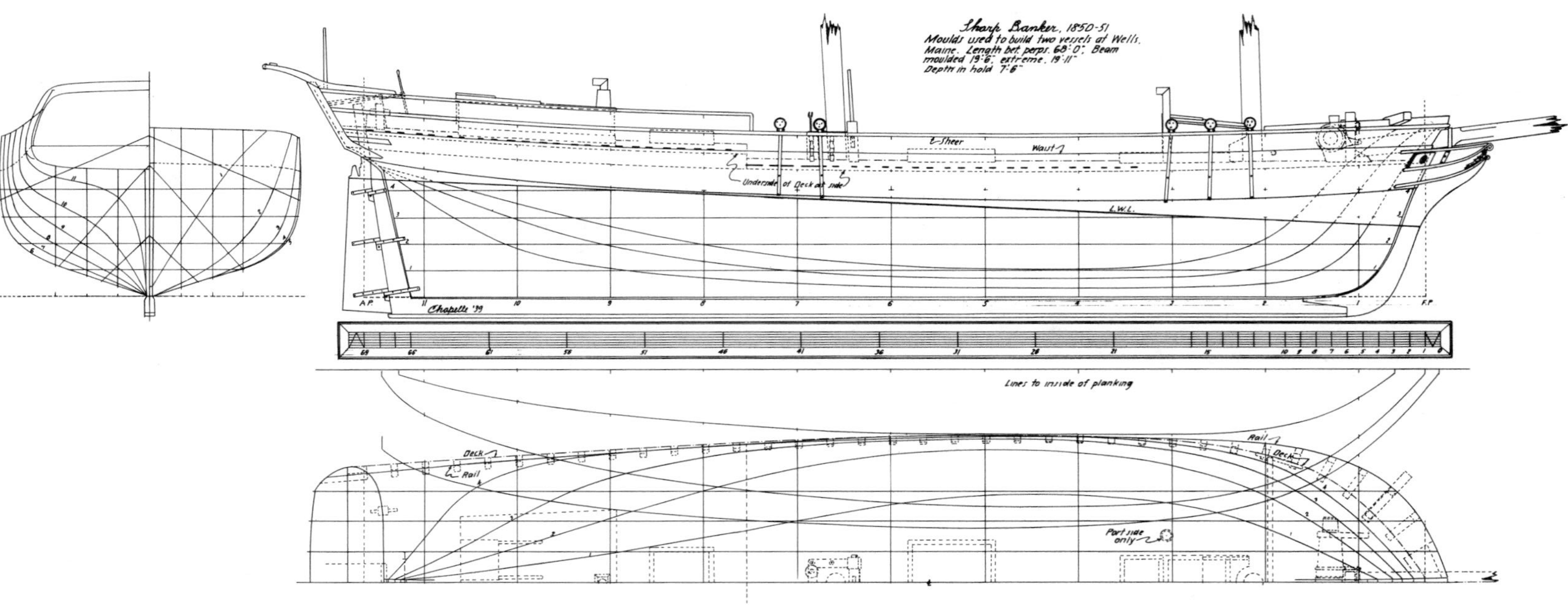
Sharp Banker, 1850-51
Moulds used to build two vessels at Wells, Maine. Length bet. perps. 68'0", Beam moulded 19'6", extreme, 19'11"
Depth in hold 7'6"
Sheer
Waist
Underside of Deck at side
L.W.L.
A.P.
F.P.
Chapelle '39
Lines to inside of planking
Deck
Rail
Port side only

PLATE 34. Unidentified Maine salt banker, 1850–1851, half-model

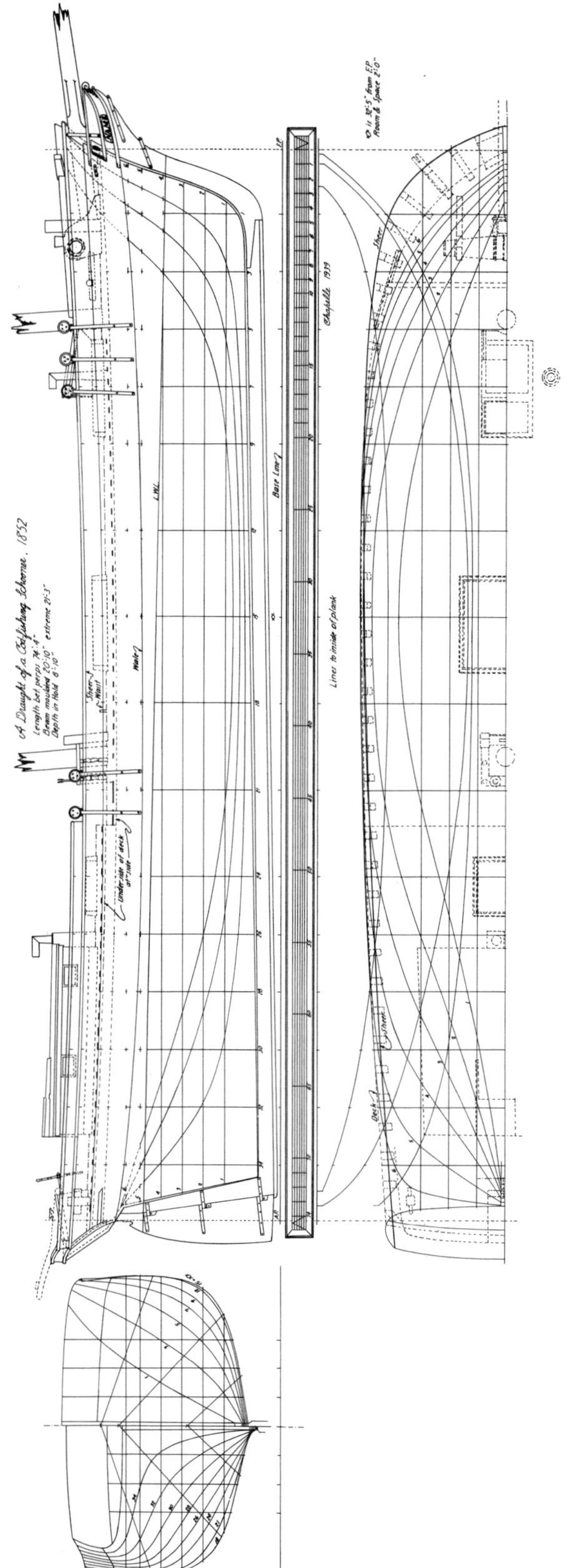

A Draught of a Codfishing Schooner, 1852
Length bet. perps 74'-4"
Beam moulded 20'-10" extreme 21'-3"
Depth in Hold 8'-10"
Sheer
Waist
Wale
LWL
Underside of deck at side
Base Line
Chapelle 1939
Liners to inside of plank
Sheer
Deck

PLATE 35. Newburyport banker, 1852, half-model

built in 1858; the *Benjamin S. Wright*, built in 1859; the *Mary B. Dyer*, built in 1860 along with a sister ship, the *H. & R. Atwood.* All were built for the Cape Cod fishery but were owned in Boston. The *R. R. Higgins* was stated to have been designed and built by Donald McKay's son, Cornelius W. McKay, as a "model craft that would outsail any vessel belonging to either Cape Ann or Cape Cod," according to Richard C. McKay, grandson of Donald McKay.* The *R. R. Higgins* differed in model from the other three to the extent that it appears probable that someone else (Donald McKay is the most likely candidate) designed the sisters *Dyer* and *Atwood* as well as the *Wright.*

Plate 36 shows the lines of the *Dyer* and *Atwood*, traced from a drawing made in 1889 by John L. Frisbee, mentioned earlier as the instructor in night trade schools in Charlestown and South Boston, where marine drafting, modeling, and ship and boat design were taught. This drawing and those of the *Benjamin S. Wright* and of the *R. R. Higgins* were in Frisbee's reference files. It is not known where or how he obtained the originals that he copied. Most of the drawings in his file had identification, but the McKay plans were exceptions.

Plate 36 shows a clipper schooner having marked sheer, straight keel, moderate drag, upright sternpost, short counter, elliptical transom set to a strong rake, much curved athwartships. Stem rabbet was straight and raking with hard curve at forefoot. Entrance was short, strong shoulders, very hollow from above LWL to forefoot.

The run was long and very fine, the straight buttock lines were very noticeable. The midsection was formed with moderately rising straight floors carried well outboard with a rather quick turn in the bilge and very marked tumble home amidships.

Though the *Wright* and the other McKay schooners were good-looking vessels they do not appear to have attracted any attention to the eastward. Some of the McKay schooners did not remain in the fisheries very long, becoming packets and West Indian traders.

A more typical fishing schooner design of the early 1860s is shown in Plate 37; this is the *Charlotte Brown* built at Essex by Joseph Story. Launched in 1860, this vessel was a modified clipper sharpshooter compromise in model. She was 83′-0″ moulded length at rail cap, 78′-10″ between perpendiculars, 22′-6″ moulded beam, 22′-10″ extreme beam, 7′-0″ depth in hold. She drew almost 8 feet loaded for sea.

Like many of the clipper schooners, the *Charlotte Brown* had a straightish sheer, low freeboard, slightly raking sternpost, short counter, strongly raking, broad elliptical transom, straight, raking stem rabbet, straight keel with

* Richard C. McKay, *Some Famous Sailing Ships and Their Builder, Donald McKay* (New York and London, 1928), p. 357. This book is not to be relied upon.

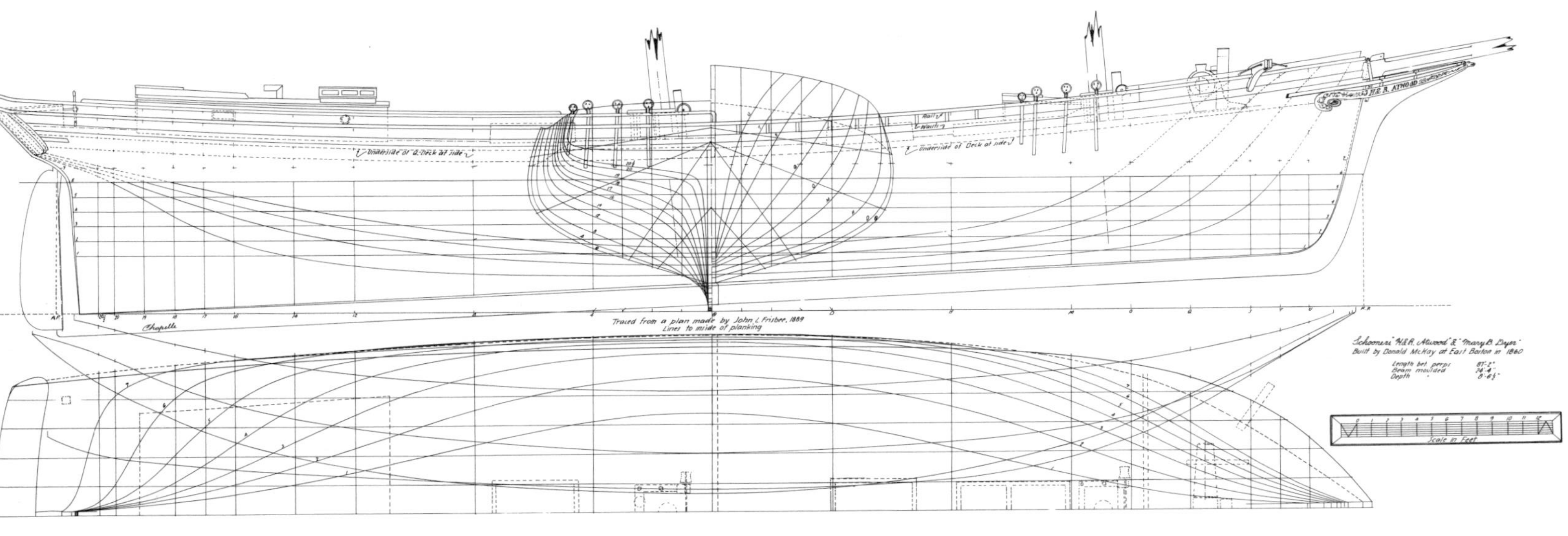
Schooners "H.&R. Atwood" & "Mary B. Dyer"
Built by Donald McKay at East Boston in 1860
Length bet. perps 87'-2"
Beam moulded 24'-4"
Depth " 8'-6½"
Scale in Feet
Traced from a plan made by John L. Frisbee, 1889
Lines to inside of planking
Underside of Q. Deck at side
Underside of Deck at side
Chapelle

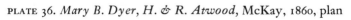

PLATE 36. *Mary B. Dyer, H. & R. Atwood*, McKay, 1860, plan

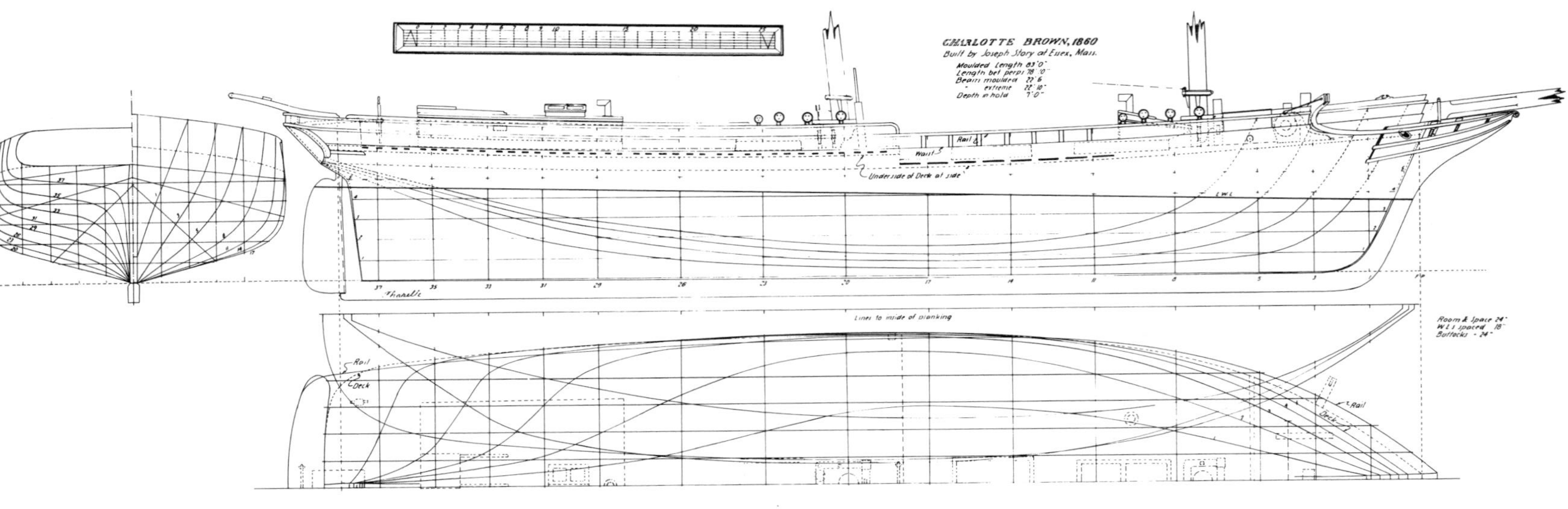
CHARLOTTE BROWN, 1860
Built by Joseph Story at Essex, Mass.
Moulded Length 83'0"
Length bet perps 78'0"
Beam moulded 22'6
" extreme 22'10"
Depth in hold 7'0"
Rail
Waist
Underside of Deck at side
LWL
Lines to inside of planking
Room & Space 24"
WLs spaced 18"
Buttocks - 24"
Deck

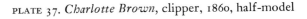

PLATE 37. *Charlotte Brown*, clipper, 1860, half-model

very moderate drag. The midsection was formed with rising straight floors carried well outboard, with a quick turn in the bilge. The entrance was long, sharp, and slightly concave at load line, just abaft the stem. The run was very long with some straight to the buttocks. The *Brown* had a long head, fitted with trails and headrails, in the style popular when she was built.

Vessels built to this model would have great power to carry sail, up to the point where their bulwark rail caps went underwater. At this heel, the skipper began to reduce sail, for a little beyond this they would reach the point where the vessels might capsize or swamp. Because of their form and ballasting, it took strong winds to heel these schooners very much, and up to that point they were very fast indeed. But on the wind in a gale they were not very weatherly nor safe in clawing off a leeshore. Running in heavy weather required attention and care, for some of the clippers would broach if driven too hard on this point of sailing. The number of vessels lost in the fisheries was steadily rising to the disastrous levels reached after 1870.

When the Civil War ended in 1865, the New England fishing fleet was depleted and required new vessels. There is not space here to examine the state of the fisheries then affected by treaties with Britain dealing with American fishing rights off the Canadian coasts, the economics of the fisheries, importation of fish into the United States, bounties and political action. It is sufficient for the purpose here to show that a revival in schooner construction started in 1865, but with no great change in proportions and dimensions in the new vessels' designs.

In 1865 Boston fishermen of Irish origin began experiments with the beam trawl used in the North Sea. For this purpose they had the small schooner *Sylph* built by Dennison J. Lawlor at East Boston, Massachusetts. The trawl gear was found to be uneconomical and was discarded, the schooner then was employed as a market fisherman for which the *Sylph*'s speed fitted her very well. Plate 38 shows this vessel's distinctive model. She was 55′-8½″ between perpendiculars, 17′-1″ moulded beam, 17′-5″ extreme beam, and 6′-4″ depth in hold. She drew 9′-8″ at post, but only 4′-3″ at forefoot.

The *Sylph* had much sheer, straight keel with unusually great drag for a New England fisherman of this time. Her sternpost was nearly vertical, with a short counter and an elliptical transom curved athwartship and set with a strong rake. The stem rabbet was also upright above the load line, moderately curved below. She was very sharp-ended, having a long, markedly concave entrance and a long, fine run with some straight in the buttocks where they crossed the load line. The midsection had slightly hollow rising floors and a high, well-rounded bilge with much tumble home in the topside. Compared to her contemporaries, she was a safe and very fast weatherly schooner, but of very small capacity. The *Sylph* had a mainmast 54′-0″ deck to cap, foremast 52′-0″ deck to cap, bowsprit 27′-0″ total length, or 17′-0″ knightheads

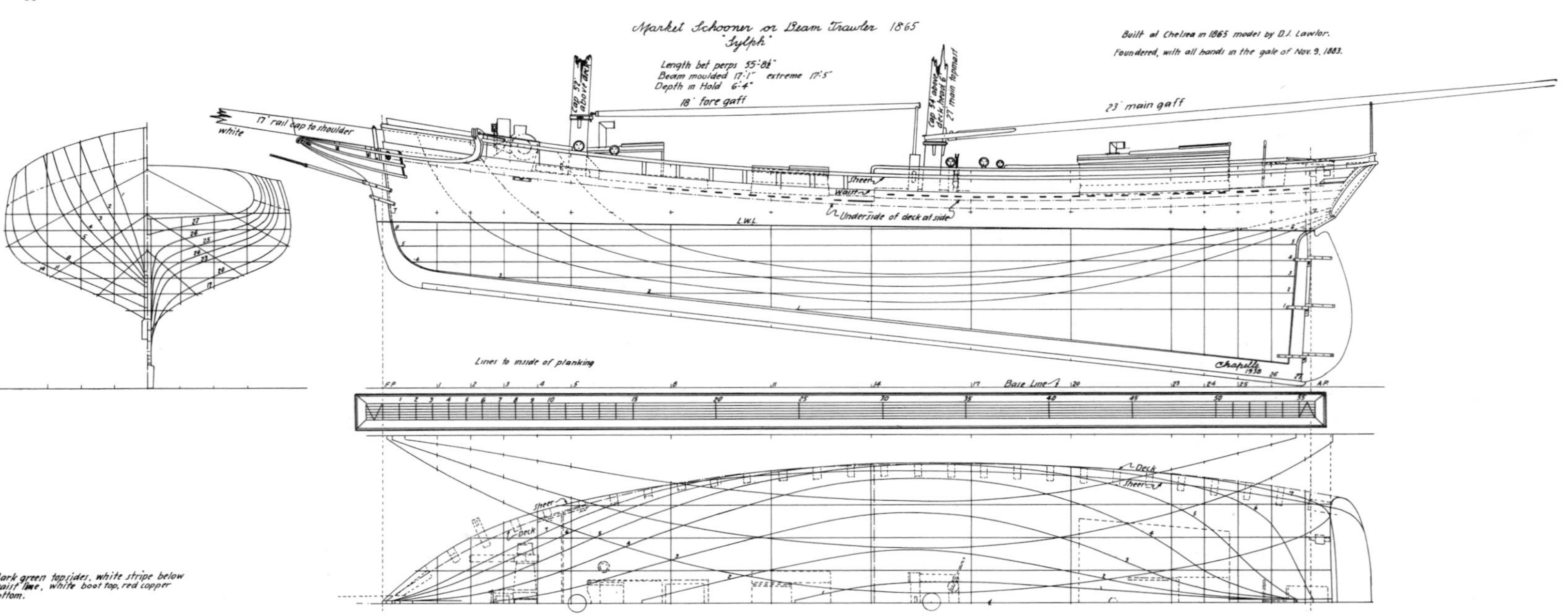
Market Schooner or Beam Trawler 1865
"Sylph"
Length bet perps 55'-8½"
Beam moulded 17'-1" extreme 17'-5"
Depth in Hold 6'-4"
18' fore gaff
23' main gaff
Built at Chelsea in 1865 model by D.J. Lawlor.
Foundered, with all hands in the gale of Nov. 9, 1883.
cap 52' above deck
cap 54' above deck, head 6'
27' main topmast
17' rail cap to shoulder
white
Sheer
Waist
Underside of deck at side
LWL
Lines to inside of planking
Chapelle 1938
Base Line
F.P.
A.P.
Deck
Sheer
Dark green topsides, white stripe below waist line, white boot top, red copper bottom.

PLATE 38. *Sylph*, beam trawler, 1865, half- and rigged-models to shoulder of pole. The foreboom was 19′-0″ long, fore gaff 18′-0″, main-boom 47′-0″, main gaff 23′-0″, and the main-topmast was 27′-0″ long, including 5′-0″ doubling. She was ballasted entirely with pig iron.

Rock ballast was carried in New England fishing schooners into the 1880s. Some of the rock ballast was actually bog ore, taken from the Essex River, but granite was most common. Because of the bulk required for rock ballast, schooners designed for its use were less sharp in midsection than vessels intended for iron ballast. This matter will receive attention later.

In 1866 Lawlor designed and built the *Thomas E. Evans* at Chelsea, Massachusetts for a Boston market fishing schooner. She proved to be very fast and remained a fisherman for only a short time; she then became a packet in the Bay of Honduras. She strongly resembled *Sylph* in model but was a more powerful vessel, having pronounced hardness in the bilges, which would increase her power to carry sail in strong winds.

Plate 39 shows the lines of the *Evans*. She had much sheer and a straight keel having a great amount of drag. Her sternpost was vertical with a short counter and an elliptical transom curved athwartship and set at a sharp rake. Her stem rabbet was straight and slightly raking. She had very fine ends, the entrance slightly concave abaft the stem and long, the run was long and very straight in the buttocks. The midsection was formed with rising slightly hollow floors and a very hard high bilge, with slight tumble home in the topside. She was 56′-4″ between perpendiculars, 17′-8″ moulded beam, 18′-0″ extreme beam, 6′-8½″ moulded depth. Her rig was the same plan as that of the *Sylph*, and of the same dimensions, except that her masts were 3′-0″ longer.

These vessels show the development of a design idea in which an original design was developed in following models to give more power and speed, apparently very successfully in these schooners. The plan and data show that a safe vessel was sought by use of relatively great draft or depth. Power to carry sail was increased by use of the hard bilges. The rig of these schooners had a single headsail, the same as the rig of the earlier sharpshooters. The nose pole became an "improvement" when lengthened and fitted as the "pole bowsprit" into the Edward Burgess-designed *Carrie E. Phillips*, built twenty-one years later. Also, these Lawlor schooners had the greater depth that was to be the objective in the first "improved" schooners in 1885.

Another noted fisherman built by Lawlor at Chelsea, Massachusetts, in 1866, from his own design, was the *Sarah H. Cressy*. This schooner, shown in Plate 40, was a modified clipper in model; she was shallow but with more deadrise than in the average clipper of her date. The *Cressy* proved to be a very fast sailer but was only a slight improvement in weatherliness and safety, over the average in her type. The *Cressy* was 71′-2″ between perpendiculars, 21′-2″ moulded beam, and 7′-8½″ moulded depth—keel rabbet to underside

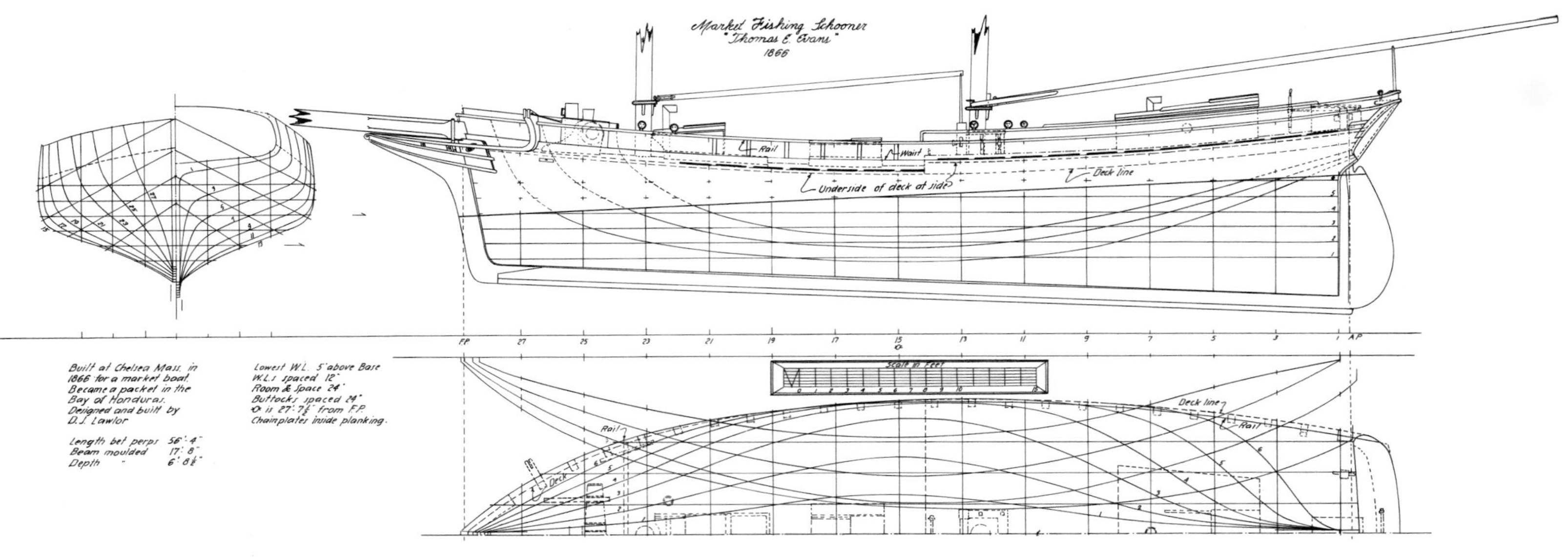
Market Fishing Schooner
"Thomas E. Evans"
1866
Rail
Wait
Deck line
Underside of deck at side
Scale in Feet
Deck line
Rail
Deck
Built at Chelsea Mass. in
1866 for a market boat.
Became a packet in the
Bay of Honduras.
Designed and built by
D. J. Lawlor
Length bet perps 56'-4"
Beam moulded 17'-8"
Depth 6'-8½"
Lowest W.L. 5' above Base
W.L.s spaced 12"
Room & Space 24"
Buttocks spaced 24"
⊕ is 27'-7½" from F.P.
Chainplates inside planking.

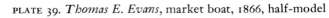

PLATE 39. *Thomas E. Evans*, market boat, 1866, half-model

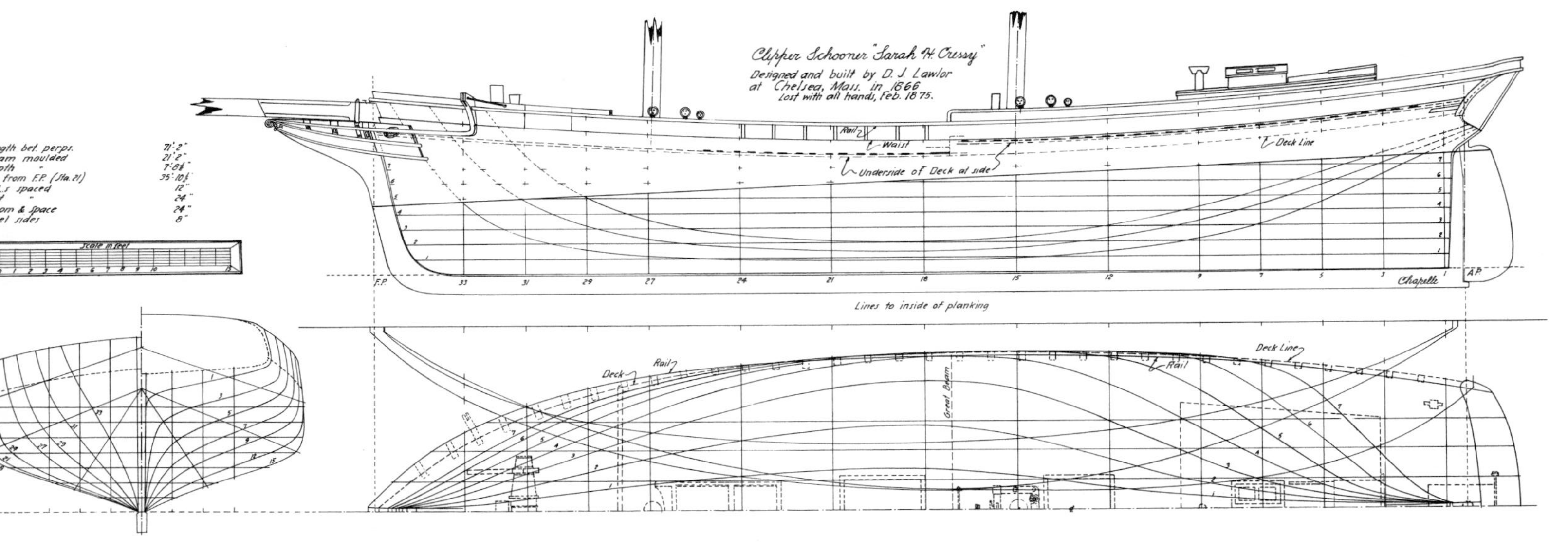
Clipper Schooner "Sarah H. Cressy"
Designed and built by D. J. Lawlor
at Chelsea, Mass. in 1866
Lost with all hands, Feb. 1875.
Length bet. perps. 71' 2"
Beam moulded 21' 2"
Depth " 7' 8½"
⊙ from F.P. (Sta. 21) 35' 10½"
W.L.s spaced 12"
But " 24"
Room & Space 24"
Keel sides 8"
Scale in feet
Rail
Waist
Underside of Deck at side
Deck Line
F.P.
A.P.
Chapelle
Lines to inside of planking
Deck
Great Beam

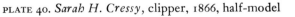

PLATE 40. *Sarah H. Cressy*, clipper, 1866, half-model

of deck plank at side. This schooner had marked sheer, straight keel with more than usual drag in a clipper, vertical sternpost with short counter. The transom was elliptical, strongly curved athwartship and sharply raked. The stem rabbet was straight, from well below the load line to the rail cap, and slightly raked. Like the *Sylph* and *Evans*, the stem was graced with a long head, complete with trails and headrails. The ends were very fine; the entrance was long, concave and sharp, with hollow just abaft the stem at load line and below. The run was long, straight in the buttocks with moderate fore-and-aft camber at quarterbeam. The midsection was formed with marked rise of straight floor, for a vessel of her proportions and type. The rise was carried well outboard to a hard bilge with some tumble home in the topside. This vessel was lost with all hands in February 1875.

Another clipper fisherman, highly regarded as a good example of the type, was the *Lizzie E. Choate* built at Ipswich in 1866. She was a large vessel for her time and type, 90′-3″ between perpendiculars, 24′-1½″ moulded beam, 9′-10½″ moulded depth. She was commanded by Joseph W. Collins and engaged in the mackerel fishery in 1866–1867, and freighting oysters from the Chesapeake to Boston in the winter of 1867. In 1868 the *Choate* was sold, to enter the West Indian fruit trade out of New York. She capsized and foundered in a gale on February 7 with the loss of all except three hands, who were rescued from the waterlogged hulk. Collins had left her prior to to this last voyage to the Indies. The loss of this schooner, which he knew well, was one of the incidents that led Collins to begin the crusade for improved fishing schooner models in the 1880s.

The *Choate*, shown in Plate 41, had slight sheer, straight keel with slight drag, nearly vertical sternpost with a short counter and elliptical transom, strongly raked and heavily curved athwartship. The stem rabbet was slightly flaring and slightly raked. The entrance was long, sharp, and concave, with much hollow in the level lines abaft the forefoot. The run was long, but somewhat full with very short straight buttocks right aft. The midsection was formed with moderately rising, straight floors reaching well outboard, a low, hard bilge, and vertical topside. The half-model of this schooner is in the U.S. National Museum of History and Technology, USNM 160112, and is on the unusual scale, for a fishing schooner half-model, of ⅓ inch = 1 foot. Collins considered the *Choate* a very fast sailer and, until her loss, a good vessel for the mackerel fishery.

The practice of building a number of fishing schooners on a single half-model has been mentioned. In 1867 a clipper schooner named *Theresa D. Baker* was launched at Essex from the yard of James and McKenzie. This vessel was much admired, and fourteen schooners were built on the *Baker*'s moulds between 1867 and 1889. The half-model, shown in Plate 42, was deposited in the Peabody Marine Museum of Salem by John James, one of

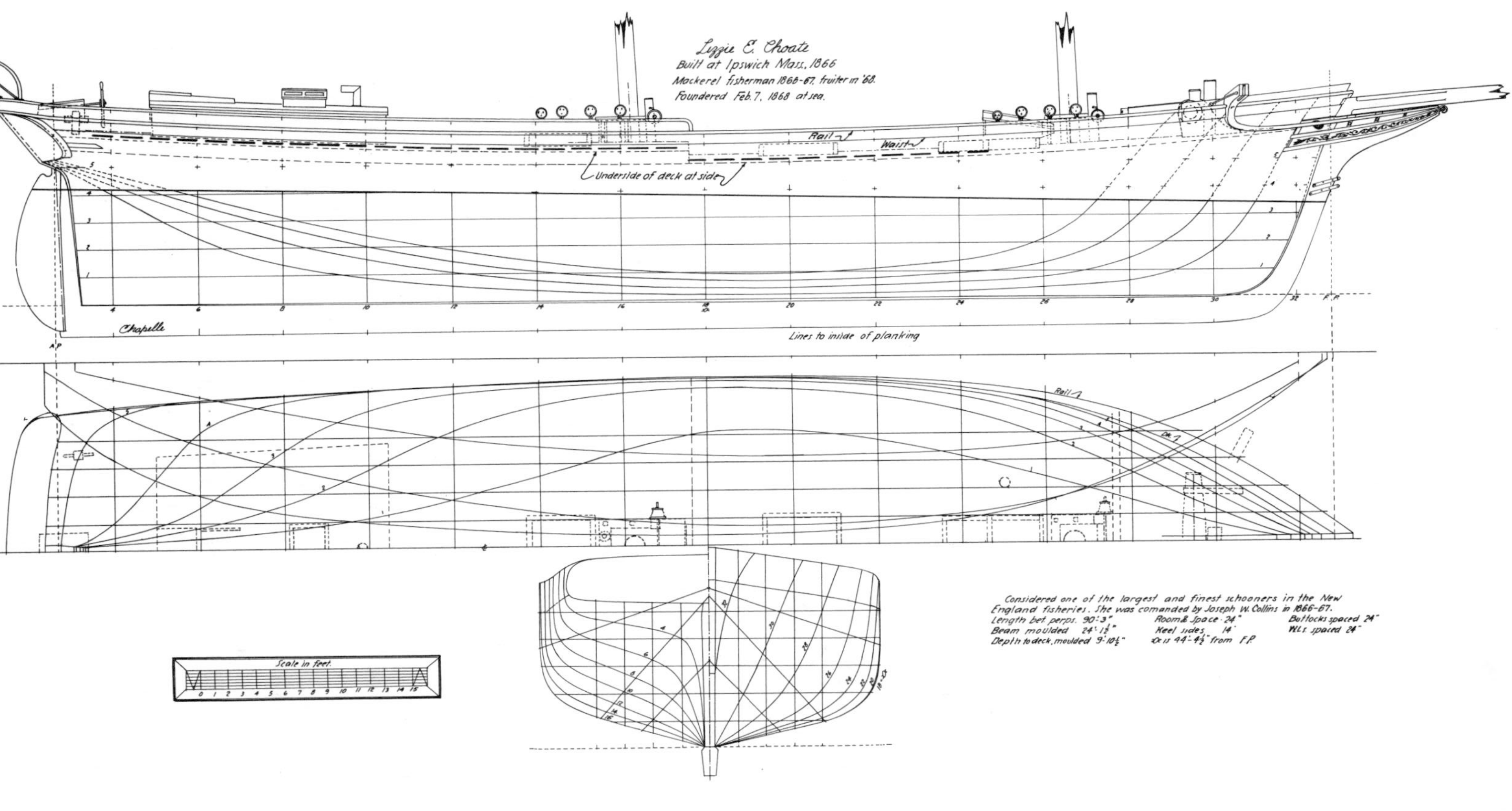
Lizzie E. Choate
Built at Ipswich Mass. 1866
Mackerel fisherman 1866-67. fruiter in '68.
Foundered Feb. 7. 1868 at sea.
Rail
Waist
Underside of deck at side
Chapelle
Lines to inside of planking
Considered one of the largest and finest schooners in the New England fisheries. She was comanded by Joseph W. Collins in 1866-67.
Length bet. perps. 90'-3"
Beam moulded 24'-1½"
Depth to deck, moulded 9'-10½"
Room & Space 24"
Keel sides 14"
⊗ is 44'-4½" from F.P.
Buttocks spaced 24"
W.L.s spaced 24"
Scale in feet.

PLATE 41. *Lizzie E. Choate*, clipper, 1866, half-model

the builders, in 1908. Names of some of the schooners supposedly built on the *Baker*'s moulds are written on the half-model. But, as stated on Plate 42, the Custom House registers show that the named schooners on this plan were all 23′-0″ moulded beam, or a little more, whereas the half-model is for a vessel only 21′-6″ moulded beam. Therefore, in spite of the strong evidence of the builder and the names written on the model, its identification must be considered doubtful. The most that can yet be said about the identification is that the model shown in Plate 42 may have been much like the *Baker*.

The schooner Plate 42 would be 75′-8″ between perpendiculars, 21′-1″ moulded beam, and 7′-2″ moulded depth. She has moderate sheer for her type, straight keel with slight drag, nearly vertical sternpost with a short counter, slightly longer than usual in her type and supposed date. She had the usual elliptical transom, slightly curved athwartship and strongly raked. Her stem rabbet was straight and well raked, adorned with the standard long head. Her entrance was long, sharp and slightly hollow at forefoot. The run was long, with moderate length of straight buttock right aft. The midsection was formed as common in the type, straight with very moderately rising floor carried well outboard, low, hard bilge, with nearly vertical topside. It should be observed that this model shows no outstanding features that would explain numerous sister ships being built on this model.

Fishing schooners hailing out of Cape Cod ports were numerous after 1845. These vessels were employed in the Georges Bank fishery, or in the mackerel fishery, or in freighting oysters from the Chesapeake to Wellfleet or other Cape Cod ports. By 1867 there were many Cape Cod vessels of relatively large size for the period. A good example of these was the *Lucy M. Jenkins* (Plate 43), employed in the mackerel and oyster business out of Wellfleet. The *Jenkins* was built at Essex by Joseph Story in 1867 and was 82′–11″ moulded length at main rail cap, 77′–4½″ between perpendiculars, 22′–0″ moulded beam, and 8′–5″ moulded depth. In model she belonged to the clipper type having a rather straight sheer, straight keel with little drag, slightly raking sternpost, short counter, elliptical transom, sharply raking and moderately curved athwartship; straight raking stem rabbet, long head, sharp entrance, slightly concave abaft forefoot, long run, fine with straight buttocks. The midsection was shaped with slightly rising straight floor carried well outboard, low, full round bilge, marked tumble home in topside. The vessels of this size usually drew 8 to 9 feet ready for sea, 21 to 30 inches freeboard to main deck at break.

The Georges Bank fishery was most profitable in winter and the best fishing grounds were on the east side of the bank. Strong tidal currents swept across the banks producing tide rips and in gales the seas broke heavily in the miles of shoal water of the Georges. Vessels anchored on this bank when fishing. With gales from the easterly quadrant, schooners anchored on the

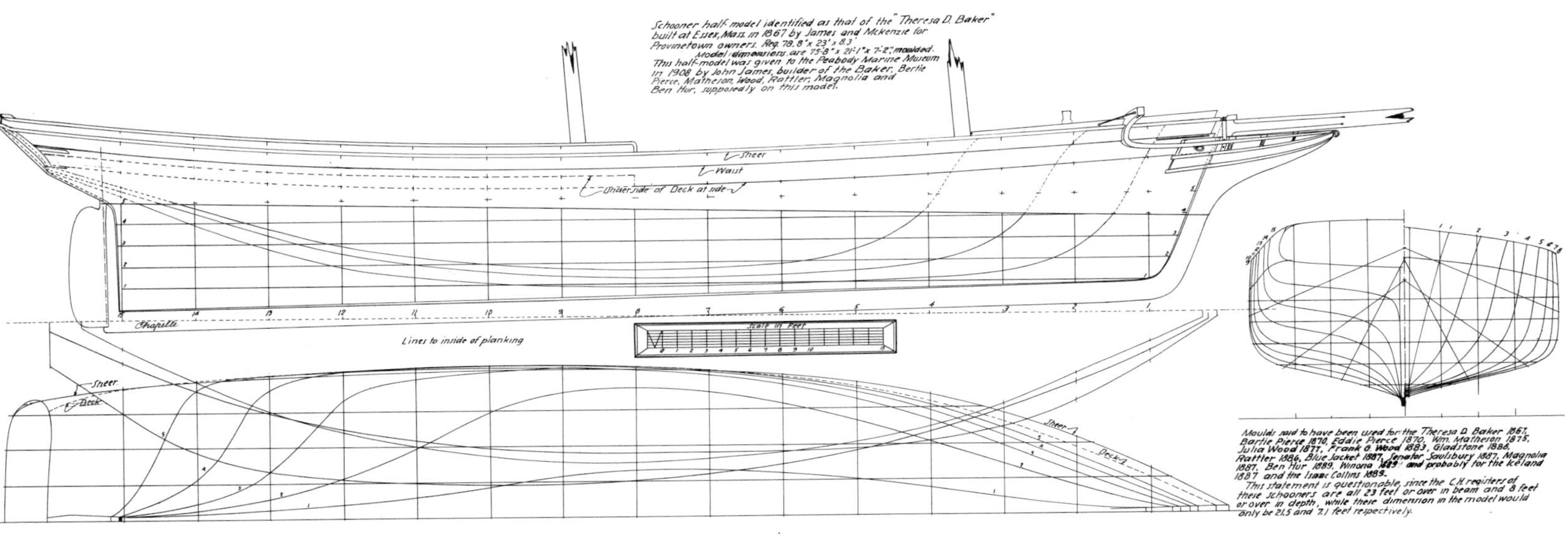
Schooner half model identified as that of the "Theresa D. Baker"
built at Essex, Mass. in 1867 by James and Mckenzie for
Provinetown owners. Reg. 78.8' x 23' x 8.3'
Model dimensions are 75'-8" x 21'-1" x 7'-2", moulded.
This half-model was given to the Peabody Marine Museum
in 1908 by John James, builder of the Baker, Bertie
Pierce, Matheson, Wood, Rattler, Magnolia and
Ben Hur, supposedly on this model.
Sheer
Waist
Underside of Deck at side
Chapelle
Lines to inside of planking
Scale in Feet
0 1 2 3 4 5 6 7 8 9 10
Sheer
Deck
Sheer
Deck
Moulds said to have been used for the Theresa D. Baker 1867,
Bartie Pierce 1870, Eddie Pierce 1870, Wm. Matheson 1875,
Julia Wood 1877, Frank G. Wood 1883, Gladstone 1886,
Rattler 1886, Blue Jacket 1887, Senator Saulsbury 1887, Magnolia
1887, Ben Hur 1889, Winona 1889 and probably for the Iceland
1887 and the Isaac Collins 1889.
This statement is questionable, since the C.H. registers of
these schooners are all 23 feet or over in beam and 8 feet
or over in depth, while these dimension in the model would
only be 21.5 and 7.1 feet respectively.

PLATE 42. *Theresa D. Baker*, clipper, 1867, half-model

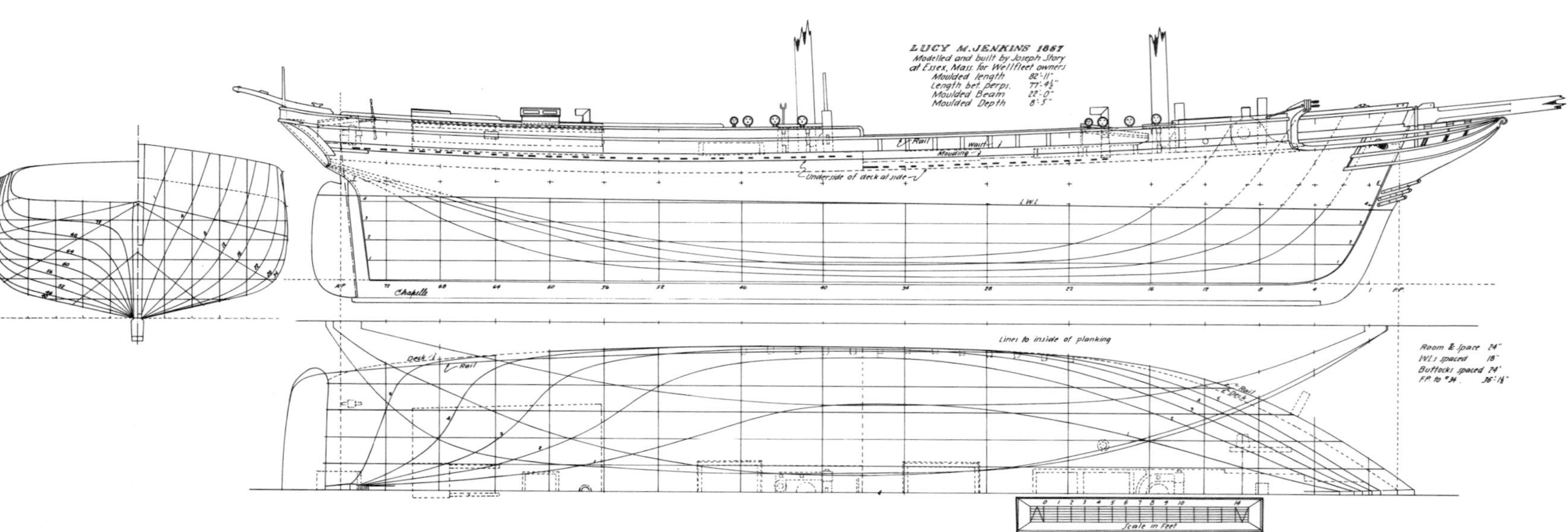
LUCY M. JENKINS 1867
Modelled and built by Joseph Story
at Essex, Mass. for Wellfleet owners
Moulded length 82'-11"
Length bet. perps. 77'-4½"
Moulded Beam 22'-0"
Moulded Depth 8'-5"
Rail
Waist
Moulding
Underside of deck at side
LWL
Chapelle
Lines to inside of planking
Deck
Rail
Room & Space 24"
WL's spaced 18"
Buttocks spaced 24"
F.P. to #34 36'-1½"
Scale in Feet

PLATE 43. *Lucy M. Jenkins*, clipper, 1867, half-model

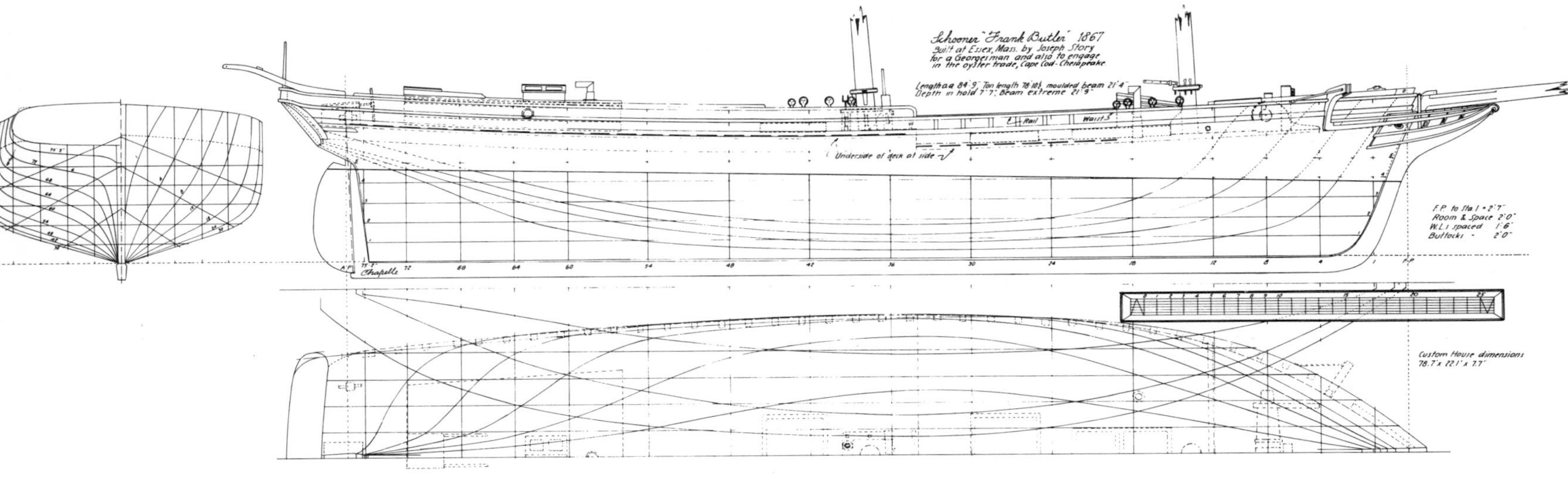

Schooner "Frank Butler" 1867
Built at Essex, Mass. by Joseph Story
for a Georgesman and also to engage
in the oyster trade, Cape Cod - Chesapeake
Length a.a. 84'9", Ton length 78'10½", moulded beam 21'4"
Depth in hold 7'7", Beam extreme 21'9"
Rail
Waist
Underside of deck at side
F.P. to Sta. 1 = 2'7"
Room & Space 2'0"
W.L.s spaced 1'6"
Buttocks - 2'0"
Custom House dimensions
78.7' x 22.1' x 7.7'
Chapelle
A.P.
F.P.

PLATE 44. *Frank Butler*, Georges Banker, 1867, half-model

best fishing grounds were on a lee shore of breaking seas and shoals.

After the Civil War the number of vessels fishing on this bank increased steadily. The result was that the vessels anchored closer together and into rather shoal water in search of good berths. If a heavy winter northeaster, usually accompanied with snow and low temperatures, should strike in, the clipper-type schooners were generally unable to claw off so remained at anchor, hoping to ride out the storm. If their anchors dragged or their anchor cable parted, they drifted into the shoals and broke up in the often tremendous surf. In the process, they often collided with nearby vessels and all either broke up immediately or drifted on to the shoals with the same end to schooners and crews. The Georges Bank winter fishery was the most dangerous to vessels and should have been carried on with only weatherly schooners capable of working to windward in gale weather, which had been one of the more endearing qualities of the old pinky. However, the New England fishermen continued to risk lives and property by the retention of the clipper fishing schooner of the type shown in Plate 44, in the Georges Bank fishery. This is the schooner *Frank Butler* built at Essex by Joseph Story in 1867 especially for the Georges Bank fishery. She was also intended for the occasional occupation of oyster freighting.

The *Frank Butler* was 80′-9″ moulded length at rail cap, 78′-10½″ between perpendiculars, 21′-4″ moulded beam, 21′-9″ extreme beam, and 7′-7″ depth in hold. She was built for Cape Cod owners. She had the rather straight sheer that distinguished many vessels of her type, and a straight keel having slight drag. Her sternpost was nearly vertical, with the short counter, elliptical transom sharply raked and rounded athwartship. The stem rabbet flared forward slightly with marked fore rake. The entrance was long, sharp, and slightly concave abaft the forefoot. The run was long with straight buttocks of much length. The midsection shows long straight floor of moderate deadrise, a firm bilge and very slight tumble home. The loaded draft was about 8′-3″.

The 1860s produced no very outstanding changes in design, except for the *Sylph* and the *Evans*. These were too small, and their services in the fisheries were too short, for them to become well known enough to influence New England fishing schooner design in any way. It should be noticed, however, that some fishing schooner designers were well aware of the advantages of deeper draft and greater range of safe heel.

Chapter Four

1870–1885

After the Civil War the North Atlantic fisheries were very profitable. By 1870 the number of New England fishing schooners, most of which were of the clipper model, had greatly increased. The clipper was by then employed in the dangerous Georges Bank fishery, with little modification of a model that originally was used almost entirely in the summer mackerel fishery. Though the clipper Georgesman was slightly more burdensome than the clipper mackerel schooner, the Georges Banker had little or no improvement in range of stability, that is, in the angle of heel from which a vessel could recover.

The growth of the New England fisheries continued to make Gloucester and Boston the leading fishery ports and Essex the leading schooner-building town. However, the Maine fishery ports and shipbuilding towns were not very far behind Cape Ann. Essex, Boston, and Gloucester were setting the fashion in fishing schooners; their vessels were considered to be the most advanced in model, rig, and construction.

One of the leading designers of New England fishing vessels after 1860 was Dennison J. Lawlor, a native of St. John, New Brunswick, Canada. He served his shipwright apprenticeship at St. John and upon completing it came to Boston seeking employment; this was sometime about 1845. The earliest half-model bearing his name that has yet been found and identified is dated 1849. He appears to have become an established designer in the early 1850s, operating a shipyard in Chelsea, Massachusetts. In the 1860s he designed a number of fishing schooners, some of which he built in his own yard; the others were built in various yards on Massachusetts Bay. As has been stated, he designed the *Sylph* and the *Thomas E. Evans*, in 1865–1866, of unusual depth for their size and date.

Lawlor had become very active by 1865; he had designed pilot boats, tugs, brigantines, fishing schooners, steamships, and fishing steamers. One of his notable designs was the *U.S. Grant,* intended for the pursuit of the Confederate cruiser *Alabama* but not completed in time for this service. A clipper auxiliary steamer, the *Grant* was built by Tobey and Littlefield at Portsmouth, New Hampshire; paid for by merchant's subscriptions, in 1864. Renamed *Meteor,* she took part in the war between Chile and Peru and was destroyed to prevent capture. The design of the *Grant* was competitive; Lawlor won over William H. Webb, Henry Steers, and other prominent designers.

Lawlor also designed and built numerous yachts, steam and sail; by 1883 he belonged to the "cutter crank" faction in the controversey between supporters of the American, shoal, centerboard sloop and the deep-draft, heavily ballasted cutters that began in the early 1880s.

Plate 45 shows a Lawlor design for a Boston market schooner, the *Actress,* built by J. M. Brooks and Son at East Boston, Massachusetts, in 1871. This schooner soon earned a reputation for fast sailing and was much admired. A sharpshooter with more rise in floor then usual, wide and shoal, the *Actress* was somewhat shallower than were the earlier sharpshooters and was not a very safe vessel. However, many of the small market fisherman of the 1860–1880 period worked so close to home that they could usually run to shelter upon the approach of a gale, so were not normally exposed to severe conditions.

The *Actress* measured 65′-8″ between perpendiculars, 18′-8″ beam moulded, and 7′-2″ depth moulded. Her Custom House measurements were 62′ x 20′ x 7′. The plan shows a very fine-lined schooner designed with a flush deck and with rather straight sheer, straight keel with moderate drag, nearly upright sternpost, short counter; high, shoal, raking wide transom, curved athwartship. The stem rabbet raked strongly forward with slight flare. The entrance was long, sharp, and slightly concave close to the stem. The run was very long with straight buttocks. The midsection had moderate rise of floor with hollow garboards; the bilge was rather hard, with marked tumble home above. The rig was that of a sharpshooter, without fore-topmast and jib-boom.

The lines of another design by Lawlor are shown in Plate 46: the *Helen M. Foster* of Boston built at Scituate, Massachusetts, in 1871. The *Foster* was designed as a large market fisherman. Sailing out of Boston she soon gained a reputation for ability to carry sail and for speed. In general, she was a powerful vessel, very slightly deeper than the most of her size, type, and class. She was designed to be 70′-7″ between perpendiculars, 20′-10″ moulded beam, and 7′-6½″ moulded depth.

The *Helen M. Foster* had a marked sheer, straight keel with moderate

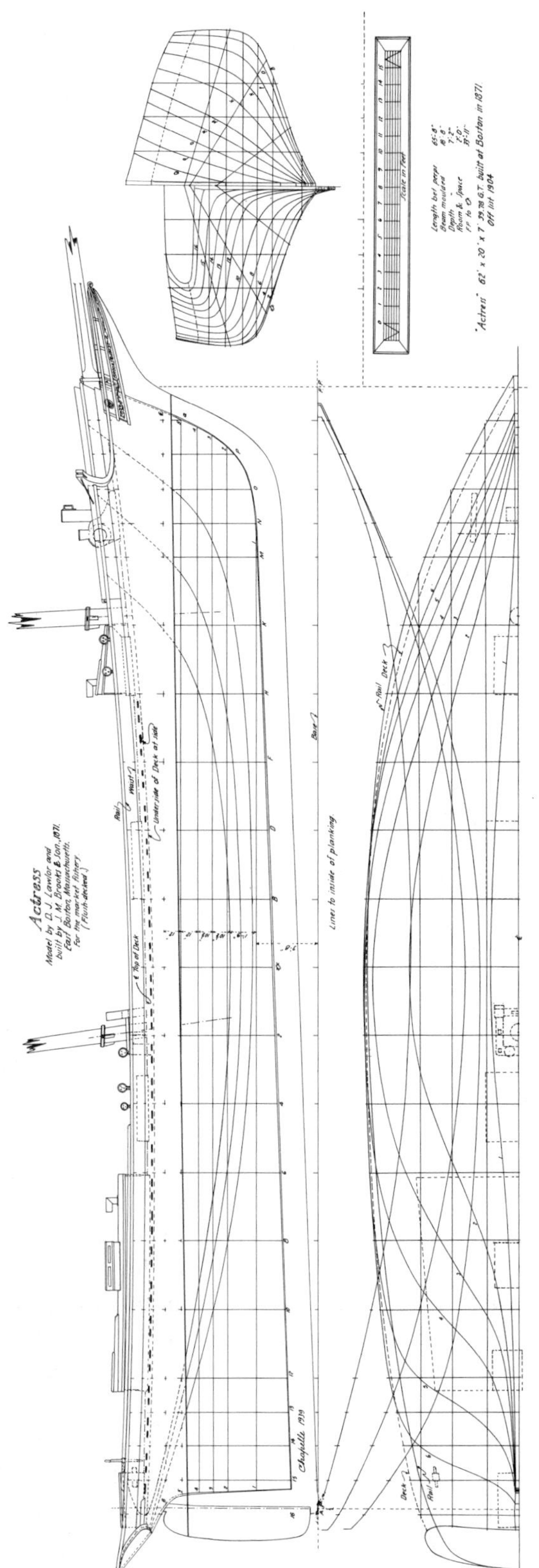
Actress
Model by D. J. Lawlor and
built by J. M. Brooks & Son, 1871.
East Boston, Massachusetts.
For the market fishery
(Flush-decked)
Lines to inside of planking.
Chapelle 1939
Scale in feet
Length bet perps 65'-8"
Beam moulded 18'-8"
Depth 7'-2"
Room & Space 2'-0"
FP to ⊙ 33'-11"
"Actress" 62' x 20' x 7' 39.78 G.T. built at Boston in 1871
Off list 1904

PLATE 45. *Actress*, 1871, half-model

drag, vertical sternpost, a short counter, with the wide, shallow elliptical transom strongly curved athwartship and sharply raked. The stem rabbet raked forward and flared somewhat. The entrance was long, sharp, and slightly concave just abaft the forefoot. The run was not exceptionally long, but was formed with straight buttocks running a short distance forward of their intersections with the after load line.

This form of run shows the characteristic that often marked Lawlor's designs: the retention of the same deadrise angle for the length of the straight quarterbeam buttock in the after sections in the body plan. This form of run was not original with Lawlor; it is to be seen in the plans of many fast-sailing vessels as far back as 1800. There appears to be no evidence that there was an established theory regarding this characteristic among master shipwrights before Lawlor's time.

The constant angle of deadrise, in such vessels as fishing schooners, could exist only outboard of the tuck in the afterbody sections and inboard of the turn of the bilge. Some designs show this treatment of constant deadrise in all afterbody sections, without much regard to the length of the run.

It has been observed that by combining constant deadrise—in the submerged portions of the body plan, sections in the run—with straight buttocks, a plane was produced, port and starboard, tilted upward outboard and toward the stern. It was claimed that these planes produced a less-resistant form than would warped planes formed by the changing angles in the deadrise. In recent years a variant in this theory has produced the hull form called "monohedron" used extensively in fast displacement motorboats.

The evolution of the counter in fishing schooners encouraged the use of straight buttocks, as their use made it easy to fair the counter and afterbody. Archer Poland, son of the Gloucester shipbuilder Daniel Poland, lofted vessels built on Cape Ann and vicinity for about thirty years. His practice was to fair counter and run in the drawing of the half-model, using two buttocks: 2′-0″ and 4′-0″ out. If these showed curves in the counter they were made straight and the outlines of the lifts in the afterbody were altered to fit the straight lines which usually were carried forward of the tuck of the counter for varying distances. This usually made the quarterbeam buttock straight well into the afterbody, very often conforming with the constant angle of deadrise theory. The constant angle of deadrise was not always carried to the transom. With wide, shallow transoms there was a change required in deadrise between load line and transom. This led to the use of the V-stern, the transom having the same or very nearly the same deadrise as the sections in the afterbody.

It has been a common assumption that the designers of the fishing schooners were mere whittlers who formed their half-models wholly by eye and guess. It is true that the last builders of sailing fishermen were businessmen

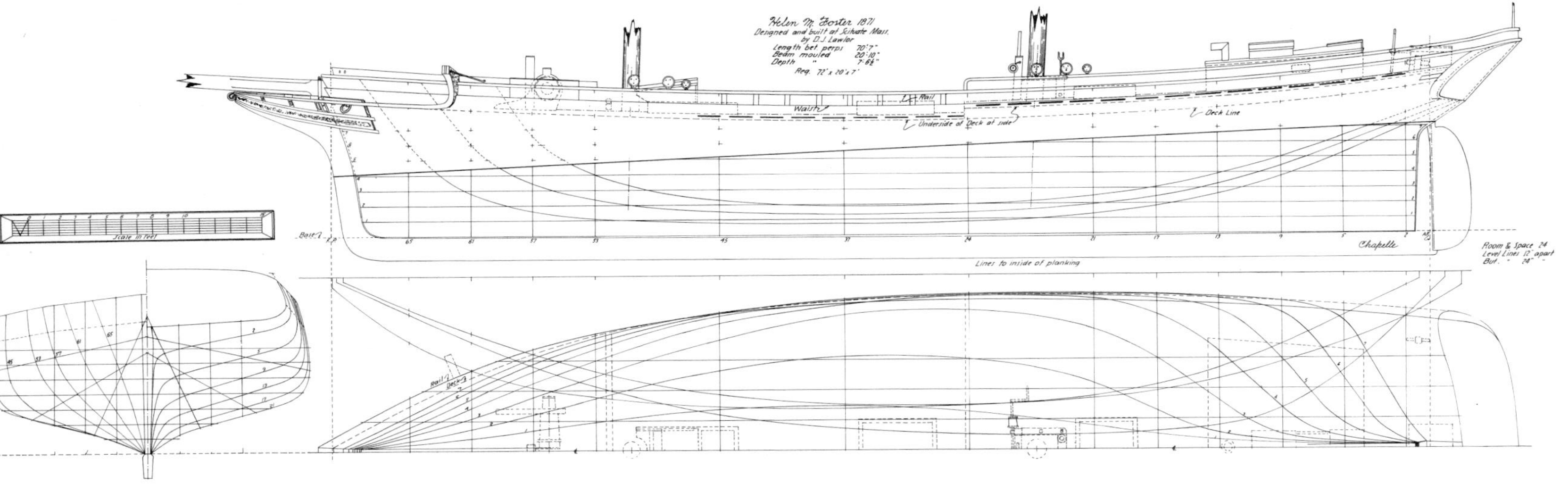
Helen M. Foster 1871
Designed and built at Scituate Mass.
by D.J. Lawlor
Length bet. perps 70'7"
Beam moulded 20'10"
Depth " 7'6½"
Reg. 72' x 20' x 7'
Waist
Rail
Underside of Deck at side
Deck Line
Lines to inside of planking
Room & Space 24
Level Lines 12" apart
But. " 24" "
Chapelle
Scale in feet
Base
Rail
Deck

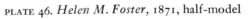

PLATE 46. *Helen M. Foster*, 1871, half-model

who did not attempt to design, depending upon modelers and naval architects of local reputation. However, throughout the last half of the nineteenth century there were designers who used the half-model, with or without accompanying detailed drawings. Indeed, the model was long accepted as a "scientific" mode of design for yachts—and for boats and vessels. It must be remembered that the most advanced practices in naval architecture in this period, so far as sailing craft were concerned, were in yachts and that there was little scientific publication relating to naval architecture. Of what little there was, hardly anything was applicable to fishing schooner design until the 1870s. English books on yacht design then appeared in America, beginning with Philip P. Marretts' *Yachts and Yacht Building, being a Treatise on the Construction of Yachts and Matters Relating to Yachting.* This was first published in 1856, with a second edition published in 1876.

Next was Dixon Kemp's *Yacht Designing, A Treatise on the Practical Application of the Scientific Principles upon which are based the Art of Designing Yachts,* published in London in 1876. While these books became known to some of the fishing schooner designers, most designers were indoctrinated in the recent design practices by magazine and newspaper pundits, and some had received technical education from a trade school and from reading the English books.

At Charlestown, Massachusetts there was a trade school, usually referred to as the "Charlestown Free School," which was established in the late 1870s, apparently. Here marine drafting and elementary shipbuilding were taught. John L. Frisbee, master shipwright of the Brooks' shipyard, East Boston, taught here for many years. He was a superior shipwright and teacher who attracted students from as far away as Nova Scotia and Virginia. He was succeeded by Albert S. Greene, a Boston Navy Yard draftsman, who was interested in yacht design and who trained at least one Boston newspaper yachting editor in this field.

Magazines covering yachting appeared in the 1870–1880s. Of these, *Forest and Stream,* established in 1870, was for years the most influential. It was a "sporting magazine" and had a staff of editors. Its first yachting editor was Charles Kunhardt, a U.S. Naval Academy graduate, class of 1870. He was also an amateur yacht designer and a caustic and prolific writer on yacht design. This journal was soon engaged in the hot controversy over the superiority of the wide, shallow, centerboard American yachts versus the deep, narrow, keel English yachts—Kunhardt writing in behalf of the latter. This magazine and its published plans of yachts, its comments and technical competence soon made it the standard reference to most persons interested in sailing craft. Since yachts were built by both Essex and Gloucester schooner builders, it is not surprising that they knew *Forest and Stream* and had very strong opinions on its policies, with positions on the keel/centerboard controversy.

The Boston newspapers also had marine reporters and yacht experts who, in summer, reported the racing results and, in winter, on the features of the yachts then building. One was "Dolly" A. G. McVey, who became an amateur designer and an outspoken critic of professional designers.

Plate 47 shows the lines of the market schooner *Nimbus*, a clipper model built at Gloucester, Massachusetts by John Bishop in 1872. She was wrecked on Cape Negro, Nova Scotia in the winter of 1878, during a violent snow storm. While quite unsuited for winter fishing, or for Newfoundland voyages in winter, vessels of this type were so employed throughout the 1870s and into the 1880s. The *Nimbus* was 75′-4″ moulded length at rail cap, 70′-1″ between perpendiculars, and 7′-0″ depth of hold. Her best trim was reported to be 8′-2″ draft at post, 7′-0″ forward.

She had marked sheer, straight keel with slight drag, nearly vertical sternpost; short counter, wide shallow, strongly raking transom, curved somewhat athwartship. Her stem rabbet was straight, raking forward. She had the standard billet and long head of the fishing schooners of her period. The midsection was formed with moderately rising straight floors carried well outboard, a hard turn of the bilge with slight tumble home in the topside. The *Nimbus* was very well built and was considered the model of her type when she was launched.

In 1874 the schooner *Howard* (Plate 48) was modeled by William A. Burnham and built by him at Essex. This vessel, intended for the cod and halibut fisheries, proved to be a good sailer and sea boat and also of a then profitable size for these fisheries. Because of these characteristics, thirty vessels were claimed to have been built on her moulds, seven of which had their names written on the half-model.

The *Howard* was 67′-7″ between perpendiculars, 20′-4″ moulded beam, and 8′-0″ moulded depth. The lines show a small schooner having moderate sheer, straight keel with small drag, nearly upright post, short counter; wide, unusually deep transom for the type and date. It raked sharply and was strongly curved athwartship. The stem rabbet was straight and raking, with billet and the standard form of long head. The midsection had straight, moderately rising floors; low, well-rounded bilges, slight tumble home in the topside. The entrance was convex and moderately sharp and long. The run was long, with short straight buttocks close to the after load line. Vessels of this type were employed extensively in the Gulf of St. Lawrence fisheries in the '70s.

Two more vessels typical of the clipper class in the 1870s are shown in Plate 49. The sisters *Bunker Hill* and the *Grace L. Fears* were built at Essex

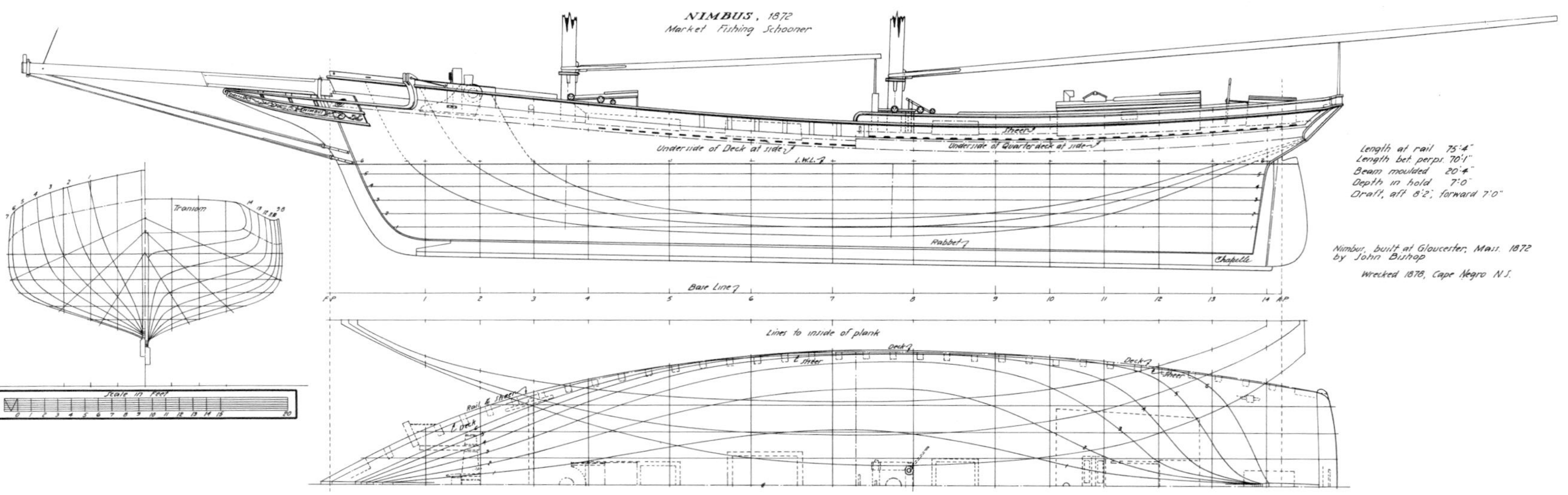
NIMBUS, 1872
Market Fishing Schooner
Length at rail 75'4"
Length bet. perps. 70'1"
Beam moulded 20'4"
Depth in hold 7'0"
Draft, aft 8'2"; forward 7'0"
Nimbus, built at Gloucester, Mass. 1872 by John Bishop
Wrecked 1878, Cape Negro N.S.
Underside of Deck at side
Underside of Quarter deck at side
Sheer
L.W.L.
Rabbet
Base Line
Lines to inside of plank
Deck
Rail & Sheer
Transom
Scale in Feet
Chapelle

PLATE 47. *Nimbus*, market boat, 1872, plan

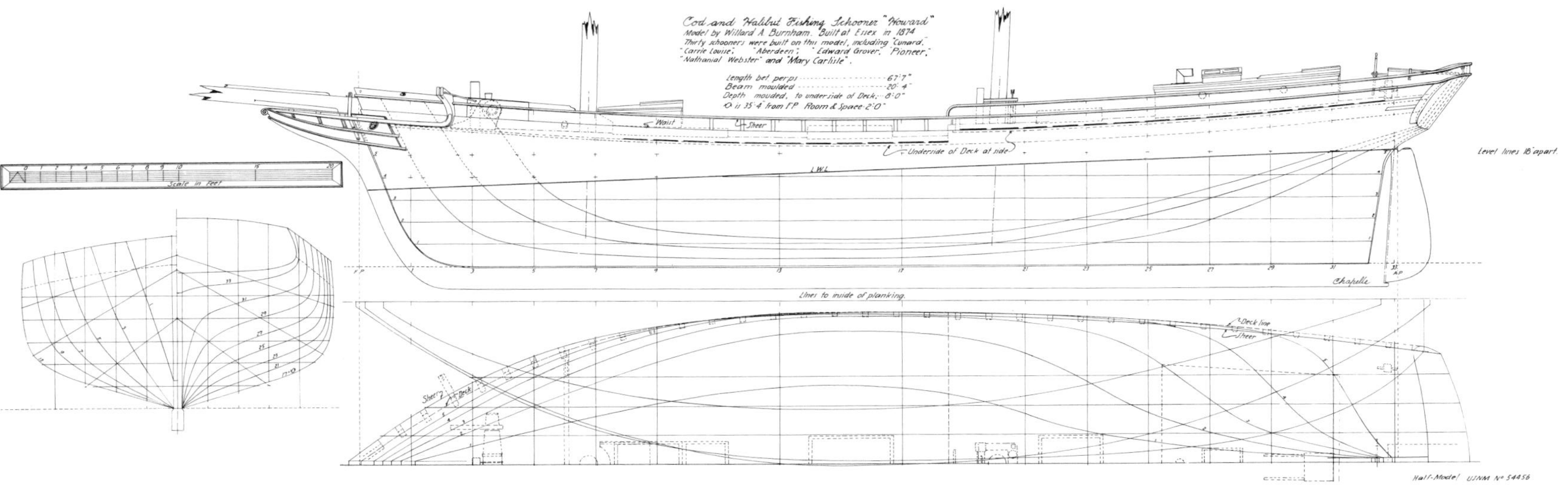
Cod and Halibut Fishing Schooner "Howard"
Model by Willard A. Burnham. Built at Essex in 1874
Thirty schooners were built on this model, including "Cunard,"
"Carrie Louise," "Aberdeen," "Edward Grover," "Pioneer,"
"Nathanial Webster" and "Mary Carlisle".
Length bet. perps .... 67'7"
Beam moulded .... 20'4"
Depth mouded, to underside of Deck ... 8'0"
⊕ is 35'4" from F.P. Room & Space 2'0"
Waist
Sheer
Underside of Deck at side
LWL
Level lines 18" apart.
Lines to inside of planking.
Deck line
Sheer
Sheer
Deck
Chapelle
Scale in Feet
Half-Model USNM № 54456

PLATE 48. *Howard*—30 vessels built on this model, 1874, half-model

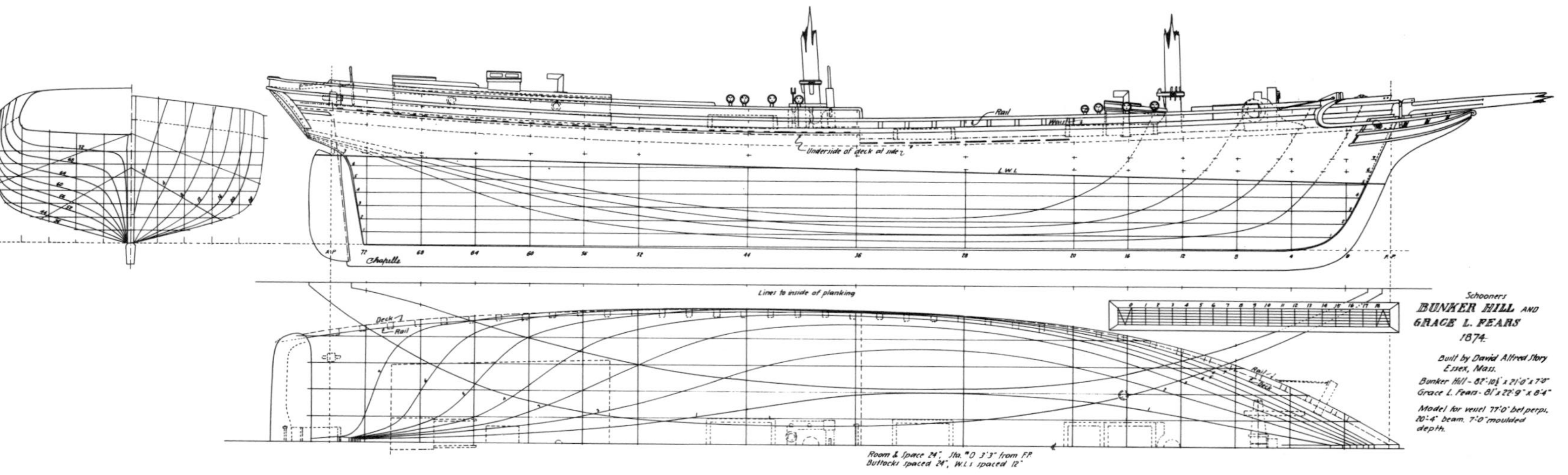
Schooners
BUNKER HILL AND
GRACE L. FEARS
1874
Built by David Alfred Story
Essex, Mass.
Bunker Hill - 82'-10½" x 21'-0" x 7'-0"
Grace L. Fears - 81' x 22'-9" x 8'-4"
Model for vessel 77'-0" bet perps.
20'-4" beam, 7'-0" moulded
depth.
Room & Space 24", Sta. "0 3'3" from F.P.
Buttocks spaced 24", W.L.s spaced 12"
Lines to inside of planking
Underside of deck at side
Rail
L.W.L.
Deck
Chapelle

PLATE 49. *Bunker Hill, Grace L. Fears,* 1874, half-model

in 1874 by David Alfred Story. Their half-model shows vessels designed to be 77′-0″ between perpendiculars, 20′-4″ beam moulded, and 7′-0″ moulded depth. The registers give *Bunker Hill*, 82′-10½″ x 21′-0″ x 7′-0″, and *Grace L. Fears*, 81′-0″ x 22′-9″ x 8′-4″. It appears as though two frames had been added amidships. The moulds of these sisters were said to have been used to build three other vessels, but these have not been identified.

These schooners had rather slight sheer, straight keel, with moderate drag, slightly raking post, short counter, rather deep transom, wide and slightly rounded athwartship with strong rake. The stem rabbet was straight and raking, with billet and long head. The entrance was long and sharp, the run was straight in the buttocks and long.

The "raking midsection" shown in Plate 49 was a common characteristic in the clipper model fisherman earlier than 1870. This was formed by staggering the point of maximum beam, in each level or "waterline" in the half-breadth plan, upward from the keel and toward the stern. This allowed the use of longer entrance and run than would otherwise be possible. The raking midsection permitted the entrance and run to overlap slightly amidships.

The midsection in the body plan of these schooners was shaped with rising straight floor, carried well outboard, a low and rather hard turn of the bilge and slight tumble home in the topside. These schooners may be said to represent the most popular model in the New England fisheries in the 1860s and '70s, as the many plans and half-models that have survived testify.

The construction of schooners especially for the salt-cod fisheries had produced rather more burdensome vessels than the mackerel and Georges Bank clippers: two-masted and nearly 90 feet tonnage length, with hull forms having rather flat floors; low, hard bilges and slight tumble home in the topside, the bankers became somewhat similar to coasting schooners, but rather sharper in the ends. The Georgesmen of this period were still intermediate, between salt banker and clipper, but this distinction was gradually disappearing as the Georgesmen, on the average, grew slowly larger. The trend was toward the design of schooners to be employed as all-around vessels that could be used in both the mackerel and Georges fisheries, and for the Gulf of St. Lawrence fisheries as well, or for the Newfoundland herring voyage in winter, or for the salt-fish fishery.

The salt bankers had not been much influenced in design by this trend during the 1870s and early 1880s. These vessels made long voyages with smaller crews than were usually employed in the other important fisheries. Provincetown had become a center of the salt-bank fishery and burdensome vessels characterized her fleet. In 1875 Provincetown owners had a three-masted banker built at Essex by John James and Company, named *Lizzie W. Matheson*. Her model was made in Essex. This schooner is shown in Plate 50. She had a long, low, raised quarterdeck, 9 inches high in the usual fish-

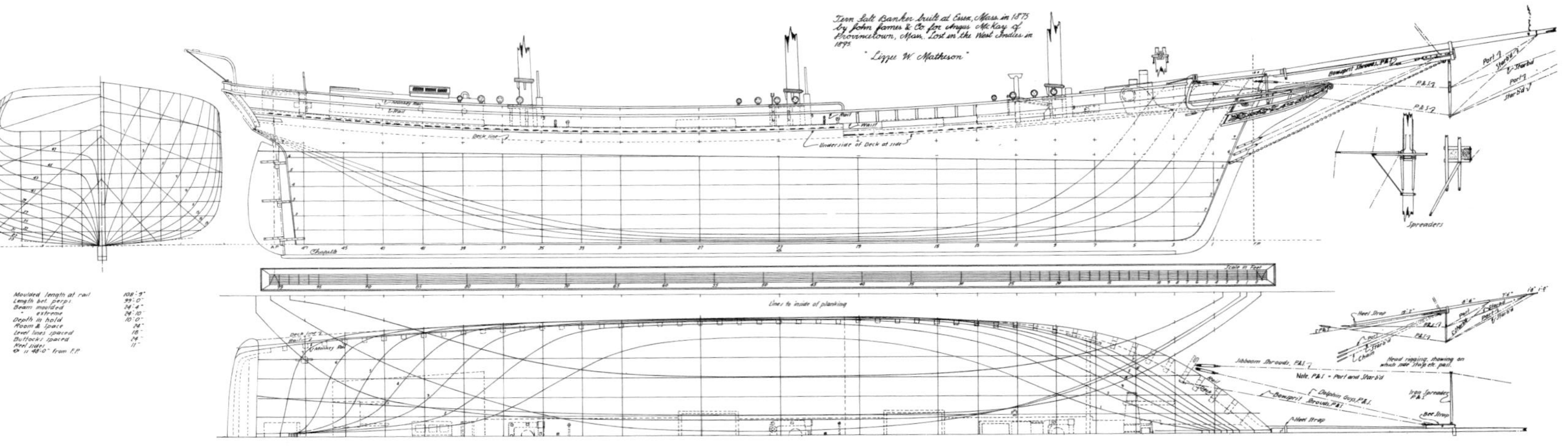
Tern Salt Banker built at Essex, Mass. in 1875 by John James & Co. for Angus McKay of Provincetown, Mass. Lost in the West Indies in 1895.
"Lizzie W. Matheson"
Moulded length at rail 108'-9"
Length bet. perps. 99'-0"
Beam moulded 24'-4"
" extreme 24'-10"
Depth in hold 10'-0"
Room & Space 24"
Level lines spaced 18"
Buttocks spaced 24"
Keel sides 11"
Spreaders
Lines to inside of planking
Scale in Feet

PLATE 50. *Lizzie W. Matheson*, tern, 1875, half-model and plans ing schooner style, with the great beam forward of the mainmast. Her model produced a vessel 108′-9″ moulded length at main rail cap, 99′-0″ between perpendiculars, 24′-10″ moulded beam, 10′-0″ depth in hold.

The *Matheson* had moderate sheer, straight keel with small drag, slightly raking sternpost, short counter, strongly raking, wide transom, curved athwartship. The stem rabbet raked and flared, the entrance was rather short and convex, but with slight hollow in the level lines close abaft the stem rabbet below the load line. The run was rather long for a burdensome hull, and the buttocks were distinctly straight. The midsection shows very slight rise in the straight floor which was carried very far outboard. The bilge was low and hard with slight tumble home above. In rig the *Matheson* was more fishing schooner than coaster.

This schooner proved profitable, seaworthy, and a good sailer. As a result she was followed by other three-masters, all built by the James yard at Essex. They were the *Willie A. McKay*, built in 1880; the *Henry S. Woodruff* in 1886; the *Arthur V. S. Woodruff* in 1888; and the *Cora S. McKay*, also built in 1888. The last two may have been sister ships. The tern schooners (the old name of three-masted schooners) did not appeal to Gloucester and Boston fishermen so no more were built at Essex until World War I and these were largely employed as salt-fish carriers rather than as bankers, by their Canadian owners. One tern fishing schooner was built at Bath, Maine, in the 1880s, and two three-masted knockabout schooners were built during World War I, one at Essex and one in Nova Scotia.

In 1877 the sole centerboard schooner built for the North Atlantic fisheries was launched at Gloucester. This was the *Augusta E. Herrick* modeled and built by Daniel Poland, who was an active schooner builder at Gloucester in the '70s. The *Herrick* was an extreme clipper, having a low quarterdeck with the "break," or "great beam," forward of the mainmast. The latter was off-center to starboard, with the centerboard off-center to port, in order to balance the hull and rig by placing the centerboard far enough aft. This was not original in the *Herrick*, of course, for it was used in many centerboard schooners built from Virginia northward. The *Herrick* proved to be a very fast sailer on a reach or running off, but was not very weatherly. Essex connoisseurs in schooner design thought that her centerboard was too small, the case having been shortened by order of the owner while under construction, it was claimed.

The *Herrick* was designed to be 95′-6″ moulded length at main rail cap, 89′-0″ between perpendiculars, and 24′-0″ moulded beam. The dimensions were intended to produce a shoal-draft schooner to work out of some shallow Maine ports. The schooner was long and low in appearance, having very moderate sheer, straight keel with little drag, slight rake to the sternpost, a long counter for the date, sharply raking transom, wide and rather shallow

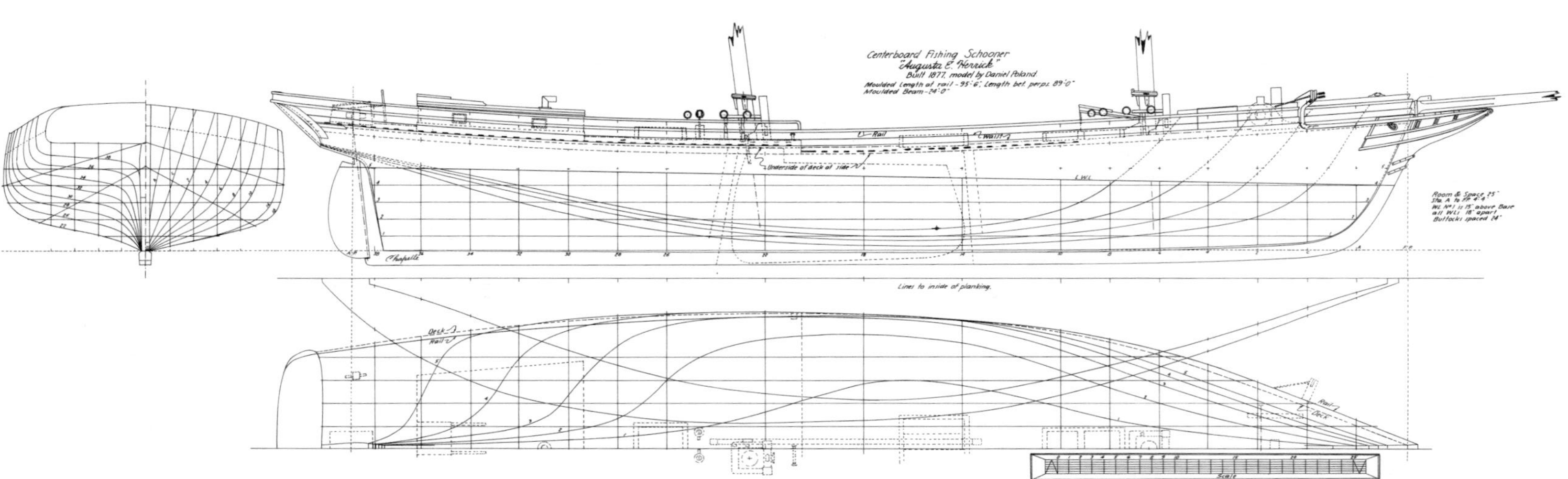
Centerboard Fishing Schooner
"Augusta E. Herrick"
Built 1877, model by Daniel Poland
Moulded Length at rail - 95'6", Length bet. perps. 89'0"
Moulded Beam - 24'0"
Room & Space 25"
Sta. A to F.P. 4'4"
WL No 1 is 15" above Base
all WLs 18" apart
Buttocks spaced 24"
Rail
Waist
Underside of deck at side
LWL
Lines to inside of planking.
Deck
Rail
Scale
Chapelle

PLATE 51. *Augusta E. Herrick*, centerboard, 1877, half-model with some curve athwartship. The stem rabbet raked and was straight above the load line, much cut away below. The entrance was long and sharp with slight hollow in the forefoot. The run was unusually long with very straight buttocks. A raking midsection was used, that in the body plan had slightly rising, straight floors carried well outboard, low and very hard turn of the bilge with marked tumble home in the topside.

It should be emphasized that the Gloucester and Essex builders were well acquainted with the centerboard, for a number of centerboard schooners and sloops had been built for the oyster fisheries, the stone trade, and for other coastal trades since 1850.

By the 1870s the mode of construction of fishing schooners had become pretty well standardized for given sizes of vessels. A schooner about 85′-0″ at rail and 21′-6″ moulded beam, had a keel 15 to 24 inches deep, including a 4- to 6-inch worm shoe, siding 10 to 12 inches. The sternpost sided 15 inches at head, 10 to 12 inches at heel. Post sided 15 inches at rudder port, 10 to 12 inches at heel. The horn timber sided about 15 to 18 inches, the knee of the sternpost 4 feet 3 inches high, about 12 to 14 feet long on keel. The keelson was 10 to 12 inches square. The stem knee was about the same as for the sternpost but usually its length on the keel was less due to fore rake. Frame futtocks (double frames) sided 6 to 7 inches at heel, with floor 8 to 10 inches deep over keel, the moulding was usually about 12 inches at keel and 4 to 5 inches at deck plank-sheer. One timber at each frame forms the rail stanchion siding 5 inches and moulding 3 inches, bulwarks 22 to 24 inches high, often a little higher forward—as much as 30 inches in some cases. In later years the frames were cut off at plank-sheer and the stanchions, siding 4½ to 5 inches at heel and moulding 4½ inches at head, were inserted between frames. Deck beams sided 8 to 9 inches and moulded from 7 to 8 inches at ℄ to 5 inches at ends. Clamps were 3 to 4 inches thick, 6 to 9 inches deep. Beam knees sided 5 inches, moulded 10 inches at throat. Carlines 4 x 6 inches. Ceiling in hold 2 inches thick, with bilge stringers 3 inches. Planking outboard 2¼ to 2½ inches, 3 inches wales dubbed smooth. Garboard sometimes 3 to 4 inches thick, dubbed fair to the bottom plank. Deck 2½ to 3 inches thick, main railcaps 2½ to 3½ inches thick, monkey railcap 2 to 2½ inches thick. Fastenings, galvanized wrought iron spikes and rod, oak treenails. Hatch coamings 2½ to 3 inches thick, cabin trunk sides 2½ to 3 inches thick.

The workmanship in this period was very good and many of the fishing schooners were "long, low and handsome." Hemp shrouds and stays sometimes gave an impression of clumsiness however, particularly in the head gear when bowsprit and jibboom were fully rigged. The clipper schooners had an extraordinary reputation for sailing very fast. In the 1870s a number of successful vessels have been identified, of which no half-models have yet been found. The *Lizzie J. Jones* was an extreme clipper whose performance attracted attention. She was built in 1875. The *John D. Long* and the *Paul Revere* were built on her model. *Oceanus* and the *George A. Upton*, both also built in 1875, were considered outstanding clippers. Similarly, schooners built earlier: in 1860 the *Olive G. Tower* was an extreme clipper of great reputation as a sailer, and other vessels were built on her lines. In 1861 the noted *John Somes*, an extreme clipper sharpshooter was built, and the schooners *Rushlight*, *George J. Clark*, *Amelia Cobb*, *Monitor*, *John Nye*, and *Fanny Nye* were later built on her lines. The *Somes* was modeled by Aaron Burnham. These vessels seem to have been selected for praise by Gloucester writers, because of their great speed, rather than for any contribution of safety or for any innovation in design characteristics. The rather inadequate descriptions of the *Lizzie J. Jones*, *Oceanus*, and the *Olive G. Tower* show them to have been typical of the clippers illustrated in the examples already described here.

The losses of vessels and fishermen in the 1860s and 1870s became horrifying after 1860. The following record speaks for itself:

1862: 19 schooners lost, 162 men
1869: 16 schooners lost, loss of life not reported
1871: 20 schooners lost, 140 men
1873: 31 schooners lost, 181 men
1875: 15 schooners lost, 122 men
1876: 29 schooners lost, 212 men
1879: 29 schooners lost, 249 men

These were the years of heavy losses; the years 1872, 1874, 1877, 1878 were not wholly free of losses, of course. The foregoing is sufficient to show how dangerous the fisheries had become, with 1879 being the most disastrous year. But losses were to continue heavy into the late 1880s, as will be seen. For the present, it is enough to point out again that the fisheries had become very prosperous and as a result there was a steady increase in the number of vessels engaged in fishing on Georges Bank in winter. As the Bank was notorious for heavy weather and dangerous shoal water, and as the best fishing was usually to windward of the Bank—making it a lee shore in effect—it would normally be expected that some losses would occur through collisions in winter gales and snowstorms on Georges, for example. Yet the huge amount of vessel property lost and the number of lives that perished could not long be disregarded. There was delay in this, however, because owners and masters of fishing schooners had taken great pride in their fast, handsome vessels and were naturally reluctant to accept criticism of their model and performance. Nevertheless, the shoal hulls of the fishing clippers were becoming a target for growing criticism. From 1845 to 1880 the dimensions of the sharpshooter clipper schooner had increased from vessels 60 to 68 feet long, 17 to 18 feet beam and 7 to 8 feet depth, to vessels 85 to 95 feet long, 21 to 25 feet beam, and 7 to 8 feet 8 inches depth. Why did depth remain so restricted, as compared to the great increases in beam and length dimensions?

The reason was in the extensive shallow areas and obstructions in Gloucester Harbor, particularly at the berthing slips and their approaches. There were, therefore, sound economic and practical reasons for the lack of enthusiasm among Gloucester vessel owners for the proposal to replace the shoal vessels with deep ones. As far back as the 1850s there had been some efforts by the fishing interests to get Congress to appropriate funds for clearing the outer harbor of boulders and a pinnacle rock, building breakwaters, and dredging out the slips and their approaches, but without any very satisfying results. In 1879 Gloucester fishing schooners were generally limited to 9 to 10 feet except for a few that had deep-water berths.

The 1870s had produced no marked improvement in the fundamental type of fishing schooner except for a few that had a little more depth than usual, such as some of Lawlor's small, market schooners of the 1860s—*Sylph* and *Evans*, for example. But these vessels were built for the Boston fleet where no serious depth of water problems existed.

In the early 1880s heavy losses of vessel property—and therefore of lives—continued. Gloucester lost 12 vessels and 115 men in 1882, 17 vessels and 209 men in 1883, 16 schooners and 131 men in 1884, 12 vessels and 34 men in 1885, 26 schooners and 136 men in 1886. As the schooners increased in size, their crews became larger and so loss of life increased markedly though the number of vessels lost might not.*

In the spring of 1882 letters critical of the popular model of fishing schooners began to appear in the *Cape Ann Advertiser* of Gloucester. The first letter was published March 3, 1882, signed by "Skipper," and expressed strong doubts of the seaworthiness of the clipper schooner fisherman. It later developed that this letter was written by Joseph William Collins, then employed by the U.S. Fish Commission, an establishment of the Smithsonian Institution.

This letter was followed by an editorial in the *Advertiser*, dated March 24, 1882, calling attention to the criticisms. On April 8, 1882, Collins wrote a long letter from Washington, D.C., published in the *Advertiser* on April 14. In it he detailed the alleged faults of the clipper schooner and made certain proposals.

Collins was born at Isleboro, Maine, August 8, 1839, the son of David and

*I am indebted to Mr. Joseph E. Garland, Mr. Julian Hatch, Mr. Paul B. Kenyon, and Mr. Robert F. Brown, all of Gloucester, for their generous assistance in the examination of Gloucester port conditions and their effects upon proposed improvements in schooner models in the 1880s.

Eliza B. (Sawyer) Collins. He received a primary education in the local country school; when he was ten years old he shipped on a fishing schooner. He educated himself by reading and study at home and at the age of twenty-three he became a skipper. In 1860 he moved to Gloucester where he became a successful fisherman, especially in the mackerel fishery. Among the vessels he commanded were the *Lizzie F. Choate* and the *Alice G. Wonson*, both large and highly regarded clipper schooners. He was temporarily employed by the U.S. Fish Commission in 1879–1880, becoming a permanent member of the Commission's staff in 1882. Between then and 1892, Collins became an active writer on practical fishing subjects, including improved fishing vessels. During his career in Washington he published seventy-nine articles, some of which were of book size. At the time his correspondence began to be published in the *Cape Ann Advertiser* he was engaged in setting up preliminary requirements for a research schooner smack for the Fish Commission. Collins had begun to have half-models and plans made for such a vessel. It is not clear how he proceeded in this but it is known he had the aid of some competent designers in the years between 1882 and 1885. These included one of the Bishops of Gloucester, U.S. Naval Constructor Samuel H. Pook and, to an extensive degree, Dennison J. Lawlor of Boston and Chelsea. Lawlor prepared the lines of the final design of the smack, named *Grampus* when launched in 1886, but Collins was the responsible supervisor of construction and filling. He resigned from the Commission's staff in 1892 and became editor of *The Fishing Gazette* and later president of the Commercial Fisheries Association. He was U.S. Commissioner for the International Fisheries Exposition at Bergen, Norway, in 1898, and prepared an excellent catalog of the exhibits. He became Chairman of the Massachusetts Fish and Game Commission in 1899 and held this appointment until his death in 1904.

With his background he was able to write about the schooners with great authority. In his long letter published April 14, 1882, Collins devoted much attention to the question of the seaworthiness of the then popular clipper model—comparing it unfavorably with that of the old pinkies. He showed a marked inclination for the English fishing cutters used in the North Sea which, he claimed, were far more safe than the clipper schooners. This probably did not help win support among any "patriots" in the centerboard *vs.* keel controversy.

In this letter the first reference to the problems of Gloucester harbor is made. Collins wrote, "I am aware that objections may be urged against the adoption of deep vessels, such for instance as the shallowness of Gloucester Harbor, the additional cost of building such crafts, etc., but I will not stop here to discuss the objections since they are of little importance if the advantages I have indicated above can be secured by a new departure. Safety of life and property should supersede all other considerations and will." Collins' statement made it plain that so practical a subject as available depth of water would not be recognized in his discussion.

A number of replies to Collins' letter followed in the *Advertiser*, one opposing and others supporting Collins. The opposing letter signed by "Sea Horse," published April 21, 1882, was not an effective rebuttal. It was followed by letters published in the *Advertiser* on April 28 and May 5, 1882, and later still by letters published in the same paper on January 25, February 1, 8, and 15, 1884. These were signed by "Vidas," whose contributions to the discussions show that he was an experienced shipbuilder and designer. No certain identification of "Vidas" can be made, but his competence in the discussion and his support of Collins' general position might suggest that "Vidas" was D. J. Lawlor. At any rate, "Vidas" showed not only technical judgment but also practical common sense in his presentation of requirements for a safe, fast vessel. The discussion by this contributor contained many interesting ideas and much historical material.

With regard to the shoal harbor at Gloucester he wrote, "We shall need, before that time [when deep schooners could replace shoal] the breakwater on Dog Bar so that the deeper waters of the outer harbor can be utilized for wharves for our vessels of greater draught of water. And it is time that some move be made to secure an appropriation by Congress for this purpose." He also mentions in one of his letters the schooner *Onward*, that some years previous (August 2, 1867) had been completely turned over and righted, with loss of masts, spars, and bulwarks, but which had survived and had been towed home. (This seems to have been the case in which the galley stove covers burned discs on the overhead in the forecastle. One other such case of rolling completely over and righting is known. The *Helen G. Wells* had such an accident on November 10, 1897.)

"Vidas" discussed the hull form that an improved design should have—sufficient deadrise in the midsection to give a righting arm when heeled deck-to, or more, and the transom should be narrower and softer in the quarters than in existing vessels. He also recognized the importance of light weight aloft and of the problems of calculating stability. He strongly criticized the very long, wedge-shaped forebody seen in some clippers, and also was critical of short, full runs, which he says had been adopted from yacht designs.

"Vidas" also mentioned proper ballasting and securing ice and fish in the hold so that they could not shift in a knockdown. He recommended revival of the old fashion of putting ashore the fore-topmast and jibboom of a schooner fitting for winter fishing.

Collins had two letters published May 12 and 19 in 1882, but did not contribute further to the discussion. Though Collins should be credited with raising the question of seaworthiness in the clipper schooners, it is apparent that "Vidas" carried the burden of describing the numerous specific characteristics that were technically required in an improved type.

The discussion, in 1884, declined in importance to opinions of how to survive severe storms in existing vessels, such as riding out storms at anchor on the Banks instead of immediately seeking sea-room and deep water, the use of oil, or a sea anchor.

There was no immediate action in the production of deep-draft fishing schooners between 1880 and 1883, though by the end of this period Collins had collected half-models and plans of schooner smacks, in what seems to have been an informal competition for the design of the schooner smack for the Fish Commission. Among the designers were one of the Bishops of Gloucester, Lawlor of Chelsea, and the naval constructor Samuel H. Pook, of Washington, D.C.

Though the inshore fisheries had declined in importance after 1865, small schooners were still being built for this fishery at Gloucester, Essex, and in Maine and Nova Scotia. This class of vessel, called schooner boat, was usually under 55 feet on deck or just under the small market schooner in size. Sloops, called sloop boats, were also used in these inshore fisheries. The small market schooner or schooner boat may be said to have replaced the pinkies in New England fisheries.

Plate 52 shows an example of the type of schooner boat built at Gloucester and Essex in the 1870s and 1880s. These were usually flush-decked with very moderate sheer, and had a long, straight keel with slight drag, nearly upright sternpost, short heavy-appearing counter, a wide transom curved athwartship, and heavy quarters. The stem rabbet was straight and raking forward above the load line. A long head was fitted, with fiddlehead, and headrails, of the then popular style.

The midsection was formed with strongly rising floor having slight hollow, a rather quick turn of bilge, slight tumble home in the topside. The midsection form resembled that of some of the more extreme sharpshooters of the 1850s. The entrance was long, sharp, and convex except just abaft the forefoot where there was a very slight hollow. The run was quite long, with straight buttocks. In arrangement they followed their big sisters—forecastle forward, trunk cabin aft, wooden pumps just abaft the midsection, but usually they had only a main hatch amidships. In rig, they followed the existing fishing schooner rigging except that they usually did not fid a fore-topmast nor did they carry a jibboom; in fact they retained the common rig of the early sharpshooters.

The schooner boat shown in Plate 52 has a designed Custom House length of 39′-7½″ between perpendiculars, 14′-1″ moulded beam, 5′-3″ depth in hold. The model for this schooner boat was made by Daniel Poland, Jr., a partner in the Gloucester shipyard of Poland and Woodbury, and was built

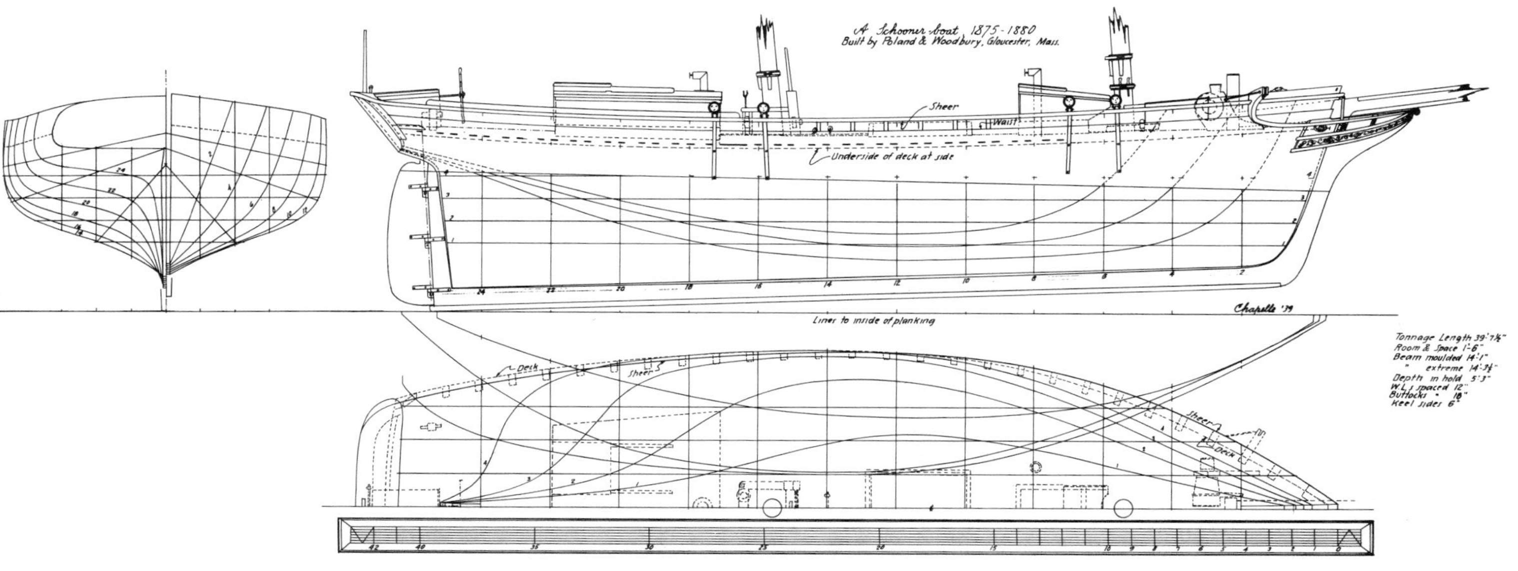
A Schooner boat 1875-1880
Built by Poland & Woodbury, Gloucester, Mass.
Sheer
Waist
Underside of deck at side
Chapelle '39
Liner to inside of planking
Tonnage Length 39'-7½"
Room & Space 1'-6"
Beam moulded 14'-1"
" extreme 14'-3½"
Depth in hold 5'-3"
W.L.s spaced 12"
Buttocks " 18"
Keel sides 6"
Deck
Sheer

PLATE 52. Schooner boat, about 1880, half-model

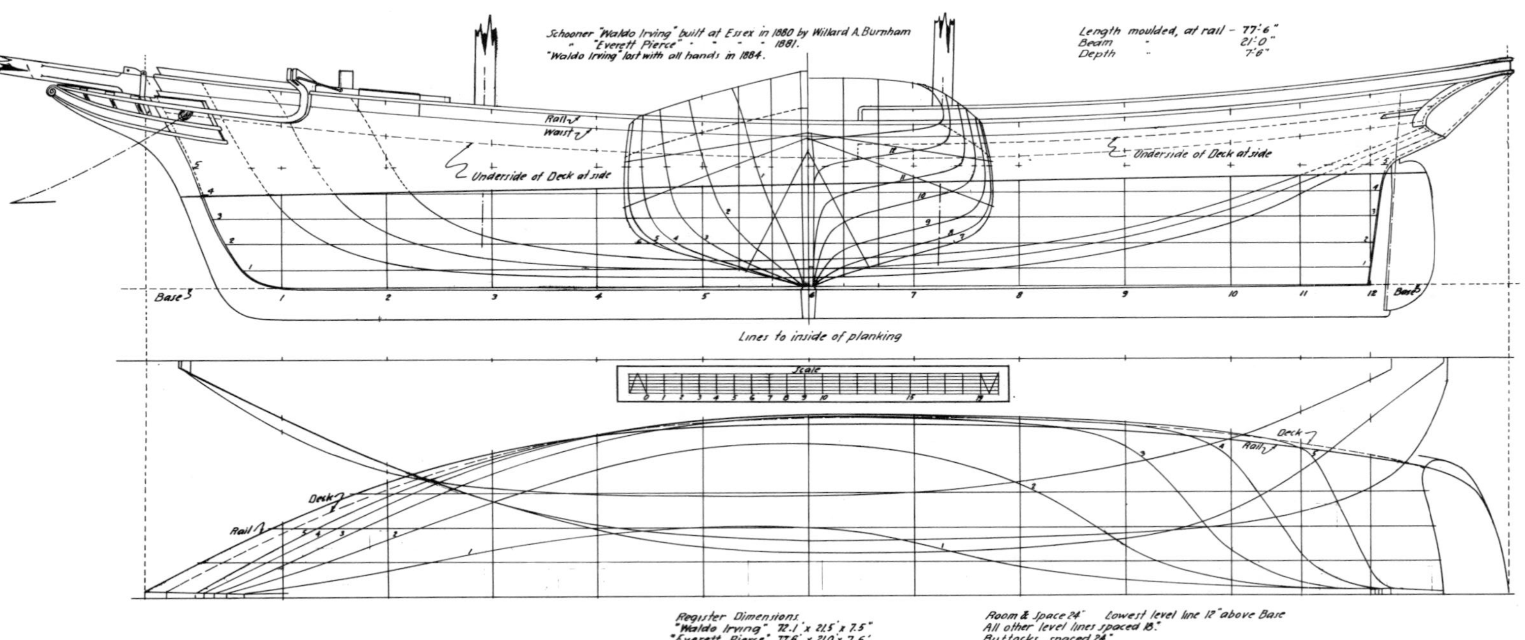
Schooner "Waldo Irving" built at Essex in 1880 by Willard A. Burnham
" "Everett Pierce" " " " 1881.
"Waldo Irving" lost with all hands in 1884.
Length moulded, at rail - 77'6"
Beam " 21'0"
Depth " 7'6"
Rail
Waist
Underside of Deck at side
Underside of Deck at side
Base
Base
Lines to inside of planking
Scale
Deck
Rail
Deck
Rail
Register Dimensions
"Waldo Irving" 72.1' x 21.5' x 7.5"
"Everett Pierce" 77.6' x 21.0' x 7.6'
Room & Space 24" Lowest level line 12" above Base
All other level lines spaced 18."
Buttocks spaced 24"

PLATE 53. *Waldo Irving*, 1880, *Everett Pierce*, 1881, half-model about 1880 in this yard, but the name of the boat was not found in the scant Poland records.

Plate 53 shows the modified clipper schooner that had come into use in the Georges Bank fishery. This model was used to build two vessels. The first was the *Waldo Irving*, built in 1880 at Essex; 72.1′ x 21.5′ x 7.5′ (new measurement). This schooner was lost with all hands in 1884. The schooner *Everett Pierce* was built at Essex in 1881; the model lengthened about 5′-0″. The model for these schooners was made by Willard A. Burnham, who was also their builder. The model was for a schooner 77′-6″ moulded length at main rail cap, 21′-0″ moulded beam, and 7′-6″ moulded depth.

The model showed marked sheer, straight keel with little drag, upright sternpost, rather long counter for the date, with a deep, wide transom much curved athwartship. The stem rabbet had a slight flare, raking forward above the load line. The entrance was long and sharp, with hollow abaft the forefoot. The run was rather short but well formed. In general, this model was of the fast carrier type. The midsection was formed with very moderate rise of straight floor carried well outboard, a low, rather hard turn of bilge, and marked tumble home in the topside.

The Provincetown model of two-masted salt bankers that had developed in the 1870s and 1880, which has been mentioned in the discussion of the design of the *Lizzie W. Matheson,* is well illustrated in the *Leon S. Swift* (Plate 54). This vessel was built by Tarr and James in 1881 at Essex. She was a sharp-ended carrier designed to be 95′-0″ Custom House length between perpendiculars, 103′-0″ moulded length at main rail cap, 24′-8″ moulded beam, 10′-0″ moulded depth. A handsome vessel of her type, she had a moderate sheer, straight keel with little drag, nearly vertical sternpost, and the counter was rather long for her type and date, with a raking, wide transom, moderately curved athwartship. The stem rabbet was raking and flared, above the load line, curved below. The vessel had the long head, with the double headrails, that the James yard usually fitted to the large Provincetown bankers, seen earlier in the *Matheson.* The entrance was long and sharp with some hollow just abaft the stem rabbet at load line and below. The midsection shows slightly rising straight floors carried outboard to the quarterbeam, a full, round bilge with very moderate tumble home in the topside.

Though the salt banker was primarily a carrier, the *Swift* seems to show that a trend toward the clipper in these bankers had occurred, after the *Matheson* was modeled. This drift toward a fast sailer may have been the result of a demand for an all-around fishing vessel suitable for both the salt bank and Georges Bank fisheries as well as for the mackerel fishery. This could be met by not only a sharper model than was thought de-

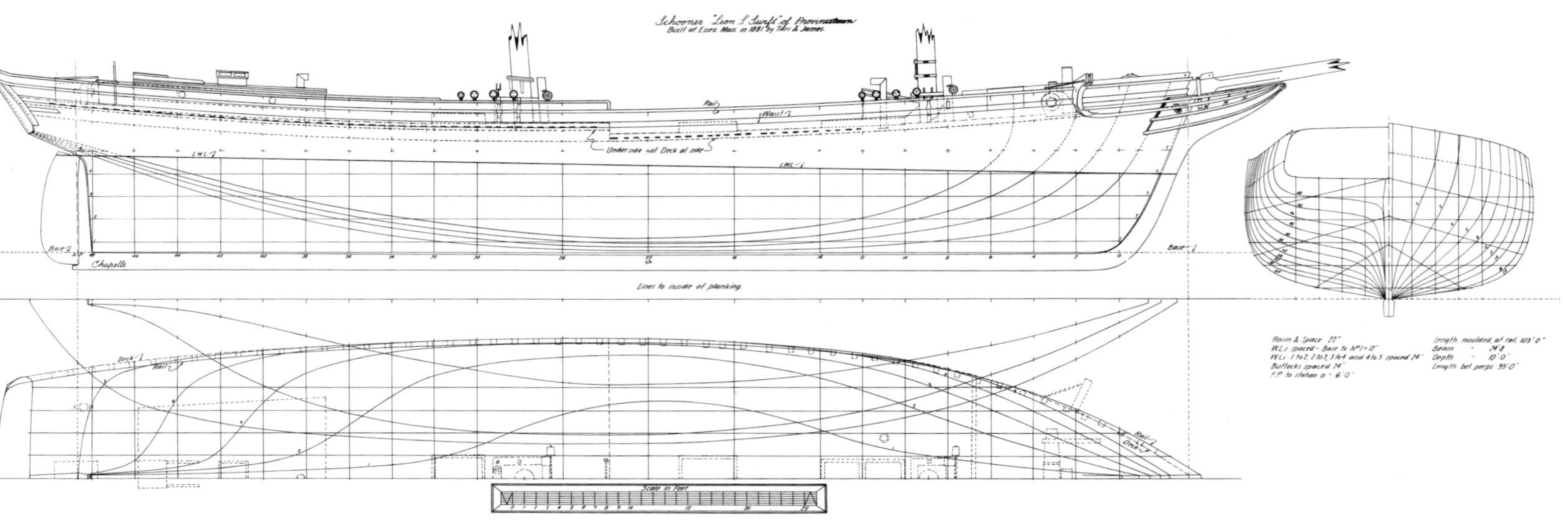
Schooner "Leon S Swift" of Provincetown
Built at Essex Mass. in 1881 by Tarr & James.
Rail
Waist
LWL
Underside of Deck at side
Base
Chapelle
Lines to inside of planking.
Deck
Rail
Scale in Feet
Room & Space 22"
W.L.s spaced - Base to No 1 = 12"
W.Ls 1 to 2, 2 to 3, 3 to 4 and 4 to 5 spaced 24"
Buttocks spaced 24"
F.P. to station 0 - 6'0"
Length, moulded, at rail, 103'0"
Beam - 24'8
Depth - 10'0"
Length bet. perps. 95'0"

PLATE 54. *Leon S. Swift*, 1881, mould loft plan

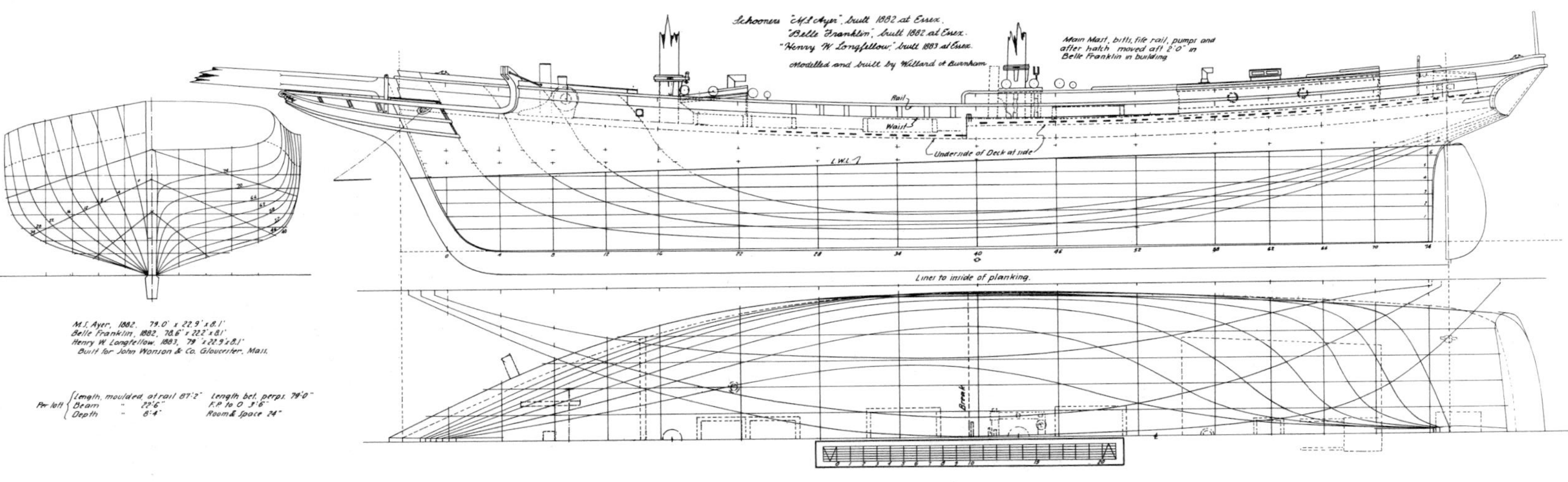
Schooners "M.S. Ayer", built 1882 at Essex.
"Belle Franklin", built 1882 at Essex.
"Henry W. Longfellow," built 1883 at Essex.
Modelled and built by Willard A. Burnham
Main Mast, bitts, fife rail, pumps and after hatch moved aft 2'0" in Belle Franklin in building
Rail
Waist
Underside of Deck at side
L.W.L.
Lines to inside of planking.
Break
M.S. Ayer, 1882, 79.0' x 22.9' x 8.1'
Belle Franklin, 1882, 78.6' x 22.2' x 8.1'
Henry W. Longfellow, 1883, 79' x 22.9' x 8.1'
Built for John Wonson & Co. Gloucester, Mass.
Per loft
Length, moulded, at rail 87'2"
Beam " 22'6"
Depth " 8'4"
Length bet. perps. 79'0"
F.P. to 0 3'6"
Room & Space 24"

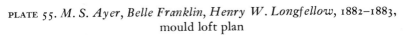

PLATE 55. *M. S. Ayer, Belle Franklin, Henry W. Longfellow*, 1882–1883, mould loft plan

sirable in earlier years in a banker, but also by an increase in size of vessel as well.

Plate 55 shows the lines of a half-model from which three schooners were built in 1882–1883. The model was made by Willard A. Burnham, who built the three schooners at Essex. These vessels were clippers of the class popular in the mackerel and Georges Bank fisheries, of the shallow model. The schooners *M. S. Ayer* and *Belle Franklin* were launched in 1882, the *Henry W. Longfellow* in 1883.

This model showed moderate sheer, straight keel with little drag, upright sternpost, a longer counter than was common earlier, a wide and rather deep transom strongly curved athwartship, a raking, straight stem rabbet, sharp, concave, and long entrance, and a long run with straight buttocks. The midsection had moderate deadrise, a quick turn in the bilge and very little tumble home above. It will be noticed that schooners of this class were somewhat pinched in forward at deck and rail. The model produced schooners 87′-2″ molded length at main rail cap, 79′-0″ length between perpendiculars, 22′-6″ moulded beam, and 8′-4″ moulded depth. These dimensions, it should be noted, were uncommonly close to the Custom House measurements.*

The clipper schooner *Edward P. Boynton* was built on the lines shown in Plate 56 at Essex in 1883. This model was also identified as that on which the schooner *Mary Fernald* had been built in 1875 at Gloucester by Poland and Woodbury. Daniel Poland, partner in this firm, built the *Boynton* at Essex after the Gloucester partnership had failed. These vessels were intended for the mackerel fishery and for the frozen herring trade with Newfoundland.

The lines show a schooner having moderate sheer, straight keel with slight drag, nearly vertical sternpost, counter of moderate length with raking, wide transom strongly curved athwartship. It is noticeable that the clipper schooners commonly had heavy quarters, considered necessary to allow the hull of bear the very large mainsails that were popular in the period under discussion. The stem rabbet was straight above the forefoot and well-raked forward. The entrance was long, concave, and very sharp at deck and rail. The run was very long and had straight buttocks. The midsection had moderately rising floor with slight hollow outboard of the garboard, a quick turn in the bilge, some tumble home in the topside. These schooners were very fast sailers. They were 77′-3½″ moulded length at main rail cap, 22′-6″ moulded beam, and 8′-5″ moulded depth. The Custom House dimensions of the *Fernald* were 78′ x 22.8′ x 7.8′; the *Boynton* measured 78′ x 22.8′ x 8′ (new measurement).

* *M. S. Ayer*, 79.0′ x 22.9′ x 8.1′; *Belle Franklin*, 78.6′ x 22.2′ x 8.1′; *Henry W. Longfellow*, 79.0′ x 22.9′ x 8.1′ (new measurement).

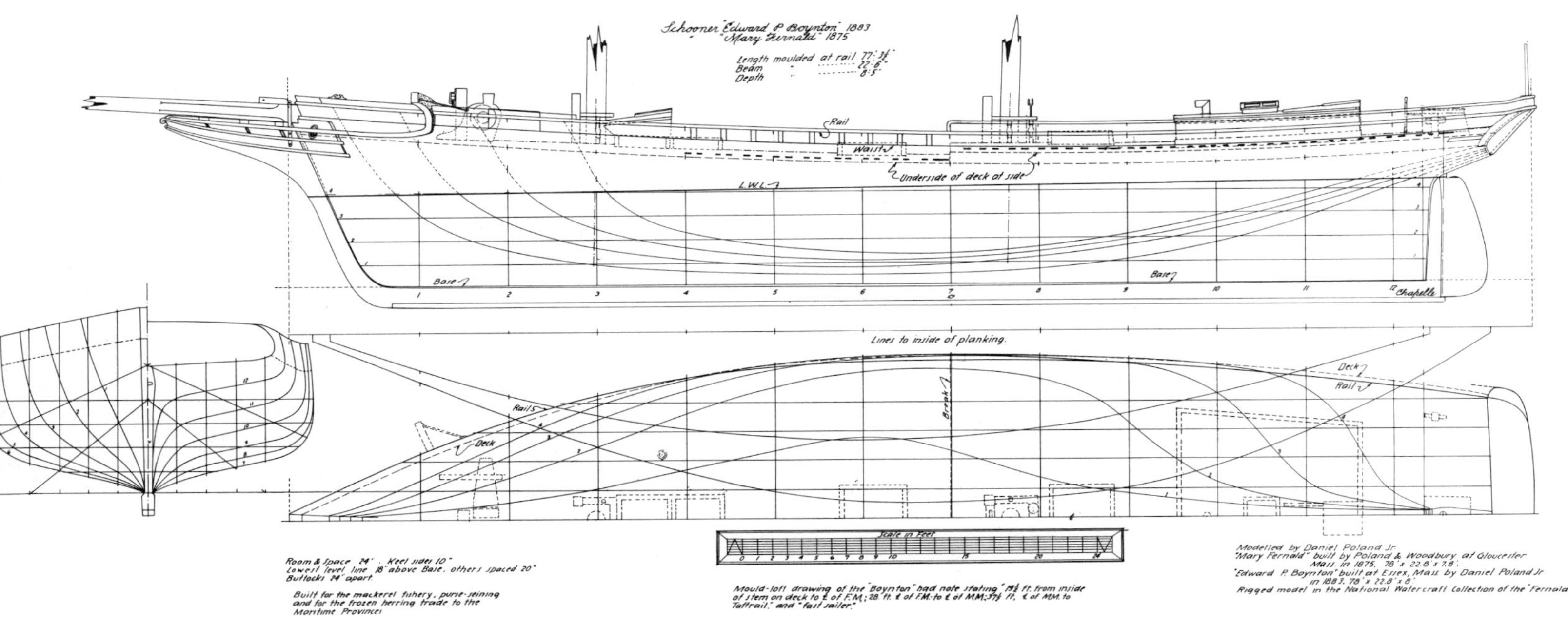
Schooner "Edward P. Boynton" 1883
" "Mary Fernald" 1875
Length moulded at rail 77'-3½"
Beam " .... 22'-6"
Depth " .... 8'-5"
Rail
Waist
Underside of deck at side
LWL
Base
Chapelle
Lines to inside of planking.
Deck
Rail
Rails
Break
Scale in Feet
Room & Space 24". Keel sides 10"
Lowest level line 18" above Base, others spaced 20"
Buttocks 24" apart.
Built for the mackerel fishery, purse-seining
and for the frozen herring trade to the
Maritime Provinces
Mould-loft drawing of the "Boynton" had note stating "19½ ft. from inside
of stem on deck to ℄ of F.M.; 28 ft. ℄ of F.M. to ℄ of M.M.; 37½ ft. ℄ of M.M. to
Taffrail." and "fast sailer."
Modelled by Daniel Poland Jr.
"Mary Fernald" built by Poland & Woodbury at Gloucester
Mass. in 1875. 78' x 22.8' x 7.8'.
"Edward P. Boynton" built at Essex, Mass. by Daniel Poland Jr.
in 1883. 78' x 22.8' x 8'.
Rigged model in the National Watercraft Collection of the "Fernald"

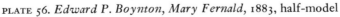

PLATE 56. *Edward P. Boynton, Mary Fernald*, 1883, half-model

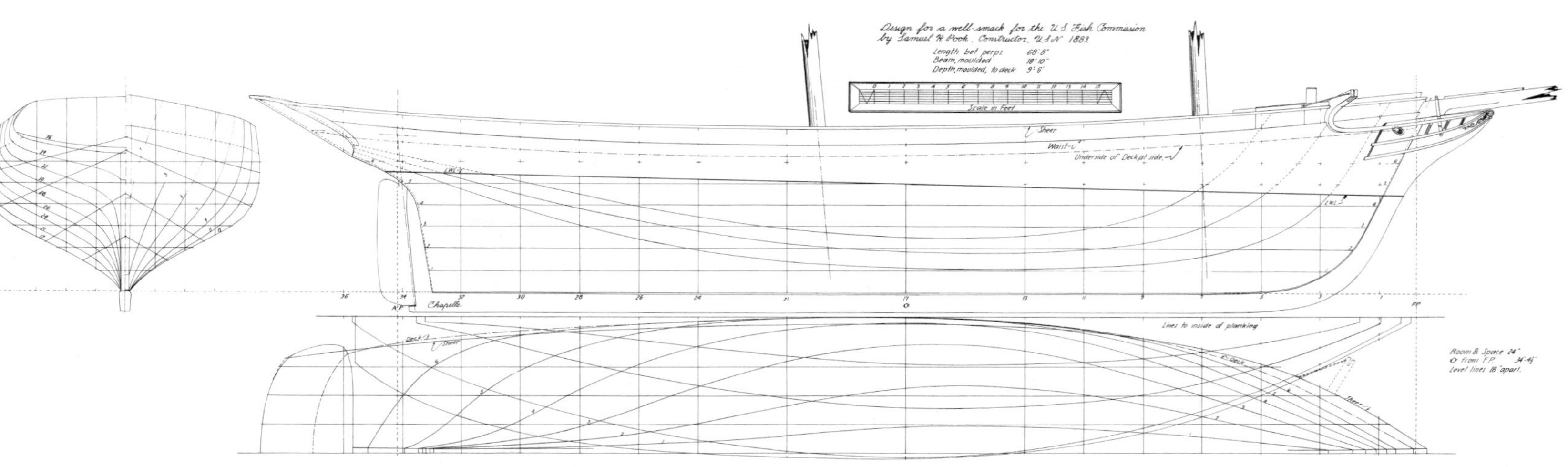
Design for a well-smack for the U.S. Fish Commission
by Samuel H. Pook, Constructor, U.S.N. 1883
Length bet perps. 68'8"
Beam, moulded 18'10"
Depth, moulded, to deck 9'6"
Scale in Feet
Sheer
Waist
Underside of Deck at side
Lines to inside of planking
Room & Space 24"
⊙ from F.P. 34'4½"
Level lines 18" apart.
Chapelle

PLATE 57. Pook-designed smack, 1883, half-model

The competitive designs for the U.S. Fish Commission's schooner smack have been mentioned. The design by Samuel H. Pook, naval constructor, is represented by a half-model in the U.S. National Museum of History and Technology, Smithsonian Institution, Washington, D.C., and its lines are shown in Plate 57. The design was made for Collins in 1883, at Washington. The dimensions were to be 68′-8″ between perpendiculars (Custom House measurement), 18′-10″ moulded beam, and 9′-6″ moulded depth. The moulded length at main rail cap was 78′-10″. The model shows flush deck and main rail but, had the design been used, it would have had the usual fisherman raised quarterdeck and monkey rail employed in the Fish Commission's *Grampus.*

The lines show a schooner having moderate sheer, straight keel with very moderate drag, slightly raking sternpost, a long counter for this period, a sharply raking rather wide transom strongly curved athwartship. The stem rabbet had strong fore rake with slight flare above the load line, with a well-rounded forefoot. The entrance was long, sharp, and slightly convex, the run was long with straight buttocks of moderate length. The midsection showed marked deadrise with hollow floor, high, firm turn of bilge, and strong tumble home. The design would have produced a fast, seaworthy schooner had it been built. Pook was the designer of many of the clipper ships of the 1850s including the famous *Red Jacket,* so a superior design would have been expected of him.

In 1884 Dennison J. Lawlor modeled a fishing schooner to be built at Essex for a New York owner. This was the *George B. Douglas,* reputed a fast sailer. She was of the shallow, clipper type and intended for the mackerel fishery (Plate 58). This schooner had a moulded length at main rail cap of 90′-4″, 22′-4″ moulded beam, and moulded depth (rabbet to underside of main deck at side) of 9′-2″. She had a strong sheer, a straight keel with marked drag for a clipper model, vertical sternpost, short counter, strongly raking, wide transom with a great deal of curvature athwartship. The stem rabbet flared and raked forward, with a rather short head and billet. The entrance was long, sharp, and markedly hollow. The run was very long with straight buttocks and had constant deadrise in the afterbody until just forward of the transom. The midsection had hollow, rising floor with strong deadrise, a very hard turn of the bilge, much tumble home in the topside. The quarters were very heavy. The *Douglas* was said to have been the last clipper-type fishing schooner designed by Lawlor.

The same year he modeled the *Douglas* he designed the *Roulette,* the real forerunner of the deep-draft schooners that Collins had proposed. Lawlor was operating a yard in East Boston and was building a large schooner yacht at this time. When he had completed her he began building *Roulette* on speculation. A poor businessman, he over extended himself financially and

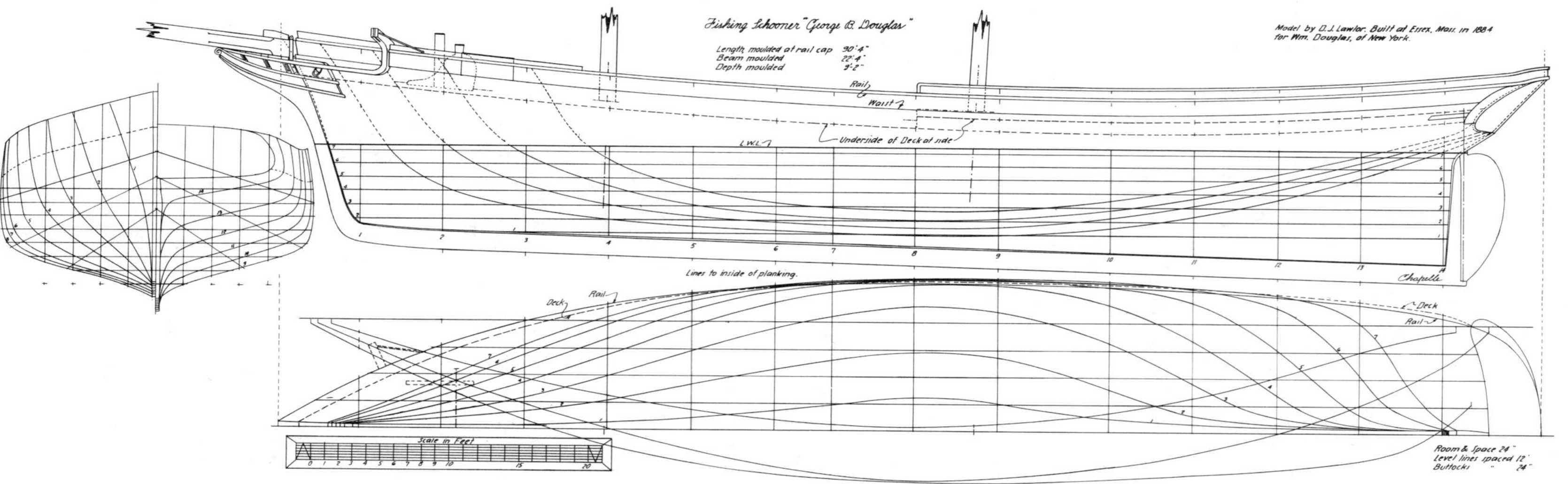
Fishing Schooner "George B. Douglas"
Length moulded at rail cap 90'4"
Beam moulded 22'4"
Depth moulded 9'2"
Model by D. J. Lawlor. Built at Essex, Mass. in 1884
for Wm. Douglas, of New York.
Rail
Waist
LWL
Underside of Deck at side
Lines to inside of planking.
Chapelle
Deck
Rail
Deck
Rail
Scale in Feet
Room & Space 24"
Level lines spaced 12"
Buttocks " 24"

PLATE 58. *George B. Douglas*, 1884, half-model

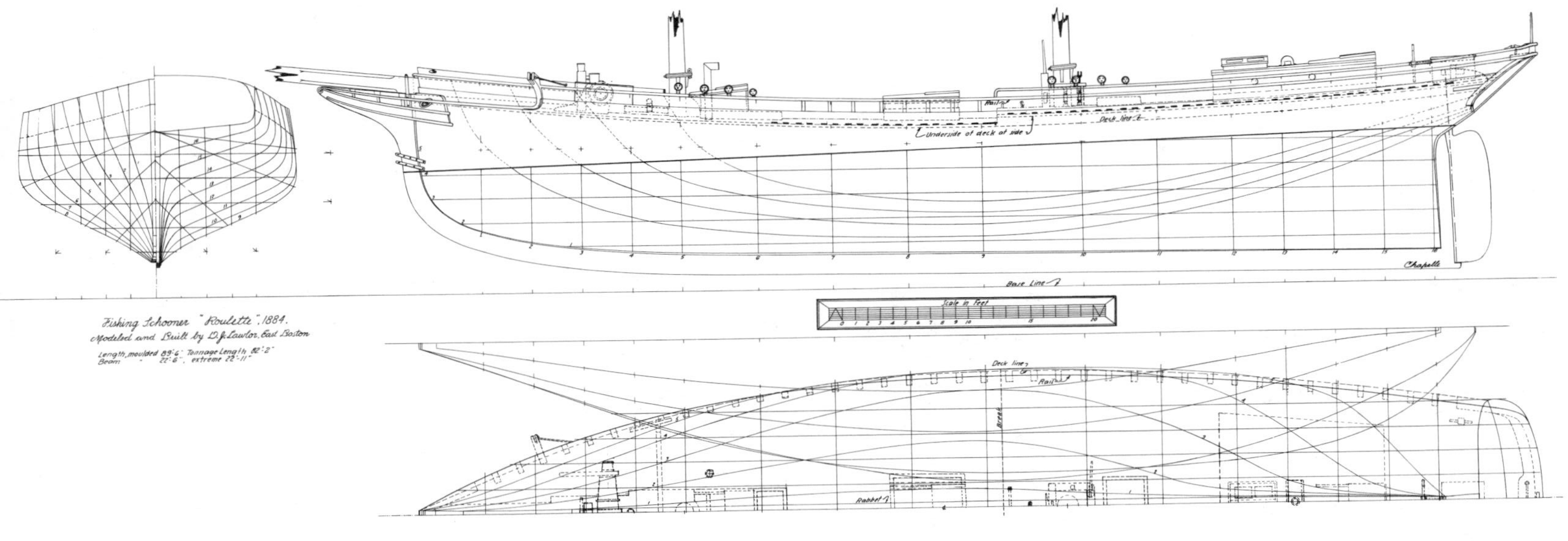
Fishing Schooner "Roulette", 1884.
Modeled and Built by D. J. Lawlor, East Boston
Length, moulded 89'-6" Tonnage Length 82'-2"
Beam " 22'-6", extreme 22'-11"
Underside of deck at side
Deck line
Rail
Base Line
Scale in Feet
0 1 2 3 4 5 6 7 8 9 10 15 20
Chapelle
Break
Rabbet
Deck line
Rail

PLATE 59. *Roulette*, 1884, rigged-model, half-model

used some of the timber left over from the yacht. The result was a lawsuit in which he lost the *Roulette* and closed his yard.

Plate 59 shows the lines of this noted schooner, the half-model of which is in the U.S. National Museum of History and Technology. *Roulette* was 89′-6″ moulded length at main rail cap, 22′-6″ moulded beam, with a designed tonnage length of 82′-2″. Her moulded depth was 10′-2″.

The *Roulette* had marked sheer, straight keel with much drag, vertical sternpost, short counter, a sharply raking transom well-curved athwartship, but she had rather heavy quarters though the stern was not excessively wide. The stem rabbet was nearly vertical above the load line but the forefoot was much rounded. The entrance was long and sharp with much hollow just abaft the stem rabbet below the deck. In spite of her upright stem she carried a long head and billet. The run was long with straight buttocks, but these were not of much length. The midsection was formed with sharply rising floor, a hollow garboard, a hard turn of the bilge, and strong tumble home in the topside. The run showed constant deadrise, with the after three stations having a slight, gradual change.

Roulette usually worked out of Boston and became famous locally for speed and weatherliness particularly in blowing weather. She drew 11 to 12 feet in ready-for-sea condition.

The *Douglas* and the *Roulette* was not the only schooners designed by Lawlor in 1884. That fall and winter he modeled the straight-stem schooners *A. S. & R. Hammond* and *Arthur D. Story*, both built at Essex and launched in early 1885.

Plate 60 shows the lines of the schooner *A. S. & R. Hammond:* 87′-5″ moulded length at main rail cap, 21′-4″ moulded beam, and 8′-6″ moulded depth. This vessel had a marked and graceful sheer, straight keel with much drag, and with forefoot much rounded off. She had a nearly upright short sternpost, rather long and somewhat heavy counter, a sharply raking transom, narrow for her date and well-rounded athwartship. Her depth forward was much reduced by having a cutaway forefoot and she had the nearly straight, upright stem of the steamboat or tugboat that had long been popular in Boston and New York pilot schooners. The entrance was long, sharp, and somewhat concave just abaft the rabbet and below deck. The midsection was formed with strongly rising floors, slightly hollow in the garboard, a somewhat hard turn of the bilge, and marked tumble home in the topside. She drew about 10 feet in service. A heavily canvassed vessel, the *Hammond* was considered fast but, like so many fast fishermen, she did not enter any of the races in her time, so won no great fame by her speed.

The building of the Fish Commission smack was delayed, in the final period, by bungling that Collins could not prevent. The initial stages had

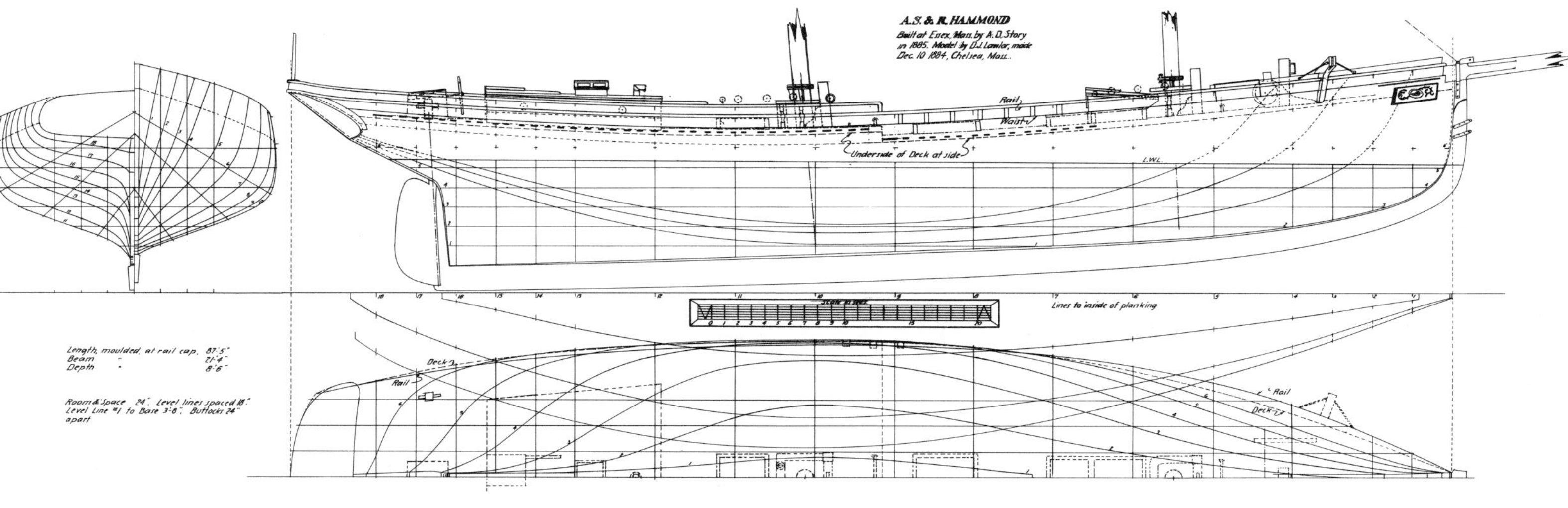
A.S. & R. HAMMOND
Built at Essex, Mass. by A. D. Story in 1885. Model by D.J. Lawlor, made Dec. 10 1884, Chelsea, Mass..
Rail
Waist
Underside of Deck at side
L.W.L.
Lines to inside of planking
Deck
Rail
Length, moulded, at rail cap. 87'5"
Beam " 21'4"
Depth " 8'6"
Room & Space 24". Level lines spaced 18". Level Line #1 to Base 3'-8". Buttocks 24" apart

PLATE 60. *A. S. & R. Hammond*, 1884, half-model

proceeded rapidly—as Collins later acknowledged—for Lawlor prepared model specifications and plans, laid down the vessel, and produced the moulds. The vessel's hull and spars were contracted for by Robert Palmer and Sons of Noank, Connecticut, in the late fall of 1885. Boats, sails, and much of the fittings and gear were purchased independently. Launching was on Tuesday, March 23, 1886, but the vessel was not ready for sea until June 5, 1886. The cause of much of the delay was the selection and purchase of a steam windlass, boiler, pumps, piping, etc., which was left to the naval officer who commanded the Commission's steamer *Albatross*. He selected and had installed much too heavy gear for the schooner to bear. After trials these were removed and replaced by a fisherman's wooden windlass. Procurement of equipment for laboratory and special requirements also caused some delay.

While these delays were being met, the plumb-stem schooner *Arthur D. Story* (laid down, some weeks after the *Grampus*, in the A. D. Story yard at Essex) had been launched, fitted, and made a round trip to northern Nova Scotia and was about ready to sail for Iceland on the day *Grampus* was launched.

Though the credit for the design of the *Grampus* has heretofore been given entirely to Collins, it is fully apparent that Lawlor was the actual hull and rig designer. How much Lawlor contributed to the published letters in the Gloucester newspapers cannot be estimated, unless he were "Vidas," which seems possible. Certainly, Lawlor had the technical skill to specify each characteristic required, to produce the desired vessel, and Collins did not.

Chapter Five

1885–1890

Collins' effort to arouse interest in an improved model of fishing schooner had attracted some favorable comment. He had displayed the half-model and plan of the new smack in Gloucester in the fall of 1885. The building of three "improved" schooners—the *John H. McManus*, 88.3′ x 24.4′ x 10.9′; the *Arthur D. Story*, 85.0′ x 23.3′ x 9.6′; and the *A. S. & R. Hammond*, 78.7′ x 21.7′ x 8.5′ register dimensions—gave added support. However, the shoal slips and berths in Gloucester Harbor were apparently a discouraging influence for there was no immediate sign that there were many owners ready to build deep-draft schooners. As to the speed of the three new schooners, the owners and skippers apparently decided to wait and see, as they were doing with regard to *Roulette*.

The lines of the *Grampus* (Plate 61) carried the imprint of D. J. Lawlor: much sheer, rather long, straight keel, nearly vertical sternpost, short counter, heavily raked transom of moderate width, strongly curved athwartship, nearly vertical stem rabbet above the load line, strongly curved below. The entrance was long, sharp, and concave just abaft the stem. The run was long and straight, or nearly so, in the buttocks, with some constant angle of deadrise in the afterbody. The midsection showed a hollow garboard (carried well forward), straight rise outboard of the garboard to quarterbeam, fairly hard turn of the bilge, marked tumble home in the topside.

Some innovations were claimed by Collins: the transom was narrower than usual in a Lawlor model of this period, giving softer quarters and a greater increase in hull depth than Lawlor had given *Roulette*. Alterations in the standard clipper rig were also made: the foremast was shortened, the jumbo stay was brought to the gammon iron, and the jumbo boom dis-

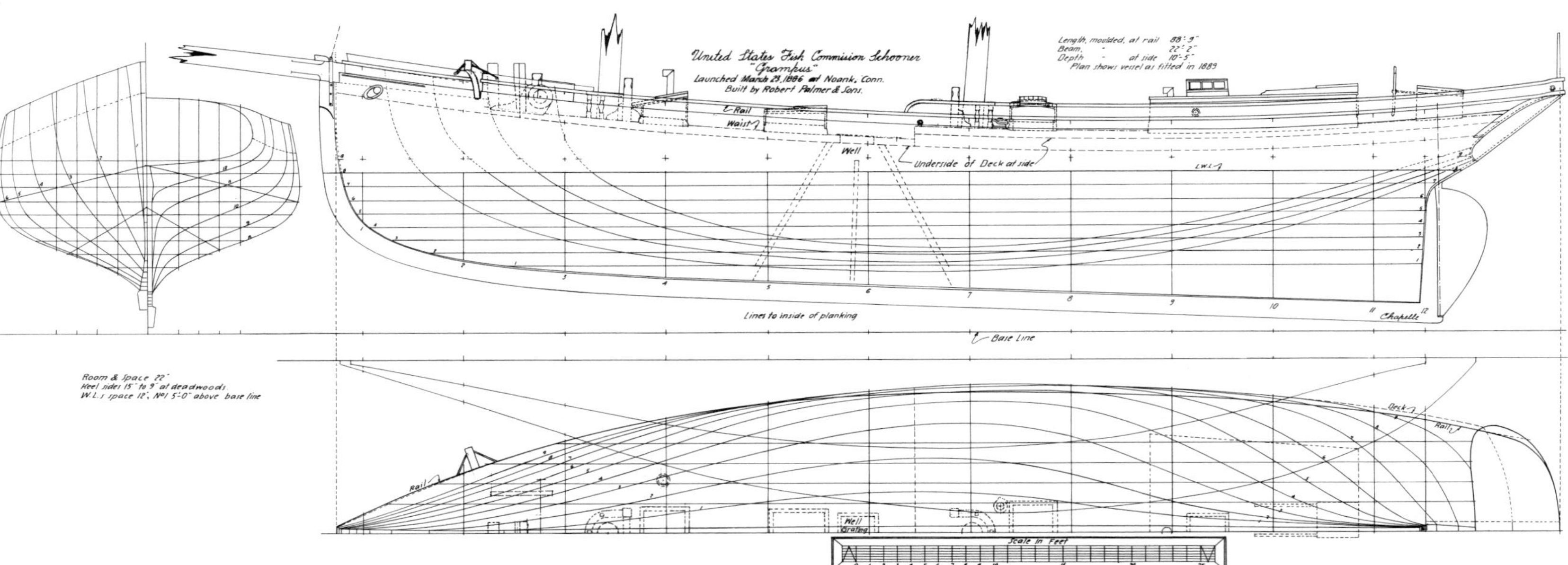
United States Fish Commission Schooner
"Grampus"
Launched March 23, 1886 at Noank, Conn.
Built by Robert Palmer & Sons.
Length, moulded, at rail 88' 9"
Beam - 22' 2"
Depth - at side 10'-5"
Plan shows vessel as fitted in 1889
Rail
Waist
Well
Underside of Deck at side
LWL
Lines to inside of planking
Chapelle
Base Line
Room & Space 22"
Keel sides 15" to 9" at deadwoods
W.L.s space 12", No 1 5'-0" above base line
Deck
Rail
Well
Grating
Scale in Feet

PLATE 61. *Grampus*, smack, 1885, plans

carded. The jibstay was brought to the bowsprit cap. These changes produced a double-headsail rig—forestaysail and jib, with a jib topsail and fore-topmast staysail. The jumbo bonnet was also discarded and iron-strapped blocks were used.

Other departures from the standard clipper fishing-schooner rig were the use of iron wire standing rigging throughout and the chain plates fastened outside of planking, let in nearly flush. The long head used in the *Roulette* was also discarded to save weight and the plumb stem of the pilot schooners adopted.

The plans published in the official report were captioned "Plans of the U.S. Fish Commission Schooner *Grampus* designed by J. W. Collins" in spite of the acknowledgment of Lawlor's very extensive contribution made in the body of the report.

Though the lines plan would produce what appears to have been the hull of a very fast schooner, so far as can now be judged, the performance of the vessel was not very satisfactory, for changes in the rig were numerous very early in her career. There were alterations in the mainboom and gaff immediately after trials and there were numerous other changes in 1888 and again in 1891. In the original rig the bowsprit was square between the knightheads, round outboard. In 1891 the jibboom was discarded and a pole bowsprit was fitted, round at the knightheads. The forestaysail stay was moved outboard a few feet, forward of the gammoning, and a bobstay for it was fitted, also a bonnet was made in the jib. It is quite certain that the original rig was not properly balanced, so that the vessel did not steer well. This was not a rare problem in fishing schooners, for the calculations of centers of effort and of lateral plane were not usually made in this period. The numerous departures in rig of the new schooner made the old rule-of-thumb methods of proportioning sails and spars obsolete.

The *Grampus* measured 90′–0″ overall, or 88′–9″ moulded length at rail cap, the extreme beam was 22′-9″, or 22′-2″ moulded, depth from top of keel to top of main deck beam, 11′-1″, or 10′-5″ moulded depth at side, and her bulwarks were 26″ high. The quarterdeck was 9″ above the main deck. She was nearly a foot deeper than the *John H. McManus* and about 1′-6″ deeper than the *Arthur D. Story*.

The *Arthur D. Story* (Plate 62) had marked sheer, straight keel with moderate drag, nearly vertical sternpost, heart-shaped transom set at a sharp rake on a very short counter projecting aft of the sternpost barely enough to clear the rudder box. The transom was immersed slightly. The schooner had a "tugboat stem," nearly straight and upright but with a slight tumble home. The forefoot was well rounded. The entrance was long, sharp, and hollow. The run was moderately long and there was a short, straight line in the buttocks. The midsection was formed with a strongly

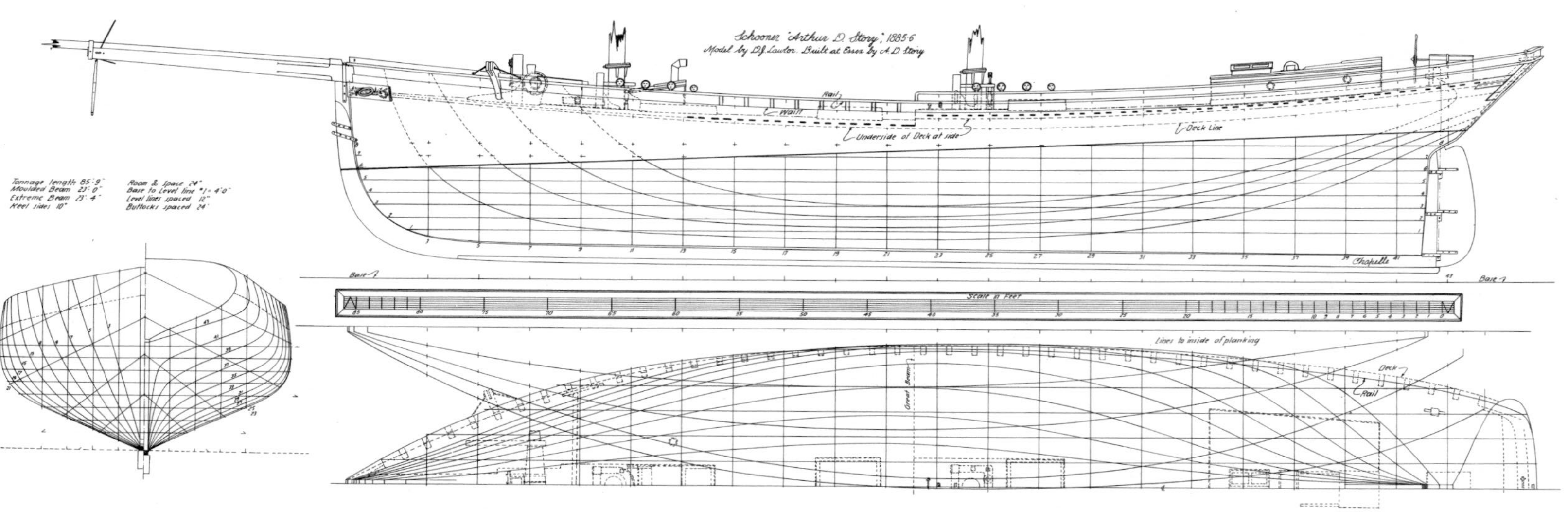
Schooner "Arthur D. Story", 1885-6
Model by D.J. Lawlor. Built at Essex by A.D. Story
Rail
Wail
Underside of Deck at side
Deck Line
Chapelle
Base
Scale in Feet
Lines to inside of planking
Great Beam
Deck
Rail
Tonnage length 85'-9"
Moulded Beam 23'-0"
Extreme Beam 23'-4"
Keel sides 10"
Room & Space 24"
Base to Level line #1 = 4'-0"
Level lines spaced 12"
Buttocks spaced 24"

PLATE 62. *Arthur D. Story*, 1885, mould loft plan

rising straight floor, a high, hard turn of the bilge, and much tumble home in the topside. The original rig was that of the old clipper, with jibboom. This vessel was 93′-6″ moulded length at main rail cap, moulded beam 23′-0″, and 9′-9″ moulded depth at side. She drew about 11′-4″ ready for sea. She was lost at sea, date unknown. The plan or the half-model of the *John H. McManus* has not been found.

In 1883 a designer appeared who became an outstanding modeler of fishing schooners: George Melville McClain, usually called "Mel McClain." He was a successful fisherman who took up schooner design as a hobby. The first schooner built to one of his models is claimed to have been the banker *Henry Dennis*, launched in 1883, but McClain had made half-models, beginning about 1880, that may have been used to build some schooners prior to 1883.

McClain was born in Bremen, Maine, in 1843. As a fisherman he commanded thirty-five different vessels in a span of fifty-six years, some of which he had modeled. It is certain that over one hundred schooners were built to his designs, counting sister ships of original models. The information found shows that between 1890 and 1894 at least fifty-five vessels were built to his designs. This was the most active period in his designing career. The list given here is incomplete since the sister ships of some built to McClain's designs cannot be identified. Among these were many vessels built on the moulds of the *I. J. Merritt Jr.*, *Lottie S. Haskins*, *Senator Lodge*, and *Marguerite Haskins*. McClain's designs will be discussed shortly.

Vessels Designed by George Melville McClain

1880 Model in MHT, Smithsonian for a clipper schooner, said to have been made by McClain.

1883 *Henry Dennis*

1884 *Robin Hood, James and Ella, Loring B. Haskell, Ralph L. Hodgdon*

1885 No vessel listed in this year in available records.

1886 *I. J. Merritt Jr., Mayflower*

1887 *George F. Edmunds, Puritan*

1888 *Masconomo*

1889 *Nellie G. Adams, Joseph Johnson, Louise J. Kenny*

1890 *Eliza Campbell, Volunteer, Lottie S. Haskins, Henry M. Stanley, Clara R. Harwood, Maggie Wells, Susan L. Hodge, Golden Hope, Parthia, Rose Cabral*

1891 *Caviare, American, Maggie and May, Edith M. Prior, Nereid, Columbia, Gladiator, Minerva, Lizzie B. Adams, Edith McInnis, Yosemite, Grayling, Mildred V. Lee*—lost with all hands.

1892 *Rienzi, Elsie F. Rowe, Clara M. Littlefield, Meteor, Ruth M. Martin, Mable D. Hines, Elector, Almeida, Albert Black, Edward A. Rich (Pioneer) Thalia*

1893 *Nellie Bly, Bertha M. Bailey, Elmer Randall, Mertis H. Perry, Mary Cabral, Marguerite Haskins, Helen G. Wells, Lewis H. Giles, Fortuna, Senator Lodge*

1894 *M. Madeline, Ralph Russell, Fortuna II, Flora L. Nickerson, Evelyn L. Smith, Effie M. Morrissey, Bessie M. Devine, Kearsarge, Alice M. Parsons*

1895 *Pauline, Hattie L. Trask, Virginia, Georgia Campbell*

1896 *Annie Greenlaw, George E. Lane, Bessie M. Devine*

1897 *Lena and Maud, A. S. Caswell*

1898 *Esther Anita*

1899 *Blanche, Golden Road, Niagara, Corsair, Titania, Henrietta G. Martin, Volant, John J. Flaherty*

1900 *Helen Miller Gould, Angelina, Dreadnaught, Tacoma, Illinois, Senator Gardner*

1901 *Alice M. Guthrie, Irene and May, Mary E. Harty, Victor*

1902 *Harriet Babson, Winifred, Veda M. McKown, Eglantine*

1903 *Mary E. Coomey, Avalon, Nokomis, Lafayette*

1904 *Hazel R. Hines*

1905 *Arthur James*

1906 *Good Luck*, round-stem profile

There were a number of centerboard schooners built at Essex for the oyster fisheries of Cape Cod. A good example is shown in Plate 63, the *Mary J. Stubbs*, built at Essex in 1886 by Tarr and James. The model of this schooner was probably made by Washington Tarr. The plan shows a centerboard schooner 66′-0″ moulded length at rail cap, 21′-8″ moulded beam, and 5′-6″ depth in hold. The working draft was about 5′-6″. A sister ship, the *Jenny Stubbs*, was built at the same time in the same yard.

This schooner had a rather straight sheer, straight keel with very little drag, slightly raking sternpost, with a short counter and a shallow, elliptical transom set at a strong rake. The stem rabbet raked forward slightly, with

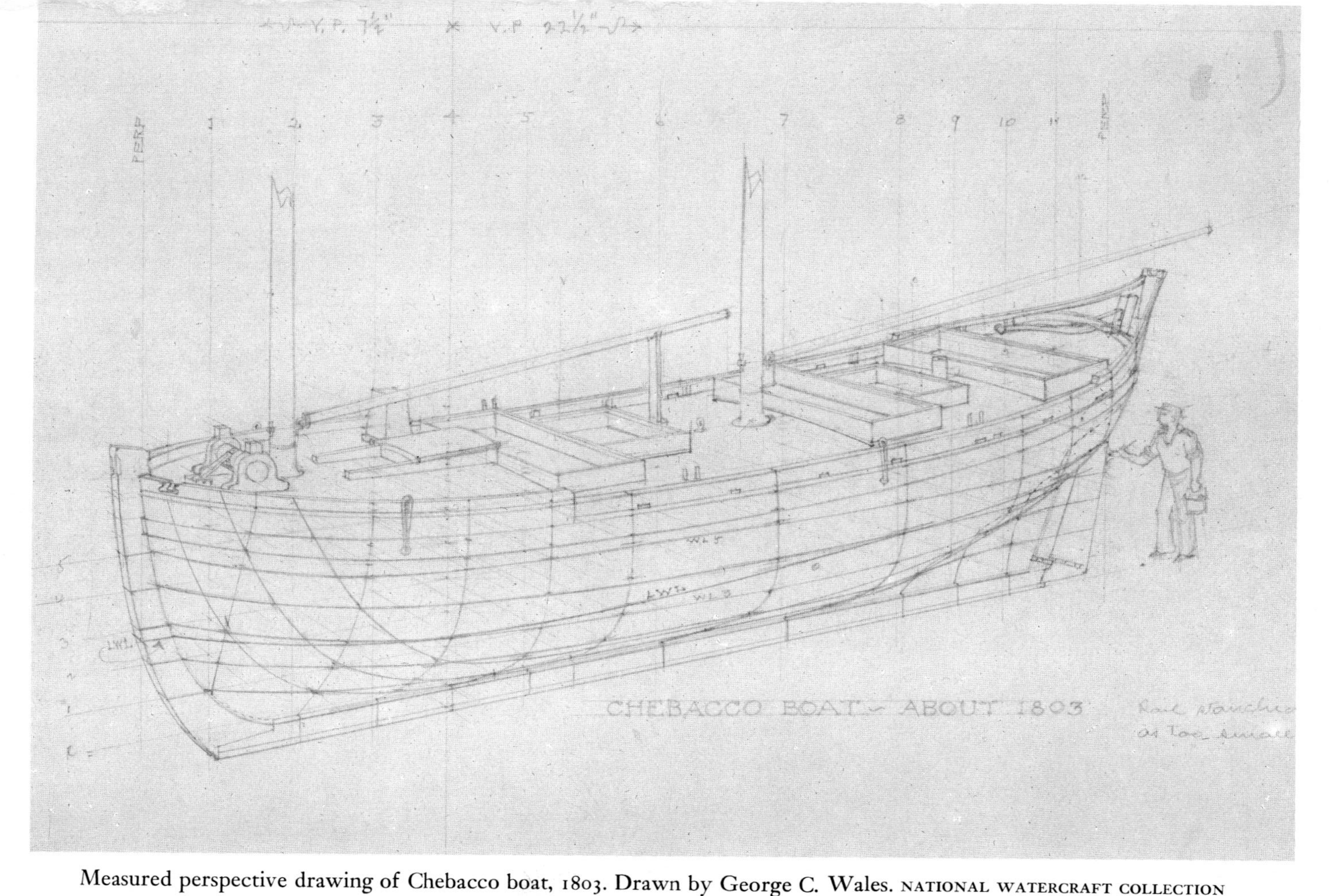
CHEBACCO BOAT— ABOUT 1803
PERP
1
2
3
4
5
6
7
8
9
10
11

Measured perspective drawing of Chebacco boat, 1803. Drawn by George C. Wales. NATIONAL WATERCRAFT COLLECTION

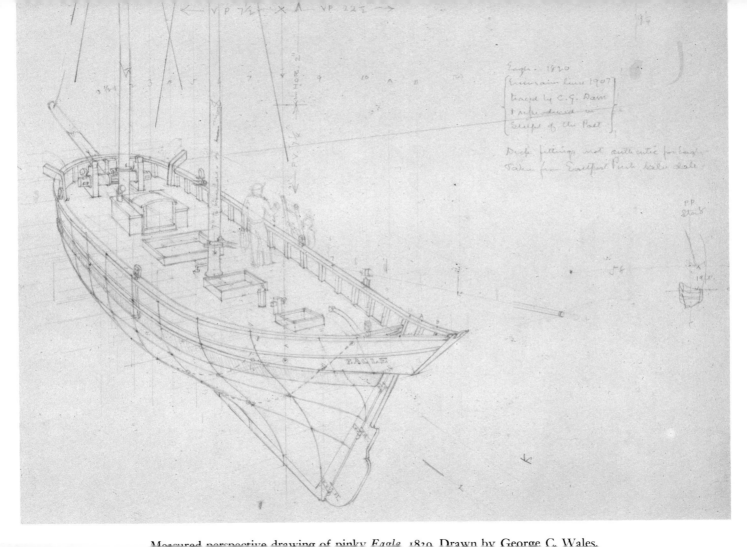

Measured perspective drawing of pinky *Eagle*, 1820. Drawn by George C. Wales.

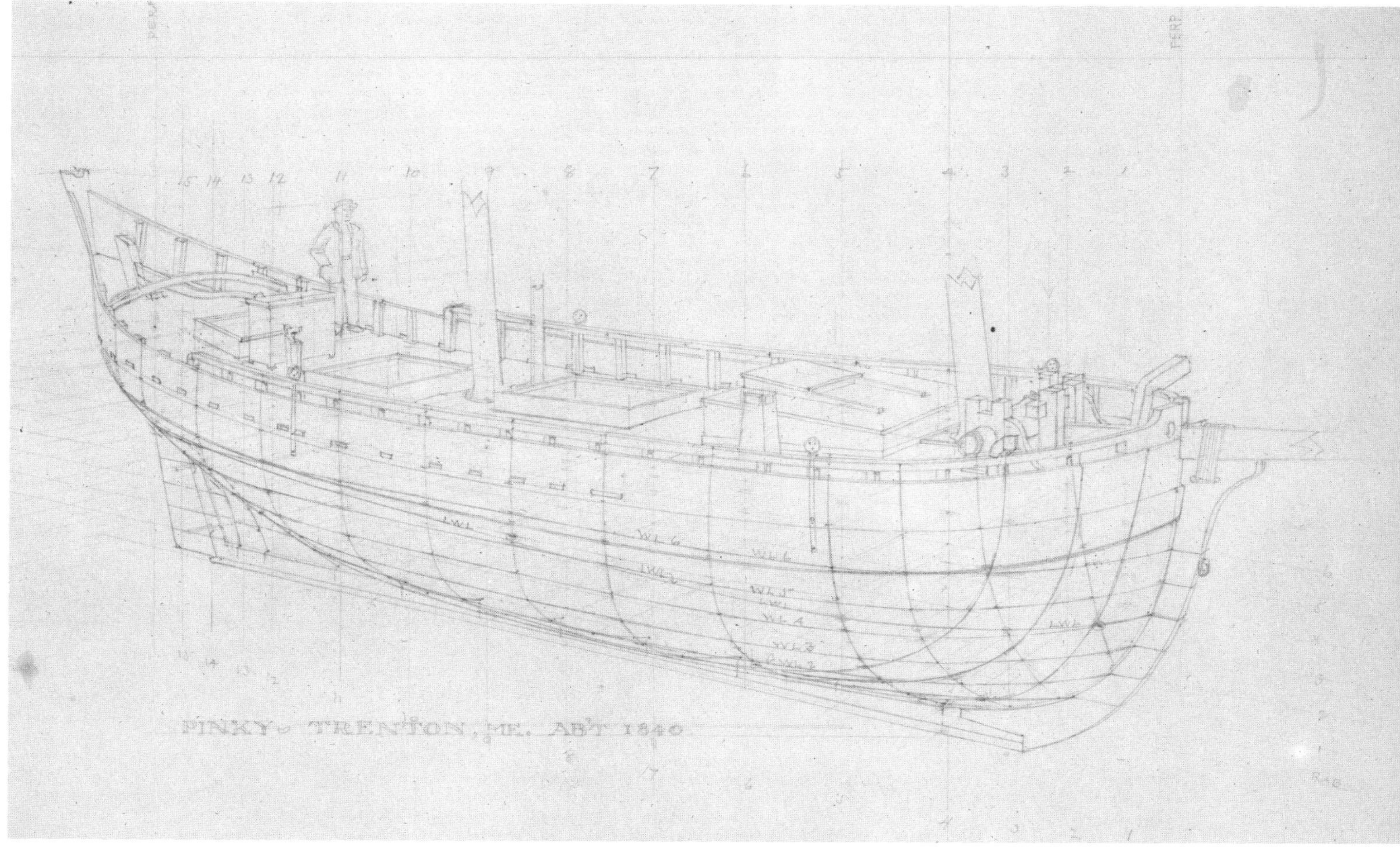
PINKY TRENTON, ME. ABT 1840

Measured perspective drawing of the Maine pinky *Trenton*, about 1840. Drawn by George C. Wales.

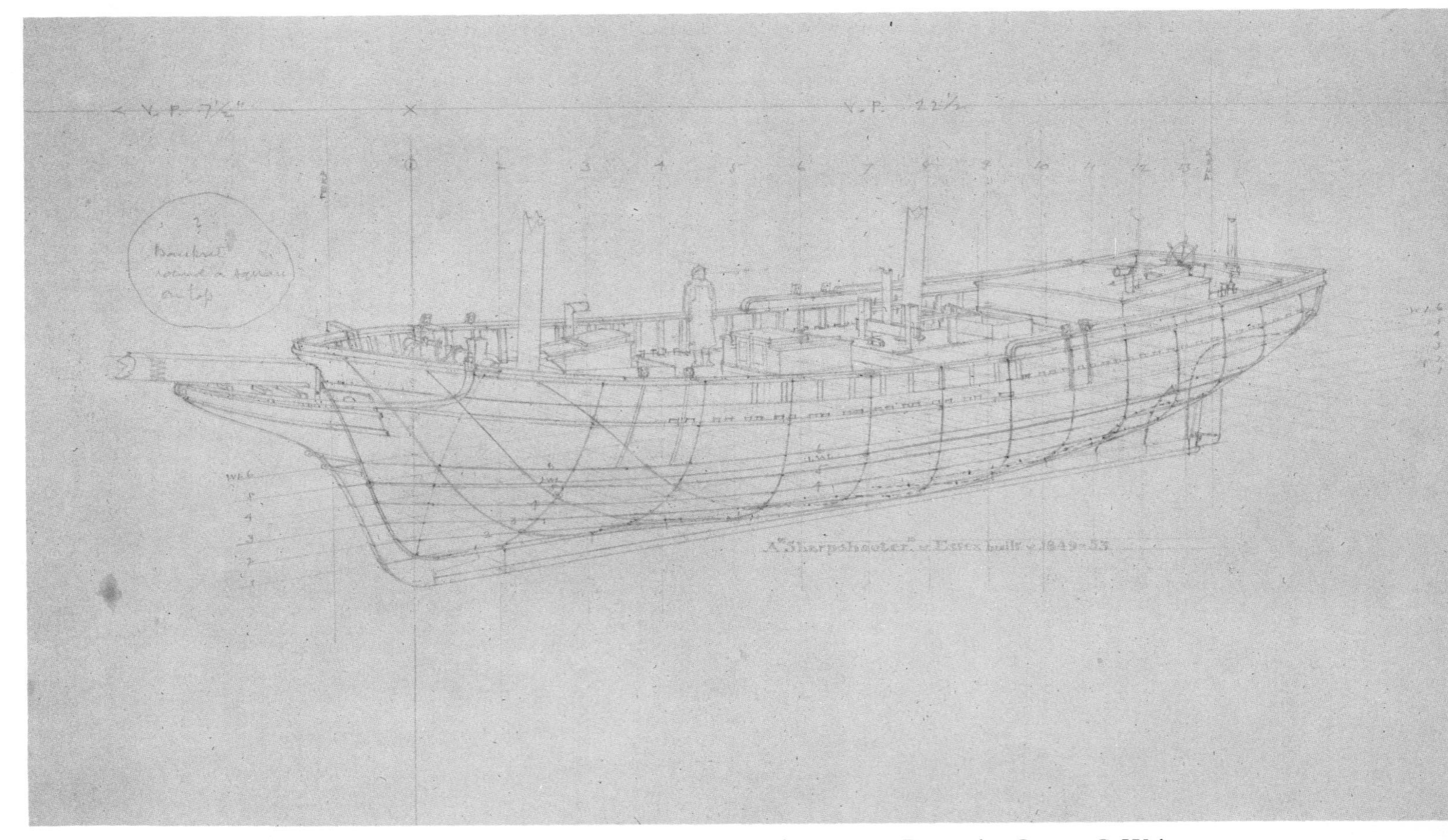
A "Sharpshooter" – Essex built – 1849–53

Measured perspective drawing of a sharpshooter of 1849–1853. Drawn by George C. Wales.

"WE'RE HERE" ESSEX BUILT 1858
LWL

Measured perspective drawing of sharpshooter schooner *We're Here*, 1858. Drawn by George C. Wales

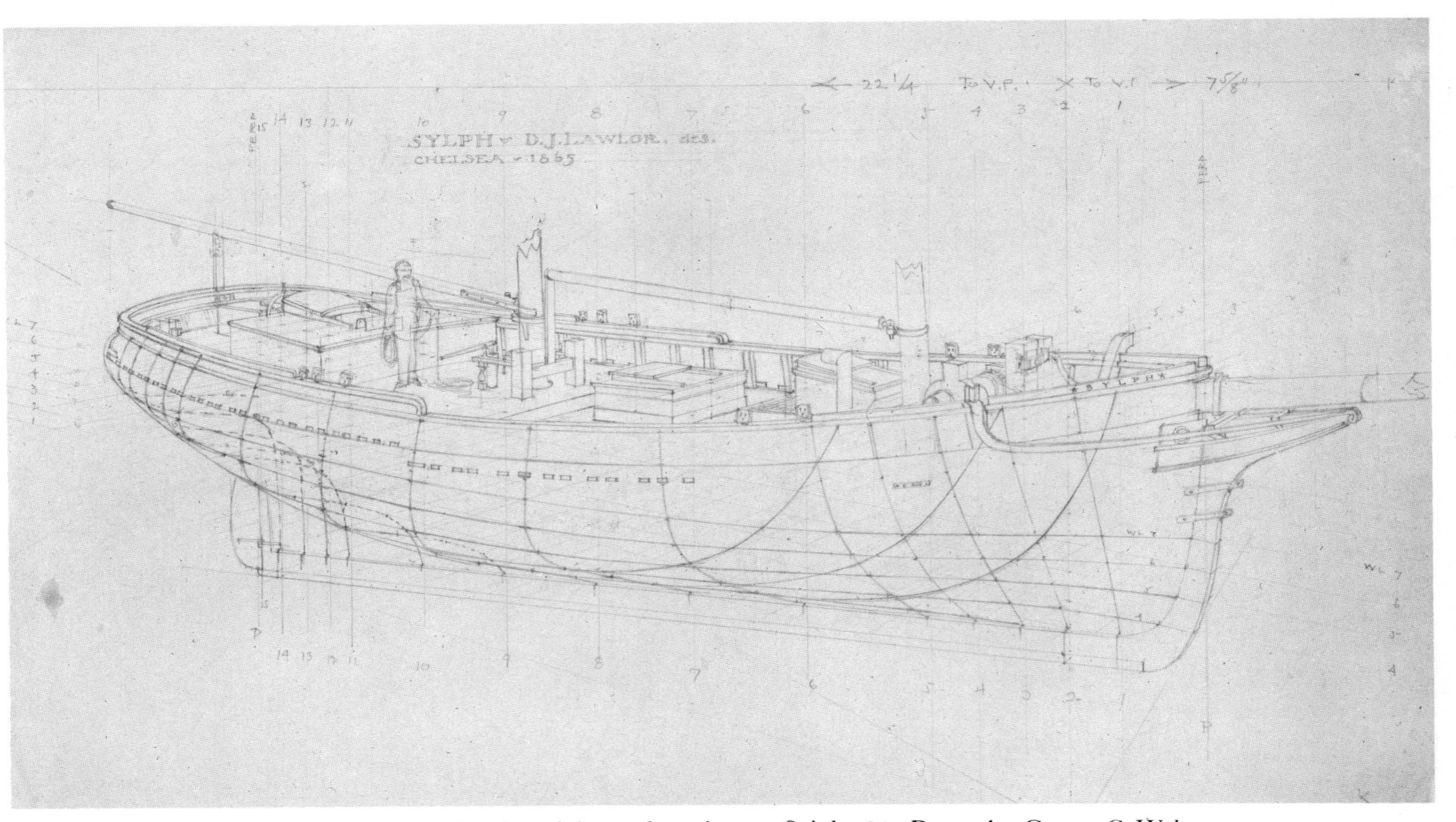
SYLPH D.J. LAWLOR. des.
CHELSEA 1865
22 1/4 TO V.P. TO V.P. 7 5/8"

Measured perspective drawing of the market schooner *Sylph*, 1865. Drawn by George C. Wales.

[Left] Schooner *Sea Flower* off Portsmouth Harbor, New Hampshire, July 5, 1837.

[Right] Schooner *Sarah Franklin* at Bass Harbor, Maine, 1891. S. G. WORTH, U.S. FISH COMMISSION

Carrie Phillips in background, *I. J. Merritt, Jr.* in foreground. CHARLES SAYLE

[Left] Schooner *Harry Belden*, Gloucester. Built in 1889 at Essex. This photograph shows the altered rig—a spike bowsprit in place of original bowsprit and jibboom. CHARLES SAYLE

[Right] *Fredonia* in dry dock while being fitted as a yacht and coppered. SMITHSONIAN INSTITUTION

Thalia. PHOTOGRAPH COURTESY OF MR. GILES M. S. TOD

Schooner *Volant*, Gloucester. Built in 1899 at Gloucester. CHARLES SAYLE

Helen B. Thomas, first knockabout. CHARLES SAYLE

Fishing schooner *Constellation.*

Shepherd King in 1903. SOCIETY FOR THE PRESERVATION OF NEW ENGLAND ANTIQUITIES

Fishing schooner *Thomas A. Cromwell.*

Fishing schooner *Elizabeth Howard* as a knockabout in 1916. FROM GORDON THOMAS GLASS PLATE

Fishing schooner *Columbia* of Gloucester, 1923. FROM P. MORRIS COPY NEGATIVE

Fishing knockabout schooner *Arcas*, 1913, bound south.

Boston fishing schooner *Shamrock*, 1922. FROM E. LEVICK PHOTOGRAPH

Fishing schooner *Elsie* of Gloucester, September 1929.

Fishing schooner *Sadie M. Nunan*, coming out of Portland, Maine. FROM PAUL STUBING PHOTOGRAPH

Halibut schooner *Squanto* passing Ten Pound Island, Gloucester.

Clipper schooner *Belle J. Neal* of Gloucester, about 1880. THE MARINERS' MUSEUM, NEWPORT NEWS, VIRGINIA

E. A. Herrick, centerboard Gloucester fishing schooner, showing clipper rig used in many schooners, 1855–1885. CHARLES SAYLE

Fishing schooner *Effort* in a fresh northwest wind, taken from Mamane Island off Monhegan Island, Maine. FROM PAUL STUBING PHOTOGRAPH

Fireboard of Marblehead neck and harbor, showing early fishing schooners out of Marblehead, about 1790. In the Lee Mansion, Marblehead, Massachusetts. PHOTO BY STANLEY P. STEVENS

[Left] Lewis H. Story. D. FOSTER TAYLOR

[Top right] Fishing schooner, 1920s. A. D. Story Yard, Essex, Massachusetts. CHARLES SAYLE

[Lower right] Fishing vessel, 1920s. A. D. Story Yard, Essex, Massachusetts. CHARLES SAYLE

Rudder for fishing schooner, 1920s. A. D. Story Yard, Essex, Massachusetts. CHARLES SAYLE

Schooner *Henry Ford*, A. D. Story Yard, Essex, Massachusetts. LEWIS H. STORY

[Left] Fishing schooner *Mystic*, James Yard, Essex, Massachusetts, 1925. Construction details, windlass. CHARLES SAYLE

[Right] Fishing schooner *Mystic*, James Yard, Essex, Massachusetts, 1925. Construction details, windlass. CHARLES SAYLE

Fishing schooner *Mystic*, James Yard, Essex, Massachusetts, 1925. Construction details, windlass. CHARLES SAYLE

Fishing schooner *Mystic*, James Yard, Essex, Massachusetts, 1925. Construction details, windlass. CHARLES SAYLE

Fishing schooner *Mystic*, James Yard, Essex, Massachusetts, 1925. Construction details, anchor davit. CHARLES SAYLE

Fishing schooner *Mystic*, James Yard, Essex, Massachusetts, 1925. Construction details, pumps. CHARLES SAYLE

Belle Franklin, early 1880s clipper fishing schooner, on the ways at Willard Burnham shipyard, Essex, Massachusetts. PHOTOGRAPH FROM U. S. NATIONAL MUSEUM

Schooner building at Essex, Massachusetts, shipyard of Willard A. Burnham, Jr., about 1895. HOWARD I. CHAPELLE

Sylvanus Smith wharf, Gloucester, 1880 or 1890, showing *Thetis* of Gloucester in foreground. CHARLES SAYLE

Sadie M. Nunan of Gloucester, about 1927. Forty-six foot schooner *Audrey and Theo* just beyond. CHARLES SAYLE

John J. Fallon, a knockabout on *Shepherd King*'s moulds, slightly altered as to sheer and bow. PEABODY MUSEUM OF SALEM

Jury bowsprit on schooner *M. A. Baston* (built at Newburyport) after a collision, showing bow of the *Ethel B. Jacobs* (built at Essex), both here at Gloucester, Massachusetts. PHOTOGRAPH FROM U. S. NATIONAL MUSEUM

Clipper bow, *Fredonia*-model schooner under construction at John Bishop's shipyard, Gloucester, Massachusetts, about 1890–95. PHOTOGRAPH FROM U. S. NATIONAL MUSEUM

Deck of new knockabout schooner *Marechal Foch*, 1919.

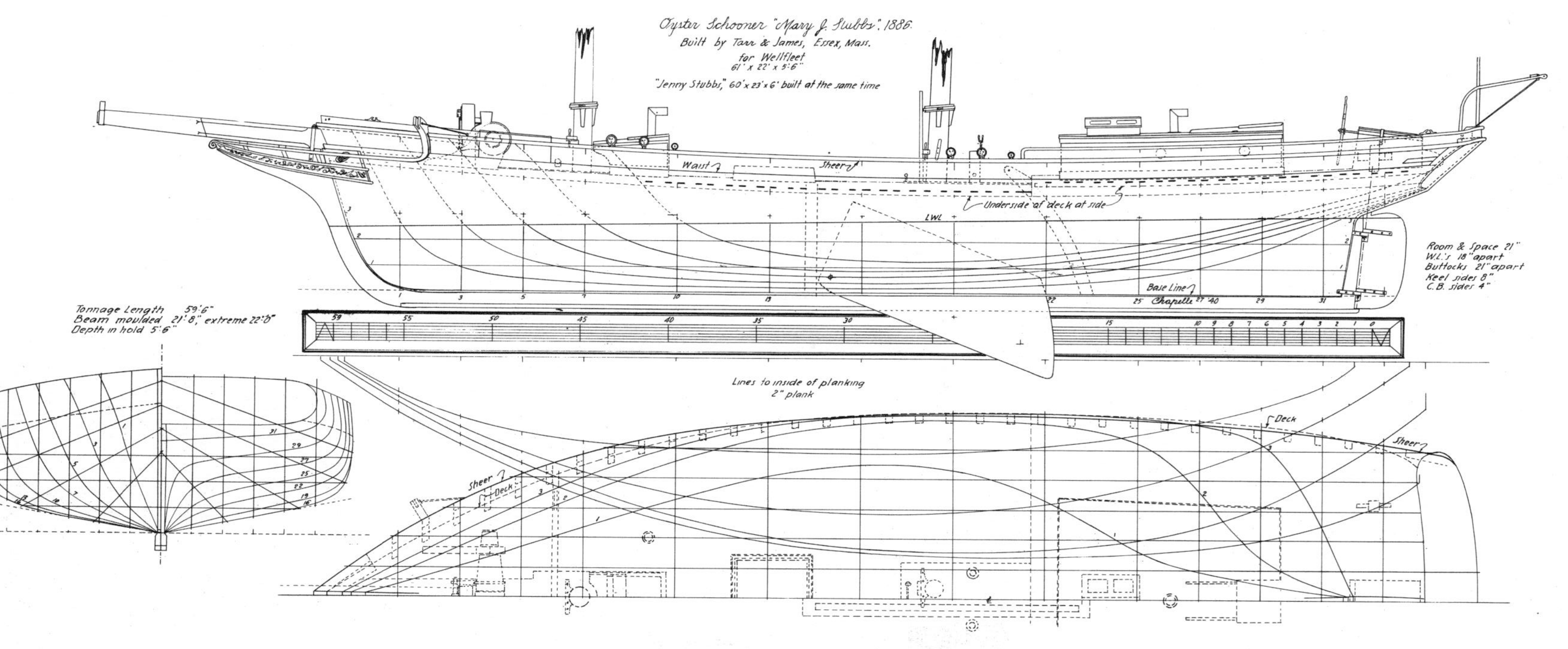

Oyster Schooner "Mary J. Stubbs". 1886.
Built by Tarr & James, Essex, Mass.
for Wellfleet
61' x 22' x 5'6"
"Jenny Stubbs," 60' x 23' x 6' built at the same time
Waist
Sheer
Underside of deck at side
LWL
Base Line
Chapelle
Room & Space 21"
W.L.'s 18" apart
Buttocks 21" apart
Keel sides 8"
C.B. sides 4"
Tonnage Length 59'6"
Beam moulded 21'8", extreme 22'0"
Depth in hold 5'6"
Lines to inside of planking
2" plank
Deck
Sheer

PLATE 63. *Mary J. Stubbs*, 1886, mould loft plan

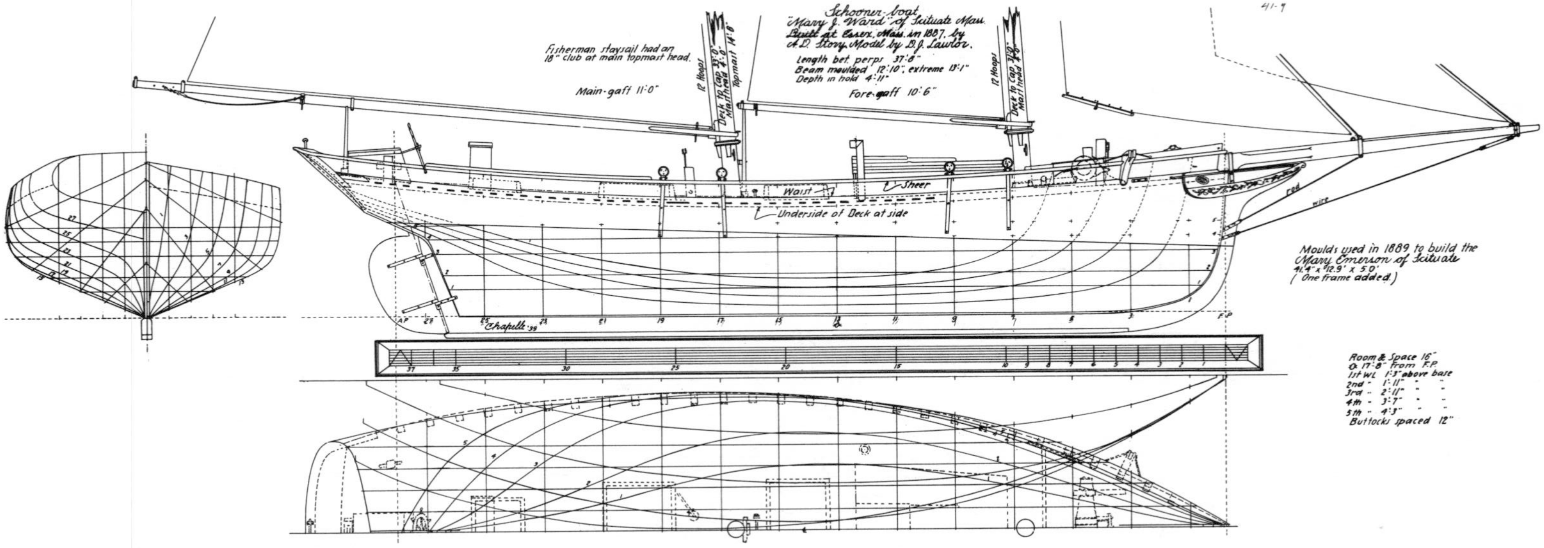

PLATE 64. *Mary J. Ward*, 1887, half-model

the forefoot well rounded. The entrance was long, sharp, and convex. The run was long and the buttocks were straight for a short distance. The schooners had the usual long head with rails and billet. The midsection had slightly rising, straight floors, a hard turn in the bilge, and slight tumble home in the topside. These schooners often worked without fore-topmasts and jibboom, but otherwise were rigged as clippers.

The centerboard and cases were off-center, the board coming down right alongside the keel, through the garboard on the port side. The *Stubbs* schooners had short quarterdecks, but many of the oyster schooners were flush-decked. Most of the Essex-built oystermen were for Wellfleet owners, but a few went to Long Island Sound. The oystermen were often given the reputation of being fast sailers.

A small inshore fishing schooner of this period is shown in Plate 64. This is the Lawlor-designed schooner boat *Mary J. Ward*, built at Essex, Massachusetts, in 1887 for a Scituate owner. The sister schooner *Mary Emerson* was built off the *Ward*'s moulds in 1889, having "one frame added." The *Mary J. Ward* was an excellent sailer and is credited with outsailing the famous Boston pilot boat *Hesper*. It should be noticed that this claim was made by a number of vessels—when the pilots did not realize that there was a race taking place.

The *Ward* was a flush-decked schooner having a rather strong sheer, straight keel with moderate drag, raking sternpost, short counter, elliptical transom sharply raked, nearly upright stem rabbet above load line, much rounded below. A light long head was used, with trails and billet head, the supporting iron-rod headrails having just appeared in new fishing schooners. The entrance was long, sharp, and slightly hollow close to the stem rabbet. The run was long and fine, with straight buttocks of moderate length. The midsection was formed with slightly hollow floors carried well outboard; high, hard turn of the bilge, and no tumble home in the topside.

The rig was up-to-date when these two schooners were built, fisherman's topmast staysail, main gaffsail, main gaff-topsail, fore gaffsail, forestaysail and jib, pole bowsprit 8-sided at knightheads. The jibstay was well outboard of the gammoning. No fore-topmast was carried, nor was there a fore gaff-topsail, or jib topsail.

The *Mary J. Ward* was 41′-9″ moulded length at rail cap, 12′-10″ moulded beam, and 4′-11″ depth in hold. The *Emerson*'s Custom House dimensions were 41.4′ x 12.9′ x 50.0′ (new measurement).

Not all of the vessels built in 1887 were on "improved" models, of course. The schooner *Carrie D. Knowles* (Plate 65) was built by Tarr and James at Essex, Massachusetts, in 1887 for Provincetown owners. She was of the old clipper model, 96′-9″ moulded length at rail cap, 24′-8″ moulded beam,

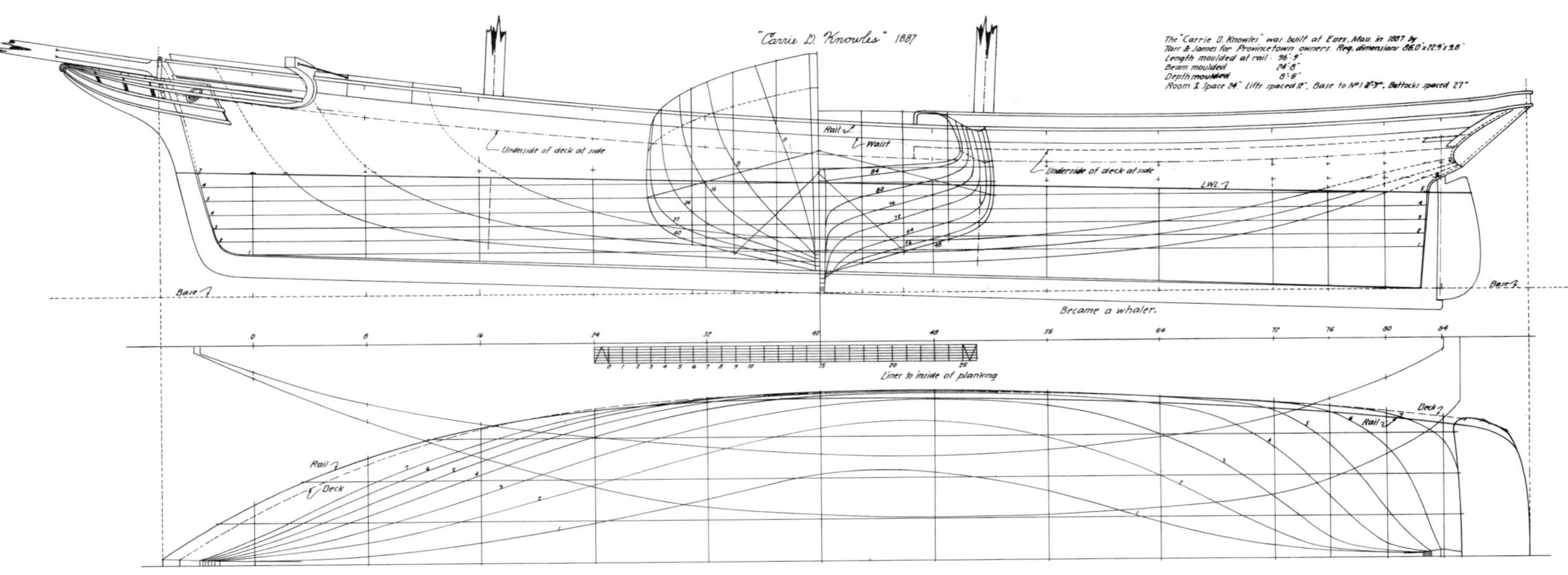
"Carrie D. Knowles" 1887
The "Carrie D. Knowles" was built at Essex, Mass. in 1887 by
Tarr & James for Provincetown owners. Reg. dimensions 86.0' x 22.9' x 9.8"
Length moulded at rail - 96'-9"
Beam moulded 24'-8"
Depth moulded 8'-6"
Room & Space 24". Lifts spaced 12", Base to No 1 2'-3". Buttocks spaced 27"
Rail
Waist
Underside of deck at side
Underside of deck at side
LWL
Base
Base
Became a whaler.
Liner to inside of planking
Rail
Deck
Rail
Deck

PLATE 65. *Carrie D. Knowles*, 1887, mould loft plans

8′-6″ moulded depth. The *Knowles* was considered a very fast sailer and eventually became a whaler.

This vessel had the strong sheer (that marked some of the last of the clippers), straight keel with some drag, nearly vertical sternpost, short counter, rather large elliptical transom sharply raked; slightly raking stem rabbet, flaring outboard a little; among angular forefoot with small rounding, and long head with double headrails. The run was long and fine with long straight buttocks. The entrance was long, very sharp, and concave. The midsection had moderately rising straight floor carried well outboard; low, hard bilge and strong tumble home in the topside.

It was in this same year, 1887, that a very distinguished vessel appeared, the *Carrie E. Phillips* (Plate 66). This was the first fishing schooner designed by Edward Burgess, of Boston, Massachusetts. Burgess had designed the America's Cup defenders *Puritan* (1885), *Mayflower* (1886), and *Volunteer* (1887), as well as a number of successful small sailing yachts. In his short professional career of seven years he designed 137 vessels and small craft, including three pilot boats (sisters), six fishermen (four on two designs), and one three-masted coasting schooner. He had become famous almost "overnight," but weakened by overwork, he died of typhoid fever on July 31, 1891, at the early age of forty-three.

The *Carrie E. Phillips* was built by Arthur D. Story at Essex, Massachusetts, in 1887. She was a plumb-stem vessel having moderate sheer, a deep, rockered keel, strongly raked sternpost, short counter with a modified V-transom, well rounded at the quarters. The entrance was long, sharp, and slightly convex; the run was long, without straight buttocks but with very slight rounding. The midsection had very rising and slightly hollow floor, slack well-rounded bilge, and slightly flaring topside becoming vertical at rail. Her length at rail cap was 104′-5″, the extreme beam was 24′-6″, and the depth in hold was 11′-0″. The tonnage length was 95′-0″.

The *Phillips* had been credited with many "firsts," but these are difficult to verify due to the lack of reliable records. She was the first fishing schooner to have a pole bowsprit, round at knightheads, and bowsprit shroud spreaders. Her chain plates were inside the planking in the old fashion. She had a double-headsail rig, iron catheads or anchor davits fitted with jib and jib-topsail fairleads. Though the *Grampus* specifications show she was not the first vessel in New England to have wire standing rigging, iron diaphram pumps, iron-strapped blocks, double headsails, and iron water tanks, the *Carrie E. Phillips* was, however, an extreme design for the period. Her very sharp ends, great deadrise and depth, remarkably deep keel outside of the keel rabbet, and strong rocker in the keel profile, hollowed sternpost, and strap pintles and gudgeons were departures from contemporary fishing schooners.

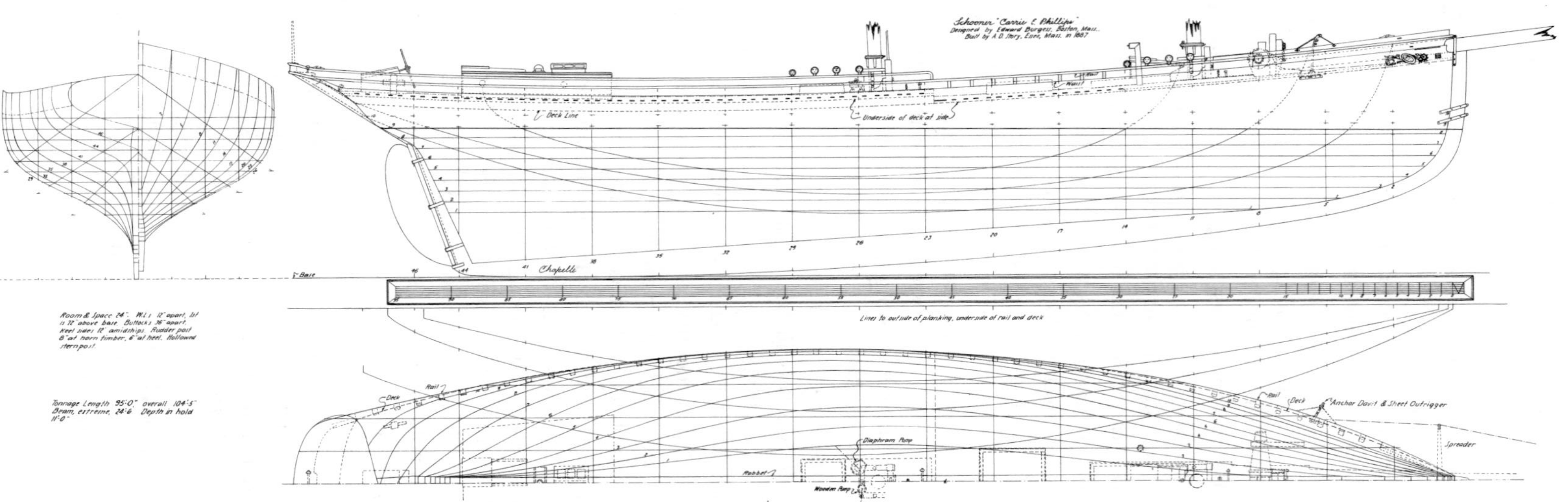
Schooner "Carrie E. Phillips"
Designed by Edward Burgess, Boston, Mass.
Built by A. D. Story, Essex, Mass. in 1887
Deck Line
Underside of deck at side
Waist
Chapelle
Base
Lines to outside of planking, underside of rail and deck
Rail
Deck
Anchor Davit & Sheet Outrigger
Spreader
Diaphram Pump
Wooden Pump
Rabbet
Room & Space 24". W.L.s 12" apart, 1st is 72" above base. Buttocks 36" apart. Keel sides 12" amidships. Rudder post 8" at horn timber, 6" at heel. Hollowed sternpost.
Tonnage Length 95'0" overall 104'5" Beam, extreme, 24'6 Depth in hold 11'0"

PLATE 66. *Carrie E. Phillips*, 1887, plan

Whether or not she had many "firsts," her general design seems to have attracted much attention, and to have hastened the acceptance of innovations in design, construction, rigging, and fittings in the fishing fleet. The *Phillips* was a very fast vessel to windward and carried sail very well in strong winds. The performance of this vessel and the fame of her designer combined to attract intense interest so that it was the *Phillips*, rather than the *Grampus*, that was the influential vessel in the introduction of innovations. The *Phillips* was lost August 23, 1899.

The first design of a fishing schooner by McClain that is identified is of the *Puritan* (Plate 67). This plumb-stem schooner was built in Essex in 1887 by Moses Adams for the Banks fisheries. In addition to the mould loft drawing of her lines found at Essex, a good scale model of her exists in the Cape Ann Historical Society collection.

The *Puritan* had moderate sheer, straight keel with little drag; short, raking sternpost, short counter and a deep, heart-shaped transom, the bottom of which was below her load line. The stern was rather narrow and the quarters were much rounded. The forefoot was rounded and there was a short rocker in the keel forward. The stem had a slight tumble home above the load line, tugboat fashion. The entrance was long, sharp, and

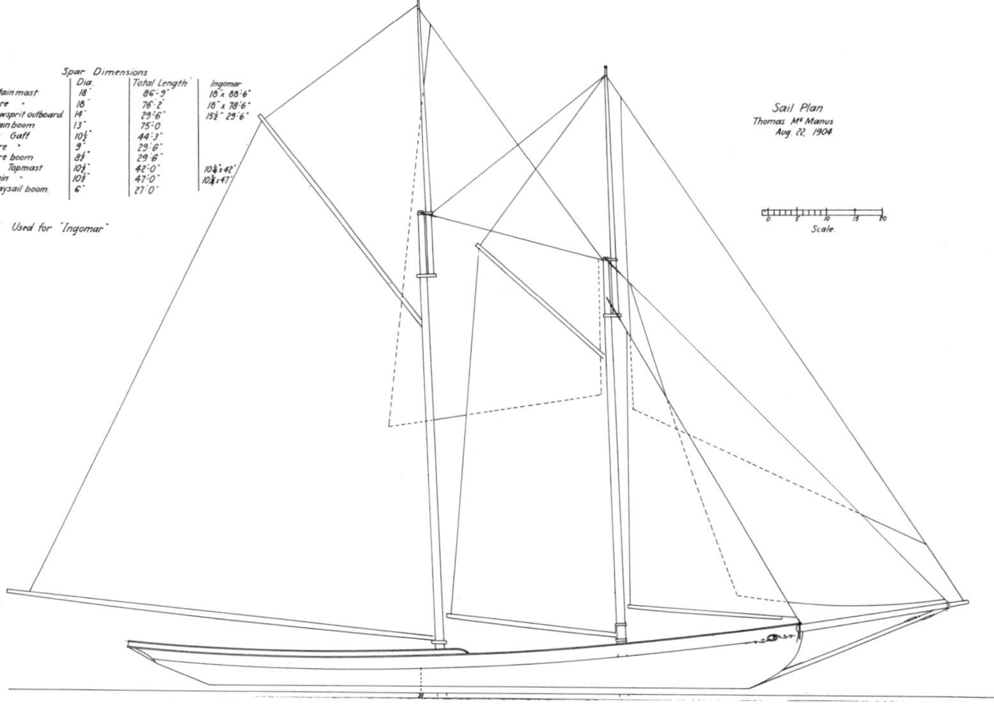
Spar Dimensions
Dia.
Total Length
Ingomar
Main mast 18" 86'-9" 18" x 88'-6"
Fore " 18" 76'-2" 18" x 78'-6"
owsprit outboard 14" 29'-6" 15½" 29'-6"
ain boom 13" 75'-0
" Gaff 10½" 44'-3"
ore " 9" 29'-6"
ore boom 8½" 29'-6"
" Topmast 10½" 42'-0" 10¼"x42'
ain " 10½" 47'-0" 10¾"x47'
taysail boom 6" 27'-0"
B. Used for "Ingomar"
Sail Plan
Thomas McManus
Aug. 22, 1904
0 5 10 15 20
Scale.

FIGURE 4

PLATE 67. *Puritan*, 1887, half-model

concave; there was marked hollow in the forefoot just abaft the stem rabbet from the load line downward. The run was fine and of moderate length. The midsection showed small deadrise in the straight floor, which was carried well outboard, a full, low, round bilge with slight tumble home in the upper topside.

The *Puritan* was 80′-5″ moulded length at rail, 82′-0″ overall, 22′-0″ moulded beam, and 9′-2″ depth in hold, and she drew about 9′-2″. She was a fast carrier in design and was considered to be well designed for her work. She had a pole bowsprit, square in the knightheads, with her forestay brought to the bowsprit a few feet forward of the gammoning. The old wooden catheads were retained. The *Puritan* carried no fore-topmast nor irons for one, so had no fore gaff-topsail nor jib topsail. This schooner was lost at Canso, Nova Scotia, September 18, 1895.

Plate 68 shows the lines of the schooner *J. H. Carey* modeled and built by Joseph Story at Essex, Massachusetts, in 1888. Her Custom House measurements were 85.6′ x 23.0′ x 9.0′. The schooner *Shenandoah*, 86.4′ x 24.0′ x 9.2′, was built on the *Carey*'s moulds, with gammon knee or clipper bow, in 1889, and another schooner, unidentified, in 1890. In these the foremost moulds were slightly altered. The *Shenandoah* was lost in a collision with the schooner *Addie M. Lawrence*, August 27, 1912.

The *Carey* was 88′-7″ moulded length at rail, 20′-10″ moulded beam, 9′-6″ moulded depth at side. She had much sheer, a straight keel with moderate drag, slight rake in the sternpost, a counter of moderate length, rather deep and strongly raking transom, a well-rounded forefoot, and a slightly raking and curved stem. The run was formed with long, straight buttocks, and the entrance was long, sharp, and slightly convex. The midsection had moderately rising straight floor carried well out, a rounded but rather hard turn of the bilge, and moderate tumble home in the upper topside. The *Carey* had a spike bowsprit square in the knightheads.

Little could be found concerning the *Carey*'s sailing qualities but her near sister ship, *Shenandoah*, was said to have been a smart sailer in blowing weather and very weatherly. The *Carey* sailed from Gloucester for the Grand Banks August 20, 1895 and was never heard from.

Very few fishing schooners had "plain stems" nearly straight and raking forward and, like the *Carey*, those that did usually seem to have been altered from the clipper bow. A few were altered to the plain, raking stem after their long heads had been knocked off or severely damaged by a sea or by collision.

In this year, 1888, a notable schooner was launched, on a design by D. J. Lawlor. This was the *Susan R. Stone* (Plate 69), a powerful vessel and a great sailer. She was built by Arthur D. Story at Essex. The register dimensions of the *Stone* were 94.0′ x 25.0′ x 10.2′. The next year, 1889, the even

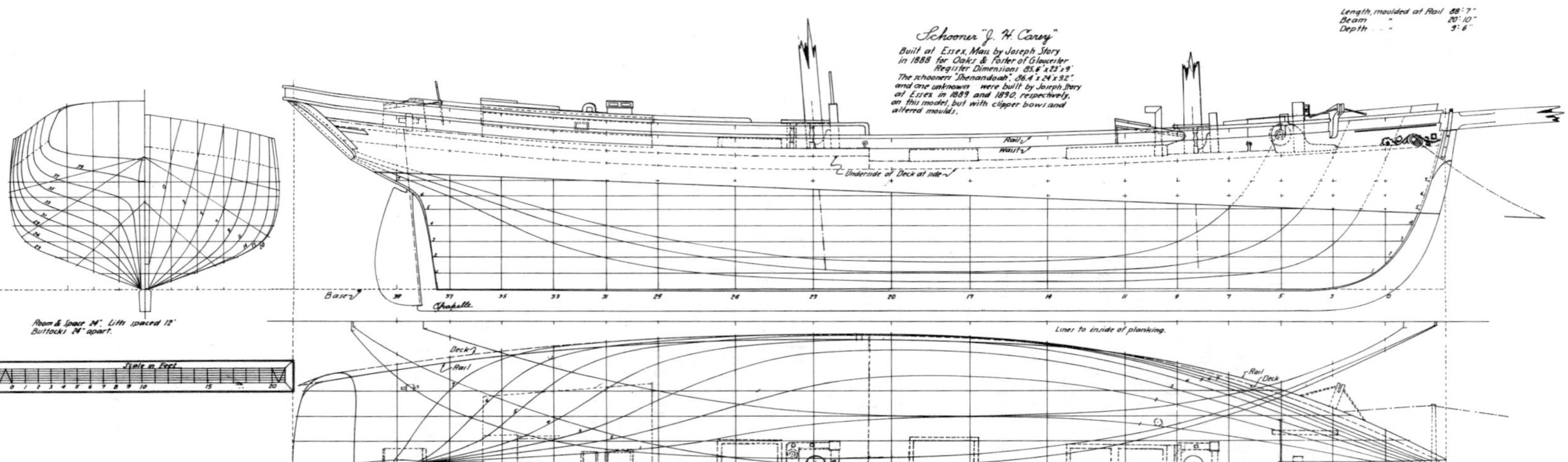

Schooner "J. H. Carey"
Built at Essex, Mass by Joseph Story in 1888 for Oaks & Foster of Gloucester
Register Dimensions 85.6' x 23' x 9'
The schooners "Shenandoah", 86.4' x 24' x 9.2', and one unknown were built by Joseph Story at Essex in 1889 and 1890, respectively, on this model, but with clipper bows and altered moulds.
Length, moulded at Rail 88' 7"
Beam " 20' 10"
Depth " 9' 6"
Rail
Waist
Underside of Deck at side
Base
Chapelle
Lines to inside of planking.
Deck
Rail
Room & Space 24". Lifts spaced 12"
Buttocks 24" apart.
Scale in Feet

PLATE 68. *J. H. Carey*, *Shenandoah*, 1888, half-model

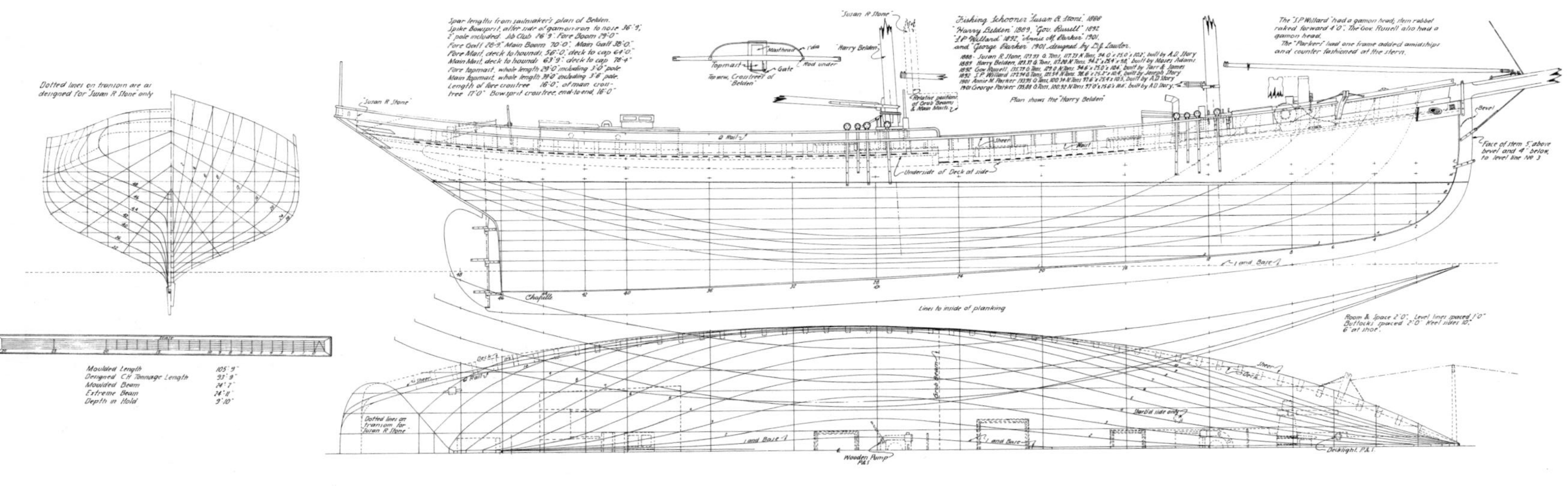
Dotted lines on transom are as designed for "Susan R Stone" only
Moulded Length 105' 9"
Designed CH Tonnage Length 93' 9"
Moulded Beam 24' 7"
Extreme Beam 24' 11"
Depth in Hold 9' 10"
"Susan R Stone"
Spar lengths from sailmaker's plan of Belden.
Spike Bowsprit, after side of gamon iron to nose 36' 9", 2' pole included. Jib Club 26' 9". Fore Boom 29' 0"
Fore Gaff 28' 9". Main Boom 70' 0". Main Gaff 38' 0".
Fore Mast, deck to hounds 56' 0", deck to cap 64' 0".
Main Mast, deck to hounds 63' 9", deck to cap 78' 4"
Fore topmast, whole length 29' 0" including 3' 0" pole
Main topmast, whole length 39' 0" including 3' 6" pole.
Length of fore crosstree 16' 0", of main crosstree 17' 0". Bowsprit crosstree, end-to-end, 16' 0"
Masthead
Topmast
Gate
Rod under
Top view, Crosstrees of "Belden"
"Harry Belden"
Relative positions of Grub Beams & Main Masts.
Fishing Schooner "Susan R. Stone" 1888
"Harry Belden" 1889, "Gov. Russell" 1892
"J.P. Willard" 1892, "Annie M. Parker" 1901,
and "George Parker" 1901 designed by D.J. Lawlor.
1888 - Susan R. Stone, 123.93 G. Tons, 117.73 N. Tons, 94.0' x 25.0' x 10.2', built by A.D. Story
1889 Harry Belden, 123.37 G. Tons, 117.20 N. Tons, 94.2' x 25.4' x 9.8', built by Moses Adams
1892 Gov. Russell, 135.73 G. Tons, 129.0 N. Tons, 94.6' x 25.0' x 10.4', built by Tarr & James
1892 J.P. Willard 172.94 G. Tons, 121.54 N. Tons, 98.6' x 25.2' x 10.4', built by Joseph Story
1901 Annie M. Parker 133.95 G. Tons, 100.34 N. Tons 97.6' x 25.4' x 10.5', built by A.D. Story
1901 George Parker 135.88 G. Tons, 100.92 N. Tons 97.0' x 25.6' x 10.6', built by A.D. Story.
Plan shows the "Harry Belden"
The "J.P. Willard" had a gamon head; stem rabbet raked forward 4' 0". The "Gov. Russell" also had a gamon head.
The "Parkers" had one frame added amidships and counter fashioned at the stern.
Rail
Sheer
Waist
Underside of Deck at side
Bevel
Face of stem 5" above bevel and 4" below, to level line No. 3
Lines to inside of planking
Room & Space 2' 0". Level lines spaced 1' 0". Buttocks spaced 2' 0". Keel sides 10", 6" at shoe.
Chapelle
Dotted lines on transom for Susan R Stone
Wooden Pump P&S
Grub Beam
Deadlight, P&S.

PLATE 69. *Susan R. Stone, Harry L. Belden,* 1888–1889, plan more noted *Harry L. Belden* was built to the same design by Moses Adams at Essex with minor changes in the stern at taffrail and in the positions of the mainmast and quarterdeck break. The register dimensions of the *Belden* were 94.2′ x 25.4′ x 9.8′. This schooner won the "Fisherman's Race that Blew," in 1892 because of her power to carry sail, her weatherliness, and speed. Her sail-carrying power, in this race, was increased by the cargo of fish she had on board, which she had not had an opportunity to unload before the race started. She had a number of rig changes in her active life.

In 1892, another schooner, the *Governor Russell*, was built on this design; her register dimensions were 94.6′ x 25.0′ x 10.4′. The *Russell*, fitted with a small gammon knee head, was built by Tarr and James at Essex. In the same year Joseph Story built another schooner on the *Stone*'s design, the *S. P. Willard*, register dimensions, 98.6′ x 25.2′ x 10.4′. In the *Willard* the stem was raked forward about four feet and fitted with a gammon knee head, with altered moulds right forward.

In 1901, the *Stone*'s design was used by Arthur D. Story to build the sister ships *Annie M. Parker* and *George Parker*. The register dimensions of the *Annie* were 97.6′ x 25.4′ x 10.5′; those of the *George* were 97.0′ x 25.6′ x 10.6′. In building these schooners a frame was inserted amidships and a short counter and elliptical transom were added, with some alterations in the aftermost moulds.

The *Belden* was 105′-9″ moulded length at rail, 24′-7″ moulded beam, and 9′-10″ depth in hold.

The *Belden* had strong sheer, straight keel with drag in the afterbody, rockered keel in a long sweep to a well-rounded forefoot, with tugboat stem above, having marked tumble home. The sternpost was short, slightly raked, topped with a deep V-transom, strongly raked. The transom was rather heart-shaped with well-rounded quarters, and its bottom was on a short horn timber thus forming a short counter which was partly immersed. The entrance was long, fine, and concave, with the hollow just abaft the stem rabbet. The run was of moderate length with straight buttocks well aft. The midsection was formed with marked hollow in the garboard sharply rising straight floor carried well out, a high and hard turn of the bilge with moderate tumble home in the upper topside. The hull form illustrated in the plan (Plate 69) is one of great initial stability, for the size of the schooner, giving extraordinary power to carry sail which, in turn, permitted great speed to be obtained in blowing weather.

Plate 70 shows another plumb-stem schooner of good qualities, the *Hustler*, built at Essex in 1889 by Tarr and James and said to have been modeled by Washington Tarr. This was a schooner 95′-3″ moulded length at rail cap, 23′-2″ moulded beam, 9′-1″ moulded depth at side; register dimensions were 84.0′ x 23.7′ x 9.2′.

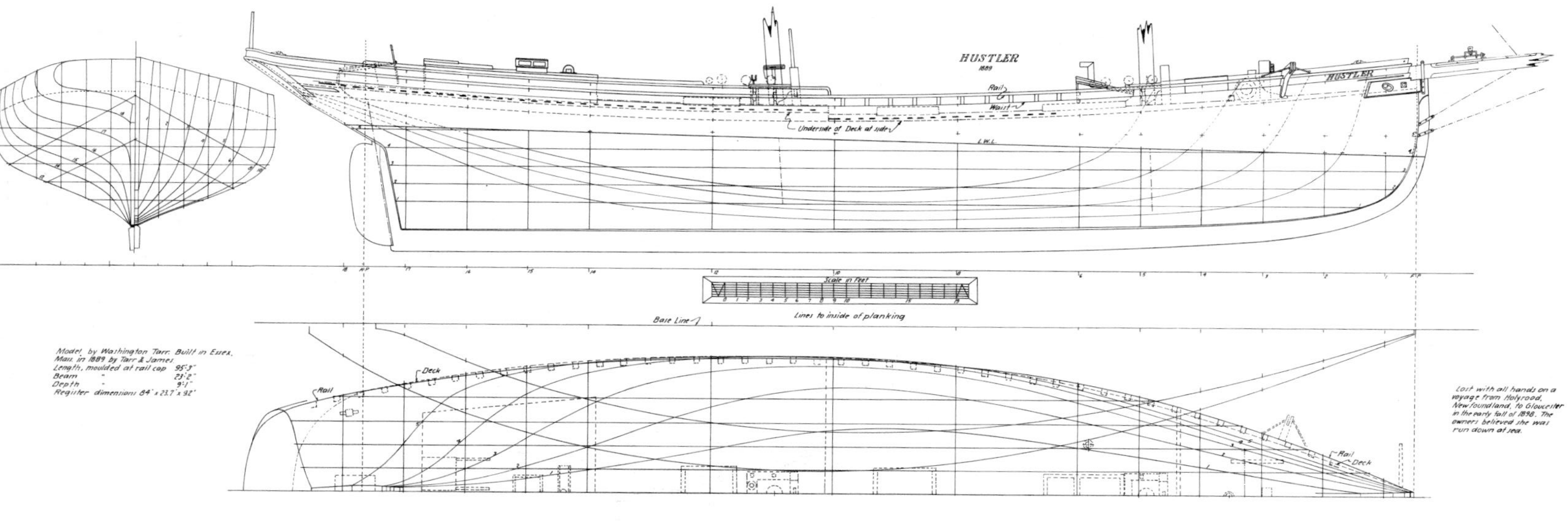
HUSTLER
1889
HUSTLER
Rail
Waist
Underside of Deck at side
L.W.L.
Scale in Feet
Lines to inside of planking
Base Line
Deck
Rail
Rail
Deck
Model by Washington Tarr. Built in Essex,
Mass. in 1889 by Tarr & James.
Length, moulded at rail cap 95'-3"
Beam " 23'-2"
Depth " 9'-1"
Register dimensions 84' x 23.7' x 9.2'
Lost with all hands on a
voyage from Holyrood,
Newfoundland, to Gloucester
in the early fall of 1898. The
owners believed she was
run down at sea.

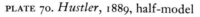

PLATE 70. *Hustler*, 1889, half-model

The *Hustler* had a graceful sheer, straight keel with some rocker forward and a well-rounded forefoot, tugboat stem with some tumble home above the load line. The sternpost was short and somewhat raking, with a shallow V- or heart-shaped transom and short counter. The run was rather short but formed with short straight buttocks. The entrance was long, with the water or level lines straight for a short distance abaft the stem rabbet. The midsection shows slightly hollow, rising floor with moderate deadrise, rounded high bilge, and slight tumble home above. This vessel had a pole bowsprit with forestay band outboard of the gammon iron. At the knightheads the bowsprit was square. This vessel had no fore-topmast nor ironwork for one. She was reputed to be a fair sailer and a good seaboat. She was lost with all hands in the early fall of 1898 and believed to have been run down by another vessel, as the *Hustler* was a new, strong, well-fitted schooner.

A smaller plumb-stem schooner, designed by Tarr, and built by Tarr and James at Essex in 1889 was the *Nickerson* (Plate 71). According to a very elderly member of the owner family, when the schooner was approaching completion and it could be seen that she was a handsome vessel, a violent argument arose over which member of the family she was to be named after. Finally, in desperation, she was named *Nickerson* "for the whole damned family."

This schooner had a graceful sheer, a straight keel with little drag but well rockered forward with a well-rounded forefoot and a tugboat stem with moderate tumble home above the load line. The sternpost raked a little and was rather short. The counter was long for the period, with a shallow, sharply raking, heart-shaped transom. The entrance was long, sharp, and slightly concave near the stem at forefoot. The run was well proportioned with short, straight buttocks. The midsection shows sharply rising and almost straight rise of floor carried well out, a firm bilge, and upright topside. The *Nickerson* was 67′-10″ moulded length at rail, 18′-7″ moulded beam, 7′-5″ moulded depth at side; register dimensions were 59.4′ x 18.5′ x 6.5′. The vessel sprung a severe leak and was lost twenty miles off the coast of Nova Scotia on September 4, 1928. The crew was saved.

The sister schooners *Fredonia* and *Nellie Dixon* (Plate 72) were launched in 1889, built from a design by Edward Burgess. The former was built at Essex by Moses Adams and for sometime after her launch she served as a yacht for J. Malcolm Forbes. The *Nellie Dixon* was also built by Moses Adams, but at East Boston. The register dimensions were 101.9′ x 23.4′ x 9.1′ for the *Dixon;* 101.9′ x 23.6′ x 10.3′ for the *Fredonia.* Strictly speaking they were not true sister ships; the differences are shown in Plate 72. In some plans of the *Fredonia*, she is shown to have had small trailboards and knees, but Lew Story, who remembered her, always insisted that she had a

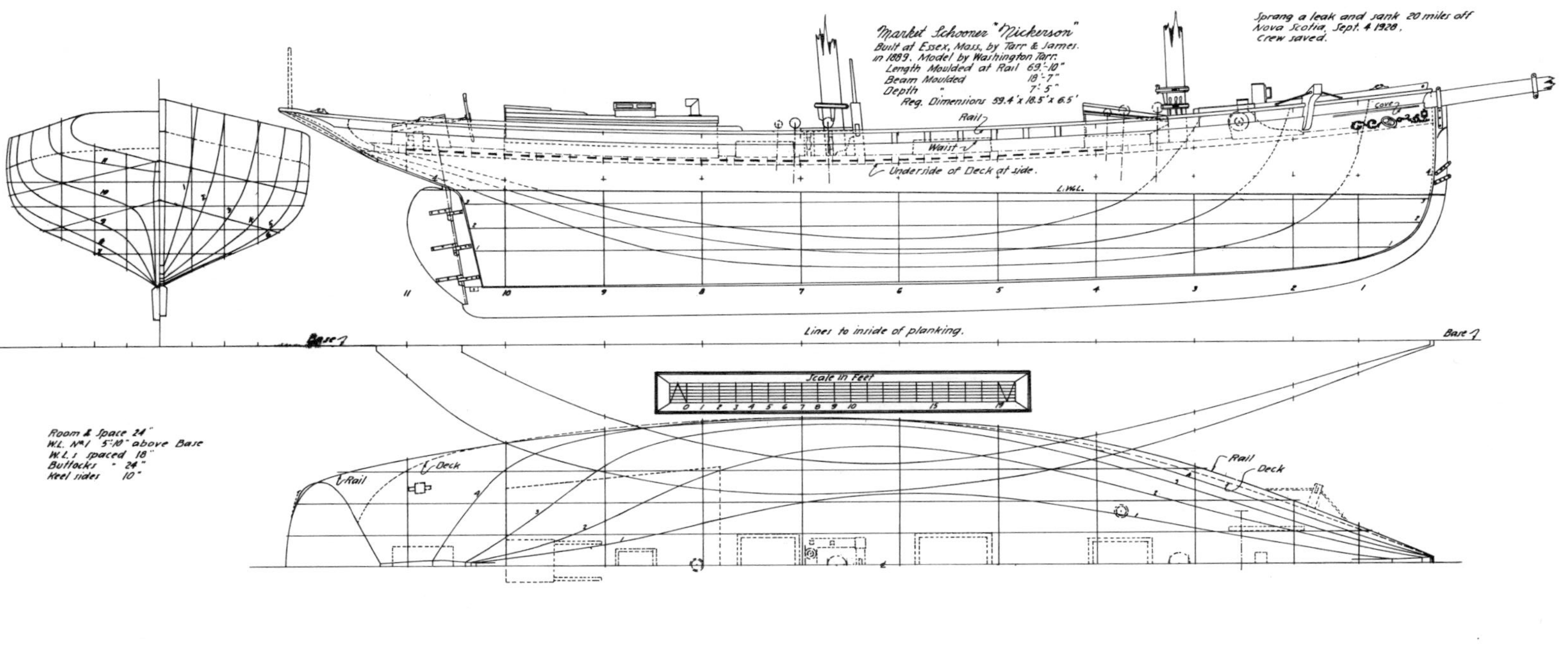
Market Schooner "Nickerson"
Built at Essex, Mass., by Tarr & James.
in 1889. Model by Washington Tarr.
Length Moulded at Rail 69'-10"
Beam Moulded 18'-7"
Depth " 7'-5"
Reg. Dimensions 59.4' x 18.5' x 6.5'
Sprang a leak and sank 20 miles off
Nova Scotia, Sept. 4 1920,
crew saved.
Rail
Waist
Underside of Deck at side.
L.W.L.
Lines to inside of planking.
Base
Scale in Feet
Room & Space 24"
W.L. No 1 5'-10" above Base
W.L.s spaced 18"
Buttocks " 24"
Keel sides 10"
Rail
Deck

PLATE 71. *Nickerson*, 1889, half-model

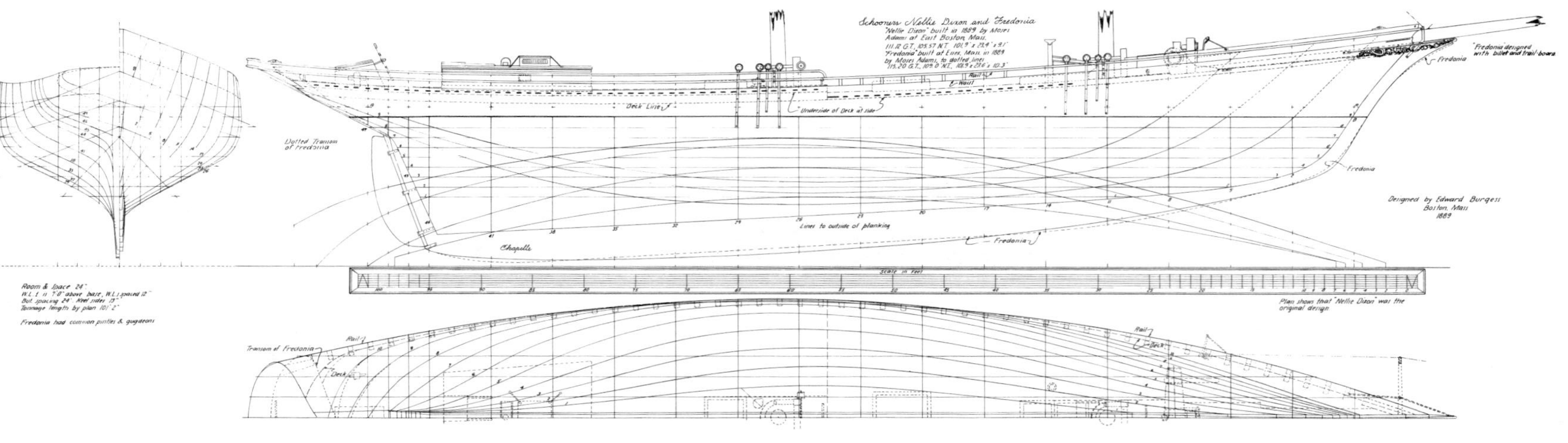
Schooners Nellie Dixon and Fredonia
"Nellie Dixon" built in 1889 by Moses Adams at East Boston Mass.
111.12 G.T., 105.57 N.T. 101.9' x 23.4' x 9.1'
"Fredonia" built at Essex, Mass. in 1889 by Moses Adams, to dotted lines
115.20 G.T., 109.0' N.T., 101.9' x 23.6' x 10.3'
"Fredonia" designed with billet and trail-boards
Designed by Edward Burgess
Boston, Mass
1889
Dotted Transom of Fredonia
Deck Line
Underside of Deck at side
Rail
Waist
Lines to outside of planking
Fredonia
Chapelle
Scale in Feet
Room & Space 24"
W.L. 1 is 7'0" above base, W.L.s spaced 12"
But. spacing 24". Keel sides 13"
Tonnage length by plan 101' 2"
Fredonia had common pintles & gudgeons
Plan shows that "Nellie Dixon" was the original design.
Transom of Fredonia
Deck

PLATE 72. *Fredonia, Nellie Dixon*, 1889, plan

plain gammon knee and scroll; this is born out by a recently obtained photograph of the schooner in drydock. The *Dixon* had billet and scroll, as shown in Plate 72. She went fishing right after her launch.

The design of these schooners was often referred to as the "*Fredonia* model," apparently because this name was applied to these schooners by Boston journalists. The name *Fredonia* model identified not only these schooners, designed by Burgess, but, as will be seen, it also identified the general hull form of all schooners having the same approximate profile.

From the original drawing of the lines of the *Dixon* and *Fredonia*, it is obvious that the *Dixon* was the original design—in solid lines—while the *Fredonia*'s lines are superimposed on it, in dotted lines. The alterations were of little scope; the only one that is of any great moment is the reduction in the stern overhang, in which the *Fredonia*'s transom was shifted forward and the rise of the horn timber increased a little, thus shortening the length at rail cap from the *Dixon*'s 114′-10″ to *Fredonia*'s 112′-5″. These schooners had the common pintles and gudgeons, without the hollowed sternpost used in the *Phillips*. The chain plates were outside the planking, *Fredonia* had less depth to her keel outside the rabbet than the *Dixon*'s 44 inches. Both vessels had their outside keels and shoes bolted on when hauled out after launch and fitting out.

The design for these two schooners showed a moderate, graceful sheer; a slightly rockered keel, but a straight keel rabbet carried forward from the sternpost about 48 feet, then rockered. The forefoot had much rounding, with a gammon knee head fitted, and with a small billet the *Fredonia* had a rather florid carved scroll, and a single wire bobstay. She was also coppered when used as a yacht.

The sternpost had much rake, above which was a short counter and a rather small, heart-shaped transom. The run was long and somewhat convex, without straight buttocks, but with very little rounding. The entrance was long and very sharp with a slight hollow in the forefoot. The midsection was formed with a much hollowed garboard, a sharp rise of floor carried straight well outboard, a high and rather hard turn of the bilge, and strong tumble home in the topside. In these vessels Burgess seems to have been somewhat influenced by the then scientific "wave-line theory," in so far as the entrance was designed very sharp and long, with the run a bit full and short.

Like the *Carrie E. Phillips*, these two schooners were reputed to be fast and weatherly and good sail-carriers. As seems to have been usual, the really fast vessels of great reputation were rarely entered in the fishermen races, so their comparative performances can only be guessed at.

The *Fredonia* was swept by a heavy sea that raised her great beam 2 inches off the maindeck, through which she filled rapidly and sank. One man was lost overboard and another fatally injured out of the twenty-three-man crew. The survivors were taken off by a steamer on December 18, 1896.

It has been shown that the years between 1884 and 1890 had been times in which extensive changes had been made in the models, rigs, and fittings of the North Atlantic fishing schooners. Slowly, a trend began to develop toward deeper, more seaworthy and weatherly vessels which were yacht-like and fast on all points of sailing. It is worthy of comment that Gloucester's shoal harbor was never adequately improved, for there still are numerous shoal berths and obstructions in the harbor at the present time. The large schooners using the harbor were often grounded at normal low tides, with occasional damage to their hulls. This happened to the *Gertrude L. Thebaud* in the 1930s.

The trend, therefore, favored the port of Boston and eventually led to a great expansion in the Boston fleet in the late 1890s and early 1900s and a gradual decline in the number of vessels working out of Gloucester.

The *Fredonia* model became the fashionable type of fishing schooner with astonishing rapidity, utilized in not only the designs of fishing schooners but in small fishing craft—the "Friendship sloop" for example. The popularity of the *Fredonia* model led to some confusion; many presumed that this name meant a vessel built on the lines of the *Fredonia*. So far, no evidence has been found to show that unidentified vessels were built on the Burgess plans, but the journalistic use of the name presents a large number of instances where it was applied to the schooners by other designers. These vessels had the rocker in the keel, cutaway forefoot and gammon knee head that were to be seen in *Fredonia*, but that was usually about as far as any "copying" of her seems to have gone. Hence the *Fredonia* model had become a type name, like sharpshooter or clipper, and no longer meant any sister ships of the *Fredonia* that may have existed.

Chapter Six

1890–1900

The vessels built in 1890 included some fine examples of designs by George M. McClain. One of these was the *Lottie S. Haskins*, an almost legendary schooner because of her sailing qualities. Not only was she an all-around fast sailer but she also worked unusually well. It was said of her that she would tack under almost any condition, except in a dead calm.

Her designer beat her into Gloucester harbor under her fisherman staysail alone and then sailed her into a slip, to show her handiness.

The *Lottie S. Haskins* (Plate 73) was built by Tarr and James at Essex, Massachusetts, and her designer held shares in her; he also commanded her for some time. She was a *Fredonia* model and her register dimensions were 70.5′ x 20.4′ x 8.5′. Her moulded length at main rail was 107′, moulded beam, 19′-10″, and 8′-11″ moulded depth at side.

She had moderate and graceful sheer, straight keel, with marked drag to about amidships, then rocketed to the forefoot, which was formed with a marked gripe. The sternpost was rather short and much raked. The counter was short and the strongly raking transom was quite deep, but the extreme rake of the transom prevented it from having a heavy appearance. The stem rabbet flared and raked strongly, the gammon knee was quite short and the billet small. As was then becoming the fashion, she had bowsprit shroud spreaders and the iron headrails supposed to have been introduced by *Fredonia*. The entrance was long, with a marked hollow in the forefoot; the run was straight in the buttocks but not very long; the midsection being at the gream beam. This section was formed with a moderately hollow floor having sharp rise, giving a high and somewhat hard turn of the bilge. There was a good deal of tumble home in the topside abaft midlength.

A number of vessels are supposed to have been built on the model of the

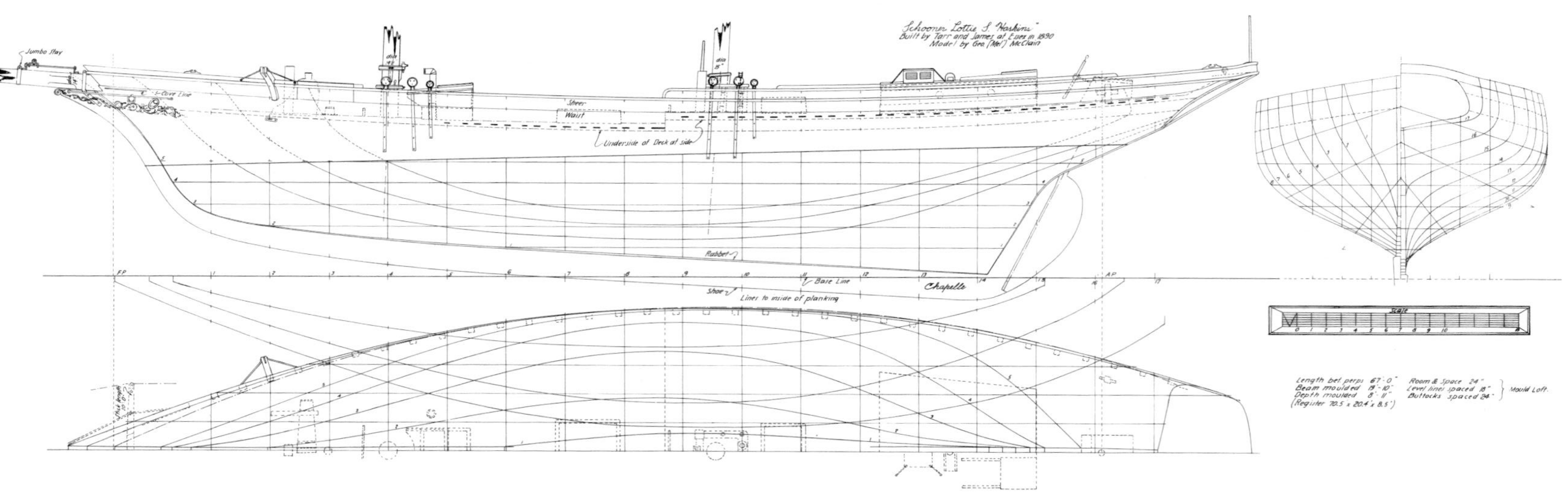
Schooner "Lottie S. Haskins"
Built by Tarr and James at Essex in 1890
Model by Geo. (Mel) McClain
Jumbo Stay
Sheer
Waist
Underside of Deck at side
Rabbet
Base Line
Shoe
Lines to inside of planking
Chapelle
FP
AP
Scale
Length bet. perps 67'-0"
Beam moulded 19'-10"
Depth moulded 8'-11"
(Register 70.5 x 20.4' x 8.5')
Room & Space 24"
Level lines spaced 18"
Buttocks spaced 24"
Mould Loft.

PLATE 73. *Lottie S. Haskins*, 1890, plans

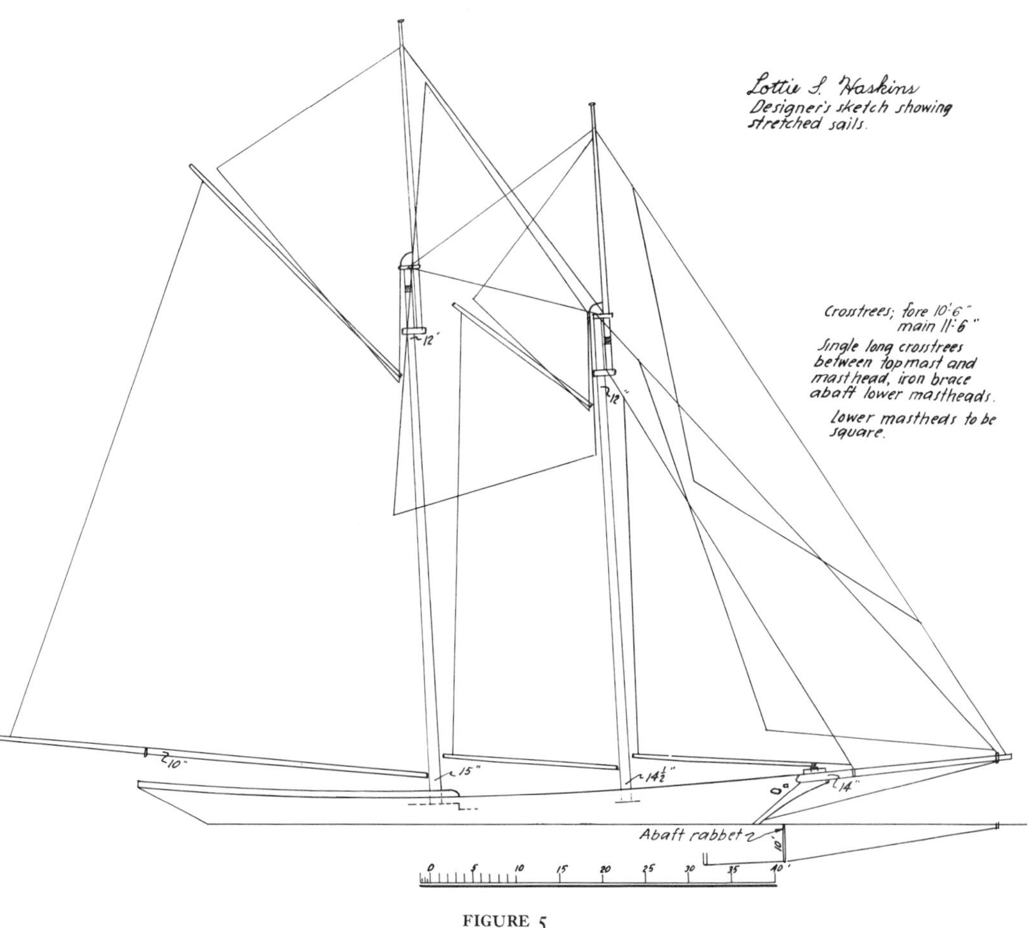
Lottie S. Haskins
Designer's sketch showing stretched sails.
Crosstrees; fore 10'6"
main 11'6"
Single long crosstrees between topmast and masthead, iron brace abaft lower mastheads.
Lower mastheads to be square.
12'
12"
10"
15"
14½"
14"
Abaft rabbet
10'
0 5 10 15 20 25 30 35 40'

FIGURE 5

Lottie S. Haskins, including the *Henry M. Stanley*, *Clara R. Harwood*, *Minerva*, *Alameida*, *Mertis Perry*, *Mary Cabral*, *Lizzie B. Adams*, and *Evelyn L. Smith*, all launched between 1890 and 1893. Listings of sister ships like this are usually based on newspaper reports of launchings and are not wholly reliable.

Another vessel of great reputation, launched in 1890, was the *Senator Lodge* (Plate 74) designed by McClain and built at Essex by A. D. Story. Her model was exhibited at the Chicago Worlds Fair, 1892–1893. The claim has been made that twenty-five schooners were built on her model; these included *Corsair*, *Dreadnaught*, *Kearsarge*, *Esther Anita*, *Titania*, *Tacoma*, and *Virginia*. But mould loft drawings show that *Dreadnaught*, *Tacoma*, and *Illinois* were sisters; the original model of these appears to have been first used for *Dreadnaught* and was an original design, not a sister ship of the *Lodge*. Under such circumstances it is as yet impossible to identify many of the vessels built on the *Lodge*'s model, or to be certain about any of the vessels named here. The *Senator Lodge* was lost December 10, 1893.

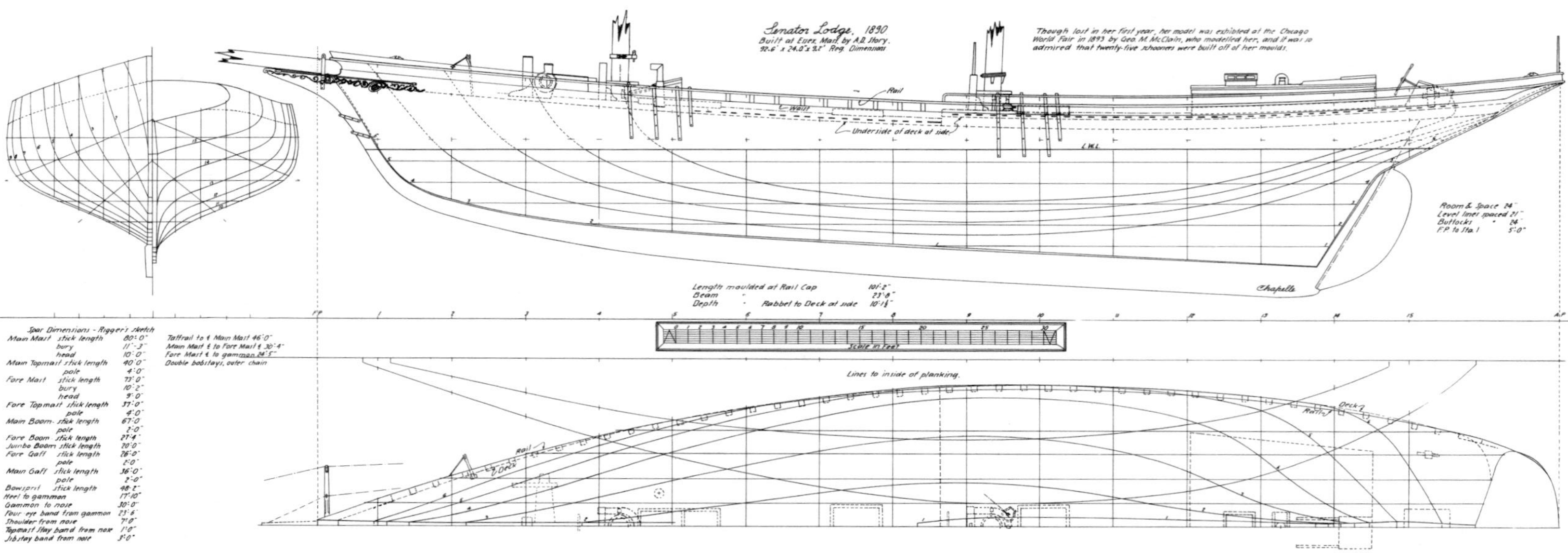

Senator Lodge, 1890
Built at Essex, Mass. by A.D. Story.
92.6' x 24.0" x 9.2" Reg. Dimensions
Though lost in her first year, her model was exhibited at the Chicago World Fair in 1893 by Geo. M. McClain, who modelled her, and it was so admired that twenty-five schooners were built off of her moulds.
Rail
Waist
Underside of deck at side
L.W.L.
Room & Space 24"
Level lines spaced 21"
Buttocks " 24"
F.P. to Sta. 1 5'-0"
Length moulded at Rail Cap 101'-2"
Beam " 23'-8"
Depth " Rabbet to Deck at side 10'-1½"
Chapelle
Scale in Feet
Lines to inside of planking.
Deck
Rail
Spar Dimensions - Rigger's sketch
Main Mast stick length 80'-0"
bury 11'-3"
head 10'-0"
Main Topmast stick length 40'-0"
pole 4'-0"
Fore Mast stick length 73'-0"
bury 10'-2"
head 9'-0"
Fore Topmast stick length 37'-0"
pole 4'-0"
Main Boom stick length 67'-0"
pole 2'-0"
Fore Boom stick length 27'-4"
Jumbo Boom stick length 20'-0"
Fore Gaff stick length 26'-0"
pole 2'-0"
Main Gaff stick length 36'-0"
pole 2'-0"
Bowsprit stick length 48'-2"
Heel to gammon 17'-10"
Gammon to nose 30'-0"
Four eye band from gammon 23'-6"
Shoulder from nose 7'-0"
Topmast Stay band from nose 1'-0"
Jibstay band from nose 3'-0"
Taffrail to ℄ Main Mast 46'-0"
Main Mast ℄ to Fore Mast ℄ 30'-4"
Fore Mast ℄ to gammon 24'-5"
Double bobstays, outer chain

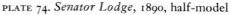

PLATE 74. *Senator Lodge*, 1890, half-model

The *Lodge* had a strong, graceful sheer; the keel rabbet was straight, with strong drag, from the sternpost forward to about midlength. From here forward there was much rocker to a somewhat cutaway fore gripe. The stem was finished off with a gammon knee, scroll, and small billet. The sternpost raked heavily and was short. The counter was short and heavy and sharply raked at horn timber to form a straight line from tuck to taffrail, so that the sharply raking, heart-shaped transom lined up with the horn timber. The entrance was long, sharp, and slightly hollow in the forefoot. The run was long, straight in the buttocks for a short distance and fine. The midsection showed a slightly hollow, sharply rising floor, a high, hard bilge with much tumble home in the topside. The *Lodge* was 101′-2″ moulded length at rail, 23′-0″ moulded beam, and 10′-1½″ moulded depth at side; her register dimensions were 92.6′ x 24.0′ x 9.2′.

This vessel was a good example of McClain's treatment of the hull features of what can be described as his versions of the *Fredonia* model in 1890. He produced a vessel having a little less depth in proportion to beam than in the Burgess crack. It may perhaps be said that McClain was more conservative than Burgess. The transom and counter of the *Senator Lodge* were very nearly the same as those of the *Fredonia*, but so shaped as to maintain some borderline straight in the buttock lines.

Another successful McClain model was that for the schooner *Rose Cabral* (Plate 75), built by Tarr and James at Essex in 1890. Her register dimensions were 86.6′ x 23.9′ x 9.1′ and she was a *Fredonia* model, 101′-0″ moulded length at rail cap, 23′-2″ moulded beam, and 10′-0″ moulded depth at side. She was considered very weatherly and was a fast sailer to windward.

She had moderate sheer, straight rabbet on the keel with drag from the sternpost to about midlength, forward of which it was rockered. She had a small fore gripe and gammon knee head with scroll and billet. Like the others just described she had a raking and heavily flared stem rabbet above the load line. Her sternpost raked and she had a *Fredonia* counter and transom. Her entrance was long, sharp, and hollowed in the fore gripe. The run was rather short and steep but with some straight in the buttocks, making the run quite fine, but somewhat different from *Fredonia* and the *Lodge*. The midsection had slightly hollow, sharply rising floor with a high, hard turn of the bilge and much tumble home in the topside.

With the cutaway fore gripe hull and rocker in the keel, the sail plans could show short foremasts but required long bowsprits and mainbooms. The long bowsprits necessitated shroud spreaders. This style of rig was used throughout most of the 1890s. In this period the old jumbo forestaysail had become entirely obsolete and the double headsail was the standard rig.

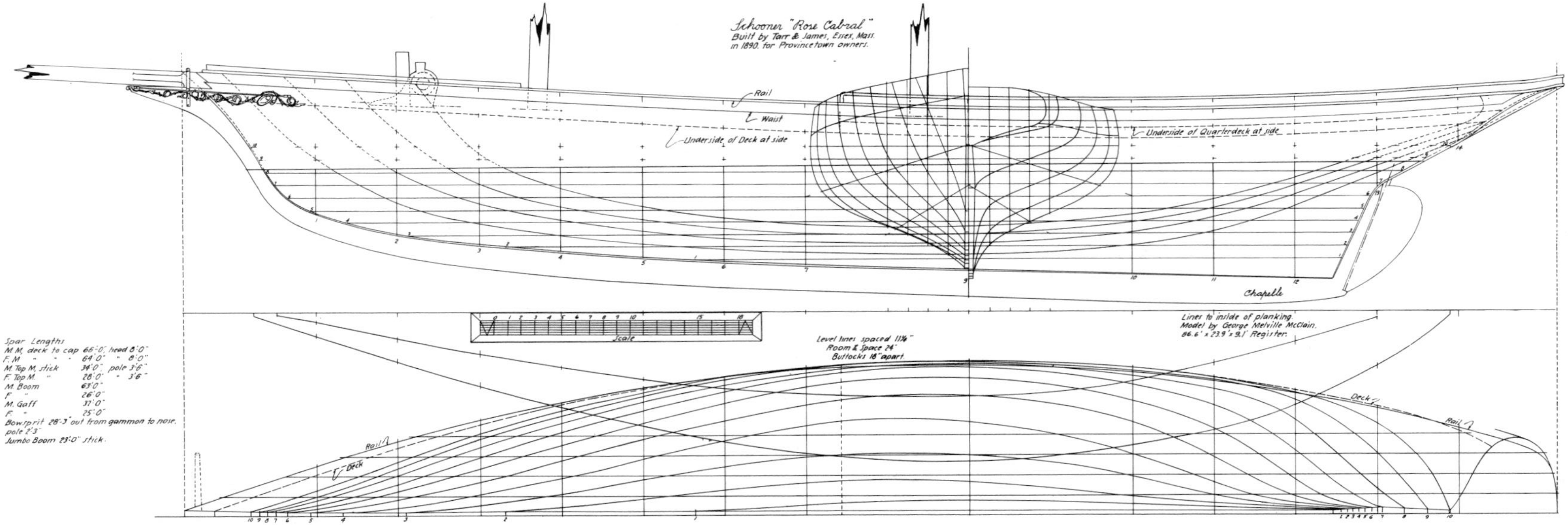

Schooner "Rose Cabral"
Built by Tarr & James, Essex, Mass.
in 1890. for Provincetown owners.

Rail

Waist

Underside of Deck at side

Underside of Quarterdeck at side

Chapelle

Spar Lengths
M.M. deck to cap 66'-0", head 8'-0"
F.M. " " " 64'-0" " 8'-0"
M. Top M. stick 34'-0", pole 3'-6"
F. Top M. " 28'-0" " 3'-6"
M. Boom 63'-0"
F. " 26'-0"
M. Gaff 37'-0"
F. " 25'-0"
Bowsprit 28'-3" out from gammon to nose.
pole 2'-3"
Jumbo Boom 23'-0" stick.

Scale

Level lines spaced 11¼"
Room & Space 24"
Buttocks 18" apart.

Lines to inside of planking.
Model by George Melville McClain.
86.6' x 23.9' x 9.1' Register.

Deck

Rail

PLATE 75. *Rose Cabral*, 1890, half-model

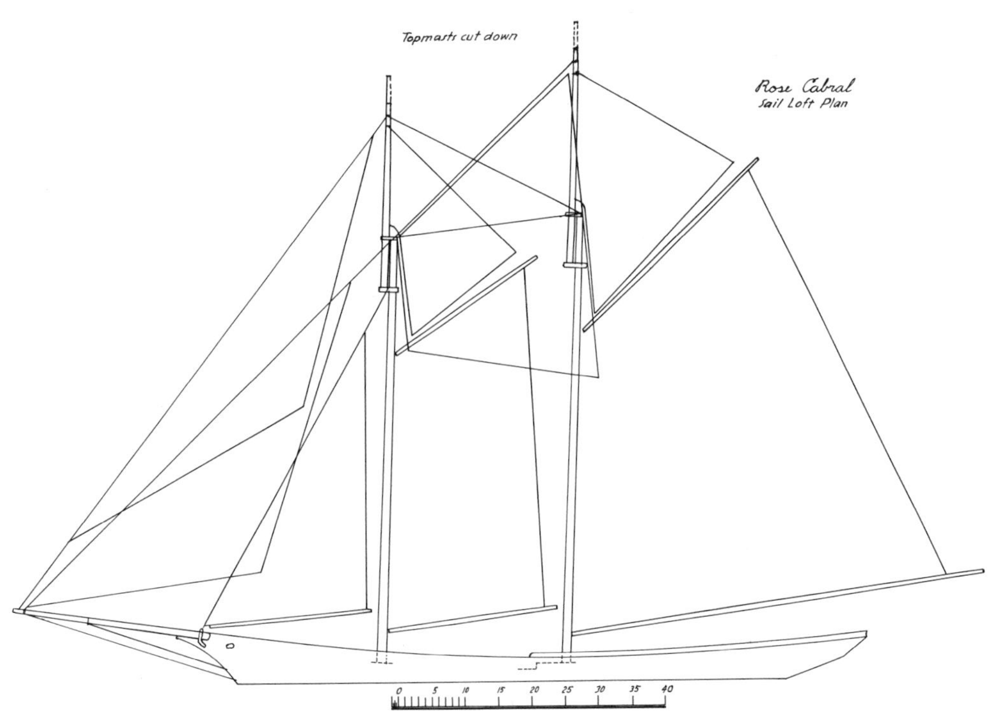
Topmasts cut down
Rose Cabral
Sail Loft Plan
0 5 10 15 20 25 30 35 40

FIGURE 6

Plate 76 is the plan of the schooner *Eliza B. Campbell*, built at Essex by Moses Adams in 1890. The schooner *Alva*, built in 1892, may have been on this model by McClain. The *Eliza B. Campbell* had jibboom, dolphin striker, and bowsprit spreader when launched. The *Campbell*'s register dimensions were 88.4′ x 23.9′ x 9.8′, and she was 97′-5″ moulded length at rail cap, 23′-2″ moulded beam, and 10′-9″ moulded depth. The *Campbell* had rather strong sheer, straight keel rabbet from sternpost forward to nearly under the foremast, rockered forward of this, with a rather deep forefoot for a McClain design. The stem had the gammon knee, scroll, bowsprit shroud spreader, and billet. The sternpost was short, with much rake, the counter was therefore deep at the tuck, with the horn timber rising sharply to the transom, which was heart-shaped and sharply raked. The stem was heavily flared forward and raked. The entrance was long, very sharp, and hollow at the fore gripe. The run was rather short and steep, with straight buttocks. The midsection was formed with slightly hollow, sharply rising floor carried well out, with a high, hard turn of the bilge, and moderate tumble home in the topside. These schooners were handsome and good carriers. Other vessels are thought to have been built on this model, but so far none have been identified with certainty.

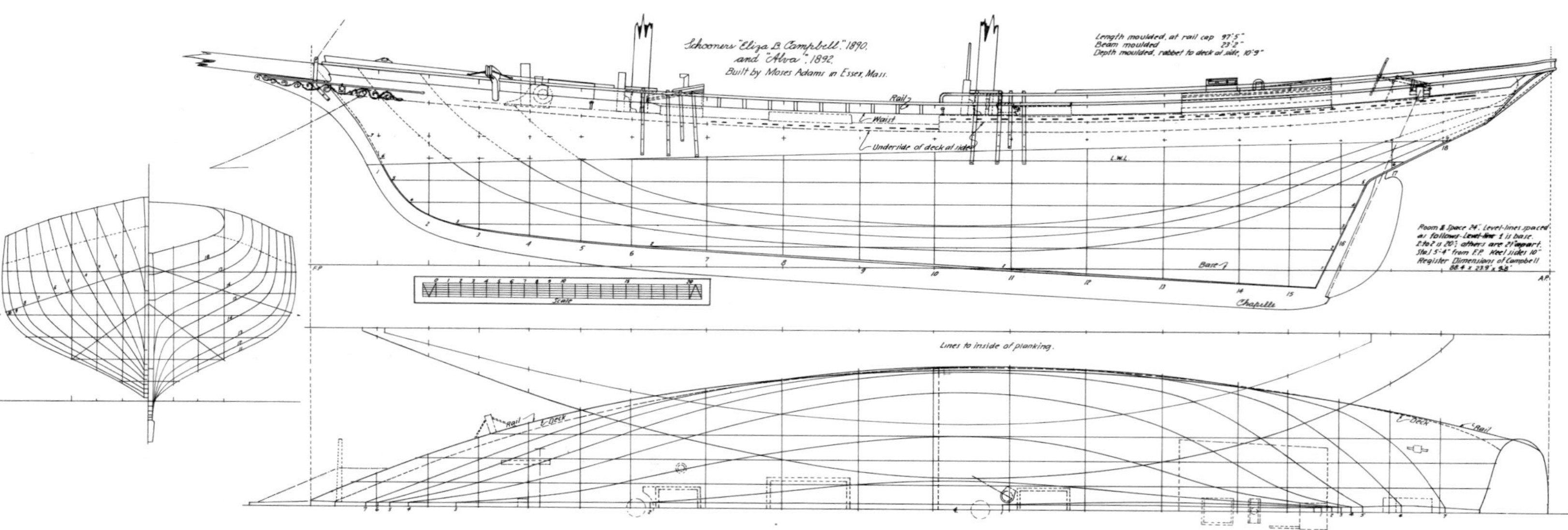
Schooners "Eliza B. Campbell", 1890.
and "Alva", 1892.
Built by Moses Adams in Essex, Mass.
Length moulded, at rail cap 97'5"
Beam moulded 23'2"
Depth moulded, rabbet to deck at side, 10'9"
Rail
Waist
Underside of deck at side
L.W.L.
Room & Space 24". Level-lines spaced
as follows - 1 is base.
1 to 2 is 20"; others are 21" apart.
Sta. 1 5'-4" from F.P. Keel sides 10"
Register Dimensions of Campbell
88.4 x 23.9' x 9.8'
F.P.
A.P.
Base
Scale
Chapelle
Lines to inside of planking.
Rail
Deck

PLATE 76. *Eliza B. Campbell*, 1890, *Alva*, 1892, half-model

Plate 77 is the plan of Burgess' sister ships, *Gloriana* and *Harvard* which were built in 1891 at Essex by Tarr and James. The register dimensions were: *Gloriana*, 96.0′ x 23.2′ x 10.0′; *Harvard*, 95.4′ x 23.6′ x 10.4′. Both of these vessels were supposed to have been built on the lines of *Fredonia*, but this is not true. The *Harvard* and *Gloriana* were launched after Burgess' death. The *Harvard* achieved a reputation as a fast sailer—both were weatherly and well balanced. In 1930 the *Harvard* became a school ship of the United States Nautical Training School, Boston, Massachusetts. Their rig is shown in Fig. 7.

The design showed a moderate, graceful sheer, straight keel rabbet with some drag, carried forward from the sternpost to nearly the foremast, then rockered into a rather shallow forefoot, thence faired into a strongly raking straight stem rabbet having a small gammon knee head, scroll, billet, and bowsprit shroud spreader. The sternpost raked and there was a short counter with a rather shallow, sharply raking, heart-shaped transom. The horn timber did not fair into the transom, as on the earlier Burgess-designed schooners, and the counter was much like that in most of the modeled fishing schooners. The entrance was long, sharp, and slightly convex as the stem was approached. The run was long and fine and the buttocks were nearly straight. The midsection had a straight, sharply rising floor, a high and rather soft turn of the bilge. The topside had very little tumble home, with slight flare between load line and plank-sheer. These schooners were 102′-0″ length at rail, 23′-4″ beam, and 11′-0″ depth at side. Lines of these vessels were to outside of planking, as built.

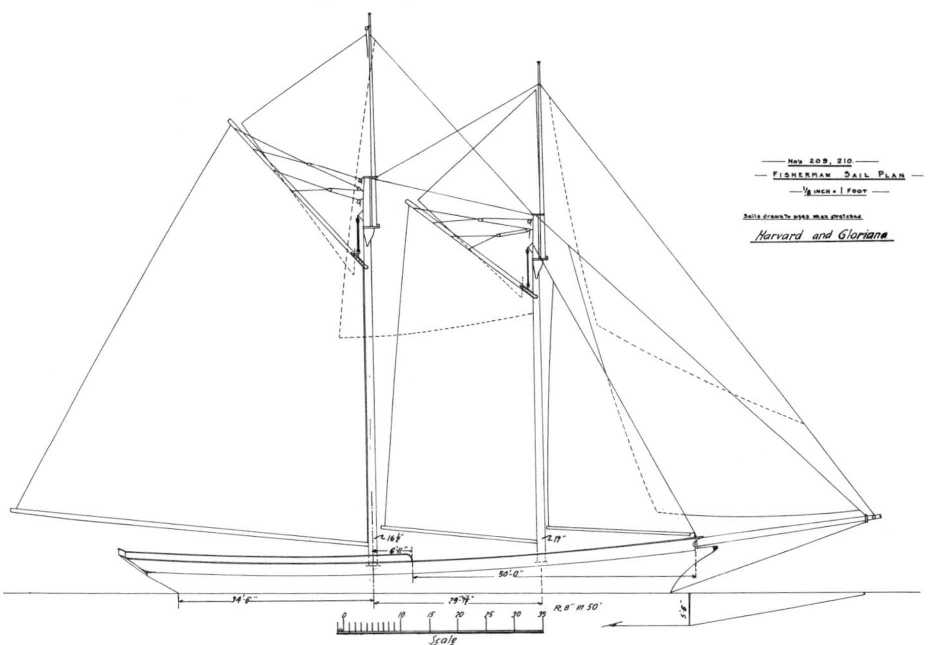
No's 209, 210.
Fisherman Sail Plan
1/8 inch = 1 foot
Harvard and Gloriana
50′-0″
Scale

FIGURE 7

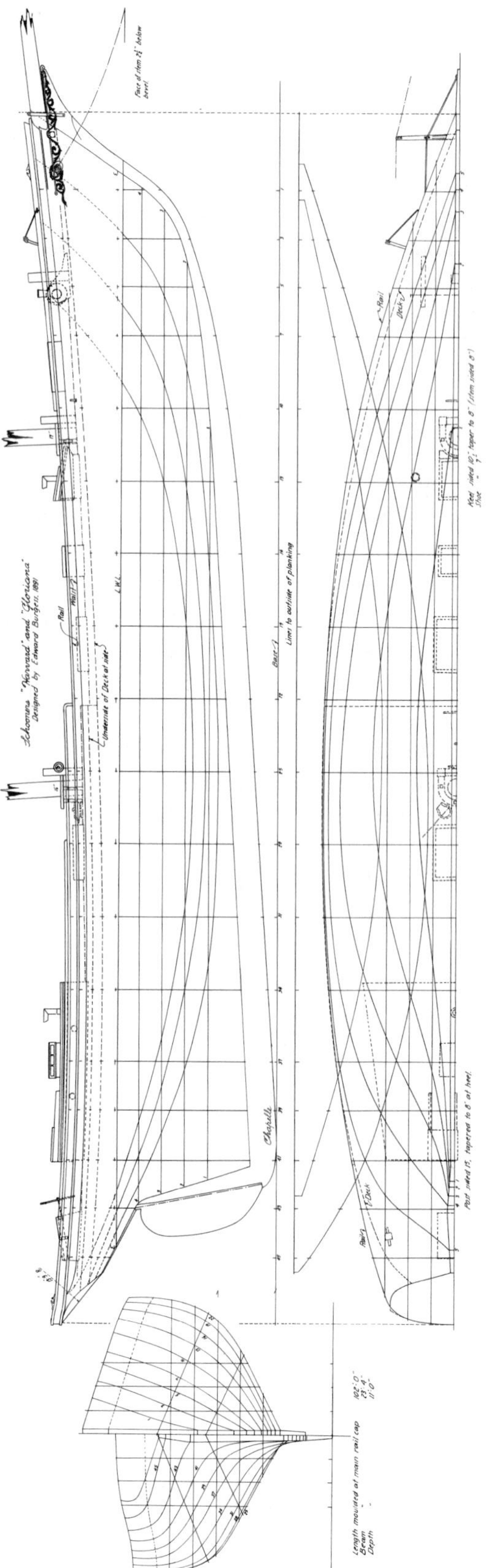
Schooners "Harvard" and "Gloriana"
Designed by Edward Burgess 1891
Rail
Underside of Deck at side
L.W.L.
Lines to outside of planking
Chapelle
Rail
Deck
Length moulded at main rail cap 102'-0"
Beam 13'-4"
Depth 11'-0"

PLATE 77. *Gloriana, Harvard,* 1891, plan, offsets

Another Burgess-designed schooner is shown in Plate 78, the *Emma and Helen* built by Moses Adams at Essex, Massachusetts, in 1891. This vessel, it can be seen immediately, was quite different than the other Burgess-designed schooners. Long, low, narrow, and rather shoal, she probably was intended for a smart sailing carrier. Unfortunately nothing has been found concerning the reasons for this departure from the relatively deep schooner models of the '90s. The register dimensions of the *Emma and Helen* were 84.7′ x 23.0′ x 9.2′, and she was 116′-6″ from taffrail to face of billet, 23′-0″ extreme beam. The tonnage length in the register does not agree with the design; the tonnage length of the latter was about 101.9′ by scale, due, perhaps, to a misprint, or error in entering the dimensions in the published registers.

The *Emma and Helen* had a rather straight sheer, long, straight keel rabbet with slight drag running from sternpost to nearly under the windlass, a sweep up forward to the stem rabbet, which was straight and sharply raking above the load line. The sternpost rabbet raked sharply and so did the transom, as the vessel had a *Fredonia* counter, but shallower than in that schooner. The transom was heart-shaped, its rake making it appear rather shallow. The entrance was long, slightly convex and very sharp. The run was short, rising rather sharply with short straight buttocks. The body was carried well fore-and-aft. The midsection showed a moderately rising straight floor, a well-rounded bilge, and slight tumble home.

In view of the difference in tonnage length between the lines plan and the published register, it should be stated that there is as yet no evidence to support the apparent possibility of an error in identification of the plan. This vessel was on the register at least as late as 1906.

The schooner *Yosemite* (Plate 79) was modeled by McClain and built by A. D. Story at Essex in 1891. She was said to have been the deepest schooner designed by McClain. Her register dimensions were 97.8′ x 23.2′ x 11.5′, and she was 107′-7″ moulded length at rail cap, 22′-10″ moulded beam, and 11′-10″ moulded depth at side. Her draft loaded was about 14 feet. This schooner was very weatherly, a good sailer, and at her best in heavy weather, according to the son of her first captain. This seems a reasonable description, for she had the appearance of being a powerful vessel well able to carry sail in blowing weather.

The *Yosemite* had a rather marked and graceful sheer, a long, straight keel rabbet with drag carried forward from the sternpost almost to the foremast. From here the rabbet rockered upward, fairing into a shallow fore gripe, thence into a straight, strongly raking stem rabbet. She had the usual gammon knee head, scroll, billet, and bowsprit spreader. The short sternpost raked strongly—the counter was of the *Fredonia* type, short and deep with horn timber in line with the transom ℄ in profile. The entrance

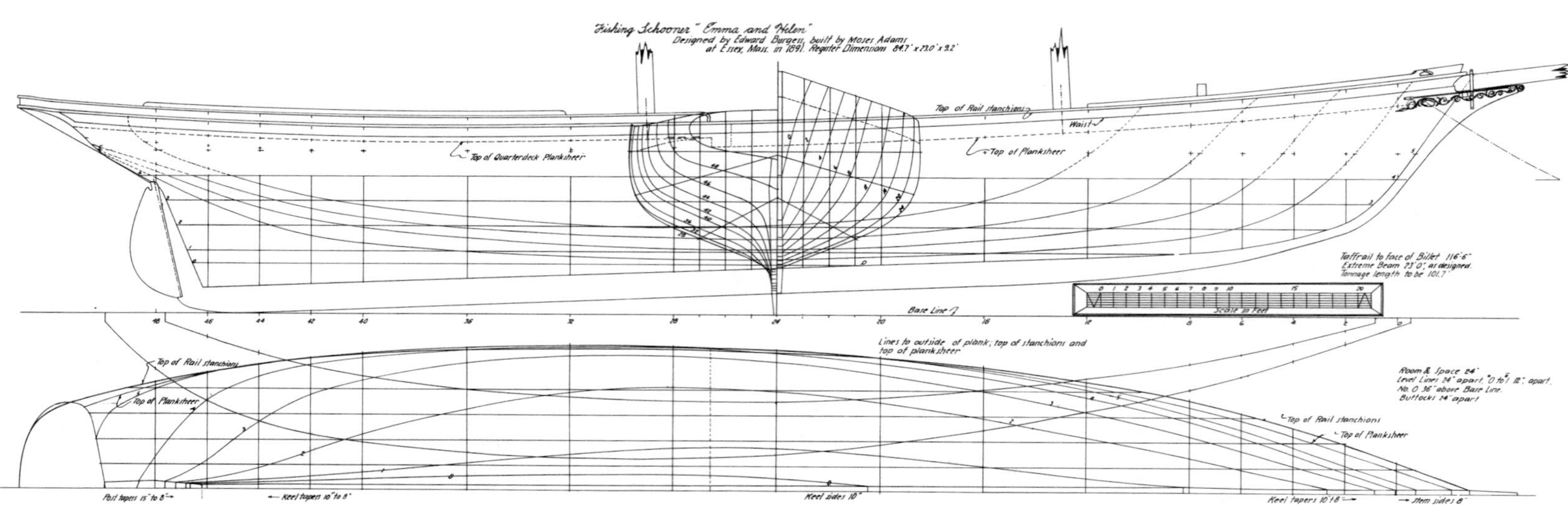
Fishing Schooner "Emma and Helen"
Designed by Edward Burgess, built by Moses Adams at Essex, Mass. in 1891. Register Dimensions 84.7' x 23.0' x 9.2'
Top of Rail stanchions
Waist
Top of Plank sheer
Top of Quarterdeck Plank sheer
Taffrail to face of Billet 116'6"
Extreme Beam 23'0", as designed.
Tonnage length to be 101.7'
Scale in Feet
Base Line
Lines to outside of plank; top of stanchions and top of planksheer
Room & Space 24"
Level Lines 24" apart, "0 to 1" 12" apart.
No. 0 36" above Base Line.
Buttocks 24" apart
Top of Rail stanchions
Top of Planksheer
Post tapers 15" to 8"
Keel tapers 10" to 8"
Keel sides 10"
Keel tapers 10" to 8"
Stem sides 8"

PLATE 78. *Emma and Helen*, 1891, plan, offsets

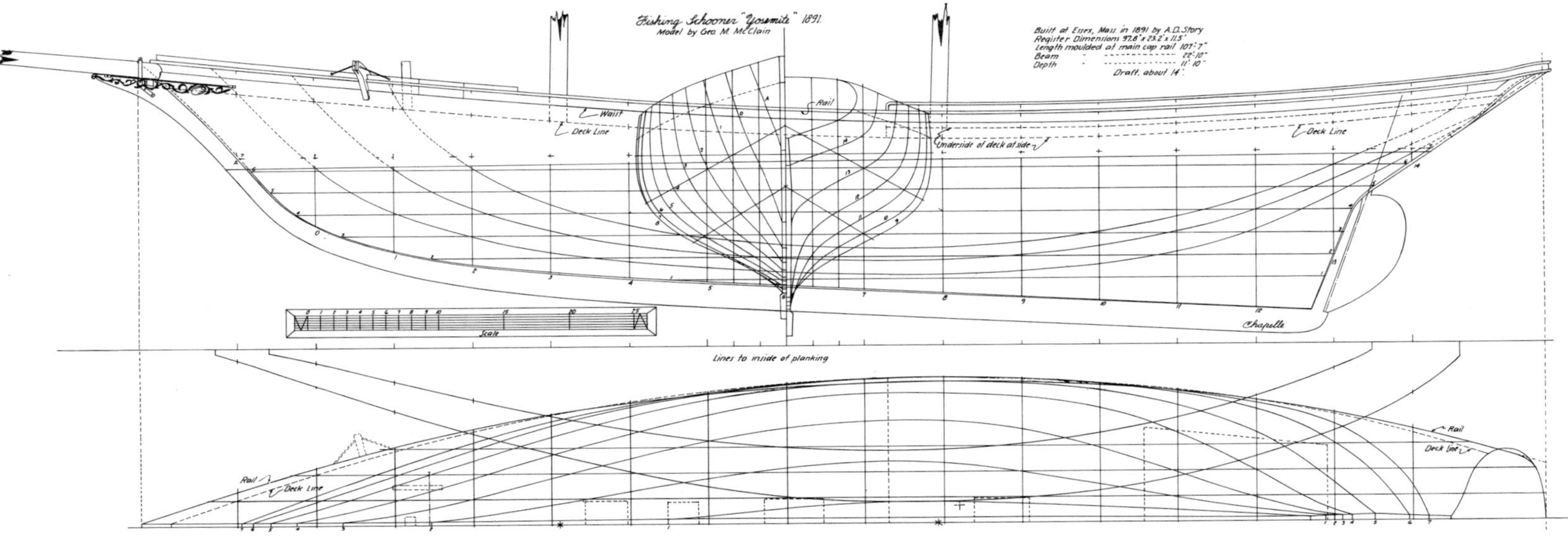
Fishing Schooner "Yosemite" 1891.
Model by Geo. M. McClain
Built at Essex, Mass. in 1891 by A.D. Story
Register Dimensions 97.8' x 23.2' x 11.5'
Length moulded at main cap rail 107'-7"
Beam - 22'-10"
Depth - 11'-10"
Draft, about 14'.
Rail
Waist
Deck Line
Underside of deck at side
Deck Line
Scale
Chapelle
Lines to inside of planking
Rail
Deck Line
Rail
Deck Line

PLATE 79. *Yosemite*, 1891, half-model

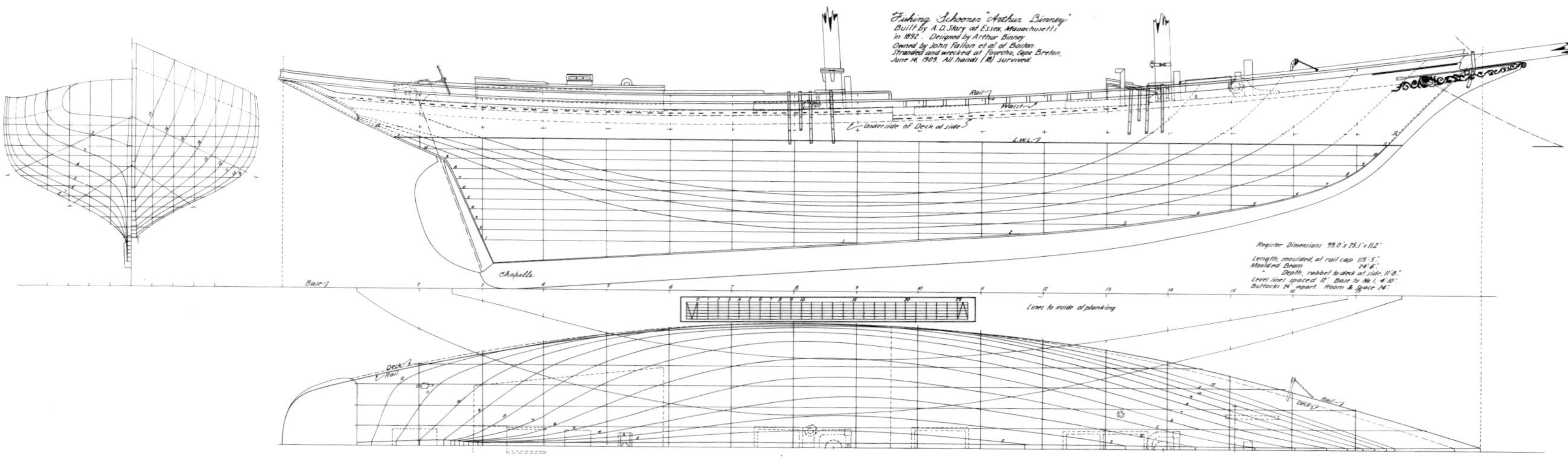
Fishing Schooner "Arthur Binney"
Built by A.D. Story at Essex, Massachusetts
in 1892. Designed by Arthur Binney
Owned by John Fallon et al. of Boston.
Stranded and wrecked at Fourchu, Cape Breton,
June 14, 1909. All hands (18) survived.
Rail
Waist
Underside of Deck at side
L.W.L.
Chapelle
Base
Register Dimensions 99.0' x 25.1' x 11.2'
Length, moulded, at rail cap 115'-5"
Moulded Beam 24'-6"
" Depth, rabbet to deck at side, 11'-8"
Level lines spaced 12" Base to No. 1, 4'-10"
Buttocks 24" apart. Room & Space 24"
Lines to inside of planking
Deck
Rail

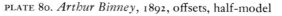

PLATE 80. *Arthur Binney*, 1892, offsets, half-model

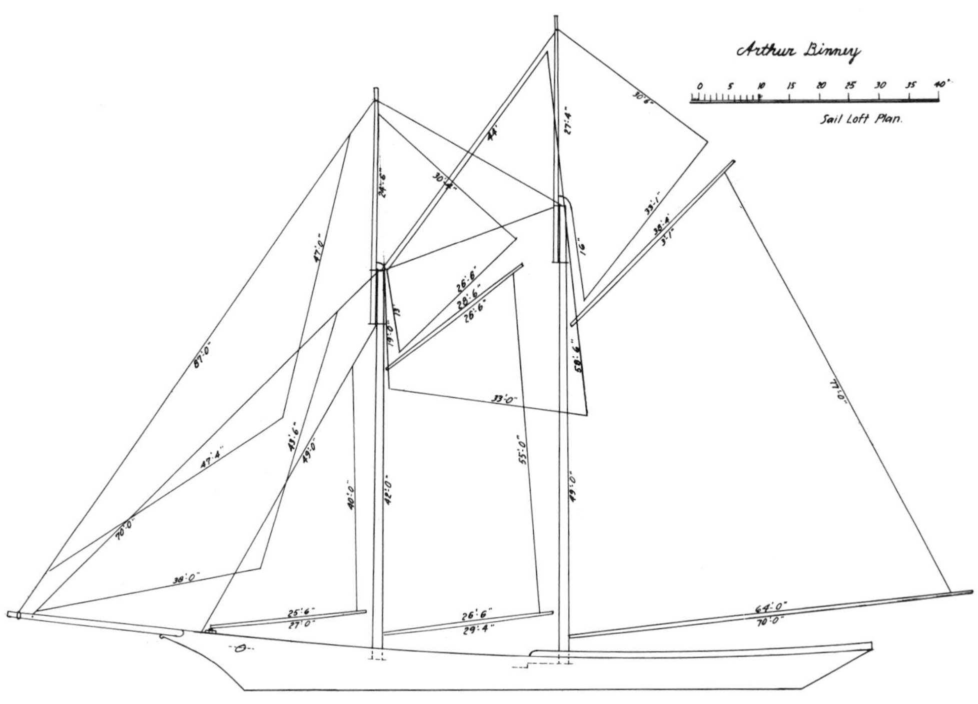
Arthur Binney
0 5 10 15 20 25 30 35 40'
Sail Loft Plan.
87'0"
47'4"
70'0"
38'0"
40'0"
42'0"
33'0"
55'0"
49'0"
58'6"
77'0"
25'6"
27'0"
26'6"
29'4"
64'0"
70'0"

FIGURE 8

was long and sharp, with slight hollow in the fore gripe. The run was rather short, with a slight straight in the steep buttocks. The midsection was formed with hollow sharply rising floor carried well outboard, a high, well-rounded turn of the bilge, and some tumble home in the topside. The *Yosemite* was a handsome schooner and much admired.

The schooner *Arthur Binney* (Plate 80) was designed by the successor to Edward Burgess, Arthur Binney, in 1892 and was built by A. D. Story in that year. Arthur Binney had at least fifteen fishing schooners built to his designs. Of these vessels, plans of four and one half-model have been found. The half-model was made from a plan and was used as an office decoration, as was then customary in many designers' offices. Little has been published about Binney and his work. The year he took over the Burgess practice, 1891, he designed the large schooner *Mary G. Powers*, register dimensions 109.0′ x 25.0′ x 10.8′, which was built at Essex in 1892. The surviving plans of fisherman are all for large schooners. The *Powers* was very much like *Fredonia* in appearance but larger. The *Arthur Binney* was the smallest of the schooners whose dimensions are known. Arthur Binney also designed some coasting schooners, besides many yachts. The fishermen designed by Binney were the just mentioned *Mary G. Powers* (designed in 1891, built in 1892); *Arthur Binney*, 1892 (99′ x 25.1′ x 11.2′); *Maggie Sullivan*, 1893 (107.5′ x 25′ x 11.0′); *Mary G. Whalen*, 1894; *Francis Whalen* (110.5′ x

25.3′ x 11.2′); *Edna Wallace Hopper*, 1901 (107.5′ x 25.2′ x 11.2′); *Benjamin F. Phillips*, 1901 (110.8′ x 25.8′ x 11.5′); *Independence I*, 1901 (107.7′ x 25.2′ x 11.2′); *Katherine & Ellen* (register as *Catherine & Ellen*), 1902 (113.6′ x 26.7′ x 11.5′); *Constellation*, 1902; *Saladin*, 1902; *Independence II*, 1904 (111′ x 25.4′ x 11.8′); *Athlete*, 1906 (107.4′ x 25′ x 11.6′); *Ellen & Mary*, 1912 (109.7′ x 25.5′ x 12.2′); and *Mary*, 1912 (113.8′ x 25.7′ x 12′). All of these vessels, whose dimensions are given, were built at Essex.

Plate 80 shows a schooner having marked sheer, straight keel rabbet, with heavy drag, running from the sternpost to a little forward of the fore end and under the main hatch, curving up forward to a small fore gripe with strongly raked, straight stem rabbet. The *Binney* had a fish (halibut?) for a figurehead and such a head is roughly sketched on the *Power*'s sail plan. The schooner had gammon knee head and bowsprit shrouds spreader. The sternpost rabbet raked sharply. The counter was longer than in the *Fredonia* but the horn timber lined up with the transom ℄ as in that schooner, giving a somewhat heavy appearance to the counter. The entrance was long, sharp, and slightly hollow at the forefoot. The run was long, with short straight

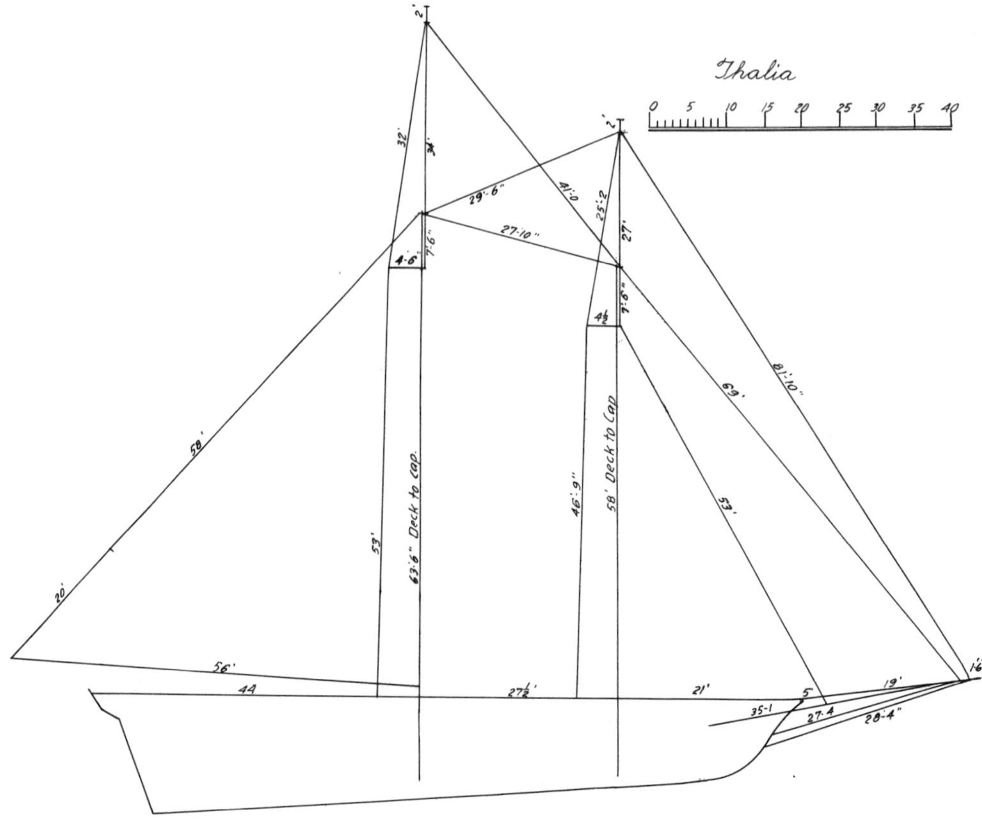
Thalia
0 5 10 15 20 25 30 35 40
2'
32'
29'-6"
27-10"
41'-0
25'-2
27'
4-6
7-6"
4½
7-6"
81'-10"
69'
58'
53'
63'-6" Deck to cap.
46'-9"
58' Deck to Cap
53'
20'
56'
44
27½'
21'
35-1
5'
27-4
28-4"
19'
1-6

FIGURE 9

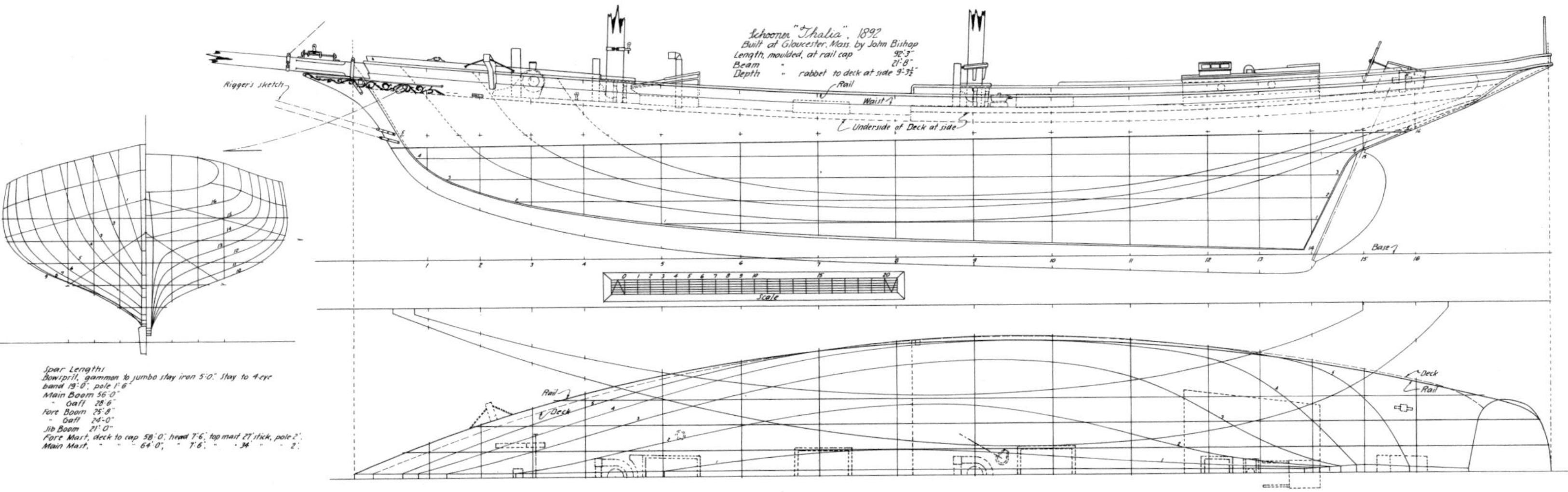
Schooner "Thalia", 1892
Built at Gloucester, Mass. by John Bishop
Length, moulded, at rail cap 92'-3"
Beam " 21'-8"
Depth " rabbet to deck at side 9'-3½"
Rail
Waist
Underside of Deck at side
Rigger's sketch
Base
Scale
Deck
Rail
Spar Lengths
Bowsprit, gammon to jumbo stay iron 5'-0", Stay to 4-eye band 19'-0", pole 1'-6"
Main Boom 56'-0"
" Gaff 28'-6"
Fore Boom 25'-8"
" Gaff 24'-0"
Jib Boom 21'-0"
Fore Mast, deck to cap 58'-0", head 7'-6", top mast 27' stick, pole 2'.
Main Mast, " " " 64'-0", " 7'-6", " " 34' " " 2'.

PLATE 81. *Thalia*, 1892, mould loft lines

buttocks. The midsection had a hollow, sharply rising floor carried outboard with a well-rounded turn of the bilge. There was a slight tumble home in the topside. This vessel sailed well and was a good sea boat, and carried her rig easily, according to statements of two of her crew. The *Binney* was 115′-15″ moulded length at rail cap, 24′-6″ moulded beam, and 11′-8″ moulded depth at side.

The schooner *Thalia* (Plate 81) was built by John Bishop at Gloucester, Massachusetts, in 1892 from a model by George M. McClain. Her register dimensions were 81.8′ x 22.0′ x 9.0′; she was 92′-0″ moulded length at rail cap, 21′-8″ moulded beam, 9′-3½″ moulded depth at side. Judging by the numerous designs of schooners by McClain that have survived, by about 1892 he had developed the combination of features that came to characterize most of his work. These features are illustrated in *Thalia:* moderate sheer, straight keel rabbet with very moderate drag carried forward from the sternpost to under the main hatch, then rockered up to the shallow fore gripe, thence to a strongly raked stem rabbet with slight flare. The sternpost raked strongly and the counter was usually quite long with a sharply raked, rather shallow, oval, or elliptical, transom. The appearance of the counter was commonly by now much lighter and well proportioned, compared to the *Fredonia* style of counter. The entrance was long, sharp, with a very slight hollow in the forefoot. The run was also long and fine, with some straight in the buttocks. The midsection was formed with marked hollow in the garboard and much rise outboard; a high and easy bilge with much tumble home in the topside.

The Bishop brothers, Hugh and John, had built schooners at Gloucester as early as 1872. They had a reputation for building very fine schooners. Some are known to have been modeled by Hugh Bishop, others by McClain or by Thomas A. Irving of Gloucester and Essex, who built vessels in the 90s and early 1900s on his own account. Irving built small schooners and many sloop boats, but he also built some large schooners in the boom years of the '90s and early 1900s. He was an expert modeler.

John Bishop built about 150 vessels at Gloucester between 1881 and 1912. He died November 2, 1912, at Gloucester. Hugh Bishop died at Roxbury, Massachusetts, December 26, 1915, aged sixty-three. At times Hugh operated a shipyard at Gloucester but at other times he was foreman for his brother. Tom Irving died at Gloucester on October 16, 1917, aged eighty-five, having lived in Gloucester for sixty-seven years. Irving built over twenty large schooners besides schooner and sloop boats. In the 1870s Poland and Woodbury (Daniel Poland, Jr. and Charles C. Woodbury) built at Gloucester, as did David Alfred Story, who retired in 1881. His yard was taken over by Bishop and Murphy and became the John Bishop shipyard in 1890. Leonard B. McKenzie built eight schooners and a schooner boat at Gloucester between 1901 and 1910, then removed to Essex where he built several vessels before he died. Numerous builders operated in the city and small vessels were often built on the wharves and launched sideways into the slips.

Returning to the *Thalia*, her lines are for a somewhat shallower hull, in proportion to beam, than the Burgess schooners or the earlier McClain vessels.

Plate 82 shows a schooner laid down in 1892 and launched in 1893 from John Bishop's yard at Gloucester. This was the *Vigilant*, having the following register dimensions: 89.0′ x 22.5′ x 9.8′. She was 96′-2″ moulded length at rail cap, 22′-0″ moulded beam, and 11′-7″ moulded depth at side. It is not known who made her model. She had the reputation of being a fast, light-weather sailer and of being a very handy schooner.

The *Vigilant* had marked sheer, short, straight keel rabbet, running from sternpost forward to the midsection, the rest formed in a long sweep fairing into a curved stem rabbet. The stem had a gammon knee head formed into a "swan-breast bow" with billet, scroll, and bowsprit spreader. The use of the "swan-breast bow" was due to the rounded stem rabbet and cutaway forefoot, when deadwood outside the stem rabbet was made small, as in the *Vigilant*. A very small number of fishing schooners had this style of stem profile in the 1890s and early 1900s, but usually the reverse curve in profile was so slight as to be hardly noticeable. The sternpost

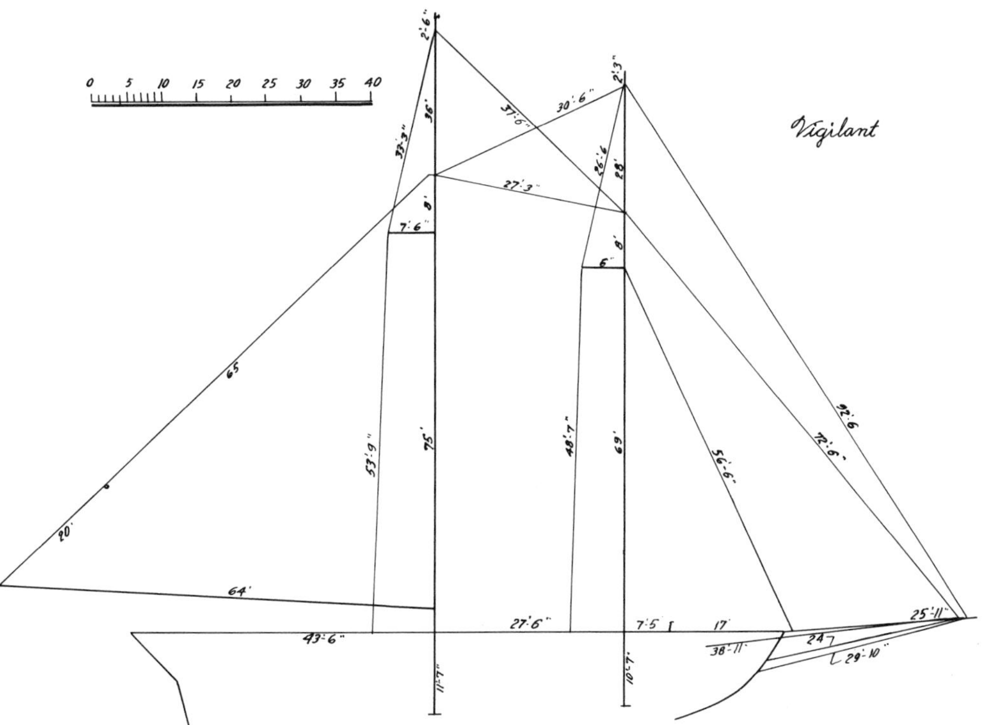

0 5 10 15 20 25 30 35 40
Vigilant
2′6″
2′3″
36′
33′3″
37′6″
30′6″
26′6″
28′
27′3″
8′
7′6″
8′
6″
65
20′
53′9″
75′
48′7″
69′
55′9″
72′6″
92′6″
64′
43′6″
27′6″
7′5
17′
25′11″
38′11″
24
29′10″
11′7″
10′7″

FIGURE 10

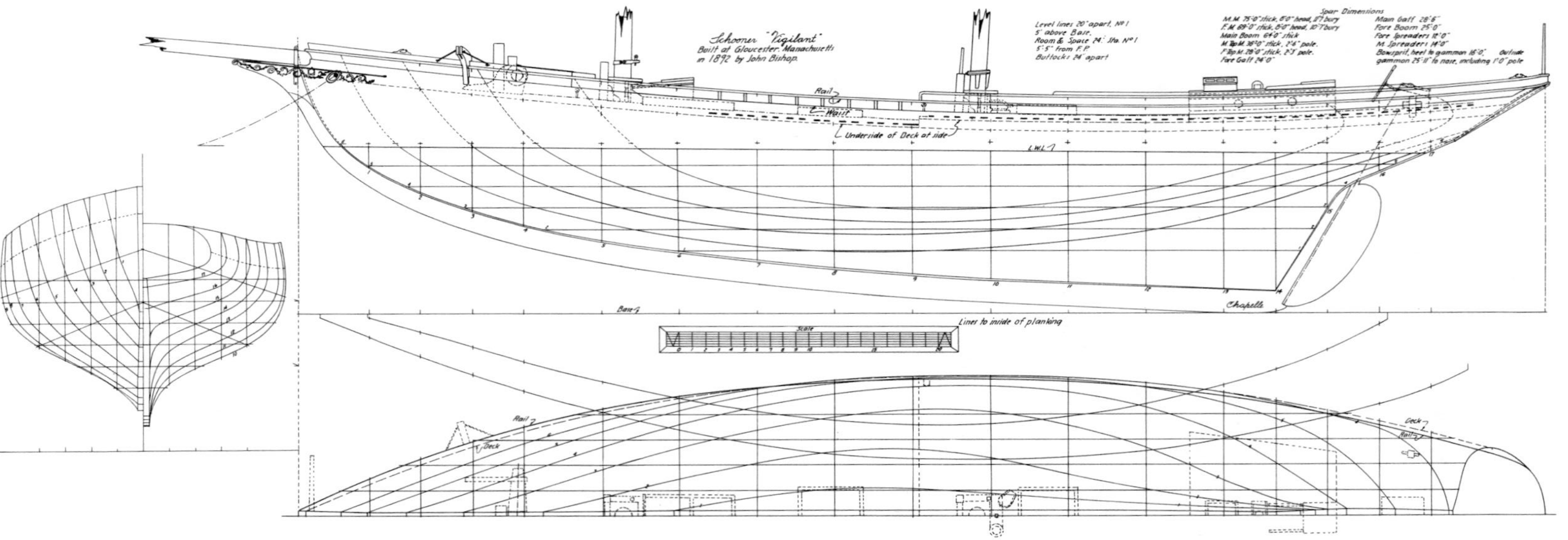
Schooner "Vigilant"
Built at Gloucester, Massachusetts
in 1892 by John Bishop.
Level lines 20" apart, No 1
5' above Base.
Room & Space 24". Sta. No 1
5'-5" from F.P.
Buttocks 24" apart
Spar Dimensions
M.M. 75'-0" stick, 8'-0" head, 11'7 bury
F.M. 69'-0" stick, 8'-0" head, 10'7 bury
Main Boom 64'-0" stick
M. Top M. 36'-0" stick, 2'-6" pole.
F. Top M. 28'-0" stick, 2'-3" pole.
Fore Gaff 24'-0"
Main Gaff 28'-6"
Fore Boom 25'-0"
Fore Spreaders 12'-0"
M. Spreaders 14'-0"
Bowsprit, heel to gammon 16'-0", Outside
gammon 25'-11" to nose, including 1'-0" pole
Rail
Waist
Underside of Deck at side
L.W.L.
Base
Chapelle
Lines to inside of planking
Scale
Deck
Rail

PLATE 82. *Vigilant*, 1893, mould loft lines

rabbet of the *Vigilant* was quite short and therefore the counter was slightly heavy-appearing, but a large, sharply raking, elliptical transom lessened somewhat the heaviness of the counter profile. The entrance was long, sharp, and convex, except for a very slight hollow in the lower part of the forefoot. The run was formed with some straight in the buttocks, faired from the counter. The midsection had a hollow, sharply rising floor, a rather high, full round bilge with much tumble home in the topside.

The schooner *Viking* (Plate 83) was also built by John Bishop at Gloucester and launched in 1893. The designer of this schooner has not been identified. Register 76.0′ x 20.6′ x 8.6′.

This vessel had a lively sheer, straight keel rabbet with small drag, running from sternpost to a little forward of midlength, then carried forward in a long sweep to fair into a rather deep forefoot, thence to a nearly straight, raking stem rabbet. The stem was fitted with gammon knee head, having a billet and scroll, and bowsprit spreaders. The sternpost rabbet had moderate rake and the counter was long and partly submerged as was common in this period. The transom was large, elliptical, and well raked. The entrance was long, sharp with a faint hollow in the forefoot. The run was also long, fine with rather straight buttocks. The midsection had sharply rising, slightly hollow floor carried well out, well-rounded, high turn of the bilge, and some tumble home in the topside. Little has been found about the qualities of this schooner.

Plate 84 shows the schooner *Helen G. Wells* which achieved notoriety by being completely rolled over the full 360 degrees and surviving. This vessel was designed by George M. McClain and built at Gloucester by Thomas A. Irving in 1893. Her register dimensions were 91.2′ x 24.8′ x 9.4′. She was 96′ moulded length on the rail and 22′-6″ moulded beam. She was a relatively deep vessel having moderate sheer, straight keel rabbet, with moderate drag carried forward to about amidships with a sweep up to a rather deep forefoot and strongly flaring stem rabbet. She had gammon knee head, billet, scroll, and bowsprit spreader. The sternpost had a strongly raked rabbet, rather short, but with quite a long counter heavily submerged, and a large heart-shaped transom. The entrance was long, very sharp, and quite hollow in the deep forefoot. The run was long with prominent straight in the buttocks. The midsection had a rising slightly hollow floor, high turn on the bilge, which was moderately hard, with moderate tumble home in the topside.

The *Helen G. Wells* was anchored on the Grand Banks on November 10, 1897. She parted her cable in a strong northwest gale and was immediately put under riding sail, reefed fore, and jumbo. She was then struck by an enormous sea and rolled over, bottom-up. The two men on deck aft saw the sea approaching and had just got into the cabin and had closed the

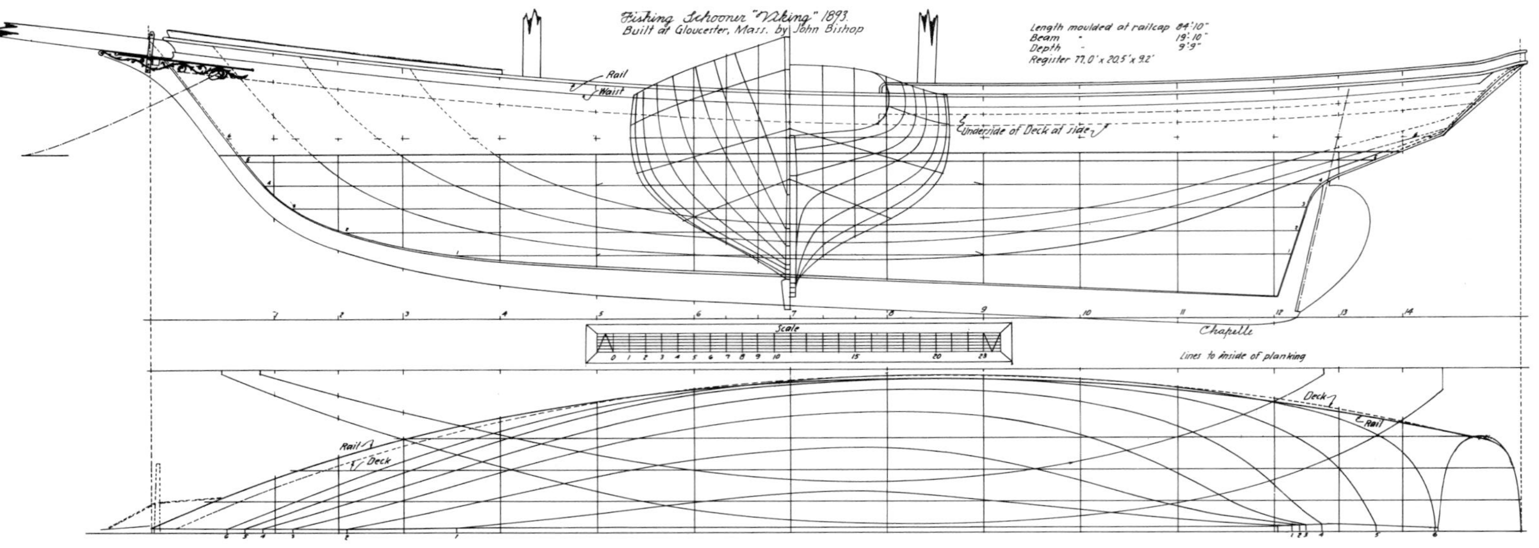
Fishing Schooner "Viking" 1893.
Built at Gloucester, Mass. by John Bishop
Length moulded at railcap 84' 10"
Beam - 19' 10"
Depth - 9' 9"
Register 77.0' x 20.5' x 9.2'
Rail
Waist
Underside of Deck at side
Chapelle
Scale
Lines to inside of planking
Deck
Rail
Rail
Deck

PLATE 83. *Viking*, 1893, mould loft lines

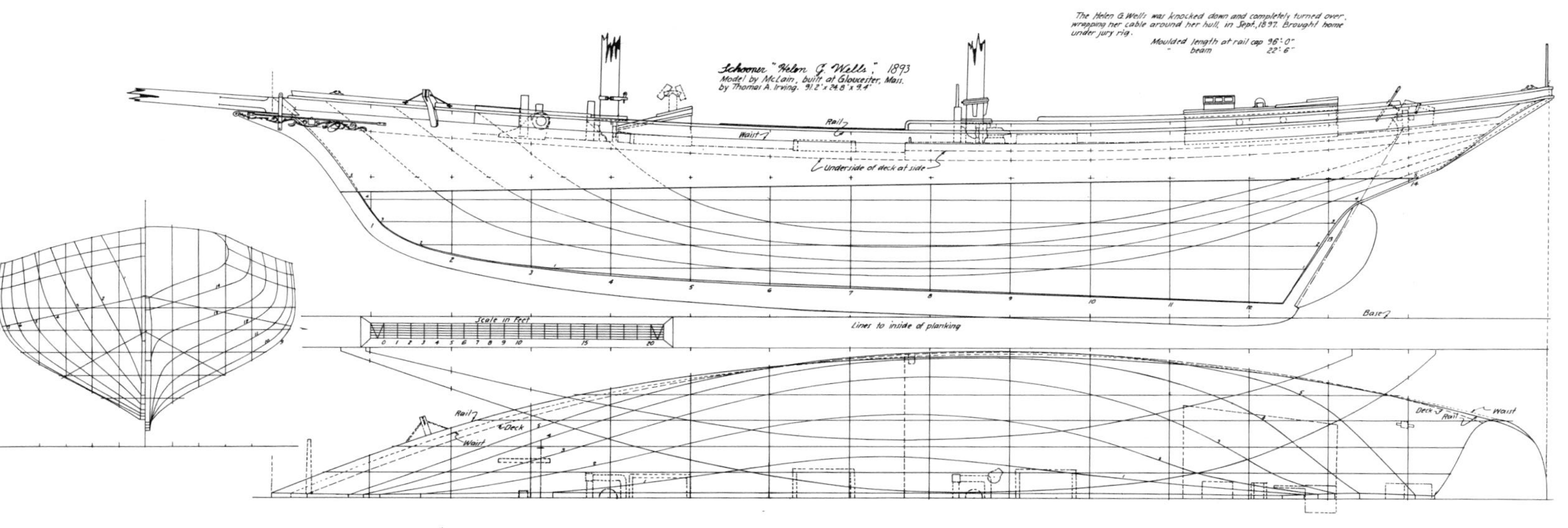

Schooner "Helen G. Wells," 1893
Model by McLain, built at Gloucester, Mass.
by Thomas A. Irving. 91.2' x 24.8' x 9.4'
The Helen G. Wells was knocked down and completely turned over, wrapping her cable around her hull, in Sept. 1897. Brought home under jury rig.
Moulded length at rail cap 96' 0"
" beam 22' 6"
Rail
Waist
Underside of deck at side
Base
Lines to inside of planking
Scale in Feet
0 1 2 3 4 5 6 7 8 9 10 15 20
Deck
Rail
Waist

PLATE 84. *Helen G. Wells*, 1893, mould loft lines

slide hatch when the wave struck her. She wrapped her cable, which had been coiled on deck after it broke, completely around her but she stayed afloat and was towed into St. John, Newfoundland, in a very poor condition. She was repaired and refitted and employed in the New England fisheries until she was sold to Havana, Cuba, in 1915*.

The *Wells* was a fast sailer and handled very well. The accident to this vessel caused McClain to tell a reporter that no practical fishing schooner could be designed that would not be knocked down when hit by one of these freak seas, no matter how deep her hull. Such monster waves were undoubtedly the cause of many fishing schooners going "missing" in the days of sail.

The noted light-weather flier *Marguerite Haskins* (Plate 85) was designed by McClain and built at Essex by Tarr and James in 1893. Her register dimensions were 92.4′ x 24.8′ x 9.4′ and she measured 102′-1½″ moulded length at rail, 24′-0″ moulded beam, and 10′-6″ rabbet to deck at side. This schooner had a moderate, graceful sheer, straight keel rabbet from post to about midlength with much drag, sweep up forward to a rather shallow forefoot and faired into a slightly flared, raking stem rabbet. The sternpost rabbet raked markedly and the counter was of the *Fredonia* type, but longer and shallower than in the Burgess schooner. This style of counter, with the very raking heart-shaped transom, appeared shallow because of its sharp rake. This seems to have been a variant of the *Fredonia*'s counter, to be seen in some of McClain's models and employed in place of the counter seen in *Thalia*. In general, the counters were becoming longer and lighter in this period.

The entrance was long and sharp with slight hollow in the forefoot. The run was long and fine, with the short, straight buttocks that came to mark most of the McClain models that have survived. The midsection had much hollow in the floors, carried well outboard with high, well-rounded bilge and much tumble home in the topside. When the *Haskins* first came out she had a small bust of a girl for a figurehead. This schooner was much admired for her beauty, and her speed in light weather, and her weatherliness. Fig. 11 shows the rig of the *Haskins*, which was well proportioned so as to permit a variety of sail combinations to be used. Fig. 12 shows rigger's sketch of the *Haskins*.

In 1894 J. Horace Burnham of Essex "cut" a model for a sharp schooner, from which Arthur D. Story built two schooners that year, the *Boyd and Leeds* and the *Pythian*, register dimensions 79.2′ x 21.2′ x 8.5′. These vessels proved to be very fast and seaworthy and attracted much attention, and as

* Letter of Charles F. Sayle to author, December 18, 1970.

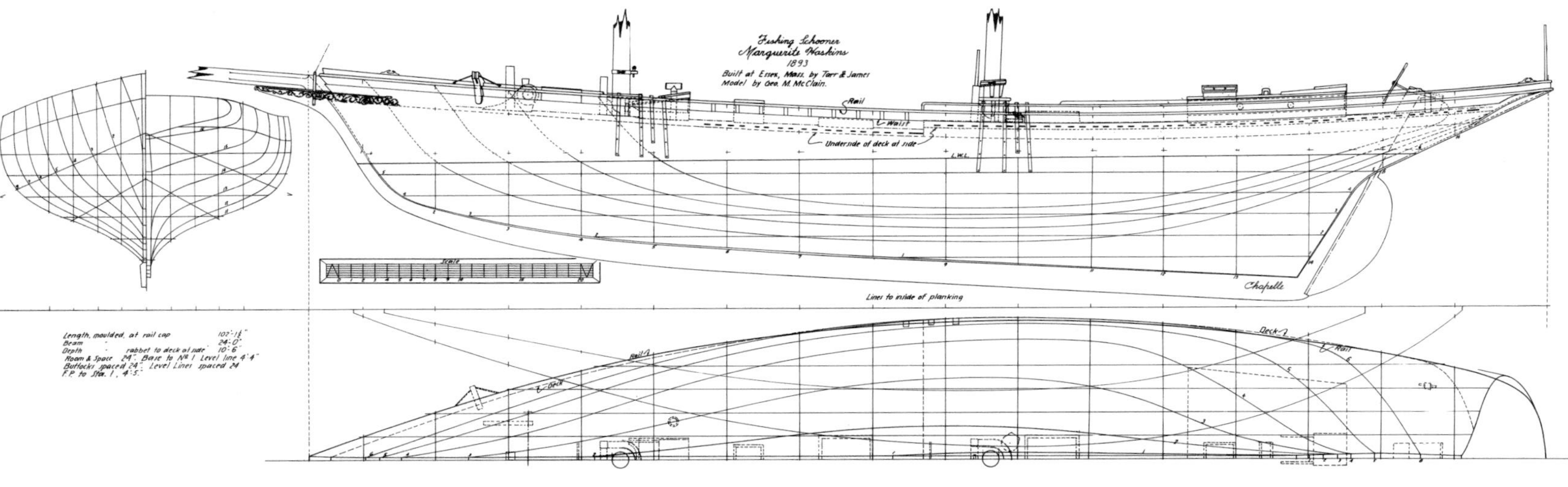
Fishing Schooner
Marguerite Haskins
1893
Built at Essex, Mass. by Tarr & James
Model by Geo. M. McClain.
Rail
Waist
Underside of deck at side
L.W.L.
Scale
Chapelle
Lines to inside of planking
Length, moulded, at rail cap 102'-1½"
Beam " 24'-0"
Depth " rabbet to deck at side 10'-6"
Room & Space 24". Base to No. 1 Level line 4'-4"
Buttocks spaced 24". Level Lines spaced 24
F.P. to Sta. 1, 4'-5"
Deck
Rail

PLATE 85. *Marguerite Haskins*, 1893, half-model

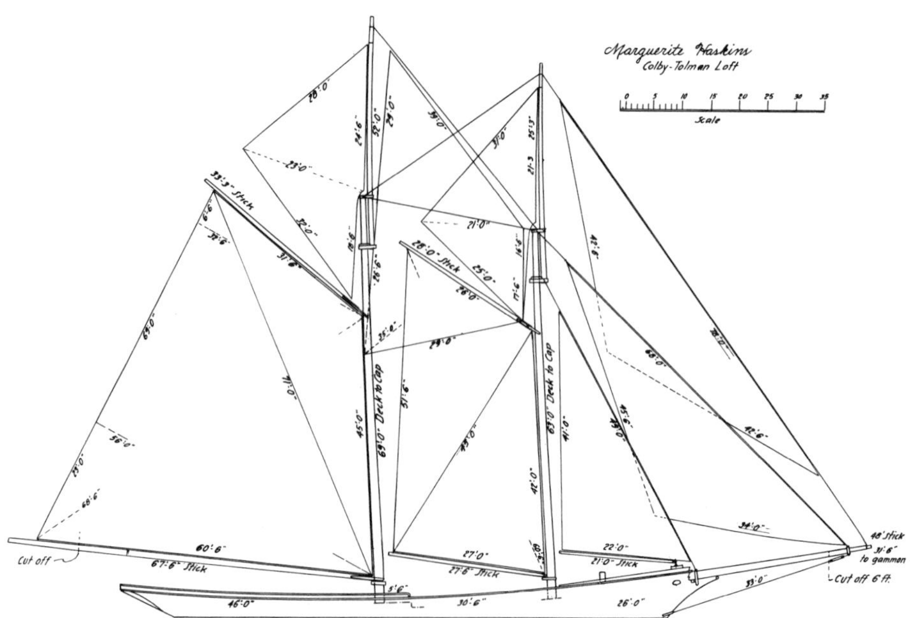
Marguerite Haskins
Colby-Tolman Loft
Scale
69'0" Deck to Cap
63'0" Deck to Cap
67'6" Stick
Cut off
Cut off 6 ft.
to gammon

FIGURE 11

FIGURE 12

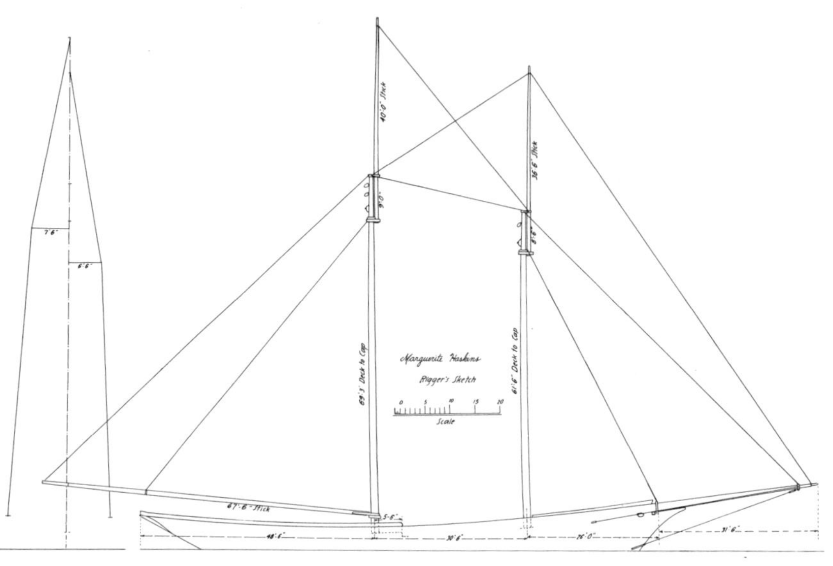
Marguerite Haskins
Rigger's Sketch
Scale
69'3" Deck to Cap
61'6" Deck to Cap

a result fifteen more vessels were built on this model (Plate 86) between 1894 and 1907. The names and register dimensions of these schooners and the names of their builders are given on the plan.

The Burnham model, which strongly resembled a Baltimore clipper, produced schooners having slight sheer and straight keel rabbet with moderate drag. The forefoot was well rounded with a convex curve in the stem rabbet above the load line. The sternpost rabbet raked strongly and the counter was relatively long for the date of design. The transom raked sharply and was heart-shaped. The entrance was long, very sharp, and with some hollow at forefoot. The run was not very long but with some straight in the buttocks. The midsection had strongly rising, straight floor, a high and rather hard turn of the bilge, with some tumble home in the topside. The Burnham design was fitted with gammon knee head, billet, scroll, and iron headrails. The bowsprit spreaders were used in the vessels built in 1894 and 1895, but were discarded in those built soon thereafter. The rigs of the first two schooners built on the Burnham model are also shown in Figures 13 and 14.

The appearance of the Baltimore clipper model at so late a period and in so many sister ships requires comment. It can be seen, in the many published plans, that this type has been used extensively with some variation in width-depth proportion, and in the rakes of stem and sternpost. Capacity also varied, of course, but the popularity of the model was always greatest in relatively light displacement vessels. Hence the clipper model was often employed in vessels carrying small or light cargoes—such as market fishermen, fruiters, and packets—or in vessels carrying no cargo—such as yachts and pilot boats. The well-known design characteristics of the Baltimore clipper can still be seen in some cruising yachts. The model, as usually employed, produced a weatherly, fast, sea-worthy vessel—often good performers in light and moderate weather. By the use of much beam and hard bilges, a variant could be produced that would sail and work well in heavy weather. With such characteristics, the Baltimore clipper fitted the requirements of fishing schooner design, as shown in the sharpshooters and in the later *Boyd and Leeds* and her sisters. This is not to say that some other hull forms would not serve equally well, however. It was the owner's, or builder's, or designer's selection that governed the hull form used in building, whether it was a variant of the Baltimore clipper model or a variant of the *Fredonia* model.

The *William H. Rider*, built at Essex, Massachusetts, in 1895 by John Prince Story, was the last fishing schooner fitted out at Gloucester to have iron stern davits. Plate 87 shows this vessel as designed; she was apparently lengthened two frame spaces (4′-0″) in lofting, giving register dimensions as follows: 80.6′ x 20.6′ x 9.0′. It is not known who made her model. As de-

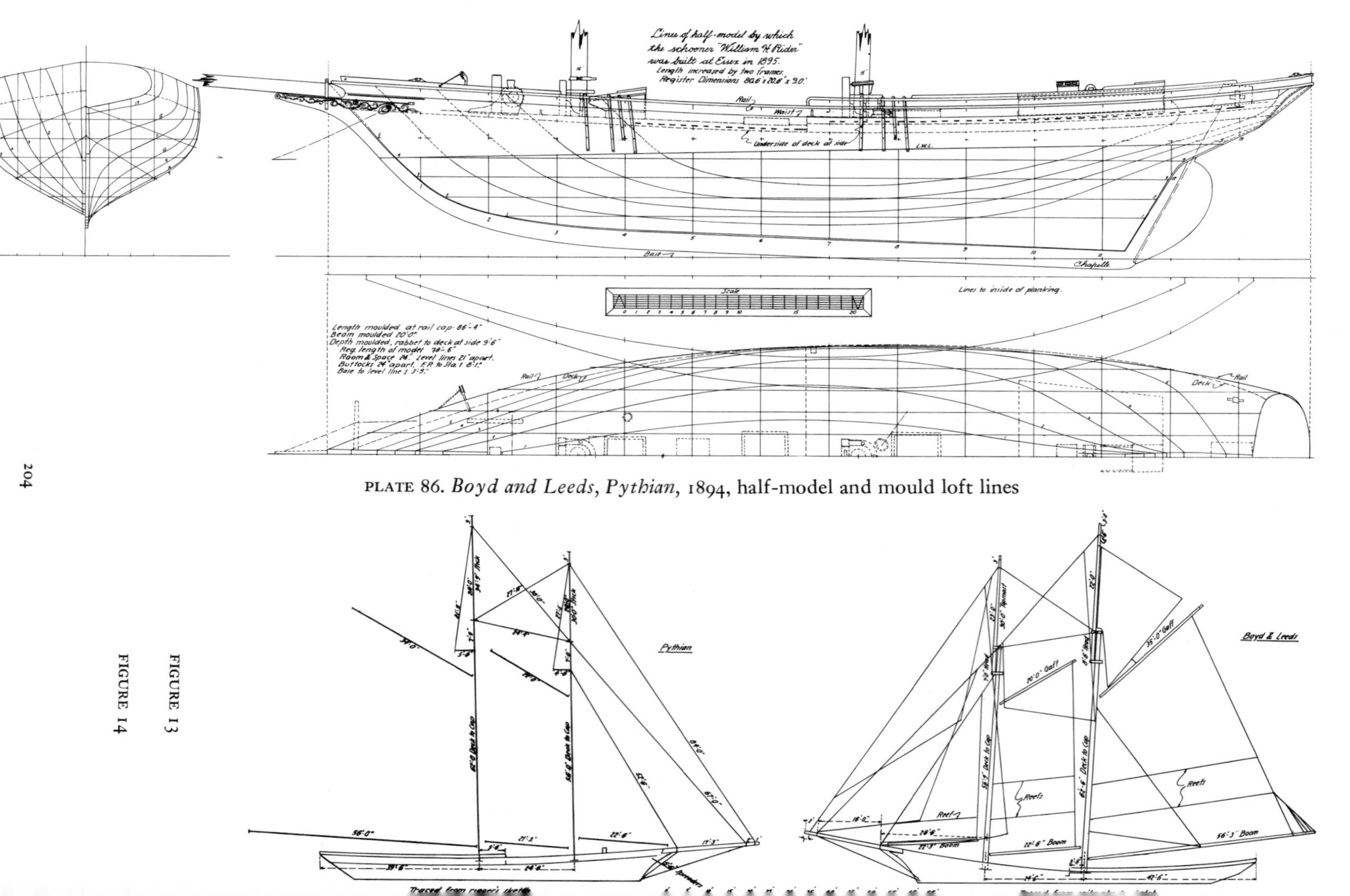
Lines of half-model by which
the schooner "William H. Rider"
was built at Essex in 1895.
Length increased by two frames.
Register Dimensions 80.6' x 20.6' x 9.0'
Rail
Waist
Underside of deck at side
L.W.L.
Base
Chapelle
Lines to inside of planking.
Scale
Length moulded at rail cap 86'-4"
Beam moulded 20'0"
Depth moulded, rabbet to deck at side 9'6"
Reg. length of model 78'-6"
Room & Space 24". Level lines 21" apart.
Buttocks 24" apart. F.P. to Sta. 1 6'-1".
Base to level line 1 3'-9".
Deck
Pythian
62'-0" Deck to Cap
56'-6" Deck to Cap
56'-0"
21'-3"
22'-6"
17'-3"
34'-0"
52'-6"
67'-0"
64'-0"
Traced from rigger's sketch
Boyd & Leeds
35'-0" Gaff
20'-0" Gaff
30'-0" Topmast
22'-0"
56'-9" Deck to Cap
62'-6" Deck to Cap
Reefs
Reef
16'-0"
22'-3" Boom
22'-6" Boom
56'-3" Boom
24'-6"
42'-6"
PLATE 86. *Boyd and Leeds*, *Pythian*, 1894, half-model and mould loft lines

FIGURE 13

FIGURE 14

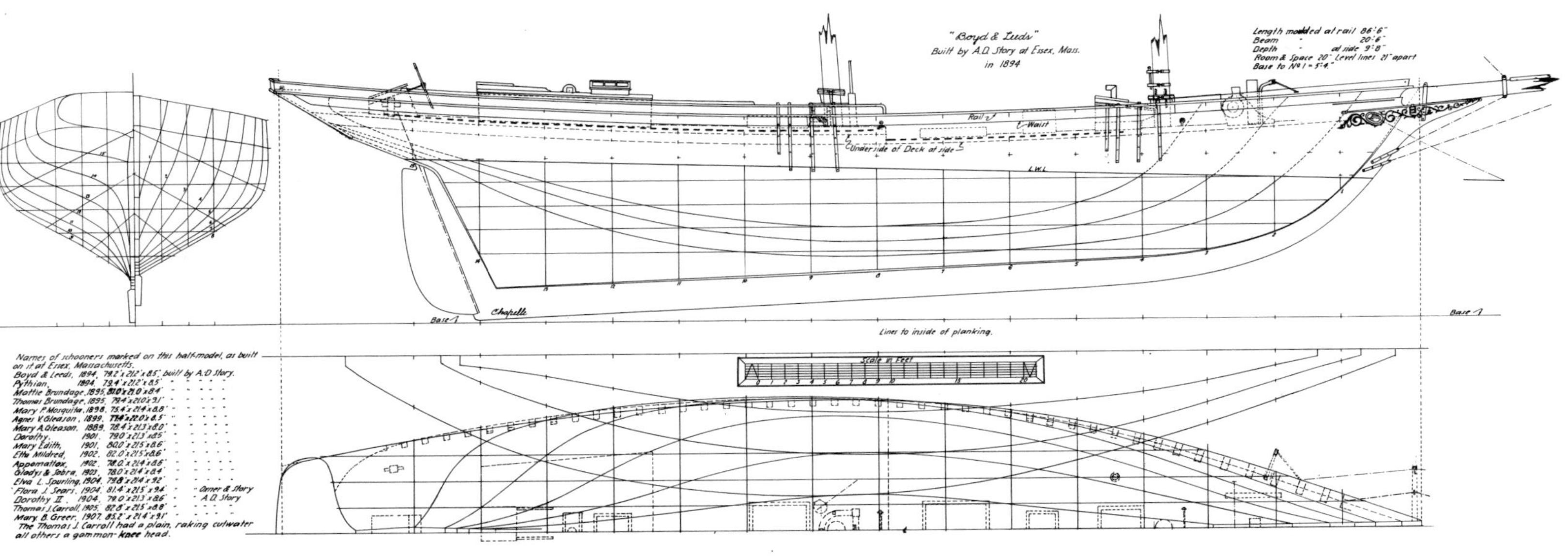
"Boyd & Leeds"
Built by A.D. Story at Essex, Mass.
in 1894
Length moulded at rail 86'6"
Beam - 20'6"
Depth - at side 9'8"
Room & Space 20" Level lines 21" apart
Base to No 1 = 5'4"
Rail
Waist
Underside of Deck at side
LWL
Base
Chapelle
Lines to inside of planking.
Scale in Feet
Names of schooners marked on this half-model, as built on it at Essex, Massachusetts.
Boyd & Leeds, 1894, 79.2' x 21.2' x 8.5', built by A.D. Story.
Pythian, 1894, 79.4' x 21.2' x 8.5'
Mattie Brundage, 1895, 81.0' x 21.0' x 8.4'
Thomas Brundage, 1895, 79.4' x 21.0' x 9.1'
Mary P. Mosquita, 1898, 75.4' x 21.4' x 8.8'
Agnes V. Gleason, 1899, 77.4' x 22.0' x 8.5'
Mary A. Gleason, 1889, 78.4' x 21.3' x 8.0'
Dorothy, 1901, 79.0' x 21.3' x 8.5'
Mary Edith, 1901, 80.0' x 21.5' x 8.6'
Etta Mildred, 1902, 82.0' x 21.5' x 8.6'
Appomattox, 1902, 78.0' x 21.4' x 8.6'
Gladys & Sabra, 1903, 78.0' x 21.4' x 8.4'
Elva L. Spurling, 1904, 79.8' x 21.4' x 9.2'
Flora J. Sears, 1904, 81.4' x 21.5' x 9.4' - Orner & Story
Dorothy II, 1904, 79.0' x 21.3' x 8.6' - A.D. Story
Thomas J. Carroll, 1905, 82.8' x 21.5' x 8.8'
Mary B. Greer, 1907, 85.2' x 21.4' x 9.1'
The Thomas J. Carroll had a plain, raking cutwater all others a gammon-knee head.

PLATE 87. *William H. Rider*, 1895, mould loft lines

signed, she had marked sheer, straight keel rabbet, with a little drag carried forward from the post to under the forecastle companionway, faired into a long sweep upward to the much-rounded forefoot, thence into a raking stem rabbet that was nearly straight. The sternpost rabbet was strongly raked and a counter of moderate length, with a sharply raked elliptical transom, finished the stern. The stem had the fashionable gammon knee head. The entrance was long and sharp with slight hollow in the forefoot. The run was of moderate length, with some straight in the buttocks. The midsection shows a sharply rising, straight floor, a high, firm bilge with practically no tumble home in the topside. She was 86′-4″ moulded length at rail (as designed), 20′-0″ moulded beam, and would have measured about 76′-6″ for Custom House length and 9′-6″ moulded depth at side. The builder said this vessel sailed and worked very well without being an outstanding performer. A photograph of the *Rider* on the ways, ready to launch, was used in making the Town Seal of Essex.

Plate 88 is the lines of the schooner *William A. Morse*, built at Essex, Massachusetts, in 1896 by Tarr and James. This vessel was a heavy-weather sailer, and was another variant of the *Fredonia* model. Her designer is unknown. The register dimensions of the *Morse* were 82.6′ x 22.6′ x 8.8′. She was 90′-6″ moulded length at rail cap, 22′-0″ moulded beam, and 9′-8″ moulded depth at side.

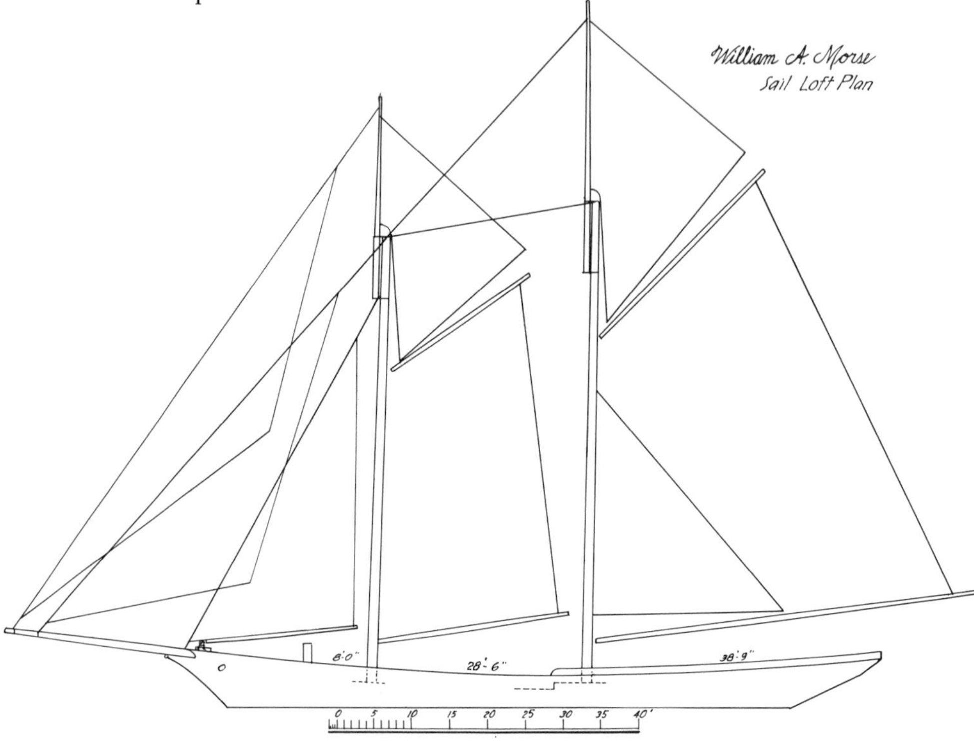
William A. Morse
Sail Loft Plan
8:0"
28:6"
38:9"
0 5 10 15 20 25 30 35 40'

FIGURE 15

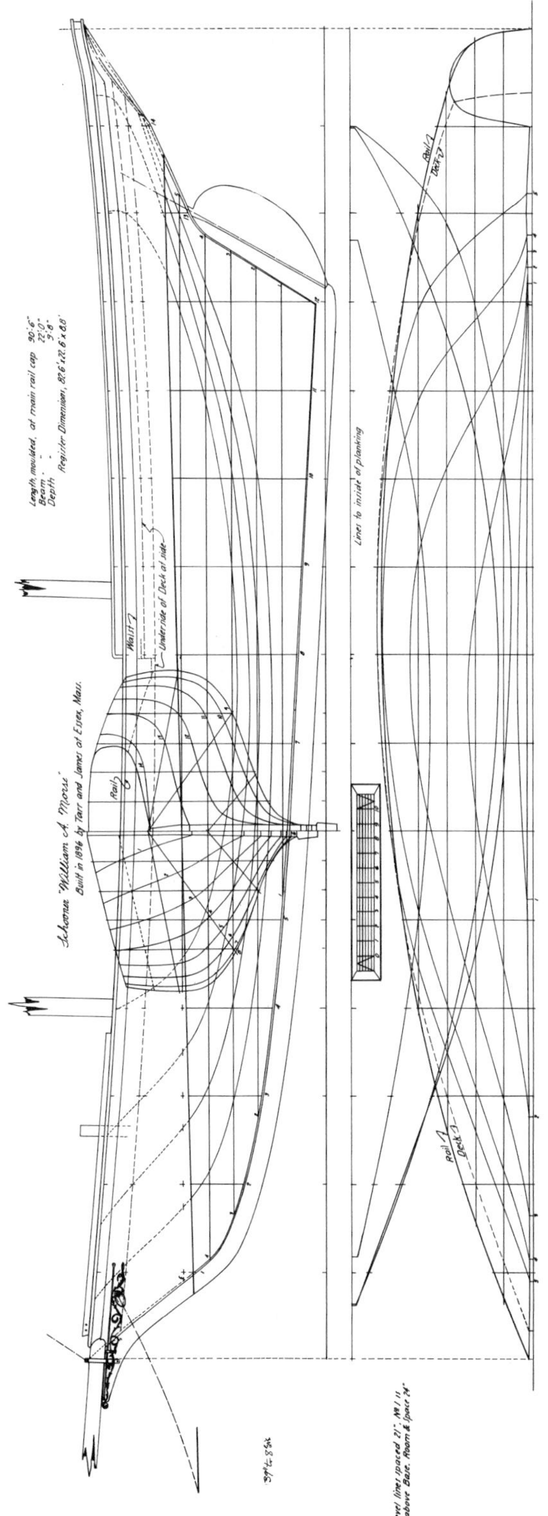
Schooner "William A. Morse"
Built in 1896 by Tarr and James at Essex, Mass.
Length, moulded, at main rail cap 90'6"
Beam " " 22'0"
Depth 9'8"
Register Dimension, 82.6 x 22.6 x 8.8
Waist
Underside of Deck at side
Rail
Lines to inside of planking
Rail
Deck
Rail
Deck
Level lines spaced 21". No. 1 11
3' above Base. Room & Space 24"

PLATE 88. *William A. Morse*, 1896, mould loft lines

The *Morse* had moderate sheer, straight keel rabbet, with a little drag from sternpost forward to about mid-length, then with a long sweep up to a cutaway forefoot to a nearly straight raking stem rabbet. The stem had the gammon knee, scroll, billet, and iron rod headrail or brace; the bowsprit spreader was omitted as the bowsprit was not as long as in the earlier schooners. The sternpost rabbet raked sharply, with a rather short, light counter and strongly raking elliptical transom. The entrance was long, sharp, with much hollow in the forefoot. The run was long, fine, with some straight in the buttocks. The midsection had a hollow, rising floor, with a rather hard bilge and a good deal of tumble home in the topside. The *Morse* was spoken of as a handsome schooner.

Plate 89 is the schooner *Volant*, built from a model by George M. McClain at Gloucester in 1899 by John Bishop. Her register dimensions were 85.9′ x 23.0′ x 9.6′. She was 95′-8″ moulded length at rail cap, 23′-0″ moulded beam, and 10′-3″ moulded depth at side. Her sheer was somewhat slight, the keel rabbet was straight from sternpost forward to about midships, with moderate drag, thence it swept up in a long sweep to a marked forefoot and faired into a straight, well-raked stem rabbet. The sternpost rabbet raked strongly, the counter was of medium length. The elliptical transom raked sharply, giving the stern a pleasingly light appearance. The entrance was long, sharp, and quite hollow in the forefoot. The run was of moderate length, with some straight in the buttocks. The midsection had a little hollow in the floor, a high, moderately hard turn of the bilge, with tumble home in the topside. She was remembered by some old fishermen and ship

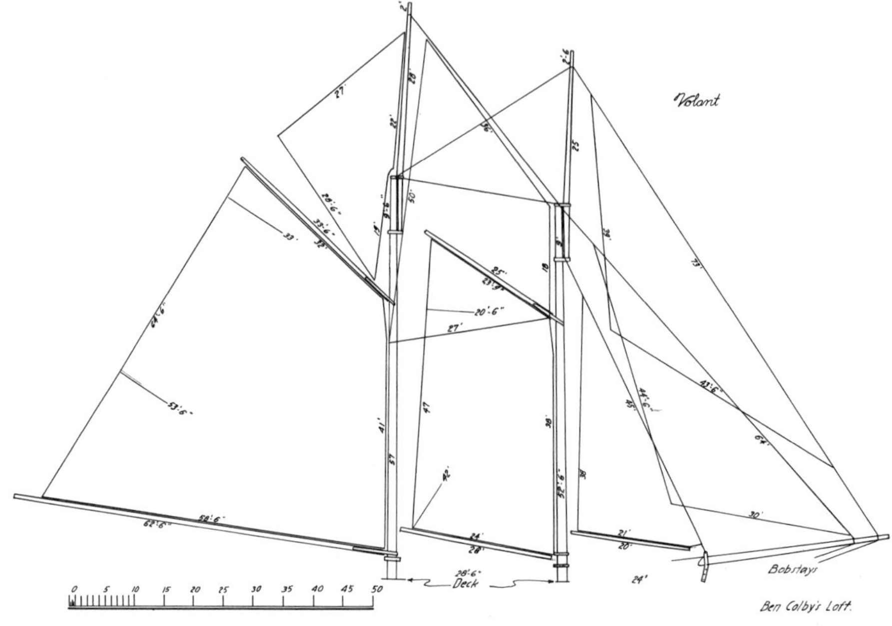
Volant
Bobstays
28′-6″
Deck
Ben Colby's Loft
0 5 10 15 20 25 30 35 40 45 50

FIGURE 16

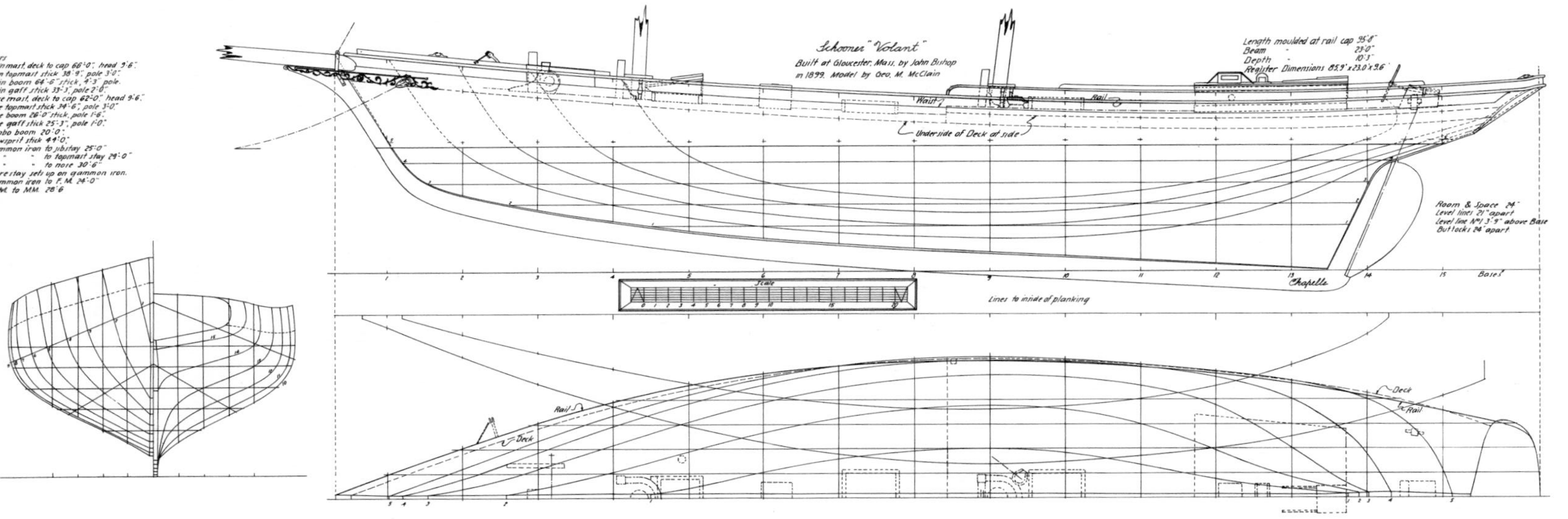

Spars
Main mast, deck to cap 66'-0", head 9'-6".
Main topmast stick 38'-9", pole 3'-0".
Main boom 64'-6" stick, 4'-3" pole.
Main gaff stick 33'-3", pole 2'-0".
Fore mast, deck to cap 62'-0" head 9'-6".
Fore topmast stick 34'-6", pole 3'-0".
Fore boom 26'-0" stick, pole 1'-6".
Fore gaff stick 25'-3", pole 1'-0".
Jumbo boom 20'-0".
Bowsprit stick 44'-0".
Gammon iron to jibstay 25'-0"
" " to topmast stay 29'-0"
" " to nose 30'-6"
Forestay sets up on gammon iron.
Gammon iron to F.M. 24'-0"
F.M. to M.M. 28'6
Schooner "Volant"
Built at Gloucester, Mass. by John Bishop
in 1899. Model by Geo. M. McClain
Length moulded at rail cap 95'-8"
Beam - 23'-0"
Depth - 10'-3"
Register Dimensions 85.9' x 23.0' x 9.6'
Waist
Rail
Underside of Deck at side
Room & Space 24"
Level lines 21" apart
Level line No. 1 3'-9" above Base
Buttocks 24" apart
Base
Scale
Chapelle
Lines to inside of planking
Rail
Deck
Deck
Rail

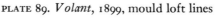

PLATE 89. *Volant*, 1899, mould loft lines

carpenters as a very good vessel as well as a handsome one. She had the fashionable billet, gammon knee head, and scroll.

A number of vessels, in the 1890s, were modeled by yacht builders. A fine example of design by one of these is shown in Plate 90. This powerful schooner, named *Anglo-Saxon*, was modeled by Archibald ("Archie") Fenton, of Manchester, Massachusetts—a very competent yacht designer—and built by Tarr and James at Essex. She had a short life, being wrecked on the coast of Nova Scotia, November 24, 1903, so little is known of her qualities. As far as one may judge by her lines today the vessel was weatherly and probably a fast sailer, with great power to carry sail. It was the opinion of some vessels managers at Gloucester, who were acquainted with the vessels designed by yacht builders, that some schooners were fast but their great power to carry sail made them too stiff, causing them to be expensive to operate and hard on their spars and rigging. In the 1890s and early 1900s carrying a heavy press of sail on all occasions was common practice among fishing skippers. One of these hard-driving skippers lost five sets of spars during his career, with even greater damage to rigging and sails. This characteristic of many fishing skippers was the result of the work of a great short-story writer, James B. Connolly, whose tales of the Gloucester fishermen attracted widespread attention during this period. Connolly glorified and publicized hard-driving skippers, so that a reputation for being a sail carrier became much sought after, though the result was sometimes an exhibition of recklessness. Sail carrying was a more important matter in the evolution of the fishing schooner than has been acknowledged. A reputation for hard-driving required a vessel that had been strongly built, sparred, rigged, and fitted. Coming at a time when the design of fishing schooners was reaching a high level in maximum seaworthiness and speed, the hard-driving required a vessel of great strength—the whole resulting in some of the finest seagoing schooners that were ever built.

The *Anglo-Saxon* was one of many examples of a schooner designed to meet the demands of a hard-driving skipper. She had moderate sheer, a straight keel rabbet with small drag running from the sternpost forward to about midlength, then sweeping up in a long curve to a deep but somewhat cutaway forefoot. This faired into a straight, strongly raked stem rabbet, having the usual gammon knee head, billet, scroll, iron headrail, and its supports. The sternpost rabbet raked sharply also, with a rather deep, partly submerged counter at the tuck having an elliptical, much-raked transom. The deadrise was carried into the counter to reduce pounding; this was the prime reason for the long retention of the heavy, short counter in many instances.

The entrance was long and sharp, without any hollow at the forefoot.

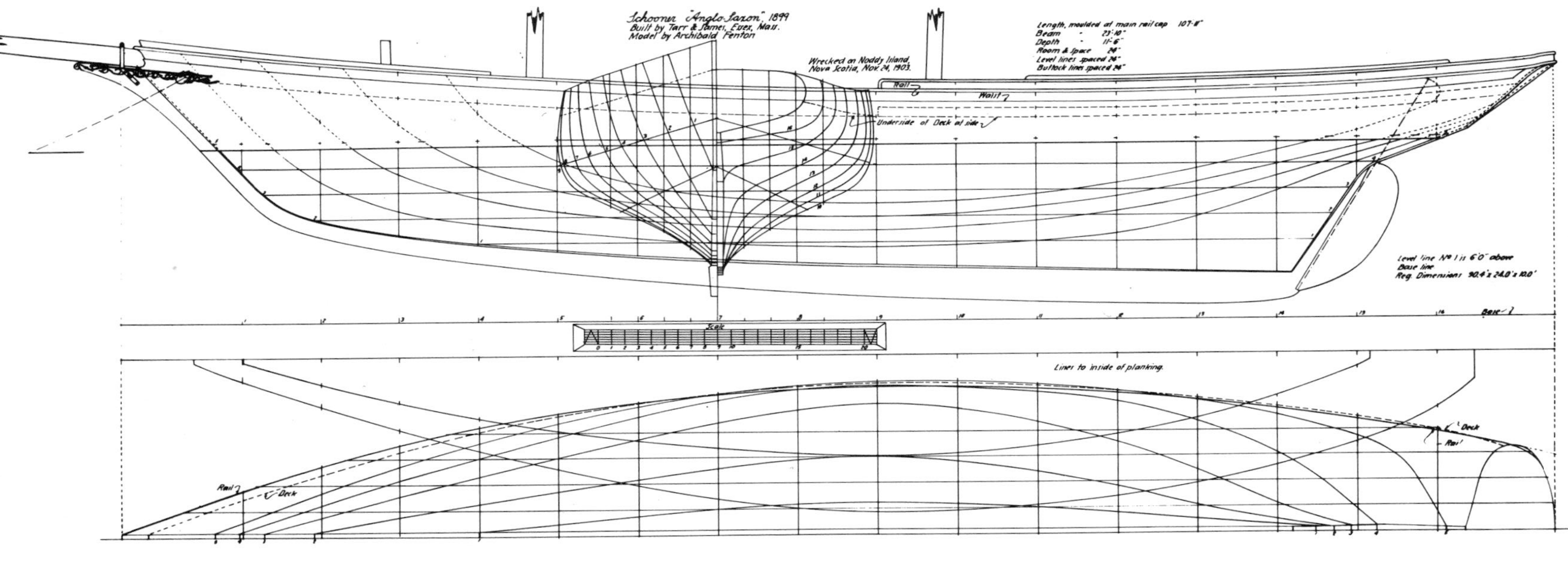

Schooner "Anglo-Saxon," 1899
Built by Tarr & James, Essex, Mass.
Model by Archibald Fenton
Wrecked on Noddy Island, Nova Scotia, Nov. 24, 1903.
Length, moulded at main rail cap 107'-11"
Beam - 23'-10"
Depth - 11'-6"
Room & Space 24"
Level lines spaced 24"
Buttock lines spaced 24"
Rail
Waist
Underside of Deck at side
Level line Nº 1 is 6'0" above Base line
Reg. Dimensions 90.4' x 24.0' x 10.0'
Base
Scale
Lines to inside of planking.
Deck
Rail

PLATE 90. *Anglo-Saxon*, 1899, half-model

In the *Anglo-Saxon* the run was unusually long for the period, beginning almost under the great beam and running to the transom in a long sweep, coming straight in the buttocks before the tuck of the counter was reached. The midsection was formed with hollow floor, a high and hard turn in the bilge and much tumble home in the topside. The register dimensions of the *Anglo-Saxon* were 90.4′ x 24.0′ x 10.0′; 107′-11″ moulded length at rail cap, 23′-10″ moulded beam, and 11′-6″ moulded depth at side.

The size of fishing schooners increased in the 1890s, as may be seen in the vessels built after 1885 and shown here in plans. An increase in the number of vessels built for Boston owners occurred in the last years of the 1890s and continued into the 1900s.

In the years between 1885 and 1895, the Gloucester fleet was built up as follows:

Year	*Number of New Vessels*
1885	20
1886	16
1887	20
1888	18
1890	22
1891	39
1892	23
1893	32
1894	20
1895	11

In the spring of 1896 Gloucester had 95 vessels for the fresh-fish market, 79 vessels handlining on Georges, 51 dory trawling on the Grand Banks, 3 vessels in the salt-halibut fishery, 15 vessels mackerel seining, 20 vessels in the frozen herring trade, 42 in the fresh-halibut fishery with *60 vessels to fit out.*

Chapter Seven

1900–1908

In 1892, two fishing schooners, sister ships, were launched at Essex, Massachusetts. They were designed by Thomas F. McManus, the son of the prominent Boston sailmaker John H. McManus, who had made sails for the Boston-owned *America*'s Cup defenders. Thomas had become a fish broker, with an office on Atlantic Avenue in downtown Boston. He had also become an admirer and friend of Dennison J. Lawlor and was well acquainted with Edward Burgess. He attended the trade school for shipwrights at Charlestown, Massachusetts, and he had become an enthusiastic amateur designer.

The sister ships were the *James S. Steele* and *Richard C. Steele.* These schooners were much cut away forward, having bows very much like that of Herreshoff's famous racing sloop *Gloriana.* For fishing schooners they had small displacement, which limited their inside ballast to an excessive extent. In fact, they were probably too much like yachts and were somewhat tender. The *James S. Steele*, mackerel fishing, with the crew on deck cleaning a deck-load of fish, was suddenly hit by a squall and knocked flat. The crew and fish went overboard, and had not the men been able to get into the seine boat and dory towing astern, there would have been another *Marie Celeste*, for the schooner had at once righted and then had continued on her course.

A small half-model of these schooners is in the National Watercraft Collection, U. S. N. M. 310887. This is on ¼″ = 1′-0″ scale and was given to the collection by Thomas F. McManus. Unfortunately McManus' plan files were apparently left in his cottage at Scituate, Massachusetts, when the family vacated it after his death in the 1930s, so the plans of these and many other schooners were lost. The *James S. Steele*'s register dimensions

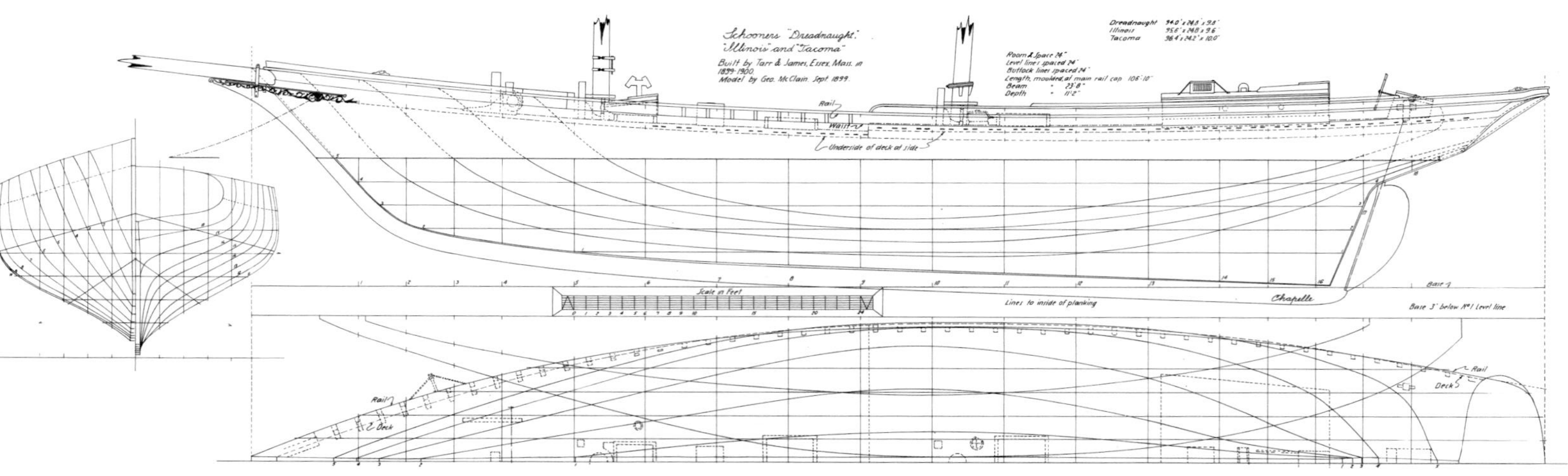

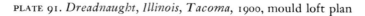

PLATE 91. *Dreadnaught, Illinois, Tacoma,* 1900, mould loft plan

were 88.0′ x 23.0′ x 10.4′. The *Richard C. Steele* does not appear in the 1892 register.

The model shows vessels 98′-6″ moulded length at main rail, 21′-6″ moulded beam, and about 13′-6″ draft. The keel was strongly rockered, without any straight in the shoe. The sternpost raked sharply, and the counter was noticeably long and narrow ending in a very small V-shaped transom. The stem rabbet faired into the keel rabbet in an overhanging fore rake, having a small gammon knee head. The sheer was rather great, the entrance was long and fine, slightly convex in the forefoot, the run was very fine with straight buttocks. The midsection had much hollow in the floor, a high but slack turn of the bilge, and much tumble home in the topside.

By about 1901 McManus had established himself as a designer of fishing schooners, helped by the expansion of the Boston and South Shore fishing fleet that began in the late 1880s. His designs, which followed the *Steeles*, usually had a rockered keel without any straight in the shoe, and a rounded bow profile without a gammon knee but with a small scroll around the hawse casting. As many of these schooners had Indian names, they were called "Indian Headers" by fishermen. McManus' career will be discussed later.

Plate 91 shows the three sister schooners *Dreadnaught*, *Illinois*, and *Tacoma*, designed by McClain in September 1889 and built at Essex in 1900 by Tarr and James. These were on a conservative design and the register dimensions of the three were: *Dreadnaught*, 94.0′ x 24.8′ x 9.8′; *Illinois*, 95.6′ x 24.8′ x 9.6′; and *Tacoma*, 96.4′ x 24.2′ x 10.0′. The loft drawing was for a schooner 106′-10″ moulded length at rail cap, 23′-8″ moulded beam, and 11′2″ moulded depth at side. The sheer was very moderate (McClain's extant designs show that some of them had relatively small sheer), the keel rabbet was straight, with moderate drag from post to midlength, thence rising in a long gentle sweep to a noticeably deep forefoot and then faired into a strongly raked straight stem rabbet. The rake of the sternpost was great, the counter was rather short and deep, the elliptical transom was sharply raked and was also somewhat deep. Part of the counter was submerged. The entrance was long, sharp, but slightly convex. The run began under the mainmast, and the buttocks were straight for a short distance forward of the tuck. The midsection had sharply rising floor, with some hollow, carried well outboard with a hard turn in the bilge and marked tumble home in the topside. The design produced a powerful schooner capable of great speed in strong winds.

The Binney-designed *Benjamin F. Phillips* is shown in Plate 92. She was a large, powerful schooner built at Essex, in 1901 by A. D. Story; her register dimensions were 110.8′ x 25.8′ x 11.2′. By scaling Binney's plan,

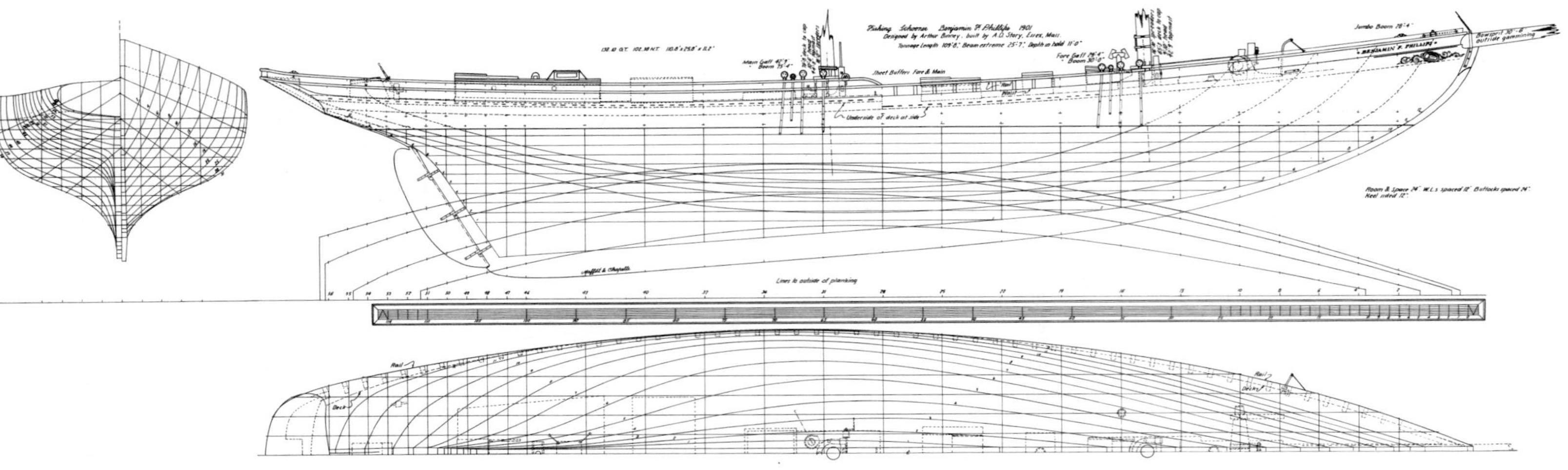
Fishing Schooner Benjamin F. Phillips 1901
Designed by Arthur Binney, built by A.D. Story, Essex, Mass.
Tonnage Length 109'8," Beam extreme 25'7," Depth in hold 11'0"
138.10 G.T. 102.38 N.T. 110.8' x 25.8' x 11.2'
Main Gaff 40'9"
" Boom 75'4"
Sheet Buffers Fore & Main
Fore Gaff 28'4"
" Boom 30'0"
Jumbo Boom 28'4"
Bowsprit 30'-8" outside gammining
BENJAMIN F. PHILLIPS
Underside of deck at side
Rail
Waist
Room & Space 24" W.L.s spaced 12" Buttocks spaced 24"
Keel sided 12"
Lines to outside of planking
Rail
Deck

PLATE 92. *Benjamin F. Phillips*, 1901, plan

these would be 109′-8″ x 25′.7″ x 11.0′. There is a fine rigged scale model of this schooner in the Peabody Museum of Salem, that was made for Arthur Binney.

The *Benjamin F. Phillips* had a graceful sheer, the keel rabbet was straight from the sternpost to underneath the forecastle ventilating hatch with heavy drag faired in a strong sweep into the curved stem rabbet. The fore overhang thus formed was short. The sternpost raked sharply, the counter was partly submerged, rather short and had the deadrise carried to a much-raked, elliptical transom, heavily curved athwartship. The entrance was long, sharp, without hollow. The run began under the mainmast and had some straight in the buttocks near the tuck. The midsection showed a hollow floor carried well outboard, a rather slack turn of bilge, and almost no tumble home in the topside. The *Phillips* had the reputation of being a fast sailer as well as a handy vessel.

The *Ida S. Brooks* (Plate 93) was built by Hugh Bishop at Gloucester in 1901. The designer is unknown but probably was Irving. The register dimensions were 80.0′ x 21.6′ x 8.6′. She was 90′-1″ moulded length at rail cap, 20′-11″ moulded beam, and 10′-0″ moulded depth at side. She had a handsome sheer, a straight keel rabbet with some drag from sternpost to under the mainmast, then carried forward in a long, gentle sweep to the stem rabbet which was curved and raking. A slight swan-breasted cutwater

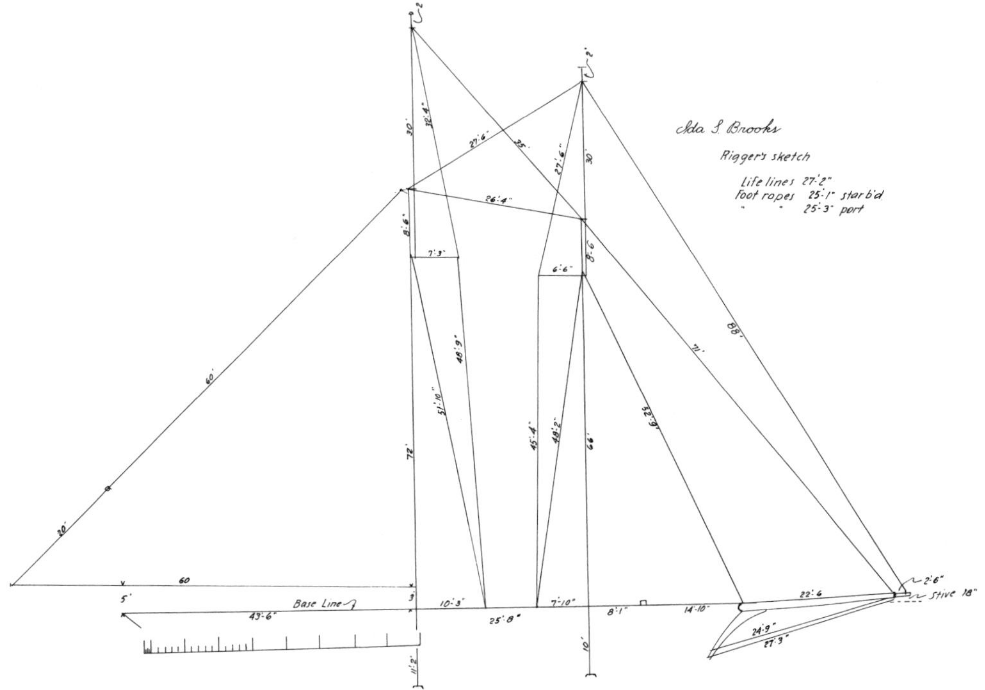
Ida S. Brooks
Rigger's sketch
Life lines 27'2"
Foot ropes 25'1" starb'd
" " 25'3" port
Base Line
Stive 18"

FIGURE 17

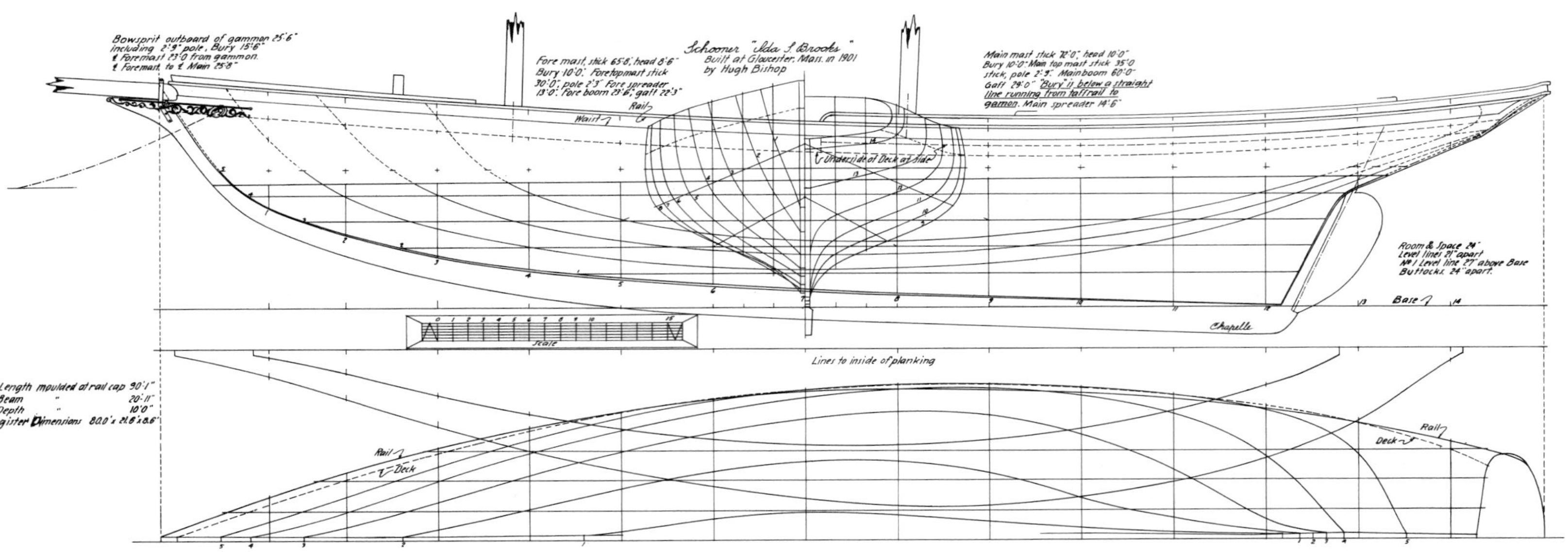
Bowsprit outboard of gammon 25'6"
including 2'9" pole, Bury 15'6"
℄ Foremast 23'0 from gammon.
℄ Foremast to ℄ Main 25'8"
Fore mast, stick 65'8", head 8'6"
Bury 10'0". Foretopmast stick
30'0", pole 2'3" Fore spreader
13'0". Fore boom 23'6", gaff 22'3"
Schooner "Ida S. Brooks"
Built at Gloucester, Mass. in 1901
by Hugh Bishop
Main mast stick 72'0", head 10'0"
Bury 10'0" Main top mast stick 35'0
stick, pole 2'9". Mainboom 60'0"
Gaff 29'0" "Bury" is below a straight
line running from taffrail to
gamon. Main spreader 14'6"
Rail
Waist
Underside of Deck at side
Room & Space 24"
Level lines 21" apart
No 1 Level line 27" above Base
Buttocks 24" apart.
Base
Scale
Chapelle
Lines to inside of planking
Length moulded at rail cap 90'1"
Beam " 20'11"
Depth " 10'0"
Register Dimensions 80.0' x 21.6' x 8.6'
Rail
Deck
Rail
Deck

PLATE 93. *Ida S. Brooks*, 1901, mould loft plan

with billet, scroll, iron headrail with iron strap brace athwartship, was employed; the sternpost raked sharply, and the counter was rather long with the tuck well submerged ending in a sharply raking, elliptical transom. The entrance was long, very sharp with a slight hollow in the forefoot. The run began under the mainmast with marked straight in the buttocks. The midsection had hollow in the garboard with the floor sharply rising and carried well outboard. The bilge was firm with no tumble home in the topside until abaft the mainmast. The *Ida S. Brooks* was a successful vessel and was considered a very handsome schooner.

Plate 94 was a design drawn April 23, 1901, by Thomas F. McManus for a large fishing schooner. The schooner *Lizzie M. Stanley* was built from this design by Tarr and James at Essex. Register dimensions were 103.0′ x 24.8′ x 10.0′; 116′-4″ moulded length at rail cap, 23′-8″ moulded beam, and 12′-0″ moulded depth at side scaled dimensions.

McManus designed few schooners with the gammon knee cutwater, preferring the rounded bow profile. He was not a very good draftsman at this time and later, during his active years, often employed students or apprentice draftsmen in preparing a design. Only lines drawings, on ⅜″ = 1′-0″ scale, offset tables and ⅛″ = 1′-0″ scale sail plans were furnished; the usual fee was $25.00. In the case of the *Lizzie M. Stanley* the drafting was poor, with some inaccurate fairing or projections, for McManus had not had enough practice to be accurate in preparing lines plans. Among the marine draftsmen apprentices McManus employed was Walter J. McInnis, who later was partner in the well-known Boston firm of naval architects, Eldredge and McInnis, Inc.

The *Lizzie M. Stanley* had a rather straight sheer, and a straight keel rabbet from the sternpost to under the mainmast, then sweeping up to a shallow but marked forefoot, thence it faired into a strongly flaring stem rabbet. The cutwater was of moderate length, having a stylized eagle head from which the scroll carried aft to abaft the hawse casting. Iron headrails and athwartship metal braces were employed. The sternpost raked strongly, the counter was of the *Fredonia* form, with a rather large, strongly raking U-shaped transom. The horn timber faired into the transom ℄, *Fredonia* fashion. The keel shoe rockered its full length, from sternpost to forefoot. This fashion, taken from yachts, caused some accidents in hauling out on marine railways, the rocker permitting a schooner to "fall down" forward after she came out of the water on the marine railway carriage. This movement sometimes knocked out the bilge blocks, allowing the vessel to fall sideways as well. Hence the rockered-keel-and-shoe fashion had a short period of popularity, beginning in Edward Burgess' time (1887–1891) and ending about 1903–1904. Crowninshield had reintroduced the straight keel shoe, with angular break in the profile forward—again an adap-

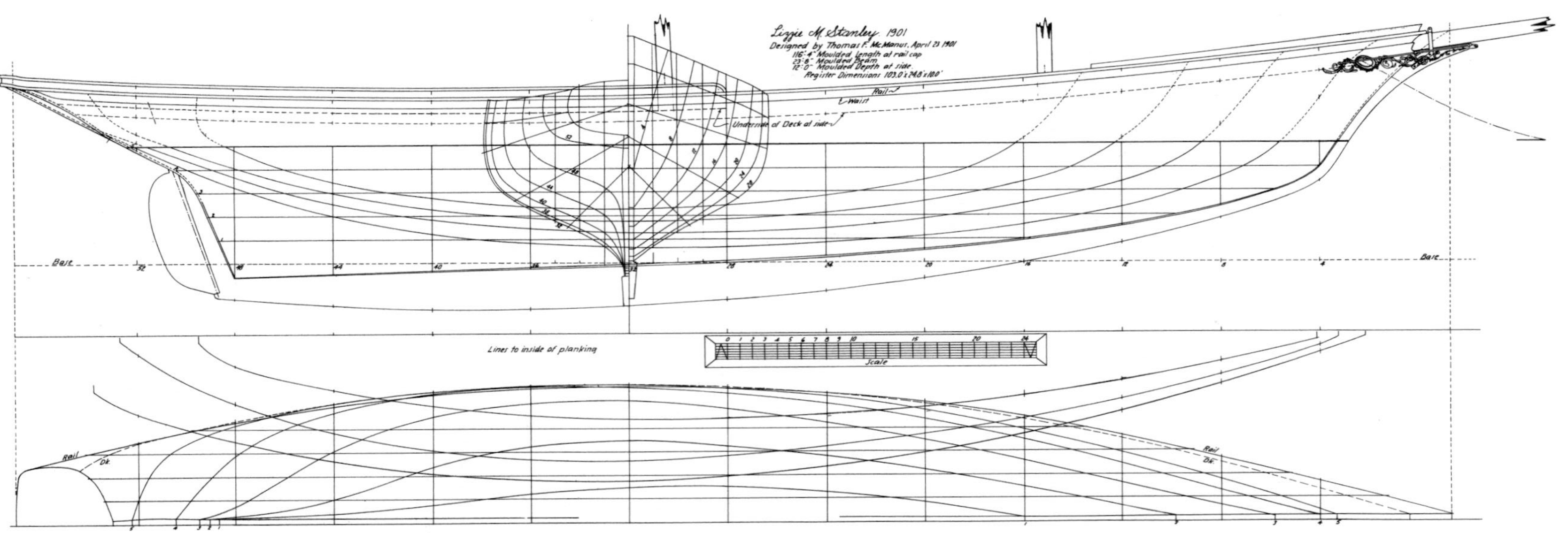
Lizzie M. Stanley 1901
Designed by Thomas F. McManus; April 23 1901
116'4" Moulded length at rail cap
23'8" Moulded Beam
12'0" Moulded Depth at side.
Register Dimensions 103.0' x 24.8' x 10.0'
Rail
Waist
Underside of Deck at side
Base
Lines to inside of planking
Scale
Rail
Dk.

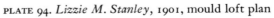

PLATE 94. *Lizzie M. Stanley*, 1901, mould loft plan

tion of yacht design practice—in 1900 in the *Rob Roy*. The Crowninshield profile became known as the "fisherman profile" in yachts of the 1920s.

The entrance of the *Lizzie M. Stanley* was long, sharp, and nearly convex. The run was rather short, full, and with very little straight length to the buttocks. The midsection had a slightly hollow floor rising sharply and carried well outboard, a high, easy bilge with very slight tumble home in the topside. The forebody of this vessel seems pinched-in at the planksheer and at the main rail, an undersirable feature affecting dryness on deck when on the wind. If a vessel developed a reputation for being wet and uncomfortable she became difficult to man and was usually sold out of the New England fisheries within a couple of years.

The McClain-designed schooner *Victor* is shown in Plate 95. She was the second large schooner in the New England fisheries to be fitted with an auxiliary gasoline engine when building. The first was the *Helen Miller Gould*, also a McClain model. The *Victor*, built by Tarr and James at Essex, was launched in March 1901. Some of the early vessels fitted with auxiliary engines had their shafts and propellers off-center alongside the sternposts with the wheel well up in the tuck. However, very early in the installation of power in fishing schooners, two sternposts were used, with the propeller aperture between them formed with blocking above and below the aperture. The rudder was hung on the after post, known in the

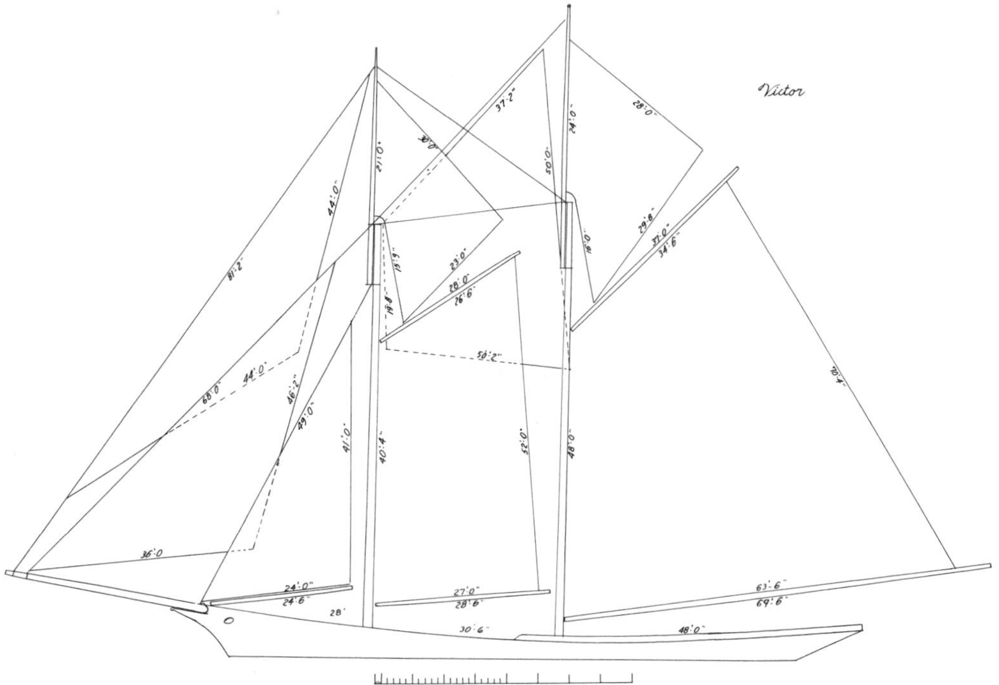
Victor

FIGURE 18

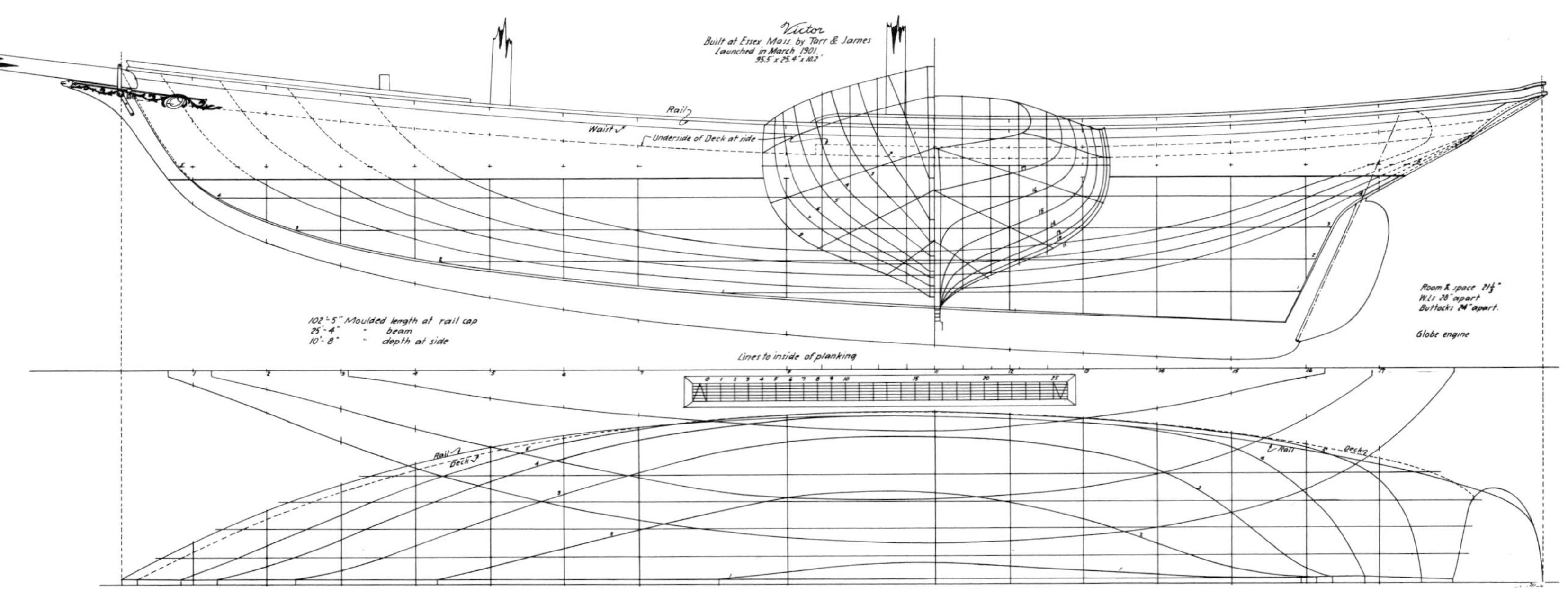
Victor
Built at Essex Mass. by Tarr & James
Launched in March 1901.
95.5' x 25.4' x 10.2'
Rail
Wait
Underside of Deck at side
102'-5" Moulded length at rail cap
25'-4" " beam
10'-8" " depth at side
Lines to inside of planking
Room & space 21½"
W.Ls 28" apart
Buttocks 24" apart.
Globe engine
Rail
Deck
Rail
Deck

PLATE 95. *Victor*, 1901, mould loft plan

Essex yards as the "prick post." It has not been determined how the *Victor*'s propeller and shaft were fitted.

The true sailing qualities of the auxiliary schooners, fitted with engines when launched, could not be ascertained due to the drag of the propeller. The early installations were often faulty. Some had inadequate engine beds resulting in misalignment and failures in the thrust bearings and stuffing boxes. There were also gasoline fires and explosions, causing loss of some vessel property and of life. Nevertheless, the advantages of auxiliary power were obvious. From 1901 on, the number of engines installed steadily increased. For a time, the unrealiability of the gasoline engine installations delayed the development of all-power fishing vessels. Steam fishing vessels were tried in the 1880s and '90s, but were found to be uneconomical in the then existing North Atlantic fisheries. The gradual conversion of the bulk of the fishing schooners to auxiliaries evenutally led to the increasing suppression of sail, with the engine becoming the paramount propulsion by 1925. The complete suppression of sail followed the introduction of the heavy oil engines and the appearance of the diesel trawlers and seiners after 1930, though a "riding sail" was utilized in some vessels well into the 1930s.

The early installations in auxiliaries were attempts to employ engines in schooners with minimum changes in sailing hull forms, and with full sail power. The result was a relatively expensive vessel in which the employment of full sail power alone, or the employment of engine power alone, would leave expensive sources of power unemployed. In this rspect, the auxiliary fishing schooner followed a course that had been fully explored in auxiliary merchant vessels, which had proven to be uneconomical in earlier years.

The *Victor* was designed as a full sail-powered vessel having the following register dimensions: 95.5′ x 25.4′ x 10.2′; she was 102′-6″ moulded length at rail cap, 25′-4″ moulded beam, and 10′-7½″ moulded depth at side. She had much sheer, a straight keel rabbet from the sternpost to about under the great beam, and rockered from there foreward, fairing into a shallow cutaway forefoot and strongly raking and curved stem rabbet. Her entrance was long and very sharp with some hollow just abaft the stem. The run was rather short but with some straight to the buttocks. Her midsection shows some hollow in the garboards, strongly rising, curved floor, well-rounded bilge, and much tumble home in the topside. Fig. 18 shows the sailmaker's plan of her rig, which was a powerful one. With her beam, she would have been a very stiff vessel under sail.

Thomas F. McManus spent much of his spare time around the fish piers in the 1890s as his interest in the improvement of fishing schooners increased. Stories of fishermen lost overboard in heavy weather were often heard on the piers, many being washed off the bowsprits when the footropes parted or sail stops broke. McManus noticed that in spite of the dangerous conditions inherent in working on the bowsprit, the footropes, back ropes, and sail stops were often in poor condition through lack of proper maintenance. The average fisherman was not a seaman trained in marlinspike seamanship, and the maintenance of rigging was usually attended to by professional riggers only when the vessels were fitting out, or after a failure in service—and the latter had to be critical. Hence, McManus thought it impractical to expect any important improvement in standing rigging maintenance.

In the 1890s some New England yachtsmen developed small keel sloops, with outside ballast, of a very seaworthy type in which there could be comfortable sailing even in rough water. These sloops often had very short bowsprits, or sometimes none at all. In a reaction against the lightly built, weak, and uncomfortable racers of the period, the seaworthy sloops attracted much attention. They were knicknamed "knockabouts," particularly those having no bowsprits.

This feature had been confined to small sailing craft but, in 1900, McManus saw it as a possible solution of the safety problem. He therefore pre-

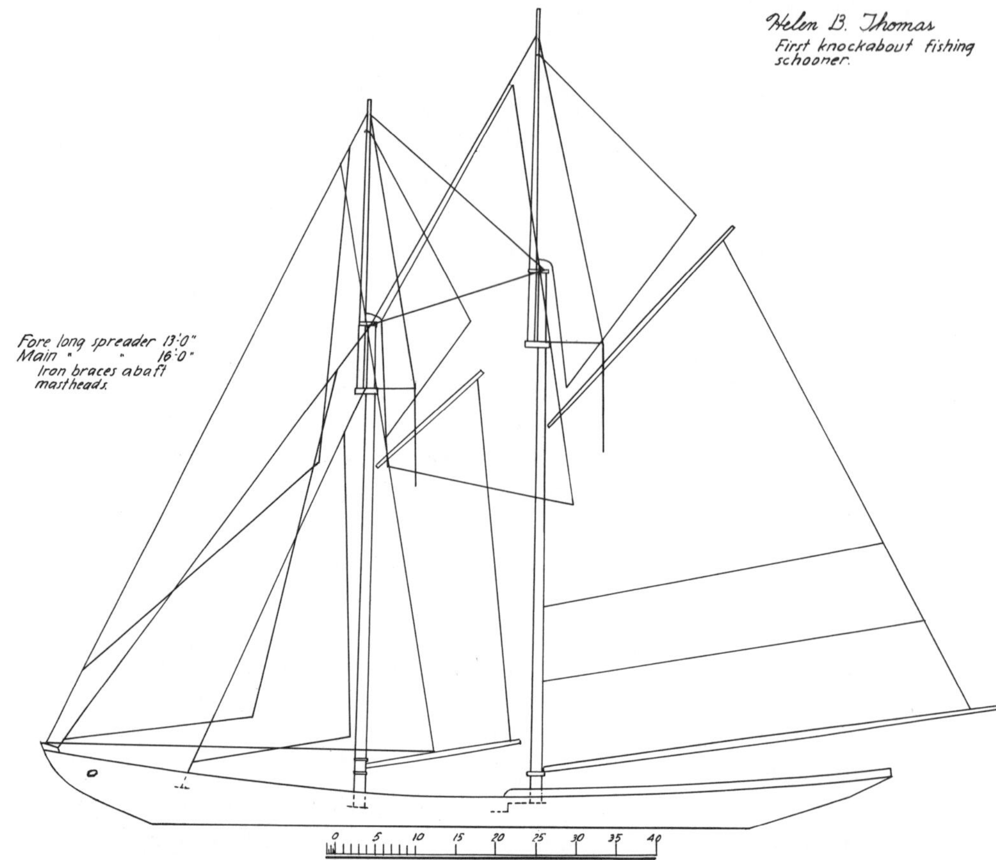
Helen B. Thomas
First knockabout fishing schooner.
Fore long spreader 13'0"
Main " " 16'0"
Iron braces abaft mastheads.
0 5 10 15 20 25 30 35 40

FIGURE 19

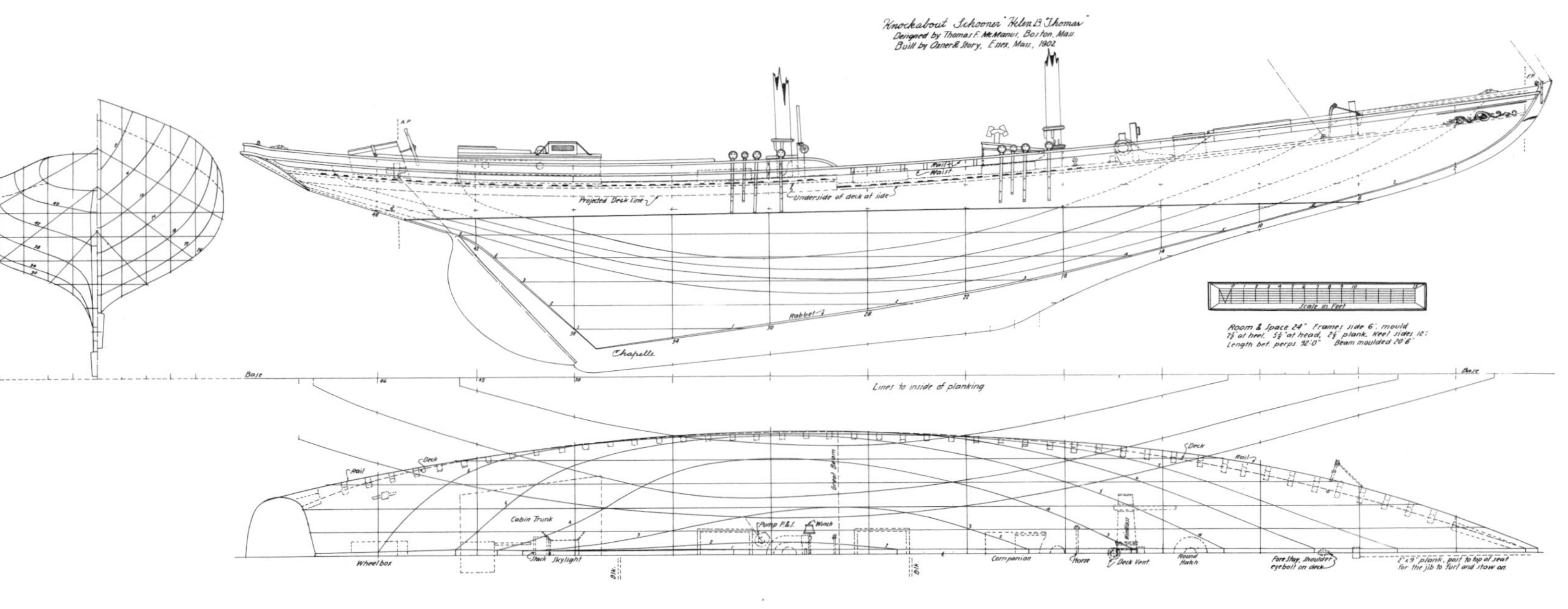
Knockabout Schooner "Helen B. Thomas"
Designed by Thomas F. McManus, Boston, Mass.
Built by Oxner & Story, Essex, Mass., 1902
Scale in Feet
Room & Space 24" Frames side 6", mould
7½" at heel, 5½" at head, 2½" plank. Keel sides 12"
Length bet. perps. 92'0" Beam moulded 20'6"
Projected Deck Line
Underside of deck at side
Rail
Waist
Rabbet
Chapelle
Base
Lines to inside of planking
Deck
Rail
Cabin Trunk
Wheelbox
Stack
Skylight
Blk.
Great Beam
Pump P.&S.
Winch
Companion
Horse
Deck Vent.
Windlass
Round Hatch
Fore Stay, Shoulder eyebolt on deck
2"x9" plank, post to top of seat for the jib to furl and stow on.

PLATE 96. *Helen B. Thomas*, 1901, plan

pared a design of a fishing schooner that had no bowsprit. Plate 96 shows this design. The design was really that of a fishing schooner, with the forebody drawn out forward to where the fore end of a bowsprit would be, so as to get the head stays far enough forward to give balance to the rig. He placed a half-model and the plans in the window of his office and tried to interest fishing vessel owners and skippers in this rather radical design. He argued that men were often washed off the bowsprit in heavy weather even when footropes were sound, and he also pointed out that the bowsprit was a prime nuisance in the slips and subject to damage. McManus found it very difficult to find anyone who would have a vessel built to the knockabout design until the fall of 1901. Then Captain William Thomas of Portland, Maine, and Cassius Hunt decided to have the knockabout built at Essex by Oxner and Story. She was built that winter, named the *Helen B. Thomas*, and launched in the spring of 1902. In building, McManus' plans were not followed in all respects. For instance, in the original design the heights of the bulwarks were least at stem and stern, reducing the amount of sheer at the main rail cap. In building, the bulwarks were of equal height for their whole length, spoiling the appearance of the vessel somewhat. This departure was corrected to some extent by trimming the vessel by the head.

The *Helen B. Thomas* was 105′-6″ moulded length at rail cap, 20′-6″ moulded beam, and 10′-1½″ moulded depth at side. Her register dimensions were 94.2′ x 21.6′ x 9.2′. According to her offsets she actually measured 92′-0″ between perpendiculars.

This vessel was a fast sailer and very handy. She was exceptionally quick in stays and was well balanced. She tacked in twenty to twenty-five seconds in smooth water.

The *Helen B. Thomas* had very marked sheer, a short, straight keel with much drag, and a very long fore rake. The sternpost raked sharply and the counter was long with a rather small transom. The stem had much overhang, strongly resembling the stem of many yachts of this period. The run was long with straight buttocks and the entrance was also long and somewhat convex. The midsection was formed with a little hollow in the garboard, rising curved floor, slack bilge, and some tumble home in the topside. The hull form was, in general, very yacht-like. Though the *Thomas* was entered in at least one fisherman race, she had only moderate success. The schooner fanciers at Boston and Gloucester claimed that she was not sailed very hard.

The knockabouts with long overhangs like those of the *Thomas*, had one rather serious handicap. By the very nature of their design they had small bodies for their length and their cost was greatly influenced by their overall length. Hence, for their hold capacity, they were structurally expensive schooners. This was apparently one of the chief causes for a rather slow increase in their number from 1902 to 1906.

An article on the *Thomas* was published in *Marine Engineering* magazine in 1902 (Vol. 17, June), from which the following specifications were taken: keel sided 12″; frames moulded 7½″ at heel and 5½″ at head, sided 6″ and spaced about 18″ ℄ to ℄. Plank 2½″ oak, treenailed; main deck beams 8″ x 8″ oak, crown about 4½″; half beams 6″ x 6″ oak, one between each pair of main beams. Deck 3″ x 5″, 60 tons of pig iron ballast. Cabin finished bright, about 11′-6″ to 11′-8″ in length; four berths. Forecastle extends to about 12′-0″ abaft the foremast; fifteen berths in two tiers, eight on portside and seven on the starboard side.

Fore and main shrouds, three on a side, wormed and parcelled, two served, 2¾″ circular iron wire, lanyards hemp of the same size or one size larger. Forestay or jumbo 3″ iron, jib stay 2¾″ iron, balloon jibstay 1½″ steel. Fore 2 main-topmast backstays or shrouds 1¾″ iron. Lanyards same size or one size larger. Preventer flying backstays 1½″ iron. Spring stays 2¾″ iron. Main-topmast stay, 1¾″ iron. Pull-back stay from fore-topmast 1¾″ iron. Pull-back stay from fore-topmast 1¾″ iron.

Mainsail and jib	No. 2 cotton duck
Foresail and jumbo	No. 1 cotton duck
Riding sail	No. 1 cotton duck
Fore and main topsails	No. 8 cotton duck
Balloon jib	6 oz. cotton duck
Fisherman staysail	8 oz. cotton duck

She carried her chain box on the starboard side of the fore companionway, and usually carried five dories on each side.

The schooner *Harriet W. Babson* (Plate 97) was designed by McClain and built in 1902 by Tarr and James at Essex. She was a burdensome schooner for a *Fredonia* type, and was an average performer, apparently at her best in strong winds. She only lasted about a year, being wrecked on Ram Island, near Boothbay, on January 18, 1903. Her register dimensions were 100.0′ x 25.0′ x 10.5′; she was 110′-7″ moulded length at rail cap, 24′-0″ moulded beam, and 10′-10″ moulded depth, from rabbet to underside of main deck at side, just forward of the great beam.

The *Babson* had a graceful, rather strong sheer, the keel rabbet was straight from sternpost forward to about midlength, having moderate drag, and was rockered forward to fair into a cutaway forefoot, and a curved, raking stem rabbet. The sternpost rabbet had much rake and the counter, partly submerged, was long, ending in a raking, elliptical transom. The

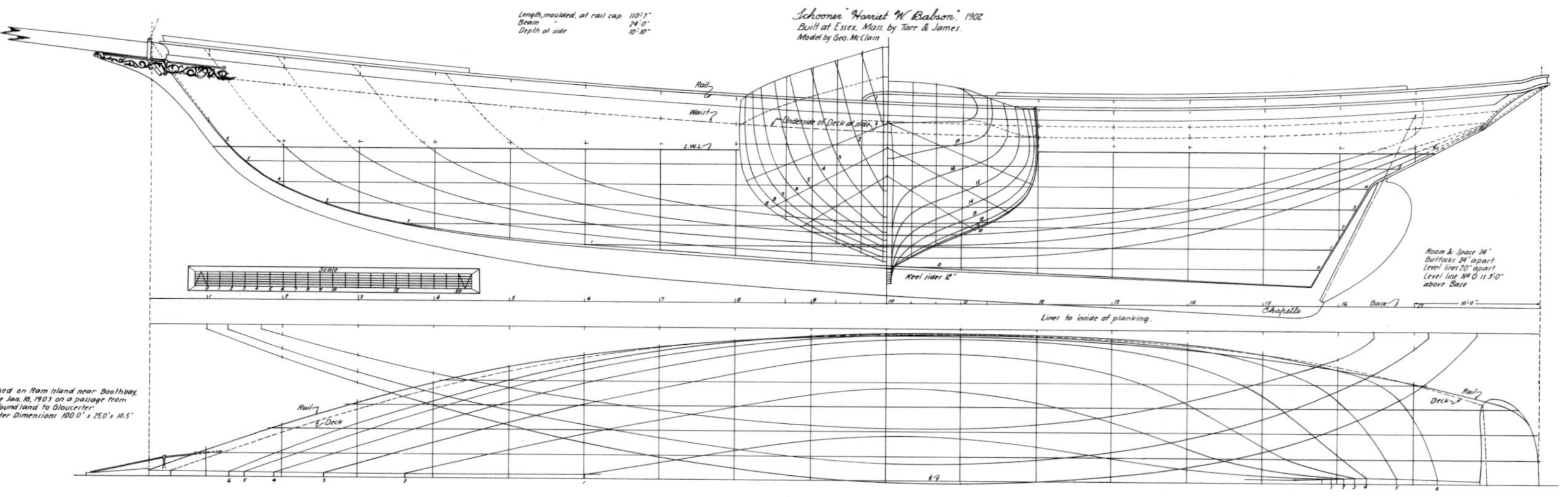
Schooner "Harriet W. Babson" 1902
Built at Essex, Mass. by Tarr & James.
Model by Geo. McClain
Length, moulded, at rail cap 110'-7"
Beam " 24'-0"
Depth at side 10'-10"
Rail
Waist
Underside of Deck at side
L.W.L.
Keel sides 12"
Scale
Lines to inside of planking.
Chapelle
Base
10'-0"
Room & Space 24"
Buttocks 24" apart
Level lines 20" apart
Level line No 0 is 3'-0" above Base
Wrecked on Ram Island near Boothbay, Maine Jan. 18, 1903 on a passage from Newfoundland to Gloucester.
Register Dimensions 100.0' x 25.0' x 10.5'
Rail
Deck

PLATE 97. *Harriet W. Babson*, 1902, half-model

keel shoe was rockered its full length in the current fashion. The entrance was long, sharp, and slightly convex. The run was long and fine, with very little straight in the buttocks. The midsection was formed with a rising, almost straight floor (there was, in fact, an almost imperceptible hollow in the midsection floor), full well-rounded turn of bilge with some tumble home in the topside.

The *Babson,* when compared with many of McClain's designs, again shows how the *Fredonia* type could be manipulated to produce either a fast carrier or a fast sailer.

The schooner *Benjamin W. Latham* was a good example of McManus' work in 1902 (Plate 98). This vessel was designed for a Noank, Connecticut, owner and was built at Essex by Tarr and James in 1902–1903. She had marked sheer, keel rabbet straight from sternpost to under the midsection, with moderate drag. Forward of the midsection the keel rabbet curved upward to the well-rounded stem rabbet. The sternpost had much rake and the counter was long, partly submerged, with a narrow, sharply raking elliptical transom. The bottom of the keel was straight, from a little forward of the sternpost, with some drag, the fore end being nearly under the foremast heel. Here a gripe was formed and the stem was then carried forward and upward to form an Indian Head, or round stem. This keel form gave

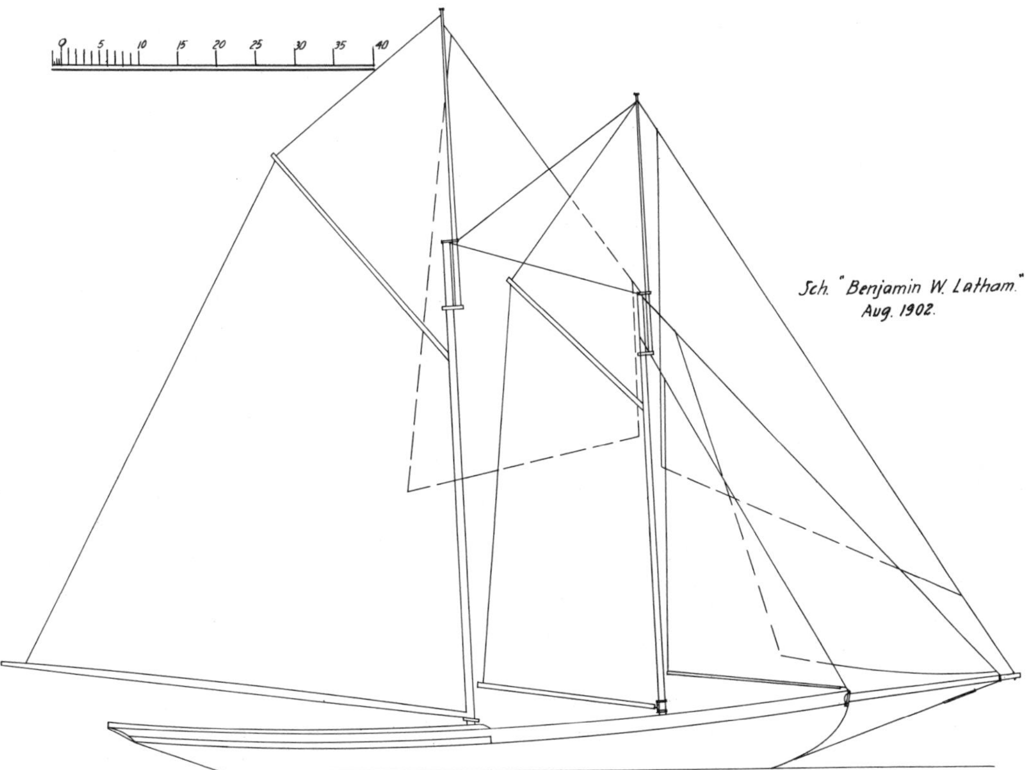
0 5 10 15 20 25 30 35 40
Sch. "Benjamin W. Latham"
Aug. 1902.

FIGURE 20

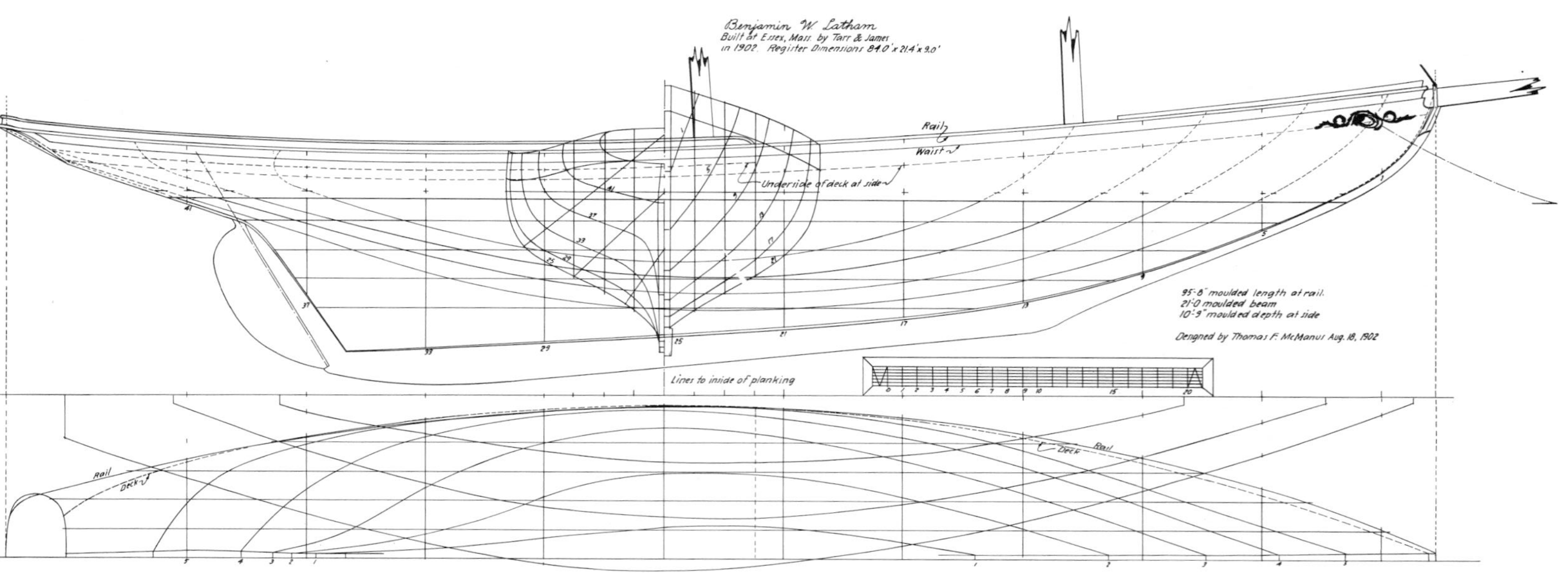
Benjamin W. Latham
Built at Essex, Mass. by Tarr & James
in 1902. Register Dimensions 84.0' x 21.4' x 9.0'
Rail
Waist
Underside of deck at side
95'-8" moulded length at rail.
21'-0 moulded beam
10'-9" moulded depth at side
Designed by Thomas F. McManus Aug. 18, 1902
Lines to inside of planking
Rail
Deck
Rail
Deck

PLATE 98. *Benjamin W. Latham*, 1902, plan

all the advantages claimed for the rockered keel but without the hauling difficulties that were described earlier. It appears to have been a form introduced in 1900 by the Boston naval architect Bowdoin B. Crowninshield, whose work will be examined shortly. The *Latham* had a sharp, convex entrance and a well-formed run with markedly straight buttocks. The midsection showed slightly hollow, sharply rising floor, a high and somewhat hard bilge, and sight tumble home in the topside. The *Latham*'s register dimensions were 84.0′ x 21.4′ x 9.0′, and she was 95′-8″ moulded length at rail cap, 21′-0″ moulded beam, and 10′-9″ moulded depth at side. According to her designer, this vessel was intended for fast sailing.

Plate 99 is the lines of the *Emily Cooney*, built at Essex by Oxner and Story in 1902; register dimensions were 77.6′ x 21.0′ x 9.4′. She was 89′-5″ moulded length at rail cap, 21′-6″ moulded beam, and 10′-11″ moulded depth at side. The plan of this vessel seems to have been made by Archer Poland, the Essex loftsman. It was roughly drawn, using the "2-and-4-foot-out" buttocks often used by McManus and Poland in their lines plans. It is possible that this plan is a revision of a McManus design, but this may be unwarranted speculation. At any rate, the drawing of her lines shows a very handsome schooner having a graceful, strong sheer, well-rockered keel and keel rabbet, carried in a long sweep to a curved, raking stem having a very short bow overhang for the *Cooney*'s period. The sternpost raked sharply and the counter was long, partly submerged, with a small elliptical sharply raking transom. The entrance was sharp, long, and slightly convex. The run was rather short with straight buttocks. The midsection showed a slight hollow in the sharply rising floor, a slack, much-rounded bilge, and some tumble home in the topside. A number of McManus' designs from 1899 to 1906 showed the short bow overhang seen in the *Cooney*.

The sister schooners *Matchless* and *Flora Nickerson* (Plate 100) were Indian Headers built at Essex in 1902. These vessels were built by Tarr and James, the design was prepared by McManus in March 1902. The register dimensions were: *Matchless*, 93.7′ x 23.6′ x 10.6′; and *Flora Nickerson*, 94.3′ x 23.9′ x 10.6′. The design called for 93′-3″ tonnage length, 23′0″ moulded beam, and 11′-6″ moulded depth at side.

The plan shows a schooner having much sheer, with keel and keel rabbet rockered and having a curved stem of a form once called a "rater bow" because it was used in yachts belonging to classes or "rates." These yachts showed stem profiles having a slight knuckle and coming nearly straight and upright in profile, about as shown in the two schooners being described. The sternpost raked a good deal and the counter was partly submerged, with a very raking, heart-shaped transom. The entrance was long, sharp, and faintly convex. The run had straight buttocks and was fine and long.

Schooner "Emily Cooney"
Built at Essex, Mass. by Oxner and Story
in 1902. Register Dimensions 77.6' x 21.0' x 9.4'
89'-5" moulded length at rail cap.
21'-6" " beam
10'-11" " depth at side

Rail
Waist
Underside of Deck at side
Rabbet
Shoe
Chapelle
Base
Lines to Inside of planking
Deck
Rail

Designer unknown; plan found in the Poland mould loft.

Scale in Feet

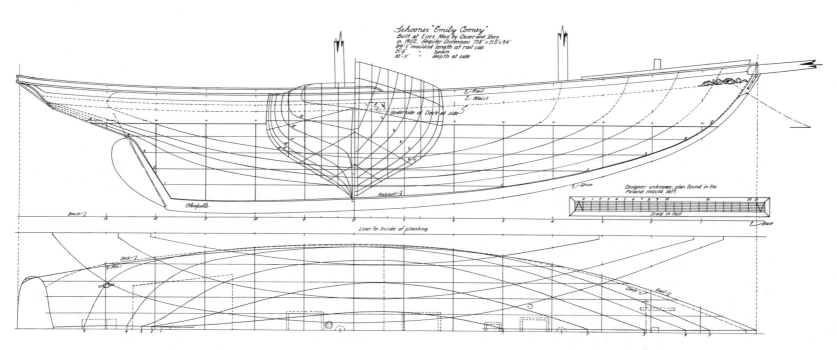

PLATE 99. *Emily Cooney*, 1902, mould loft plan

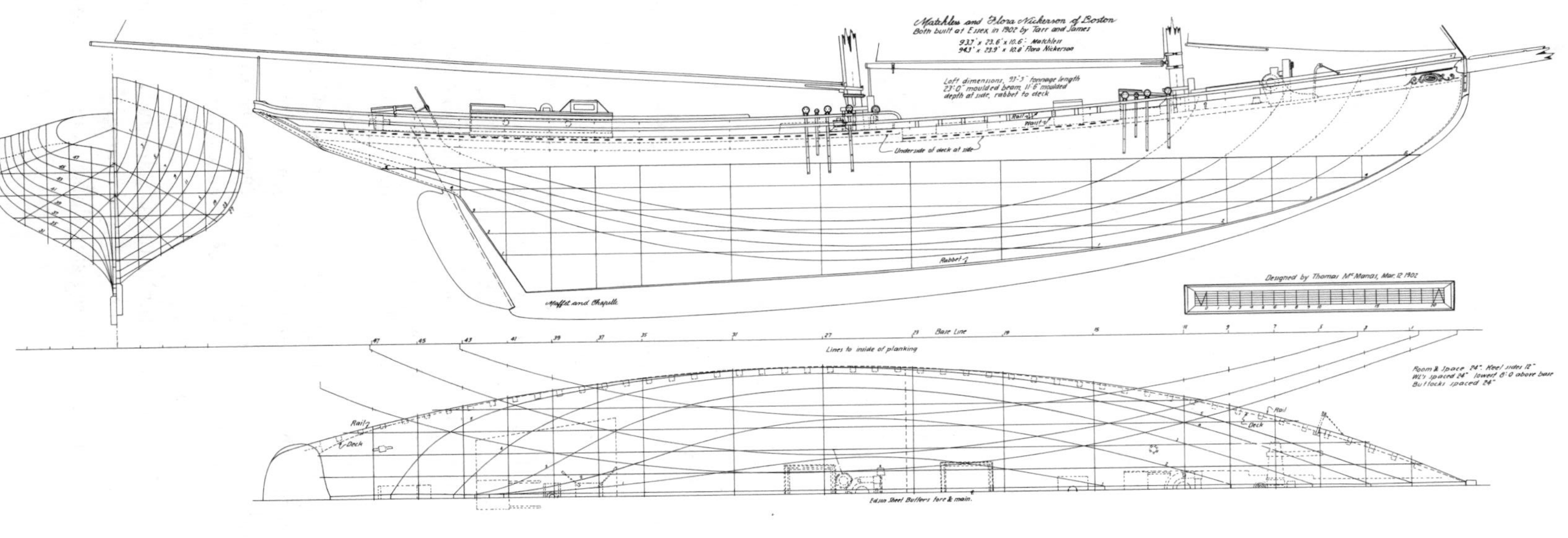
Matchless and Flora Nickerson of Boston
Both built at Essex in 1902 by Tarr and James
93.7' x 23.6' x 10.6' - Matchless
94.3' x 23.9' x 10.8' Flora Nickerson
Loft dimensions, 93'-3" tonnage length
23'-0" moulded beam 11'-6" moulded
depth at side, rabbet to deck
Rail
Waist
Underside of deck at side
Rabbet
Moffet and Chapelle
Designed by Thomas McManus, Mar. 12 1902
Base Line
Lines to inside of planking
Room & Space 24". Keel sides 12"
WL's spaced 24" lowest 6'-0 above base
Buttocks spaced 24"
Rail
Deck
Edson Steel Buffers fore & main.

PLATE 100. *Matchless*, *Flora Nickerson*, 1902, plan

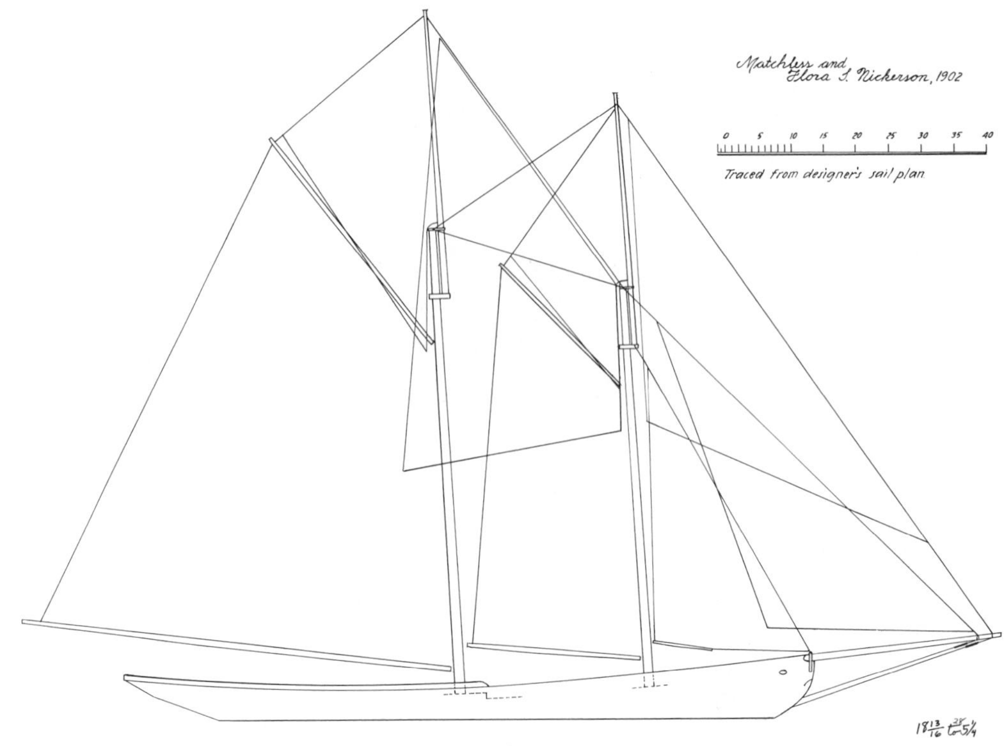
Matchless and Flora S. Nickerson, 1902
0 5 10 15 20 25 30 35 40
Traced from designer's sail plan

FIGURE 21

The midsection was formed with slightly hollow, strongly rising floor, a slack bilge, and some tumble home.

McManus' designs of fishing schooners known as Indian Headers first appeared in 1898. They were a series of designs for vessels having Indian names and round-bow profiles of the "rater" form, with short bow overhangs as trimmed in service. They all had spike bowsprits. Indian Headers included the schooners *Juniata*, *Mattakeesett*, *Samoset*, *Massasoit*, *Manomet*, *Tecumseh*, *Seaconnet*, *Squanto*, *Onato*, *Quannapowatt*, and *Manhasset*, all built between 1898 and 1904. By 1904 a great many schooners having Indian Heads had other names than those of Indian origin and the term went gradually out of use, though Indian names continued to appear in fishing schooners after 1904.

As early as 1902 McManus had begun to design vessels with well-rounded, slack bilges—in his large schooners, at least. This was to produce vessels that were not so stiff under sail in strong winds as to cause loss in spars, rigging, and sails. The club on the foot of the forestaysail of the schooners was a fad of short duration in the early 1900s.

Plate 101 shows the lines used to build three schooners: the *Avalon* in 1903, the *Hazel R. Hines* in 1904, and the *Arthur James* in 1905, all in the Tarr and James yard at Essex. The register dimensions were as follows:

Avalon, 100.0′ x 24.7′ x 10.4′; *Hazel R. Hines*, 101.0′ x 25.0′ x 10.8′; and the *Arthur James*, 103.4′ x 24.8′ x 10.6′. The design showed 111′-0″ moulded length at rail cap, 23′-4″ moulded beam, and 10′-6″ moulded depth at side. These beautiful schooners were modeled by George M. McClain. The *Arthur James* apparently had one frame added and she was entered in one Fisherman Race, having a reputation of being a very fast sailer. *Avalon* was run down and sunk off Highland Light, October 29, 1927.

These schooners had very moderate sheer, with straight keel rabbit from sternpost to a little forward of the great beam, rockered up forward to a shallow forefoot, and faired into a curved raking stem rabbet. The sternpost raked, with a rather short counter and a strongly raked, heart-shaped transom. The entrance was very sharp, slightly convex, and long. The run was very long and fine, with straight buttocks. The midsection had moderately hollow, sharply rising floor, very slack and easy turn of bilge, and very little tumble home in the topside. Like many fishing schooners built from 1900 to 1905, the gammon knee and billet or eagle-head cutwaters were fitted to these vessels.

The difficulty of judging the speed and performance of fishing schooners is shown in the sister ships *Cavalier* and *Lucania* (Plate 102). The design for these vessels was made by McManus, and is dated December 9, 1903. The *Cavalier* was built at Essex in 1904 by Tarr and James; her register dimensions were 105.2′ x 25.0′ x 11.2′. The *Lucania* was built at Gloucester

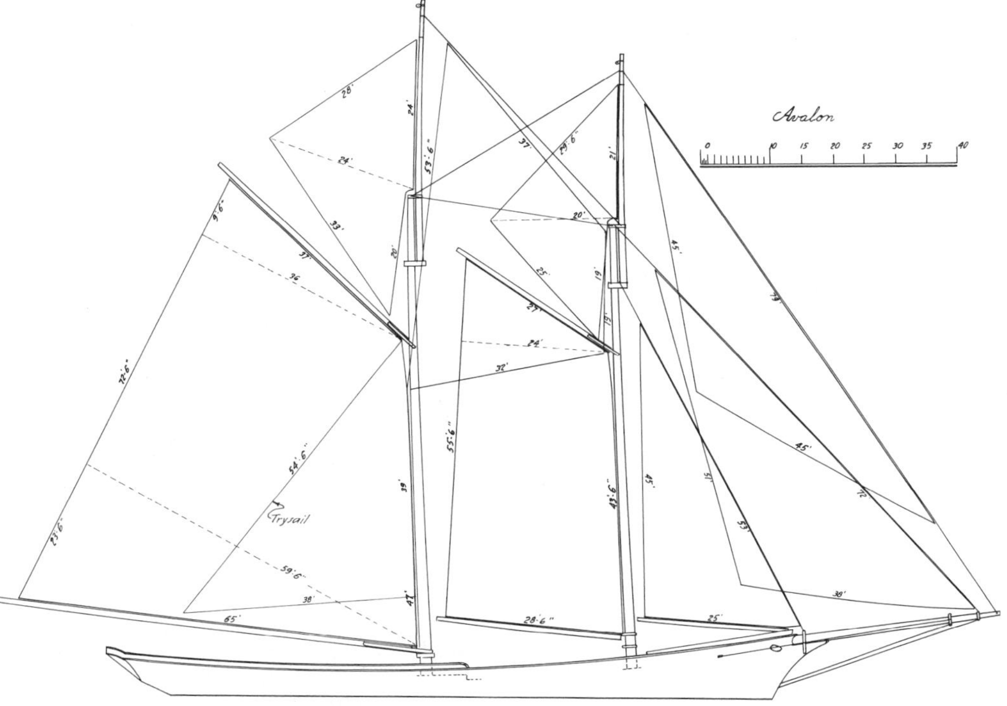
Avalon
0 10 15 20 25 30 35 40
Trysail

FIGURE 22

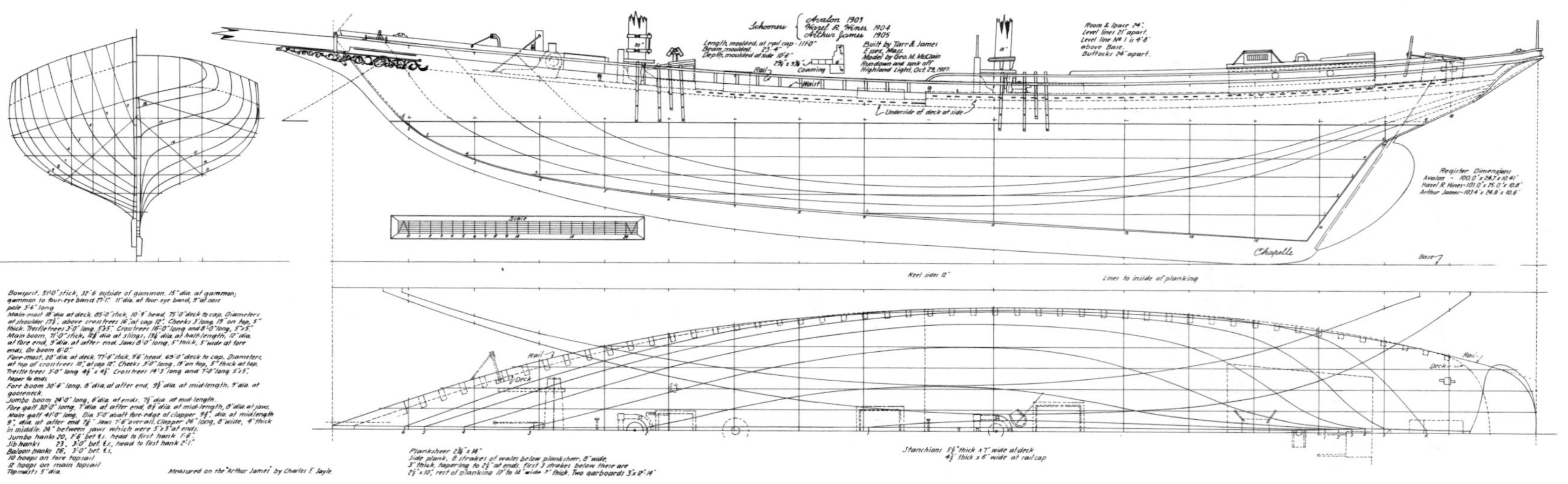
Schooners { Avalon 1903 / Hazel R. Hines 1904 / Arthur James 1905
Length, moulded, at rail cap - 111'0"
Beam, moulded. 23'-4"
Depth, moulded at side 10'6"
Built by Tarr & James
Essex, Mass.
Model by Geo. M. McClain
Rundown and sunk off
Highland Light, Oct. 29, 1927.
Room & Space 24".
Level lines 21" apart.
Level line No 1 is 4'-8"
above Base.
Buttocks 24" apart.
Rail
Coaming
Waist
Underside of deck at side
Register Dimensions
Avalon - 100.0' x 24.7 x 10.41'
Hazel R. Hines - 101.0' x 25.0' x 10.8'
Arthur James - 103.4' x 24.8' x 10.6'
Scale
Chapelle
Base
Keel sides 12"
Lines to inside of planking
Rail
Deck
Bowsprit. 51'-0" stick, 32'-6 outside of gammon. 15" dia. at gammon; gammon to four-eye band 27'-1." 11" dia. at four-eye band, 9" at nose pole 3'-6" long
Main-mast 18" dia at deck, 85'-0" stick, 10'-9" head, 75'-0" deck to cap. Diameters at shoulder 17½", above crosstrees 16", at cap 12". Cheeks 3' long, 19" on top, 5" thick. Trestletrees 3'-0" long, 5"x5". Crosstrees 16'-0" long and 8'-0" long, 5"x5".
Main boom, 71'-0" stick, 12½" dia at slings, 13¼" dia. at half-length, 12" dia. at fore end, 9" dia. at after end. Jaws 8'-0" long, 5" thick, 5" wide at fore ends. On boom 6'-0."
Fore-mast, 20" dia. at deck, 77'-6" stick, 9'6" head, 69'-0" deck to cap. Diameters, at top of crosstrees 16", at cap 12". Cheeks 3'-0" long, 19" on top, 5" thick at top. Trestle trees 3'-0" long 4½" x 4½". Crosstrees 14'-3 long and 7'-0" long 5"x5", taper to ends.
Fore boom 30'-6" long, 8" dia. at after end, 9½" dia. at mid-length, 9" dia. at gooseneck.
Jumbo boom 24'-0" long, 6" dia. at ends, 7½" dia. at mid-length.
Fore gaff 30'-0" long, 7" dia. at after end, 8½" dia. at mid-length, 8" dia. at jaws.
Main gaff 41'-0" long. Dia. 5'-0" abaft fore-edge of clapper 9½", dia. at midlength 9", dia. at after end 7½". Jaws 7'-6" over-all. Clapper 26" long, 8" wide, 4" thick in middle. 24" between jaws which were 5"x5" at ends.
Jumbo hanks 20, 2'-6" bet. ℄s. head to first hank 1'-6".
Jib hanks 23, 3'-0" bet. ℄s., head to first hank 2'-1."
Baloon hanks 26, 3'-0" bet. ℄s.
10 hoops on fore topsail
12 hoops on main topsail
Topmasts 5" dia.
Measured on the "Arthur James" by Charles F. Sayle.
Planksheer 2¾" x 14"
Side plank, 8 strakes of wales below planksheer, 8" wide, 3" thick, tapering to 2½" at ends. first 3 strakes below these are 2½" x 10", rest of planking 12" to 14" wide 2" thick. Two garboards 3" x 12"-14"
Stanchions 5½" thick x 7" wide at deck
4½" thick x 6" wide at railcap

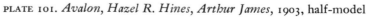

PLATE 101. *Avalon, Hazel R. Hines, Arthur James*, 1903, half-model

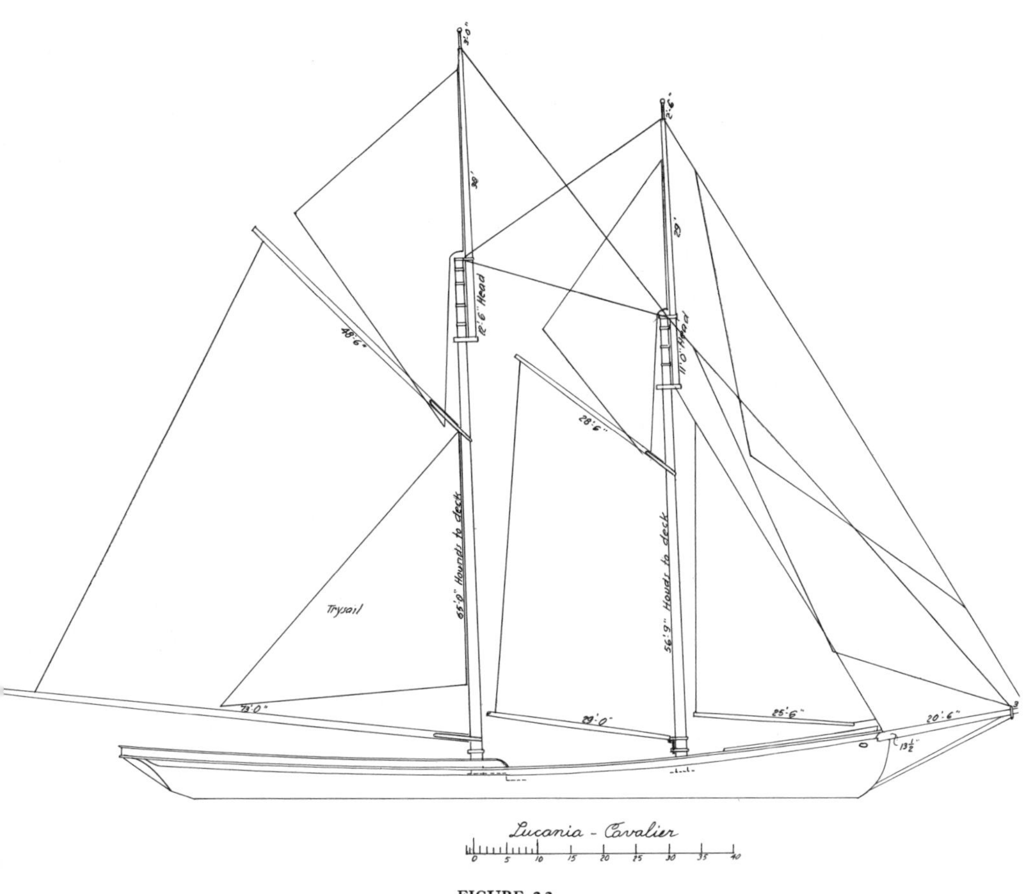
30'
29'
12'6" Head
11'0" Head
48'6"
28'6"
Trysail
65'9" Hounds to deck
56'9" Houds to deck
29'0"
25'6"
20'6"
Lucania - Cavalier
0 5 10 15 20 25 30 35 40

FIGURE 23

in 1904 by John Bishop; her register dimensions were 108.9′ x 25.0′ x 11.8′. They were to be 117′-2″ moulded length at rail cap, 24′-6″ moulded beam, and 12′-4″ moulded depth at side. It was claimed that the same moulds were used for both vessels. The *Cavalier* had a great reputation for catching fish but was not considered a very fast sailer. But the *Lucania* was given a reputation for being a very fast sailer. The rigs of these vessels were the same, except the masts of the *Lucania* were about two feet taller than those of *Cavalier*. The skipper of the *Lucania*, for much of her career, seems to have been a good sailor and helmsman. It is apparent that no sound judgment can be made of the relative speeds of these schooners, for there are too many factors that cannot be measured. In this case it might that *Lucania* was longer by one frame, as is suggested by the register dimensions. Next, there is the matter of the able master of the *Lucania*, probably no skipper of equal skill sailed the *Cavalier*. Finally there is the small extra power of *Lucania's* rig, produced by the loftier masts. Although there is no certainty that perfect, or near-perfect, hull form will insure a very fast sailer, in fact, a very good skipper was usually the deciding factor in establishing the reputation of a vessel for fast sailing.

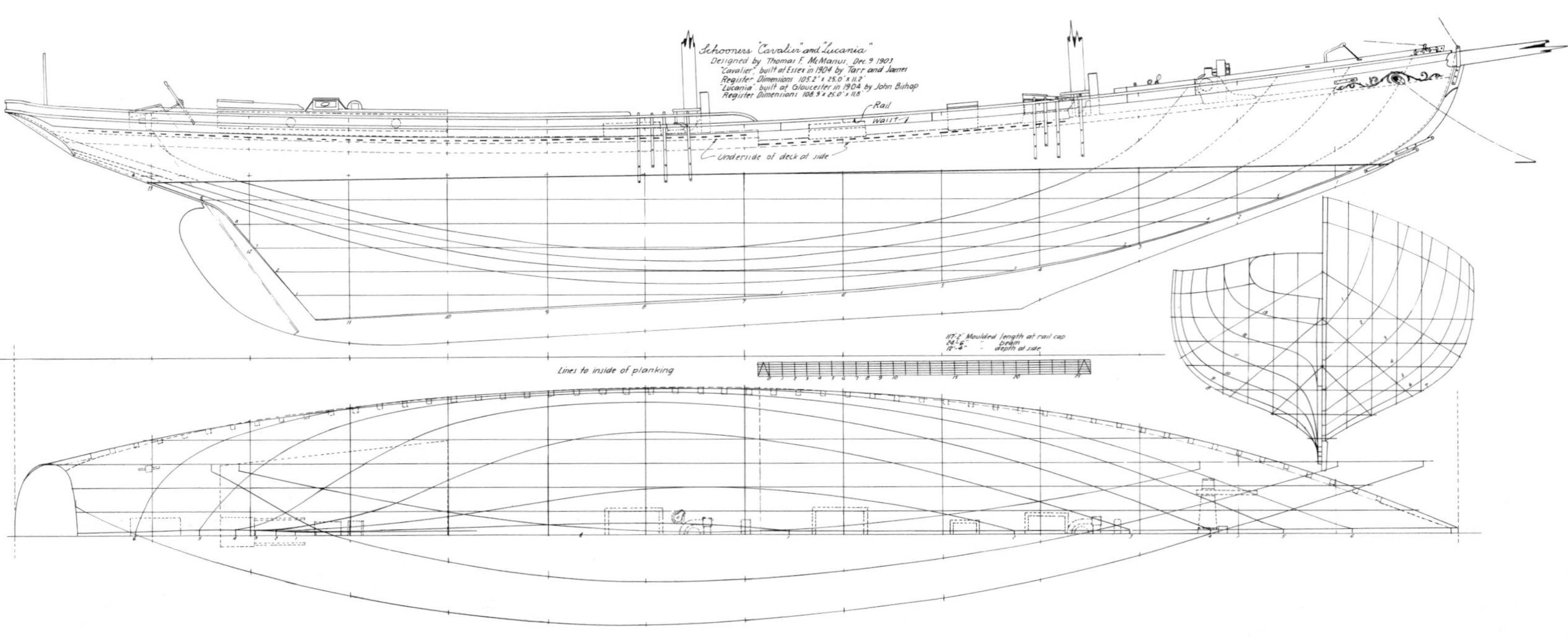
Schooners "Cavalier" and "Lucania"
Designed by Thomas F. McManus, Dec. 9 1903
"Cavalier", built at Essex in 1904 by Tarr and James
Register Dimensions 105.2' x 25.0' x 11.2'
"Lucania" built at Gloucester in 1904 by John Bishop
Register Dimensions 108.9' x 25.0' x 11.8'
Rail
Waist
Underside of deck at side
117'-2" Moulded length at rail cap
24'-6" " beam
12'-4" " depth at side
Lines to inside of planking

PLATE 102. *Lucania*, *Cavalier*, 1903, mould loft plan

The design of *Cavalier* and *Lucania* produced an Indian Header having marked sheer, straight keel rabbet from sternpost rabbet to about under the great beam, swept up forward to a curved stem having very short fore overhang. The sternpost rabbet raked sharply, and there was a rather long counter with a very raking elliptical transom. The entrance was long, sharp, and with a slight hollow in the upper part of the bow abaft the rabbet. The run was long and fine with straight in the buttocks. The midsection had hollow and sharply rising floor, easy, full-rounded bilge, and very little tumble home in the topside. This design shows the Crowninshield keel with deep gripe at fore end of the straight keel shoe.

The sister schooners *Nokomis* and *Lafayette* are shown in Plate 103; their model was the work of McClain. The *Nokomis* was built at Essex by Tarr and James in 1903, the *Lafayette* was built at Gloucester in the same year. The register dimensions of *Nokomis* were 57.0′ x 17.0′ x 7.2′, those of the *Lafayette* were 61.0′ x 17.2′ x 7.0′—two frame spaces having been added to the *Lafayette.* The model measured 60′-4″ moulded length at rail cap, 15′-10″ moulded beam, and 7′-4″ moulded depth at side. There can be no question as to the identity of the half-model of the *Nokomis* for it was in the James yard until the shipyard was burned, in the 1940s and the differences between register and model dimensions must be charged to careless measuring for register.

This design was for a small *Fredonia*-type schooner having a rather straight sheer, a straight keel rabbet from sternpost to under the great beam with little drag, then swept up forward to a shallow forefoot and to the raking and flaring stem rabbet. The cutwater was decorated with the eagle head and scroll. The keel shoe was straight from just forward of the sternpost to under the great beam, thence in a long sweep to the forefoot and stem profile. The sternpost had moderate rake, the counter was of the *Fredonia* type with a small, heart-shaped transom raked to the angle of the bottom of the counter. The entrance was long, very sharp, with some hollow abaft the stem rabbet. The run was of moderate length with short straight lines in the buttocks. The midsection showed hollow, sharply rising floor, a rather hard turn in the bilge, and tumble home in the topside. These handsome, small schooners were said to have sailed well; the *Nokomis* was lost at sea with all hands in a severe summer gale of hurricane force.

Plate 104 shows another clipper-bow fishing schooner designed by McManus in 1903, the *Ida M. Silva.* This schooner was of the *Fredonia* type; the register dimensions were 70.3′ x 19.7′ x 9.0′. She was built by Oxner and Story at Essex in 1903.

The firm of Oxner and Story was established in 1901 by Edwin H. Oxner, a Nova Scotian shipwright who had come to Essex in the 1890s and had married a local girl. His partner was a member of one of the Story families

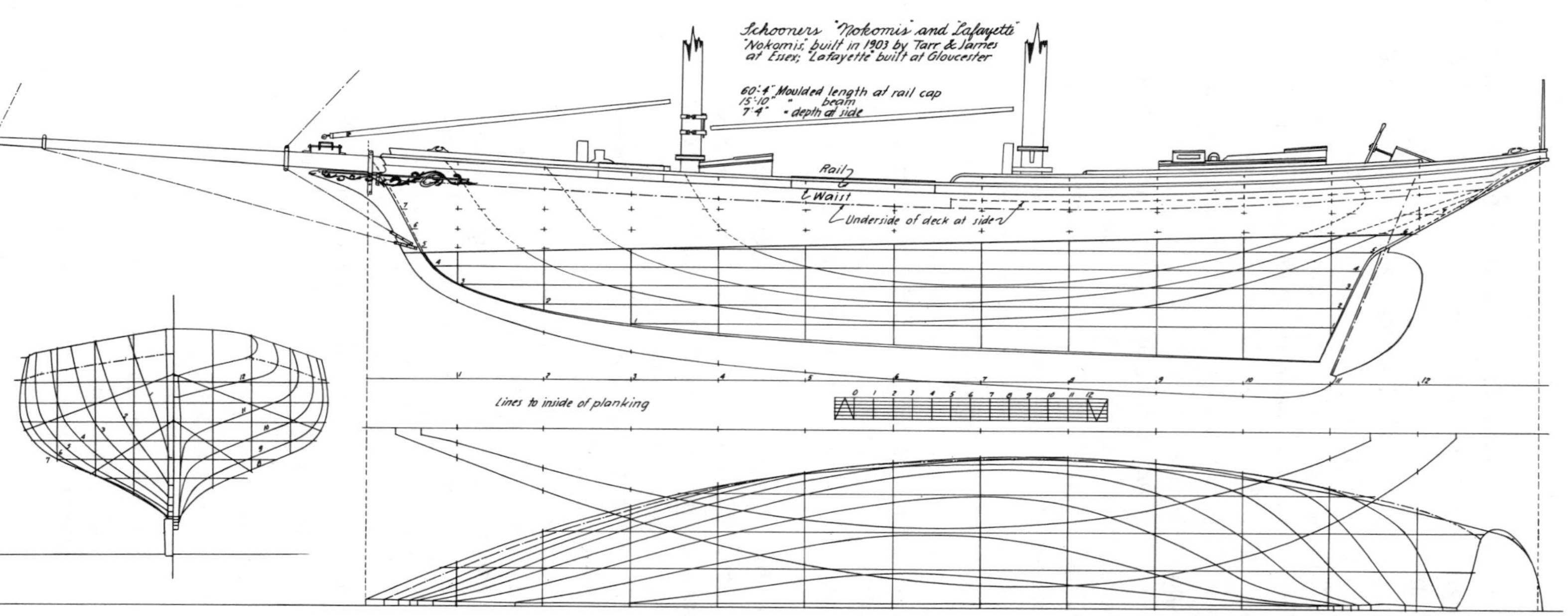
Schooners "Nokomis" and "Lafayette"
"Nokomis" built in 1903 by Tarr & James at Essex; "Lafayette" built at Gloucester
60'4" Moulded length at rail cap
15'10" " beam
7'4" " depth at side
Rail
Waist
Underside of deck at side
Lines to inside of planking

PLATE 103. *Nokomis*, *Lafayette*, 1903, mould loft plan

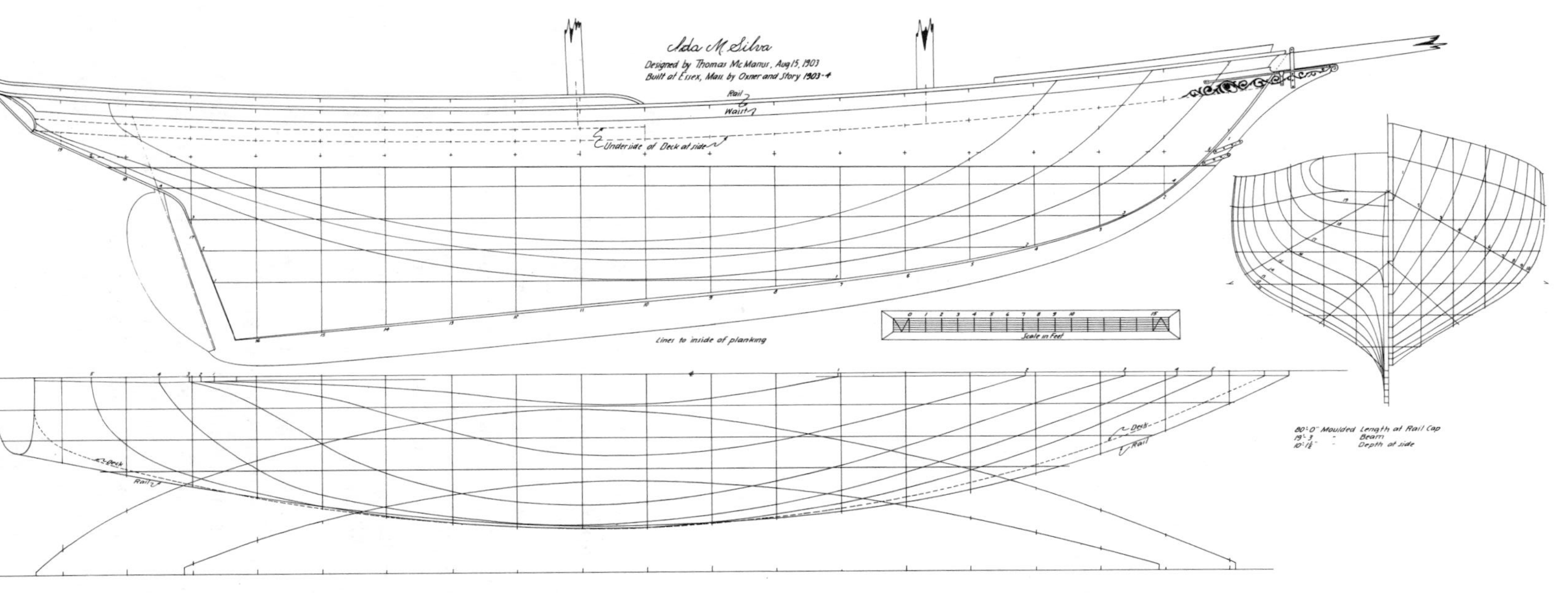
Ida M. Silva
Designed by Thomas McManus, Aug 15, 1903
Built at Essex, Mass by Oxner and Story 1903-4
Rail
Waist
Underside of Deck at side
Lines to inside of planking
Scale in Feet
Deck
Rail
80'0" Moulded Length at Rail Cap
19'3" - Beam
10'1½" - Depth at side

PLATE 104. *Ida M. Silva*, 1903, plan

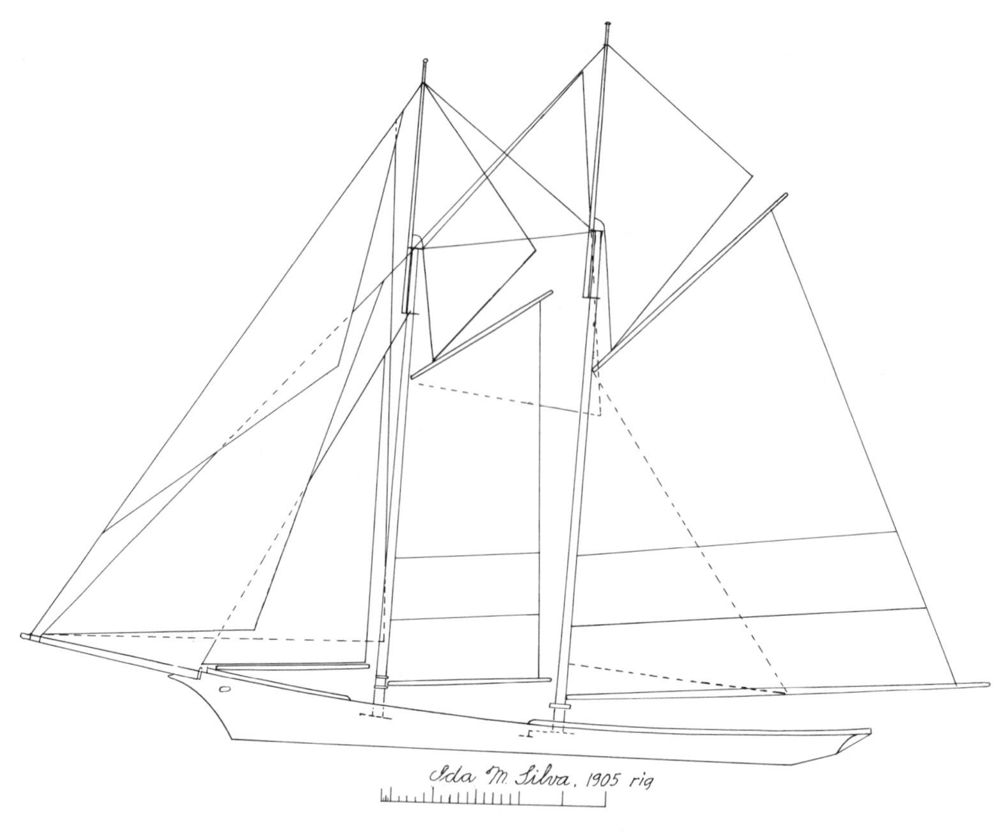
Ida M. Silva, 1905 rig

FIGURE 24

of Essex, a baker by trade. Between the year of founding, 1901, and the year of failure, 1907, the Oxner and Story yard built fifty-one vessels.

The *Ida M. Silva* had a strong sheer, a straight keel rabbet with much drag from the sternpost to about mid-length; from here it curved upward to a well-rounded forefoot and to a curved, raking stem rabbet. The sternpost had moderate rake, the counter was rather short and partly submerged. The transom was elliptical and moderately raked. The entrance was slightly convex and sharp, the run was short and with very little straight in the buttocks. The midsection had almost straight rise of floor with a very slight hollow. The bilge had an easy turn, and there was moderate tumble home in the topside. The *Silva* was said to have worked well and had about average speed under sail.

The McManus-designed schooner *Quannapowatt* (Plate 105) was an Indian Header built at Gloucester by Hugh Bishop during the winter of 1902–1903. She was representative of the popular McManus-designed schooners of her era: 108′-6″ moulded length at rail cap, 23′-2″ moulded beam, and 12′-1″ mould depth at side. Her register dimensions were 92.0′ x 23.6′ x 11.0′. This vessel had a strong sheer, rockered keel rabbet fairing into a long sweep into a short overhang round stem rabbet. The keel shoe faired

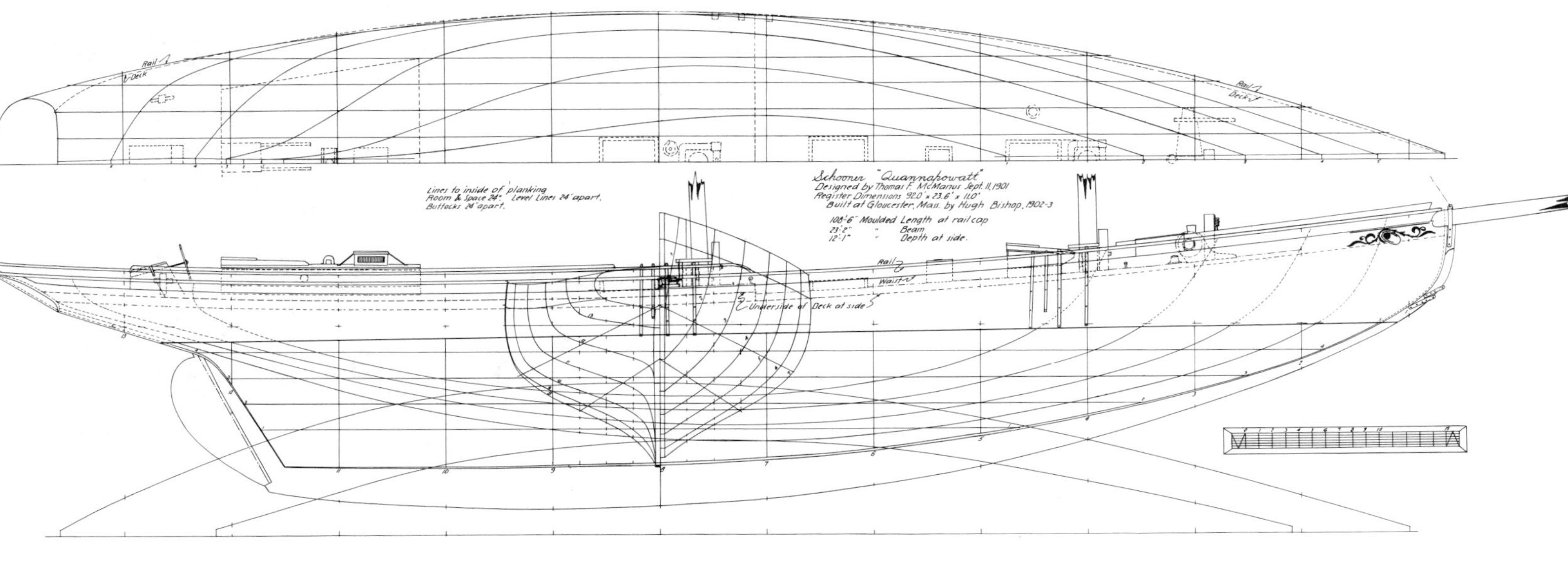
Rail
Deck
Rail
Deck
Lines to inside of planking
Room & Space 24". Level Lines 24" apart.
Buttocks 24" apart.
Schooner "Quannapowatt"
Designed by Thomas F. McManus Sept. 11, 1901
Register Dimensions 92.0' x 23.6' x 11.0'
Built at Gloucester, Mass. by Hugh Bishop, 1902-3
108'-6" Moulded Length at rail cap
23'-2" " Beam
12'-1" " Depth at side.
Rail
Waist
Underside of Deck at side

PLATE 105. *Quannapowatt*, 1903, plan

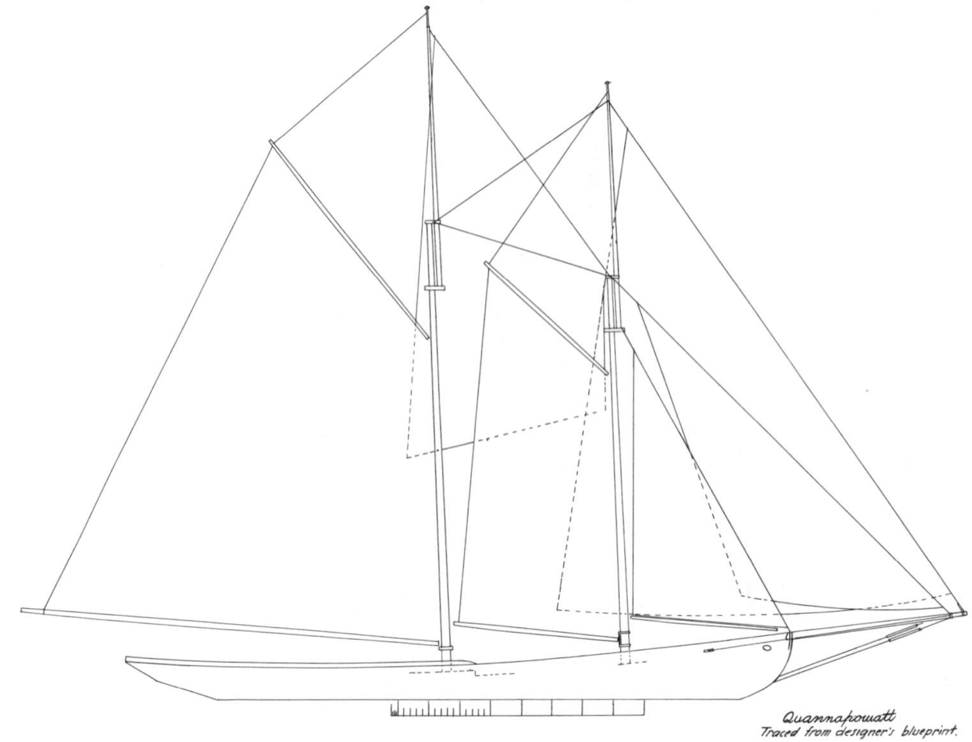
Quannapowatt
Traced from designer's blueprint.

FIGURE 25

into the face of the stem without a break. The sternpost raked strongly and the counter was long, rather light, and partly submerged. The elliptical transom was rather small and sharply raked. The entrance was very slightly convex, sharp, and long. The run was long, fine, and straight in the buttocks. Like most of the fishermen of this period, the *Quannapowatt* was trimmed a little by the head, compared to the trim shown in the designer's plan, with much less freeboard at deck amidships. The midsection showed sharply rising floor with very little hollow, an easy turn of the bilge, and tumble home in the topside.

In addition to Edward Burgess and Arthur Binney there was another yacht designer who influenced fishing schooner design. This was the Boston designer Bowdoin B. Crowninshield, a member of a prominent Boston family and a Harvard graduate. As a youngster he sailed the family's racing yachts and earned a reputation of being one of the leading racing helmsman.

In 1894 he had become so interested in yacht design that he went to work as draftsman for John R. Purdon, a well-known Boston yacht designer and builder. After working for Purdon for a year and a half, Crowninshield set up as a yacht designer and naval architect on January 1, 1897. Beginning with yacht design, he became interested in commercial vessel design. He was the designer of the only seven-masted schooner ever built, the *Thomas W.*

Lawson, and turned out plans for a number of other commercial schooner designs, including three-masters and one five-master. In addition, beginning in 1900 he produced seventeen fishing schooners designs from which at least thirty vessels were built. Crowninshield is best known in yachting history as the designer of Thomas W. Lawson's *America*'s Cup defender-candidate *Independence.* Though unsuccessful, her design exhibited much original thought and she showed great speed at times.

The first fishing schooner Crowninshield designed was the *Rob Roy,* built at Essex in 1900 by A. D. Story. This vessel was the subject of a magazine article in which her plans were published—lines, sail plan, structural plans, and scantlings (*Marine Engineering,* Vol. 6, May 1901). The article described the *Rob Roy* as a schooner 110′-6″ overall, 23′-7″ extreme beam, and 13′-4″ draft. The midsection had a sharp rise of straight floor, an easy turn in the high bilge, and slight tumble home in the topside. She had the short, straight keel with much drag and a cutaway profile that at one time became known as the "fisherman profile" in yachts. The *Rob Roy* is credited with 12½ knots—a realistic claim for the size of this vessel (excessive claims have been made for 14 to even 16 knots in vessels of equal length).

Among the vessels built to Crowninshield's designs were *Tartar, Harmony, Fame, Hope, Stranger, Arbutus,* and *Rush. Tartar*'s plans were published in *The Transactions of the Society of Naval Architects and Marine Engineers* (Vol. 15, 1907) "Wooden Sailing Ships," by B. B. Crowninshield.

Crowninshield employed some competent draftsmen, one of whom became a well-known Boston yacht designer, the late John G. Alden, from Troy, New York, a Harvard drop-out.

The Crowninshield influence was shown in the shape of fishing schooner profiles: short, straight keels with marked drag; long, light counters; and long forward overhangs. In his paper on "Wooden Sailing Ships" he speaks of the influence of a fine run on steering, and his plans show very straight buttocks. Many of the Crowninshield-designed schooners were built for Boston fishing vessel owners, whose fleets were in a period of expansion at this time. He also produced designs for the Gulf of Mexico red snapper fishery. Most of the Gulf schooners were built almost entirely of longleaf Georgia yellow pine, which seems to have lasted better in the warm Gulf waters than the standard shipbuilding timbers of the northern states.

A good example of a Crowninshield design was the *Harmony* (Plate 106). This vessel was built in 1903 at Essex by Oxner and Story. Her register dimensions were 99.5′ x 24.6′ x 11.6′. She was 113′–9″ moulded length at rail cap, 23′-10″ moulded beam, and 12′-1″ moulded depth at side. The *Harmony* belonged to the fast carrier class, having a long body for a vessel of such great lengths of bow and stern overhangs. She had a strong, graceful sheer, the short, straight keel that characterized the Crowninshield fishermen,

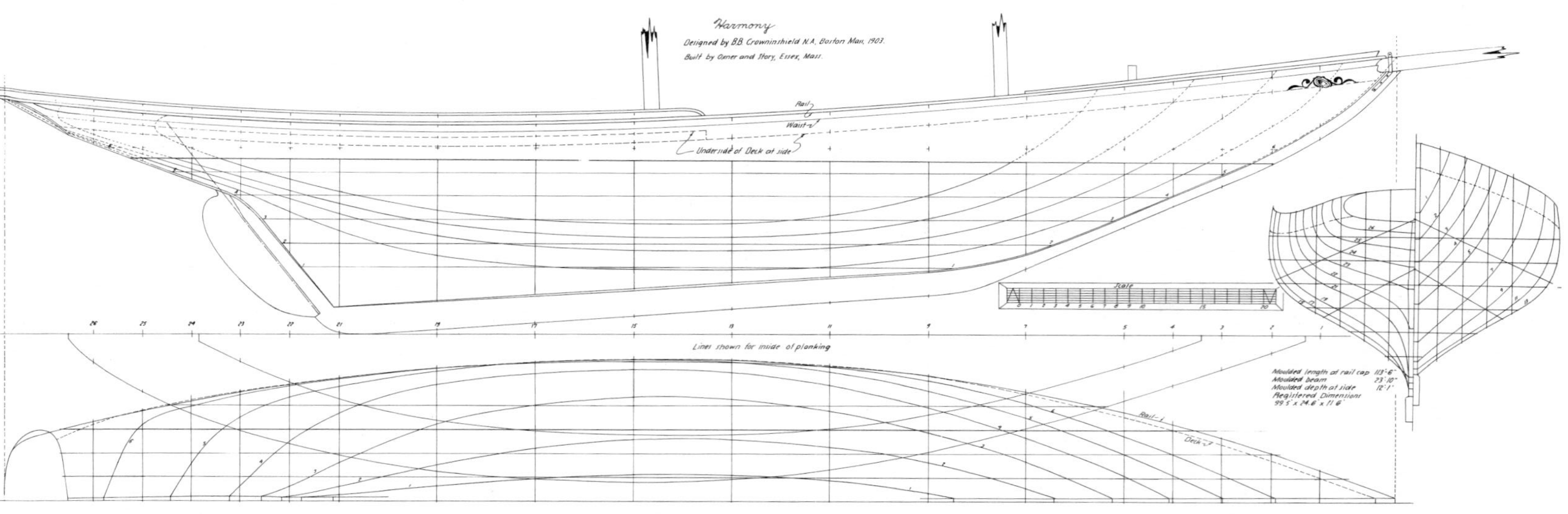
Harmony
Designed by B.B. Crowninshield N.A. Boston Mass. 1903.
Built by Oxner and Story, Essex, Mass.
Rail
Waist
Underside of Deck at side
Scale
Lines shown for inside of planking
Moulded length at rail cap 113'-6"
Moulded beam 23'-10"
Moulded depth at side 12'-1"
Registered Dimensions
99.5' x 24.6' x 11.6'
Rail
Deck

PLATE 106. *Harmony*, 1903, plan

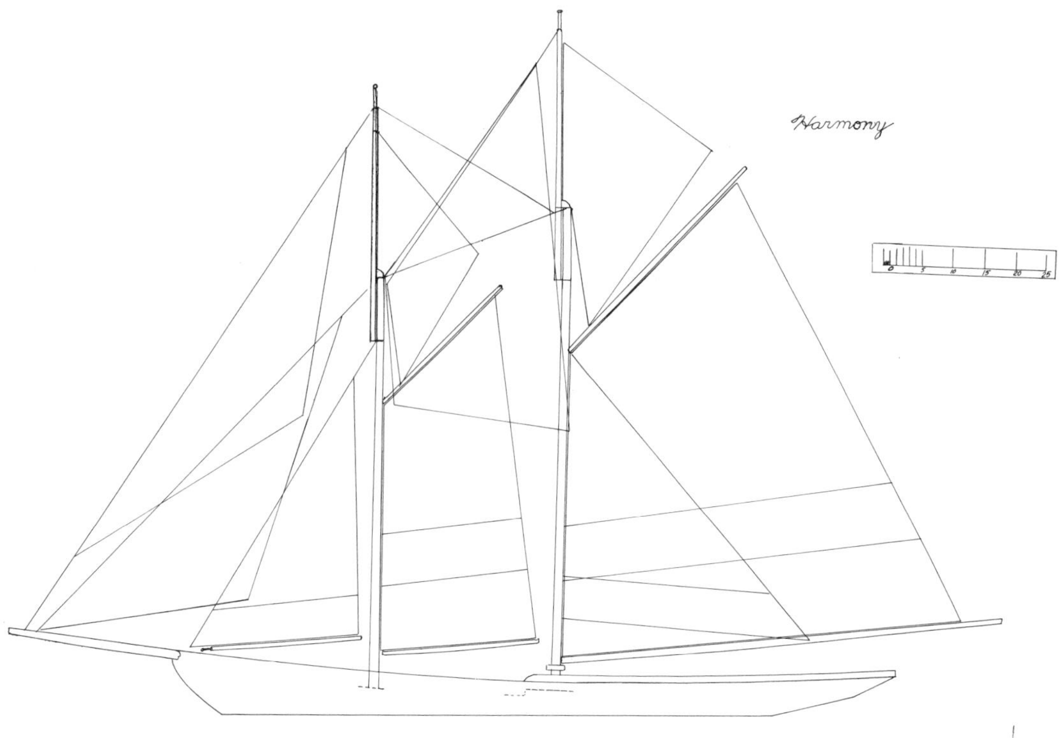
Harmony
0
5
10
15
20
25

FIGURE 26

with a long, partly submerged counter, long fore overhang with cutaway profile, and well-raked sternpost. The entrance was rather long and fine with slightly convex water lines. The run was of moderate length, with some straight to the buttocks. The midsection had somewhat hollow, sharply rising floor, a well-rounded bilge with marked tumble home above.

A smaller Crowninshield schooner was the *Stranger*, built at Essex in 1903. This vessel (Plate 107) was 73.6′ x 19.4′ x 9.0′ registry dimensions, and 83′-10½″ moulded length at rail cap, 19′-2″ moulded beam, and 9′-6″ moulded depth at side. The lines of the *Stranger* were used, but with the deck made flush, to build the schooners *Emelia Gloria*, 76.5′ x 20.0′ x 9.2′ register, and *Virginia Lyons*, 74.2′ x 19.6′ x 9.0′ register; both built at Essex by Oxner and Story in 1903.

The plan shows a schooner having a graceful sheer, a short straight keel with marked drag, the rabbet and the keel faired into a long overhanging bow, the sternpost sharply raked, the counter long, light, and partly submerged. The transom raked sharply and was elliptical in shape. The entrance was long and rather full in the waterlines, probably to prevent the long overhanging stem and forebody from trimming the vessel by the bow. The run was long and fine with some straight in the buttocks. The midsection was formed with slightly hollow, sharply rising floor, slack bilge, and some

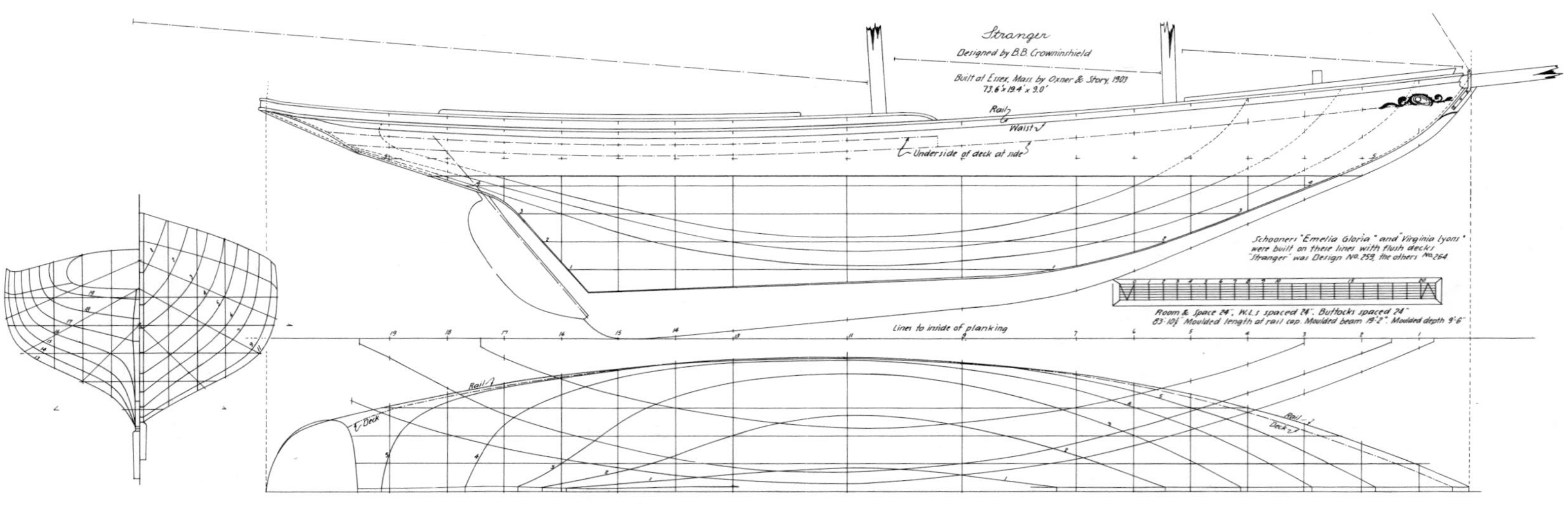
Stranger
Designed by B.B. Crowninshield
Built at Essex, Mass by Oxner & Story, 1903
73.6' x 19.4' x 9.0'
Rail
Waist
Underside of deck at side
Schooners "Emelia Gloria" and "Virginia Lyons" were built on these lines with flush decks
"Stranger" was Design No. 259, the others No. 264
Room & Space 24". W.L.s spaced 24". Buttocks spaced 24"
83'-10½" Moulded length of rail cap. Moulded beam 19'-2". Moulded depth 9'-6"
Lines to inside of planking
Rail
Deck

PLATE 107. *Stranger*, 1903, plan

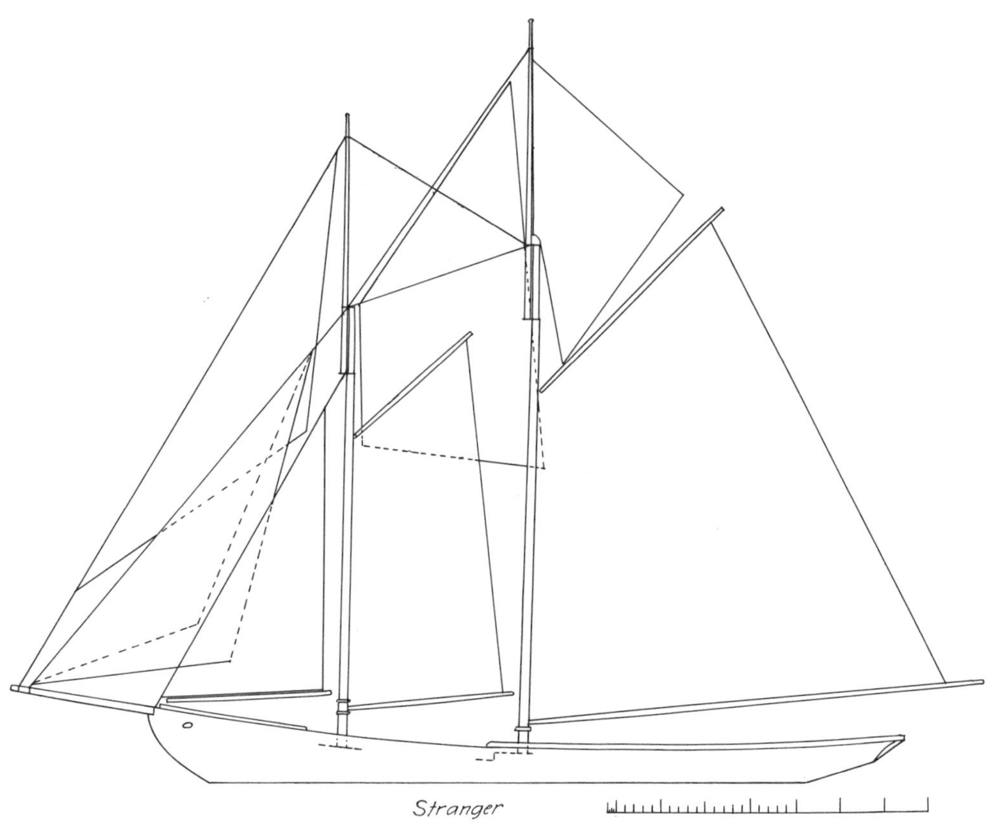
Stranger

FIGURE 27

tumble home in the topside. This was considered to be a handsome schooner, designed to sail fast.

Another example of Crowninshield's design was the *Arbutus* (Plate 108), design dated December 15, 1903. This schooner has not been traced in the registry and may have been foreign-built. She was a vessel 84′-9″ moulded length at rail, 21′-0″ moulded beam, and 10′-4½″ moulded depth at side. Arbutus had a graceful, moderate sheer, the "fisherman profile" keel and fore rake, a strongly raking sternpost with a long, light counter partly submerged. The transom, sharply raking, was elliptical. The entrance was of moderate length, convex, and the run was long and fine with very straight buttocks. The midsection showed sharply rising and hollow floor, a rather hard bilge with tumble home in the topside. Evidently this vessel was intended to sail fast; it is regrettable that she could not be traced.

Plate 109 shows the knockabout *Shepherd King*, built at Essex by Oxner and Story in 1904. She was the second knockabout to be launched, for McManus could not get another knockabout built, after the *Helen B. Thomas* was launched in 1902, until the *Thomas A. Cromwell* went down the ways

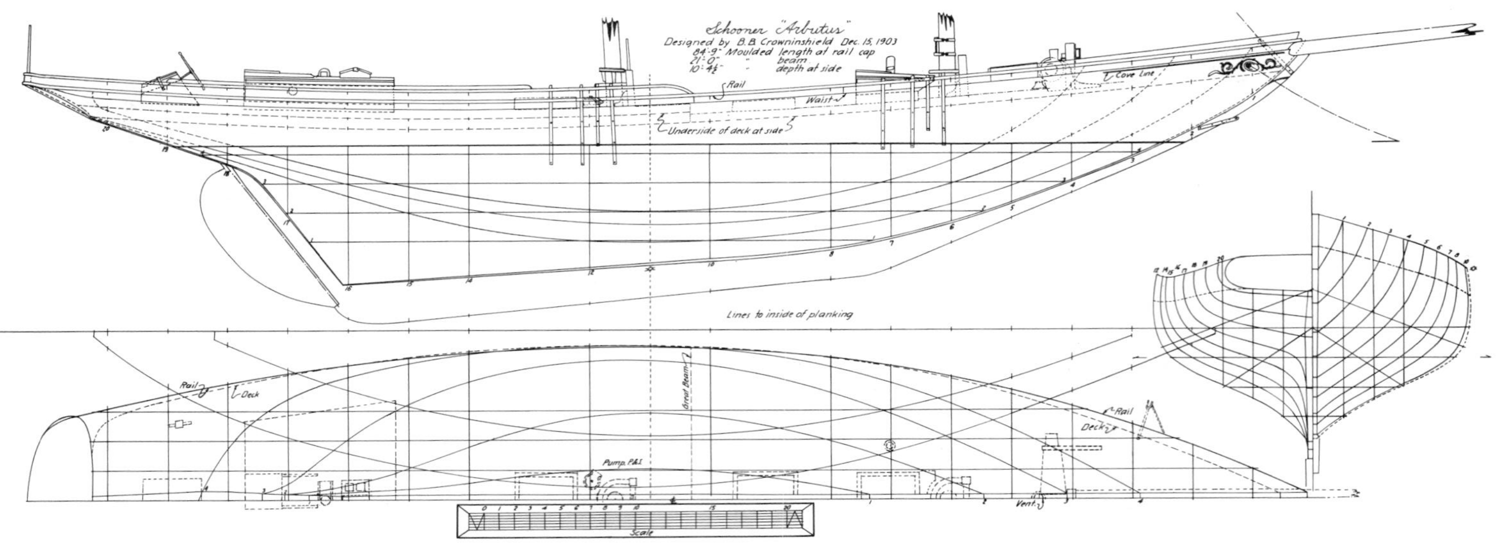
Schooner "Arbutus"
Designed by B.B. Crowninshield Dec. 15, 1903
84'-9" Moulded length at rail cap
21'-0" " beam
10'-4½" " depth at side
Rail
Waist
Cove Line
Underside of deck at side
Lines to inside of planking
Rail
Deck
Great Beam
Pump P&L
Rail
Deck
Vent.
Scale

PLATE 108. *Arbutus*, 1903, plan

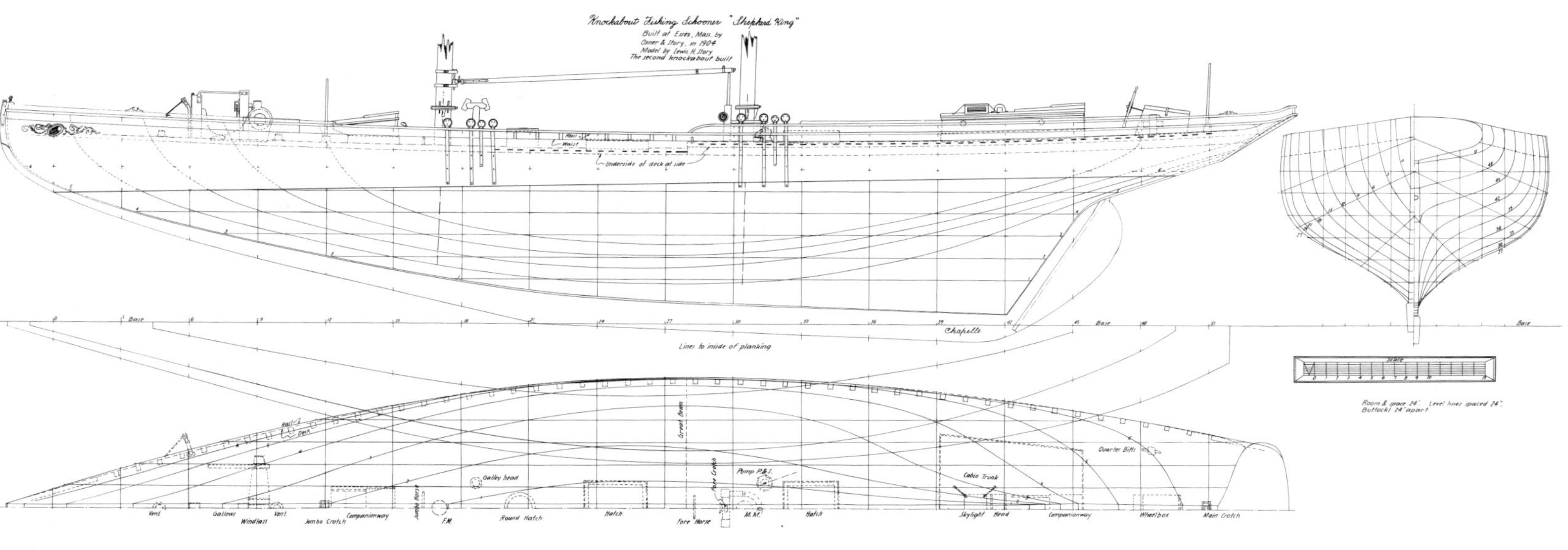
Knockabout Fishing Schooner "Shepherd King"
Built at Essex, Mass. by
Oxner & Story, in 1904
Model by Lewis H. Story
The second knockabout built
Underside of deck at side
Waist
Rail
Base
Chapelle
Lines to inside of planking
Scale
Room & space 24". Level lines spaced 24".
Buttocks 24" apart.
Rail
Deck
Great Beam
Galley head
Fore Crotch
Pump P.&.I.
Cabin Trunk
Quarter Bitts
Vent
Gallows
Windlass
Vent
Jumbo Crotch
Companionway
Jumbo Horse
F.M.
Round Hatch
Hatch
Fore Horse
M.M.
Hatch
Skylight
Head
Companionway
Wheelbox
Main Crotch

PLATE 109. *Shepherd King*, 1904, mould loft plan

in 1905. All of these early knockabouts were built by Oxner and Story. The *Arethusa* was the first knockabout built by Tarr and James, in 1907, and *Victor and Ethan* was the first knockabout built by A. D. Story, also in 1907. *Pontiac* was the first knockabout built at Gloucester; John Bishop launched her in 1906.

The *Shepherd King* was modeled by Lewis H. Story, incorporating the ideas of Edwin Oxner. As a result she was quite different from the *Helen B. Thomas*, having a "rater" bow with tumble home in its upper profile, a rather straight sheer and, as trimmed, she had very short bow and counter overhangs. The keel profile was that introduced by Crowninshield: a short straight keel with much drag, running from a strongly raking sternpost to a little abaft the foremast and with a marked angular gripe there. The fore rake then ran in a straight, rising line, then gradually curving, to fair into a curved profile stem. The counter was long, partly immersed and rather light, with a sharply raking heart-shaped transom. The entrance was long, slightly concave near the stem rabbet, and sharp. The run was moderate in length, with straight buttocks. The midsection was formed with hollow, strongly rising floor, a high and well-rounded bilge with much tumble home in the topside. The *Shepherd King* was much more burdensome than the *Helen B. Thomas* and a more economical vessel to build. She turned out to be a very fast and weatherly vessel in heavy weather. Her register dimensions were 100.0′ x 23.3′ x 12.2′, and she berthed nineteen men. She was 113′-7″ moulded length at rail cap, 23′-8″ moulded beam, and 13′-4″ moulded depth at side.

Beginning in 1907 a number of knockabouts were laid down at Essex and Gloucester. Most of the new vessels were built and trimmed to produce a short bow overhang. McManus retained a long bow overhang in his designs for a while, gradually shortening it under economic pressure caused by the overall length cost estimates used by the builders and the waste of forecastle space in the long bow overhang.

Plate 110 is the lines of the Indian Header *Onato*, built in 1904 at Essex by Oxner and Story. Her register dimensions were 101.0′ x 24.6′ x 11.8′, and she was 106′-0″ moulded length at rail cap, 24′-2″ moulded beam, and 12′-7″ moulded depth at side.

This vessel was burdensome and designed as a fast carrier by McManus. She had a marked sheer, fully rockered keel with a strongly raked sternpost and a partly immersed counter with a heavily raked heart-shaped transom. The entrance was long, sharp, and slightly convex, the run was rather short but with short straight buttocks. The midsection had moderately rising floor having slight hollow, and a full round bilge with some tumble home in the topside. This vessel was designed to be easy on her spars and rigging in heavy weather, as is shown by her midsection shape. She was a very satis-

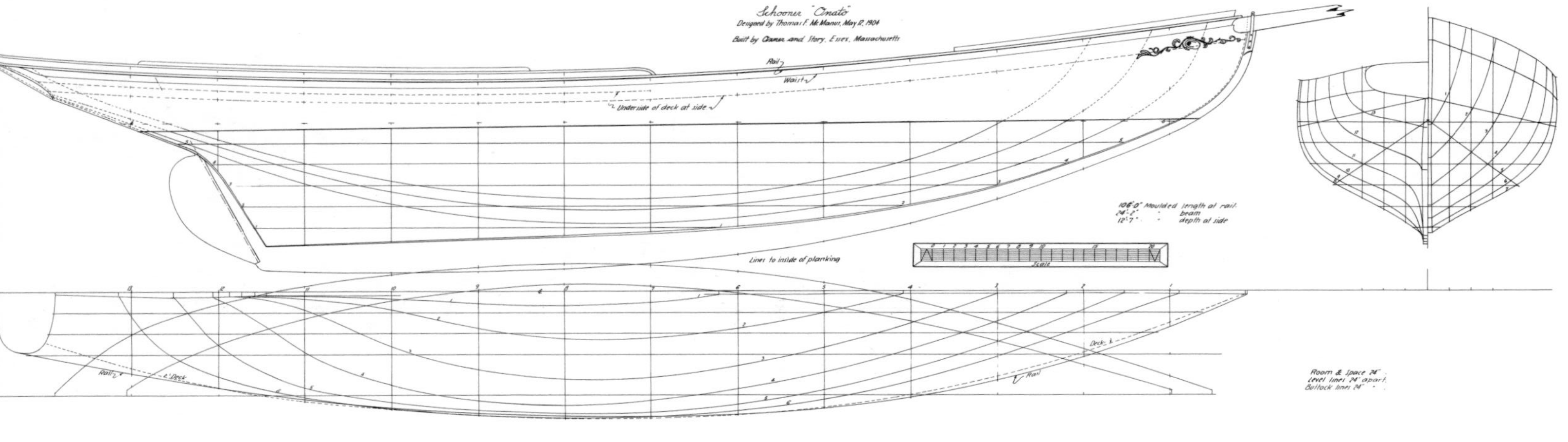
Schooner "Onato"
Designed by Thomas F. McManus, May 12, 1904
Built by Oxner and Story, Essex, Massachusetts
Rail
Waist
Underside of deck at side
Lines to inside of planking
106'-0" Moulded length at rail.
24'-2" " beam
12'-7" " depth at side
Scale
Deck
Rail
Room & Space 24".
Level lines 24" apart.
Buttock lines 24" " .

PLATE 110. *Onato*, 1904, plan

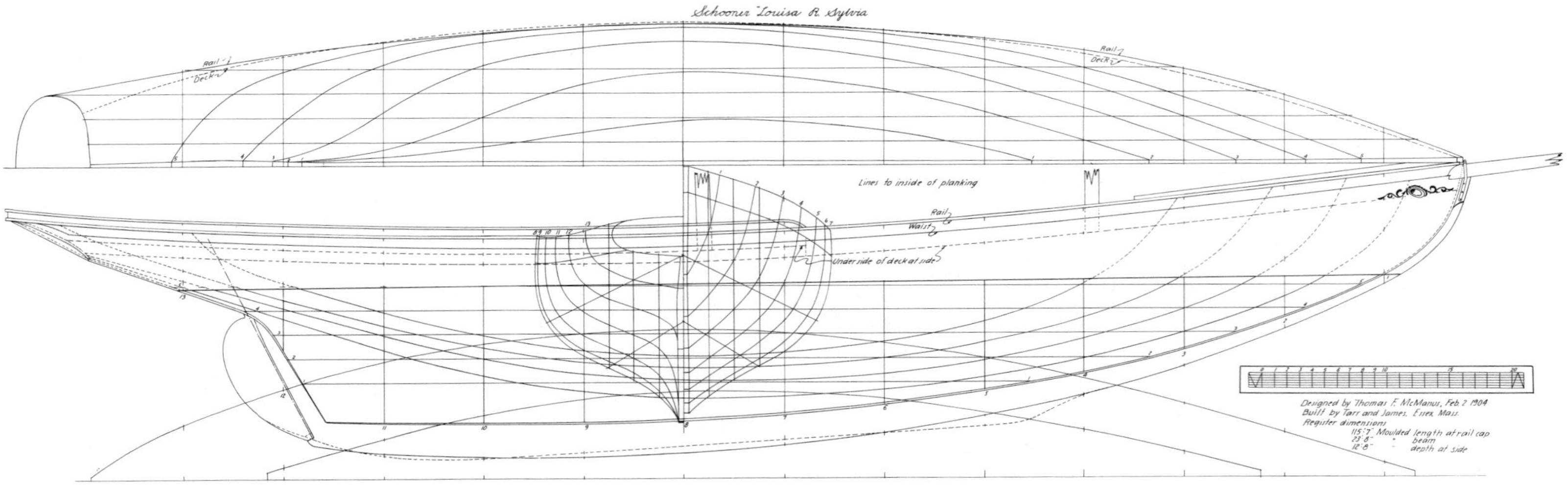
Schooner "Louisa R. Sylvia"
Rail
Deck
Rail
Deck
Lines to inside of planking
Rail
Waist
Underside of deck at side
Designed by Thomas F. McManus, Feb. 2 1904
Built by Tarr and James. Essex, Mass.
Register dimensions
115'-7" Moulded length at rail cap
23'-8" " beam
12'-8" " depth at side

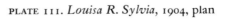

PLATE 111. *Louisa R. Sylvia*, 1904, plan

factory fishing vessel. Though she had no reputation for being fast she was able to reach about 13 knots, running free—very good for her length. It was said she was not usually sailed very hard.

The schooner design titled "*Louisa R. Silvia*" or *Silva* (Plate 111) was built at Essex in 1904 by Tarr and James. She was designed by McManus in early 1904. Her register dimensions were 101.0′ x 24.4′ x 11.4′, and her moulded length at rail cap was 115′-7″, her moulded beam was 23′-8″, and her moulded depth at side was 12′-8″. Her name as printed in the register was *Louisa R. Silva,* which would be her correct name. This schooner, though large, was sharper than the *Onato* and was designed to sail fast, though not given great sail-carrying power. The alterations shown in the keel profile, converting the original fully rockered keel into a "fisherman's profile," shows that more than one schooner may have been built to these lines.

The *Silva* had marked sheer, fully rockered keel, strongly raking sternpost, long, sweeping fore rake fairing into the Indian Header round stem without a knuckle. The counter was long and light, with a strongly raked elliptical transom. The entrance was long, sharp, and convex. The run was long, with long straight to the buttocks. The midsection had rising hollow floor, round, rather slack bilge with a little tumble home in the topside. Not a powerful vessel, the *Silva* could be expected to sail fast in moderate weather and to be useful in the mackerel fishery.

The schooner *Ingomar* (Plate 112) was designed by McManus in June 1904. Her register dimensions were 104.8′ x 25.7′ x 11.0′; she berthed twenty men. She was 116′-0″ moulded length at rail cap, 25′-0″ moulded beam, and 12′-2″ moulded depth at side. This was a good working vessel, capable of sailing fast, and she was also very weatherly. She was built by Tarr and James at Essex in 1904–1905. This schooner had much sheer, a rockered keel fairing into a round stem without a fore gripe common in most of the Indian Head type. The sternpost raked sharply, the counter was long and partly immersed. The elliptical transom was small and heavily raked. The entrance was long, sharp, and very slightly convex. The run was long, fine, and the buttocks were straight for some distance. The midship section had slightly hollow, sharply rising floor, a full round bilge bordering on slackness, and tumble home topside. Like the *Silva,* the *Ingomar* sailed very well in moderate conditions but was the more powerful of the two.

W. Starling Burgess, naval architect was a son of Edward Burgess, and designed many yachts, becoming one of the leading practitioners in the art. In 1905 he designed his first fishing schooner, the very large *Elizabeth Silsbee* (Plate 113) which was built by A. D. Story in that year. She was a big vessel, register dimensions being 116.6′ x 26.0′ x 11.6′, and she was 133′-7″ length under the rail cap, 25′-5″ extreme beam, and 15′-5″ depth, rabbet to rail cap. The *Silsbee* was designed as an auxiliary, having a 300 h.p. "Standard" gaso-

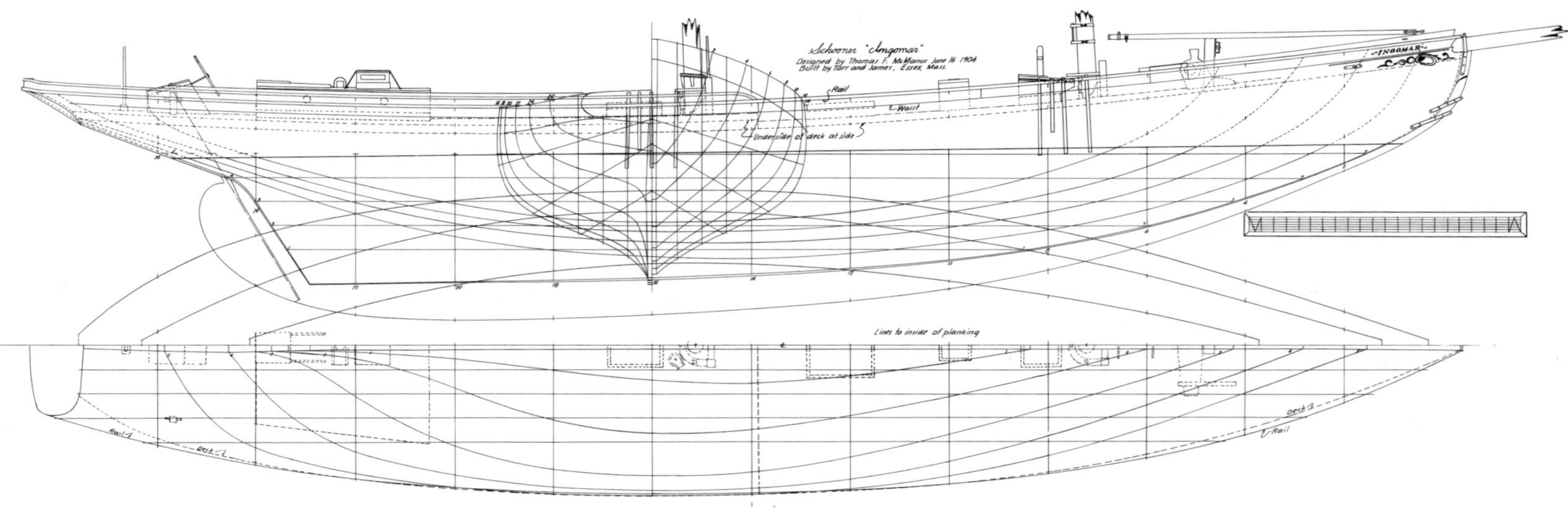
Schooner "Ingomar"
Designed by Thomas F. McManus June 16 1904
Built by Tarr and James, Essex, Mass.
"INGOMAR"
Rail
Waist
Underside of deck at side
Lines to inside of planking
Deck
Rail

PLATE 112. *Ingomar*, 1904, plan

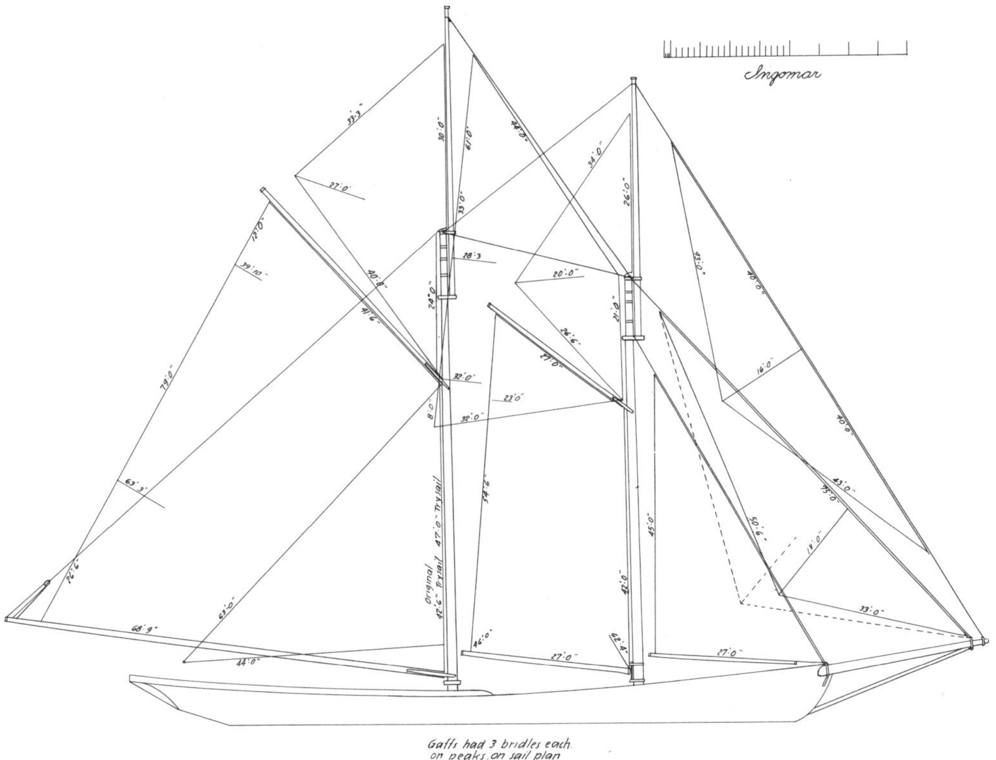
Ingomar
Original
42'6" Trysail
47'0" Trysail
Gaffs had 3 bridles each
on peaks, on sail plan

FIGURE 28

line engine. The lack of experience with engines is shown not only by the very impractical propeller aperture shown in the plan but also by the record of engine breakdowns. The *Silsbee* was supposed to have been a potentially fast sailer but was sadly handicapped by the drag of her propeller so her capabilities were never satisfactorily tested, as far as can be learned.

The *Silsbee* had rather small sheer, a straight keel with drag, "fisherman profile" fashion, but with the fore rake brought to the marked forefoot of her clipper bow. The sternpost had small rake, with a large deadwood abaft the post in which the propeller aperture was cut. To remove the propeller for a repair, the shaft—made in two lengths with two couplings—had to have the couplings removed and the inboard short length shaft unshipped, then the tail shaft slid forward to clear the aperture. Also, the rudder had to be unshipped, for to remove the tail shaft it had to be slid aft through a hole in the prick post. Alignment was difficult to maintain as the engine beds were too short.

This schooner had a long counter with a sharply raked elliptical transom. Her entrance was long and sharp, with a slight hollow near the stem. The run was very long and fine, with straight buttocks.

The midsection showed very hollow, sharply rising floor with a high

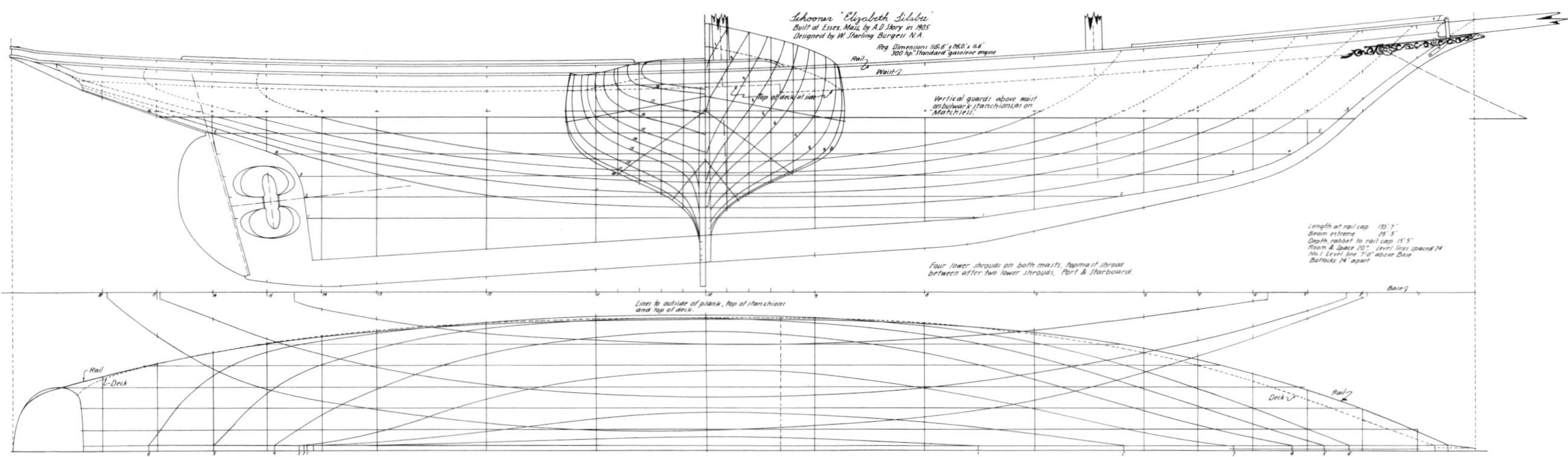
Schooner "Elizabeth Silsbee"
Built at Essex, Mass. by A.D. Story in 1905
Designed by W. Starling Burgess N.A.
Reg. Dimensions 116.6' x 26.0' x 11.6'
300 hp "Standard" gasolene engine
Rail
Waist
Top of deck at side
Vertical guards above waist on bulwark stanchions, as on "Matchless."
Length at rail cap 133' 7"
Beam extreme 25' 5"
Depth, rabbet to rail cap 15' 5"
Room & Space 20". Level lines spaced 24"
No. 1 Level line 7' 0" above Base
Buttocks 24" apart
Four lower shrouds on both masts, topmast shroud between after two lower shrouds, Port & Starboard.
Base
Lines to outside of plank, top of stanchions and top of deck.
Rail
Deck
Deck
Rail

PLATE 113. *Elizabeth Silsbee*, 1904, plan

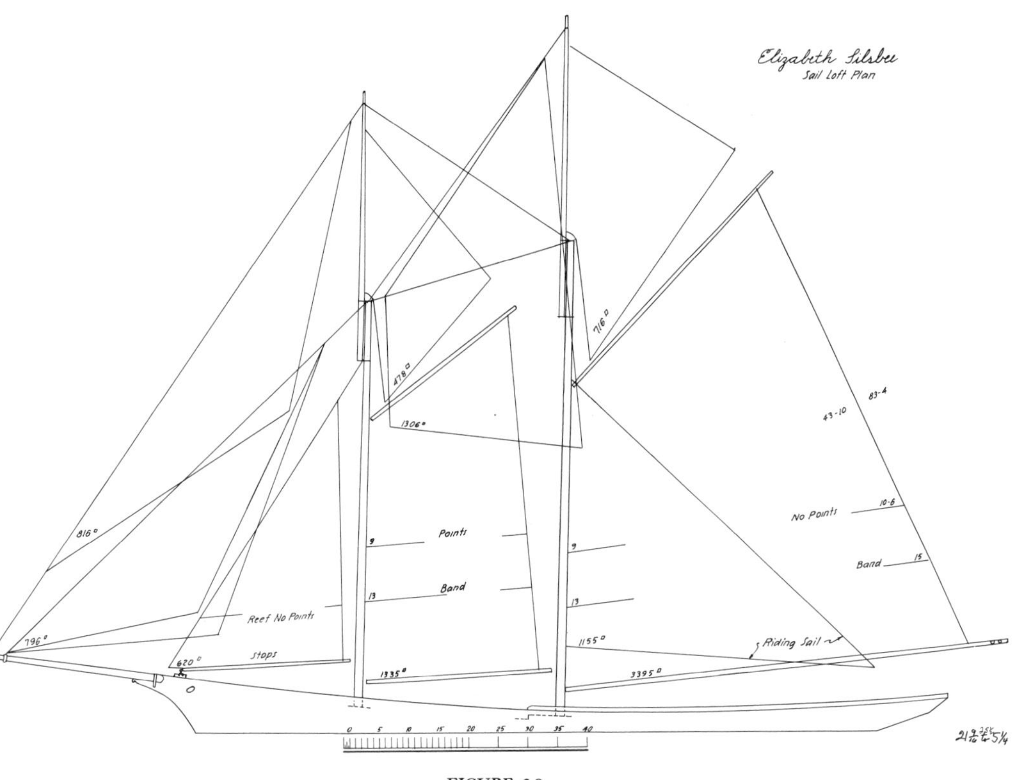

Elizabeth Silsbee
Sail Loft Plan
Points
Band
Reef No Points
Stops
No Points
Band
Riding Sail

FIGURE 29

and rather hard turn of the bilge, and strong tumble home in the topside. The great hollow in the floor in the wake of the garboards had been used in a few earlier fishing schooners, as we have seen, but in the *Silsbee* the hollow was more marked than in the earlier fishermen.

The use of such midsections was occasionally seen in fishermen since it raised the center of buoyancy, giving greater effect to the ballast and a long righting arm, as well as somewhat greater initial stability if properly proportioned. However, it was usually accompanied by a reduction in displacement and a loss of cargo capacity, compared with a midsection having the normal rising straight floor.

The third knockabout to be built at Essex was the *Thomas A. Cromwell* (Plate 114), designed by McManus. This was a long-ended knockabout built by Oxner and Story at Essex in 1905. Her register dimensions were 109.9′ x 24.5′ x 11.6′, and she had a moulded length at rail cap of 127′-3″, moulded beam 24′-0″, and a moulded depth of 12′-8″ at side. This schooner was designed to be a fast sailer but she does not appear to have been driven hard enough to have earned the reputation of being an unusually smart sailer. She was, in many respects, a development from the design of the *Helen B. Thomas*, having less sheer and, generally, a more attractive hull, but still with wasted space in the ends.

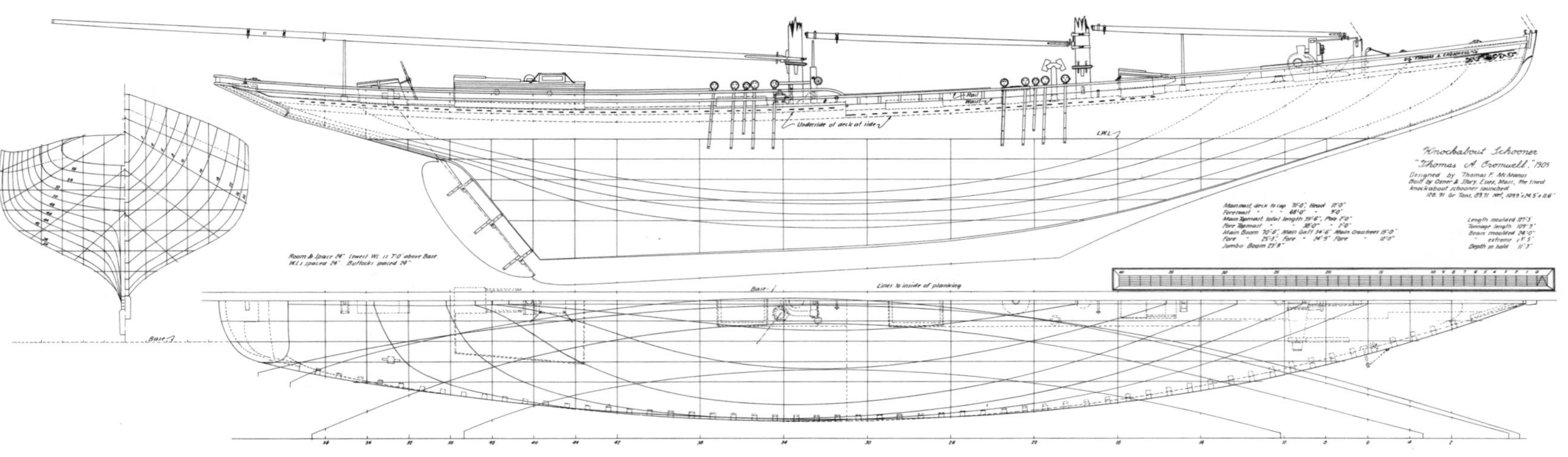
Knockabout Schooner
"Thomas A. Cromwell," 1905
Designed by Thomas F. McManus
Built by Oxner & Story, Essex, Mass., the third
knockabout schooner launched
128.91 Gr Tons, 83.71 Net, 109.9' x 24.5' x 11.6'
Mainmast, deck to cap 71'0", Head 17'0"
Foremast " " " 68'0" " 9'0"
Main Topmast, total length 39'6", Pole 7'0"
Fore Topmast " " 38'0" " 7'0"
Main Boom 70'6", Main Gaff 34'6", Main Crosstrees 15'0"
Fore " 25'3", Fore " 24'9" Fore " 12'0"
Jumbo Boom 23'9"
Length moulded 127'3"
Tonnage length 109'9"
Beam moulded 24'0"
Depth in hold 11'3"
LWL
Underside of deck at side
Room & Space 24" Lowest W.L. is 7'0" above Base
W.L.s spaced 24". Buttocks spaced 24"
Base
Lines to inside of planking

PLATE 114. *Thomas A. Cromwell*, 1905, plan

The *Cromwell* had a graceful, lively sheer and, considering her date of build, an unusually long straight keel with heavy drag, of the "fisherman profile" type. The fore rake joined the keel, almost under the foremast, in a deep gripe. The fore rake faired into the stem in a "rater" bow. The sternpost raked sharply and the counter was very long for a fisherman. The elliptical transom raked a great deal. The entrance was long, sharp, and convex, the run was quite fine, with long straight buttocks enhanced by the long counter. With this long counter, the *Cromwell* killed her captain. While the vessel was hove-to and pitching in a heavy swell with a little sternway, the master fell overboard off the taffrail. Sternway brought him under the counter and this came down on him, giving him a fatal blow on the head.

The midsection of the *Cromwell* was formed with much hollow in the garboard, strong rise in the floor, a rather quick turn of the bilge with small tumble home in the topside.

The plan shown in Plate 115 was used to build the schooner *Clintonia* in 1907, designed by McManus in February 1904. *Clintonia* was built by John Bishop in Gloucester. It was rumored that the bow was filled out, beyond what is shown in the lines, and that this design was also used to build the famous *Oriole* in 1908, used with a knockabout bow added to build the "Gray Ghost" *Elizabeth Howard* in 1916. By superimposing the tracings of the lines of the two schooners, it could be seen that *Clintonia* was the smaller vessel by nearly 6′-0″ but, in general, the body plans were almost the same except that *Clintonia* was sharper in the forebody, but the afterbody sections were, surprisingly, almost alike. It seems possible that the plan of the *Clintonia* was an original design that was progressively altered, producing not sister ships but rather closely related designs. Hence the design of *Oriole* may have developed from the 1904 design that apparently was used to build *Clintonia*. *Oriole*, said to have made the speed of 16 knots on one occasion, will be examined again later, along with the *Elizabeth Howard*.

The schooner in Plate 115 had moderate sheer, a rockered keel having a little straight in the shoe for docking purposes. The fore rake was in a long up sweep to fair into the round Indian Header stem. The sternpost raked sharply, the counter was rather deep at the tuck but finished with a relatively small heart-shaped transom, strongly raked. The entrance was sharp with a very slight convexity in the upper waterlines. The run was moderately fine with short straight line buttocks. The midsection was formed with a good deal of rise in the floor with a very slight hollow, firm bilges, and a little tumble home in the topside. The relatively fine forebody probably produced some trim by the head, as was usual in McManus designs.

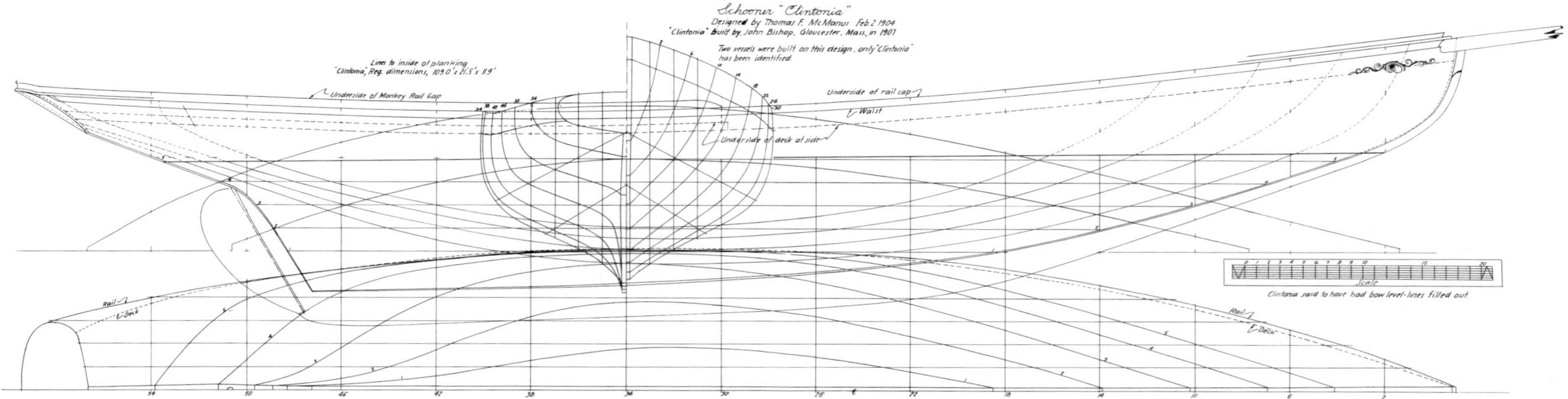

Schooner "Clintonia"
Designed by Thomas F. McManus Feb. 2 1904
"Clintonia" Built by John Bishop, Gloucester, Mass., in 1907
Two vessels were built on this design, only "Clintonia" has been identified.
Lines to inside of planking
"Clintonia", Reg. dimensions, 109.0' x 21.5' x 11.9'
Underside of Monkey Rail Cap
Underside of rail cap
Waist
Underside of deck at side
Rail
Deck
Scale
Clintonia said to have had bow level-lines filled out.

PLATE 115. *Clintonia*, 1905, plan

Chapter Eight

1908–1935

Canadian fishing schooners, out of Nova Scotian ports, resembled New England schooners, from at least as early as the 1880s. Due to economic conditions, they were often less well-fitted, but they were commonly on very good models. By 1920 the Nova Scotia fishing schooners were often much larger than the average Gloucesterman, with more freeboard but usually with less proportionate depth. Originally their ballast consisted entirely of stone, but by the early years of the twentieth century many had some pig iron ballast as well as stone.

The Canadian builders and fishermen watched the development of the Gloucestermen, occasionally adopting some feature or detail that seemed useful to them. In a few instances they obtained New England half-models or plans. Plate 116 shows a design by Crowninshield that was intended for mixed ballast and possibly for construction in Nova Scotia. The effect of mixed iron and stone ballast was to raise the center of gravity, compared to that of a vessel with all iron ballast, and this reduced stability as well as power to carry sail. The need to stow stone ballast as low as possible was obvious and the designer commonly employed moderate deadrise with straight, rising floor; often stone ballasted schooners had more than average beam for their length and depth. In the case of the schooner in Plate 116, Crowninshield employed a little hollow in the midship section floor, with a hard bilge.

The design was for a vessel 83′-0″ moulded length at rail cap, 20′-5″ moulded beam, and 9′-1″ moulded depth at side. She was to have a graceful sheer, a rather long portion of her keel was to be straight, with the long fore rake and overhanging stem favored by Crowninshield. The sternpost raked sharply and the counter was long, partly submerged, and had a

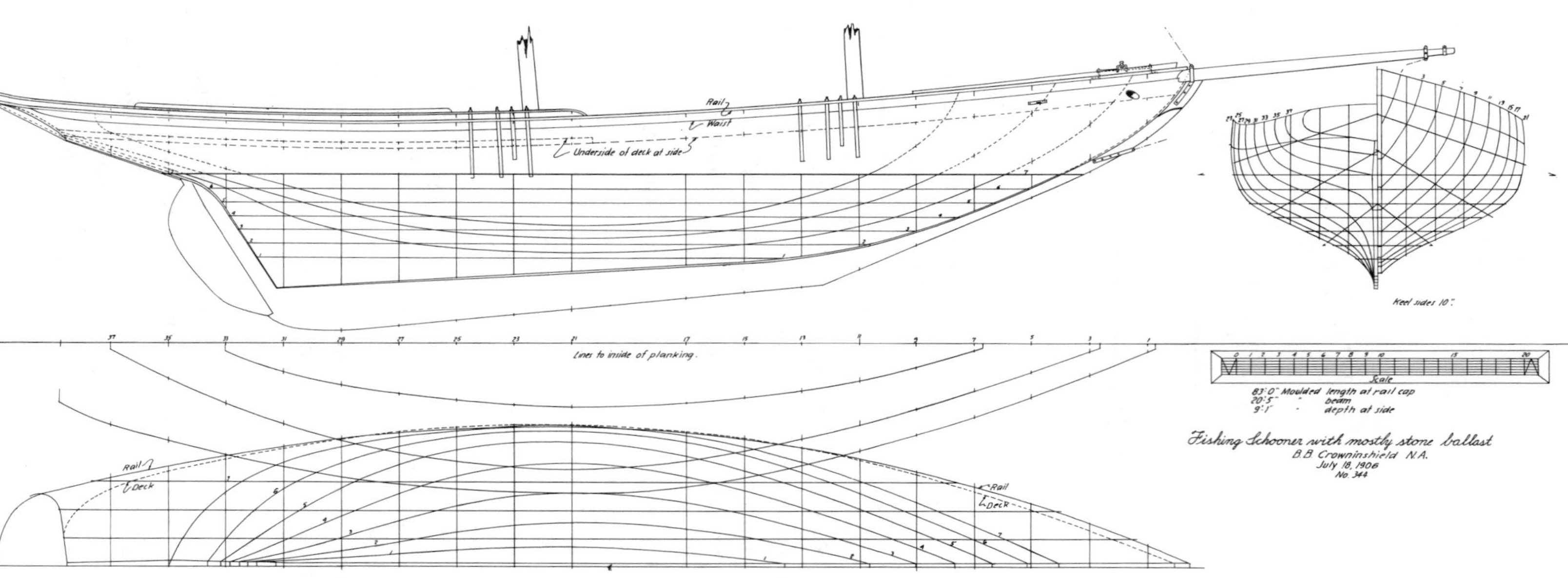
Rail
Waist
Underside of deck at side
Keel sides 10"
Lines to inside of planking.
Rail
Deck
Rail
Deck
Scale
83'0" Moulded length at rail cap
20'5" " beam
9'1" " depth at side
Fishing Schooner with mostly stone ballast
B.B Crowninshield N.A.
July 18, 1906
No. 344

PLATE 116. Crowninshield's stone-ballasted schooner, 1905, plan sharply raked elliptical transom. The entrance was convex and moderately long; the run was fine with some straight in the buttocks. The design would produce a rather yacht-like schooner. Unfortunately no record has yet been found of her name and port of hail.

As mentioned earlier, Thomas Irving modeled some of the schooners built by John Bishop and other builders. Irving used half-models, two of which won prizes at the international fishery exhibition in 1883, and he may have modeled the tern schooner *Lizzie Matheson.* He also built rigged scale models as a hobby. His models, whether builders' or rigged scale models, were made with thin lifts, giving them great accuracy.

Plate 117 shows the schooner *Juno,* modeled by Irving and built by John Bishop at Gloucester in 1905. Her designed dimensions were 104′-0″ moulded length at rail cap, 23′-4″ moulded beam, and 11′-0″ moulded depth at side. The *Juno* had rather straight sheer, a long, almost straight keel with much drag running from sternpost almost to the foremast position, then fairing up to a short-overhang round stem. Then sternpost had much rake and the counter was long and light, having a strongly raked elliptical transom. The entrance was long and sharp with no hollow or concavity; the run was of moderate length with much straight in the buttocks. The midsection had sharply rising floor with a little hollow in the garboard and outboard. The bilge was high and firm, the tumble home above was marked. This was a conservative design for her date, by then short keels with long fore rakes had become popular. *Juno*'s register dimensions were 96.0′ x 24.0′ x 10.8′; she berthed nineteen hands. Her home port was Boston, when launched, and she was said to have been a good sailer, particularly in moderate weather.

As has been shown (Plate 25), a number of centerboard schooners, designed as oyster dredges, were built at Essex and Gloucester. Plate 118 shows the last of these to have been built on Cape Ann. From this model the Schooners *May F. Patterson* and *Julia Davis* were built by A. D. Story in 1907 at Essex for Greenport, New York, owners. Their register dimensions were: *May F. Patterson,* 64.0′ x 22.5′ x 6.4′, berthing five; *Julia Davis* (No. 2), 69.0′ x 22.3′ x 5.7′ (built in 1908, the first *Julia Davis* having been sunk in a collision on her way to Greenport for delivery). The model of these schooners was furnished by the owners and designer's name has not been discovered.

This type of oyster dredge had developed from clipper-bow centerboard schooners soon after 1895. "Modernization" of the schooner-dredge type consisted of an increase in average size, the adaption of the curved, overhang stem, and a longer counter. These changes occurred on the eastern oyster grounds of New Jersey, on eastern Long Island Sound, and on Narragansett Bay. The Chesapeake and southern fisheries found the old schooner

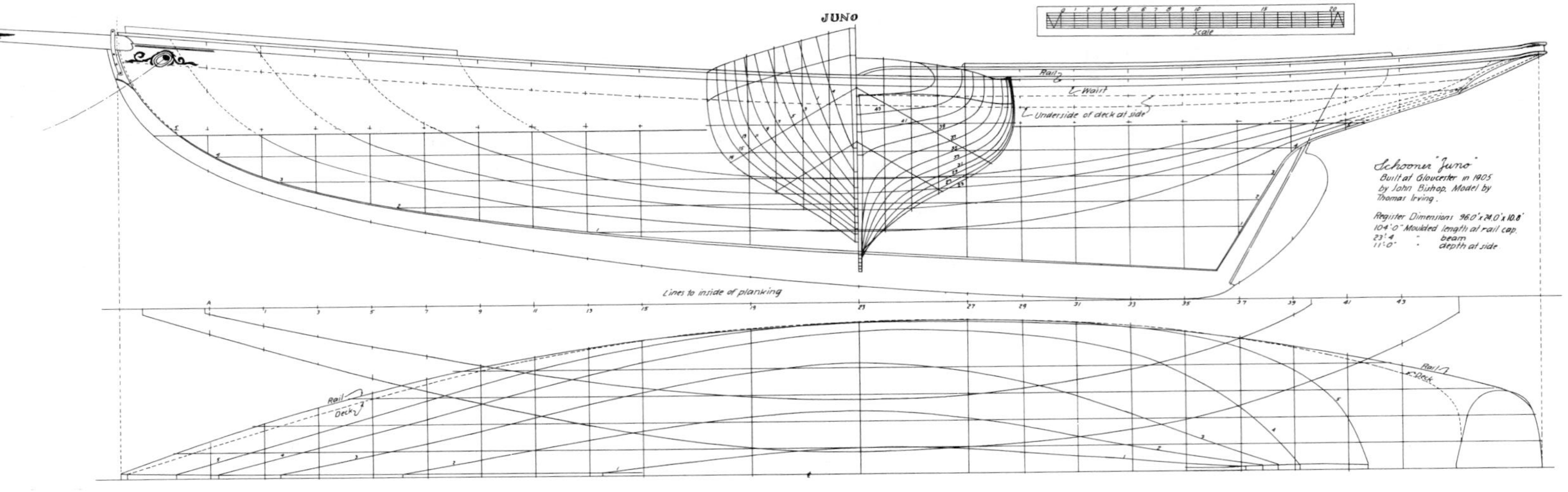
JUNO
Scale
Rail
℄ Waist
℄ Underside of deck at side
Schooner "Juno"
Built at Gloucester in 1905
by John Bishop. Model by
Thomas Irving.
Register Dimensions 96.0' x 24.0' x 10.8'
104'0" Moulded length at rail cap.
23'4 " beam
11'0" " depth at side
Lines to inside of planking
Rail
Deck

PLATE 117. *Juno*, 1905, half-model

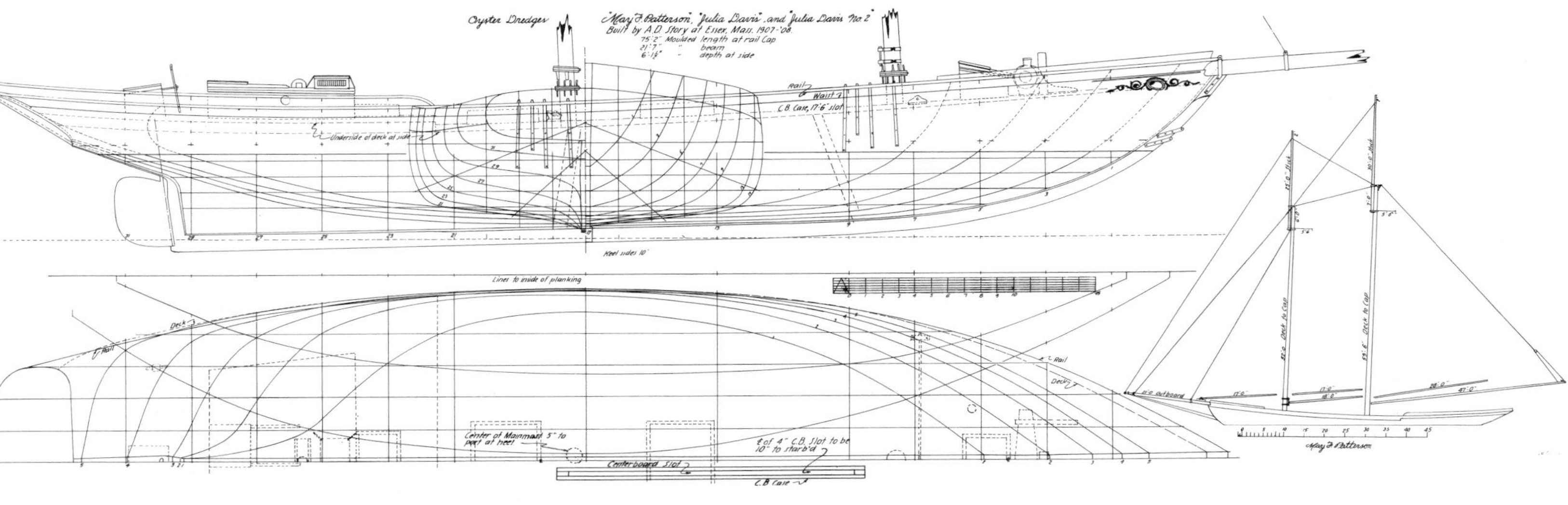
Oyster Dredger
"May F. Patterson", "Julia Davis", and "Julia Davis No. 2"
Built by A.D. Story at Essex, Mass. 1907-'08.
75'2" Moulded length at rail Cap
21'7" " beam
6'1½" - depth at side
Rail
Waist
C.B. Case, 17'6" slot
Underside of deck at side
Keel sides 10"
Lines to inside of planking
Deck
Rail
Center of Mainmast 5" to port at heel
℄ of 4" C.B. Slot to be 10" to starb'd
Centerboard Slot
C.B. Case
Deck to Cap
May F. Patterson

PLATE 118. *May Patterson*, 1907, mould loft plan

dredges adequate for a while, since these fisheries were becoming small-craft grounds employing skipjacks, the old round-bottom sloops and bugeyes and log canoes, or, as on the North Carolina grounds, sharpies, some schooner-rigged. The schooner dredges were remarkable in developing into suitable and satisfactory craft very early, and what evolution occurred was in superficial details, as was noted earlier (Plate 25). The New Jersey-designed schooners built after 1910 were often relatively large vessels of a little over 100′-0″ moulded length at main rail, 23′-0″ to 24′-0″ moulded beam and having some deadrise, and drawing about 7′-0″ with centerboard raised. These vessels were pole-masted, setting only fore and main gaffsails, a large forestaysail with a club on its foot and a small jib set on a short pole bowsprit.

The schooner shown in Plate 118 had moderate sheer, with a short raised quarterdeck, straight keel with slight drag running from the sternpost to the forward end of the centerboard slot, then curved upward in a long easy sweep to fair into a short-overhang curved stem. The sternpost had a very small rake; the counter was rather deep, of moderate length, with a large, sharply raking elliptical transom. The entrance was markedly convex and rather short; the run was long, with some straight in the buttocks near the sternpost. The midsection had very slight straight deadrise, carried very far outboard with a very hard turn to the bilge and with some tumble home in the topside. As was often the case in American centerboard schooners, the centerboard case was placed off-center and the mainmast was also off-center on the opposite side. The centerboard lanyard was an iron rod, the arrangement permitted this to be carried aloft to the mainmast trestletrees by a tackle at the head of the rod.

Due to their light draft (the Essex-built schooners drew about 6′-0″) and relatively light displacement, many of the oyster schooner dredges sailed very fast and were very weatherly in the conditions in which they worked. The eastern oyster schooners seem to have carried topmasts and gaff-topsails throughout most of their existence. The schooners built on the lines of the *May F. Patterson* measured 75′-2″ moulded length at main rail cap, 21′-7″ moulded beam, and 6′-1½″ moulded depth at side, as lofted.

The slow increase in the number of knockabouts built for the New England fisheries picked up speed after 1905. Plate 119 shows the lines of the McManus-designed knockabout *Pontiac*, built by John Bishop at Gloucester in 1906 as previously mentioned (page 252). She appears to have been one of the early knockabouts in which McManus employed the short bow overhang, the advantages of which had been made apparent by the *Shepherd King*. Register 96.0′ x 23.7′ x 11.0′.

The *Pontiac* had a graceful, strong sheer, a straight keel with much drag running from the heel of the sternpost to nearly under the heel of the

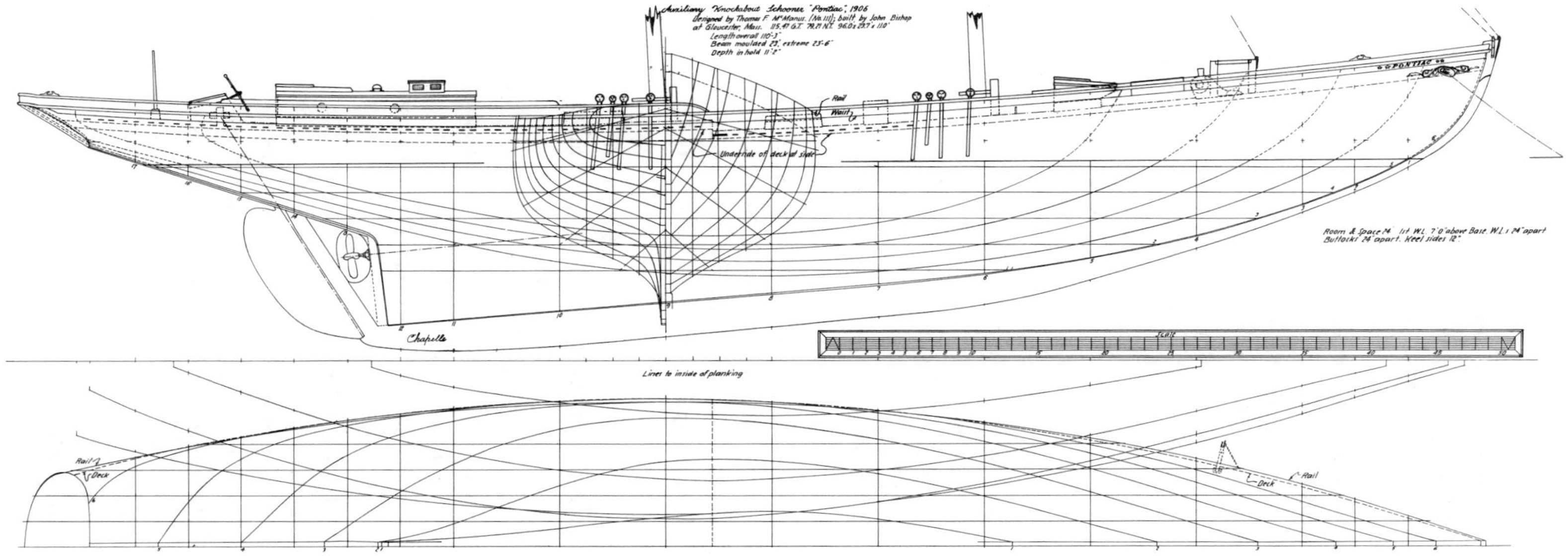

PLATE 119. *Pontiac*, 1906, plan

foremast, then sweeping up to fair into a short-overhang round bow. Because the *Pontiac* was designed to be an auxiliary fisherman, McManus gave her a long deep counter so as to locate the propeller well under the stern overhang. The transom raked sharply and was elliptical. The entrance was long and very sharp; the run had much straight in the buttocks producing a long and fine afterbody. The midsection showed a slightly hollow, much rising floor, a round, easy bilge, and marked tumble home in the topsides. This schooner model soon became McManus' standard treatment of the design of knockabouts. There were troubles for the designers of the knockabouts; some carried too much weather helm due to attempts to carry huge mainsails with very long mainbooms and headsails that were too small or too short in the foot. It was eventually recognized that the knockabout rig could be balanced by increasing the hoist in both gaffsails, and shortening the mainboom a few feet. The center of effort was often slightly abaft the center of lateral plane in these large schooners, but there were numerous exceptions, apparently.

Another difficulty was the fore-and-aft trim of a knockabout. Most of the launchings of McManus' knockabouts, and of some of the bowsprit schooners, put the vessel afloat down by the head. It does not seem that McManus ever ordered trim ballast to be stowed prior to the launch. The cause of faulty trim was obvious, of course; the loss of displacement in the forebody to obtain the yacht-like cutaway forefoot, and the placing of a relatively full midsection abaft the true midlength. Ballasting in such a case, particularly with iron and stone ballast, could be very difficult. Placing inboard ballast in the run helped mostly in controlling fore-and-aft trim, but it was not very effective in gaining stability. This was due to the rise of the deadwood in the afterbody to support the after cant timbers, which not only gave little room for ballast but also raised the ballast and its center of gravity higher aft than amidships. In short, inboard ballast needed to be concentrated amidships in these fishing schooners to be effective. The yachtsman's basic measurement—load waterline length—meant nothing to the fisherman nor to the schooner builder, so usually there was no line of reference. Often the schooners were overballasted at Gloucester—sitting deep in the water and not uncommomly out of fore-and-aft trim, that is to say down by the head. Pictures of some schooners under sail show that they either were ballasted by the head or were so sharp forward as to lack displacement there to such an extent that they could not be properly trimmed by shifting some ballast aft. The overballasting seems to have grown out of the hard-driving of the schooners, where stability—particularly initial stability—was of prime importance.

The launching of a knockabout that came to rest down by the head was said by two witnesses to have embarrassed McManus so much that he left the yard without a word. This happened once with the Charleston pilot schooner and again with the *Elizabeth Howard*. In modeling the *Louise Howard*, Adams (the builder) gave his design a little more bearing forward, in proportion, but also used some trim ballast right aft.

Plate 120 is the lines of the large knockabout *Arethusa*, designed by McManus and built by Tarr and James at Essex in 1907. A large, short-ended knockabout, she had the reputation of being very fast and weatherly. On one occasion she easily escaped from a Canadian fishery patrol steamer by hard sailing. With a bowsprit added and with the forecastle companionway moved to abaft the foremast from its original position forward of the foremast, she became a well-known rum runner during the Prohibition Era and there many more claims of her speed were made. She was 127′-3″ moulded length at main rail cap, 25′-0″ moulded beam, and 13′-2″ moulded depth at side Her register dimensions were 114.0′ x 25.6′ x 12.5′, and she berthed twenty. Figure 30 shows the finally developed rig of a large knockabout.

The *Arethusa* was much like the *Pontiac* in model. The former had a strong graceful sheer, a straight keel with much drag running from the heel of the sternpost to underneath the foremast where an angular gripe was

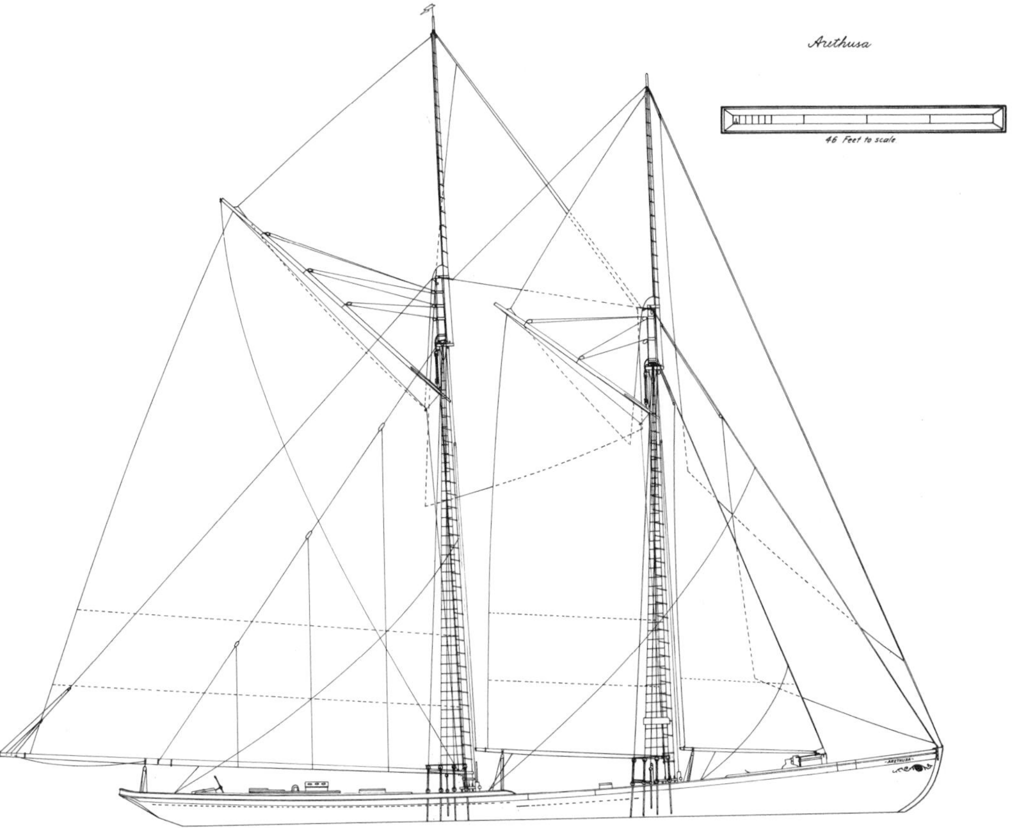
Arethusa
46 Feet to scale

FIGURE 30

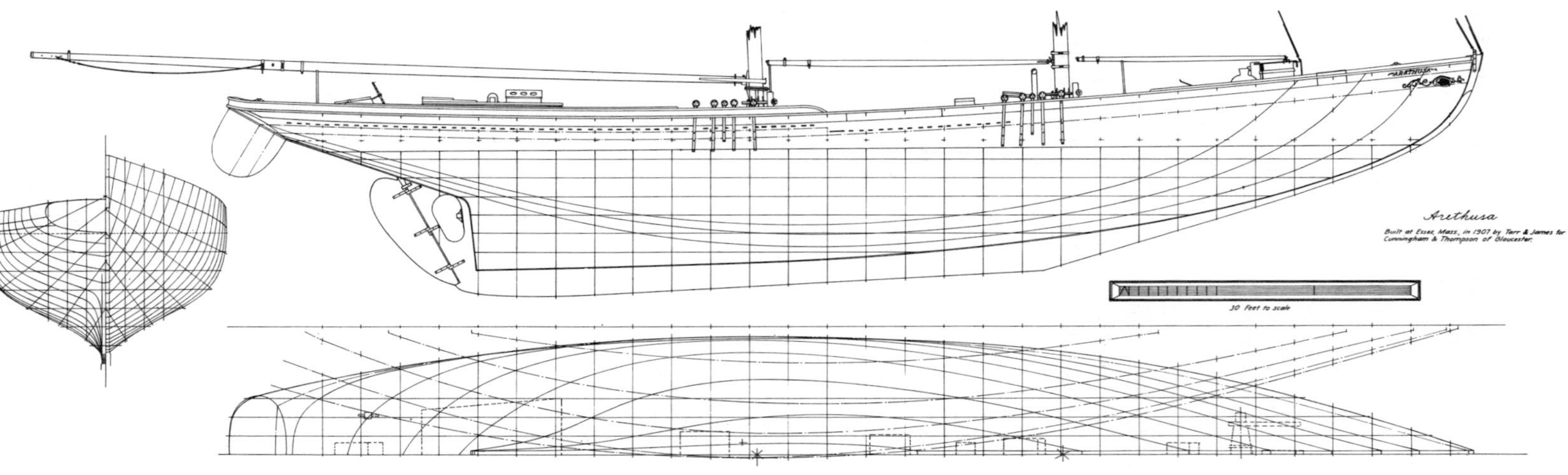
"ARETHUSA"
Arethusa
Built at Essex, Mass., in 1907 by Tarr & James for
Cunningham & Thompson of Gloucester.
30 Feet to scale

PLATE 120. *Arethusa*, 1907, mould loft plan

formed. From this, it rose in a long easy sweep to fair into the short-overhang curved stem. The sternpost was set at a slight rake. The counter, being designed for an auxiliary fishing schooner, was very long and heavy, with a very sharply raking elliptical transom. The entrance was long, sharp, and very slightly hollow abaft the stem rabbet.

The run was quite long with much straight to the buttocks. The midsection had hollow garboards, much rise of floor, fair and rather easy bilge, with slight tumble home in the topside. This schooner represented the final step in the improvement of the knockabout; within ten years her decline as a sailing type was to become apparent and the sailing vessels gradually became motor "draggers" (trawlers) with spars cut down or unshipped entirely.

It was an accepted belief at Gloucester that the McManus-designed schooner *Oriole* (Design No. 132, March 28, 1908), built at Essex by Tarr and James, had sailed at a speed of 16 knots. This is an excessive claim of speed for a vessel of the length of the *Oriole*, and for a commercial sailing vessel. For the purposes here, it is only necessary to say that the *Oriole* was a vessel with an accepted record of having much exceeded the speed-length ratio that she would normally be expected to reach. The history of the *Clintonia* and *Oriole* design has been given on page 261. The plan of the *Oriole* shows some apparent relationship to a design made in 1904 by McManus, used to build the *Clintonia* in 1907. This matter will be discussed below with regard to the *Elizabeth Howard*.

In 1917 Frank C. Adams, a shipbuilder of East Boothbay, Maine, went to Boston with Captain Howard of Portland, Maine, to see Tom McManus. They wished to build to the *Oriole* lines but wanted a knockabout schooner. It was decided to lengthen the *Oriole* lines by the bow. The *Oriole* was a large vessel for an American fishing schooner, having the following register dimensions: 115.5′ x 25.0′ x 12.0′. She was 127′-0″ moulded length at main rail cap, 25′-1″ moulded beam, and 13′-1″ moulded depth at side. Since the *Oriole* had a normal raking sternpost, the prick post would have to be added as the new vessel was to be an auxiliary. This required a small change in the vicinity of the sternpost. The changes were drawn, except that offsets of *Oriole*, a sketch of the mode of lengthening stem, and a hull profile on a small scale were all that Adams received. Plate 121 shows the lines of *Oriole* as plotted for the mould-loft by means of the offsets and the sketches. The small dash lines show the new vessel's lines and the unbroken lines show *Oriole*. This made the new vessel, the *Elizabeth Howard*, 148′-8″ moulded length at main rail cap; otherwise she maintained the same moulded dimensions as the *Oriole*. It is a matter for thought that the *Howard* obtained a reputation as a fast sailer in moderate and light winds—certainly the claim for *Oriole* shows plainly that she was a heavy-weather sailer.

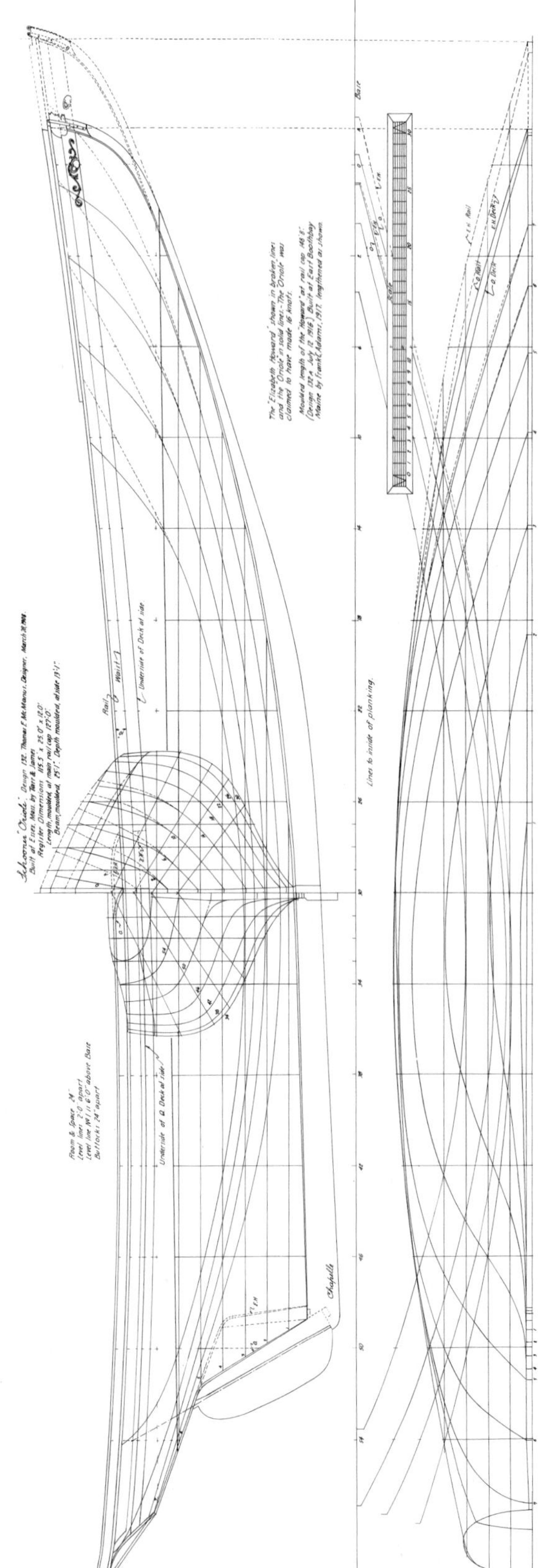
Schooner "Oriole". Design 132. Thomas F. McManus, Designer. March 28, 1908.
Built at Essex, Mass. by Tarr & James
Register Dimensions 115.5' x 25.0' x 12.0'
Length, moulded, at main rail cap 127'-0"
Beam, moulded, 25'-1". Depth moulded, at side 13'-1"
The "Elizabeth Howard" shown in broken lines and the "Oriole" in solid lines.-The "Oriole" was claimed to have made 16 knots.
Moulded length of the "Howard" at rail cap 148'-8".
(Design 132 A July 12 1916) Built at East Boothbay Maine by Frank C. Adams, 1917. lengthened as shown.
Room & Space 24"
Level lines 2'-0" apart
Level line No. 1 is 6'-0" above Base
Buttocks 24" apart
Rail
Waist
Underside of Deck at side
Underside of Q. Deck at side
Lines to inside of planking.
Base
Scale
Chapelle

PLATE 121. *Oriole, Elizabeth Howard*, 1908, mould loft plan

There is no need to describe the lines of the *Howard* here since a description of *Oriole* is the proper source.

The *Oriole* was a large schooner having a strong sheer, a short straight keel with much drag running from the heel of the sternpost to just forward of the design midsection, thence sweeping up to the round stem in a long, easy sweep, hardening on the stem to give somewhat of a "rater bow." The sternpost raked sharply and was retained as the prick post in the *Howard.* The counter was of moderate length and not heavy. The elliptical transom raked sharply. The entrance was long and sharp, the midsection being abaft the midlength of the hull. The run was also long, fine, and with some straight in the buttocks but not to any unusual degree. The midsection shows very hollow garboard and floor, a rather firm turn of bilge, and some tumble home in the topside. The body plan of *Oriole* does not suggest any very marked power to carry sail nor anything unusual to support a claim for 16 knots speed. The alterations made in the lines to build the *Elizabeth Howard* had no departures in her underbody from *Oriole* except for the minor change in the fairing at the sternpost. No deck layouts for these two vessels were found, nor any masting sketch. The *Elizabeth Howard* was not employed in fishing in her early years, rather she was freighting salt fish from Newfoundland. Her racing career has been fully published during the fishermen races and needs no attention here. The changes made in her for racing were said to have been the shifting of the foremast and addition of a bowsprit, with sails cut to match. There was the usual question of whether or not the alterations increased her sailing speed. Some who had sailed in her before and after the alterations claimed she was faster as a knockabout—a similar opinion existed regarding *Arethusa.*

Plate 122 shows lines and much detail of the knockabout *Rhodora* and of an unidentified schooner built on her lines. The ticked lines show *Rhodora* as built; she was an auxiliary schooner. She was originally pole-masted and bald-headed, but was resparred with topmasts, as shown in the spar table of lengths. She was a short-bow overhang knockabout designed by McManus on October 3, 1908 and built by Arthur D. Story at Essex in 1910. Her register dimensions were 103.9′ x 23.5′ x 11.0′. She was 117′-3″ overall, 102′-3″ between perpendiculars, 23′-0″ moulded beam, 23′-6″ extreme beam. It is to be noted that the design was made in the early fall of 1908 but apparently it was two years before the design was used to build a vessel.

The design shown in Plate 122 had a graceful sheer with a good deal of spring, a short, straight keel with much drag running from the sternpost to almost under the foremast, where an angular gripe was formed. From here the keel rose to a round stem, ending in an easy sweep in the fore rake. The original design shows a strongly raking sternpost, long and rather light

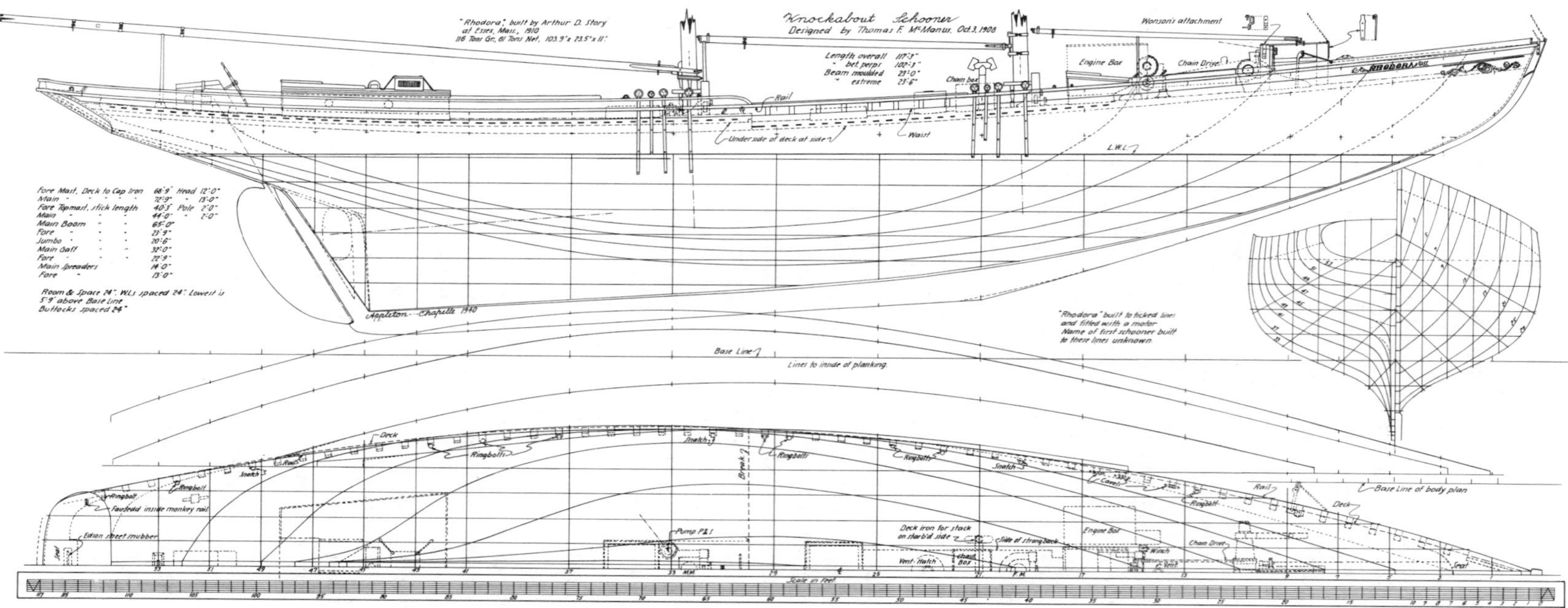
Knockabout Schooner
Designed by Thomas F. McManus. Oct. 3, 1908
"Rhodora", built by Arthur D. Story
at Essex, Mass., 1910
116 Tons Gr., 81 Tons Net, 103.9' x 23.5' x 11.'
Length overall 117'-3"
" bet. perps 102'-3"
Beam moulded 23'-0"
" extreme 23'-6"
Wonson's attachment
Engine Box
Chain Drive
Chain box
Rail
Waist
Underside of deck at side
L.W.L.
Fore Mast, Deck to Cap Iron 68'-9" Head 12'-0"
Main " " " " " 72'-9" " 13'-0"
Fore Topmast, stick length 40'-3" Pole 2'-0"
Main " " " 44'-0" " 2'-0"
Main Boom " " 65'-0"
Fore " " " 23'-9"
Jumbo " " " 20'-6"
Main Gaff " " 32'-0"
Fore " " " 22'-9"
Main Spreaders 14'-0"
Fore " 13'-0"
Room & Space 24". W.L.s spaced 24". Lowest is
5'-9" above Base Line
Buttocks spaced 24"
Appleton—Chapelle 1940
"Rhodora" built to ticked lines
and fitted with a motor
Name of first schooner built
to these lines unknown.
Base Line
Lines to inside of planking.
Base Line of body plan
Deck
Rail
Ringbolt
Snatch
Break
Fairlead inside monkey rail
Edson sheet snubber
Pump P&S
Deck iron for stack on starb'd side
Side of strongback
Vent. Hatch
Chain Box
Engine Box
Chain Drive
Winch
Scale in Feet

PLATE 122. *Rhodora*, 1908, mould loft plan

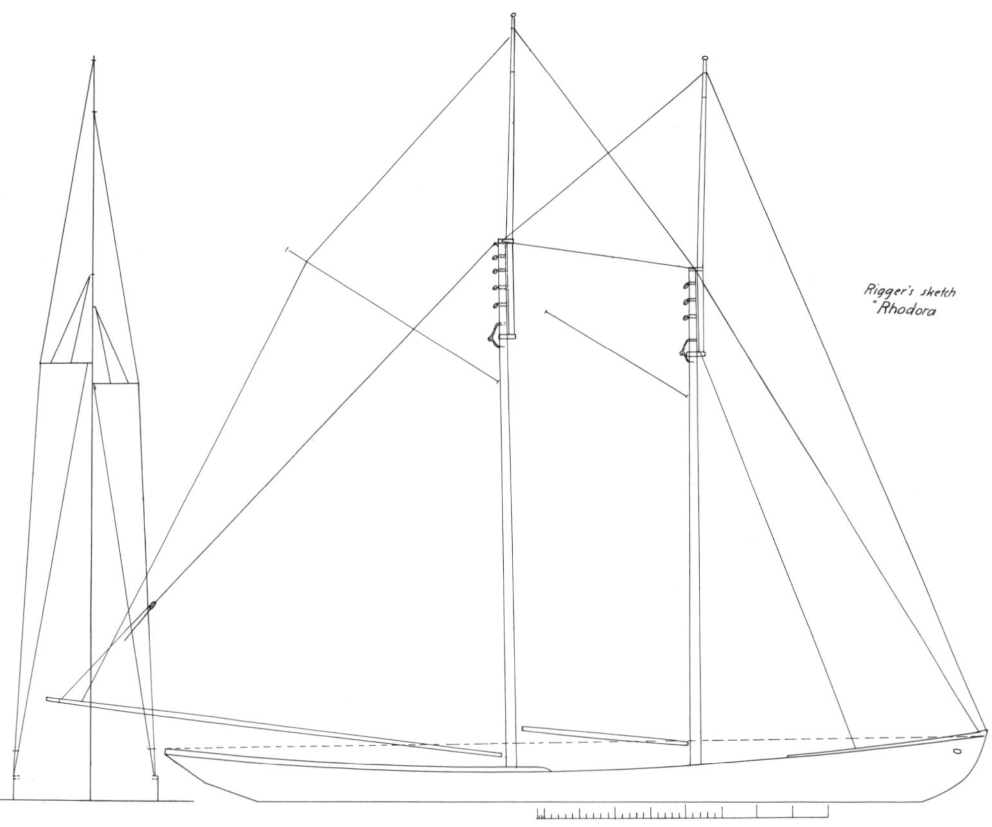
Rigger's sketch
"Rhodora

FIGURE 31

counter, partly submerged, with a very raking elliptical transom. The entrance was long and sharp, and the run was of moderate length with straight buttocks. The midship section had a very hollow garboard, moderate rise in floor, and a firm bilge with tumble home in the topside. The alterations made for *Rhodora* included fairing off the angular fore gripe and refairing the tuck to fit a short sternpost forward of the original sternpost, which became the prick post, allowing room for an aperture. This lengthened the counter. The plan shows the deck arrangement and fittings of the vessel when she was surveyed in the winter of 1938–1939 at Gloucester. The *Rhodora* was credited with a range in speed up to 14 knots. She was eventually sold to Newfoundland, where she was wrecked in 1953.

Plate 123 is the lines of the second knockabout built on the model of the *Shepherd King* (Plate 109), the *Aspinet.* The third knockabout on this model was the *John J. Fallon;* the *Aspinet* and *Fallon* were built at Essex in 1928 by Tarr and James. These two vessels were given more sheer than the *King* and had a very marked rater bow. Otherwise they were like that

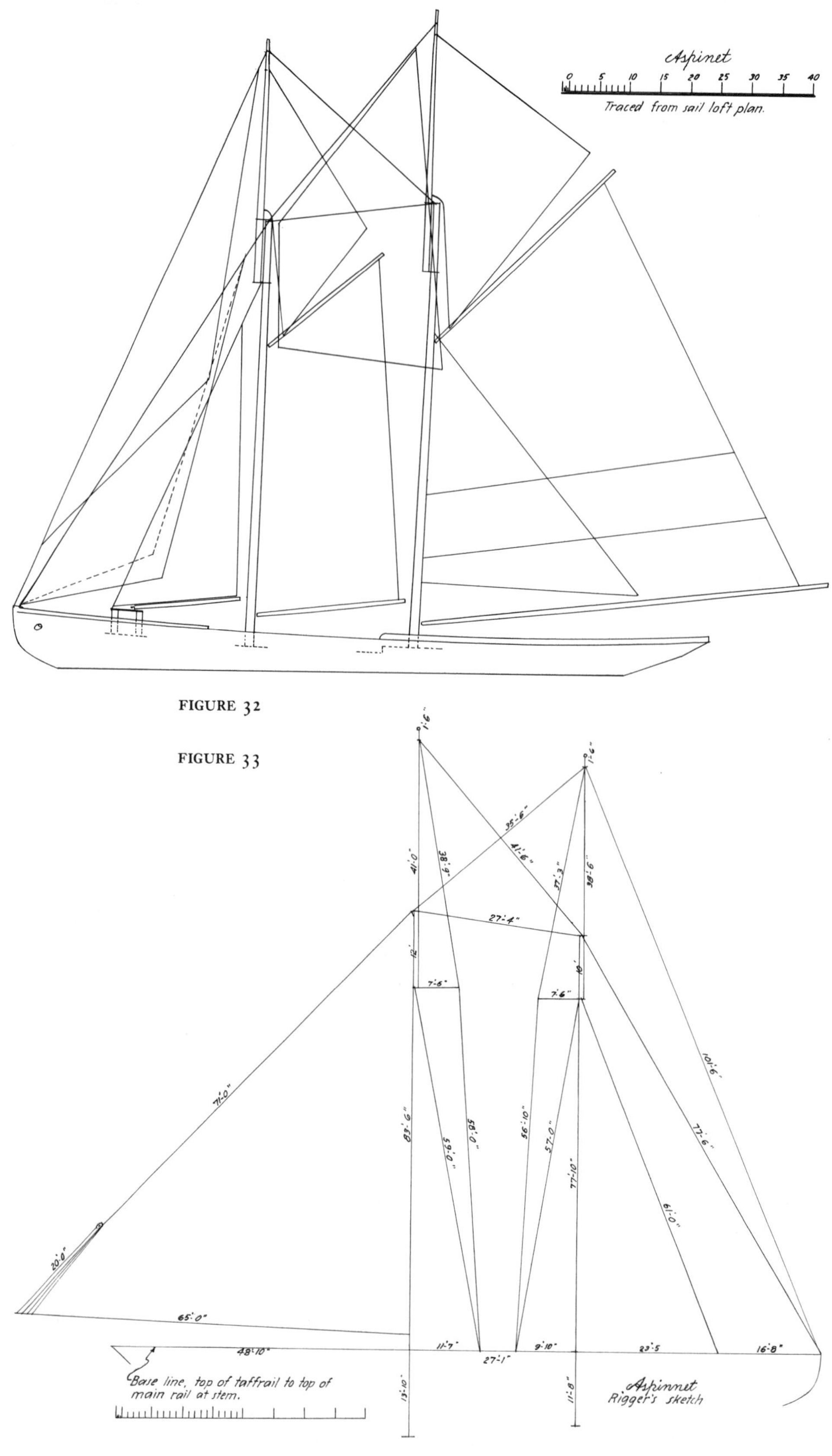
Aspinet
0 5 10 15 20 25 30 35 40
Traced from sail loft plan.
1'-6"
1'-6"
35'-6"
41'-0"
38'-9"
41'-6"
37'-3"
38'-6"
27'-4"
12'
10'
7'-6"
7'-6"
71'-0"
101'-6"
83'-6"
59'-0"
58'-0"
56'-10"
57'-0"
77'-10"
77'-6"
61'-0"
20'-0"
65'-0"
48'-10"
11'-7"
27'-1"
9'-10"
23'-5
16'-8"
Base line, top of taffrail to top of main rail at stem.
13'-10"
11'-8"
Aspinnet
Rigger's sketch

FIGURE 32

FIGURE 33

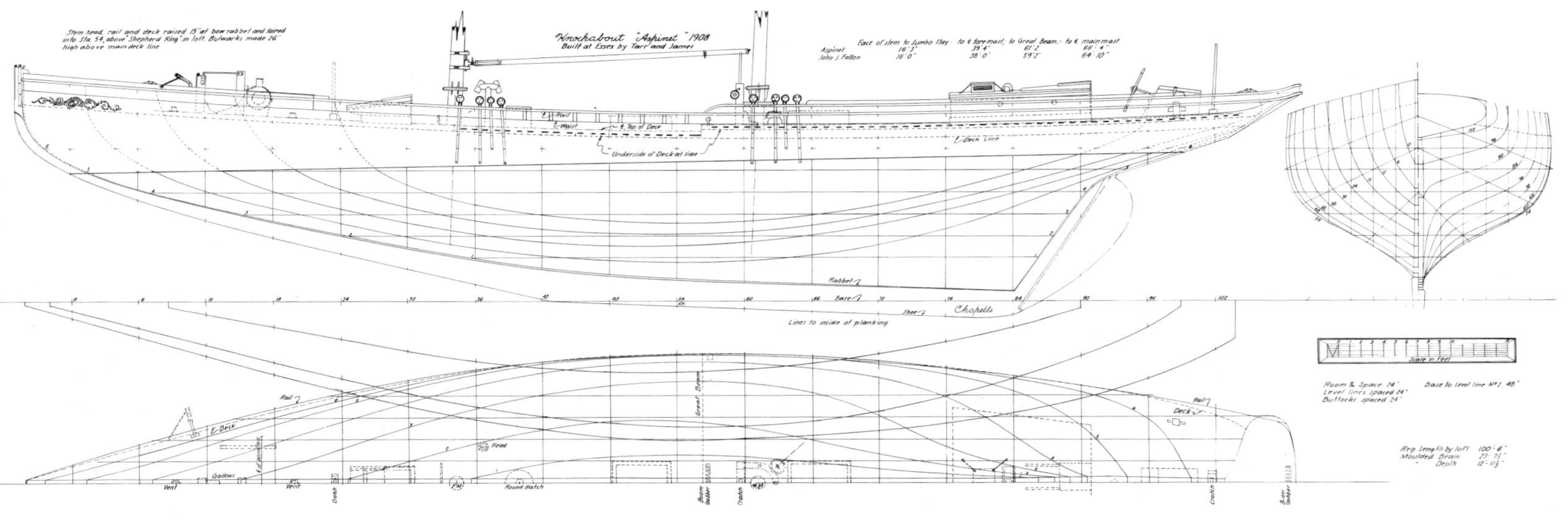
Stem head, rail and deck raised 15" at bow rabbet and faired into Sta. 54, above "Shepherd King" in loft. Bulwarks made 26" high above main deck line
Knockabout "Aspinet" 1908
Built at Essex by Tarr and James
Face of stem to Jumbo Stay · to ℄ foremast; to Great Beam, - to ℄ mainmast
Aspinet 16' 3" 39' 4" 61' 2 66' 4"
John J. Fallon 16' 0" 38' 0" 59' 2" 64' 10"
Rail
Waist
Top of Deck
Underside of Deck at side
Deck Line
Rabbet
Base
Sheer
Chapelle
Lines to inside of planking
Scale in Feet
Room & Space 24"
Level lines spaced 24"
Buttocks spaced 24"
Base to level line No 1. 48"
Reg. Length by loft 100' 6"
Moulded Beam 23' 7½"
" Depth 12' 11½"
Deck
Great Beam
Head
Gallows
Vent
Crotch
Round Hatch
Boom Gabber
Boom Gabber

PLATE 123. *Aspinet*, 1908, mould loft plan

vessel in nearly all respects. Later, two more vessels were built on the moulds of the *Shepherd King*—the *Virginia* (1926) and the *Rainbow* (1929)—but with some midship moulds omitted so as to produce power draggers 80.5′ and 89.3′ registered length, respectively. Both were built at Essex by John F. James and Son. All of the vessels built with the *King*'s moulds were owned by Jacob O. Brigham, except the *Fallon* which was owned by John J. Fallon. The port of hail for all was Boston, Massachusetts. In the reduction in length, the beam of the two smaller vessels was reduced also. Though apparently successful draggers, the *Virginia* and *Rainbow* were odd in appearance, seeming to have ends too sharp for the full midsections employed.

The *Aspinet* and the *John J. Fallon* were very smart sailers, particularly so in blowing weather. There is no need to describe the *Aspinet* and *Fallon* for they were like the *Shepherd King* in all respects, except for the stem profile and the increased amount of sheer forward. The register dimensions of the vessels were: *Shepherd King*, 100′ x 23.3′ x 12.2′; *Aspinet*, 102.5′ x 23.7′ x 12.2′; *John J. Fallon*, 103.0′ x 24.0′ x 12′; *Virginia*, 80.5′ x 21.2′ x 9.7′; and *Rainbow*, 89.3′ x 21.6′ x 10.0′

The placing of the jumbo sheet horse in knockabouts forward of the foremast, as in *Aspinet*, were a hazard for men entering and leaving the forecastle companionway, for the threshing of the sheet and its blocks could deal a fearful blow. In some vessels the companionway was placed as close as possible to the foreside of the foremast with the sheet block very close to the foreside of the companionway. However, this sometimes produced a poor lead for the jumbo sheet. Hence some knockabouts were built with the forecastle companionway abaft the foremast and the jumbo sheet forward of the foremast. A number of knockabouts, like *Arethusa*, were altered after launch to give this deck layout. The position of the forecastle companionway was affected in one way or another by the lengths of forecastle or fish hold desired, so the matter was not just a question of safety. Coming so late in the evolution of the New England fishing schooners, the final positions of forecastle companionway and of the jumbo sheet were never fully settled, apparently.

A large McManus-designed knockabout was built by A. D. Story at Essex in 1909 and named *Virginia*. This schooner, shown in Plate 124, was 115′-2″ moulded length at rail cap, 22′-6″ moulded beam and her registry dimensions were 102.2′ x 23.0′ x 10.2′. The *Virginia* was another good example of a short-bow overhang sailing knockabout of McManus' design. The schooner had a handsome sheer, a straight keel rabbet running from the strongly raking sternpost to beneath the main hatch, then fairing in a long and very easy sweep to the curved profile stem. The counter was of moderate length with a sharply raked heart-shaped transom. The en-

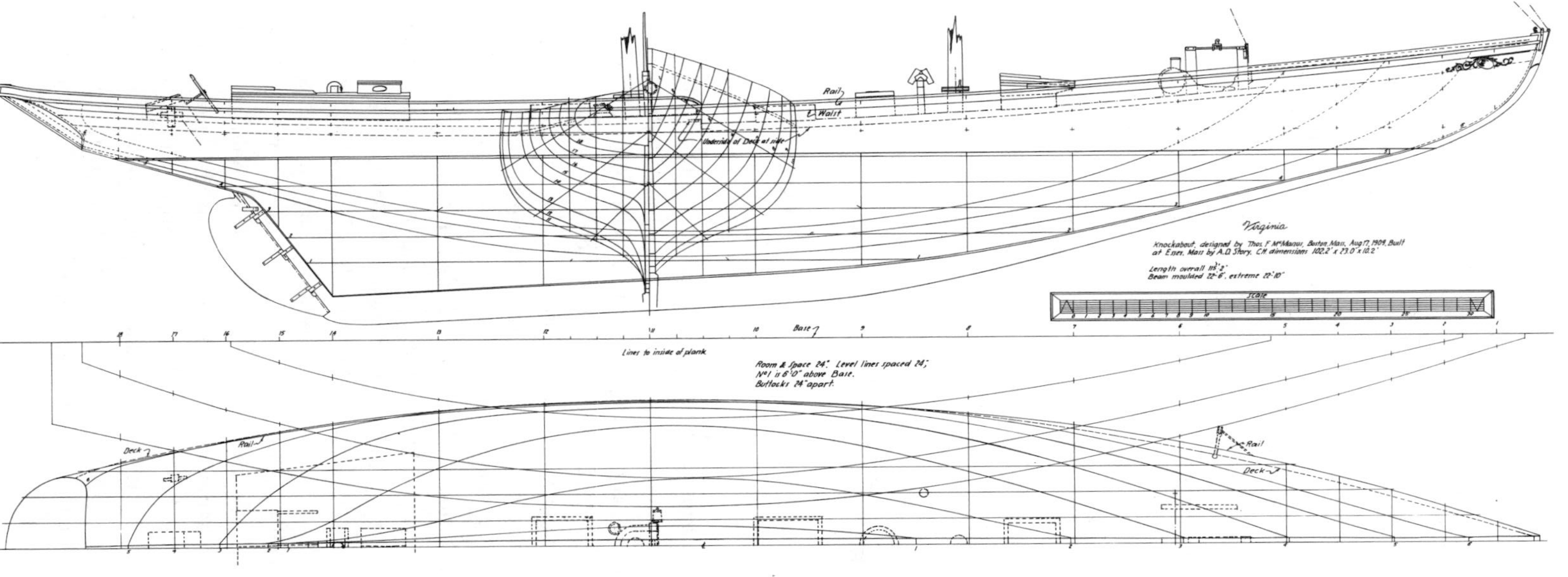
Virginia
Knockabout, designed by Thos. F. McManus, Boston, Mass., Aug 17, 1909. Built at Essex, Mass by A.D. Story. C.H. dimensions 102.2' x 23.0' x 10.2'
Length overall 115'-2"
Beam moulded 22'-6", extreme 22'-10"
Scale
Rail
Waist
Underside of Deck at side
Base
Lines to inside of plank
Room & Space 24". Level lines spaced 24";
No 1 is 6'-0" above Base.
Buttocks 24" apart.
Deck
Rail
Rail
Deck

PLATE 124. *Virginia*, 1909, mould loft plan

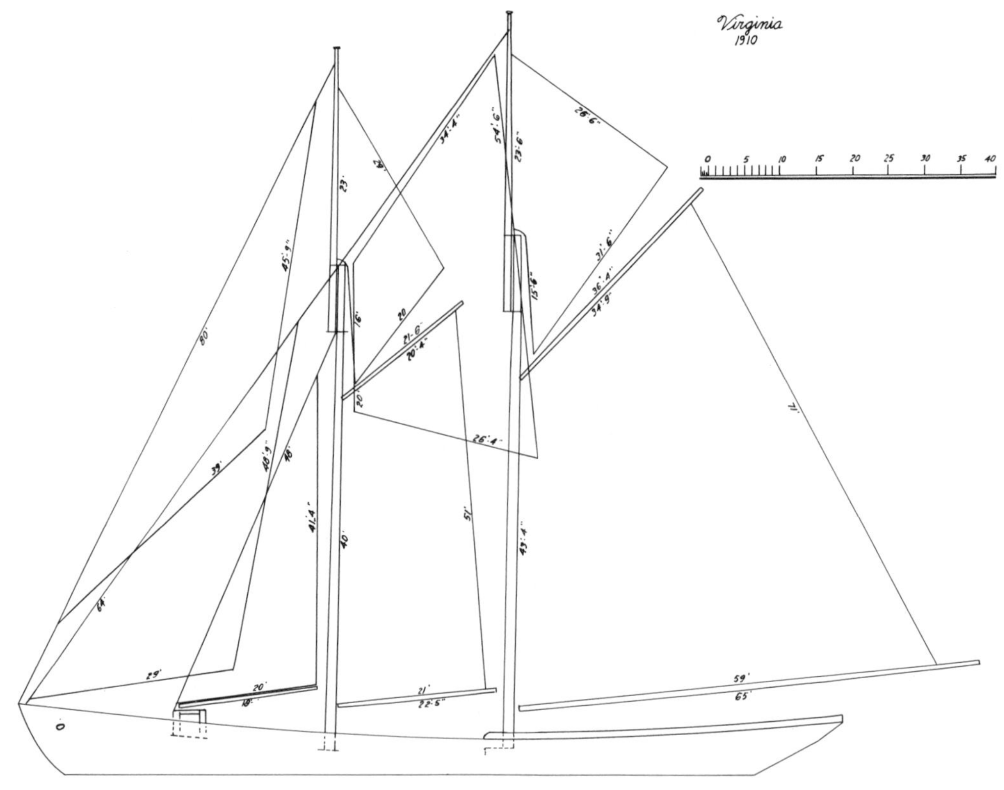
Virginia
1910
0 5 10 15 20 25 30 35 40

FIGURE 34

trance was long and sharp, with a very slight hollow in the L.W.L. just abaft the stem rabbet. The run was long with straight buttocks carried well forward, producing a fine run. The form of the midsection followed McManus' then common practice: hollow garboard, rising straight floor, full, easy bilge with tumble home in the topside, to give a vessel with an easy roll, not hard on her spars and rigging yet capable of fast sailing in moderate to strong winds.

The evolution of McManus' Indian Header type of schooner produced a variety of related hull forms by 1909–1910. Plate 125 shows the lines used, apparently, to build at least two schooners fitted for power installation. The identity of these schooners has been based on date and dimensions given in the register. It seems quite certain that they may have been the *Stiletto*, built in Gloucester in 1909–1910, 105.0′ x 24.8′ x 11.7′ register dimensions, and the *Sylvania*, 105.6′ x 24.8′ x 11.6′, built in the same yard as *Stiletto*, and at the same time, by John Bishop. It cannot be determined which schooner was built according to the broken lines. Both of these schooners were notable sailers and were admirable sea boats.

McManus identified the design as "No. 153," but he kept no record of the names of the vessels a numbered design represented. Also, some designs

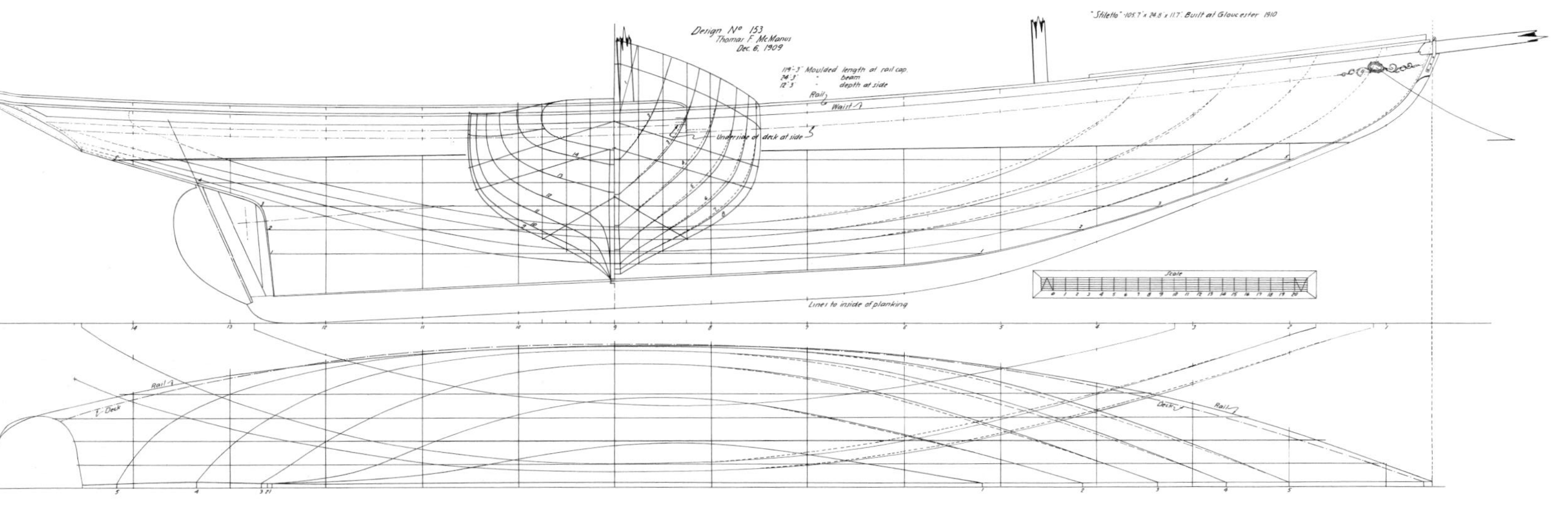
Design No 153
Thomas F. McManus
Dec. 6, 1909
119'-3" Moulded length at rail cap.
24'-3" " beam
12'-3" " depth at side
Rail
Waist
Underside of deck at side
"Stiletto" 105.7' x 24.8' x 11.7'. Built at Gloucester 1910
Scale
Lines to inside of planking
Rail
Deck

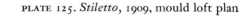

PLATE 125. *Stiletto*, 1909, mould loft plan

have been found without design numbers. The only resort was to attempt identification by means of comparisons of scaled register dimensions, dates of build and design, names of builders and owners.

This schooner design was for a vessel having a graceful sheer, a straight keel rabbet having very moderate drag and running from a short sternpost forward to beneath the main hatch position; from here the rabbet rose in a slight sweep to fair in with a short-overhang curved stem rabbet, somewhat of the rater bow form. The counter was long, to make room for the prick post, and had a sharply raking elliptical transom. The entrance was long, sharp, and very slightly convex, shown in unbroken lines for the original design and in broken lines for a later revision. The broken lines included waterlines in the half-breadth plan, buttocks in the sheer plan, and section modifications in the body plan. The run was long and easy with long, straight buttocks. The propeller aperture is shown without fairing or fairing blocking, both of which must have been used in construction. The midsection was formed with only a slight hollow at the garboard and steeply rising straight floor carried well out and up to a high, rather quick turn of bilge, with a little tumble home in the topside. Though designed as an auxiliary, this schooner was intended to sail fast and to be easy on her rig and gear.

These schooners were 119′-3″ moulded length at rail cap, 23′-0″ moulded beam, and 12′-3″ depth at side.

McManus' reputation as a fishing schooner designer had become well known in both Maine and in the Canadian Maritime Provinces by 1910. The Canadian schooner builders had been well informed on New England fishing schooner design as early as 1886, and in 1892 the Canadian fishery patrol schooner *Kingfisher*, register dimensions 100.0′ x 24.0′ x 10.0′, was built at Shelburne, Nova Scotia on the then latest *Fredonia* model; she was equal in speed and performance to some of the better New England vessels of the period. After 1900 a few designs were purchased in New England, including some by McClain, Crowninshield, and McManus. As mentioned earlier, designs suitable for partial rock ballasting were in demand and some of the purchased designs were ordered with this as a requirement. It seems evident that this was sometimes done in the hope of finding a design superior to the provincial vessels, then in the Canadian fisheries, yet suited for the partial rock ballasting.

In the fall of 1910 McManus received an order for such a design from the Newfoundland fishing company owned by the Hollet family. This schooner was built by the Shelburne Shipbuilding Company, at Shelburne, Nova Scotia, in 1911; James Hardy was the master builder in this yard. The Shelburne shipyards built many vessels for Newfoundland owners, most of them coasters. In fact, the Shelburne yards' reputations were more for building fine coasting schooners than for building fishing schooners.

The vessel built by the Shelburne Shipbuilding Company was named the *Gordon M. Hollet* and is shown in Plate 126. She was 106′-4″ moulded length at rail cap, 23′-10″ moulded beam, and 11′-5″ moulded depth at side. The *Hollet* had a graceful sheer, a long, straight keel rabbet carried to forward of the midsection, fairing in a long sweep up to a very short-overhang round stem. A number of Canadian half-models of fishing schooners suggest that many of the Canadian designers favored a very short-overhang stem (almost a plumb bow) in 1900–1912, such as is shown in the *Hollet*. The stern was formed by a raking sternpost, a rather long counter, and a very raking elliptical transom. The entrance was long and sharp with a slight hollow about the loadline, just abaft the stem rabbet. The run was long with very straight buttocks carried well forward. The midsection had a very slight hollow in the garboard, a short rising straight floor, and an easy turn in the bilge with slight tumble home in the topside. Inquiry produced little information on the performance of the *Hollet* except for the usual claim that she was a good sailer and sea boat.

Much of the Nova Scotia fishing schooner building was carried on in small yards like those at Essex. The number of fishing schooners built in these yards became very large, over 200 vessels by 1900. The Canadians carried on an extensive cod fishery—"banking"—and their vessels grew in size until, by the time World War I began, vessels about 110 feet moulded length at rail cap became common. Auxiliary power was late in appearing in the Canadian schooners.

The auxiliary knockabout had now become the New England fishing schooner type. Carrying full sail power on a fast hull, the typical knockabout was fitted with a powerful oil engine, which lessened the danger of fuel oil or gasoline fires and explosions. It therefore might be said that the knockabout was the acme in the long evolution of the New England fishing schooner.

Plate 127 is the plan of the knockabout *Gertrude DeCosta*, built at Essex by Tarr and James in 1912. The plan from which this plate was drawn was a rather roughly drawn set of lines in pencil. McManus often complained that his designs were "stolen"; that is to say, a design was purchased from him and a vessel built, then if the vessel were successful or outstanding, other vessels were built "on the moulds" without any design royalties being paid to him. Alterations in design would naturally take place in this stage and this was probably done in the mould loft if the alterations were more than adding a frame space or two. As a result, when McManus tried to recover the plans and offsets, he was not completely successful, though he managed to reduce the number of plans that would otherwise have survived. Moulds made from his designs were often retained in the loft, or in

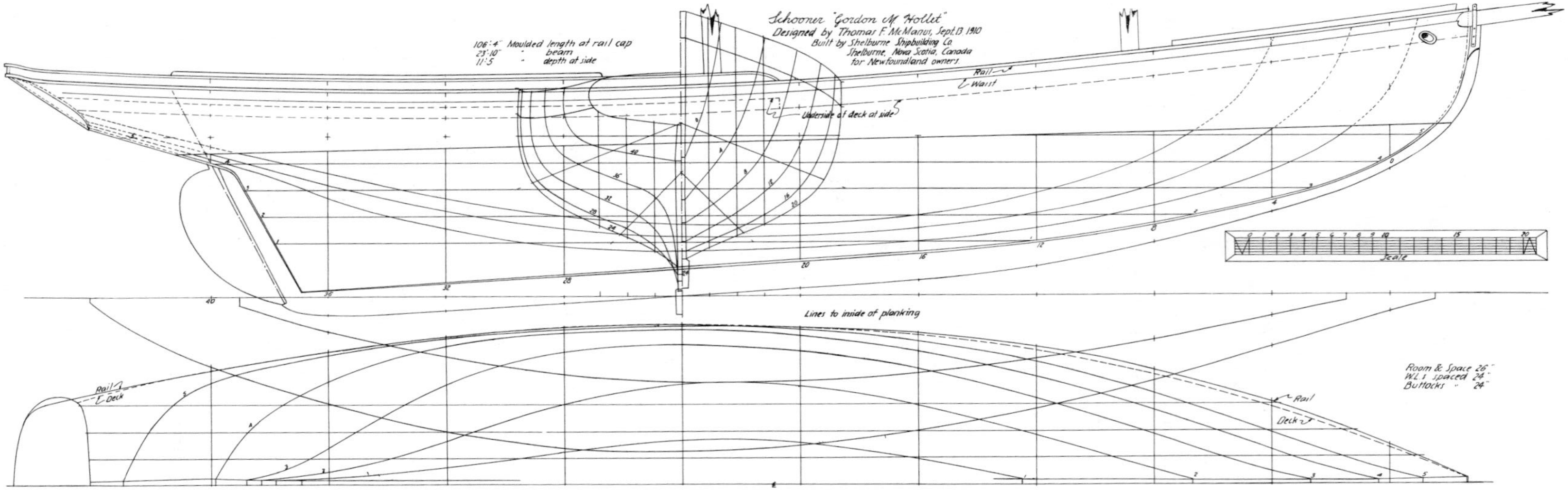

Schooner "Gordon M. Hollet"
Designed by Thomas F. McManus, Sept. 13. 1910
Built by Shelburne Shipbuilding Co.
Shelburne, Nova Scotia, Canada
for Newfoundland owners.

106'-4" Moulded length at rail cap
23'-10" " beam
11'-5 " depth at side

Rail
Waist
Underside of deck at side
Scale
Lines to inside of planking
Rail
Deck
Room & Space 26"
W.L.'s spaced 24"
Buttocks " 24"

PLATE 126. *Gordon M. Hollet*, 1910, plan

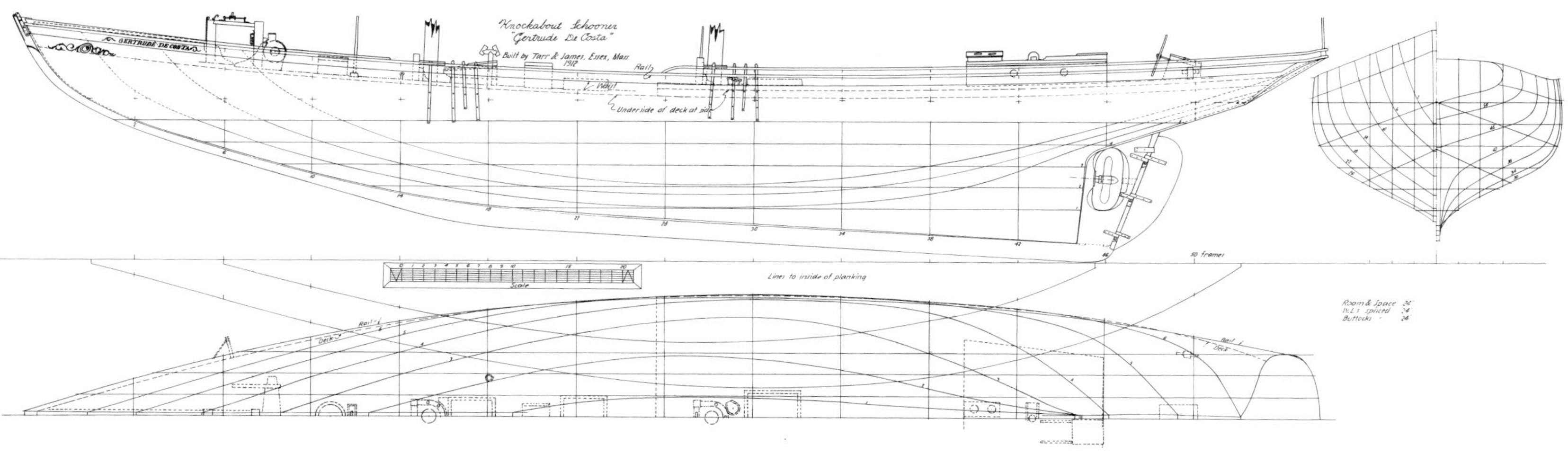
Knockabout Schooner
"Gertrude De Costa"
Built by Tarr & James, Essex, Mass
1912
GERTRUDE DE COSTA
Rail
Underside of deck at side
50 frames
Lines to inside of planking
Scale
Room & Space 24
Buttocks 24

PLATE 127. *Gertrude DeCosta*, 1912, mould loft plan

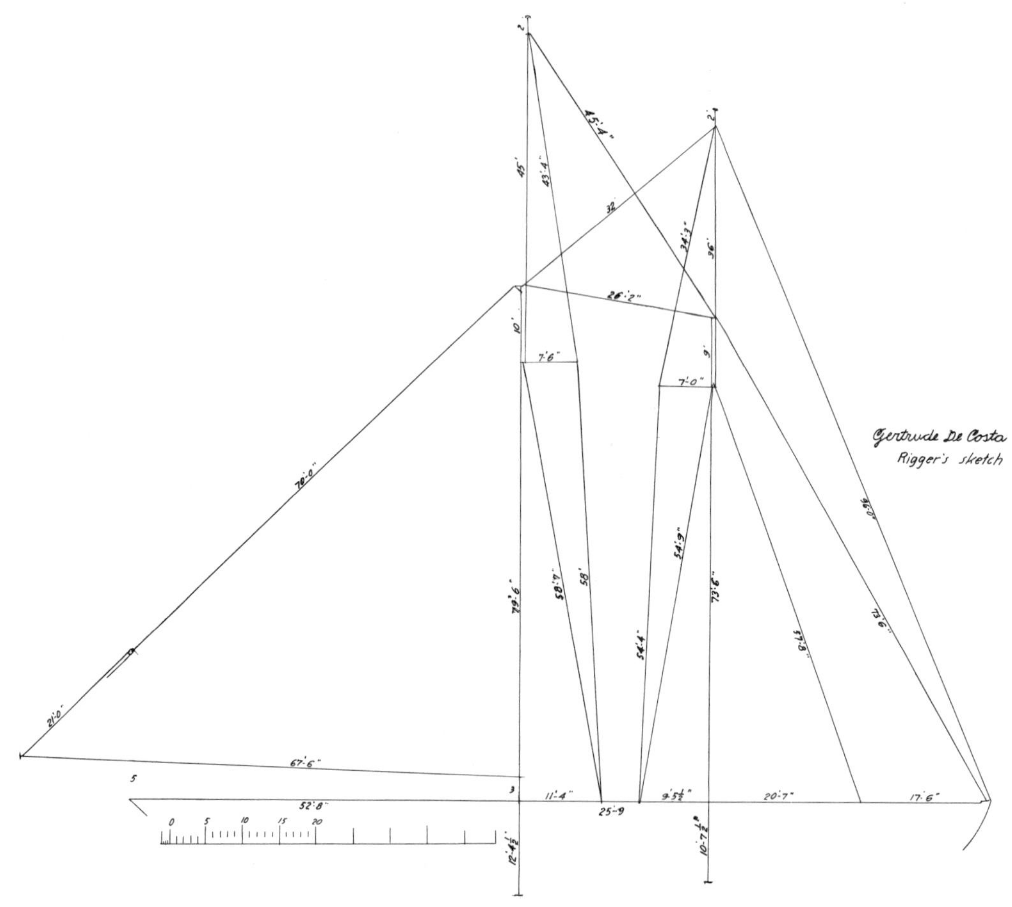
Gertrude De Costa
Rigger's sketch
45'
43'4"
32'
36'
26'2"
10'
7'6"
9'
7'0"
21'0"
67'6"
52'8"
11'4"
25'9
20'7"
17'6"
79'6"
58'
54'4"
0
5
10
15
20

FIGURE 35

the shipyards, and some of these moulds were turned over to McManus, but moulds were too large and awkward to store, so full sets of moulds were often available for unauthorized use. Due to long-established practices, the ownership of the "building rights" to designs was and is very difficult to establish and retain. McManus produced a master model which he and others made the point of departure, as we have seen had been the case with the *Fredonia* model.

The *Gertrude DeCosta* had a graceful sheer, a straight keel running from the sternpost to beneath the after fore chains, and then rising in an almost straight fore rake to fair into a short-overhang curved stem. The fore gripe was faired off in a short sweep. The sternpost was almost upright with raking prick post abaft, and the usual blocking to permit fairing of the aperture. The counter was long and partly immersed, with short, straight buttocks so drawn as to give room for the engine beds and stringers under the quarterdeck just forward of the fore end of the cabin trunk. The entrance was long and sharp and slightly convex. The run was of adequate length but the body was carried farther aft than was common in sailing fishing schooners. The midsection had only slight hollow in the garboard, with long, rising, straight floor outboard. The bilge was well rounded and easy, with tumble home in the topside. The vessel first had topmasts but these were soon struck and she became pole-masted in effect, like most of her type. Register 102.5′ x 23.0′ x 8.6′.

A few knockabouts of great size for two-masted schooners were launched in New England right after the outbreak of World War I. Plate 128 shows one of these, the *Louise Howard,* built at East Boothbay, Maine, in 1917–1918 by Frank C. Adams, who also modeled her as an enlarged and improved *Elizabeth Howard.* An earlier knockabout, the *Catherine*, built in 1915 at Essex by A. D. Story, was the nearest rival of the *Louise Howard.* The *Catherine* was 120.6′ x 25.2′ x 12.4′, while the *Louise* was 129′-2″ x 26′-5½″ x 12′-4″. In truth, however, the *Louise Howard* does not appear to have been engaged in fishing but spent most if not all of her short career in freighting salt and cured fish from Newfoundland to the West Indies; she was wrecked at Fort Macon, Morehead City, North Carolina, April 14, 1921. The *Elizabeth Howard* was wrecked on Porter's Island, Nova Scotia, in November 1923.

The *Howard* had a graceful sheer, a straight keel running from the vertical sternpost to beneath the main hatch, then fairing up in a long, easy sweep to a short-overhang curved stem. The stern was built with prick post and aperture, having a long, partly immersed counter with a sharply raking elliptical transom. The entrance was long, sharp, and slightly convex. When the *Elizabeth Howard* was launched, it will be remembered that she came to rest by the head, so Adams modeled the *Louise* with a slightly fuller entrance in proportion. The run was long, fine, with straight buttocks carried a little forward of the tuck of the counter. The midsection was formed with a slight hollow at the garboard, long, rising, almost straight floor carried well outboard, a high, much-rounded bilge with slight tumble home in the topside. No comment on the performance of this vessel is available.

Prior to 1900 the few large fishing schooners built in New England were little over 100 foot tonnage length. Due to the availability of large timber. the strength of these vessels was not a problem in construction. A rough standard range of scantling had been established by the New England fishing schooner builders, based upon traditional structural practices. This utilized oak and yellow pine timbers in one piece up to at least 75 feet in length and squaring to 15″ x 15″ at the head. Timber 36″ x 36″ might be had. To obtain speedy construction, the builders usually filled up the fore and after deadwoods with a few pieces of large timber, rather than employing a

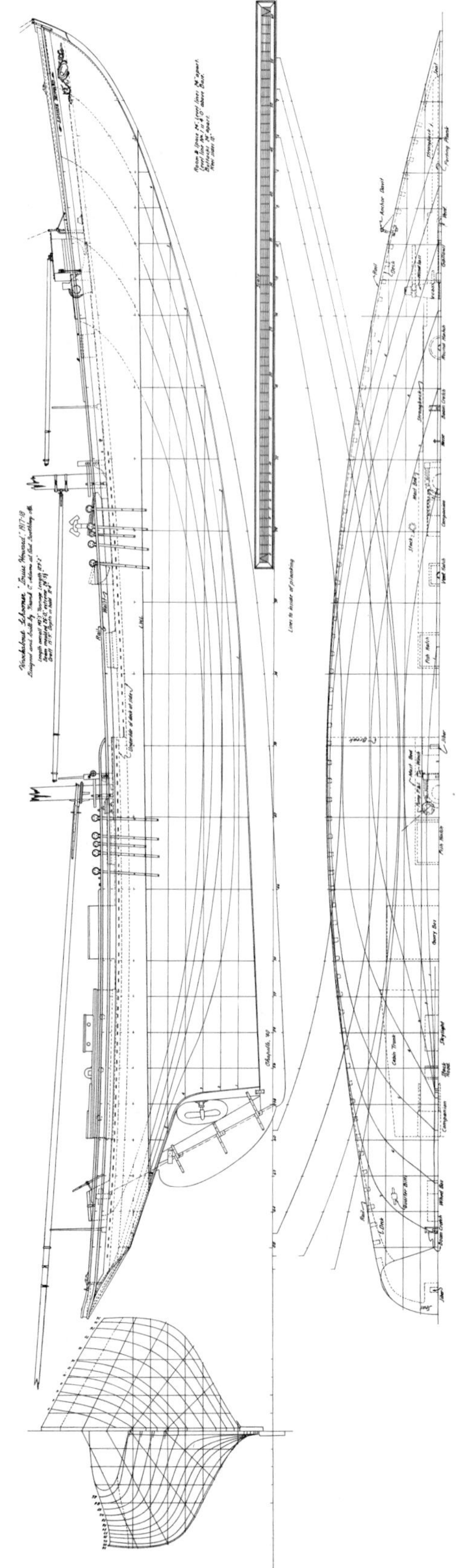

PLATE 128. *Louise Howard*, 1917, mould loft plan

great number of small pieces. Scarphs were, naturally, quite long, as were the faying surfaces. Longitudinals—keel, keelson stringers, clamps, and wales—were the longest possible from the readily available stock.

In the 1890s the New England builders began to have difficulty and expense in obtaining large timbers, first in masts and then in structural timber. As a result, there was a gradual decrease in timber dimensions, leading to the use of many small timbers in the structure. This in turn led to short scarphs and faying surfaces, without a decrease in labor costs.

At the same time there was a growing increase in the size of some New England schooners; the tonnage lengths ranged from 115 to 125 feet. By 1910 such vessels could only be built by use of many timbers, smaller in scantlings than in earlier years. The result was that the frame of a large schooner was built with numerous, but relatively small, timbers requiring more numerous, but small, fastenings. Wooden vessels built of many small timbers and fastenings, in the traditional manner, began "working" and then, in a short time, leaked and became hogged and weak. A different mode of construction had then to be developed, based on lamination in some degree. This the New England builders did not have time to develop in the 1900s and the results were to be seen in the last of the sailing fishing schooners, and in the racer, particularly.

The Canadians experienced much the same gradual change, but later than the New Englanders. A plentiful supply of timber, not of the species considered prime shipbuilding timber in the United States, however, of which large scantlings could be obtained, delayed the day of reckoning. It should be noted that shipbuilding timber was so squandered in World War I that large wooden shipbuilding was practically cut to a half within ten years after the war. A similar condition arose in World War II, when prime timber was used for pallets, concrete form timber, and in other work where low-grade timber would have been sufficient. Laminated construction was eventually developed in small craft, but too late to be fully understood, so that other materials—fiber glass, ferro-concrete, etc.—have replaced wood to a large degree.

The racing of fishing schooners, prior to the Canadian "international" challenge in 1920, had not produced vessels especially designed to race. All contenders were out-and-out fishing schooners, whose owners, or skippers, or backers, thought them fast and would foot the costs of fitting out. In such informal races as these there were no measurement limitations or rules; it was boat-for-boat, in which the larger fishing schooners usually won easily, as would be expected. But formal racing, as required by the Canadian challenge, led to a "deed of gift" and to measurement limitations that would determine a vessel's eligibility to race. As a result of the first two international races, both competitors began building vessels whose primary requirement was that they be eligible to race, not that they be good and economical fishing vessels. In the background was the fact that fishing vessels most suited for Canadian fisheries were large, say 130 to 150 feet in length on main rail cap, while the economical size of the New England vessels was in the range of about 110 to 125 feet; a scant few of the Boston fleet were 125 to 130 feet long.

In 1921 the schooner *Yankee* (Plate 129) was built by A. D. Story at Essex; the model was furnished by Edward Perkins of Essex and was for a schooner 125′-0″ moulded length at main rail, 25′-4″ moulded beam, and 12′-11″ moulded depth at side. The vessel was sailed in a number of trials in 1921 but was erratic, sometimes showing bursts of speed, but never a consistent performer. There was neither time nor money to "tune up" the vessel, though she had a competent skipper. After her disappointing performance as a racer she was converted into a "schooner dragger" power fisherman.

In the fall of 1923 the schooner *Shamrock* was laid down by A. D. Story at Essex for the O'Hara Brothers of Boston on the model of the *Yankee*. Shifts in mast positions, a deepening of the fore gripe, and lengthening of the counter to have been the few alterations made. The measurements of the *Shamrock* were 130′-0″ moulded length at main rail, 25′-4″ moulded beam, and 12′-11″ moulded depth at side. This vessel, too, failed in the trials for a lack in tuning-up, and probably funds; the vessel then became a schooner dragger.

Plate 129 shows a vessel having a rather small amount of sheer, long, straight keel with the fore gripe nearly underneath the after end of the forecastle, then rising in a long, nearly straight sweep to the overhanging round stem. The run was formed with a nearly vertical, short sternpost and the now usual prick post, with a long, deeply immersed counter having a raking heart-shaped transom. The straight buttocks were carried to a little forward of the tuck of the counter. The entrance was rather short, sharp, and somewhat convex. The midsection had a slight hollow in the garboard, a strongly rising, slightly curving, floor, with a high, slack bilge with marked tumble home above.

It was claimed by the skippers that these two vessels would have sailed very fast if some changes in spars and rig as well as trim could have been made. The *Yankee* had some lee helm which led to the shifts in positions of the masts in building *Shamrock*.

The development of the Canadian fishing schooners cannot be fully explored here for lack of space and also for a lack of sufficient research. As a general statement, their evolution was nearly parallel to the course of development seen in American schooners after about 1885. There were some departures from the New England vessels in deck arrangements,

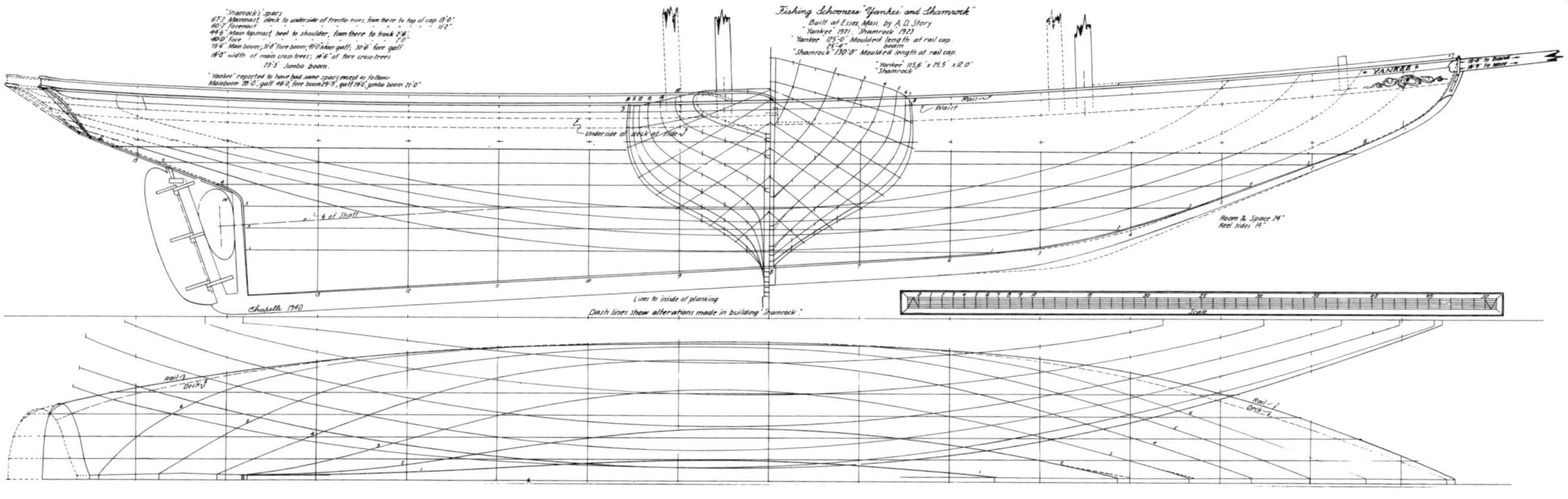
"Shamrock's" spars
67'7" Mainmast, deck to underside of trestle-trees, from there to top of cap 13'0"
60'7" Foremast " " " " " " " " " " " 11'2"
44'6" Main topmast, heel to shoulder; from there to truck 2'6"
40'0" Fore " " " " " " " " " 2'0"
75'6" Main boom; 31'6" Fore boom; 41'0" Main gaff; 30'6" fore gaff
16'0" width of main cross-trees; 14'6" of fore cross-trees
23'3" Jumbo boom.
"Yankee" reported to have had same spars except as follows-
Mainboom 78'0", gaff 46'0", fore boom 29'9", gaff 29'0", jumbo boom 21'0"
Fishing Schooners "Yankee" and "Shamrock"
Built at Essex, Mass. by A. D. Story
"Yankee" 1921, "Shamrock" 1923
"Yankee" 125'-0" Moulded length at rail cap.
25'-4" " beam
"Shamrock" 130'0" Moulded length at rail cap.
"Yankee" 115,6" x 25,5" x 12.0"
"Shamrock"
Rail
Waist
Underside of deck at side
YANKEE
Room & Space 24"
Keel sides 14"
℄ of Shaft
Lines to inside of planking
Dash lines show alterations made in building "Shamrock."
Chapelle 1940
Scale
Rail
Deck

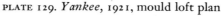

PLATE 129. *Yankee*, 1921, mould loft plan

windlasses, pumps, winches, and in hull, deck, and spare ironwork, also in deck furniture. The Canadians tended toward large, fast-sailing carriers (having a load draft of about 12 feet) that could be used for fishing and in the Newfoundland herring and salt-fish trades to the West Indies. The draft limitation was imposed by West Indian anchorages.

Beginning with the first series of races, the defeat of the Canadian *Delawana* by the Gloucester schooner *Esperanto* led the Canadians to build the schooner *Bluenose* in the Smith and Rhuland yard at Lunenburg, Nova Scotia, from the design of a young Halifax naval architect, William J. Roué. This was a vessel reported to have been 143′-0″ overall, or 130.2′ register length, and her lines, shown in Plate 130, obtained by the courtesy of her designer, verify the reported length. It has been alleged that the vessel departed from the design and that it was due to these departures that this vessel sailed very fast. A personal investigation and much testimony from other builders, fishermen, vessel owners, and yachtsmen who visited the yard during construction agree that the sheer and main deck were raised forward of the break in the deck, beginning here at zero increase of height in sheer and main deck and gradually increasing to the height of 16 inches at the rabbet of the stem for both sheer and deck. The purpose

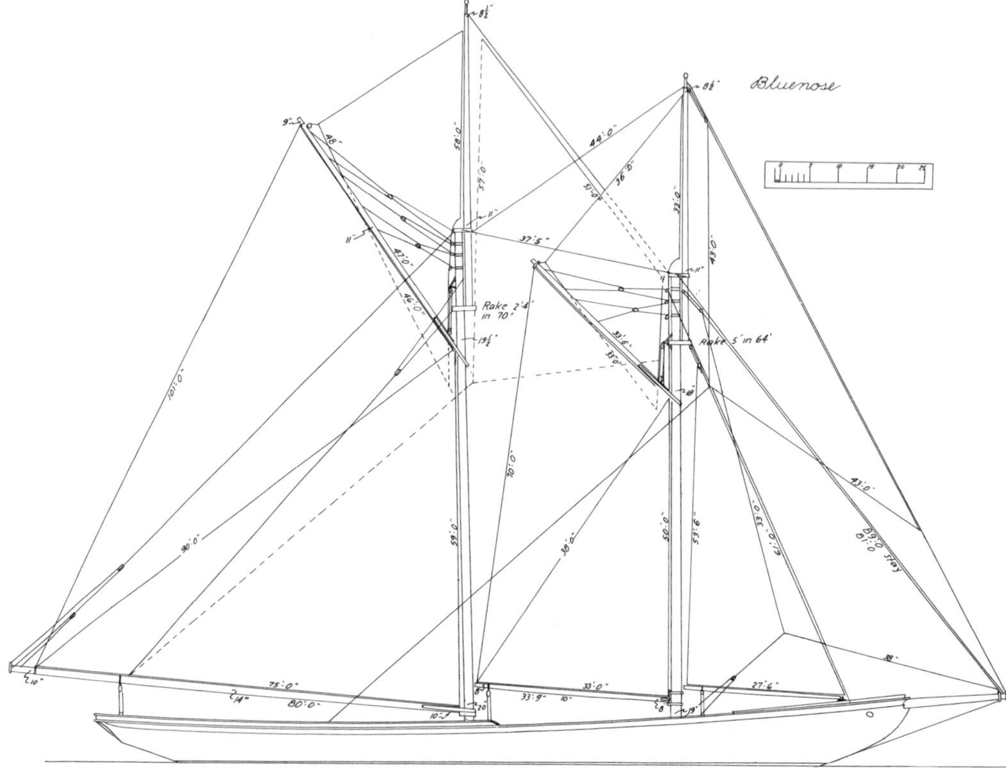
Bluenose
Rake 2′4″ in 70′
Rake 5′ in 64′

FIGURE 36

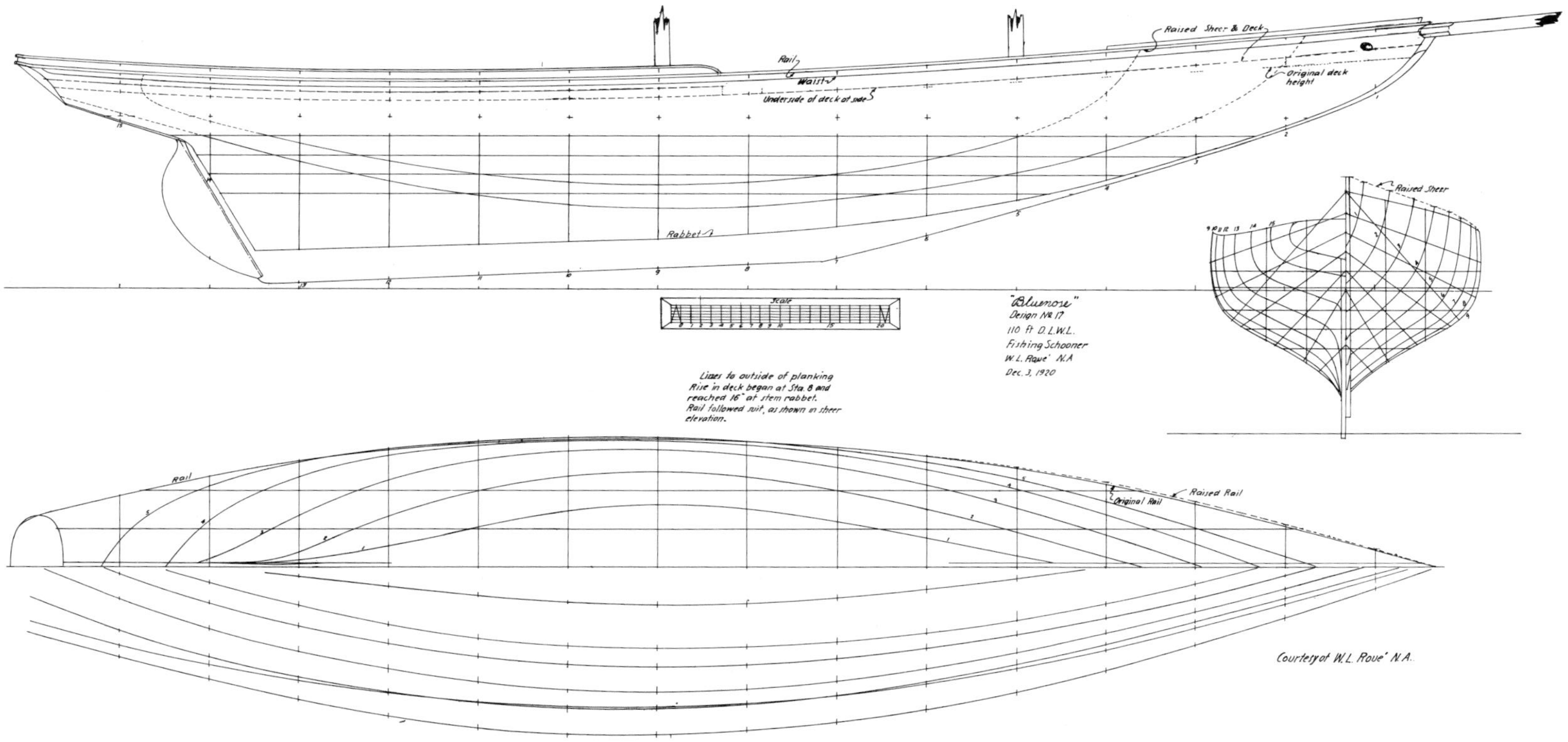

Raised Sheer & Deck
Rail
Waist
Underside of deck at side
Original deck height
Rabbet
Raised Sheer
Scale
"Bluenose"
Design № 17
110 ft D.L.W.L.
Fishing Schooner
W. L. Roué N.A
Dec. 3, 1920
Lines to outside of planking
Rise in deck began at Sta. 8 and reached 16" at stem rabbet.
Rail followed suit, as shown in sheer elevation.
Rail
Raised Rail
Original Rail
Courtesy of W. L. Roué N.A.

PLATE 130. *Bluenose*, 1920, plan

was to produce more headroom forward in the forecastle. So far as available evidence is concerned, it seems fully apparent that no other change occurred, intentionally at least, while the vessel was building, or fitting out. Indeed, there was the statement of three witnesses that Smith, one of the owners of the Smith and Rhuland yard, said to Roué on launching day that if the vessel were unsuccessful Roué would be responsible, if successful he, Roué, would get the credit. In short Smith washed his hands of the schooner. There remains the question of how closely she followed the designer's lines. It was the practice of some Canadian builders to loft every third or fourth frame, leaving the intermediate ones to educated guessing. If this were done in *Bluenose* she might have been off the lines in some places, perhaps as much as 2 inches; enough to affect performance but almost impossible to find without the use of templates—which would be impractical under the circumstances. It has therefore been argued that the failure of the Canadians to produce as fast a sailer as the *Bluenose* in another fishing schooner was due to their not having the lines of the vessel as actually built. But it is a well-known fact that sister ships rarely sailed alike, for relatively unimportant individual variations in rig, smoothness of bottom, and precise displacement might effect performance equally as much as small variations in hull lines.

At any rate, the *Bluenose* was built to race and to fit the official measurements for competitors in the International Fishing Schooner Races, and fitness for fishing, though required, was relatively superficial.

The *Bluenose* is shown in Plate 130 with deck and sheer raised forward, she was 143′-0″ long under the main rail cap, 27′-0″ extreme beam, and 14′-6″ depth at side. She had a marked sheer as altered, and this is shown in the Plate, a short, straight keel having small drag and running forward almost to Section 7, then rising in a long, almost straight fore rake to a rather long-overhang bow. The stern was formed with a strongly raking post and a fairly long counter with raking heart-shaped transom. The entrance was long and sharp, the run was long, with some straight in the buttocks. The midsection had some hollow in the sharply rising floor, a high and rather hard bilge, with some tumble home in the topside. The *Bluenose* was a powerful vessel well able to carry sail in the hands of her captain, who was an aggressive, unsportsmanlike, and abusive man, but a prime sailor.

A typical Canadian fishing schooner of the pre-racing period, designed for fishing, is shown in Plate 131. This was the schooner *Artisan*, built in 1911 at Shelburne, Nova Scotia, by John McKay. She is believed to have been designed by her builder who had attended the Charlestown, Massachusetts, Free School. This vessel was 118′-6″ moulded length at rail cap, 26′-0″ moulded beam, and 12′-4″ moulded depth at side. Her register dimen-

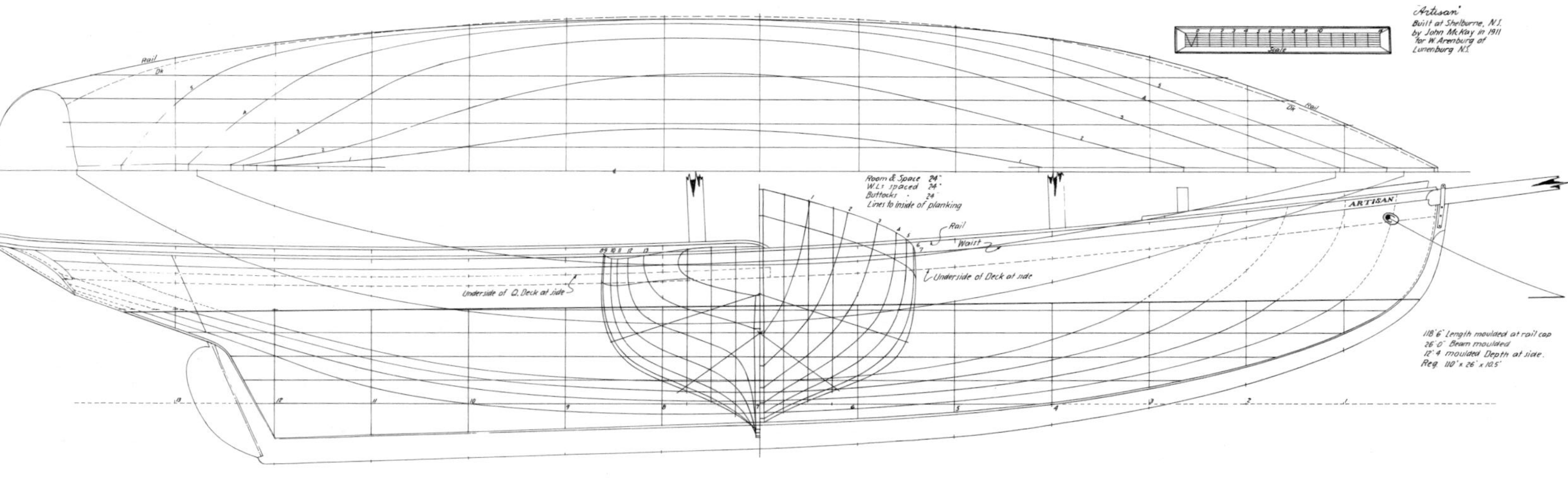
"Artisan"
Built at Shelburne, N.S.
by John McKay in 1911
for W. Arenburg of
Lunenburg N.S.
Scale
Room & Space 24"
W.L.s spaced 24"
Buttocks " 24"
Lines to inside of planking
Rail
Waist
Underside of Deck at side
Underside of Q. Deck at side
ARTISAN
118'6" Length moulded at rail cap
26'0" Beam moulded
12'4" moulded Depth at side.
Reg. 110' x 26' x 10.5'

PLATE 131. *Artisan*, 1911, half-model

sions were 110.0′ x 26.0′ x 10.5′. It will be noticed that she had an almost "straight stem"; the very short fore overhang that has been mentioned earlier in Canadian schooners.

The *Artisan* had a lively sheer, a long, straight keel having moderate drag running forward to a little more than half-length, then sweeping up in a long curve to fair into a very short-overhang curved stem. The sternpost had marked rake and was rather short. The counter, partly immersed, was moderately long, rather heavy, and having a sharply raking heart-shaped transom. The entrance was long, sharp, and very slightly concave just abaft the stem. The run was rather long, with some straight in the buttocks. The midsection showed a slight hollow in rising floor, a well-rounded, easy bilge, and some tumble home in the topside. This vessel was designed as a fast carrier, and could be used in the Newfoundland salt-fish trade, as well as for a fisherman.

A later Nova Scotia fishing schooner is shown in Plate 132. This is the large banker *Sylvia Mosher*, built by John McLean and Sons in their yard at Mahone Bay, Nova Scotia, in 1925. This was 133′-3″ moulded length at main rail cap, 25′-11″ moulded beam, and 11′-10½″ moulded depth at side. The vessel was the design of Charles McLean and was fairly typical of his fishing schooner models. The *Sylvia Mosher* was a very fast sailer; though not intended as a racer, she was expected to take part in the Canadian elimination races and so was to be a candidate for the Canadian entry in the International Fishing Schooner Races in 1926. However, the *Sylvia Mosher* was lost with all hands, twenty-eight men, in the early fall hurricane of 1926, on Sable Island. The big schooner *Sadie Knickle* was also lost in this storm.

The McLean yard was noted for the superior construction and finish of their vessels. This yard not only designed and built vessels for provincial owners, but also operated a small fleet of fishing schooners in the early years of the yard's existence. In the age of sailing fishermen, 1900–1926 the McLean yard built twenty-three fishing schooners besides many other vessels, including tern schooners, freighters, rum-runners, draggers, and government craft. Another yard at Mahone Bay that was active in building sailing fishing schooners was the Burgoyne Brothers, one of whom, David, was a talented vessel designer. Among the outstanding Nova Scotian designers was Robie McLeod. It said of him that when he found that his sons refused to follow the shipbuilder's trade, he burned his models, so very few examples of his work have survived. McLeod designed vessels ranging from square-riggers (topsail schooners, brigantines, and a few barks to fishing schooners and steamers.

The *Sylvia Mosher* had rather straight sheer for her length, a long, straight keel having some drag running from the sternpost forward to nearly beneath the foremast, forming a fore gripe, then fairing upward in

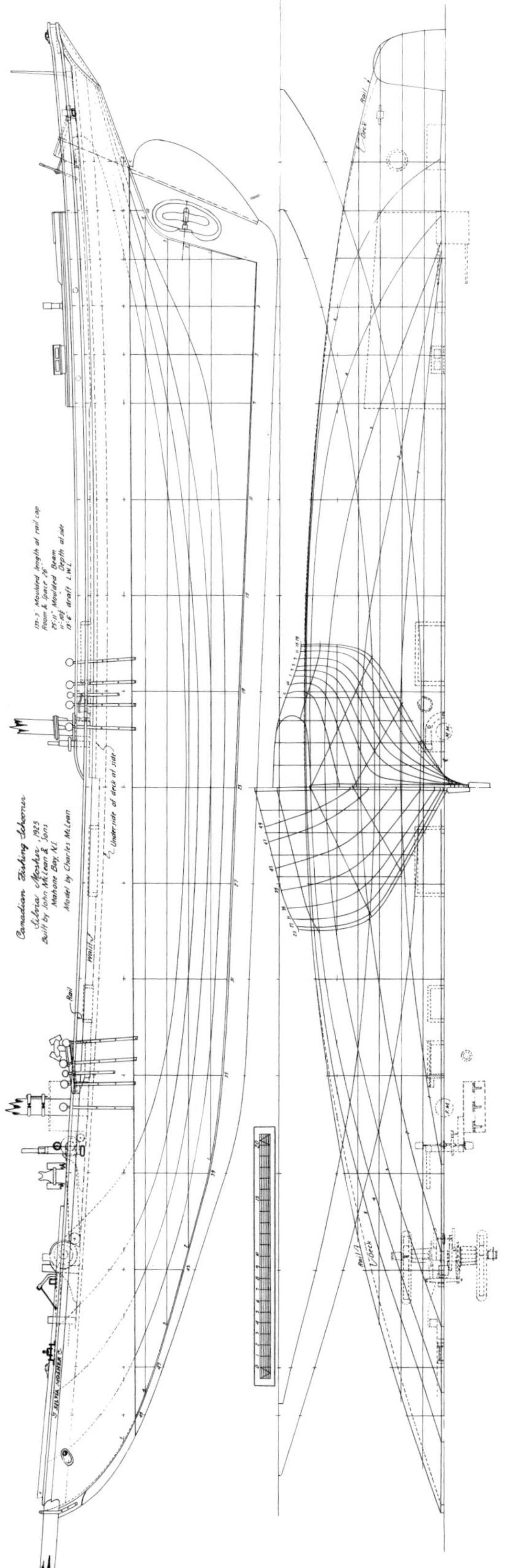

PLATE 132. *Sylvia Mosher*, 1925, half-model, plan

a long sweep to fair into a short-overhang bow. The entrance was long and sharp, the run quite long with straight buttocks. The post had moderate rake and a prick post was used with aperture blocking, but this was not shaped as in New England vessels. The counter was partly immersed, with sharply raking elliptical transom. The midsection had sharply rising straight floors carried far outbroad, a high and rather hard turn of bilge, with nearly vertical topside.

Once power began to be installed in Canadian vessels, about 1912, the auxiliary fishing schooner became very common in the Canadian fisheries. The *Mosher*'s deck layout, taken from the designer's plan, was probably very much like that of *Bluenose.*

The defeat of the McManus-designed fishing schooner *Elsie* by the *Bluenose* in 1921 had been the result of the disqualification of the new American schooner *Mayflower,* on the grounds that she was a yacht masquerading as a fishing schooner. This vessel had been designed by W. Starling Burgess and built in 1920–1921 by John F. James and Son at Essex. She was 7 inches longer overall than *Bluenose,* narrower by 3 inches but with a designed draft 2 inches deeper, especially designed to race and to meet *Bluenose* on even terms. But the *Mayflower* had some radical departures. For one thing she had some wire-rope running rigging and even sported a wholly unnecessary dolphin striker hung from her stem just above her stem bevel and below the bottom of the gammon iron. This was enough to cause comment, but a feud between Gloucester and Boston fishermen seems to have been the real reason for banning the *Mayflower.* It was charged at Gloucester that she was intended to make a few superficial fishing trips and then she would be sold to become a yacht, and the Canadians refused to race against her. The result was that *Mayflower* never had a chance to try her speed in a formal race and ended her days as a West Indian freighter after a short career as a fishing vessel.

Therefore elimination races had to be held, in which a few of the old sailing schooners were entered. The *Elsie* was the winner in these races, went to Halifax to meet *Bluenose* and was beaten. The latter was 143 feet long overall, the *Elsie* was 124 feet overall. It was obvious, of course, that New England fishermen would have to find a new and larger vessel before they could hope to beat *Bluenose.* Again a group of fishermen combined to have a new, large, fast schooner built and again Burgess prepared the design. The new schooner, *Puritan,* was built at Essex by James and was launched March 15, 1922. The new vessel had a "family resemblance" to *Mayflower.* Plate 133 shows the *Puritan* with the deck arrangement as measured in the vessel. The *Mayflower* had an ugly, chopped-off counter stern making the transom almost upright. *Puritan*'s lines show her counter mutilated also, but

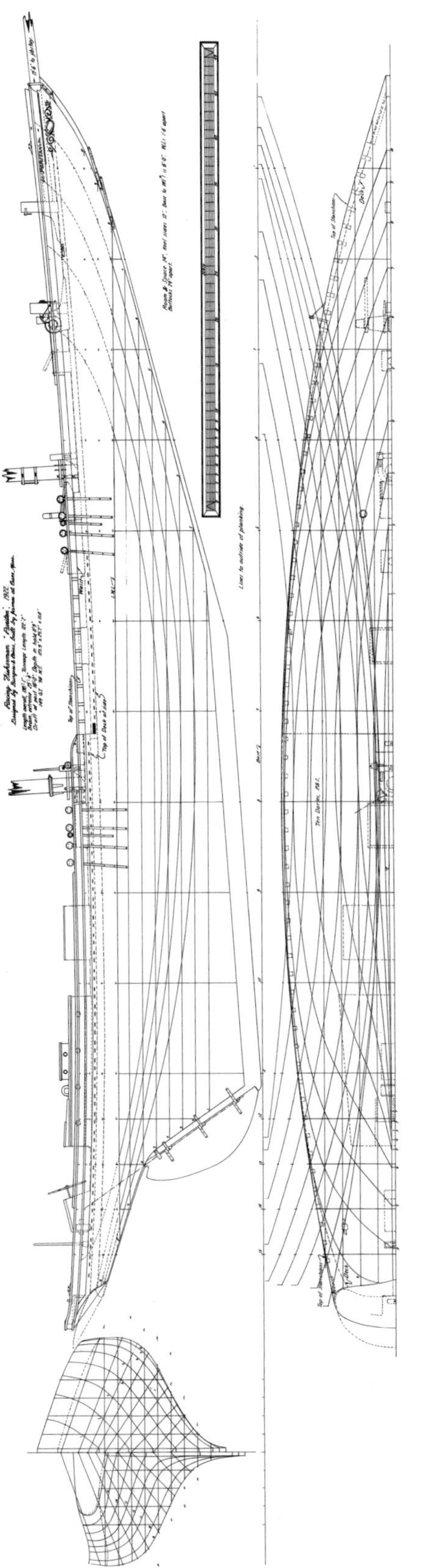

PLATE 133. *Puritan*, 1921, plan

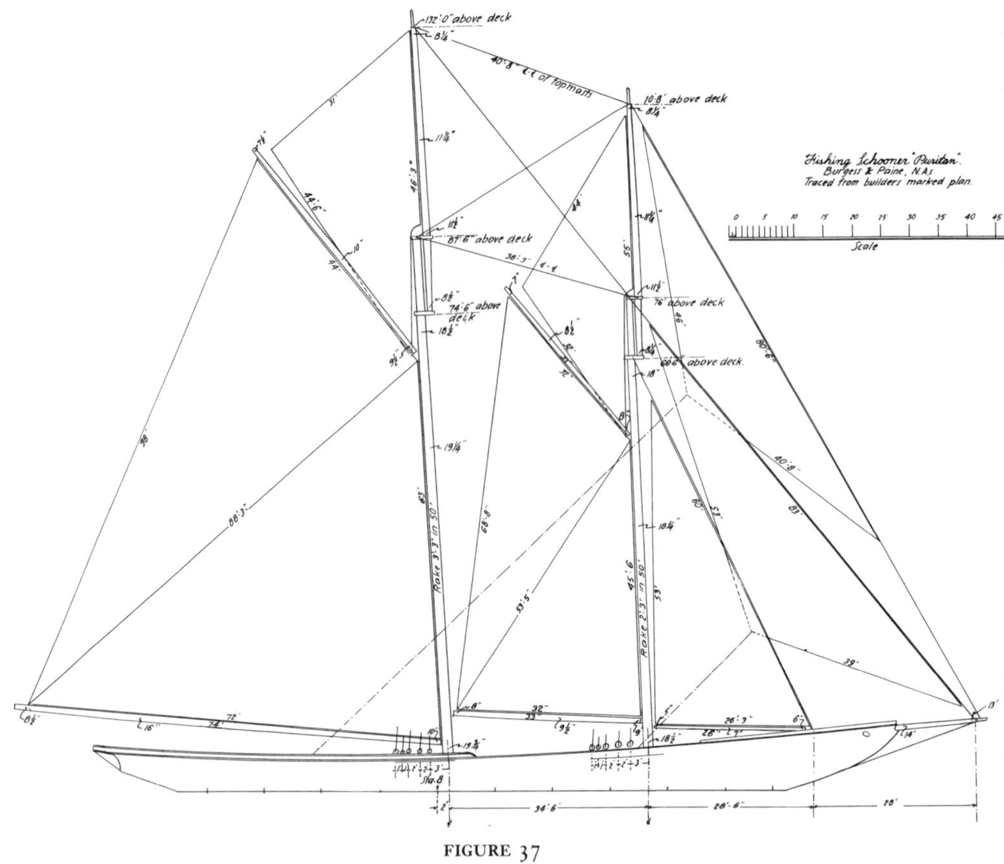
Fishing Schooner "Puritan".
Burgess & Paine, N.As
Traced from builders' marked plan.
Scale

FIGURE 37

with much rake in the new transom. It appears that the counter was chopped off to bring her overall length from over 140′ to 138′-1″.

Mayflower measured 143′-9″ on the main rail cap, 25′-8″ beam, and was intended to draw about 17′. The tonnage length was 130.5′. *Puritan* measured 138′-1″ on the main rail cap, 25′-4″ extreme beam, and her tonnage length was 123.9′. She drew about 16′-0″ in racing trim.

The plan shows a schooner having a handsome sheer, a straight keel with much drag running from the sternpost forward to about midlength, then rising in a slightly curved fore rake to fair into a long-overhang curved stem. The sternpost raked sharply; the counter was long, well immersed, and originally finished in a sharply raking, heart-shaped transom. This has been altered to reduce the rake and shorten the counter. The entrance was long, sharp, and convex. The run was also long, with long straight buttocks. The vessel was marked by her very easy lines and was of light displacement for her dimensions. The midsection had a hollow, sharply rising floor, a high and rather firm bilge, with tumble home in the topside.

The *Puritan* beat *Mayflower* in an impromptu brush, and in her very short life the *Puritan* showed that she was a very fast sailer. She is credied with a speed of 15 knots by the press. On her third fishing trip, June 17, 1922, she overran her time and distance and became a total loss on the northwest bar of Sable Island; all but one of the crew were saved.

At the time *Puritan* was building in James' yard at Essex, A. D. Story was at work on a big racing schooner designed by McManus. This vessel was launched almost a month after *Puritan*, on April 11, 1922. *Puritan* had gone off the ways on March 15. The new racer was named *Henry Ford.* McManus took special care to gather up all blueprints of his plans of the *Ford*, so no plans of her have yet been found. The *Ford* was 139 feet overall, 4 feet shorter than *Bluenose* and exactly the same overall length as *Puritan.* Photographs show that the *Ford* resembled *Bluenose* but had sharper bow sections. The defeat of the *Ford* by the *Bluenose* was a noxious affair in which the sail plan of the *Ford* was repeatedly reduced by the race committee, to the point where her mainsail would not stand properly. There is no purpose to be served by recounting the history of each of the races, but all of those in which the Canadian Captain Walters sailed were distinguished by a complete lack of sportsmanship and by much bickering.

In 1923 new races were proposed and a group of fishermen and businessmen had Burgess and Paine design a new racing schooner to be built by A. D. Story at Essex. It was first suggested that a sister of *Puritan* be built, but finally it was settled that a new design be used. The *Columbia* (Plate 134) was the result. This was a schooner 140′-8″ length on main rail, 25′-0″ depth

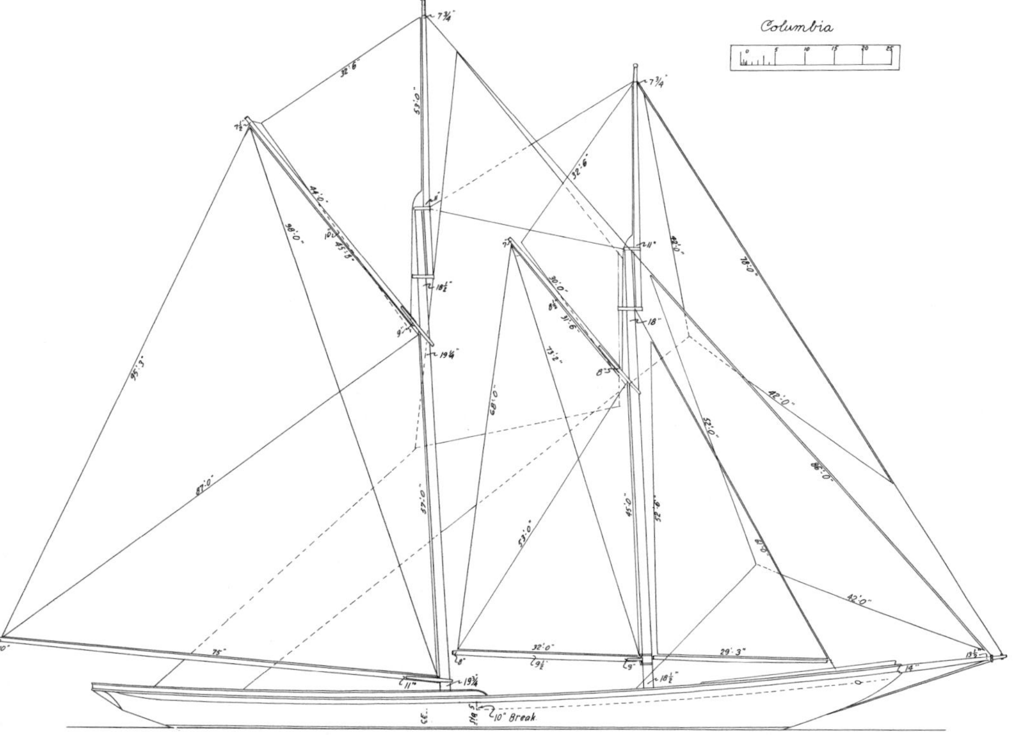
Columbia
10" Break

FIGURE 38

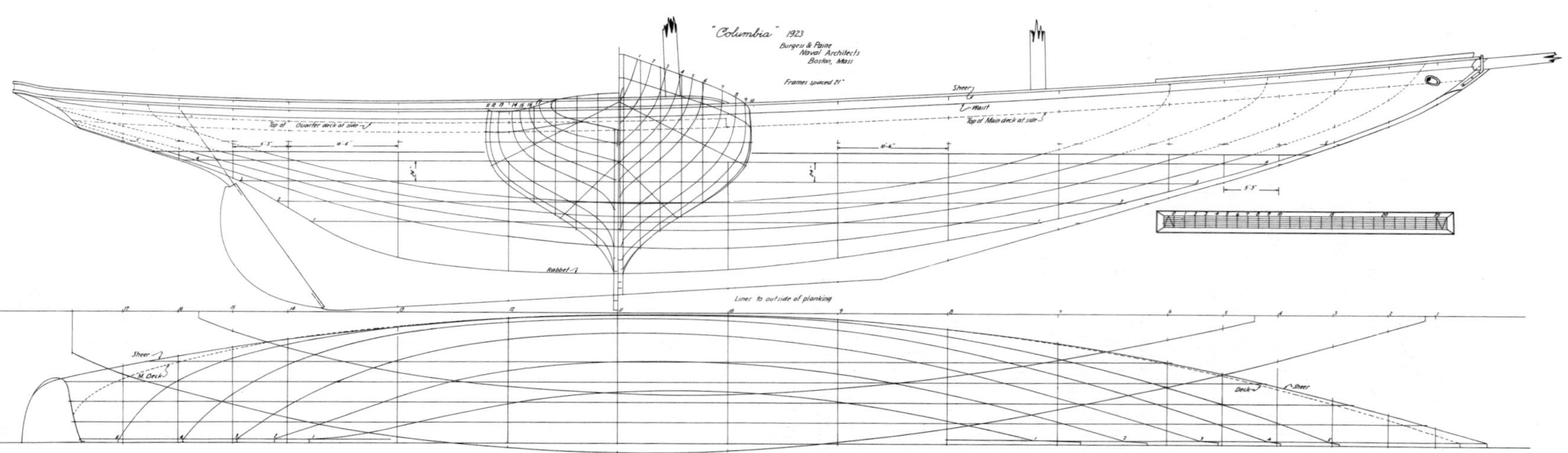
"Columbia" 1923
Burgess & Paine
Naval Architects
Boston, Mass
Frames spaced 21"
Sheer
Waist
Top of Main deck at side
Top of Quarter deck at side
Rabbet
Lines to outside of planking
Sheer
M. Deck
Deck
Sheer

PLATE 134. *Columbia*, 1923, plan

at side. The vessel as measured for her races was reported to have been 141′-3″ overall, 25.8′ beam, and drawing 15′-8″. *Columbia* had a peculiar keel rabbet; it was heavily curved and crossed the stern deadwood well above the base line to fair, in a reverse curve, into the counter. This style of rabbet has been used on yachts, usually small, but was most unusual in a large commercial vessel like the *Columbia.* One serious objection to this would be that the bottom plank gave little support to the deadwood when the vessel grounded out. Another is that, in a large vessel like *Columbia,* the rabbet crosses the numerous seams in the deadwood and each seam crossing requires caulking and stopwaters that are, at best, subject to occasional leakage. Altogether, there are elements of weakness in this construction, and no practical advantage for it can be advanced.

The *Columbia* had a graceful sheer, a short keel or exterior deadwood or skeg of varying depth, straight on the bottom, from the sternpost running forward to a point somewhat beyond midlength with a strong, almost straight fore rake to fair into a long, somewhat pointed stem profile. The sternpost and exposed deadwood supporting it mark the stern; the counter is long, parly immersed, and ending in a sharply raking heart-shaped transom. The entrance is long, slightly convex, and sharp. The run is distinguished by long, straight buttocks and is fine. Fairing pieces surround the rudder stock and port in the tuck. The midsection was marked by hollow garboard, carried into the rising floor that was carried well outboard. The bilge was high and firm with tumble home in the topside.

Columbia was designed by the short-lived partnership of Burgess and Paine; there is some uncertainty as to which of the two dominated in the design, but it was probably Starling Burgess who was responsible for the plans. This vessel damaged her rudder stock in launching through carelessness in the yard and the injury was not discovered until the schooner had lost a series of races. After a rather disappointing racing career, the *Columbia* was lost with all hands in the storm of August 24, 1927, off Sable Island.

On January 3, 1928, a large Canadian trawler working off Sable Island fouled her gear, and in attempting to clear herself in darkness she raised the wreck of a large schooner to the surface. Turning her searchlight on the wreck, the vessel could be seen plainly and many of the crew of the trawler were certain the wreck was the *Columbia.* In a few moments the trawling cable broke and the wreck settled beneath the surface. This took place in an area where there are many wrecks.

The last schooner was built for the International Fishing Schooner Races was the *Gertrude L. Thebaud,* built in Essex by A. D. Story in 1929. She was designed by Frank Paine, of the firm Paine, Belknap and Skene. Her construction was supervised to some extent by Ben Pine, who had skippered many of the racing fishermen. Plate 135 shows the lines of the schooner; a

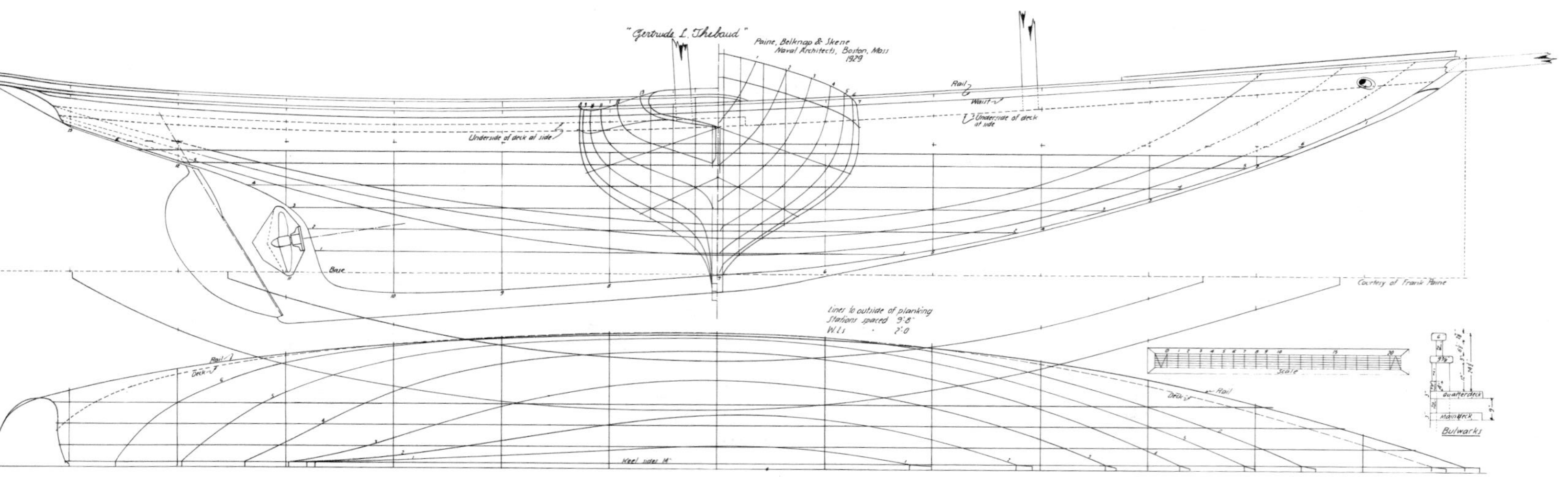
"Gertrude L. Thebaud"
Paine, Belknap & Skene
Naval Architects, Boston, Mass
1929
Rail
Waist
Underside of deck at side
Underside of deck at side
Base
Courtesy of Frank Paine
Lines to outside of planking
Stations spaced 9'8"
W.L.s " 2'0
Rail
Deck
Keel sides 14"
Deck
Rail
Scale
Quarterdeck
Maindeck
Bulwarks

PLATE 135. *Gertrude L. Thebaud*, 1925, plan

vessel having a graceful sheer, a straight keel having strong drag running forward to the midsection, then curving upward in a gentle sweep to fair into the rather long-overhang curved stem. The stern, prick post, and aperture fairing blocks were fitted Canadian fashion and the keel rabbet curved upward as it approached the sternpost, and so showed some stern deadwood. The counter was long, partly immersed, and ended in a sharply raking heart-shaped transom. The entrance was long and convex, the run was long with straight buttocks carried a little forward of the tuck. The midsection had a noticeably hollow garboard, almost straight, and there was a strongly rising floor, a firm bilge, and tumble home in the topside. The *Gertrude L. Thebaud* was 132′-7″ on the main rail cap and was 115.8′ x 25.2′ x 12.2′ tonnage dimensions.

There were some difficulties in the shipyard when the *Thebaud* was building. The builder, A. D. Story, was not well so one of his sons was acting foreman. Through inexperience errors were made in placing the masts and as a result the designer made the yard shift the masts. The vessel, after launch, was found to be tender; 10 feet were cut off the topmast lengths and ballast added. It was also found that the schooner had some lee helm when all sail was set. In grounding out in the slip at Ben Pine's wharf the

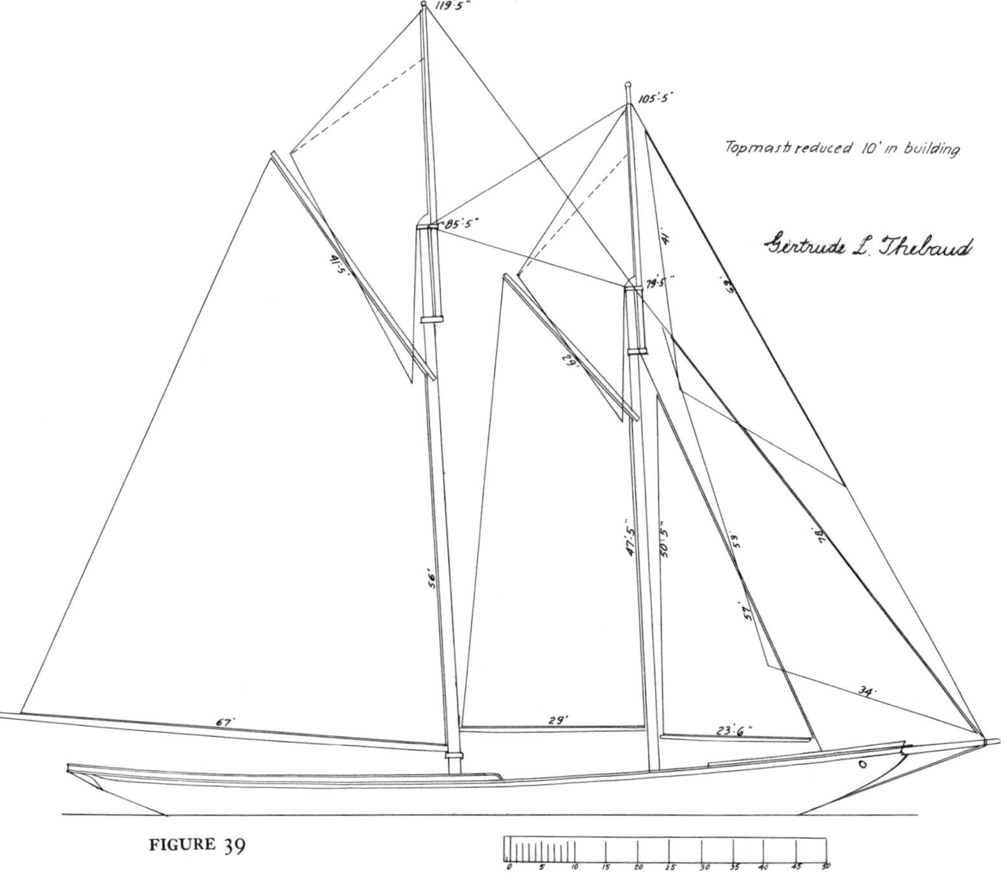
119'5"
105'5"
Topmasts reduced 10' in building
85'5"
Gertrude L. Thebaud
79'5"
41'5
41'
62'
47'5"
50'5"
53'
78'
56'
57'
34'
67'
29'
23'6"
0 5 10 15 20 25 30 35 40 45 50

FIGURE 39

schooner started her prick post which caused a troublesome leak. The *Thebaud* was no match for *Bluenose* in any but light weather.

By this time the sailing schooner was solely a racer, for the fisheries demanded power vessels. A sailing fishing schooner could no longer be manned. Soon the same conditions applied to the Canadian vessels—the day of sail had passed.

Candidates for the defense or challenge of the International Fishing Schooner Race appeared in the Canadian elimination trials, but most vessels failed to be successful because they were too small, or required too much tuning up, or too many alterations that were too expensive. The vessels were not well handled in the elimination races.

A tragic case was the *Keno*, shown in Plate 136. This vessel was built by John McLean and Sons at Mahone Bay, Nova Scotia, in 1923 for Captain Albert Himmelman, a clever sailor who liked to race. Charles McLean modeled this vessel under the supervision of Captain Himmelman. In completing the builder's model, McLean expressed the opinion that the vessel was too sharp to carry sail with mixed stone and iron ballast. Himmelman insisted on building on the model, however. When the vessel was completed she showed great speed in moderate winds, though she was somewhat tender. She fitted out for a trip and left port in company with an American schooner and neither was ever seen again.

Keno was 139′-6″ moulded length on the main rail cap, 25′-4″ moulded beam, and 13′-1″ depth at side, scaled from the half-model.

The plan shows a schooner having moderate sheer, straight keel with some drag running to a little forward of midlength and then fairing upward in a long fore rake to fair into a curved stem. The stern post raked sharply and the counter, partly immersed, was long with a very raking elliptical transom. The entrance was long and very sharp; there was a very slight hollow just abaft the stem in the load line. The run was long, very fine, with long straight buttocks. The midsection had hollow in garboard and floor. The latter ran well outboard, giving a high and rather hard turn of bilge with a little tumble home in the topside. The name *Keno* means a throw of dice in which all dice show 5; supposedly a very lucky throw.

Another candidate for challenging the *Bluenose* is shown in Plate 137, the schooner *Haligonian* designed by William Roué and built at Shelburne, Nova Scotia, in 1925. The new schooner was expected to beat the *Bluenose*, but failed by a narrow margin; this disappointment may have been due to the skipper of the *Bluenose* being the better racing sailor. Local authorities thought the masts should have been shifted aft. *Haligonian* was 145′-6″ on the main rail cap, 27′-6″ beam, and had a designed draft of about 16′, the required draft in the racing rule.

The schooner shown in Plate 137 had a marked sheer, a straight keel

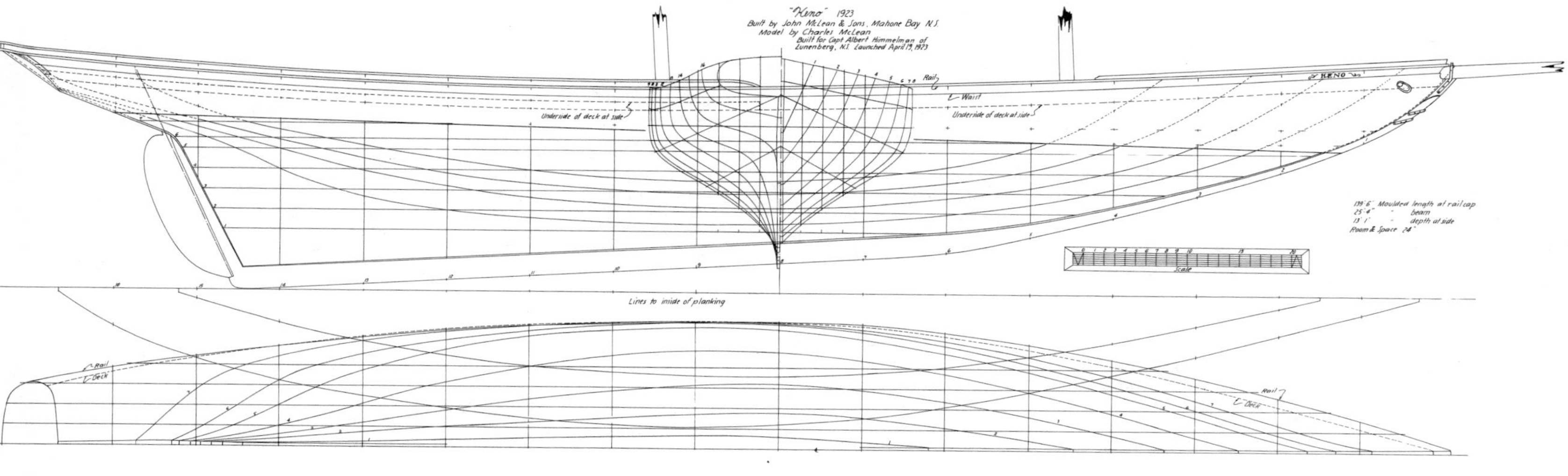
"Keno" 1923
Built by John McLean & Sons, Mahone Bay N.S.
Model by Charles McLean
Built for Capt Albert Himmelman of
Lunenberg, N.S. Launched April 19, 1923
Rail
Waist
Underside of deck at side
Underside of deck at side
KENO
139' 6" Moulded length at railcap
25' 4" " beam
13' 1" " depth at side
Room & Space 24"
Scale
Lines to inside of planking
Rail
Deck
Rail
Deck

PLATE 136. *Keno*, 1925, half-model

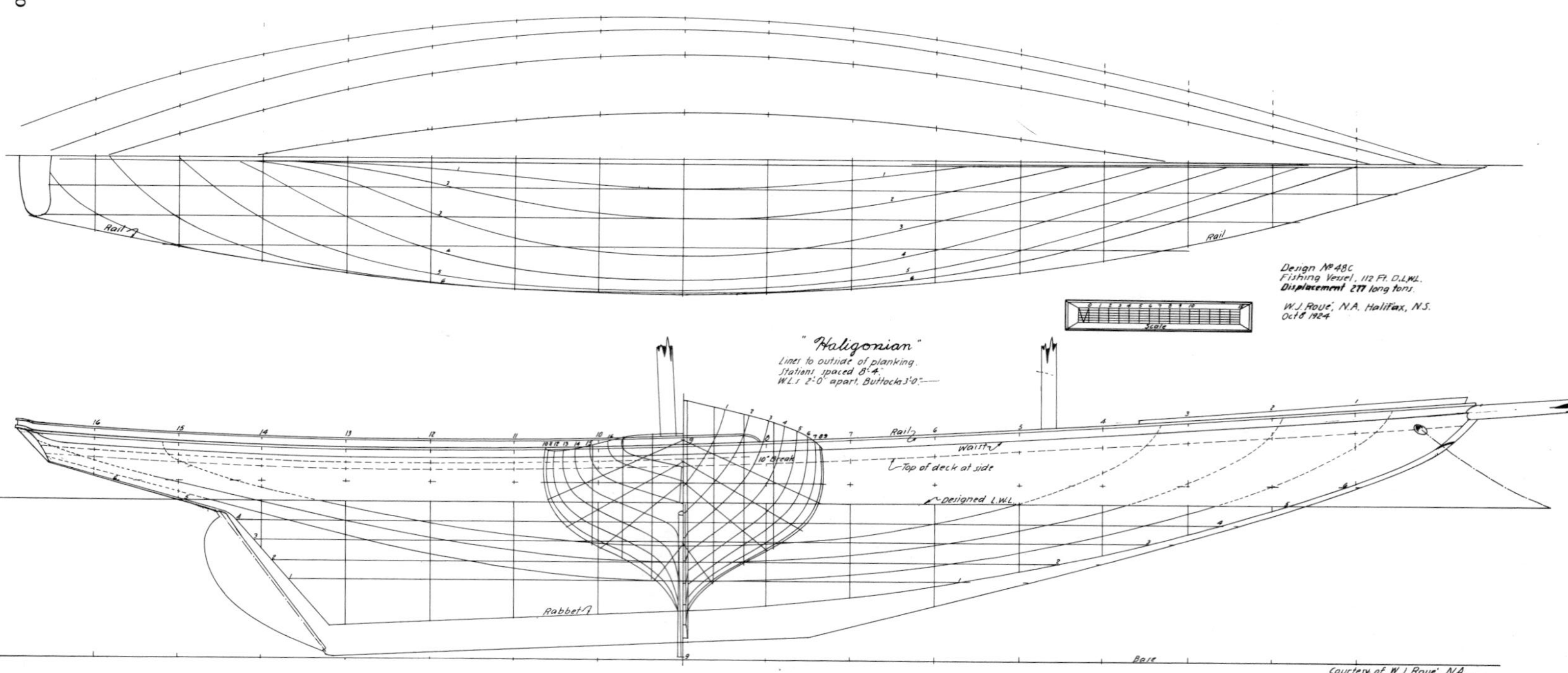
Design No 48C
Fishing Vessel, 112 Ft. O.L.W.L.
Displacement 277 long tons.
W.J. Roué, N.A. Halifax, N.S.
Oct 8 1924
Scale
"Haligonian"
Lines to outside of planking.
Stations spaced 8'-4".
W.L.s 2'-0" apart, Buttocks 3'-0"
Rail
Waist
Top of deck at side
Designed L.W.L.
10" Break
Rabbet
Base
Courtesy of W.J. Roué, N.A.

PLATE 137. *Haligonian*, 1924, plan

with much drag running forward to point a little forward of midlength, thence rising in a long fore rake or a gentle sweep to fair into the long-overhang bow. The sternpost raked strongly, the counter was long and ended in a raking heart-shaped transom. The entrance was sharp and slightly convex; the run was long and very fine with long straight buttocks. The midsection was formed with a hollow garboard, rising floor carried well out, a firm turn of bilge, and some tumble home in the topside.

These designs by Roué, the *Bluenose* and *Haligonian*, were unusual in being drawn on ¼″ = 1′-0″ scale. However, Roué was a very skilled draftsman so his drawings were undoubtedly precise. Offsets closer than ½ inch would be very difficult to take off the plans nevertheless.

The "racing fishermen," designed primarily to meet the requirements of international racing, have been held up as the finest examples of the Gloucester fishing schooners that were ever built. Though handsome and fast, only five such vessels were ever built in New England—*Mayflower*, *Puritan*, *Henry Ford*, *Columbia*, and *Gertrude L. Thebaud*—and four or five were built in Nova Scotia—*Bluenose*, *Canadia*, *Keno*, and *Haligonian* come to mind. The Canadians may have had more "hopefuls," but elimination races weeded out the prospects, in the early races at least, and also any whose measurements did not conform with the racing rule dimensions, *Canadia* for example.

The racing requirements encouraged the maximum size of fishing schooner being used, 140 to 150 feet overall. The Canadians had such vessels in their fishery, but the average fishing schooner was much smaller in the New England fishery. However, as a result of the first race, the Canadians built a new, very large fishing schooner, the *Bluenose*, and her launch caused the New Englanders to built a contender, the *Mayflower*, as has been recounted.

Both of the contenders were committed, therefore, to the new racing type. These new vessels were purely sailing craft of large dimensions for two-masted fore-and-aft schooners, coming into existence in a period when motors, in auxiliaries, were driving sail from both the Canadian and the New England fisheries. The sailing schooner was obsolete, in fact, by 1920.

No wonder, then, that the racing schooners actually taking part in the international races—and some that were unsuccessful candidates—were economic failures, requiring subsidies to allow them to exist in both racing and fishery, without complete conversion to power.

The racer produced no important factor that was new in 1920. Examination of the designs here of fishing schooners, built earlier, show that all the factors in the design of the racers, except size, of course, had been utilized eighteen to twenty years earlier by McManus, Crowninshield, and others. The elements included light displacement for given dimensions, relatively long overhangs, hollow garboards with hollow extending up into the floors, fine entrance and run; in short the elements used in the designs of fast, seagoing schooner yachts from 1895 to 1920.

The only important factor not used in racing fishermen, outside ballast, was used in two schooners designed by McManus in 1898. These were the *Massasoit* and *Juniata:* 58.4′ x 17.8′ x 7.6 and 85.0′ x 23.0′ x 10.0′, respectively. The reasons for not using outside ballast in fishing schooners was, first, the cost, for structure would have to be altered to get the additional strength in deadwood, keel, keelson, and frames that would be needed to employ much outside ballast. In McManus' schooners the outside ballast was in a large exterior keel above the rather deep shoe; not as low as possible. Secondly, the outside ballast would increase initial stability, whereas the soft-bilge McManus schooners were intended to reduce initial stability, to reduce failures in rigging and spars.

It is apparent that the last all-sail schooners, like *Elsie*, *Stiletto*, and similar vessels, along with the full-rigged knockabouts, were the final stages in the evolution of the New England and Canadian fishing schooner, or "Gloucesterman." The racer was, at best, no more than a special and technically minor adaptation of the bowsprit-fitted fishing schooner of the earliest years of the century. She had no relation to fishing schooner design, either as a descendant or as a parent. By the time the last racer was built, her type was obsolete and the quality of construction decadent. The end of the sailing fishing schooner was at hand.

Notebook on Details of Gloucester Fishing Schooners

(Those pages from the author's notebook that had no drawings have been set in type without changes.)

The sketches and notes that follow were taken from rough drawings and data obtained during the years between 1932 and 1939 at Essex, Gloucester, and Boston. This material was sought with the purposes of recording not only the evolution of the Gloucester fishing schooner, but also the evolution of her rig and fittings, so far as was then possible.

The result is presented here, which contains my own observations, measurements, and sketches, as well as those of friends. Especial acknowledgment must be made to Mr. Edward S. Bosley, who not only donated a large amount of drawings and notes on details of hardware, fittings, and rig but also took time to examine and to criticize my notes and sketches. I have therefore been able to add a great deal of skillful research to what I had attempted. I also had the aid of Mr. Charles F. Sayle, who had served on some of the last fishing schooners to carry the full schooner rig. From him I received sketches and notes, as well as a large number of photographs of deck and rig details that have been most helpful. I must also acknowledge the aid I received from the late Lewis H. Story, the late David F. Taylor, and the shipsmiths, shipwrights, master shipbuilders, vessel managers, riggers, and sailmakers whose many contributions are in the pages that follow. Contributors are identified by their initials.

The period in which my research was done was a time when the sailing fishing schooner was making her final appearance. No longer could topmasts and topsails be seen, and the rig most employed was jumbo, foresail, and riding sail. In but two vessels, in 1933, there were no engines. The remaining vessels were fully powered and sailing gear was being rapidly discarded and junked. Except for a few, the old schooners remaining in the fisheries were of a medium size. There was but one "schooner boat" and one "sloopboat" left at Gloucester, and neither working in 1933. This state of the fishing fleet gave a limited area for surveys of fittings aboard vessels, though there was much hardware and vessels' gear ashore. This made it easy to find fittings and hardware to be measured, but left many questions as to use and purpose of some objects, particularly where rigging was concerned. It was not until Mr. Sayle and Mr. Bosley came to my aid that all of these questions were finally answered.

Documents and publications relating to the building of fishing schooners were found to be very scarce, and usually unreliable when found. Old marine catalogs were of some assistance, but a very great part of the fishing schooner hardware was made to "fit the work" by the local shipsmiths. It was rare, then, to find a fitting that could be described by a catalog listing.

Specifications, block lists, and hardware illustrations were also difficult to find and, when found, they were often incomplete or otherwise unsatisfactory. The two published sources that were utilized were the *Report of the Commissioner, for 1887, Part XV, U.S. Commission of Fish and Fisheries*, Government Printing Office, Washington, D.C., 1891, pp. 437–462. This is a full description of the Commission's schooner "Grampus," with plans and specifications. An earlier schooner was described in the *Report on the Shipbuilding Industry of the United States* by Henry Hall, special agent, U.S. Bureau of the Census, Tenth Census, Vol. 8, Washington, D.C., Government Printing Office, 1884, pp. 13–18. This is a fairly complete specification of a 75-ton clipper schooner, probably a fishing schooner, built about 1875. These publications had little on hardware or fittings. Fragments of blueprints showing some fittings for the 1891 rigging of "Grampus" were found, but these were suspect as not being typical of fishing schooners of this date.

It was not possible to examine all of the ironwork of a single schooner, but it was possible to obtain a composite survey of typical fittings and gear for the period of evolution. For the periods before 1885 it was necessary to turn toward contemporary rigged scale models, of which there were a number. The earliest were in the 1850s. These models required careful selection, because of a lack of documentation in some models and because of unskillful repairs in others. While such a source is not wholly reliable, comparison of models of a given period and, where available, of photographs in the same period makes it possible to establish most of the rigging and fitting used after about 1885.

One troublesome factor was the inability to work out a precise scale that would relate the dimensions of fittings to size of vessels. Comparisons of fittings with hull dimensions of vessels in the same period did not prove satisfactory due to lack of details of many fittings of varying sizes. Experience and judgment seem to have guided the shipsmith in this matter, each having his own ideas.

Though I have copied sketches made by others, any errors found by the reader are my responsibility. It has been found that there were variations in many fittings and also in rigging details. Even with the limitations imposed by the small number of vessels that were available, this was soon apparent and prevented any conclusions as to which of the variants was the most common or typical in many instances.

The date of change in gear, rigging, and hardware that will be given are, in most cases, only approximate.

The sketches used are often drawn out of scale. This was usually done where dimensions were lacking, or where the sketch was to illustrate a principle or method.

It has been a surprise to find such complexity in the rig of a two-masted gaffsail schooner. However, much of this was the result of size and the requirements of the schooner's work and evolution.

IRON-STOCK ANCHOR

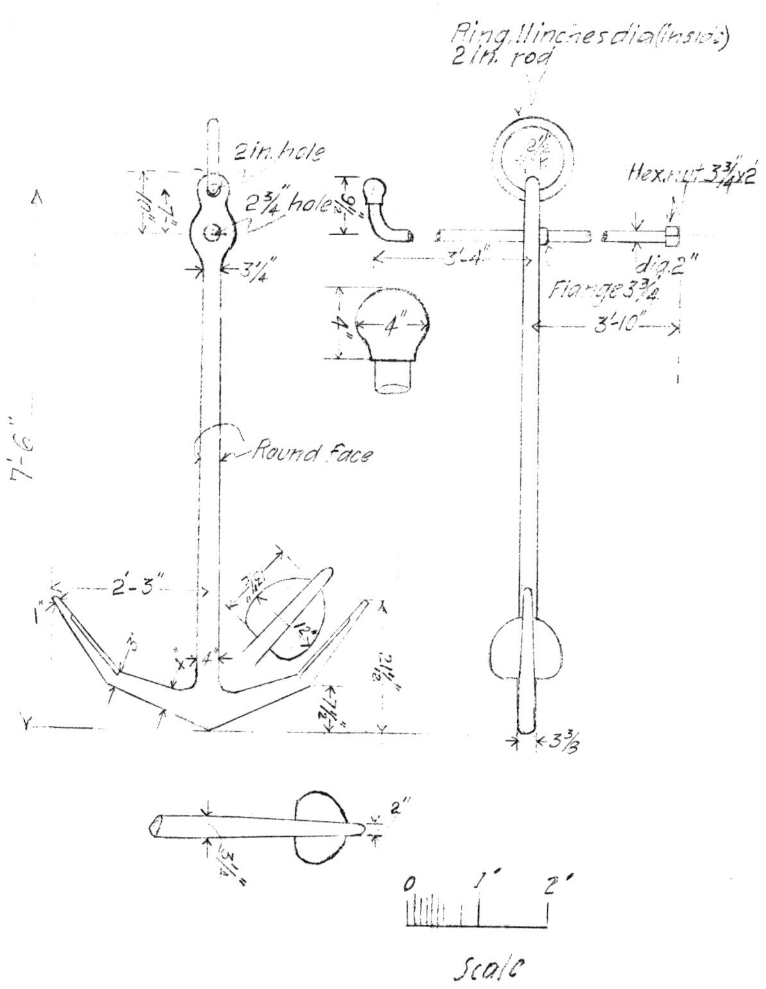
2 in. rod
2 in. hole
2¾" hole
3¼"
3'-4"
Hex. nut 3¾" x 2
dia. 2"
Flange 3¾
3'-10"
4"
Round face
7'-6"
2'-3"
1"
2"
0
1'
2'
Scale

ANCHOR (BANK)

9'-10" from ℄ of hole for ring
to bottom of anchor.

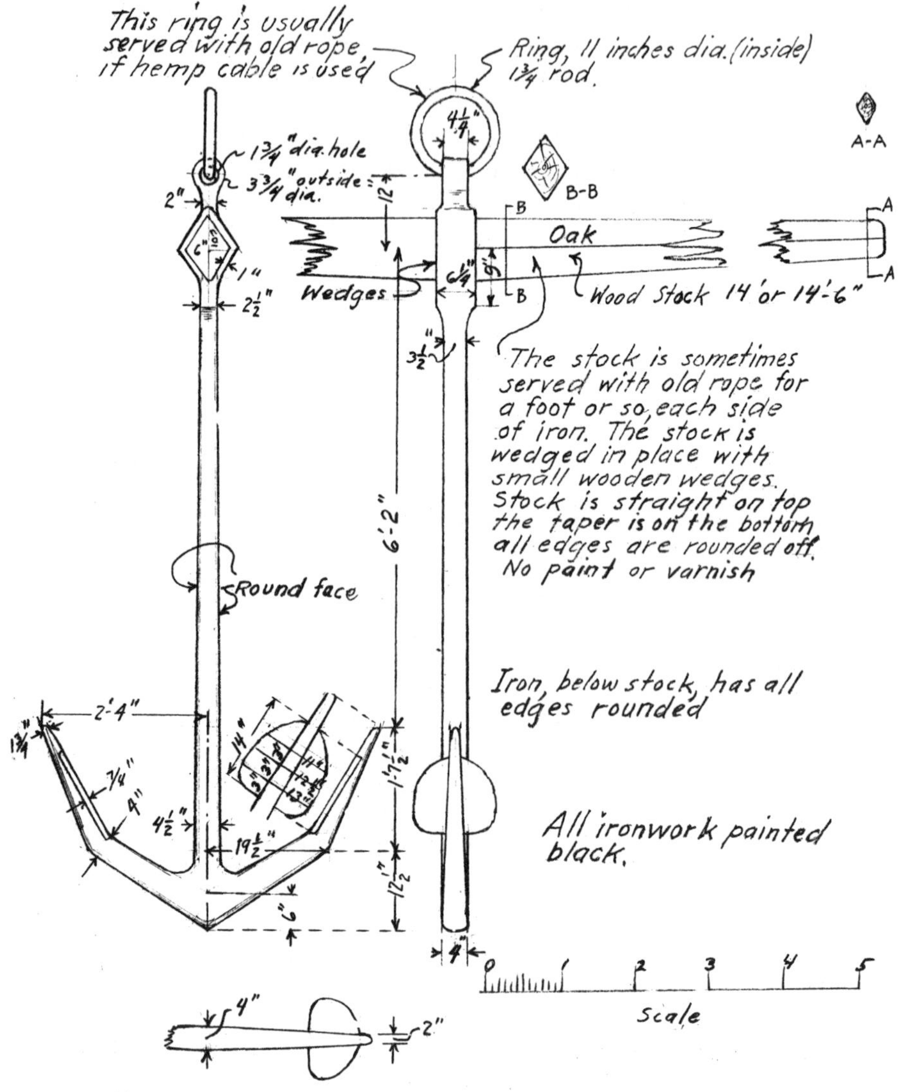
This ring is usually served with old rope, if hemp cable is used
Ring, 11 inches dia. (inside) 1¾ rod.
4¼"
A-A
B-B
1¾" dia. hole
3¾" outside dia.
12"
2"
6"
10"
Oak
1"
Wedges
6¼"
9"
Wood Stock 14' or 14'-6"
2½"
3½"
The stock is sometimes served with old rope for a foot or so, each side of iron. The stock is wedged in place with small wooden wedges. Stock is straight on top the taper is on the bottom all edges are rounded off. No paint or varnish
6'-2"
Round face
Iron, below stock, has all edges rounded
2'-4"
1¾"
14"
1'-7½"
¾"
4"
4½"
19½"
All ironwork painted black.
12½"
6"
4"
0 1 2 3 4 5
Scale
4"
2"

ANCHOR STOWAGE

The large banks anchor was used only on the banks. This anchor was taken apart and stowed on deck forward of the windlass. The stock was lashed alongside the anchor, which was secured with flukes aft, crown forward. The anchor davit was unshipped and secured underneath the anchor. The iron anchor, used in harbors, was usually stowed on the rail abaft the anchor davits, if it were to be used often, with the anchor davit in place. The same stowage was used in vessels having wooden catheads, but these could not be unshipped and stowed, of course. Anchors were sometimes lashed to windlass bitts when not required soon, stowed thus, outboard of bitts, on the warping head.

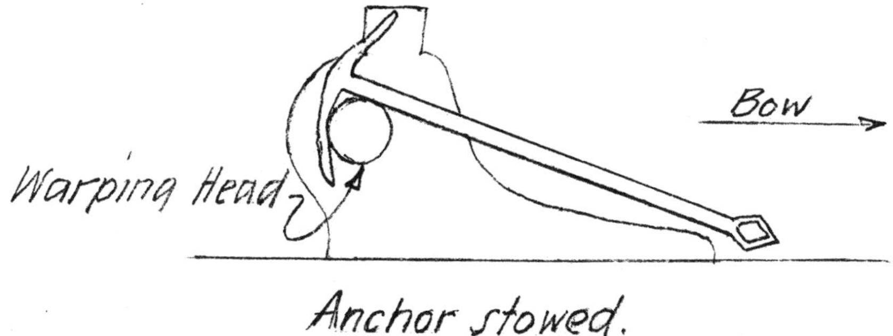
Bow
Warping Head

Anchor stowed.

ANCHOR CHAIN AND CABLE

Hemp cable, used in the Georges and Newfoundland banks fisheries, was carried on deck in two coils. These were on each side of the forecastle companionway. The starboard coil was the smaller, so that it would fit clear of the jumbo horse and the galley stack.

After 1900, the ventilation hatch, next abaft the forecastle companionway, was often constructed round and the cable could be coiled around it. This feature seems to have first appeared in Crowninshield-designed schooners, but cable stowage this way had a very short popularity.

Chain cable was not used on the banks, but only for harbor service, so only a relatively small amount was carried, usually in a chain box on deck, abreast the foremast. (See "Chain Box.")

Cables 300-400 fathoms long and 8″-9″ in circumference were carried for halibut fishing ("Banks").

ANCHOR CHAIN *"ADMIRALTY"*

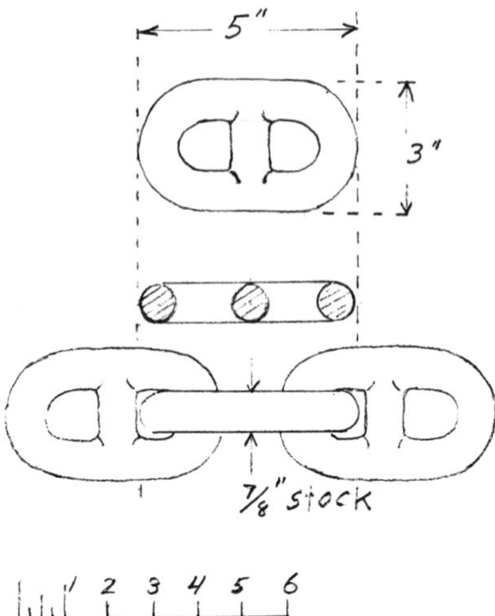
5"
3"
7/8" stock
1 2 3 4 5 6
6 inches

As used on schooners above 75' tonnage length. Small Schooners used smaller chain, often plain chain 3/4" stock, 4 1/4" x 2 1/2" links.

"Philip P. Manta"

ANCHOR DAVITS

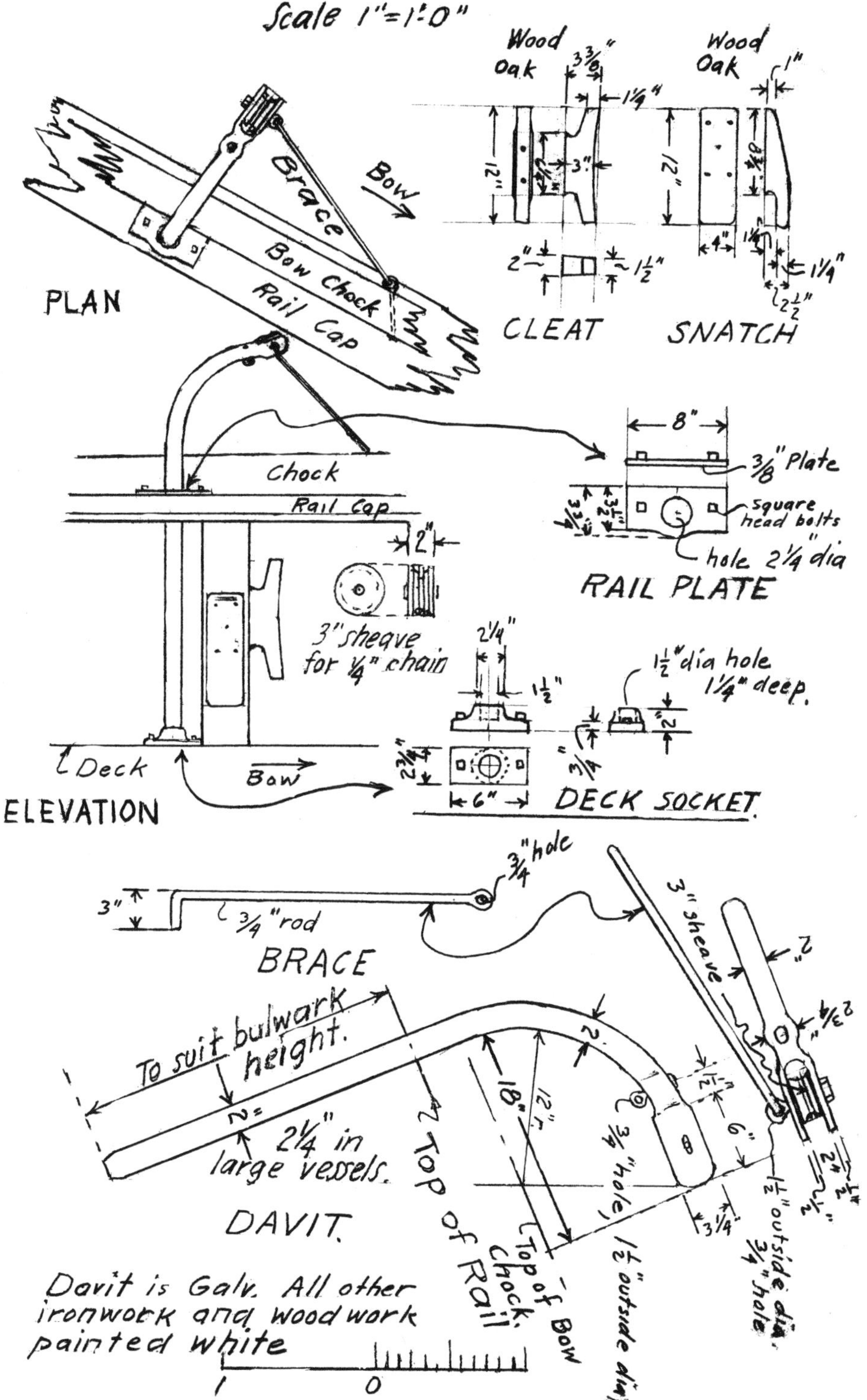

Scale 1"=1'-0"
Wood Oak
Wood Oak
Brace
Bow
Bow Chock
Rail Cap
PLAN
CLEAT
SNATCH
Chock
Rail Cap
3/8" Plate
square head bolts
hole 2 1/4" dia
RAIL PLATE
3" sheave for 1/4" chain
1 1/2" dia hole 1 1/4" deep.
Deck
Bow
ELEVATION
DECK SOCKET
3/4" hole
3/4" rod
BRACE
3" sheave
To suit bulwark height.
2 1/4" in large vessels.
Top of Rail
Top of Chock
Top of Bow
3/4" hole
1 1/2" outside dia
1 1/2" outside dia.
3/4" hole
DAVIT.
Davit is Galv. All other ironwork and wood work painted white
1
0

ANCHOR DAVITS (NOTES)

Location of anchor davits noted in surveys were: "Elsie"—7′ forward of the center line of windlass barrel; "Philip P. Manta"—just abaft the third bulwark stanchion, counting the aftermast hawse timber as 1.

On knockabouts, davits were from abreast to about 18″ forward of the foremost timber of the jumbo gallows frame. Padding, where anchor spoon works, had fore-end abreast foreside of windlass barrel. Padding 4′ long. Another vessel had fore-end of padding opposite the ℄ of windlass barrel.

ANCHOR SPOON (NOTES)

In raising the anchor, when it was brought to the hawse pipe, the cathead fall was passed through the ring by which it was brought to the cathead and the fall belayed. The flukes were then hooked, using the "fishhook" (an iron hook on a short piece of line having a spliced eye in its end), and hauled up by means of the masthead tackle, which was hooked into the spliced eye. The anchor was brought horizontal and then the spoon was inserted underneath the flukes, between the flukes and the rail, and was thus brought up to the bow chock rail. By bearing down on the inboard end of the spoon the anchor was brought over and landed on deck.

ANCHOR SPOON FROM "ELSIE"

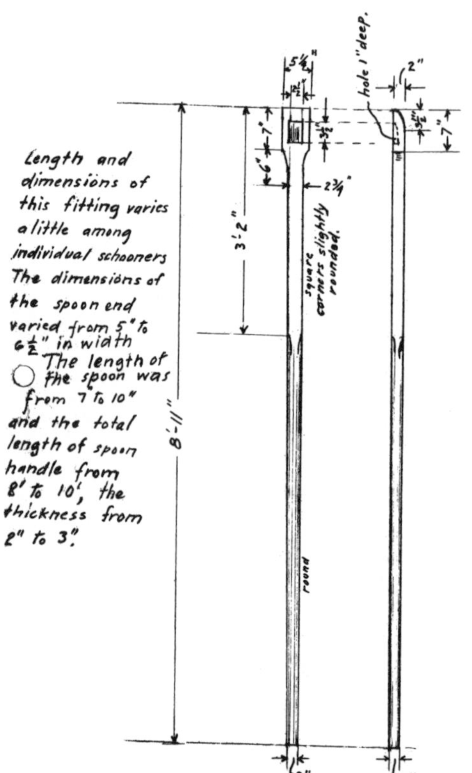
Length and dimensions of this fitting varies a little among individual schooners The dimensions of the spoon end varied from 5" to 6½" in width The length of the spoon was from 7 to 10" and the total length of spoon handle from 8' to 10', the thickness from 2" to 3".
5¼"
hole 1" deep.
2"
7"
6"
2¾"
3'-2"
square corners slightly rounded.
8'-11"
round
2"
2"

The spoon was made of a 3″ oak plank, about 9′ or 10′ long, spade-shaped. The handle was usually chamfered off a little, but sometimes it was made wholly round. The spade was about 5″-6½″ wide and about 7″-8″ long. The top of the spade was hollowed about 1″ deep and the tip of the underside of the spade was rounded.

See sketch of the anchor spoon found on "Elsie."

ANCHOR GEAR (NOTES)

Catting and stowing anchor: The anchor was raised and brought to the hawse with the cable. The hawser ring was hooked with the "fishhook" and the tail of this was spliced over a thimble or to a large ring, into which the hook of the jumbo top lift tackle was hooked. With this the anchor was brought up and aft (the cable being slacked simultaneously). Then, when the fishhook was within reach, the cat stopper was passed through the hawser ring, thence up and over the cathead sheave, then under the snatch and belayed on cleat or rail stanchion. Now the anchor was hanging from the cathead. The fishhook was disengaged and used to catch an anchor fluke, and with the jumbo top lift tackle the crown of the anchor was brought to the top of the rail. The anchor could now be lashed to the rail with a shank painter to a ringbolt centered at the padding of the bulwarks. If to be stowed on deck, the anchor was pried over the rail with the anchor spoon, so that it could be brought inboard. [E.S.B., L.H.S.]

The fishhook was made with a large hook of 1⅛″ iron rod shaped to form a hook having a shank 10″-20″ long. The hook was 9″-10″ across the mouth. At the top of the shank, a 2″ i. d. eye was formed standing at right angle to the hook. Into this was spliced a piece of 3¾″ circ. manila, about 8′ long with the other end of the rope finished with a thimble spliced in, or with the rope spliced to a ring about 3″ or 4″ diameter. [I.D.]

The cat stopper was made about 4′ of ¼″ chain, one end hooked into ringbolt under the cathead arm. The other end was shackled to a thimble spliced to 3¾″ circ. manila rope, the other end of which was well whipped. This rope was about 5′-6′ long.

APERTURES
GENERAL ARRANGEMENT

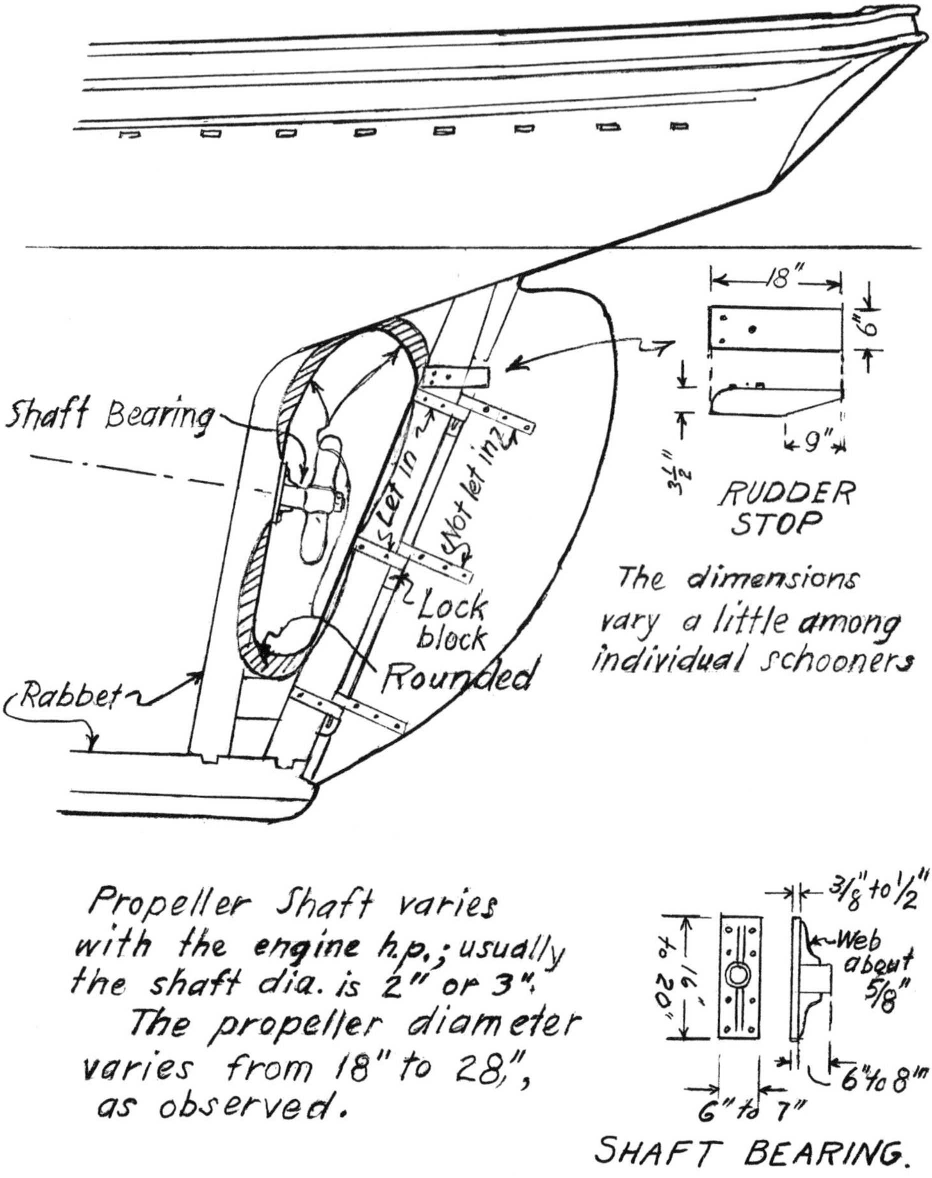

Shaft Bearing

Let in

Not let in

Lock block

Rounded

Rabbet

18"

6"

$3\frac{1}{2}$"

9"

RUDDER STOP

The dimensions vary a little among individual schooners

Propeller Shaft varies with the engine h.p.; usually the shaft dia. is 2" or 3". The propeller diameter varies from 18" to 28", as observed.

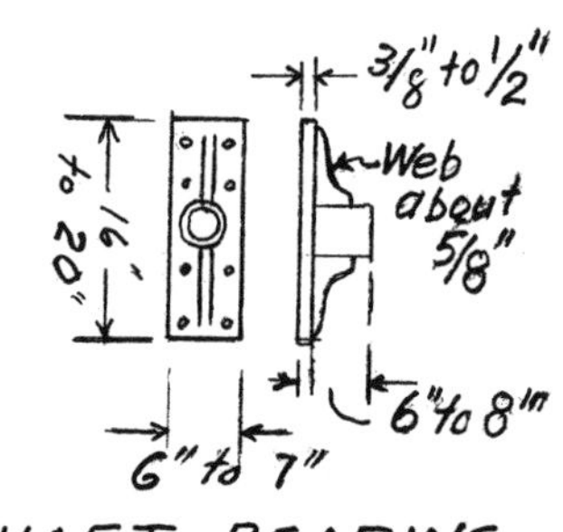

3/8" to 1/2"
Web about 5/8"
16" to 20"
6" to 8"
6" to 7"

SHAFT BEARING.

BACKROPES (BOWSPRIT)

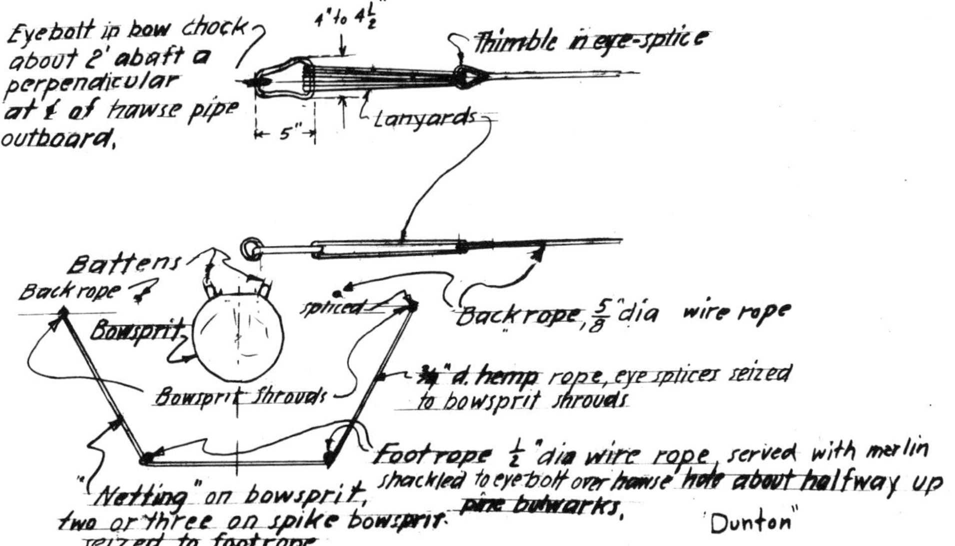
Eyebolt in bow chock about 2' abaft a perpendicular at ℄ of hawse pipe outboard.
4" to 4½"
Thimble in eye-splice
Lanyards
5"
Battens
Back rope
Bowsprit
spliced
Back rope, ⅝" dia wire rope
¾" d. hemp rope, eye splices seized to bowsprit shrouds
Bowsprit shrouds
Foot rope ½" dia wire rope, served with merlin shackled to eye bolt over hawse hole about halfway up pipe bulwarks.
"Netting" on bowsprit, two or three on spike bowsprit seized to foot rope
"Dunton"

BACKROPES (BOWSPRIT)

Backropes of "Philip P. Manta" were ⅝″ dia. wire rope.

Backropes secured to the bow rail chock about 2′ abaft ℄ of hawse, and to bowsprit jibstay wye forward.

MAST BANDS

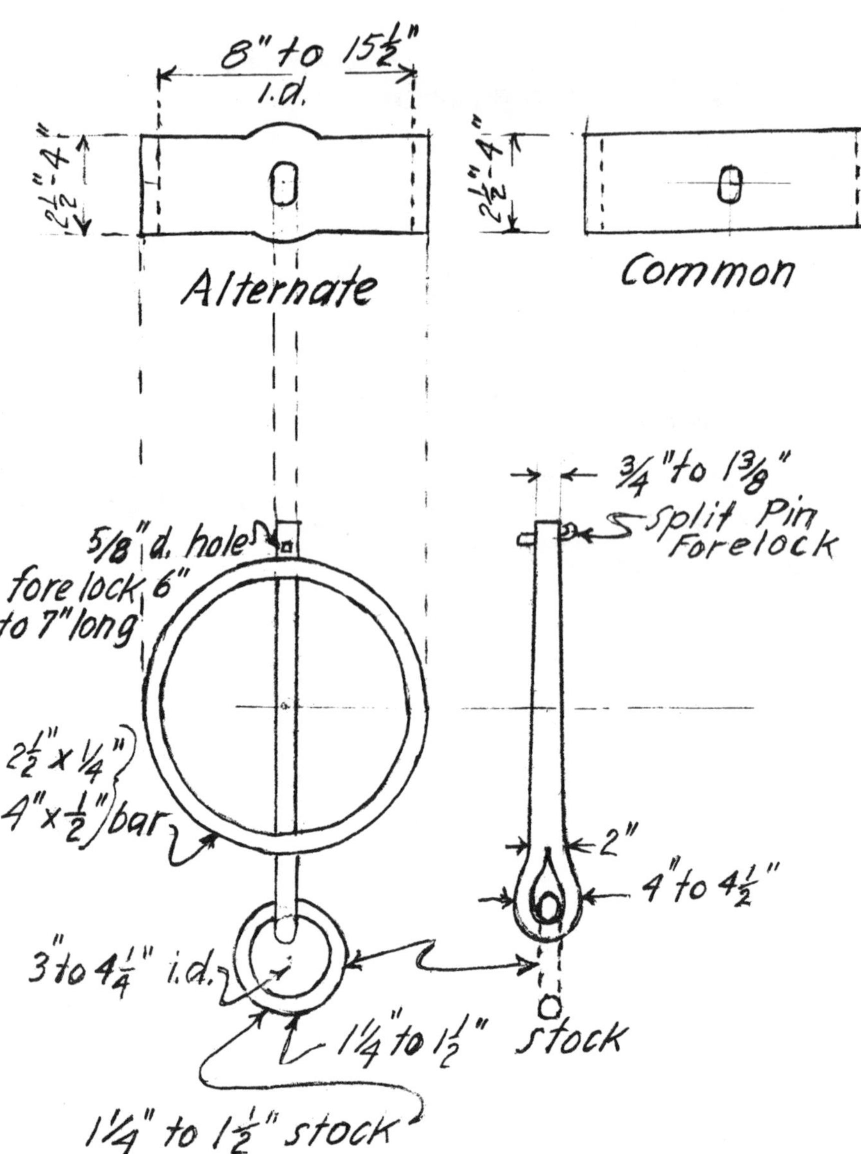

8" to 15½"
i.d.
2½"-4"
Alternate
2½"-4"
Common
¾" to 1⅜"
Split Pin Forelock
5/8" d. hole
fore lock 6" to 7" long
2½" x ¼"
4" x ½" bar
2"
4" to 4½"
3" to 4¼" i.d.
1¼" to 1½" stock
1¼" to 1½" stock

Not to scale

BAILS AND BANDS
FOREMAST

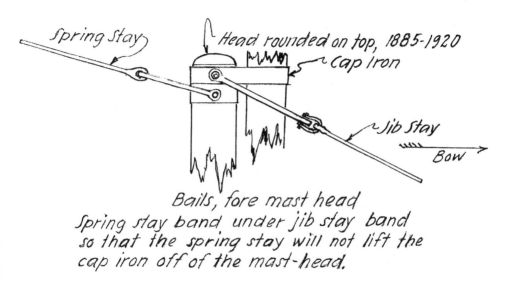

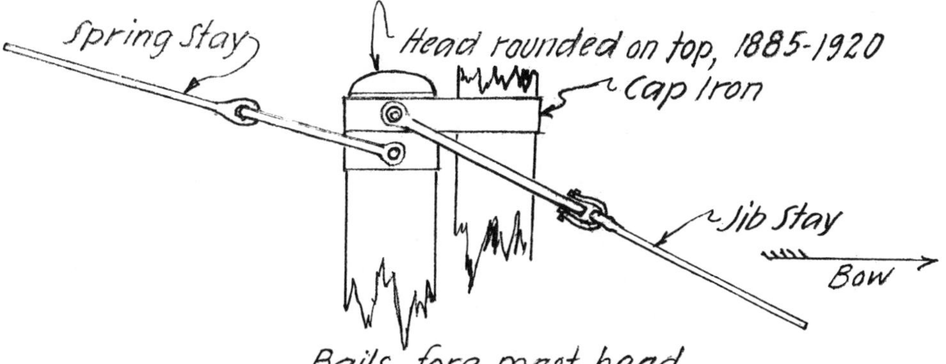
Spring Stay
Head rounded on top, 1885-1920
Cap Iron
Jib Stay
Bow

Bails, fore mast head
Spring stay band under jib stay band so that the spring stay will not lift the cap iron off of the mast-head.

BAIL—FOREMAST SPRINGSTAY BAIL, ETC.

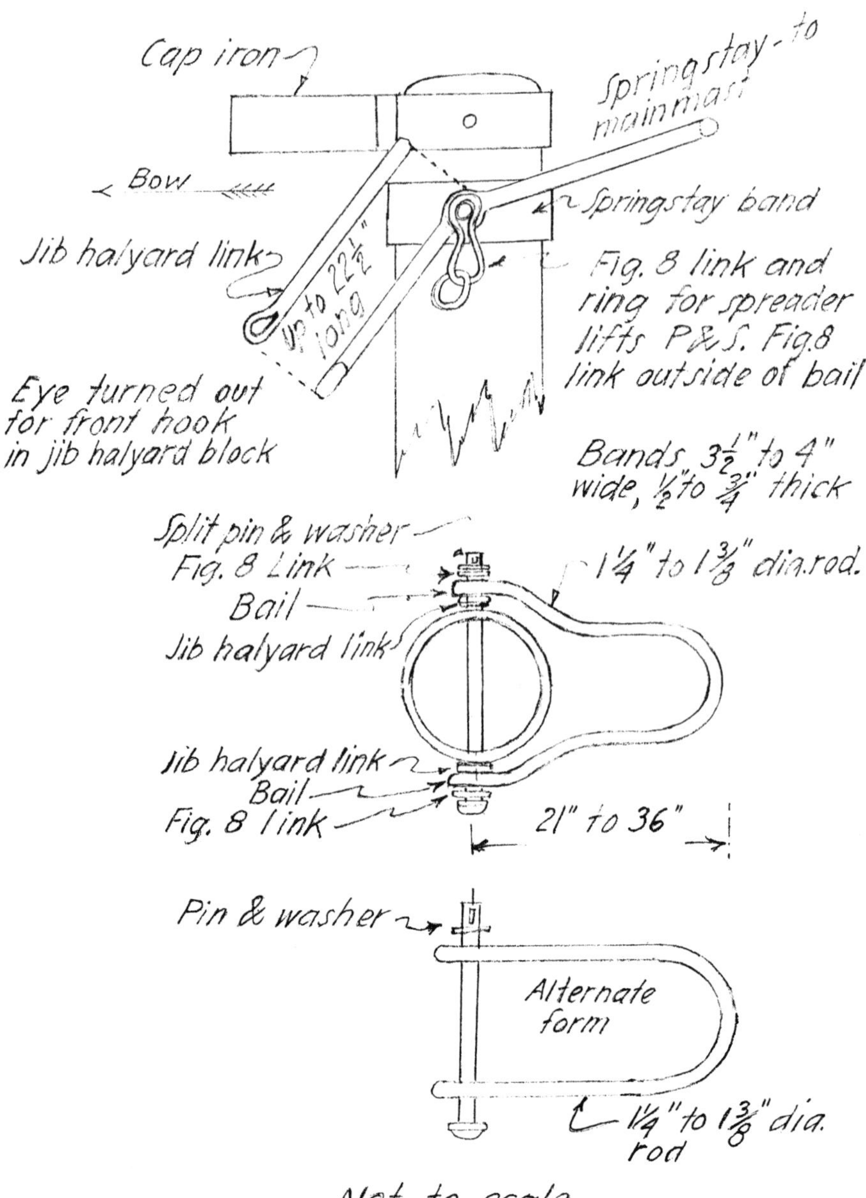
Cap iron
Springstay-to mainmast
Bow
Springstay band
Jib halyard link
Up to 22½" long
Fig. 8 link and ring for spreader lifts P&S. Fig. 8 link outside of bail
Eye turned out for front hook in jib halyard block
Bands 3½" to 4" wide, ½" to ¾" thick
Split pin & washer
Fig. 8 Link
Bail
Jib halyard link
1¼" to 1⅜" dia. rod.
Jib halyard link
Bail
Fig. 8 link
21" to 36"
Pin & washer
Alternate form
1¼" to 1⅜" dia. rod
Not to scale

BALLAST (NOTES)

Schooners up to the 1880s were ballasted with rock, some of which was iron ore. Much of this came from Essex River. Pig iron ballast became the standard ballast after 1890, or thereabouts. The ballast was taken out of the schooners at intervals and washed, and the hold cleaned. This practice began with stone ballast and continued with pig iron, for a dirty hold contaminated fish.

The iron ballast might be mixed with stone—the lower tier being iron, with stone in the upper tier. Sometimes the iron ballast was crowned upward along the vessel's center line, with rock filling the wings. Stringers laid athwartship, over the ballast, were secured in the wings, covered with plank laid fore-and-aft and spiked to the stringers. The fish pens and dividing-boards were built on this flooring leaving a narrow passageway along the center line of the hold. Care was taken to secure the ballast so that it could not shift. [L.H.S.]

Rock ballast was employed in Nova Scotia schooners until the end of sail. Only two fishing schooners are known to have been built with outside ballast. One was the "Massasoit," designed by McManus and built in 1898. The amount of outside ballast was small, however. The other schooner was the "Juniata," built the same year and the larger of the two.

In the last few years of schooner building, boiler punchings and concrete were used to top of floors to give clear limbers, and to form a "ground tier" of permanent ballast. Concrete was also used as a sole or floor in the fishhold.

BATTENS (WOOD), RAIL, DECK, AND BOWSPRIT

Two oak battens 2″ x 2″ were spiked, one on each side, to the top of the bowsprit, in which sail stops were secured. In spike bowsprits, the top was often flattened; in the older bowsprits the cross-sections were more U-shaped. The battens ran fore-to-aft from a little abaft the bowsprit shoulders, or bees, to within 2′ or 3′ of the gammoning. The flat top of the spike bowsprits was retained only to 1905.

Eight to ten oak battens, spaced about 1″–1½″ apart edge-to-edge, 2″ wide, and 1½″ thick, were spiked on deck, running from the hawse block, at the inboard end of the chain hawse hole (usually port side) in line with lead of chain to under the windlass barrel. These protected the deck in working the chain. Some schooners had them for both hawses.

In old vessels, four to six oak battens were spiked on the quarterdeck parallel to the break, and their length that of the width of the mainmast bed. They were about 1½″ x 2″. One was placed closely afore and one closely abaft the foresheet horse, the other spaced from near the mainmast bitts to the great beam. These protected the deck from the lower fore sheet block, but when iron stropped blocks appeared they were replaced by iron straps and bars. A similar condition was in the protective battens on the main rail over the transom, where wooden battens were replaced.

Wooden battens 1¼″ x 1½″, spiked fore-and-aft on deck, ran from the after-end of the trunk cabin to abreast the fore-end of the wheel box, spaced 1⅛″ apart edge-to-edge. These gave footing for the helmsman, and were on both sides of a tiller. With wheel steering they were on the starboard side only, eight to ten in number.

BEAMS, DECK (NOTES)

The deck beams of fishing schooners, 1845–1930, crowned about 5 inches in 24 feet. The beams were sawn to mould about a quarter of an inch to the foot crown, or about 4 inches in 24 feet. Often, after being sawn to moulded crown, they would be stacked in the shipyard for two or three weeks, or even longer. With this treatment some of the beams would lose a little of their crown. As a result, the beams were forced to crown by securing them in place and then bringing them to proper crown by shoring and dubbing.

First the beams were fitted in place and fastened to clamps and shelves. A piece of decking was used to fair the beams. The piece of the greatest length available was laid on the beams and clamped to the "high" ones. The other beams were then shored up from the keelson to bring them up to the batten, that is, the crown of the "high" beams, and all beams, were then dubbed fair with the adze. The carlins were fitted and faired. When the deck framing had been brought to crown (it was the intent to work in a little "spring" into all beams, as this prevented the deck from becoming too flat with age) the permanent shores were fitted and driven.

The permanent shores had a tenon or round spur on the upper ends which fitted into sockets or holes in the underside of the beams. The lower ends of the shores were fitted to long grooves on the top of the keelson which allowed the stanchions or shores to have their heels driven fore-to-aft to obtain the desired crown and tension. The shores were all double and had what the Essex ship carpenters called "half-tenons" at their heels. (See sketch.) [L.H.S.]

The James yard at Essex used ¼″ crown for each foot of beam but other builders used a little more crown, say 4½″ crown in 24′ beam. [L.H.S.]

BEAMS (DECK)

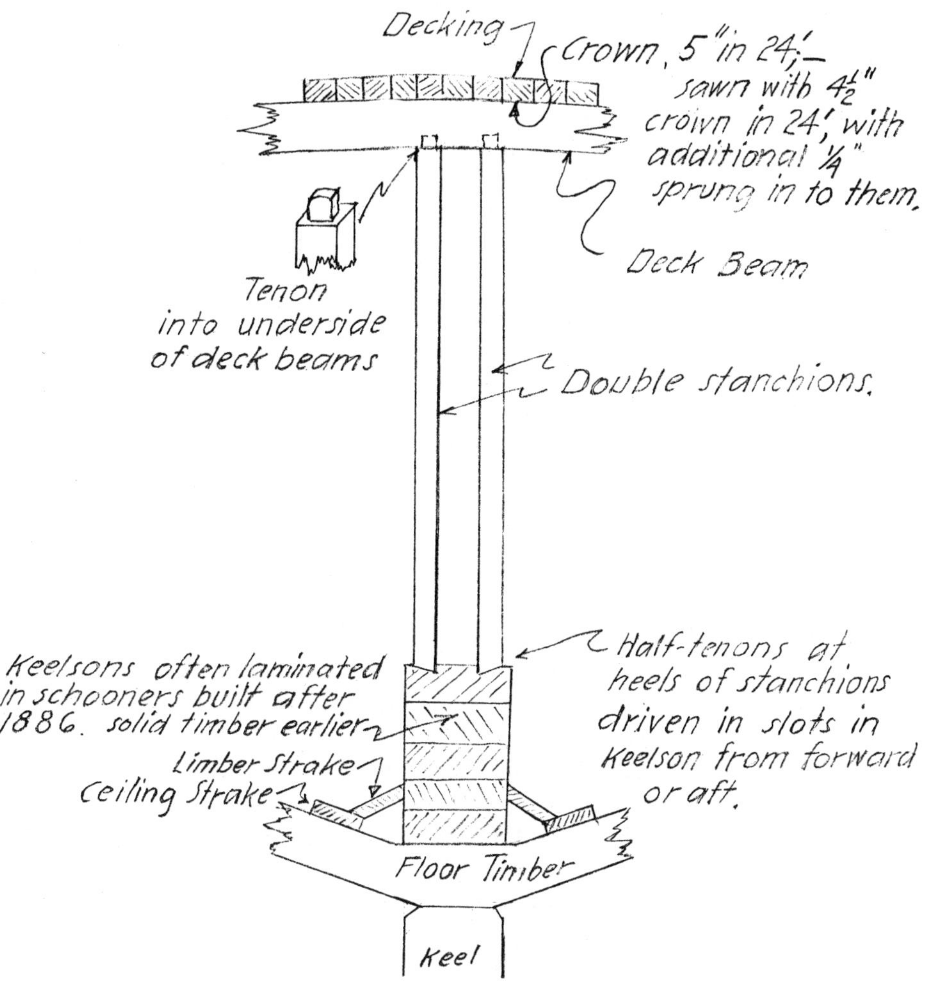
Hold Stanchions
to spring crown into the deck beams.
Decking
Crown, 5" in 24;—
sawn with 4½"
crown in 24', with
additional ¼"
sprung in to them.
Deck Beam
Tenon
into underside
of deck beams
Double stanchions.
Keelsons often laminated
in schooners built after
1886. solid timber earlier
Half-tenons at
heels of stanchions
driven in slots in
Keelson from forward
or aft.
Limber Strake
Ceiling Strake
Floor Timber
Keel

BEES (NOTES)

Bee holes in the bowsprit were 2½″-3½″ dia. depending on the size of the vessel; if a single fore or jumbo stay were used, as was common in most fishing schooners under 75′ registered length, having hemp rigging, the single stay was passed through the bee hole, in the center line of the bowsprit, and if there were a jibboom, this was placed on the upper port quarter of the bowsprit, to clear the stay. The forestay then led down to the inner bobstay plates on the cutwater and then turned on itself, on top of the stay, and was secured by three seizings, parcelled and served, then covered with a rawhide boot. The outer bobstay was of chain after about 1845. This was set up with hearts and lanyards, or was merely set up as taut as possible by the riggers.

If the jibboom was on the center line of the bowsprit, there would be two forestays, crossed and seized to form an eye aloft, brought to the bowsprit bees in two legs. The legs were seized together above the jibboom, high enough to allow the legs to clear that spar. Each leg, below this seizing, passed through its bee hole in the bee block, on each side of the bowsprit, and thence to the bobstay plates on each side of the cutwater.

The holes in the bee blocks were staggered a couple of inches so that the port bee hole was slightly abaft the starboard hole. The port leg was carried to the uppermost pair of bobstay plates. The lowermost, or outer, bobstay was chain, set up with hearts and lanyards at its outer end. The legs forming bobstays set up at the bobstay plates in the same manner as the single forestay. The hanks of the jumbo stays were large enough to ride on the two legs seized together above the jibboom.

The bee blocks were through bolted to the bowsprit and were from 24″-30″ long, 6″-7″ wide and from 2¾″-4″ thick. The ends were rounded off. The fore-end butted against the bowsprit cap iron. In the period between 1855 and 1885 the bowsprit shroud chain plates were fitted on the outside of the bee blocks and secured with the bee block bolts, upset in countersunk holes in the chain plates. The fore-ends of the chain plates followed the rounding of the bee blocks and overlapped and seated on top of the bowsprit cap iron. Here it was through-bolted: its bolt passing through chain plates extended a few inches abaft the bee blocks formed in an eye to receive its bowsprit shroud. Chain plates were ⅜ to ¾ of an inch thick, 2½″-5″ wide.

The bee blocks were often on the profile ℄ of the bowsprit, but if the bowsprit was U-shaped in cross-section out to the cap, the bee blocks had their tops flush with the top of the bowsprit.

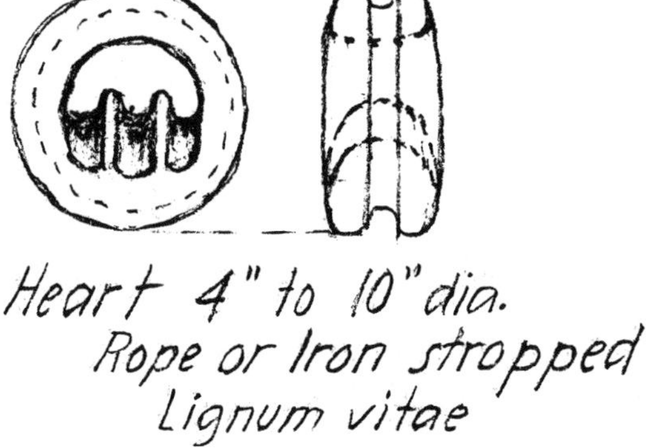

Heart 4″ to 10″ dia.
Rope or Iron stropped
Lignum vitae

BELAYING PINS

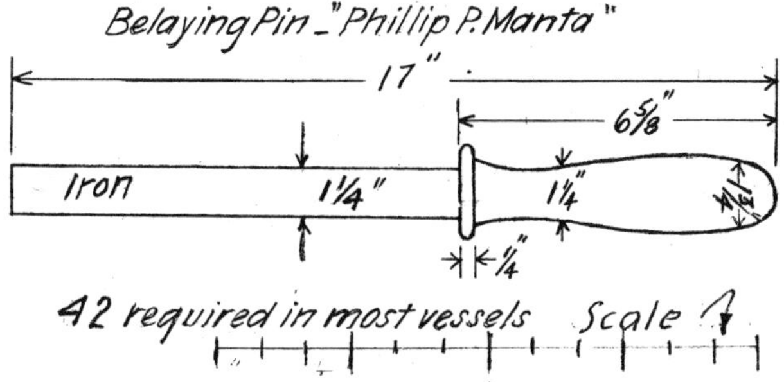
Belaying Pin - "Phillip P. Manta"
17"
6⅝"
Iron
1¼"
1¼"
¼"
42 required in most vessels
Scale

List of belaying pins and distribution, 1892
3 pins in breast hook
2 pins in fore boom jaws, Omit if there is a fore boom gooseneck
6 pins in fore chains, rail cap, 3 on each side
10 pins in main chains, rail cap, 5 on each side
6 pins in foremast fife rail
6 pins in mainmast fife rail
2 pins in rail, main topmast staysail sheets
2 pins in rail, jib topsail sheets
4 pins on stern seat
2 pins in mainboom jaws
43 pins required, locust or iron, or both.

BELAYS, TYPICAL FISHING SCHOONER, 1905–1925

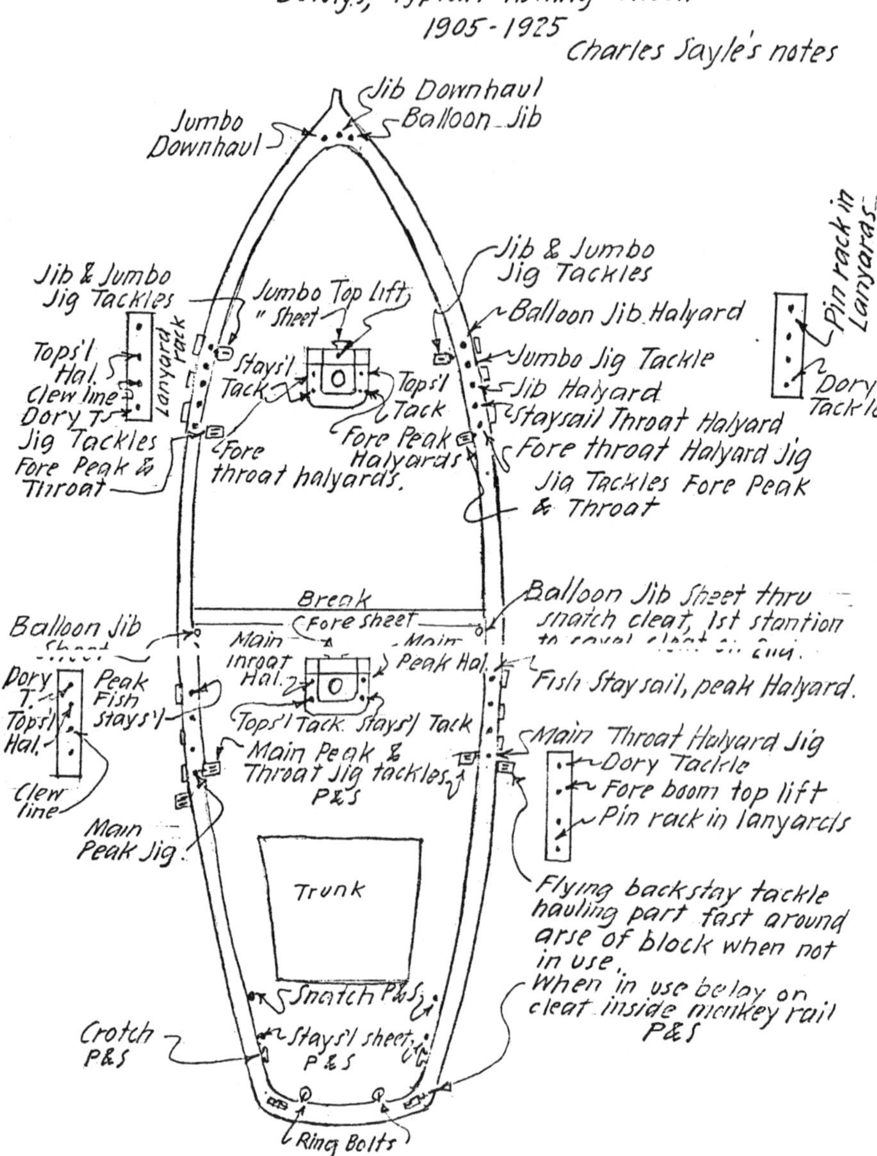
Belays, typical fishing schooner
1905 - 1925
Charles Sayle's notes
Jib Downhaul
Balloon Jib
Jumbo Downhaul
Jib & Jumbo Jig Tackles
Balloon Jib Halyard
Jumbo Jig Tackle
Jib Halyard
Staysail Throat Halyard
Fore throat Halyard Jig
Jig Tackles Fore Peak & Throat
Pin rack in Lanyards
Dory Tackle
Jib & Jumbo Jig Tackles
Tops'l Hal.
Clew line
Dory T.
Jig Tackles Fore Peak & Throat
Lanyard rack
Jumbo Top lift
" Sheet
Stays'l Tack
Tops'l Tack
Fore Peak Halyards
Fore throat halyards.
Break
Fore sheet
Balloon Jib Sheet thru snatch cleat, 1st stantion
Balloon Jib Sheet
Main throat Hal.
Main Peak Hal.
Fish Staysail, peak Halyard.
Dory T.
Tops'l Hal.
Clew line
Peak Fish stays'l
Tops'l Tack
Stays'l Tack
Main Peak & Throat Jig tackles. P&S
Main Throat Halyard Jig
Dory Tackle
Fore boom top lift
Pin rack in lanyards
Main Peak Jig.
Trunk
Flying backstay tackle hauling part fast around arse of block when not in use.
When in use belay on cleat inside monkey rail P&S
Snatch P&S
Stays'l sheet P&S
Crotch P&S
Ring Bolts

Jig tackle falls made fast around
arse of block sometimes
Pins not used here were used
Fish hoisting tackles etc..

BELAYS, RUNNING RIGGING, 1900

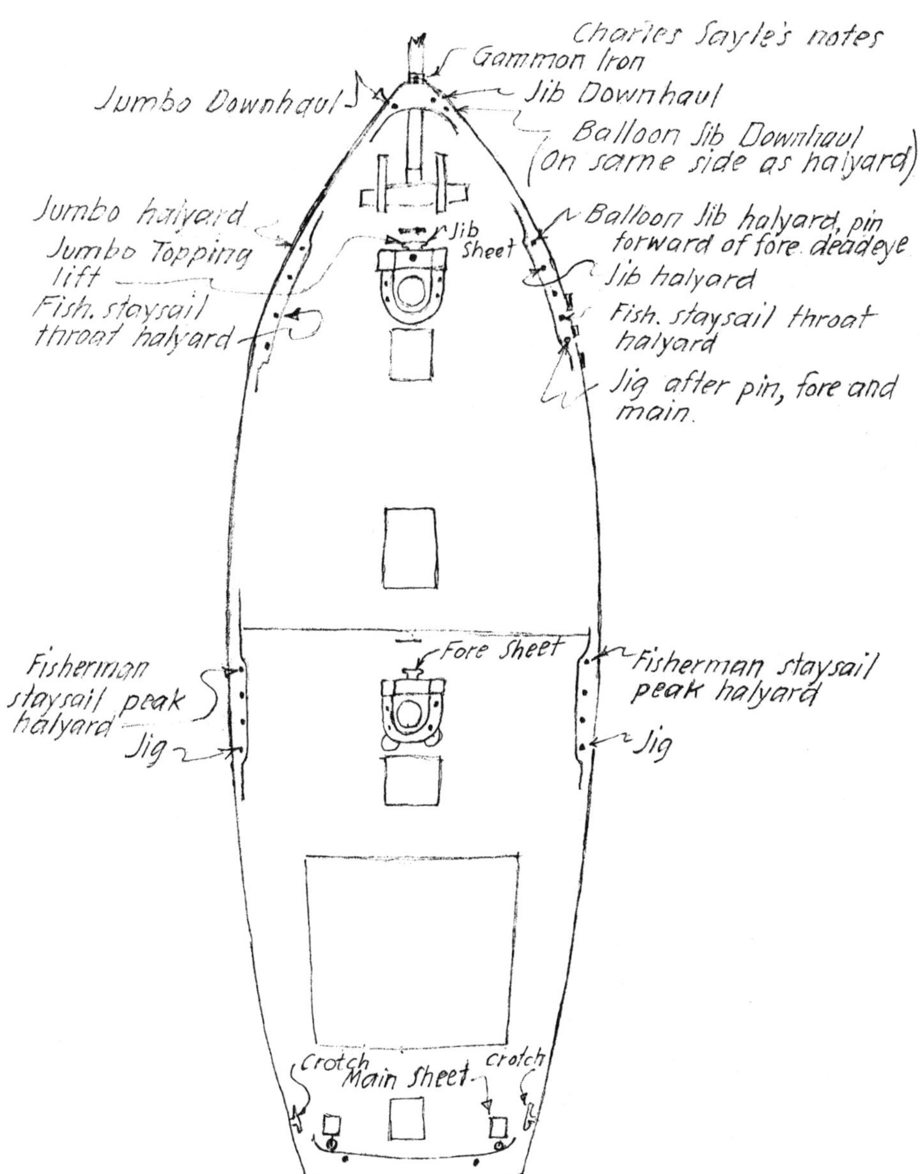
Charles Sayle's notes
Gammon Iron
Jumbo Downhaul
Jib Downhaul
Balloon Jib Downhaul
(On same side as halyard)
Jumbo halyard
Jumbo Topping lift
Jib Sheet
Balloon Jib halyard, pin forward of fore deadeye
Jib halyard
Fish. staysail throat halyard
Fish. staysail throat halyard
Jig after pin, fore and main.
Fore Sheet
Fisherman staysail peak halyard
Fisherman staysail peak halyard
Jig
Jig
Crotch
Main Sheet
Crotch

BELAYS, RUNNING RIGGING, 1900

The hauling part of jig tackles belayed on pins in main rail at shrouds, or in the arse of the lower block.

Topsail halyards belay to portside, first pin in pin racks in shroud lanyards, clew lines (downhauls) belayed to second pin in racks.

Dory tackles belay to pin racks in shroud lanyards.

Foreboom topping lift to first pin, starboard pin rack in shroud lanyards.

Topsail sheets to starboard side, second pin in fife rails, tacks to pins in mainboom jaws.

Flying backstay falls belayed around arse of lower block when not in use. Made fast to cleat on inside of monkey rail next to a ringbolt on deck, where they hooked when running off. Staysail sheet leads outside main shrouds, through snatch cleat under mainboom, about one-third of a boom length from jaws, thence to pin boom jaws.

Staysail tack line was often brought around the foreside of the foremast and belayed on opposite side from that the sail was set on—this hauled the tack farther forward and brought it closer to the mast.

Peak and throat halyards, main and sometimes fore, belayed thus: fall brought down under snatch cleat on mast bitts, thence up and around bitt, over fall of halyard followed with two or three turns around after pin in fife rail.

PIN BELAYS, RUNNING RIGGING, 1900 (NOTES)

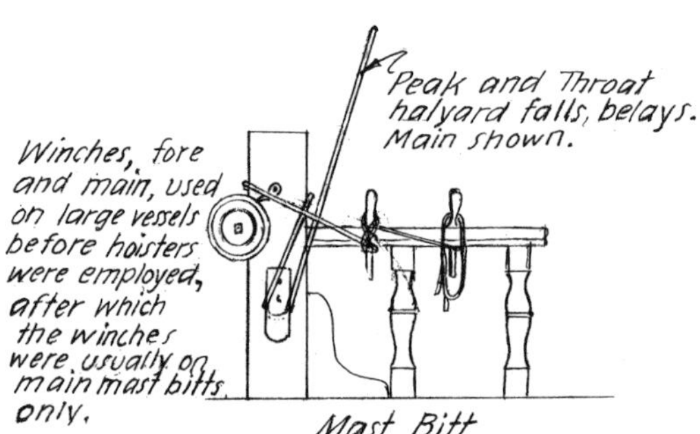
Peak and Throat
halyard falls, belays.
Main shown.
Winches, fore
and main, used
on large vessels
before hoisters
were employed,
after which
the winches
were usually on
main mast bitts
only.
Mast Bitt

Snatch cleat and kevel (or cleat) on bulwark stanchions abaft after corners of cabin trunk used to belay staysail sheets when on the wind. Some vessels carried the balloon jib sheets to a snatch and kevel nearly abreast fore end of cabin trunk. C.S.

BELAYING PINS

Details from the schooner PHILIP P. MANTA.

Not to scale.

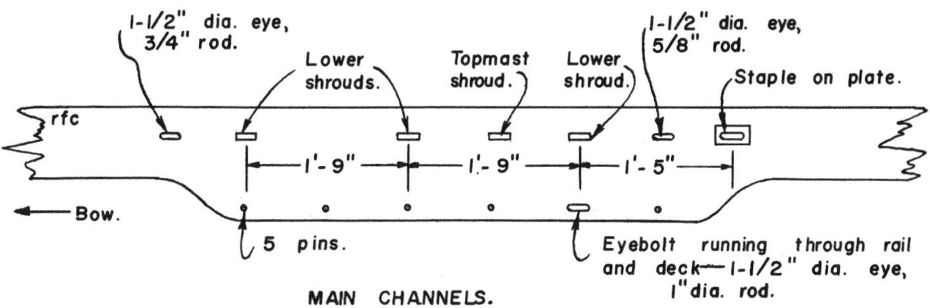
1-1/2" dia. eye,
3/4" rod.
Lower
shrouds.
Topmast
shroud.
Lower
shroud.
1-1/2" dia. eye,
5/8" rod.
Staple on plate.
rfc
1'- 9"
1'- 9"
1'- 5"
Bow.
5 pins.
Eyebolt running through rail and deck—1-1/2" dia. eye, 1" dia. rod.

MAIN CHANNELS.

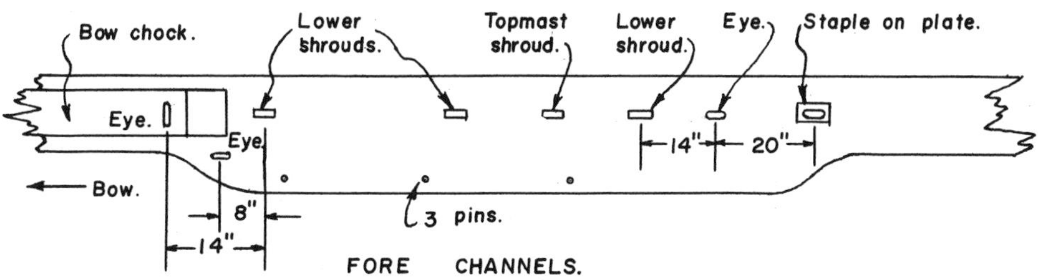
Bow chock.
Lower
shrouds.
Topmast
shroud.
Lower
shroud.
Eye.
Staple on plate.
Eye.
Eye
14"
20"
Bow.
8"
14"
3 pins.

FORE CHANNELS.

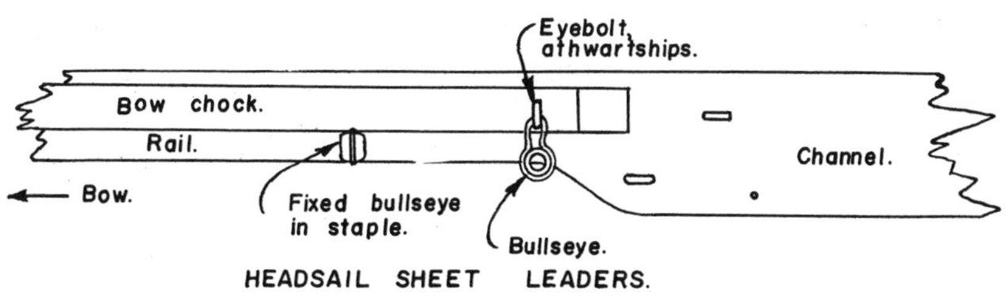
Eyebolt,
athwartships.
Bow chock.
Rail.
Channel.
Bow.
Fixed bullseye
in staple.
Bullseye.

HEADSAIL SHEET LEADERS.

BELAYING PINS RACK,
"MARY T. FALLON"

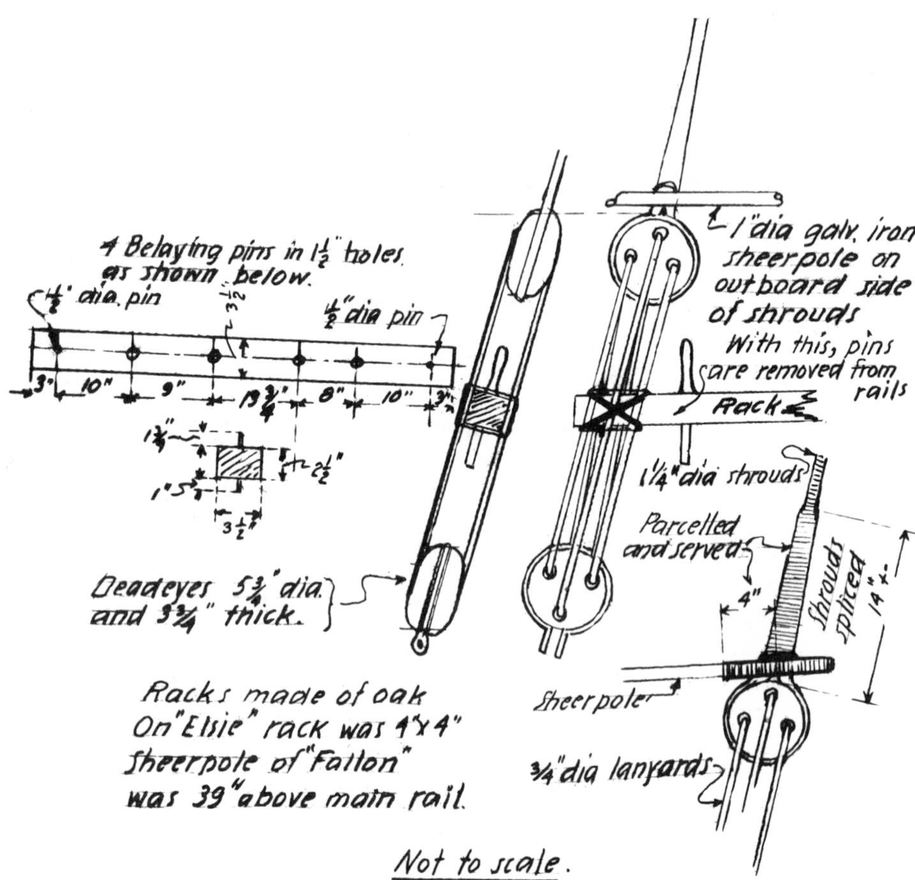
4 Belaying pins in 1½" holes as shown below.
½" dia. pin
½" dia pin
3½"
3"
10"
9"
13¾"
8"
10"
3"
1¾"
2½"
1"
3½"
1" dia galv. iron sheerpole on outboard side of shrouds
With this, pins are removed from rails
Rack
1¼" dia shrouds
Parcelled and served
4"
Shrouds spliced
14"±
Deadeyes 5¾" dia. and 3¾" thick.
Racks made of oak
On "Elsie" rack was 4"x4"
Sheerpole of "Fallon" was 39" above main rail.
Sheerpole
¾" dia lanyards
Not to scale.

Sheerpoles served about 4" each way from shrouds. Shrouds served and parcelled. Topmast shroud deadeyes 4½" dia, 3" thick. Shrouds served and parcelled, with canvass, only at splice, in this vessel.

BILLET, *1840–1885*

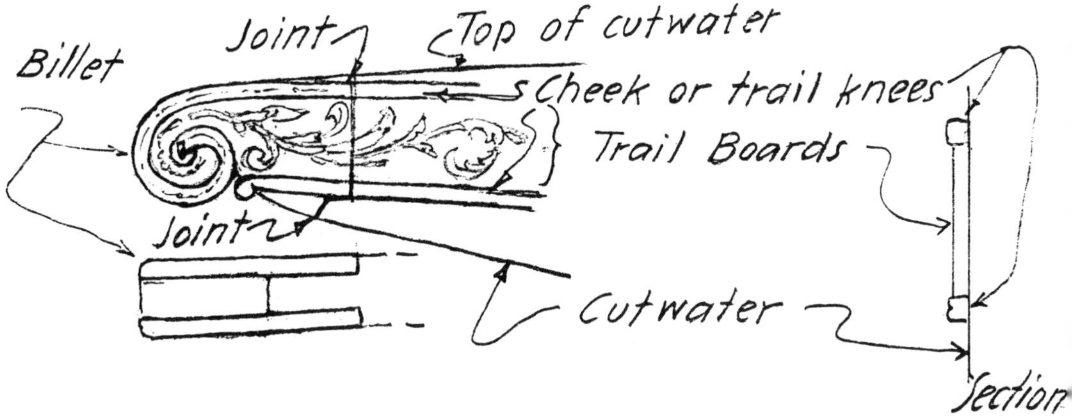
Billet
Joint
Top of cutwater
Cheek or trail knees
Trail Boards
Joint
Cutwater
Section

Billets carved out of white pine, with carving to fair into trailboards. Carving stylized foliage, of maple or oak branches. Billet fairs into cheek knees also. Billet usually of three pieces, two the thickness of the cutwater outboard end. Usually billet was accompanied by head rails and brackets before 1889.

Billets and head rails went out of style during the late 1880s, replaced by a simplified billet carved out of the cutwater, with a foliage scroll carved in the sides of the cutwater and in the planking, and carried around abaft the hawse castings. The last clipper bow schooners usually had a stylized eagle's head with scroll. The billets of fishing schooners were usually small and were sometimes over before 1865. Large billets were fitted in bankers (these were round), through the '70s and '80s. In the 1890s billets became very small, though round, and some gammon knee cutwaters ended in what was almost a point.

BITTS (WINCHES)

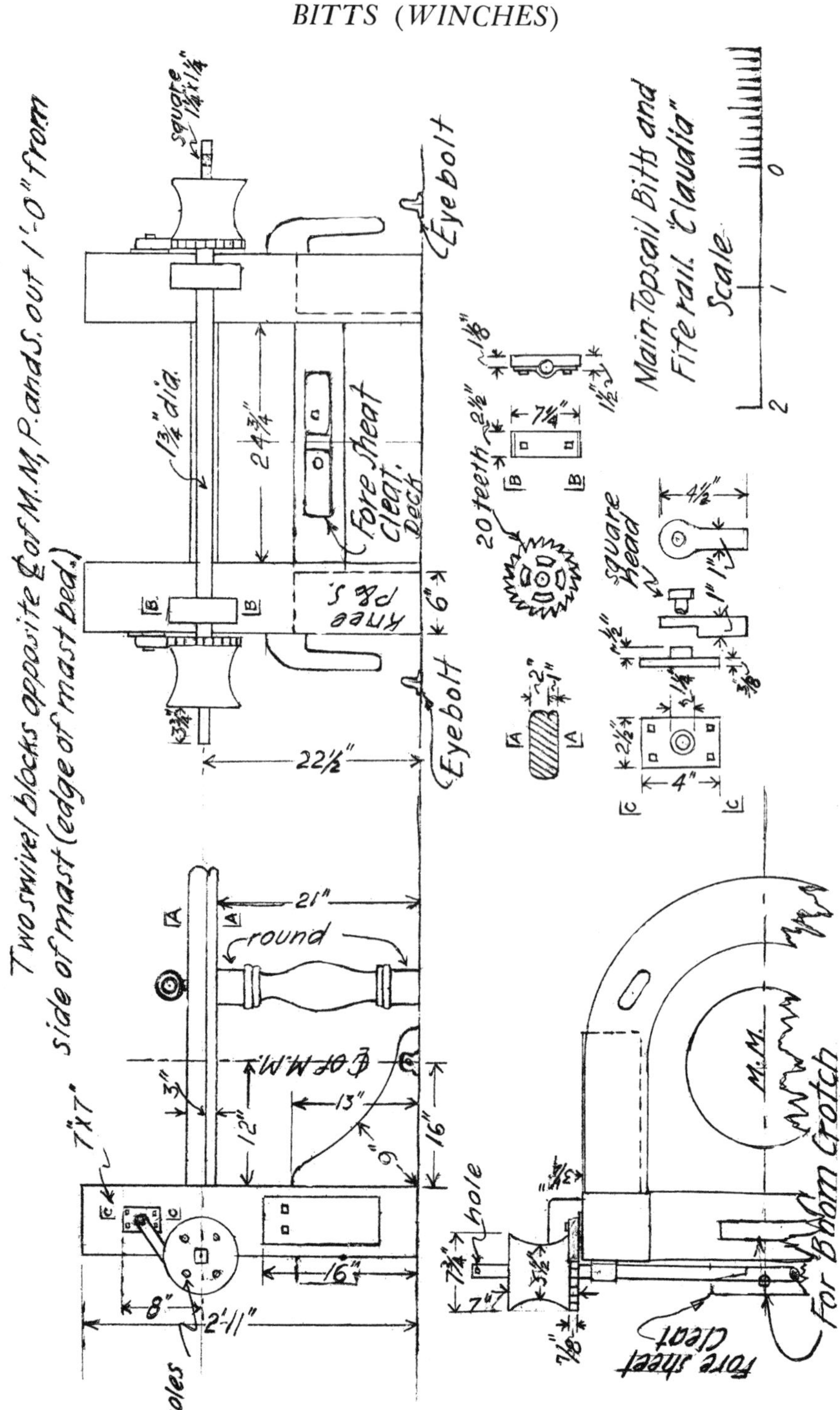

Two swivel blocks opposite ℄ of M.M, P. and S. out 1'-0" from side of mast (edge of mast bed.)
Main Topsail Bitts and Fife rail. "Claudia"
Scale
Eyebolt
Eyebolt
Fore Sheet cleat. Deck
knee P&S.
20 teeth
square head
round
℄ of M.M.
M.M.
For Boom Crotch
fore sheet cleat
hole
holes

MAIN TOPSAIL BITTS

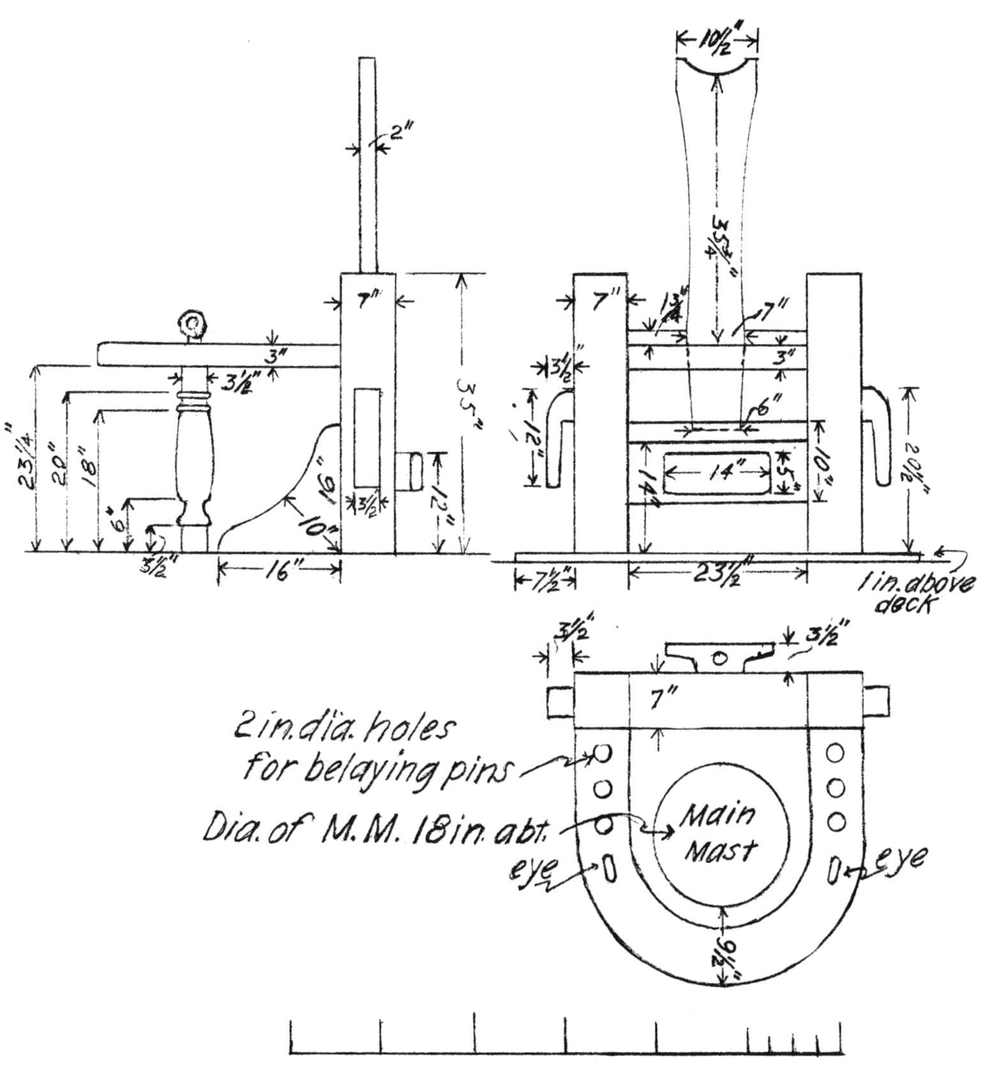
2"
7"
3"
3½"
35"
23¼"
20"
18"
6"
3½"
16"
10"
3½
12"
16"
10½"
35¾"
7"
1¾"
7"
3"
3½"
6"
12"
14"
5"
10"
14"
20½"
7½"
23½"
1 in. above deck
3½"
3½"
7"
2 in. dia. holes for belaying pins
Dia. of M.M. 18 in. abt.
Main Mast
eye
eye
9½"

MAIN TOPSAIL BITTS
SCHOONER "A.D. STORY," EX "MARY"

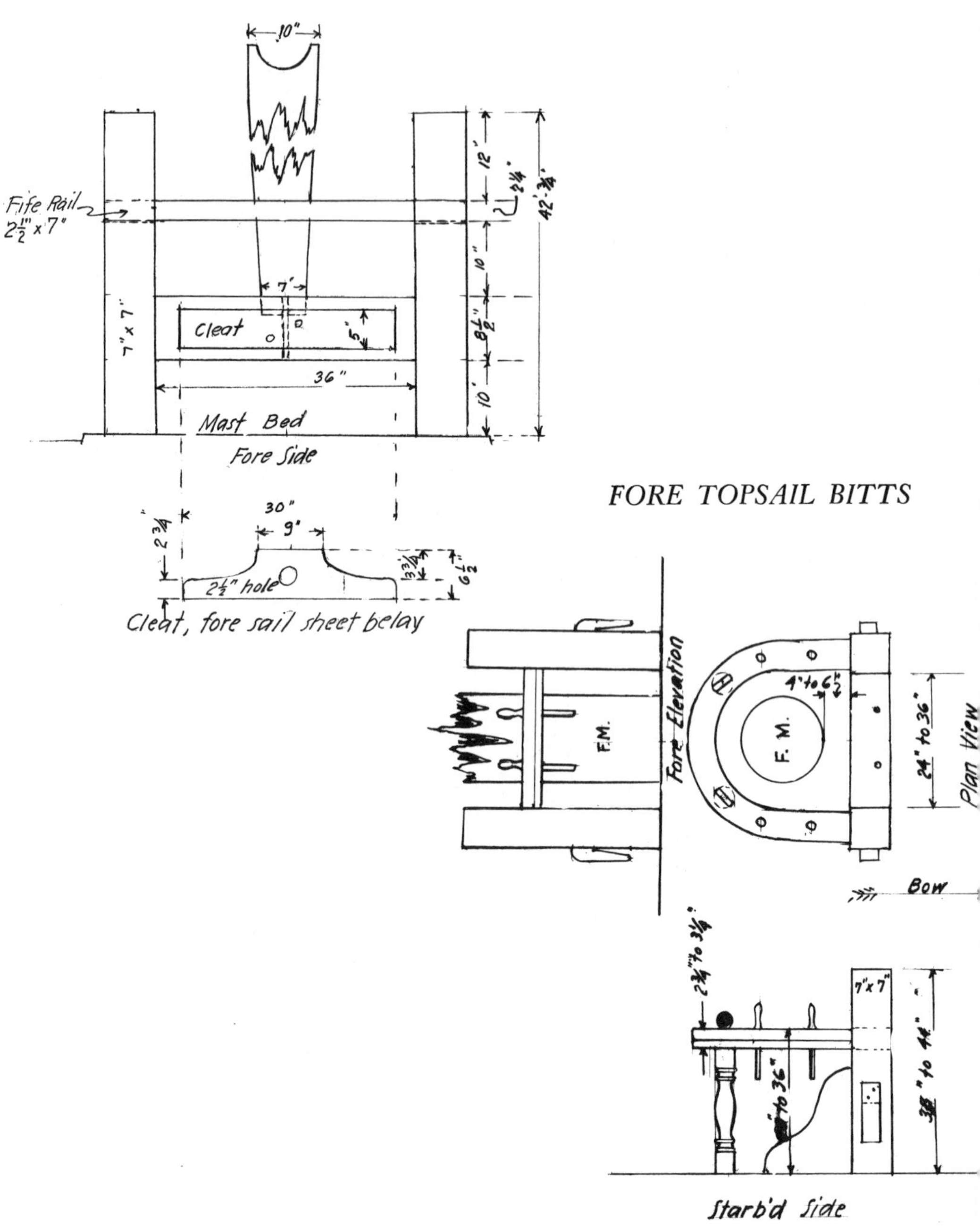

10"
12"
2¼"
42"-¾"
Fife Rail
2½" x 7"
7"
10"
7" x 7"
Cleat
5"
8½"
36"
10"
Mast Bed
Fore Side
30"
9"
2¾"
2½" hole
3¾"
6½"
Cleat, fore sail sheet belay
FORE TOPSAIL BITTS
F.M.
Fore Elevation
4" to 6½"
F. M.
24" to 36"
Plan View
Bow
2¾" to 3¼"
7" x 7"
to 36"
38" to 44"
Starb'd Side
Based on "Philip P. Manta"
Heights same as on main tops'l bitt.

BLOCKS (SCHEDULE)

Blocks on "Dunton": throat halyards, main-gaff double block 14″ x 10″ shell, 10″ thick. Hook 1¾″ stock. Blocks on trestletrees: single to starboard, double to port. Foremast, peak blocks on gaff 14″ x 10″, 5½″ thick, singles, two blocks. Fore throat on gaff 14″ x 10½″, 12″ thick, triple block, two double blocks aloft. Jumbo sheet block 8″ x 5½″, 6¼″ thick. Two singles on deck, one double on boom. Two single blocks on mast cheeks for jumbo halyard. Three single blocks on mast for forepeak, two doubles on mast for throat halyards. Two singles for fore-gaff peak. One treble on fore-gaff for throat. Two double blocks to post, one single to starboard for main throat, on mast. Three singles at masthead for main peak. Large double for throat on gaff. [C.S.]

Many large schooners had three peak halyard blocks on the foremast and four on the main. On the foremast the eyes of the wyes were arranged thus:

Top block—1″ to starboard of ℄.

Middle—1″ to port of mast ℄.

Lowest—3″ to port of mast ℄. On the mainmast the top block was 4″ to starboard of mast ℄, the second block was 4″ to port of mast ℄, the third was 1″ to port of the mast ℄, and the lowest block was 4″ to port of the mast ℄.

Deck fairlead on mainsheet of the knockabout "Adventure" had a round steel plate, 18½″ in dia. of ¼″ plate with an eyebolt at center, eye 1¼″ i.d. and standing 4″ above the plate. Lead block 8″ x 6″ single.

"Ethel Penny," knockabout; foremast, throat block three sheaves: peak blocks, lower one sheave, top block two sheaves. Mainmast, throat three sheaves; peak blocks, lowest two sheaves, middle one sheave, top block one sheave.

Blocks on masts are all hooked into lines in the wyes and the hooks all open away from the mast.

BLOCKS (SCHEDULE FOR HALYARDS) ED BOSLEY

Main throat halyards: two doubles on heart iron near trestletrees. On gaff a double to port and a single to starboard, both hooked to spectacle iron in links near gaff jaws.

Fore throat halyards: two doubles on mast, as on main, one triple hooked to ring in links in gaff jaws.

Main peak halyard: four singles hooked to ringbolts in masthead, three singles banded to gaff.

Fore peak halyard: three singles hooked to ringbolts in masthead, two singles banded to gaff.

Jib halyard: two singles, one on each side of fore masthead hooked to links on pin through springstay bail; one single with sister-hooks at head of jib.

Jumbo halyard: two singles, hooked to eyebolts under trestletrees (front hooks and eyebolts athwartship), one single with sister-hooks at head of sail.

Jigs: fore and main peak halyards and jib halyard have their jigs on port side.

Fore and main throat halyards and jumbo halyard have their jigs on the starboard side.

BLOCK LISTS

Schooners "Elk," "Avalon," and "Arthur James"	SIZE OF BLOCKS
Fore and main halyards and sheets	12″
Jigs	8″
Crotch tackles	6″
Jumbo and jib halyards	10″
Jumbo sheet	8″
Jumbo jig	7″
Jib jigs	6″
Reef tackle	6″
Fore- and main-boom tackles	10″
Balloon jib halyard	6″
Fore- and main-gaff topsail halyards	6″
Fore- and main-gaff topsail sheets	6″
Fisherman staysail peak halyards	7″
Fisherman staysail throat halyards	7″ or 8″
Flying backstays	7″ or 8″

These schooners were 100′ on deck, 113′ overall, 24′-9″ beam—launched in 1903. Partial block list for size comparison.

BLOCK LIST, "GRAMPUS," 1885

Blocks, ash, lignum vitae sheaves, iron or patent bushings, galv. iron strapped, inside of the shell of the block. A few blocks to be made with lignum vitae shells—in some iron sheaves are required.

MAINSAIL	*No.*	*Size*	*Bushing*
3-fold main peak	1	12″	Pat.
Single-fold main peak	2	12″	Pat.
3-fold main throat	1	12″	Pat.
2-fold main throat	1	12″	Pat
3-fold main sheet	1	12″	Pat
2-fold main sheet-lignum vitae	1	12″	Pat
Single-fold runner, main boom top. lift	1	7″	Pat.
Single-fold upper main boom top. lift	1	8″	iron
Single-fold main peak whips	2	7″	iron
Single-fold main peak downhaul	1	5″	iron
2-fold main crutch tackles	2	7″	iron
Single-fold main crutch tackles	2	7″	iron
2-fold main boom tackle	1	9″	Pat.
Single-fold main boom tackle	1	9″	Pat.
2-fold main reef tackle	1	6″	Pat
Single-fold main reef tackle	1	6″	Pat

FORESAIL	*No.*	*Size*	*Bushing*
3-fold forepeak	1	12″	Pat.
Single-fold forepeak	2	12″	Pat.
2-fold forethroat	2	12″	Pat.
2-fold foresheet	1	11″	Pat.
Single-fold foresheet, lig. vitae	1	11″	Pat.
Single-fold foreboom top. lift	2	8″	Pat.
Single-fold forepeak whips	1	7″	iron
Single-fold foreboom tackle	1	7″	iron

FORESTAYSAIL			
Single-fold forestaysail halyards	1	9″	Pat.
Two-fold forestaysail halyards	1	9″	Pat.
Single-fold forestaysail downhaul	1	7″	Pat.
Single-fold lig. vitae (round) staysail sheet	1	8″	iron
Single-fold top lift blocks	2	8″	Pat.

JIB			
Single-fold jib halyards	2	9″	Pat.
Single-fold jib downhaul	1	6″	Pat.
Single-fold lig. vitae (round) sheet	2	7″	Pat.

FLYING JIB

Single-fold flying jib halyards	2	7″	Pat.
Single-fold flying jib downhaul	1	5″	Pat.
Single-fold flying jib (round) sheet	2	6″	Pat.

JIB TOPSAIL

Single-fold jib topsail halyards	2	6″	Pat.
Single-fold jib topsail downhaul	1	5″	Pat.

FORE AND MAIN GAFF TOPSAIL

Single fold gaff-topsail sheets	2	7″	Pat.
Single-fold gaff-topsail halyards	1	6″	iron
Single-fold gaff-topsail clew lines	4	4″	iron
Cleats on gaffs with sheaves	2	4″	iron

MAINSTAYSAIL

Single-fold staysail halyards			
Staysail tack club	2	7″	iron

MISCELLANEOUS

Locust belaying pins	18		
Iron belaying pins	4		
Parrel trucks for gaffs			
Deadeyes—shrouds		6″	
Hearts for jibstays and guys	4	4½″	
Gilded trucks, balls	2		
Riding sail hoops with hooks	11		
Dory tackle blocks, rope straps, single	3	6″	Pat.
Two-fold davit tackle blocks	2	8″	Pat.

BLOCK LIST "GRAMPUS," 1885

	No.	*Size*	*Bushing*
Single-fold main-topmast backstay	2	7″	iron
Two-fold main-topmast backstay	2	7″	iron
Two-hole fairleaders for gaff-topsail gear.			

The "Grampus" block list, prepared for this 90′ overall schooner in 1885, differs little from those of later date. Running rigging sizes, in fishing vessels, were determined by what could be grasped with the hand. This gave a wide range in strength since tackles were used wherever the load was great. The blocks used in running rigging were not closely graduated in size nor in the diameters of rope they would handle. In fact, vessels on the general model of "Grampus" were notoriously harder on spars, running and standing rigging and on blocks than larger schooners built ten to twenty years later. This was due to basic changes in hull form, which can be seen in the plans. This was the factor that prevented spar and rigging sizes from increasing in any direct proportion with increased hull dimensions.

Hence the block sizes given for "Grampus" could be used for schooners ranging in size from about 85′ to 110′, tonnage length, 1885 to about 1912, but the number of sheaves in some blocks would increase, with an increase in hull dimensions, to obtain greater power that would be required.

BLOCK LIST
"COLUMBIA," 152 TONS

Six brass fairleads on spreaders

Foresail: two 14″ singles—specials on peak (fixed eye)

Halyard peak: three 14″ singles on masthead with shackles

peak jig tackles: two 9″ doubles, one with becket and thimble
one with shackle

sheet: one 12″ double with sliding shackle
one 12″ single with shackle and becket

boom tackle: one 8″ double with hook
one 8″ single with hook, becket, and thimble

foreboom toplift: one 8″ single with wire thimble
one 8″ single with rope thimble

Balloon jib, halyards: one 8″ single with front hook and becket
one 8″ single with sister hook

downhaul: one 6″ single

Fisherman staysail halyard throat: one 9″ single with shackle

halyard peak: one 8″ single, front hook and double swivel, upper
two 8″ singles with Coleman hooks, lower

Jib halyard: two 12″ singles with front shackles, upper
one 12″ single with sister-hooks, lower

jig: two 8″ singles, one with shackle, one with becket and thimble, upper

downhaul: one 6″ single

Jumbo halyard: two 12″ singles with front shackles, upper
one 12″ single with sister-hooks, lower

jig: two 8″ singles, one with shackle, one with becket and thimble

sheet: one 10″ on boom, two 10″ singles on deck, so sheet can straddle hoister chain to windlass, with shackles and one with becket
downhaul: one 6″ single
toplift: two 8″ singles, one with wire thimble, one with rope thimble

Foresail halyard: two 14″ double with front shackles
throat: one 14″ triple with shackle—on gaff
jig: two 9″ doubles, one with becket and thimble, one with shackle

Fore-topsail halyard: one 8″ single with front hook and becket
one 8″ single with sister-hook, lower
topsail sheet under throat of gaff, starboard side
one 7″ single, iron strap

end of gaff: one 7″ single when fishing
one 7″ double when racing

Mainsail halyard peak: four 14″ singles, front shackles, masthead
three 14″ singles specials (fixed eye) on gaff

jig: one 9″ double with becket and thimble, upper
one 9″ double with shackle, on rail

halyard, throat: two 14″ doubles with front shackles, aloft
one 14″ double, extra heavy front hook, gaff
one 14″ single, extra heavy front hook, gaff

jig: one 9″ double with becket and trimble, upper
one 9″ double with shackle on rail

sheet: one 14″ triple with sliding shackle, upper
one 14″ double oblong block with becket and heavy shackle

Two crotch tackles, each with one 8″ single hook and becket
one 8″ double with hook

Boom tackle: one 10″ double with short hook and becket
one 10″ single with long hook and becket

Reef tackle: two 6″ doubles, one with hook and becket
one with hook

Main toplift: one 10″ double with rope thimble
one 12″ single with rope thimble

Main-gaff topsail: one 8″ single with front hook and becket

halyard: one 8″ single with sister hook
sheet: one 7″ single with becket and shackle
one 7″ single with sister hook, on sail
one 7″ single under throat of gaff, starboard side, with iron strap

Main-gaff topsail: one 8″ single with front hook and becket
Two flying or preventer backstays, topmast, fore,
one 8″ double with shackle
one 8″ single with hook and becket } on each stay

Two flying or preventer backstays, topmast, main
one 8″ double with shackle
one 8″ double with hook and becket } on each stay

Four dory tackles: two 7″ singles with rope thimbles on each tackle

BLOCK SIZES

Size of Sheave	*Dia. of Rope*	*Length of Shell*
inches	*inches*	*inches*
1¾ x ½ x ⅜	⅜	3
2¼ x ⅝ x ⅜	½	4
3 x ¾ x ⅜	9/16	5
3½ x 1 x ½	⅝ or ¾	6
4¼ x 1 x ½	¾	7
4¾ x 1⅛ x ⅝	⅞	8
5½ x 1⅛ x ⅝	⅞	9
6¼ x 1¼ x ⅝	1	10
7¼ x 1¼ x ¾	1	11
8 x 1⅜ x ¾	1⅛	12
9 x 1½ x ¾	1⅛	13
9½ x 1⅝ x ⅞	1¼	14
10 x 1⅝ x ⅞	1¼	15
11 x 1¾ x ⅞	1⅜	16

Sheave dimensions are diameter of sheave, width of sheave and diameter of pin.

(*From Merriman table of vessel blocks*)

BLOCK FITTINGS FROM 1890 CATALOG

Gloucester-made blocks were more angular in the shell than was usual in those made elsewhere, and were about this pattern.

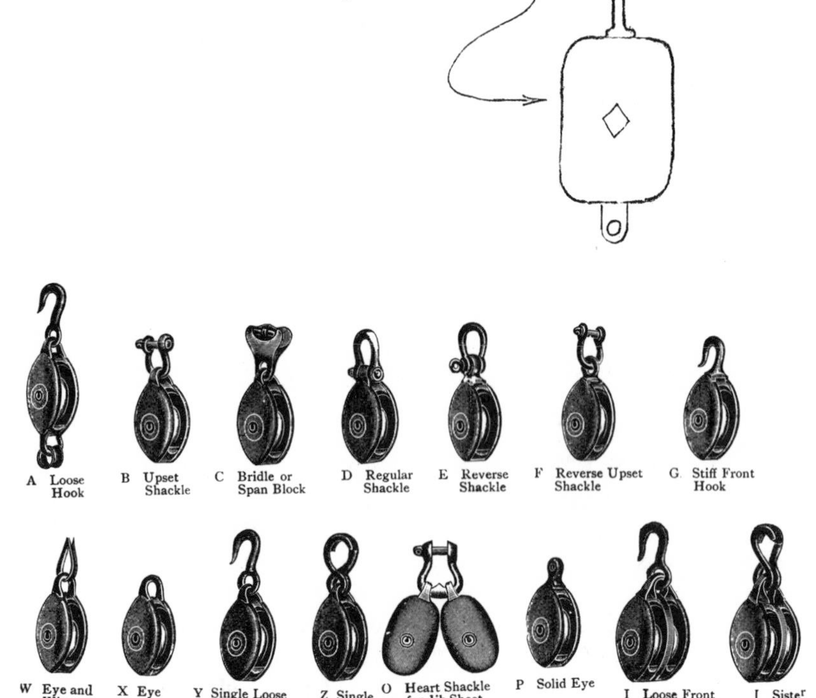
A Loose Hook
B Upset Shackle
C Bridle or Span Block
D Regular Shackle
E Reverse Shackle
F Reverse Upset Shackle
G Stiff Front Hook
W Eye and Wire Thimble
X Eye
Y Single Loose Front Hook
Z Single Sister Hook
O Heart Shackle for Jib Sheet to Side
P Solid Eye
I Loose Front Hook
J Sister Hook

L Ring

BLOCKS, HALYARD

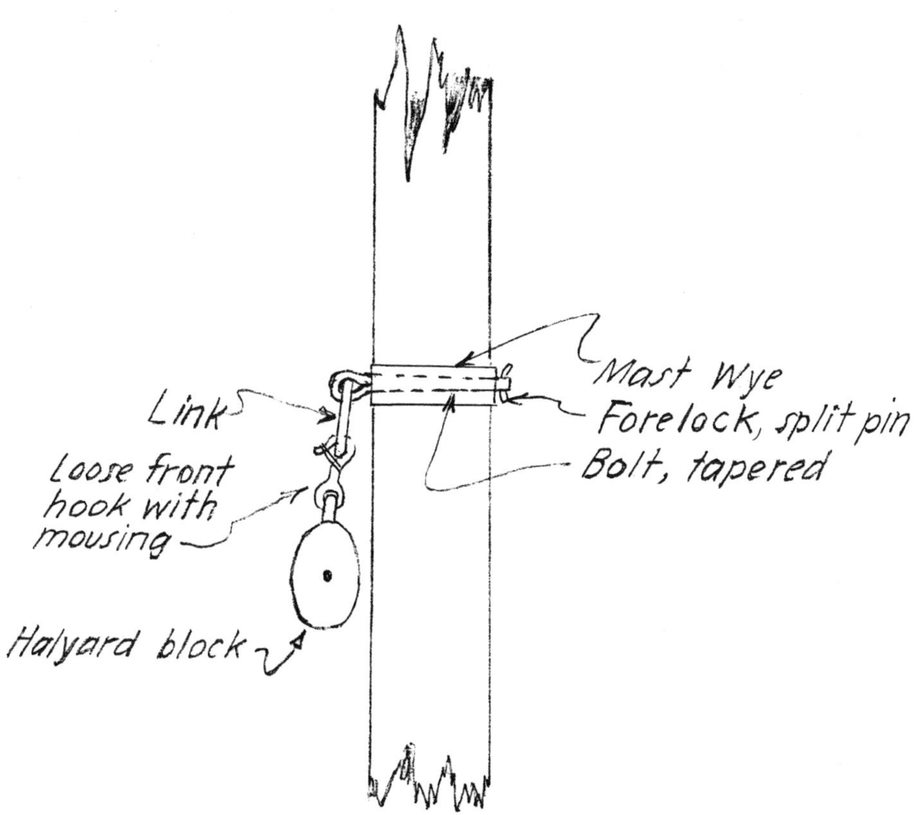
Mast Wye
Forelock, split pin
Bolt, tapered
Link
Loose front hook with mousing
Halyard block

Hooks to have open ends facing away from the masts.

BLOCKS, MASTHEAD

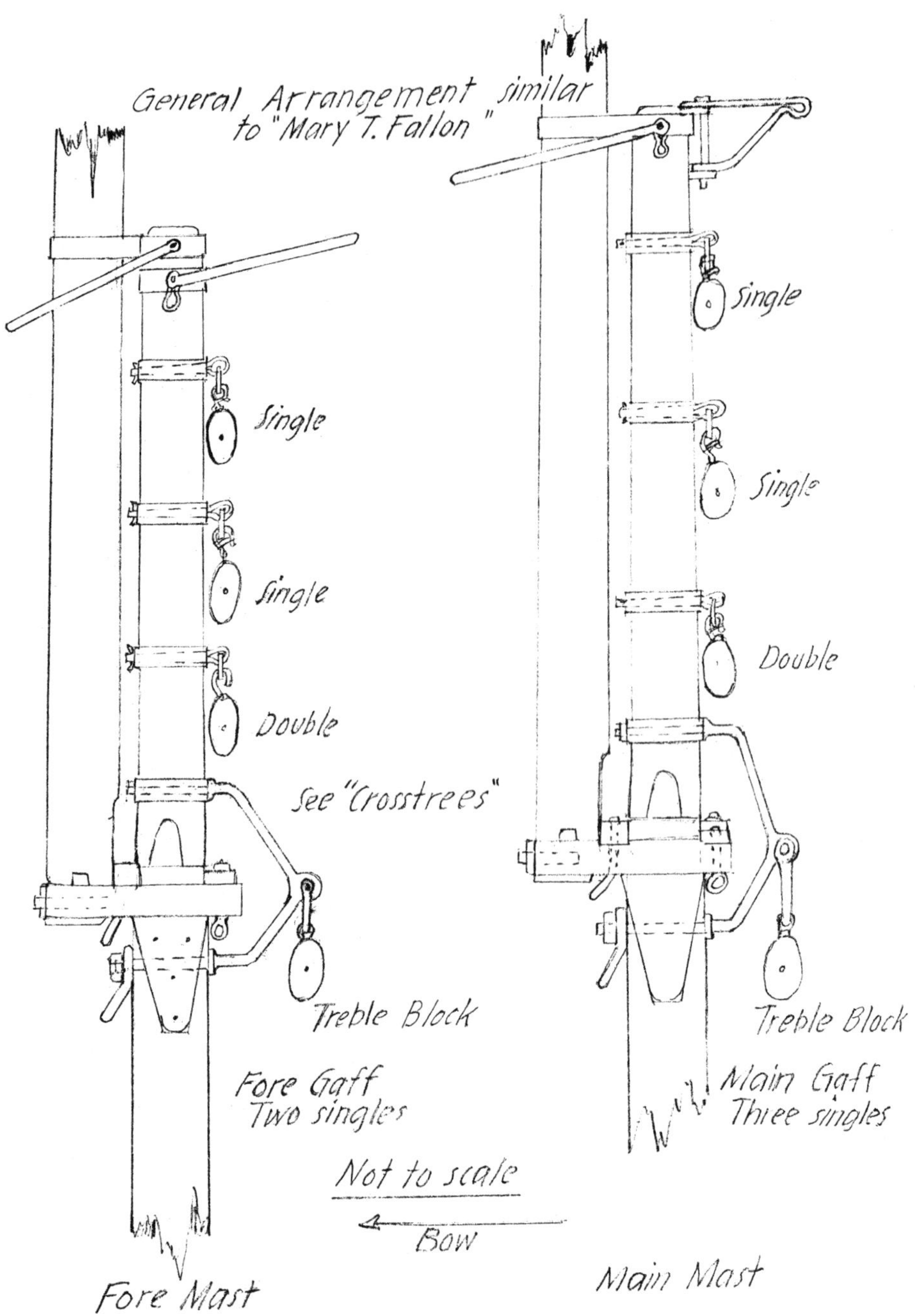
General Arrangement similar to "Mary T. Fallon"
Single
Single
Double
See "Crosstrees"
Treble Block
Fore Gaff
Two singles
Single
Single
Double
Treble Block
Main Gaff
Three singles
Not to scale
Bow
Fore Mast
Main Mast

BLOCKS, MASTHEAD

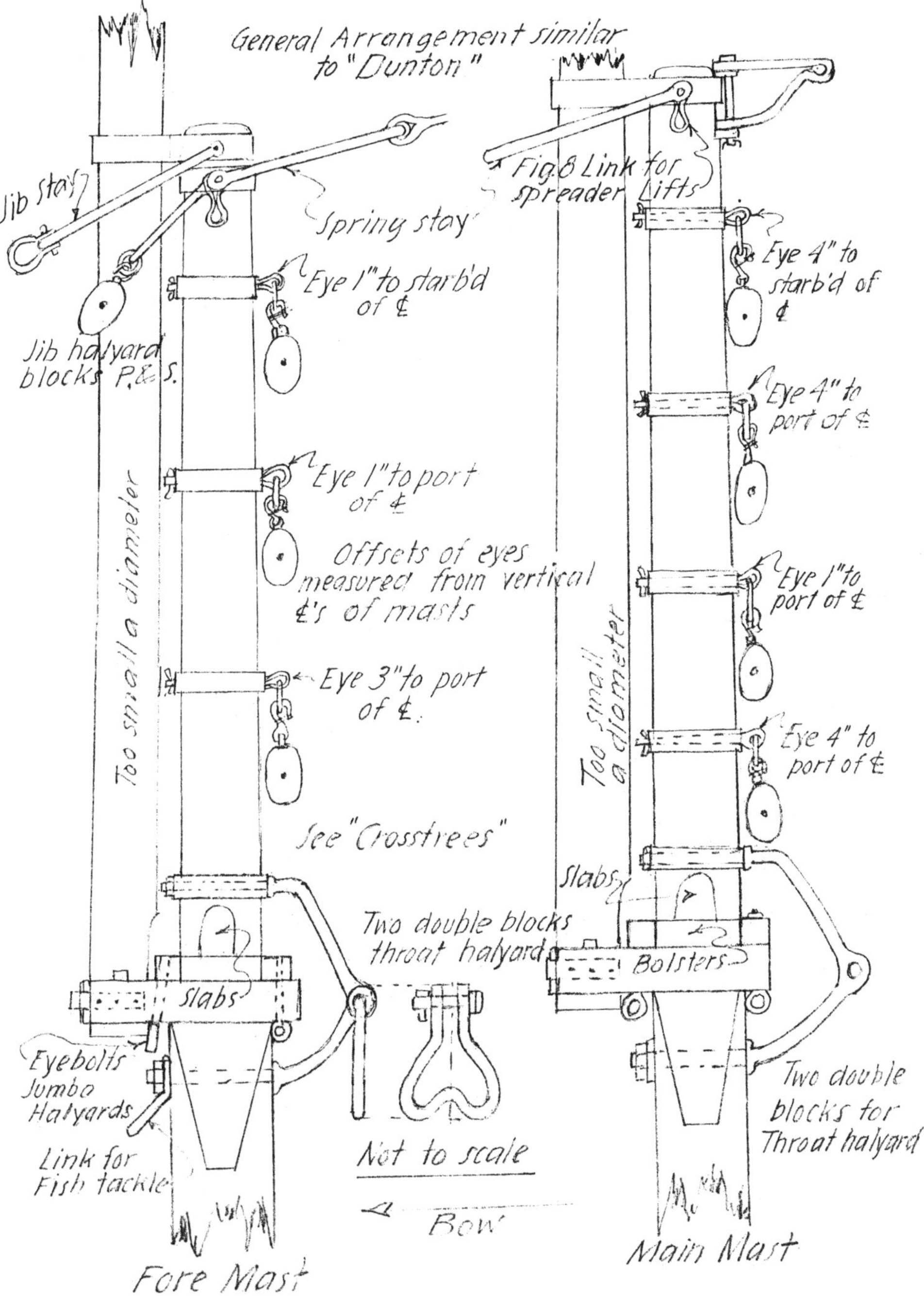
General Arrangement similar to "Dunton"
Jib stay
Spring stay
Fig.8 Link for spreader Lifts
Eye 1" to starb'd of ¢
Jib halyard blocks P.&S.
Eye 4" to starb'd of ¢
Eye 4" to port of ¢
Eye 1" to port of ¢
Offsets of eyes measured from vertical ¢'s of masts
Eye 1" to port of ¢
Too small a diameter
Eye 3" to port of ¢.
Too small a diameter
Eye 4" to port of ¢
See "Crosstrees"
Slabs
Two double blocks throat halyard
Bolsters
Slabs
Eyebolts Jumbo Halyards
Link for Fish tackle
Two double blocks for Throat halyard
Not to scale
Bow
Fore Mast
Main Mast

BOBSTAYS (NOTES)

Schooners had one to three bobstays, the outer one was chain, the inner the forestay extensions. Both were set up with hearts or deadeyes, and lanyards under the bowsprit. When wire rope standing rigging came into use in 1885, turnbuckles were employed. Many variations in bowsprit rigging appeared in the early 1890s.

"Carrie Phillips" claimed to be the first fishing schooner to be fitted with a spike bowsprit and its simplified gear; she introduced extensive use of spar ironwork. This schooner had two bobstays, led to separate bands or wyes on the bowsprit. Two sets of bobstay plates on the stem. These were 32″ or 34″ long, 3″ or 3¼″ wide, in pairs.

The chain bobstays, in many clipper schooners in the 1880s, set up to a band just forward of the forestay bee hole on the bowsprit. The bobstays, above the load waterline, were tarred, wrapped with canvas, and then covered with rawhide. On the stem, above the waterline, a piece of oak about 6′ long, was secured on each side. These were to protect the banks anchor cable from chafe and were fitted to bankers only. Small deadeyes or hearts with landyards set up the bowsprit rigging, until wire rope came into use. Three bobstays were employed only with hemp standing rigging, when a double fore or jumbo stay was used. (See "Bowsprit with Jibboom," "Bees," and "Bowsprit Ironwork.")

Wire rope for standing rigging was introduced prior to 1885. In that year "Grampus" specifications required "galvanized wire rope," which was quite stiff to handle.

A
Oak
A
6′-0″±
"Chafing Stick"
Cut out to fit over bobstay plat and bolts
5″
3″

A wire rope bobstay was the same dia. as the jibstay, and was set up with a turnbuckle under the bowsprit in a heavy wye. At the bobstay chain plates a closed shackle was placed between the two parts on the stem. A thimble was placed in the fore-end of the closed shackle. The bobstay end was passed around the round thimble and then brought forward on top of the stay and seized, "cutter fashion." As the bowsprits shortened in the late

1890s, the bobstays were often spliced at the chain plates, as they could easily be taken up with very little stretch.

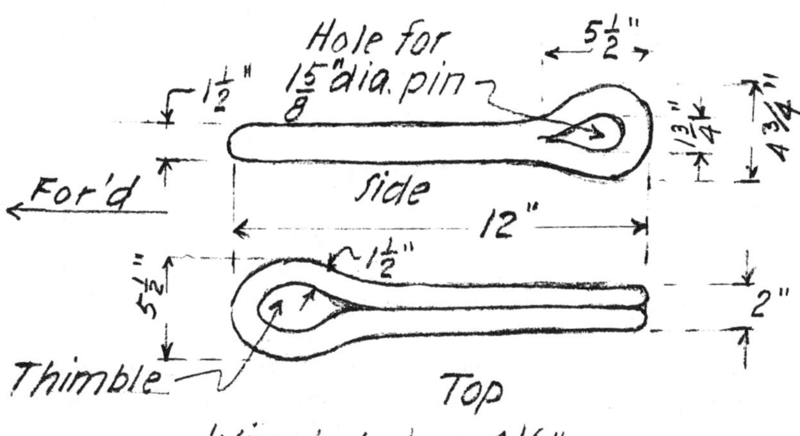
Hole for
15/8" dia. pin
5 1/2"
1 1/2"
1 3/4"
4 3/4"
For'd
Side
12"
1 1/2"
5 1/2"
2"
Thimble
Top
Wire bobstay 4 1/4"
circ. with thimble
in closed shackle

BOLSTERS, SLABS

Bolsters were fitted on top of the trestletrees on each side of the masthead so that the shrouds would not be cut, nor be cramped, where they pass over the trestletrees.

The bolsters were of oak. So were the "slabs," fastened on each side of the masthead above the bolsters, to keep the shrouds from cutting into the soft pine masthead.

BONNETS

Bonnets were carried on Gloucester fishing schooners as late as 1895. Vessels having the large jumbo, built before 1885 or thereabouts, had bonnets on that sail. When the double-head rig replaced the large jumbo, some schooners had bonnets on their jibs.

It cannot be determined now how the lacing was rove at luff and leach cringles. The top of the bonnet had closely spaced loops of line along it, which were passed through grommets in the sail, along the roping and secured, chain fashion. This lacing was usually worked from luff and leach, with two long loops at the midlength of the bonnet that were tied.

To remove the bonnet, the knot was untied and the loops unrove automatically. First, however, an auxilliary sheet was attached to the cringle of the sail just above the bonnet and then set up, the regular sheet (or sheets) was taken off. Apparently two tacks were used, one on the bonnet and one on the sail. Thus, the bonnet could be removed from the sail very quickly, but was unhandy to reset. On jibs the release knot seems to have been at the luff of the bonnet, so that it could be reached without lowering the sail, which was done to reset the bonnet, or if the release knot could not be reached. A bonneted sail was heavily patched in the wake of the lacing.

Chain lacing
Loops passed through one another in succession.
for releas
knot

HATCH, "BOOBY"
(*SEE DETAIL SKETCHES*)

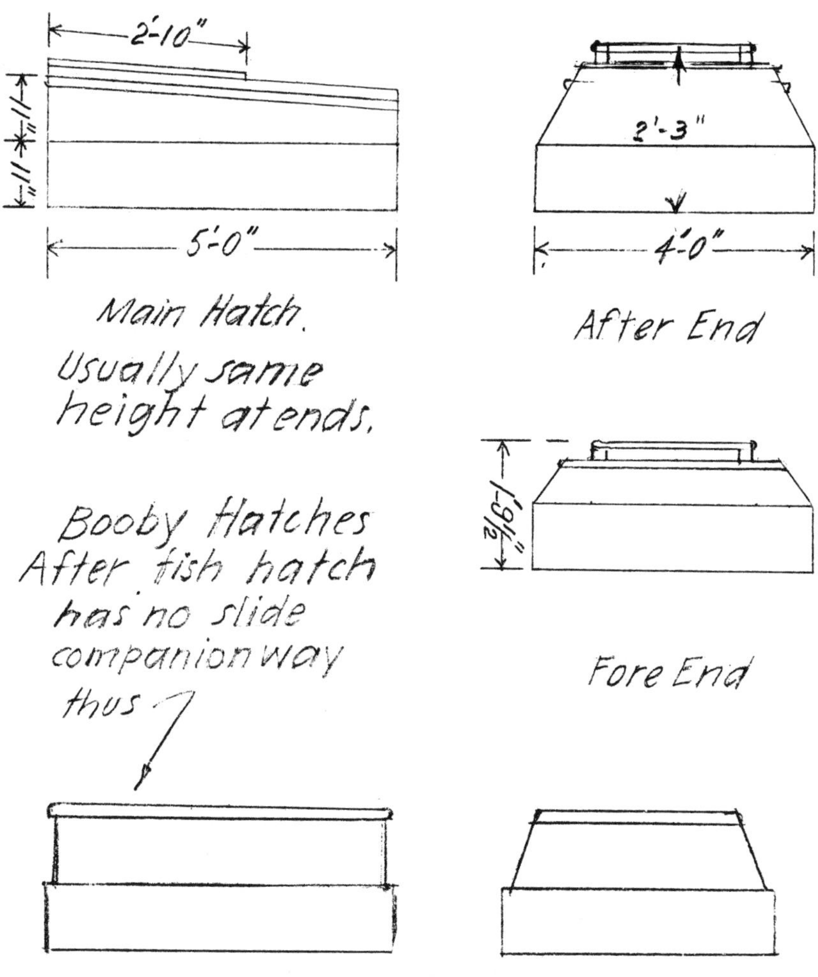
2'-10"
11"
11"
5'-0"
Main Hatch.
Usually same height at ends.
2'-3"
4'-0"
After End
1'-9½"
Booby Hatches
After fish hatch
has no slide
companionway
thus
Fore End

BOOBY HATCHES

Booby hatches were fitted on vessels intended for winter fishing on the banks.

Booby hatches had slide companionways on the afterside; quite a few had slide companionways on both ends. In the latter case the slides had two grooves so that one cover could slide under the other. Slides of the booby hatches were double-planked with ⅞″ boards. Quarter-rounds on each corner, backed by oak corner-posts. Slides of oak secured to hatch roamings by ringbolts and lashings inside, as a rule. [L.H.S.]

BOOBY HATCH FOR FISH HATCHES

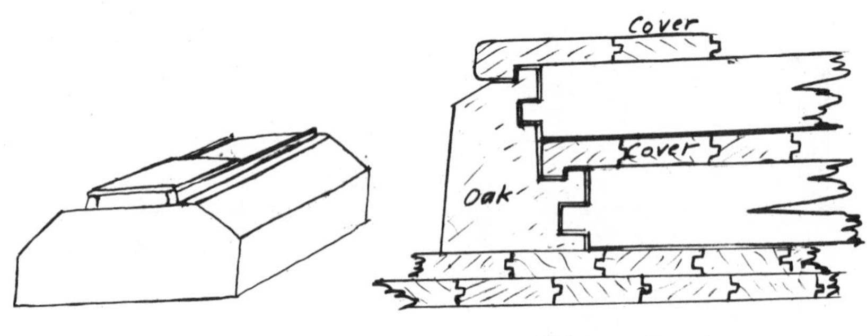
Cover
Cover
Oak
Slides for Booby Hatches LHS

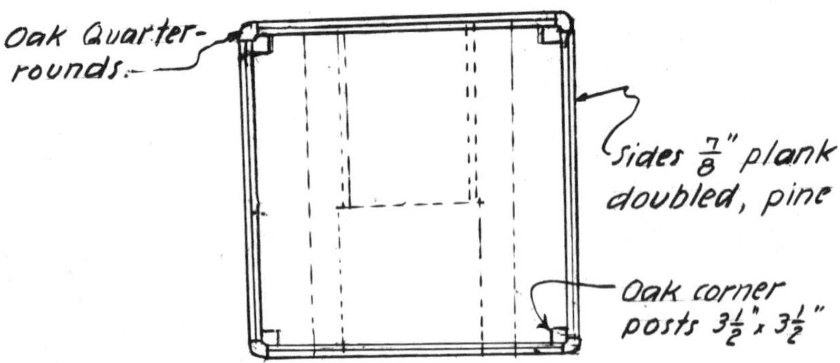
Oak Quarter-rounds.
Sides 7/8" plank doubled, pine
Oak corner posts 3½" x 3½"

Booby hatch over fish hatch; had slide-hatch at after end, sometimes at fore end also. each slide-hatch had double tops, or covers, which slid one under the other. LHS.

Clamp bolt
Sheet Wye
Double with loose front hook
Wye band
Main Boom
Long, loose side hook single with becket
Eyebolt
Belay, pin
on port side

BOOM GUY OR BOOM TACKLE

Boom guys were carried on mainbooms, sometimes on foreboom also. Their purpose was to hold the booms outboard when running before the wind the vessel rolling. They were made up of a single-sheave block with becket and with a long, loose side hook. This was hooked into an eyebolt under boom a little abaft the mainboom jaws. A double-sheave block, with loose front hook, was hooked into a two-eared wye; clamp bolt under boom just forward of mainboom sheet wye, and the hook moused. The tackle rove as follows: from single-sheave block becket to over the double-sheave block, thence to under the single-sheave block, thence to over double-sheave, with fall leading aft to belay on pin in port side of jaws, for the mainboom guy, and to belay on a wooden cleat on one side of the foreboom, for the fore guy.

To guy the mainboom, the single block was unhooked and brought to the rail near the aftermost fore shroud and hooked into a staple on the rail cap. The fall was then led off and set up, then belayed on the pin in the boom jaws. The foreboom guy led to a staple on the bow chock rail, just abaft the pad on the bulwarks there; the fall belaying on a cleat on the side of the foreboom. Racers sometimes had pendants for guys to hook into, to avoid overhauling the tackles, which were very long on a large schooner.

BOWS

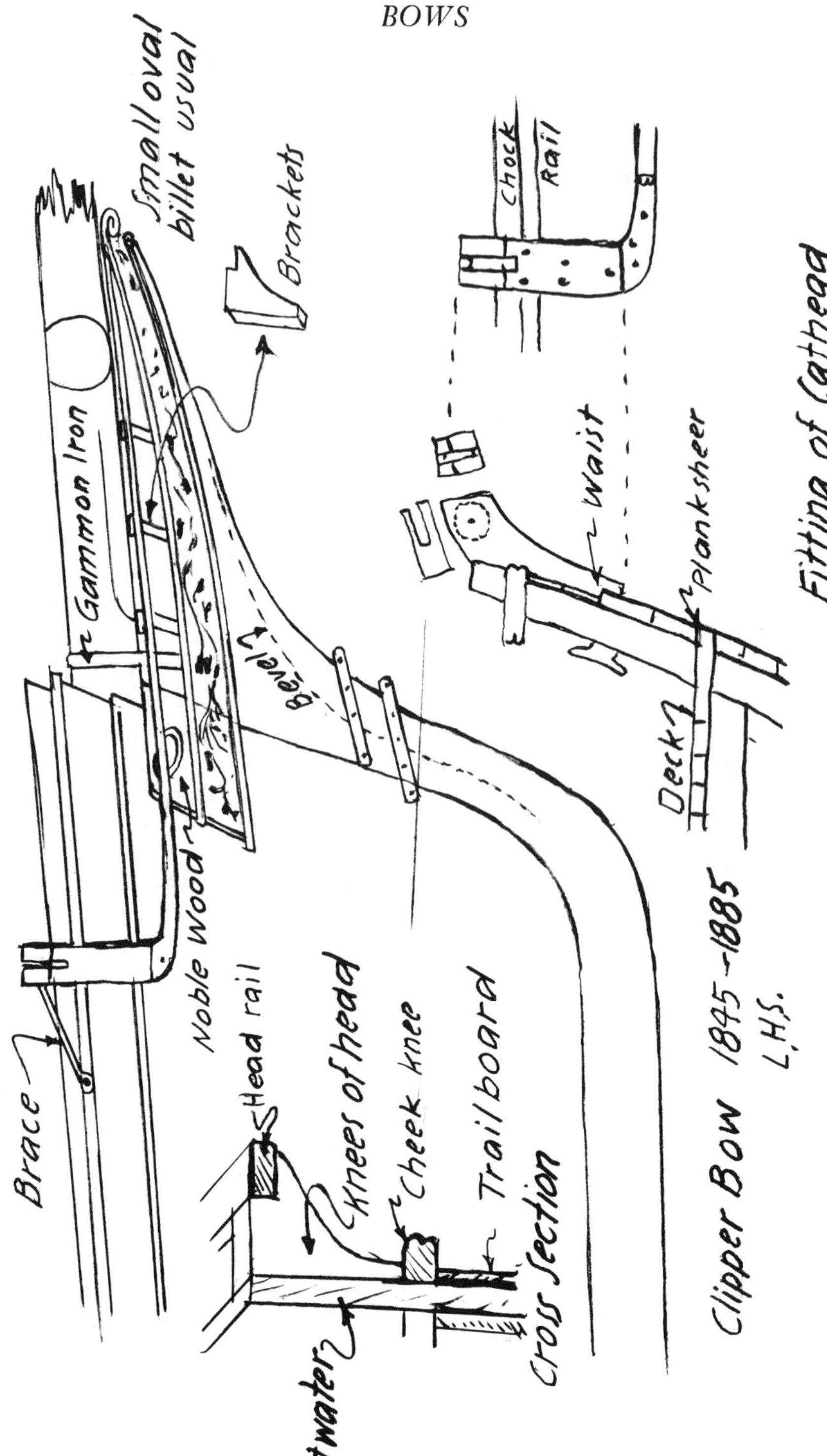
Small oval billet usual
Brackets
Chock
Rail
Gammon Iron
Waist
Planksheer
Fitting of Cathead
Bevel
Deck
Noble Wood
Brace
Head rail
Knees of head
Cheek knee
Trailboard
Cross Section
Cutwater
Clipper Bow 1845–1885
L.H.S.

BOWS

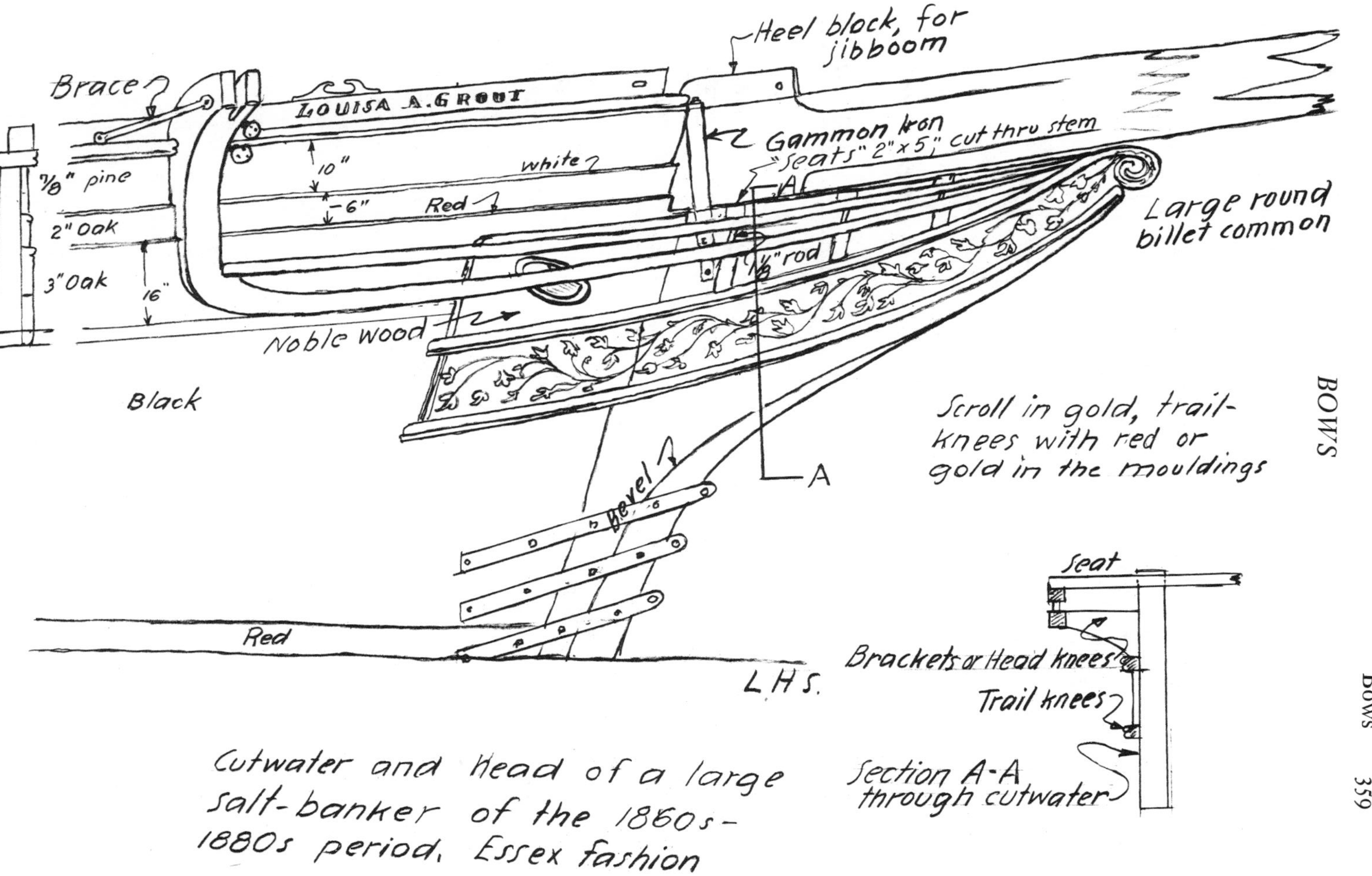
Heel block, for jibboom
Brace
LOUISA A.GROUT
Gammon Iron
"Seats" 2" x 5" cut thru stem
A
white
10"
6"
Red
7/8" pine
2" Oak
3" Oak
16"
rod
Large round billet common
Noble wood
Black
Scroll in gold, trail-knees with red or gold in the mouldings
Bevel
A
Seat
Red
Brackets or Head knees
L H S.
Trail knees
Section A-A through cutwater

Cutwater and head of a large salt-banker of the 1860s–1880s period. Essex fashion

BOWS

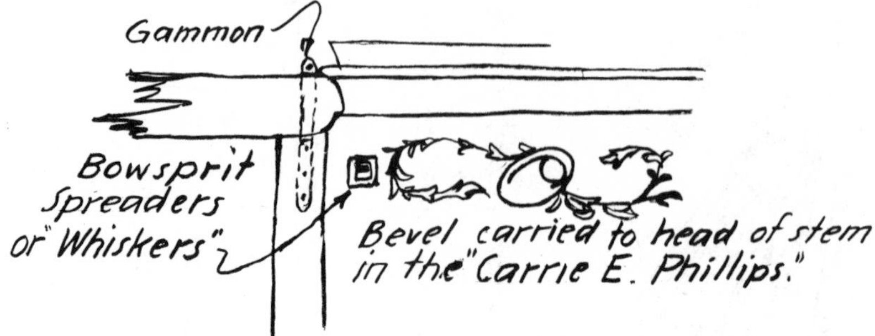
Gammon
Bowsprit Spreaders or "Whiskers"
Bevel carried to head of stem in the "Carrie E. Phillips."
Sketch of bow scroll used on a "plumb-stemmer," 1885
LHS

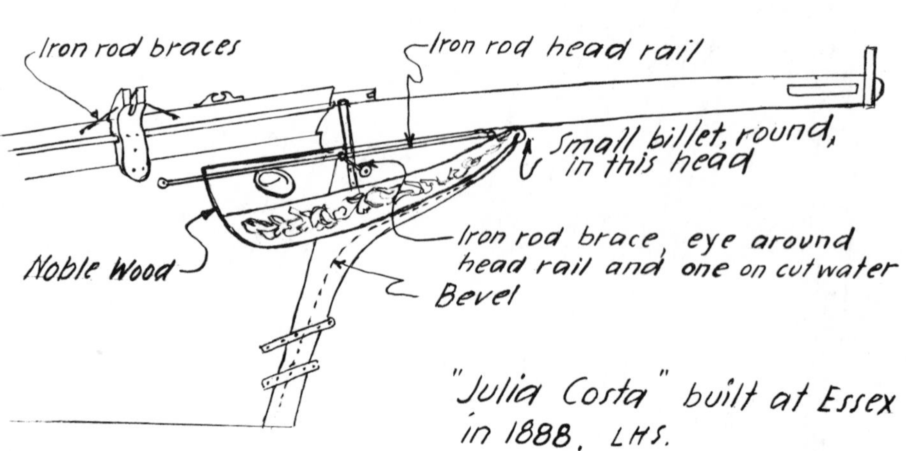
Iron rod braces
Iron rod head rail
Small billet, round, in this head
Iron rod brace, eye around head rail and one on cutwater
Noble Wood
Bevel
"Julia Costa" built at Essex in 1888. LHS.

A few schooners were built with this head

BOWS

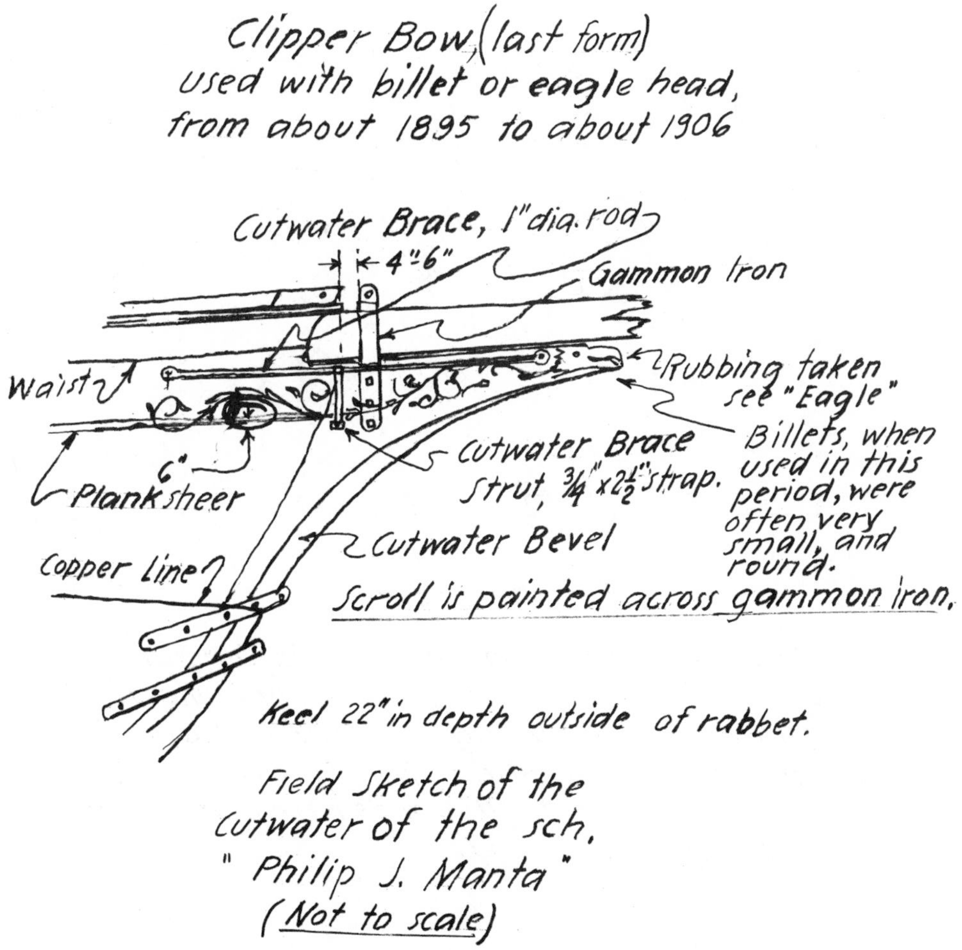

Clipper Bow, (last form)
used with billet or eagle head,
from about 1895 to about 1906

Cutwater Brace, 1" dia. rod

4"-6"

Gammon Iron

Rubbing taken
see "Eagle"

Waist

Billets, when used in this period, were often very small, and round.

6"

Cutwater Brace Strut, 3/4" x 2 1/2" strap.

Planksheer

Cutwater Bevel

Copper Line

Scroll is painted across gammon iron.

Keel 22" in depth outside of rabbet.

Field Sketch of the
Cutwater of the sch.
"Philip J. Manta"
(Not to scale)

BOW
VARIATION RETAINING TRAILBOARDS, 1886

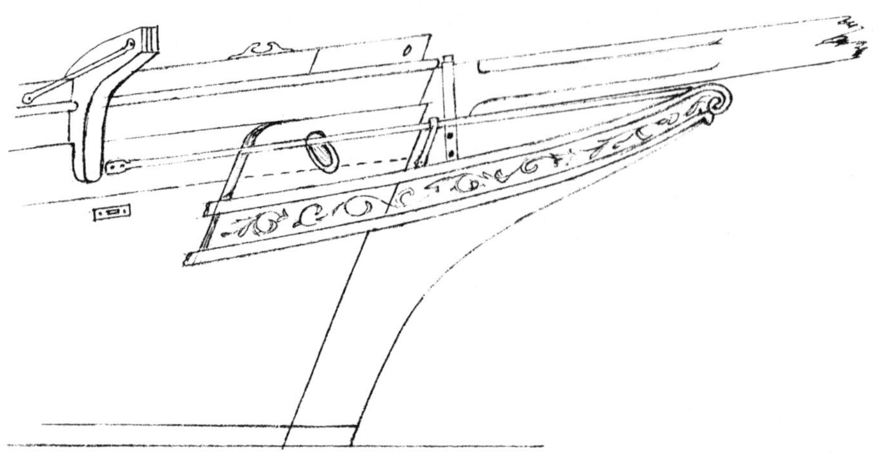

Numerous variations in the clipper bow appeared in 1885-1890, usually retaining trail-boards but employing simplified headrails of wood or iron. These had short periods of some popularity but trailboards were going rapidly out of fashion by 1887.

BOWS
(MISCELLANEOUS NOTES)

The bows of fishing schooners changed little in the period between 1845 and 1885. The cutwater was rather long and beaked, supported by trail knees and mouldings, with carved trailboards between, in addition, the cut-water received support from head rails, one on each side. These butted the billet, or fiddle-head, forward, and faired up, in a sharp, quick curve, to the underside of the catheads. The head rails rested on brackets athwarthship, three in number. The top of the cutwater, from top of billet to underside of bowsprit at stem rabbet, was straight. 5″-8″ plank "seats" were secured athwartship, ends to top of head rails, passing under the bowsprit through cutwater, placed over the brackets.

In the 1860–1880s period, some large bankers had double head rails, as shown in the sketch of the "Louisa A. Grout." The schooners in the period between 1845 and 1885 had noble-woods.

Nearly all schooners in this period had simple carved billets; the figurehead was very rare. Occasional departures appeared; three schooners designed by Donald McKay and built in 1860 had trail boards in the form of ribbons, without trail knees. The head rails were straight, of wood, without brackets. Eagle or animal figureheads were used.

Between 1880 and 1900 there were many changes in the bows of New England fishing schooners, particularly in the short period between 1885 and 1895. Beginning in 1885, the straight, upright stem of the New York and Boston pilot boats was introduced—first with bowsprit jibboom rig, then with pole bowsprit rig in 1887. The noblewood was retained in the straight, or plumb, stemmers; except for the Edward Burgess-designed "Carrie E. Phillips," launched in 1887, in which it was omitted. This vessel introduced many innovations besides the long, pole bowsprit. One was bowsprit shroud spreaders or "whiskers." These were of wood; in the straight stem vessels the spreaders were passed through the bows athwartships just below the cove line of the waist, a little abaft the stem rabbet. There was not room, in the straight stem, for both spreader and gammon iron outside the stem rabbet.

This was a British idea, used to give spread to the shrouds of the long pole bowsprit, in a very narrow hull, such as the British cutter yacht of the 1880s had become. When the cutter was imported by American yachtsmen (the "cutter cranks") the bowsprit whiskers were retained. Burgess was a moderate "cutter crank" so, in adopting the long pole bowsprit he naturally employed the "whiskers" of the cutter.

Two years after the "Carrie E. Phillips" came out, Burgess designed the near-sister ships "Nellie Dixon" and "Fredonia," having clipper cutwaters with billets carved into the cutwaters followed by a scrool cut into cutwater and planking. This would have allowed the whiskers to be cut through the cutwater, clear of the gammoning, but Burgess followed the "Phillips" in placing the whiskers abaft the stem rabbet. The general acceptance of "whiskers" in fishing schooners was due to Burgess' designs.

BOWS
(*MISCELLANEOUS NOTES—IRON HEAD RAILS*)

Burgess' prestige was very great, for he had been successful in the design of "America's" Cup defenders. When the "Nellie Dixon" was building in Boston and the "Fredonia" in Essex, they both were carefully watched by fishermen having new vessels under construction, so some copying resulted. This led to some rather weird combinations. For example, the "Norumbega," built by Moses Adams in 1890, had a rather short bowsprit of the pole type, round in the knighthead, with whiskers, but there was also a jibboom, complete with spreaders and dolphin striker, in the old style.

The long pole bowsprit did not remain popular, for it was a man-killer in heavy weather. When the bowsprit was shortened, there was no excuse for whiskers, so they went out of favor also, in the mid-nineties.

Most of these schooners that had "whiskers" had them outside the stem rabbet, with gammon iron farther out if they had clipper bows of the gammon-knee type. In straight-stem schooners the whiskers were in the bows, and passed through the noble-woods. The clipper-bow schooners had an iron head rail, bolted to the cutwater, on each side, just abaft the billet. This canted outboard so that it crossed over the top of the whiskers, about halfway out. Here it was staple-bolted. At this point it was bent so that the after eye could be bolted to the waist, just below the cow line and 2′-3′ abaft the hawse casting ℄. The bolts here generally went through stanchions, as well as the waist planking.

When the whiskers were omitted, the iron head rails were as just described, except for the iron braces in place of the whiskers. These straps ran from each side of the cutwater where the braces were bolted, thence to the head rail where they were welded. The iron head rail was commonly bent here, but in some cases the rail was straight, when viewed from above. This would have been controlled by the fullness of the bows. The head rail was commonly straight in profile, parallel to the waist cove line.

The clipper gammon-knee cutwater was replaced in the fishing schooners by the overhanging, curved stem profile that had appeared in the late 1890s. The amount of overhang varied; in the early examples the amount was rather great, as represented in the Crowninshield designs. But schooners designed by Binney and McManus had short-bow overhangs; some of McManus's designs had stem profiles having very short overhangs and moderate curves above the load waterline.

With the appearance of the knockabout schooners, the bow overhang was very great; the McManus prototype was fundamentally an ordinary schooner with her projecting stem carried out to about where such a vessel's pole bowsprit would end. As the cost of these vessels was based on total length of hull, the bow overhang was much shortened in later knockabouts, giving more capacity than in the first vessels of this type.

BOWS
IRON HEAD RAILS AND BRACES

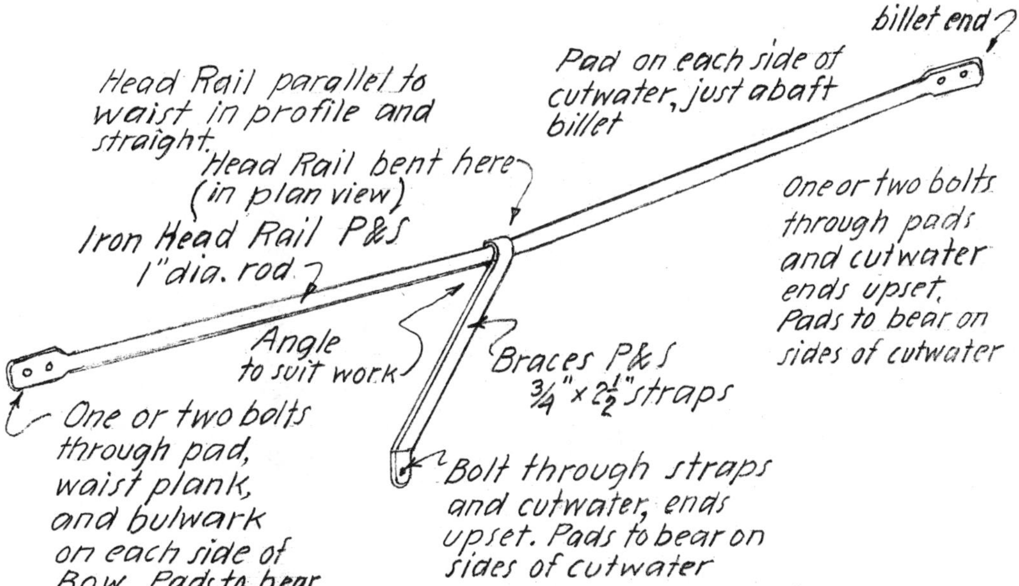

Head Rail parallel to waist in profile and straight.
Head Rail bent here (in plan view)
Iron Head Rail P&S 1" dia. rod
Pad on each side of cutwater, just abaft billet
billet end
One or two bolts through pads and cutwater ends upset. Pads to bear on sides of cutwater
Angle to suit work
Braces P&S $\frac{3}{4}$" x $2\frac{1}{2}$" straps
One or two bolts through pad, waist plank, and bulwark on each side of Bow. Pads to bear on the waist plank.
Bolt through straps and cutwater, ends upset. Pads to bear on sides of cutwater

Angle of brace varied; in some schooners it was almost at right angles to the sides of the cutwater, nearly level with the rod head rail. In others it was set at an angle to the cutwater as shown. This seems to have been done so the pads of the braces would clear the gammon iron on the cutwater and was not the usual practice at Essex. The head rail was always straight from end to end in profile.

See "Head Rails"

BOWS

UNUSUAL HEAD RIG

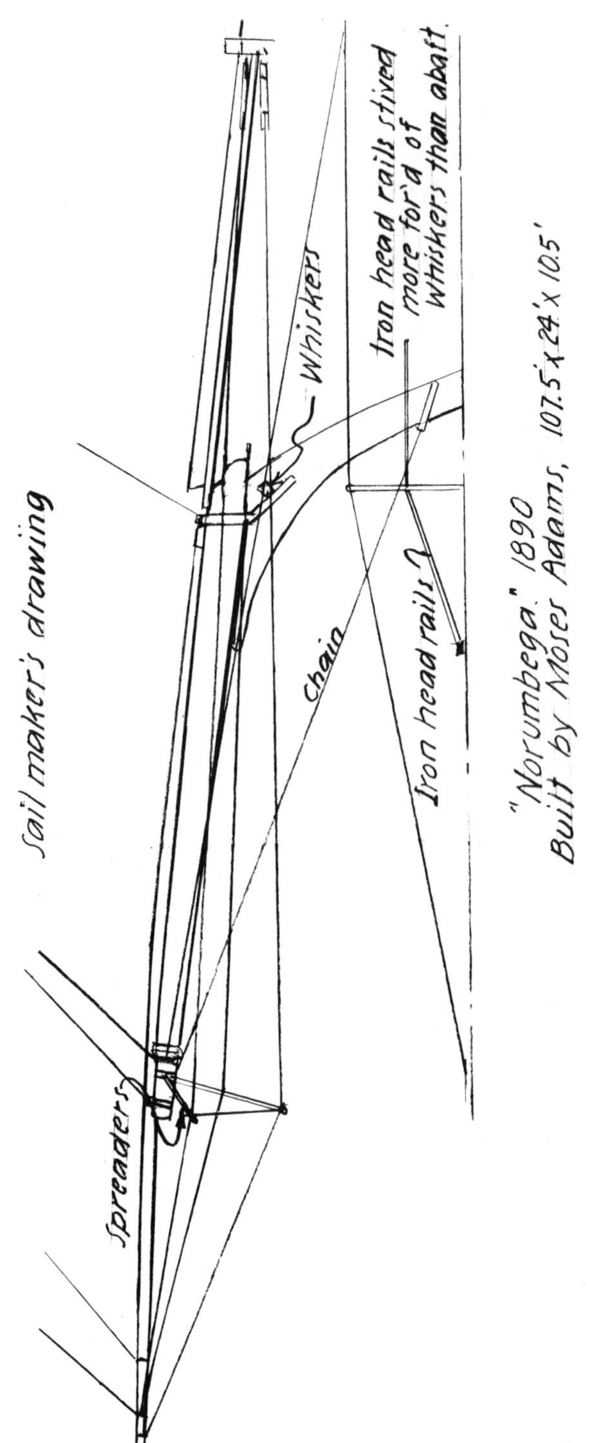
Sail maker's drawing
Whiskers
Iron head rails stived
more for'd of
Whiskers than abaft.
Chain
Iron head rails
Spreaders
"Norumbega." 1890
Built by Moses Adams, 107.5' x 24' x 10.5'

BOWSPRIT WITH JIBBOOM, 1855–1875 (SEE "SCHOONER RIG DETAILS—BUILT BETWEEN 1855 AND 1865")

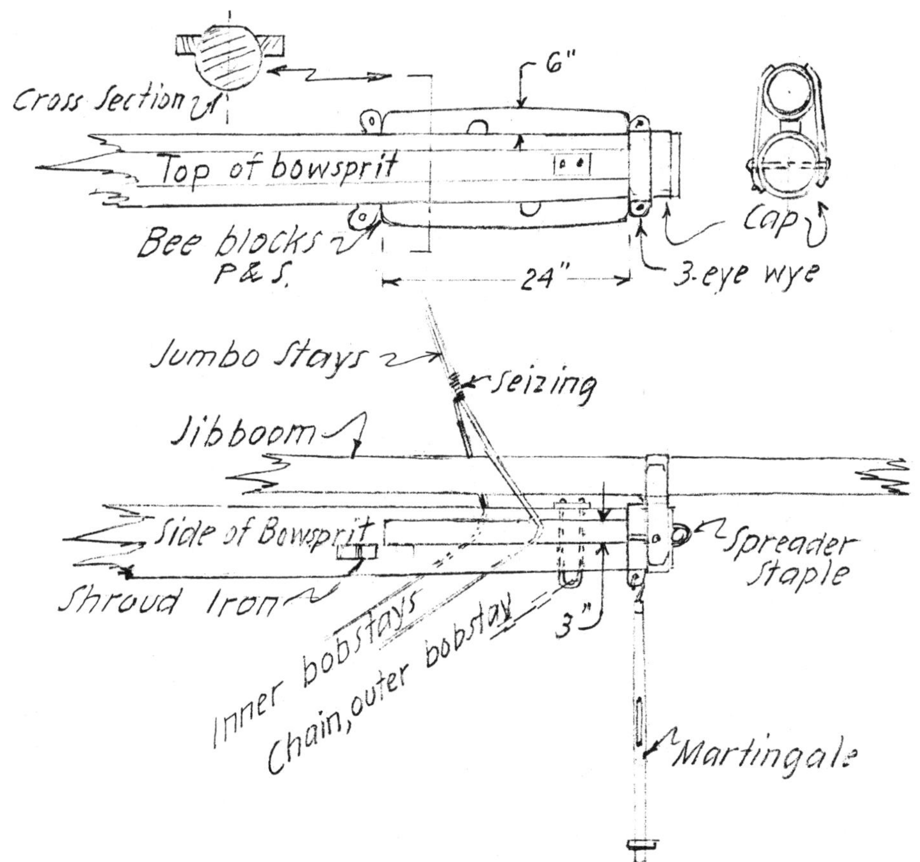
Cross Section
6"
Top of bowsprit
Cap
Bee blocks
P&S.
24"
3-eye wye
Jumbo Stays
Seizing
Jibboom
Side of Bowsprit
Spreader
Staple
Shroud Iron
Inner bobstays
Chain, outer bobstay
3"
Martingale

Common 2-Jumbo stay rigging of 1855-1875, however there were numerous variations in detail. Jumbo hanks rode on both stays, above seizing.

Not to scale

BOWSPRIT AND JIBBOOM, 1855–1885
SINGLE JUMBO STAY

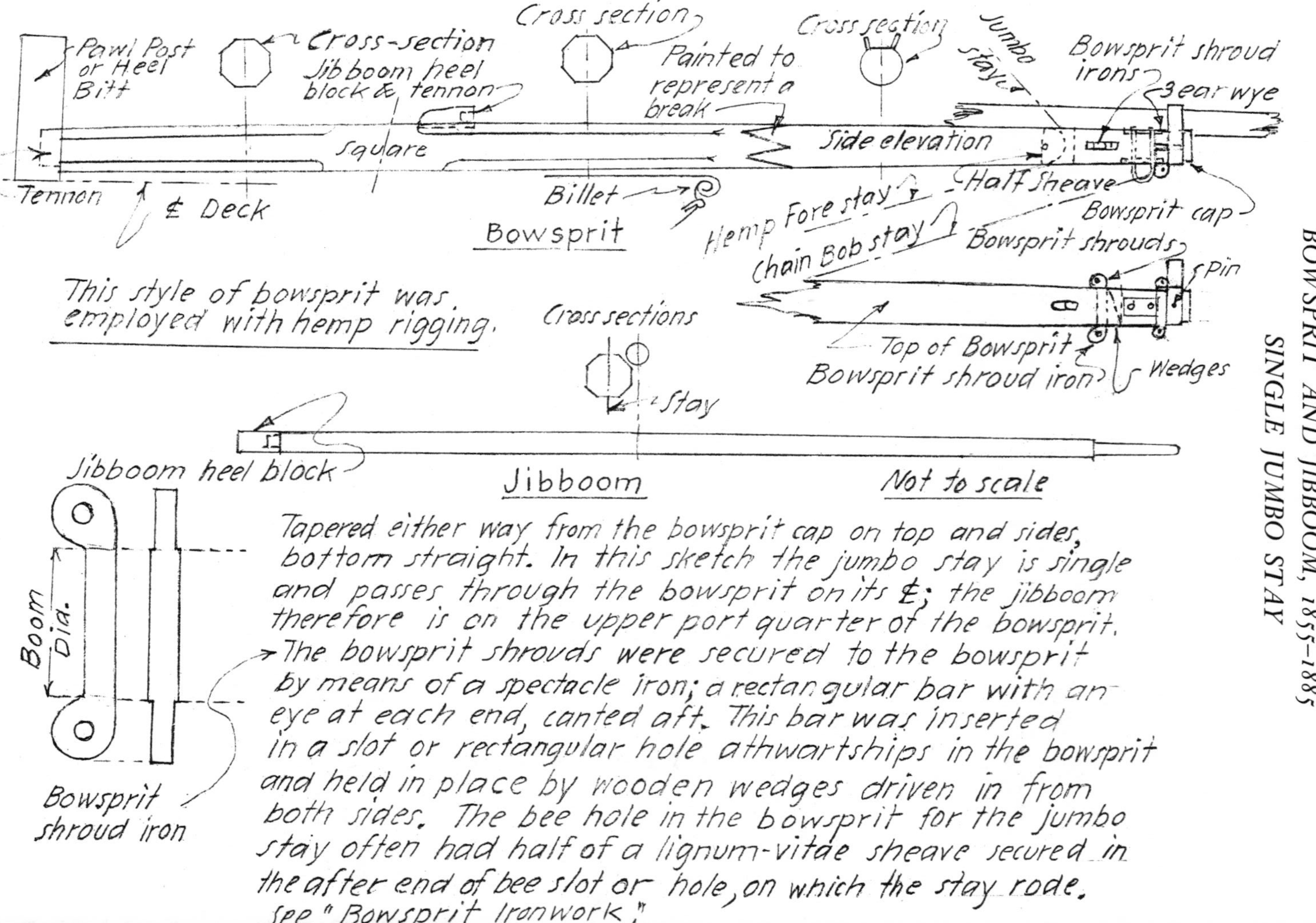
Pawl Post or Heel Bitt
Cross-section Jibboom heel block & tennon
Cross section
Painted to represent a break
Cross section
Jumbo stay
Bowsprit shroud irons
3 ear wye
Side elevation
Square
Tennon
℄ Deck
Billet
Bowsprit
Hemp Fore stay
Half Sheave
Bowsprit cap
Chain Bob stay
Bowsprit shrouds
Pin
This style of bowsprit was employed with hemp rigging.
Cross sections
Stay
Top of Bowsprit
Bowsprit shroud iron
Wedges
Jibboom heel block
Jibboom
Not to scale
Boom Dia.
Bowsprit shroud iron
Tapered either way from the bowsprit cap on top and sides, bottom straight. In this sketch the jumbo stay is single and passes through the bowsprit on its ℄; the jibboom therefore is on the upper port quarter of the bowsprit.
The bowsprit shrouds were secured to the bowsprit by means of a spectacle iron; a rectangular bar with an eye at each end, canted aft. This bar was inserted in a slot or rectangular hole athwartships in the bowsprit and held in place by wooden wedges driven in from both sides. The bee hole in the bowsprit for the jumbo stay often had half of a lignum-vitae sheave secured in the after end of bee slot or hole, on which the stay rode.
See "Bowsprit Ironwork."

BOWSPRIT, 1888–1894 *(SPIKE)*

Between 1888 and 1894 the spike bowsprit was often square at the knight-heads, but round (with a slight flat top) outboard. This appears to have been particularly true of the clipper-bow schooners. A large number of these had the forestay set up a few feet forward of the gammon. The bowsprit was then square from heel to about 2′-0″ outboard of gammon, then 8-sided for a couple of feet, to near the jumbo stay band where it was worked round. If the jumbo sail had a boom the length of the foot, its runner or tack horse fitting was placed between the gammon and the jumbo band. An example of this is shown in the plan of the "Lottie S. Haskins."

The bowsprit made for such a rig was occasionally round inboard; square only for about 2 or 3 feet either way from the gammon. Some were 8-sided inboard, instead of round.

The flat top of the spike bowsprit disappeared when bowsprits were shortened in the McManus schooners in the late 1890s.

[C. A., L. H. S.]

BOWSPRIT, 1888–1894 *(SPIKE)*

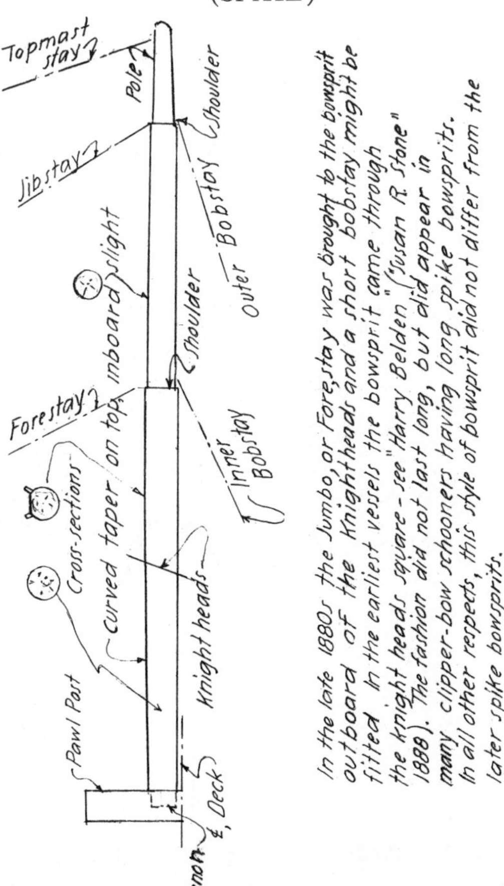
Topmast stay
Pole
Shoulder
Jibstay
Outer Bobstay
slight
inboard
Shoulder
Forestay
Curved taper on top
Cross-sections
Inner Bobstay
Knight heads
Pawl Post
℄, Deck
Tenon
In the late 1880s the Jumbo, or Forestay was brought to the bowsprit outboard of the Knightheads and a short bobstay might be fitted. In the earliest vessels the bowsprit came through the knight heads square - see "Harry Belden" ("Susan R. Stone" 1888). The fashion did not last long, but did appear in many clipper-bow schooners having long spike bowsprits. In all other respects, this style of bowsprit did not differ from the later spike bowsprits.

BOWSPRIT, 1898–1930 (SHORT SPIKE)

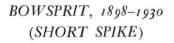

Pawl or Sampson Post.
Knight heads
Cross section whole length
Tapered in a curve on top only, knight heads to pole
℄, Deck
Tennon
Not to scale.
Side elevation
Shoulder
Pole
Bottom straight, no taper

Spike bowsprits had very slight taper from knightheads to pawl post. All taper on top of stick, bottom straight, outboard. Round in knightheads. Stick flat on top, outboard, sides tapered. In the 1880s, triangular pieces of wood were fitted to spike bowsprits at knightheads to make the bowsprit square where it passed through the bulwarks.

Hole for spike bowsprits in bulwarks was scribed with a fish-hook shaped iron, having a sharp point on the short leg. The distance between the legs was half the diameter of the bowsprit hole. A small guide hole was bored in the stem-head. The long leg was inserted in the guide hole and, revolving the tool, the bowsprit hole could be scribed, outside on the planking with the pointed leg. The bowsprit hole could then be cut out with chisels and gouges. The hawse-holes were scribed with a similar tool and then cut to fit the hawse castings in like manner. The "Carrie E. Phillips" was the first to be fitted with a bowsprit round at knightheads. The flat top of the bowsprit was changed to round when the long spike bowsprit was replaced with the short spike bowsprit about 1906.

Charles Andrews
L.H.S.

BOWSPRITS (NOTES)

The plumb-stem schooner "A. D. Story," which had been launched in 1886, some weeks before the U. S. Fish Commission's schooner "Grampus," had the jibboom rig of her time, having the large jib, or jumbo. "Grampus" appears to have been the first of this class of fishing schooners to be rigged with a forestaysail, with its stay shackled to the gammon iron. She thus had four headsails, forestaysail, jib, flying jib, and jib topsail. When she was rerigged in 1891 she was given a pole, or "spike," bowsprit with forestay shackled to a wye a few feet outboard of the gammon iron.

The size of the bowsprits, when they were square at the gammon iron, was determined by the depth from the underside of the rail cap to the line of the top of the quarterdeck planksheer projected to the stem. A vessel of 70 to 80 feet length would have a bowsprit 18 inches square at gammon iron, or thereabouts.

A photograph of a spike bowsprit dated 1894 shows a wye at outer end of pole with eyes top and bottom, one two-eye wye, with eyes top and bottom, at shoulder, and a four-eye wye on its fore side, bringing two eyes together at the shoulder. It shows the forestay shackled into the bowsprit wye just forward of the billet; the wye having ears and clamp bolts top and bottom.

The "Carrie E. Phillips," 1886, claimed to be the first fisherman to have a spike bowsprit, and introduced other new features.

Sharpshooters did not have much stive in their bowsprits and these either lined up with the sheer or were nearly parallel with the load line, with hog at outboard end. This was true of some clipper schooners.

Photograph of sch. "I. H. Higgins," 1882, shows 4-eye wye at bowsprit end with cap iron for jibboom just abaft of it, acting as a backing band to the 4-eye wye which probably took the shrouds and outer bobstay.

Five evenly spaced lines ran athwartship under the bowsprit, from shroud to shroud, of ¾" dia. manila or hemp. These served to keep the jib from falling into the water when the sail was being lowered for furling. When schooners carried the big jib or jumbo more sail stops were required, as well as "net lines."

Bowsprits were made straight on the bottom with the taper on top and sides, 1845–1930.

John Prince Story, master ship carpenter, stated that schooners built for the salt banks fisheries, and for freighting winters from Cape Cod, had more stive in their bowsprits than regular fishermen.

Cleats on the bowsprit were 2¼" x 2". The cleats ran from about 10"-12" abaft the bowsprit shoulder wye to 3"-6" forward of the foreside of gammon iron.

Some vessels had their bowsprits much hogged down forward. In such cases the hog was cut into the bowsprit when it was being made. This was rare in New England vessels, but common on the Chesapeake.

BOWSPRIT IRONWORK (MISCELLANEOUS NOTES)

The "Mary T. Fallon" had one wye at bowsprit shoulders, turnbuckles on shrouds at their outer ends. Photographs of schooners building at Gloucester in 1875 show the bowsprit cap iron, or "jibboom band" with a two-eye wye abaft it. At about the location of the bee hole for the forestay, there was a rope strop around the bowsprit. The bowsprit cap iron had a bolt through it athwartship to hold the cap in place.

The bowsprit shrouds were secured to the bowsprit by an iron fitting made of a 2″ x 1½″ bar having an eye at each end, spectacle-fashion. A hole was cut athwartship in the bowsprit, a little abaft the cap iron, large enough to allow the fitting to be pushed through it. The fitting was then forced aft in the hole, with the eyes on both sides facing aft to take the shrouds. The fitting was secured by wedges driven from each side, P. & S., on the foreside of the fitting. This seems to have been in use as early as 1855 as an alternate to bee chainplates. (See "Bees," "Bowsprit and Jibboom.")

When the forestay came inboard, as in "Elsie," it was secured to the bowsprit by a wye made of 1″ x 3¼″ bar, with ears and clamping bolts, into which the stay was shackled. The wye was in two parts so that it could be fitted with the bowsprit in place, hence it clamped top and bottom.

BOWSPRIT RIGGING IRONWORK

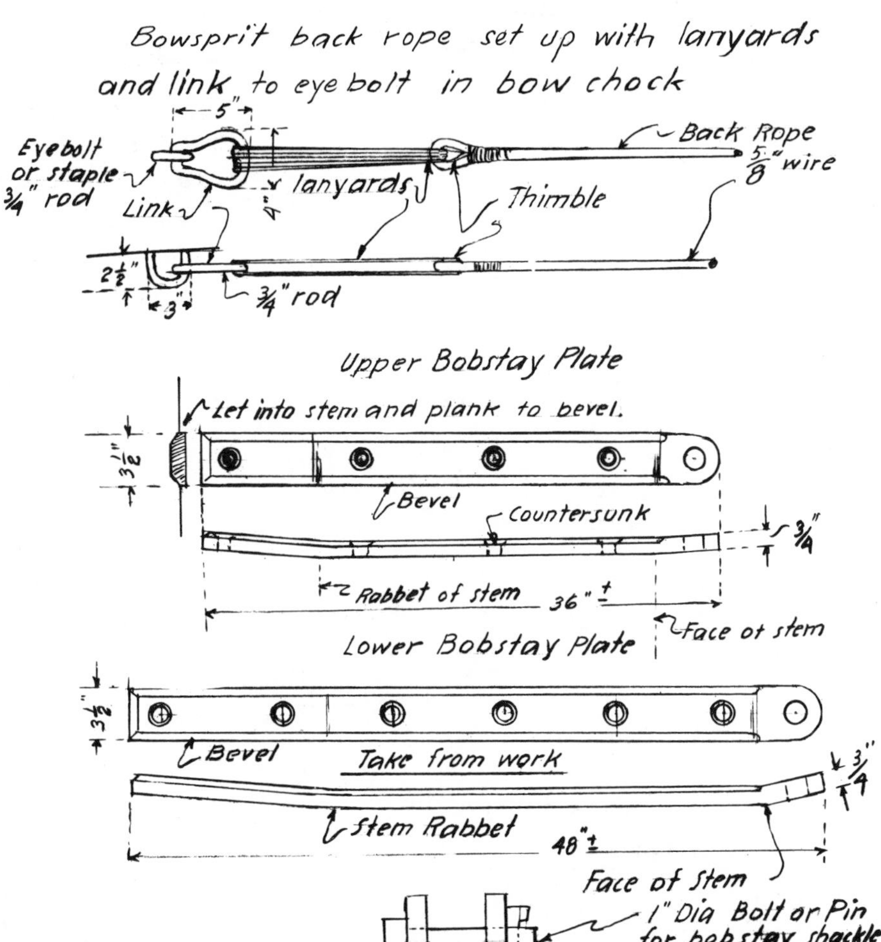
Bowsprit back rope set up with lanyards and link to eye bolt in bow chock
5"
Eyebolt or staple
3/4" rod
Link
4"
lanyards
Thimble
Back Rope
5/8" wire
2½"
3"
3/4" rod
Upper Bobstay Plate
Let into stem and plank to bevel.
3½"
Bevel
Countersunk
3/4"
Rabbet of stem
36" ±
Face of stem
Lower Bobstay Plate
3½"
Bevel
Take from work
3/4"
Stem Rabbet
48" ±
Face of Stem
1" Dia Bolt or Pin for bobstay shackle with forelock, (split pin)

BOWSPRIT RIGGING IRONWORK

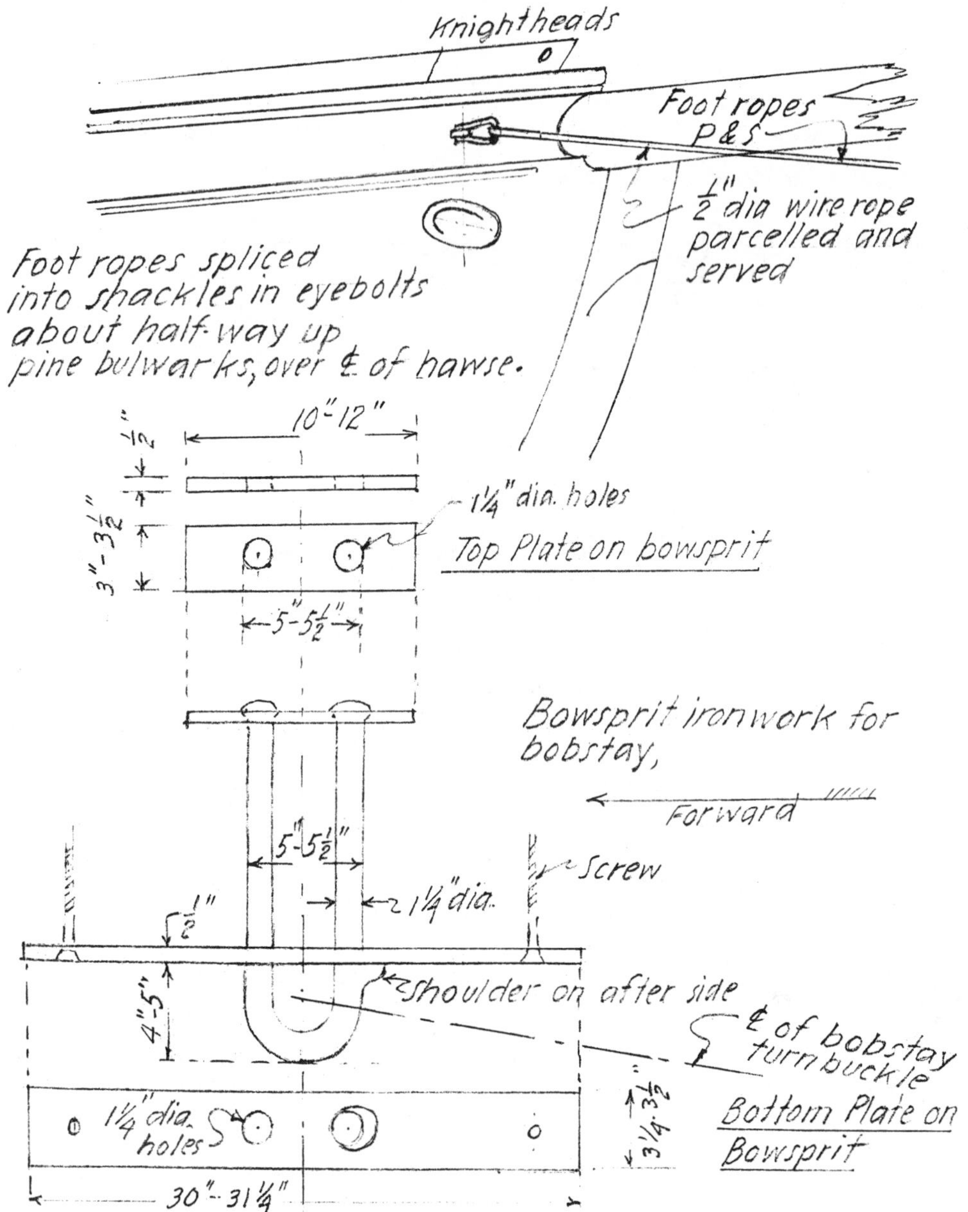

Knightheads
Foot ropes P&S
1/2" dia wire rope parcelled and served
Foot ropes spliced into shackles in eyebolts about half-way up pine bulwarks, over ℄ of hawse.
10"-12"
1/2"
3"-3 1/2"
1 1/4" dia. holes
Top Plate on bowsprit
5-5 1/2"
Bowsprit ironwork for bobstay,
Forward
5"-5 1/2"
Screw
1/2"
1 1/4" dia.
4"-5"
Shoulder on after side
℄ of bobstay turnbuckle
3 1/4-3 1/2
1 1/4" dia. holes
Bottom Plate on Bowsprit
30"-31 1/4"

Not to scale

Amended to Bosley's notes and to Chapelle & Taylor. Waters

BOWSPRIT RIGGING IRONWORK (SPIKE)

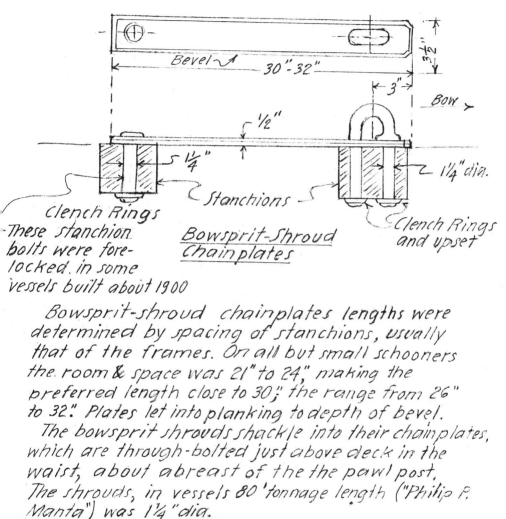

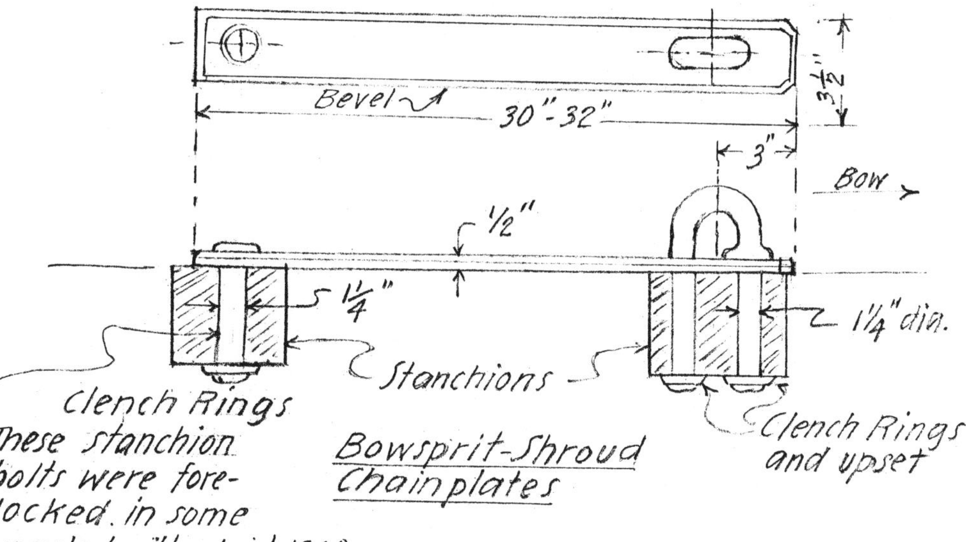
Bevel
30"-32"
3½"
3"
Bow
½"
1¼"
1¼" dia.
Stanchions
Clench Rings
-These stanchion bolts were fore-locked. in some vessels built about 1900
Clench Rings and upset
Bowsprit-Shroud Chainplates

Bowsprit-shroud chainplates lengths were determined by spacing of stanchions, usually that of the frames. On all but small schooners the room & space was 21" to 24", making the preferred length close to 30", the range from 26" to 32". Plates let into planking to depth of bevel.

The bowsprit shrouds shackle into their chainplates, which are through-bolted just above deck in the waist, about abreast of the the pawl post. The shrouds, in vessels 80' tonnage length ("Philip P. Manta") was 1¼" dia.

"Elsie" chainplates were 31" x $3\frac{1}{2}$" x $\frac{1}{2}$" or $\frac{5}{8}$".

BOWSPRIT IRONWORK, 1920–1930

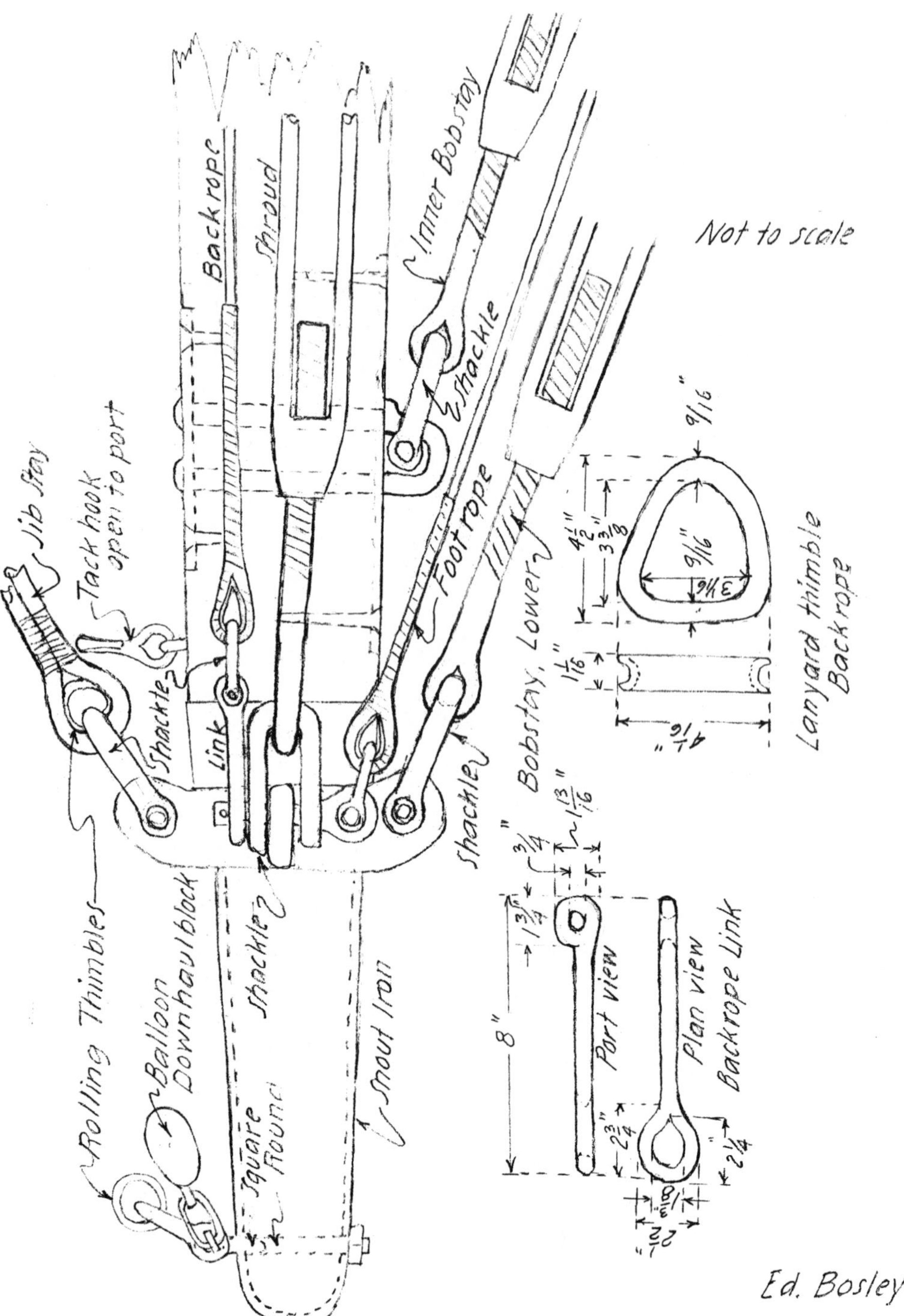

Not to scale
Backrope
Shroud
Inner Bobstay
Shackle
Footrope
Bobstay, Lower
Shackle
Jib Stay
Tack hook open to port
Shackle
Link
Shackle
Rolling Thimbles
Balloon Downhaul block
Square
Round
Snout Iron
Lanyard thimble Backrope
Port view
Plan view Backrope Link
Ed. Bosley

BOWSPRIT IRONWORK

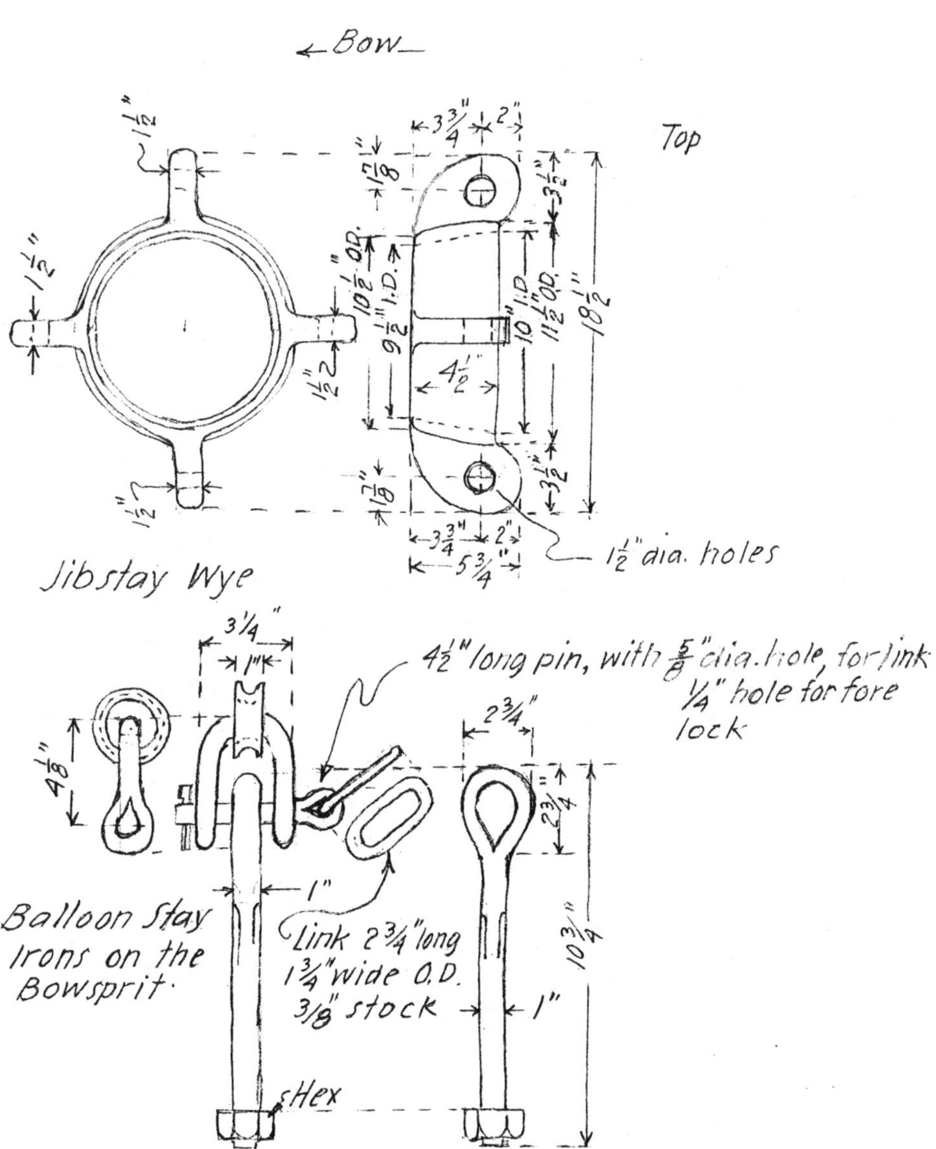

← Bow
Top
1½" dia. holes
Jibstay Wye
4½" long pin, with 5/8" dia. hole, for link
¼" hole for fore lock
Link 2¾" long
1¾" wide O.D.
3/8" stock
Balloon Stay
Irons on the
Bowsprit.
Hex

Ed. Bosley

BOWSPRIT IRONWORK
(SPIKE BOWSPRIT)

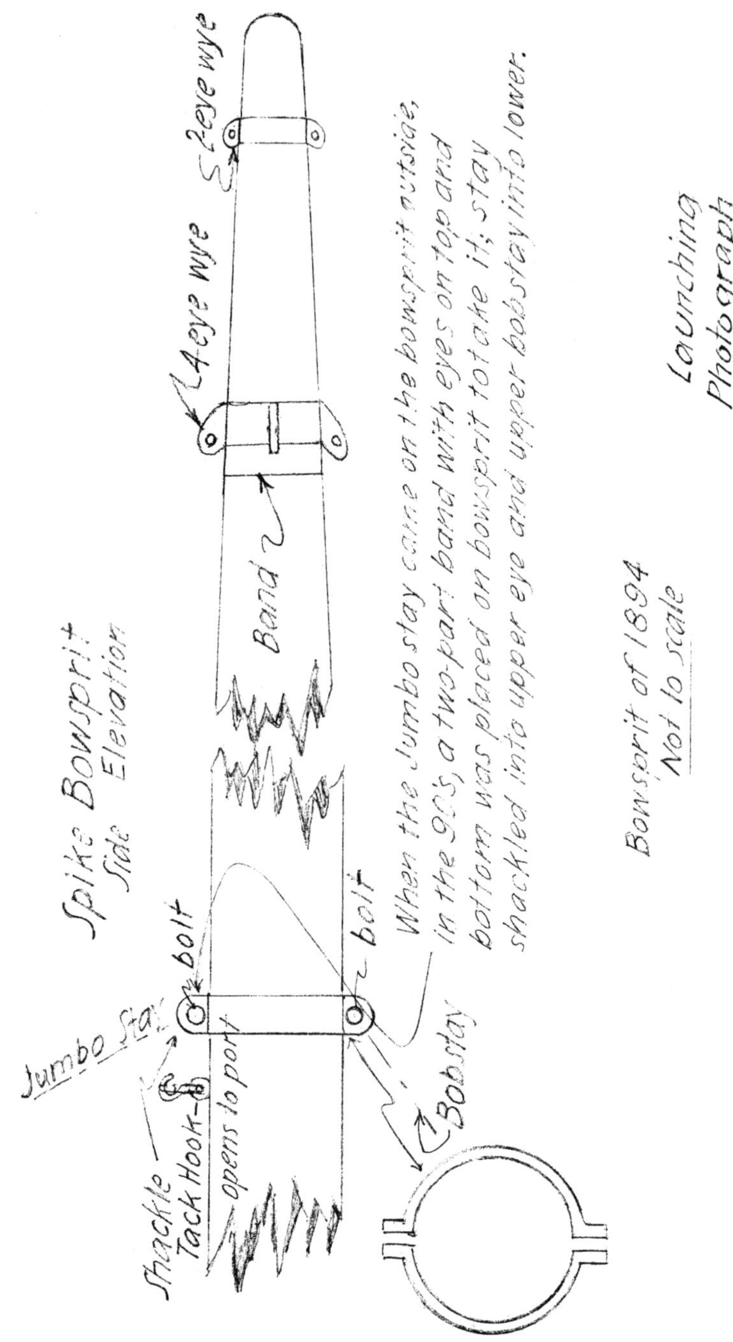
2eye wye
4eye wye
Band
Spike Bowsprit
Side Elevation
bolt
bolt
Jumbo Stay
Shackle
Tack Hook—opens to port
Bobstay
When the Jumbo stay came on the bowsprit outside, in the 90's, a two-part band with eyes on top and bottom was placed on bowsprit to take it; stay shackled into upper eye and upper bobstay into lower.
Launching Photograph
Bowsprit of 1894
Not to scale

BOWSPRIT IRONWORK, SKETCH NO. 1
SPIKE BOWSPRIT, 1890–1936

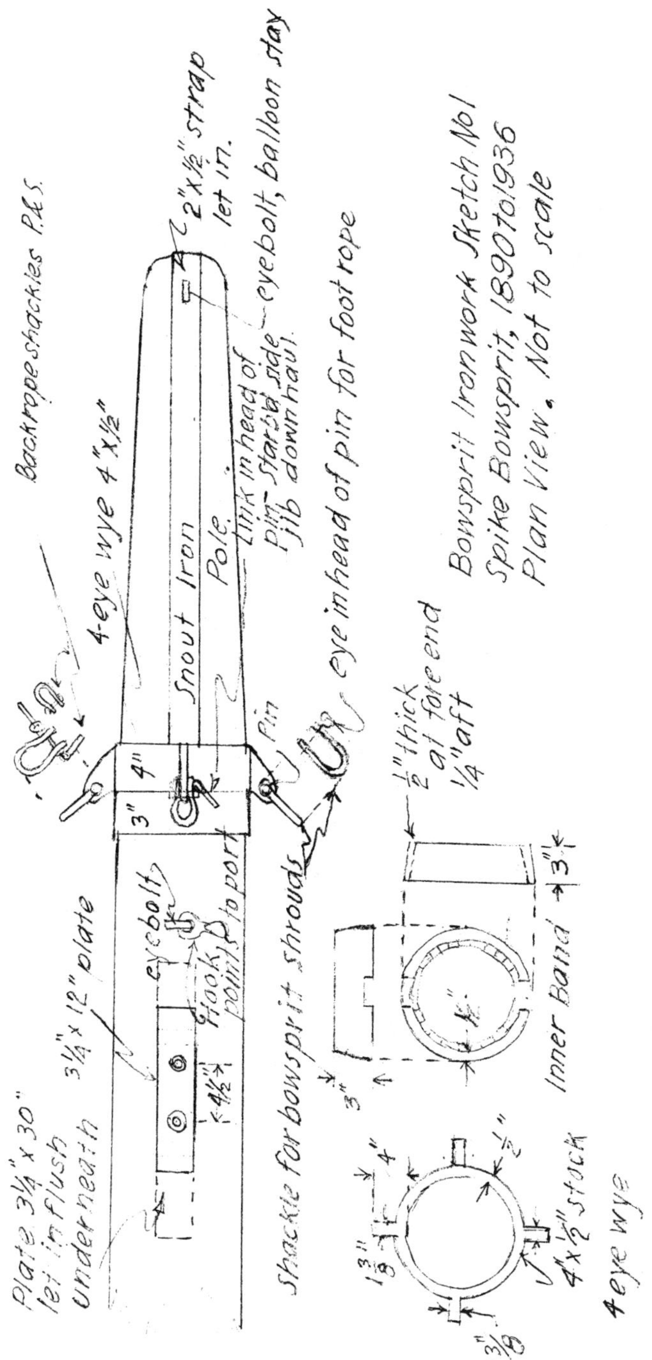
Backrope shackles P.&S.
4-eye wye 4"x½"
2"x½" strap let in.
eyebolt, balloon stay
Link in head of pin - Starbd side jib downhaul.
eye in head of pin for foot rope
Snout Iron
Pole
Pin
Bowsprit Ironwork Sketch No 1
Spike Bowsprit, 1890 to 1936
Plan View. Not to scale
½" thick at fore end
¼" aft
Inner Band
Plate 3¼" x 30" let in flush underneath
3¼ x 12" plate
eyebolt
Hook points to port
Shackle for bowsprit shrouds
4 x ½" stock
4 eye wye

BOWSPRIT IRONWORK, SKETCH NO. 2

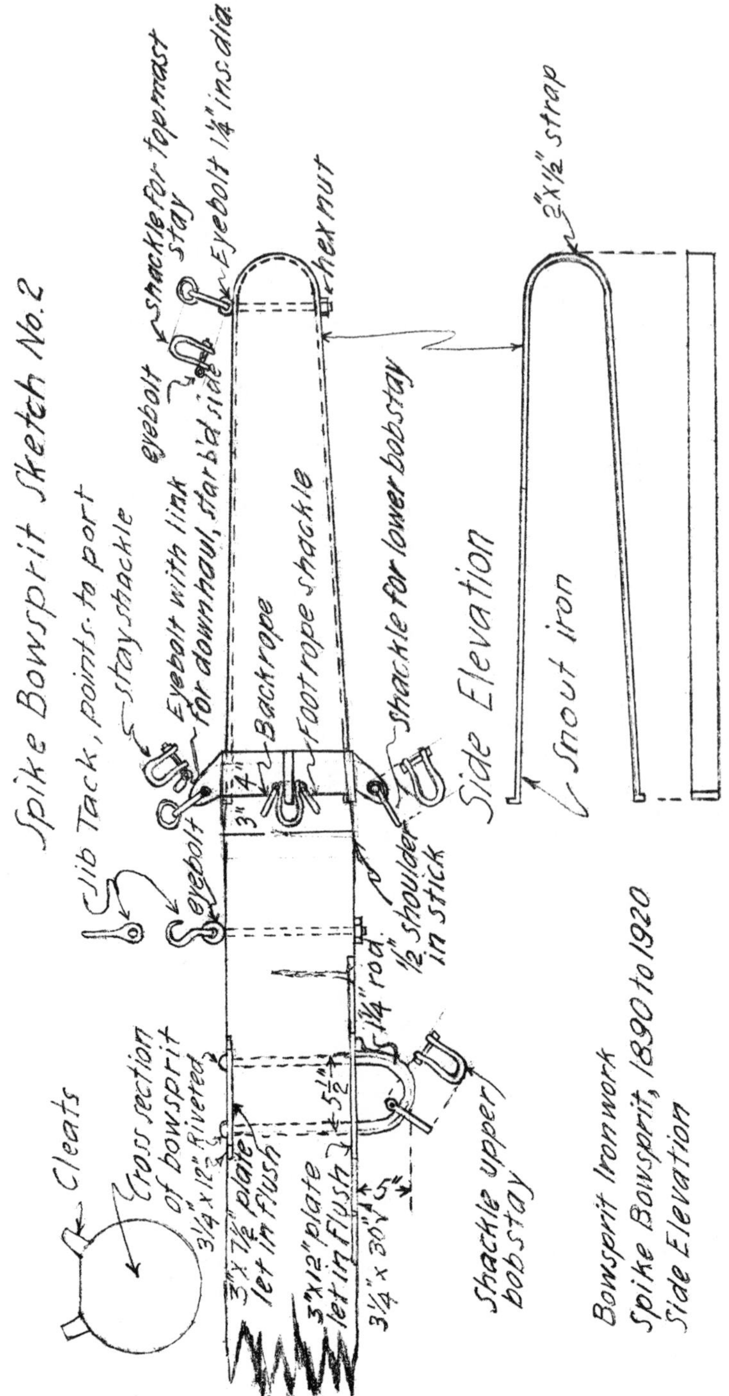

Spike Bowsprit Sketch No. 2
Jib Tack, points to port
stay shackle
eyebolt
Eyebolt with link for downhaul, starb'd side
eyebolt
shackle for topmast stay
Eyebolt 1¼" ins. dia.
hex nut
Backrope
Footrope shackle
Shackle for lower bobstay
3"
4"
½" shoulder in stick
1¼" rod
Side Elevation
Snout iron
2"X½" strap
Cleats
Cross section of bowsprit
3¼ x 12" Riveted
3"x 7½" plate let in flush
3"x12" plate let in flush
5½"
5"
3¼" x 30"
Shackle upper bobstay
Bowsprit Ironwork 1890 to 1920
Bowsprit Ironwork
Spike Bowsprit
Side Elevation

SPIKE BOWSPRIT, 1890–1920
BOWSPRIT SAIL STOPS

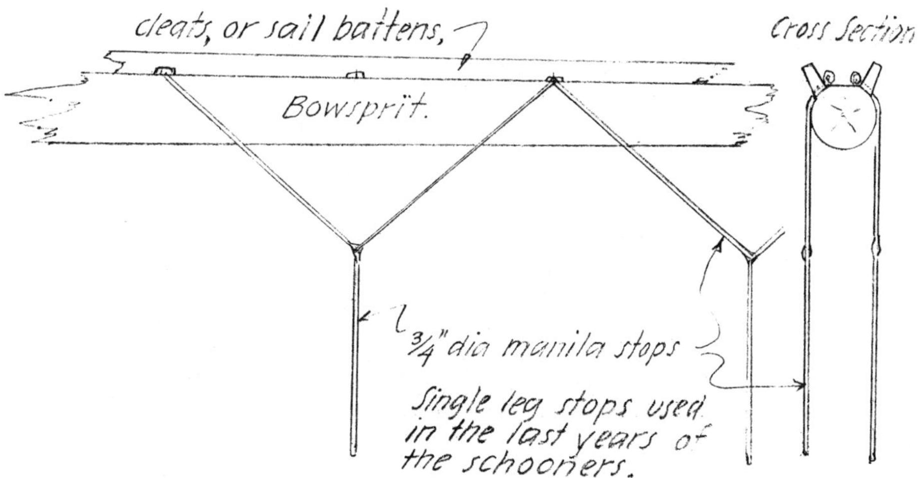
cleats, or sail battens,
Cross Section
Bowsprit.
3/4" dia manila stops
Single leg stops used in the last years of the schooners.

Sail stops on bowsprit serve to secure the furled jib and are permanently rove off. They have two legs each, passed through holes in the cleats and held by stop knots on the inside of the cleats. There were usually four on a side, eight in all, spaced 2' to 3' apart. The legs were long enough to lap a little on the top of the furled sail, the tails were used in pairs, port and starboard, to form the lashings. Because of the shape of the furled jib, the forward stops would be a little longer than the after ones. The legs were used as they gave almost continuous support to the furled sail along the sides. In small schooners, the stops were single pieces of rope, spaced 2'- 2'-6" without legs.

BOWSPRIT SHROUDS (MISCELLANEOUS NOTES)

Thomas McManus and others stated that the condition of bowsprit shrouds, footropes, net lines, and backropes, was often allowed to deteriorate, through neglect in fitting out, to the extent that loss of life resulted. This opinion led McManus to introduce the knockabout fishing schooner in 1902.

BREAST HOOK OR "SEAT"

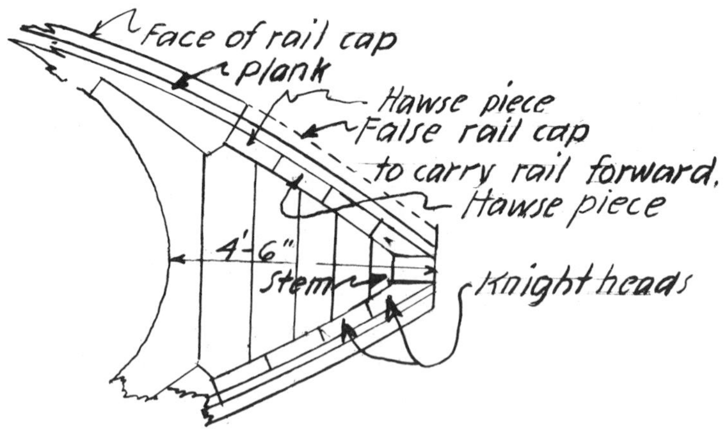
Face of rail cap
plank
Hawse piece
False rail cap
to carry rail forward.
Hawse piece
4'-6"
Stem
Knight heads

Mary T. Fallon" 1901
75.5' x 21.6' x 9.0'

Breast hooks or "seats" were from about 4' to 6' in length; the latter in very sharp-ended vessels. Jibboom-tack horse was mounted on the seat in many schooners having a spike bowsprit, with fore-stay set up on gammon iron.

Thickness of seat timbers determined by thickness of rail cap. Chock rail covers heads of Hawse pieces and Knight heads in this schooner.

BREAST HOOKS OR "SEATS"
(NOTES)

The fore seat of the "Mary E. O'Hara" was 46" fore-and-aft. In the "J. M. Marshall", knockabout it was 3'-4" from after face of stem to after end of seat, or 5'-1" from stem band. In the knockabout "Rhodora" it was 6'-0" from stem rabbet to after end of seat.

Aft, a seat was formed over the transom by widening the main rail-cap, inside of the monkey rail. Athwartship, this seat crowned with the main rail, or nearly parallel with the deck. The sketch below shows the after seat of the "Ethel Penny." The after seat of the knockabout "Rhodora" measured 2'-6" from inside of Monkey Rail at ℄, the mainsheet buffer table was 18" fore-and-aft from the fore edge of seat and 4'-0" athwartships. See "Mainsheet Buffer."

The stern seats ranged from 1'-3" to 2'-6" inside of Monkey Rail in the schooners observed.

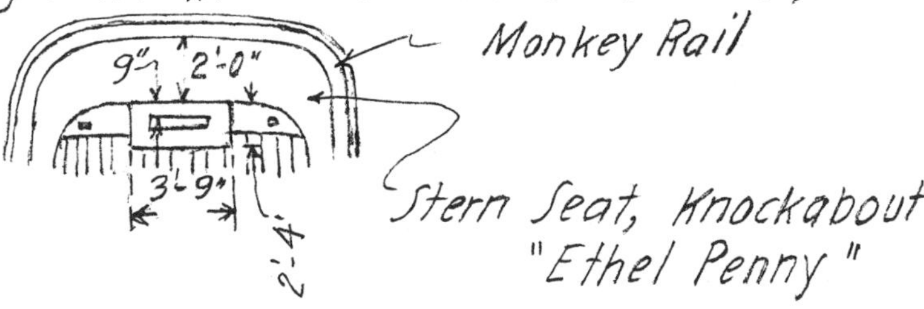
Monkey Rail
9"
2'-0"
3'-9"
2'-4"
Stern Seat, Knockabout "Ethel Penny"

Before 1885, or thereabouts, the after seat was not much over 1'-3" fore-and-aft, the crown very moderate.

"BULL NOSE" MOULDING

Standard moulding used in Essex-built fishing schooners, 1850-1906

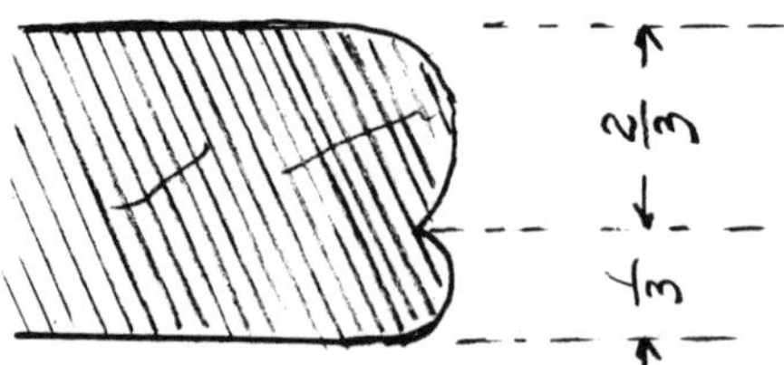

Moulding used in rail caps, trail knees, etc.

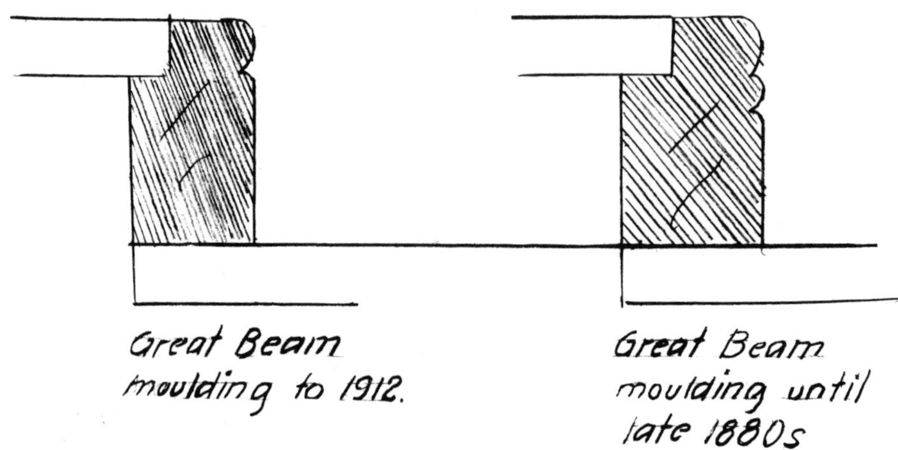

Great Beam moulding to 1912.

Great Beam moulding until late 1880s

BULWARKS

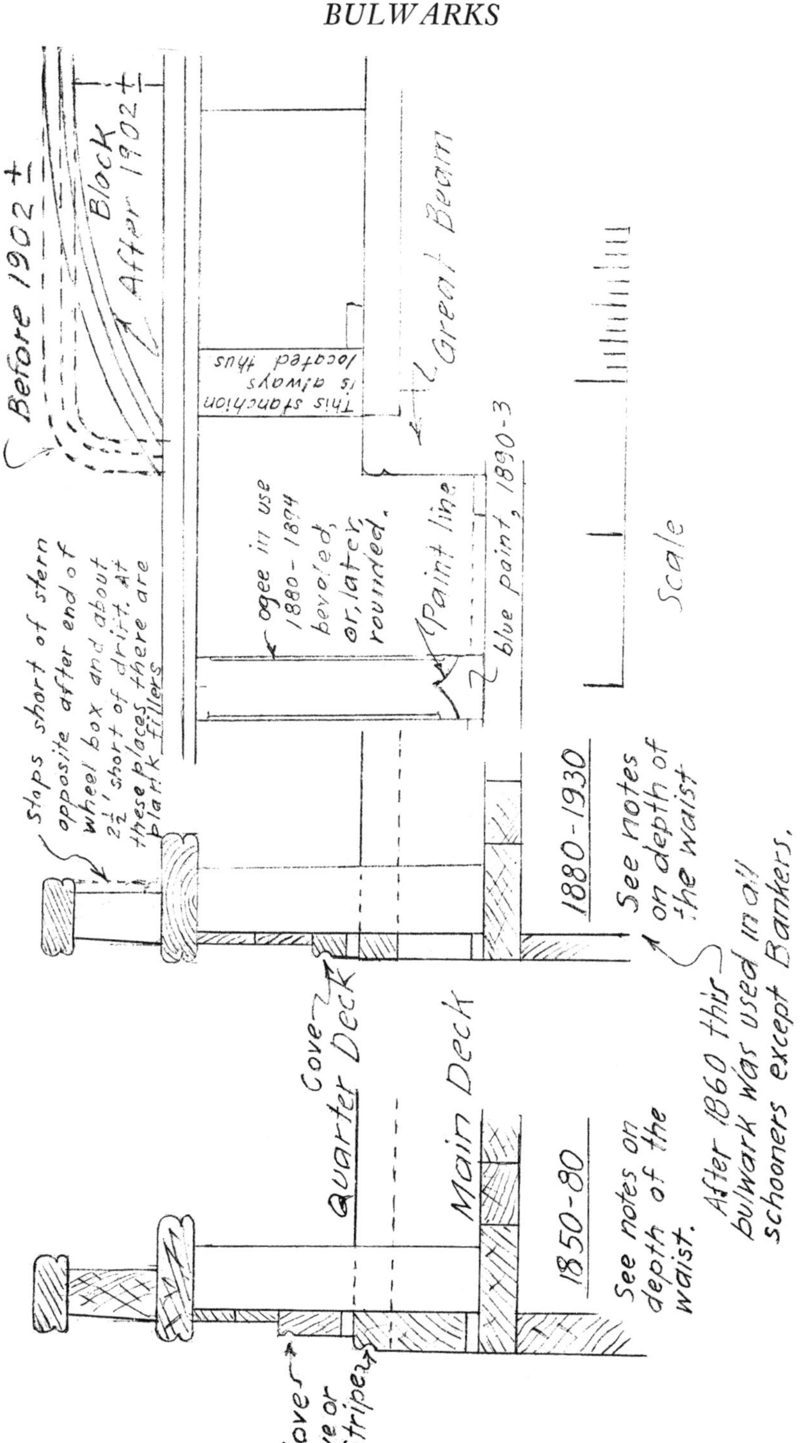
Before 1902 ±
Block
After 1902 ±
Great Beam
This stanchion is always located thus
ogee in use 1880-1894 beveled, or, later, rounded.
Paint line
blue paint, 1890-3
Scale
Stops short of stern opposite after end of wheel box and about 2½' short of drift. At these places there are plank fillers
1880-1930
See notes on depth of the waist
Cove
Quarter Deck
Main Deck
1850-80
See notes on depth of the waist.
After 1860 this bulwark was used in all schooners except Bankers.
Cove
Cove or Stripe

BULWARKS

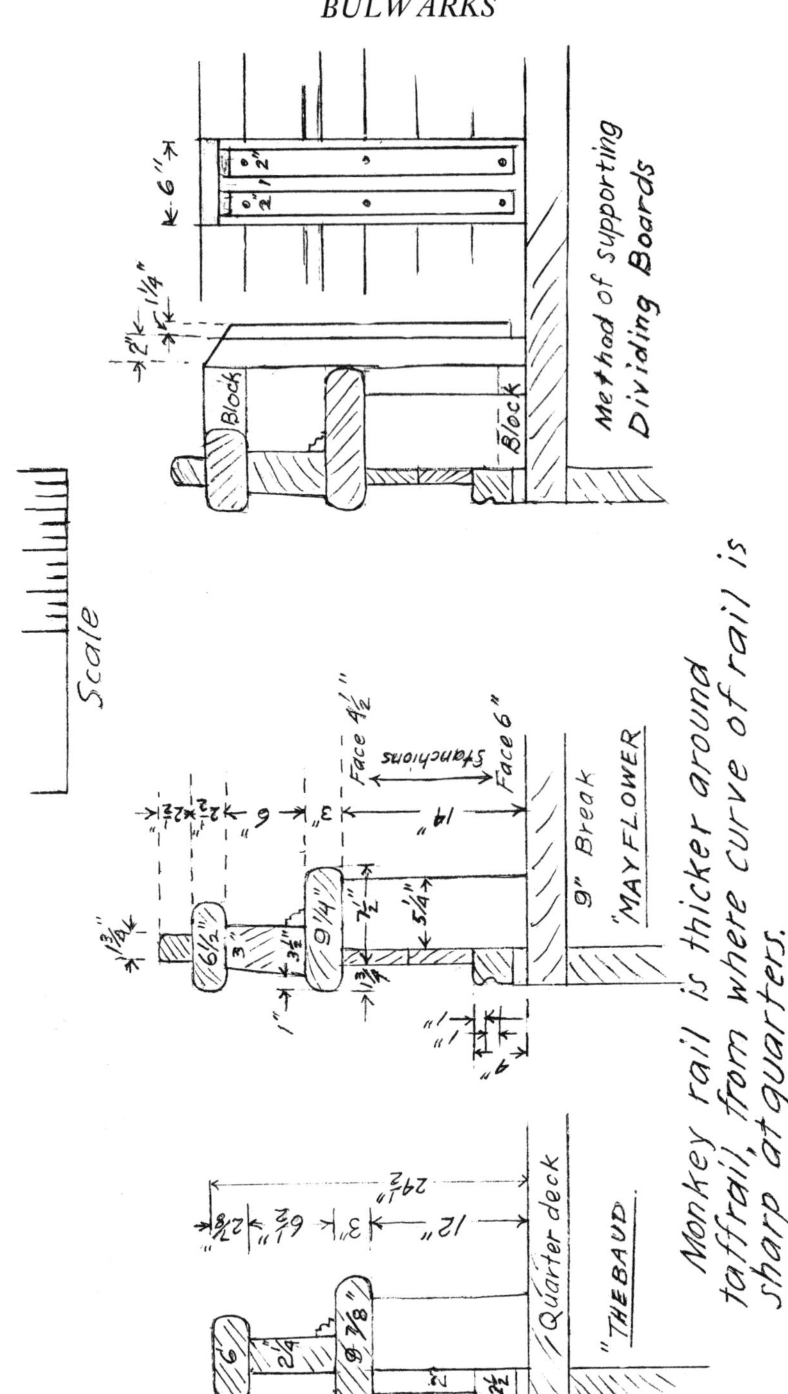

Method of supporting Dividing Boards
Block
Block
Scale
Stanchions
Face 4½"
Face 6"
9" Break
"MAYFLOWER"
Quarter deck
"THEBAUD"
Monkey rail is thicker around taffrail, from where curve of rail is sharp at quarters.

BULWARKS

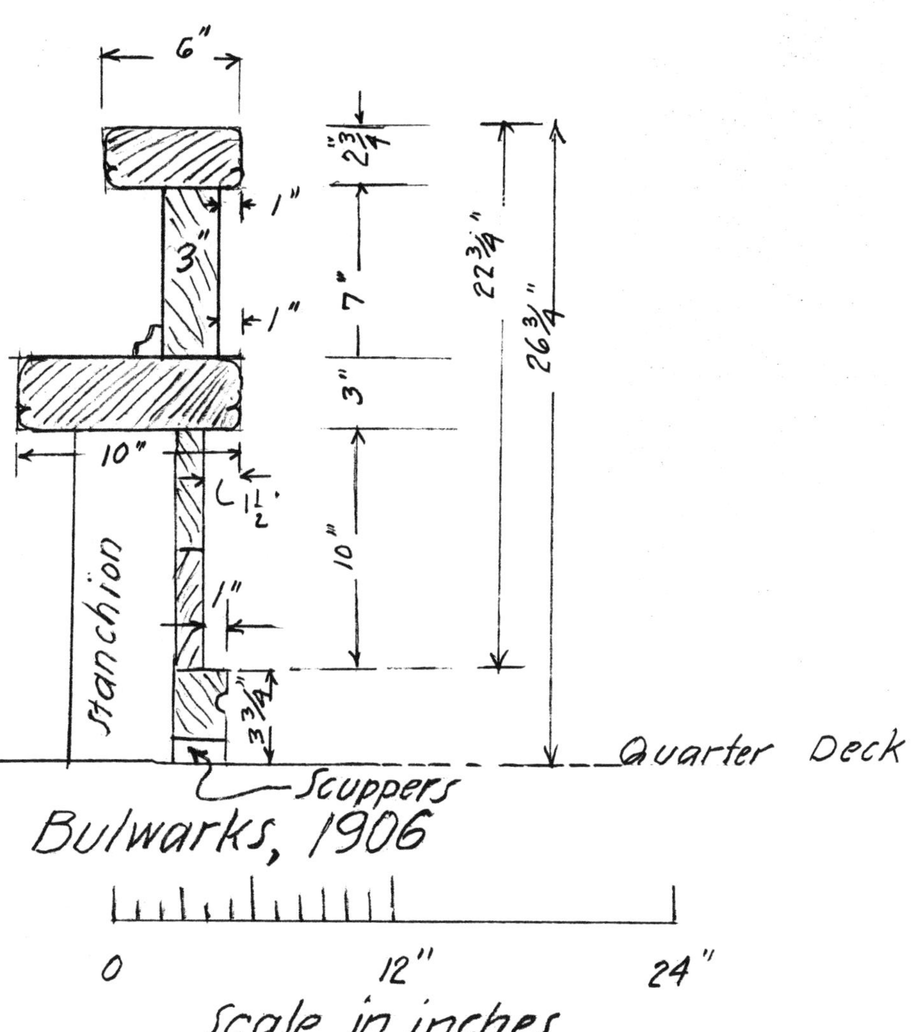
6"
2¾"
1"
3"
7"
1"
22¾"
26¾"
3"
10"
1½"
10"
1"
Stanchion
3¾"
Quarter Deck
Scuppers
Bulwarks, 1906
0
12"
24"
Scale in inches

BULWARKS (NOTES)

The bulwark stanchions of the knockabout "Natalie Hammond" moulded 5″ at deck, 4½″ at rail, siding 6″.

Main rail cap of "Elsie" was 3″ thick.

Depth of pine bulwark, rail cap to waist was 6⅝″ ("Elsie").

Quarterdeck rail cap was 6⅜″ wide, and the rail was 6⅜″ high, above main rail. The chock rail on top of the quarterdeck rail began 21″ from the ℄ of the after chain plate (mainmast) and ran aft to a point abreast the boom crotch ("Elsie").

"Elsie" had a bulwark stanchion placed exactly opposite the after-end of the cabin trunk.

The pine bulwarks of a banker like the "Grout" were probably 9″ or 10″ deep under the rail cap. Sometimes they used pine in one width, but the James Yard usually used three planks of matched pine, beaded. The oak waist might be 17″ to 18″ high, in two strakes. Some bankers had a bead worked on the top of the waist instead of a cove. James usually used the bead on large bankers. "Adventure," knockabout, had stanchions with inboard corners bevelled off.

Bulwark stanchions of fishing schooners, built after 1850 at least, appear to have been placed between the frames, rather than being made a part of the frames. The stanchions were therefore spaced the same as the frames, in theory at least, but the measurements of the stanchions taken from five schooners showed such irregularities in spacing as to indicate that only the stanchions at the great beam and in the wake of the chain plates were very carefully located.

"Bulwarks of schooners in the 1870s and early 1880s has waists some 15″-17″ in depth (above the plank-sheer). Then the pine bulwarks were 8″-10″ deep. Bead lines or coves were usually painted stone or chrome yellow. Early vessels, before 1870, had white coves. The waist then ended straight at the fashion piece with no upsweep in the waist.

Some vessels built in the 1870s and early 1880s, had a red bead over the quarterdeck scuppers and a white or yellow stripe or band on the quarterdeck plank-sheer and both carried forward to the bow. The Provincetown three-masters were so finished.

The depth of the pine bulwarks has been about 10″ since about 1906. Earlier vessels often had pine bulwarks 7″-9″ in depth with the waist perhaps about 16″ deep above the maindeck plank-sheer, with a ¾″ cove in the top of the waist.

In a Gloucester-built schooner of about 1875, the quarterdeck plank-sheer band faired to the level of the underside of the bowsprit at the stem rabbet.

Bulwarks of the "Grampus," smack, deck to top of rail cap 26″, height of quarterdeck 9″ (1885).

Bulwarks of the knockabout "Ethel B. Penny" were 23″ high, from main deck to top of rail.

Bulwarks of the "Mary T. Fallon" (1901)—thickness of bulwarks 1″ plank; waist 2¼″ stock." [L.H.S.]

(See "Waist.")

The bulwarks were usually of constant height, 24″-27″, but in the 1860s, '70s, and '80s the bankers often had bulwarks 30″-33″ high. When knockabouts first appeared, a few were built with more sheer in the deck line than at the main rail. This might give 18″ bulwarks at bow and stern, with 24″-26″ bulwarks amidship.

Occasionally a builder's half-model, of earlier date than the knockabouts, shows this departure. But this feature in a model might not appear in the vessel. This happened in the first knockabout, the "Helen Thomas." McManus had much more sheer in the deck line than in the rail cap, which produced an attractive design, but the builders fitted the "Thomas" with bulwarks of constant height, as shown in the plan here. This gave the vessel excessive sheer and height of rail at stem. See Plate 96.

BULWARKS

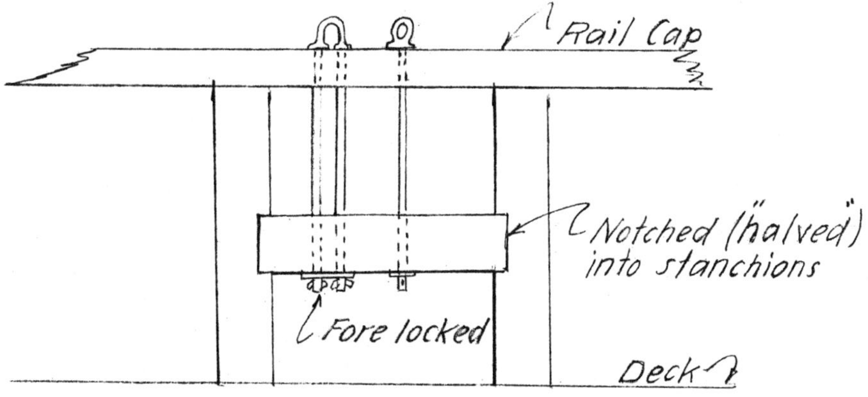
Rail Cap
Notched ("halved") into stanchions
Fore locked
Deck

Method of fitting staples and eyes in rail cap between stanchions, where heavy strains will be encountered. Used only in wake of the shrouds.

BULWARKS

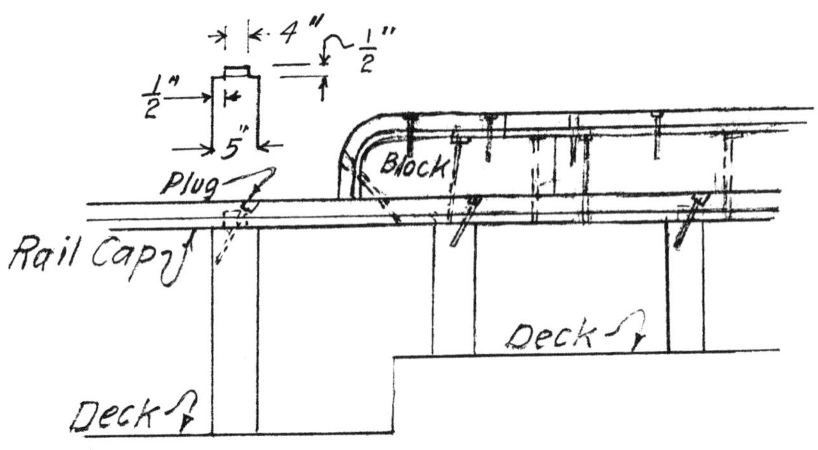
4"
1/2"
1/2"
5"
Plug
Block
Rail Cap
Deck
Deck

Method of spiking rail caps to stanchions. Spike driven as shown, at an angle, head countersunk, and plugged. Heads of stanchions tennoned. Monkey rail cap similarly spiked to quarter-deck log rail. Stanchions were fastened, near their heels by two treenails, passing through clamps, stanchion, and sheer strake. In case of injury, the treenails could be bored out and the damaged stanchions removed, without disturbing the sound timbers.

CABIN TRUNKS

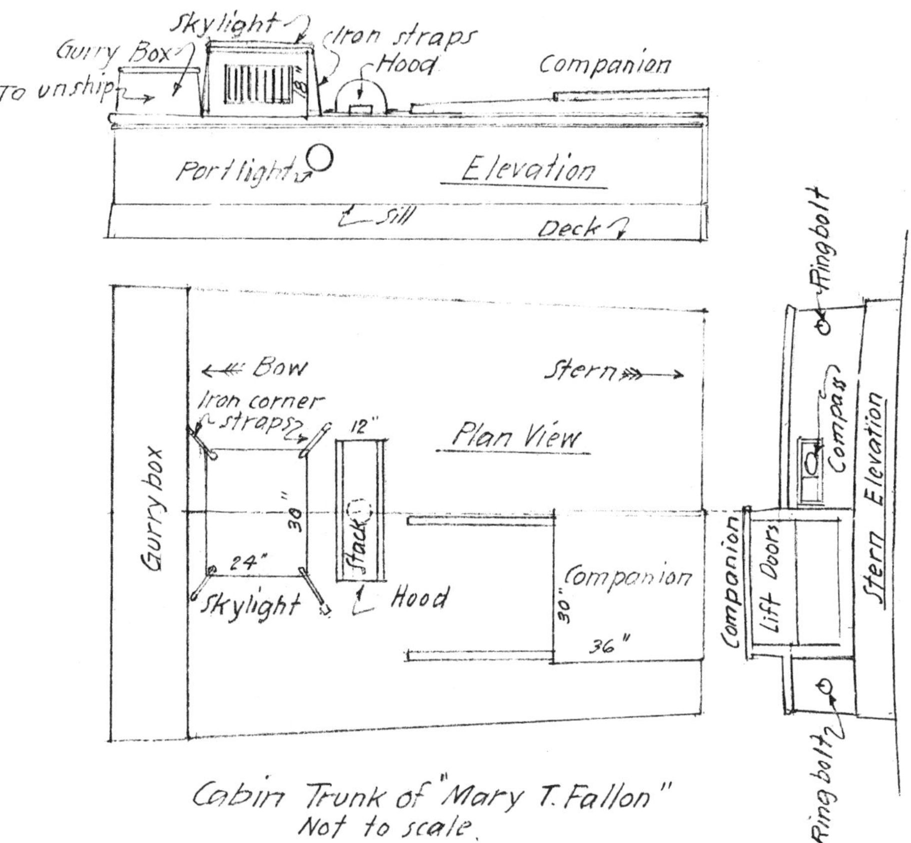
Skylight
Iron straps
Gurry Box
Hood
Companion
To unship
18"
Portlight
Elevation
Sill
Deck
Bow
Stern
Iron corner straps
12"
Plan View
Gurry box
30"
24"
Stack
Skylight
Hood
Companion
30"
36"
Companion
Lift Doors
Ringbolt
Compass
Stern Elevation
Ringbolt

Cabin Trunk of "Mary T. Fallon"
Not to scale.

CABIN TRUNKS, "ELSIE"

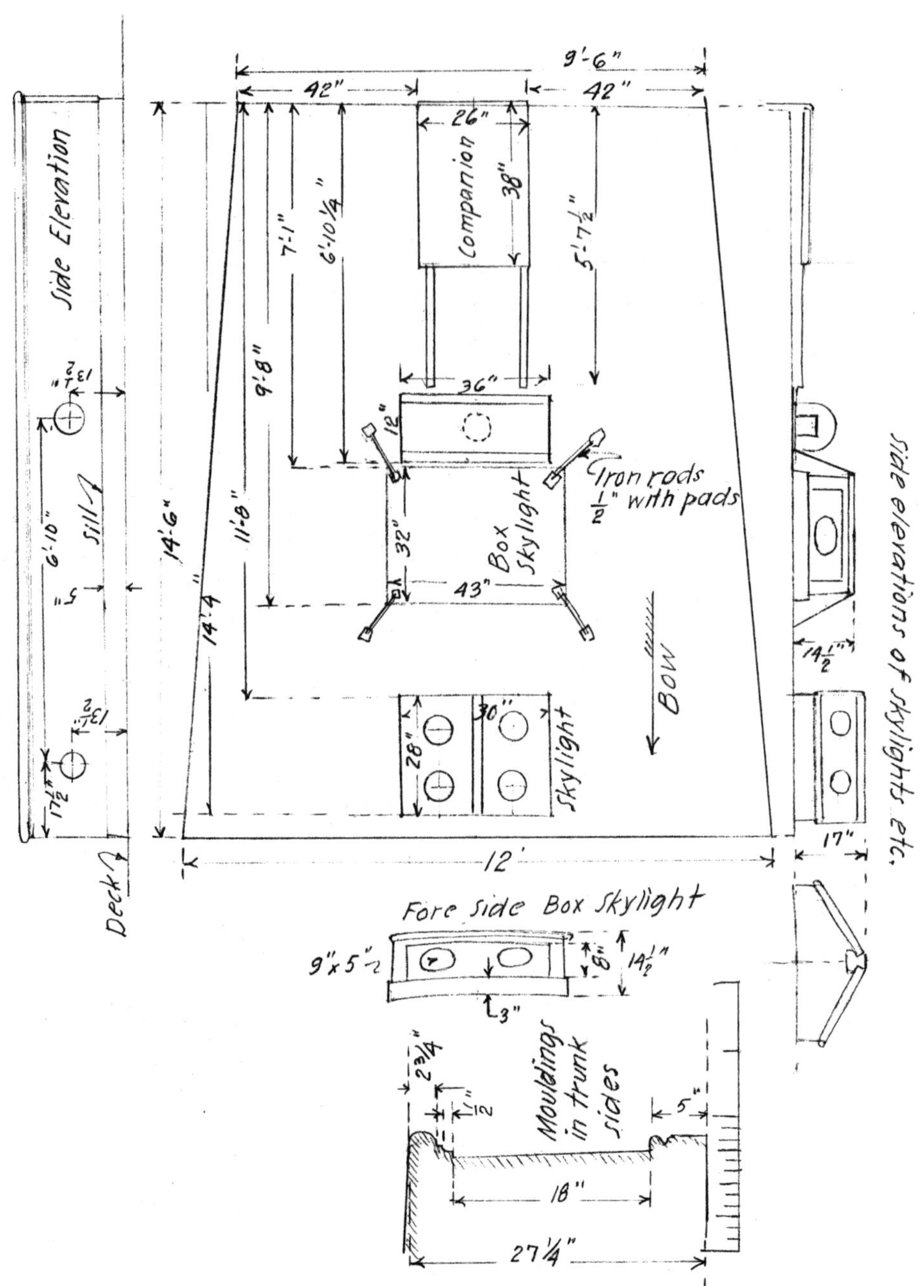
Side Elevation
Sill
Deck
Companion
Box Skylight
Iron rods 1/2" with pads
Skylight
BOW
Side elevations of skylights etc.
Fore Side Box Skylight
9"x 5 1/2"
Mouldings in trunk sides
9'-6"
42"
42"
26"
38"
36"
12"
32"
43"
28"
30"
12'
14'6"
14'4"
11'8"
9'8"
7'1"
6'10 1/4"
5'7 1/2"
6'10"
13 1/2"
17 1/2"
5"
14 1/2"
17"
8"
3"
2 3/4"
1/2"
5"
18"
27 1/4"

CABIN TRUNKS
(*MISCELLANEOUS NOTES*)

Cabin trunks were built with the sides straight and parallel, as nearly as possible, to the bulwarks. Since the vessel's after bulwarks came nearer together in all schooners, as the transom was approached, the cabin trunks were narrower aft than forward. In old vessels with wide transoms, this was less apparent than in the later, narrow-transom vessels. Also, the trunks were moved farther forward as counters were made longer in overhang.

"Columbia's" cabin trunk was 18′ long, the fore-end was 12′ wide, the after-end 10′ wide. The common range of length in trunks was 12′-15′. The heights of the sides of the trunks was 27″-30″. There was usually two portlights on each side of the trunks. A few schooners did have parallel-sided trunks; the knockabout "Oretha F. Spinney" was so built.

In the knockabout "Gertrude De Costa" the alleyways alongside the cabin trunks were 53″ wide at the fore-end (outside of trunk side to inside of waist planking in the bulwarks) and 45″ at the after-end, which was about 25′ from the taffrail.

Cabin trunk roof beams were generally about 6″ x 6″; 24″-30″ on centers. The crown was slight, somewhere about 3″ in 12′.

In old vessels, of earlier date than 1885, the trunks appear short and almost square and hardly show above the quarterdeck rail in photographs.

The cabin trunks of the "Grampus," 1886, was 27½″ high, 15′-0″ long. The fore-end was 14′-7″ wide, the after-end 12′-6″ wide. "Grampus" was 90′-0″ overall, 81′-6″ on the waterline. She was designed and laid down in early 1885.

The "cutting up boards" on top of the cabin trunk of the knockabout "Adventure" extended along the sides of the roof for its full length. These were 2″ x 8″ hardwood plank.

The cabin companionway was usually to port of the ℄ of the trunk cabin, sometimes as much as the width of the companionway.

CABIN TRUNKS
CONSTRUCTION OF SLIDING DOORS, ETC.

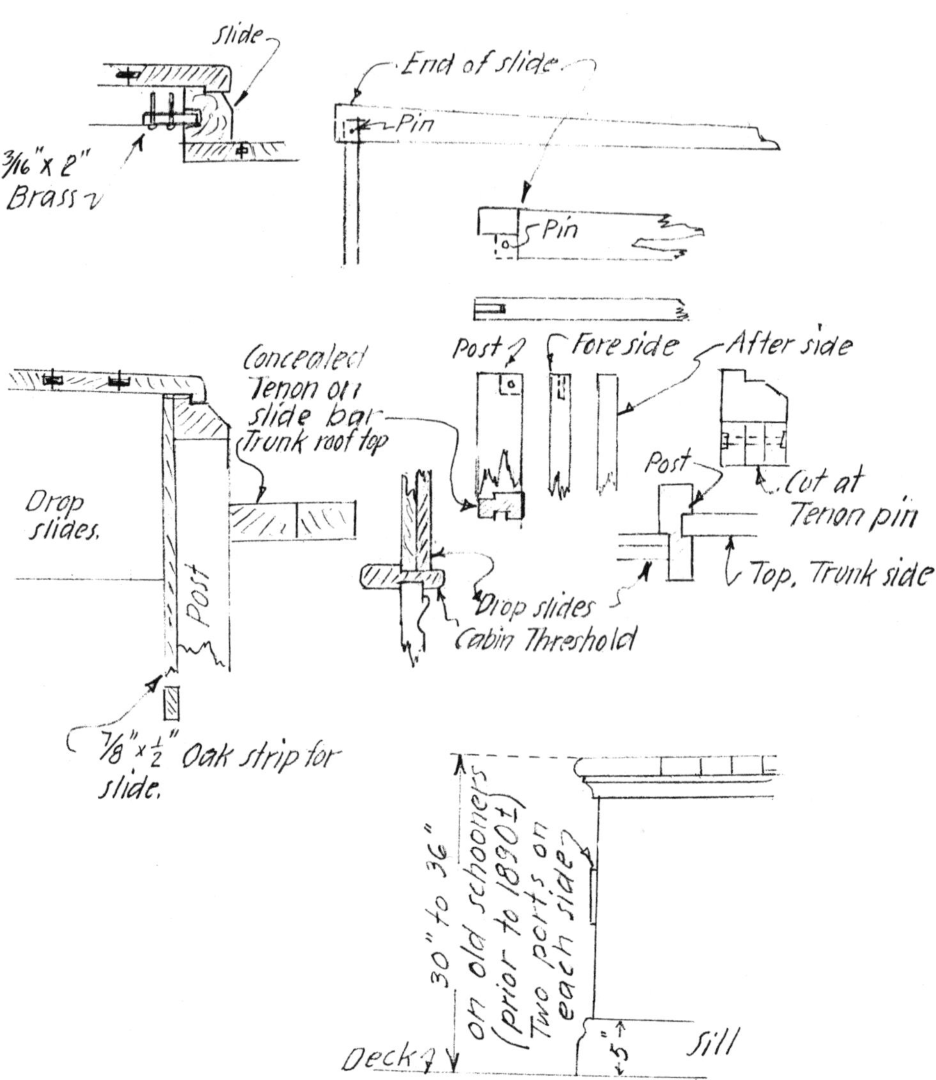
Slide
3/16" x 2"
Brass
End of slide
Pin
Pin
Concealed
Tenon on
slide bar
Trunk roof top
Post
Fore side
After side
Drop
slides.
Post
Post
Cut at
Tenon pin
Top, Trunk side
Drop slides
Cabin Threshold
7/8" x 1/2" Oak strip for
slide.
30" to 36"
on old schooners
(prior to 1890±)
Two ports on
each side
Deck
5"
Sill

CABIN TRUNKS

Length of cabin trunk on "Phillip P. Manta"
12'-8"; Sides $28\frac{1}{2}$" high. After end 5'-9" forward
of ℄ of rudder post at deck.

Bow

Top of cabin trunk, in 1875, shown in photographs.

CANT FRAMES

"Cants" were frames which had their heels butted against the sides of the deadwood at bow and stern. In the days of very full-ended craft the heels of the cant frames were bevelled so that they radiated somewhat, like spokes in a wheel, closely spaced at heel and wider spaced at head. "Square frames" were those whose floor timbers could cross the keel and they were at right angles to the hull's center line, of course.

When schooners became very sharp-ended, it was considered that canting bow and stern frames was no longer necessary, but they retained the old name. The square frames were carried into the ends as far as the deadwoods there would permit. There were five or six pairs of cants at the bow and the same number in the stern—some very sharp vessels had seven pairs (1890).

CARVINGS

Carving was never extensive nor ornate on North Atlantic fishing schooners and was confined to billets, trailboards, name and hail boards, and stern boards. In the 1870s and 1880s the trailboards and billets occasionally exhibited somewhat intricate treatment of foliage but, in general, fishing schooners had sparse scrolls and small billet heads. The scrolls and name and hail boards had incised carving and were either gilded or painted yellow. The first fisherman registered in the Gloucester Custom House as having a figurehead is the "Viola," built at Essex in 1832 (68′-2″ x 18′-6″ x 7′-11″). However, "Viola" is described as having a billet when registered in 1839. Billets appeared in the registers after 1883. The schooner "Laura and Eliza," built at Essex that year, was a square stern vessel with billet (53′-10″ x 16′-1″ x 6′-7½″). By 1832 billet heads were numerous in the Gloucester registers.

Many billets were oval when small, before 1860. Rather large billets appeared in the bankers, 1855–1885; these were round.

CAP IRON AND BAIL

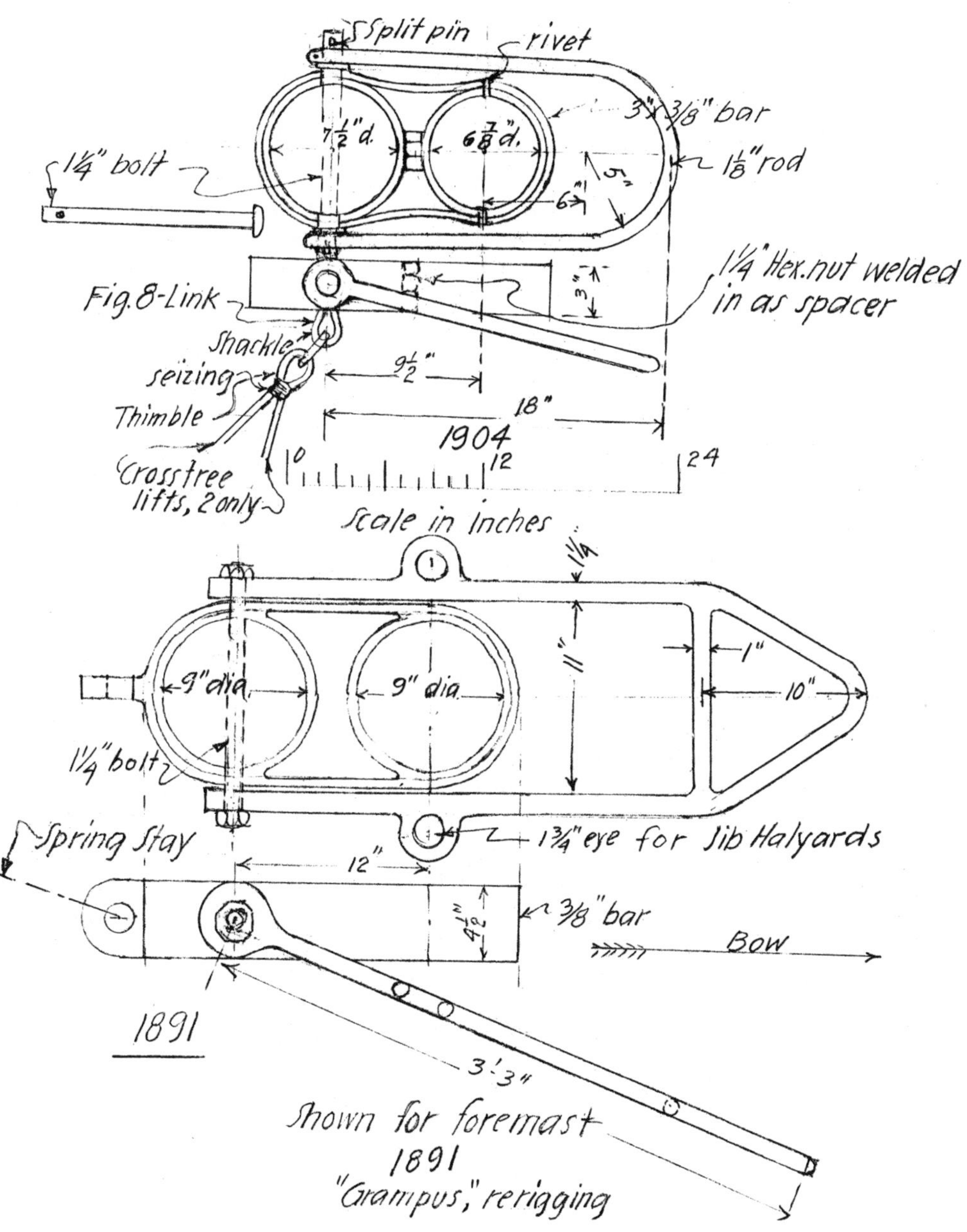

Split pin
rivet
7 1/2" d.
6 7/8" d.
3"x 3/8" bar
1 1/8" rod
1 1/4" bolt
5"
6"
1 1/4" Hex. nut welded in as spacer
Fig. 8-Link
3"
Shackle
seizing
9 1/2"
Thimble
18"
1904
Crosstree lifts, 2 only
0
12
24
Scale in inches
1 1/4
11"
1"
9" dia.
9" dia.
10"
1 1/4" bolt
Spring Stay
1 3/4" eye for Jib Halyards
12"
4 1/2"
3/8" bar
Bow
1891
3' 3"
Shown for foremast
1891
"Grampus," rerigging

CATHEADS (NOTES)

Prior to about 1845, catheads were fashioned of large knees, having a long and short arm. The long arm was inside the bulwarks, on the inboard face of a stanchion and through-bolted to outside of planking. The short arm reached outboard 24″-30″ with an iron sheave in the outer end. Later, with the introduction of the long head, the catheads were formed of small knees and were secured outside the bulwarks abreast stanchions and through-bolted. The knees were shaped to stand nearly vertical, with the heel of the lower arms faired into the after-ends of the head rails in a short, hard curve. In the 1850s the lower arms were hewn to a curve toward the bow and, in profile, the after-ends of the head rails appeared to sweep up the heel of the catheads in a more graceful curve. Viewed from outboard, the catheads appeared to cut through the bow chocks.

With the long head, the catheads had an iron brace abaft them, to the rail. This was of ½″ or ¾″ dia. iron rod with pads at each end. One end fitted under the head of the axle-bolt of the cathead, which was on its afterside. The other pad was bolted to the outboard face of the bow chock, or of the main rail cap, about 30″-36″ abaft the catheads. Until the head rails, trail-boards and knees of the head ceased to be used, iron braces were usually fitted on the after side of the catheads.

With the omission of the head rails, which began about 1885, the catheads were fashioned of small knees fastened outside bulwarks and through-bolted to inside of a stanchion. The lower arms of these catheads reached down on to the waist, almost to the plank-sheer. This form of cathead usually had iron rod braces afore and abaft it. As long as the schooners carried jibbooms the jibboom shrouds were set up with hearts, or small deadeyes, and lanyards on the foresides of the catheads. This style of cathead was employed from about 1884 to well into the 1890s, being gradually replaced, after 1885, by the iron anchor davit, fitted to unship. In the 1890s, iron anchor davits, fitted as sheet outriggers for jib and jib-topsail sheets were tried, but did not become popular and soon disappeared. The iron anchor davit always had its brace on the foreside, out of the way when the anchor was being brought to the rail. (See "Anchor Davit.")

The changes in the catheads were related to changes in the head rigging and spars, of course.

CATHEAD GEAR
FISH HOOK AND CAT STOPPER

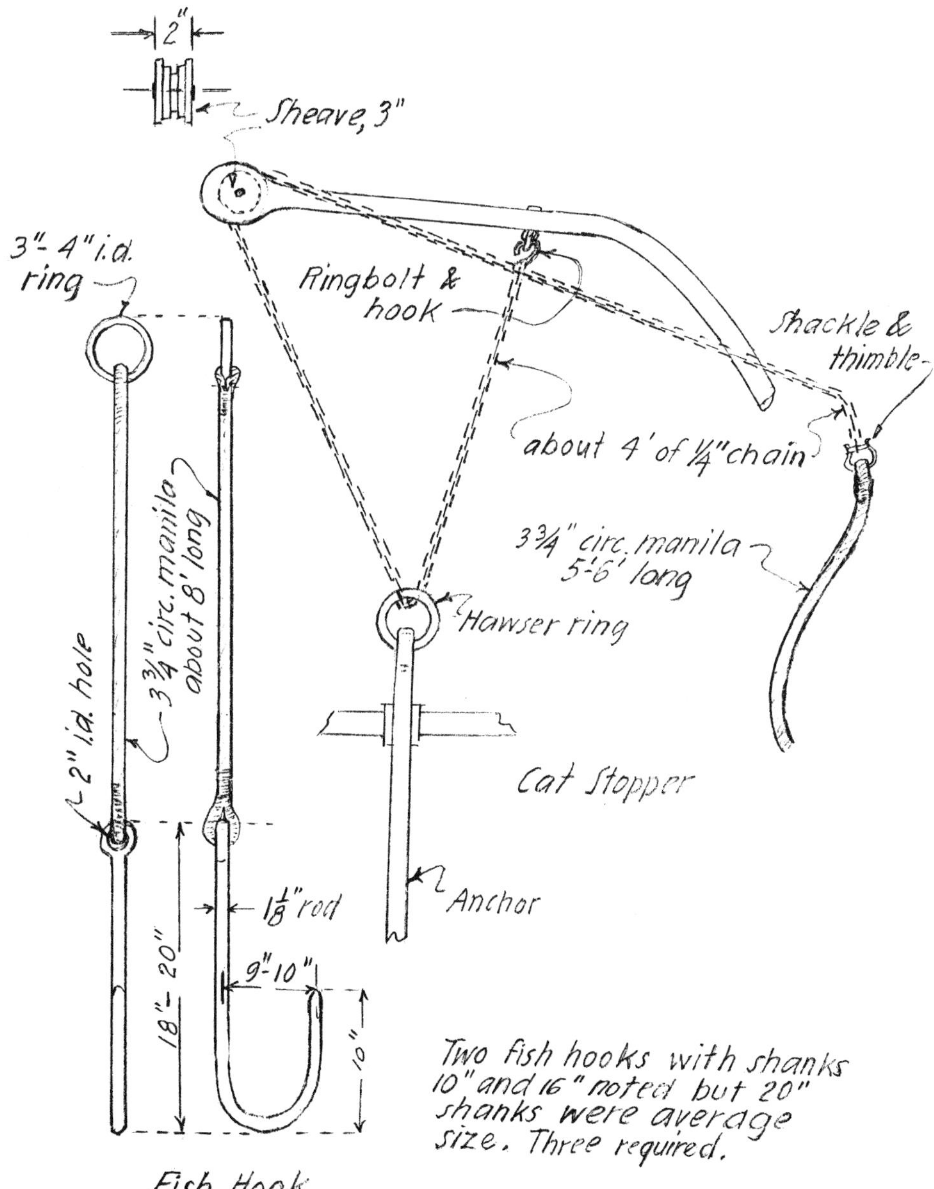
2"
Sheave, 3"
3"-4" i.d. ring
Ringbolt & hook
Shackle & thimble
about 4' of 1/4" chain
3 3/4" circ. manila about 8' long
3 3/4" circ. manila 5'-6' long
Hawser ring
2" i.d. hole
Cat Stopper
1 1/8" rod
Anchor
18"-20"
9"-10"
10"
Two fish hooks with shanks 10" and 16" noted but 20" shanks were average size. Three required.
Fish Hook

CENTERBOARDS

So far as yet discovered, only one North Atlantic fishing schooner had a centerboard. This was the "Augusta E. Herrick" designed and built by Poland and Woodbury at Gloucester, in 1877. She measured 90.6′ x 24.7′ x 7.6′. She was modelled by Daniel Poland, Jr., one of the partners in the building yard.

She was said to have sailed very fast, except when on the wind, where she did not do well. It was claimed that this was due to her centerboard being too small.

Essex builders launched a number of centerboard schooners for the New England oyster fisheries in the '80s and '90s, all relatively small vessels. Their models were usually made in Essex, however.

CHAFING MATS (NOTES)

Chafing mats were sometimes fitted to the topping lifts of fishing schooners. A long mat was fitted at the masthead, reaching from a little below the crane to a little below the gaff, when hoisted, with three evenly spaced short mats below.

When fitting for a winter voyage to Newfoundland for herring, lazyjacks were rigged, on which chafing mats were secured. In this case no chafing mats were fitted to the topping lift, apparently. The amount of chafing gear used seems to have varied with the period. Vessels fitted after 1886–1890 had fewer chafing mats than those fitted earlier.

Chafing gear was of rope yarns, made up into "baggy winkle" and wrapped around lift or jacks for the desired lengths.

CHAFING MATS ON LAZYJACKS

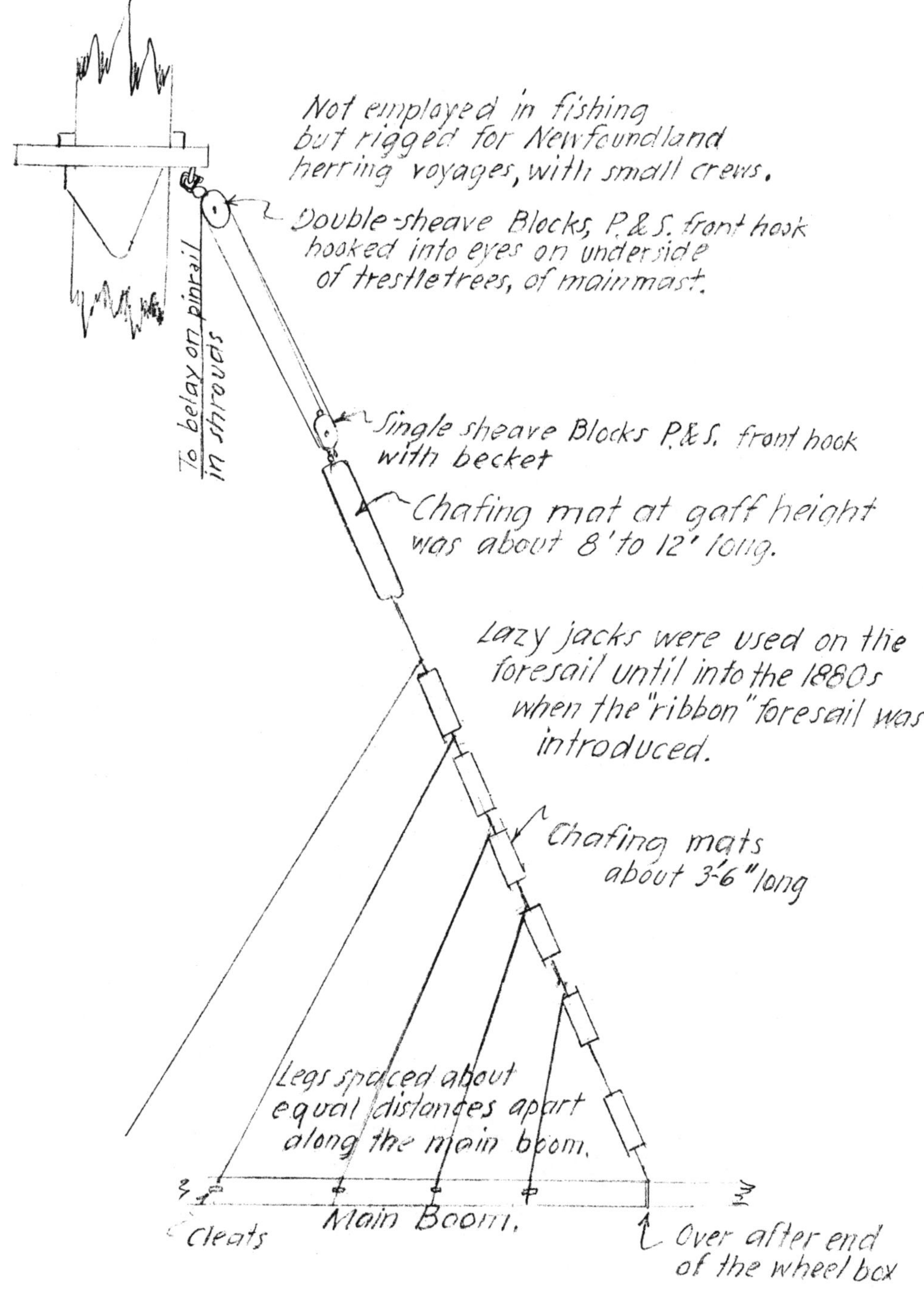
Not employed in fishing
but rigged for Newfoundland
herring voyages, with small crews.
Double-sheave Blocks, P.&S. front hook
hooked into eyes on underside
of trestletrees, of mainmast.
To belay on pinrail
in shrouds
Single sheave Blocks P.&S. front hook
with becket
Chafing mat at gaff height
was about 8' to 12' long.
Lazy jacks were used on the
foresail until into the 1880s
when the "ribbon" foresail was
introduced.
Chafing mats
about 3'6" long
Legs spaced about
equal distances apart
along the main boom.
Main Boom.
Cleats
Over after end
of the wheel box

CHAIN BOXES

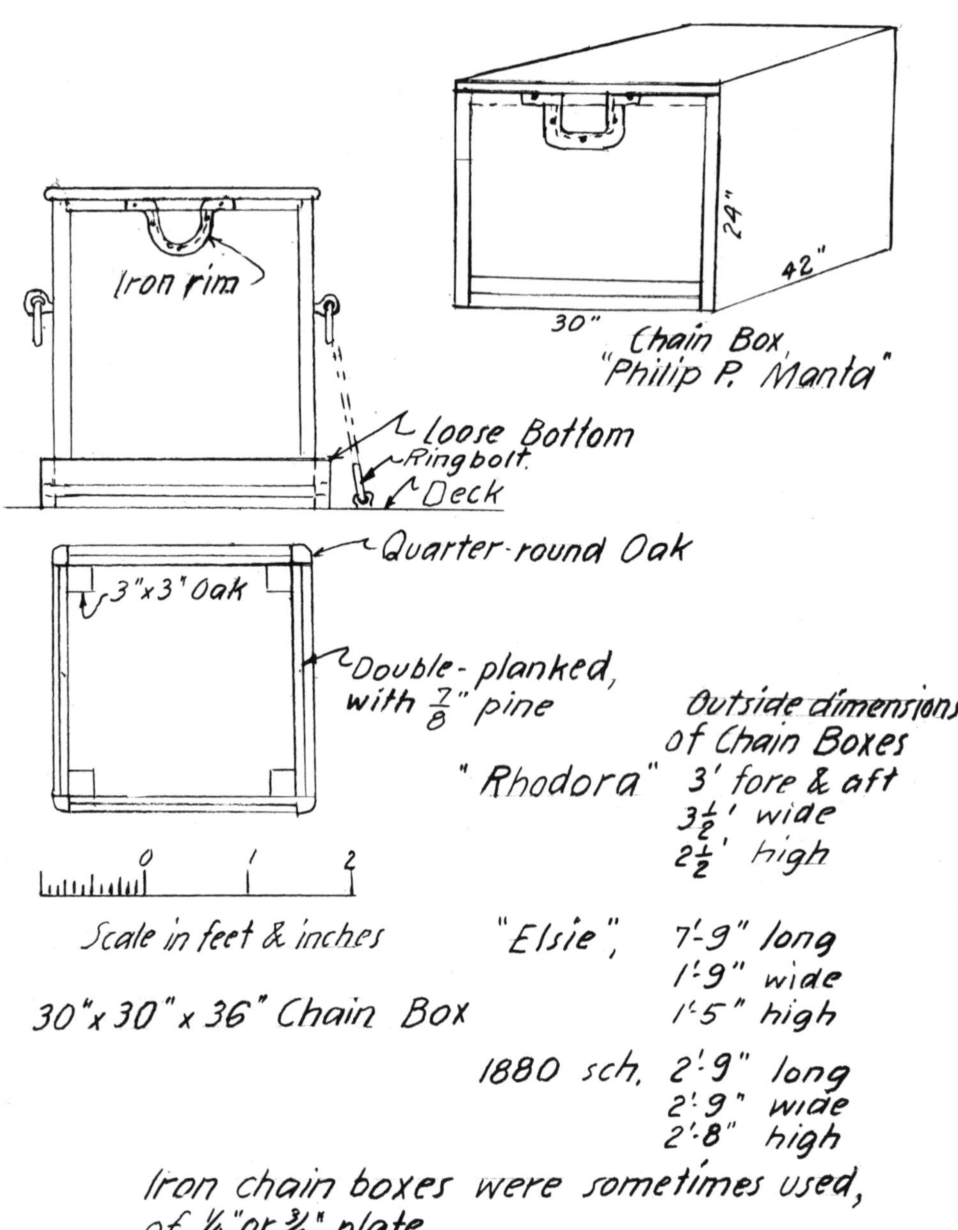
Iron rim
24"
42"
30"
Chain Box,
"Philip P. Manta"
Loose Bottom
Ringbolt.
Deck
Quarter-round Oak
3"x3" Oak
Double-planked,
with 7/8" pine
Outside dimensions
of Chain Boxes
"Rhodora" 3' fore & aft
3½' wide
2½' high
0 1 2
Scale in feet & inches
"Elsie", 7'-9" long
1'-9" wide
1'-5" high
30"x 30" x 36" Chain Box
1880 sch. 2'-9" long
2'-9" wide
2'-8" high
Iron chain boxes were sometimes used,
of ¼" or ⅜" plate.

CHAIN PLATES

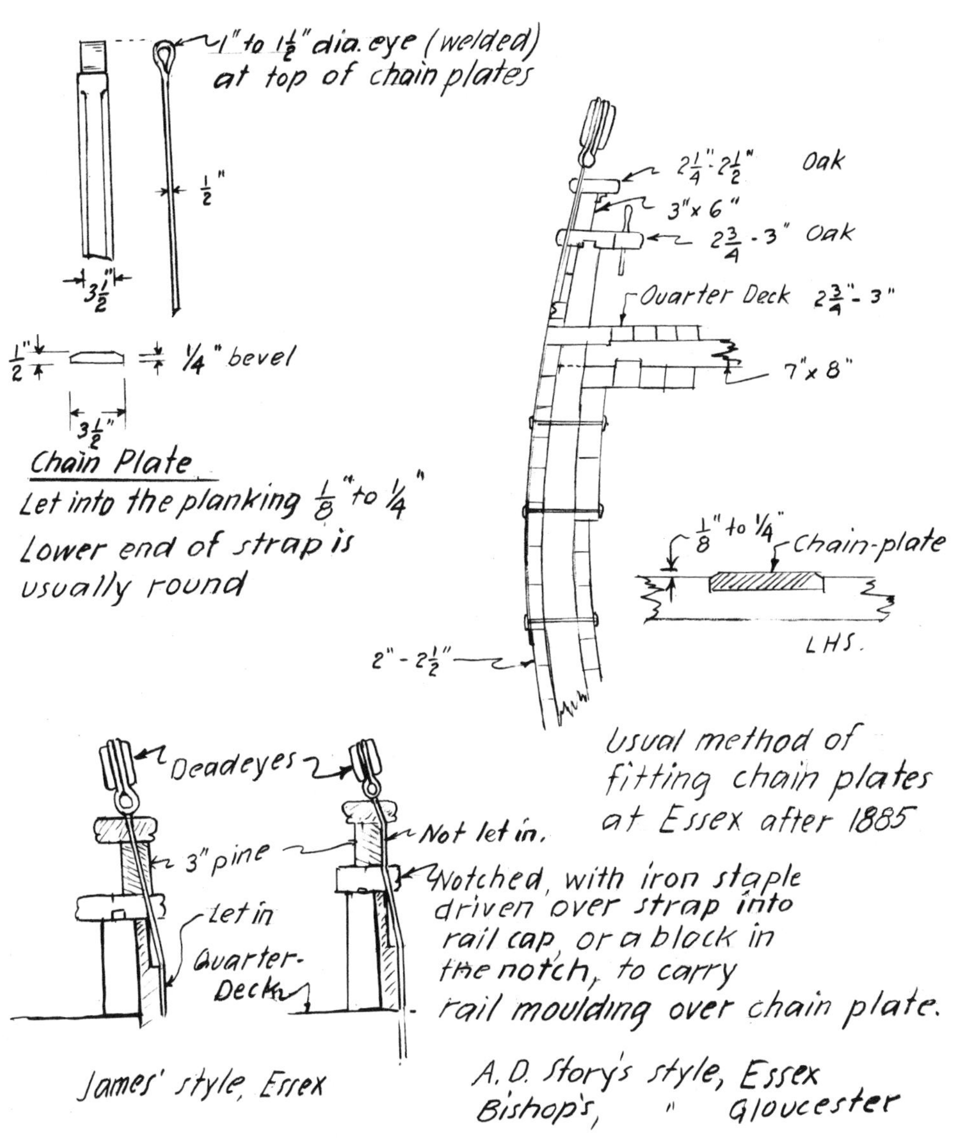
1" to 1½" dia. eye (welded) at top of chain plates
½"
3½"
½"
¼" bevel
3½"
Chain Plate
Let into the planking ⅛" to ¼"
Lower end of strap is usually round
2¼"-2½" Oak
3"x 6"
2¾-3" Oak
Quarter Deck 2¾"-3"
7"x 8"
⅛" to ¼"
Chain-plate
LHS.
2"-2½"
Usual method of fitting chain plates at Essex after 1885
Deadeyes
3" pine
Let in
Quarter-Deck
Not let in.
Notched, with iron staple driven over strap into rail cap, or a block in the notch, to carry rail moulding over chain plate.
James' style, Essex
A. D. Story's style, Essex
Bishop's, " Gloucester
Not to scale

CHAIN PLATES

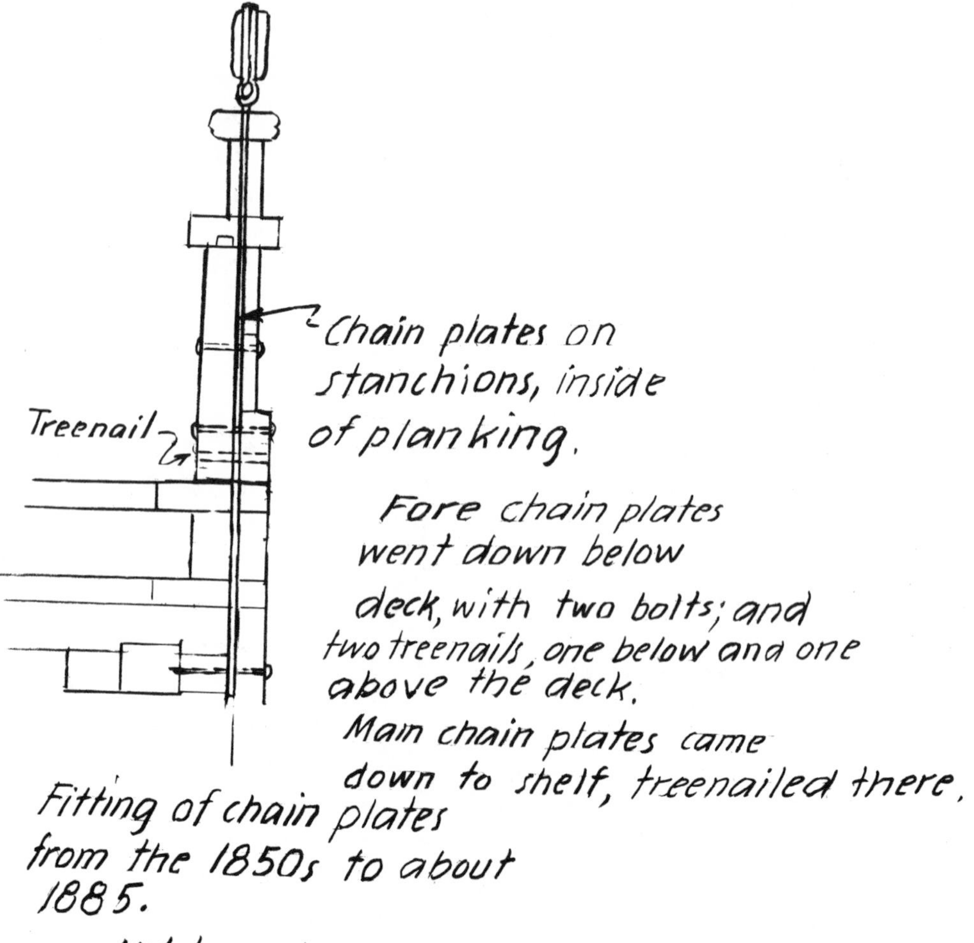
Chain plates on stanchions, inside of planking.
Treenail
Fore chain plates went down below deck, with two bolts; and two treenails, one below and one above the deck.
Main chain plates came down to shelf, treenailed there.

Fitting of chain plates from the 1850s to about 1885.

Not to scale

CHAIN PLATE FITTINGS

Staple bolts and eyebolts abaft aftermost chainplates

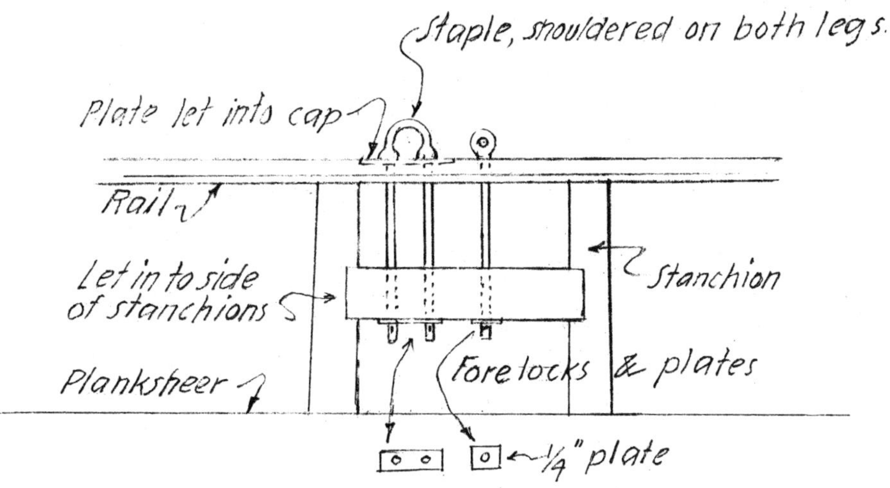
Staple, shouldered on both legs.
Plate let into cap
Rail
Let in to side of stanchions
Stanchion
Planksheer
Fore locks & plates
1/4" plate

Not to scale.

Often used for topmast backstays, when not set up at the break. Main boom tackle pendant hooked in this staple when off the wind.

CHAIN PLATES (NOTES)

Where the chain plates cross the top of the waist, the waist plank was notched a little for the chain plate in order that it might bear on the pine bulwark plank above the waist.

Chain plates of "Puritan" (1887) and "Julia Costa" (1888) were outside the planking, and this was also true of "Grampus" (1885). It seems apparent that the abandonment of the old practice of placing chain plates on the frames inside the planking occurred before 1885, for by 1886–1888 it was standard practice to place chain plates outside the hull planking. The old practice of putting the chain plates inside the plank seems to have been introduced in the 1850s at Essex and Gloucester.

Passing the chain plates through the main rail cap and through the monkey rail and cap, as practiced by the James Yard, was once common practice at Essex.

When the chain plates were inside the planking, the fore chain plates reached down below the deck, the others went only a little below the top of the waist. The chain plates were fastened with bolts through the waist, chain plate and stanchion, and the stanchions had two treenails through stanchion and plank below. One vessel went twenty years before it was discovered, during a repair, that only one treenail was holding a shroud stanchion. The Bishop shipyards in Gloucester usually fitted the chain plates as A. D. Story did, all outside the planking. [L.H.S., J.P.S., A.D.S., E.F.]

"CHECKER" OR DIVIDING BOARDS

One at each end of cabin trunk and one in the middle. The boards are 2" thick.

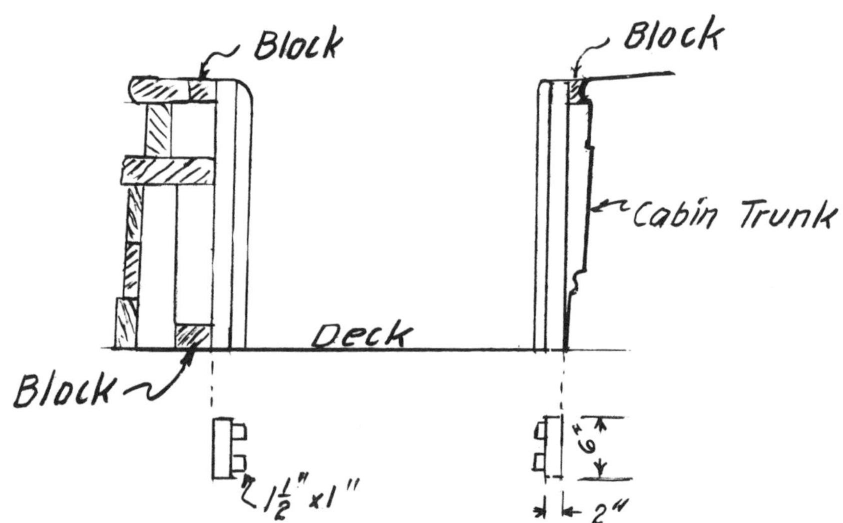
Block
Block
Cabin Trunk
Deck
Block
6"
1½"x1"
2"

CHOCKS, IRON

Four iron chocks, galvanized, were fitted, two at the bow, on the bow chock rail and two aft, one on each quarter on the quarterdeck rail cap. The after chocks were made with a bend so that their bases followed the curve of the rail cap at the quarters.

Bow chocks were located a little forward of the catheads or anchor davits, or about half way between davit and ℄ of hawse pipe. Stern chocks line up with quarter bitts, parallel to ℄ of vessel.

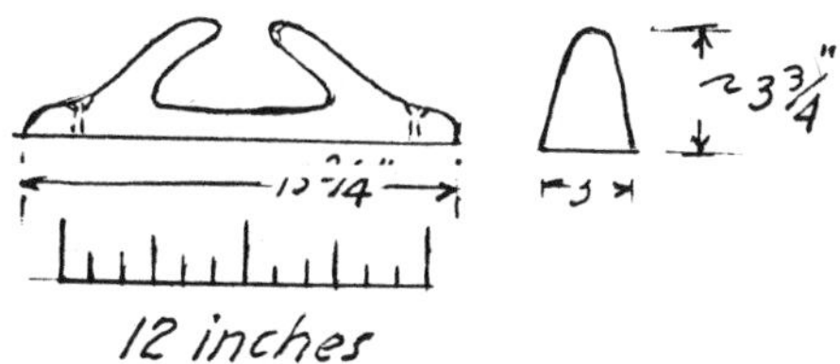
3¾"
12 inches

CHOCK RAILS AND BULWARK PADS

The bow chock rail was of oak, running from the afterside of the knightheads to within 4″-8″ of the foreside of the foremast swifter chain plate. The top of the knightheads were usually cut off about 4″-4½″ high above the top of the main rail cap. The top of the bow chock faired into the top of the knightheads. Gradually reducing in height, it ended 3″ high, cut off perpendicularly at its after-end. It was usually rounded off in plan view here. The bow chock rail was about 3½″ thick. In knockabouts the chock rail capped both knightheads, and hawse timbers, running to the stem, tapering aft with the after-end about 6′-10′ forward of the formast swifter chain plate, the dimensions as given above. Chocks spiked to rail caps, to protect the rail cap and chock rail from damage in boarding the anchor, iron straps, ½″ x 1½″ and 36″-48″ long, were nailed to the rail cap and chock rail, two to the top of the chock rail and one inside, as close to the top as possible. Hatch nails were used to secure those. A wooden filler piece, 36″-48″ long, was nailed to the outside of the chock rail and to the outer top of the main rail cap. A plank pad was fitted between the waist and the underside of the rail cap; this was as long as the upper pad and straps. Sometimes an iron strap was nailed to the outboard face of the main rail cap. The fore-ends of the pads and straps were about 48″-54″ abaft the anchor davits, or catheads.

The after chock rails ran from a point 12″-18″ abaft the aftermost main shroud chain plates to abreast the mainboom crotch or after-end of the wheelbox. These were 3″-4″ high, 2½″ thick. The ends rounded down in profile, square in plan. These chock rails were spiked to the monkey rail.

In schooners, built prior to about 1910, the space between the waist and the underside of the rail cap, extending from the first stanchion of the bulwarks forward of the great beam to the first stanchions abaft the aftermost chain plates of the foremast shrouds, was protected by vertical fenders. These were of oak 2½″-3″ wide, 1½″-1¾″ thick, placed outside each stanchion and spiked through all. After about 1910 these were replaced by a plank pad running from 12″ forward of the great beam to 10′-15′ forward and covering the pine bulwarks from waist to main rail cap.

CHOCK RAILS

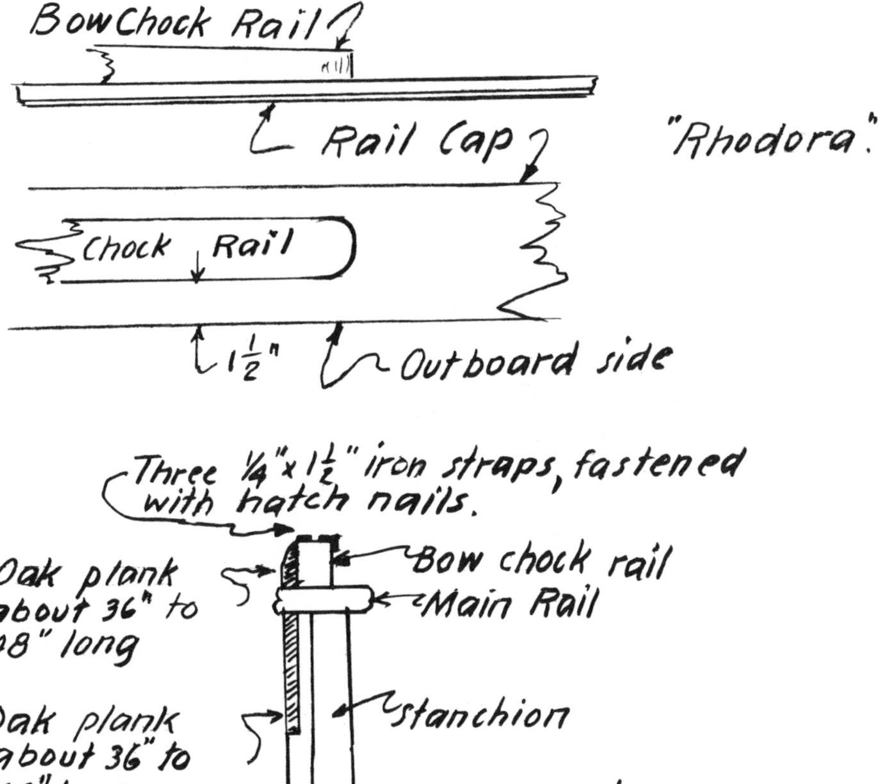
Bow Chock Rail
Rail Cap
"Rhodora."
Chock Rail
1½"
Outboard side
Three ¼" x 1½" iron straps, fastened with hatch nails.
Bow chock rail
Main Rail
Oak plank about 36" to 48" long
Stanchion
Oak plank about 36" to 48" long
Deck

Pads or fillers between rail cap and waist, and on outside of bow chock, with iron strapping, to protect planking-damage in catting the anchor. Fore-ends of pads and strapping were about 48" to 54" abaft the catheads.

CLEW IRON

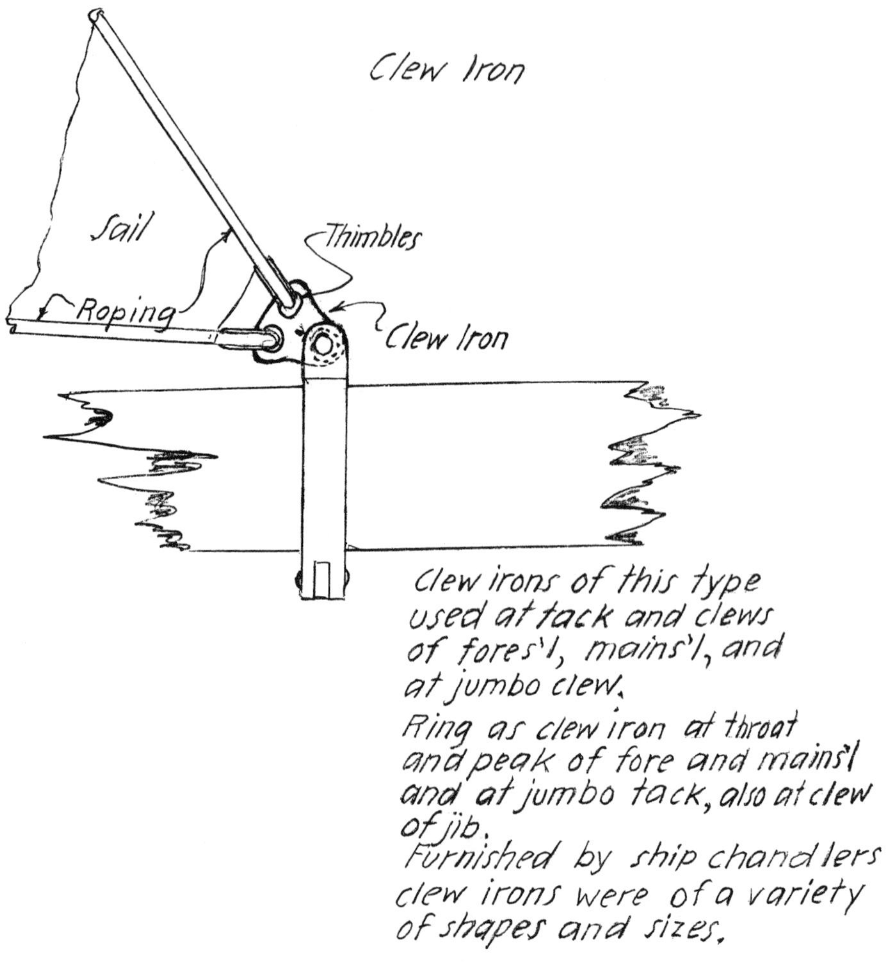
Clew Iron
Sail
Thimbles
Roping
Clew Iron
Clew irons of this type used at tack and clews of fores'l, mains'l, and at jumbo clew.
Ring as clew iron at throat and peak of fore and mains'l and at jumbo tack, also at clew of jib.
Furnished by ship chandlers clew irons were of a variety of shapes and sizes.

CLIPPER BOWS (NOTES)

Headwork, like that of the "Julia Costa" (1888), was fitted to some fishing schooners, but this fashion was short-lived—three or four years. The "Costa's" head may have been inspired by the old yacht "America's" head.

The simple billet and scroll gammon knee came into fashion in the early 1890s, following the cutwater of "Fredonia" of 1889, or rather of her near sister, the "Nellie Dixon." This, in its initial stage of development, projected 7′ to 7′-9″ forward of the stem rabbet at billet height and was braced by an iron rod on each side. These ran from a little abaft the billet carving to the hull a little abaft the hawse casting. The rods were bolted at each end and were nearly parallel to the waist cove line; the rods were straight in profile.

The introduction of the bowsprit shrouds spreader in 1887 led to their use with the gammon knee cutwater. Placed either through the cutwater close to the stem rabbet, it could be used to stiffen the rod braces, the "iron head rails." These were passed over the spreader and were fastened to it, at about halfway outboard. This usually required the rods to be slightly bent at the spreader, in plan view. When the spreaders were discarded, in the middle '90s, iron bar spreaders, one on each side of the stem and through-bolted, were used. (See "Bows.")

In the late 1890s, the projection of the small billet or the eagle-head, from the stem rabbet was often reduced to 4′-9″ to 5′-0″ by 1903. Some measurements taken from schooners show that the "Mary T. Fallon," built in 1901, had a head projecting 6′-5″; the "Philip P. Manta," built in 1902, had a head projecting 6′-3″; the "Avalon," built in 1903, had a head projecting 5′-3″. These may be taken as about average lengths for the schooners above 90′ tonnage length. There is evidence that this range of length of cutwater was not strictly adhered to, however, for photographs show that some schooners built 1890–1896 had short cutwaters, while some later vessels had long heads. The rake or flare of the stem rabbet would determine the length of the cutwater to some degree, perhaps. The greater the flare of the stem rabbet, the shorter the head might then be a satisfactory rule. Actually, this was a matter of artistic design so might be a matter of "eye" on the part of the man "setting the head."

There was a period before 1885 when the builders' name was placed on the trailboards in an oval frame of carved vines, just forward of the stem rabbet. This disappeared with the trailboards in the 1880s.

The noble-wood went out of use with the appearance of the gammon knee head in the early 1890s.

The last fishing schooner built in Essex with a clipper bow was the "Athlete" (1906) designed by Arthur Binney, according to some authorities. In 1906 the round-stem "Good Luck" was launched, the last schooner designed by George Melville McClain.

Some of the gammon knee clipper-bow schooners had no real billet, the cutwater ending a very small half-circle in which the scroll began ("Ethel B. Jacobs").

COMPANIONWAYS, FORECASTLE

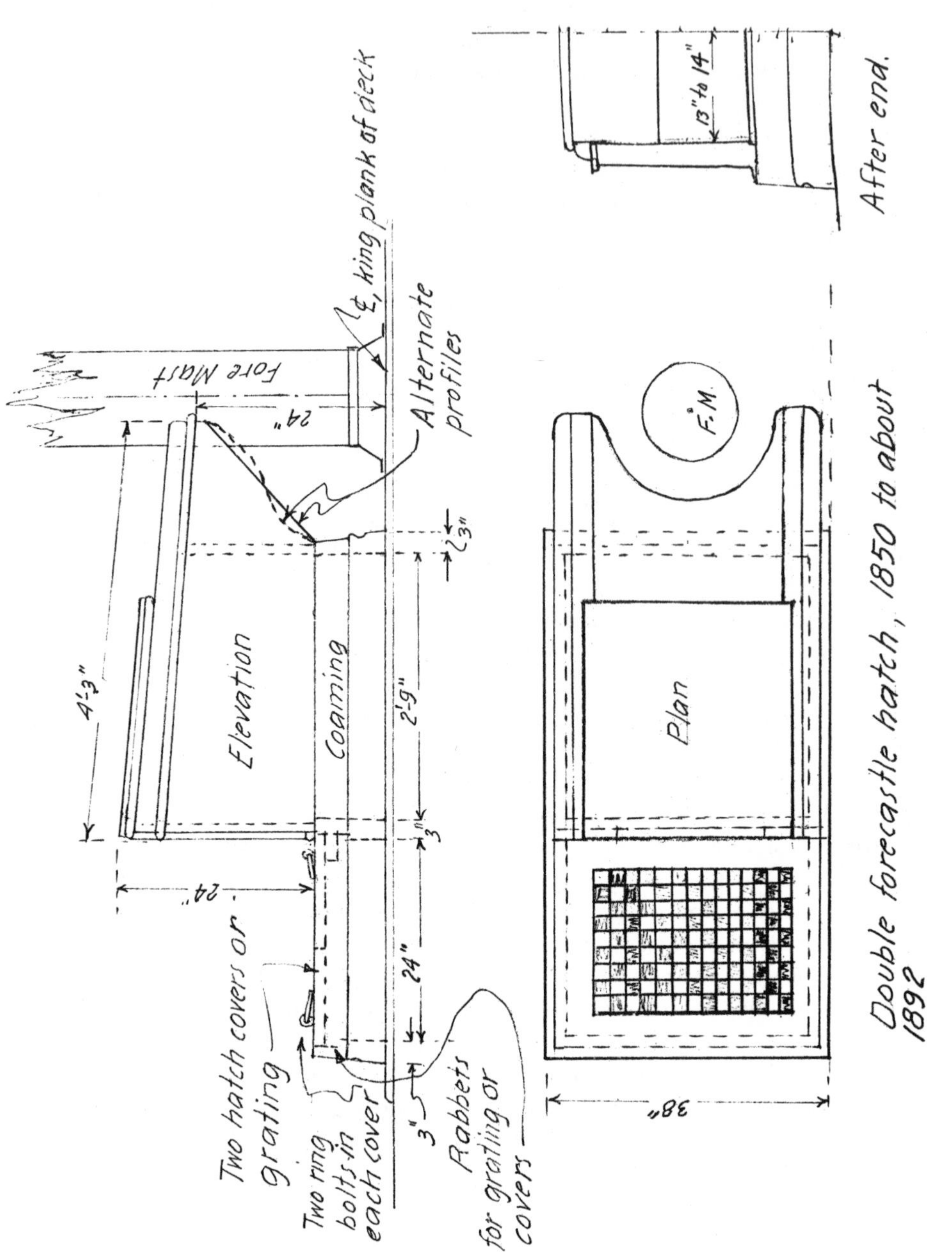
Fore Mast
℄, king plank of deck
Alternate profiles
24"
4'-3"
Elevation
Coaming
2'-9"
3"
24"
Two hatch covers or grating
Two ring bolts in each cover
Rabbets for grating or covers
13" to 14"
After end.
F.M.
Plan
38"
Double forecastle hatch, 1850 to about 1892

COMPANIONWAYS, FORECASTLE

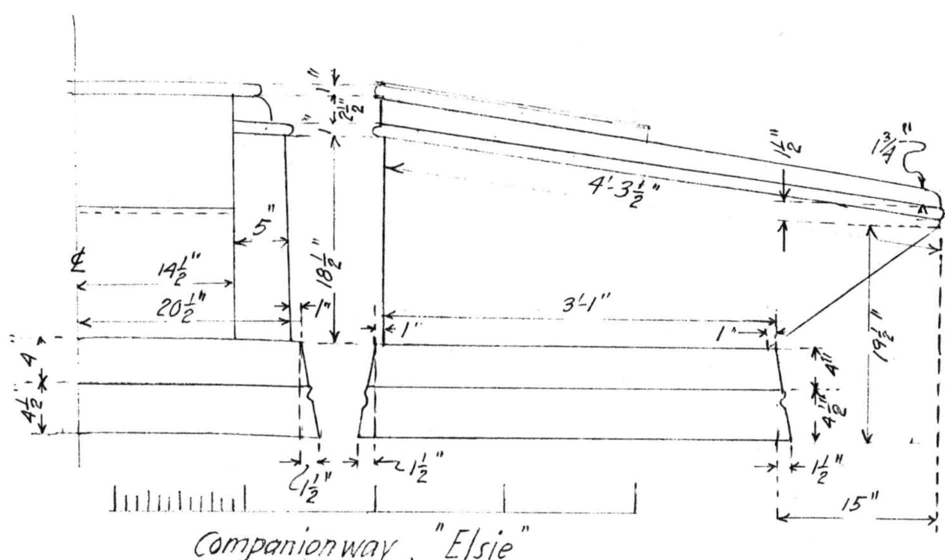
3'-1"
15"

Companionway, "Elsie"

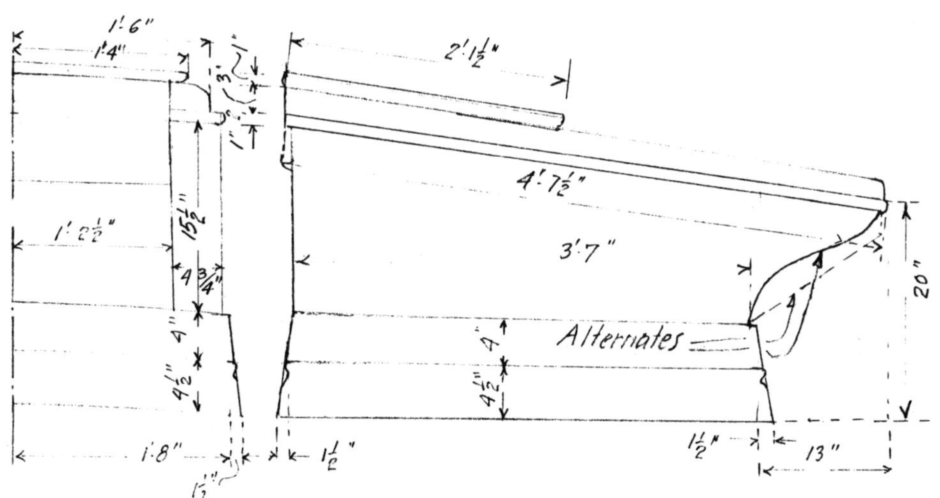
3'7"
Alternates
20"
13"

Companionway, 1891 (1885-1901)
Dimensions vary in all companionways to some extent.

COMPANIONWAYS, FORECASTLE

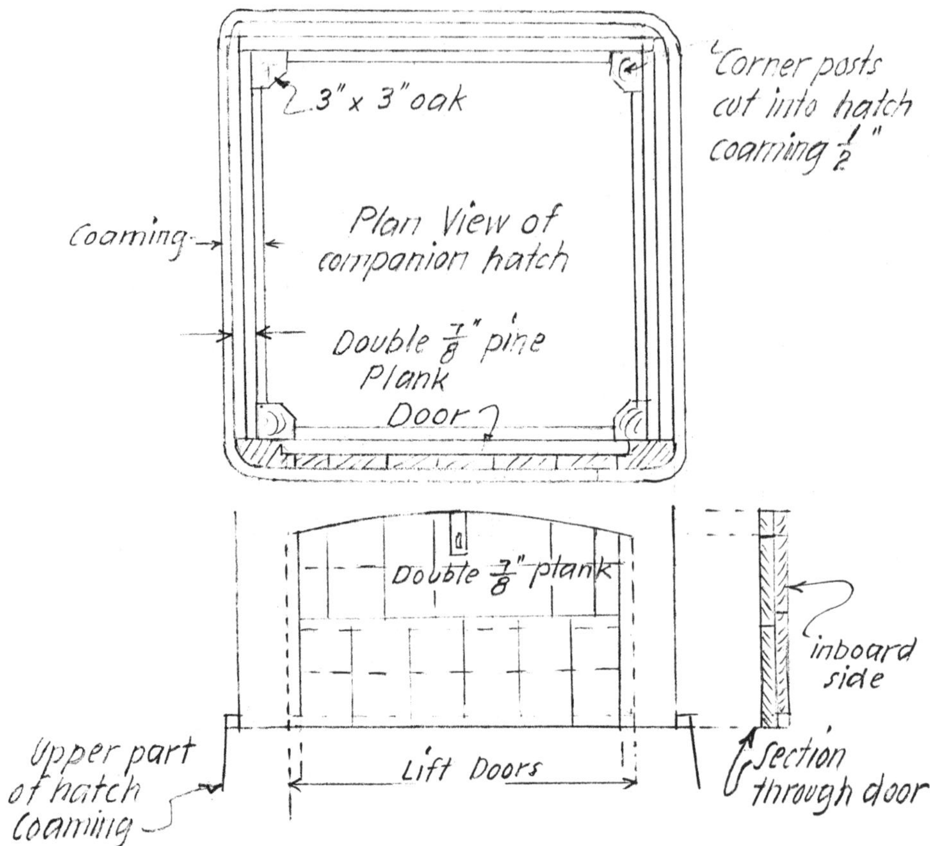
Corner posts cut into hatch coaming 1/2"
3" x 3" oak
Plan View of companion hatch
Coaming
Double 7/8" pine Plank Door
Double 7/8" plank
inboard side
Upper part of hatch Coaming
Lift Doors
Section through door

Lift doors made of two skins, inner horizontal, outer vertical, with hasp on hatch cover; lock on upper section of door.

COMPANIONWAYS, FORECASTLE

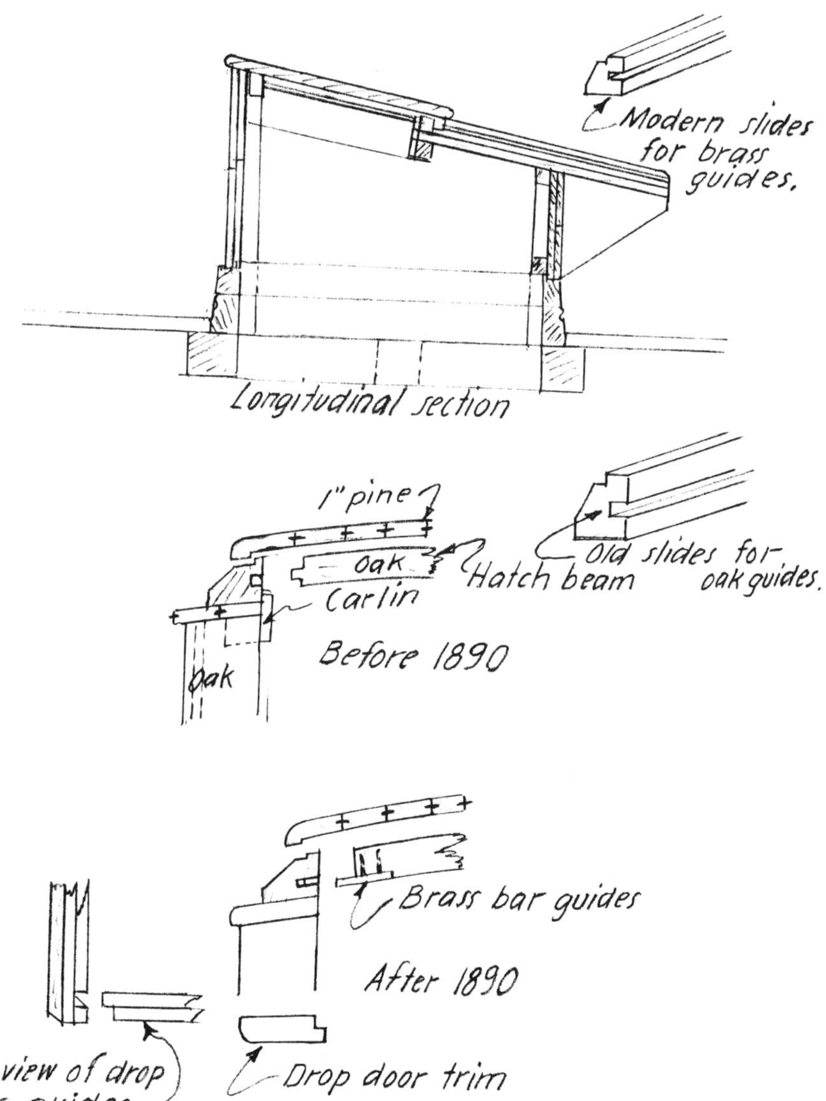
Modern slides for brass guides.
Longitudinal section
1" pine
oak
Hatch beam
Old slides for oak guides.
Carlin
Before 1890
oak
Brass bar guides
After 1890
Plan view of drop door guides
Drop door trim

COMPANIONWAYS, FORECASTLE (NOTES)

The double or combination forecastle hatch consisted of a sliding top companionway and a small, low, supply hatch immediately abaft the threshold of the companionway lift doors. The sills included both hatches. The supply hatch was no higher than the sills and was fitted with a grating to unship and two plank covers, to bar from below. This hatch was used to pass supplies down to the galley; at sea it was barred and caulked.

The companionway hatch was placed close abaft the foremast; the fore-end of the top was hollowed at the center so that the sliding cover came against the mast when fully open. In the early vessels the companionway was smaller than in later schooners.

The combination hatch was rarely used in the market or mackerel fishermen but often fitted in vessels intended for any of the offshore banks fisheries. The dimensions of these hatches varied somewhat, vessel to vessel. In the '90s, when large schooners became common, the combination hatch was replaced by the single hatch companionway and a small hatch was built some feet abaft the companionway, between this and the main hatch.

COMPASS

Gloucester schooners, before 1840, had dry compasses, in which the card was balanced on a needle. The box in which is was mounted was 7″-9″ square and 3″ deep. [L.H.S.] The compass was in a box binnacle, or stand, on deck as was usual in the pinkies, lighted with whale oil lamps.

When cabin trunks became popular, in the 1840s, the spirit compass came into use, placed inside the afterend of the trunk, in a glazed, oval port, covered outside with a sliding cover, moving athwartship. A lamp alongside, on the compass, was on the starboard side of the cabin trunk companionway, and often the latter was off-center to port as much as its width.

This compass mounting proved so satisfactory that it remained in use to the end of the schooners in the fisheries.

COUNTER

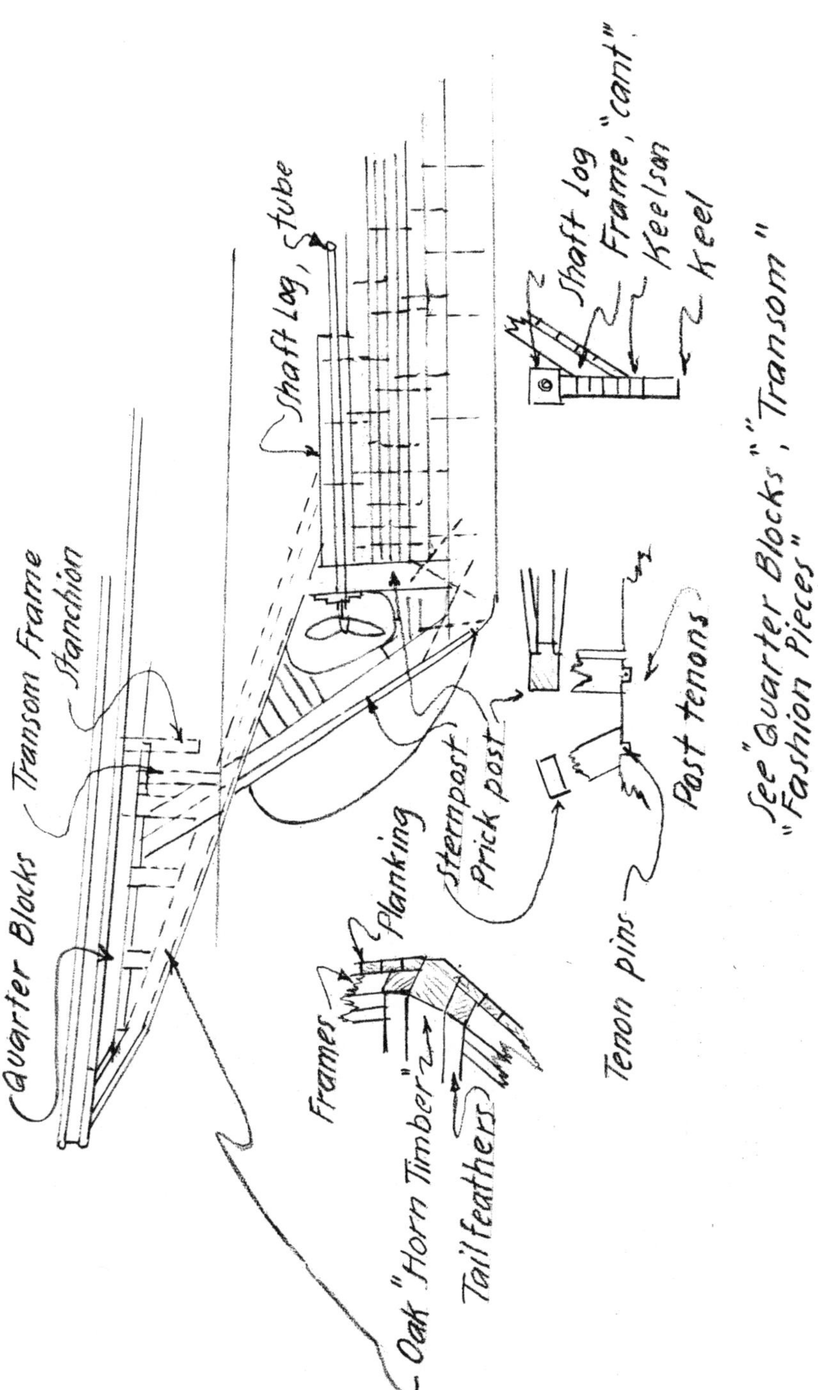
Quarter Blocks
Transom Frame
Stanchion
Shaft Log, tube
Shaft log
Frame, "cant"
Keelson
Keel
Planking
Sternpost
Prick post
Post tenons
Frames
Oak "Horn Timber"
Tail feathers
Tenon pins
See "Quarter Blocks", "Transom"
"Fashion Pieces"

COUNTER

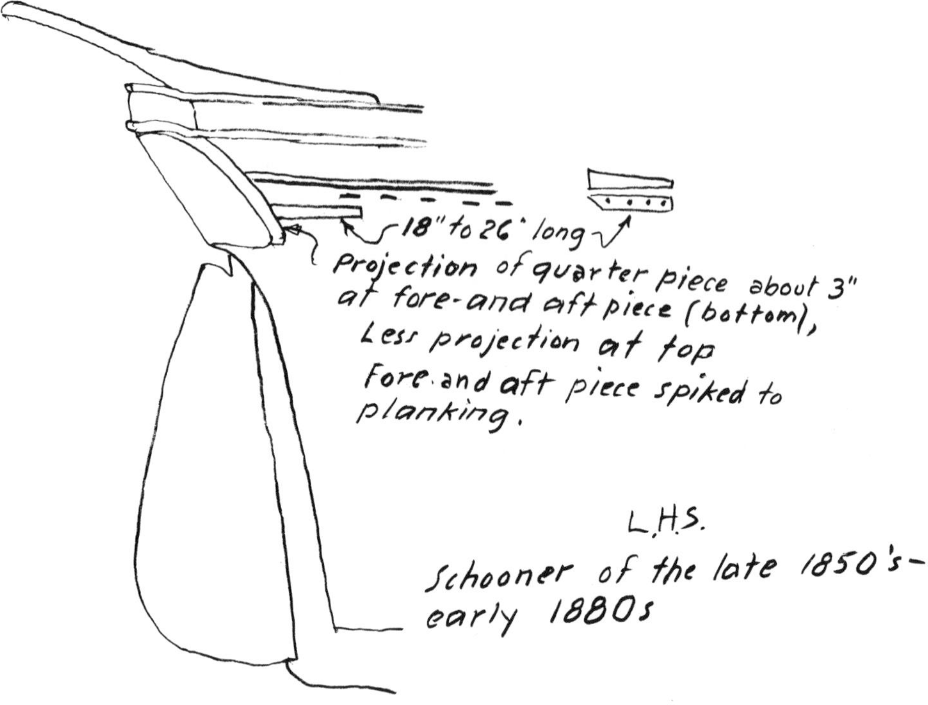
18" to 26" long
Projection of quarter piece about 3" at fore-and aft piece (bottom),
Less projection at top
Fore and aft piece spiked to planking.
L.H.S.
Schooner of the late 1850's–early 1880s

COUNTER

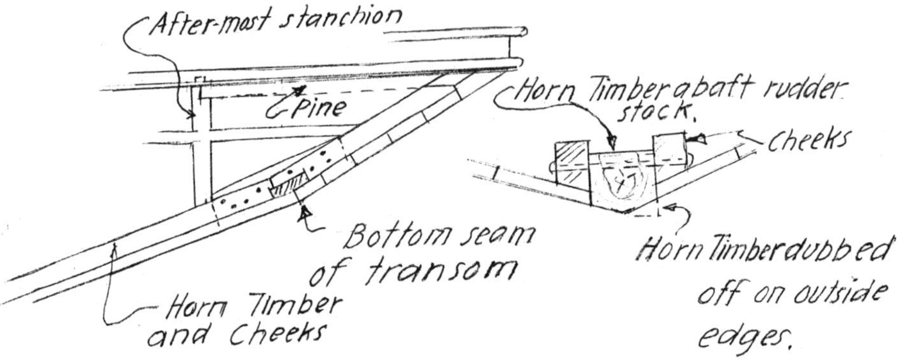
After-most stanchion
Pine
Bottom seam of transom
Horn Timber and Cheeks
Horn Timber abaft rudder stock.
Cheeks
Horn Timber dubbed off on outside edges.

Planking of transom mitred into side planking after fashion pieces went out of use. See "Fashion Pieces," "Quarter Blocks," "Transom."

COVE LINES

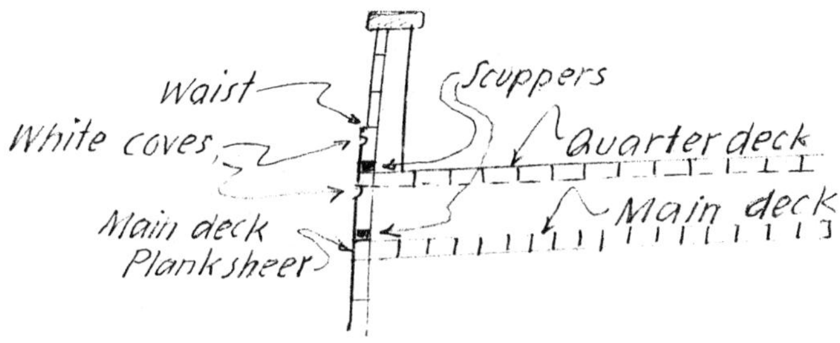
Waist
White coves
Scuppers
Quarter deck
Main deck
Main deck
Planksheer

After painted bands, multicolored, went out of fashion, coves about 3/4" wide were cut into the planking. One cove was an inch or thereabouts below the waist line and well above the quarterdeck scuppers. The lower cove had its top along the lower edge of the planksheer of the maindeck. They were both painted white in the 1860s and 1870s. In the 1880s the upper cove was painted stone or chrome yellow. Discharge from the quarterdeck and maindeck scuppers stained these coves, so the fashion did not last long. In the late 1880s the cove just below the waist line alone survived, painted yellow. This practice continued to the end of schooner construction at Essex.

CROSSTREES (NOTES)

Until the mid-80s, two straight crosstrees were employed, with futtocks and two topmast shrouds a side. In addition, the topmast backstay and outrigger were carried. The crosstrees were much shorter than they became with the later types of crosstrees. In 1885 the crosstrees were one-third the topmast length; trestletree to shoulder. In a few vessels the fore spreader on each mast was placed forward of the topmast heel, but schooners of the 1870s and early 1880s appear to have commonly had the fore-crosstrees between lower masthead and topmast heel, with short trestletrees.

In schooners rigged permanently without fore-topmasts, as in the "sharpshooters" of the late 1840s and 1850s, no fore-crosstrees were used but short trestletrees were fitted to hold the standing rigging aloft on the foremast.

It is apparent that a variety of crosstrees were employed during the late 1880s and in the 1890s. Most variation was in the forms of the iron braces with the long crosstrees, as far as can now be determined.

In the early 1900s, the long crosstrees were 15′ long, the short after-crosstrees, 7′-6″, in a 95′ (registered length) schooner's mainmast. On the foremast the long crosstrees were 14′ long, the short crosstrees were 7′ long in a vessel of this size.

The crosstrees tapered on the bottom. The after short crosstrees on each mast had no taper, as a rule, on the fore and after sides in the 1900s. But earlier, in the 1890s, photographs show taper. The long crosstrees were sometimes straight on the afterside; all taper was on the foreside. Some had a slight curve, say 1½″ setback at the ends. In a 95′ vessel, the long crosstrees were 5″ fore-and-aft and 4″ thick. The outboard ends were about 3″-3½″ fore-and-aft, due to taper, and about 3½″ thick. These dimensions are for a vessel having 40′ topmasts; if she had 50′ topmasts the crosstrees would be about 1′-0″ longer than with the 40′ topmast. With the long and short crosstrees the length of the short crosstree was one-half that of the long crosstree plus the diameter of the lower masthead at trestletrees.

The iron brace used in place of the short crosstrees, with the single, long crosstrees was of 1″-1¼″ rod flattened into a strap, about ½″ x 1¾″, extending across the trestletrees abaft the masthead and outboard to the peak halyard fairlead, say 8″-12″ from the outboard faces of the trestletrees, P. & S. The ends of the braces were formed into pads about 1¾″ x 3½″ to take two bolts each. Three bolts secured the brace abaft the masthead to the blocking and the two trestletrees. Metal fairleads were pivot-bolted to the brace, about 6″ from the outboard face of each trestletree, P. &. S. standing clear so they could swing.

The big racing schooners like "Columbia" had lifts to the ends of the short crosstrees. "Columbia's" long crosstrees were 15′-6″ long, the short were 6′-6″ on the mainmast; the long 13′-0″ and the short 6′-3″ on the foremast.

CROSSTREES, END BRACES OR "STRUT"

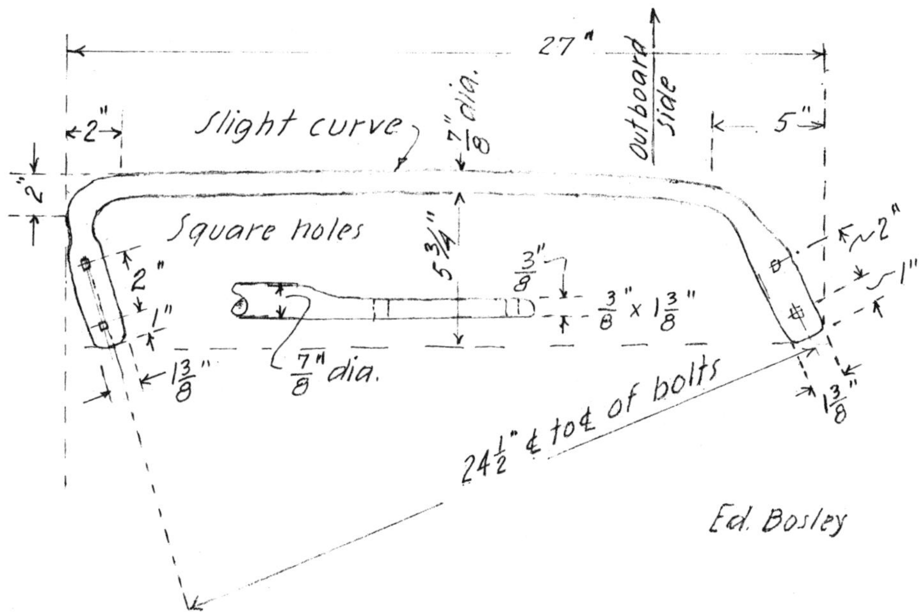
27"
Outboard side
2"
5"
Slight curve
7/8" dia.
2"
Square holes
5 3/4"
2"
1"
3/8"
3/8" x 1 3/8"
~2"
~1"
1 3/8"
7/8" dia.
24 1/2" ℄ to ℄ of bolts
1 3/8"
Ed. Bosley

Braces of this type fitted to long and short crosstrees. Angles at which pads stand to brace determined by fitting to work. The rod usually has a slight bow outboard, Port and Starb'd braces required for each mast 3/8" dia. shouldered eyebolts fitted to braces for lifts.

CROSSTREES FOR HEMP RIGGING

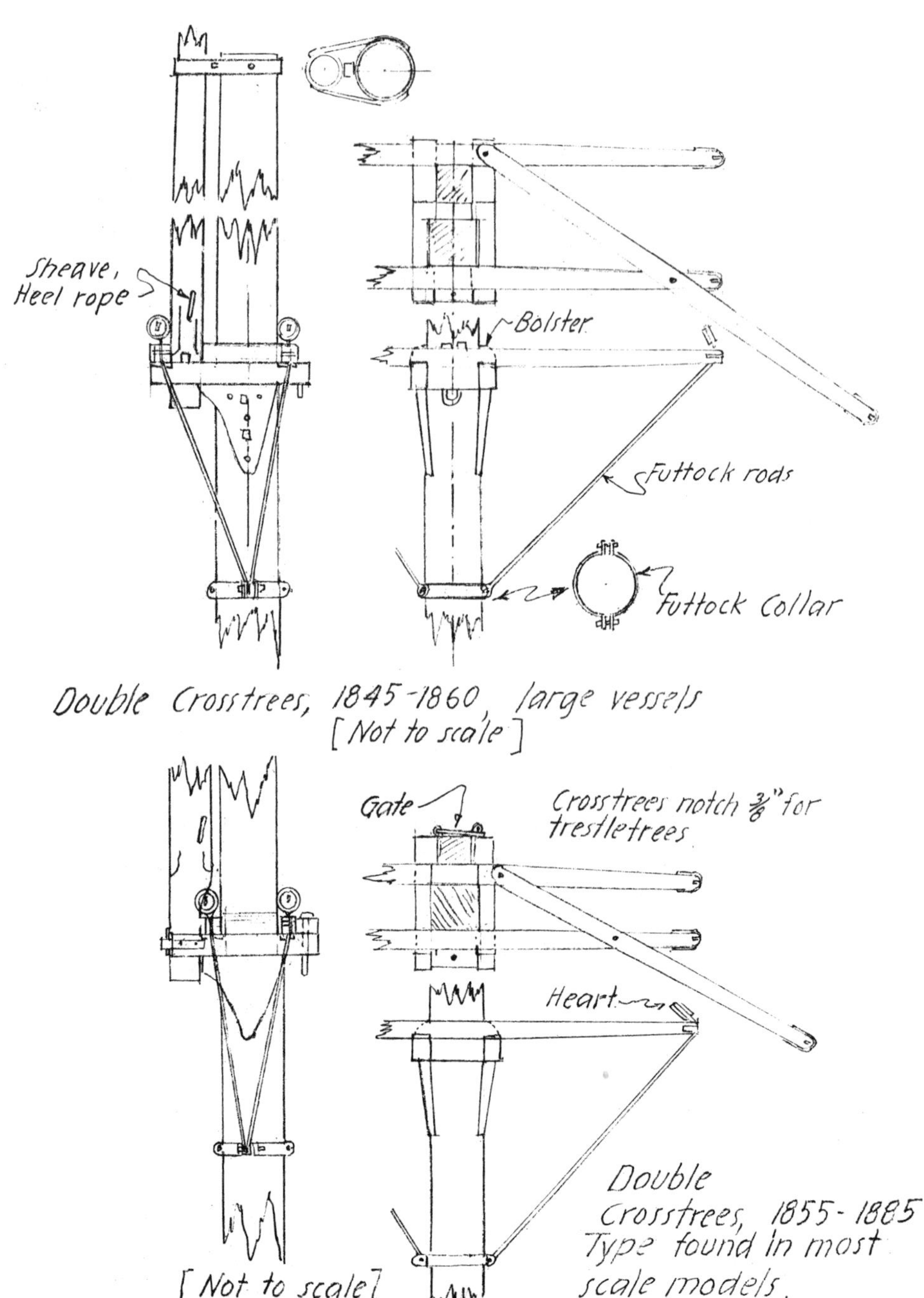
Sheave,
Heel rope
Bolster
Futtock rods
Futtock Collar
Double Crosstrees, 1845-1860, large vessels
[Not to scale]
Gate
Crosstrees notch 3/8" for
trestletrees
Heart
Double
Crosstrees, 1855-1885
Type found in most
scale models.
[Not to scale]

CROSSTREES, SINGLE LONG

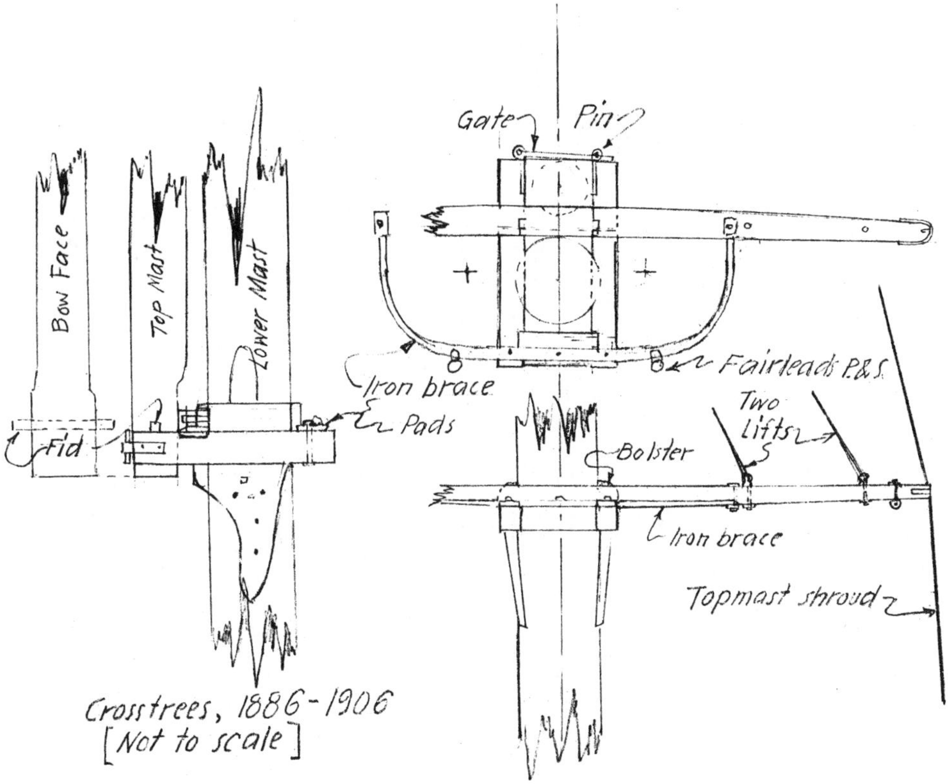

Crosstrees, 1886-1906
[Not to scale]

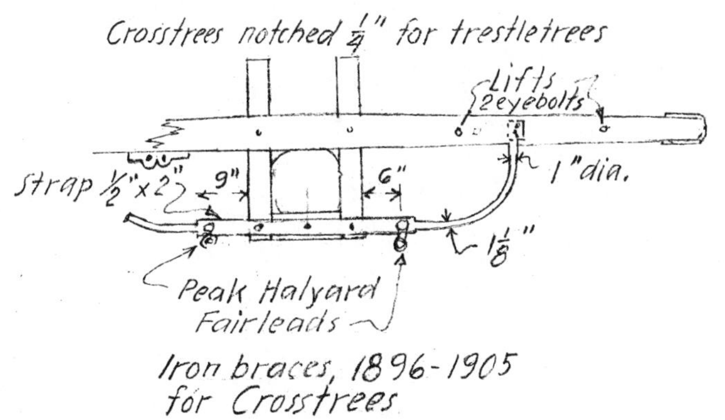
Crosstrees notched 1/4" for trestletrees
Lifts
2 eyebolts
1" dia.
Strap 1/2"x2"
9"
6"
1 1/8"
Peak Halyard
Fairleads

Iron braces, 1896-1905
for Crosstrees

CROSSTREES, SINGLE LONG, 1887–1930

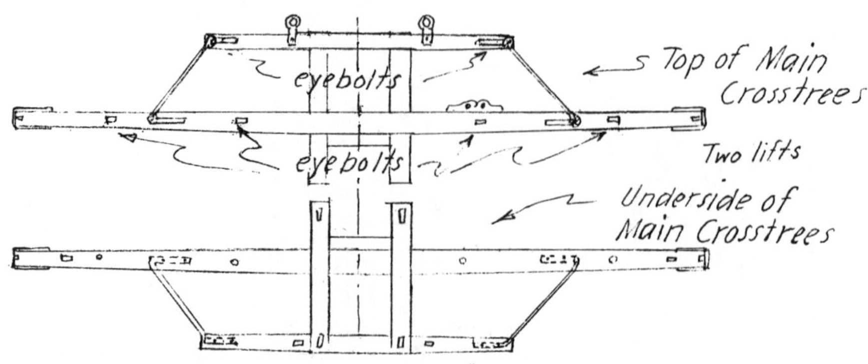
eyebolts
Top of Main Crosstrees
eyebolts
Two lifts
Underside of Main Crosstrees

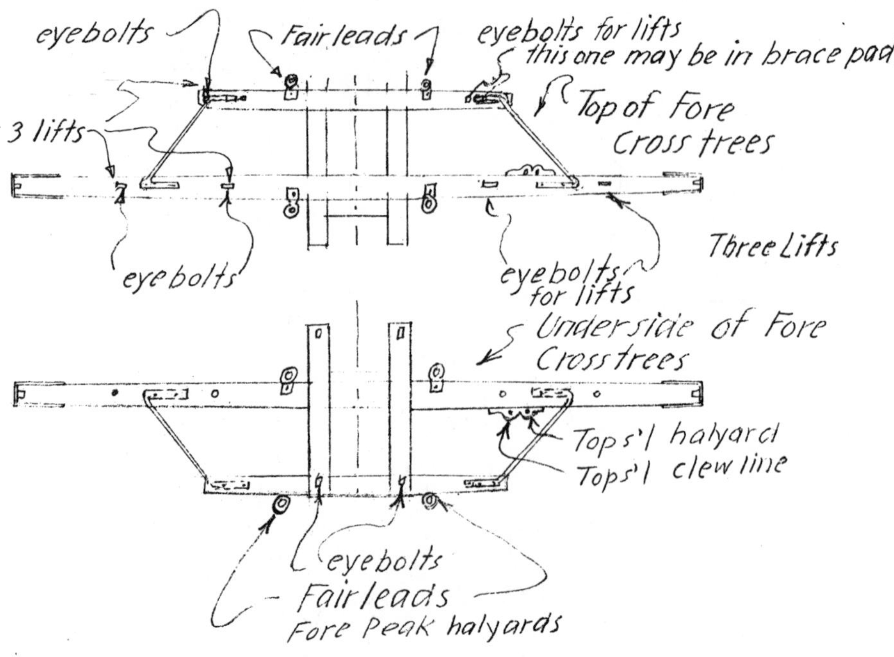
eyebolts
Fair leads
eyebolts for lifts
this one may be in brace pad.
Top of Fore Cross trees
3 lifts
eyebolts
Three Lifts
eyebolts for lifts
Underside of Fore Crosstrees
Tops'l halyard
Tops'l clew line
eyebolts
Fairleads
Fore Peak halyards

Not to scale

CROSSTREES, SINGLE LONG, 1900–1930

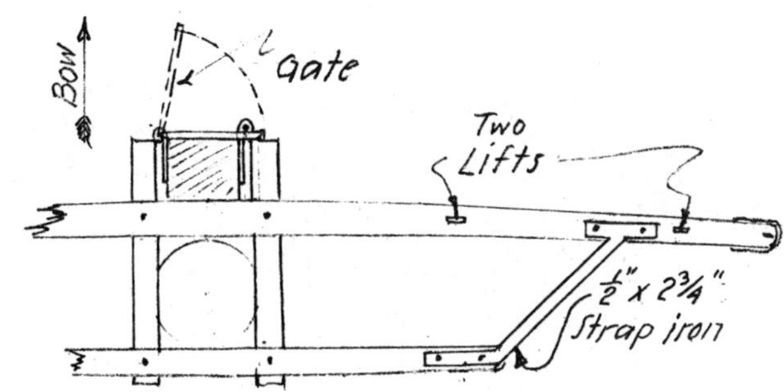
Bow
Gate
Two
Lifts
½" x 2¾"
Strap iron

Single long Crosstrees, 1901-1912
Crowninshield
[Not to scale]

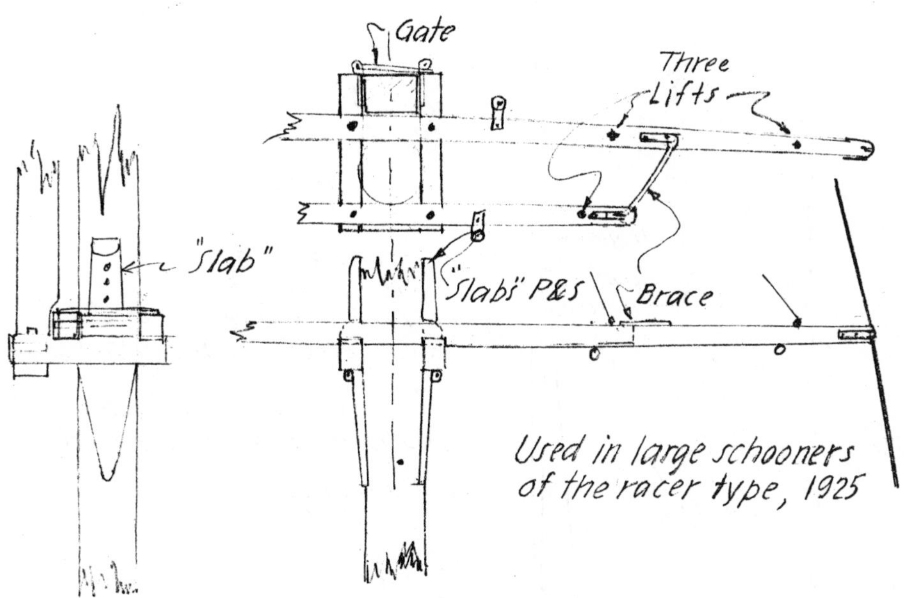
Gate
Three
Lifts
"Slab"
"Slabs" P&S
Brace
Used in large schooners
of the racer type, 1925

[Not to scale]

CROSSTREES

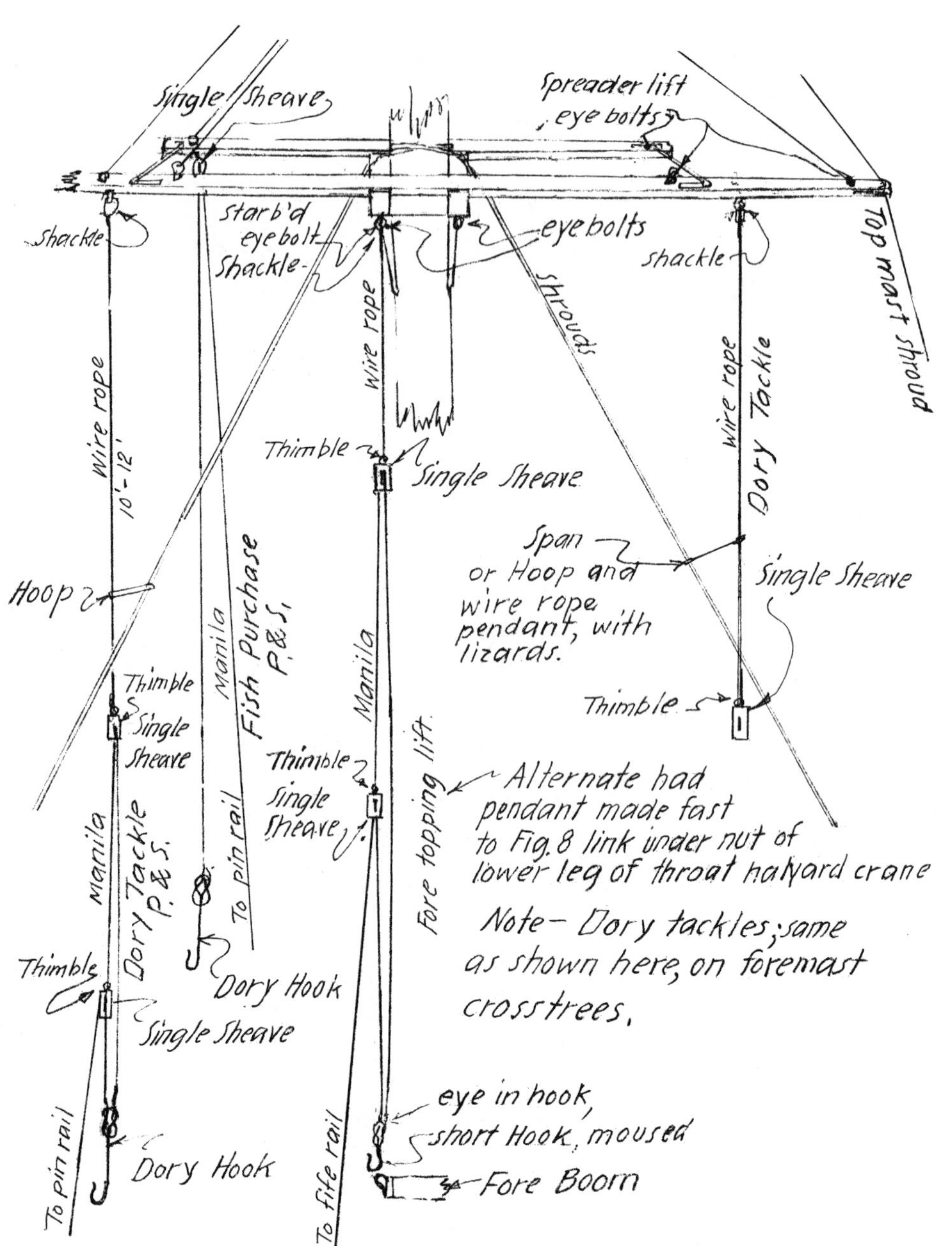

Single Sheave
Spreader lift eye bolts
Shackle
Starb'd eye bolt
Shackle
eye bolts
shackle
Top mast shroud
wire rope
10'-12'
Shrouds
wire rope
wire rope
Dory Tackle
Thimble
Single Sheave
Span or Hoop and wire rope pendant, with lizards.
Single Sheave
Hoop
Manila
Fish Purchase P.&S.
Manila
Thimble
Thimble
Single Sheave
Thimble
Single Sheave
Alternate had pendant made fast to Fig. 8 link under nut of lower leg of throat halyard crane
Manila
Dory Tackle P.&S.
To pin rail
Fore topping lift
Note— Dory tackles, same as shown here, on foremast crosstrees.
Thimble
Dory Hook
Single Sheave
eye in hook, short Hook, moused
To pin rail
Dory Hook
To fife rail
Fore Boom

CROSSTREE IRONWORK

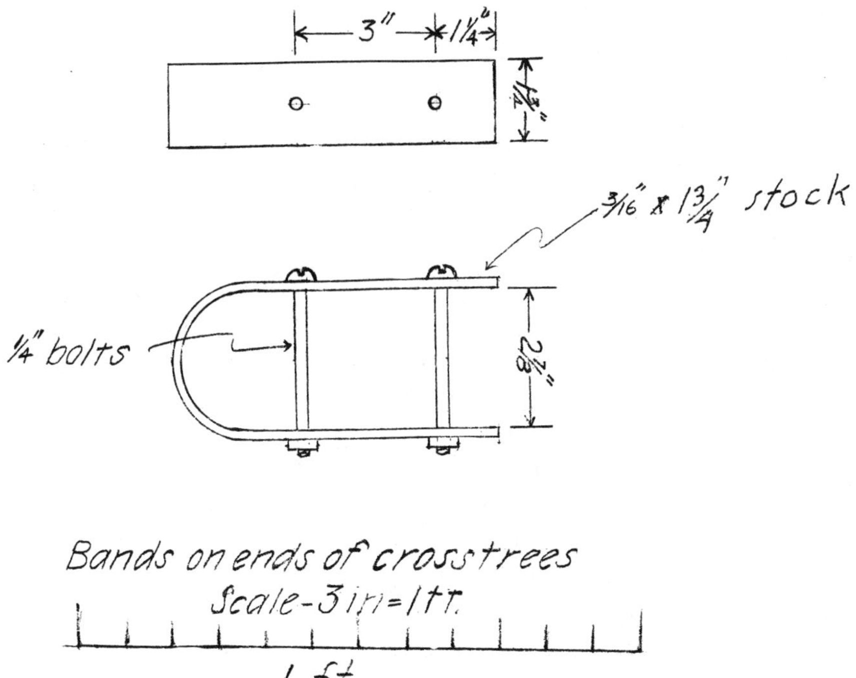
3"
1¼"
1¾"
3/16" x 1¾" stock
¼" bolts
2⅞"
Bands on ends of crosstrees
Scale-3 in=1 ft.
1 ft.

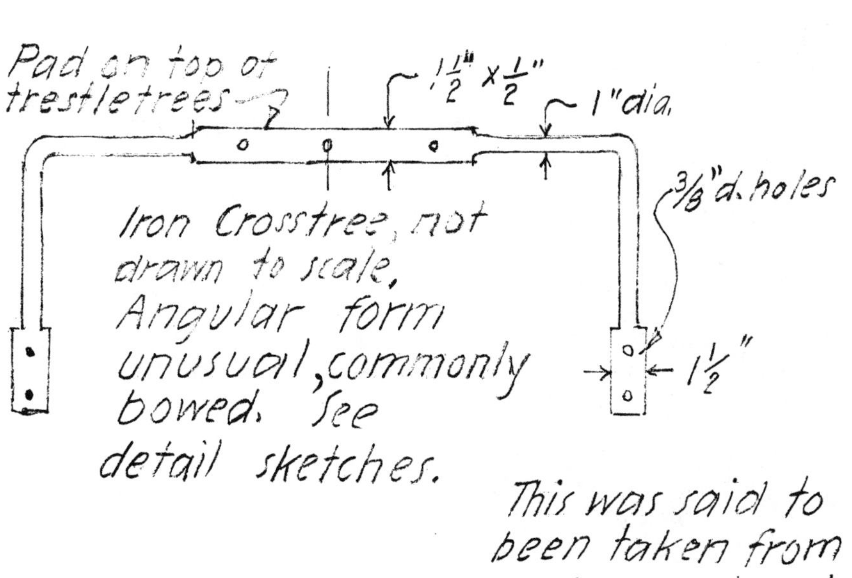
Pad on top of trestletrees
1½" x ½"
1" dia.
⅜" d. holes
1½"
Iron Crosstree, not drawn to scale, Angular form unusual, commonly bowed. See detail sketches.
This was said to been taken from a schooner-boat.

CROSSTREE LIFTS

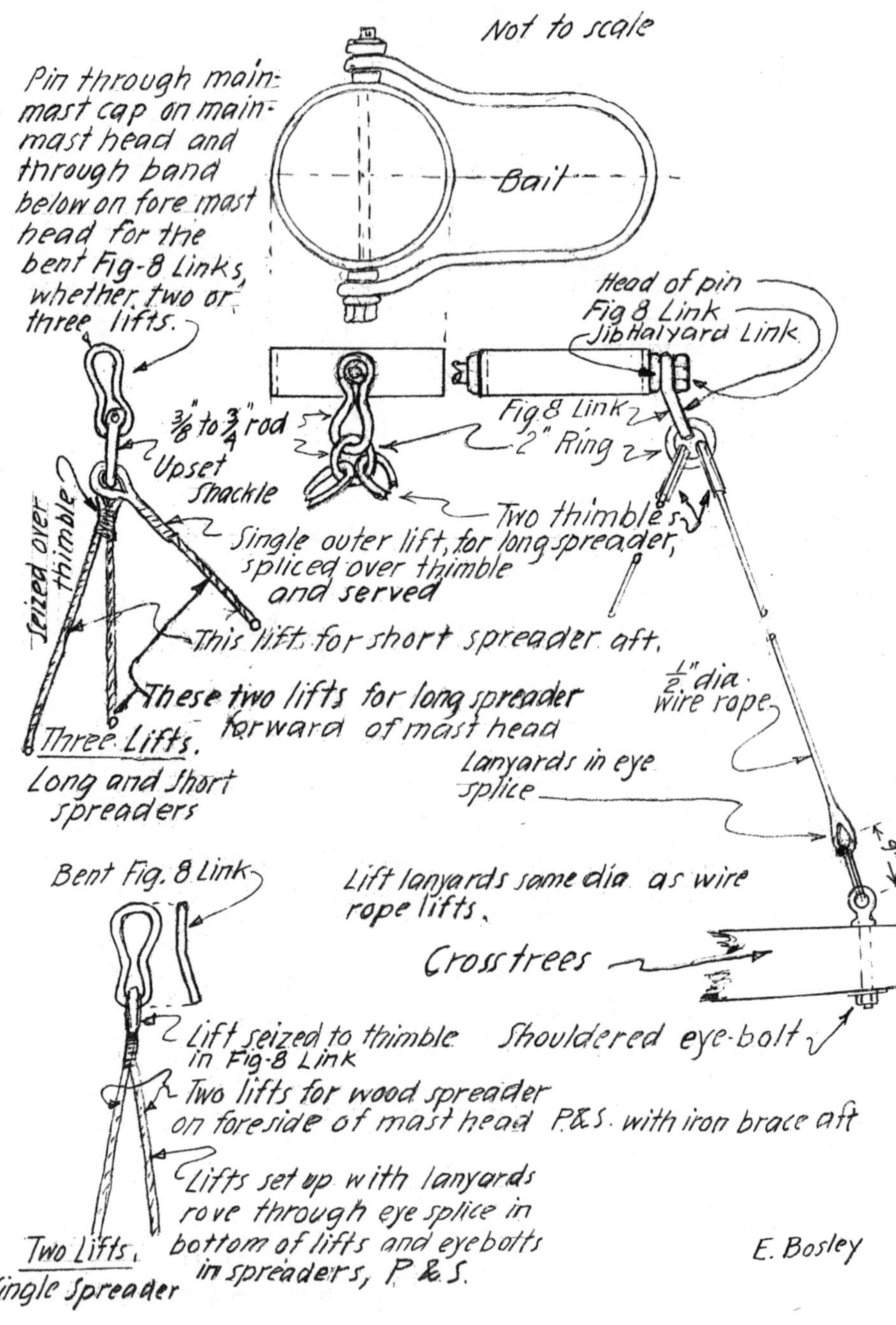
Not to scale
Pin through main-mast cap on main-mast head and through band below on fore mast head for the bent Fig-8 Links, whether two or three lifts.
Bait
Head of pin
Fig 8 Link
Jib Halyard Link
3/8" to 3/4" rod
Upset Shackle
Fig 8 Link
2" Ring
Seized over thimble
Two thimbles
Single outer lift, for long spreader, spliced over thimble and served
This lift for short spreader aft.
These two lifts for long spreader forward of mast head
1/2" dia wire rope
Three Lifts.
Long and Short spreaders
Lanyards in eye splice
9"
Bent Fig. 8 Link
Lift lanyards same dia as wire rope lifts.
Crosstrees
Lift seized to thimble in Fig-8 Link
Shouldered eye-bolt
Two lifts for wood spreader on foreside of mast head P&S. with iron brace aft
Lifts set up with lanyards rove through eye splice in bottom of lifts and eyebolts in spreaders, P & S.
Two Lifts.
Single Spreader
E. Bosley

CROSSTREE LIFTS
FIGURE-8 LINK FITTING AT MASTHEAD

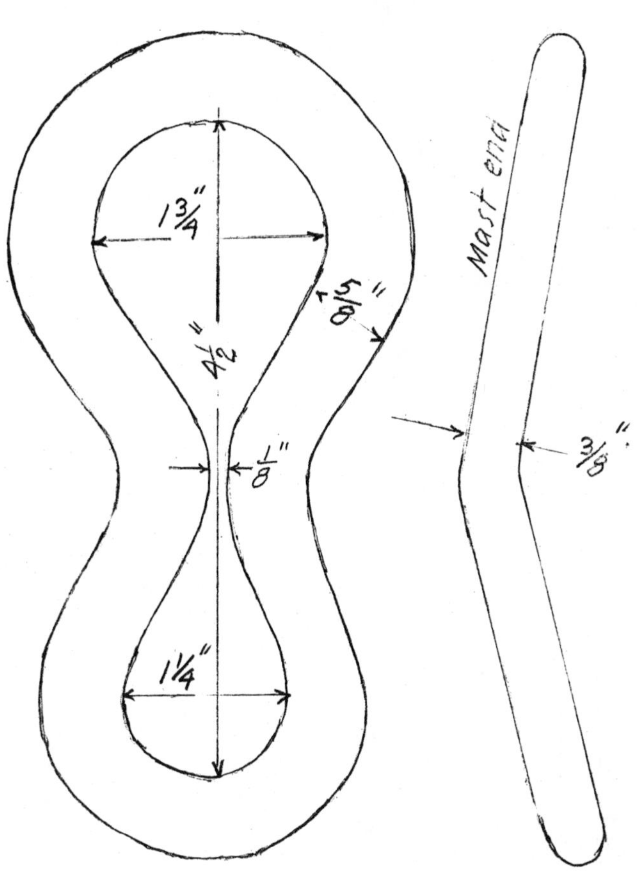
1¾"
⅝"
4½"
⅛"
1¼"
Mast end
⅜"

CROTCHES, BOOM, "ELSIE"

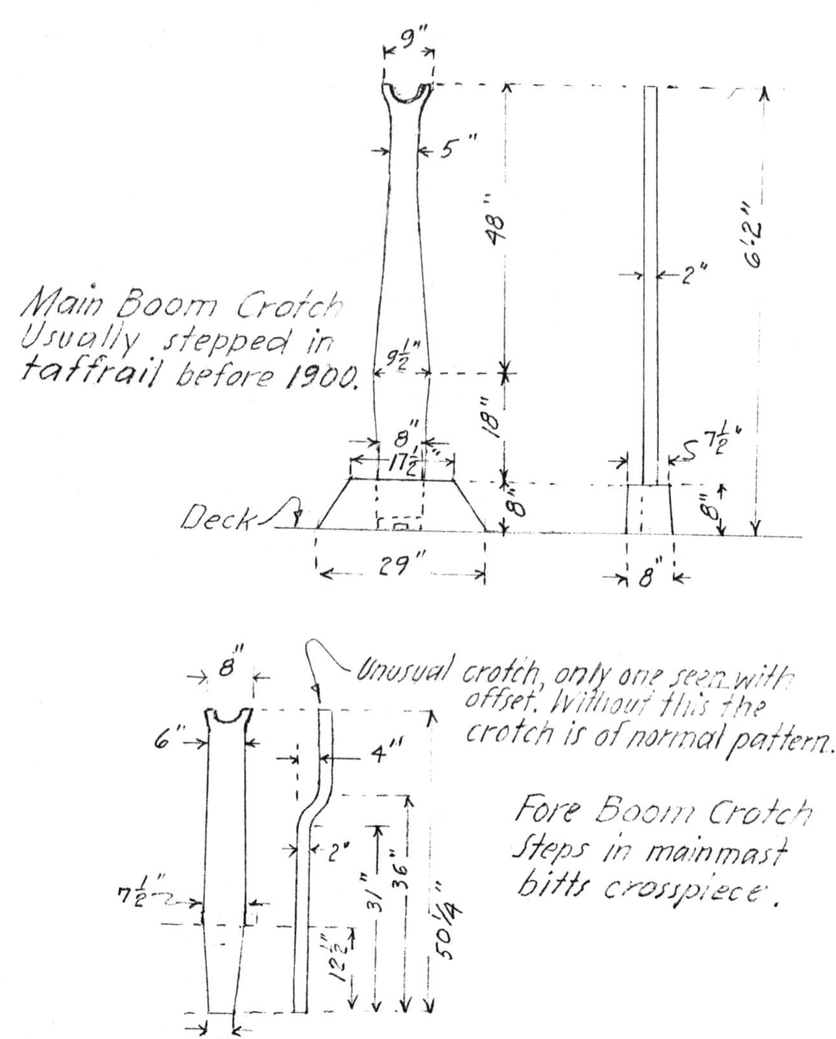
9"
5"
48"
6'2"
2"
Main Boom Crotch
Usually stepped in
taffrail before 1900.
9½"
18"
8"
17½"
7½"
Deck
8"
29"
8"
8"
Unusual crotch, only one seen with
offset. Without this the
crotch is of normal pattern.
8"
6"
4"
Fore Boom Crotch
Steps in mainmast
bitts crosspiece.
2"
31"
36"
50¼"
7½"
12½"
5"

Fore boom of "Elsie" did not extend as close to the main mast as usual, hence the offset in the fore boom crotch.

CROTCH TACKLES

When the mainboom was in its crotch, like the other booms, it was secured by setting the sheet up hard. But, because of its size and weight, the mainboom was fitted with crotch tackles as well. These tackles were made up with one double block fitted with a loose hook and one single, with loose hook and becket. The single block hooked into the sheet horse on the mainboom, the double hooked into an eyebolt on deck, in the quarters. Its fall belayed on a wooden cleat on the inside of the monkey rail near the eyebolts. Port and starboard tackles were required, of course. Instead of these tackles, some large schooners were rigged with two chain pendants, one hooked into the mainboom sheet horse, and one hooked into deck eyebolts, set up with a turnbuckle between the pendants. P. & S. forebooms were sometimes fitted with crotch tackles, but these were rarely carried rigged on the foreboom. Jumbo booms could be secured by the sheet.

CURVATURE OF THE MASTS RAKE

Masts of fishing schooners were usually stayed with the mastheads pulled forward about 1′-2′ from the masts' center lines, with all sail lowered. The purpose was to produce a taut forestay and jibstay, and also springstay, with sails hoisted. Topmasts were sprung forward in proportion, to tauten jibtopsail stay. The bowsprit, if one existed, would be hogged down for the same purpose. With sails hoisted, the masts became nearly straight and slightly raked.

Mainmasts raked more than foremasts, but rakes were moderate after 1860.

DAVITS (NOTES)

Iron stern davits were used on fishing schooners from the mid-50s until the early '90s. All of the old Grand and Georges Bankers carried a yawl boat in these davits. These boats were built in Essex and Gloucester. Though primarily rowboats, some were fitted to sail, having a single sprit sail.

The davits were 3″ diameter, tapered to about 2¾″ diameter just inside the sheaves, of which there were two, with an eye about 20″ inboard. The inboard end of the davit was stepped in a chock on the monkey rail, with the heel of the davit carried through the rail cap. This had a scupper hole bored through the cap outboard. The chock was countersunk about half the depth of its base. There were two rod braces, one from an eye on the inboard side of the davit, forward of the sheaves a bit. This hooked into an eyebolt on top of the monkey rail cap about 18″ either side of the hull ℄. A second brace, also leading from inboard of the sheaves, led to an eyebolt on top of the monkey rail cap near the chock. The davit could be readily unshipped. A plank, for lashing the yawl, was bolted to the davits just inside the sheaves (with staple bolts) running from davit to davit. The last schooner built in Essex, fitted for davits, was the Georgesman "William Ryder" launched in 1895—built by John Prince Story.

DAVITS (WOODEN)

Wooden stern davits were fitted in fishing schooners from colonial times and continued in use until the mid-1850s, when iron davits began to be used. Wooden davits were secured on top of the monkey rail, as shown in the diagramatic sketch below, and were made of 6″ to 8″ oak, with a 2″ x 6″ to $2\frac{1}{2}$″ to 10″ plank for yawl-boat stops. In the passage to the banks, the yawl was often carried upside-down on the top of the davits and lashed. Fitted on hand-liners. Sketch taken from model.

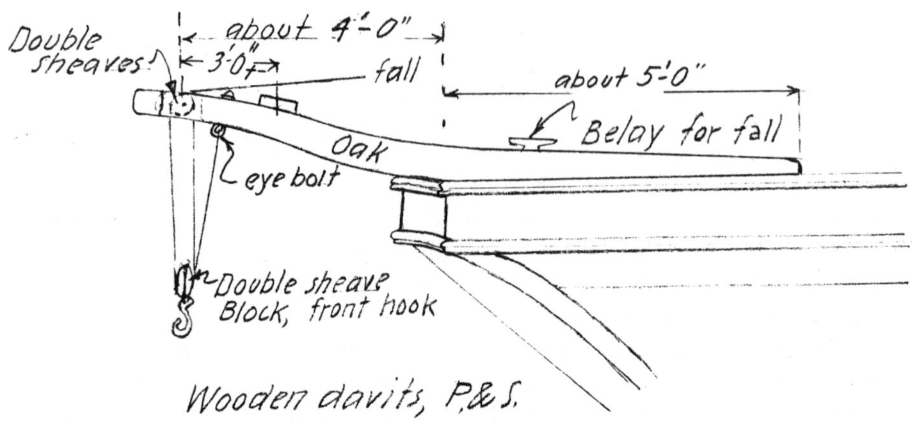
Double sheaves
about 4'-0"
3'0"
fall
about 5'0"
Belay for fall
Oak
eye bolt
Double sheave Block, front hook

Wooden davits, P.& S.

DAVITS
CARRIED FOR HAND-LINE FISHING ONLY

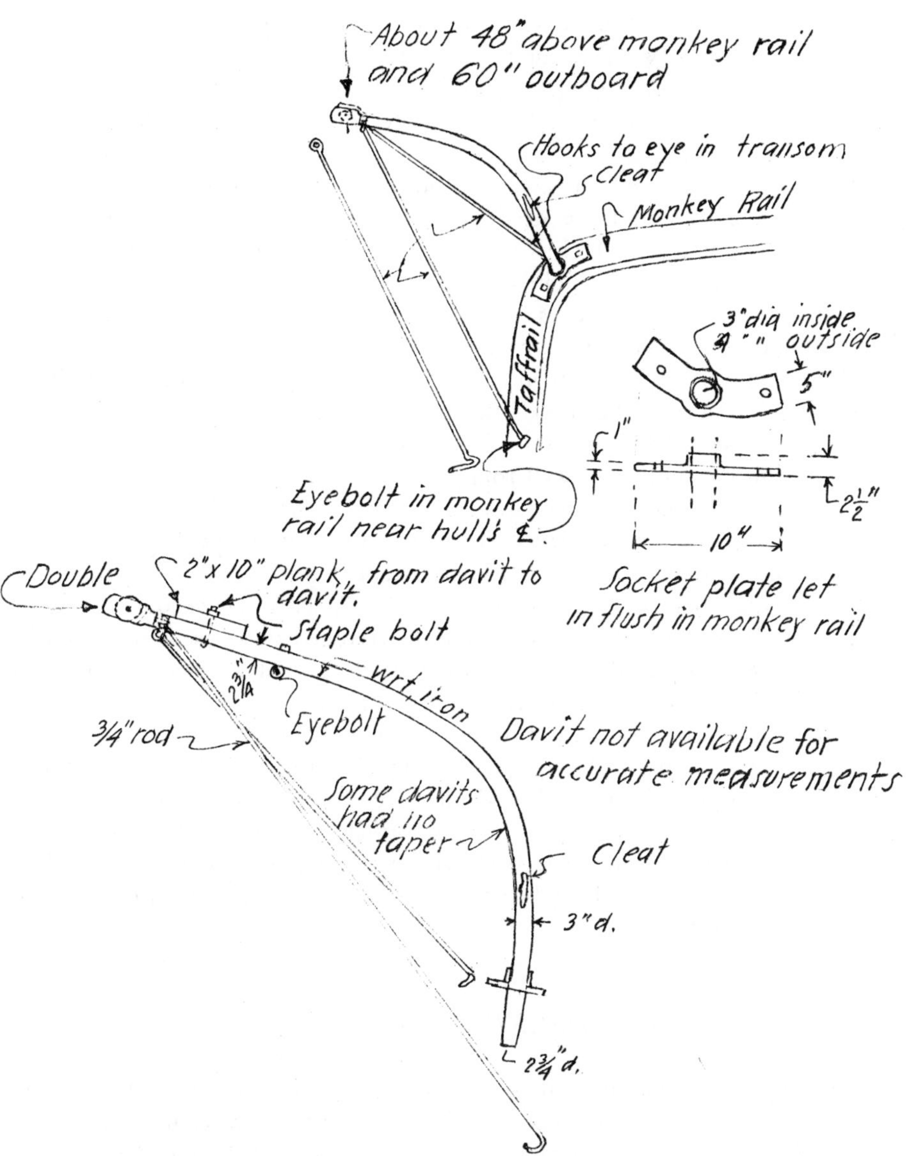
About 48" above monkey rail
and 60" outboard
Hooks to eye in transom
Cleat
Monkey Rail
Taffrail
3"dia inside
4" " outside
5"
1"
2½"
10"
Socket plate let
in flush in monkey rail
Eyebolt in monkey
rail near hull's ℄.
Double
2"x 10" plank, from davit to
davit.
Staple bolt
2¾"
wrt. iron
Eyebolt
¾" rod
Davit not available for
accurate measurements
Some davits
had no
taper
Cleat
3" d.
2¾" d.

DEADEYES AND LANYARDS (NOTES)

Deadeyes and lanyards were used at Essex and Gloucester for shrouds and headrigging until into the 1860s. Then turnbuckles came slowly into use for bobstays, and for bowsprit shrouds. Deadeyes in the shrouds remained in general use to the end of the schooners in the fisheries.

The diameters of some deadeyes measured were:

"Mary T. Fallon": 6″, for lower shrouds (1901).

"Natalie Hammond": 6½″ for lower shrouds, topmast shrouds 5½″ diameter (1913)

"L.A. Dunton": 7″ for lower shrouds, topmast shrouds 5″ (1923)

The thicknesses of these deadeyes respectively were: 7″ diameter, 4½ thick; 6″ diameter, 4″ thick; 6½″ diameter, 3¾″ thick; 5½″ diameter, 3″ thick; 7″ diameter, 4½″ thick; 5″ diameter, 3½″ thick.

The lower-shroud deadeyes had double scores in their circumference, going around them, less 3″ on bottom, to take ¾″ or ⅞″ diameter iron strop. This deadeye had nearly flat inboard and outboard faces. The upper deadeyes had no score at the top of their circumference for 3 to 4 inches, but were single-scored for the rest of the distance. The inboard and outboard faces of this deadeye were well-rounded.

The lanyard holes of these deadeyes were about 1¼″ diameter, taking ¾″-1″ diameter hemp lanyard stuff, well treated with Copenhagen tar, four strands and no heart. From top of lower deadeye to the bottom of the upper deadeye, the distance was from 2′-4″ to 2′-10″, when the shrouds were set up. Later four strands tarred manila well stretched were used for lanyards. Hole in the upper deadeye for Matthew Walker knot not scored. Hole on inboard side, left side of deadeye looking outboard.

The size of deadeyes used in fishing schooners did not follow any precise rule. Large schooners, above 110′ tonnage length, had 7″-7½″ diameter, deadeyes in lower shrouds; 5″-5½″ diameter for topmast shroud deadeyes. Smaller vessels had 6″-6½″ deadeyes for lower shrouds and 4½″-5″ deadeyes for topmast shrouds. Large vessels that had deadeyes only 6″-6½″ in diameter, in the lower shrouds, and 5″ diameter in topmast shrouds, were found in two instances.

DECKING (NOTES)

In fishing schooners built before 1845, deck plank was wider than it was after that date. As the schooners were full forward and wide at the transom, wide plank (say 5″-7″ wide) laid parallel to the hull ℄ would create no difficulty along the waterways. By tapering a few of the plank toward the bow, the necessity of notching, or "nibbing" plank-ends into the waterways would be reduced to a minimum. In the 1850s narrow deck plank became the fashion. The plank on the main deck, 4″ to 5″wide and 3″ thick, (finished dimensions 3¾-4¾", 2¾" thick) was laid parallel to the hull ℄, but the quarterdeck plank was laid parallel to the sides of the cabin trunk, commonly almost parallel to the waterway and bulwarks of that deck. Forward, the main deck was nibbed where it butted against the waterways. However, parallel to the hull ℄, and extending about 2′ either side of it, was a belt of thicker plank, about ¾" to 1" thicker than the decking; the "strongback," or "mast bed." The mast bed was usually as wide as the forecastle companionway, or 8" wider, but forward of the foremast, or under the windlass barrel, it stepped down in width by cutting short the outside strakes of the bed. The wide center plank, 10"-12" wide, was carried to the stem under the bowsprit. The strongback was not nibbed, as a rule, at the bow. There seems to have been no rigid practice in planning the arrangement of deck planking.

The planking of the deck of the "Philip P. Manta" was laid parallel to the ℄ on the main deck. On the quarterdeck, the outboard six planks on each side were tapered aft and were parallel to the inside of bulwark planks. No nibbing was employed. Deck plank was 3½" wide, 28 planks on the quarterdeck, king plank on trunk top. Waterways were 10" wide. On the "L.A. Dunton," the quarterdeck plank was 3¾" wide, 4⅝" wide on main deck. The great beam was 4½" wide from face to rabbet butts of quarterdeck planking. "Elsie's" decks were not nibbed.

In the "Mary T. Fallon" the main deck plank was not nibbed. Planking 2½" wide, 2" thick. Quarterdeck plank nibbed into king plank.

The "Mary E. O'Hara" had main and quarterdeck plank nibbed into waterways.

Decking of knockabout "Ethel B. Penny" was 4" wide. Ten strakes ran to knightheads. No king plank aft. Plank butts notched into opposite butts on ℄.

Main deck plank on "Adventure" nibbed a little amidship. Strongback ran aft to the companionway, as wide as this hatchway. Strongback was of four 8" planks and one 12" plank at ℄; top of strongback 1" above rest of deck. The deck of knockabout "Rhodora" laid with strongback running from foremast bed to main hatch and was 2" narrower on each side than the companionway. Mainmast bed was the same width as the main hatch inside and ran aft to the trunk.

Decking oiled; waterways and strongback painted white or blue in 1934. Seams pitched until after 1908, when seam compounds were used.

Probably most vessels had 3" x 4" deck plank laid flat for deck, on edge for mast beds, etc. Measured thickness variations were due to use of commercial sizes and to "joinering-off" in finishing the decks. Some very large schooners had deck plank 5½" to 6" wide, with mast beds 1" thicker than deck.

DECKING
NIBBING USED AT ESSEX

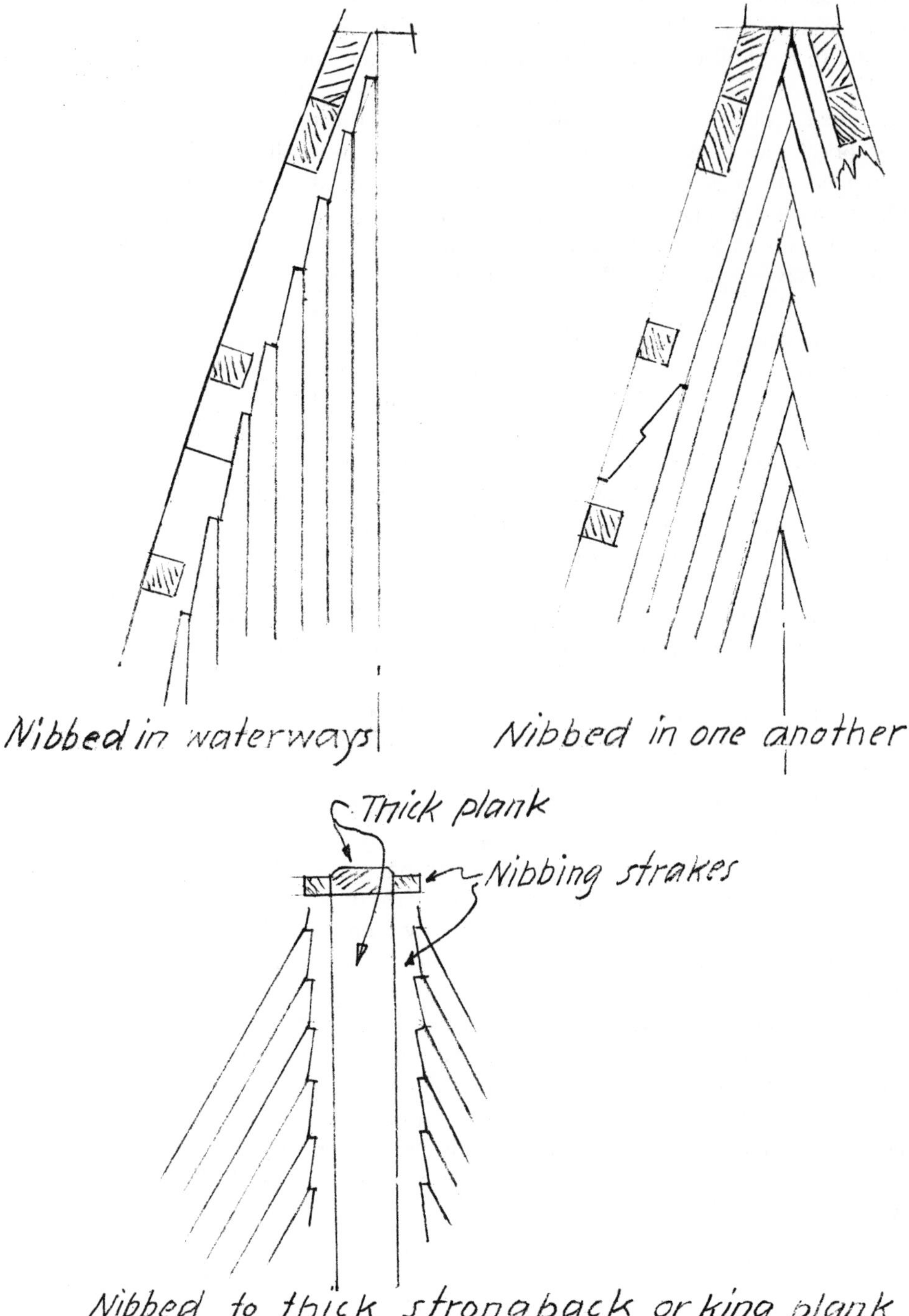

Nibbed in waterways

Nibbed in one another

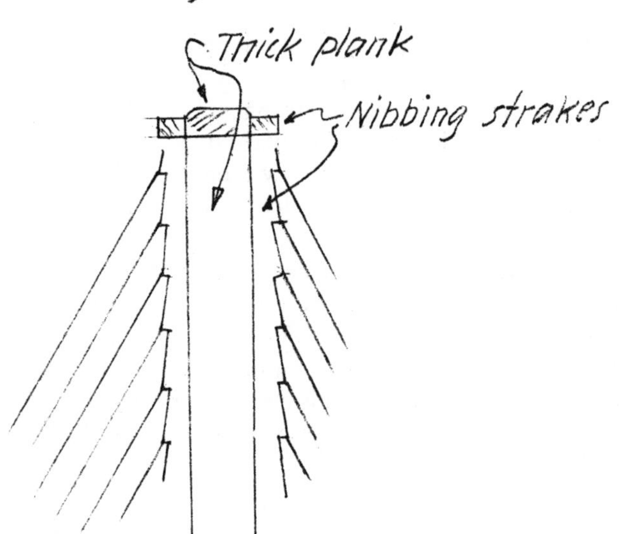
Thick plank
Nibbing strakes

Nibbed to thick strongback or king plank

DECKING
"ETHEL PENNY," KNOCKABOUT

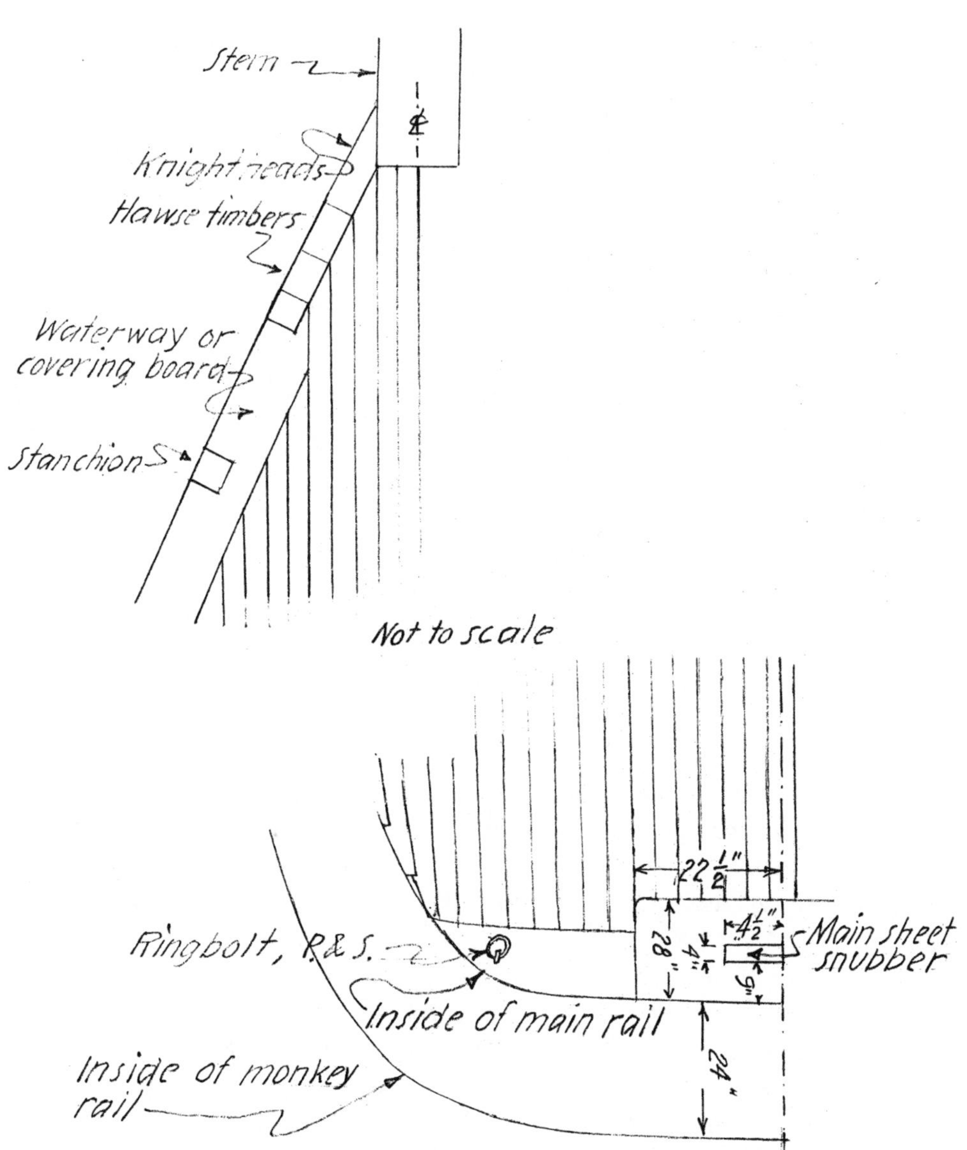
Stem
Knightheads
Hawse timbers
Waterway or covering board
Stanchions
Not to scale
Ringbolt, P.&S.
Inside of main rail
Inside of monkey rail
22 1/2"
28"
4 1/2"
4"
9"
24"
Main sheet snubber

DECKLIGHTS

Decklights were introduced in Gloucester schooners in the early 1850s. Up until 1900 decklight frames were octagon-shaped, as well as round, on the outside; some had prism glass.

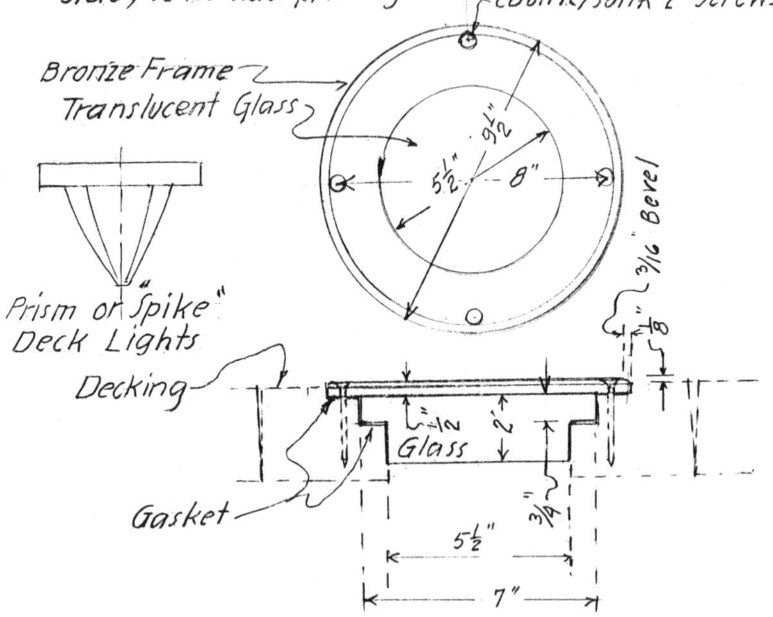

Countersunk 2" Screws
Bronze Frame
Translucent Glass
9½"
5½"
8"
3/16" Bevel
Prism or "Spike" Deck Lights
1/8"
Decking
1/2"
2"
Glass
3/4"
Gasket
5½"
7"

General arrangement – One alongside pawl bitts, foreside, port or starb'd. One alongside companionway usually to port, or alongside galley hatch. In a few instances measured there were two lights; one each side, between companionway and galley hatch. Also two decklights were placed abaft cabin trunk, one each side clear of cabin door. No decklights under 5" opening diameter were observed.

"Grampus," 1885, had eight 9" decklights, 1½" thick, brass rings set in white lead.

DEVIL'S CLAW

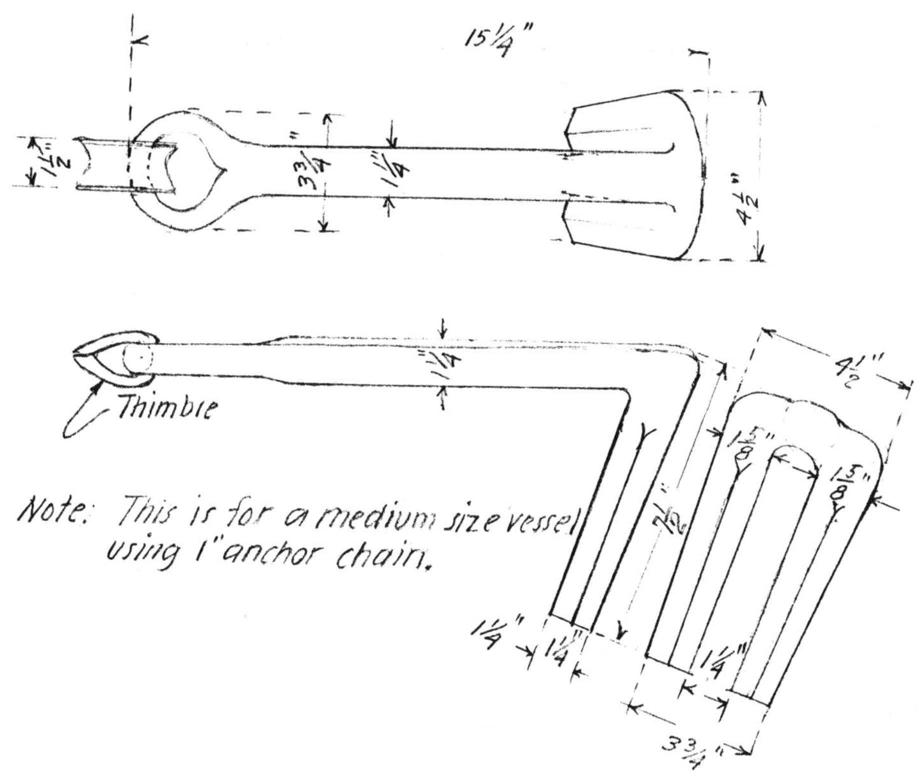
15¼"
1½"
3¾"
1¼"
4½"
Thimble
1¼"
4½"
1⅝"
7½"
1⅝"
Note: This is for a medium size vessel using 1" anchor chain.
1¼"
1¼"
1¼"
3¾"

Used to grab chain of anchor inboard hawse.
Had manila tail to secure claw to pawl post.
"Elsie" had Devil's Claw but did not see it rigged.

H.I.C.

DOLPHIN STRIKERS OR MARTINGALES, 1850–1885

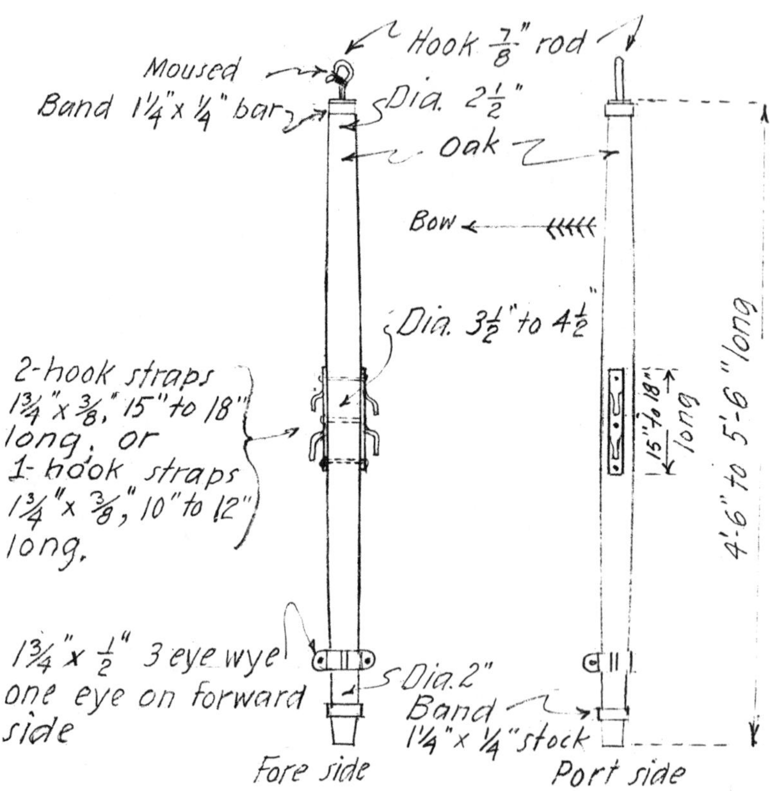
Hook 7/8" rod
Moused
Band 1¼"x ¼" bar
Dia. 2½"
Oak
Bow
Dia. 3½" to 4½"
2-hook straps 1¾"x ⅜," 15" to 18" long, or 1-hook straps 1¾"x ⅜," 10" to 12" long.
15" to 18" long
4'-6" to 5'-6" long
1¾"x ½" 3 eye wye one eye on forward side
Dia. 2"
Band 1¼"x ¼" stock
Fore side
Port side

Turned to curved tapers toward each end from mid-length. Martingales raked forward at the bottom, in Gloucestermen.

DOLPHIN-STRIKER GUYS

The dolphin striker, or martingale, was held from swinging athwartship by guys of hemp rope before 1885; of flexible wire rope afterward. These were spliced into wye at heel of the dolphin striker, on each side. The guys led to the ends of the iron jibboom spreader at bowsprit cap iron, where they were usually seized into the eyes made for them on the spreader.

DORIES (NOTES)

Dories most commonly used on fishing schooners were the "banks dory," about 14′ to 15′ long on the bottom, 18′ to 19′-6″ long on the gunwale, 4′-10″ to 4′-11″ wide on the bottom and 1′-8″ to 1′-9″ depth. These boats had removable thwarts so would nest in a stack. They were usually stowed on the main deck in two stacks, abreast the main hatch and close to it, allowing about 24″ between dories and inside of bulwarks. They were sometimes stowed on top of the fish-pen boards ("checkerboards"). The lashing ringbolts were located in fitting out, not at the building yards.

Hand liners usually fished "single-dory," that is, one man to a dory. For such an operation the dories were 13′ on the bottom, as a rule. "Columbia" once had four nests of dories on her main deck, two nests a side. This was twenty-four dories all told, as her nests contained six dories, hand lining. The knockabouts "Rhodora" and "Arethusa" each carried ten dories or at most twelve, which was the usual number for average-size vessels in New England after 1900, dory trawling.

Dories were built in very large numbers in Amesbury and Salisbury for over forty-five years. Hiram Lowell and Sons of Amesbury stocked dories on Whalen's Wharf in Gloucester, as did the noted Higgins and Gifford firm of the latter port. A. D. Story ran a dory shop in Gloucester off Vincent Street in the late '80s, but could not compete. In the 1870s some dories were built in Medford and in Newburyport. Shelbourne, Nova Scotia, was noted for building fine dories, as well as vessels, in the twentieth century.

DORY HOOK

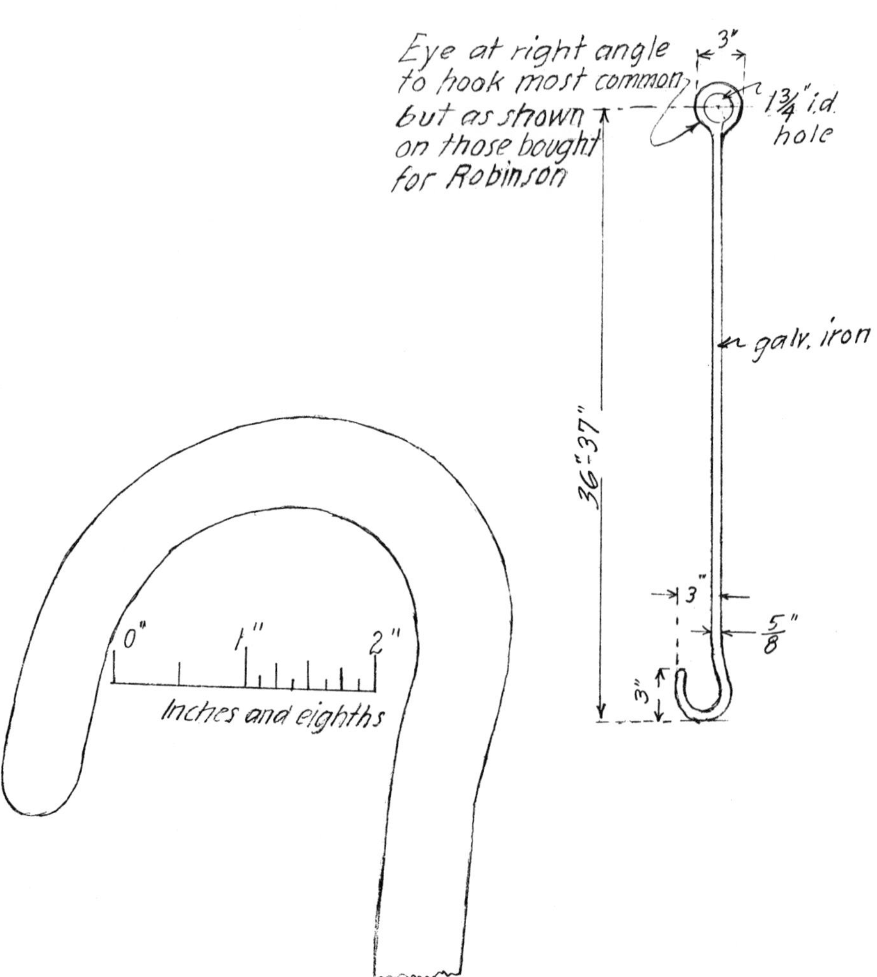
Eye at right angle
to hook most common,
but as shown
on those bought
for Robinson
3"
1¾" i.d.
hole
galv. iron
36"-37"
3"
5/8"
3"
0"
1"
2"
Inches and eighths

DOWNHAULS (NOTES)

Rolling thimble

Downhaul blocks, all 6", on starb'd side of stay for jib, on port side for jumbo and ballooner.

oval link on pin, forelocked.

Jib, jumbo or balloon stay:- rolling thimble

Shackle to suit, eye bolt (balloon) wye (jib) plate on port (jumbo)

E.B.

"Ballooner" (jib topsail)—a line attached to head cringle of sail, led through three or four thimbles (seized to hanks) then to block on bowsprit, at shoulder, which is hooked to a rope strop passed around bowsprit. The fall was belayed to pin on bow "seat." A small rope-stropped block with becket around bowsprit was sometimes used here.

Jib downhaul was like that of the ballooner except downhaul block was hooked, or shackled, into jibstay wye or stay shackle on starboard side of bowsprit.

Jumbo downhaul—a line secured to halyard block, with sister-hooks at head of sail, and with two half-hitches and bitter end seized. Led through three or four hanks (rings) or through thimbles lashed to them, then to a block shackled to the large shackle of the gammoning on the port side, if the stay set up there. When the stay set up outside the stem and gammon iron, the downhaul block was secured by a strop or becket around the bowsprit, or by a shackle. In winter this block was replaced by a lignum vitae fairlead secured to the bowsprit close to the stay by a becket.

(See "Gaff-topsails" for downhaul or clew line.)

Fore-gaff downhaul, a single line turned into eye in end of the gaff and seized. Fall led to foreboom made fast with becket around boom.

Main-gaff downhaul—really flag halyards—line rove through single-sheave block hooked into eye at end of gaff and moused. Both falls secured with beckets. A "becket" here was a short piece of line with an eye spliced into each end; lacing line was used in these eyes to secure the beckets.

"Columbia" and some others had main-gaff downhaul fast to peak of the gaff, lower end secured to throat halyard block link at gaff jaws; these came down within reach, where downhaul could be cast off and used to control gaff so as to furl the mainsail.

DRIFTS

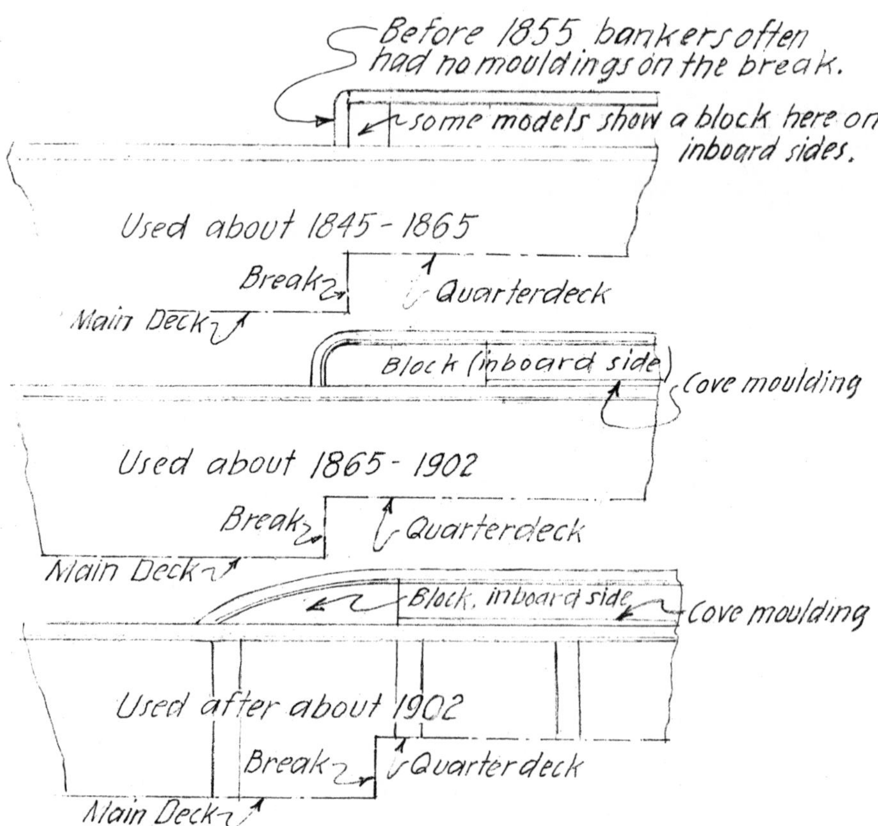
Before 1855 bankers often had no mouldings on the break.
some models show a block here on inboard sides.
Used about 1845 - 1865
Break
Quarterdeck
Main Deck
Block (inboard side)
Cove moulding
Used about 1865 - 1902
Break
Quarterdeck
Main Deck
Block, inboard side
Cove moulding
Used after about 1902
Break
Quarterdeck
Main Deck

At the "Great Beam", or break in the deck, there was a break in the rail, from main to quarter deck, as shown above, in three stages of evolution. The beginings and endings of the periods of use are approximate for changes were not sudden.

EAGLE HEAD

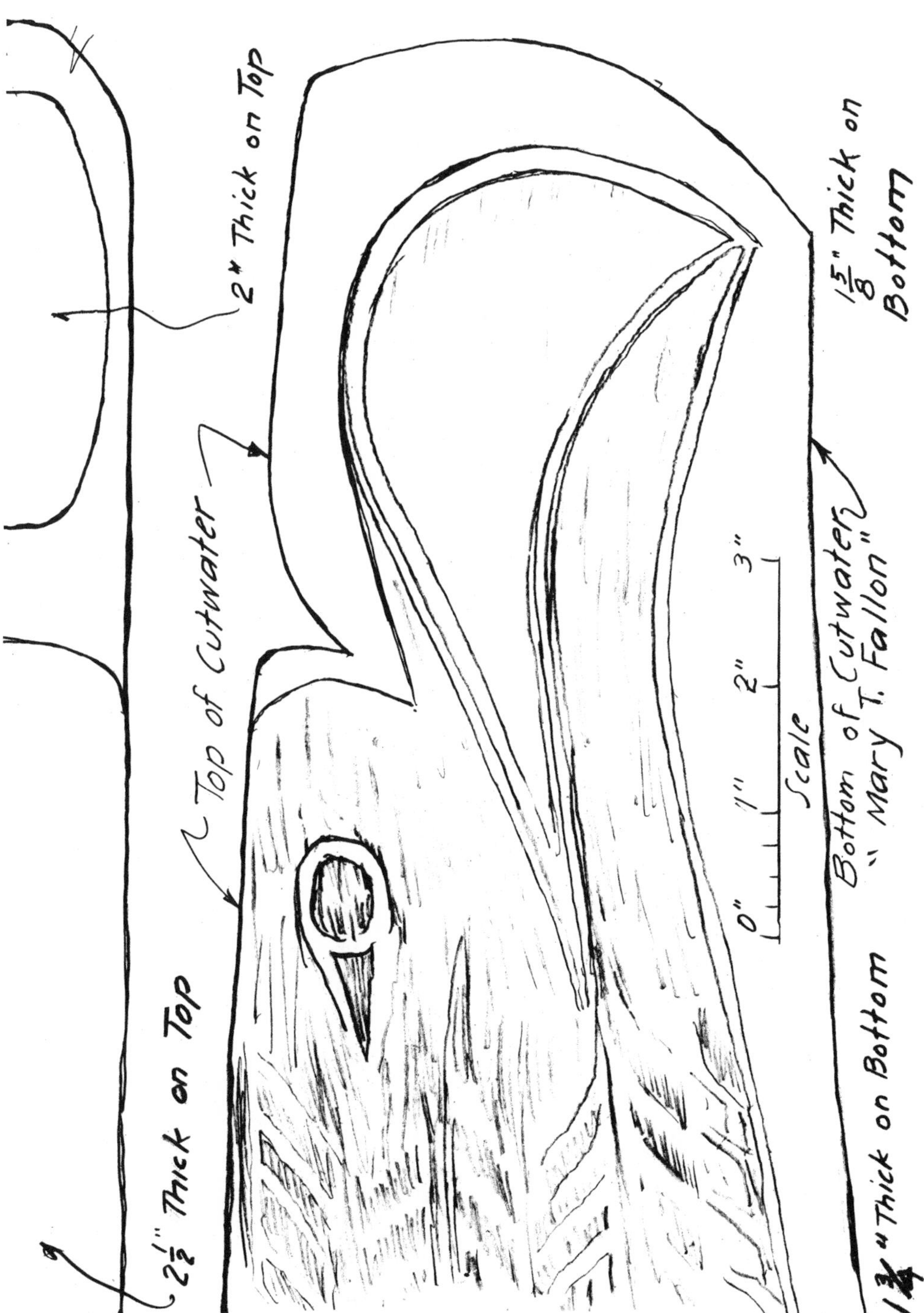
2½" Thick on Top
2" Thick on Top
Top of Cutwater
1⅝" Thick on Bottom
Bottom of Cutwater
"Mary T. Fallon"
Scale
0" 1" 2" 3"
1¾" Thick on Bottom

EYEBOLTS, RINGBOLTS, ETC. (DECK AND INSIDE OF BULWARKS)

On deck:

"Philip P. Manta"

1—on ℄, close abaft main hatch
1—on ℄ just abaft foreside galley hatch
1—P. & S. opposite middle of galley hatch
1—P. & S. opposite after-end of main hatch
1—P. & S. on great beam, halfway up, 3′-0″ inside of bulwark planking.
On bulwarks, beginning at first stanchion abaft hawse:

"Philip P. Manta," identified by number.

on No. 3—snatch chock abaft davit,
on No. 3 & 4—staple on chock, between
on No. 6 & 7—eye between
on No. 7—ringbolt
on No. 9—wooden cleat, vertical
on No. 10—snatch chock
on No. 14—ringbolt
on No. 17—ringbolt
on No. 20—ringbolt
on No. 21—ringbolt
Cat stopper cleat omitted, should be on No. 3 or close to davit

on No. 22—snatch chock
on No. 23-25—main chains, chain shrouds, one low just forward of chain plate (after)
on No. 27—ringbolt
on No. 33—ringbolt
on No. 34—snatch chock
on No. 39—cleat, wood, vert.
on No. 40—cleat, wood, vert.
on No. 41—large ringbolt
large ringbolt in counter 12″ inside of bulwarks

FAIRLEADS, LIGNUM VITAE

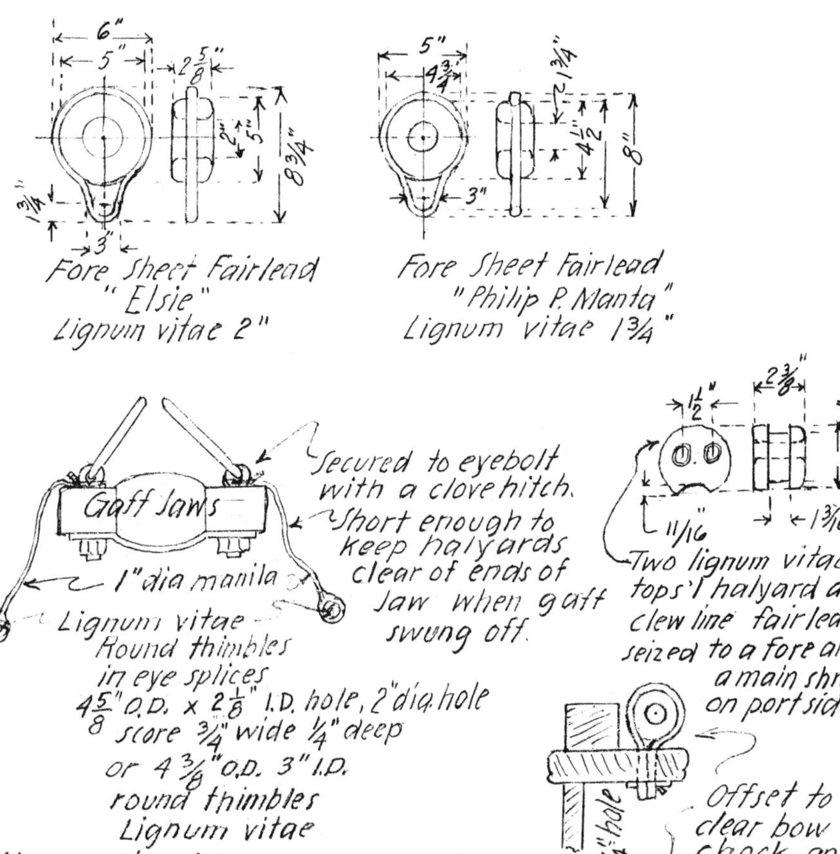

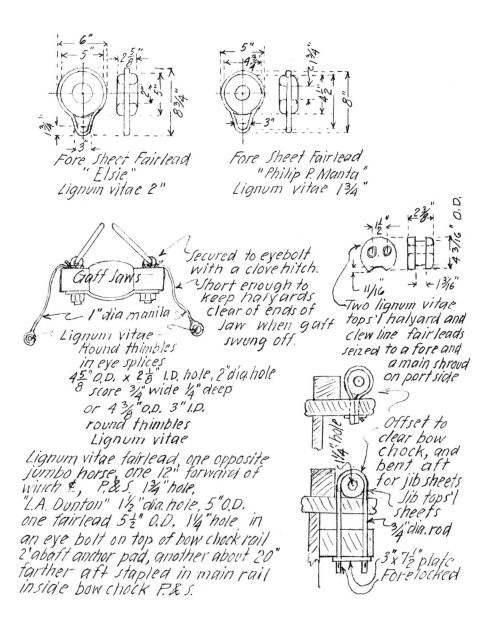

Fore Sheet Fairlead
"Elsie"
Lignum vitae 2"
Fore Sheet Fairlead
"Philip P. Manta"
Lignum vitae 1¾"
Gaff Jaws
Secured to eyebolt with a clove hitch.
Short enough to keep halyards clear of ends of Jaw when gaff swung off.
1" dia manila
Lignum vitae Round thimbles in eye splices
4 5/8" O.D. x 2 1/8" I.D. hole, 2" dia. hole score ¾" wide ¼" deep
or 4 3/8" O.D. 3" I.D. round thimbles Lignum vitae
Two lignum vitae tops'l halyard and clew line fairleads seized to a fore and a main shroud on port side
1¼" hole
Offset to clear bow chock, and bent aft for jib sheets
Jib tops'l sheets
¾" dia. rod
3" x 7½" plate Forelocked

Lignum vitae fairlead, one opposite jumbo horse, one 12" forward of winch ℄, P.&S. 1¾" hole.
"L.A. Dunton" 1½" dia. hole, 5" O.D. one fairlead 5½" O.D. 1¼" hole in an eye bolt on top of bow chock rail 2' abaft anchor pad, another about 20" farther aft stapled in main rail inside bow chock P.&S.

FAIRLEADS (METAL)

Two fairleads of this type were bolted to the top of each short crosstree (or to iron brace with single crosstree) about 6″ outboard of the outboard sides of the trestletrees. The fairleads pivoted on the crosstrees or braces. There were two on the forespreader of the foremast (one on each side) for the jib halyards, usually on foreside of the spreader. In the "Thebaud" E. Bosley found she had short links for her jib halyard blocks so the halyards came down farther aft than usual, so the fairleads were turned around and were fitted on the afterside of the forespreader.

The peak halyards were led through fairleads, abaft the lower mastheads.

FAIRLEADS (METAL)

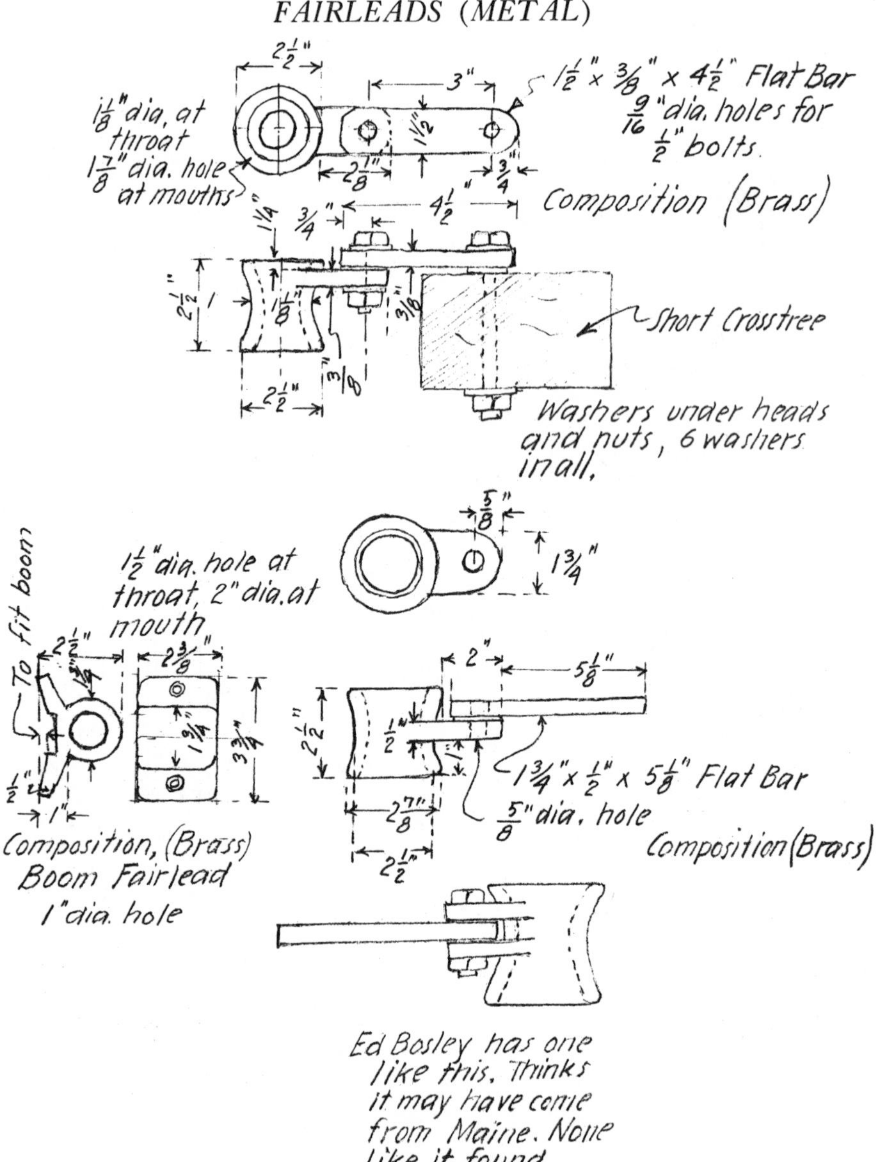
1½″ × ⅜″ × 4½″ Flat Bar
9/16″ dia. holes for ½″ bolts.
1⅛″ dia. at throat
1⅞″ dia. hole at mouths
Composition (Brass)
Short Crosstree
Washers under heads and nuts, 6 washers in all.
1½″ dia. hole at throat, 2″ dia. at mouth
To fit boom
Composition, (Brass) Boom Fairlead 1″ dia. hole
1¾″ × ½″ × 5⅝″ Flat Bar
⅝″ dia. hole
Composition (Brass)
Ed Bosley has one like this. Thinks it may have come from Maine. None like it found.

FASHION PIECES OLD STYLE

It was shipbuilding practice (long before the earliest technical records of the American schooners exist) to protect the ends of the transom, or counter, planking with a timber shaped to the side of the hull and covering the exposed ends of the transom planking, where this planking laps over the after-ends of the side planking. This was necessary to protect the transom plank, in the topside, in coming into contact with wharves, or other vessels, or piles.

Up into the late 1880s, this timber, known as a "fashion piece," was made of a natural crook that was shaped to the hull, at the outboard ends of the transom plank. It was of oak, about 5″ wide in side elevation, and ran from the bottom of the main rail cap, where it was only about 1½″ thick, to the place where it crossed the plank-sheer. Here it was increased in thickness to about 3″-3½″. From here it continued down the edge of the transom to where it began to tuck under the stern, or transom. Here it ended, being reduced to 1¼″-1½″ thick. Just below the plank-sheer, a fore-and-aft timber was spiked on the planking. Its after-end butted against the fashion piece, with its face thick enough so that it would come flush there. The fore-and-aft piece was parallel to the plank-sheer and was 18″-20″ or 22″ long, with its fore-end about 1¼″ thick. This piece was about 3½″-4½″ wide on its outboard face and it protected the fashion piece from being torn off by a glancing blow from forward. The precise date that the fashion piece went out of style cannot be established now, but it probably was about 1887–1890. (See "Counter.")

FASHION PIECES, LATER STYLE
(SEE "COUNTER")

Influenced by yacht practices, perhaps, some time around 1887-88 the fashion pieces became about 10"-12" long; enough to run from underside of main rail to waist line, and only about 1¼" to 1¾" thick. Forward of the fashion piece fore-and-aft plank was applied over the "pine bulwarks" (above the waist) and the waist line made to appear as though it curved up to main rail at the fore side of the fashion piece.

The upward sweep began at the after bulwark stanchion, which was about 18"-24" forward of the quarter block. These protected the transom plank at the quarters where the transom was widest.

a. Deck Rail
False knee
Main Rail
Waist
Cove
Planksheer
Waist sweeps up — A.D. Story
" straight aft, — James
Foreside of fashion piece, (plank)
Transom plank mitred into side planking.

The fashion pieces survived only as protective planks applied over the top of the side planking at the transom above the quarter-deck planksheer.

FIFE RAILS 1845–1890
(*SEE "BITTS"*)

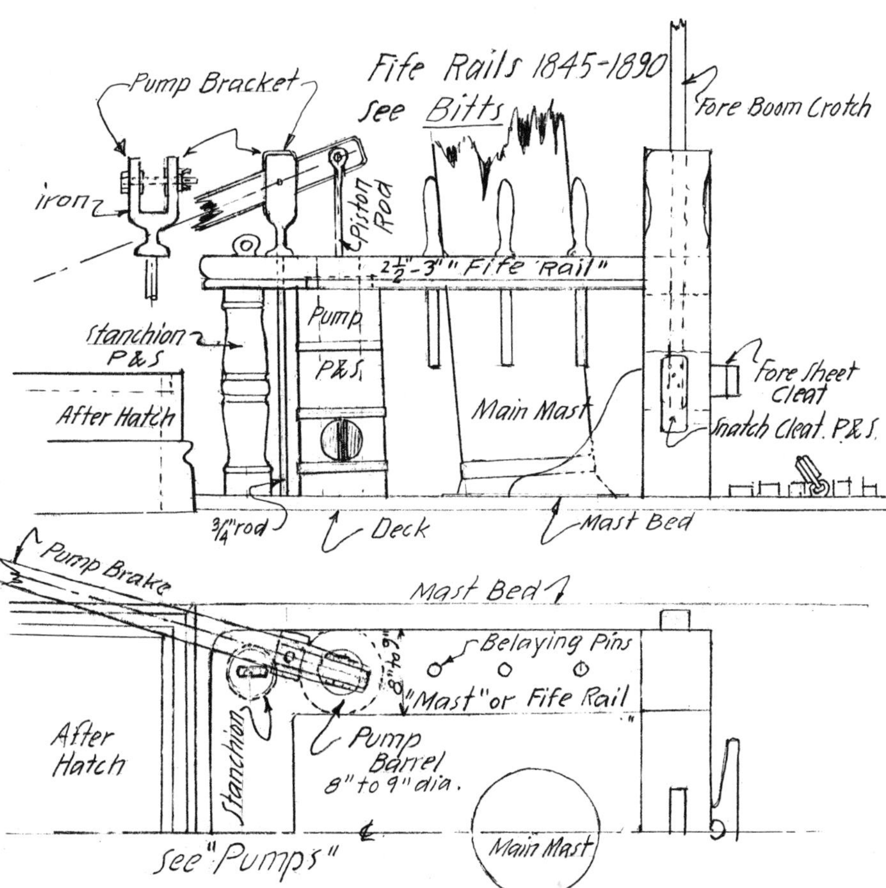
Fife Rails 1845-1890
See Bitts
Pump Bracket
Fore Boom Crotch
iron
Piston Rod
2½"-3" "Fife Rail"
Stanchion P&S
Pump
P&S
After Hatch
Main Mast
Fore Sheet Cleat
Snatch Cleat. P&S.
¾" rod
Deck
Mast Bed
Pump Brake
Mast Bed
Belaying Pins
8" to 9"
"Mast" or Fife Rail
After Hatch
Stanchion
Pump Barrel 8" to 9" dia.
See "Pumps"
Main Mast

Fife Rails and Bitts were combined with wooden piston pumps at the main mast in fishing schooners, as shown here. There were slight variations; the outside dia. of the wooden pump barrels was from 8" to 9", with bores 3" to 4" dia. The barrels were iron strapped (to prevent checking) at irregular intervals. The shape of the brackets varied with the maker. The pump barrels were made at Essex, using primitive lathes and long augers. The pump barrels were wedged with cedar rather than caulked.

MAIN FIFE RAIL AND BITTS
BOOM SADDLE, MAIN MAST

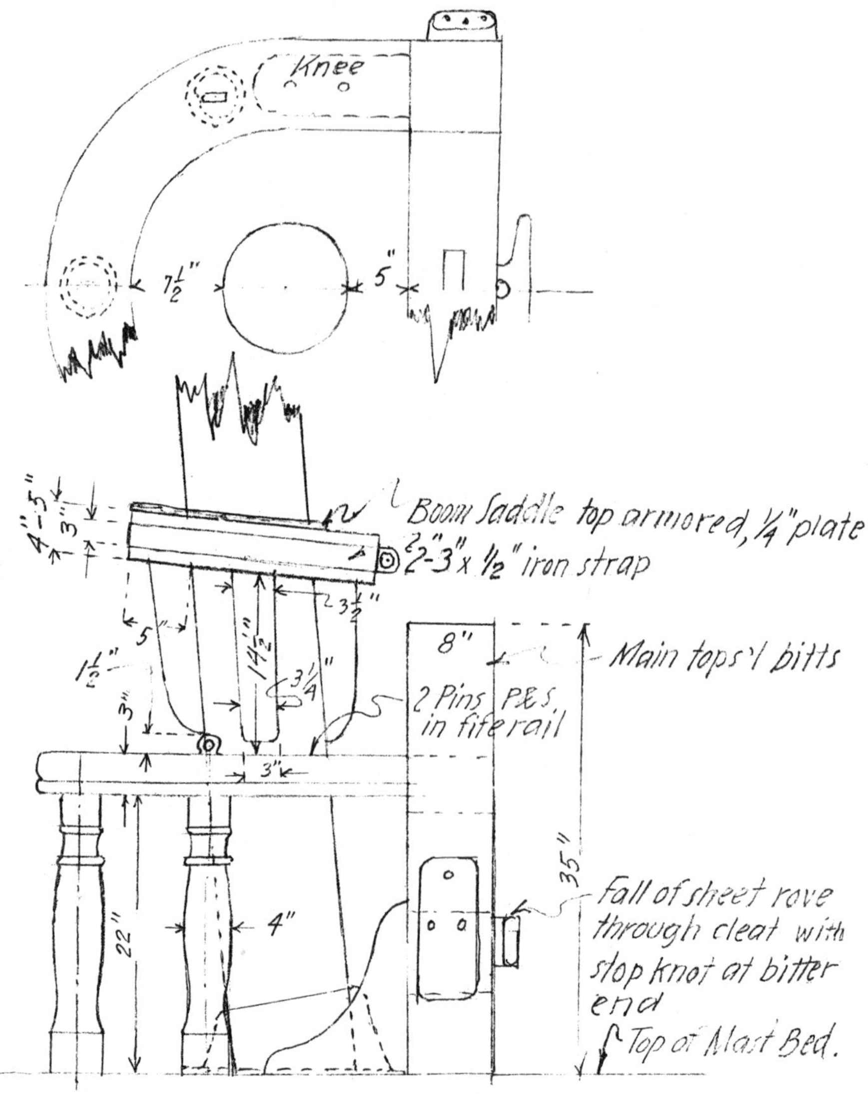
Knee
$7\frac{1}{2}$"
5"
4"-5"
3"
Boom Saddle top armored, ¼" plate
2"-3" x ½" iron strap
5"
$3\frac{1}{2}$"
14"
$1\frac{1}{2}$"
$3\frac{1}{4}$"
3"
8"
Main tops'l bitts
2 Pins P&S in fife rail
3"
35"
22"
4"
Fall of sheet rove through cleat with stop knot at bitter end
Top of Mast Bed.

Type of Fife Rail and Boom Saddle used on the main mast since the 1880s. Saddles, with boom jaws, were used on fore and main as late as 1882, in a few Gloucester schooners.

FIGURE-8, TWISTED LINK

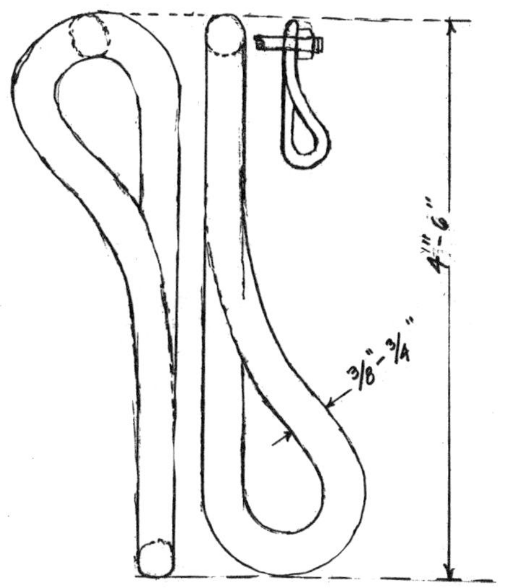
4"-6"
3/8"-3/4"

FIGURE-8 LINK
USED FOR CROSSTREE LIFTS, ETC.

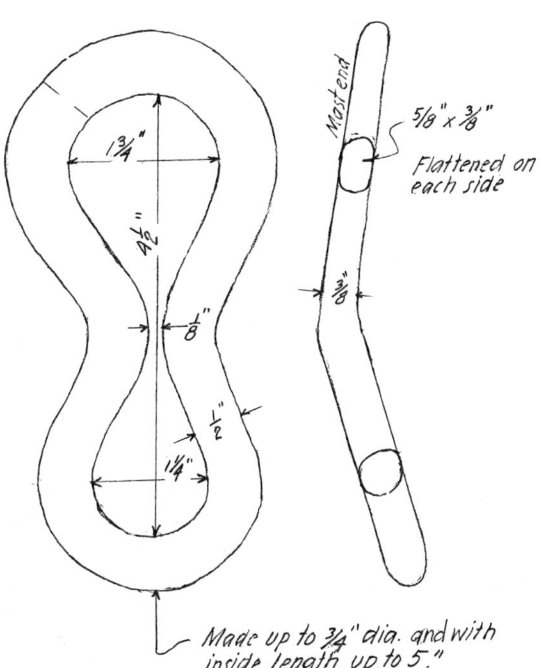
1 3/4"
4 1/2"
1/8"
1/2"
1 1/4"
Mast end
5/8" x 3/8"
Flattened on each side
3/8"
Made up to 3/4" dia. and with inside length up to 5."

FISHERMAN STAYSAIL PEAK HALYARDS

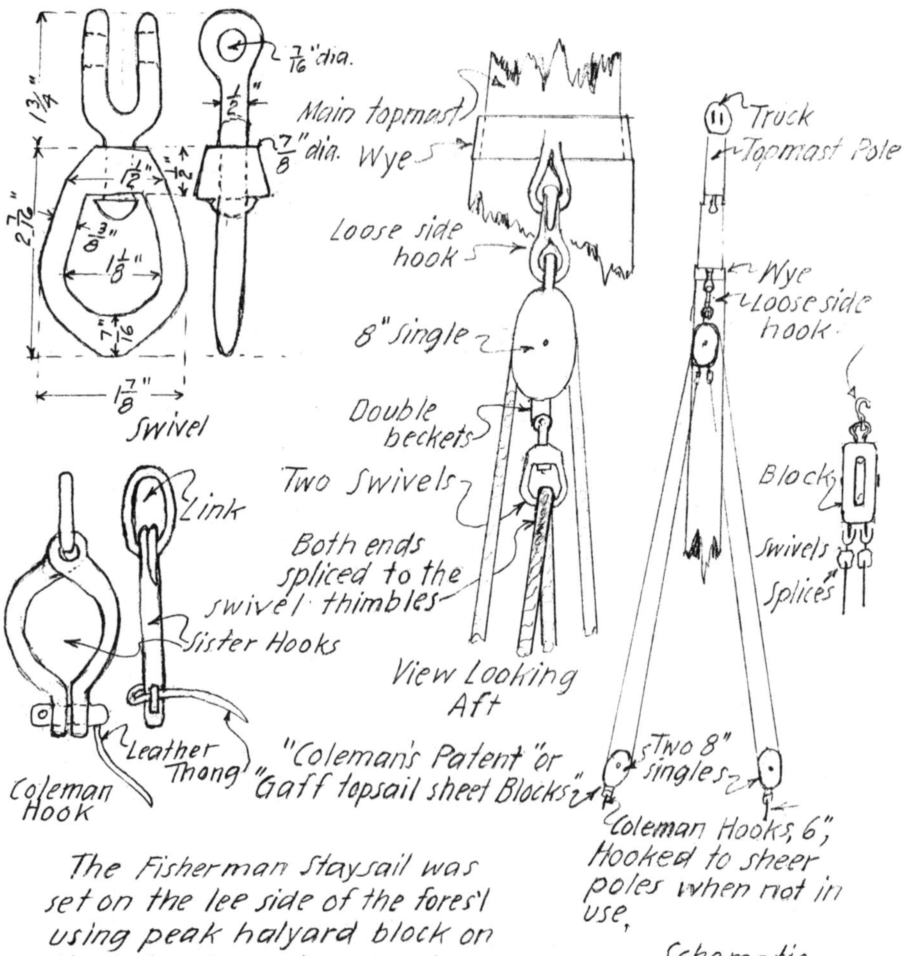
1 3/4"
2 7/16"
1/2"
1 1/2"
3/8"
1 1/8"
7/16"
1 7/8"
Swivel
7/16" dia.
1/2"
7/8" dia.
Main topmast
Wye
Loose side hook
8" single
Double beckets
Two Swivels
Both ends spliced to the swivel thimbles
View Looking Aft
Truck
Topmast Pole
Wye
Loose side hook
Block
Swivels
Splices
Link
Sister Hooks
Leather Thong
Coleman Hook
"Coleman's Patent" or "Gaff topsail sheet Blocks"
Two 8" singles
Coleman Hooks, 6", Hooked to sheer poles when not in use.
Schematic
E. Bosley

The Fisherman Staysail was set on the lee side of the fores'l using peak halyard block on that side. In coming about or jibing, the staysail had to be shifted to the new lee side of the spring stay and fore gaff to prevent chafe. There fore it was lowered to deck, the peak blocks inter changed in the head cringle. The throat halyard was cast off, the other end of it made fast to the throat cringle and the sail was ready to hoist on the lee side of spring stay and gaff.

FISHERMAN STAYSAIL PEAK, THROAT HALYARDS, SHEET AND TACK

The fisherman staysail had two halyards, main (peak) and fore (throat). The sail had to be lowered in tacking or jibbing as it had to be carried on the lee side of the springstay and foresail.

The throat halyard had a single block hooked to a link in thimble on foremast head springstay bail, on after side of foremast head.

Peak halyard had single block on foreside of main-topmast head, hooked into eye on wye.

Throat halyard made fast to cringle of sail at throat and led through the block at foremast head, with fall belayed to pin in the rail cap.

Peak halyard led from peak cringle of sail through block at main-topmast head. Fall belayed to pin in main rail cap.

The tack was a pendant about 2′-0″ long; in the free end of this was a snap hook large enough to snap around the staysail's throat halyard. A wooden grab hook was often used in place of the snap hook. In addition, another tack was secured to the tack cringle of the sail, belayed to a pin in the fife rail at foremast. The rigging of the tacks permits control of the sail in raising or lowering and hardening of luff.

The sheet is a single piece of line passed through the clew cringle of the sail, crossed at the center of the bight and seized to form port and starboard sheets. These belayed well aft, near the quarters, but belay was largely controlled by cut of the staysail.

The staysail halyards are knotted in the sail cringles to allow quick release for dipping sail.

FISHERMAN STAYSAIL, GRAB HOOK

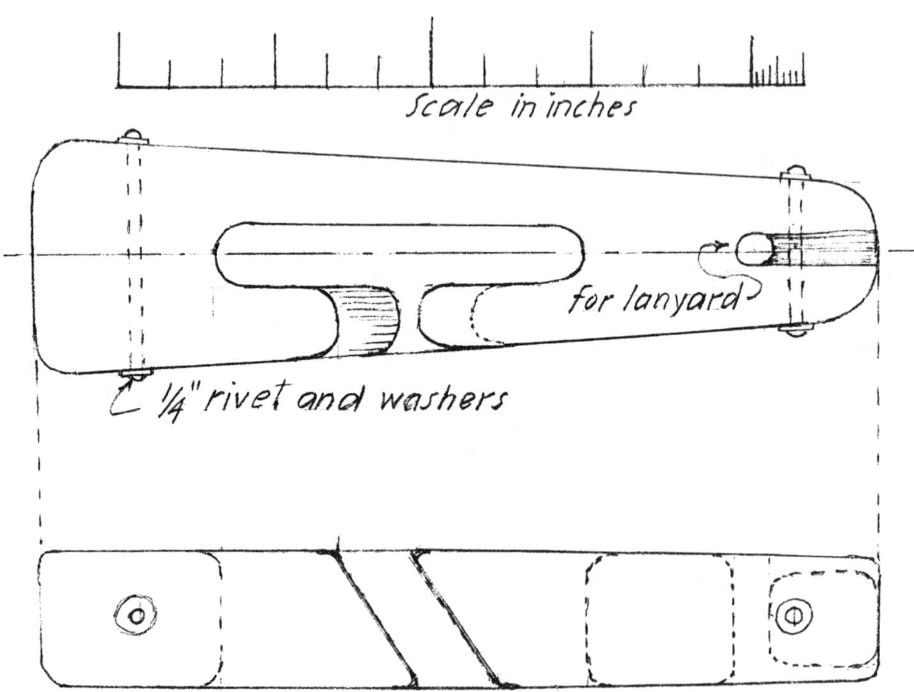
Scale in inches
for lanyard
1/4" rivet and washers

Oak grab hook used to keep tack of fisherman staysail stretched forward. A short lanyard was spliced through hole and bent to staysail tack cringle
Snatch portion of grab hook was hooked to th
fore throat (or fore peak) halyard fall of the foresail to flatten the luff of the staysail. C.S.

FISHERMAN STAYSAIL

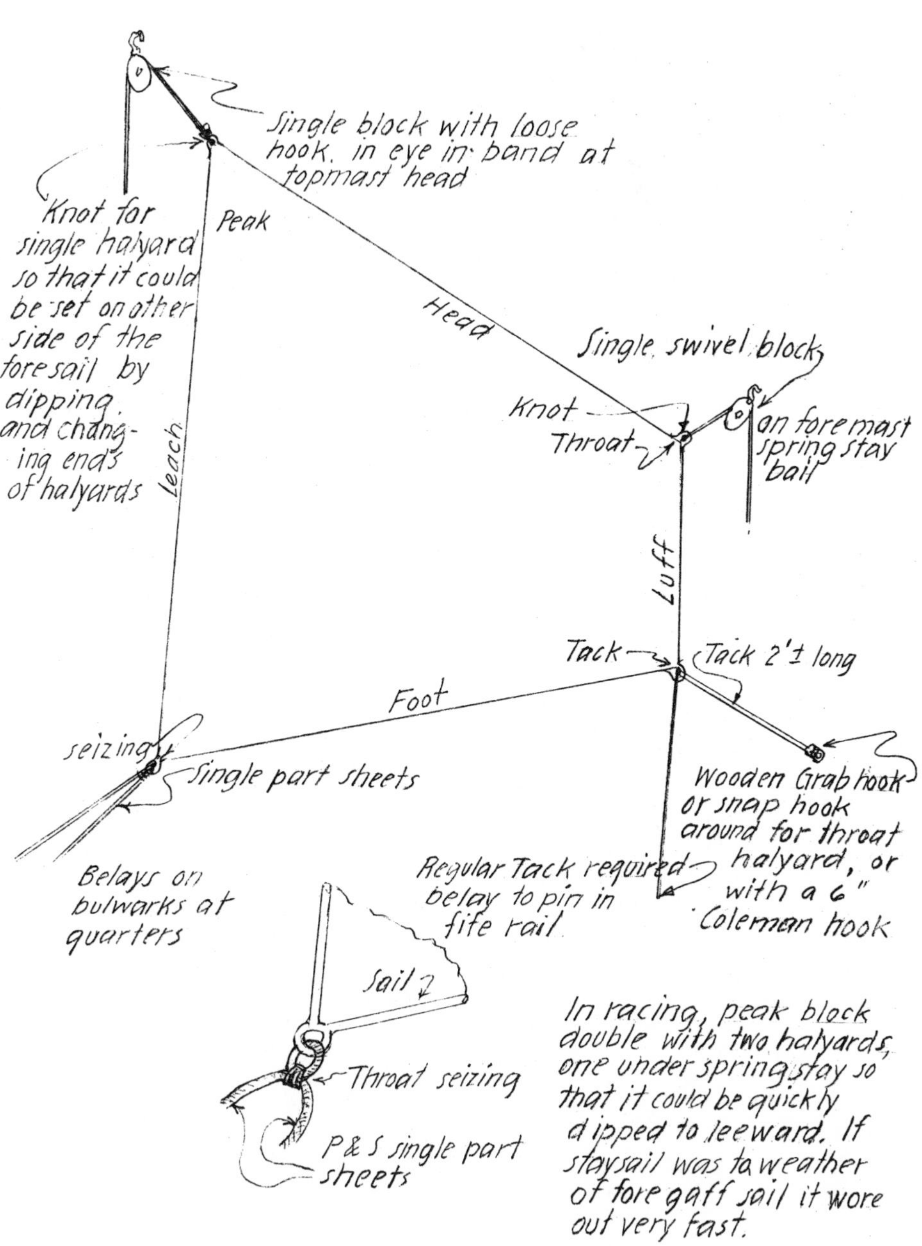
Single block with loose hook. in eye in band at topmast head
Knot for single halyard so that it could be set on other side of the foresail by dipping and changing ends of halyards
Peak
Head
Leach
Single swivel block
Knot
Throat
on foremast spring stay bail
Luff
Tack
Tack 2'± long
Foot
seizing
Single part sheets
Belays on bulwarks at quarters
Wooden Grab hook or snap hook around for throat halyard, or with a 6" Coleman hook
Regular Tack required belay to pin in fife rail
Sail
Throat seizing
P & S single part sheets
In racing, peak block double with two halyards, one under spring stay so that it could be quickly dipped to leeward. If staysail was to weather of fore gaff sail it wore out very fast.

"FISH HOOK"
PART OF ANCHOR GEAR

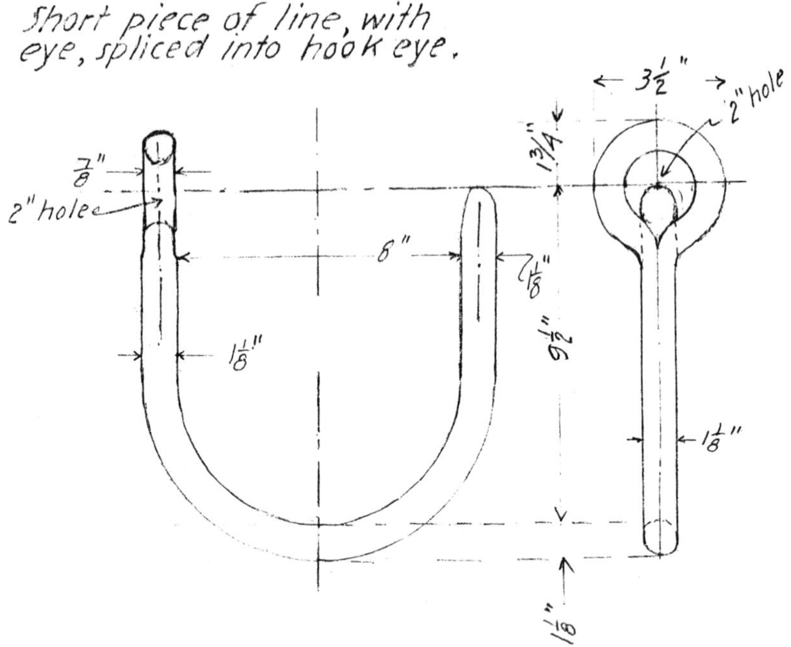
Short piece of line, with
eye, spliced into hook eye.
7/8"
2" hole
8"
1 1/8"
1 1/8"
9 1/2"
1 3/4"
3 1/2"
2" hole
1 1/8"
1 1/8"

This hook unusually short. The shank should be 18" to 22" long; crown of hook to ℄ of eye. 9 feet of 3¾" circ. manila. Spliced over 2" I.D. x 1¾" wide rope thimble in eye of hook and also at bitter end.

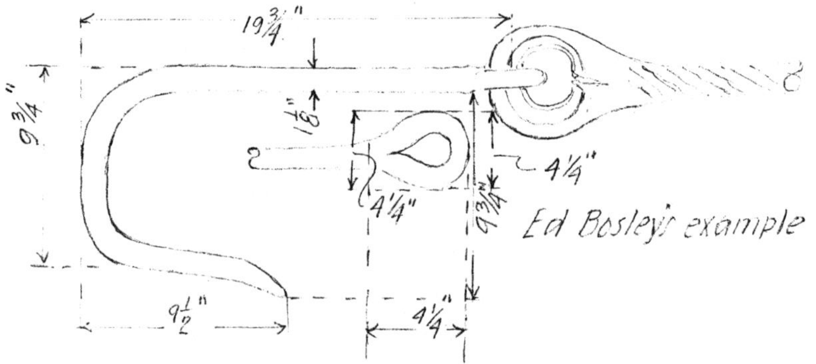
19 3/4"
9 3/4"
1 1/8"
4 1/4"
4 1/4"
9 3/4"
Ed Bosley's example
9 1/2"
4 1/4"

FISHHOLDS

Before 1890, or thereabouts, Essex-built schooners left the yards with their holds bare, except for the tight cabin and forecastle bulkheads. The ceiling was in place. Deck beams, clamps, shelves, etc., were given a coat of rosin varnish. Later the yards built the bunks, tables, stove platform, and lockers in galley. The aftercabin was likewise fitted with berths, lockers, ladder, etc., so that the initial fitting out required less time at Gloucester. Concrete soles in fishholds used after 1895. [L.H.S.]

The tight bulkheads were located a little forward of the main hatch and at the fore-end of the cabin trunk. They were made of 1½″-2″ plank. A joiner bulkhead was placed near the after-end of the cabin trunk and at the fore-end of the forecastle; under the windlass in many schooners.

FORE BOOM FITTINGS

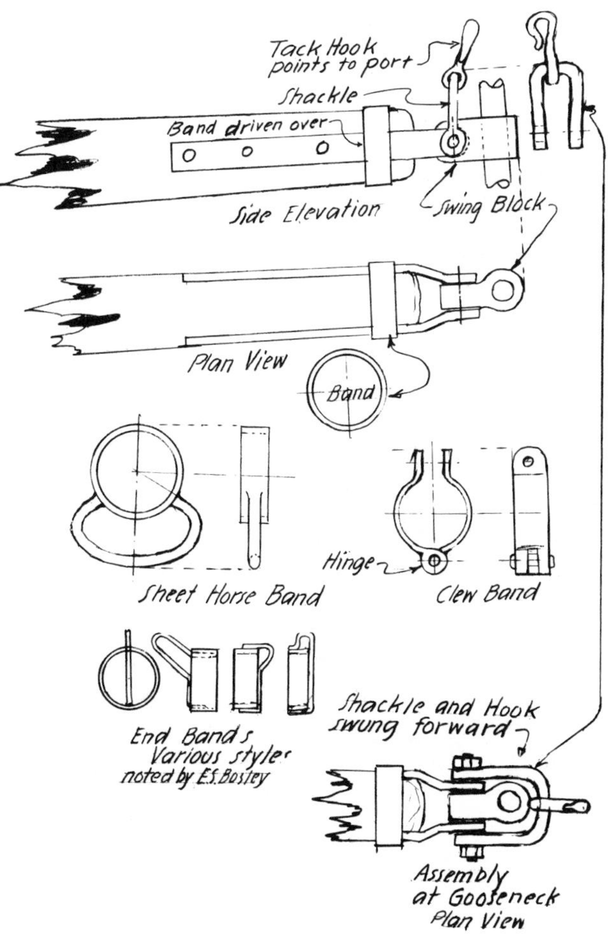
Tack Hook points to port
Shackle
Band driven over
Side Elevation
Swing Block
Plan View
Band
Hinge
Sheet Horse Band
Clew Band
End Bands Various styles noted by E.S.Bosley
Shackle and Hook swung forward
Assembly at Gooseneck Plan View

FORE BOOM FITTINGS AND FOREMAST GOOSENECK

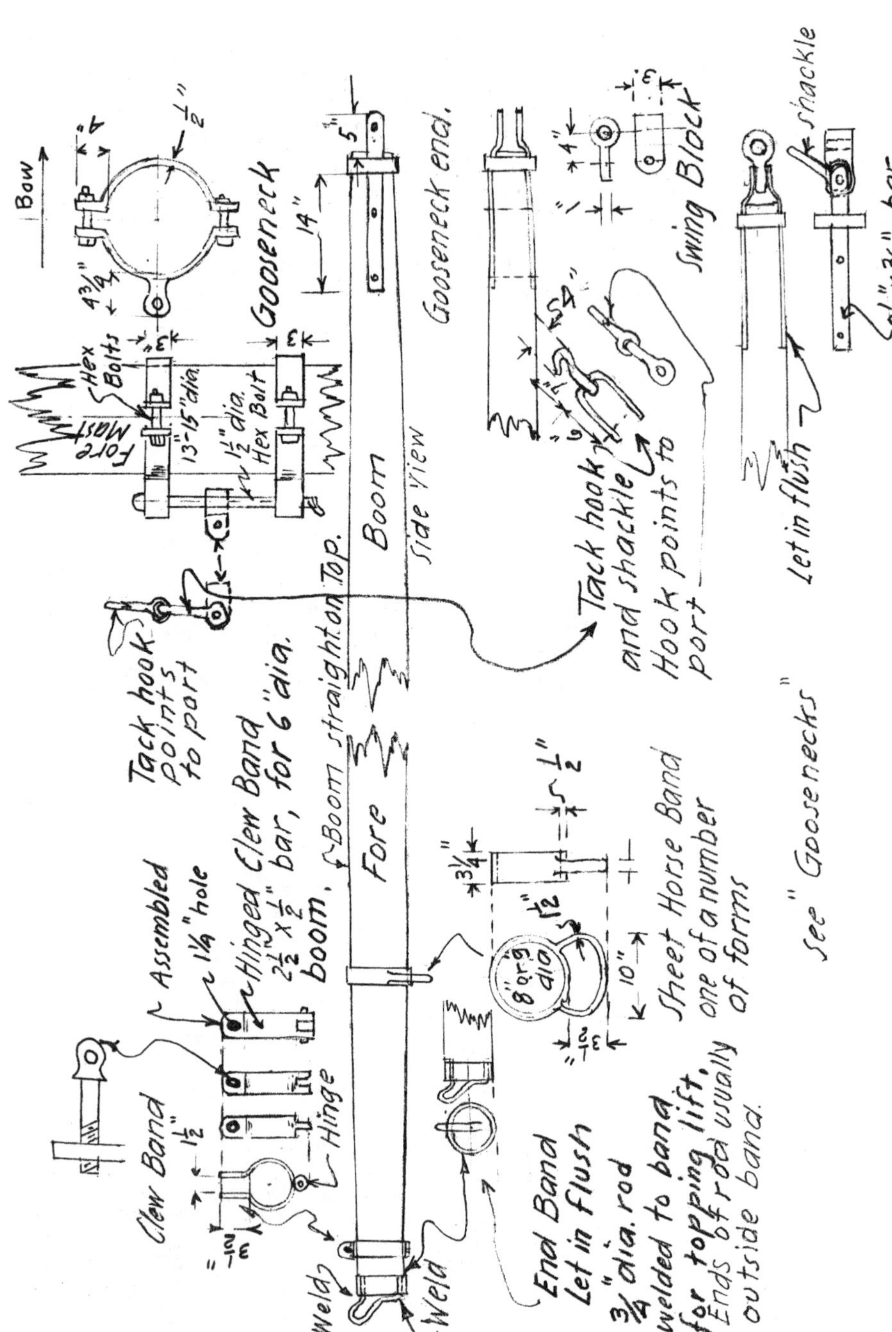
Bow
Gooseneck
Hex Bolts
Fore Mast
13"-15" dia.
1 1/2" dia. Hex Bolt
14"
5"
Gooseneck end.
Boom
Side View
Boom straight on Top.
Fore
Tack hook points to port
Tack hook and shackle
Hook points to port
Swing Block
shackle
2 1/2" x 3/4" bar
let in flush
Assembled
1 1/4" hole
Hinged Clew Band 2 1/2" x 1/2" bar, for 6" dia. boom.
Hinge
Clew Band
Weld
Weld
End Band Let in flush
3/4" dia. rod welded to band for topping lift.
Ends of rod usually outside band.
8" o.d. dia
10"
Sheet Horse Band one of a number of forms
See "Goosenecks"

FORE SHEET HORSE

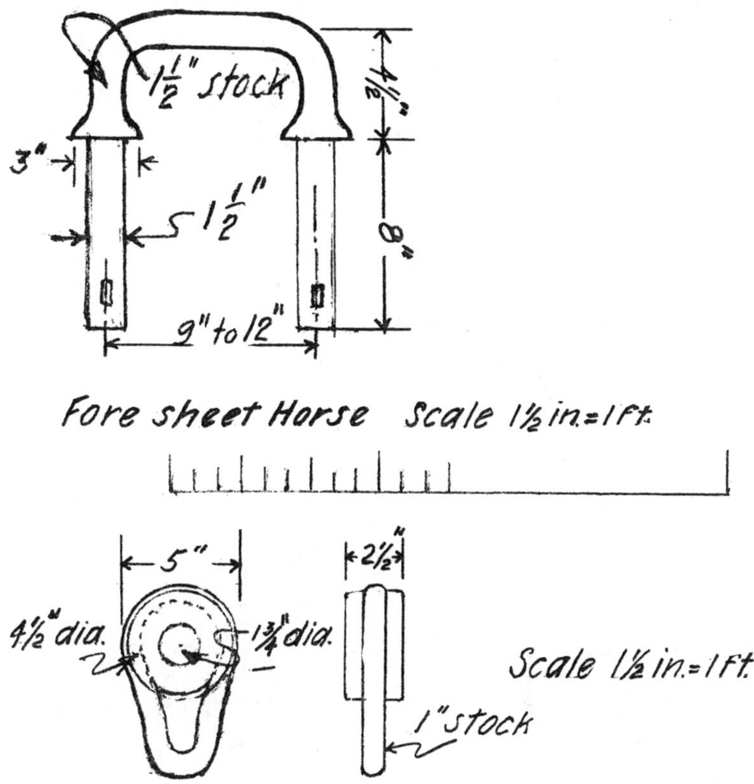
1½" stock
4½"
3"
1½"
8"
9" to 12"
Fore sheet Horse Scale 1½ in.=1 ft.
5"
2½"
4½" dia.
1¾" dia.
Scale 1½ in.=1 ft.
1" stock

Fairlead for Foresheet

FORE SHEET SLIDING SHACKLE SOMETIMES USED ON JUMBO SHEET

Fitted in various ways, as shown below, with rocker under foresheet horse, reversed with rocker on top of horse on foresheet wye, and with rockers at both ends. This fitting was used on foresheet, mainsheet, and on Jumbo sheet. Rocker was usually less round than shown here.

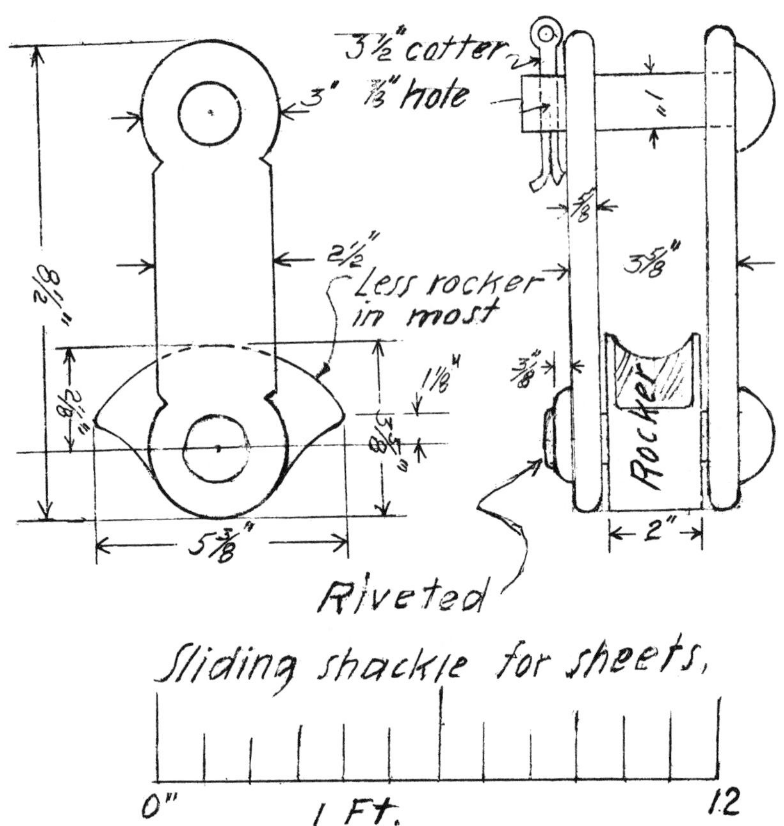
3½" cotter
3"
hole
2½"
Less rocker in most
3⅝"
1⅛"
5⅞"
8½"
Rocker
2"
Riveted
Sliding shackle for sheets.
0"
1 Ft.
12

FORE SHEET, DIAGRAMMATIC

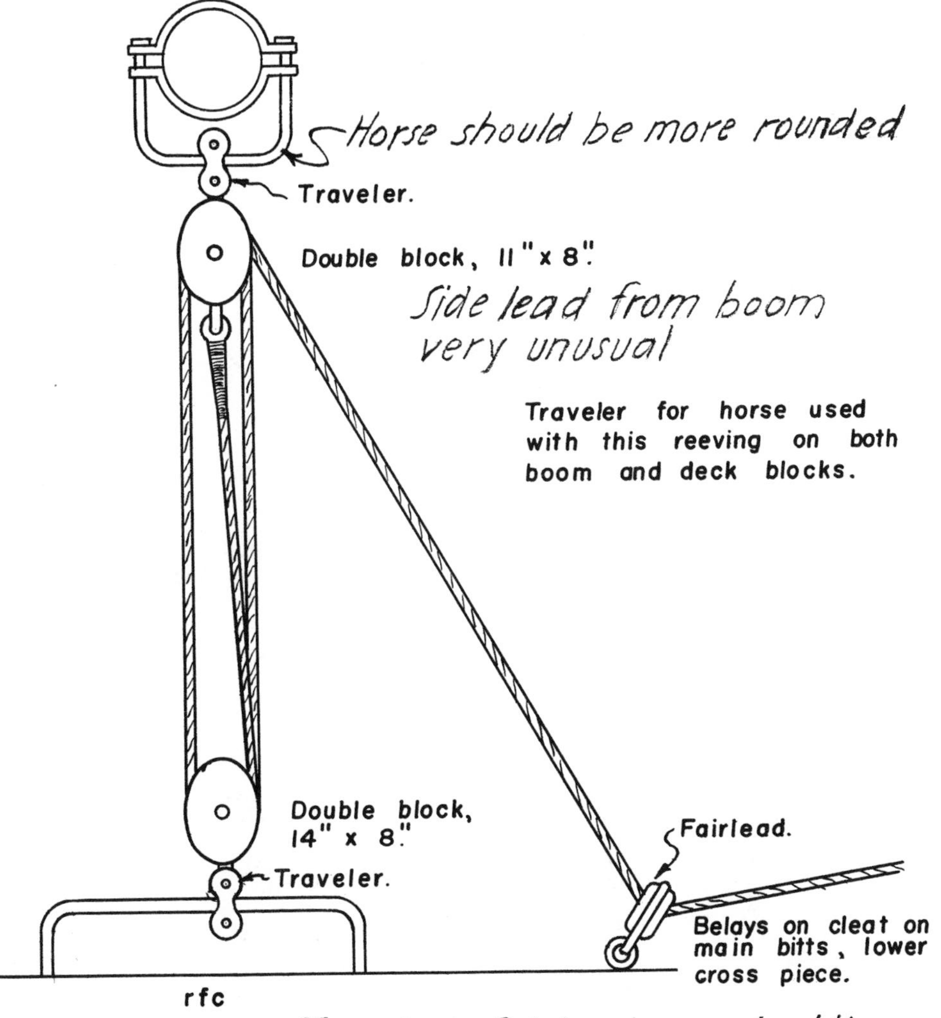
Horse should be more rounded
Traveler.
Double block, 11" x 8".
Side lead from boom very unusual
Traveler for horse used with this reeving on both boom and deck blocks.
Double block, 14" x 8".
Traveler.
Fairlead.
Belays on cleat on main bitts, lower cross piece.
rfc
Two deck fairleads used with this reeving; one abreast horse and one on ℄ forward of bitts.

FORE SHEET, DIAGRAMMATIC

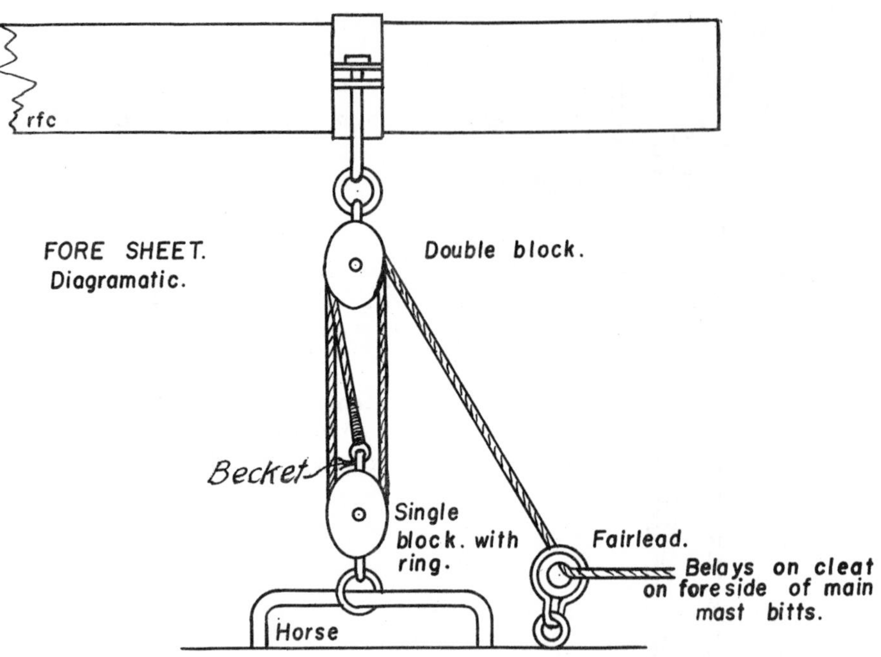
rfc
FORE SHEET.
Diagramatic.
Double block.
Becket
Single
block. with
ring.
Fairlead.
Belays on cleat
on fore side of main
mast bitts.
Horse

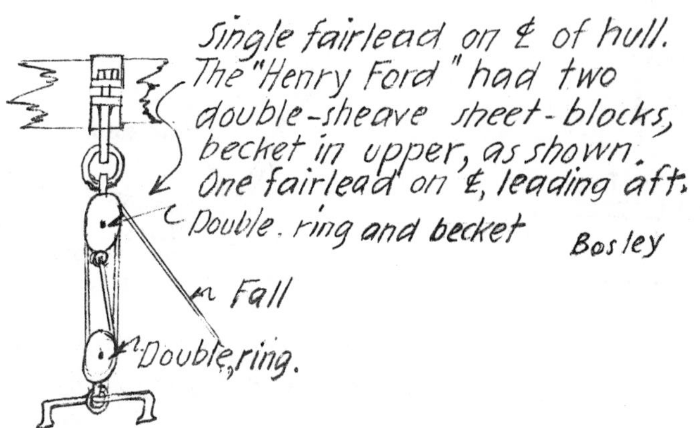
Single fairlead on ℄ of hull.
The "Henry Ford" had two
double-sheave sheet-blocks,
becket in upper, as shown.
One fairlead on ℄, leading aft.
Double. ring and becket
Bosley
Fall
Double, ring.

ARRANGEMENT OF FORE SHEET HORSE AT MAIN MAST, "ELSIE"

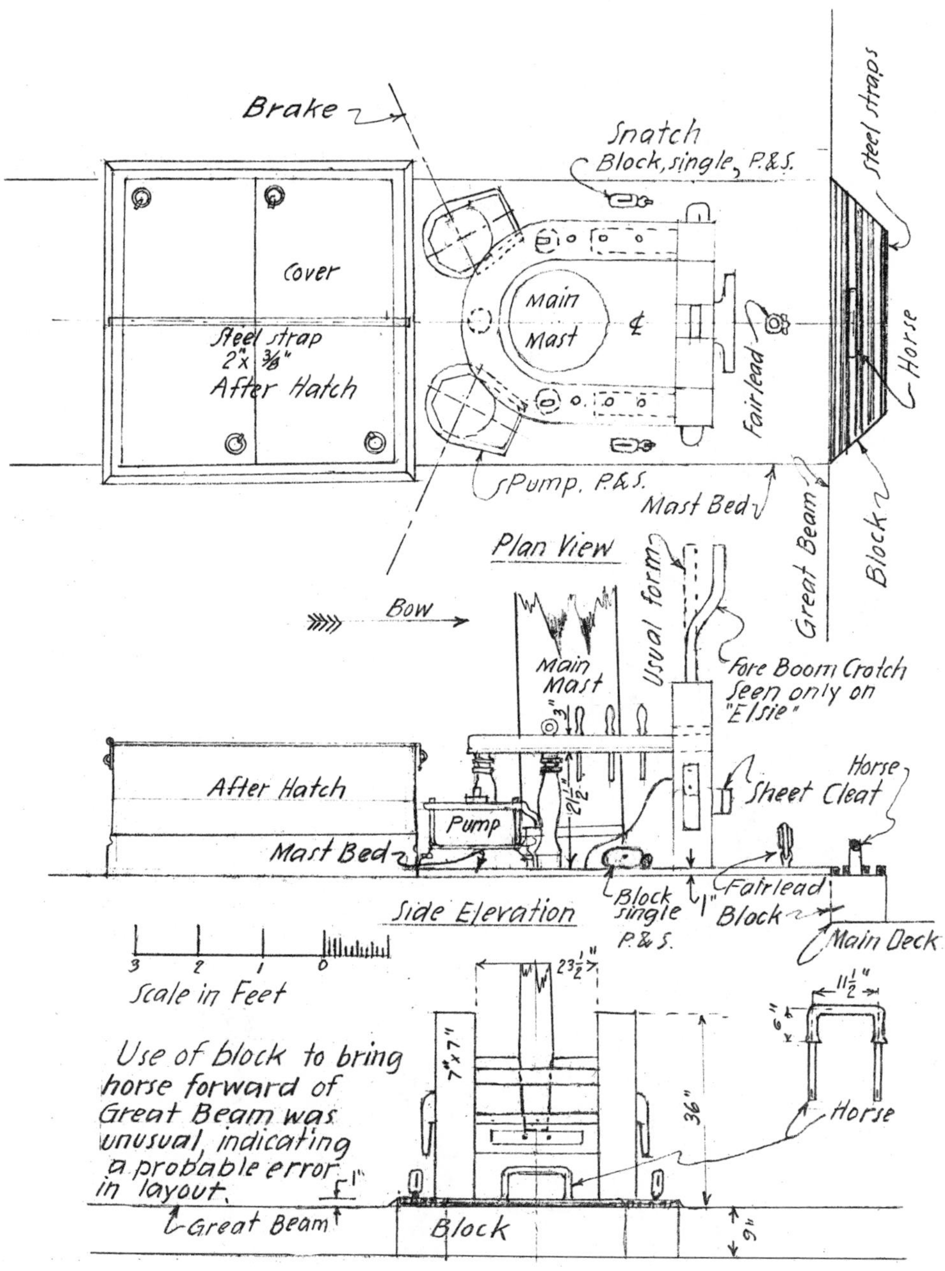

Brake
Snatch Block, single, P.&S.
Steel straps
Cover
Main Mast
℄
Steel strap 2" x 3/8"
After Hatch
Fairlead
Horse
Pump, P.&S.
Mast Bed
Great Beam
Block
Plan View
Bow
Usual form
Main Mast
Fore Boom Crotch Seen only on "Elsie"
3"
21 1/2"
After Hatch
Pump
Mast Bed
Horse
Sheet Cleat
Block single P.&S.
1"
Fairlead Block
Main Deck
Side Elevation
3 2 1 0
Scale in Feet
23 1/2"
7" x 7"
36"
11 1/2"
6"
Horse
Use of block to bring horse forward of Great Beam was unusual, indicating a probable error in layout.
1"
Great Beam
Block
9"

FRAMES

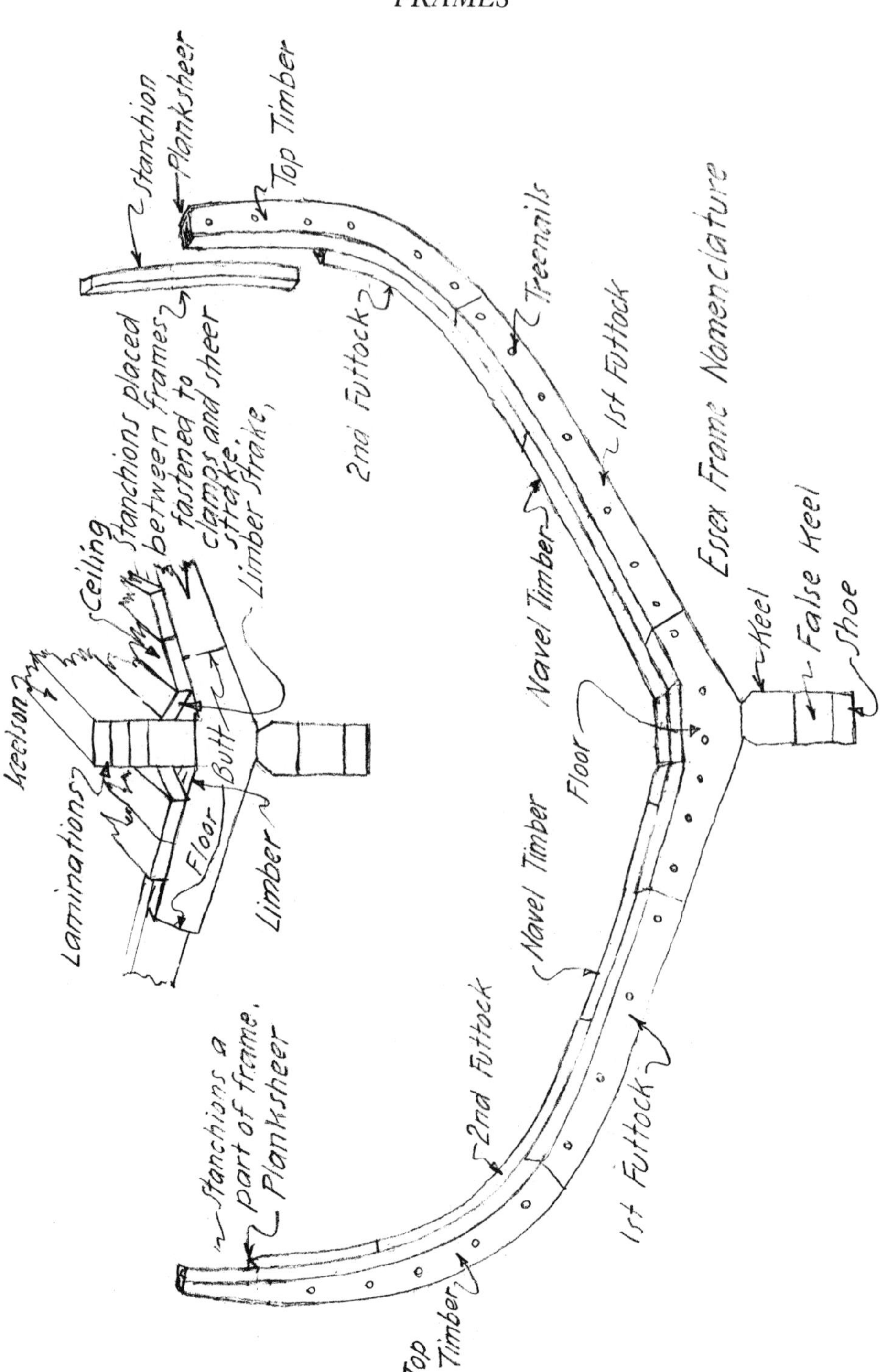

Stanchion
Planksheer
Top Timber
Stanchions placed between frames fastened to clamps and sheer strake.
Limber strake,
Ceiling
Keelson
Laminations
Floor
Butt
Limber
2nd Futtock
Treenails
1st Futtock
Essex Frame Nomenclature
Navel Timber
Keel
False Keel
Shoe
Floor
Navel Timber
2nd Futtock
1st Futtock
Stanchions a part of frame.
Planksheer
Top Timber

GAFF (MAIN), THROAT HALYARD IRONWORK

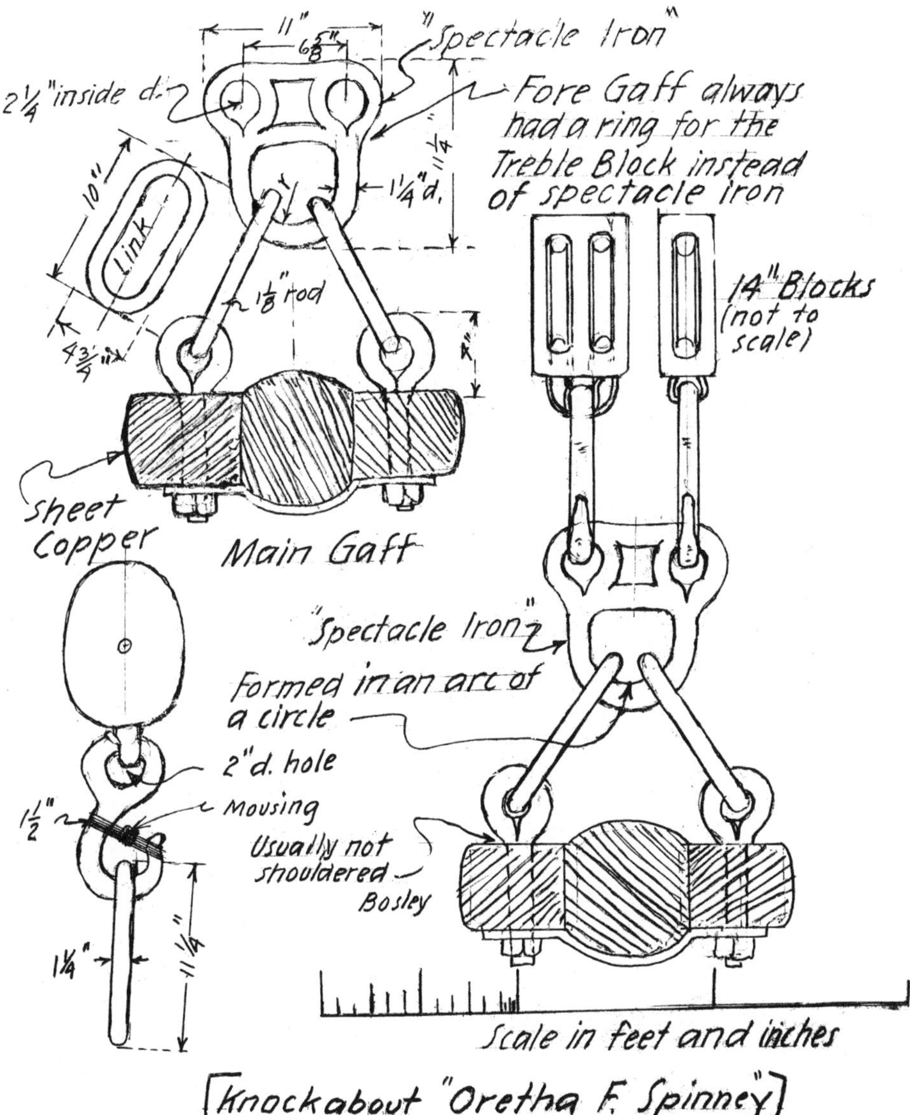
11"
6 5/8"
"Spectacle Iron"
2 1/4" inside d.
Fore Gaff always had a ring for the Treble Block instead of spectacle iron
11 1/4"
1 1/4" d.
10"
Link
1 1/8" rod
4 3/4"
4"
14" Blocks (not to scale)
Sheet Copper
Main Gaff
"Spectacle Iron"
Formed in an arc of a circle
2" d. hole
Mousing
1 1/2"
Usually not shouldered
Bosley
1 1/4"
11 1/4"
Scale in feet and inches
[Knockabout "Oretha F. Spinney"]

GAFF (MAIN), THROAT HALYARD IRONWORK

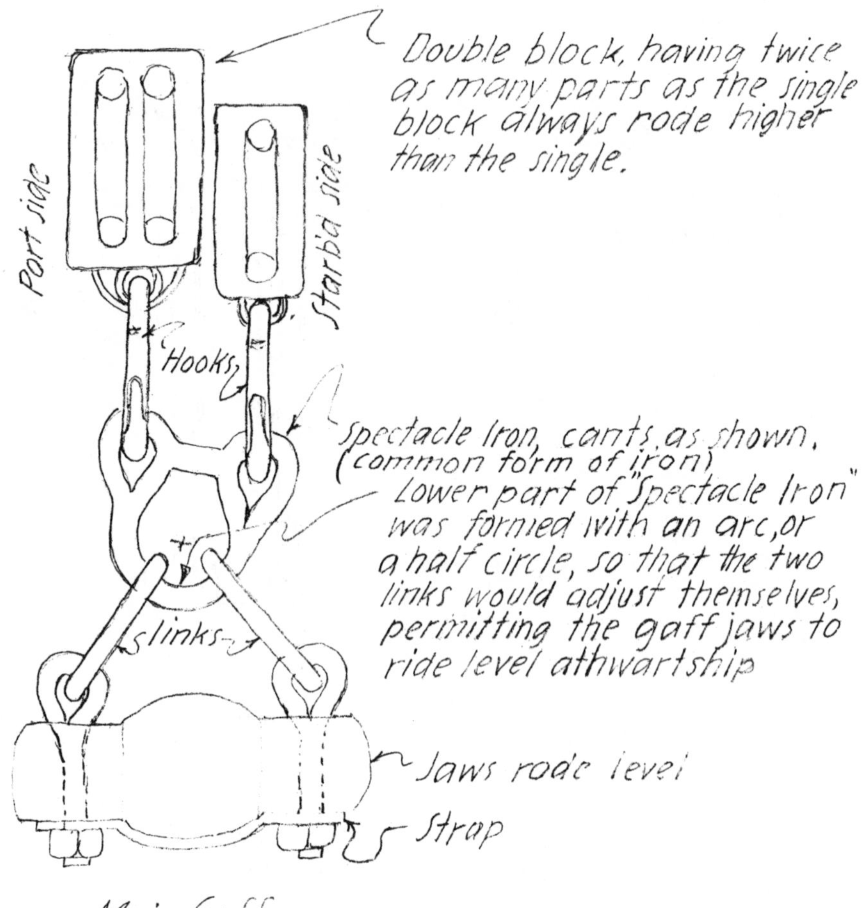
Double block, having twice as many parts as the single block always rode higher than the single.
Port side
Starb'd side
Hooks
Spectacle Iron, cants as shown. (common form of iron)
Lower part of "Spectacle Iron" was formed with an arc, or a half circle, so that the two links would adjust themselves, permitting the gaff jaws to ride level athwartship
links
Jaws rode level
Strap
Main Gaff
E.S Bosley

FORE AND MAIN GAFFS

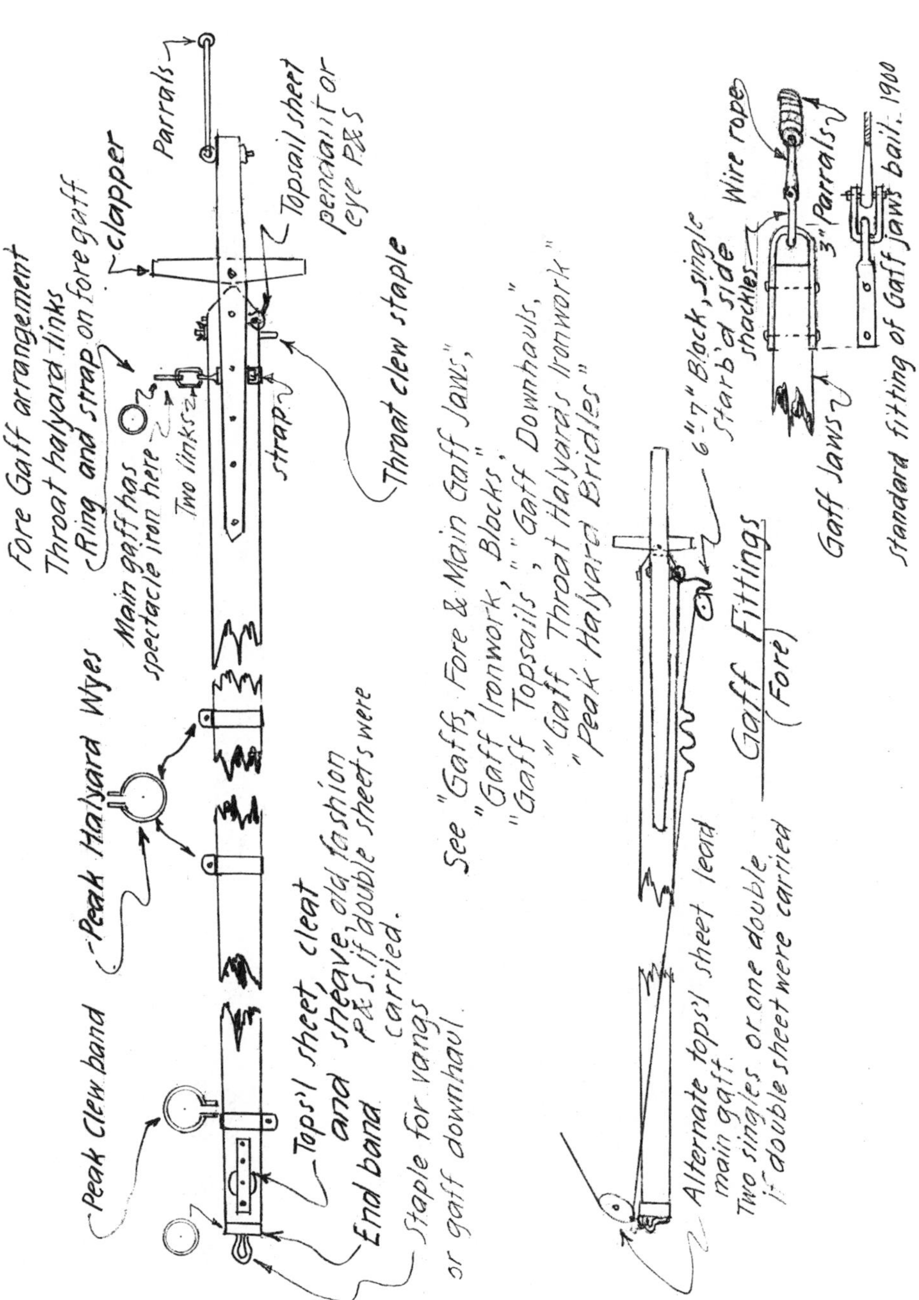
Fore Gaff arrangement
Throat halyard links
Ring and strap on fore gaff
clapper
Parrals
Topsail sheet pendant or eye P&S
Main gaff has spectacle iron here
Two links
strap
Throat clew staple
Peak Halyard Wyes
Peak Clew band
Tops'l sheet, cleat and sheave, old fashion P&S. If double sheets were carried.
End band
Staple for vangs or gaff downhaul.
See "Gaffs, Fore & Main Gaff Jaws",
"Gaff Ironwork, Blocks",
"Gaff Topsails", "Gaff Downhauls",
"Gaff Throat Halyards Ironwork"
"Peak Halyard Bridles"
Alternate tops'l sheet lead main gaff.
Two singles or one double, if double sheet were carried
Gaff Fittings (Fore)
6"-7" Block, single starb'd side
shackles
Wire rope
3" Parrals
Gaff Jaws
Standard fitting of Gaff jaws bail. 1900

FORE GAFF JAWS

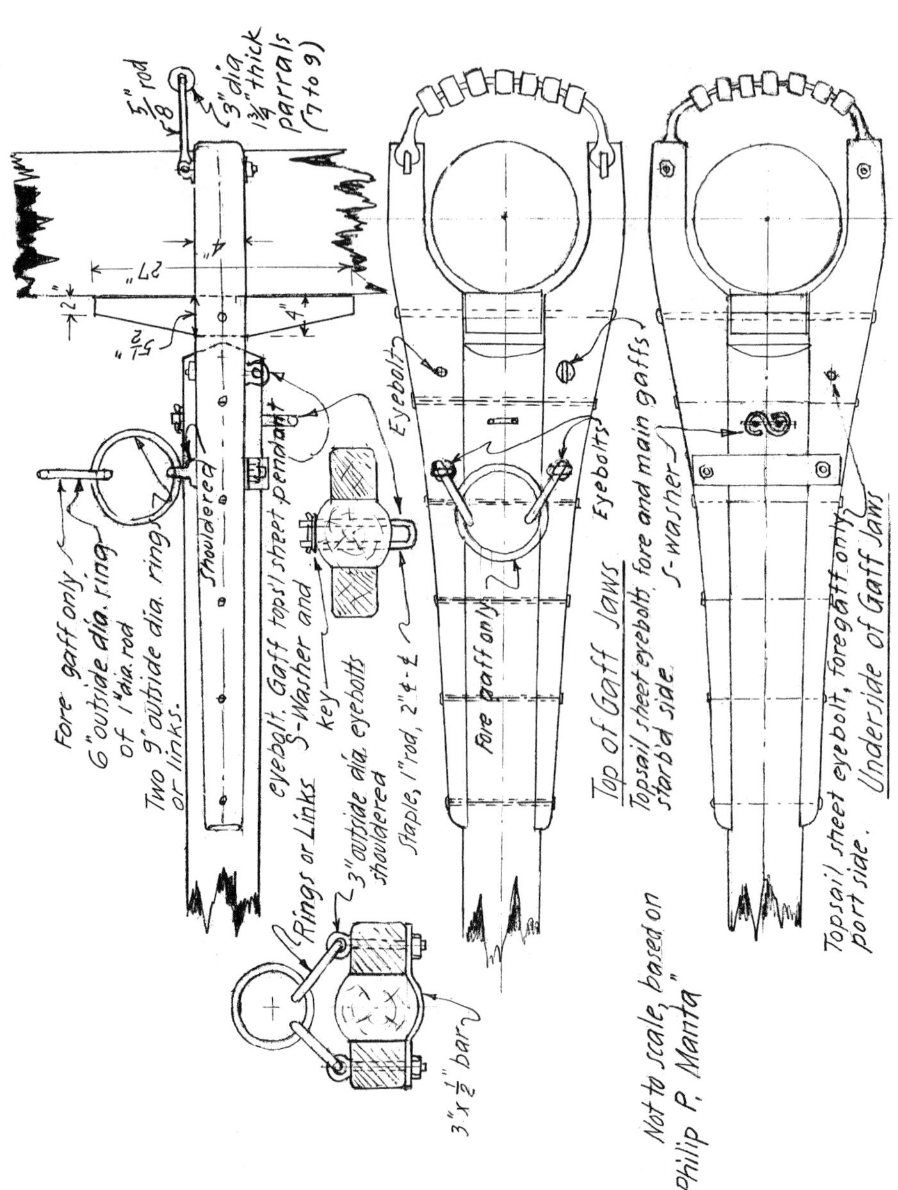

5/8" rod
3" dia. 1 3/4" thick parrals (7 to 9)
27"
4"
Fore gaff only
6" outside dia. ring of 1" dia. rod
Two 9" outside dia. rings or links.
Shouldered
eyebolt. Gaff tops'l sheet pendant
S-washer and key
Rings or Links
3" outside dia. eyebolts shouldered
Staple, 1" rod, 2" ℄-℄
3" x 1/2" bar
Eyebolt
Eyebolts
Fore gaff only
Top of Gaff Jaws
Topsail sheet eyebolts fore and main gaffs starb'd side.
S-washer
Topsail sheet eyebolt, foregaff only port side.
Underside of Gaff Jaws
Not to scale, based on "Philip P. Manta"

GAFFS, FORE AND MAIN

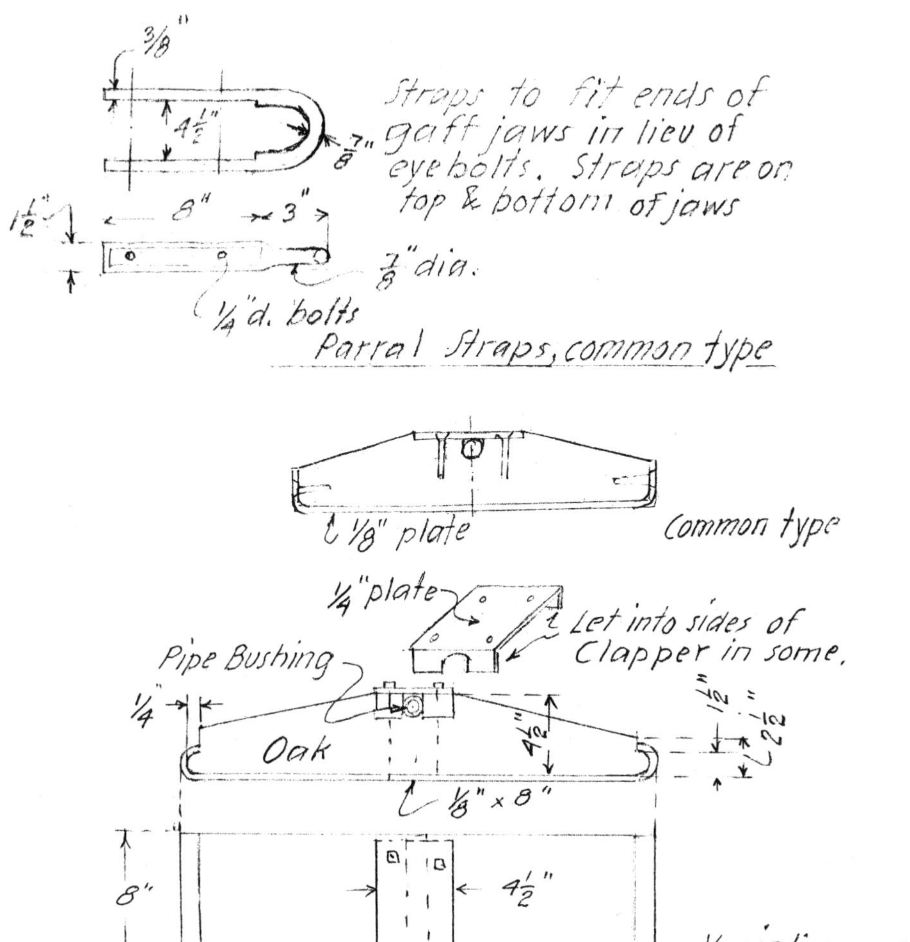

3/8"
4 1/2"
7/8"
Straps to fit ends of gaff jaws in lieu of eyebolts. Straps are on top & bottom of jaws
1 1/2"
8"
3"
7/8" dia.
1/4" d. bolts
Parral Straps, common type
1/8" plate
Common type
1/4" plate
Let into sides of Clapper in some.
Pipe Bushing
1/4"
Oak
4 1/2"
1/2"
2 1/2"
1/8" x 8"
8"
4 1/2"
Variation, one seen E.B.
27 1/2"

Clapper measured by
Edward Bosley, 1952

Most clappers not armored nor bushed in this manner, so far as could be seen.

GAFF IRONWORK, BLOCKS

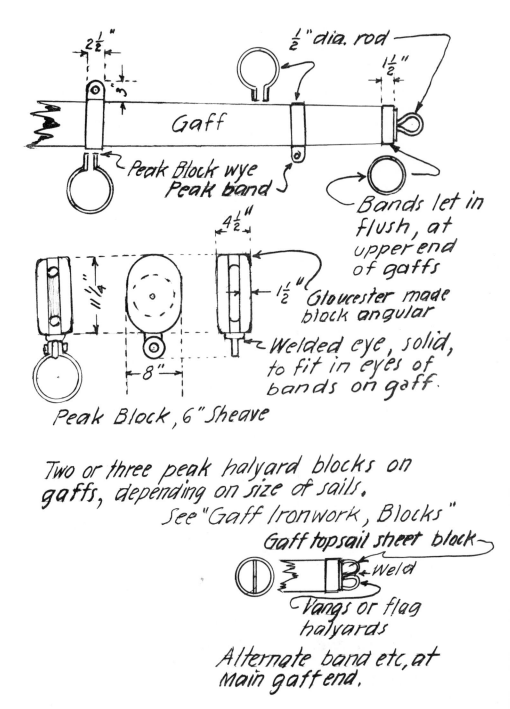

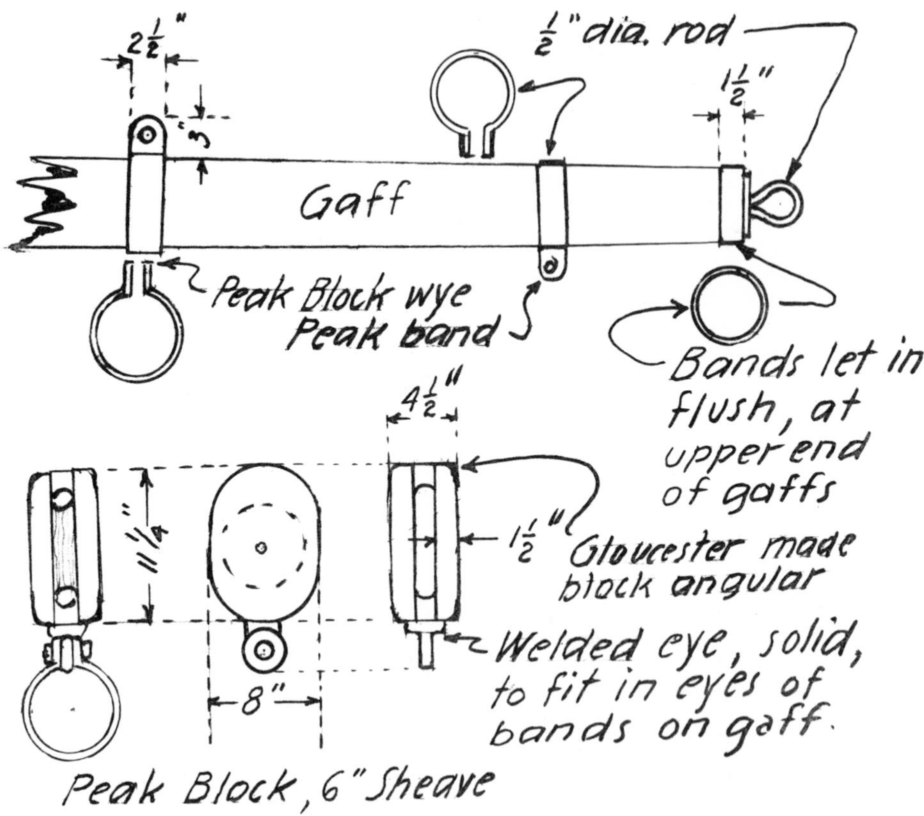
2½"
3"
½" dia. rod
1½"
Gaff
Peak Block wye
Peak band
Bands let in flush, at upper end of gaffs
4½"
11¼"
1½" Gloucester made block angular
Welded eye, solid, to fit in eyes of bands on gaff.
8"

Peak Block, 6" Sheave

Two or three peak halyard blocks on gaffs, depending on size of sails.

See "Gaff Ironwork, Blocks"

Gaff topsail sheet block

Weld

Vangs or flag halyards

Alternate band etc, at Main gaff end.

GAFF TOPSAILS

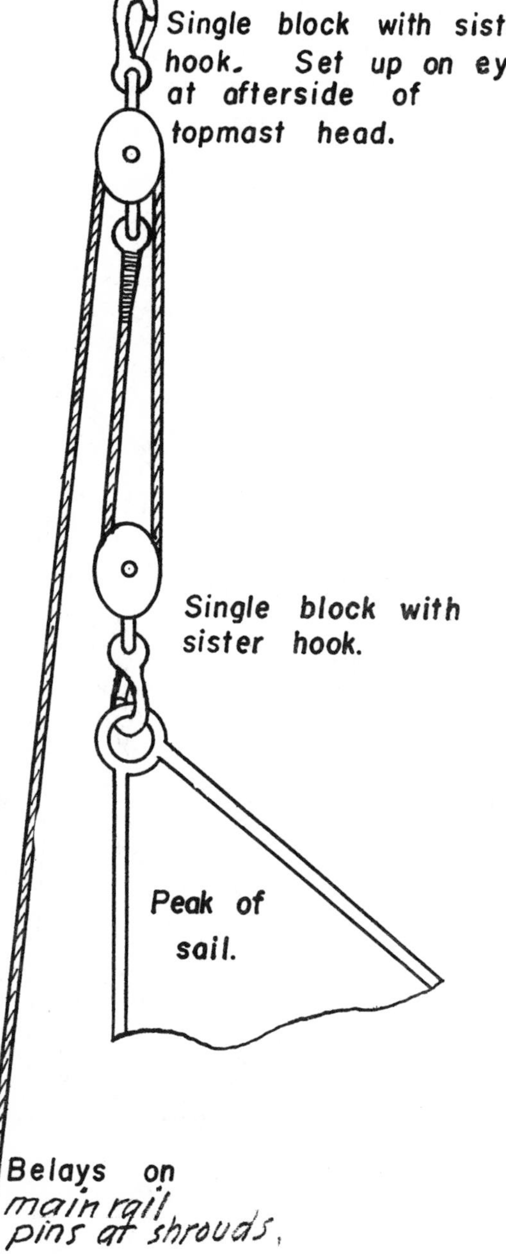
FORE and MAIN TOPSAIL HALLIARDS.
Diagramatic.
Single block with sister hook. Set up on eye at afterside of topmast head.
Single block with sister hook.
Peak of sail.
Belays on main rail pins at shrouds.

GAFF TOPSAIL SHEETS, FORE AND MAIN

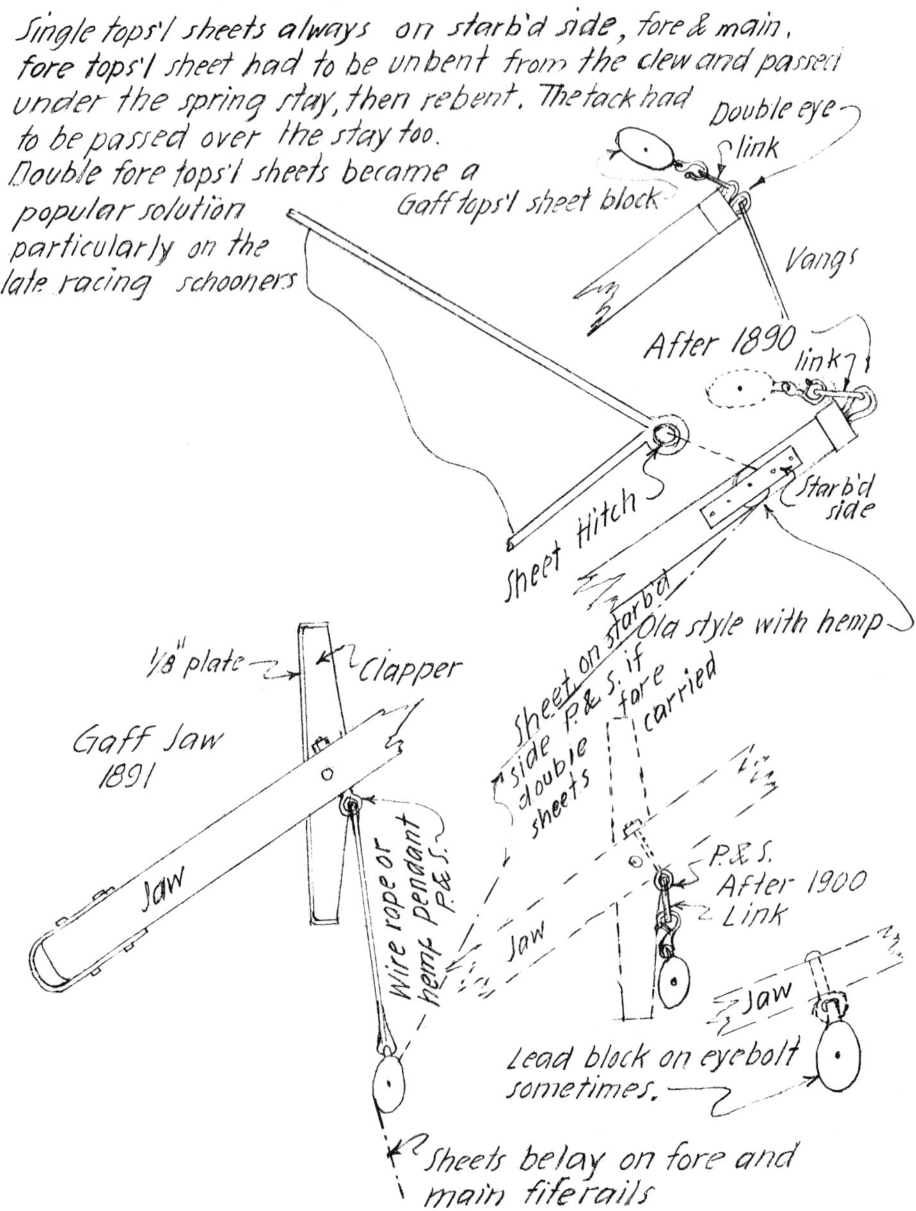
Single tops'l sheets always on starb'd side, fore & main.
fore tops'l sheet had to be unbent from the clew and passed under the spring stay, then rebent. The tack had to be passed over the stay too.
Double fore tops'l sheets became a popular solution particularly on the late racing schooners
Double eye
link
Gaff tops'l sheet block
Vangs
After 1890
link
Starb'd side
Sheet Hitch
Old style with hemp
Sheet on starb'd side P.& S. if double fore sheets carried
1/8" plate
Clapper
Gaff Jaw 1891
Jaw
Wire rope or hemp pendant P.& S.
P.& S. After 1900
Link
Jaw
Jaw
Lead block on eyebolt sometimes.
Sheets belay on fore and main fiferails

GAFF TOPSAILS, FORE AND MAIN LEADS OF CLEWLINE

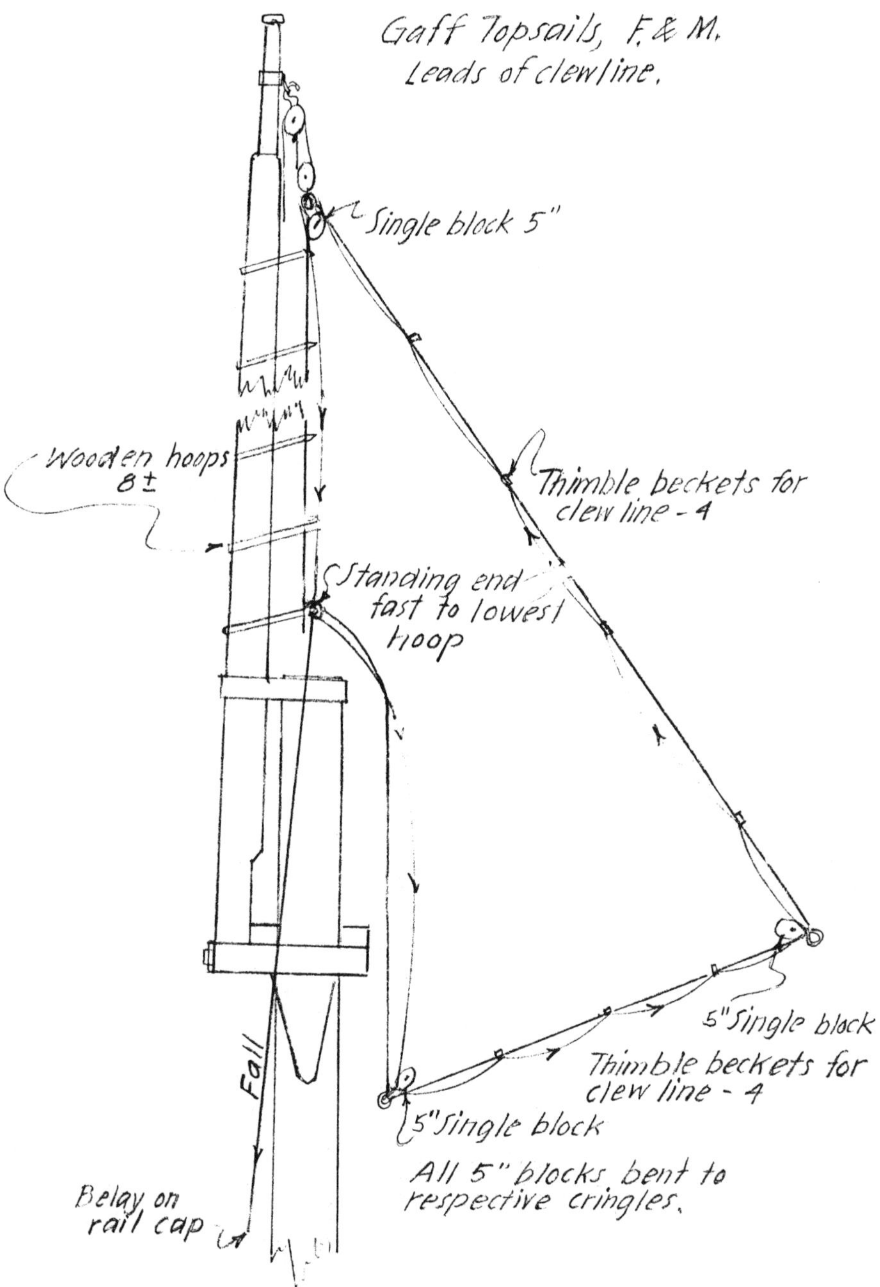
Gaff Topsails, F. & M.
Leads of clewline.
Single block 5"
Wooden hoops
8±
Thimble beckets for
clew line - 4
Standing end
fast to lowest
hoop
5" Single block
Thimble beckets for
clew line - 4
5" Single block
Fall
All 5" blocks bent to
respective cringles.
Belay on
rail cap

GAFF TOPSAIL CLEW BLOCKS

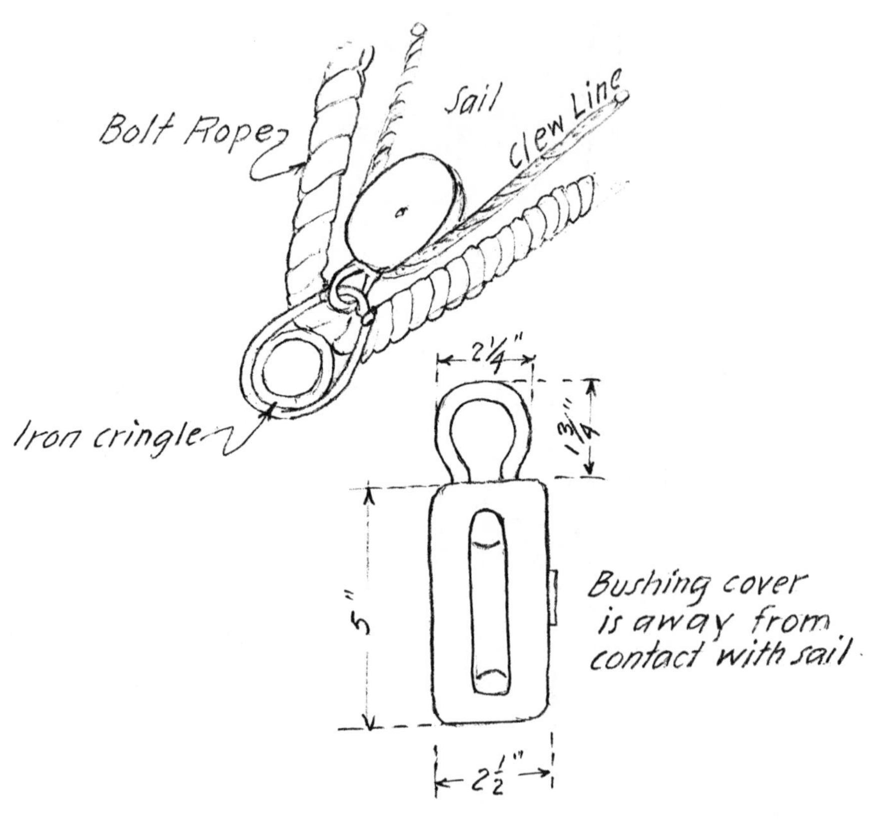
Bolt Rope
Sail
Clew Line
Iron cringle
2¼"
1¾"
5"
2½"
Bushing cover
is away from
contact with sail.

Ed Bosley

GAFF TOPSAILS

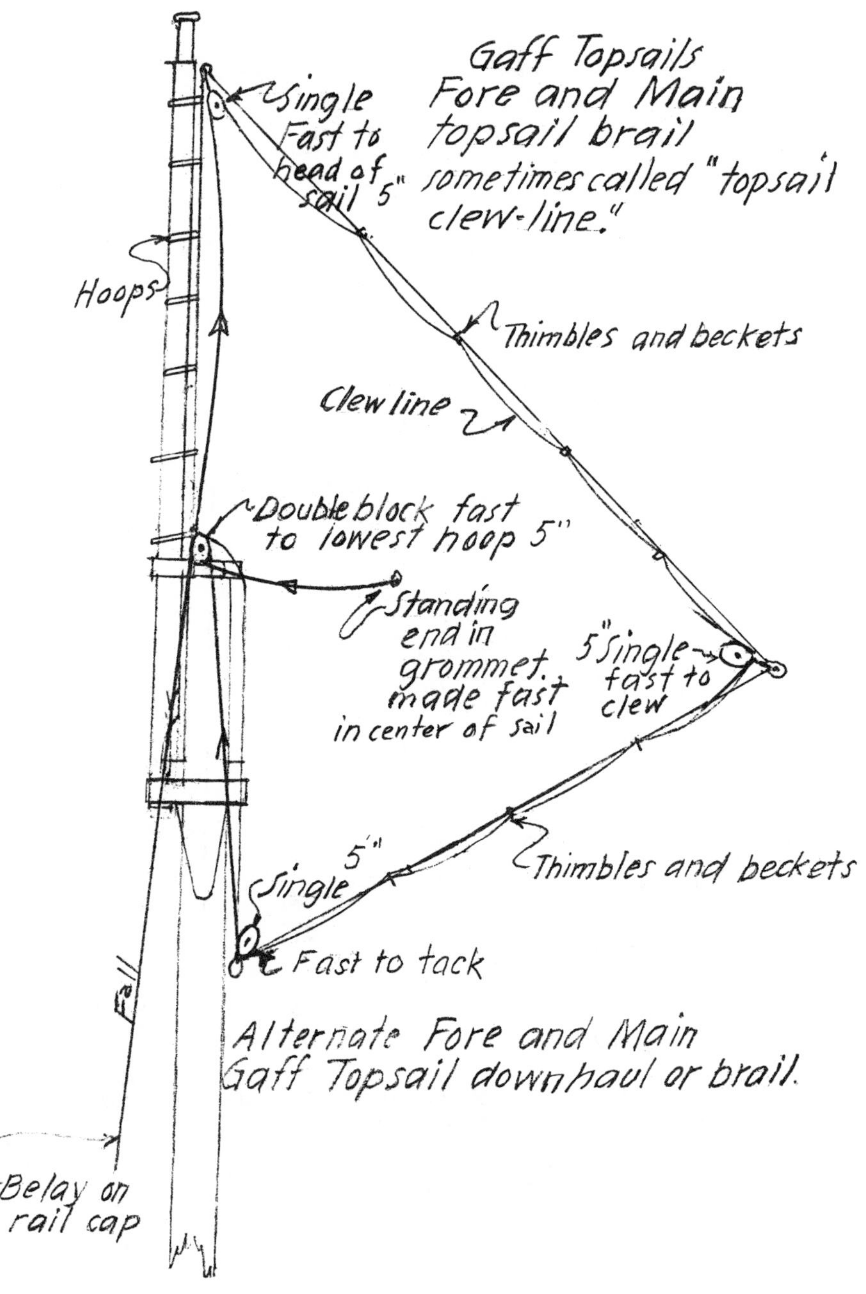
Gaff Topsails
Fore and Main
topsail brail
sometimes called "topsail
clew-line."
Single
Fast to
head of
sail 5"
Hoops
Thimbles and beckets
Clew line
Double block fast
to lowest hoop 5"
Standing
end in
grommet.
made fast
in center of sail
5" Single
fast to
clew
Thimbles and beckets
5"
Single
Fast to tack
Fall
Alternate Fore and Main
Gaff Topsail downhaul or brail.
Belay on
rail cap

GAFF DOWNHAULS OR "VANGS"

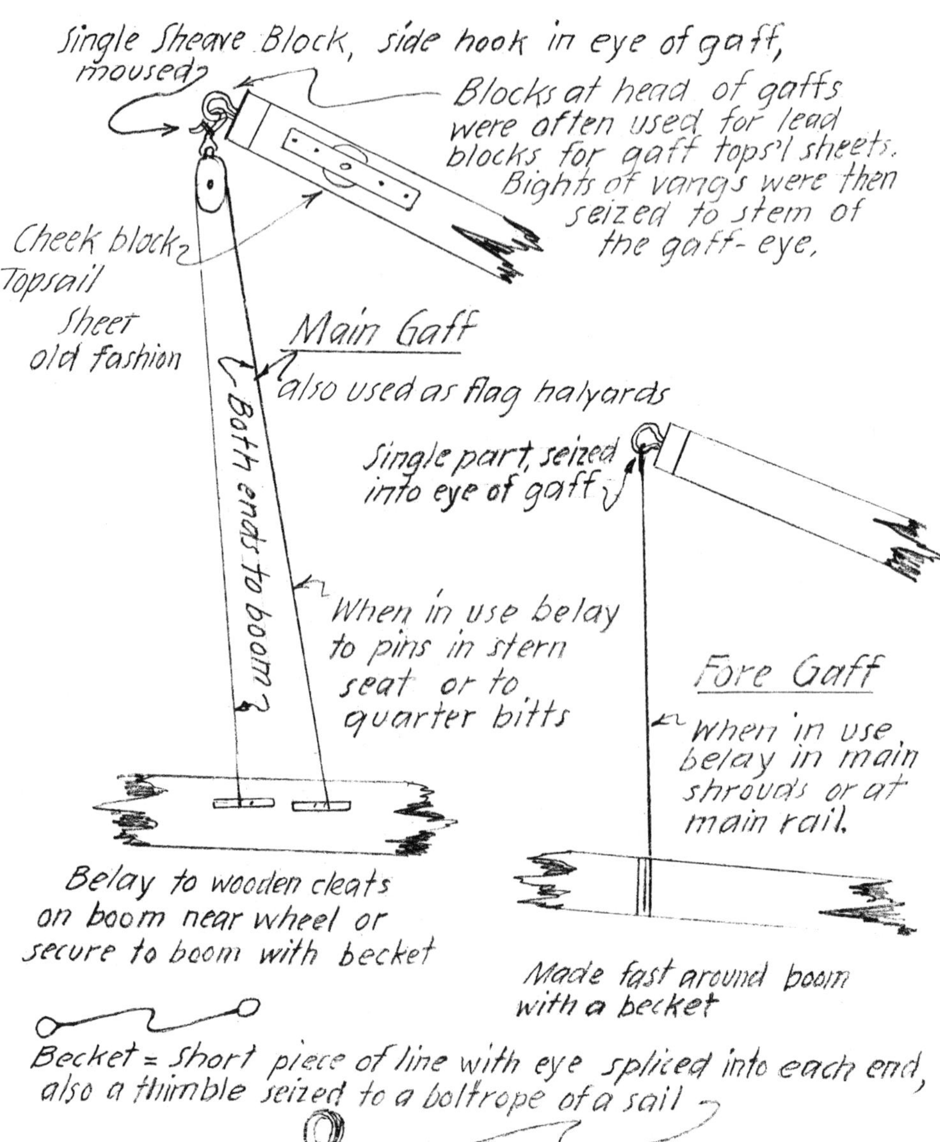
Single Sheave Block, side hook in eye of gaff, moused
Blocks at head of gaffs were often used for lead blocks for gaff tops'l sheets. Bights of vangs were then seized to stem of the gaff-eye.
Cheek block Topsail Sheet old fashion
Main Gaff
also used as flag halyards
Both ends to boom
When in use belay to pins in stern seat or to quarter bitts
Single part, seized into eye of gaff
Fore Gaff
When in use belay in main shrouds or at main rail.
Belay to wooden cleats on boom near wheel or secure to boom with becket
Made fast around boom with a becket
Becket = Short piece of line with eye spliced into each end, also a thimble seized to a boltrope of a sail

GAMMON IRON, OLD STYLE SQUARE BOWSPRIT

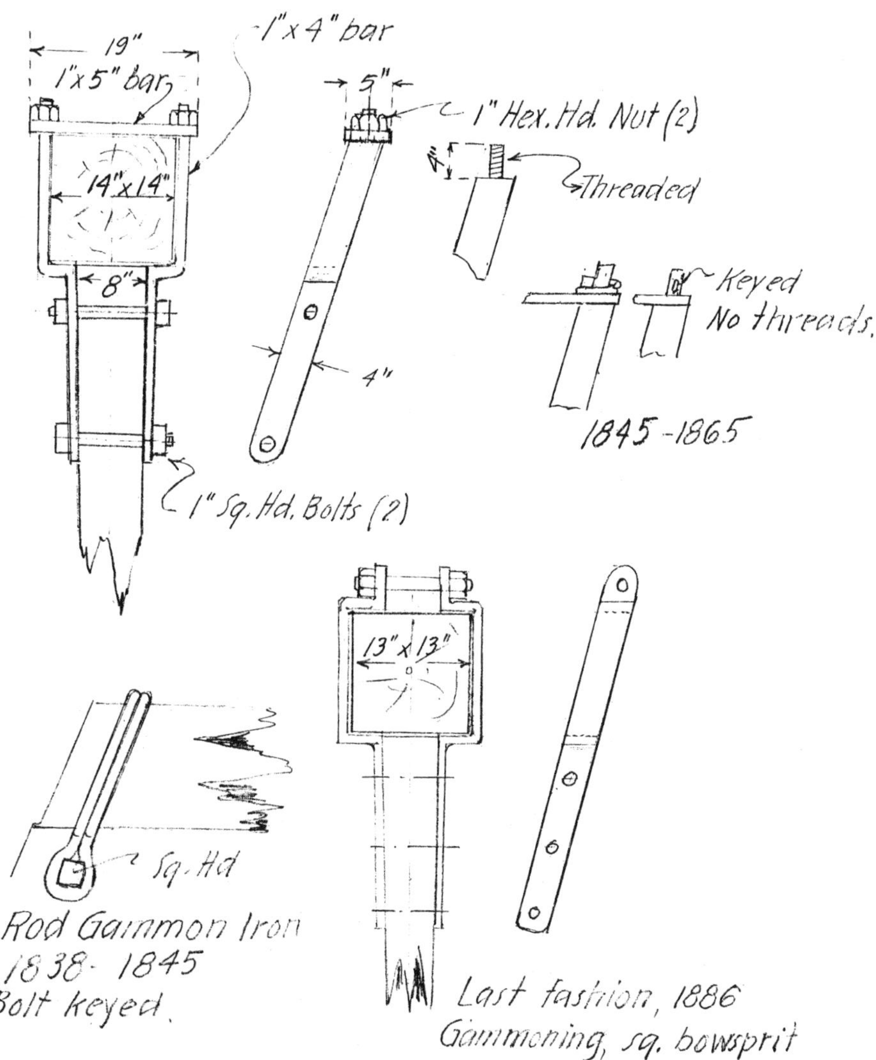
1"x4" bar
19"
1"x5" bar
5"
1" Hex. Hd. Nut (2)
14"x14"
Threaded
8"
Keyed
No threads.
4"
1845 -1865
1" Sq. Hd. Bolts (2)
13"x13"
Sq. Hd
Rod Gammon Iron
1838- 1845
Bolt keyed.
Last fashion, 1886
Gammoning, sq. bowsprit

GAMMON IRON, ROUND BOWSPRIT

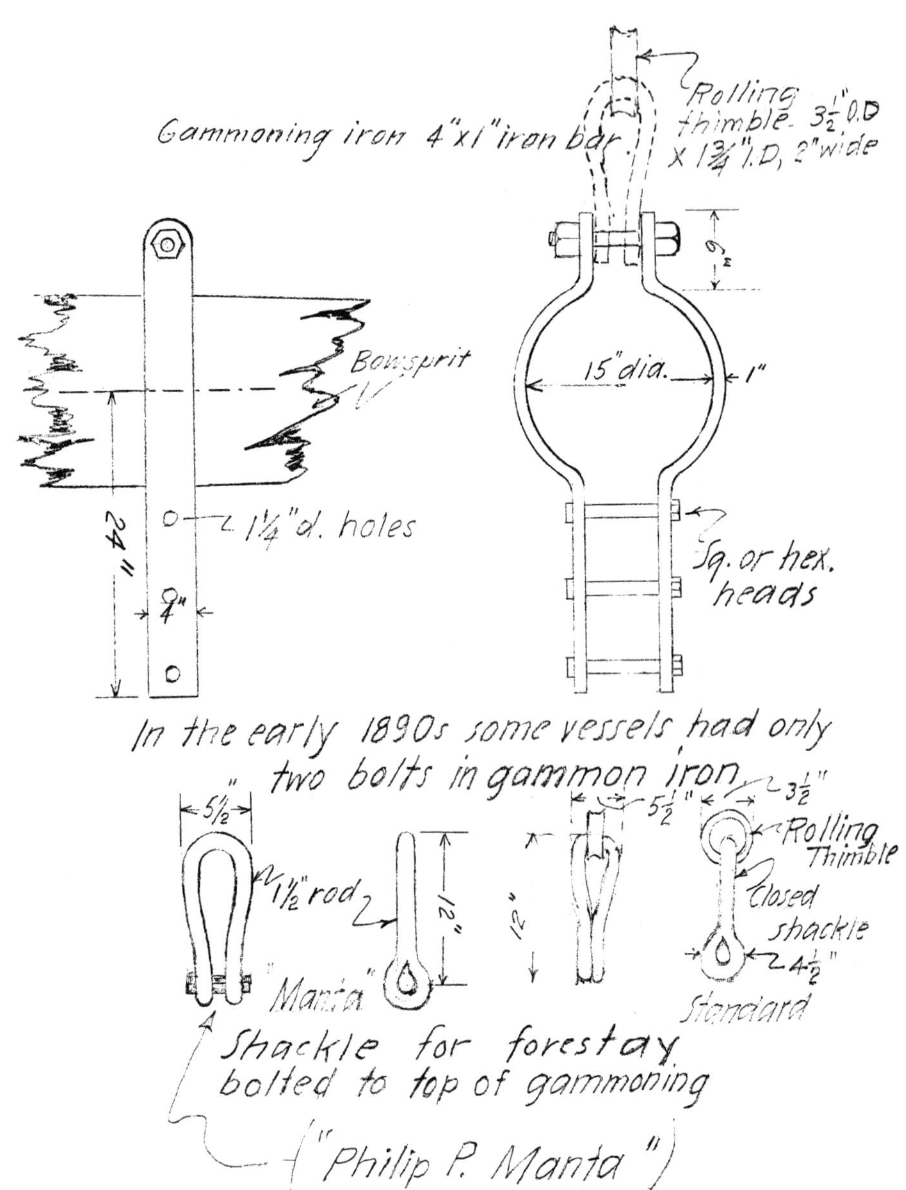

Gammoning iron 4"x1" iron bar
Rolling thimble 3½" O.D x 1¾" I.D, 2" wide
Bowsprit
15" dia.
1"
1¼" d. holes
24"
4"
Sq. or hex. heads
In the early 1890s some vessels had only two bolts in gammon iron
5½"
1½" rod
12"
"Manta"
12"
5½"
3½"
Rolling Thimble
Closed shackle
4½"
Standard
Shackle for forestay bolted to top of gammoning
("Philip P. Manta")

GAMMON IRON, "ELSIE"

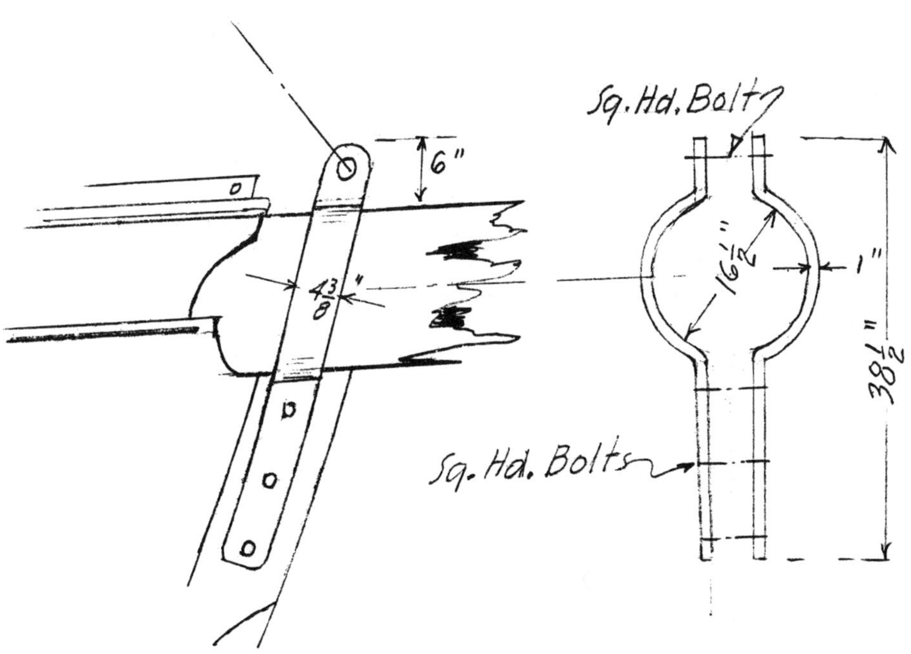
6"
Sq. Hd. Bolt
$4\frac{3}{8}$"
$16\frac{1}{2}$"
1"
$38\frac{1}{2}$"
Sq. Hd. Bolts

GOOSENECKS (NOTES)

Measurements of the heights of goosenecks on schooners will serve to show normal practices. The gooseneck of the "Mary T. Fallon" had its lower band about 12″ above the pinrail, or nearly 4′-0″ from mast bed to underside of the lower band. The bands were 24″, ℄ to ℄, on this vessel. "Ellen Marshall," knockabout, had lower band 2′-8″ above pin rail. Bands were 15″ apart, edge-to-edge, inside. "Philip P. Manta," lower band 5′-3″ above mast bed, the bands 10″ apart, edge-to-edge, inside. It is seen that, in some schooners the bands were very close together. These show the vessel is not fitted for dory-fishing. A shipsmith, Wm. Walters, said that the bands were 24″ to 30″ apart, ℄ to ℄ in a dory fisherman, with the lower band 12″ above the pin rail, or about 36″ to 38″, from mast bed to underside of lower band, in some schooners.

In the 1850s and '60s, the foremast saddles of mackerel and market schooners were heavily strapped around the outside face, using ¾″ to 1″ bar iron, 3½″ to 4″ wide. To this was welded a vertical eye, to come on the middle of the afterside of the foremast saddle. The eye was the full depth of the saddle band. The pivot bolt of the foreboom fitted into the eye on the saddle. The fore-end of the boom had straps, P & S, having eyes that came on either side of the pivot eyebolt in the saddle band. A bolt was driven through all—straps and pivot bolt—the whole forming a simple gooseneck. But with such a fitting the boom could not be raised, so could not be used in bankers.

With the boom saddle, the band had ears on both sides of the mast, port and starboard, in the type used in the 1950s and '60s, so that it could be set up if the wooden saddle shrank. Usually the saddle had belaying pins in it, clear of the swing of the boom, or, if space was lacking, one or two were placed forward of the clamping eyes.

GOOSENECKS, FORE MAST
(*SEE FORE BOOM*)

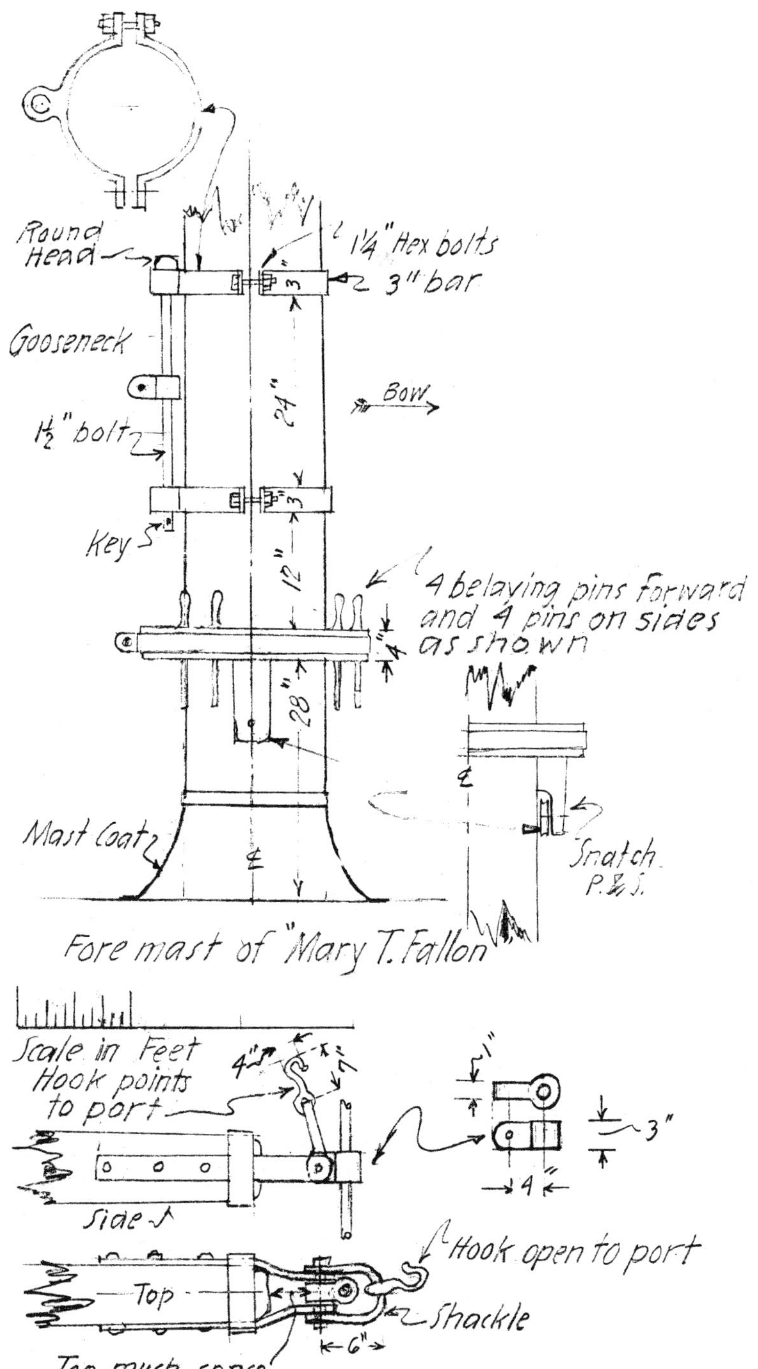

Round Head
1¼" Hex bolts
3" bar
3
Gooseneck
24"
Bow
1½" bolt
3
Key
12"
4 belaying pins forward and 4 pins on sides as shown
4"
28"
Mast Coat
Snatch P. & S.
Fore mast of "Mary T. Fallon"
Scale in Feet
Hook points to port
4"
7"
1"
3"
4"
Side
Top
Hook open to port
Shackle
6"
Too much space

GOOSENECK
(SEE FORE BOOM)

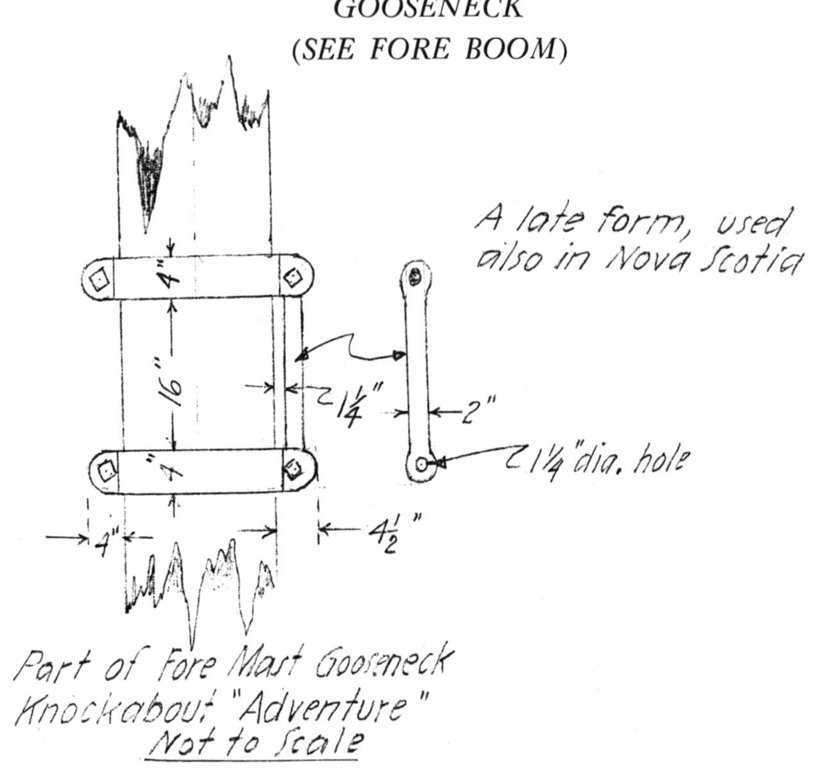
A late form, used also in Nova Scotia
4"
16"
4"
1¼"
2"
1¼" dia. hole
4"
4½"

Part of Fore Mast Gooseneck
Knockabout "Adventure"
Not to Scale

Goosenecks were introduced in the New England fishing schooners sometime in the 1880s, for the fore boom. Previously these booms were made with jaws and a saddle was fitted to the foremast. A few schooners had a circular pin rail around the mast below the saddle and, later, below the gooseneck. The fore boom had to be fitted so that it could clear stacks of dories of varying heights; hence the gooseneck had two bands spaced apart to allow the height of boom to vary, as had been possible with the old jaws, by changing the height of the foresail. This required heaving or slacking off the halyards. Gooseneck could be raised, however, if peak of gaff became so high as to foul springstay with foresail reefed.

GOOSENECK, FORE MAST SADDLE

1855–1860

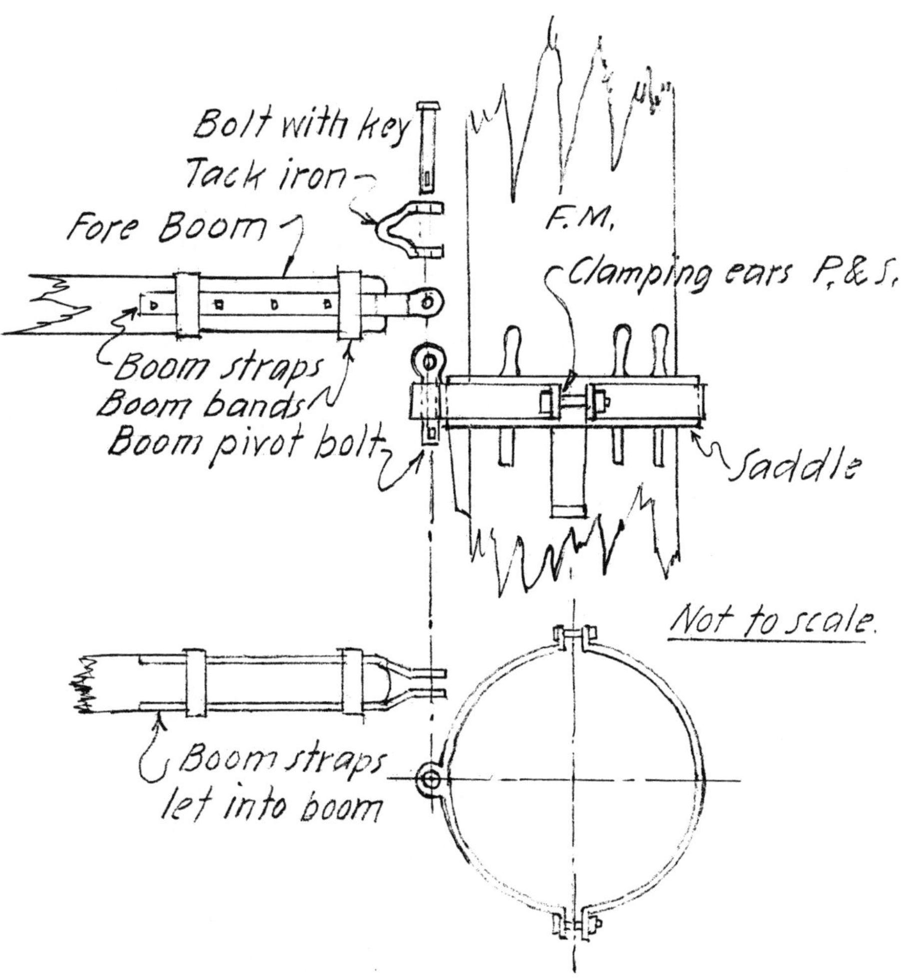
Bolt with key
Tack iron
Fore Boom
F.M.
Clamping ears P,& S.
Boom straps
Boom bands
Boom pivot bolt
Saddle
Not to scale.
Boom straps
let into boom

GREAT BEAM
(SEE "MOULDINGS")

The great beam is the timber forming the rise in the deck, from the main deck to quarterdeck. This was 9″-12″ high, usually 9″ or 10″. Some vessels had no break in the deck. The great beam was placed close to the midlength at deck level, and about 4′ to 5′ forward of the mainmast. The great beam was laid over the main deck beam on which the butts of the main deck planking ended, with the after faces of the beams and the butts of the main deck all brought flush. The top of the great beam was rabbeted at the afterside to receive the quarterdeck planking, leaving 3″ or 4″ of the top of the great beam exposed.

The ends of the great beam were cut to fit around stanchions placed to receive it. The plank-sheer aft of the beam was fitted against it in the rabbet at the top of the beam and around the stanchions. The ends of the great beam were cut to come flush with the inside of the waist plank of the bulwarks and, being covered by this planking, could not be seen from outboard.

Ringbolts, 3′ inboard of the bulwarks, on the forward face of the great beam, about halfway up, were seen on some schooners. Heavy ringbolts in the deck about 1′ inside the first stanchion, abaft that at the break, and on top of the great beam, were also observed.

Small schooners, such as market fishermen, had breaks as low as 6″; many were flush-decked but few large schooners were so built.

GURRY OR "BAIT" BOX
BAIT BOX AND CUTTING-UP BOARDS

The gurry box was always installed at Gloucester or where the vessel was fitted out. The box was usually placed between the cabin trunk and the after hatch, so that there was room to walk around it on a big vessel, though both large and small vessels often had the box in front of and against the cabin trunk. In this case the box would be as wide as the foreside of the trunk and 4′ to 5′ fore-and-aft; the height that of the cabin trunk. Square-ended boxes were used on most vessels, but *Columbia* had boxes that were beveled off on the outboard sides so that the foreside was much narrower than the afterside. [L.H.S.] In first fitting-out she had a rectangular box against the trunk. This was replaced with the one described above with a space between it and the cabin trunk. [E.S.B.]

A box on top of the cabin trunk, at its fore-end, will be occasionally seen in old photographs. This was the bait box, used to hold salted clam bait. This was employed particularly in mackerel handline fishing.

Along the sides of the trunk cabin roof 2″ to 4″ x 10″ plank were secured;

used for cutting bait. The boards were of maple and usually ran the length of the trunk. They were fastened only by corner pieces nailed to the trunk roof, as shown here, and could be unshipped (for cleaning). Commonly fitted each side of companion.

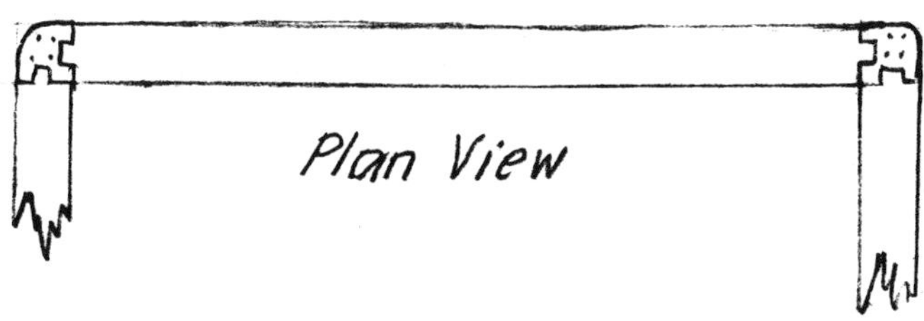
Plan View

HAIL
(*SEE "NAME BOARD"*)

During the last fifty years of the era of the sailing fishermen, they carried their name and port of hail on the monkey rail over the transom. This was arranged to extend from quarter to quarter, in 5″ or 5½″ Roman letters. The name of the port only was given, not the state. In earlier years the name and hail was painted on each side; on the monkey rail abreast the cabin trunk. A few vessels had name and hail on transom.

HARDWARE
(*SMALL*)

Small hardware, such as block fittings, latches, side lights (after 1865), lamps, lanterns, deck irons, hinges, locks, ringbolts, thimbles, sail hardware, galley and cabin stoves, etc., was purchased from ship chandlers, after 1840, at least. These were not of distinctive design, for use in the schooners, but were what was available in the fishing ports. If a piece of hardware could not be purchased a shipsmith could improvise something that would serve. As long as hearths were used, a smith could fit its ironwork, but by 1830 there were foundries in Gloucester and other ports producing stoves, anchors, and castings, and forgings as well.

HATCHES

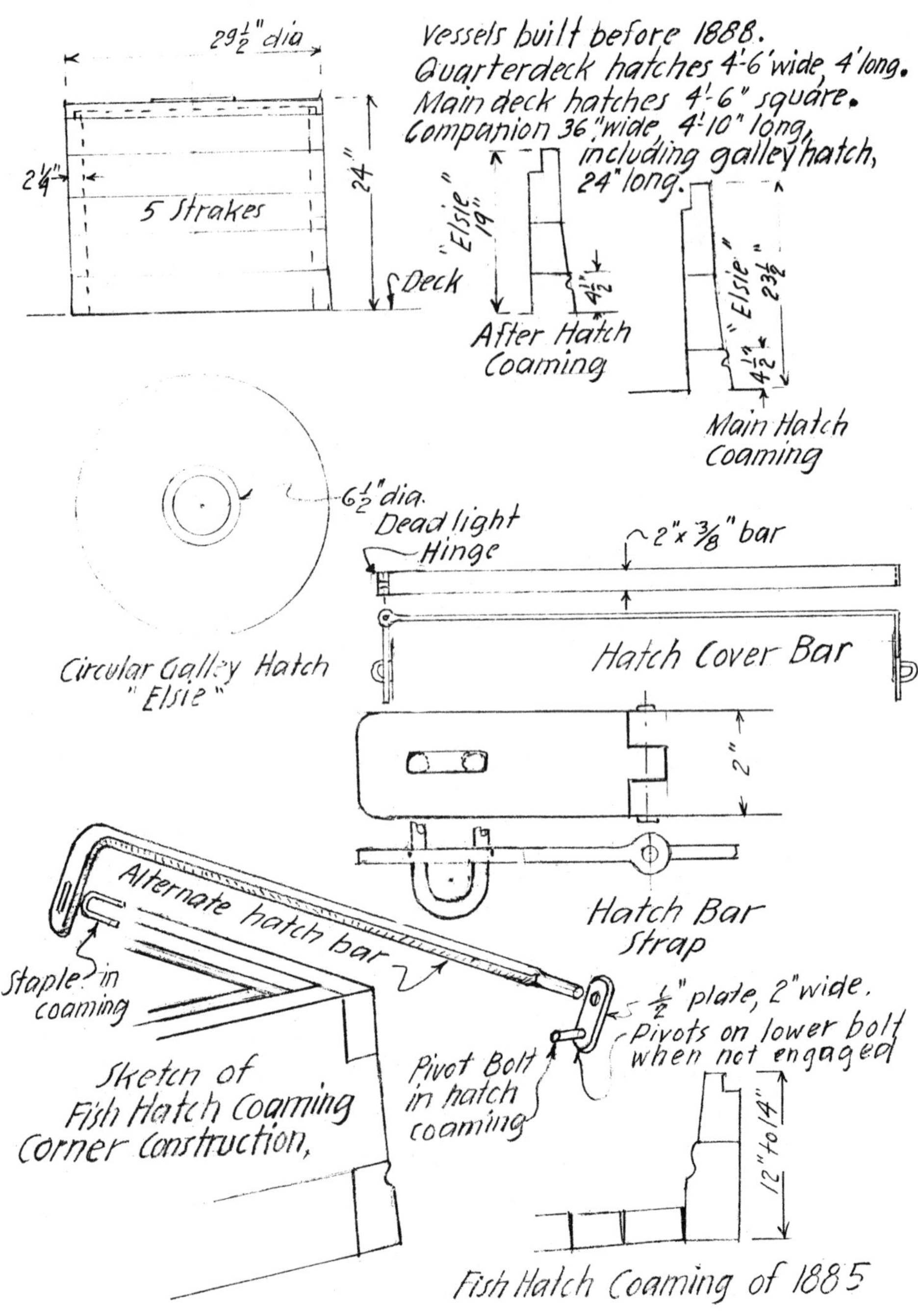

29½" dia
2¼"
5 Strakes
24"
Deck
Vessels built before 1888.
Quarterdeck hatches 4'-6' wide, 4' long.
Main deck hatches 4'-6" square.
Companion 36" wide, 4'-10" long,
including galley hatch,
24" long.
"Elsie" 19"
4½"
After Hatch
Coaming
"Elsie" 23½"
4½"
Main Hatch
Coaming
6½" dia.
Dead light
Circular Galley Hatch
"Elsie"
Hinge
2" x ⅜" bar
Hatch Cover Bar
2"
Hatch Bar
Strap
Alternate hatch bar
Staple in
coaming
½" plate, 2" wide.
Pivots on lower bolt
when not engaged
Pivot Bolt
in hatch
coaming
Sketch of
Fish Hatch Coaming
Corner Construction,
12" to 14"
Fish Hatch Coaming of 1885

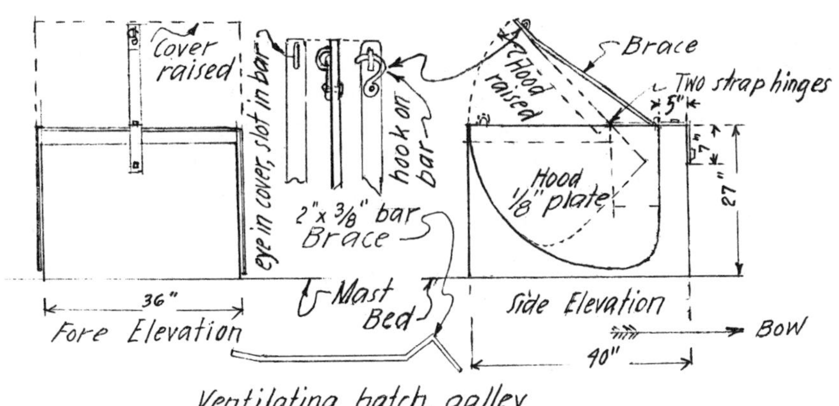
Cover raised
eye in cover, slot in bar
hook on bar
2" x 3/8" bar
Brace
Mast Bed
Brace
Hood raised
Two strap hinges
5"
7"
Hood 1/8" plate
27"
36"
Fore Elevation
Side Elevation
Bow
40"

Ventilating hatch, galley "Ellen T. Marshall", knockabout

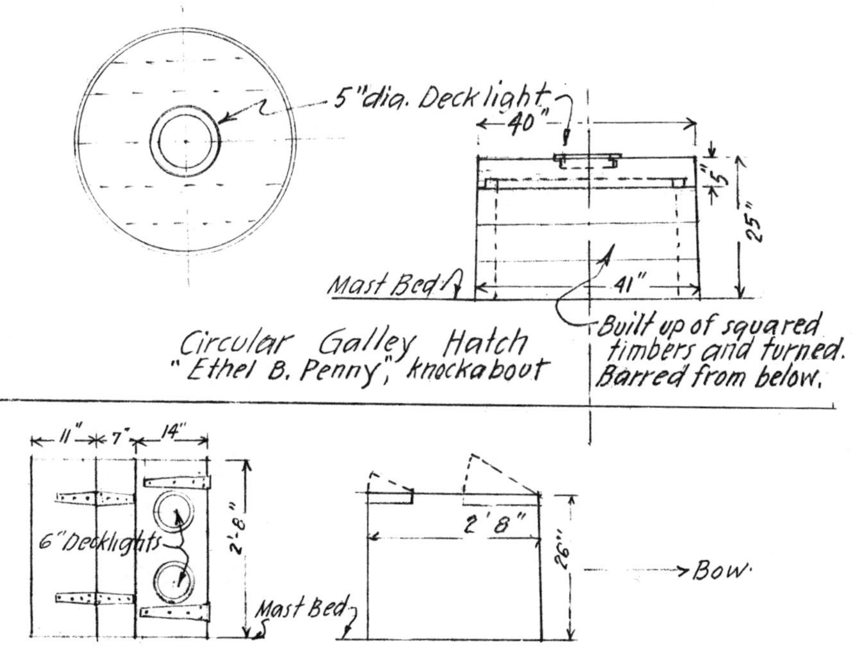
5" dia. Deck light
40"
5"
25"
Mast Bed
41"
Built up of squared timbers and turned. Barred from below.
11"
7"
14"
6" Decklights
2'-8"
Mast Bed
2' 8"
26"
Bow

Circular Galley Hatch "Ethel B. Penny", knockabout

Rectangular Galley Hatch
This type varied in dimensions and arrangement of covers and decklights.

HATCH COVERS (NOTES)

Hatch covers, for the main and quarterdeck fish hatches, were in two sections, divided athwartship, seated in rabbets cut on the inside and top of the hatch coamings. There were two ringbolts in each section. The cover was framed and planked with seams running fore-and-aft. The sections were locked in place by a steel strap, 1 ¾″ x ¼″, running fore-and-aft, on the ℄, and made in two pieces, joined by a hinge. One piece crossed the covers and bent down the outside of the coaming, secured by a hasp and staple. At the hinged end, the short piece ran down the outside of the coaming and was secured with a hasp and staple. Strap extends down coamings about 8″, to ℄ of staple, on each side.

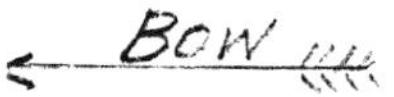
BOW

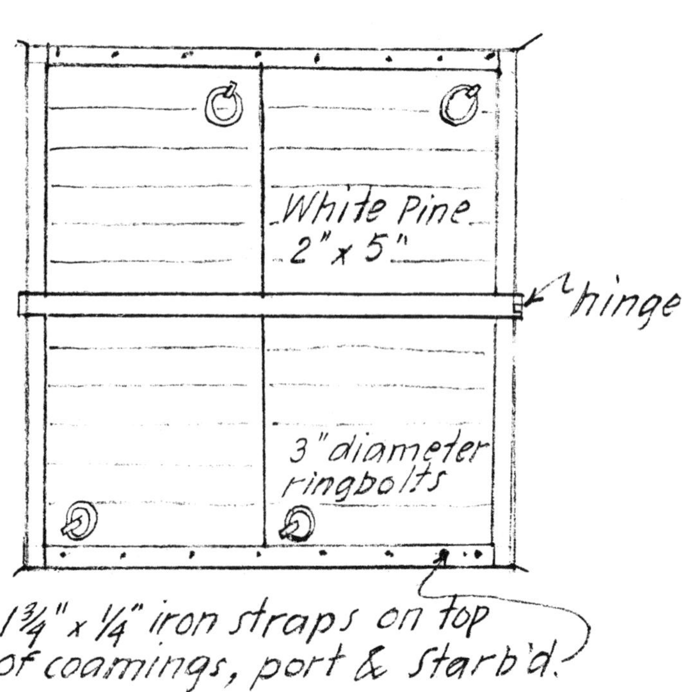
White Pine
2"x 5"
hinge
3"diameter
ringbolts
1¾"x ¼" iron straps on top
of coamings, port & starb'd.

HAWSE BLOCKS

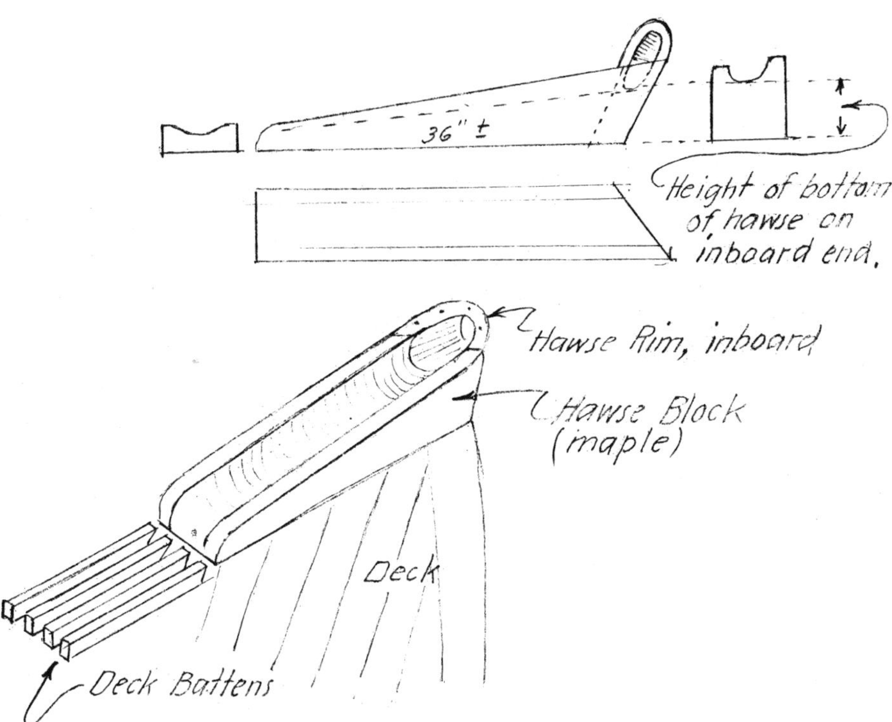
36" ±
Height of bottom of hawse on inboard end.
Hawse Rim, inboard
Hawse Block (maple)
Deck
Deck Battens

Hawse Blocks, Port & Starb'd, were fitted on deck, in line with the hawse pipes, with the fore ends of the groove in each brought to the height of the bottom of the inside of the hawse pipe.
The after ends of the blocks were about 2½" in height and the blocks were 30" to 38" long. They served to bring cable or chain from the deck battens up and over the lower inboard rim of the hawse castings. The fore-ends of the blocks fitted closely against the inboard faces of the hawse timbers, as well as against the rim of the casting.

HAWSE CASTINGS

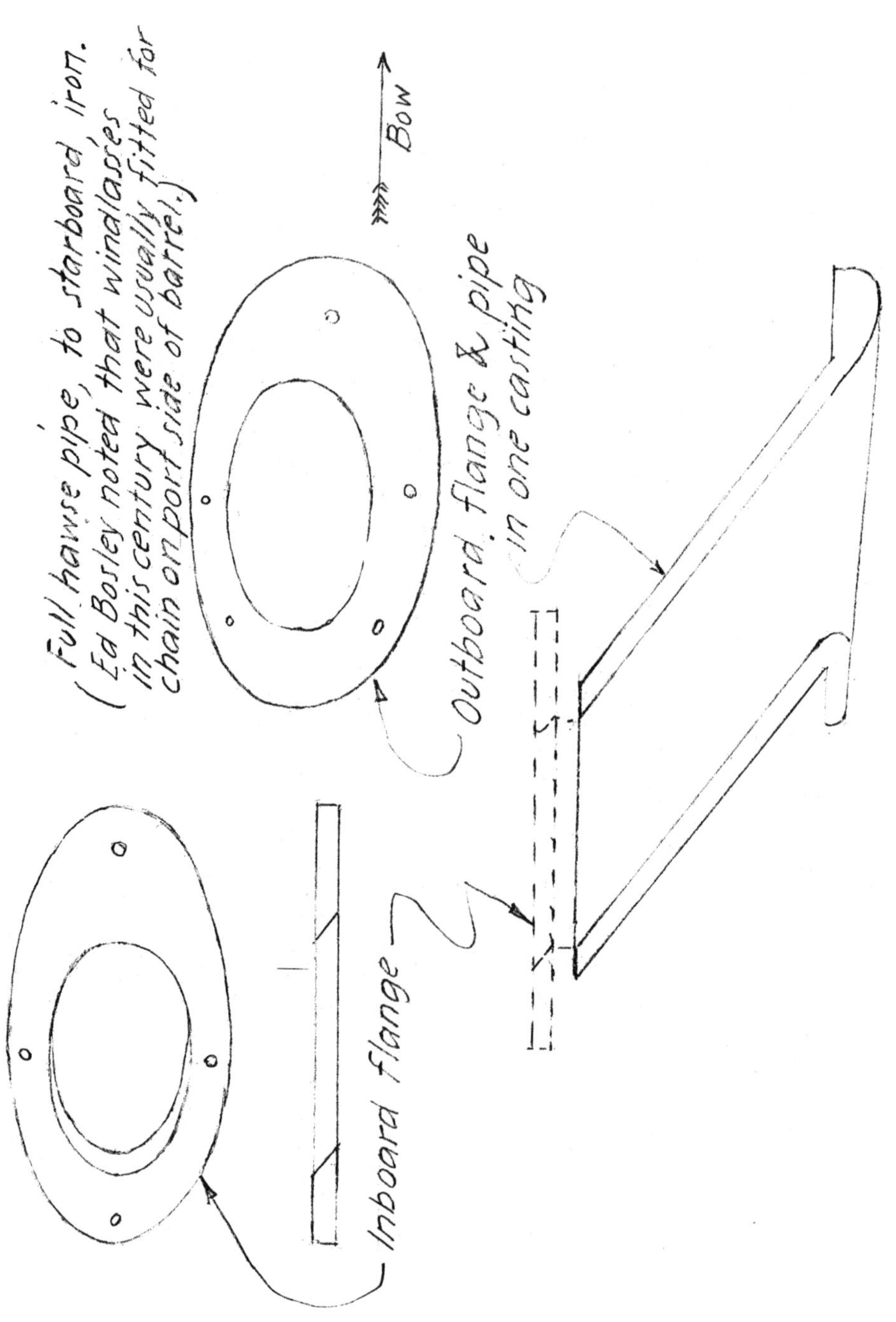
Full hawse pipe, to starboard iron.
(Ed Bosley noted that windlasses in this century were usually fitted for chain on port side of barrel.)
Bow
Outboard flange & pipe in one casting
Inboard flange

HAWSE CASTINGS

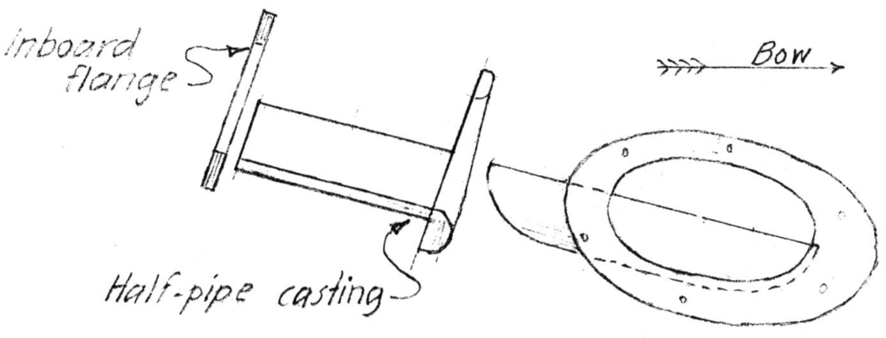
inboard flange
Bow
Half-pipe casting
Outboard flange and half-pipe

Half-hawse pipe to port, composition [brass or bronze] Note: In the present century the windlasses were fitted to handle manila cable on starb'd side of barrel in many vessels.

The diameters of the hawse hole were about 7" to 8", before 1885; in later vessels the diameters were 8" to 9". This applies to vessels over 70' on deck. In the vessels of later construction than 1885, the outboard rim and pipe were cast in one, the inside rim cast separate, with the rim covering the after edges of the pipe when fastened in place. The half-pipe castings were similarly made. The inboard rim was cast either full or half. If the latter, the top of the hawse hole was bare wood.

Dimensions of hawse castings.—"Arthur D. Story" ex "Mary", 1912 · dia. outside vertically 16" fore-and aft 24"; both to outside of ring. Hawse inboard 5" above deck (to bottom, of inside of pipe Dia, inside of pipe, 9".)

HAWSE CASTINGS (NOTES)

Location of hawse, "Elsie," foreside of flange to stem rabbet, on plank, 4′-0″. Flange 21″ x 15″, 9″ diameter hawse hole. Top of hawse rim outside, 4″ to 5″ below waist ("Gertrude De Costa," "Elsie," and "Natalie Hammond").

The depth of the outboard rim, on the fore and bottom section, increased after 1885 or thereabouts. No hawse pipes were fitted so that the inboard ends came through, or very close to, the main deck, that is, to pass through the plank-sheer. The result was that the bottom of the inside diameter of the hawse pipe was 5″-6″ above the main deck, inboard. Hawse castings were made from patterns taken from the vessel, if none that fitted a schooner under construction could be found.

In vessels built before 1845, the hawse holes were lined with heavy sheet lead, apparently.

In the placing of the hawse pipes, it was necessary to line them up athwartship so that the cable and chain would center on the windlass barrel properly, and pitch to lead fairly over the barrel from the outboard end of the hawse pipe at rim.

It is very doubtful that any fishing schooner had the hawse rims in the trailboards. "Fredonia's" lines plan shows the hawse in this position, but when she left Essex she had no trailboards. Lines of "Gloriana" and her sister ship "Harvard," show the hawse in the trailboards, but it is not established that these vessels were so fitted. "Fredonia," "Gloriana," and "Harvard" were Edward Burgess' designs. "Nellie Dixon," "Fredonia's" near-sister ship, had no trailboards.

HAWSE PIPES AND HAWSE HOLES

There seems to have been no rule for the pitch of the hawse, except to align it with the top of the windlass barrel and to center its ℄ on the windlass drum. The master carpenter usually lined up the hawse by boring a ⅝″ diameter lead-hole on each side, from inside out. An iron compass, somewhat like a fishhook, of ½″ diameter rod, was made. The short arm was filed to a sharp point. The space between the point and the ℄ of the long arm was the radius of the hawse pipe, o.d. The long arm was inserted in the lead-holes from the outside and, revolving the tool, the hawse was scribed on the planking. Reversing the tool, the holes could be scribed on the inboard sides of hawse timbers and the holes cut.

The angle, or pitch of the hawse on fishing schooners built before 1885 was somewhat more than in later schooners. The pipes were shorter in the older vessels as these had fuller bows. In these, the pitch was about 4″ to the foot. In later schooners the pitch was about 2″ or 2½″ to the foot. The iron pipes were always the complete one and the half-pipes the composition one.

Later castings had more flare downward and more rounding in the fore-end and bottom of the rim. [L.H.S.]

The inside of the hawse pipes were painted red; the yellow metal hawse was sometimes left bright. [L.H.S.]

HEAD RAILS (CLIPPER BOWS)

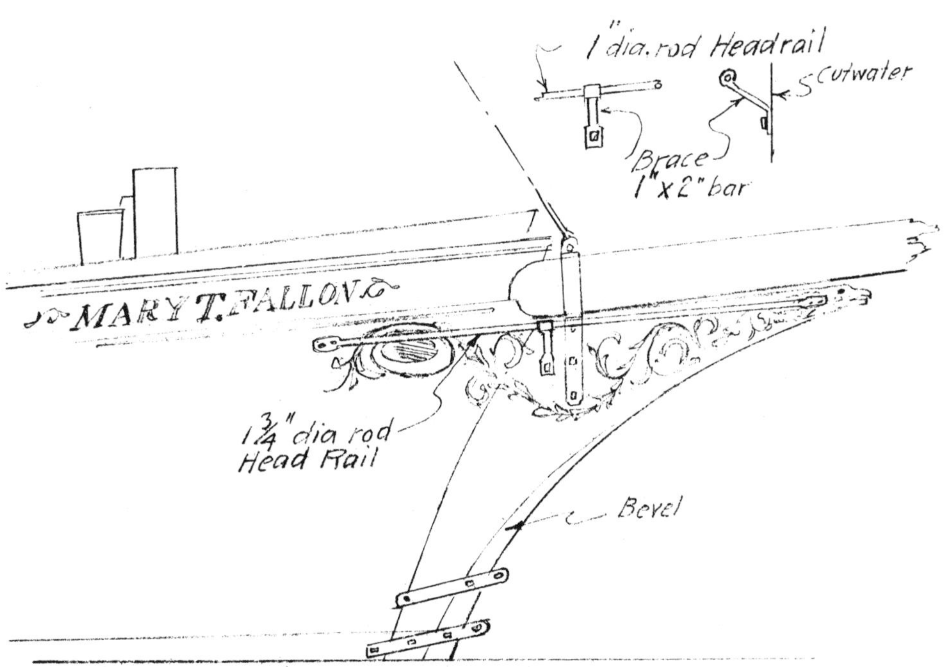
1" dia. rod Headrail
Cutwater
Brace
1"x2" bar
MARY T. FALLON
1 3/4" dia rod
Head Rail
Bevel

Last form of Clipper Bow showing iron headrail and brace. After the wooden headrails were dropped and the trail boards alone remained, the iron headrail and brace were introduced L.H.S.

HEAD RAILS, 1890s (CLIPPER BOWS)

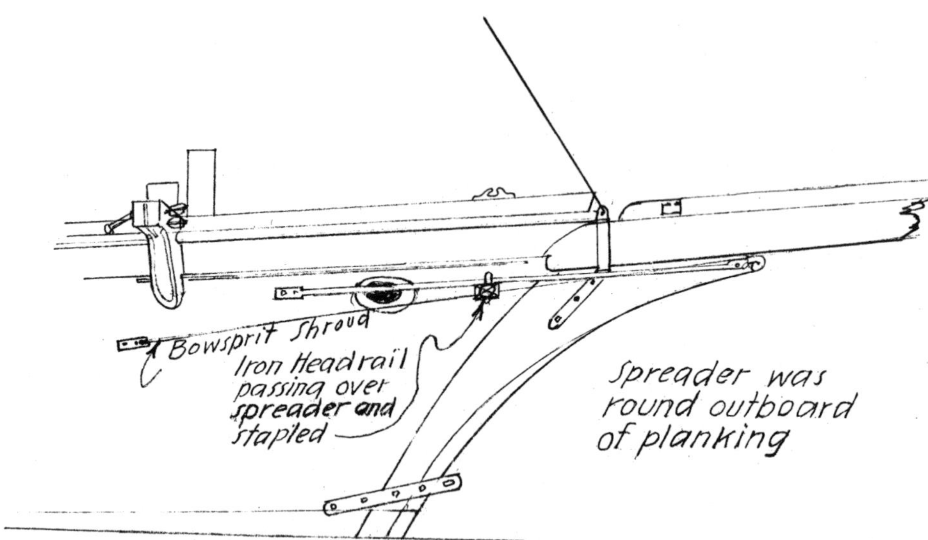
Bowsprit Shroud
Iron Headrail passing over spreader and stapled
Spreader was round outboard of planking

When the bowsprit "Whisker", or spreader was introduced, soon after 1885, the iron head rails were fitted as shown here. The whiskers were usually through the cutwater but some vessels had them through the bows as shown here.

HEAD RAILS (IRON)

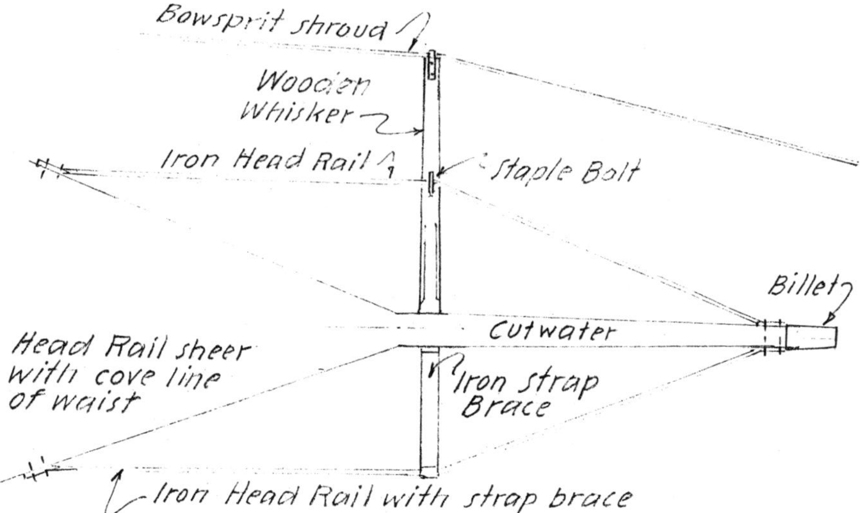
Bowsprit shroud
Wooden Whisker
Iron Head Rail
Staple Bolt
Billet
Cutwater
Head Rail sheer with cove line of waist
Iron Strap Brace
Iron Head Rail with strap brace

Iron head rails were of 1" to 1¼" rod, with pads 3"x 5" formed at each end, to take one or two bolts each. With wooden whiskers the head rail rested on top of the whiskers, secured with a suitable staple bolt. The fore pad was just abaft the billet, the after pad rested on the waist plank abaft the hawse. The rail was bent in plan as shown. When whiskers were discarded, an iron brace ½"-1" x 2"-2½" strap iron, was fitted in its place, on the side of the cutwater. This was usually level with the head rails. The iron brace was never abaft the stem rabbet, unlike the whiskers.

See "Bows"

HEAD RIGGING

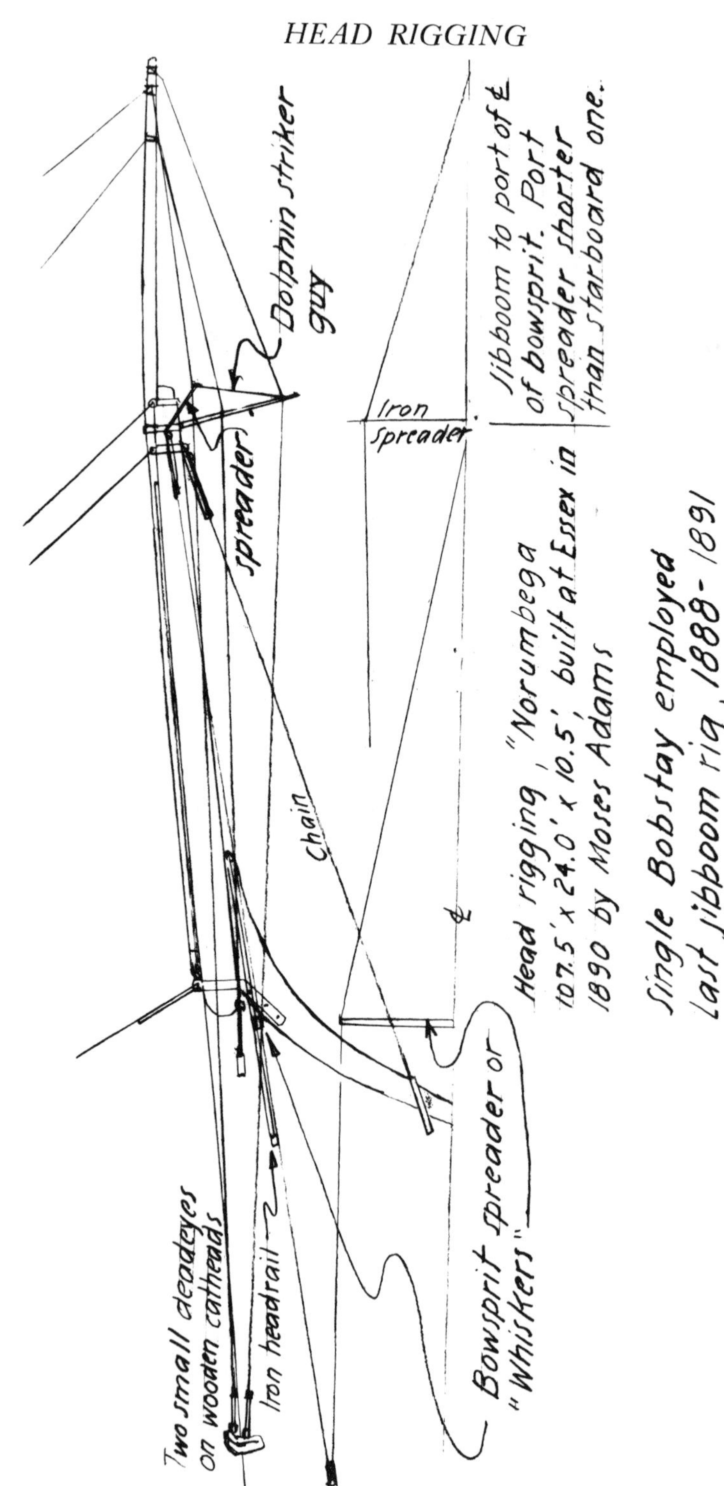
Dolphin striker guy
spreader
Iron Spreader
Jibboom to port of ℄ of bowsprit. Port spreader shorter than starboard one.
Chain
℄
Head rigging, "Norumbega" 107.5' x 24.0' x 10.5', built at Essex in 1890 by Moses Adams
Single Bobstay employed last jibboom rig, 1888-1891
Bowsprit spreader or "Whiskers"
Two small deadeyes on wooden catheads
Iron headrail

HEART IRON FOR THROAT HALYARD BLOCKS ON FORE AND MAIN MASTS

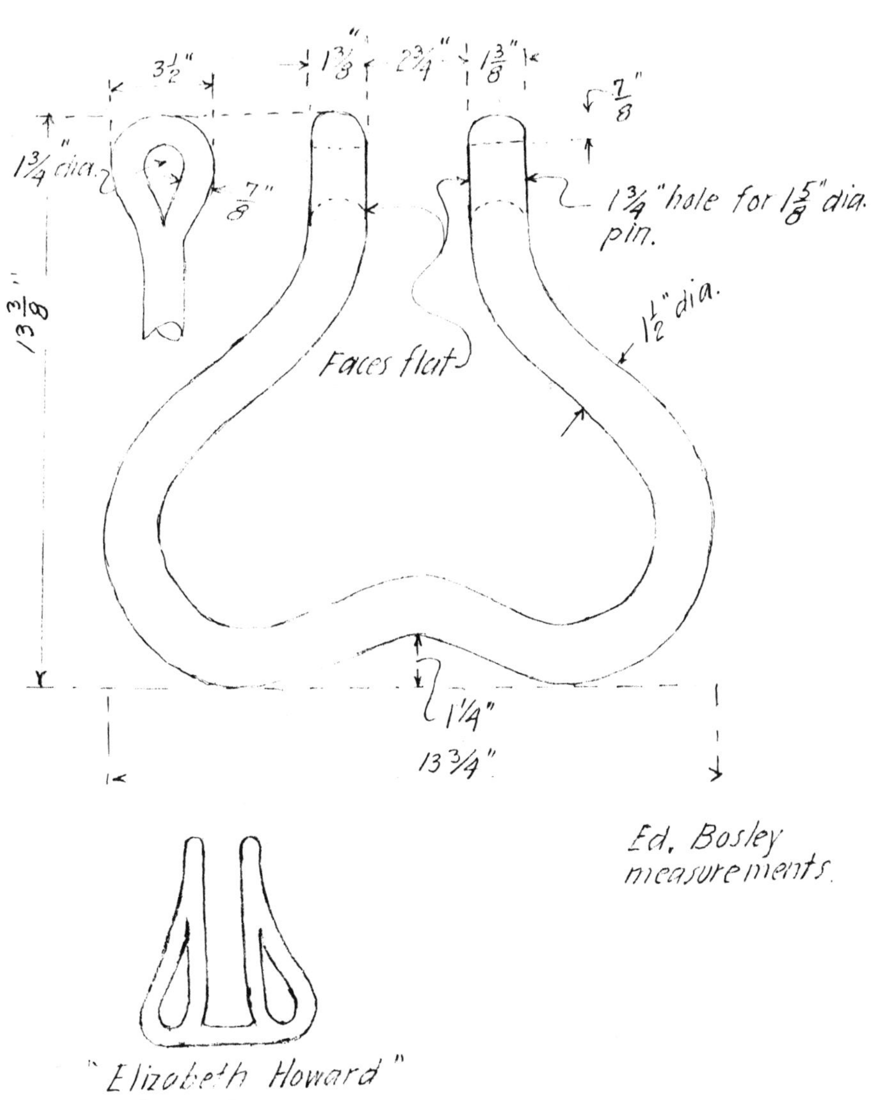
3½"
1⅜"
2¾"
1⅜"
7/8"
1¾" dia.
7/8"
13⅜"
1¾" hole for 1⅝" dia. pin.
1½" dia.
Faces flat
1¼"
13¾"
Ed. Bosley measurements.

"Elizabeth Howard" Heart Irons

HINGES

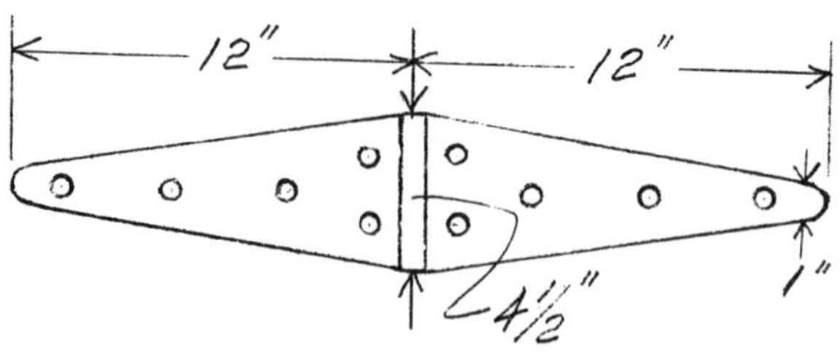
12"
12"
4½"
1"

Hinges on hatch (Fore side)

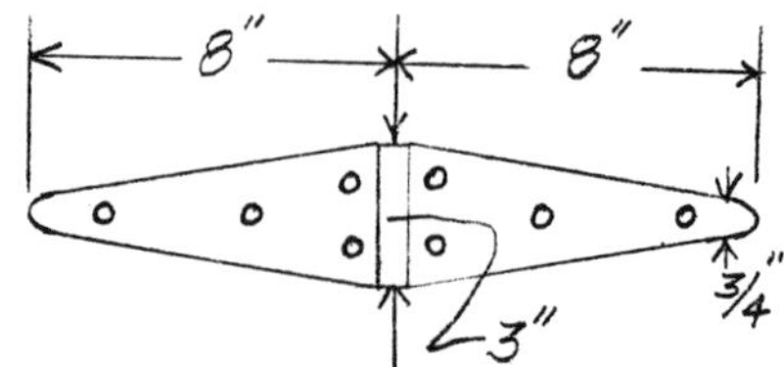
8"
8"
3"
¾"

Hinges on top of hatch

For galley hatches, etc.

HOISTING ENGINES (*NOTES*)

Though auxiliary gasoline engines for propulsion were installed as early as 1903, in fishing schooners, it was not until about 1915 that powered hoisters were fitted. In this year the first hoister is said to have been installed in a halibut fisherman. This equipment was not part of building contracts but was made and installed by Gloucester, or nearby, machine shops and foundries. As a result, no two of five installations examined were alike.

The stationary-type gasoline engine was placed in a box, on either side of the foremast bitts, extending aft from a little forward of the foremast bitts to abreast of the after-end of the companionway. The boxes were about 3′-0″ wide, 5′-0″ high and 6′-0″ long, but due to the variations in the installations, these dimensions are not very useful guides.

The hoisting engine usually drove a special ring gear on the windlass barrel, through an idler on deck which was driven by chain and sprocket, with a clutch on the engine. The winch was gear-driven, with an individual clutch. Fuel tank was usually in after-end of box, which was roughly built, in all cases that were seen. The ring gear on windlass had a metal guard over it and, sometimes, over the idler.

Hoisting engines were one-cylinder, horizontal "stationary" gasoline engines, 6-8 h.p., make-or-break ignition, until about 1915.

HORSES

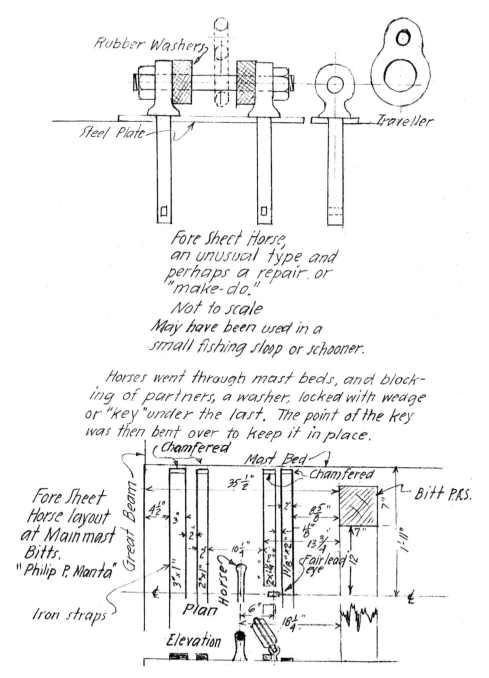

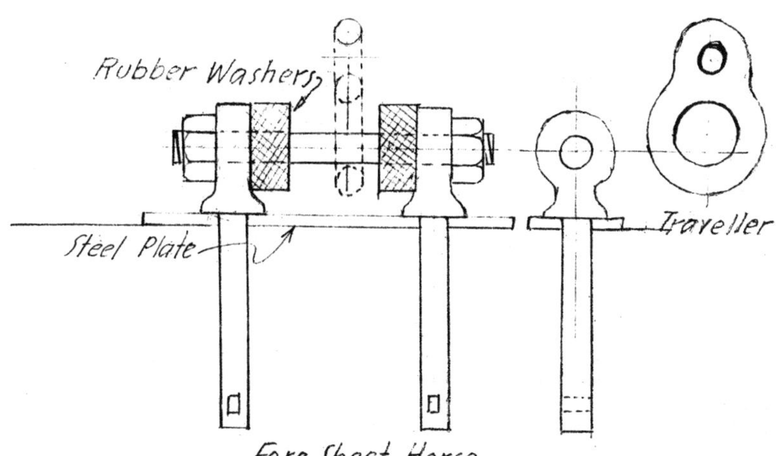
Rubber Washers
Steel Plate
Traveller

Fore Sheet Horse, an unusual type and perhaps a repair, or "make-do." Not to scale May have been used in a small fishing sloop or schooner.

Horses went through mast beds, and blocking of partners, a washer, locked with wedge or "key" under the last. The point of the key was then bent over to keep it in place.

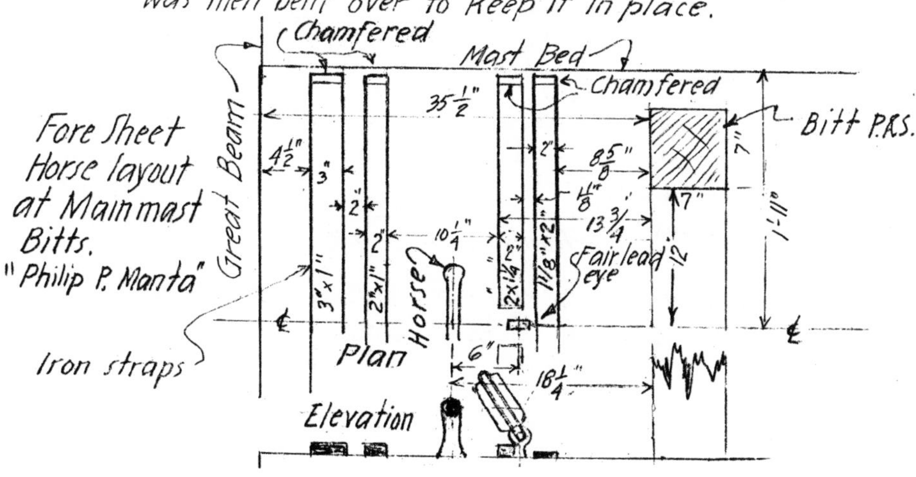
Chamfered
Mast Bed
Chamfered
Bitt P.R.S.
Fore Sheet Horse layout at Mainmast Bitts. "Philip P. Manta"
Great Beam
Horse
Fairlead eye
Iron straps
Plan
Elevation
35 1/2"
4 1/2"
3"
2"
2"
10 1/4"
2"
8 5/8"
13 3/4
7"
7"
12"
1'-11"
3"x1"
2"x1"
2x1 1/4"
1 1/8"x2"
6"
18 1/4"

HORSES FOR SHEETS

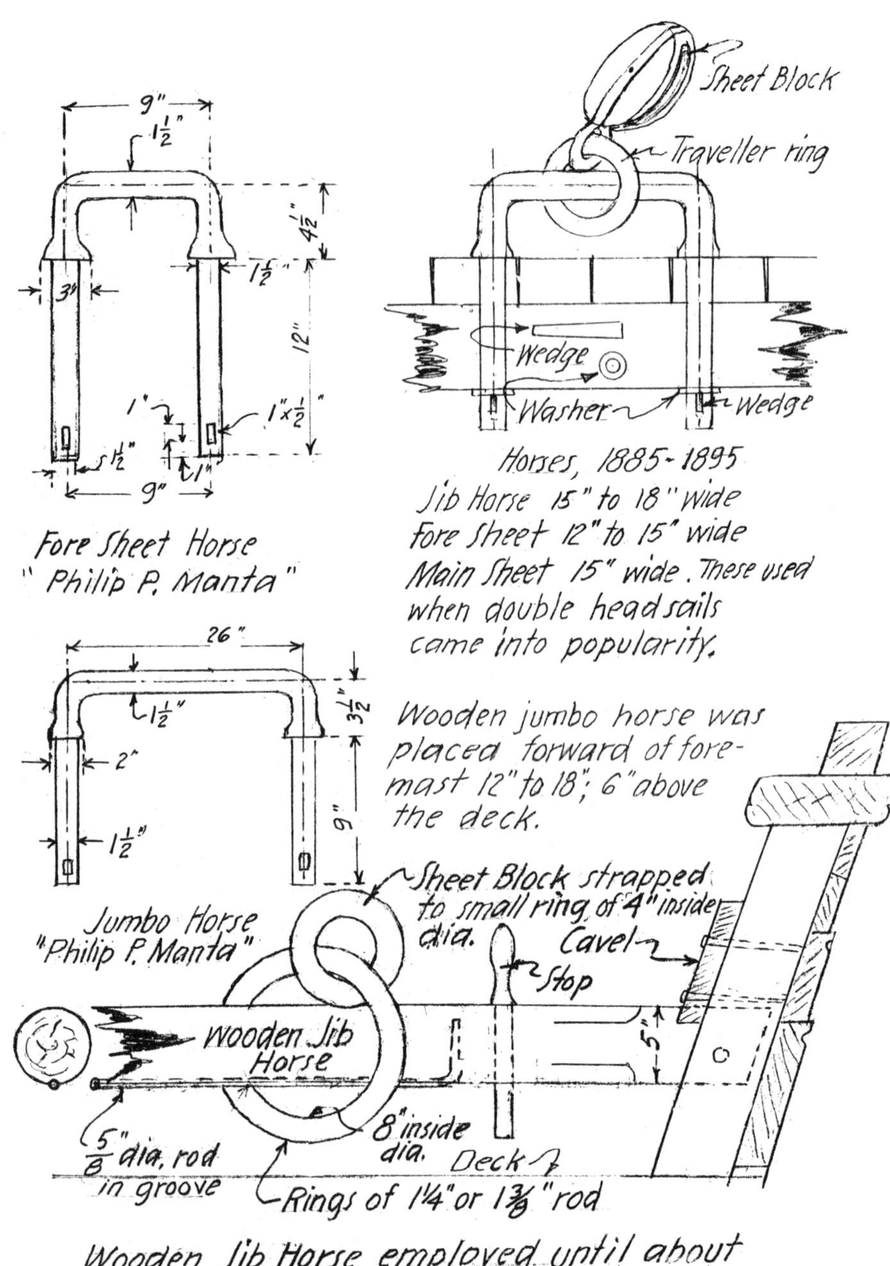
Sheet Block
Traveller ring
Wedge
Washer
Wedge
Horses, 1885-1895
Jib Horse 15" to 18" wide
Fore Sheet 12" to 15" wide
Main Sheet 15" wide. These used when double headsails came into popularity.
Fore Sheet Horse "Philip P. Manta"
Wooden jumbo horse was placed forward of fore-mast 12" to 18"; 6" above the deck.
Jumbo Horse "Philip P. Manta"
Sheet Block strapped to small ring of 4" inside dia.
Cavel
Stop
Wooden Jib Horse
8" inside dia.
5/8" dia. rod in groove
Deck
Rings of 1¼" or 1⅜" rod

Wooden Jib Horse employed until about 1885, usually of White Oak

HORSESHOES AND EMBLEMS

Horseshoes were often carried on fishing schooners "for luck." They were usually nailed to the foreside of the pawl post just above the heel of the bowsprit. Knockabouts had the horseshoe on the forepost of the gallows just below the jumbo stay iron. The horseshoes were usually nailed open end up "so that her luck would not run out." "Columbia" had the Masonic emblem between name and hail on her taffrail. The first "Bluenose" had the three-ring emblem between name and hail on her transom. "Claudia" had a horseshoe, open end down, on the foreside of her mainmast under the mainboom saddle.

JIBBOOMS WITH BOWSPRITS SQUARE AT GAMMONING

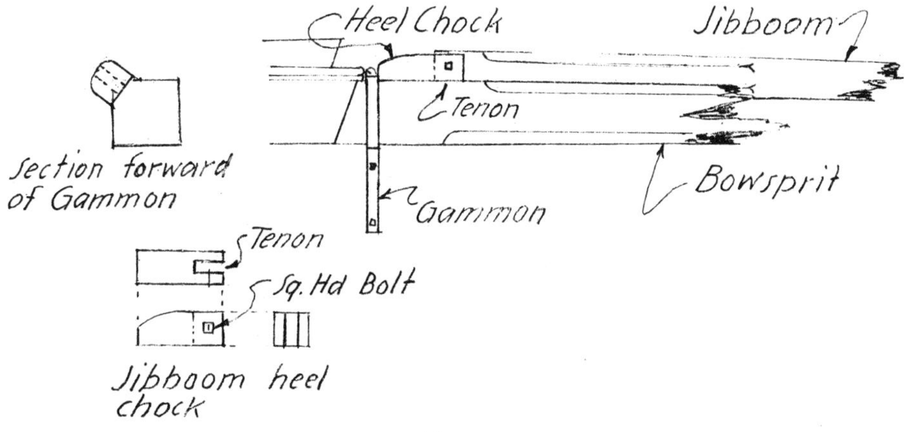
Heel Chock
Jibboom
Tenon
Section forward of Gammon
Bowsprit
Gammon
Tenon
Sq. Hd Bolt
Jibboom heel chock

Jibboom on port upper quarter of bowsprit for single head stay.

The heel of the jibboom was formed with a tenon which fitted into the heel chock where it was secured by a sq. hd. bolt driven athwartships, having washer and forelock.

The heel block butted against the fore side of the gammon iron, as a rule.

JIBBOOMS (NOTES)

The jibboom hogged down, outside of the bowsprit cap so that the ℄ of the pole came down to approximately a line projected along the underside of the bowsprit. [L.H.S.]

When the jibstay was moved inboard to the gammon in the late 1880s, the martingale, spreaders, and jibboom were retained for a time. The change was gradual, for the fore, or jumbo, stay was first moved inboard from near the bowsprit cap to a wye a few feet forward of the gammon. This seems to have been introduced in the "plumb-stemmers"; "Grampus," "A. D. Story" and "Harry Belden" were so rigged. A shift of the stay to the gammon may have been inspired by the introduction of the very raking clipper stem of the "Fredonia" model.

In a photograph made in 1875 there was one jibboom shroud set up to each cathead.

The jibboom shrouds were rigged to a three-eye wye on the jibboom pole, the bottom wye for the martingale on the jibboom pole, the bottom wye for the martingale stay. Sometimes two wyes were placed at the shoulder of the pole.

JIBBOOM SPREADERS, IRON

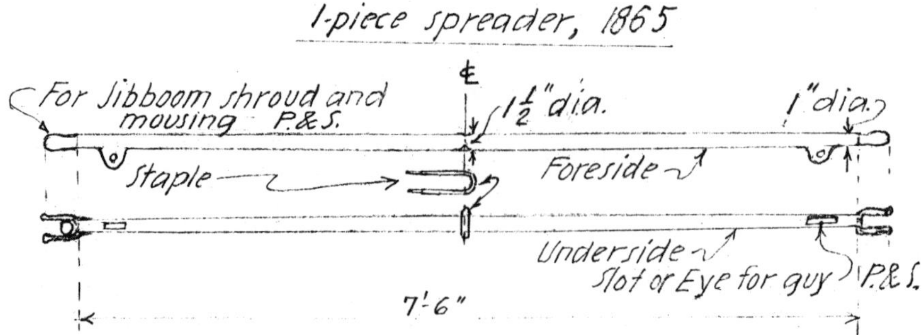
1-piece spreader, 1865
℄
For Jibboom shroud and mousing P.&S.
1½" dia.
1" dia.
Staple
Foreside
Underside
Slot or Eye for guy
P.&S.
7'-6"

Spreader, iron, secured with a large staple, 6" x 1½" of ⅝" dia. rod, driven into the fore end of the bowsprit. This type of spreader used with double fore stay.

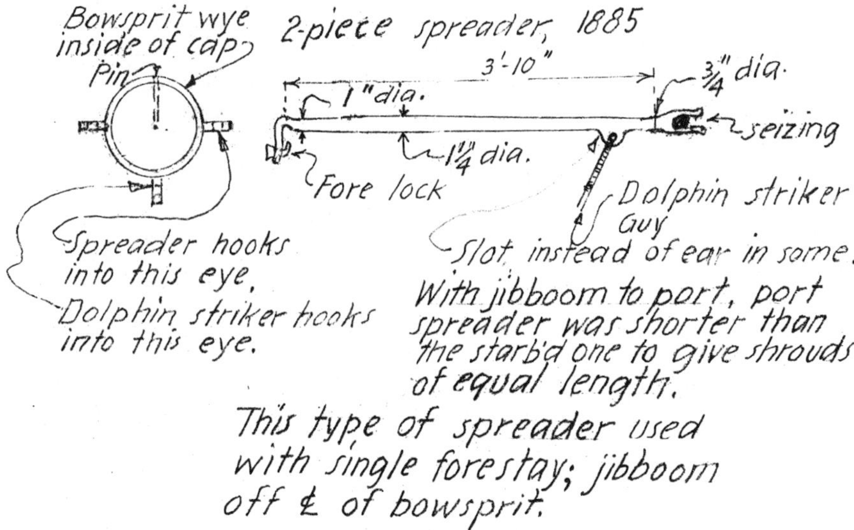
Bowsprit wye inside of cap
Pin
2-piece spreader, 1885
3'-10"
3/4" dia.
1" dia.
seizing
1 1/4" dia.
Fore lock
Dolphin striker
Guy
Spreader hooks into this eye.
Dolphin striker hooks into this eye.
Slot instead of ear in some.
With jibboom to port, port spreader was shorter than the starb'd one to give shrouds of equal length.
This type of spreader used with single forestay; jibboom off ℄ of bowsprit.
As described by smith Wm. Walters and by rigger Geo. Roberts.

JIBBOOM SPREADERS (NOTES)

Jibboom spreaders, of wrought iron, appear to have been introduced in the clipper schooners built in the early 1850s, the sharpshooters usually having no jibboom. With the double headstay and bee blocks, with shroud chain plates, it was easiest to place the spreader on the fore-end of the bowsprit, secured by a large staple driven into the end-grain. With the single stay and jibboom off-center, the bowsprit cap iron used did not allow ears for the two-arm spreader to hook into, so a three-eye wye was fitted on the afterside of the cap iron, to take the spreader arms and the dolphin striker as well. The jibboom shrouds were seized into the forks at the outboard ends of the spreader arms to prevent the arms from swinging. There were variations in the form of the spreaders, to support additional shrouds by means of hook-straps welded to the spreaders. Sometimes the bowsprit cap iron was inboard of the dolphin-striker wye instead of the arrangement shown in the sketch.

FORESTAYSAIL CLUB (JUMBO)

From the mid 1840's up until the late 1880s, schooners having the large jib were fitted to carry a club 4 to 6 ft. long at the foot of this sail. Sometimes the jib was cut straight on the foot, but in many schooners the sail was cut so that the foot, at the club, was at an angle to the rest of the foot. The large single jib always had a bonnet at the foot, about 3' to 3'-6" deep. The term "jumbo" was first applied to these big jibs, but later was applied to the fore-staysail that took the place of the big jib, when the "double-head-sail rig" appeared in 1886.

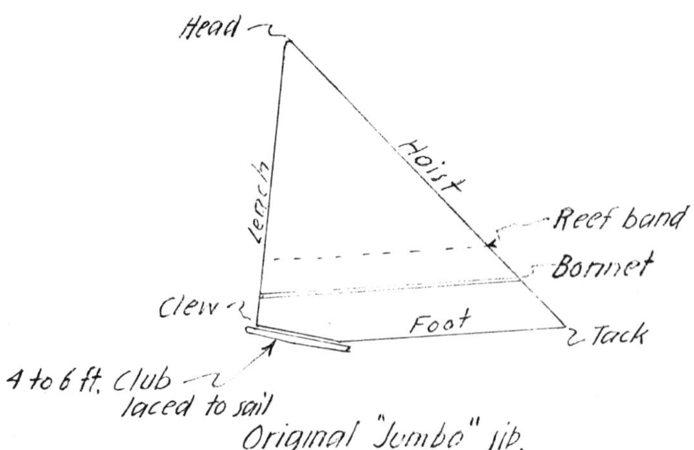
Head
Hoist
Leech
Reef band
Bonnet
Clew
Foot
Tack
4 to 6 ft. Club
laced to sail

Original "Jumbo" jib.

FORESTAYSAIL CLUB (JUMBO)

The jumbo club did not go out of use with the disappearance of the big single jib. The "Indian Headers" of 1898–1902, such as the "Manhasset" (1902), "Metamora" (1902), "Ellen C. Burke" (1902), and the first knockabout, the "Helen B. Thomas," all had clubs on the forestaysail. The "Burke" had a bridle on her club. McManus designs in this period often showed this club in the sail plans. But it was usually left to the sailmaker or the master whether a new vessel had a club or a boom. Photographs of "Indian Headers" are the only certain guides in this matter.

In this period the forestaysail had no bonnet; instead there was usually a single reefband, the jib only having the bonnet.

JIB AND JUMBO HANKS

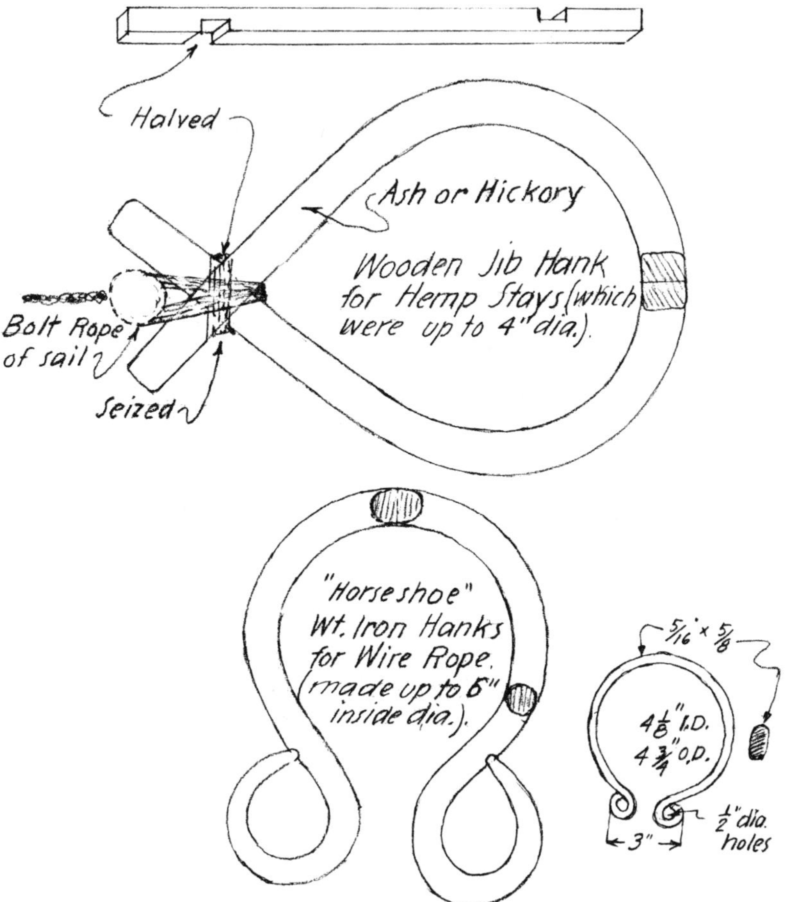
Halved
Ash or Hickory
Wooden Jib Hank
for Hemp Stays (which
were up to 4" dia.).
Bolt Rope
of sail
Seized
"Horseshoe"
Wt. Iron Hanks
for Wire Rope.
(made up to 6"
inside dia.).
5/16" x 5/8
4 1/8" I.D.
4 3/4" O.D.
1/2" dia.
holes
3"

JIB AND JUMBO HANKS

Wrought iron jib hanks came into use in fishing schooners when wire rope rigging was adopted, sometime before 1885. Rings were first employed on all

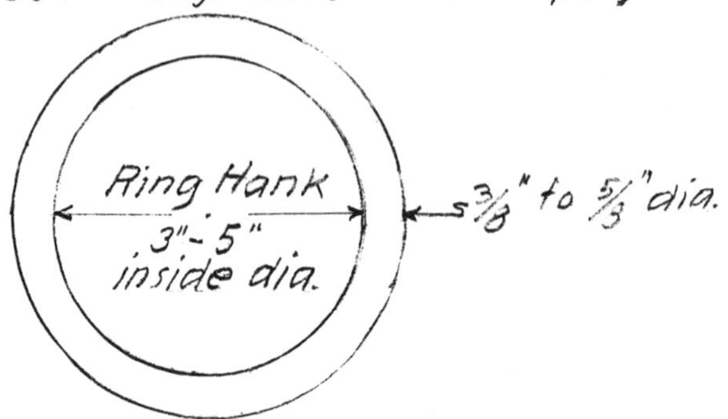
Ring Hank
3"-5"
inside dia.
3/8" to 5/8" dia.

headstays, but soon were relegated to the lowest 10 or 12 hanks on the jumbo, when the boom did not slide. In order to get slack to lower the sail either jackline and beckets, or only rings and jackline were then used. Above the ring-hanks, or where rings were not used, the horseshoe hanks were employed. Horseshoe hanks came into use about 1887-9.

The headsail hanks were spaced about 2'-0" to 2'-6" apart in schooners above 60' registered length

"Philip P. Mantor" – hanks on jib tops'l 2'-4" to 2'-6" apart hanks on jib were about 2'-2" to 2'-4" apart

"Columbia" – total of 22 hanks on jumbo, 30 on jib, 26 on jib tops'l. "Frances P. Mesquita", total of 16 on jumbo 24 on jib. "Blue Nose" 17 on Jumbo, 24 on jib, 25 on jib topsail.

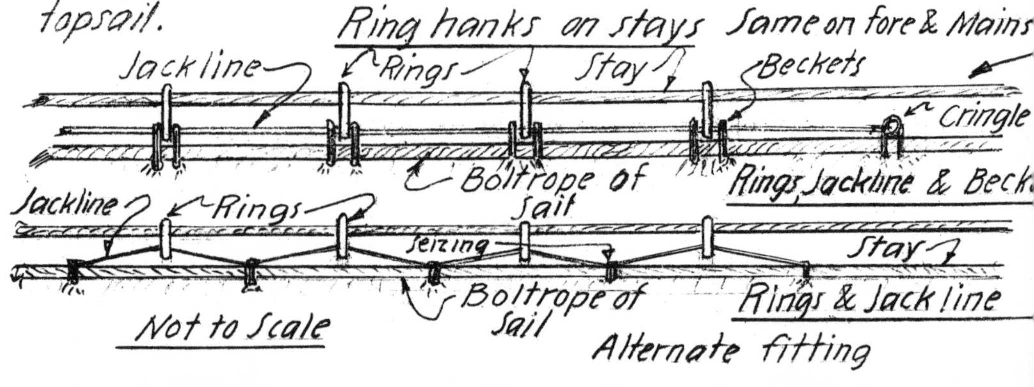
Ring hanks on stays
Same on fore & Mains
Jackline
Rings
Stay
Beckets
Cringle
Boltrope of Sail
Rings, Jackline & Beck
Jackline
Rings
Seizing
Stay
Boltrope of Sail
Rings & Jack line
Not to Scale
Alternate fitting

JIB SNAP

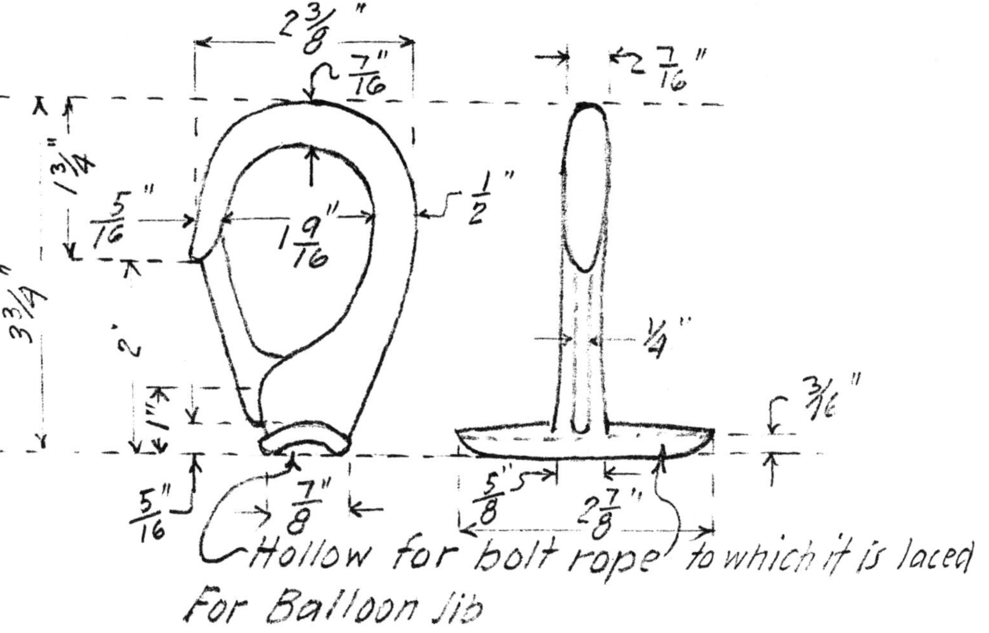
2 3/8"
7/16"
2 7/16"
1 3/4"
5/16"
1 9/16"
1/2"
1/4"
3 3/4"
2"
3/16"
1"
5/16"
7/8"
5/8"
2 7/8"
Hollow for bolt rope to which it is laced
For Balloon Jib

JIB TOPSAILSTAY

The jib topsailstay was the lightest of the headstays. It ran from the fore-topmast shoulder to an eyebolt on the bowsprit pole, very close to its nose. This eyebolt passed through both straps of the snout iron and the pole, set up under all with a nut. The bottom of the stay shackled into the eye, bow of shackle up, stay seized, after setting up over a heavy rolling thimble in shackle. The head of the stay had an eye-splice which went over the topmast pole—there was one wye having two eyes for the gaff-topsail halyard block and jib topsail block.

The main-topmast had a wye with one drop loop on foreside for staysail peak halyard. Another and smaller wye was two-thirds or three-quarters the way up the pole. This was for the main topsail halyard block only.

With the jibboom rig, the jib topsailstay ran to the shoulder of the jib-boom, of course, and its head was an eye over the fore-topmast pole.

JIB TOPSAIL (BALLOONER) RIGGING

Halyards—two single-sheave blocks, 6″-7″. Upper block hooks into wye at shoulder of fore-topmast with hook facing forward. Upper block has loose front hook and becket; lower block has sister-hooks, hooked into head of sail. Halyard leads from becket and thimble of upper block, through lower block sheave, thence to sheave in upper blocks, then down through a pivoted fairlead on foreside of the fore crosstree, the fall then belayed on a pin in the rail cap at fore shrouds.

Downhaul—single-sheave block, secured to pole of bowsprit or hooked into eye of shackle pin, upper end seized into cringle at head of sail and leads down through three or four hanks fitted with fairleads, or bullseyes, though block and then inboard to belaying, pin on the fore seat over the bowsprit, on the port side.

Sheets—made in one length of line, passed through clew iron of sail, crossed over and seized in the bight. The two sheets thus formed are port and starboard sheets. They belay on the bulwarks abaft the great beam, as determined by the cut of the sail.

Halyards—of the jib topsail, were also belayed on a pin in the rail cap, starboard side in way of shrouds, in some schooners.

JIB TOPSAIL OR BALLOONER HALYARD

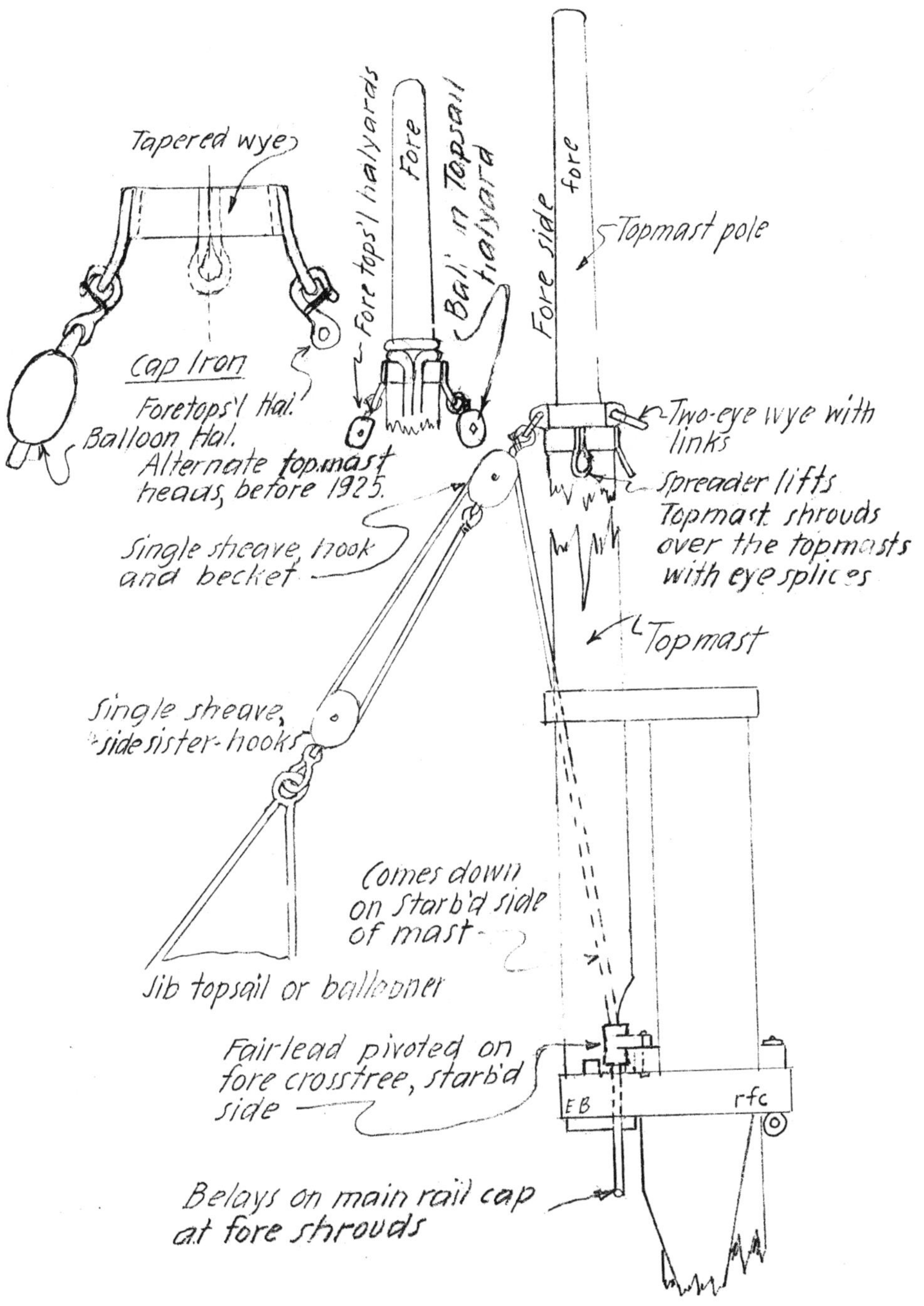
Tapered wye
Cap Iron
Foretops'l Hal.
Balloon Hal.
Alternate topmast heads, before 1925.
Fore tops'l halyards
Fore
Ball'n Topsail halyard
Fore side
fore
Topmast pole
Two-eye wye with links
Spreader lifts Topmast shrouds over the topmasts with eye splices
Single sheave, hook and becket
Topmast
Single sheave, side sister-hooks
Comes down on Starb'd side of mast
Jib topsail or ballooner
Fairlead pivoted on fore crosstree, starb'd side
EB
rfc
Belays on main rail cap at fore shrouds

JIB SHEET LEAD (BALLOON)

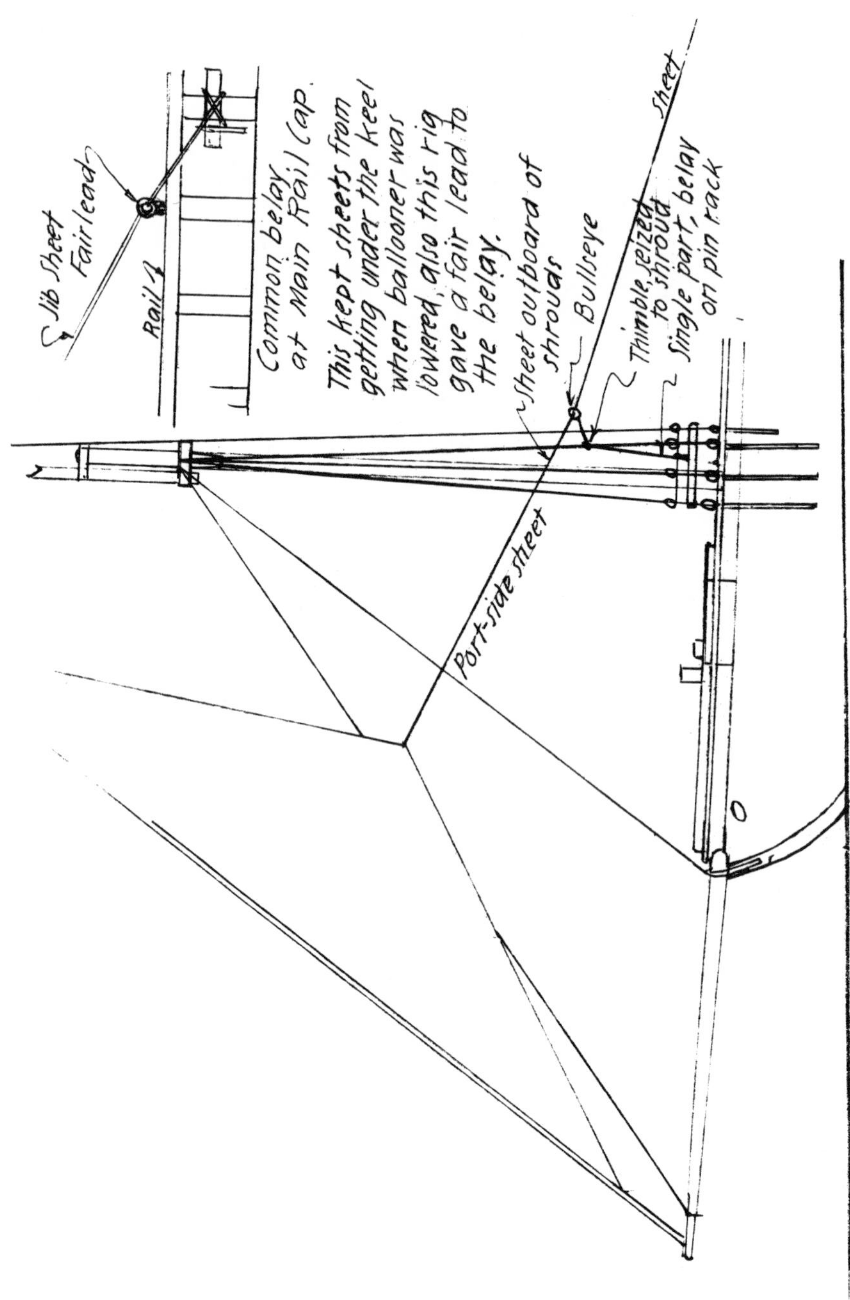
Jib Sheet
Fairlead
Rail
Common belay
at Main Rail Cap.
This kept sheets from
getting under the keel
when ballooner was
lowered, also this rig
gave a fair lead to
the belay.
Sheet outboard of
shrouds
Bullseye
Thimble, seized
to shroud
Single part, belay
on pin rack
Sheet
Port-side sheet

JIB TOPSAIL SHEETS (BALLOONER)

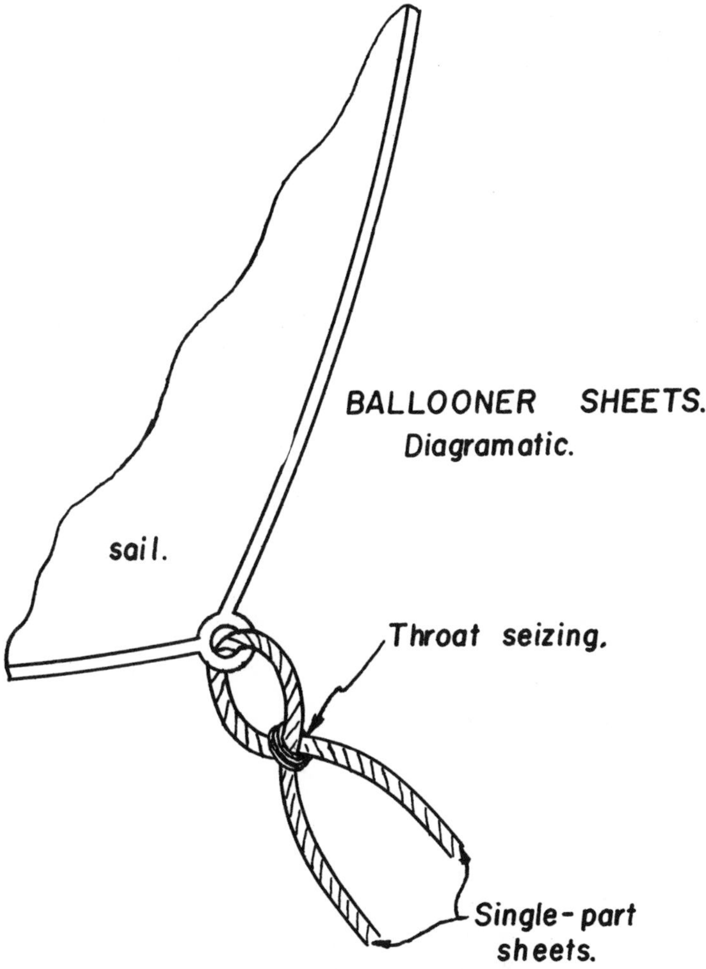
BALLOONER SHEETS.
Diagramatic.
sail.
Throat seizing.
Single-part
sheets.

Each sheet belays on pin in rail cap at break in deck.
Or, may belay further aft to a cleat on a stanchion

JIB HALYARDS (NOTES)

When the double-head sail rig was adopted in the early 1880s, the huge jumbo of earlier times was replaced by a forestaysail (the modern "jumbo") and a jib. Though these sails might be of approximately the same area, the jib was made of lighter sailcloth and had neither reefband nor boom (nor club). Therefore, its halyards had a single fall and the upper single block of the halyard hooked into the jibstay bail in many vessels, shackled in some cases, after about 1890.

Earlier, the upper block was hung at the masthead just below the cap iron. In vessels after about 1905 two blocks were hooked into links fastened on the springstay bolt through masthead, on both sides. The port end of the halyard had a jib (or "whip") on it with its lower block hooked in an eye in the rail cap, just forward of the port fore rigging. The hauling end was belayed opposite on a pin in the starboard rail cap. [E.B.]

JIB HALYARDS AND STAY

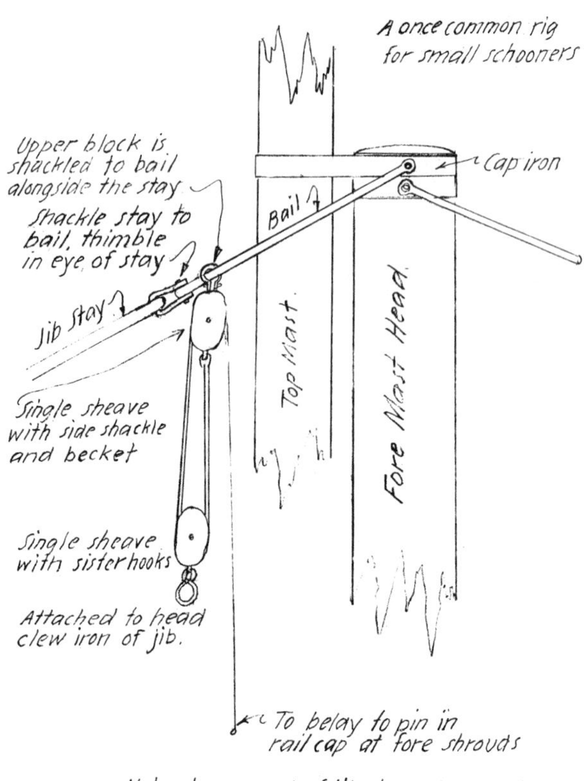
A once common rig for small schooners
Upper block is shackled to bail alongside the stay
Cap iron
Shackle stay to bail, thimble in eye of stay
Bail
Jib stay
Top Mast
Fore Mast Head
Single sheave with side shackle and becket
Single sheave with sister hooks
Attached to head clew iron of jib.
To belay to pin in rail cap at fore shrouds
Note Lower end of jib stay shackled into eye of wye on bowsprit.

JIB HALYARDS AND STAY

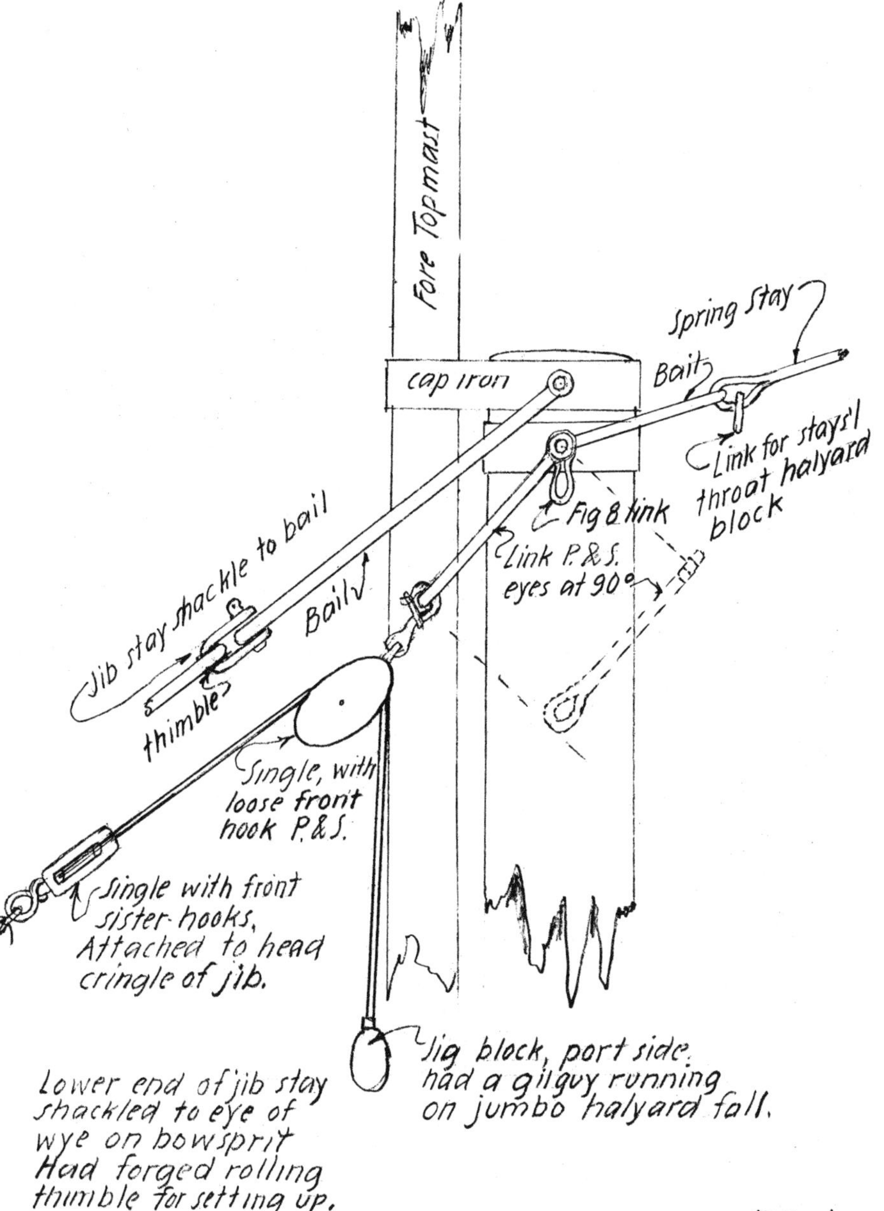
Fore Topmast
Spring Stay
cap iron
Bail
Link for stays'l throat halyard block
Fig 8 link
Link P.&S. eyes at 90°
Jib stay shackle to bail
Bail
thimble
Single, with loose front hook P.&S.
Single with front sister-hooks. Attached to head cringle of jib.
Jig block, port side. had a gilguy running on jumbo halyard fall.
Lower end of jib stay shackled to eye of wye on bowsprit Had forged rolling thimble for setting up.
E Bosley

JIB HALYARDS AND STAY (NOTES)

The methods of rigging the jib halyards varied. Apparently a once common one was to place one single-sheave block on the side of the foremasthead, just below the cap iron and bail band. A bolt through the masthead athwartship, with a Figure-8 link, was employed. The aforementioned block was hooked into the Figure-8 link and moused. The halyard led from the becket of the masthead block down and through a single-sheave block, with sister-hooks—hooked into the head iron of the jib, thence aloft and through the masthead block. The fall then belayed on the fife rail.

In large schooners the jib halyard was often double-ended, fitted with a jig. In this case two single-sheave blocks were hung on the masthead bolt and two Figure-8 links; one on port side and one on starboard side. The jig fall was generally on the port side, where the belay was on the fife rail.

The lead was from the starboard fife rail aloft through the masthead block, down to a single-sheave block sister-hooked to the head of the jib, thence aloft to the port masthead block and thence down to the head block of the jig. The jig was rove like the jumbo halyard.

An alternate rig to jib halyard is also shown, of later years, that was popular in the average-size and large schooners.

JIB SHEETS, DIAGRAMATIC

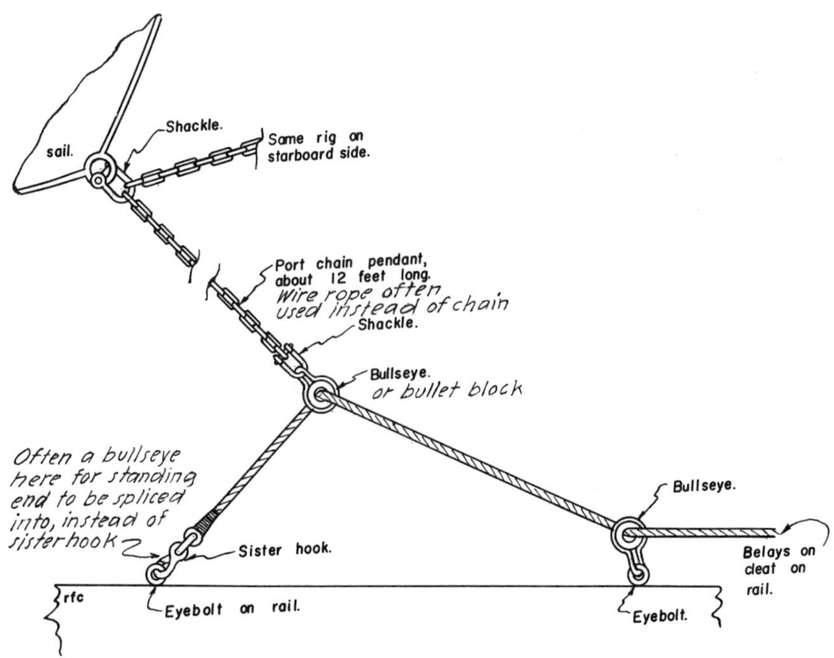
Shackle.
sail.
Same rig on starboard side.
Port chain pendant, about 12 feet long.
Wire rope often used instead of chain
Shackle.
Bullseye.
or bullet block
Often a bullseye here for standing end to be spliced into, instead of sisterhook
Bullseye.
Sister hook.
Belays on cleat on rail.
rfc
Eyebolt on rail.
Eyebolt.

JUMBO SHEET

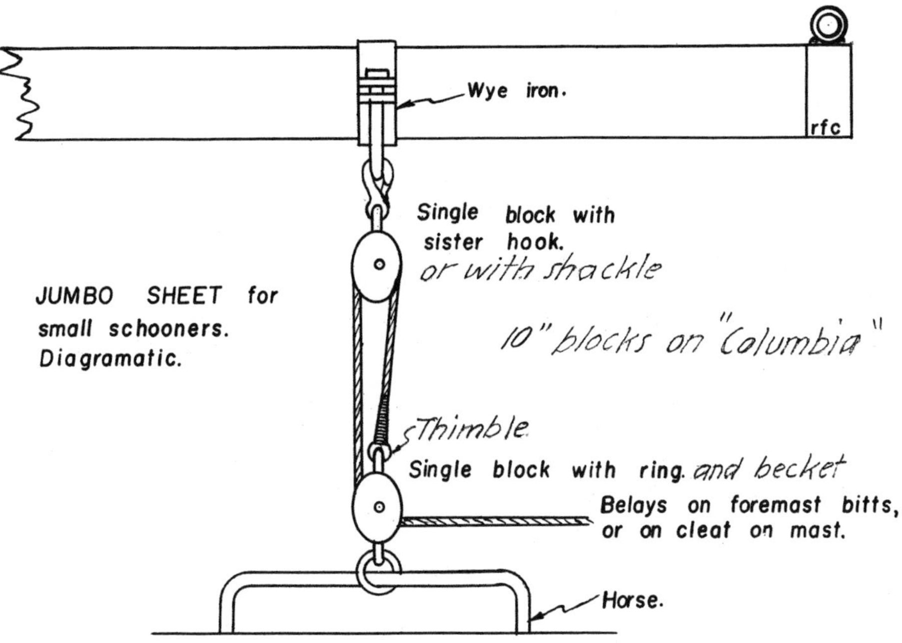
Wye iron.
rfc
Single block with
sister hook.
or with shackle
JUMBO SHEET for
small schooners.
Diagramatic.
10" blocks on "Columbia"
Thimble
Single block with ring. and becket
Belays on foremast bitts,
or on cleat on mast.
Horse.

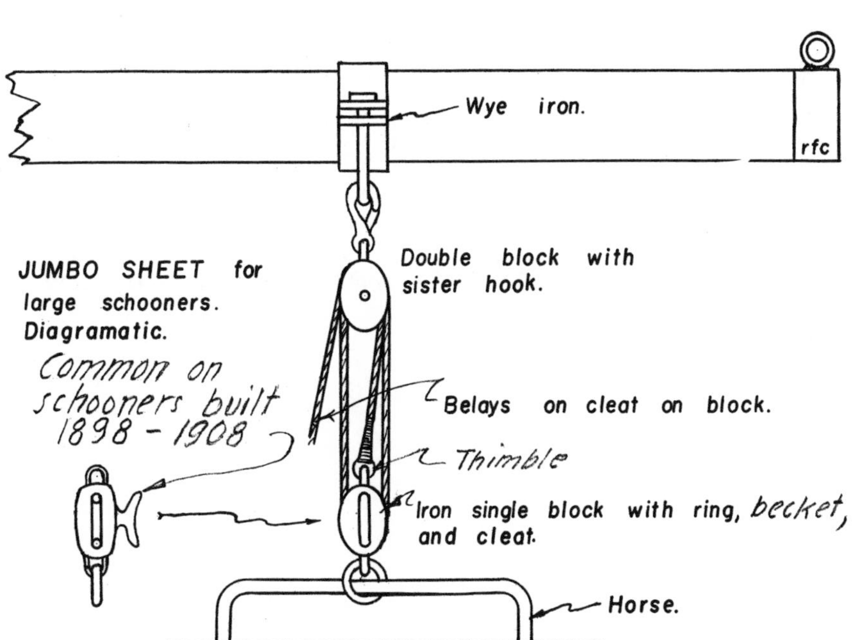
Wye iron.
rfc
Double block with
sister hook.
JUMBO SHEET for
large schooners.
Diagramatic.
Common on
schooners built
1898 - 1908
Belays on cleat on block.
Thimble
Iron single block with ring, becket,
and cleat.
Horse.

JUMBO SHEETS

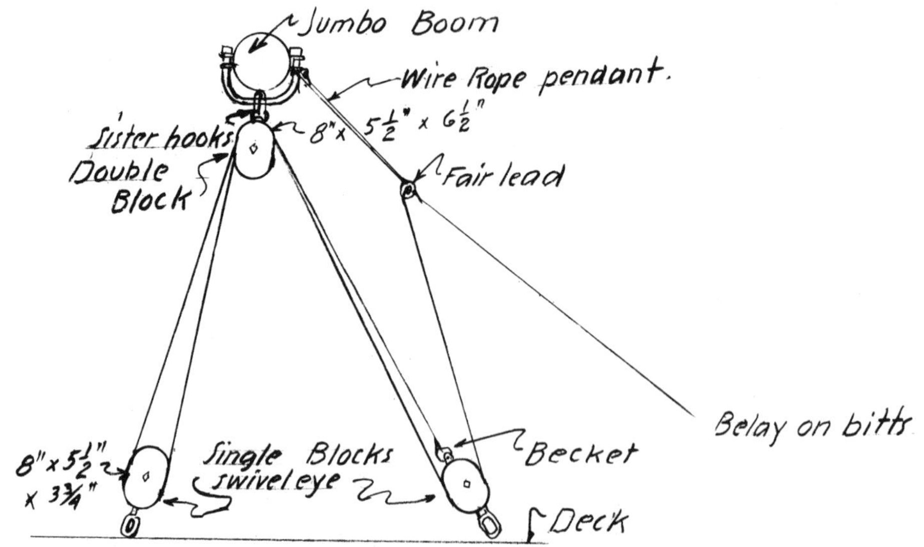
Jumbo Boom
Wire Rope pendant.
Sister hooks
8" x 5½" x 6½"
Double Block
Fair lead
Belay on bitts
Becket
8" x 5½" x 3¾"
Single Blocks swivel eye
Deck

Only vessel seen that was rigged this way was the "Dunton," 1934.

JUMBO HALYARDS (NOTES)

The jumbo halyards were rigged in various ways, depending upon the size of the sail and the period in which the vessel was built and rigged. In the days of hemp rigging, the jumbo, then the jib, was a large and heavy sail fitted with a bonnet, so the halyard was double-ended and one fall had a jig. When the double-head sail rig of more modern style was adopted, and the forestaysail became the jumbo, though relatively smaller in area, it remained a heavy sail, having a reefband and a heavy boom. As a result its halyards continued to be rigged with a jig in most vessels. Only in the small schooners were the halyards rigged with a single fall. The jumbo halyards rove like the jib halyards, in general.

JUMBO HALYARDS
SMALL SCHOONERS, 60–75 FEET

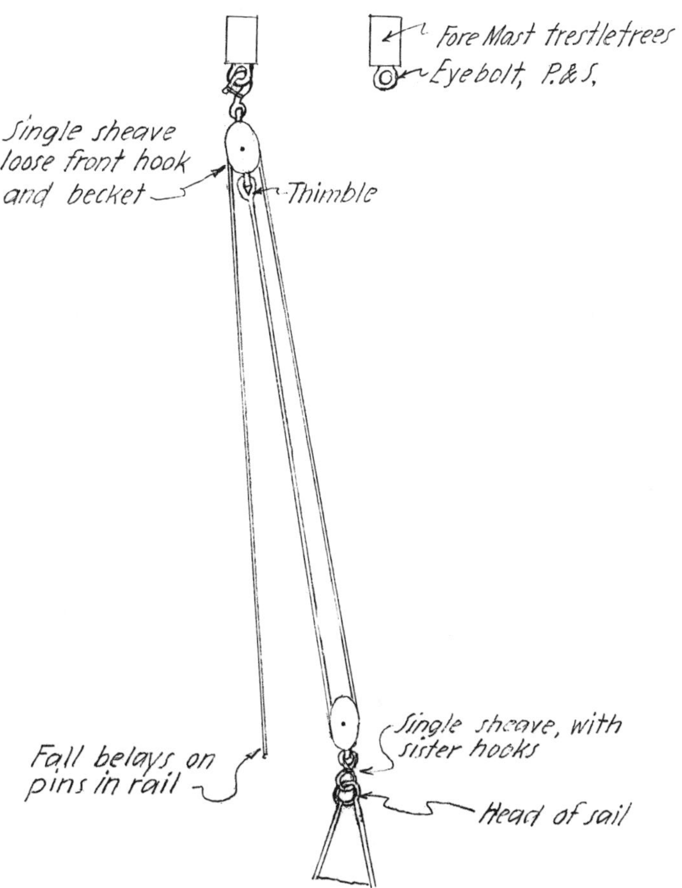
Fore Mast trestletrees
Eyebolt, P.& S.
Single sheave
loose front hook
and becket
Thimble
Single sheave, with
sister hooks
Fall belays on
pins in rail
Head of sail

JUMBO HALYARDS
SMALL SCHOONERS, 60–75 FEET

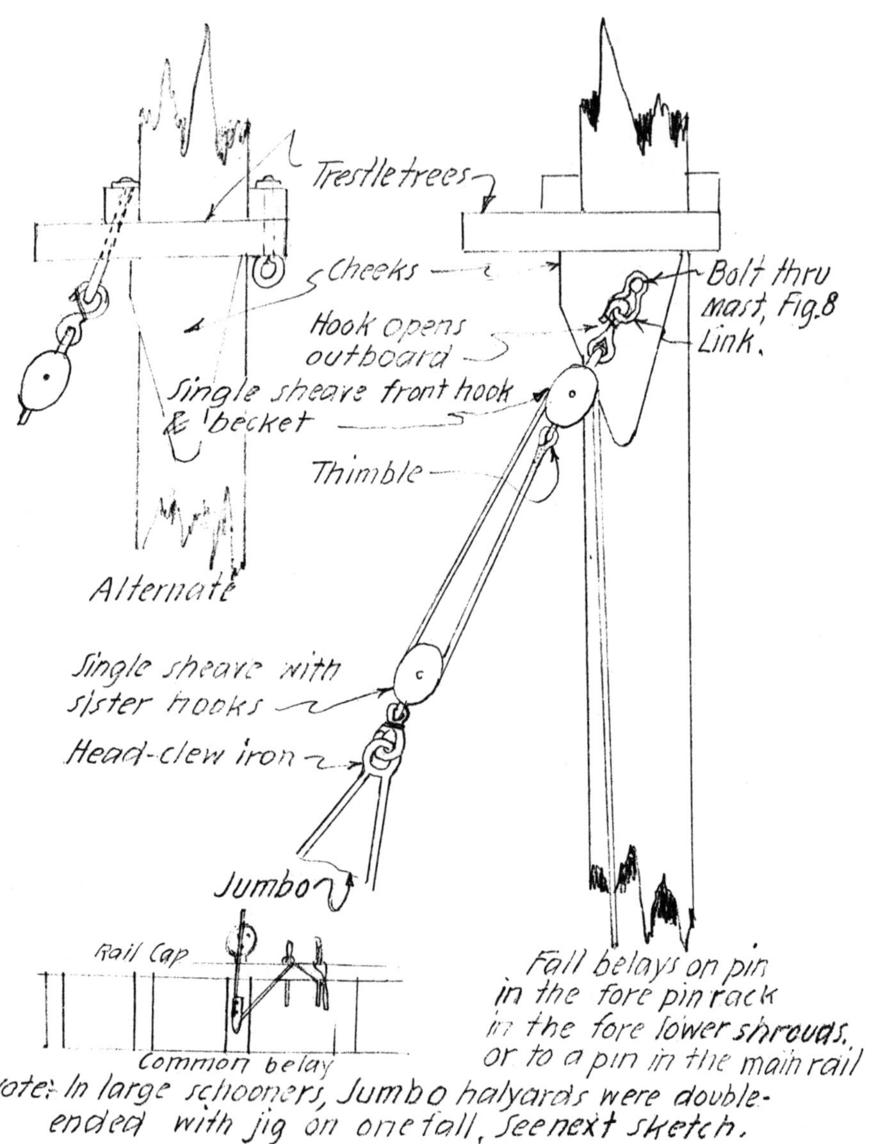
Trestletrees
Cheeks
Bolt thru mast, Fig.8 Link.
Hook opens outboard
Single sheave front hook & becket
Thimble
Alternate
Single sheave with sister hooks
Head-clew iron
Jumbo
Rail Cap
Common belay
Fall belays on pin in the fore pin rack in the fore lower shrouds, or to a pin in the main rail
Note: In large schooners, Jumbo halyards were double-ended with jig on one fall, See next sketch.

JUMBO HALYARDS FOR A LARGE SCHOONER

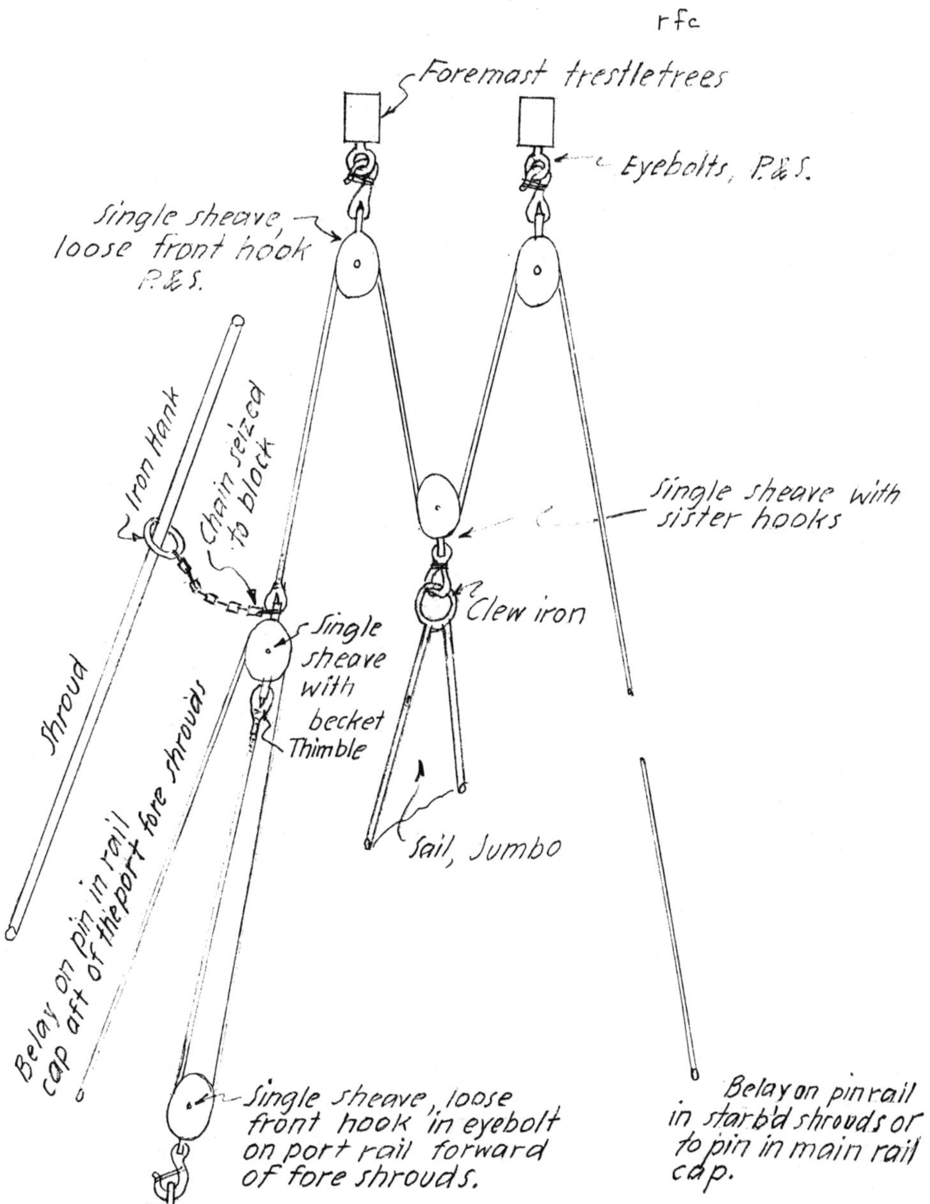
rfc
Foremast trestletrees
Eyebolts, P.&S.
Single sheave, loose front hook P.&S.
Iron Hank
Chain seized to block
Single sheave with sister hooks
Clew iron
Single sheave with becket
Thimble
Shroud
Sail, Jumbo
Belay on pin in rail cap aft of the port fore shrouds
Single sheave, loose front hook in eyebolt on port rail forward of fore shrouds.
Belay on pin rail in starb'd shrouds or to pin in main rail cap.

JUMBO HALYARD, "THEBAUD"

r.f.c

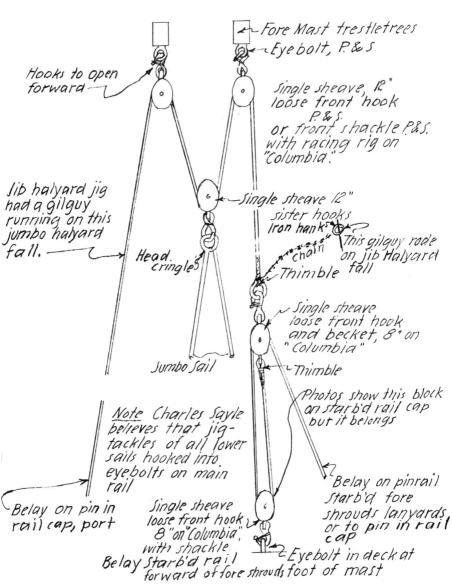

Fore Mast trestletrees

Eyebolt, P.&S.

Hooks to open forward

Single sheave, 12" loose front hook P.&S. or front shackle P.&S. with racing rig on "Columbia."

Jib halyard jig had a gilguy running on this jumbo halyard fall.

Single sheave 12" sister hooks

Iron hanks

This gilguy rode on jib Halyard fall

chain

Head cringles

Thimble

Single sheave loose front hook and becket, 8" on "Columbia"

Jumbo Sail

Thimble

Photos show this block on starb'd rail cap but it belongs

Note Charles Sayle believes that jig-tackles of all lower sails hooked into eyebolts on main rail

Belay on pinrail Starb'd fore shrouds lanyards, or to pin in rail cap

Belay on pin in rail cap, port

Single sheave loose front hook 8" on "Columbia" with shackle

Belay Starb'd rail forward of fore shrouds

Eyebolt in deck at foot of mast

JUMBO STAY

With hemp standing rigging, the jumbo stay was made up with a large eye so that the splice came well down the stay when in place. This allowed the topmast to be struck without affecting the stay.

With the coming of iron rigging, a strop (with eye at each end) became the standard, employing thimbles and shackles. The lower eye, brought to the gammon, or to a wye on the bowsprit, was made up with the end brought up inboard on itself and seized, then served. As the iron ring hanks, or any other of the iron hanks, would chafe the long seizing, a chafing bar, T-shaped, was fitted over as shown in the sketch. Iron seizing wire was used with iron rigging, of course, marlin with hemp.

JUMBO STAY

Not to scale

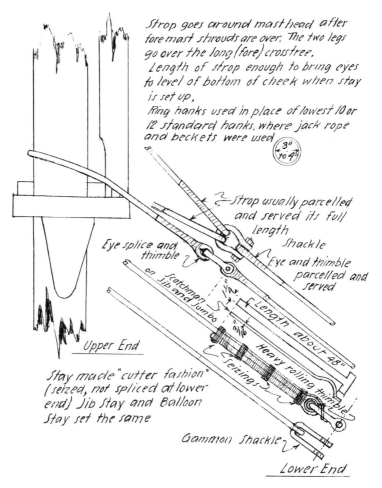

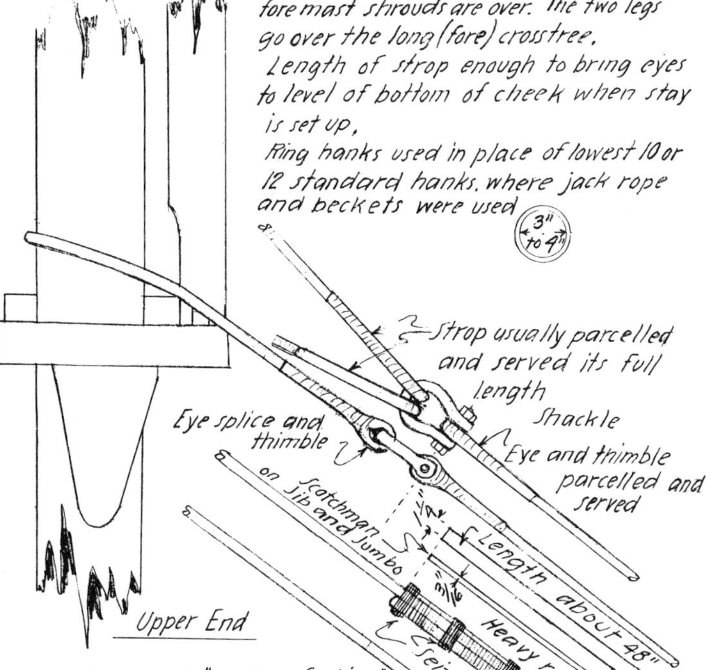
Strop goes around masthead after fore mast shrouds are over. The two legs go over the long (fore) crosstree.
Length of strop enough to bring eyes to level of bottom of cheek when stay is set up.
Ring hanks used in place of lowest 10 or 12 standard hanks, where jack rope and beckets were used
3" to 4"
Strop usually parcelled and served its full length
Shackle
Eye splice and thimble
Eye and thimble parcelled and served
on Scotchman Jib and Jumbo
Length about 48"
Heavy rolling thimble
Seizings
Upper End
Stay made "cutter fashion" (seized, not spliced at lower end) Jib Stay and Balloon Stay set the same
Gammon Shackle
Lower End

JUMBO STAY OR FORESTAY

The forestay of the "Philip P. Manta," 81′ tonnage length, built 1901, was 1¼″ diameter, plough steel wire rope. The forestay strop, or collar, went over masthead after the shrouds. The strop was parcelled and served over all. Forestay shackled into legs of the strop and into stem band, gammoning, inboard wye or bowsprit wye, outboard, according to the fashion then popular. A chafing iron was secured over the stay at lower shackle to protect it from the hanks. See last two entries. The chafing iron was sometimes called a "Scotchman." This was 1¼″-1⅜″ wide, ⅛″-³⁄₁₆″ thick and 44″-48″ long. Sometimes the cross section was worked thus on the long strap.

JUMBO TOPPING LIFT

The jumbo topping lift was employed in working ground tackle as well as for its primary purpose. It was reeved as follows: A wire pendant, 3 to 4 feet long with a sister-hook at its upper end, was hooked into a twisted Figure-8 iron link secured to the foremast by the washers and nut of the lower leg of the fore throat halyard crane. The lower end of the pendant was spliced into the thimble of a single-sheave block. Through this block was rove a line, one end of which was spliced into the thimble of a single-sheave block. From this block, the line led over the sheave of the pendant block, thence down to a short hook, which was hooked into a wye on the jumbo boom. Here the line was given a toggle-bend in the eye of the hook and then passed over the sheave of the lower block, with the fall belaying on the foreside of the fife rail of the foremast. (See next sketch.)

JUMBO TOPPING LIFT

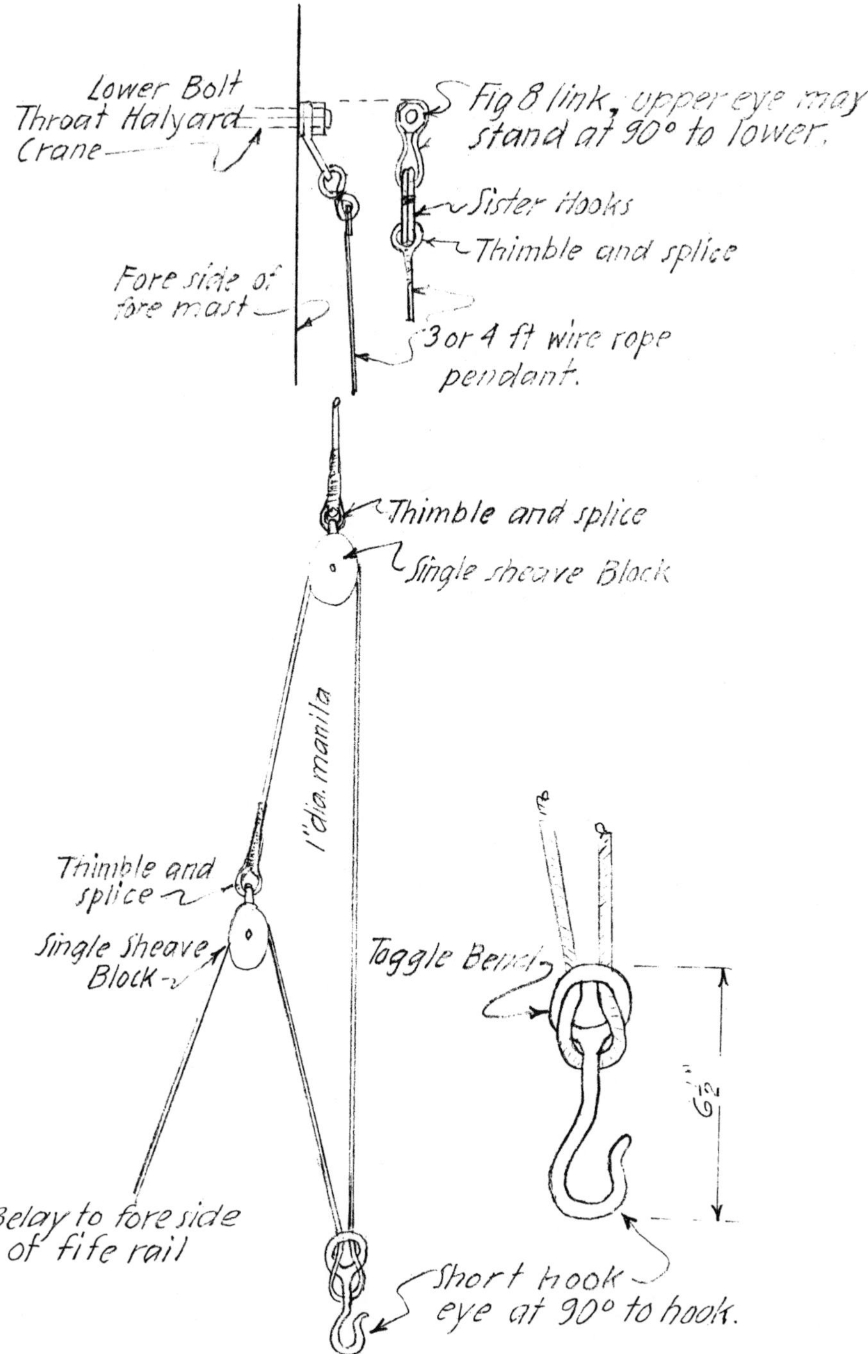
Lower Bolt
Throat Halyard
Crane
Fig 8 link, upper eye may
stand at 90° to lower.
Sister Hooks
Thimble and splice
Fore side of
fore mast
3 or 4 ft wire rope
pendant.
Thimble and splice
Single sheave Block
1" dia. manila
Thimble and
splice
Single Sheave
Block
Toggle Bend
Belay to fore side
of fife rail
Short hook
eye at 90° to hook.

JUMBO BOOM "RIDER" AND HORSE "RUNNER" (NOTES)

When the pole bowsprit became popular, and the forestay was located outboard of the gammon, the jumbo sail was usually fitted with a boom running the full length of its foot. In order to properly furl the jumbo, the boom then had to move a little, fore-and-aft. A sliding tack fitting was developed, consisting of one or two rods supported above the top of the bowsprit, fitted with a sliding tack-eye. In the period of the plumb-stemmers the fitting was between stay and gammon. But when the forestay was brought to the gammoning, the jumbo tack fitting was placed on the forward seat or on the top of the bowsprit inboard. Various names were applied to these fittings, "jumbo boom horse" seems to have been the most used at Gloucester. The double-rod horse was the most common, by far.

JUMBO BOOM "RIDER" AND HORSE "RUNNER"

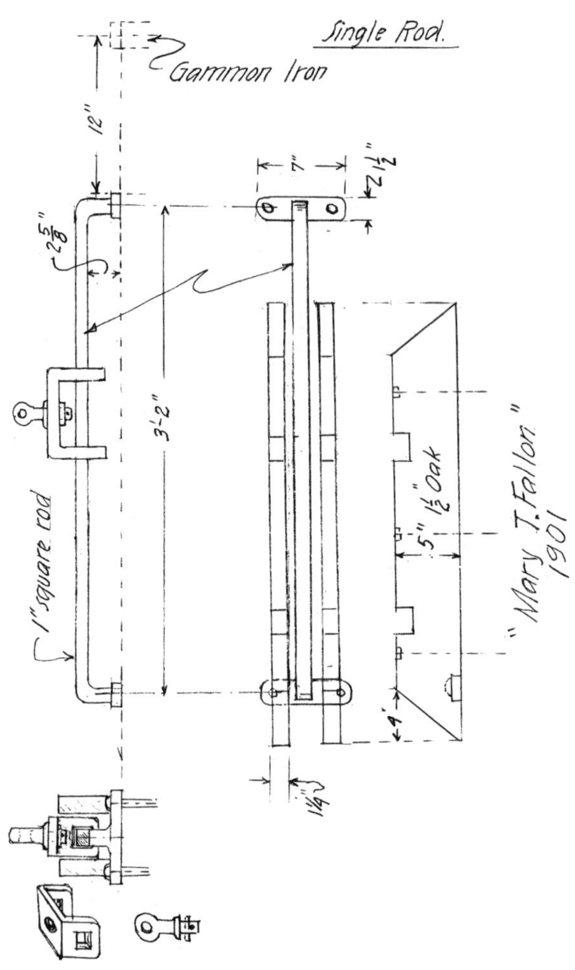
Single Rod.
Gammon Iron
12"
7"
2½"
2⅝"
3'-2"
1" square rod
5"
1½" Oak
4"
1¼"
"Mary T. Fallon"
1901

JUMBO TACK TACKLE

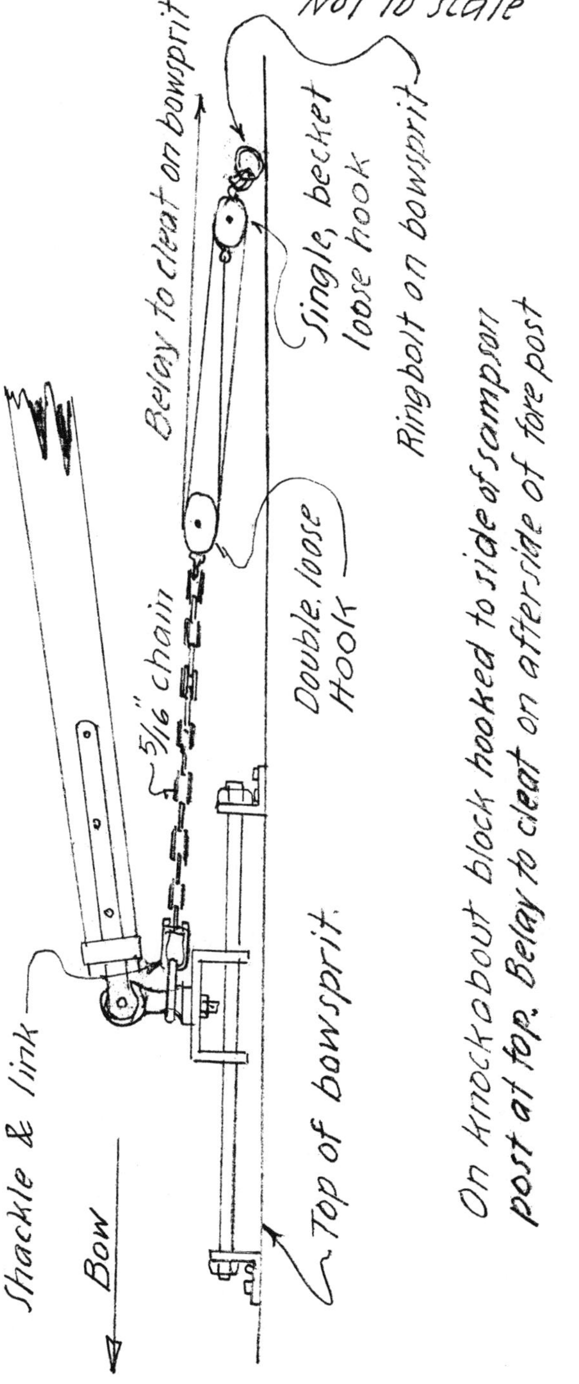

Not to scale
Belay to cleat on bowsprit
Single, becket
loose hook
Ringbolt on bowsprit
Double, loose
Hook
5/16" chain
Shackle & link
Bow
Top of bowsprit
On knockabout block hooked to side of sampson
post at top. Belay to cleat on afterside of fore post

JUMBO BOOM RIDER AND HORSE "RUNNER"

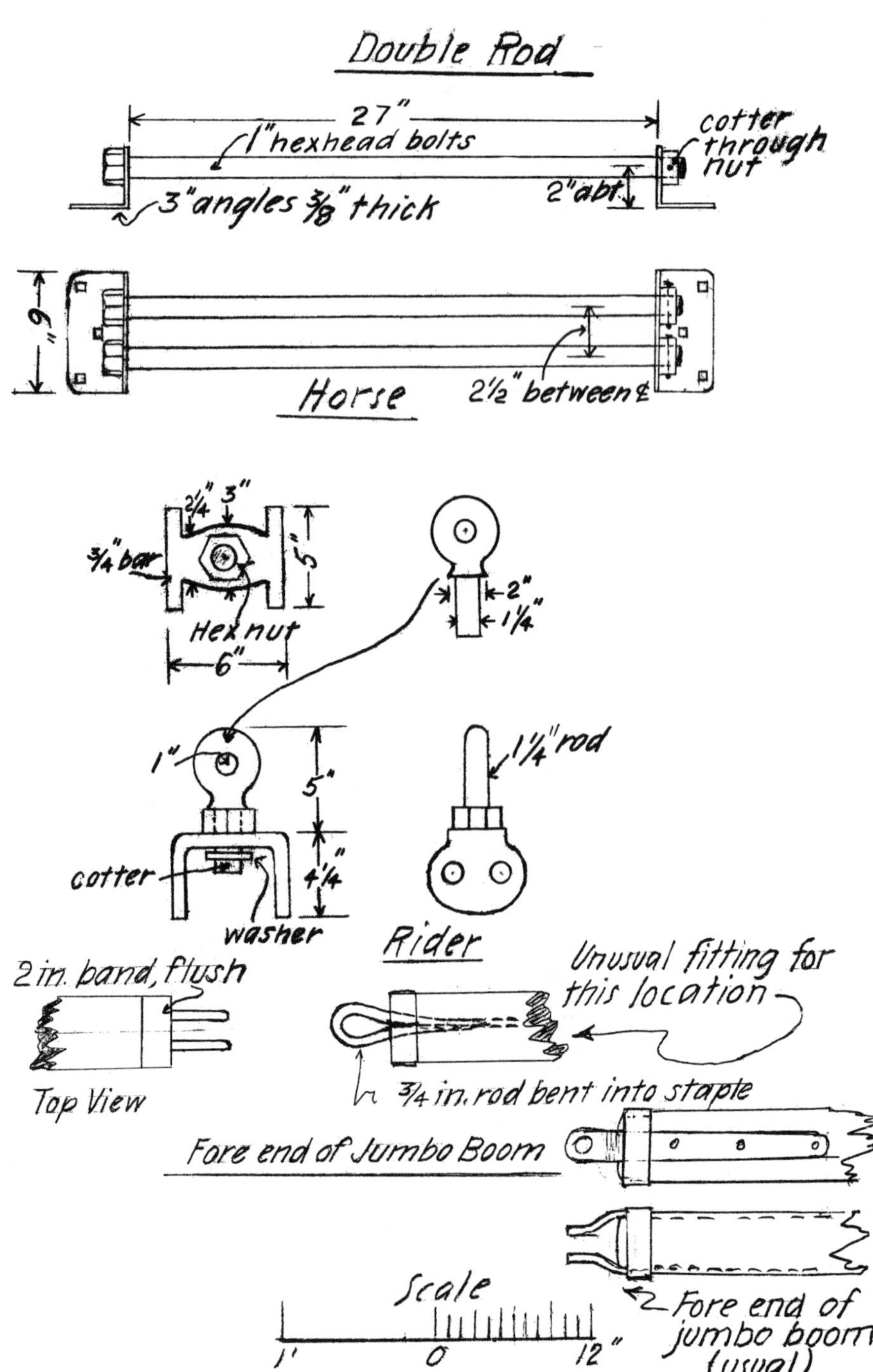

Double Rod
27"
1" hexhead bolts
cotter through nut
2" abt.
3" angles 3/8" thick
6"
Horse
2½" between ℄
2¼"
3"
3/4" bar
5"
Hex nut
6"
2"
1¼"
1"
5"
4¼"
1¼" rod
cotter
washer
Rider
2 in. band, flush
Top View
Unusual fitting for this location
3/4 in. rod bent into staple
Fore end of Jumbo Boom
Scale
1'
0
12"
Fore end of jumbo boom (usual)

KNOCKABOUT STEM IRONWORK

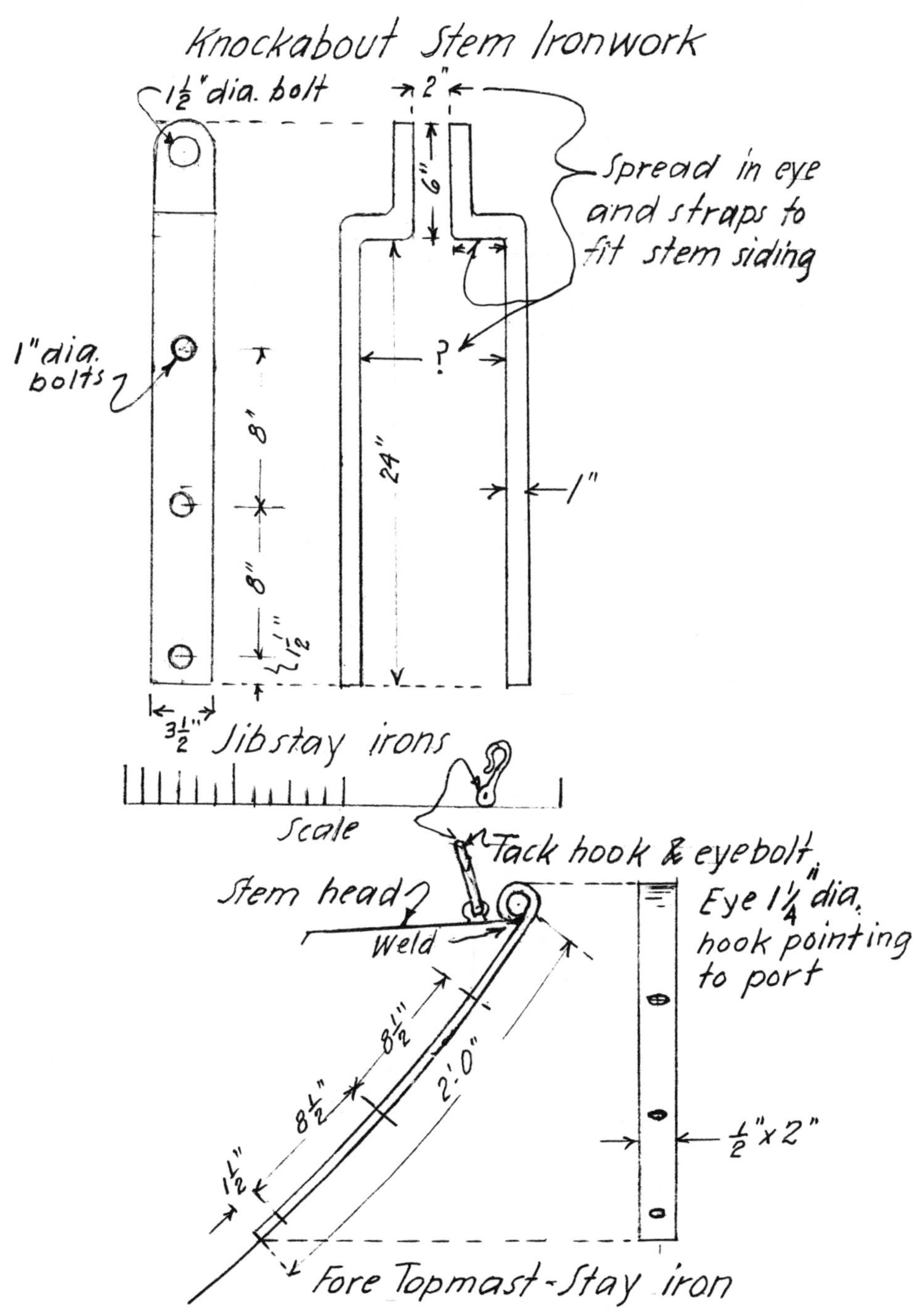

Knockabout Stem Ironwork
1½" dia. bolt
2"
6"
Spread in eye and straps to fit stem siding
1" dia. bolts
8"
8"
1½"
24"
?
1"
3½"
Jibstay irons
Scale
Tack hook & eyebolt.
Stem head
Eye 1¼" dia. hook pointing to port
Weld
8½"
8½"
1½"
2'0"
½" x 2"
Fore Topmast-Stay iron

KNOCKABOUT STEM IRONWORK

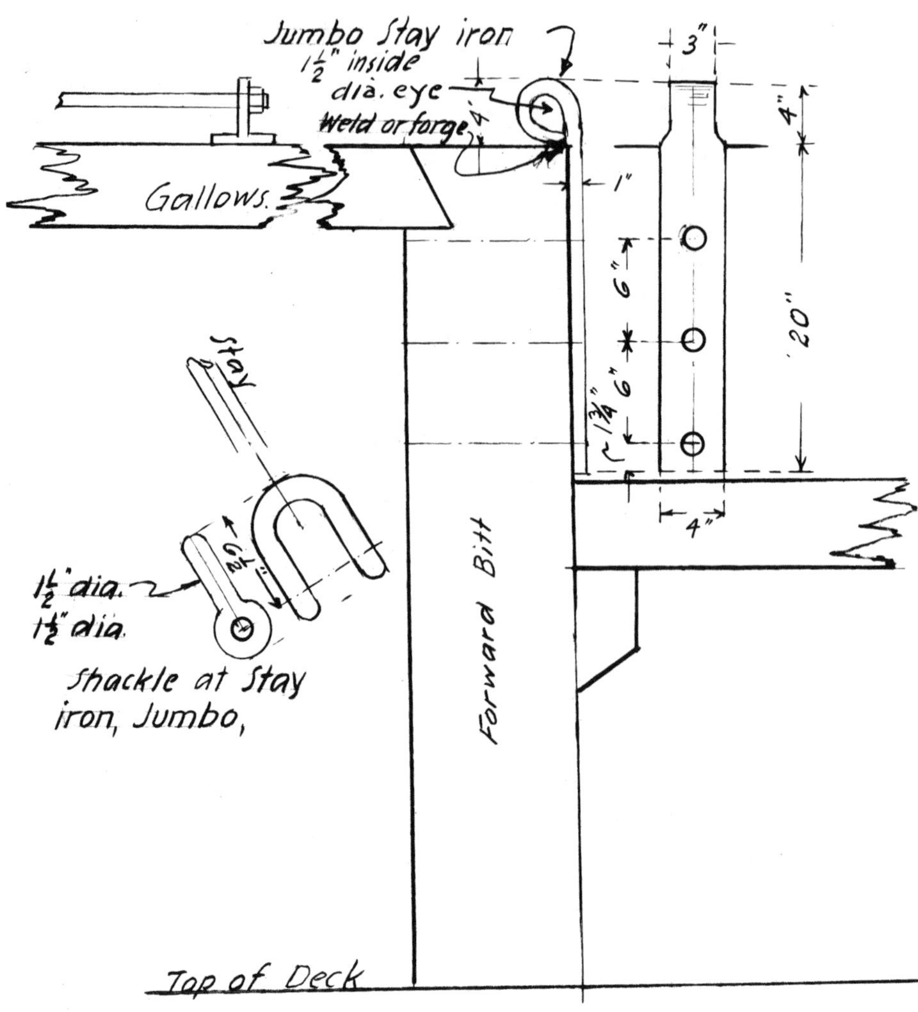
Jumbo Stay iron
1½" inside
dia. eye
Weld or forge
4"
3"
4"
Gallows.
1"
6"
6"
20"
1¾"
4"
Stay
6½"
1½" dia.
1½" dia.
Shackle at Stay
iron, Jumbo,
Forward Bitt
Top of Deck

KNOCKABOUT JUMBO BOOM RIDER, "ETHEL B. PENNY"

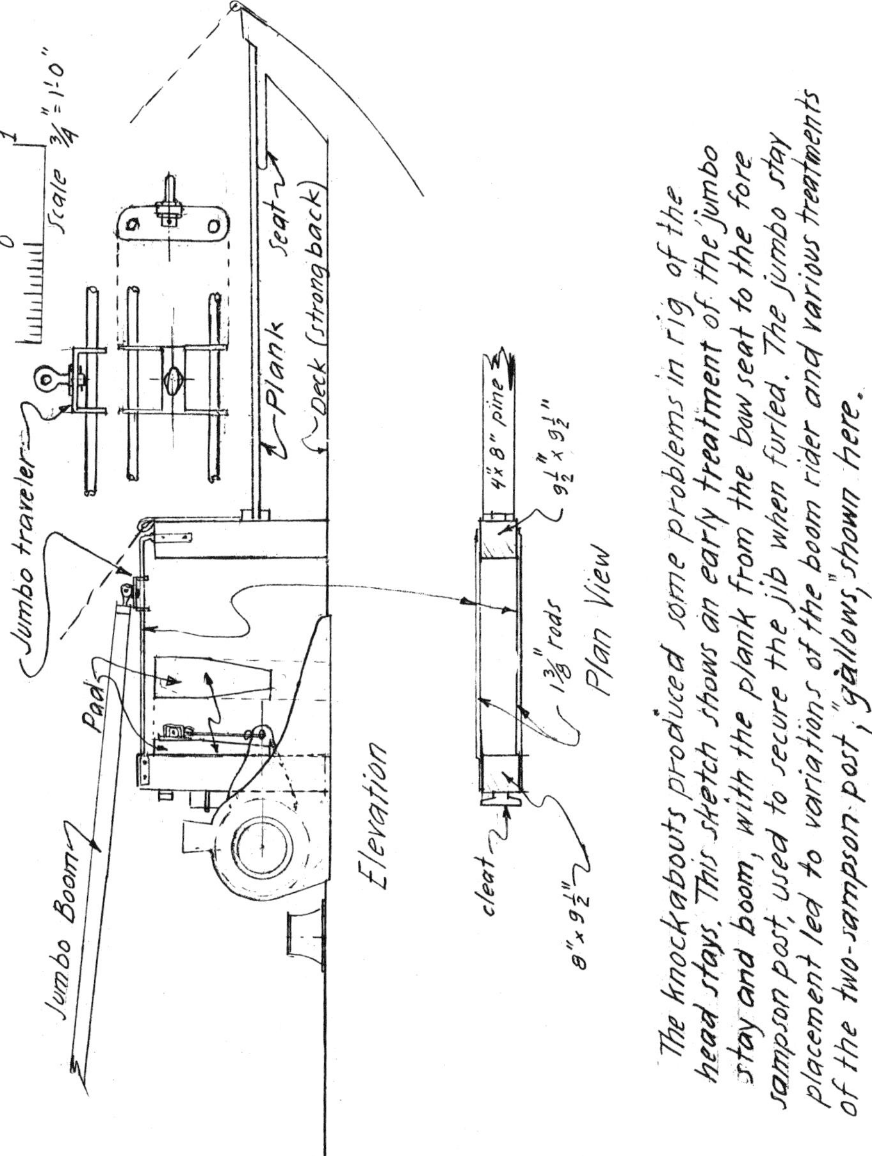
0
1
Scale 3/4" = 1'-0"
Jumbo traveler
Plank
Seat
Deck (strongback)
Pad
Jumbo Boom
Elevation
4" x 8" pine
9½" x 9½"
1 3/8" rods
Plan View
cleat
8" x 9½"
The knockabouts produced some problems in rig of the head stays. This sketch shows an early treatment of the jumbo stay and boom, with the plank from the bow seat to the fore sampson post, used to secure the jib when furled. The jumbo stay placement led to variations of the boom rider and various treatments of the two-sampson-post, "gallows," shown here.

KNOCKABOUT FORE BOOM SADDLE

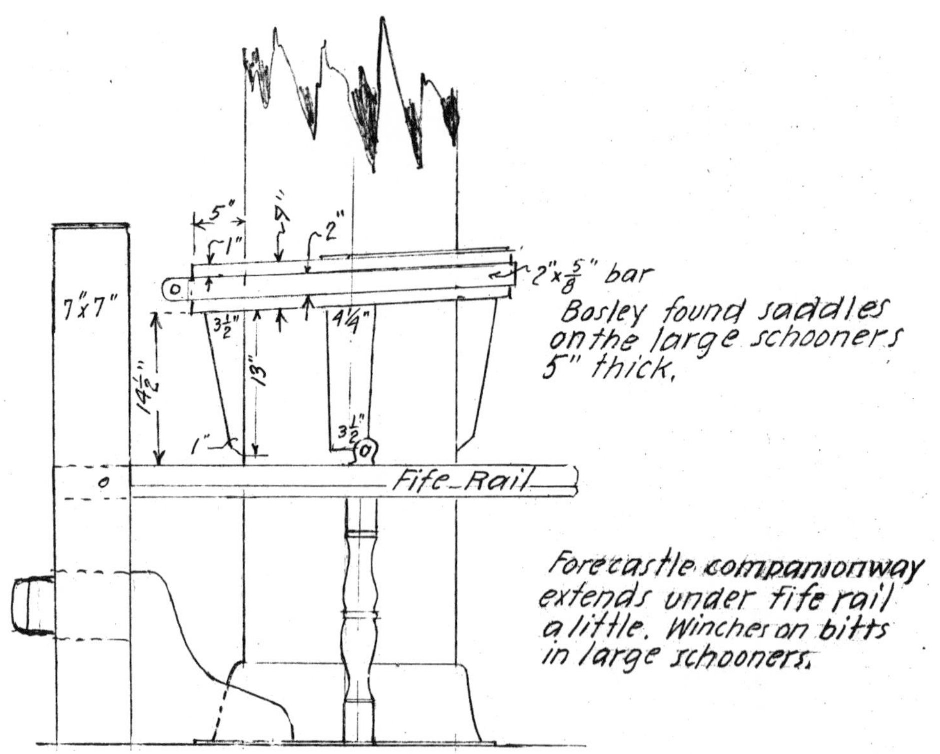
7"x7"
5"
1"
9"
2"
2"x5/8" bar
Bosley found saddles on the large schooners 5" thick.
3½"
4¼"
14½"
13"
1"
3½"
Fife Rail
Forecastle companionway extends under fife rail a little. Winches on bitts in large schooners.

Other details shown in "Main Boom Jaws & Saddle"

Boom saddles were employed on both fore and main masts of schooners built before 1875, as a rule; both booms being fitted with jaws.

KEELS

When the keel structure, outside the rabbet, was very deep and the keel narrow, as it often was after 1890, it was customary to launch on the structural keel, leaving off the false keel or keels and the shoe. These were put on when the vessel was hauled out for final painting and for fitting-out. The "Fredonia," built at Essex in 1889, was the first so treated. The total depth of her keel outside the rabbet was 46″. [L.H.S.]

KNEES

In schooners built at Essex before 1902, vertical or hanging knees were placed under beams forming the mast partners, under the beams supporting the ends of the hatches and under the beams at the ends of the cabin trunk. Lodging, or horizontal, knees and blocking were used under the plank-sheer, in the partners and on the outboard sides of hatch and cabin trunk carlines. After auxiliary engines began to be installed and spars and sail areas were reduced, the number of knees employed in new vessels declined. Hanging knees went out of use except at partners, with the advent of power.

LANYARD PEAR LINK WITH FIGURE-8 LINK

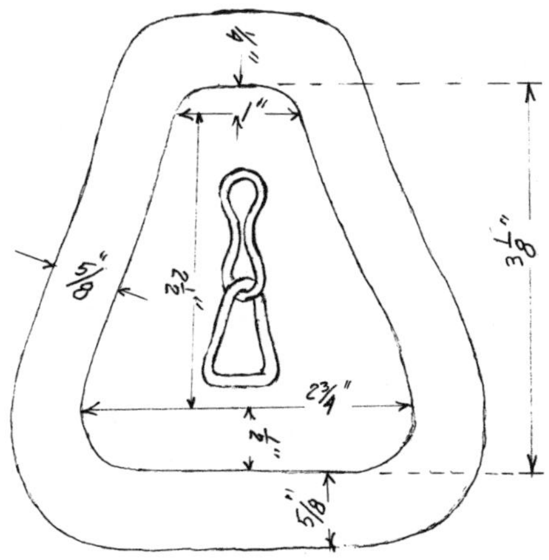

1/4"
1"
3 7/8"
5/8"
2 1/2"
2 3/4"
1/2"
5/8"

LIGHT BOXES, FITTINGS

Topmast Shrouds
Strut in the fore
rigging, underneath
Light box about $8\frac{1}{2}''$-$9\frac{1}{2}''$
at the shroud-jaws of the strut ("Elsie").

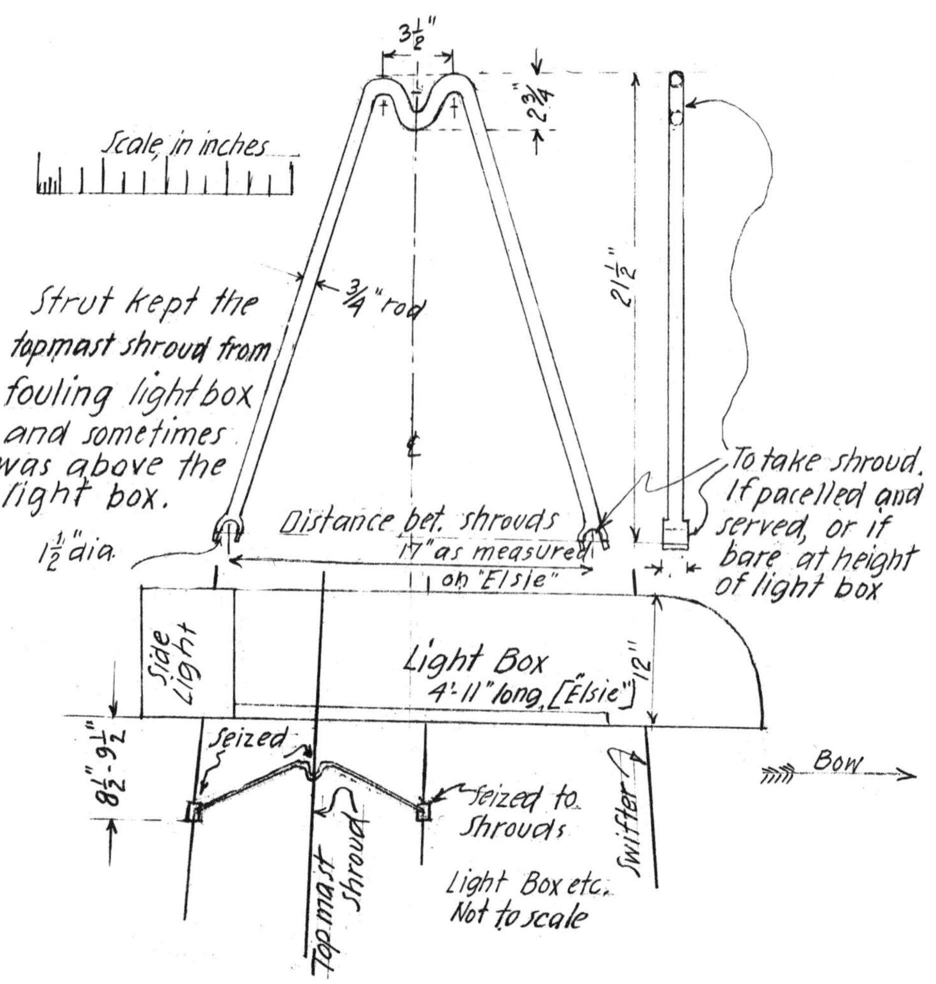
3½"
2¾"
Scale, in inches
2'1½"
Strut kept the topmast shroud from fouling light box and sometimes was above the light box.
¾" rod
To take shroud. If pacelled and served, or if bare at height of light box
1½" dia.
Distance bet. shrouds 17" as measured on "Elsie"
Side Light
Light Box 4'-11" long, ["Elsie"]
12"
8½"-9½"
Seized
Seized to Shrouds
Topmast Shroud
Swifter
Bow
Light Box etc. Not to scale

LIGHT BOX, FITTINGS

Light Boxes made of 1¼" plank. In a 100' vessel the boxes would be about 4'-6" to 5'-0" long, 8" wide and 11" deep.

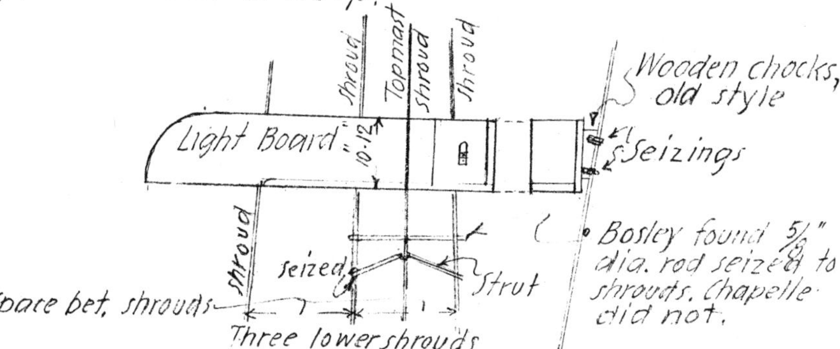
Shroud
Topmast shroud
Shroud
Light Board
10-12"
Wooden chocks, old style
Seizings
Bosley found 5/8" dia. rod seized to shrouds. Chapelle did not.
shroud
seized
Strut
Space bet. shrouds
Three lower shrouds

P. & S. painted red & green fitted to take required size of standard, kerosene side-lights. Boxes were 6' to 8' above the main rail cap.

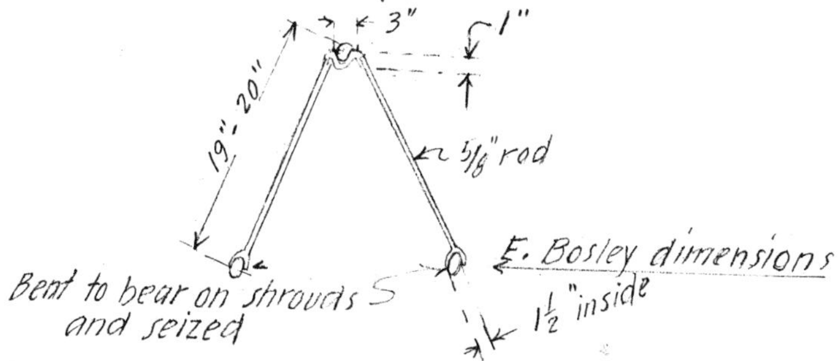
3"
1"
19"-20"
5/8" rod
E. Bosley dimensions
Bent to bear on shrouds and seized
1½" inside

Side lights were required by law in 1865.

LIGHT BOARD IRONS

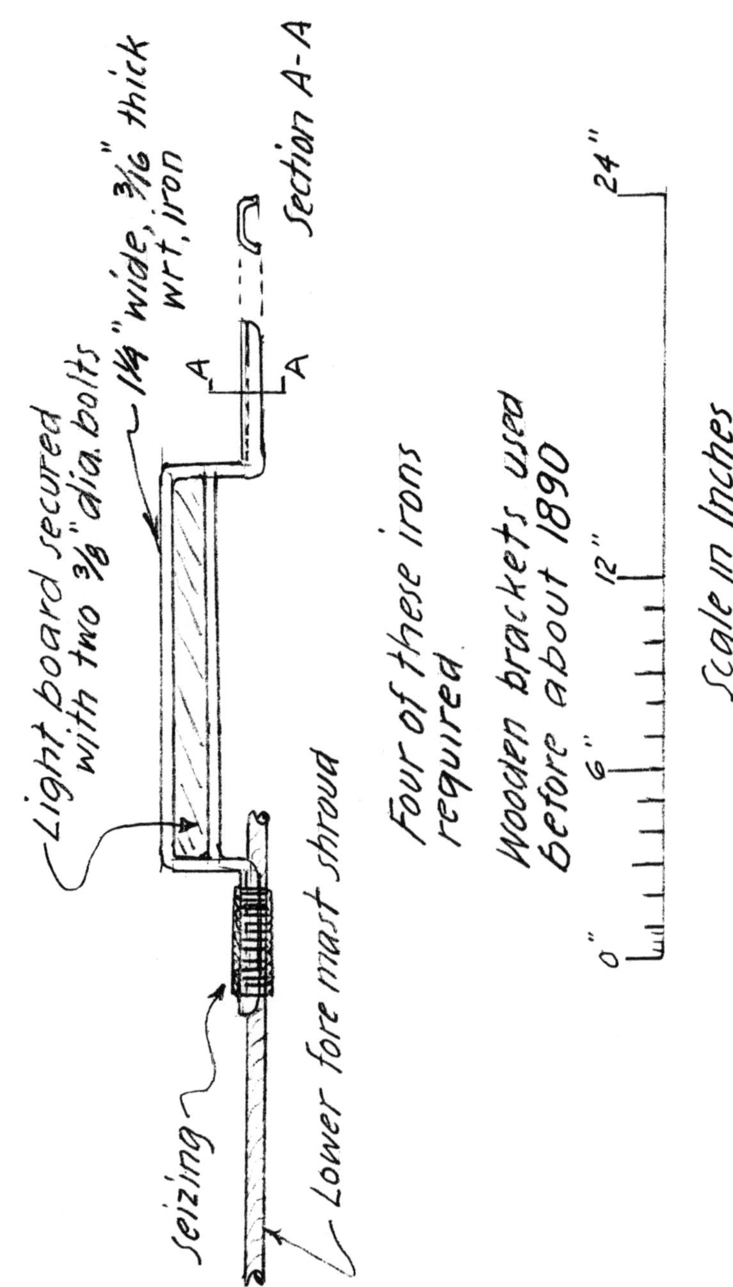
Light board secured with two 3/8" dia. bolts
1 1/4" wide, 3/16" thick wrt. iron
Section A-A
A
A
Four of these irons required
Wooden brackets used before about 1890
0"
6"
12"
24"
Scale in Inches
Seizing
Lower fore mast shroud

LIMBER

Galv. chain, in one length, was stretched fore-and-aft, P.&S., in each limber, with some slack. By pulling this back and forth the limber could be cleared.

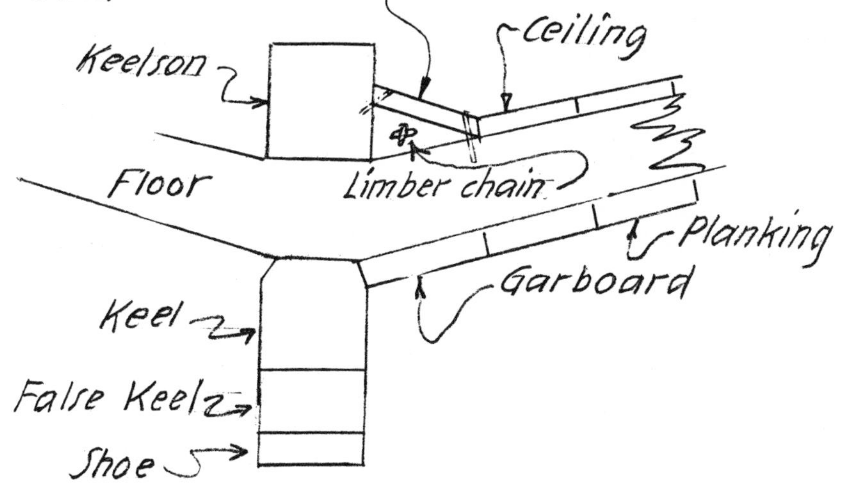
Limber strake
Ceiling
Keelson
Floor
Limber chain
Planking
Garboard
Keel
False Keel
Shoe

LIZARDS, OR *LIGNUM VITAE* FAIRLEADS

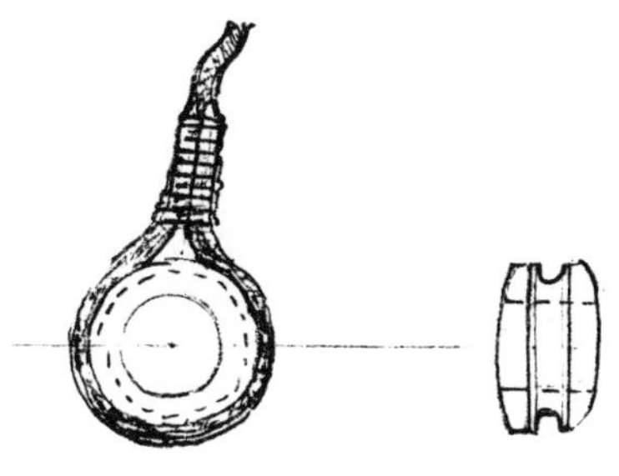

Outside dia.	$2\frac{1}{2}$"	$2\frac{3}{4}$"	3"	$3\frac{1}{2}$"	4"
Hole dia.	1"	$1\frac{1}{8}$"	$1\frac{1}{4}$"	$1\frac{3}{8}$"	$1\frac{1}{2}$"

MACKEREL POCKET BOOMS AND SEINE ROLLERS

Schooners engaged in mackerel-seine fishing had outrigger booms to support the "pocket." These were light spars having a hook-shaped iron driven in one end. Eye bolts were driven into the outboard edge of the rail caps, one just abaft the fore chainplates and just afore the after chainplates. The length of the booms was determined by the size of the pocket. The heel iron of the booms hooked into the eyes in the rail caps; guys and mast-head tackles supported the outboard ends of the booms.

Mackerel fishing schooners were fitted with a seine roller. This was a wooden roller, 6 to 8 inches in diameter, located on top of the quarterdeck or monkey rail. It was usually on the port side just abaft the main chainplates and was long enough to bring its after end slightly abaft the fore end of the cabin trunk. This was fitted to the schooners after the large seine nets and seine boats came into use.

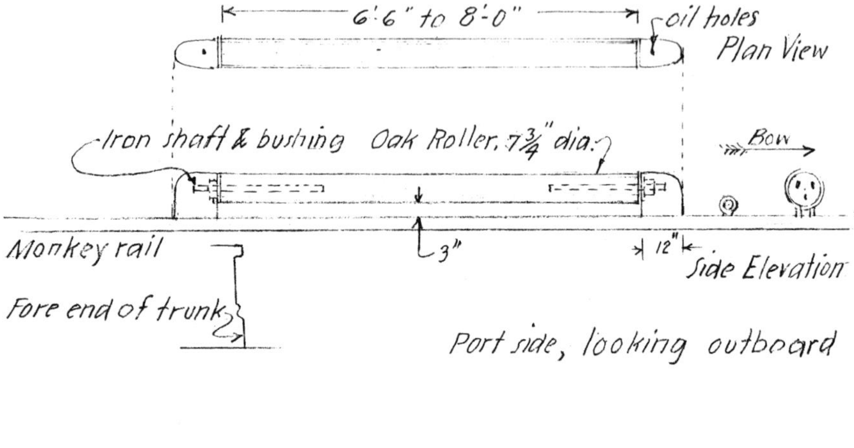

6'6" to 8'-0"
oil holes
Plan View
Iron shaft & bushing
Oak Roller, 7¾" dia.
Bow
Monkey rail
3"
12"
Side Elevation
Fore end of trunk
Port side, looking outboard

TYPICAL MAIN BOOM JAWS AND SADDLE

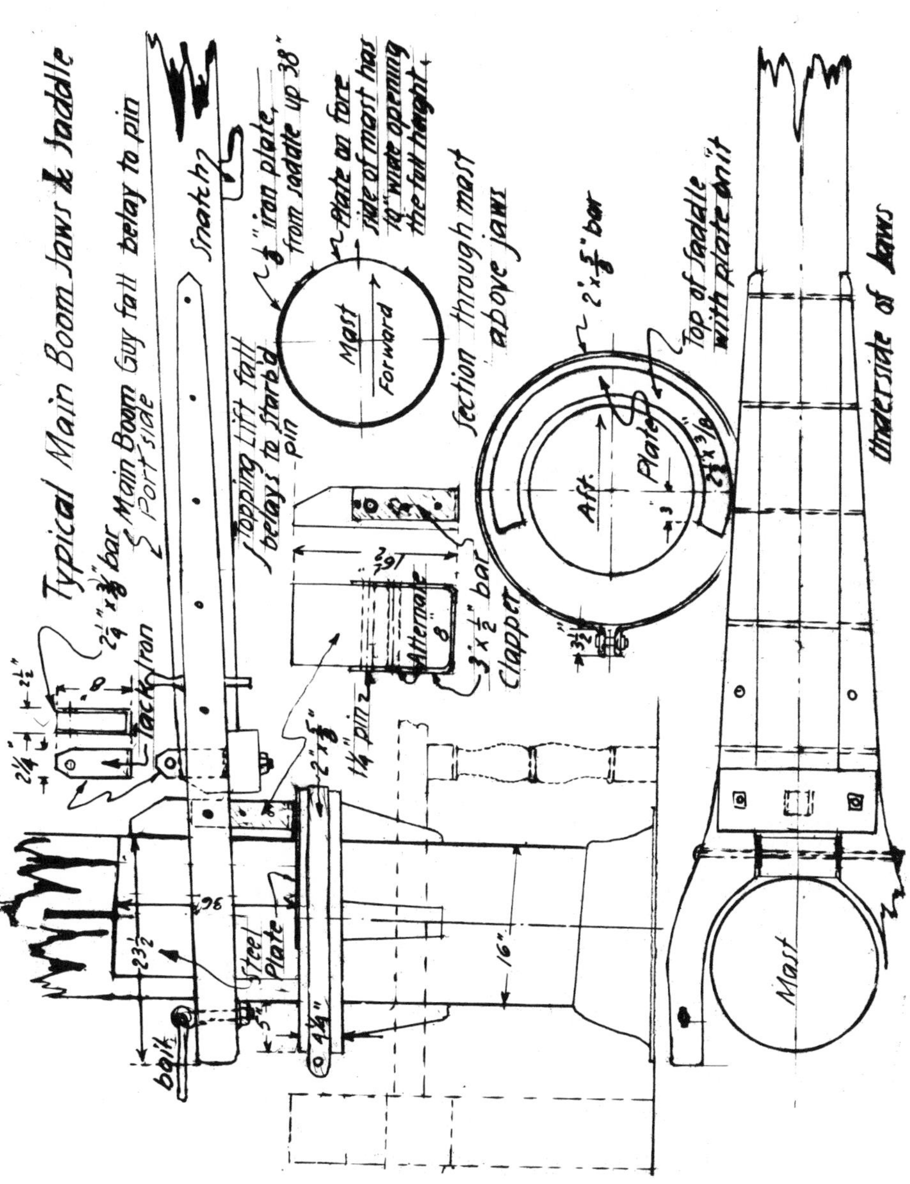
Typical Main Boom Jaws & Saddle
Main Boom Guy fall belay to pin
Port side
Snatch b
Topping Lift fall belays to starb'd pin
Mast
Forward
Section through mast above jaws
Aft
Plate
Clapper
Alternate
Tack Iron
Steel Plate
bolt
16"
Top of saddle with plate on it
Underside of Jaws
Mast

MAIN BOOM IRONWORK

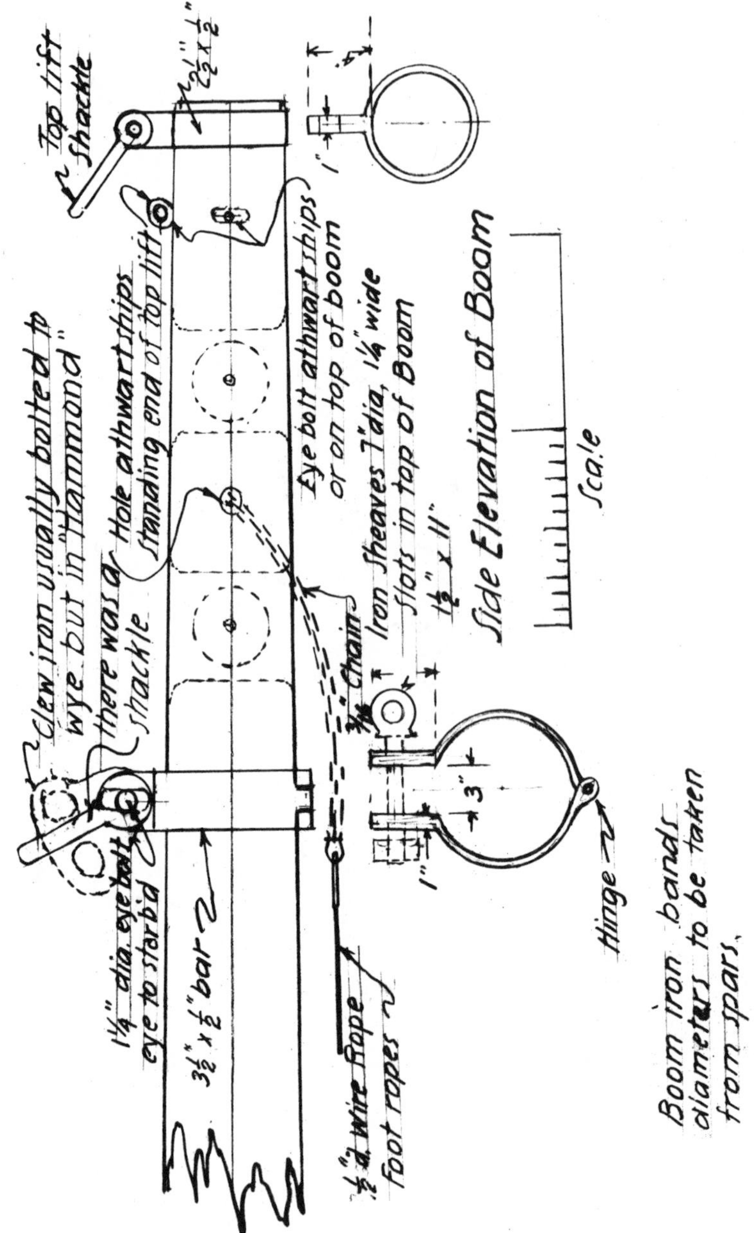
Clew iron usually bolted to wye but in "Hammond" there was a shackle
Hole athwartships standing end of top lift
Top lift shackle
2½" x ½"
1¼" dia. eye bolt eye to starbd
3½" x ½" bar
Eye bolt athwartships or on top of boom
Iron Sheaves 7" dia, 1¼ wide
slots in top of Boom
1½" x 11"
5/16" Chain
½" d. Wire Rope
Foot ropes
1"
3"
1"
Side Elevation of Boom
Scale
Hinge
Boom iron bands diameters to be taken from spars.
"Natalie Hammond" Knockabout

MAIN BOOM IRONWORK

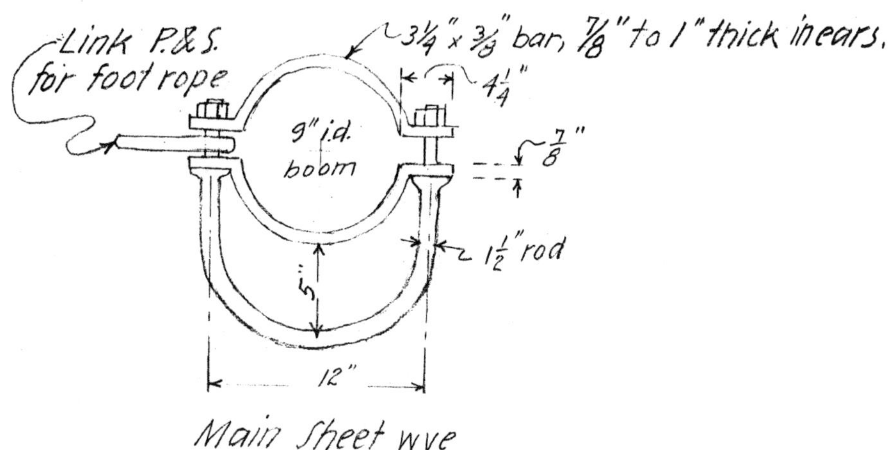
Link P.&S.
for foot rope
3¼" x ⅜" bar, ⅞" to 1" thick in ears.
4¼"
9" i.d.
boom
⅞"
1½" rod
5"
12"

Main Sheet wye
Boom Guy wye same but no horse, eye-bolts, eyes down, with links
hex nuts.

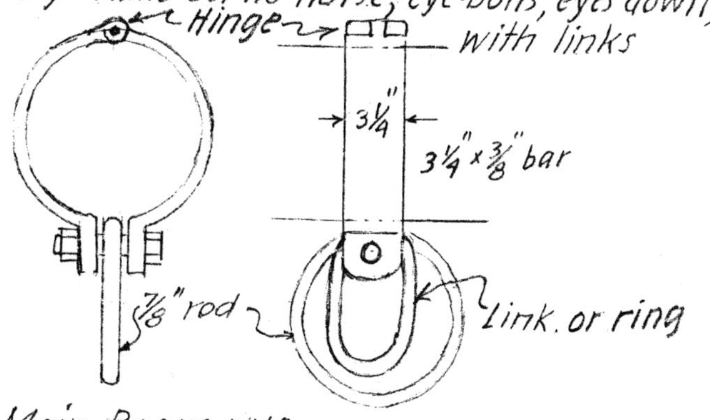
Hinge
3¼"
3¼" x ⅜" bar
⅞" rod
Link. or ring

Main Boom wye
For boom tackle, same on fore boom.

All boom bands to be chamferred thus.

MAIN BOOM IRONWORK, "NATALIE HAMMOND"

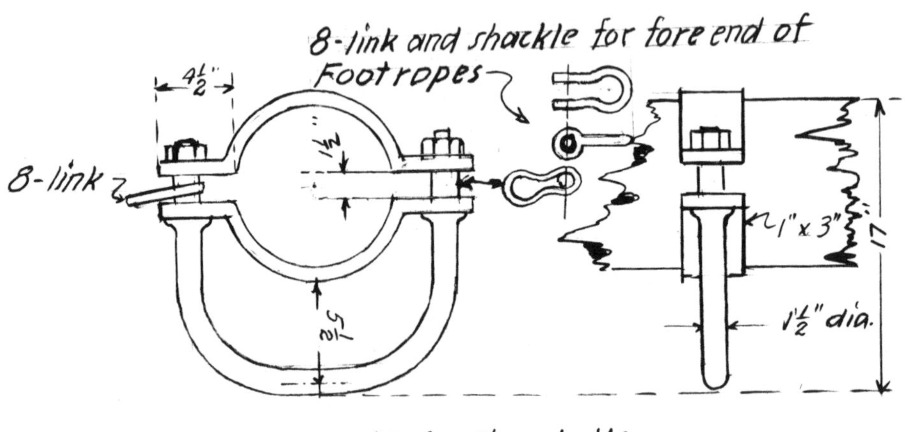
8-link and shackle for fore end of Footropes
4½"
8-link
¾"
5½"
1" x 3"
1½" dia.
17"

Main Sheet Wye
"Natalie Hammond"

MAIN BOOM IRONWORK, "NATALIE HAMMOND"

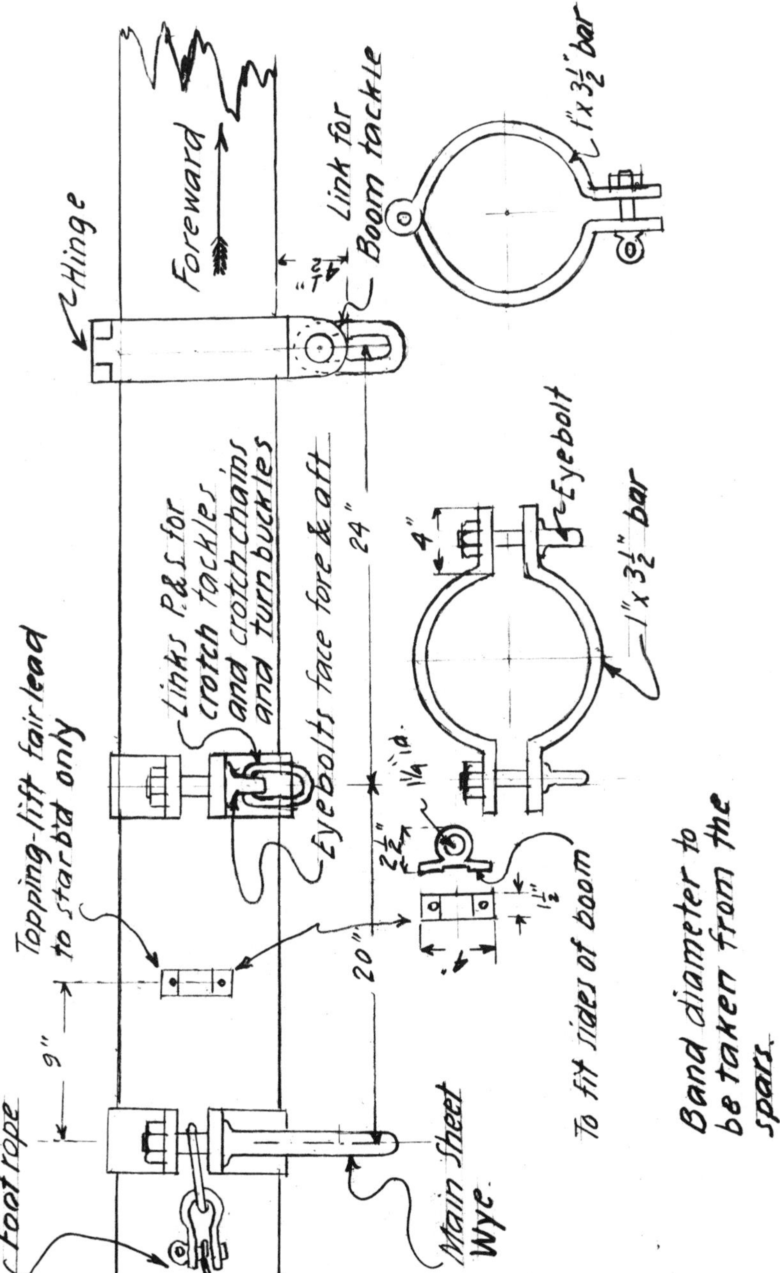

Foot rope
Main Sheet Wye
9"
20"
Topping-lift fair lead to star b'd only
Links P.&S. for crotch tackles, and crotch chains and turn buckles
Eyebolts face fore & aft
24"
1¼" dia.
2½"
4"
1½"
To fit sides of boom
Band diameter to be taken from the spars.
Hinge
Foreward
Link for Boom tackle
2½"
1"x3½" bar
Eyebolt
4"
1"x3½" bar

MAIN BOOM JAWS, "NATALIE HAMMOND"

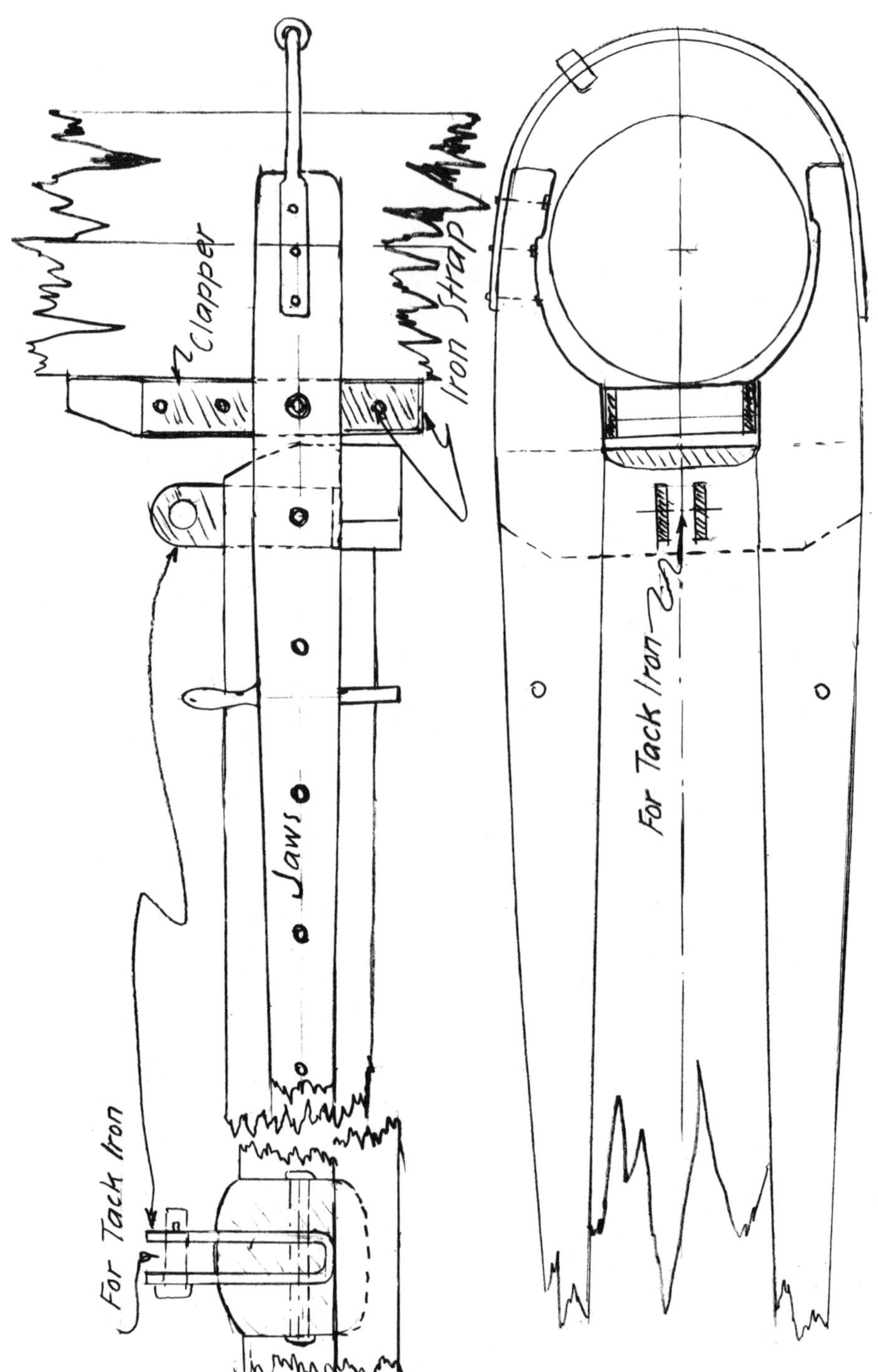
Clapper
Iron Strap
Jaws
For Tack Iron
For Tack Iron

MAINSHEET

The usual reeving of a fishing schooner, after the type reached 90′-0″ registered length, was as follows: There was a triple-sheave block on the mainboom, a double-sheave block on the ring-traveler on the horse, the block fitted with a becket. On deck, or on the inboard planking of the transom, there was a single-sheave block, or a large fairlead, on an eyebolt that was placed at the center of a circular steel plate, 3/16″ thick nailed on deck or on the plank inside the transom. This protected the deck from the block, or fairlead, when the sheet was thrashing about. If no steel plate were fitted, the lead block was surrounded by a coil of 1″ diameter rope, nailed to the deck or inside of transom, to act as a cushion.

The sheet rove thus spliced to becket on traveler block then to first sheave of boom block, thence to first sheave on traveler block, thence to second sheave on boom block, thence to second sheave on traveler block, then to third sheave on boom block, leading then to lead block or fairlead, belaying on quarter-bitt, port or starboard. If a patented snubber were used, instead of an iron horse, as employed extensively after 1892, the reeving of the sheet would not be changed. The lower or taffrail block would be frapped or, after about 1920, an old automobile tire was used instead of frapping.

In earlier and smaller schooners the traveler block was single-sheave and the boom block double-sheave. The single-sheave lower block was then on an iron ring-traveler mounted on a common iron horse, on deck or on main taffrail, with padding around a lead fairlead. The mainsheet was always abaft the wheel box.

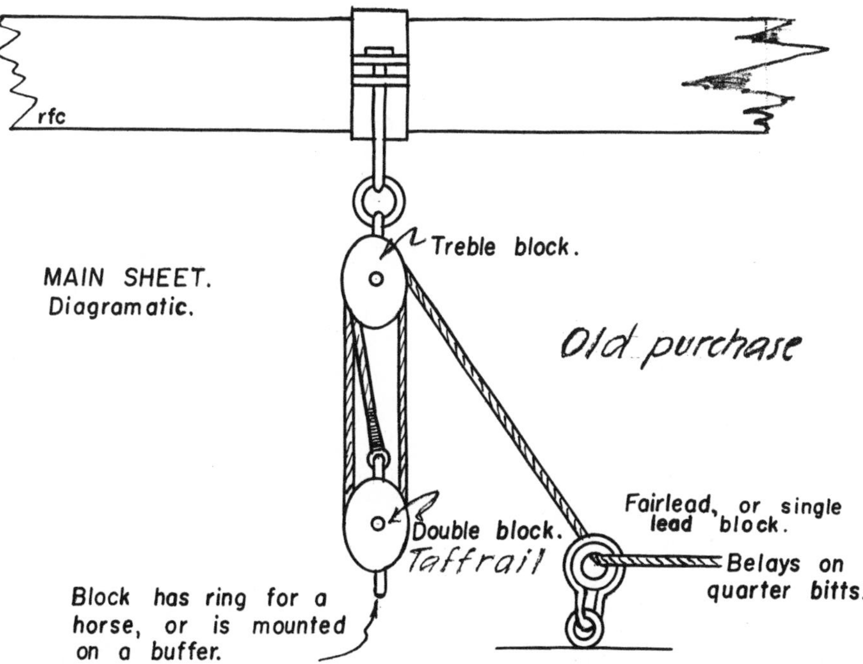
rfc
Treble block.
MAIN SHEET.
Diagramatic.
Old purchase
Fairlead, or single lead block.
Double block.
Taffrail
Belays on quarter bitts.
Block has ring for a horse, or is mounted on a buffer.

MAINSHEET
"TAFFRAIL BLOCK" (SHELL), LOWER BLOCK OF SHEET

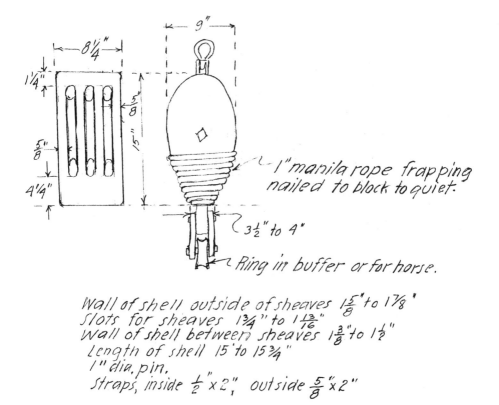

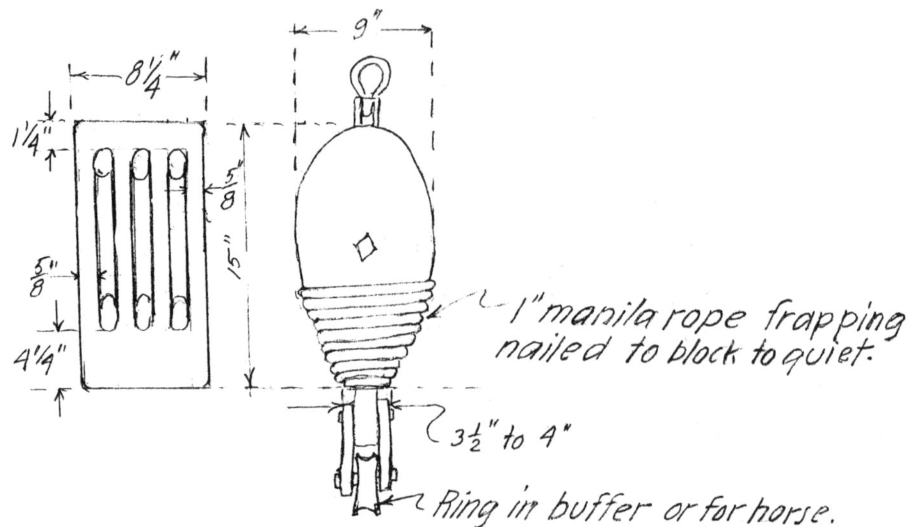
9"
8¼"
1¼"
5/8"
5/8"
15"
4¼"
1" manila rope frapping nailed to block to quiet.
3½" to 4"
Ring in buffer or for horse.

Wall of shell outside of sheaves 1 5/8" to 1 7/8"
Slots for sheaves 1¾" to 1 13/16"
Wall of shell between sheaves 1 3/8" to 1½"
Length of shell 15" to 15¾"
1" dia. pin.
Straps, inside ½" x 2", outside 5/8" x 2"

MAIN BOOM FITTINGS

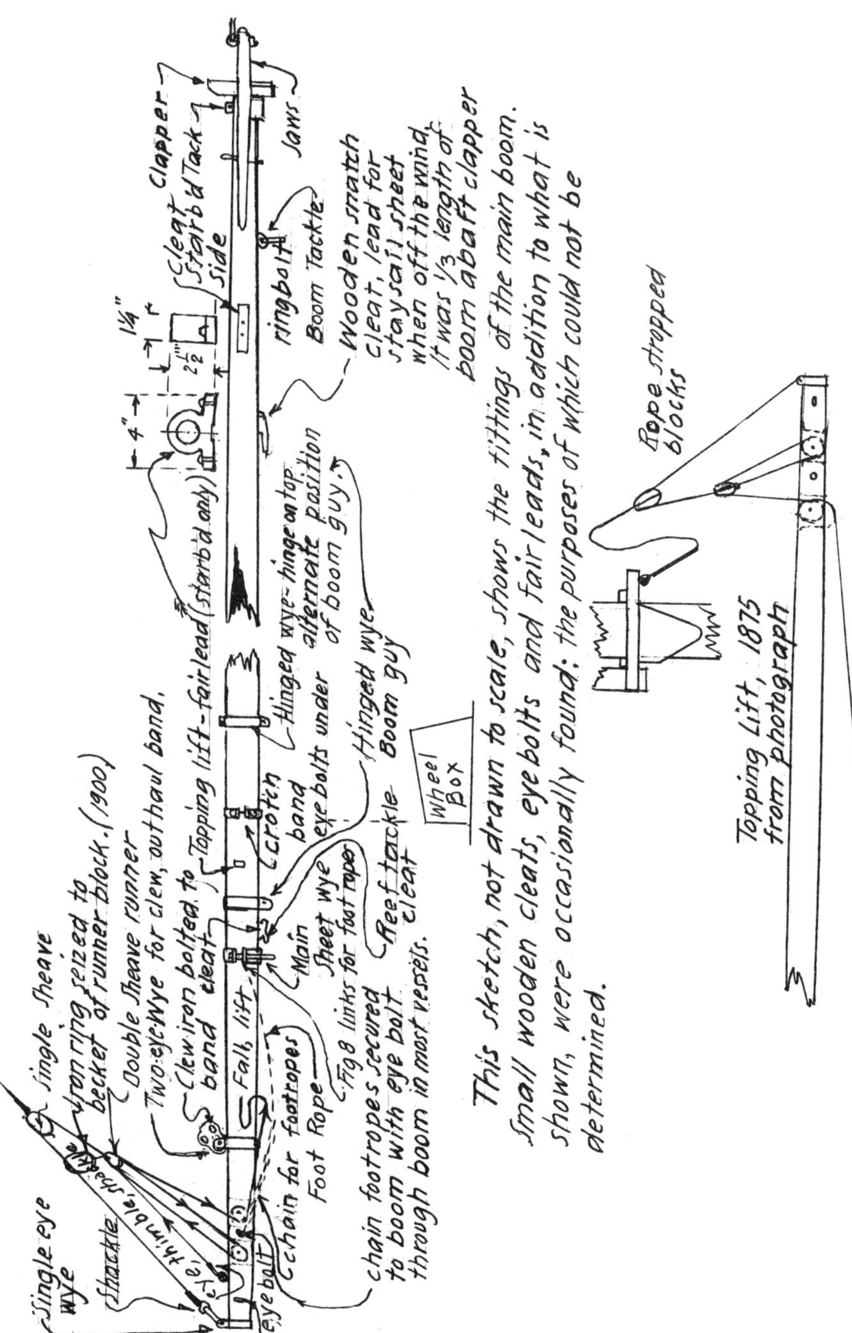
Single eye wye
Shackle
eye, thimble, shackle
Single Sheave
Iron ring seized to becket of runner block. (1900)
Double Sheave runner
Two-eye Wye for clew, outhaul band.
Clew iron bolted to band cleat
Topping lift-fairlead (starb'd only)
4"
1¼"
2½"
Cleat Starb'd Tack side
Clapper
eye bolt
chain for footropes
Fall, lift
Foot Rope
Main Sheet wye
Fig 8 links for foot rope
crotch band
eye bolts under
Hinged wye-hinge on top alternate position of boom guy.
Hinged wye Boom guy
Reef tackle cleat
chain footropes secured to boom with eye bolt through boom in most vessels.
Wheel Box
ringbolt
Boom Tackle
Jaws
Wooden snatch cleat, lead for staysail sheet when off the wind, It was ⅓ length of boom abaft clapper
This sketch, not drawn to scale, shows the fittings of the main boom. Small wooden cleats, eyebolts and fairleads, in addition to what is shown, were occasionally found: the purposes of which could not be determined.
Rope stropped blocks
Topping Lift, 1875 from photograph

MAINSHEET HORSES AND BOOM BUFFERS

Until fishing schooners approaching 100′ length on deck were being built, with rigs to match, the old iron mainsheet horses were adequate. These were 5′-6′ wide, 8″-9″ high, of 2″ wrt. iron rod, forged to the same general design used for the foresheet horses. The mainsheet horse bolts, below the flanges, passed through the decking and beam; the ends locked with washer and key, or ran through transom ceiling, frame, and plank, to lock on the after face of the transom plank, if located far enough aft. In some old schooners the horse was on the main rail cap inside the monkey rail, and locked on the outboard face of the transom. In the 1890s the horses were threaded below the flanges, with washer and a square nut. Because of the rake of the transom the washers had to be padded outside. Stops were fitted at the ends of the horses. These were oak blocks spiked inside the ends of the horses to stop the traveler ring from fouling on the end supports of the horse. Another common horse, fore and main, was made of two large, long eyebolts fitted with a rod, locked outboard of the eyes with washers and keys, with wooden block stops. The ring-traveler was usually of 1″-1½″ diameter rod. The ring was fitted with a thimble for rope-stropped blocks. These were noisy so the lower wooden sheet block was often padded with tightly wrapped rope, up to a little below the pin of the sheave, nailed to the shell, or a coiled rope mat was made around the horse, if space permitted, as described earlier. (See "Main sheet.")

As the size of the schooners and of their sail area increased, the shocks given by the huge mainsails in particular, when tacking or jibbing, caused broken spars, hull damage, or parted gear. This led to the use of the "boom buffer" produced by the Edson Corporation of South Boston, Massachusetts, in the early 1880s. The buffer employed six to eight rubber springs on a rod horse, supported by two large-shouldered eyebolts. Inside these eyes were sliding members fitted with through-bolts. A ring-traveler, for the lower sheet block, was connected to the sliding members by pairs of straps. Spacers between springs were used.

When the ring-traveler was moved from side to side, the sliding members moved to compress the rubber springs and slow the movement of the ring-traveler. Through the courtesy of the Edson Corporation, a catalog drawing for buffers is reproduced here. The design of this fitting can readily be understood. In the vessels measured that had this fitting, such as "Elsie," Nos. 6 and 7 were employed. It will be seen that the buffers rested upon a ¼″ steel plate. Usually the mainsheet buffer was located on the transom, or on the deck close to the transom, and covered with a heavy plank, or two edge-bolted planks, about 24″ wide and 48″ long supported at the outboard ends by wooden chocks about 3″ thick. The top was about 2½″ or 3″ thick and had a rectangular hole cut in it 20″ athwartship and 12″ fore-and-aft. In this the ring-traveler and its straps moved.

In the "Philip P. Manta," this cover of the buffer was 3″ plank, 6′-0″ athwartship, 28″ fore-and-aft, standing 9″ off the deck. Usually the cover top was at the level of the main rail, at the center of the transom.

The boom buffers recommended by the Edson Corporation, for use in fishing schooners, were based on L.W.L. These were for mainsheets, and were commonly Nos. 5, 6, and 7; L.W.L.s 70 to 115 feet. Buffers for the foresheets were to be one size smaller than for the mainsheet. In the mid-1890s, nearly all schooners above 85′ L.W.L., or 90′ Custom House length, had buffers on both fore and main sheets.

"Grampus," 1885, had buggers for both main and fore sheets.

EDSON PATENT BOOM BUFFER, FOR MAINSHEET

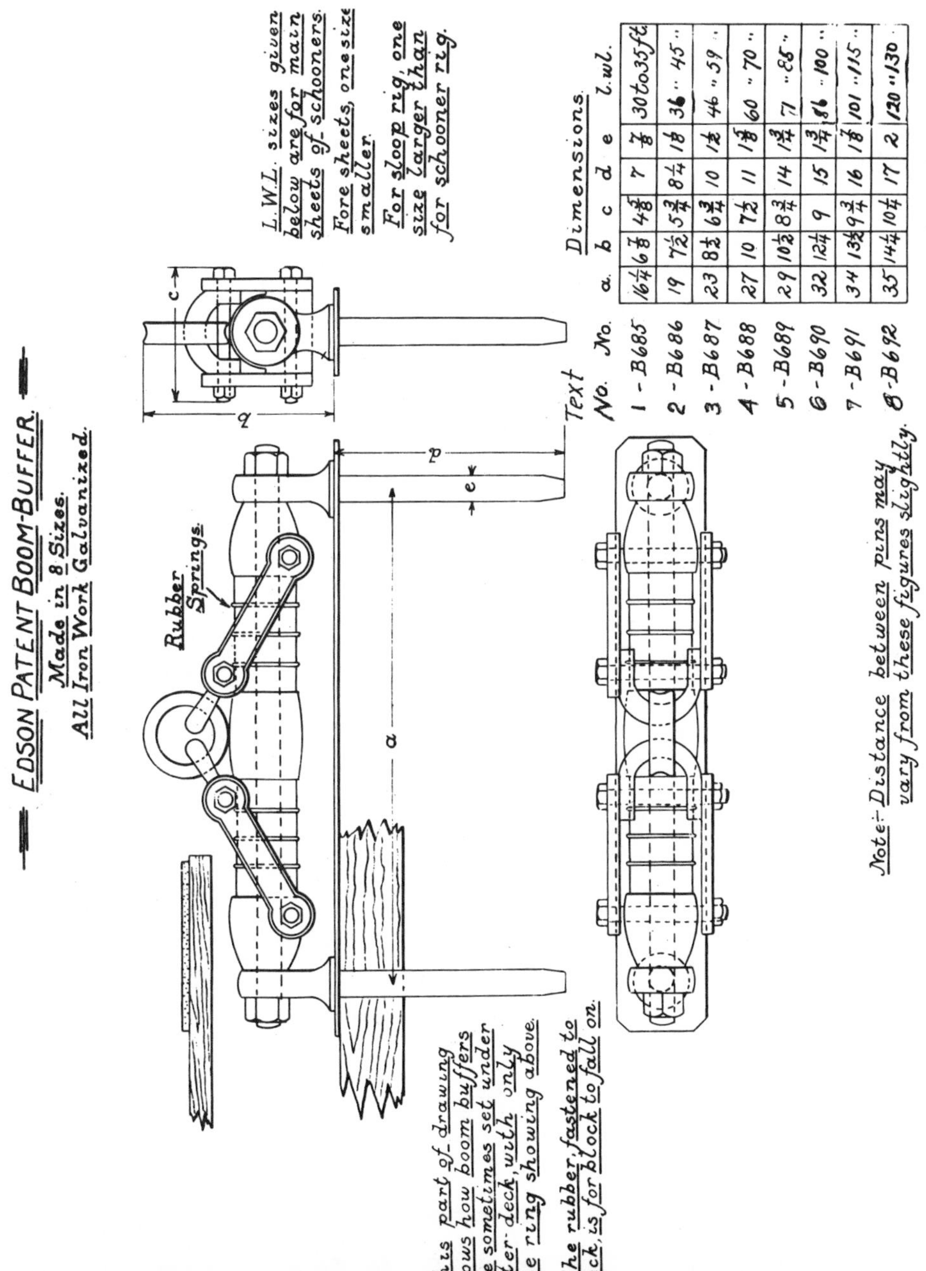
EDSON PATENT BOOM-BUFFER.
Made in 8 Sizes.
All Iron Work Galvanized.
Rubber Springs.
L.W.L. sizes given below are for main sheets of schooners.
Fore sheets, one size smaller.
For sloop rig, one size larger than for schooner rig.
a
b
c
d
e
[T]his part of drawing [sh]ows how boom buffers [a]re sometimes set under [a]fter-deck, with only [t]he ring showing above.
[T]he rubber, fastened to [d]eck, is for block to fall on.
Note:- Distance between pins may vary from these figures slightly.

Text No.	No.	a	b	c	d	e	l.wl.
1	B685	16¼	6⅞	4⅝	7	⅞	30 to 35 ft.
2	B686	19	7½	5¾	8¼	1⅛	36 " 45 "
3	B687	23	8½	6¾	10	1½	46 " 59 "
4	B688	27	10	7½	11	1⅝	60 " 70 "
5	B689	29	10½	8¾	14	1¾	71 " 85 "
6	B690	32	12¼	9	15	1¾	86 " 100 "
7	B691	34	13½	9¾	16	1⅞	101 " 115 "
8	B692	35	14¼	10¼	17	2	120 " 130

BOOM BUFFER, MAINSHEET

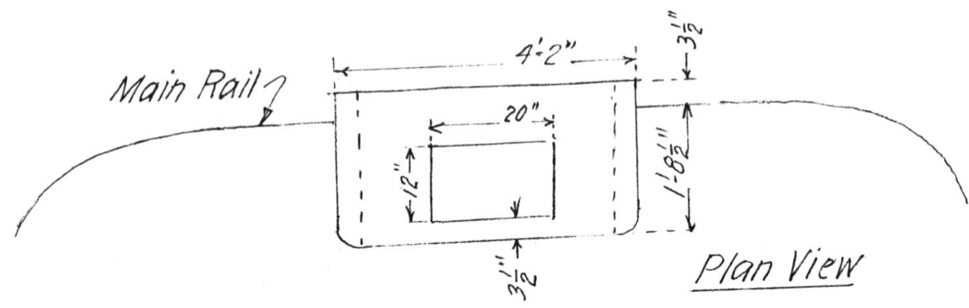
Main Rail
4'-2"
20"
12"
1'-8½"
3½"
3½"
Plan View

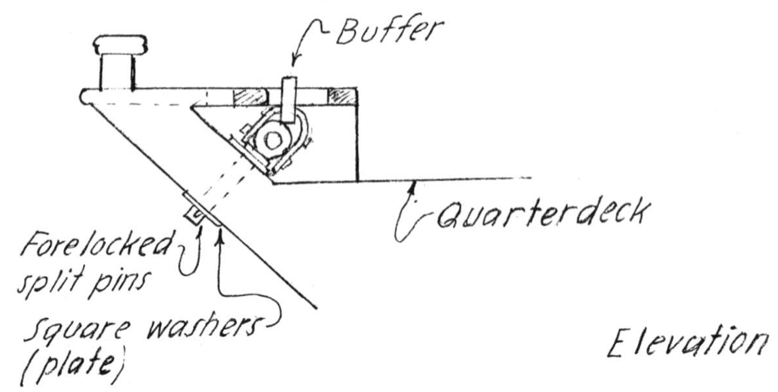
Buffer
Quarterdeck
Forelocked split pins
Square washers (plate)
Elevation

MAST BURY, HEEL AND STEP

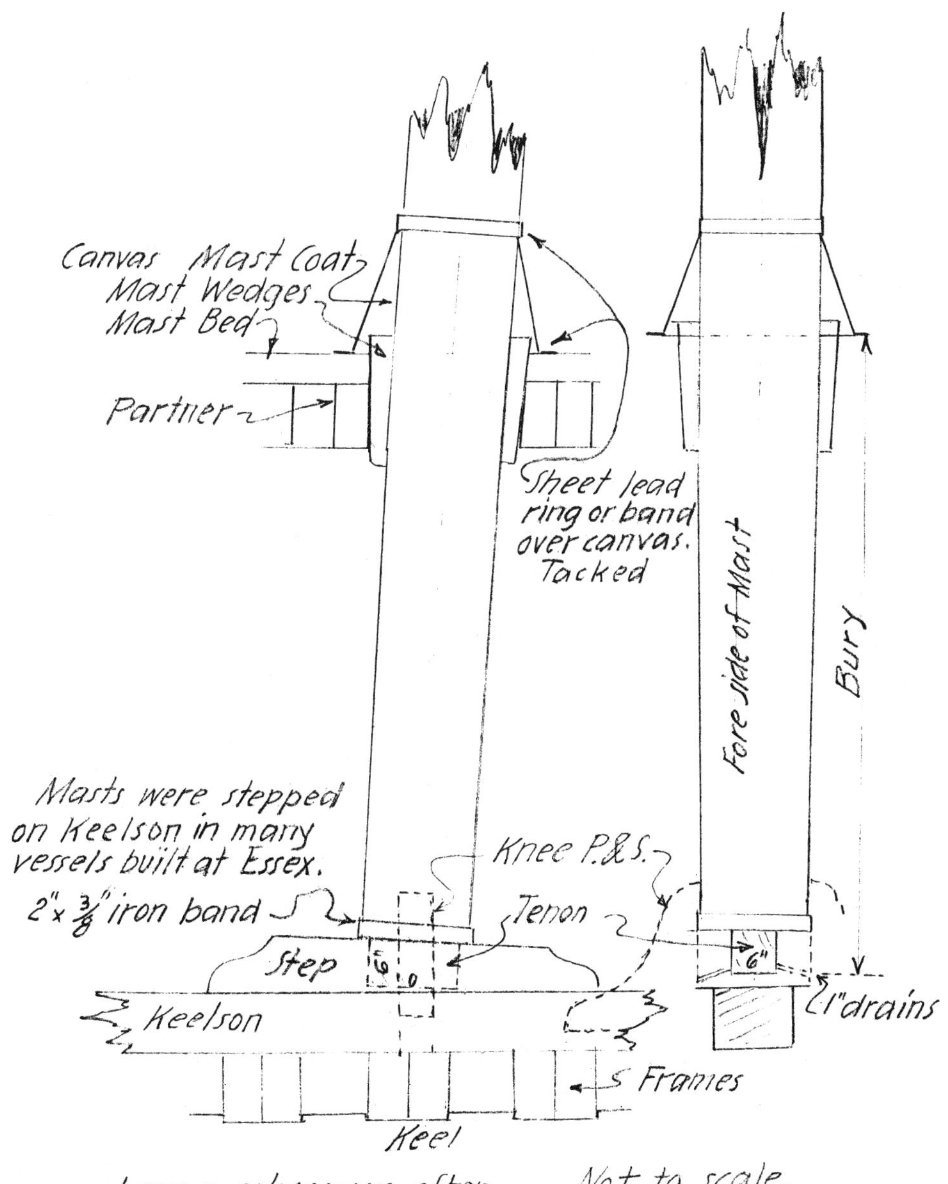
Canvas Mast Coat
Mast Wedges
Mast Bed
Partner
Sheet lead ring or band over canvas. Tacked
Fore side of Mast
Bury
Masts were stepped on Keelson in many vessels built at Essex.
Knee P.&S.
2"x 3/8" iron band
Tenon
Step
6"
1" drains
Keelson
Frames
Keel
Large schooners often had knees on each side of the heel, athwartships,
Not to scale.

MAST CHEEKS, (SEE TRESTLETREES)

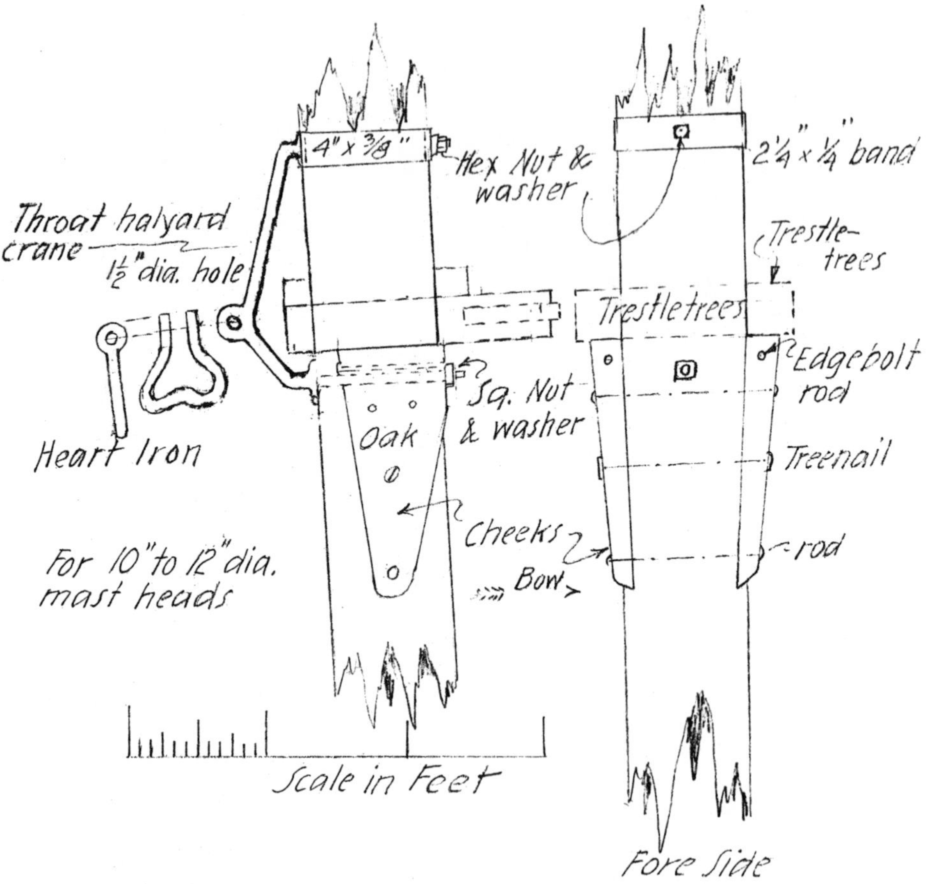

4"x 3/8"
Hex Nut & washer
2 1/4" x 1/4" band
Throat halyard crane
1 1/2" dia. hole
Trestle-trees
Trestletrees
Edgebolt rod
Heart Iron
Sq. Nut & washer
Oak
Treenail
Cheeks
rod
For 10" to 12" dia. mast heads
Bow
Scale in Feet
Fore Side

Cheeks were rather short and plain in most vessels, as shown in scale drawing above, but the "Gertrude De Costa" had them thus–

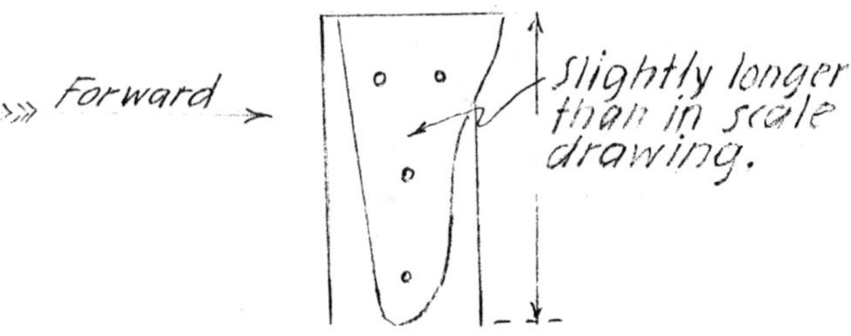
Forward
Slightly longer than in scale drawing.

MAST HEADS

The masts, above the hounds or cheeks, of fishing schooners were square in cross-section until the early 1890s.

The schooners "Harry L. Belden" and "Lottie S. Haskins" had square mast-heads; the "Belden" was built in 1889, the "Lottie S. Haskins" in 1890. In the early 1890s some vessels had oval mast-heads fitted, but by 1895 the round mast-heads had become practically the standard in fishing schooners.

The last fishing schooner to have square mast heads is said to have been "Harvard," built in 1891; designed by Edward Burgess.

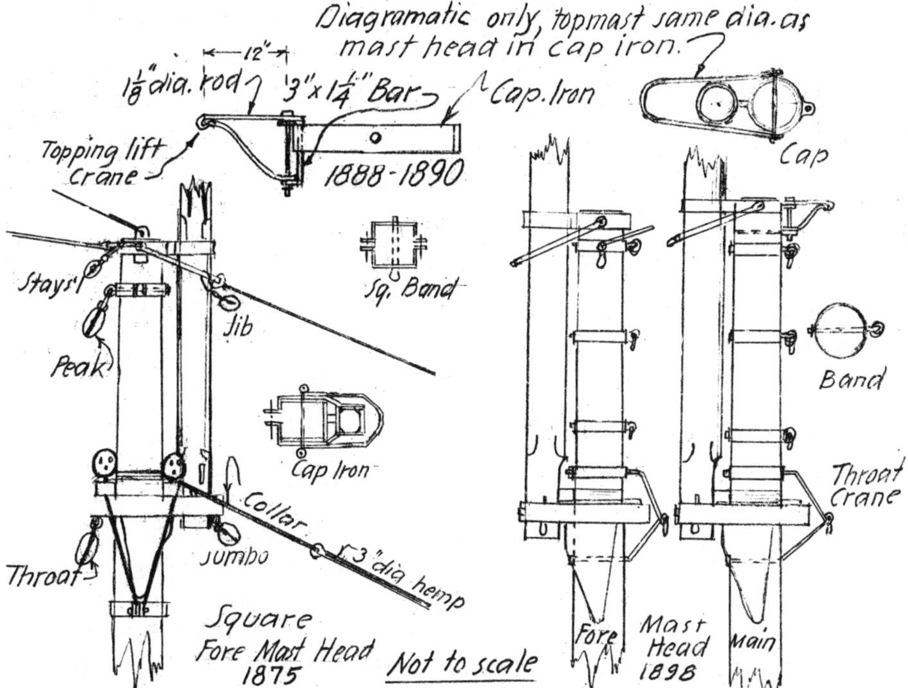
Diagramatic only, topmast same dia. as mast head in cap iron.
12"
1 1/8" dia. rod
3" x 1 1/4" Bar
Cap. Iron
Topping lift Crane
1888-1890
Cap
Sq. Band
Stays'l
Jib
Peak
Band
Cap Iron
Throat Crane
Collar
Jumbo
Throat
3" dia hemp
Square Fore Mast Head 1875
Not to scale
Fore
Mast Head 1898
Main

MASTS: DIMENSIONS, TAPER, AND PLACEMENT

The Essex sparmaker Andrews stated that before 1900 masts were about 1″ in diameter for each 4′ of stick length. But most of the later vessels had masts 1″ in diameter for each 4½′ to 5′ of stick length. Mainbooms were about 1″ diameter for 6′ of stick length. Main-goffs were about 1″ diameter for 5′ of stick length. Fore-gaffs were about 1″ in diameter for 3′ of stick length, for a trifle more. Forebooms were about 1″ diameter for 3′ of stick length. Main-topmasts were about 1″ diameter for 4½′ of stick length. Fore-topmasts were about 1″ diameter for 4¼′ of stick length. Pole bowsprits were 1½″ diameter for 1¼′-1½′ of stick length. The spares of the Crowninshield-designed fishing schooner "Tartar" were on these proportions.

Tapers of masts were not the same on all sides. The afterside of a mast should be straight from the height of its boom, above the deck, to the trestletrees. The taper of the mast would then be on the foreside andsides. However, this rule was not adhered to at Essex and Gloucester. Likewise the sides of all spars were not alike in taper. The "sail side" of gaffs, booms, and clubs was usually straight, and this was true of topmasts. The amount of taper was determined by the available timber, of course, but mast usually tapered about 2″ from boom height to underside of trestletrees. "Tartar's" mainmast was 78′ above deck, 18″ diameter at boom height, 16″ at hounds—underside of trestletrees; the length of the head was 12′. The diameter above the shoulder was about 13″-14″ and 10″-11″ at cap. The foremast was 64′ above the deck, 17″ diameter at boom, 15″ at hounds. Foremasthead 10½′ long, and about 12″ diameter at shoulder; about 10″ at cap. "Tartar's" mainboom was 72″ long, 12″ diameter and 8″ diameter at after-end, 9″ at fore-end. Her main-gaff was 42′ long, 8½″ diameter, 6″ at after-end, 7″ at jaws. The foreboom was about 27′ long, 9″ diameter; 7″ diameter at after-end, 8″ at fore-end. Her fore-gaff was 27′ long, 8″ diameter, 6″ at after-end, 7″ at jaws. The main-topmast was 49½′ long, 11″ diameter, 10½″ at heel, about 8″ at pole. The fore-topmast was 44¼′ long, 10¼″ diameter, 9¾″ at heel and about 7¼″ diameter at pole.

The pole bowsprit was 29¾′ outboard of face of stem, 16″ diameter at gammon, 8″ at pole. Below deck the masts tapered evenly on all sides; the heel, at the top of the tenon, was about 3-4″ less in diameter than at deck.

No evidence of the use of any masting rule was found. The rigs seem to have been designed "by eye" and by visual comparisons with other vessels of the same size and type. Thomas McManus furnished builders with a ⅛″-1′0″ scale sketch of the rig, but diameters were rarely given.

One experienced builder stated that the great beam was placed nearly at overall midlength. The mainmast would then be placed 3½″-4′ abaft the great beam. The foremast was placed "in accordance with the shape of the bow"—a very vague piece of information. Usually the great beam and mast positions were determined on the half-model or on its mould loft "take-off."

It is easily shown that the placement rule given above was not followed closely. The distance between great beam and ℄ of the mainmast was measured on such vessels as "Ethel B. Penny," knockabout, 4′; "Claudia," 5′-5″; "Mary T. Fallon," 2′-10″; "Mary E. O'Hara," 5′-4″. Mast positions in many vessels are shown in the plans in this work.

MAST HOOPS

Topmast Hoops 11″ I.D. × $1\frac{1}{8}$″ wide × $\frac{7}{8}$″ thick
" " 14″ I.D. × $1\frac{1}{4}$″ wide × 1″ thick
Lower Mast " , 18″ I.D. × $1\frac{1}{2}$″ wide × 1″ thick
" " " 24″ I.D. × $1\frac{3}{4}$ wide × $1\frac{1}{8}$″ thick
" " " 24″ I.D. × $1\frac{7}{8}$″ wide × $1\frac{1}{8}$″ thick

"Riggers' term "Topmast Hoops" were from 6″ to 12″ I.D. Diameter of hoops generally about one-quarter larger than mast diameter.

Copper Rivets

Ash

Two or three spare hoops were carried on each mast, at boom.

Inside dia. 6″ 7″ 8″ 9″ 10″ 11″ 12″ 14″ 16″ 18″ 20″ 22″ 24″ 28″

A 16″ hoop was $1\frac{1}{2}$″ deep, $1\frac{1}{8}$″ thick. 24″ was $1\frac{3}{4}$″ to $1\frac{7}{8}$″ × $1\frac{1}{8}$″.

Mast Hoops spaced 24″ to 36″ apart, depending on the size of the vessel, "Sailmaker's choice".

On the "Philip P. Manta's" masts there were 13 hoops on the foremast, 15 on the main. These hoops were 24″ inside dia, of ash, with three copper rivets each. Examples of the number of hoops carried are "Columbia", 1923, Fore-mast 16, main 16. "Esperanto", 1906, fore-mast 12, main 14. "Effie M. Morrissey" 1893, fore-mast 16, main 17. "Tattler," 1901, fore-mast 15, main 16. "Frances P. Mesquita", 1905, fore-mast 15, main 17. "Blue Nose" had 16 on fore, 19 on main. "Thebaud" had 18 on both masts, "Helen B. Thomas", Fore-mast 16, main 17.

MAST SHEATHING, (SEE SADDLE, MAIN BOOM)

In fishing schooners it was necessary to protect the masts from chafe where the jaws of the gaffs and of the boom rode, when under sail. Above the boom saddle and on the after side of the mast, extending a little more than half way around, was a steel plate to take the jaws. The plate was about 3'-0" high and 1/4" thick, spiked to the mast. The top of the saddle was armored in the same manner, with a half-moon shaped 3/16" plate. The boom clapper was rarely protected with steel on the face toward the mast but was on the heel of the clapper riding on the saddle armor, in most vessels.

Aloft, the masts were protected from the gaff jaws and clapper by vertical wooden sheathing (nailed to the masts) from a little below the mast cheeks, down the mast about 6' or 8'. This was of oak, about 1 1/8" x 2". The sheathing was tapered at its lower and upper ends. It was set in white lead and was kept greased. This sheathing was long enough to protect the masts from the gaffs when under full sail or with two reefs in. The gaff clappers were armored with iron plate on their mast faces and greased. The upper sheathing was not placed on a new vessel unless this were done when fitting out.

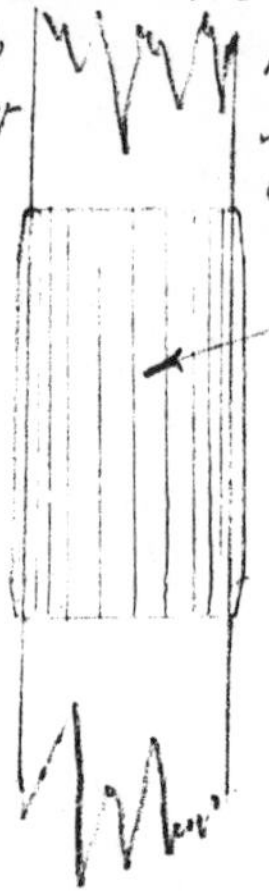

Mast sheathing aloft.

MONKEY RAIL

There were small mouldings fitted inside of the monkey rail, on the main rail, in the corner made by these two members. These began aft, about opposite the after end of the wheel box, and ran forward to about 2'-6" short of the "Drift," or Break. On the quarters, a sheet of copper covered the top of the monkey rail cap. These covered the quarter scarphs in this rail, as shown below.

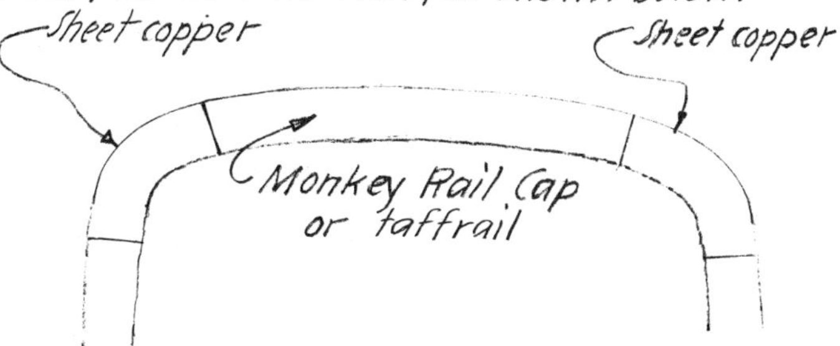
Sheet copper
Sheet copper
Monkey Rail Cap
or taffrail

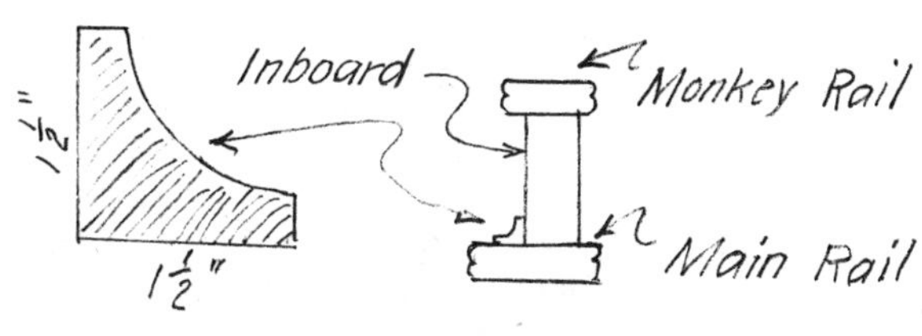
1½"
1½"
Inboard
Monkey Rail
Main Rail

Monkey Rail Moulding

The monkey rail did not tumble-home, except in the quarters and across the transom top, where a slight tumble-home might show.

NAME BOARDS

Old schooners, built before 1890, had their names painted on the bow chock-rail and on the transom. The latter was changed, with name and hail painted on the monkey rail over the transom, in the 1890s. Letters were in Roman type, of primitive design, if painted in Essex. It was not usual for the name to be painted on a new vessel at Essex, this was done at Gloucester when fitting out. The Gloucester painters had a more artistic letter form. In the early 1900s it became the practice to carve and paint the name on port and starboard name boards; the carving being incised. These boards were fastened on the pine bulwarks, above the waist, on the bow abaft the hawse. Some vessels had name board, or painted name, on the monkey rail abreast the wheel-box. Lewis H. Story carved many name boards in the 1900s, at Essex. Sometimes a star or short vine was placed afore and abaft the name. Letters were gilded in all cases.

MAO

Old Essex style

N — V-cross-section

Gloucester style

L. H. S.

NOBLE-WOOD
(SEE "BOWS")

In Essex, a wooden pad, fitted at the outboard hawse hold rims to protect the planking there from damage from the anchor (when hoisting prior to catting) was called the "noble-wood." This pad at the outboard hawse hold had been in use as early as the middle of the eighteenth century and, in fishing schooners, remained in use until the early 1890s. After the noble-wood went out of favor, the bows had only a carved scroll around the outboard hawse rim, led from the billet, as a vine.

The noble-wood, on schooners, built from 1845 to the early 1890s, had no carving on it. It ran from a little forward of the stem rabbet (the fore-end of the noble-wood bevelled off against the sides of the cutwater at stem rabbet as a rule; otherwise it rounded off at the rabbet) to the after-end of the trailboards. In plumb-stem vessels and those without trailboards, the after-end of the noble-wood was carried aft so that the hawse rim nearly centered on it, fore-and-aft. The bottom of the noble-wood rested on the top of the upper trail knee or on top of the trailboard, as in "Julia Costa." In plumb-stem vessels, and those without trails, the bottom was about 5″ below the bottom of the hawse rim, the top of the noble-wood was often in line with the bottom of the bowsprit. The thickness of the noble-wood was from about 5″ to 7″. There were two or three strakes or oak, fore-and-aft, in a noble-wood; edge-treenailed as the hawse permitted and spiked and drifted through the planking into knightheads, hawse timbers and frames, as construction dictated. The "Carrie E. Phillips" was the first fishing schooner in which the noble-woods were omitted. The top and after edges of the noble-woods were rounded-off; the bottom edge was rounded only to the extent that it projected outboard of the trail knees.

PAINT

The fashions in painting fishing schooners seem to have varied widely. As early as 1750 fishing vessels were painted bright colors—green in a variety of shades, black, yellow, blue, red, and white were used. Often the transom of a vessel was painted in different colors than the sides of the hull. Unfortunately the patterns used were not described in any contemporary source that I have yet found. Up until the 1850s there was no effective bottom paint. Lime, "white wash," covered with melted tallow was widely used. Sometimes verdigris (copper carbonate—a green, poisonous powder, not soluble in water) was mixed in the tallow, giving a gray-white—"with green streaks"—appearance to the bottom. The lime-and-tallow bottom was often described as "white bottom."

Copper antifouling bottom paint was introduced in 1851 into the United States by Watterstedt, but its use could not be verified on Cape Ann. Tarr and Wonson commenced the production and sale of antifouling paint at Gloucester in 1863. This brand quickly became popular, though the paint had to be stirred constantly when being applied. It was dark brown in color. Green bottom paint seems to have been used to some extent in the late 1840s and in the 1850s. Its composition is unknown, but it was probably a verdigris mixture. Zinc bottom paint was also used, to a very limited extent, but not at Cape Ann, apparently.

The brown copper paint became the standard antifouling paint at

Gloucester by 1880. In the 1890s—1891, 1892–1893—red copper was available and some fishing schooners had their bottoms painted with this for 2½ to 3 feet below their load lines, with the dark brown below. The red copper also was used for a "boot-top", 3 to 6 inches above the load line.

Above the waterline the topsides were painted black, green, gray and white, depending upon the period. In the 1930s the vessels had black topsides with a narrow multi-colored band at the waist. This continued into the 1840s, but dark green became popular somewhere around 1845. Soon after this, and through the 1850s, vessels appeared painted dark or emerald green from the boot-top to the waist, black above, to top of main and monkey rails, and to top of bow chocks. The multi-colored stripe went out of fashion in the late 1850s; the coves were then painted yellow, "stone yellow," or white. In the 1880s a number of fishing schooners had white or gray topsides, with yellow coves and carving. This style was probably introduced by the "Carrie E. Phillips"; it did not last long.

In 1875 most schooners had dark brown copper bottom, black topsides, yellow carvings, coves and mouldings of the head "lined off." The last meant that a very narrow band of color was painted along the lower part of the "hawk's-bill" mouldings.

The black topsides carried up to the top of the rails and bow chocks, broken only by the coves. The bowsprit was black out to the billet, or a little forward of that, where a "broken" effect was painted. Jibboom black at heel, out a short distance, say 2′, then white to bowsprit cap. Outboard of this, varnished, pole may be white or black. Masts white from deck to a foot or so above the saddle. Above this white—sometimes black, spreaders white, gaffs and all booms white. Topmasts white—sometimes pole was black. Decks oiled, with waterways and deck structures white. Bowsprit inboard white. Windlass, bitts, etc., white. Sometimes billet was white, carried up to and over the top of the rails. The foregoing is also a description of the painting of most schooners from the mid-'90s to 1910, and is the "working" painting of many schooners that had been launched with far more ornate painting schedules.

The most ornate and impractical painting schedule appeared between 1890 and 1894. This is shown in the sketch. In the years 1891–1892 and 1893, many schooners were launched that were painted as follows:

In the 1860s and '70s, the bow chock rail was commonly painted white inside and out. Also in this period, the outboard face of the monkey rail was painted white between the main and monkey rail caps. In new vessels the rail caps were varnished with this style of painting. After a short service they were usually painted black, however.

PAINT, 1891–1893

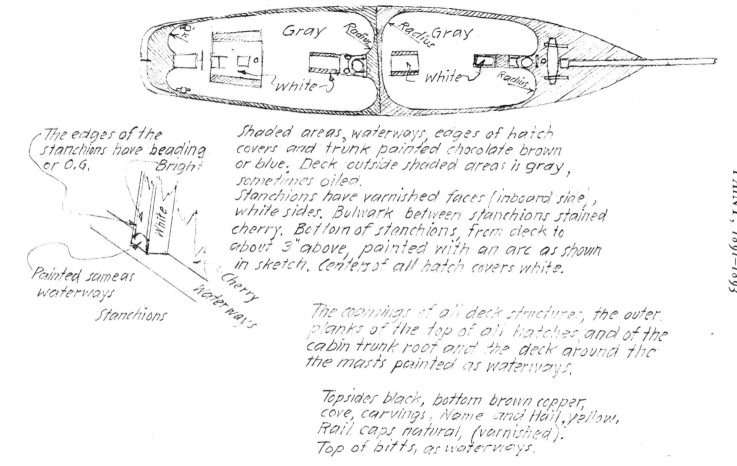

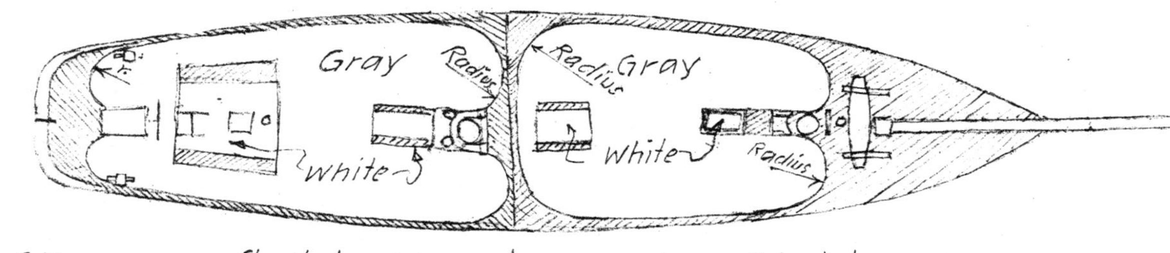
Gray
Radius
Gray
Radius
White
White
Radius

The edges of the stanchions have beading or O.G.

Bright

White

Painted same as waterways

Stanchions

Cherry

Waterways

Shaded areas, waterways, edges of hatch covers and trunk painted chocolate brown or blue. Deck outside shaded areas is gray, sometimes oiled.
Stanchions have varnished faces (inboard side), white sides. Bulwark between stanchions stained cherry. Bottom of stanchions, from deck to about 3" above, painted with an arc as shown in sketch. Centers of all hatch covers white.

The coamings of all deck structures, the outer planks of the top of all hatches and of the cabin trunk roof and the deck around the the masts painted as waterways.

Topsides black, bottom brown copper, cove, carvings, Name and Hail, yellow.
Rail caps natural, (varnished).
Top of bitts, as waterways.

PAINT, 1901–1928

Green
White
Green
Buff
White
Buff

"Avalon,"- booms, gaffs buff, mastheads, bowsprit black
"Arthur James,"- white spars, mastheads, blocks; deck gray
"Constellation,"-"Avalon;" { pea green deck, buff around windlass bitts, wheelbox; white waterways, break,
"Harvard,"-same.
"Stilletto"- gray deck; buff spars, blocks.

The inside of hawse pipe were usually painted red but yellow metal hawse rims were polished bright. Half-castings, however, were painted inside.

Bow chocks were painted white inboard, and sometimes outboard too, along with the outboard face of the main rail cap, when a vessel was new.

PAINT

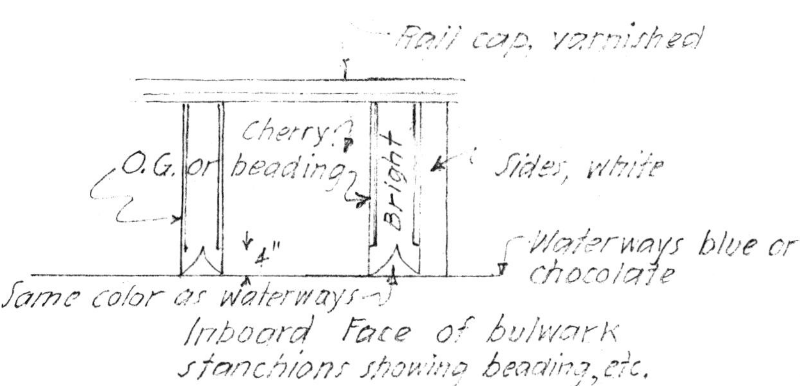
Rail cap, varnished
Cherry?
O.G. or beading
Bright
Sides, white
4"
Waterways blue or chocolate
Same color as waterways

Inboard Face of bulwark stanchions showing beading, etc.

The ornate painting scheme just described was applied to new vessels only, and this was also true of white or gray topside paint. White paint inboard was popular because deck structures painted white could be readily seen at night.

After 1895, the painting scheme reverted to the 1875 style, more or less, employing black, white - and occasionaly blue, or gray. Ornate painting schemes rarely lasted longer than a few months of service.

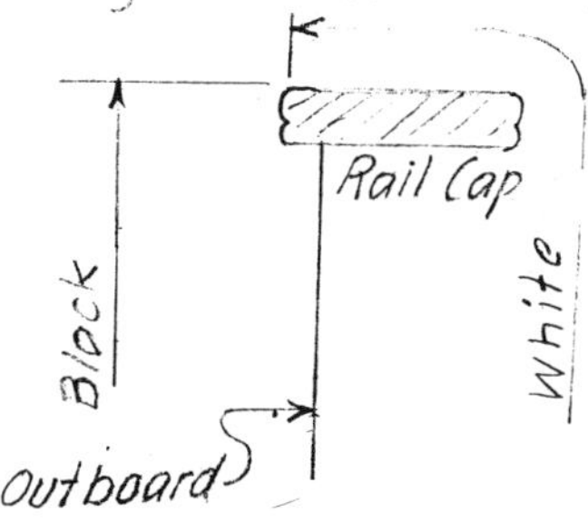
Rail Cap
Black
White
Outboard

Hulls painted dark green from boot-top to waist, black above, were common well into the 1890s.

Demarkation of inside white paint and topside black on all rail caps and on bow chock rails.

PARRALS, (SEE GAFFS, FORE AND MAIN GAFF JAWS)

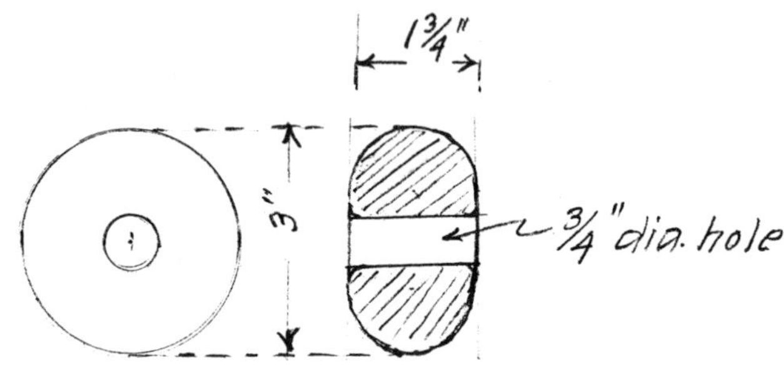
1¾"
3"
¾" dia. hole

Lignum vitea Parral.

These parrals were not used on the main boom. The parrals used on the main boom jaws were either a bail—an iron rod with eyes in each end, in eye bolts in the ends of the jaws, and bent around the main mast—or a short length of wire rope eye-spliced over thimbles in the eyebolts in the ends of the jaws and passed around the fore side of the main mast. When hemp rigging was used, the parral rope was hemp, covered with greased rawhide.

PEAK HALYARD BRIDLES

Bridles for the peak halyard blocks appear to have been introduced into the fishing schooners by Burgess, in the "Fredonia" of 1889. Their use continued into the 1900s, with vessels rigged with rigid peak blocks and bands, or with bridles, without regard to size or other known factors. Among the vessels rigged with bridles were "Esperanto," "Elk," "Mary De Costa," "Arthur James," "Henry Ford," "Squanto," "James W. Parker," "Spain," "Rose Dorothea," "Wm. M. Goodspeed," "James Steele," and "Metamora." Vessels rigged with fixed-eye blocks and bands include "Elsie," "Columbia," "Thebaud," "Helen B. Thomas," "Puritan" (racing fisherman) "Rob Roy," "Carrie E. Phillips," and "I. J. Merritt, Jr."

The bridles were of wire rope, having spliced eyes at each end that would fit the gaff snugly. These would be prevented from slipping down by small wooden cleats on the underside of the gaffs. In fishing schooners there were three "spans" or bridles on the main-gaff, with three bridle blocks, and three main masthead blocks. All were single sheave, except for the middle masthead block, which was sometimes double. Spans do not appear to have been used on the fore-gaff of a fishing schooner.

In the early bridles, fitted to "Fredonia," a bull's-eye was rove into the span before splicing the ends. The binding of the bull's-eye was turned in to form an eye into which the hook of the halyard was secured and moused. By 1896 the "flat-sheet bridle" block was available. It was thought that the bridles distributed the strains over the length of the gaff, but the use of both rigs of the halyards indicate that the bridles were not necessary. There were some who thought bridles broke gaffs; the "Henry Ford" had them removed.

PEAK MAIN-GAFF BRIDLES

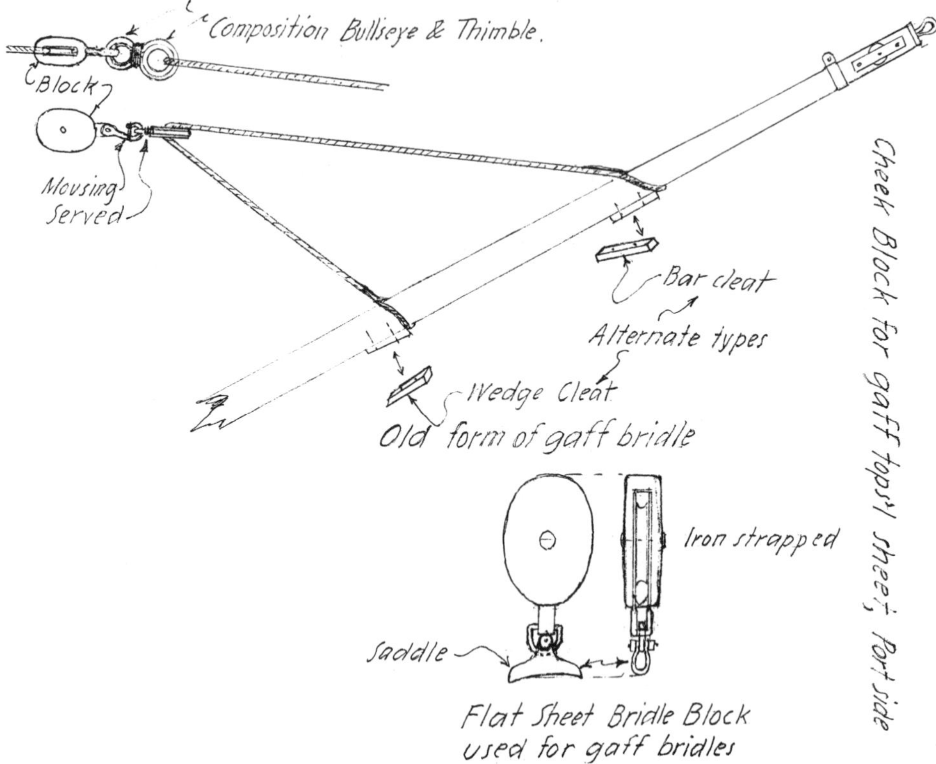
Composition Bullseye & Thimble.
Block
Mousing
Served
Bar cleat
Alternate types
Wedge Cleat
Old form of gaff bridle
Iron strapped
Saddle
Flat Sheet Bridle Block
used for gaff bridles
Cheek Block for gaff topsl sheet, port side

PENDANTS

Pendants were short pieces of line-wire rope, hemp rope, or chain secured aloft to a sail clew, with a block at the opposite end. The gaff-topsail sheet pendant was a short piece of hemp (or, later, wire) rope hooked or spliced into an eyebolt, having its eye on the underside of one arm of the gaff jaws. Spliced to the lower end was a single-sheave block, serving as a lead-block for the topsail sheet at the throats of the main- and fore-gaff sails. Other pendants were on tackles suspended from the fore and main spreaders. (See "Crosstrees.") Pendants were also fitted to serve as fittings of the jib topsail, jib and main-topmast staysails. In a few large fishing schooners, the pendants of the jib sheets were of chain. The cut of these sails determined the positions of their sheet leads and belays, and these, in turn, fixed the lengths of their sheet pendants.

PINRAILS

Many schooners had belaying pins in a wooden collar, made like a boom saddle, on the foremast. In the "Mary T. Fallon" the collar was about 36″ above the deck. The collar had eight belaying pins in it and had an iron strap around it. The mainmast pinrail was the common U-shaped form 36″ high with 8″ x 8″ bitts.

The knockabout "Ethel B. Penny" had the pin collar on the foremast 3′- 2½″ above the mast bed.

The fore pinrail of the "Philip P. Manta" had these measurements: bitts 7″ x 7″, pinrail 26″ above deck. The rail was U-shaped in plan view, 3¼″ thick, 7″ wide. Bitts 24″ apart athwartship, inboard face to inboard face. The bitt crosspiece cleared the foreside of the mast by 4″, and had two belaying pins in it for the jumbo sheet. Bitts were 39″ high above desk.

Two pins, balloon downhaul to port, jib to starboard were in the fore "seat," close to the inboard edge in the "Manta," as was common.

(See "Bitts," "Belaying Pins," "Belaying Pins Rack" for additional measurements and sketches.)

Few vessels had "square" pinrails, that is angular in plan view, after wooden pumps went out of favor. However, the "Mary E. O'Hara" had square pinrails in 1936, 29½″ above the deck, bitts 7″ x 7″, 37″ high. "Columbia" and "Henry Ford" had square pinrails; "Thebaud" had them on her mainmast only.

PLANKING (NOTES)

The number of strakes employed in planking one side of a fishing schooner above 65′-0″ registered length was from sixteen to twenty-two strakes. Photographs of schooners under construction between 1875 and 1898 show that seventeen to eighteen strakes were used, keel rabbet to underside of main deck plank-sheer. Above the top of the plank-sheer there were two strakes to the waist and from waist to main rail cap there were two more strakes, making the "pine" bulwarks. Sometime around 1890 there was a change made in the pine bulwarks and some schooners had three strakes of very narrow plank, with beaded edges, between waist and main rail cap (James' yard practice).

The knockabout schooner "Adventure" had twenty-one strakes, rabbet to plank-sheer. The widest strake was 18″, finished, with others 14″, 12″, 10″, and 8″ maximum widths, all yellow pine. The schooners in the 85′–100′ range (register) had eighteen to twenty strakes.

Top side plank seams lined off so as to almost parallel the rail sheer, the strakes appearing to have a very slight taper toward stem and stern. Stealers were usually required, placed below the load line; a shutter strake was worked in below the turn of the bilge; the planking schedule: plank topside down to chosen position of shutter strake, then to fit garboard and then plank upward and fit shutter. Both sides were planked at once, of course. Steam bending was utilized, where necessary. White oak strakes were employed if hard-bent strakes were required.

Many of the large schooners, up until the late 1890s, had wales. There were 3″ plank, in three or four strakes, fitted below the main deck plank-sheer and finished 7″ to 9″ wide. Their lower, projecting, edge was dubbed off to fair into the 2½″ plank below. Likewise, thick garboards were sometimes fitted in one to three strakes, and then dubbed fair into the bottom plank. If there was marked hollow in the frames at the keel, the garboard would be fitted rounded on the inside, hollowed on the outside. The shutter strakes usually ran the length of the hull but stealers were commonly a quarter, or less than one-third, the hull-length. The shutters were in 3 or 4 lengths.

The "Philip P. Manta" was planked with seventeen strakes garboard to plank-sheer. The garboard at the sternpost was 23½″ wide; the next strake 22″, the next strake 18″ wide. The main keel was 10½″ deep, false keel 8½″ deep and the shoe 3″ deep, the wood outside the rabbet was, therefore, 22″ deep.

Most builders' half-models show the hull form to the inside of all plank, and to the underside of all mouldings—rail, plank-sheer, etc. With these, the frame offsets can be lifted from the model, without corrections for thickness of planking. The lifts of such models are parallel to the keel rabbet in the old, straight-keel schooners. If there is much drag to the keel, however, there was an arbitrary base line, usually the top of the lowest lift. In either case there is no established load waterline. But in all cases the frame or mould sections will be perpendicular to the straight rabbet of the keel, or to the arbitrarily chosen base line, whichever is indicated.

The fishing schooner designs by naval architects are invariably drawn to show the hull form to the outside of the finished plank. This requires the projection of the inside face of the planking from the designer's lines after they are laid down on the loft floor. McManus, influenced by yachting practice, designed his fishing schooners to the outside of the plank, but on the mould loft floor his plans and offsets were often lofted as though they were intended to be to the inside of the plank. The only certain exceptions were the fishing schooners built especially for racing under a yacht-designer's supervision of construction, but there may have been others, forgotten by my informants.

The plank-sheer was made to drop over the stanchions of the bulwarks, and its outboard edge spiked to the top edge of the sheer strakes. The stanchions were not caulked at the plank-sheer but were wedged with white cedar wedges. As a result the bulwarks were not planked until the stanchions were ready and capped by the main rail cap. The plank-sheer edges of main and quarter-decks were exposed afore and abaft the great beam, of course, but were "jointered off" smooth with the planking and painted out. The plank-sheer edge of the main deck butted at the great beam, that of the quarterdeck plank-sheer likewise. The lower waist strake was carried aft to form the sheer strake of the quarterdeck. The top of the narrow scupper strake of the quarterdeck was the waist line. This faired into the top of the upper waist plank forward. Seams and butts in this construction were painted out so as not to be readily seen.

"Thebaud" had twenty-two strakes from keel rabbet to plank-sheer.

PLUMB, OR STRAIGHT, STEM

Though the nearly vertical, straight stem had been used in the Chebacco Boats and in some of the colonial, Mablehead schooners, it was out of fashion in fishing schooners from the first quarter of the nineteenth century to 1885.

The plain, unadorned, straight stern was then in use in pilot schooners, and, later, in yachts. In 1882 Joseph W. Collins, a Gloucester fishing skipper employed by the U.S. Fish Commission, began preliminary studies for the design for a well-smack schooner, for fishery research. The study was also intended to produce a swift, safe, and seaworthy schooner, the model of which would replace the shallow, unsafe clipper fishing schooner type then in use in New England fisheries. Collins had written about the shortcomings of the clipper model.

For an adviser he selected Dennison J. Lawlor, a shipbuilder and designer of Chelsea, Massachusetts, who had designed and built many fishing schooners and pilot boats. Lawlor was a strong adherent of an improved fishing schooner model; he had designed three schooners (in 1865, 1866 and in 1884) that were deeper than the clippers.

The Collins' design studies produced the well-smack schooner "Grampus," launched at Noank, Connecticut, March 23, 1886, and completed by June 5, 1886. She had a straight, upright stem, selected because of the saving in weight it represented, compared to the then-standard "long head" of the clippers, according to Collins' published report.

However, "Grampus" appeared late on the scene, delayed in construction by changes in gear and its installation. In 1884 Lawlor designed at least three straight-stem schooners: the "Arthur D. Story," "John H. McManus" and the "A. S. & R. Hammond." These vessels were completed in 1885, months before "Grampus" went to sea. In this year, the straight-stem schooners "Rattler" and "Gladstone" were launched, but these were on the "Theresa Baker" model of 1867, with long head omitted.

This flurry of building "straight-stemmers" led to a short-lived fashion for this stem profile. In 1886–1887 the "Annie B. Cannon," "Blue Jacket," "Fernwood," "Magnolia" and "Iceland" (some of these were the "Baker" model with the long head omitted) were built; also the noted "Carrie E.

Phillips," designed by Edward Burgess, and the "Puritan," designed by George Melville ("Mel") McCain were launched.

In 1887–1888 the Lawlor-designed plumb-stemmer "Susan R. Stone" was launched, along with the "Halcyon" and the "J. H. Carey," by other designers. In 1888–1889 the "Harry Beldon" was launched (a sister ship to the "Susan R. Stone"). "Ben Hur," "General Cogswell," "Isaac Collins," "Joseph B. Maguire" were plumb-stemmers that were produced by omission of the long head on the "Baker" model. Lawlor designed the "Nickerson," also launched in 1889. The "Hustler" was another straight-stem schooner launched in 1889, designed by Washington Tarr. This marked the end of the plumb-stem fashion. In 1889–1890 no straight-stem schooner seems to have been built. In 1891 the plumb-stem ketch "Resolute" was launched at Essex, built by A. D. Story. She was not a success and was re-rigged as a schooner.

In 1901 two schooners were built on the "Belden's" model, but with one frame added amidships and a counter fitted in place of the original V-transom. These were the "George Parker" and the "Annie M. Parker."

So far as can now be determined, all of the straight-stemmers had noble-woods, except the "Carrie E. Phillips" and, perhaps, the "Parkers." Some Lawlor-designed vessels had small scrolls around the hawse castings on the noble-woods.

Some of the vessels fitted as straight-stemmers by omission of the long heads had curved stem rabbets, resulting in curved stem profiles. This gave a few of them a curiously modern appearance, the "J. H. Carey" was an example of this.

PORTS, TRUNK, ETC.

Lights in the cabin trunk did not exceed two on each side, each located to give light where the skylight did not serve. Before 1885 one port a side was usual; in fact only the large schooners had two lights a side and these infrequently. The ports were 6″-7″ diameter in the clear, and fixed. After 1895 or thereabouts, the opening ports were occasionally installed. The fixed lights, before 1875, were rectangular, about 6″ x 9″, bedded in a rabbet with white lead and secured by a wooden frame outside. Sometimes the ports were square, about 6″ x 6″. Many vessels did not have any trunk ports in this period, depending upon the skylight. Round portlights came into use in the 1870s, fitted with iron, outside frames; sometimes round, but more often octagon on the outside edges. Until well into the 1880s the glass was not clear. These glass portlights were often installed in the skylight lids, instead of rectangular framed lid lights.

In "Elsie" there was a fixed, round light, in the top of the circular galley hatch, 6½″ diameter in the clear.

Rod guards, ¼″ diameter rod, were fitted only on rectangular ports and skylight lids, if at all.

PUMP (WOODEN)

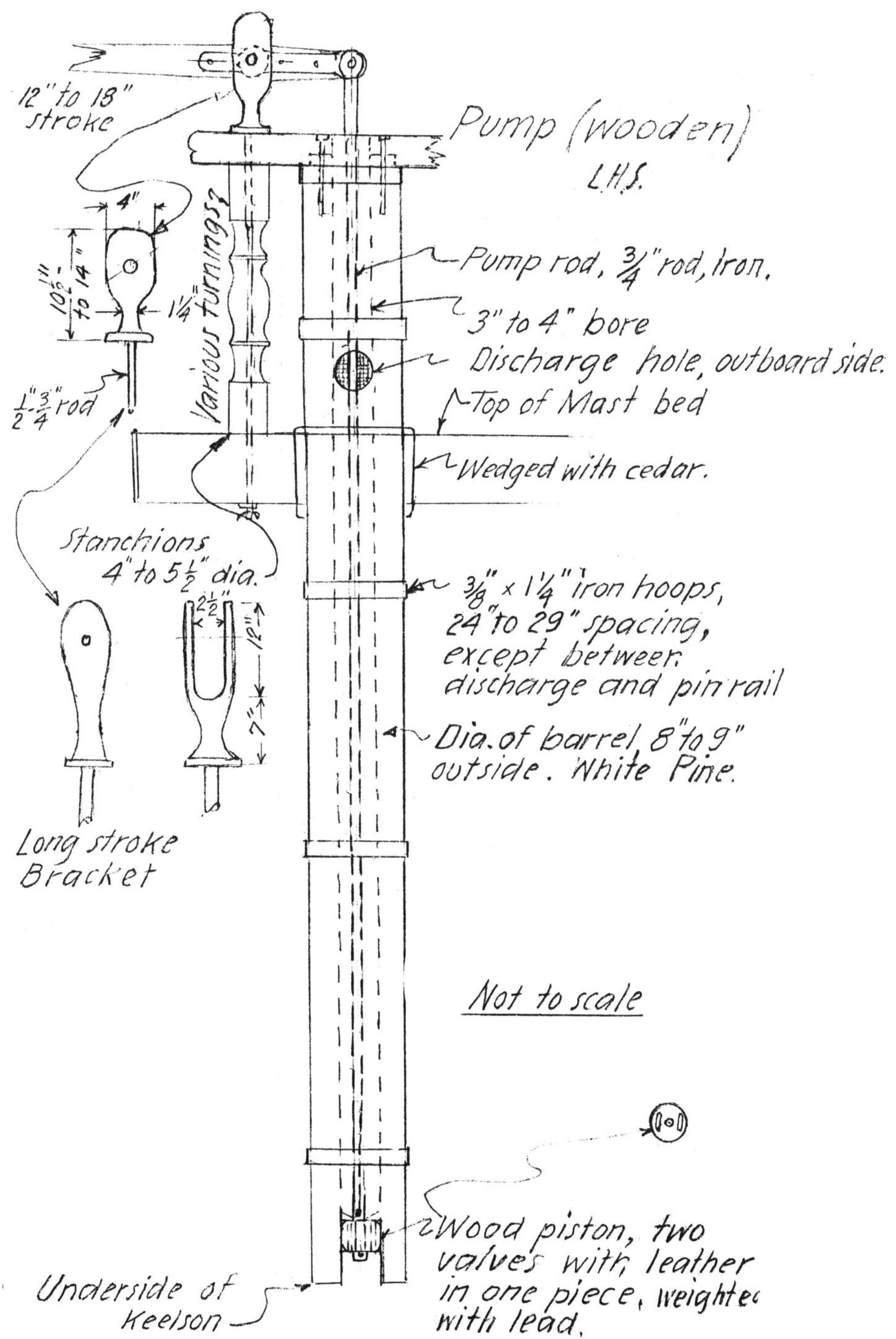
12" to 18" stroke
Pump (wooden) L.H.S.
4"
10½" - to 14"
1¼"
½"-¾" rod
Various turnings?
Pump rod, ¾" rod, Iron.
3" to 4" bore
Discharge hole, outboard side.
Top of Mast bed
Wedged with cedar.
Stanchions 4" to 5½" dia.
2½"
12"
7"
⅜" x 1¼" iron hoops, 24" to 29" spacing, except between discharge and pin rail
Dia. of barrel, 8" to 9" outside. White Pine.
Long stroke Bracket
Not to scale
Wood piston, two valves with leather in one piece, weighted with lead.
Underside of Keelson

PUMP, WOODEN

With wooden pumps, the mainmast fife rail was rectangular, or "square," in plan. Only the aftercorners were slightly rounded. The turned stanchions were usually placed to support the aftercorners, with another stanchion between the after stanchion and the bitts, port and starboard, at about midway. The pump barrel was placed inboard of the aftercorner stanchions, to have the brake pivot in the bracket in the after stanchion. The result was that the mainmast bed was wider in proportion in the vessel with wooden pumps than a vessel with iron pumps. The wooden pump barrels rested on either side of the keelson, its thickness, or width, apart. Usually the barrels were 2″ to 4″ further apart at the fife rail than they were at the keelson. These wooden pumps were efficient, so had lasted, little changed, since colonial times, though iron brakes (or "heavers") had been used extensively in America before 1800.

The barrels were in a box in the holds to protect them.

Schooners "Harry Belden," plumb-stem "Puritan," and "Lottie Haskins" had wooden pumps, according to their contemporary rigged-models.

Photographs show various positions for pumps, stanchions, and pump handles. (See "Fife Rails.")

PUMPS (DIAPHRAGM)

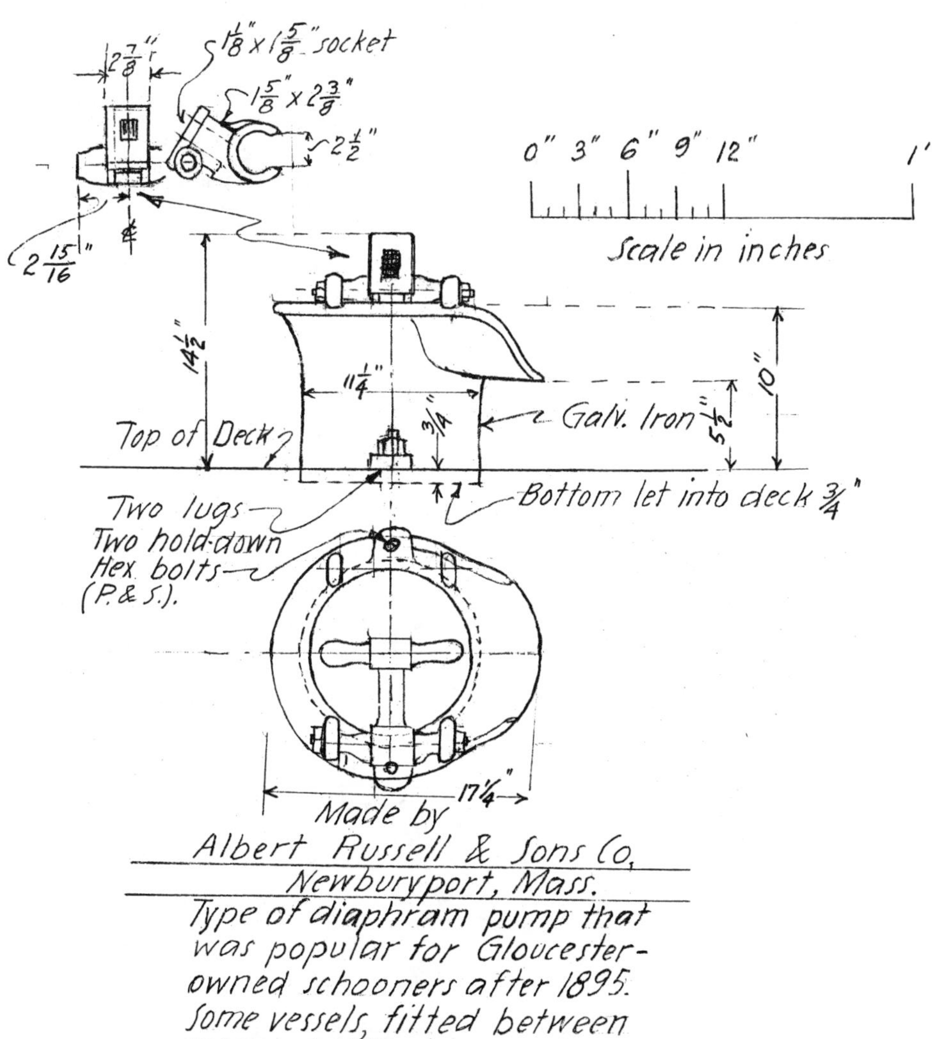

1⅛" x 1⅝" socket
2⅞"
1⅝" x 2⅜"
2½"
2 15/16"
0" 3" 6" 9" 12" 1'
Scale in inches
14½"
11¼"
3/4"
10"
Galv. Iron
5½"
Top of Deck
Bottom let into deck ¾"
Two lugs
Two hold-down Hex. bolts (P.& S.).
17¼"
Made by
Albert Russell & Sons Co,
Newburyport, Mass.

Type of diaphram pump that was popular for Gloucester-owned schooners after 1895. Some vessels, fitted between 1889 and 1895, had one Russell pump and one wooden pump, but this practice was soon abandoned.

PUMPS, EDSON NO. 2

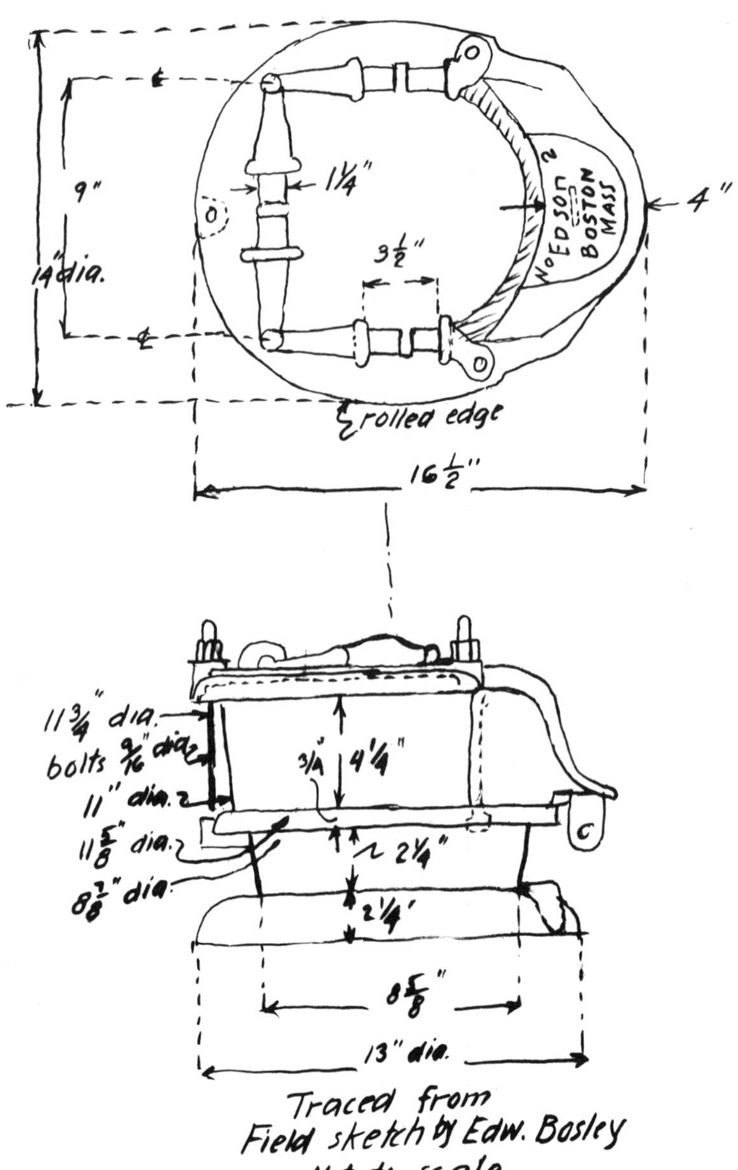
9"
14" dia.
1¼"
3½"
No EDSON 2
BOSTON
MASS
4"
rolled edge
16½"
11¾" dia.
bolts 9/16" dia.
11" dia.
11⅝" dia.
8⅞" dia.
3/4
4¼"
2¼"
2¼'
8⅝"
13" dia.

Traced from
Field sketch by Edw. Bosley
Not to scale

PUMPS, EDSON NO. 3

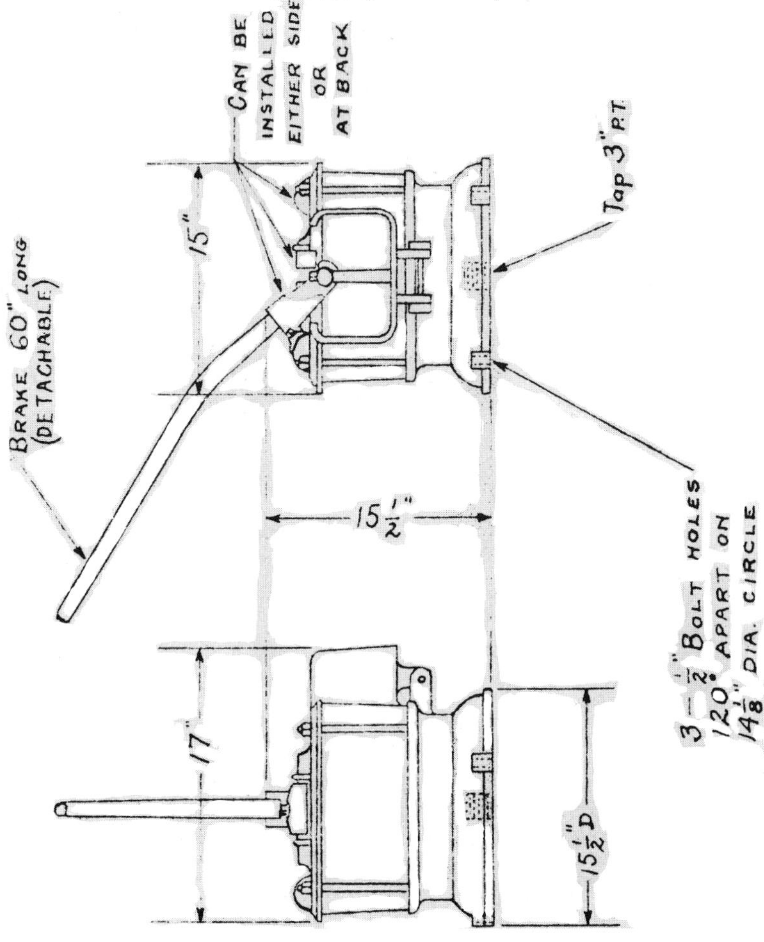
Brake 60" long
(detachable)
15"
Can be
installed
either side
or
at back
Tap 3" P.T.
15 1/2"
3 — 1/2" Bolt holes
120° apart on
14 1/8" dia. circle
17"
15 1/2" D

PUMPS, EDSON NO. 4

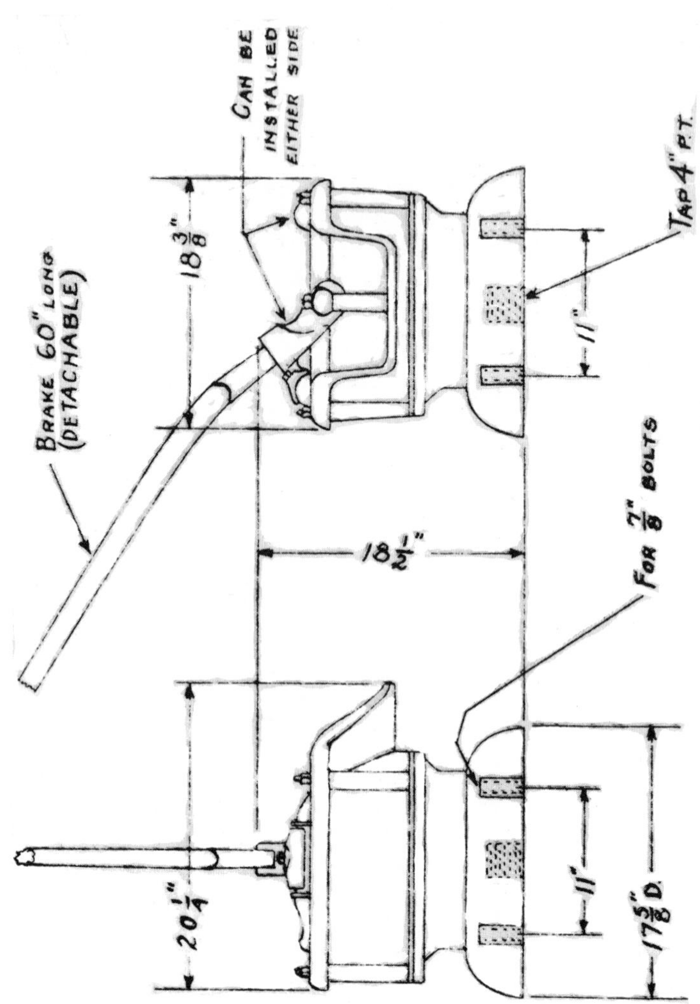
BRAKE 60" LONG (DETACHABLE)
CAN BE INSTALLED EITHER SIDE
18 3/8"
18 1/2"
11"
TAP 4" P.T.
FOR 7/8" BOLTS
20 1/4"
11"
17 5/8" D.

PUMPS (IRON DIAPHRAGM)

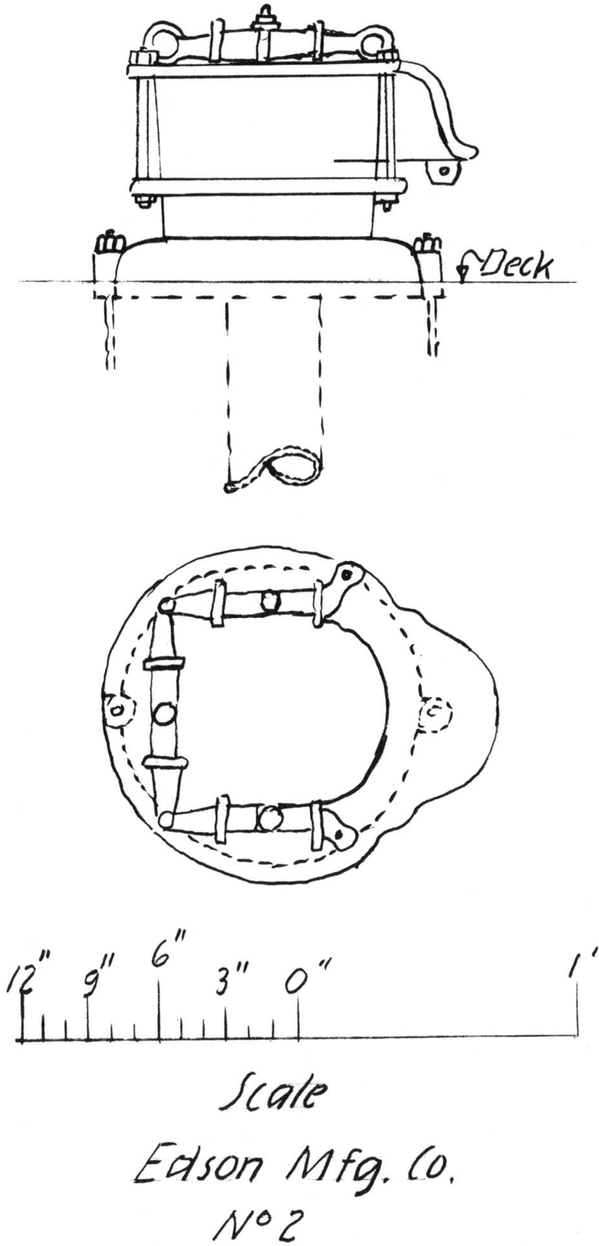
Deck
12" 9" 6" 3" 0" 1'
Scale
Edson Mfg. Co.
N° 2

PUMPS

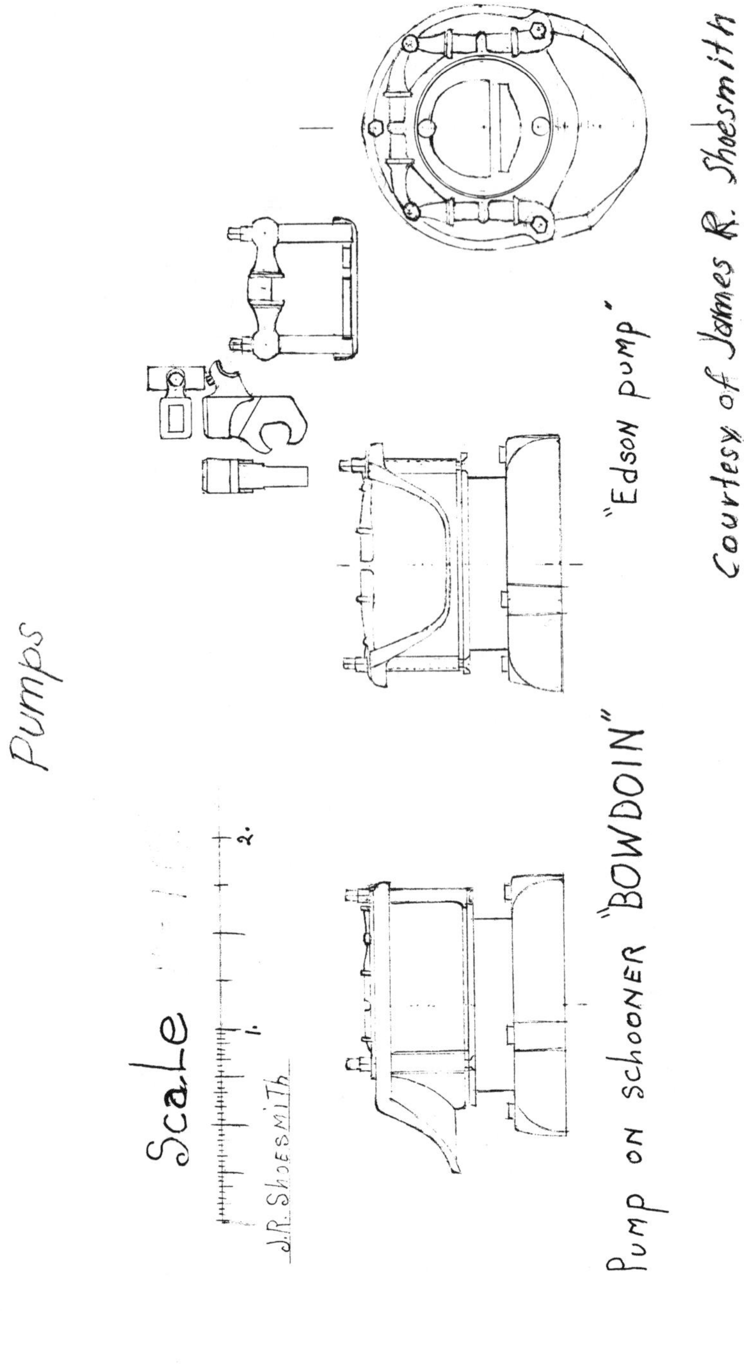

Pumps
Scale
1.
2.
J.R. Shoesmith
Pump on schooner "BOWDOIN"
"Edson pump"
Courtesy of James R. Shoesmith

PUMPS (IRON DIAPHRAGM), LOUD PATENT

BOTTOM INLET *or* BILGE PUMPS

HAND POWER

IN 1876 we manufactured the first diaphragm Bilge Pump ever made. Many thousands of our pumps are now in use on ships, barges, scows, etc., all over the world.

Since the first Pump was made, the Edson Manufacturing Company has perfected many improvements in this Pump.

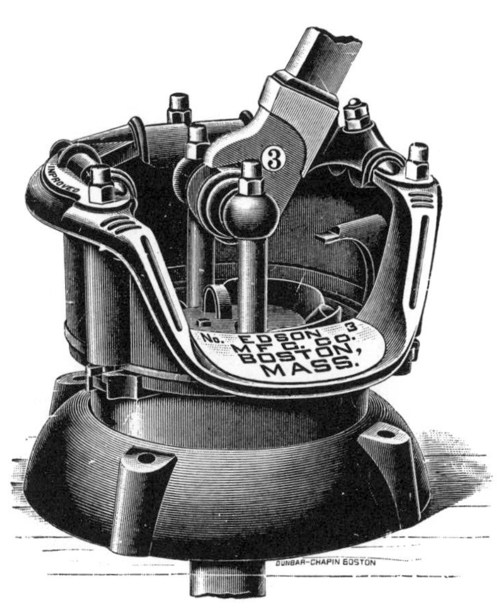
IMPROVED
No. EDSON 3
MFG. CO.
BOSTON,
MASS.
DUNBAR-CHAPIN BOSTON

Patent Pending

Note our Latest Improvements:

Hinge makes it easy for one man to open the head to insert Diaphragm. It insures head going back exactly where it belongs, with lugs properly aligned and *without displacing Diaphragm.*

Bevelled Rim around outer circumference of top of base properly centers the Diaphragm. Heretofore pump has usually been closed with Diaphragm just caught on one edge and the other projecting through; resulting in Diaphragm soon breaking down on the short side.

Groove in the top of base to receive corresponding Bead on our new Diaphragm, helps to center diaphragm and also makes a tight fit, thus insuring full suction of water instead of leakage of air through under the Diaphragm as heretofore.

MARINE DIAPHRAGM PUMPS

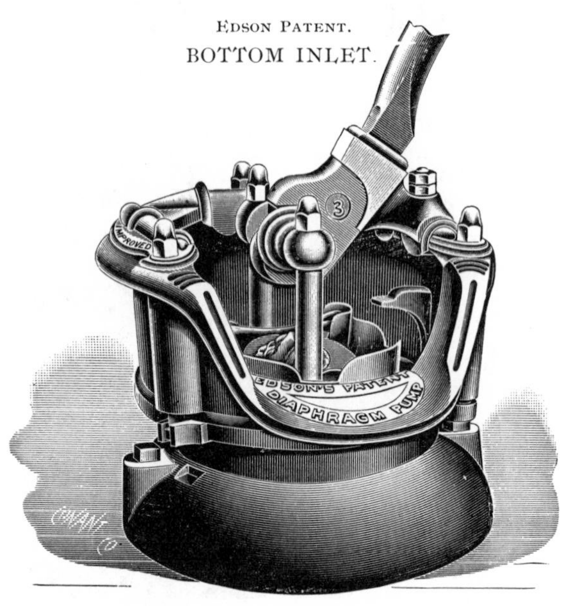
EDSON PATENT.
BOTTOM INLET.
IMPROVED
3
EDSON'S PATENT
DIAPHRAGM PUMP

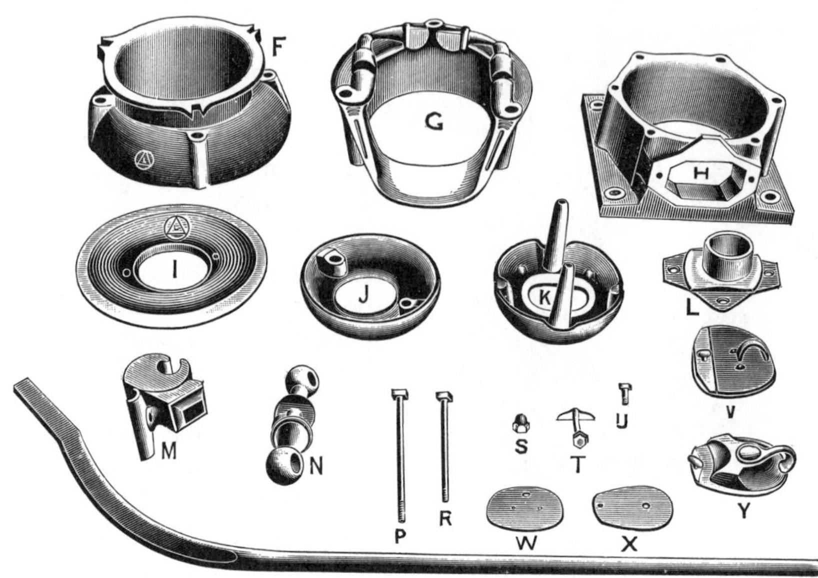
F
G
H
I
J
K
L
M
N
P
R
S
T
U
V
W
X
Y
Z

PLUNGER PUMPS, RUSSELL PATTERN

Plunger Pumps.

RUSSELL PATTERN.

H.B.BENNETT CO

Russell Pump Parts.

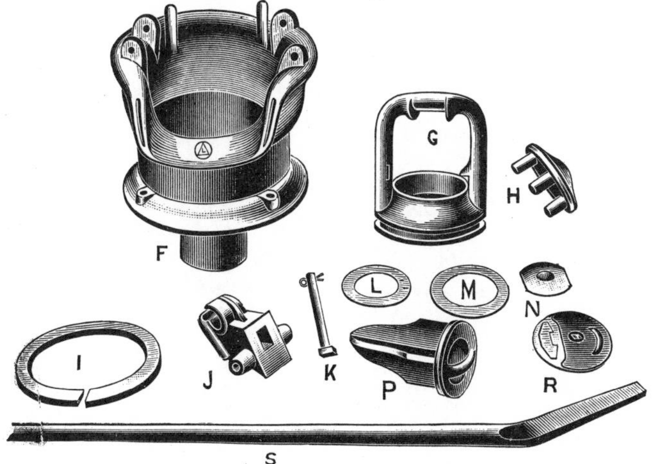
F
G
H
I
J
K
L
M
N
P
R
S

PUMPS, IRON (DIAPHRAGM AND PLUNGER)

Iron pumps, abreast of one another, were placed abaft the mainmast. Their athwartship ℄ was usually about 24″-26″ abaft the ℄ of the mainmast. There was normally about 10″-14″ from the forward side of the afterhatch to the athwartship ℄ of the pumps. The pumps, athwartship, were 28″-32″, ℄ to ℄. Sometimes the deck fittings of the pumps were in a watertight box, taking the pump discharge, which was piped forward on deck to the great beam where a cross-pipe carried the discharge overboard. The knockabout "Oretha F. Spinney" was one of the two vessels, fitted this way, that were noticed.

The suction pipes, below deck, were boxed-in, with the limber chain through the wells formed alongside of the keelson. The diaphragm pump owed much of its popularity to its ability to pump sludge and foreign matter that would plug the old wooden pumps or any of the piston type.

The deck or base fitting of these pumps was let into the top of the mast bed about three-quarters of an inch, it was noticed.

QUARTER BITTS

Quarter bitts were fitted, in the New England fishing schooners, abreast the wheel box and outboard enough to line up with the sides of the cabin trunk. They were single-post and usually had one cross-piece. The post ranged from 21" to 30" high above the quarterdeck, and from 7"x7" to 8"x8." The post was beveled on all sides to line up with the cabin trunk sides, yet fit against a deck beam. The post tumbled inboard a little at its head. Its top was covered with sheet copper.

The cross piece, at its bottom, was between 9" and 12" above deck, and passed through the post. It was about 4" deep and 2¼" to 2¾" thick. All edges of crosspiece were slightly rounded, as was the post above deck. The only schooner having two cross-pieces in the quarter bitts, that I saw, was the "Philip P. Manta", but I was told that double crosspieces were used in the late 1890s in a few vessels. Crosspieces usually had one locking bolt, which was driven through post and crosspiece.

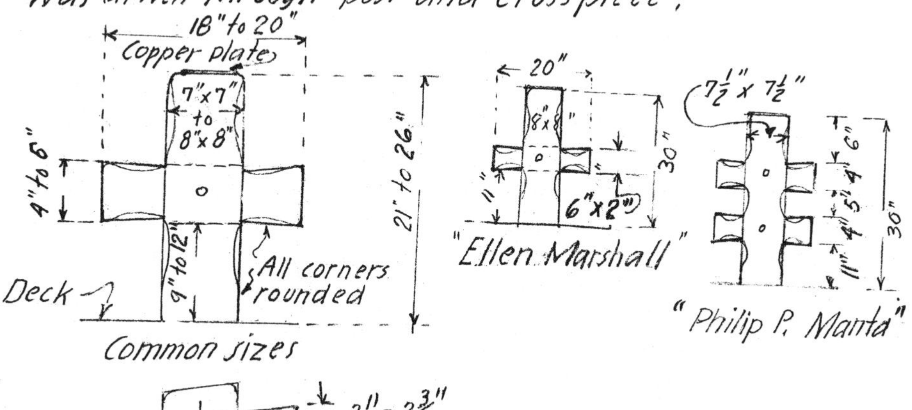

18" to 20"
Copper plate
7"x7"
to
8"x8"
4" to 6"
21" to 26"
9" to 12"
All corners rounded
Deck
Common sizes
20"
8"x8"
30"
11"
6"x2"
"Ellen Marshall"
7½" x 7½"
6"
4"
5"
4"
11"
30"
"Philip P. Manta"

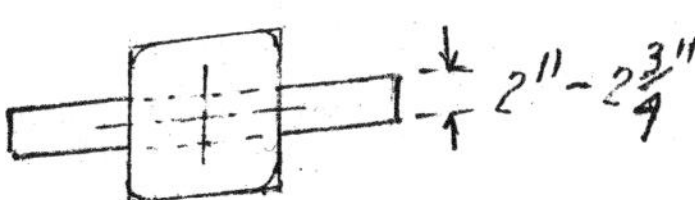

2" - 2¾"

QUARTER BLOCKS

From about 1855, tht rounding of the quarters, to fair into the top of the transom, became increasingly marked. Plank could not take the twist this required, so "quarter blocks," fitted under the main rail cap and hewn to shape, were often necessary. These were of white pine. The strake just below the main rail cap did not run to the transom but butted into a rabbet at the fore-end of the quarter blocks, where the tumble home became great enough to cause marked twist. The quarter blocks usually rested on the head of a stanchion at their fore-ends and on the after faces of the transom frame. Their depth was usually 6″-8″. The blocks were usually hidden by the fashion pieces, after about 1890.

The monkey rail, and its cap, rounded in at the quarters. Made of solid timber, hewn to curves of quarters and taffrail, it had little or no tumble home at the quarters, and little across the transom top. (See "Counter.")

RACERS
(FISHING SCHOONERS THAT ARE KNOWN TO HAVE TAKEN PART IN RACES)

YEAR	NAME	PLACE OF BUILD
1882	"Sarah H. Prior"	East Boston, Mass.
1883	"Edith Emery"	Essex, Mass.
1883	"Gertie S. Windsor"	Boston, Mass.
1884	"Emily P. Wright"	Essex, Mass.
1884	"Roulette"	East Boston, Mass.
1885	"Belle J. Neal"	Essex, Mass.
1885	"Hattie I. Phillips"	Essex, Mass.
1885	"John H. McManus"	East Boston, Mass.
1886	"I. J. Merritt, Jr."	Essex, Mass.
1886	"Wm. Parnell O'Hara"	Essex, Mass.
1886	"Sylvester Whalen"	East Boston, Mass.
1886	"William Emerson"	Boston, Mass.
1887	"Carrie H. Phillips"	Essex, Mass.
1888	"Susan R. Stone"	East Boston, Mass.
1889	"Fredonia"	Essex, Mass.
1889	"Harry L. Belden"	Essex, Mass.
1890	"Lottie S. Haskins"	Essex, Mass.
1890	"Nannie C. Bohlin"	Gloucester, Mass.
1891	"Ethel B. Jacobs"	Essex, Mass.
1891	"James G. Blaine"	Essex, Mass.
1891	"Grayling"	Essex, Mass.
1891	"Joseph Rowe"	Gloucester, Mass.

1892	"James S. Steele"	Essex, Mass.
1898	"Mattakeeset"	Essex, Mass.
1900	"Priscilla Smith"	Essex, Mass.
1900	"Navaho"	Gloucester, Mass.
1901	"Benjamin F. Phillips"	Essex, Mass.
1901	"Manomet"	East Boothbay, Me.
1902	"Helen B. Thomas"	Essex, Mass.
1902	"Philip P. Manta"	Essex, Mass.
1905	"Arthur James"	Essex, Mass.
1905	"Thomas S. Gorton"	Essex, Mass.
1905	"James W. Parker"	Essex, Mass.
1905	"Rose Dorothea"	Essex, Mass.
1905	"Francis P. Mesquita"	Gloucester, Mass.
1906	"Esperanto"	Essex, Mass.
1910	"Elsie"	Essex, Mass.
1910	"Josephine De Costa"	Essex, Mass.
1912	"Arthur D. Story" (ex-"Mary")	Essex, Mass.
1913	"Progress"	Essex, Mass.
1914	"Ralph Brown"	Essex, Mass.
1915	"Elsie G. Silva"	Gloucester, Mass.
1915	"Elizabeth Howard"	East Boothbay, Me.
1921	"L. A. Dunton"	Essex, Mass.
1921	"Mayflower" (banned)	Essex, Mass.
1921	"Yankee"	Essex, Mass.
1922	"Henry Ford"	Essex, Mass.
1922	"Puritan"	Essex, Mass.
1923	"Columbia"	Essex, Mass.
1923	"Shamrock"	Essex, Mass.
1930	"Gertrude L. Thebaud"	Essex, Mass.

[List by Lewis H. Story, taken from newspapers.]

Dates given in this list are the date of build of each vessel. It should be noted that only working fishing schooners raced until 1920, when the so-called racing fishermen came into existence.

RAIL CAPS
(SEE "BULWARKS")

The main rail caps, in schooners built in the 1880s, were commonly 3″ x 9″ (to 10″) except in small vessels. Similarly, monkey rail caps were 2½″ x 6″ (to 7″).

In the 1890s, the main rail caps were 3″ thick, the monkey rail caps were 2¼″-2½″ and the fife rails were 2½″-3″. These dimensions held good until the end of the sailing fishermen.

RATLINES

As fishing schooners had no more than three shrouds a side for each mast the ratlines ran from swifter to the aftermost shroud. The ratlines were 5/8″ to 3/4″ dia. hemp with an eye splice in each end. The lowest ratline was about 14″ above the sheerpole - the ratlines above this were about 16″ or 16½″ apart. The shrouds rattled down were served, if they were of iron wire rope. In some schooners only the starb'd fore shrouds and the port main shrouds were rattled down. The swordfishermen were fully rattled down, to topmasts, but in the other fisheries only the lower shrouds were rattled down.

The eyes of the ratlines were seized to the swifter and aftermost shroud; ratline clove hitched to the middle shroud. The eye splices in the ratlines were tucked one-and-a-half times and seized in a horizontal position. The seizing stuff was eye-spliced into the ratline eyes. The free end of the seizing stuff was passed thrice around the shroud and through its eye each time and secured in the ratline eye with the third pass. The clove hitch was on the outboard side of the shroud and the lower end of the hitch led aft.

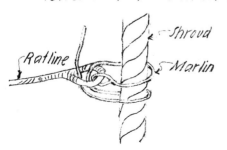

REEF TACKLE

The reef tackle was not carried rove off, as a rule, but was rigged only when reefing began, and then for the mainsail alone. It was led thus. A single-sheave 6″ block with becket and lashing eye, was secured to the reef cringle by a short rope strop and a wooden toggle. The lead was from the becket down and through a double-sheave 6″ block, side hooked into a wye on the mainboom end, then up and through the single-sheave 6″ block, then down and through the double-sheave 6″ block, with the fall carried forward to belay on a cleat or the boom, within reach of men standing on or near the mainsheet buffer, or the wheelbox. The belay cleat was on the port side of boom.

REEFING TACKLE, DIAGRAMMATIC

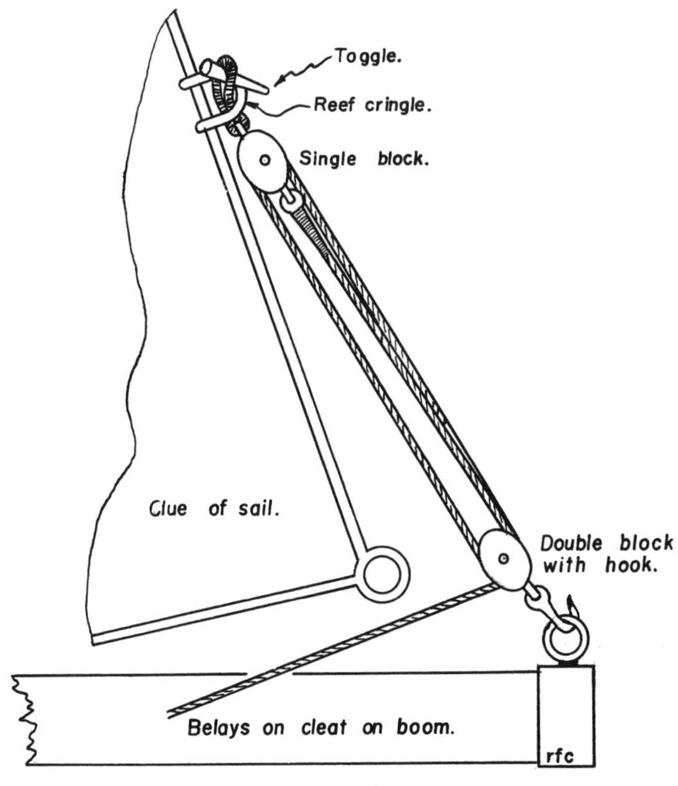
Toggle.
Reef cringle.
Single block.
Clue of sail.
Double block with hook.
Belays on cleat on boom.
rfc

Not commonly carried rove-off

RIGGING, HEMP

Until the introduction of iron and steel wire shrouds and stays into fishing schooner rigging in 1883–1884, hemp had been used for all standing rigging except the lower bobstays, which were chain. The hemp standing rigging was always tarred. The jib or forestay was about 8¾″ in circumference, the shrouds 6¾″, bowsprit shrouds and springstay 5″, flying jibstay 4½″, backstays 3″, topmast shrouds and stays 2¾″, footropes 2¾″ jib and forboom tapping-lift pendants 3-4½″.

The forestay was made up with a large eye to go over the foremast head, of sufficient size to allow the topmast to pass through when rigged. The lower end passed through the bee hole in the bowsprit and then passed over a thimble on the outer bolt of the upper bobstay chain plates on the cutwater and returned up the stay for 3½′-4′ and seized. It was then parcelled and served, finally covered with canvas and a sewn rawhide boot.

Stays and shrouds were not always spliced, often they were first cross-seized, then two or three round seizings were passed. At the lower end of a stay, if seized, the stay was returned up on itself on the inboard side, "cutter fashion." Seizing stuff was tarred hemp marlin, with a hard twist.

Double headstays were used in some clipper fishing schooners, 1855–1870; a well-made contemporary rigged scale model shows that the upper end of the stay was formed of the bight, which went abaft the masthead. The legs passed over and outside the trestletrees and also over the fore-crosstree, and were seized together 4 or 5 feet from the fore-ends of the trestletrees. The stay was parcelled and served for its full length within the eye, or loop, around the masthead, formed by the seizing. The lower end of the double stay, formed by the two legs, passed through the bee blocks on either side of the bowsprit. The jibboom was on the top and center line of the bowsprit, the legs straddling it. Close above the jibboom the two legs of the stay were seized together. All seizings on this stay were round seizings, well-tarred. The wooden jumbo hanks rode on both legs, of course.

The two legs led from their bee holes to pairs of bobstay plates on the cutwater; each leg making up on a thimble in its pair of plates and returning on top of itself, for 3 or 4 feet; seized, parcelled, served, tarried, and covered with a sewn rawhide boot. It will be seen that three pairs of bobstay plates were required with this rig; the lowest for the chain bobstay and the two above for the two legs of the stay. Old photographs show that this rigging made the bow appear cluttered and clumsy. The single stay was therefore extensively used; the double stay being used only on the large bankers after 1865, until wire rope replaced hemp for standing rigging.

Most stays leading to the mastheads were usually eye-spliced into the bails, or to links in wyes or straps, using thimbles, it was rather common practice, at one time, to use seizings at one end of a stay and an eye-splice at the other, in rigging the upper stays.

RIGGING FOR SCHOONER, 76-FOOT TONNAGE LENGTH BUILT IN 1880 (75 TONS REGISTER)

HEMP STANDING RIGGING	CIRCUMFERENCE
Jibstay	8¾″
Foremast shrouds	6¾″
Mainmast shrouds	6¾″
Bowsprit shrouds	5″
Springstay	5″
Flying jibstay	4½″
Flying jib guys	4″
Fore-topmast backstays	3″
Main-topmast backstays	3″
Fore-topmast shrouds	2¾″
Fore-topmast stay	2¾″
Main-topmast shrouds	2¾″
Main-topmast stay	2¾″
Bowsprit footropes	2¾″
Mainboom footropes	2½″
Counterstay, (fore-topmast)	2½″
Main-topgallant stay	2″
Fore-topgallant stay	2″
Flying jib footropes	2¼″
Jib topping lift	3″
Foreboom topping-lift pendant	3″
Mainboom topping-lift pendant	4½″
Main topping-lift pendant	4½″
Flying jib topping-lift pendant	3½″

Blocks: 16 doubles, 46 singles, 24-6″ and 8-4″ dia. dead eyes, 36-21″ and 16-10″ dia. mast hoops 24-24″, 30-18″ and 40-16″ circ. jib hanks, 2 trucks. Two chains, 30 to 45 fathoms each. If fitted for cod fishing, she would have 225 to 475 fathoms of the best 8½″-8¾″ manila cable and three anchors. Two were on the rails abaff the catheads and one was stowed on deck.

MANILA RUNNING RIGGING	CIRCUMFERENCE
Mainsheet	3″
Cat stoppers	3″
Main topping-lift runner	3″
Fish hook	3″
Fore and main halyards	3″
Forepeak halyards	2 ¾″
Fore throat halyards	2 ½″
Foresheet	2 ¾″
Main peak halyards	2 ¾″
Main throat halyards	2 ½″
Jib halyards	2 ½″
Jib sheet	2 ½″
Jib downhaul	2″
Main-staysail halyards	2 ½″
Main-staysail sheet	2 ½″
Mainboom tackle	2 ½″
Flying jib halyards	2 ¼″
Flying jib downhaul	1 ¾″
Jib topping lift	2 ¼″
Flying jib sheets	2 ¼″
Forestaysail halyards	2 ¼″
Topsail sheet	2 ¼″
Crotch tackles	2 ¼″
Main topping-lift fall	2 ¼″
Topsail halyards	2″
Main peak downhaul	1 ¾″
Foreboom topping lift	2″
Forepeak downhaul	2″
Topsail tack	2″
Reef tackle	2″
Main peak whip	2″
Forepeak whip	2″
Jib peak whip	2″
Jib topsail halyards	1 ¾″
Jib topsail downhaul	1 ½″
Jib topsail sheet	2 ½″
Topsail clew line	1 ¾″

This schedule was for an average-size schooner built between 1860 and 1885. The size of running rigging in vessels between 70′ and 90′ varied little. There might be ½″ to 1″ variation in the circumference of some of the standing rigging, however.

RIGGING FOR "GRAMPUS," 1885

Standing rigging is galv. iron wire. Footropes, life lines, and a few pendants are hemp. Running rigging is manila.

WIRE RIGGING	CIRCUMFERENCE
Jibstay, bobstay	4½″
Forestay, fore and main shrouds	3¼″
Springstay (triatic), preventerstay	3″
Bowsprit shrouds	2¾″
Flying jib and jumperstays	2½″
Backropes	2¼″
Inner jibboom guys, outer jumperstay fore- and main-top mast backstays foreboom and forestaysail topping lift pendants.	2″
Balloon jibstay and outer-jibboom guys	1¾″
Main-topmast stay, counterstay (from head of fore-topmast to mainmast head) fore- and main-topmast shrouds.	2″
Upper-topmast stays and belly lashing for jibboom.	1″

HEMP ROPES	CIRCUMFERENCE
Lanyards	3″
Jib footropes and lifelines	2¾″
Mainboom footropes and jibboom footropes	2½″
Ratlines	2″

MANILA ROPES	CIRCUMFERENCE
Mainboom topping-lift pendant, 4 strands	4½″
Mainboom tackle pendant, 4 strands	4″
Foreboom tackle pendant, 4 strands	3½″
Mainboom topping-lift runner	3″
Boat gripes	3″
Tarred manila lanyards, 4 strands, for fore and main rigging	3″
Tarred manila lanyards, 4 strands, for head rigging and fore-topmast backstays	2″
Mainsheet, fore and main peak halyards	3″
Fore and main throat halyards, foresheet and cat stoppers	2¾″

Jib halyards, forestaysail halyards, forestaysail sheet, jib sheet, after mainstaysail halyards, mainstaysail sheet, mainboom tackle fall, balloon jib sheet, davit tackle falls and reefearings	2½″
Forward mainstaysail halyards, flying jib halyards, flying jib sheet, foreboom tackle fall, gaff-topsail halyards, gaff-topsail sheets, crutch tackles, mainboom topping-lift fall, forestaysail topping-lift fall, maintopmast back-stay fall	2½″
Forestaysail and jib downhauls, foreboom topping-lift fall, fore and main peak downhauls, gaff-topsail tacks, reef tackle main and fore peak whips, foot lacings for sails	2″
Balloon jib halyards, flying jib downhaul, fore and main gaff-topsail clew lines and jib stops	1¾″
Head lacings for sails and sail gaskets	1½″

Pendant halyards to be of special size, cotton line, made for that purpose. (See "Block List.")

RUNNING RIGGING *"GERTRUDE L. THEBAUD"* *AND SCHOONERS OF HER APPROXIMATE SIZE* *100 TO 150 TONS*

RUNNING GEAR	CIRC.	NOTE
Main peak and throat halyards	3½″	
Mainsheet	3½″	
Forepeak and throat halyards	3½″	
Foresheet	3½″	
Fore and main jig tackles	2½″	
Main peak downhaul	2½″	
Jumbo and jib halyards	3″	
Jumbo and jib sheets	3″	
Jumbo and jib downhauls	2¼″	
Jumbo and jib jig tackles	2″	
Jumbo topping lift	2″	
Fore- and main-topsail halyards	2″	
Fore- and main-topsail sheets	2½″	
Fore and main tacks and clew lines	2″	
Balloon jib halyards	2¼″	
Balloon jib downhaul	1¾″	
Balloon jib tackware	1¾″	

Balloon jib sheets, wire pendants	1¾″	
Balloon jib sheets, manila	2″	
Fish. staysail throat halyard	2½″	
Fish. staysail peak halyard	2¾″	
Fish. staysail sheets	2¾″	or 3″ o.k.
Dory tackles	2″	
Lanyards, hemp, lower masts	3½″-3¾″	Same dia. as
Lanyards, hemp, topmasts	2¼″-2½″	wire shrouds
Main topping lift, wire	3¼″	it serves
Main topping lift, if manila	5″	
Runner, manila	3½″	
Fall, manila	2¾″	
Foreboom topping lift	2½″	
Boom tackles same as jumbo and jib halyards.		

RINGBOLTS (DECK)

Ringbolts in deck of the schooner "Philip P. Manta":

—One on deck center line just abaft main hatch.

—One on deck center line just forward of galley hatch.

—One, port and starboard opposite center of galley hatch, also one, port and starboard opposite after-end of main hatch. Ringbolts outboard of respective hatches 24″.

—One, port and starboard, on top of great beam 12″ inside bulwark stanchions.

—One port and starboard on deck, 20″ inside bulwarks stanchions, as close to after-end of deck as is possible.

ROUND (GALLEY) HATCH

The round galley hatch was apparently introduced in Crowninshield-designed schooners somewhere about 1900, though all of his designs did not show it. Its purpose seems to allow a cable to be coiled around it in a secure manner. It was built up of 3″ or 4″ plank, bread-and-butter fashion. The hatch cover had a thick glass light in it, 6″ to 10″ in diameter. The round hatch was fashionable for about 10 years, then it was replaced by a square galley hatch, about large enough to pass a flour-barrel below. This hatch had two covers, opening athwartship, with a glass light in the after cover, 6″ to 9″ in diameter. Some vessels had two lights in this hatch and ironwork to hold the cover open, to serve as a ventilator. (See "Hatches.")

RUDDER

New England fishing schooners, after 1815 were commonly fitted with the "plug-stock rudder." This type of rudder had a round stock from its head down to the upper pintle. Its center line then coincided with the fore-side of the blade. This was bevelled to permit the blade to swing without binding on the sternpost. The after face of the sternpost was hollowed above the top pintle. Below this, the timber forming the stock was formed to be part of the blade as well as the stock. (See next sketch.) The blade as formed of four or five planks, edge-bolted together and to the stock. Some taper was worked into the blade so that the trailing edge was about half the siding of the stock. As the stern post usually tapered from its head downward to the heel, so did the rudderstock. The center line of the pintles lined up with that of the stock. The rudder blade bolts were ¾″ to 1″ rod with ends upset. There were three sets of rudder braces ("pintles" and "gudgeons") equally spaced. The straps of these were let in flush into the blade but not into the sternpost. No rudder chains were used, rudder stops placed just above the upper braces were fastened to the sides of the sternpost. (See "Aperture.") The rudder lock, which prevented the rudder lifting and unshipping was a block of wood under the middle brace, as shown in the rudder sketch.

RUDDER

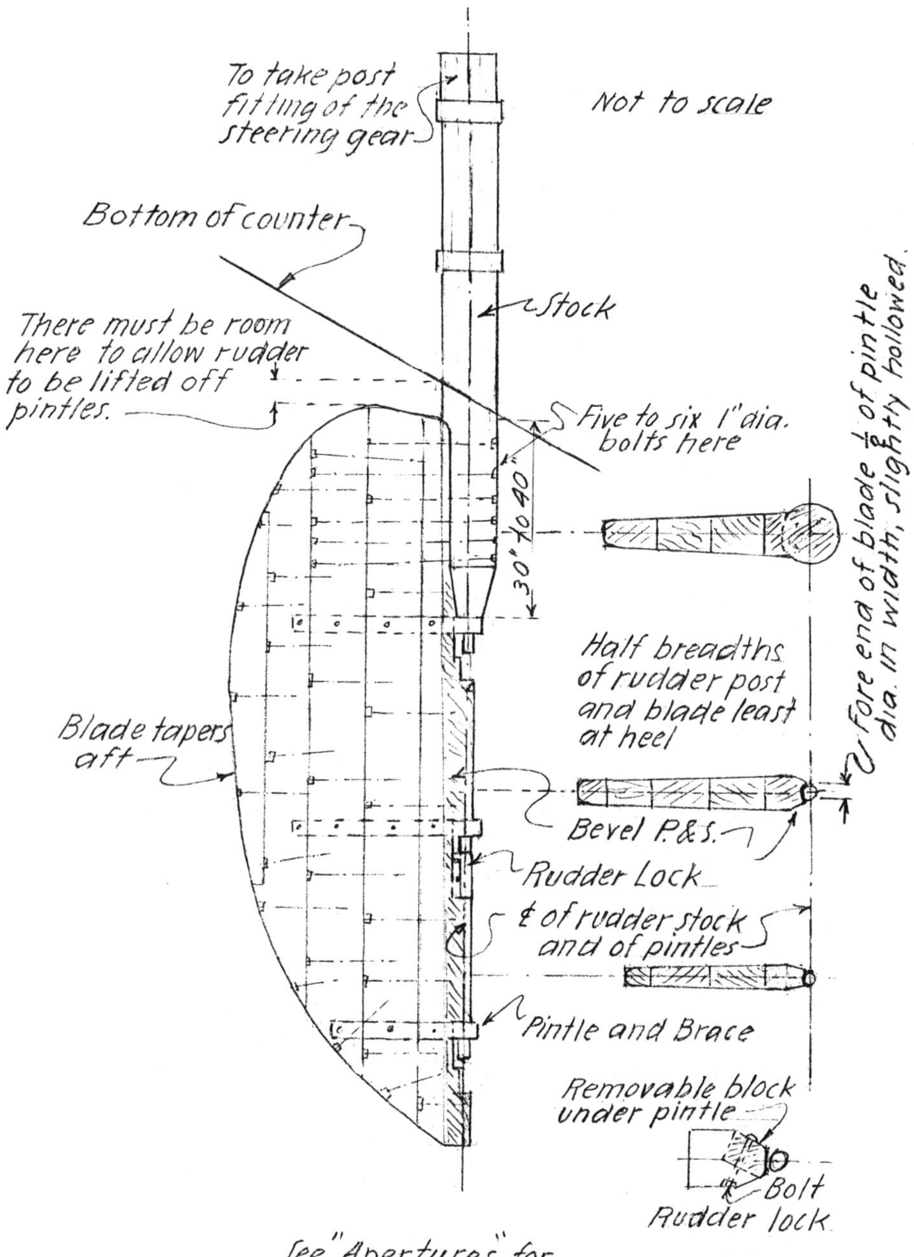
To take post fitting of the steering gear
Not to scale
Bottom of counter
Stock
There must be room here to allow rudder to be lifted off pintles.
Five to six 1" dia. bolts here
30" to 40"
Fore end of blade ½ of pintle dia. in width, slightly hollowed.
Half breadths of rudder post and blade least at heel
Blade tapers aft
Bevel P.&S.
Rudder Lock
℄ of rudder stock and of pintles
Pintle and Brace
Removable block under pintle
Bolt
Rudder lock
See "Apertures" for Rudder Stop

RUDDER AND CASE, 10-INCH STOCK, 10½-INCH BORE

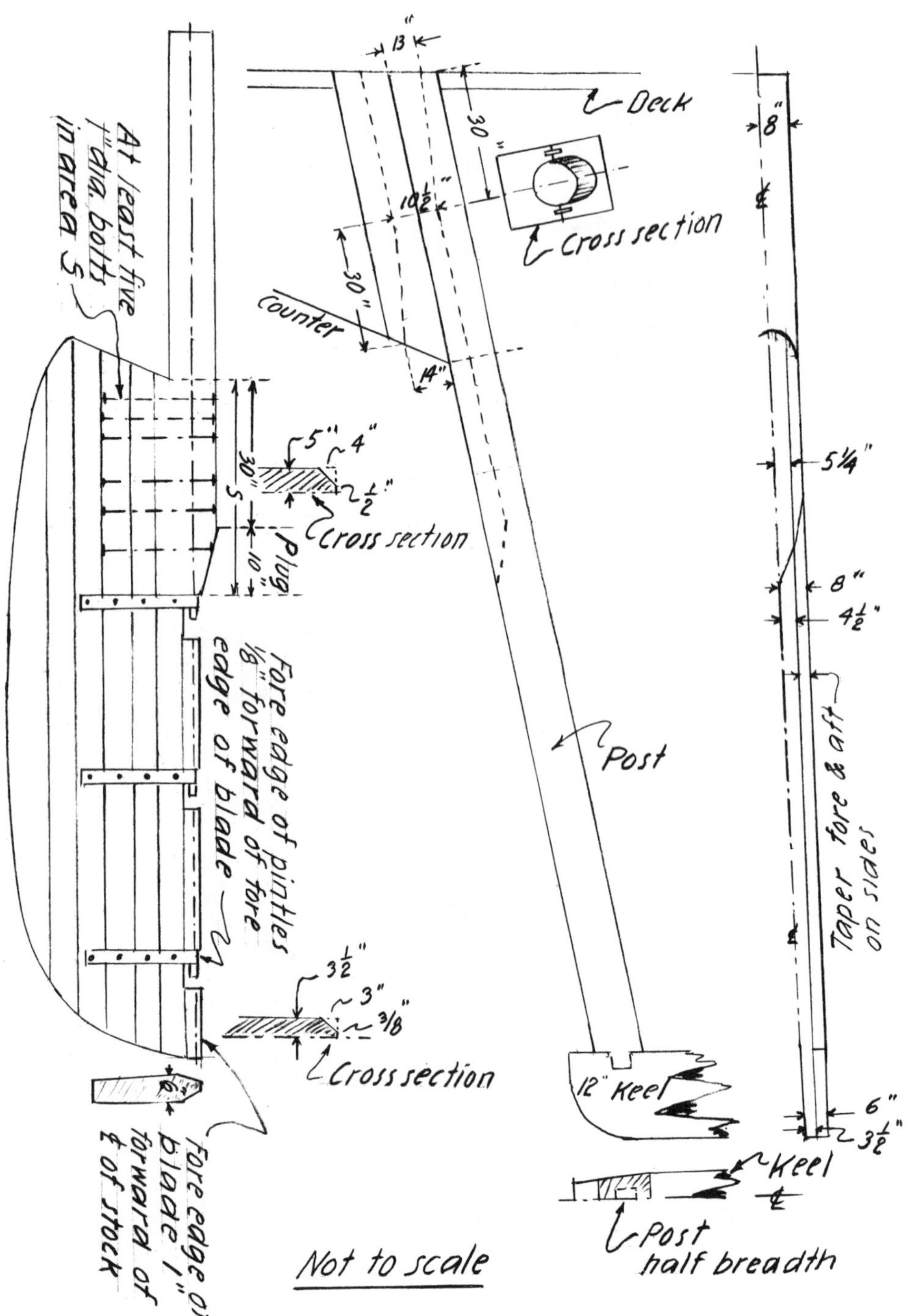

13"
Deck
30"
8"
10½"
Cross section
30"
Counter
14"
At least five 1" dia. bolts in area S
5"
4"
½"
30"
S
Cross section
Plug
10"
5¼"
8"
4½"
Post
Fore edge of pintles 1/8" forward of fore edge of blade
Taper fore & aft on sides
3½"
3"
3/8"
Cross section
12" Keel
6"
3½"
Keel
Post half breadth
Fore edge of blade 1" forward of ℄ of stock
Not to scale

RUDDER AND CASE

The rudder blade and stock were of white oak, the braces and bolts were of bronze or of yellow metal. The blade bolts were usually of iron.

The blade profile varied, and in early vessels, of before 1845, was often straight on the trailing edge and bottom. In the 1850s the curved profile became popular but in no standard shape, so far as can now be established, until into the 1890s.

Small wooden battens, nailed to each side of the blade close to the trailing edge, or on each side of the trailing edge, were occasionally seen. These were supposed to help a vessel that did not steer well. The battens were usually about ¾″ to 1″ square.

The rudder case was made of two timbers, one the sternpost, the other after half of the case. These were worked, the after face of the post hollowed for a short distance below the tuck of the counter and up to the head (deck) and the after half from tuck to head, to form the "bore." The latter was not round, but was elongated above and below, as shown in the sketch. This allowed the rudderstock to be inserted from below. The timbers of the case were splined in the counter. The plug of the stock came to rest in the tapered hollow in the post. The after piece of the case was held by the deck partners and the fore-end of the horn timber, and its cheek timbers; a drive-fit. The sternpost was tapered downward from the tuck, as was the rudder. The sides of the sternpost were tapered from the rabbet aft.

RUDDER PINTLE AND BRACE
"PINTLE AND GUDGEON"

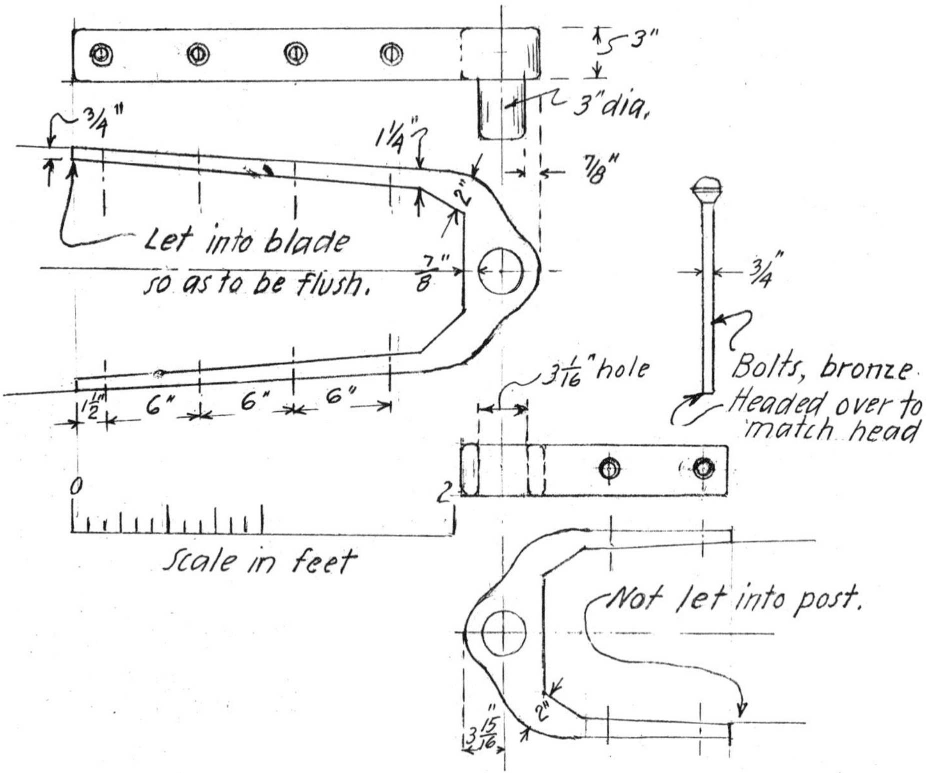
3"
3" dia.
3/4"
1 1/4"
7/8"
2"
Let into blade
so as to be flush.
7/8"
3/4"
Bolts, bronze.
Headed over to
match head
3 1/16" hole
1/2"
6"
6"
6"
0
2
Scale in feet
Not let into post.
2"
3 15/16"

Taken from large knockabout
"Adventure"

Bolts usually were through all, but braces were sometimes drilled offset, then short bolts were driven into the sternpost, or through planking into deadwood.

SADDLE, MAIN BOOM

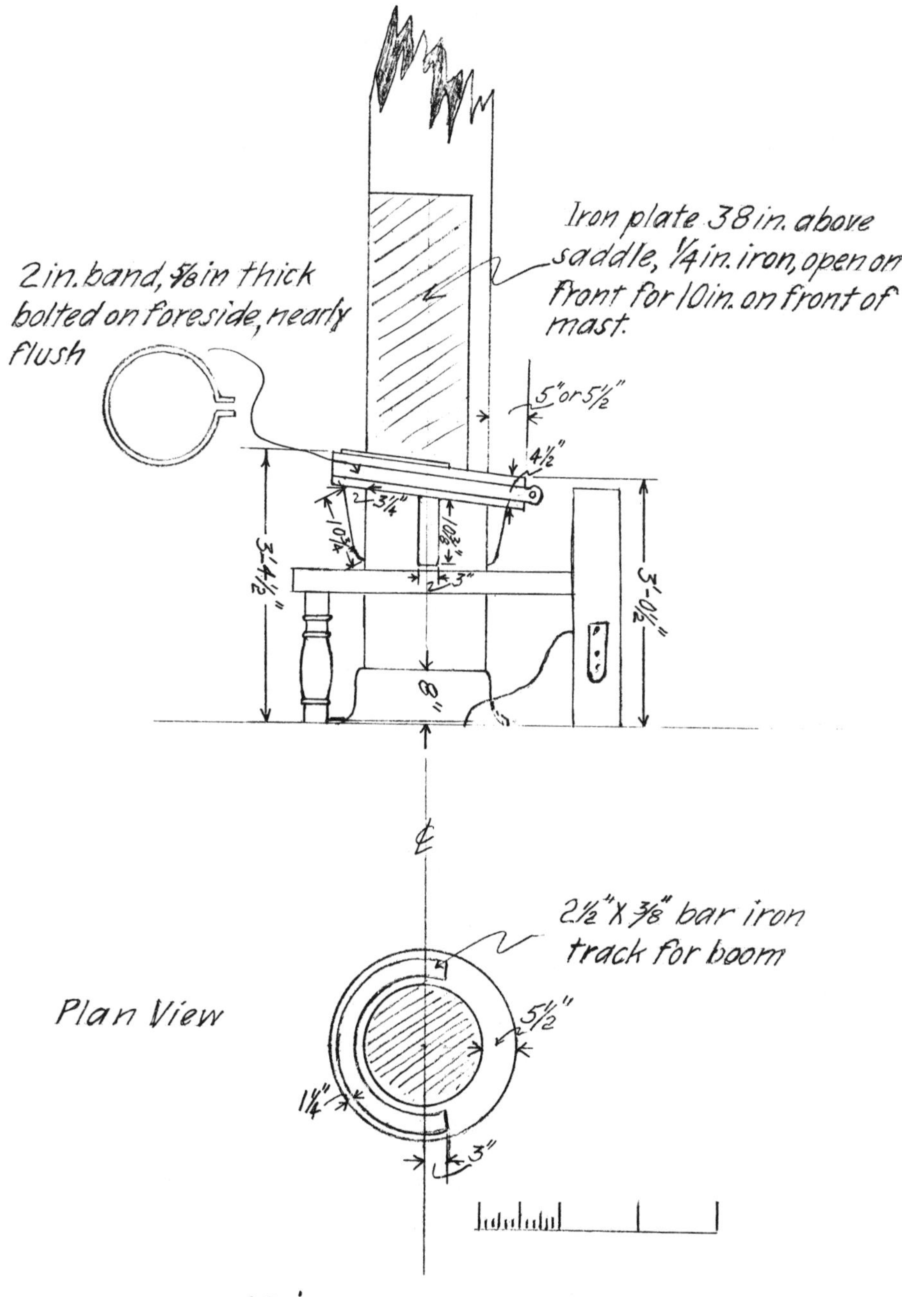
Iron plate 38 in. above saddle, 1/4 in. iron, open on front for 10 in. on front of mast.
2 in. band, 5/8 in thick bolted on foreside, nearly flush
5" or 5 1/2"
4 1/2"
2 3/4"
10 3/4"
10 3/8"
3'-4 1/2"
2 3"
3'-0 1/2"
8"
2 1/2" X 3/8" bar iron track for boom
Plan View
5 1/2"
1 1/4"
3"

Main-mast boom saddle
"Philip P. Manta."

SAIL LACINGS, ETC.

Sail lacings of 80′-100′ fishing schooners were ¾″ dia. rope on booms, spiral-turns; ⅝″ dia. rope on gaffs, turn-and-hitch (marlin hitch); jumbo lacing was ½″ dia., spiral-turns.

Ed Bosley found lacing on gaffs 2″ circ., manila, and 2¼″ circ. on booms. in large vessels. Thimbles along foot of main- and fore-sails for lacing were beckets and also beckets for jackrope along the luffs. 2″ manila clew line for topsails, 5″ clew line blocks. Smaller of the two thimbles in spectacle clew irons was for hemp sail rope, on foot of sail. Spectacle clew irons at foot of main- and fore-sail and rings at the heads. Wire cringle, parcelled at clew of jib (ring used here also, apparently). (See "Sail.")

SAILS (NOTES)

The knockabout schooner "Helen B. Thomas" was canvassed as follows:-
Main Sail No 2, Fore Sail No 1, Jumbo No 1, Jib No 2 Topsails No 8, Balloon No 6, Staysail No 10, Storm Trysail No 1.
"Grampus," 1885, medium-hard Woodbury duck 22" wide, Fore Sail, Fore Staysail, Riding Sail No 0. Main Sail and Jib No 1, Flying Jib and Sail Covers No 6, Fore and Main Gaff Topsails No 8, Main Topmast Stay Sail No 10. Balloon Jib 8 oz.
"Columbia" - Main Sail No 0. Fore Sail No 00. Jumbo No 00. Jib No 1, Gaff Topsails No 7, Balloon and Staysail No 9. Storm Trysail No 0 hard duck. Main Sail also of hard duck. Canvas sail cloth 22" wide, Seams 2" wide. Net width of cloths sewn up 20", ¾" stretch allowance.

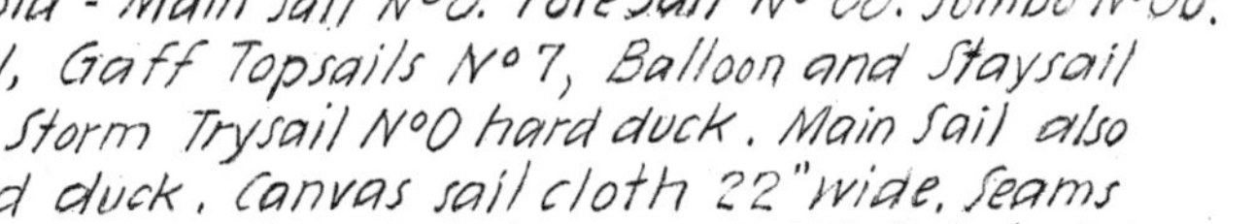

Bolt rope to port — 4" to 6" — 2" — 2" — Fore & Main.

Hemp boltropes on booms and gaffs.
Last cloth, fore & main, doubled over at leech, 4" lap at center of leech to 6" maximum at peak and clew.
Jack rope: (lace line) for lower hoops on main sail and fore sail; and on rings of jumbo and jib 1¾" circ. manila.

See "Sail Lacings, Etc."

SALT STOPS
FOR PRESERVATION OF FISHING SCHOONERS

Salt, as a preserver of wood, was used in fishing schconers in colonial times; the lack of rot in vessels carrying salt, or salt fish, having been noted. The practice of "salting" a schooner remained popular until the early 1900s.

"Stops" were placed between each pair of frames, just above the light waterline or at the bilge. The stops were of oak or pine, 1" thick, with their fore and after ends beveled. Two saw kerfs were cut, in the sides of the frames, into which the sharp ends of the stop were driven. The salt stops had to be fitted before planking and ceiling were completed. When the stops were in place, and the planking and ceiling were completed, the pockets thus formed were filled to planksheer level with salt previously used in a salt fish trip. The planksheer was finally secured over the salt. No access holes were drilled in the planksheer, but when re-salting was required access holes were drilled, and plugged when the re-salting was done.

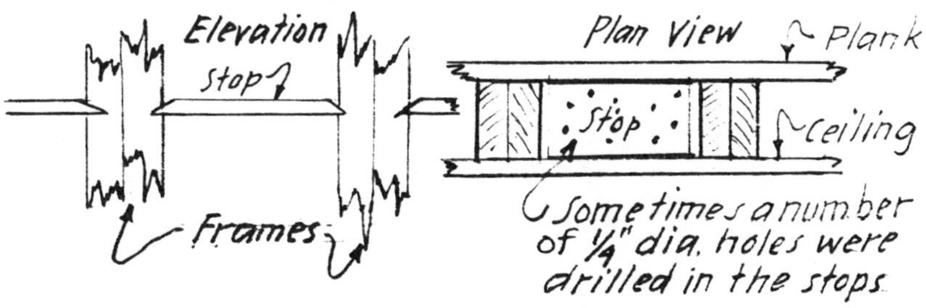
Elevation
Stop
Frames
Plan View
Plank
Stop
Ceiling
Sometimes a number of 1/4" dia. holes were drilled in the stops

SAMPSON, OR PAWL, POSTS (SEE "WINDLASSES")

The sampson, or pawl, post was a large timber stepped in a tenon in the forward deadwood. The pawl block of the windlass rode on this post and the heel of the bowsprit tenoned into it.

In "Elsie" this post was 13½″ fore-and-aft, 10¾″ wide and 50″ high above strongback of the deck. On the "Philip P. Manta" 12½″ x 12½″, 51″ high; on the "Mary E. O'Hara," 12″ x 12″, 53″ high; on the "Ellen Marshall," knockabout, 10″ x 10″, 55″ high (two posts about 3′-0″ apart, face-to-face).

The furling plank of the knockabout "Ethel Penny," from forward post to fore seat, was 3½″ x 10″.

Note: All knockabouts, except the "Helen B. Thomas," had a pawl post, with another post, "sampson," 3′ or 4′ forward of it, to support the "runner" of the jumbo boom and the furling plank, as well as the jumbo stay iron.

In the big schooners, having long fine bows like the racers, the pawl and windlass bitts were well aft to give room to work ground tackle. These vessels had a sampson post which served as the bowsprit heel bitt. The jumbo stay iron might be on this; in such a case the jumbo gooseneck might also be on this bitt.

SCHOONER RIG DETAILS (FOR SCHOONERS BUILT BETWEEN 1855 AND 1865)

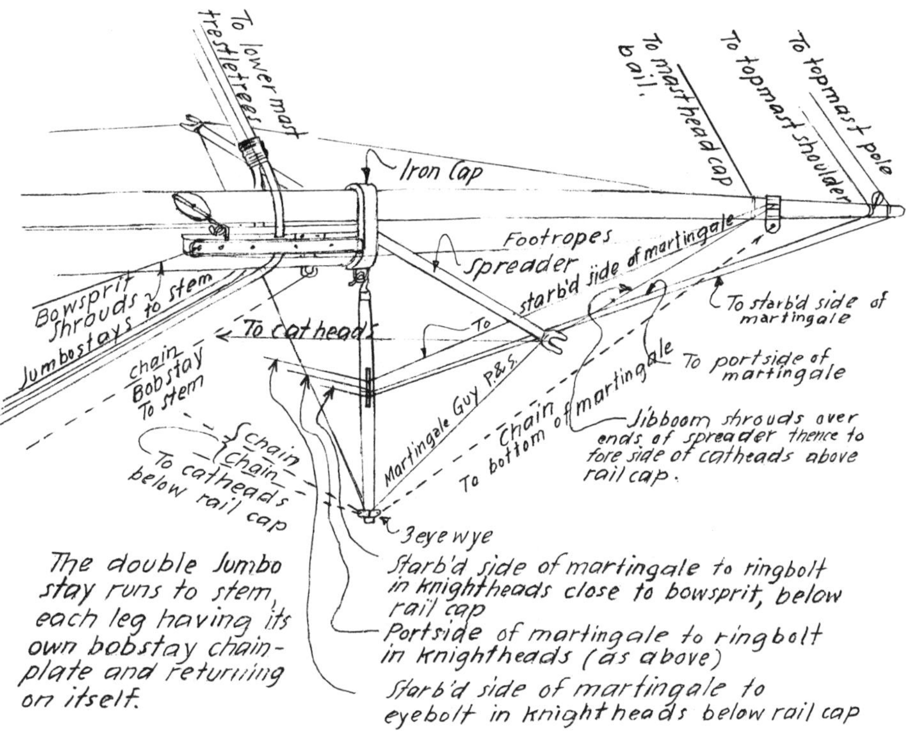
To lower mast trestletrees
To masthead cap bail.
To topmast shoulder
To topmast pole
Iron Cap
Footropes
Spreader
starb'd side of martingale
To starb'd side of martingale
Bowsprit Shrouds to stem
Jumbostays to stem
To catheads
To
chain Bobstay To stem
To portside of martingale
Martingale Guy P.&S.
Chain To bottom of martingale
Jibboom shrouds over ends of spreader thence to fore side of catheads above rail cap.
Chain
Chain
To catheads below rail cap
3eye wye
The double Jumbo stay runs to stem, each leg having its own bobstay chain-plate and returning on itself.
Starb'd side of martingale to ringbolt in knightheads close to bowsprit, below rail cap
Portside of martingale to ringbolt in knightheads (as above)
Starb'd side of martingale to eyebolt in knightheads below rail cap

Wooden bowsprit caps, iron-bound, were to be seen on fishing schooners and coasters as late as 1860, but were out of fashion as early as 1845.

The spreaders for the jibboom shrouds were of iron and were stapled to the fore end of the bowsprit.

Bowsprit shrouds set up on bee blocks by means of iron straps on outboard sides of the bee blocks, through-bolted.

3/8" × 1" slot P.&S.

2"-2¼" dia.

1¼-1½" dia

Groove for ¾" dia. staple

Iron Jibboom spreader 8'-2" long, of about 1865 (Sketch not to scale)

SCHOONER RIG DETAILS (FOR SCHOONERS BUILT BETWEEN 1855 AND 1865)

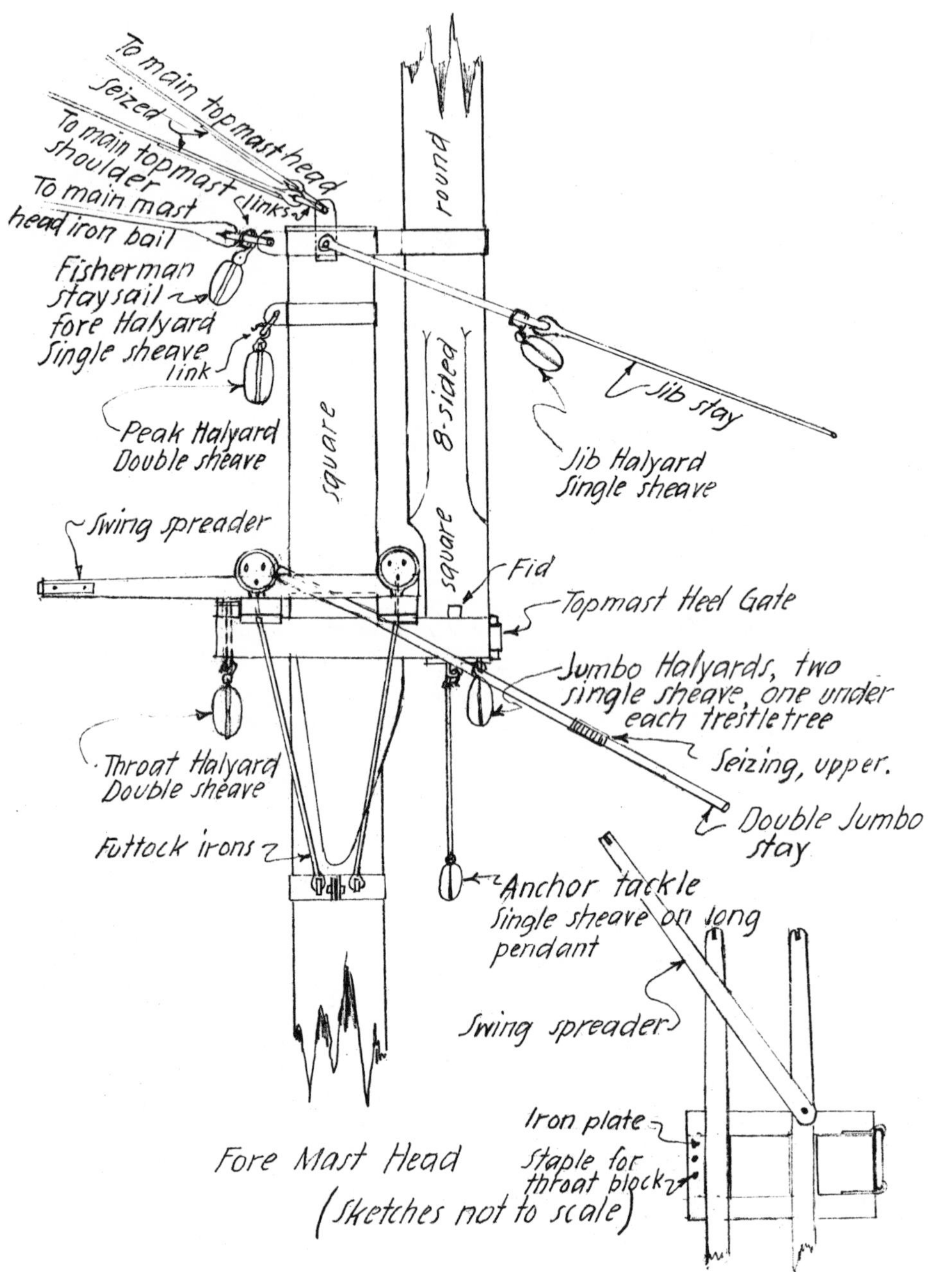

To main topmast head
Seized
To main topmast shoulder
links
To main mast
head iron bail
Fisherman staysail
fore Halyard
Single sheave
link
Peak Halyard
Double sheave
round
8-sided
square
square
Jib stay
Jib Halyard
Single sheave
Swing spreader
Fid
Topmast Heel Gate
Jumbo Halyards, two single sheave, one under each trestletree
Seizing, upper.
Throat Halyard
Double sheave
Double Jumbo stay
Futtock irons
Anchor tackle
Single sheave on long pendant
Swing spreader
Iron plate
Staple for throat block
Fore Mast Head
(Sketches not to scale)

SCHOONER RIG DETAILS (FOR SCHOONERS BUILT BETWEEN 1855 AND 1865)

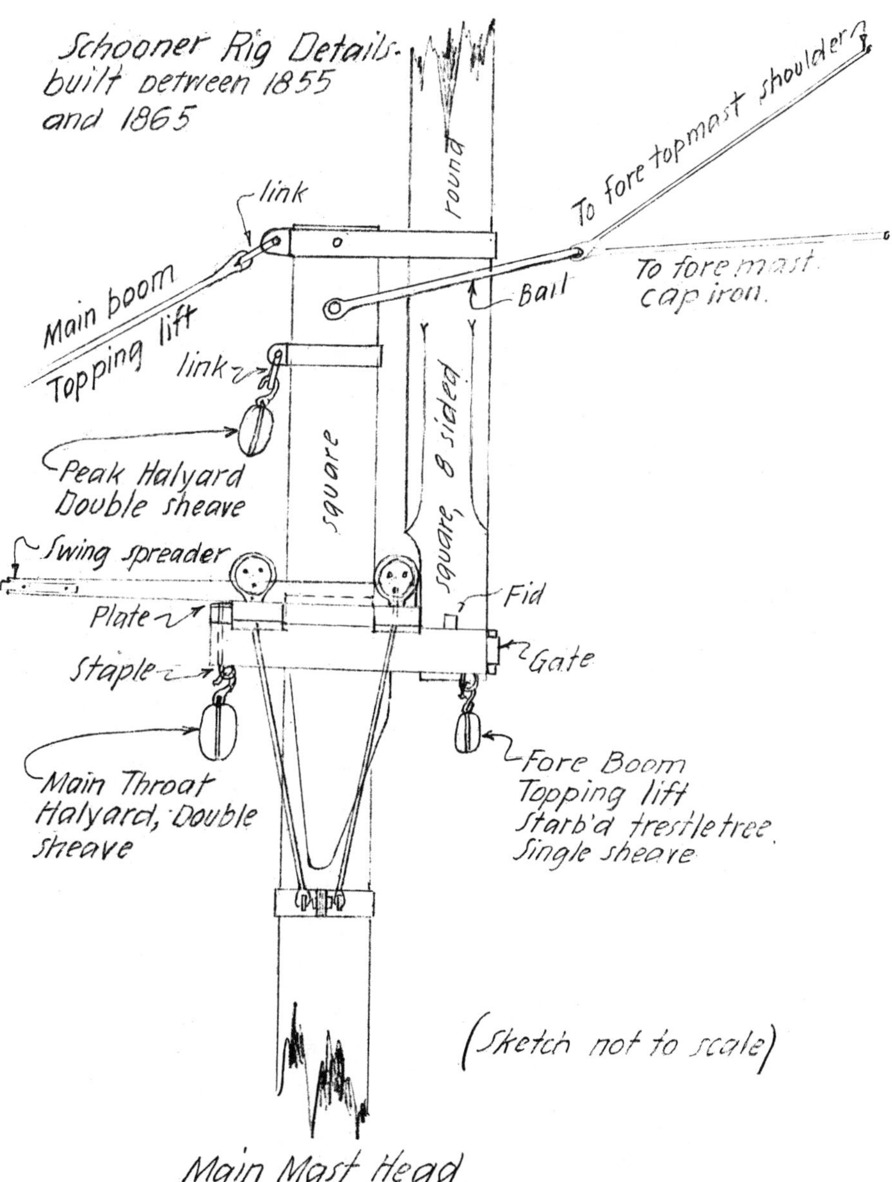
Schooner Rig Details-
built between 1855
and 1865
round
To fore topmast shoulder
link
To fore mast
cap iron.
Bail
Main boom
Topping lift
link
square, 8 sided
square
Peak Halyard
Double sheave
Swing spreader
Fid
Plate
Gate
Staple
Fore Boom
Topping lift
Starb'd trestletree
Single sheave
Main Throat
Halyard, Double
sheave
(Sketch not to scale)
Main Mast Head,

SCHOONER RIG DETAILS (FOR SCHOONERS BUILT BETWEEN 1855 AND 1865)

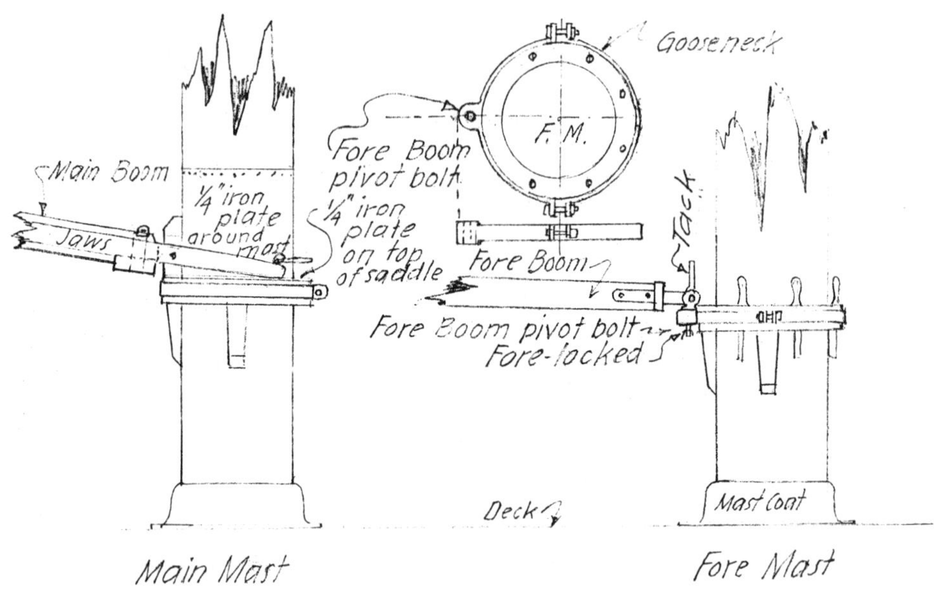
Gooseneck
F. M.
Fore Boom pivot bolt
Main Boom
1/4" iron plate around mast
Jaws
1/4" iron plate on top of saddle
Fore Boom
Tack
Fore Boom pivot bolt
Fore-locked
Deck
Mast Coat
Main Mast
Fore Mast

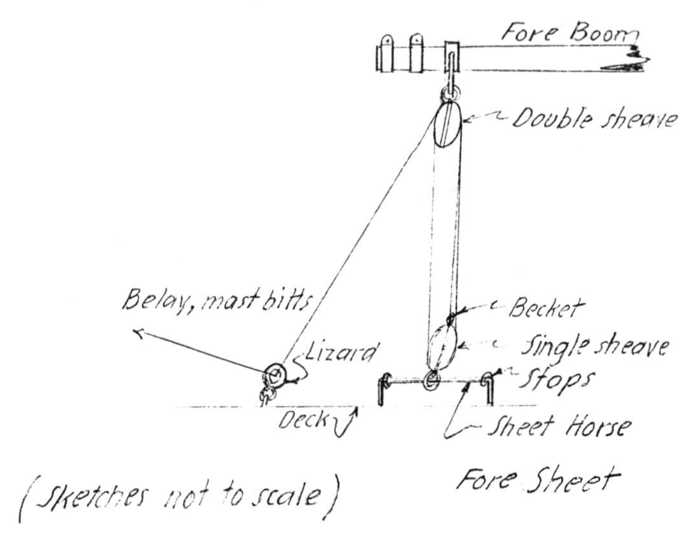
Fore Boom
Double sheave
Belay, mast bitts
Becket
Lizard
Single sheave
Stops
Deck
Sheet Horse
Fore Sheet
(Sketches not to scale)

SCHOONER RIG DETAILS (FOR SCHOONERS BUILT BETWEEN 1855 AND 1865)

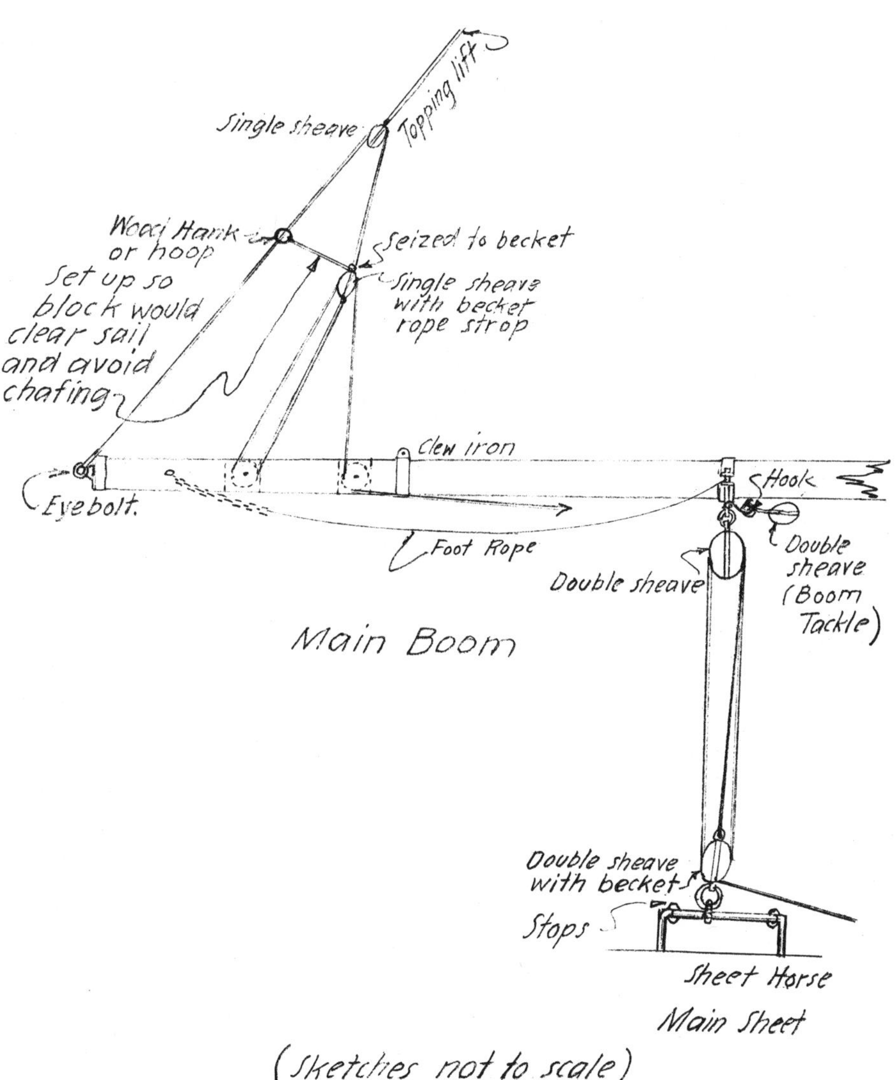
Topping lift
Single sheave
Wood Hank or hoop
Seized to becket
Single sheave with becket rope strop
Set up so block would clear sail and avoid chafing
Clew iron
Hook
Eyebolt.
Foot Rope
Double sheave
Double sheave (Boom Tackle)
Main Boom
Double sheave with becket
Stops
Sheet Horse
Main Sheet
(Sketches not to scale)

SCHOONER RIG DETAILS (FOR SCHOONERS BUILT BETWEEN 1855 AND 1865)

Three shrouds a side for each mast. Topmast shroud set up on fourth chain plate, abaft the lower shroud chain plates at rail. Swifters were abreast of a line a few inches forward of the foreside of masts at deck level. Two topmast shrouds set up on crosstrees and spider irons. Topmast shroud to rail passed over swing spreader.

Jib topsail halyard blocks, single sheave—masthead block hooked into eye of stay.

Jib halyard blocks, single sheave—masthead block hooked into eye of stay.

Jumbo halyard blocks, three single-sheave blocks, one on head of sail, one on each trestletree, close to fore-end. Double-ended halyard; jig on port fall, belays on pins in rails.

Jumbo downhaul leads through bow chock rail, starboard side, belays on bow seat. Jib downhill same except is on port side. Jib topsail downhaul same, except is on starboard side. Blocks for downhauls of jib and jib topsail on jibboom are hooked into straps on that spar. Note: it is possible these were lizards (fairleads) rather than blocks. Not clear on model due to damage and an attempt to repair. Note: Jumbo halyard jig on starboard in later years.

SCROLLS, *1885–1921*

Bow

Scroll, "Gertrude Parker"

Scroll, "Arthur D. Story" ex "Mary" 1912

Scroll, Knockabout "Natalie Hammond" 1913

Gammon

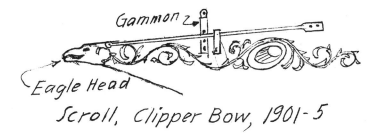

Eagle Head

Scroll, Clipper Bow, 1901-5

Scroll, "L. A. Dunton" 1921

SCROLLS

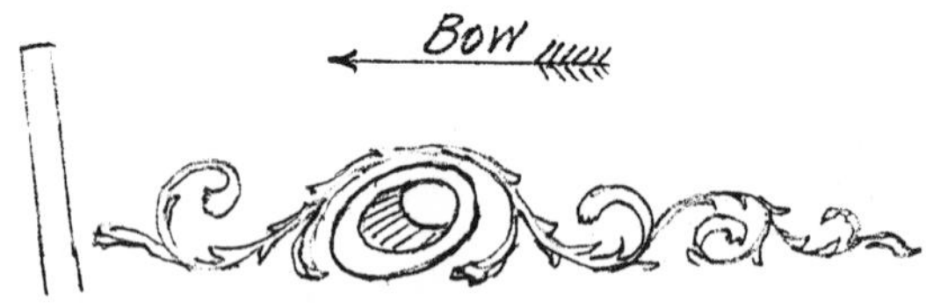
Bow

Scroll, "Ingomar" 1904

Scroll, Knockabout "Gertrude De Costa" 1912

Scroll- "through hawse"

Plumb Stem, on noble wood 1885

See "Bows"

SCUPPERS

Scuppers were usually 4½″ to 5″ long, 1″ to 1⅛″ high. Before the 1880s many schooners had long scuppers running from stanchion-to-stanchion, with each stanchion faced with a block. Pinkies and some schooners had no blocks to face stanchions, the lower edge of the waist being about 1½″ above the plank-sheer for most of its length.

After 1880, or a little earlier, short scuppers were placed on each side of the stanchions from the after stanchion at the fore chain plates to the great beam, a long scupper was placed at foreside of this beam on the main deck. On the quarterdeck, short scuppers were placed on each side of all stanchions, beginning at the afterside of the first stanchion of the quarterdeck

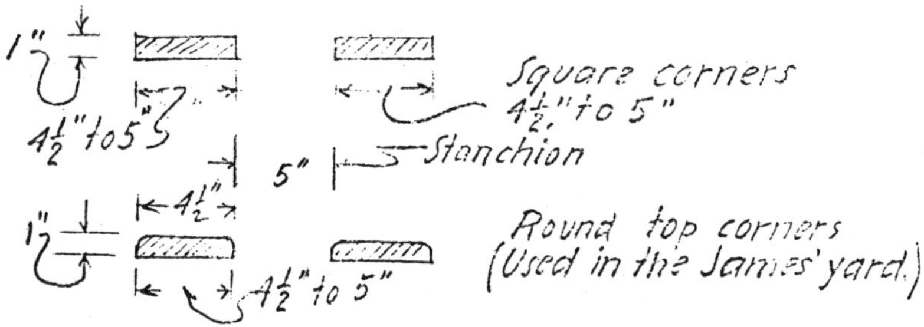
1"
4½" to 5"
Square corners
4½" to 5"
5"
Stanchion
1"
4½"
Round top corners
(Used in the James' yard)
4½" to 5"

at the great beam and running to within 2′ or 3′ of the transom.

About 1900, single short scuppers were used on the quarterdeck, placed on the afterside only, of each stanchion, but a few vessels had them only on the foreside. On the main deck the double scupper at each stanchion, with long scupper at great beam was retained.

There were schooners before 1900 that had scuppers, at the last two or three after stanchions, on the aftersides only. Some vessels had scuppers on the foresides only; these where water would pool in the bays between stanchions. Often, in vessels having scuppers at one side of stanchions, it was necessary to cut additional scuppers after the first trip. This was due to water standing alongside of one or more stanchions.

SEINE BOAT TACKLES

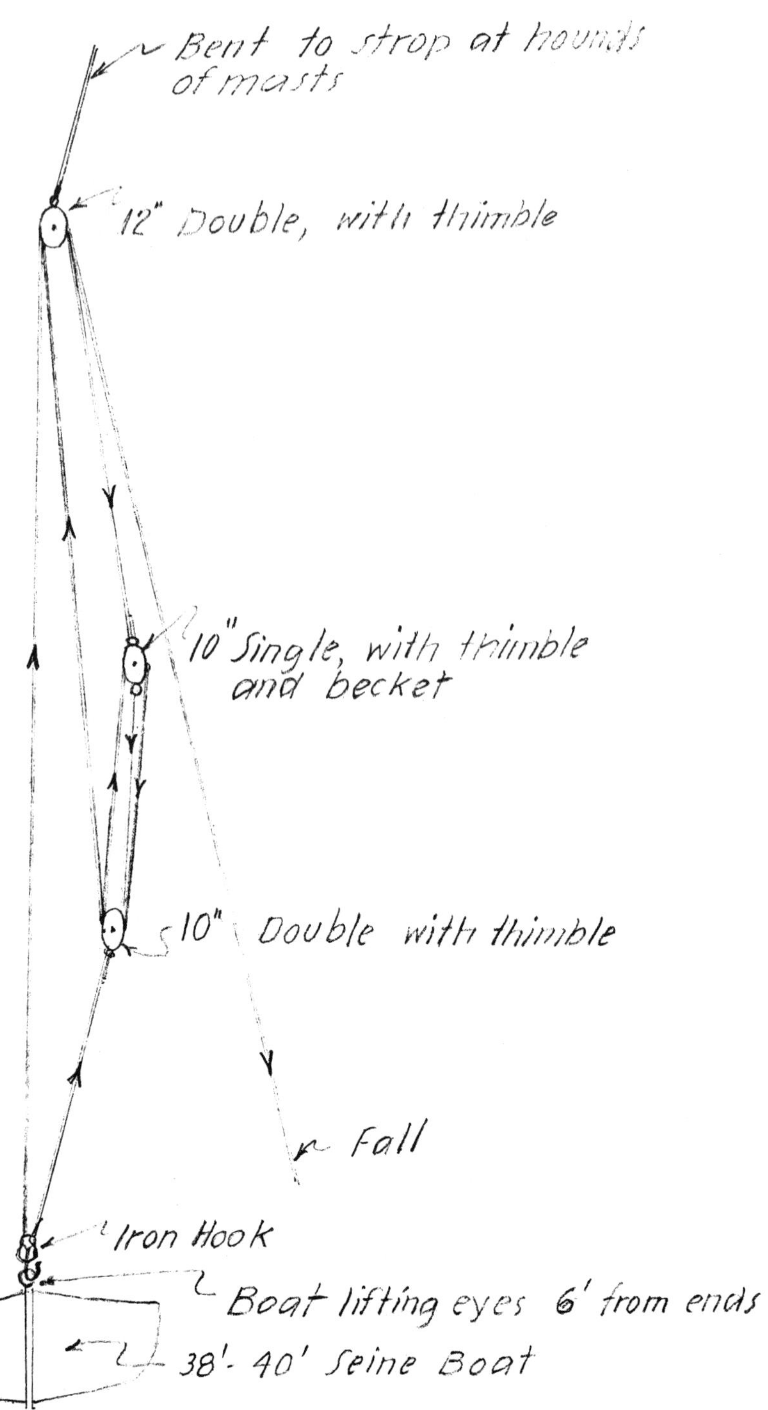
Bent to strop at hounds
of masts
12" Double, with thimble
10" Single, with thimble
and becket
10" Double with thimble
Fall
Iron Hook
Boat lifting eyes 6' from ends
38'-40' Seine Boat

SHACKLES

Though shackles had been developed for blocks and chain before 1885, it was not until about this time that they were introduced into the rigging of fishing schooners. Apparently this was part of the change to wire rope standing rigging and iron-strop blocks. Beginning with the standard shackles, a number of special shackles were developed for fishing schooners. The pin in the shackles used in rigging fishing schooners, was always forelocked or keyed. In the 1900s this took the form of a cotter-pin. Most of these shackles, not part of a block fitting, were made by the ship-smith. This was particularly

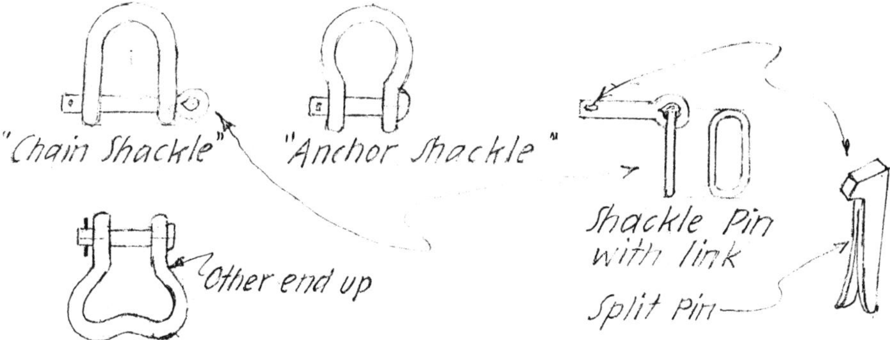
"Chain Shackle"
"Anchor Shackle"
Other end up
Shackle Pin with link
Split Pin
"Heart Shackle" usually large

true of the heart shackles used for the throat halyards, which were very large and strong. Variations in form were therefore common in these large shackles.

SHEER POLES

Sheer poles, of 1″ dia. galv. iron rod, were fitted outside the lower shrouds of each mast. They stand parallel to the rail sheer, just above the upper deadeyes of the shrouds, seized with wire over the deadeye splice and serving. The poles were secured to each of the lower shrouds and the poles were then served and tarred, sheer poles kept deadeyes in line so that they could not turn, standing parallel to the rail. (See "Deadeyes and Lanyards.")

SHROUDS, WIRE ROPE

The lower shrouds were usually three a side on fishing schooners over 70′ reg. length. The forward shroud on each mast, the "swifter," was made with a cut-eye-splice. This eye went over the masthead first, with a leg on each side, the lower ends of which were turned over the upper deadeyes of the foremost shroud on each side. If four lower shrouds were required, the swifters were put on first and last. The shrouds abaft the swifter (fore) were the starboard pair which were cut in one piece, seized to form a loop at the masthead, with the resulting two legs becoming the second and third shrouds on the starboard side. The port second and third shrouds were made the same way and this pair was placed over the masthead last, for the three chain plates.

Shrouds at the mastheads were usually served and canvas-covered down 2 to 4 feet below the underside of the trestletrees. They were spliced and served, tapered up about 14″-16″ above the tops of the upper deadeyes, also the shrouds as they pass around the upper deadeyes were canvas-covered. In most schooners, serving was carried up 13 ratlines on the foremast shrouds.

In most Crowinshield-designed schooners a masthead shroud was rigged. This spliced into two-eye wye at the masthead cap and set up on the aftermost chainplate on the main rail, while the usual topmast shroud came over the long crosstrees and set up on a chain plate at the middle of the four chain plates at the rail. With this rigging there were five chain plates at each side, at each mast. The masthead shroud broke mastheads and went out of fashion after a few years.

With wire rope rigging, the upper deadeyes of all shrouds were spliced in, with hemp rigging they were seized in, using first a throat seizing, followed two or three round seizings. The bitter ends of the hemp shrouds were capped with rawhide, leather, or canvas.

Some schooners had the lower shrouds, three to a side, served and rattled down with ratlines port and starboard on each mast. A few had only one side at each mast rattled down, say on port side at foremast, starboard at mainmast. Ratlines were spaced about 16″ apart. Hemp shrouds were coated with Copenhagen tar. Wire rope shrouds were painted black, or tarred; canvas usually painted white. With wire rope, "wire seizing," of soft iron, was employed. With hemp, "marlin" was used.

The deadeyes used in the masthead shrouds were about the same diameter as those used in the lower shrouds. With hemp rigging the deadeyes were about 1″ to 1½″ greater diameter and 1″ to 1½″ greater thickness than were deadeyes used with wire rope rigging. (See "Ratlines," "Sheer Poles," and "Deadeyes and Lanyards.")

SKYLIGHTS

There was usually one skylight on the cabin trunk, its fore-end was about 3′-0″ from the fore-end of the cabin trunk roof; placed to fit the roof beams, which were spaced about 30″ on centers.

Prior to about 1865, the majority of skylights were about 36″-38″ square, having pitched covers, each with two panes of ¼″ glass, protected by ¼″-⅜″ rods, fore-and-aft. After that date, the box-type skylight became popular. This type had a solid roof, slightly crowned, and vertical sides pierced for two rectangular panes of glass, each (port and starboard). Some vessels had panes in all four sides. Usually the glass was protected by iron rods, sometimes placed fore-and-aft, sometimes placed vertically. If the trunk cabin had opening ports in its sides, the box-type skylight did not usually open for ventilation; otherwise the fore- and after-ends of the box skylight might open outward. In all cases, the box skylight was fitted with corner guards to prevent rigging from fouling the skylight. These guards were ⅜″-½″ iron rods, having pads at the ends, placed at each corner of the top of the box skylight, at 45° to the sides of the top. Their other ends were fastened to the cabin roof, to come on a roof beam. These guards were secured with "stove-bolts," having flat countersunk heads.

In the early 1900s some skylights had the old pitched tops but with fixed, round portlights in the covers, requiring neither glass nor corner guards. These had rather low sides.

SKYLIGHTS

Skylights were usually fitted with canvas covers secured with snap buttons, or in ealier times, with draw-strings.

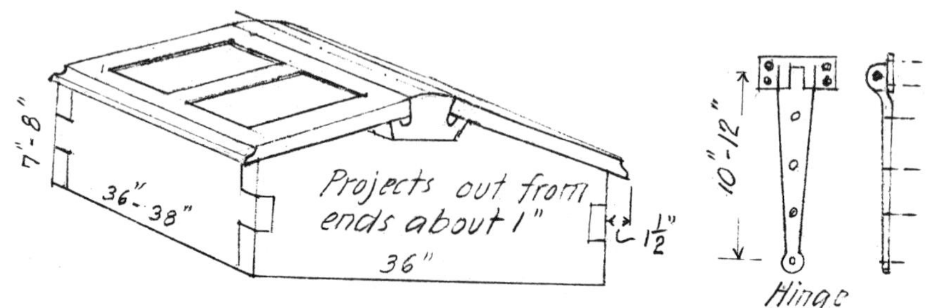
7"-8"
36"-38"
Projects out from ends about 1"
36"
1 1/2"
10"-12"
Hinge

Pitch-covers skylight, 1850-1885
Glass guards not shown

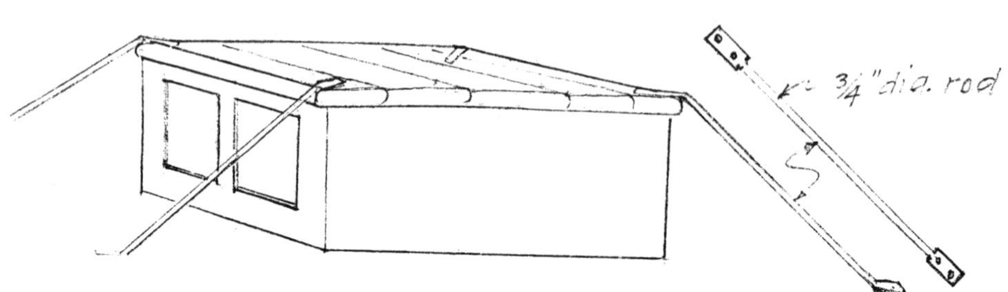
3/4" dia. rod

Box skylight with rigging guards
Glass guards not shown

SKYLIGHTS

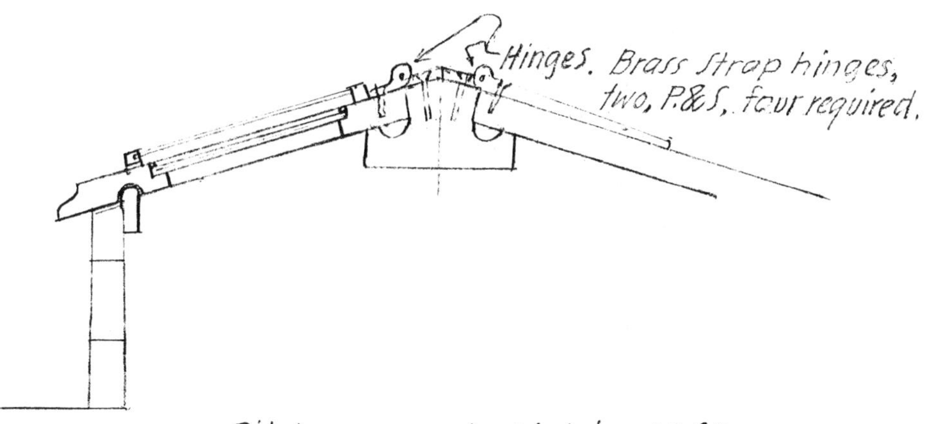
Hinges. Brass strap hinges,
two, P.&S., four required.

Pitch cover skylight 1883
As described by John Prince Story

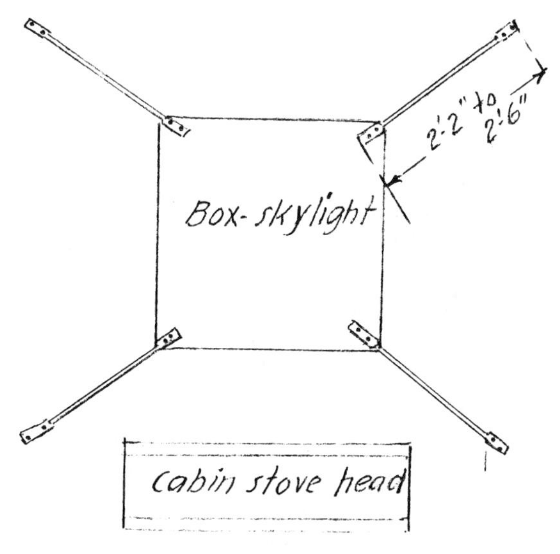
2'2" to 2'6"
Box-skylight
cabin stove head

Rigging Guards,
box skylight

SNATCH BLOCK

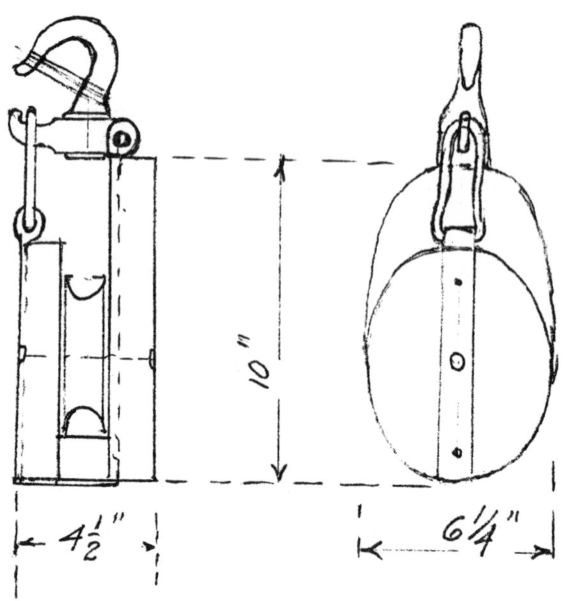
10"
4½"
6¼"

For 1¼" dia. rope.

Not usually fitted until haisting engines came into use. Placed alongside the pinrails in eyebolts.

A more primitive snatch block without lock; with the hook on long shell; was the most common type used.

SNATCH CLEATS OR CHOCKS

Most vessels used snatch cleats on rail stanchions and on mast bitts; some had these on the fore mast, under the pin collar. These were 9"–12" long, 3" x 4", shaped as shown below. The snatch cleats served as snatch hooks and as fairleads, in leading tackle falls to cleats on the bulwark stanchions belays. Mast bitt snatch cleats, and some on bulwark stanchions, served as sway hooks. Sheaves appear to have been used only when snatch cleats served as chocks under the foremast belaying pin collar.

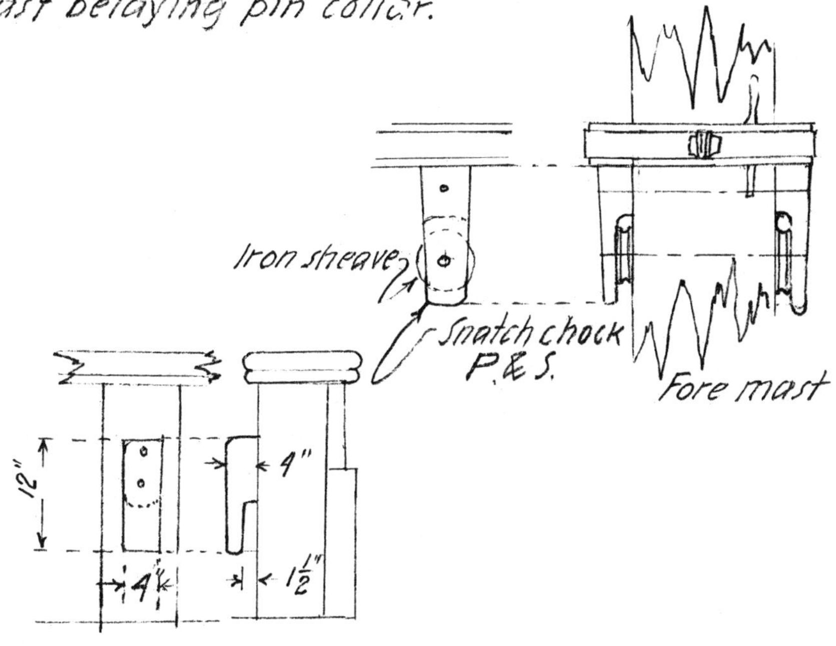
Iron sheave
Snatch chock P.& S.
Fore mast
12"
4"
4"
1½"

Rail Stanchion snatch cleats, oak

SPAR DIMENSIONS

"Grampus," length, overall 90′; length LWL 81′-6′; beam extreme, at deck, 22′-3″; beam LWL, 22′-9″; depth, from top of keel to top of main deck beam, 11′-1″; height of great beam 9″; height of bulwarks, deck to top of rail, 26″; height of cabin trunk 27½″; length of cabin trunk 15′; width of cabin trunk, fore-end, 14′-7″; after-end, 12′-6″. Net. Reg. Tonnage, 83.30 Tons. Launched 23 March, 1886.

SPAR	LENGTH	DIA.
Mainmast, deck to hounds	55′-1″	19″
Mainmast head	7′-6″	——
Main-topmast above cap	28′-6″	9″
Foremast, deck to hounds	52′-11″	19″
Foremast, head	8′-0″	——
Fore-topmast above cap	26′-0″	9″
Bowsprit outside stem	19′-0″	21″ square
Jibboom outside cap	17′-3″	9¾″
Jibboon cap to flying jibstay hole	11′-6″	——
Mainboom	58′-0″	13″
Main gaff	28′-6″	7¼″
Foreboom	23′-10″	7″
Fore gaff	24′-0″	6¼″
Swinging boat booms	20′-0″	——

Masts and bowsprit white pine, others spruce.
In 1888 the mainboom was of Oregon pine, 59′-0″, 11½″ dia.
Bowsprit square at knightheads, 15″ dia. at cap.
Main gaff in 1887, was 30′ long.
Stick lengths not given.
33′ overall seine boat, 7′-2″ beam outside plank; and 2′-6″ depth, top of keel to top of gunwale Chain cables, 1″ Admiralty, two strings, 60 fathoms each. Anchor: Two 700 lbs., Third 500 lbs., iron-stocked kedge 200 lbs.

SPECTACLE IRONS

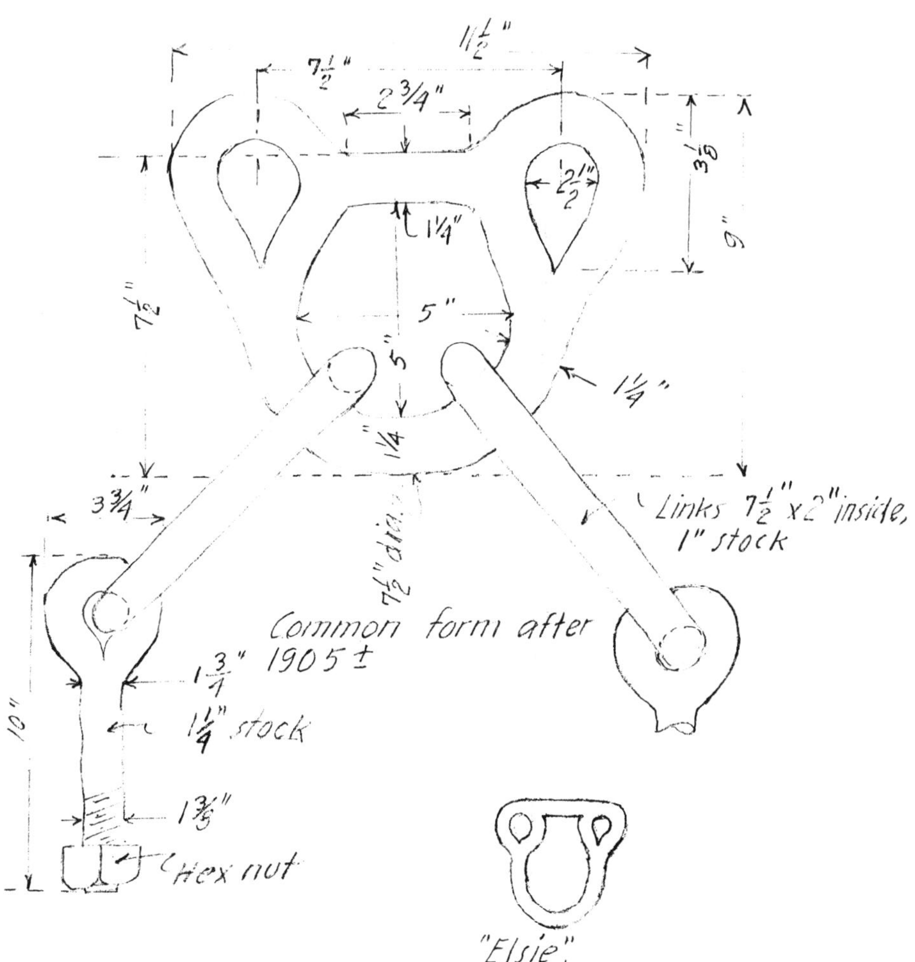
Links 7½" x 2" inside, 1" stock
Common form after 1905 ±
1¼" stock
Hex nut
"Elsie"

A number of other variations were found. See "Gaff, Throat Halyards Ironwork"

STACKS OR "HEADS"
CABIN AND GALLEY STOVES

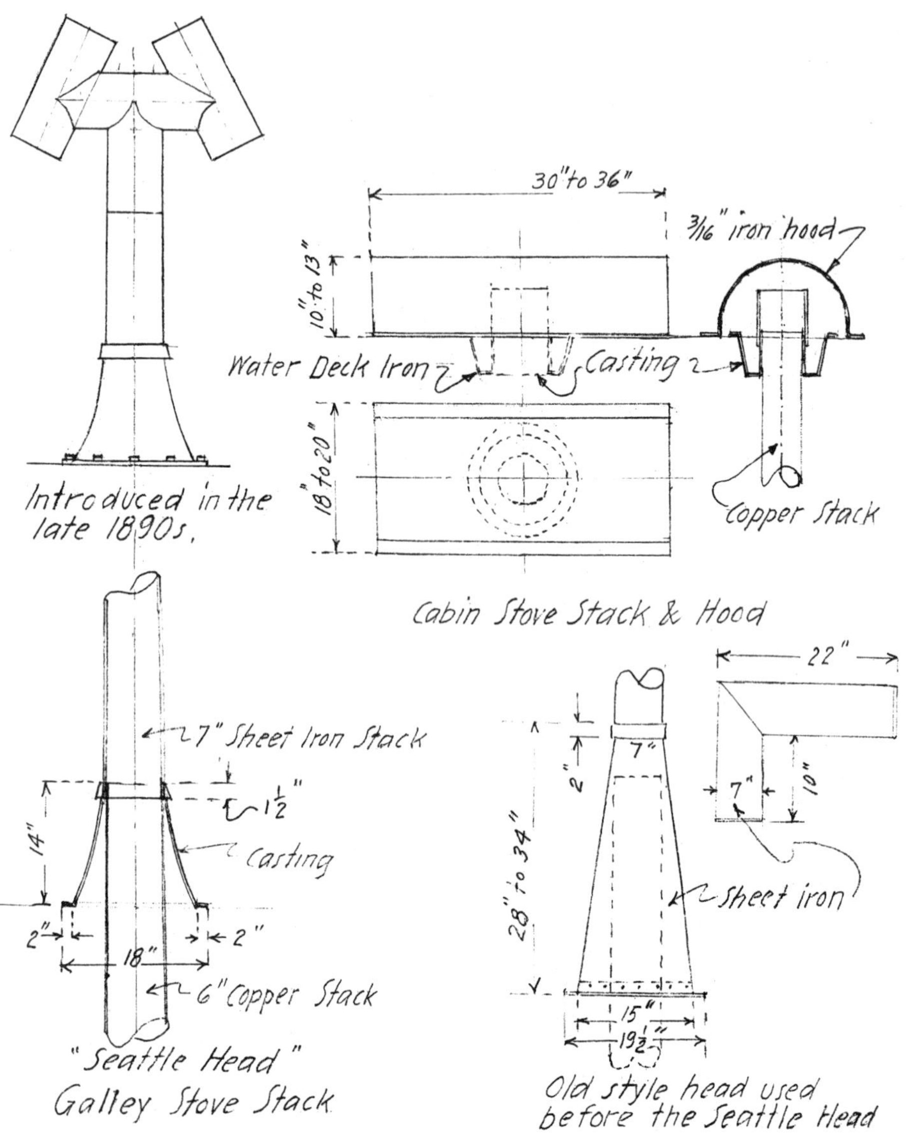

Introduced in the late 1890s.
30" to 36"
3/16" iron hood
10" to 13"
Water Deck Iron
Casting
18" to 20"
Copper Stack
Cabin Stove Stack & Hood
7" Sheet Iron Stack
1½"
14"
Casting
2"
2"
18"
6" Copper Stack
"Seattle Head"
Galley Stove Stack
22"
7"
10"
7"
2"
28" to 34"
Sheet iron
15"
19½"
Old style head used before the Seattle Head

STACK (GALLEY)

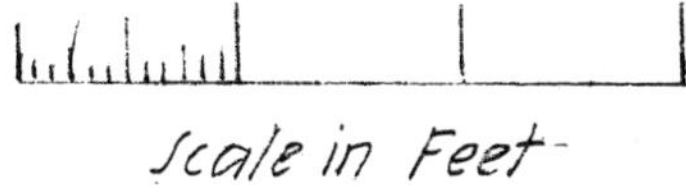
Scale in Feet

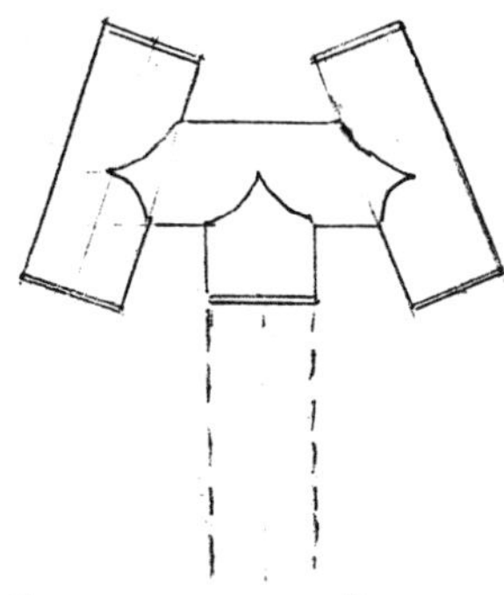

"Thebaud's" Head
Latest pattern

The total height of the galley stack must allow the foreboom to clear the stack by about 15" to 18" when the boom was squared off.

In the old head the iron-plate base came up to about 28" above the deck in some photographs taken in the late 1880s, but were near 34" earlier.

Where the stacks went through the main deck the space between casting and stove chimney was open, but in the cabin trunk it was closed by the water deck ring. For some unknown reason the stack was commonly to starboard. But, as was also true of the compass, this was not a hard and fast rule. A few of the large schooners had galley stacks P.&S, having two stoves in the galley.

STANCHIONS, RAIL (FITTINGS)

Stanchions numbered from forward aft, beginning at some stated point.
"Philip P. Manta": 6″ x 6″ at deck, 5½″ x 5½″ at rail. Stanchion No. 1, about 14″ abaft ℄ of hawse casting measured on hull ℄. All "cleats" are wooden.

1. abaft hawse
3. snatch cleat, anchor davit just abaft. See notes
4. between #3 and #4, staple and bow chock above # 4
6. eye in rail, between #6 and #7,
7. ringbolt for shank painter
9. wooden cleat
10. snatch cleat

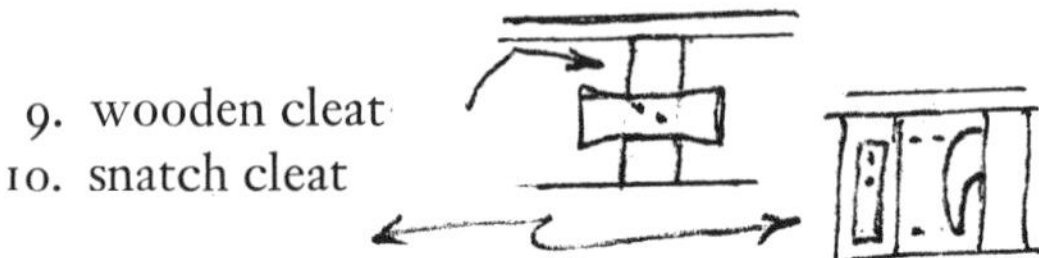

11. #10, #11, and #12 fore chain plates, a little off
12. stanchions
14. ringbolt
17. ringbolt
19. ringbolt, starboard, 5″ abaft great beam, port missing?
20. snatch cleat
21. ringbolt
22. snatch cleat
23. main chain plates, #23, #24 and #25
24. chain plates are not on stanchions. Heels
25. seem to be on top timbers of frames
27. ringbolt
33. ringbolt
34. fair lead cleat, hole instead of slot
37. cleat or cavel
39. cleat
40. cleat
41. large ringbolt 3″ inside dia. for crotch tackles or chains

stanchion

Large ringbolts in transom ceiling, 12″ inside bulwarks. 3″ inside dia. for preventers.

Notes: No. 3 stanchion has cleat on foreside, snatch cleat on inboard side. Davit heel plate on plank-sheer just abaft No. 3 stanchion. Staple in plate on top of bow chock just clear of after edge of stanchion No. 3. Iron warping chock on top of bow chock rail over stanchion No. 2. Cleats and snatches are halfway up stanchions, more or less.

Purposes of some fittings could be understood only if vessels could have been fully rigged and fitted.

Note: Cleat on fore-side stanchion No. 3 for cat stopper. Staple in plate on bow chock for foreboom tackle pendant, also for seine boat towing boom.

"Elsie": Numbers omitted in list were stanchions without fittings

No. 1. stanchion on top of great beam, going aft
No. 8. snatch
No. 9. ringbolt
No. 10. cavel or cleat
No. 11. snatch
No. 12. cavel
No. 17. ringbolt
No. 20. snatch
No. 22. cavel
No. 23. snatch
No. 24. cavel, wood fairlead over #24, on main rail inside monkey rail
No. 25. 3″ i.d. ringbolt
great beam, going forward.
Top of great beam is stanchion #0
No. 2. ringbolt, 1st stanchion on main deck.
No. 7. cavel, raised for'd, lowered aft, at a slant
No. 8. ringbolt
No. 11. ringbolt
No. 14. snatch, fore chain plate
No. 15. snatch, fore chain plate
No. 18. cavel—two fairleads over
No. 20. ringbolt
No. 24. cleat, anchor davits
No. 29. first hawse timber.

Knockabout "Ethel Penny"
No. 1. is first stanchion abaft hawse
No. 5. cavel
No. 9. ringbolt
No. 13. cavel
No. 15. eyebolt
No. 17. cavel, 18″ long
No. 18. 12″ snatch
No. 23. ringbolt
No. 27. ringbolt
No. 29. great beam
No. 35. ringbolt
No. 52. ringbolt
(The above list is not complete, some cavels were missing.)

"Rhodora," knockabout:
Stanchion No. 1—after-end hawse timbers.
Stanchions not numbered had no fittings.

No. 7. snatch
No. 8. staple, in chockrail, 7″ aft ℄ of No. 8.
No. 11. ringbolt, fairlead in rail cap over
No. 12. cavel
No. 13. Fair lead in rail cap between 12 & 13
No. 14. cavel, fairlead in rail cap 6″ for'd of ℄ of 14
No. 15. cavel
No. 16. eyebolt in rail cap over
No. 17. eyebolt in rail cap over
No. 18. snatch
No. 21. ringbolt
No. 23. ringbolt
No. 27. ringbolt
No. 28. ringbolt
No. 29. is on great beam (quarterdeck)
No. 30. snatch
No. 31. eyebolt in rail cap, 6″ forward of ℄ of 31
No. 34. staple in rail cap 12″ forward of ℄ of 34
No. 36. ringbolt
No. 39. ringbolt
No. 48. snatch
No. 51. ringbolt
No. 54. ringbolt, fair lead in main rail cap, inside monkey rail, 18″ aft of 54.

In most knockabouts the anchor davits were placed opposite the foremost post of the jumbo boom gallows. Fore-ends of pads are about opposite fore side of windlass barrel.

STAPLE BOLTS

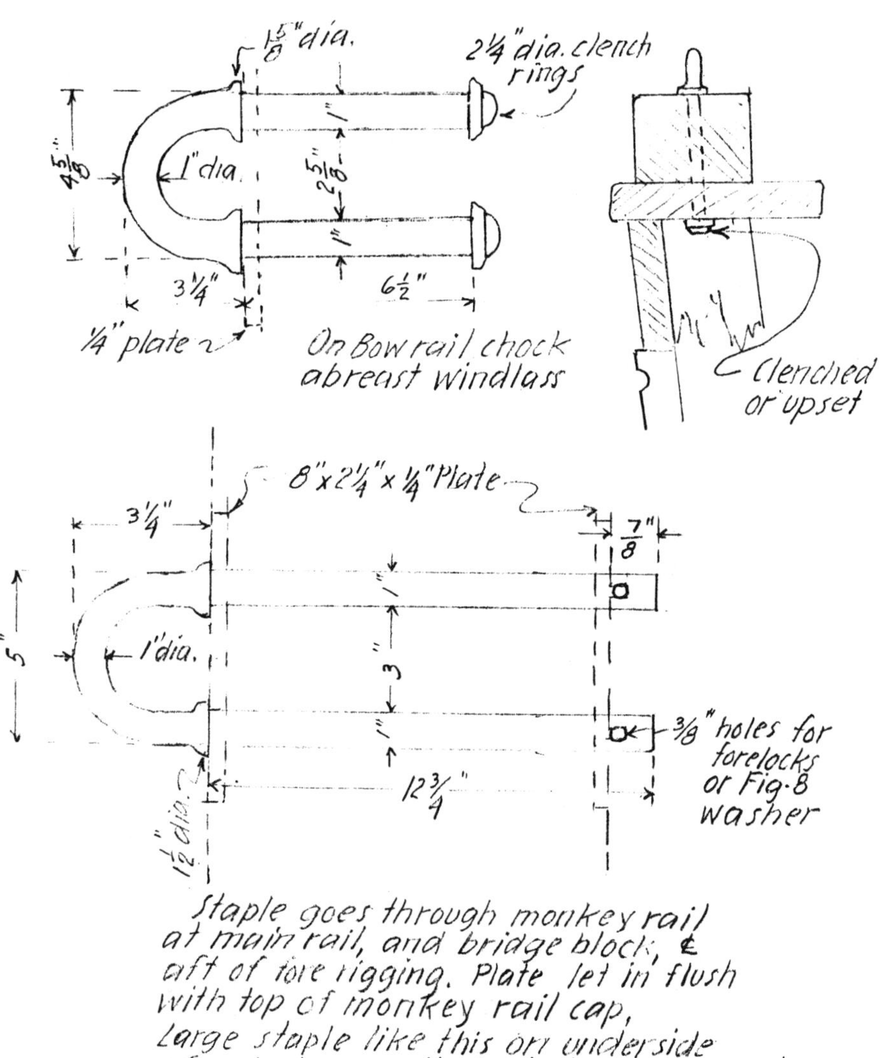
1 5/8" dia.
2¼" dia. clench rings
4 5/8"
1" dia.
1"
2 5/8"
1"
3¼"
6½"
¼" plate
On Bow rail chock abreast windlass
Clenched or upset
8" x 2¼" x ¼" Plate
3¼"
7/8"
5"
1" dia.
1"
3"
1"
3/8" holes for forelocks or Fig. 8 washer
12 3/4"
1½" dia.

Staple goes through monkey rail at main rail, and bridge block, ℄ aft of fore rigging. Plate let in flush with top of monkey rail cap, Large staple like this on underside of pole bowsprit for bobstay, (inner).

STAY LINK, MAIN-TOPMAST

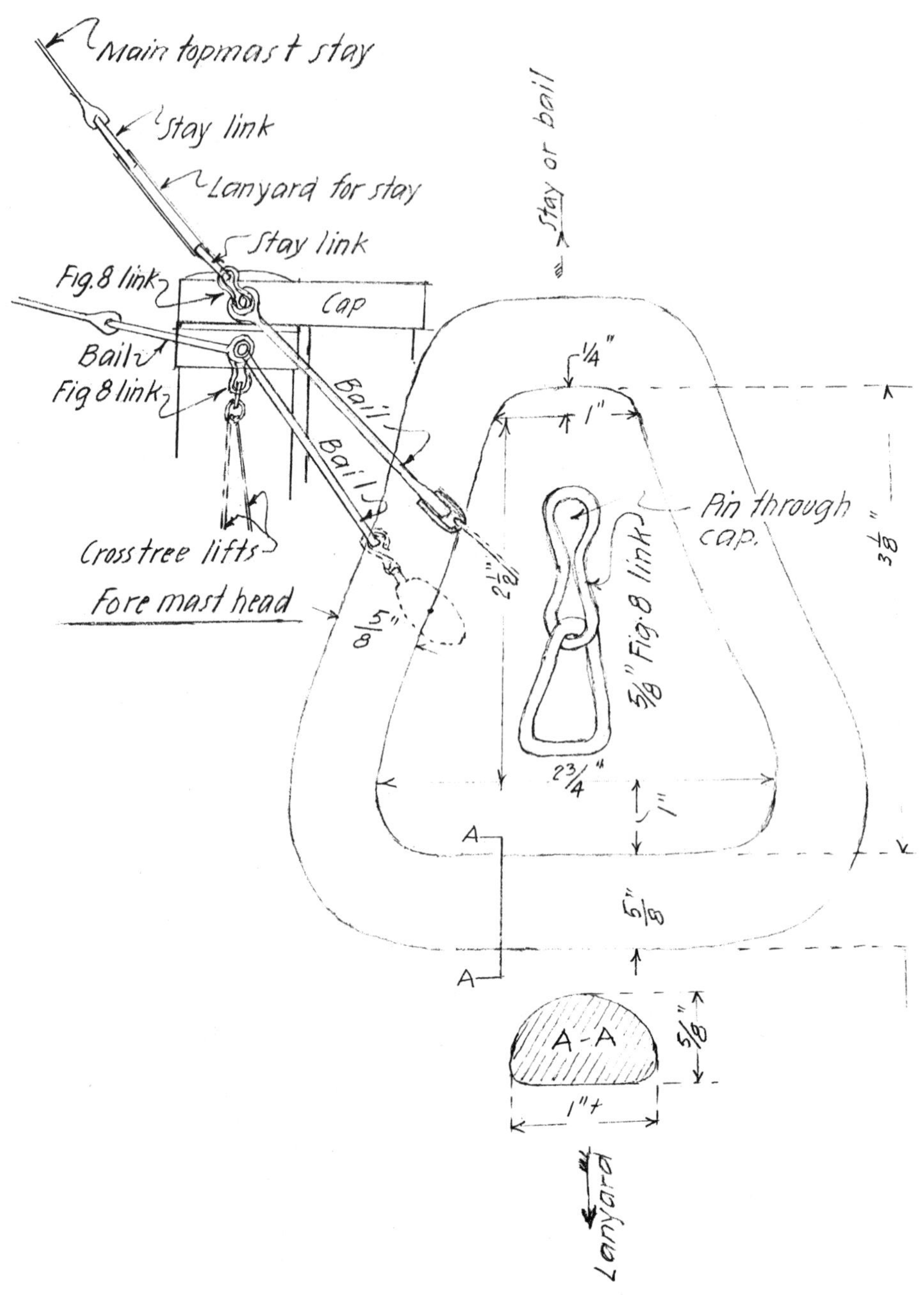
Main topmast stay
Stay link
Lanyard for stay
Stay link
Fig.8 link
Cap
Bail
Fig 8 link
Bail
Bail
Crosstree lifts
Fore mast head
Stay or bail
1/4"
1"
Pin through cap.
5/8" Fig.8 link
3 1/8"
2 1/8"
5/8"
2 3/4"
1"
5/8"
A
A
A-A
5/8"
1"+
Lanyard

STAYS
MAIN-TOPMAST STAY, SPRING STAY ("TRIATIC"), COUNTERSTAY ("PULL-BACK")

Main-topmast stay, eye-spliced at main-topmast shoulder, secured at foremast cap by eye-splice and thimble, lanyard links and lanyard, Fig. 8 link, on starboard side of foremast head, outside of the jibstay bail and underneath of head of pin through bail and cap. Pin went through masthead from starboard. Lanyard link and Fig. 8 link used to be on starboard side of main cap also, for the fore-topmast counterstay. Dropped from main cap in 1910–1920, counterstay lanyards were setup to a lanyard link in the thimble in the after-end of spring stay at bail. Stays having eye-splices in ends had thimbles in the eyes. Stay served at eye-splices for a foot or two. In the old vessels with hemp rigging the stays were eye-spliced at one end, seized at the other. The counterstay, when it first came into use was seized at mainmast cap end. Counterstays probably came into use at Gloucester in the 1840s, but this date is no more than approximate. [Bosley, Roberts.]

STEERING GEARS
(NOTES)

Tiller-steering was employed in New England fishing schooners, from colonial times until about 1845–1850. When the average size of these vessels increased in this period, a more powerful means of steering was required. For a short period, after 1850, the rope-drum and wheel, mounted on standards set on deck, was used. The tiller was short and only a few inches above the deck, abaft the drum. It was operated by tackles from the drum. This gear was the same that was used on large sailing vessels of this period. The "shincracker" gear—in which the steering-wheel drum and standards were mounted on the tiller, and travelled with it—does not seem to have been used except in pinkies and in some vessels built in Maine and on Buzzards Bay, Massachusetts, in the 1840s.

Geared steering, employing a geared quadrant on the rudderstock and a pinion on the steering wheel, had been introduced in England as early as 1794 and in the United States in 1800–1810. In 1829 U.S. Revenue Service schooners were fitted with such gears. By 1865–1870 many patents gears of this type were in use, such as "Jackson's Patent Screw Steering Apparatus" and "Van Deuzen's Patent Yielding Steering Apparatus." A few of these gears were fitted at Essex but it was thought that gears of this type were too weak and some too expensive. These gears did break teeth when under strain but this was eventually cured. However the quadrant-and-pinion steering gear was considered fit for small or light-displacement vessels, only.

The standard screw-steering gears of the New England fishing schooners came into being in the 1850s, and by 1885 three manufacturers were producing gears. These were the A. P. Stoddart and Co. and the N. Richardson Sons, both of Gloucester, and the Edson Manufacturing Company of Boston. The Edson Manufacturing Company, now at New Bedford, is the sole survivor. These gears had many variations in design, to fit the shipbuilders' needs. Edson and Richardson had gears that allowed the steering wheel to stand at a lesser angle than the rudder post when, in the early 1890s, many schooners were designed with sharply raking sternposts.

Wooden steering wheels were employed in Essex-built schooners until after 1865; since then the wheels were of galvanized iron, with wooden handgrips. The iron wheels proved stronger and more lasting, under fishing schooners' working conditions, than the more ornamental wooden wheels. The rim diameters of iron steering wheels were usually 30″ to 36″; or about 42″ to 48″ diameter over the grips in schooners over 65′ tonnage length. Iron steering wheels were introduced at Gloucester sometime about 1858–1865, apparently.

STEERING GEAR (WHEELBOXES)

The construction of the steering-gear wheelbox was controlled by the type and make of steering gear. In general, the fore-end of the wheelbox sloped or raked aft so as to parallel the ℄ of the rudderpost. In the 1890s, when the rake of the post was very great, the swivel-head fittings allowed the wheel to have less rake than the rudderpost, as has been noted. The screws of the steering gear could be forward of, or abaft, the rudderstock or post. The fore-end of the wheelbox at deck was usually 4′ to 5′ abaft the after-end of the cabin trunk and was 2′-9″ to 3′ high, measured on the rake. The after end of the wheelbox was from 2′ to 2′-3″ above the deck. The top of the wheelbox was 3′-6″ to 4′ long and 2′-4″ wide. On a schooner having a rudderstock 10″ in diameter, the fore-end of the wheelbox at deck was 14″ to 16″ forward of the ℄ of the stock.

The sides and ends of the wheelbox were of 3″ white pine, edge-bolted to deck beams and rudder port carlins. In old, short-counter vessels the after-end of the wheelbox was often on the main taffrail, or nearly flush with it. The top of the wheelbox had a framed cover, held in place by a steel strap, 1½″-1¾″ wide, ¼″ thick, as shown in the sketches.

STEERING GEARS (WHEELBOXES)

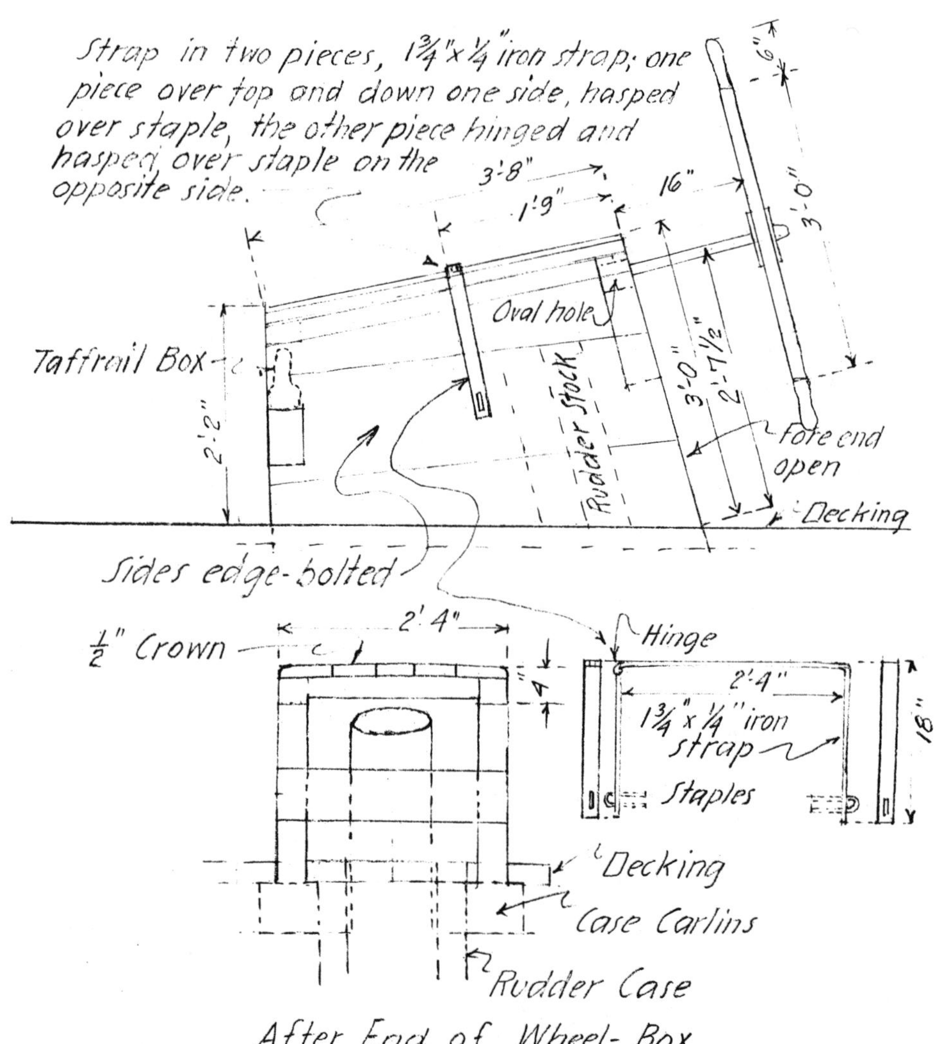
Strap in two pieces, 1¾"x¼" iron strap; one piece over top and down one side, hasped over staple, the other piece hinged and hasped over staple on the opposite side.
3'-8"
1'-9"
16"
6"
3'-0"
Oval hole
Taffrail Box
2'-2"
Rudder Stock
3'-0"
2'-7½"
Fore end open
Decking
Sides edge-bolted
2'-4"
½" Crown
4"
Hinge
2'-4"
1¾" x ¼" iron strap
18"
Staples
Decking
Case Carlins
Rudder Case

After End of Wheel-Box.

STEERING GEARS (WHEELBOXES)

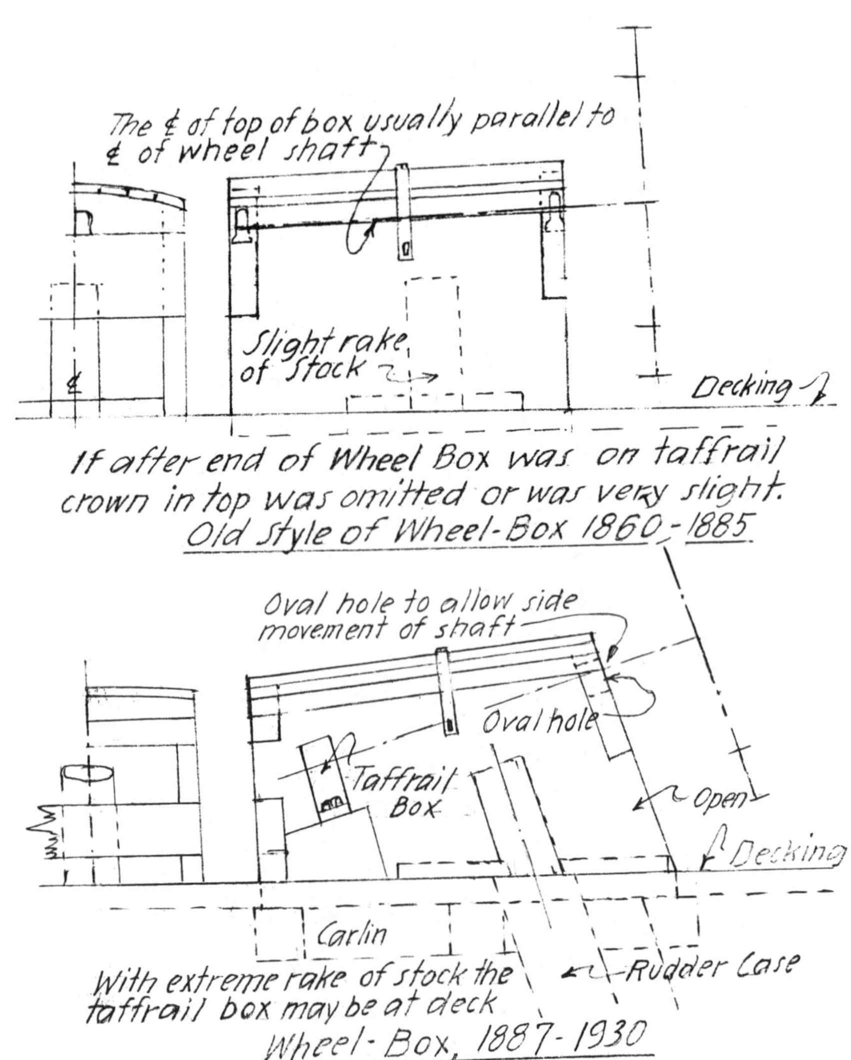

The ¢ of top of box usually parallel to ¢ of wheel shaft
Slight rake of Stock
Decking
If after end of Wheel Box was on taffrail crown in top was omitted or was very slight.
Old Style of Wheel-Box 1860-1885
Oval hole to allow side movement of shaft
Oval hole
Taffrail Box
Open
Decking
Carlin
Rudder Case
With extreme rake of stock the taffrail box may be at deck
Wheel-Box, 1887-1930

STEERING GEARS (WHEELS)

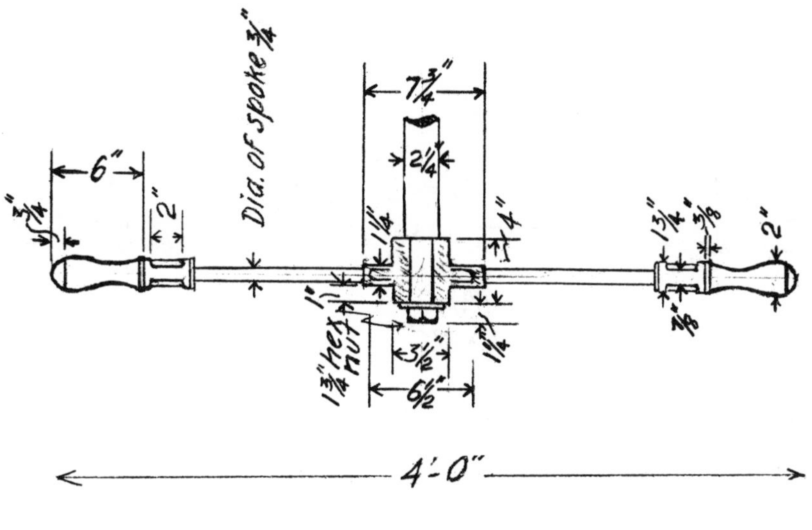
Dia. of spoke 3/4
6"
2"
3/4"
7 3/4"
2 1/4
1 1/4"
4"
1"
1 3/4" hex nut
3 1/2"
6 1/2"
1 1/4"
1 3/4"
3/8
2"
1/8"
4'-0"

Wheel of "Arthur D. Story"

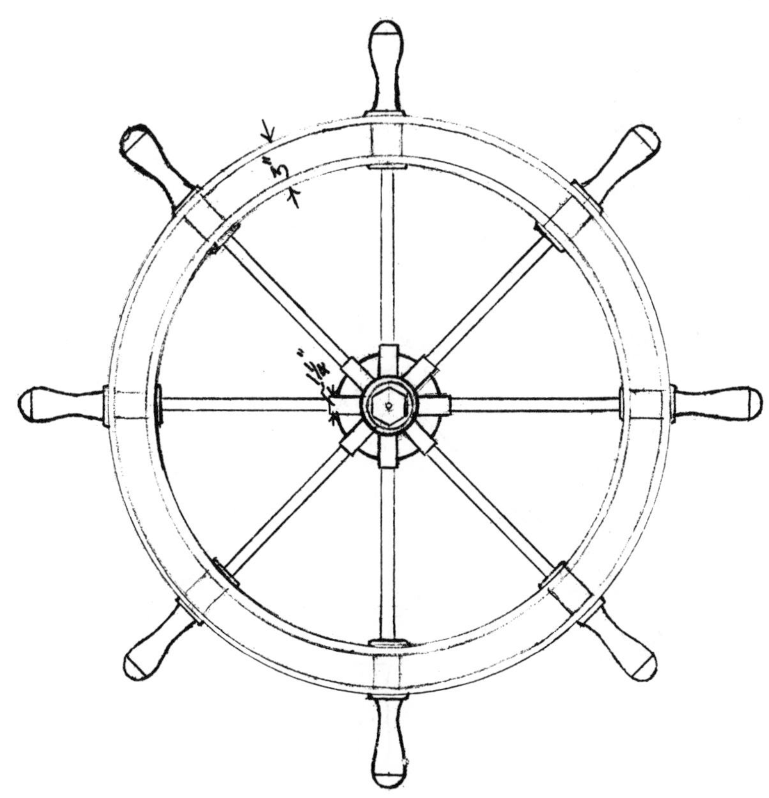
3"
1 1/4"

STEERING GEARS (WHEELS)

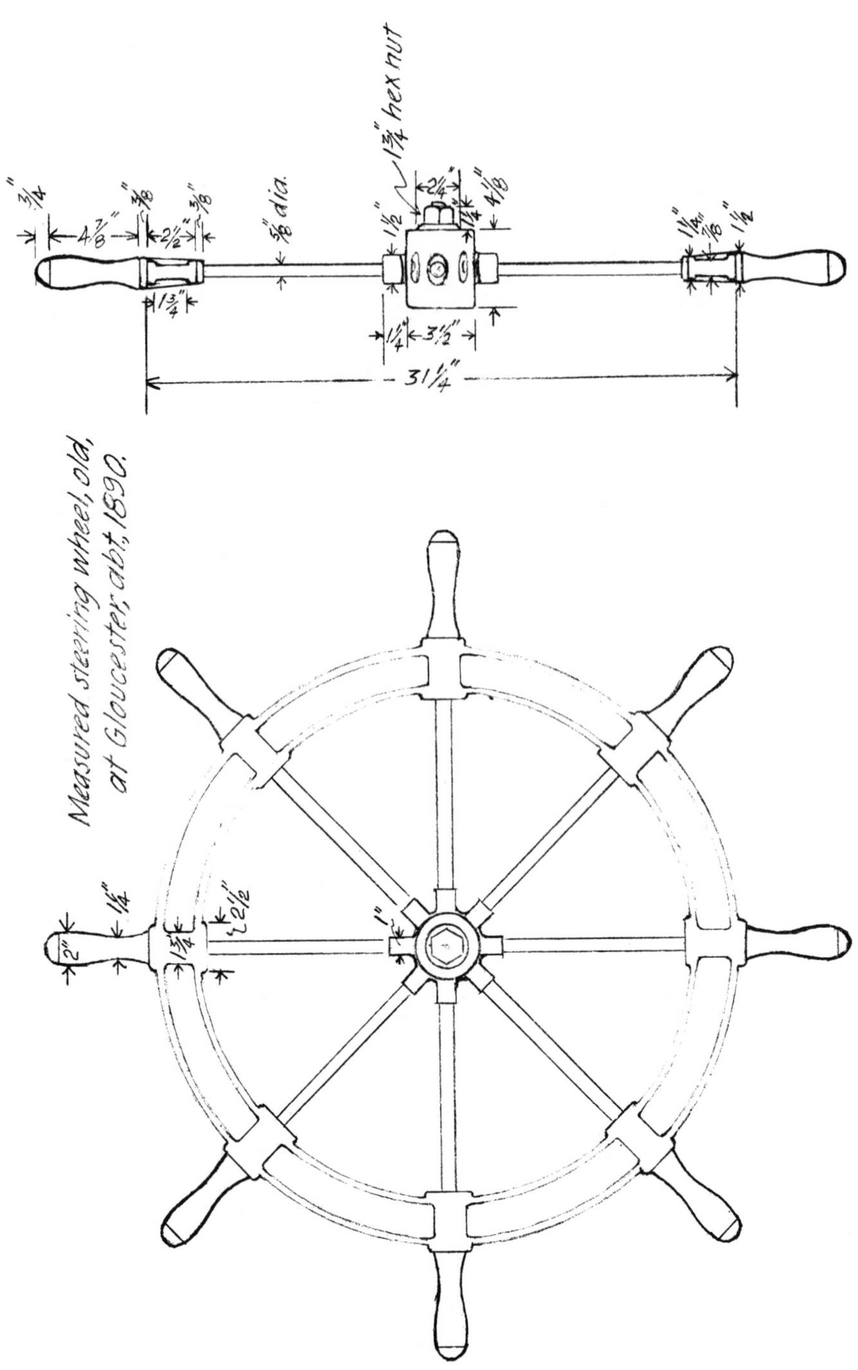
1¾" hex nut
5/8" dia.
2¼"
4⅞"
2½"
1¾"
1½"
1¼"
3½"
31¼"
Measured steering wheel, old,
at Gloucester, abt. 1890.
2"
1"

STEERING GEARS

L. ROBINSON STEERERS.

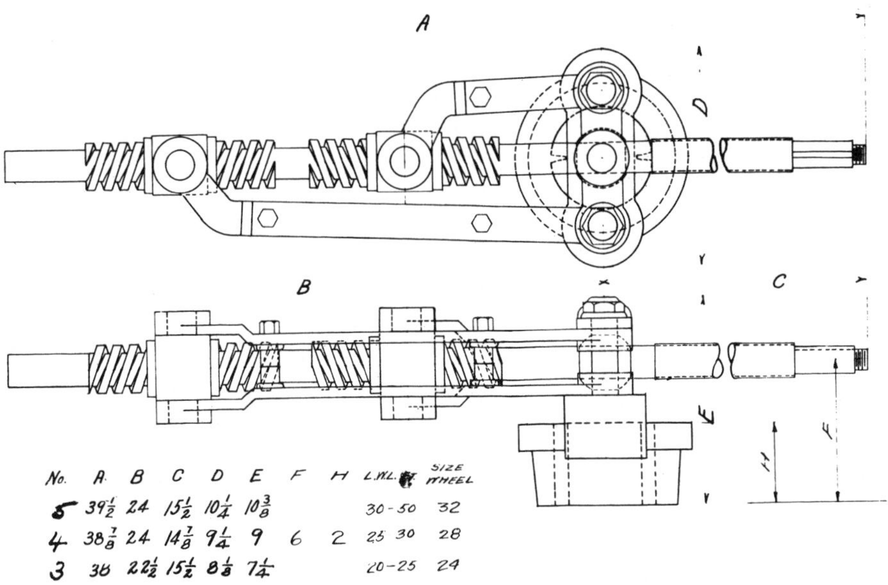
A
D
B
C
E
F
H

No.	A.	B	C	D	E	F	H	L.W.L. FT.	SIZE WHEEL
5	39½	24	15½	10¼	10⅜			30-50	32
4	38⅞	24	14⅞	9¼	9	6	2	25 30	28
3	38	22½	15½	8⅛	7¼			20-25	24

H = DISTANCE RUDDER POST PROJECTS INTO HUB

EDSON IMPROVED PATENT ROBINSON STEERER
With Split Rudder Head Hoops.

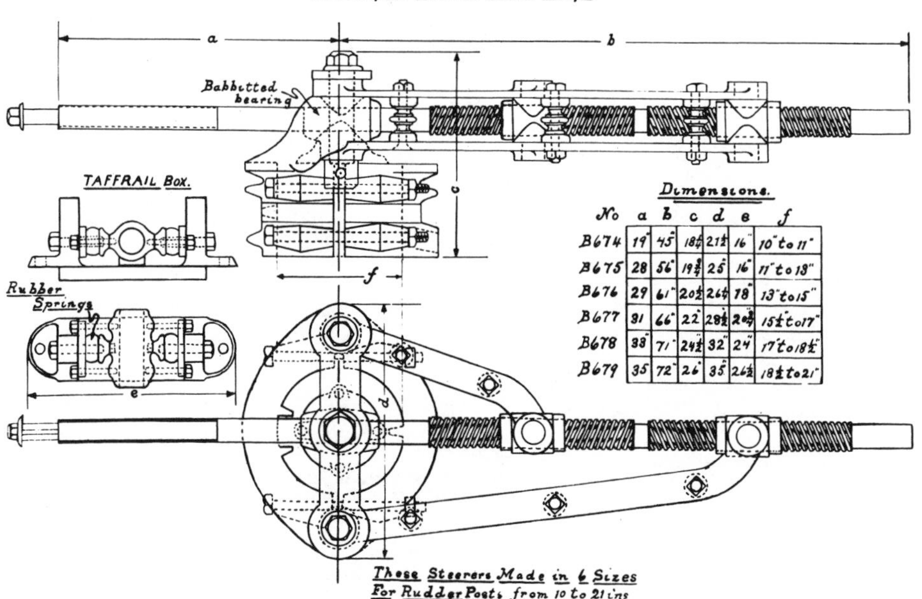
a
b
Babbitted bearing
c
TAFFRAIL BOX.
Rubber Springs
f
e
d

Dimensions.

No	a	b	c	d	e	f
B674	19"	45"	18¼	21½	16"	10" to 11"
B675	28	56"	19¾	25"	16"	11" to 13"
B676	29	61"	20½	26¼	18"	13" to 15"
B677	31	66"	22"	28½	20¾	15½" to 17"
B678	33"	71"	24½	32"	24"	17" to 18½"
B679	35	72"	26"	35"	26½	18½ to 21"

These Steerers Made in 6 Sizes
For Rudder Posts from 10 to 21 ins

STEERING GEARS

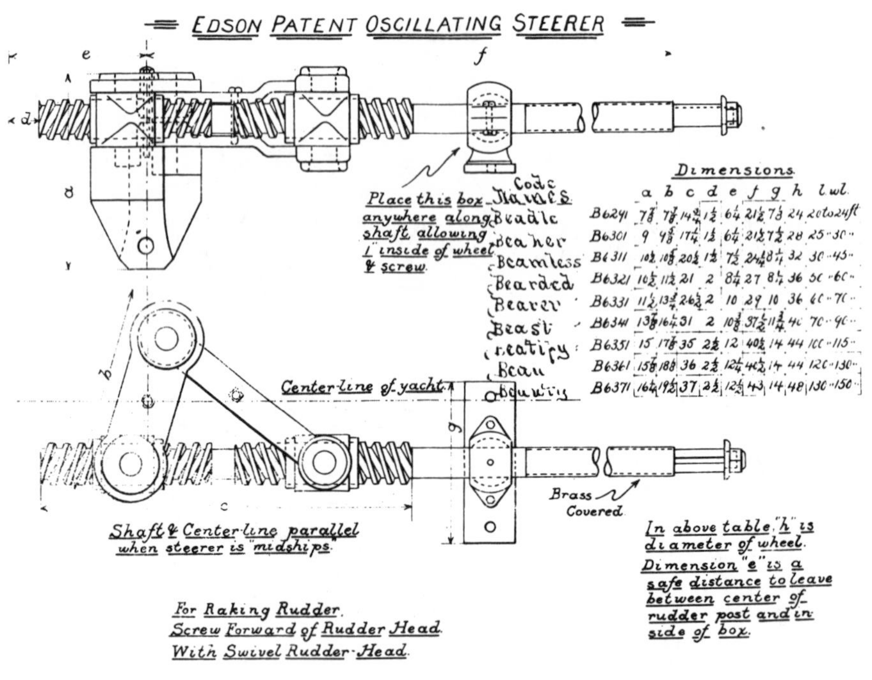
EDSON PATENT OSCILLATING STEERER
Place this box anywhere along shaft allowing 1" inside of wheel & screw.
Center-line of yacht.
Brass Covered.
Shaft & Center-line parallel when steerer is "midships".
In above table "h" is diameter of wheel.
Dimension "e" is a safe distance to leave between center of rudder post and inside of box.
For Raking Rudder.
Screw Forward of Rudder Head.
With Swivel Rudder-Head.

Dimensions

Code Names		a	b	c	d	e	f	g	h	l.w.l.
Beadle	B6241	7 7/8	7 7/8	14 3/4	1 1/2	6 1/4	21 1/2	7 3/8	24	20 to 24 ft
Beaker	B6301	9	4 5/8	17 1/4	1 1/2	6 1/4	21 1/2	7 1/2	28	25 " 30 "
Beamless	B6311	10 1/2	10 5/8	20 1/2	1 1/2	7 1/2	24 1/4	8 1/4	32	30 " 45 "
Bearded	B6321	10 1/2	11 1/2	21	2	8 1/4	27	8 1/4	36	50 " 60 "
Bearer	B6331	11 1/2	13 3/4	26 1/2	2	10	29	10	36	60 " 70 "
Beast	B6341	13 7/8	16 1/4	31	2	10 3/8	37 1/2	11 3/4	40	70 " 90 "
Beatify	B6351	15	17 7/8	35	2 1/2	12	40 1/2	14	44	100 " 115 "
Beau	B6361	15 7/8	18 3/8	36	2 1/2	12 1/4	40 1/2	14	44	120 " 130 "
Beauty	B6371	16 1/4	19 1/2	37	2 1/2	12 1/2	43	14	48	130 " 150 "

EDSON PATENT OSCILLATING STEERER

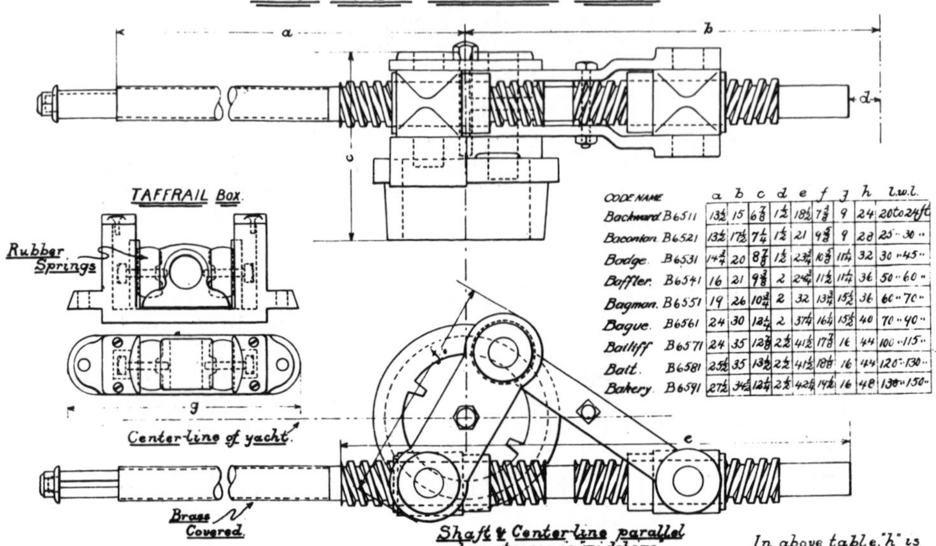
TAFFRAIL Box.
Rubber Springs
Center-line of yacht.
Brass Covered.
Shaft & Center-line parallel when steerer is "midships".

CODE NAME		a	b	c	d	e	f	g	h	l.w.l.
Backward	B6511	13 1/2	15	6 7/8	1 1/2	18 1/2	7 3/8	9	24	20 to 24 ft
Baconian	B6521	13 1/2	17 1/2	7 1/4	1 1/2	21	9 5/8	9	28	25 " 30 "
Badge	B6531	14 3/4	20	8 7/8	1 1/2	23 3/4	10 5/8	11 1/4	32	30 " 45 "
Baffler	B6541	16	21	9 3/8	2	24 3/4	11 1/2	11 1/4	36	50 " 60 "
Bagman	B6551	19	26	10 3/4	2	32	13 3/4	15 1/2	36	60 " 70 "
Bague	B6561	24	30	12 1/4	2	37 1/4	16 1/4	15 1/2	40	70 " 90 "
Bailiff	B6571	24	35	12 7/8	2 1/2	41 1/2	17 7/8	16	44	100 " 115 "
Bait	B6581	25 1/2	35	13 1/2	2 1/2	41 1/2	18 1/8	16	44	120 " 130 "
Bakery	B6591	27 1/2	34 1/2	12 1/4	2 1/2	42 1/4	14 1/2	16	48	130 " 150 "

In above table "h" is diameter of wheel.
Dimension "b" is a safe distance to leave between center of rudder post and inside of box.

Screw Aft of Rudder-head.
Made in 9 Sizes. For Rudder Posts 4 in., 5 in., etc. to 12 in. inclusive.

STEERING GEARS

TABLE OF RECOMMENDED SIZE SCREW STEERERS FOR BOATS OF 20' TO 120' WATER LINE LENGTHS

Used on sch. "Sadie Nunan"
$8\frac{1}{2}$" dia. rudder stock

WATER LINE LENGTH	SIZE STEERER
20 – 25	00
25 – 35	0
35 – 45	1
45 – 60	2
60 – 80	3
80 – 100	4
100 – 120	5

EDSON-METEOR STEERING GEAR

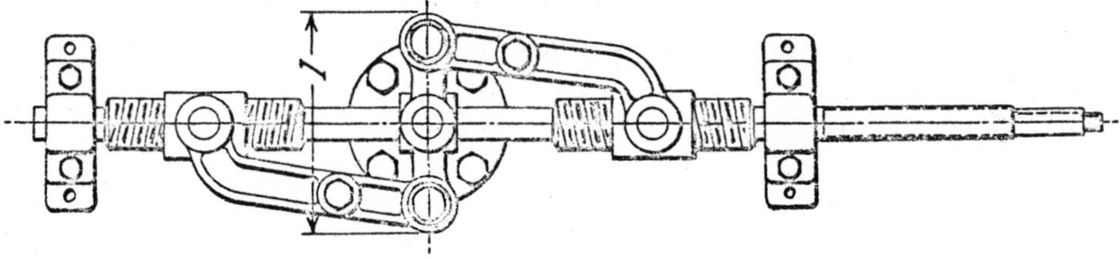
1

STEM BEVELS (NOTES)

The stem forms used on fishing schooners, built in the 1845–1885 period, had cutwaters that were slightly tapered, from the stem rabbet outboard; the siding reducing about 2″-2½″ on each side. In the wake of the gammon iron the full stem siding was maintained. At the leading edge of the cutwater the siding was reduced; from the forefoot up to 2′-3′ above the L.W.L., to 2½″-3″ in width. The bevel bearding did not fair into the taper of the cutwater; its line was abaft the leading edge of the cutwater 6″-9″, from the fore-edge of the gripe, up to above the L.W.L. for a couple of feet, and then fading to zero as it approached the underside of the lower trail moulding. (See "Bows.")

In the plumb-stemers, the cutwater tapered in siding, from the stem rabbet to the face of the stem to side about 2″-2½″. The top of this bevel was a little below the bottom of the gammon iron, and its bottom was at the fore-gripe. The "Carrie E. Phillips" had her stem beveled to the underside of the bowsprit, the sole exception known in fishing schooners.

In the gammon knee clipper bow the leading edge was bevelled as in the clipper bows of 1845–1885, except for having more taper outboard in the cutwater; making the bearding line of the bevel less obvious. In some very sharp vessels the L.W.L. faired into the taper of the cutwater for a short distance, but this was most unusual.

In the overhang curved stem, the cutwater was bevelled from stem rabbet outboard to face of stem. The top of the bevel was well below the bottom of the gammon iron. It rarely was bevelled enough to fair into the hull planking abaft the rabbet, however.

In knockabouts the top of the stem bevel on the cutwater was 14″-16″ below the top of the plank-sheer of the main deck. The top of the stem was about 2″-3″ above the top of the bow chock rail. The latter was usually about 4″ high at stem, above the top of the main rail.

The bow rabbet of knockabouts was carried up to the waistline height, the pine bulwarks were merely bevelled to meet the sides of the upper cutwater or stem.

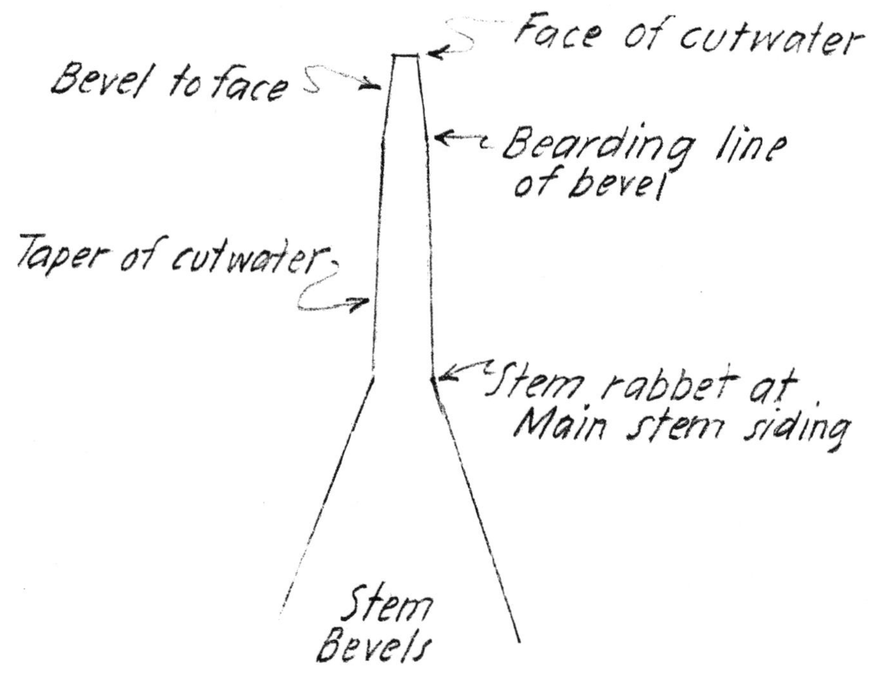
Face of cutwater
Bevel to face
Bearding line of bevel
Taper of cutwater
Stem rabbet at Main stem siding
Stem Bevels

THIMBLES FOR BOLTROPES

1¼" wide to 1 5/16" wide at points
1⅜" wide to 1½" wide at points

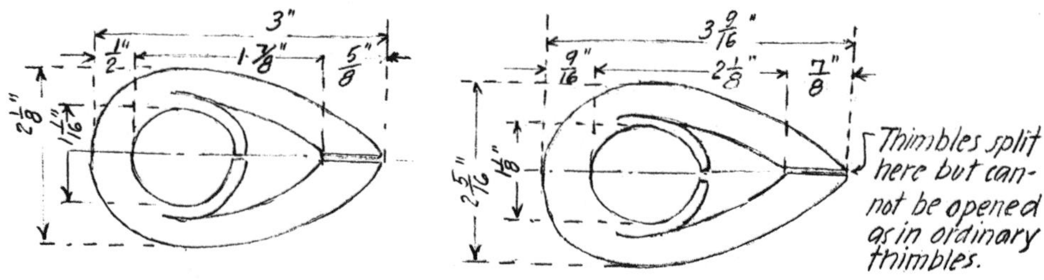
3"
1/2"
1·7/8"
5/8"
2 1/8"
1 7/16"
3 9/16"
9/16"
2 1/8"
7/8"
2 5/16"
1 5/8"
Thimbles split here but cannot be opened as in ordinary thimbles.

Hemp Thimble

Manila Thimble

Taken from 7"x7" spectacle clew iron by E. Bosley.

Manila thimble was always larger than that for hemp boltrope

THIMBLES

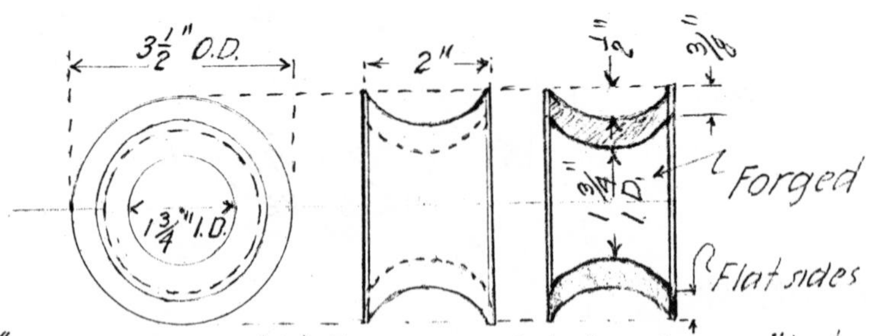
3½" O.D.
2"
½"
⅜"
1¾" I.D.
1¼" D.
Forged
Flat sides

"Rolling thimble," One on jumbo stay, One on jib stay A smaller one on balloon stay. Used to allow stay to be taken up; the thimble revolving on its pin.

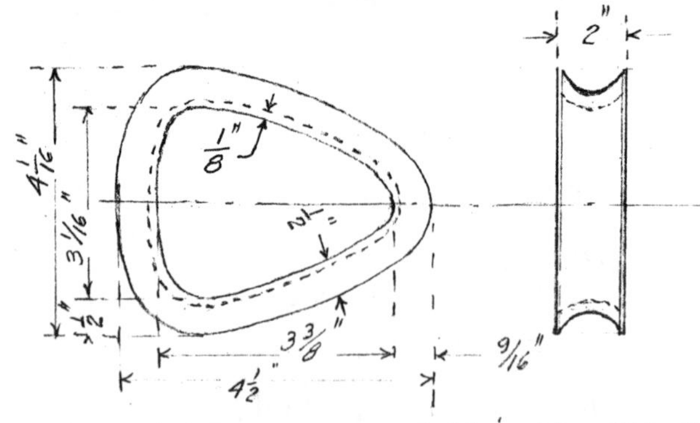
2"
4 1/16"
3 1/16"
⅛"
½"
3⅜"
4½"
9/16"

Topmast stay lanyard thimble. This form of thimble used with lanyards on back ropes on bowsprit as well as on stays,

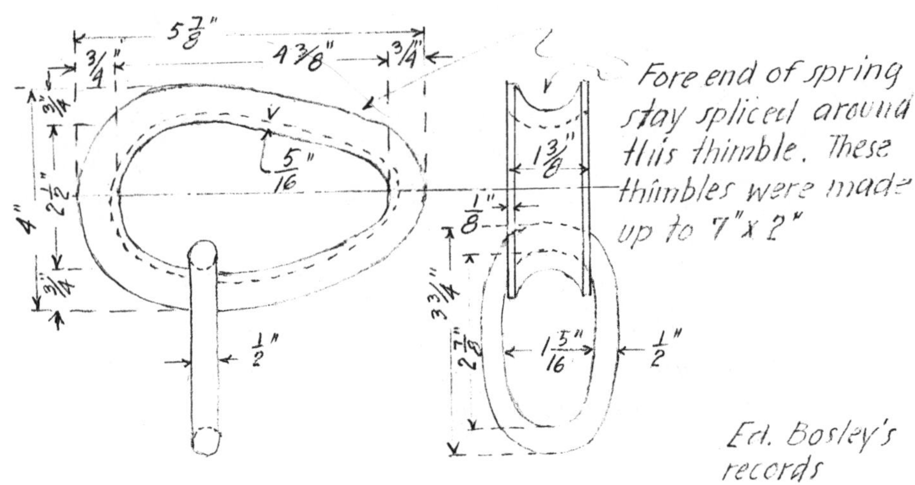
5⅞"
¾"
4⅜"
¾"
4"
2½"
5/16"
½"
Fore end of spring stay spliced around this thimble. These thimbles were made up to 7" x 2"
1⅜"
⅛"
3¼"
2⅞"
1 5/16"
½"
Ed. Bosley's records

THROAT HALYARDS BLOCK, 1880

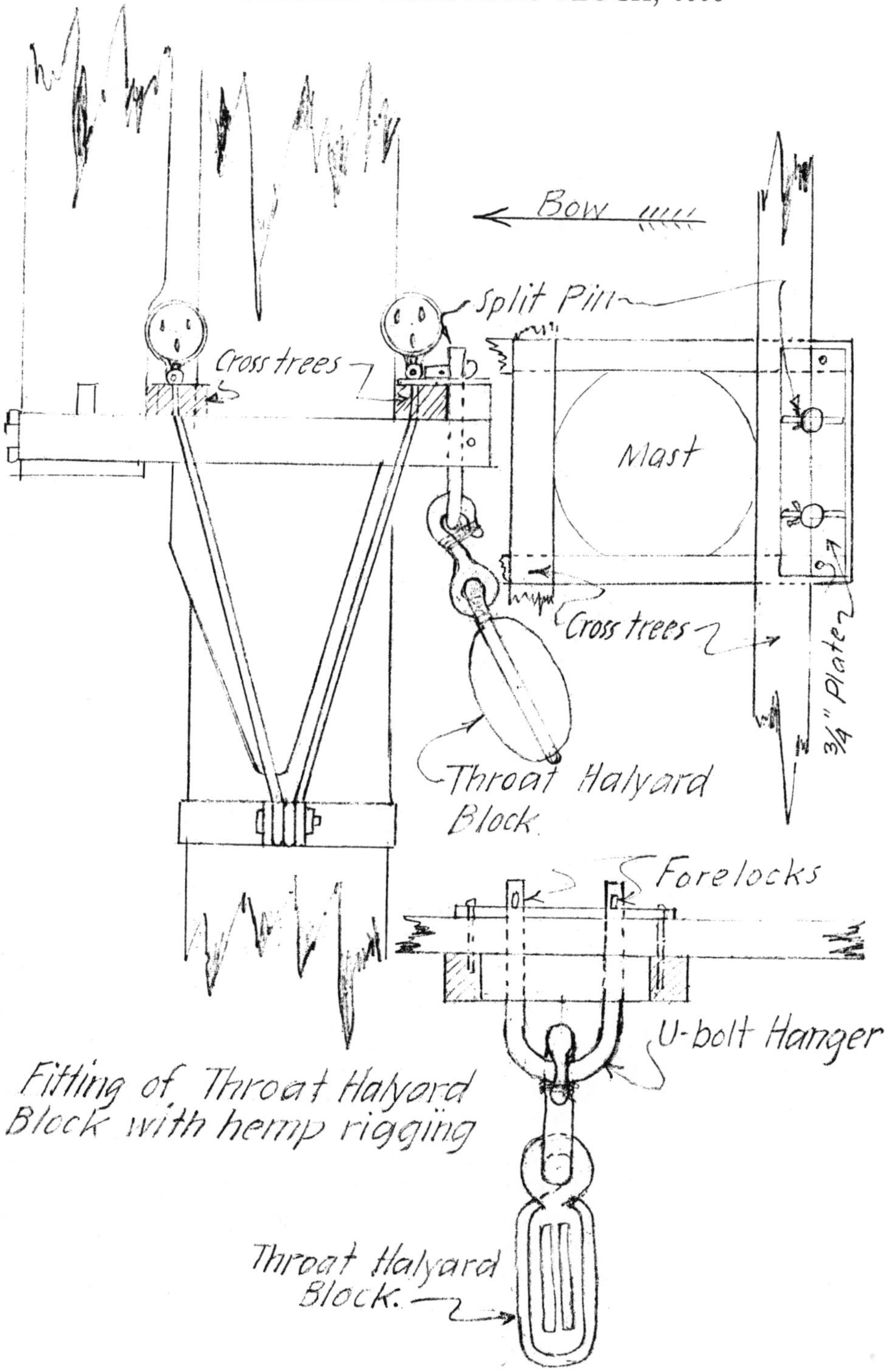

Bow

Split Pin

Cross trees

Mast

Cross trees

3/4" Plate

Throat Halyard Block

Forelocks

U-bolt Hanger

Fitting of Throat Halyard Block with hemp rigging

Throat Halyard Block.

THROAT HALYARDS 1890–1935

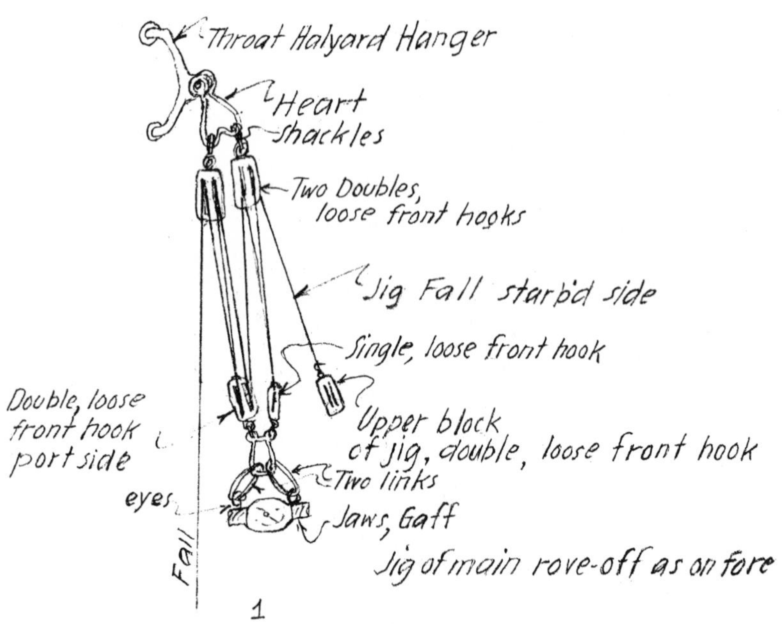
Throat Halyard Hanger
Heart
Shackles
Two Doubles,
loose front hooks
Jig Fall starb'd side
Single, loose front hook
Double, loose
front hook
port side
Upper block
of jig, double, loose front hook
Two links
eyes
Jaws, Gaff
Fall
Jig of main rove-off as on fore
1

Main throat halyard port side

Heart, only if there were two blocks
Shackle
Triple, loose front hook
Throat halyard blocks sometimes
faced athwartship.
Double, loose front hook
Ring
Upper block of jig Double, loose front
hook.
Halyard fall
Two
Links
Jig Fall
Gaff
Big schooners had double here too
with becket in upper block.
Single, loose front hook, with becket,
lower block of jig
Starb'd side

Fore throat
halyard port side

THROAT HALYARD CRANES

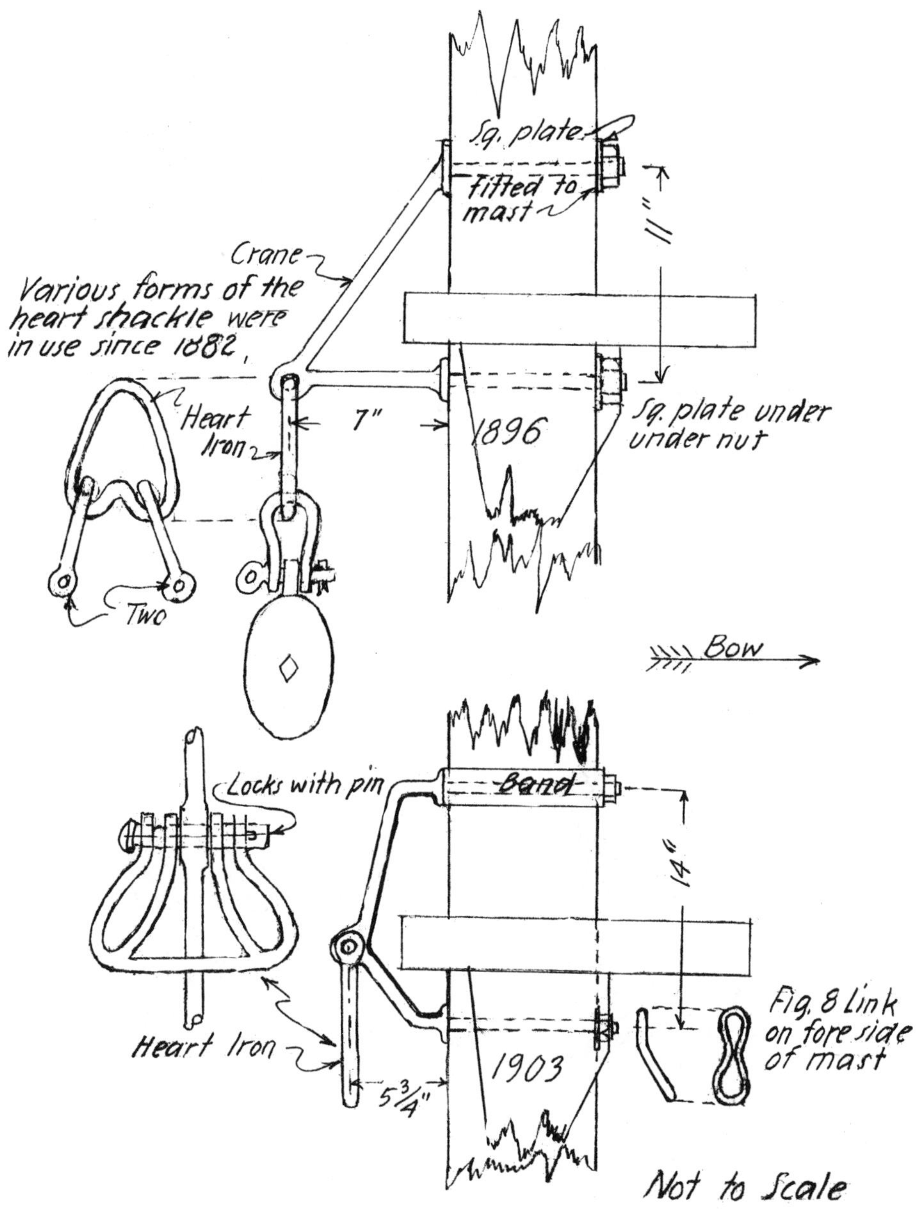
Sq. plate
fitted to mast
11"
Crane
Various forms of the heart shackle were in use since 1882.
Heart Iron
7"
1896
Sq. plate under under nut
Two
Bow
Locks with pin
Band
14"
Heart Iron
5 3/4"
1903
Fig. 8 Link on fore side of mast
Not to Scale

THROAT HALYARD CRANE FOR A VERY LARGE SCHOONER, 1900

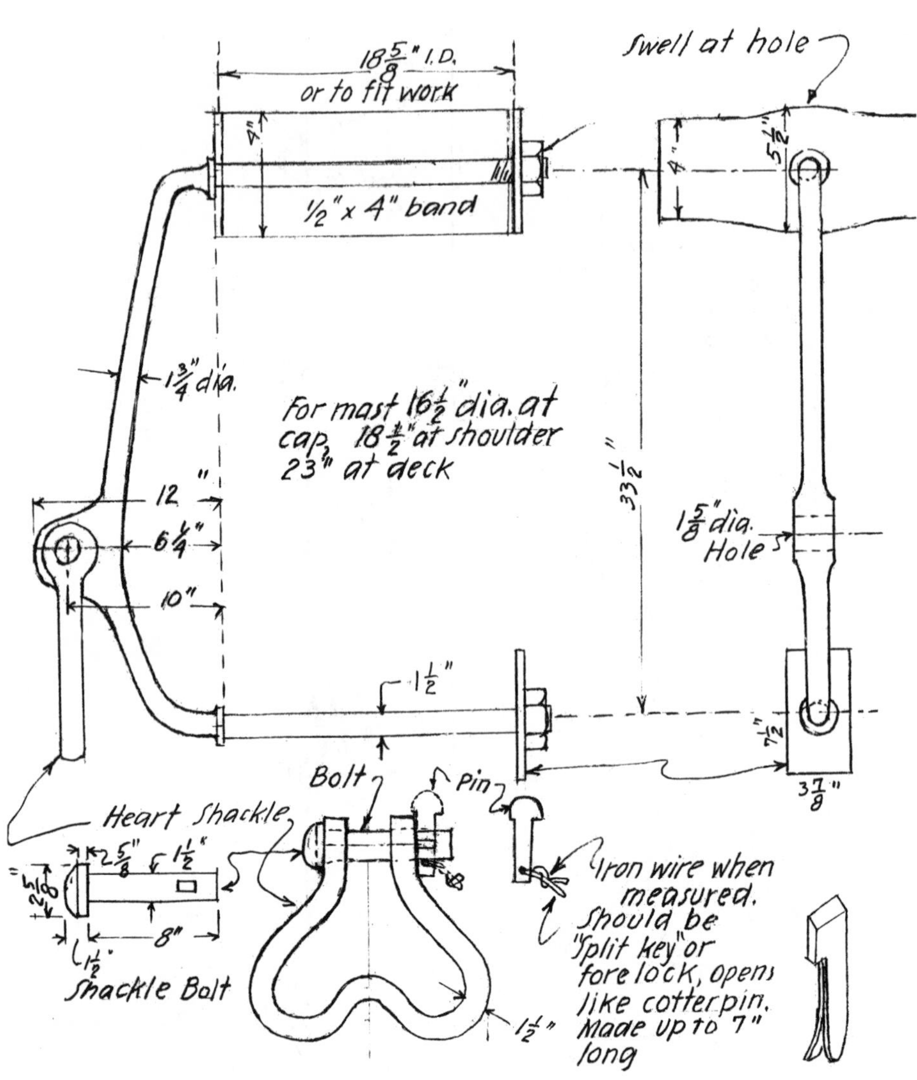
18 5/8" I.D. or to fit work
Swell at hole
4"
5 1/2"
1/2" x 4" band
1 3/4" dia.
For mast 16 1/2" dia. at cap, 18 1/2" at shoulder 23" at deck
33 1/2"
12"
6 1/4"
10"
1 5/8" dia. Hole
1 1/2"
7 1/2"
3 7/8"
Bolt
Pin
Heart Shackle
2 5/8"
1 1/2"
8"
1 1/2"
Shackle Bolt
Iron wire when measured. Should be "Split key" or fore lock, opens like cotter pin. Made up to 7" long
1 1/2"

THROAT HALYARD CRANES

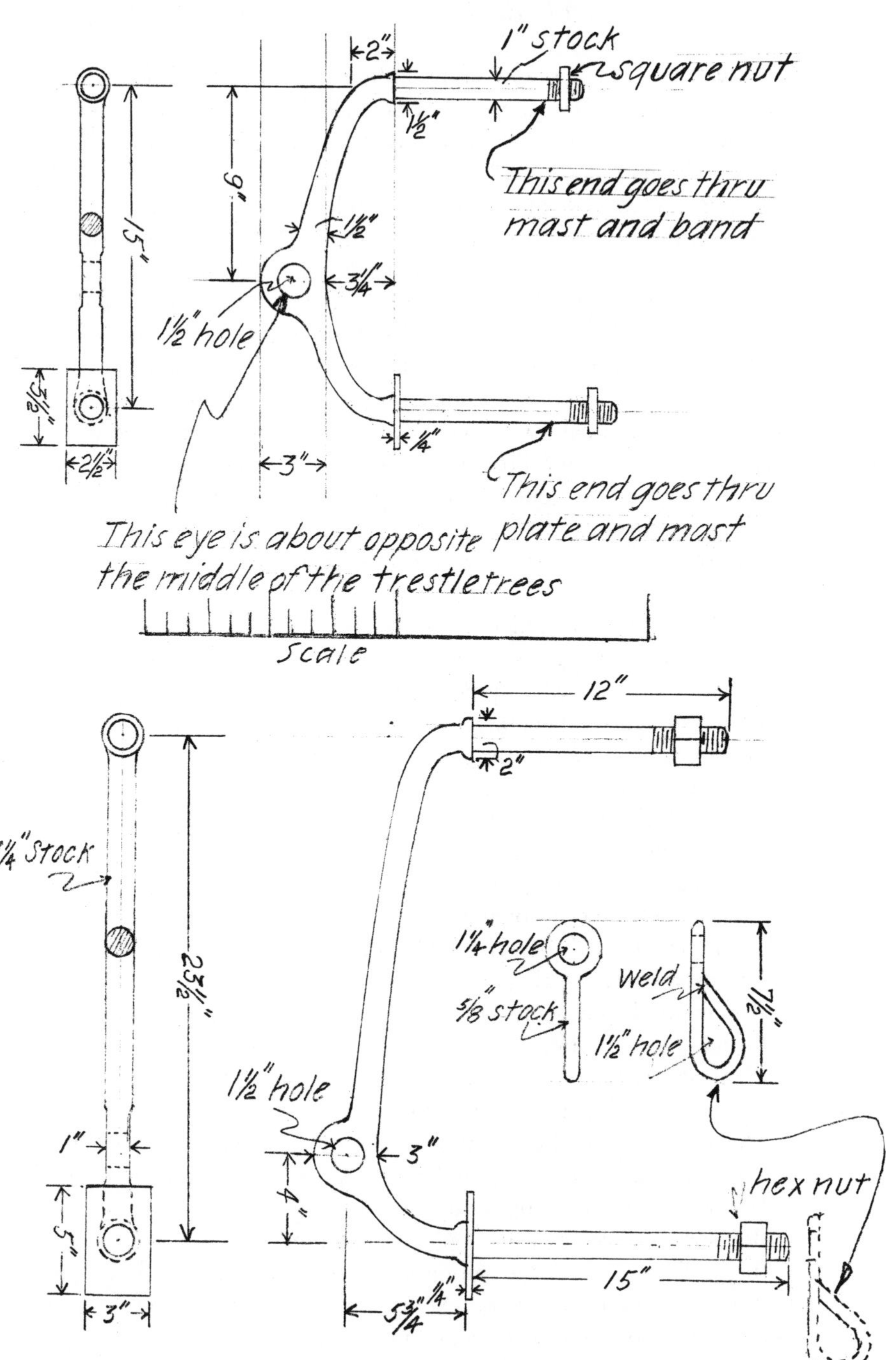
1" stock
square nut
2"
½"
This end goes thru mast and band
9"
15"
1½"
3¼"
1½" hole
3½"
2½"
3"
¼"
This end goes thru plate and mast
This eye is about opposite the middle of the trestletrees
Scale
12"
2"
1¼" stock
23½"
1¼" hole
5/8" stock
Weld
1½" hole
7½"
1½" hole
1"
3"
4"
5"
3"
hex nut
15"
5¾"
¼"

TIMBER USED IN SHIPBUILDING AT ESSEX AND GLOUCESTER

One of the reasons why shipbuilding became established in Massachusetts in colonial times was the great oak and pine forests in the colony. Pinkies and schooners were built with oak frames, keels, posts, plank, and beams; with white pine decks and deck furniture; until into the 1840s. Then southern long-leaf yellow pine, juniper, maple, birch, and spruce were employed as substitutes for the vanished oak supply. Unfortunately, the great Maine forests produced only red oak, considered poor ship timber by Massachusetts ship carpenters. This led to the importation of the yellow pine, and of Maryland and Virginia white oak, after 1865. Hence the selection of the best timbers for a schooner varied with the date of build.

From 1845 to 1865 some oak was used, with spruce or white pine top timbers, pine and oak plank were available, except during the war.

From 1865 on, the following timbers were employed:

Keel—white oak, yellow pine, maple or birch, scarphed.

Stem, stern posts—white oak.

Keelsons—yellow pine, 12″ x 12″, scarphed, red or white oak, maple or birch.

Plank—white oak, rail to bilge, yellow pine or birch below. The yellow pine or birch gave a smooth bottom.

Ceiling—oak or yellow pine, birch.

Clamps—yellow pine, birch, spruce.

Deck beams—deck frame, carlins, etc., white oak.

Knight heads—white oak.

Frames, bulwark stanchions—oak, yellow pine, spruce.

Stem apron, stern knee—oak.

Deadwoods—yellow pine, oak, maple, birch.

Great beam, hatch coamings, sills, mast or fife rails, posts, windlass bed, windlass knees, quarter bitts, all rails, chock rails, pawl post—oak.

Windlass barrel—oak.

Rudderstock and blade—oak.

Decking—white pine.

Plank-sheer, monkey rail, cabin trunk, wheelbox, fore companionway, skylights, slide hatch—white pine.

Masts, booms, gaffs, topmasts—white pine. After 1895 "Oregon Pine," or fir, masts became popular; the spars were white pine or fir. A few vessels had yellow pine masts.

Bowsprits—oak, fir, yellow pine, white pine.

In the last years of the sailing schooners, western fir, larch and long-leaf yellow pine were used very extensively in hull construction and for spars, as these timbers could be obtained in long lengths.

Vessels built at Essex for Gulf Coast owners were framed entirely with long-leaf yellow pine. Decks, etc., were of southern cedar, that is, juniper. Maine spruce was used for small spars.

TOPMAST FOR A LARGE SCHOONER, FOR PROPORTIONS ("THEBAUD")

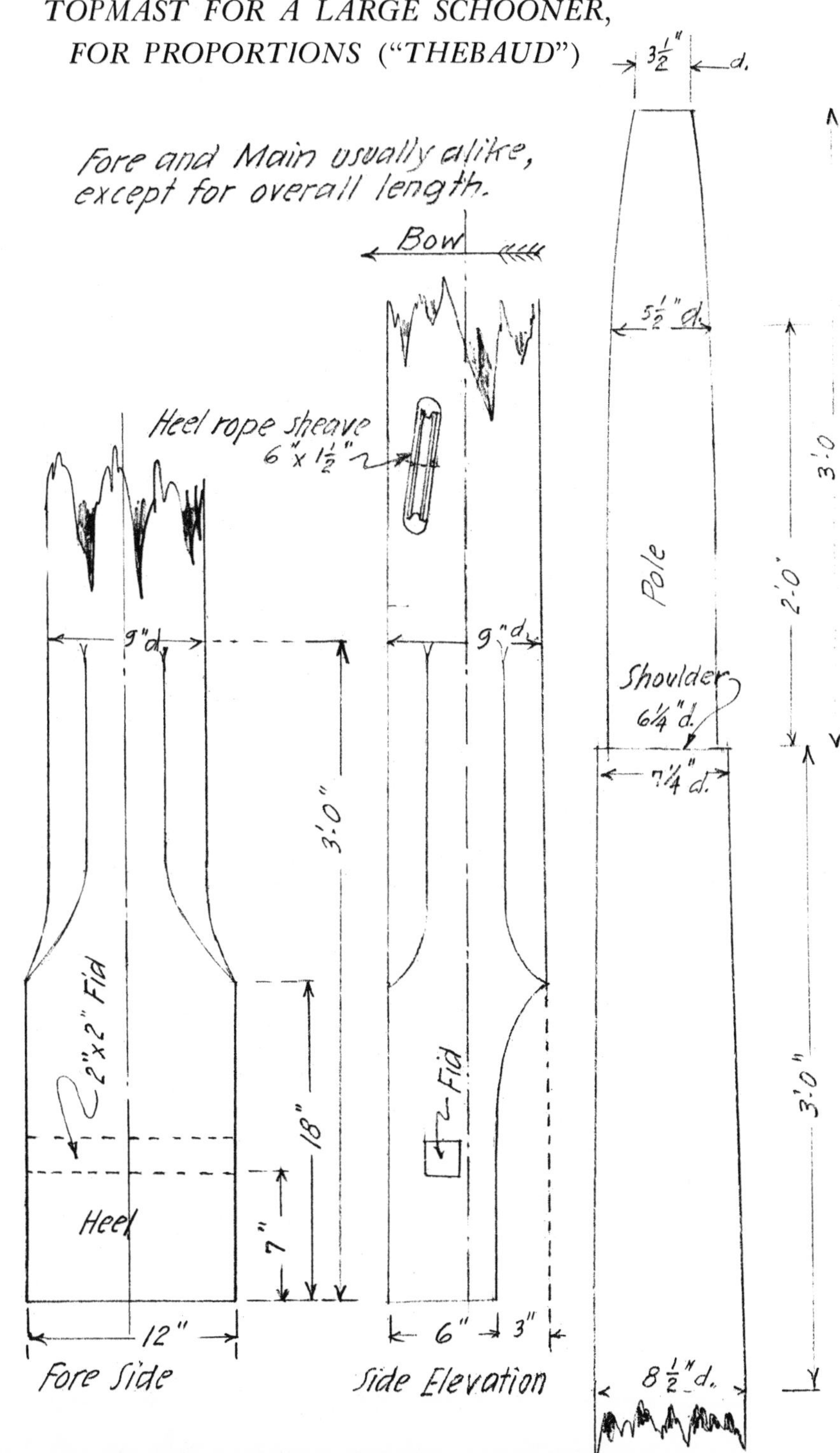
Fore and Main usually alike, except for overall length.
Bow
Heel rope sheave 6" x 1½"
3½" d.
5½" d.
Pole
Shoulder 6¼" d.
7¼" d.
8½" d.
9" d.
9" d.
3'0"
2'0"
3'0"
3'0"
2"x2" Fid
Fid
18"
7"
Heel
12"
6"
3"
Fore Side
Side Elevation

TOPMAST HEADS

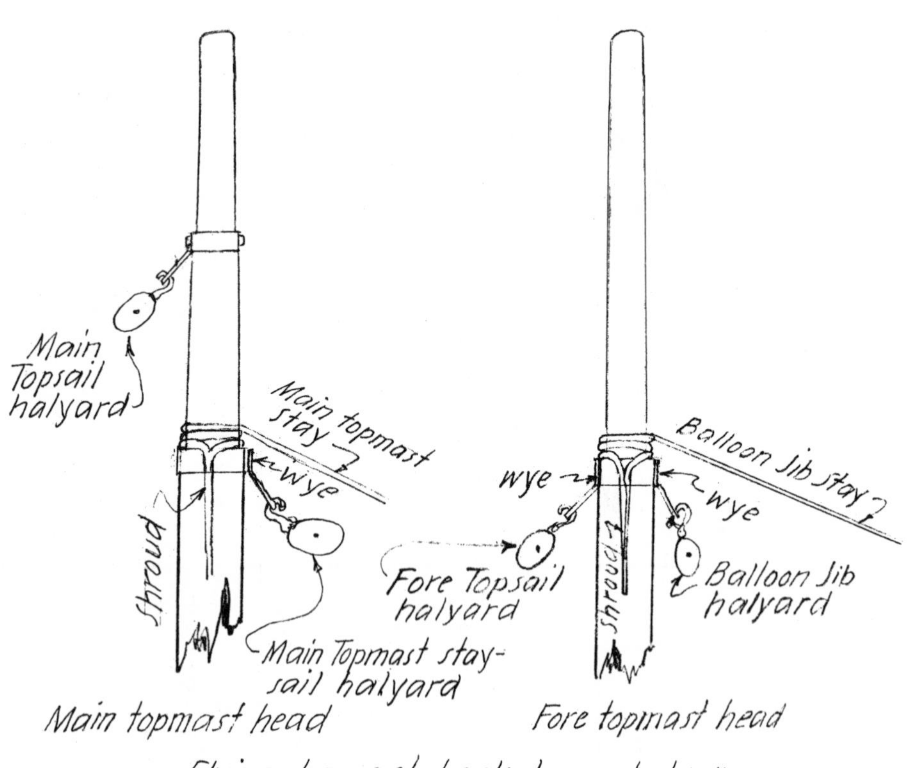
Main Topsail halyard
Main topmast stay
wye
Shroud
Main Topmast staysail halyard
Main topmast head
Balloon Jib stay
wye
wye
Fore Topsail halyard
Shroud
Balloon Jib halyard
Fore topmast head
Flying topmast backstay not shown, pendants over eyes of stays.

TOPMAST RIGGING, AT MASTHEAD

1. Shrouds go on first on shoulders { starboard 1st / port 2nd }
2. Stays go on next
3. Pull-back goes on next, foremast only
4. Preventer or flying backstay goes next on mainmast. On the large racers both topmasts usually had backstays.

Note: "Pull-back" was called "counterstay" by some riggers.

TOPMAST HEAD DETAILS, WYE AND TRUCK MEDIUM-SIZE VESSEL

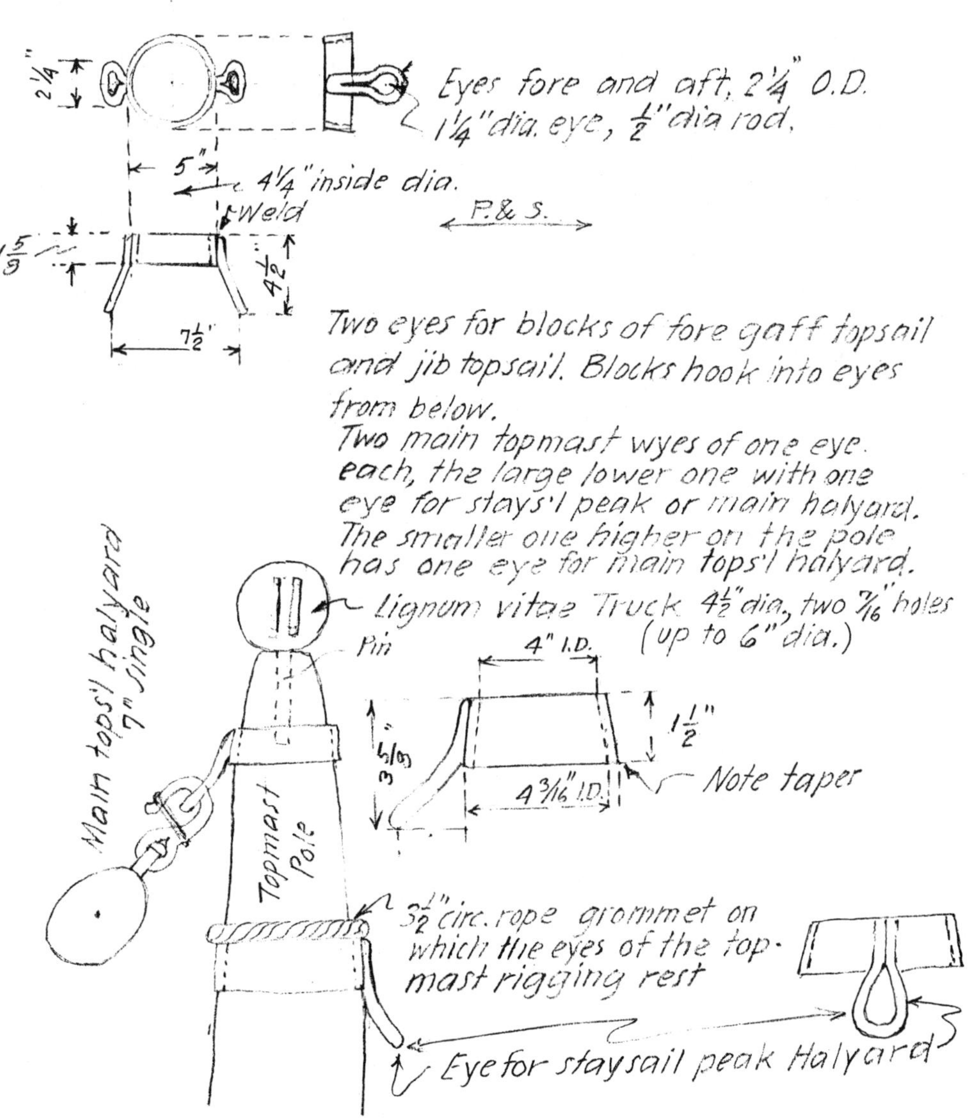
2 1/4"
Eyes fore and aft, 2 1/4" O.D.
1 1/4" dia. eye, 1/2" dia rod.
5"
4 1/4" inside dia.
Weld
P. & S.
1 5/8
4 1/2
7 1/2"
Two eyes for blocks of fore gaff topsail and jib topsail. Blocks hook into eyes from below.
Two main topmast wyes of one eye each, the large lower one with one eye for stays'l peak or main halyard.
The smaller one higher on the pole has one eye for main tops'l halyard.
Main tops'l halyard 7" single
Lignum vitae Truck 4 1/2" dia., two 7/16" holes (up to 6" dia.)
Pin
4" I.D.
1 1/2"
3 5/8"
4 3/16" I.D.
Note taper
Topmast Pole
3 1/2" circ. rope grommet on which the eyes of the topmast rigging rest
Eye for staysail peak Halyard

TOPPING LIFTS, MAINBOOM (SEE "MAINBOOM FITTINGS")

Fishing schooners, built before 1850, had single-mainboom topping lifts but the evidence is insufficient to attempt a description of their reeving. About 1850 it was common to have a long hemp or manila pendant, with a single-sheave block at its lower end, a hook at its head. The latter was hooked into an eyebolt on the underside of the after-end of a trestletree. The tail block was placed about 5′-8′ above the boom at its after-end when in sailing trim. Using this, the topping lift was reeved thus, a line was hooked into the eye of a wye at boom end, passed through the pendant block and the hauling and spliced into a single-sheave, the "runner," having a becket. The fall led from the becket down and under a sheave in the boom, up and through the runner, then down to a second sheave in the boom, a foot, or a little more, inboard of the first. This served as a lead block, the fall leading inboard and belaying on cleat on the boom near the jaw. This reeve of a topping lift appeared in a photograph as late as 1875.

Another reeving, in use at least as early as 1857, was to have the pendant hooked into a link in an eye on the afterside of the mainmast cap iron. The rest of the reeving was as described above.

TOPPING LIFTS, MAINBOOM, 1857

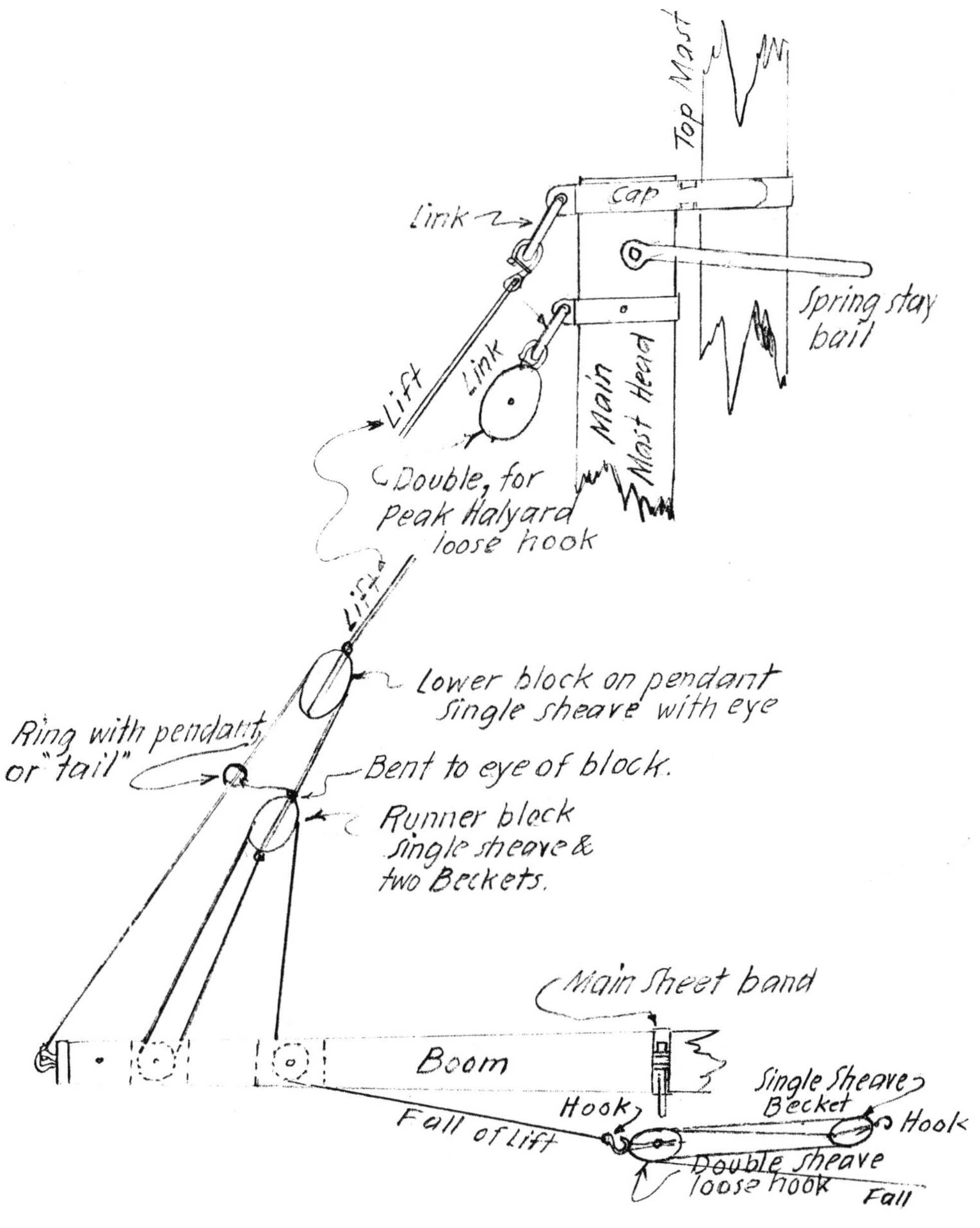
Top Mast
Cap
Link
Spring stay bail
Link
Lift
Main Mast Head
Double, for peak Halyard loose hook
Lift
Lower block on pendant Single sheave with eye
Ring with pendant or "tail"
Bent to eye of block.
Runner block Single sheave & two Beckets.
Main Sheet band
Boom
Single Sheave Becket
Hook
Hook
Fall of Lift
Double Sheave loose hook
Fall

TOPPING LIFT, MAINBOOM, 1885–1910

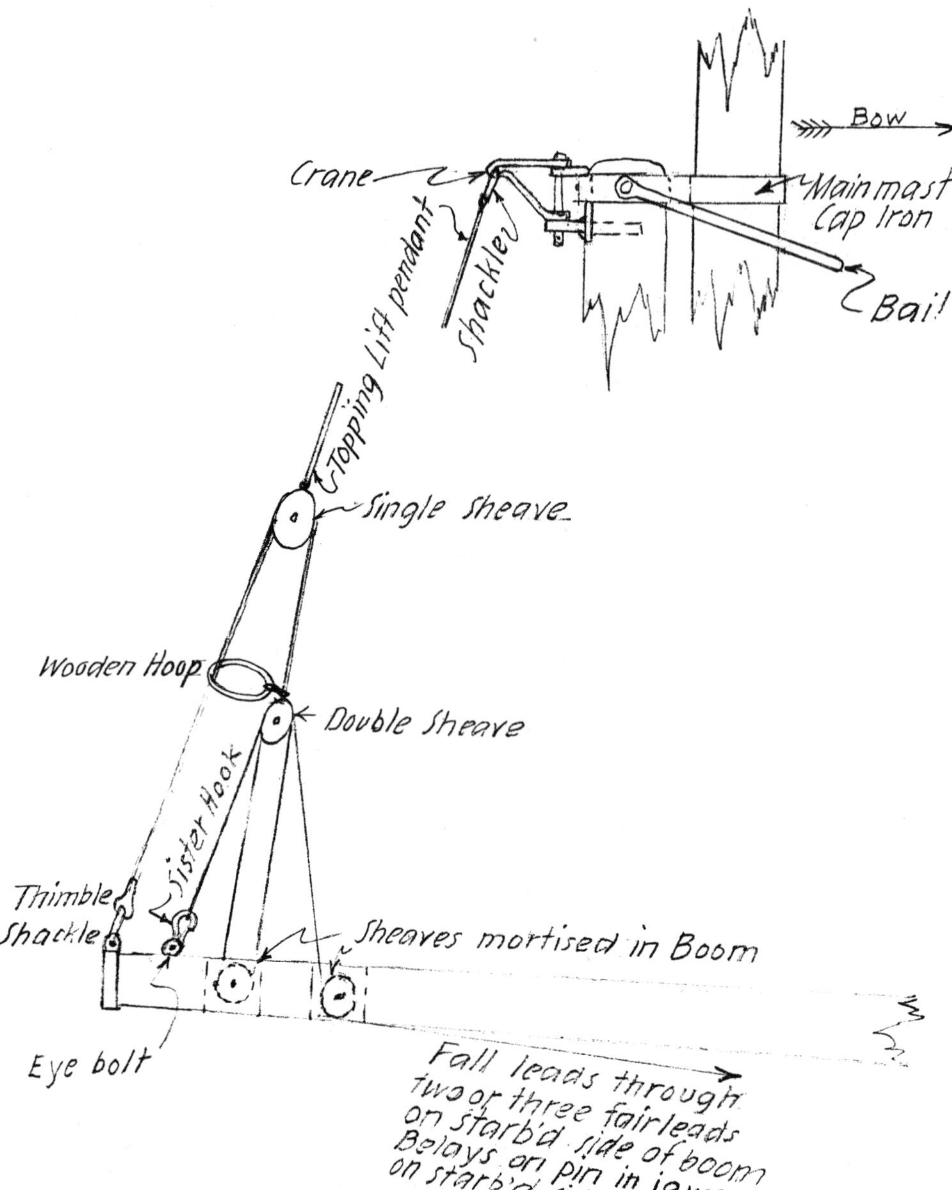
Bow
Crane
Main mast Cap Iron
Shackle
Topping Lift pendant
Bail
Single Sheave
Wooden Hoop
Double Sheave
Sister Hook
Thimble
Shackle
Sheaves mortised in Boom
Eye bolt
Fall leads through two or three fairleads on starb'd side of boom Belays on pin in jaws on starb'd side.

TOPPING LIFT, MAINBOOM
CAP IRON AND CRANE, 1887–1898

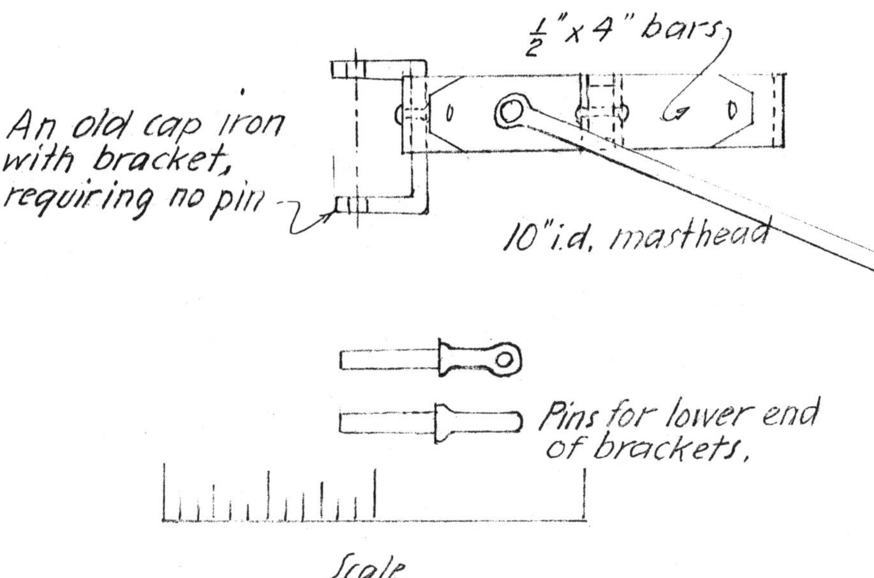

1/2" x 4" bars
An old cap iron
with bracket,
requiring no pin
10" i.d. masthead
Pins for lower end
of brackets.
Scale.

Cap irons and topping lift cranes varied in form and size. The cranes and brackets supported a great load, requiring careful workmanship, particularly in the large schooners.

TOPPING LIFT, MAINBOOM
CAP IRON AND CRANE, 1890

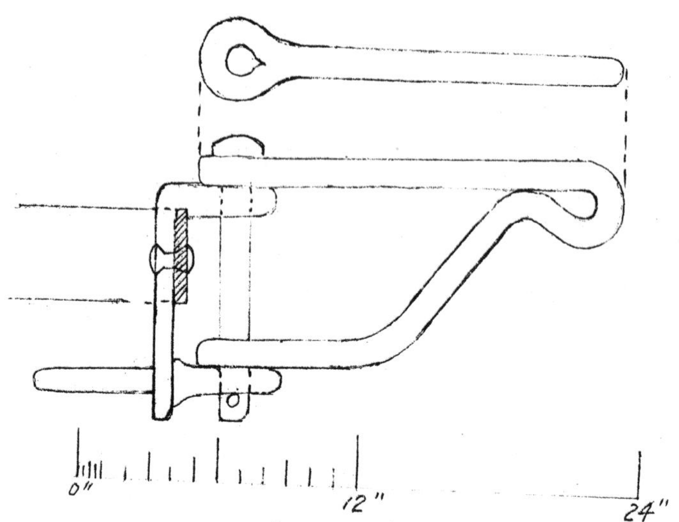

0"
12"
24"

Crane & mainmast head Cap Iron

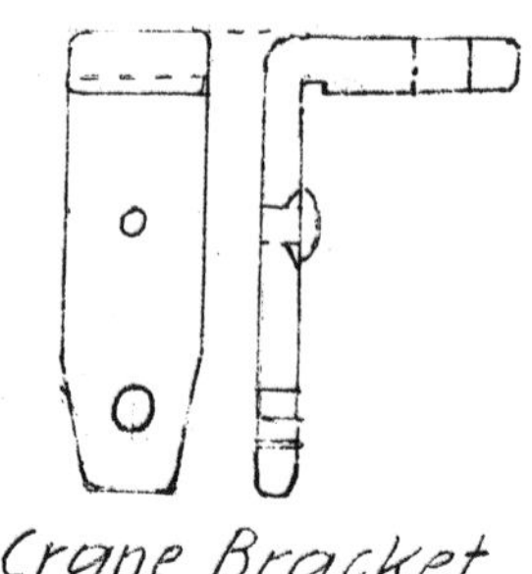

Crane Bracket.

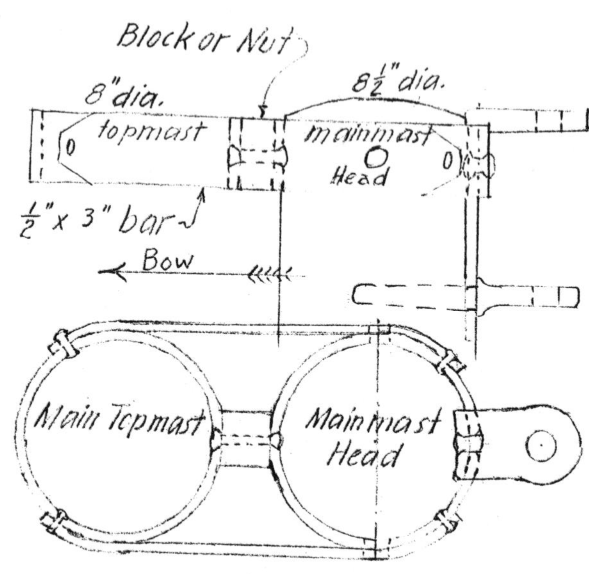

Block or Nut
8"dia.
$8\frac{1}{2}$"dia.
topmast
mainmast
Head
$\frac{1}{2}$"x 3" bar
Bow
Main Topmast
Mainmast
Head

Cap iron, $8\frac{1}{2}$"dia. mainmast head 1885–1895

TOPPING LIFT, MAINBOOM CAP IRON AND CRANE, 1900–1925 (FOR LARGE VESSEL)

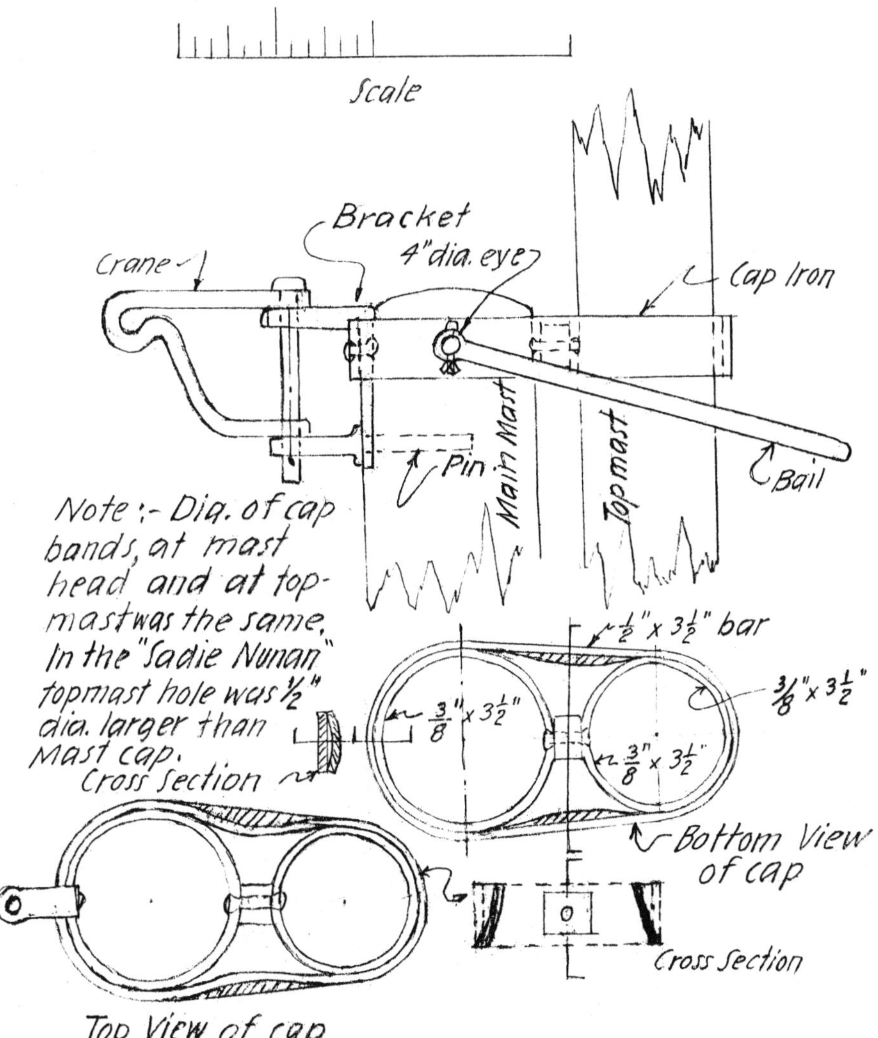
Scale
Bracket
4"dia. eye
Crane
Cap Iron
Main Mast
Topmast
Pin
Bail
Note :- Dia. of cap bands, at mast head and at top-mast was the same. In the "Sadie Nunan" topmast hole was ½" dia. larger than Mast cap.
Cross Section
½" x 3½" bar
3/8" x 3½"
3/8" x 3½"
3/8" x 3½"
Bottom View of cap
Cross Section
Top View of cap

See "Cap Iron and Bail"

TRAILBOARDS

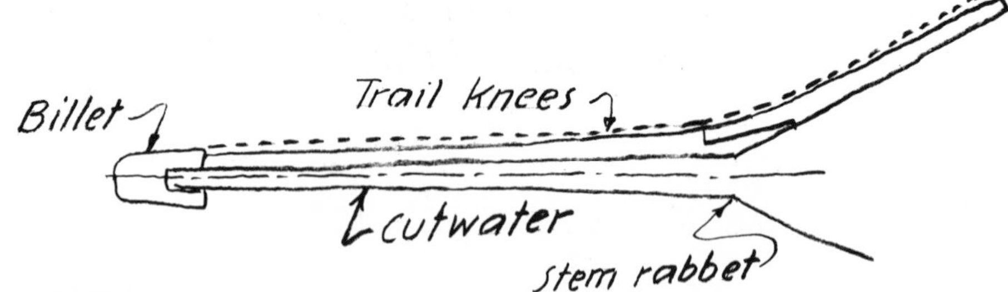
Billet
Trail knees
Cutwater
Stem rabbet

Trail Knee
Trail Board
Trail Knee
Section through Trail L.H.S.
Cutwater

Trail Boards made of 3" white pine to fit work after cutwater were bolted on and Trail Knees or "cheeks" were spiked in place. The outboard ends were reduced in thickness, to $1\frac{1}{2}$" or 2". A scarph was made at the stem rabbet, in the trail board and in each of the trail knees. In the old, full-bow vessels, pads or fillers were placed inside the trail boards at stem rabbet, or the trail was thicker than in later vessels. The trail knees were made deeper in the throat at the stem rabbet also. Essex carvers were expert in producing handsome cutwaters and "head work"; each having distinctive characteristics.

TRAILBOARDS
FITTING

In general, the Essex carvers made the trailboards narrow, whether trail knees were employed or not. The width of the after-ends of these trailboards was about one-ninth the freeboard at bow rabbet, L.W.L. to top of main rail cap. At billet, the trailboards were about half the width of their after-ends. The trailboards, at bow rabbet, were placed so that their ℄ was about mid-height of the bow freeboard. The after-ends of the trailboards were about their width, in length abaft the ℄ of the hawse hole (outboard ℄ of the hawse casting). In profile, the trailboard ℄ came almost straight abaft the bow rabbet, with some slope downward toward the stern. The sketches and plans show the many trailboards of various periods.

Trailboards, in the last years of their use on fishing schooners, were screw-fastened, to allow removal for painting, or for caulking of topside planking. [Data obtained from photographs and L.H.S.]
(See "Bows.")

TRANSOMS

Transoms, when counters came into popularity in the 1850s, were framed with knees fastened to the horn timbers. The transom frame was set up but not planked until the side planking was in place. This produced exposed grain at the ends of the transom planks that was covered by the transom fashion pieces. When the latter went out of fashion the transom planking was mitred to the side planking. The transom frame was continuous from the horn timber to deck, port and starboard, with vertical timbers fitted about 20″-24″ apart. There was a deck beam formed as the top of the transom frame. In the final evolution of the fashion piece, it became no more than a protective piece of plank, applied over the side planking at the transom.

TRESLETREES FOR A SCHOONER UNDER 80 FEET REG. (SEE MAST CHEEKS)

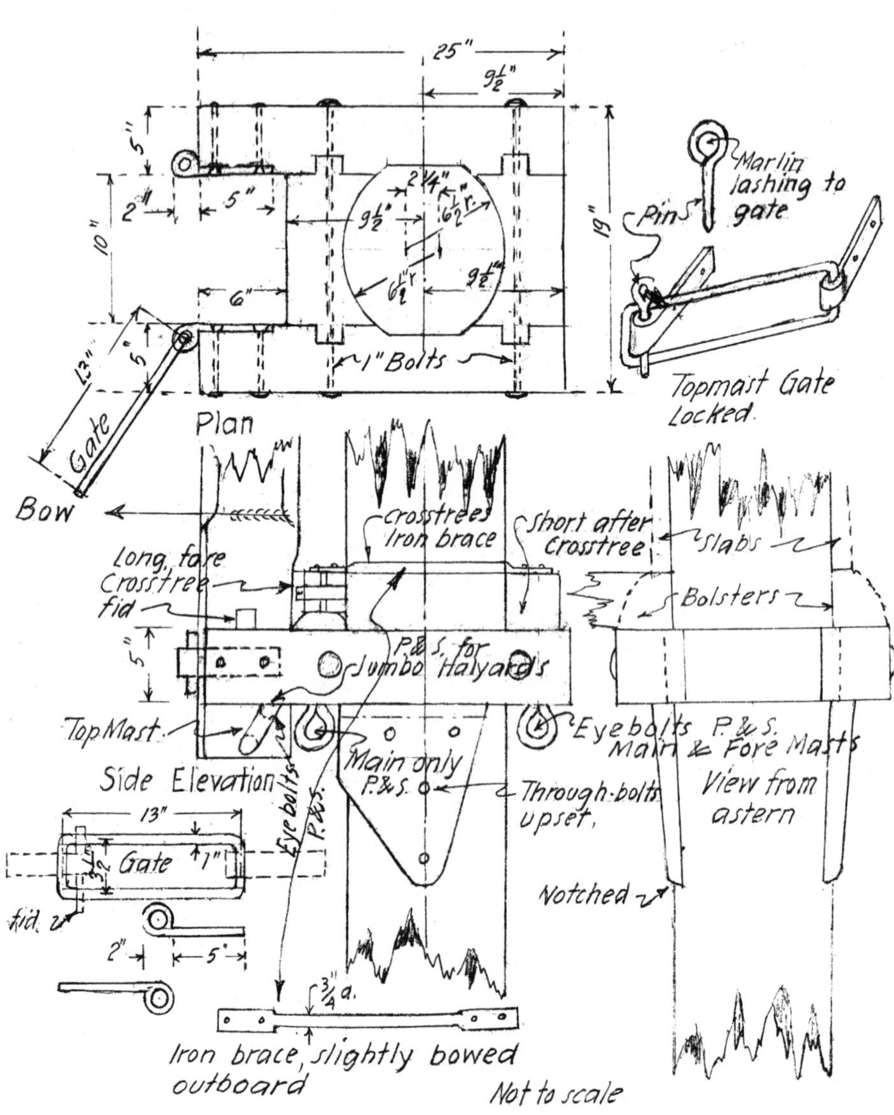
25"
9½"
5"
10"
2"
5"
2¼"
9½"
6½"r.
6½"r
9½"
6"
19"
13"
5"
Gate
1" Bolts
Plan
Bow
Marlin lashing to gate
Pin
Topmast Gate Locked
Crosstrees Iron brace
Short after Crosstree
Slabs
Bolsters
Long, fore Crosstree
fid
5"
P.&S. for Jumbo Halyards
TopMast
Eyebolts P.&S. Main & Fore Masts
Main only P.&S.
Through-bolts upset.
View from astern
Side Elevation
Eyebolts P.&S.
13"
Gate
3½
1"
fid
Notched
2"
5"
¾ d.
Iron brace, slightly bowed outboard
Not to scale

TURNBUCKLES

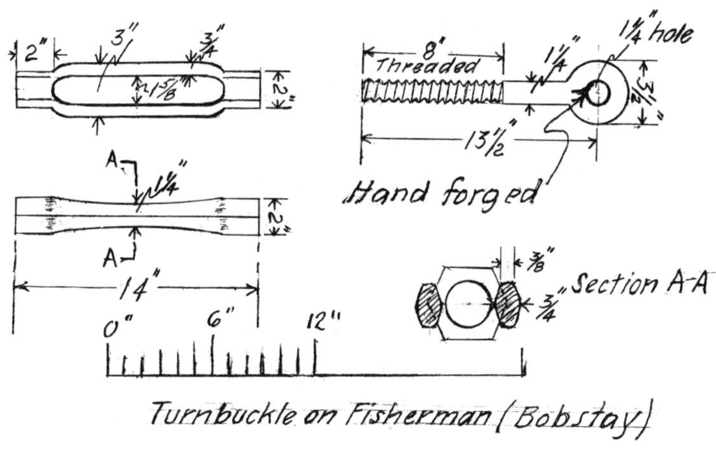
2"
3"
3/4"
1 5/8"
2"
A
1 1/4"
2"
A
14"
0"
6"
12"
8"
Threaded
1 1/4"
1 1/4" hole
3 1/2"
13 1/2"
Hand forged
3/8"
Section A-A
3/4"

Turnbuckle on Fisherman (Bobstay)

Turnbuckles were introduced into the rigging of fishing schooners in the late 1860s. They were first used to set up the chain bobstays. When wire rope was introduced in the 1880s, the inner bobstay was set up by turnbuckles in many new vessels. The turnbuckles were placed immediately under the bowsprit. Later, in the 1890s, turnbuckles were used on the bowsprit shrouds and jibboom rigging of a few vessels. Shroud turnbuckles were placed at the bowsprit pole. In a few knockabouts, turnbuckles were employed on the "balloon stay," or the topmast-head stay. Hearts and lanyards, and deadeyes, were employed in most sailing fishermen right down to 1925, however. There was a long-standing prejudice among fishermen against turnbuckles, due to "stripping" of the threads of some early turnbuckles when heavily strained.

TURNBUCKLES

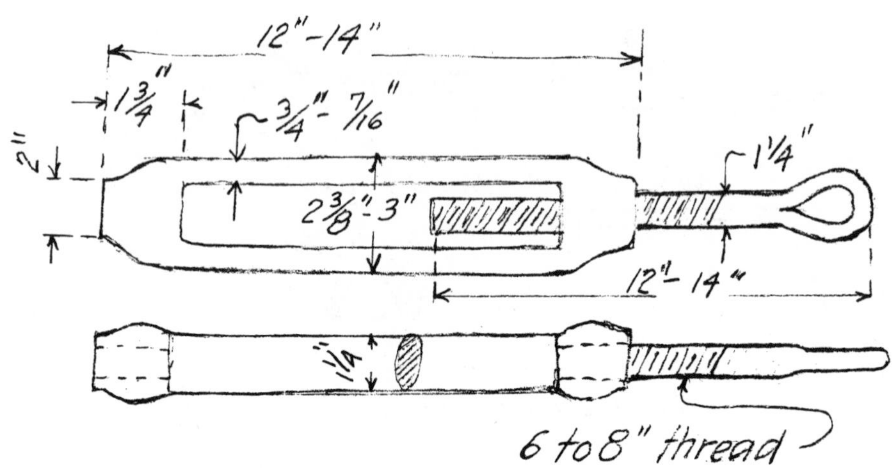
12"-14"
1 3/4"
3/4"-7/16"
2"
1 1/4"
2 3/8"-3"
12"-14"
1 1/4
6 to 8" thread

A common type of turnbuckle used for bobstay, bowsprit shrouds and crotch tackles, in various sizes. Turnbuckles for bobstays were 16" to 18" long in the body, which was 1¾" to 2" wide in the slot, and 1¼" to 1½" deep, ⅞" to 1¼" wide in the sides. The eyes were from 1⅜" to 1½" dia. rod. Eyes in both ends. Fore end shackles to heavy 4-eye wye band under bowsprit, bobstay spliced into after eye of turnbuckle over thimble.

TREENAILS

Treenails used at Essex were generally of white oak or, rarely, of locust. Before steam power appeared in Essex (in the 1880s) treenails were made by hand. The wood was sawn into blocks of the desired length, usually 24″-28″, and the ends marked off in 1¼″-1½″ squares. With axe and mallet these blocks were split into square billets. These were then driven through a tempered steel tube or die, so that a round treenail was formed by the tool; the excess wood falling outside the die. The latter was fixed in a large wooden table or bench set over a hole in the ground below it. When steam power became available, power lathes, or dowel-cutting machines, were used. Shipbuilding areas were slow in employing steam-power tools, except in the large centers of the industry, such as Boston or Portsmouth or New York. The broadaxe and adz were the important tools when heavy timber was worked, not only at Essex but also far to the eastward.

Treenails were used to fasten frame futtocks together, for thick planking, and to fasten some of the deadwood. Treenails, after being driven, were wedged with thin oak wedges that stood vertical to the grain of the plank or timber being fastened. Through-treenail-fastenings were wedged at each end. In fastening where through-bolting was not practical the point of the treenail was split and a small wedge inserted. When driven to the bottom of the hole, the wedge went home and locked the treenail in place. A 1″-1½″ dia. treenail, driven in this manner, had tremendous holding power, far exceeding that of a nail or spike of comparative length. Eight-sided treenails were used before 1840. [L.H.S.]

VENTILATORS (FORECASTLE)

Deck ventilators for the forecastle were fitted to nearly all schooners, after about 1880. These, in a variety of sizes and shapes, were placed on the ℄ of the forward deck-strongback, just under the after side of the windlass barrel. Knockabouts usually had another, about 4'0" forward of the fore side of the forepost of the jumbo gallows. These ventilators had galv. iron deck-irons, fitted with glass tops which could be replaced with a cowl head in good weather. A canvas cover could be fitted over the deck iron and glass top.

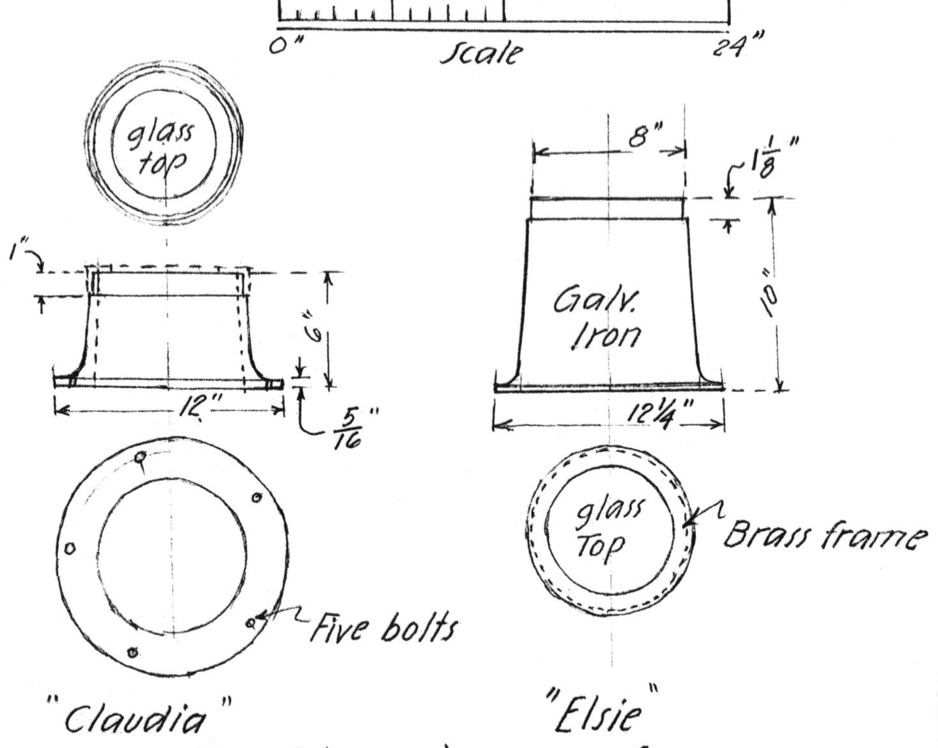
0"
Scale
24"
glass top
1"
6"
12"
5/16"
Five bolts
8"
1 1/8"
10"
Galv. Iron
12¼"
glass Top
Brass frame
"Claudia"
"Elsie"

Two of the most common forms seen in 1932-6

V-TRANSOMS

The V-transom, as first developed during the 1840s and 1850s, had the bottom of the V brought to the straight rabbet of the sternpost, with the rudderstock passing through the lower planks of the transom. This style of transom was adopted by the builders of pilot boats, yachts, Hudson River sloops, and schooners. The schooner yacht "America" had this style of transom.

To carry both the sternpost head and the rudderstock up through the lower part of the V was a difficult task requiring very careful fitting of small pieces of timber. Leaks were common. However, when the V-transom was introduced into the New England fishing schooners—apparently by Dennison J. Lawlor—the heel of the V-transom was moved aft, so as to require the "tail" or "horn timbers" and the filler piece, as developed in the construction of the true counter introduced at Essex in the early 1850s, if not earlier. The modified V-transom counter had the head of the sternpost and rudderstock a little forward of the heel of the transom. The result was a very short counter combined with a strongly raked, heart-shaped transom, well immersed. This transom stern had a short period of popularity between 1885 and 1890, and then disappeared.

V-TRANSOMS

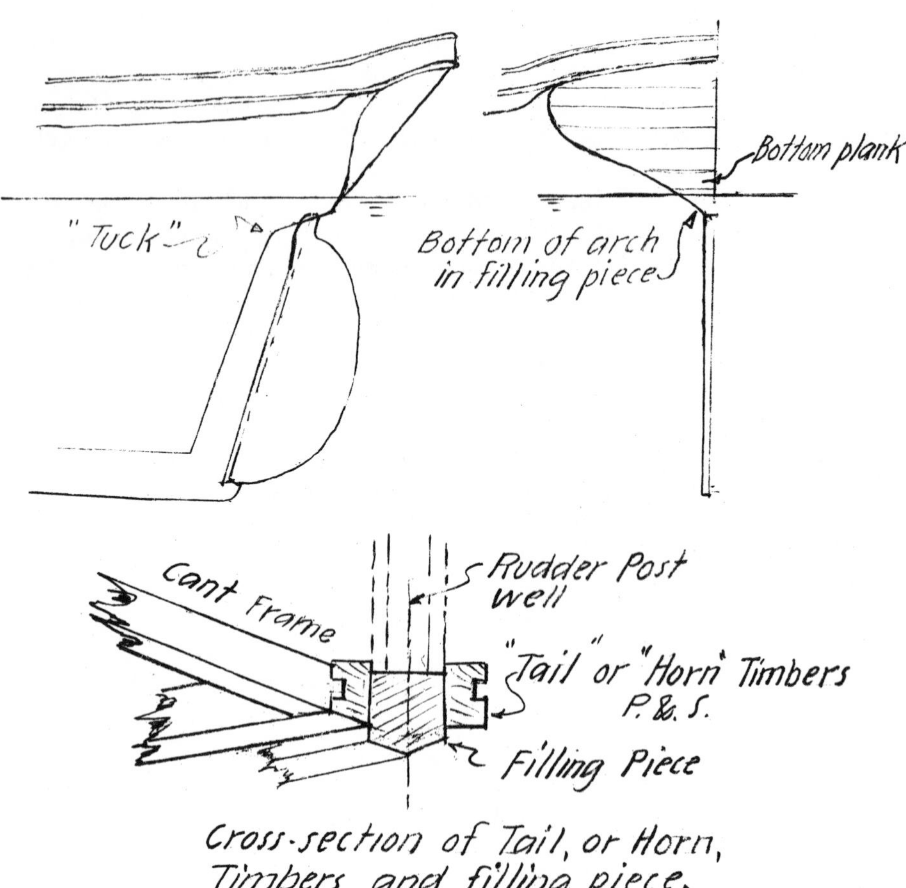

"Tuck"
Bottom plank
Bottom of arch in filling piece
Rudder Post well
Cant Frame
"Tail" or "Horn" Timbers P. & S.
Filling Piece

Cross-section of Tail, or Horn, Timbers and filling piece.

The V-Transom was usually immersed to a depth of about 2'0"; the width of the L.W.L. on the transom might be as much as 4 or 5 feet, creating some drag but not enough to be a practical resistance problem.

WAIST
(SEE "BULWARKS")
(NOTES)

In many schooners, prior to 1885, the waistline was far enough above the quarterdeck scuppers to give room for double stripes, usually red and white. The three-masted fishing schooners built by James in the 1880s had a double-stripe above the quarterdeck scuppers.

The waist, above the main deck, was 15″-17″ or thereabouts. The "pine bulwarks" were 7″-10″ deep. The cove bead was ¾″ wide.

The waistline was usually parallel to the main rail but some vessels had their waist rising slightly at the bow and stern, making the pine bulwarks shallower, forward and aft, than amidship. The height, deck to rail cap, was constant.

The waist turned up to form the plank fashion piece of the transom in schooners built by A. D. Story, but finished straight aft, to meet a plank fashion piece at an angle in schooners built by the James yard and those built by John Prince Story. Some knockabouts had lower bulwarks at ends. In large schooners the waist was of 3″ plank, and the plank below the plank-sheer was about 2½″, all dubbed fair.

A few schooners had red, white, and blue bands, or white, orange (buff) and blue in multi-bands. The waist was a little higher than usual in such cases, all of which were in the early 1850s.

WATER BUTTS AND TANKS
(NOTES)

Water was carried in barrels, in fishing schooners, until the early 1870s. Salt bankers, which remained at sea for lengthy periods, carried a large water supply, stowing the barrels under the forecastle sole, and on end at the forward fishhold bulkhead. Barrels were also carried on deck for daily use, chocked and lashed at the fore-end of the cabin trunk and alongside the forecastle companionway. Kegs were also used, stowed to occupy small spaces where barrels did not fit.

Wooden tanks, made of cypress and bound with iron rod or straps, came into favor about 1870. These were rectangular, with the longitudinal corners rounded, heads rabbeted into the inside ends of the staves, which were 1½″-2″ thick, tapered in width to produce the tank forms that were required. If the tank was tapered longitudinally, rods were used to secure the staves; strapping ¼″-1½″ was employed otherwise. The straps or rods were set up by patent clamps, usually two to a strap, top and bottom. The tanks were securely chocked. They were filled from cat-rigged waterboats in most fishing ports; these boats had manually worked force-pumps and canvas hoses. The waterboat's hose was led to the fillers of the tanks through the ventilator or galley hatch. Water was also supplied from taps on harbor piers. With tanks, the daily supply was procured with a hand pump in the galley.

For many years a tank-maker at Gloucester, named Joseph Marlin, supplied tanks to all vessels building there, or at Essex. He made patterns from the schooners under construction so that the tanks fitted closely on each side of the keelson, under the forecastle sole. These tanks were about 10′ long. As fishing schooners grew shoaler and sharper forward, the space for tanks decreased. Iron tanks replaced wooden tanks in the early 1900s, though they were disliked by the crews.

WATER BUTTS AND TANKS

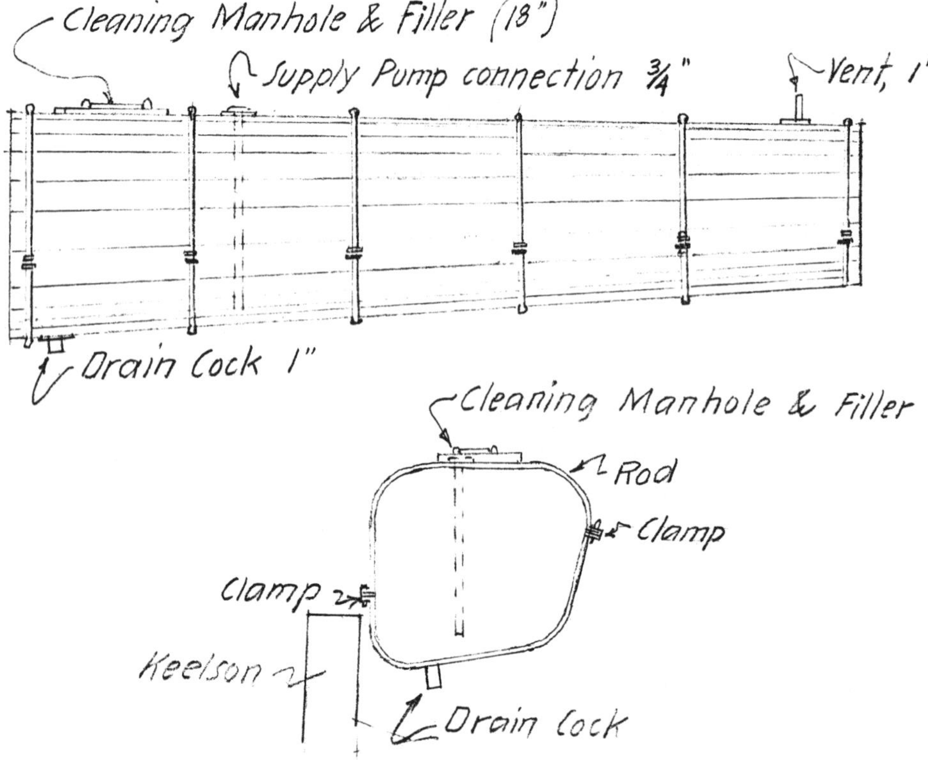
Cleaning Manhole & Filler (18")
Supply Pump connection 3/4"
Vent, 1"
Drain Cock 1"
Cleaning Manhole & Filler
Rod
Clamp
Clamp
Keelson
Drain Cock

From sketch by L.H.S., drawn from memory " Two tanks were usually fitted just forward of fore bulkhead of fore fishhold in schooners built in the 1890s" Tanks made P.& S. to fit either side of keelson.

WHISKERS (BOWSPRITS SHROUD SPREADERS)

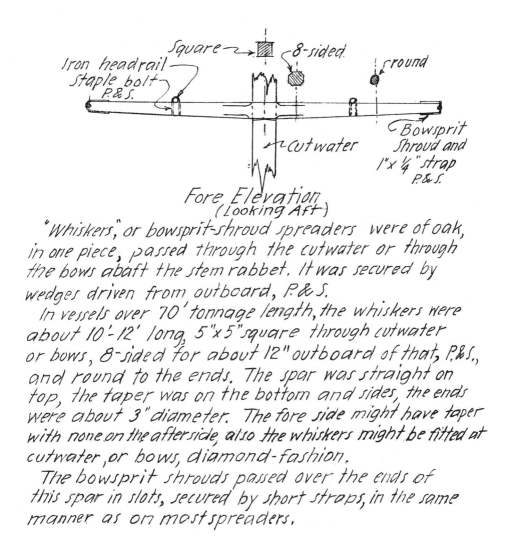

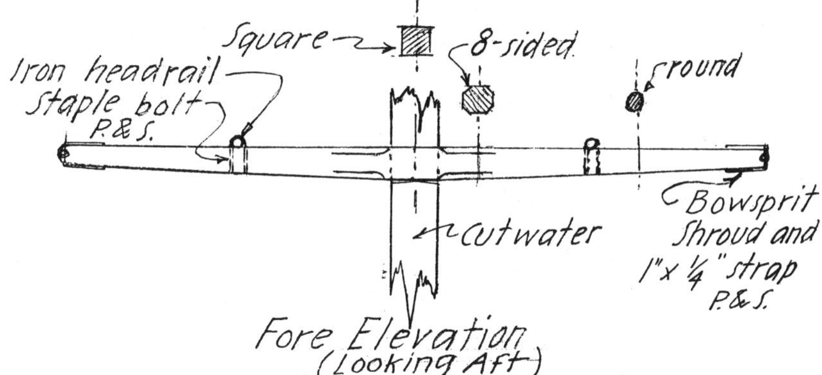
Square
8-sided
Iron headrail
Staple bolt
P.&S.
round
Cutwater
Bowsprit
Shroud and
1"x ¼" strap
P.&S.
Fore Elevation
(Looking Aft)

"Whiskers," or bowsprit-shroud spreaders were of oak, in one piece, passed through the cutwater or through the bows abaft the stem rabbet. It was secured by wedges driven from outboard, P.&S.

In vessels over 70' tonnage length, the whiskers were about 10'-12' long, 5"x 5" square through cutwater or bows, 8-sided for about 12" outboard of that, P.&S., and round to the ends. The spar was straight on top, the taper was on the bottom and sides, the ends were about 3" diameter. The fore side might have taper with none on the afterside, also the whiskers might be fitted at cutwater, or bows, diamond-fashion.

The bowsprit shrouds passed over the ends of this spar in slots, secured by short straps, in the same manner as on most spreaders.

WINCHES
(SEE "BITTS [WINCHES]")

(SEE "BITTS [WINCHES]")

Iron winches, mounted on mast bitts, were fitted to merchant vessels as early as 1764, in America. The date of their first use in fishing schooners has not been determined, but it is known that some large schooners owned in Gloucester and Boston were fitted with a mainmast bitts winch as early as 1857, at least. These fishing schooners seem to have been vessels intended for off-season voyages, where small crews were employed. By 1860 some schooners had winches on both fore- and main-mast bitts. They were chiefly used to hoist sails and, after 1906, or thereabouts, the foremast winches were fitted for power, which was used to handle anchor or sails.

The winches were of the standard type, galvanized steel, having drums about 8″ maximum diameter, 5½″-6″ minimum diameter, and 6″-6½″ wide, plus 1″ for pawl teeth. The pawl was pivoted on the outside of the bitt posts. The shaft was 1½″-1¾″ dia. and was fitted for hand-cranks, to ship at the ends, outside of the drums. The drums were about 3′-3″ apart, pawl to pawl. The winch-shaft was about 22½″-28″ above the mast beds. Snatch blocks were usually placed abreast the masts, hooked into eyebolts in the mast beds. The snatch cleats on the bitts at the masts were used for belaying only.

WINDLASS BITTS, CHEEKS, AND KNEES SHOWING SOME OF THE VARIOUS PATTERNS

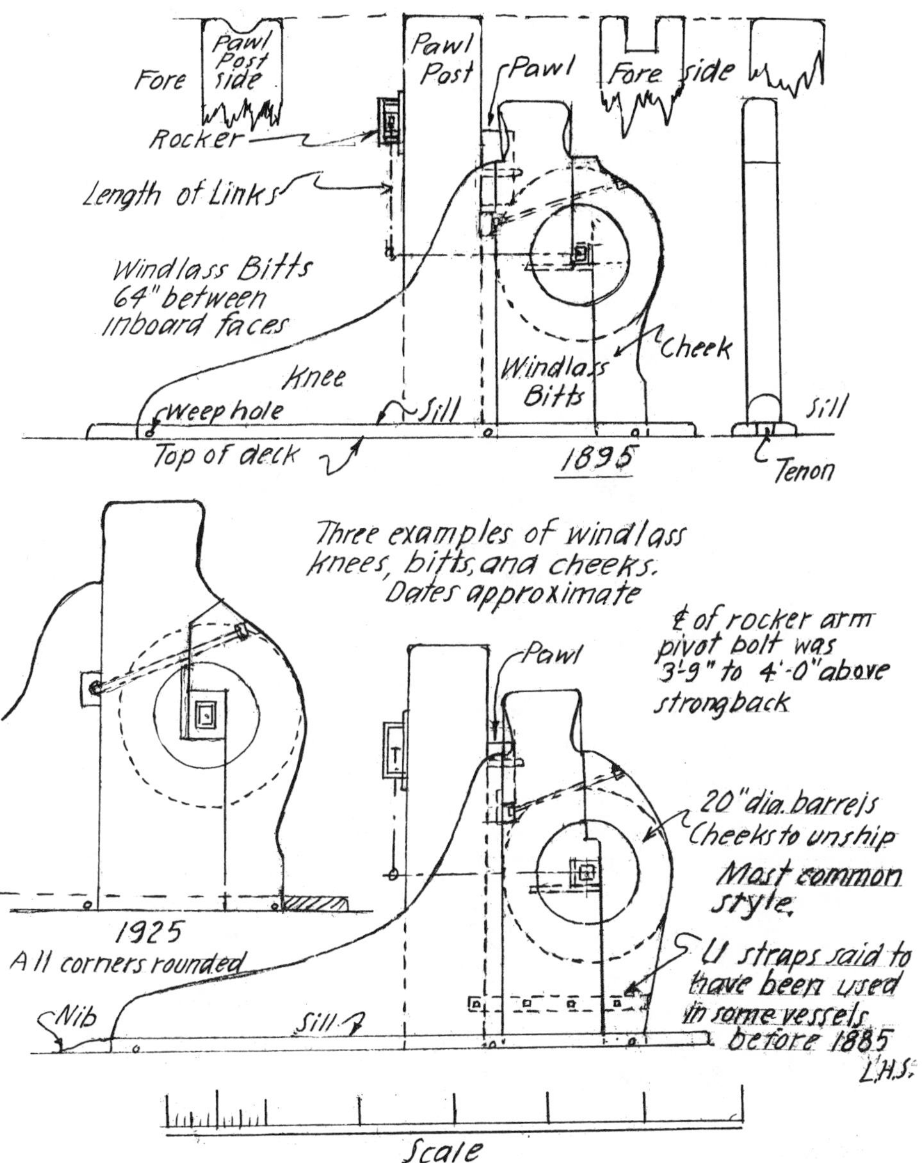
Fore
Pawl Post side
Pawl Post
Pawl
Fore side
Rocker
Length of Links
Windlass Bitts 64" between inboard faces
Knee
Sweep hole
Sill
Windlass Bitts
Cheek
Sill
Top of deck
1895
Tenon
Three examples of windlass knees, bitts, and cheeks. Dates approximate
℄ of rocker arm pivot bolt was 3'-9" to 4'-0" above strongback
Pawl
20" dia. barrels
Cheeks to unship
Most common style.
1925
All corners rounded
Nib
Sill
U straps said to have been used in some vessels before 1885
L.H.S.
Scale

WINDLASS, BOLTING OF BITTS

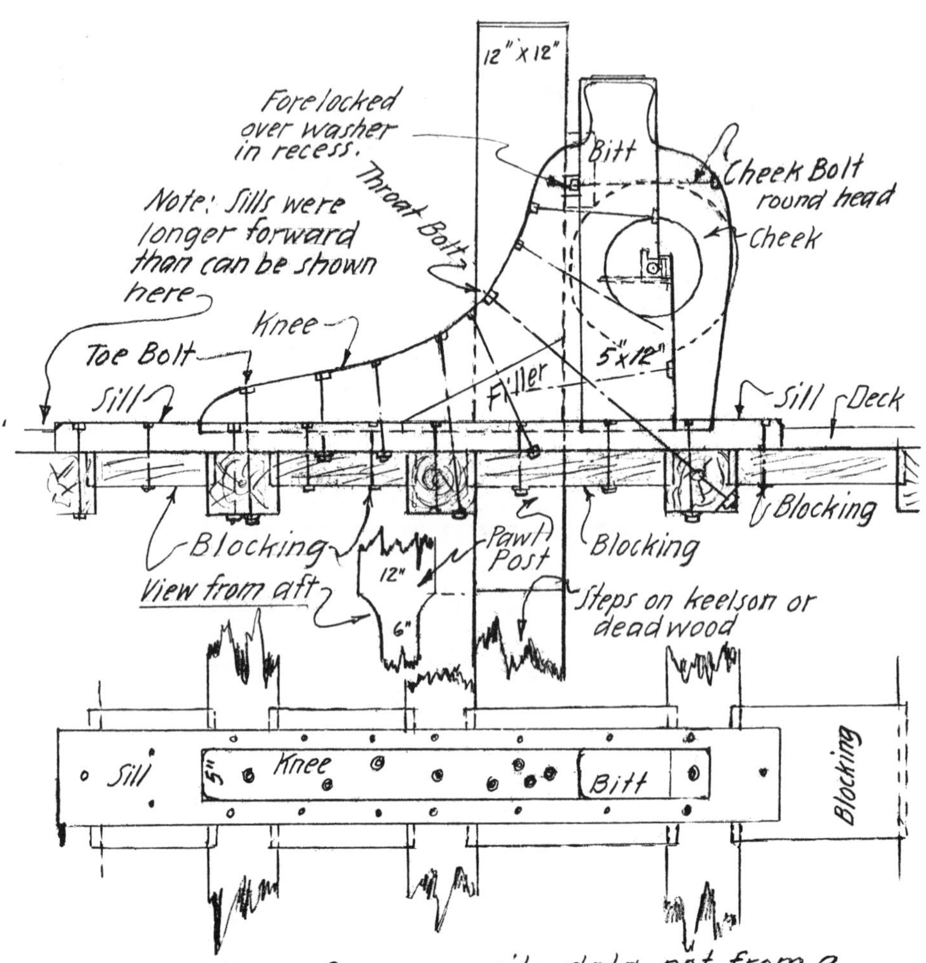
Not to scale
12" x 12"
Forelocked over washer in recess.
Bitt
Cheek Bolt round head
Throat Bolt
Cheek
Note: Sills were longer forward than can be shown here
Knee
Toe Bolt
5"x12"
Filler
Sill
Sill
Deck
Blocking
Blocking
Pawl Post
Blocking
Blocking
12"
View from aft
6"
Steps on keelson or deadwood
Sill
5"
Knee
Bitt
Blocking
Drawn from composite data, not from a single vessel. Built up knees common after about 1915, due to lack of large stock

WINDLASS, ORTHOGRAPHIC VIEW

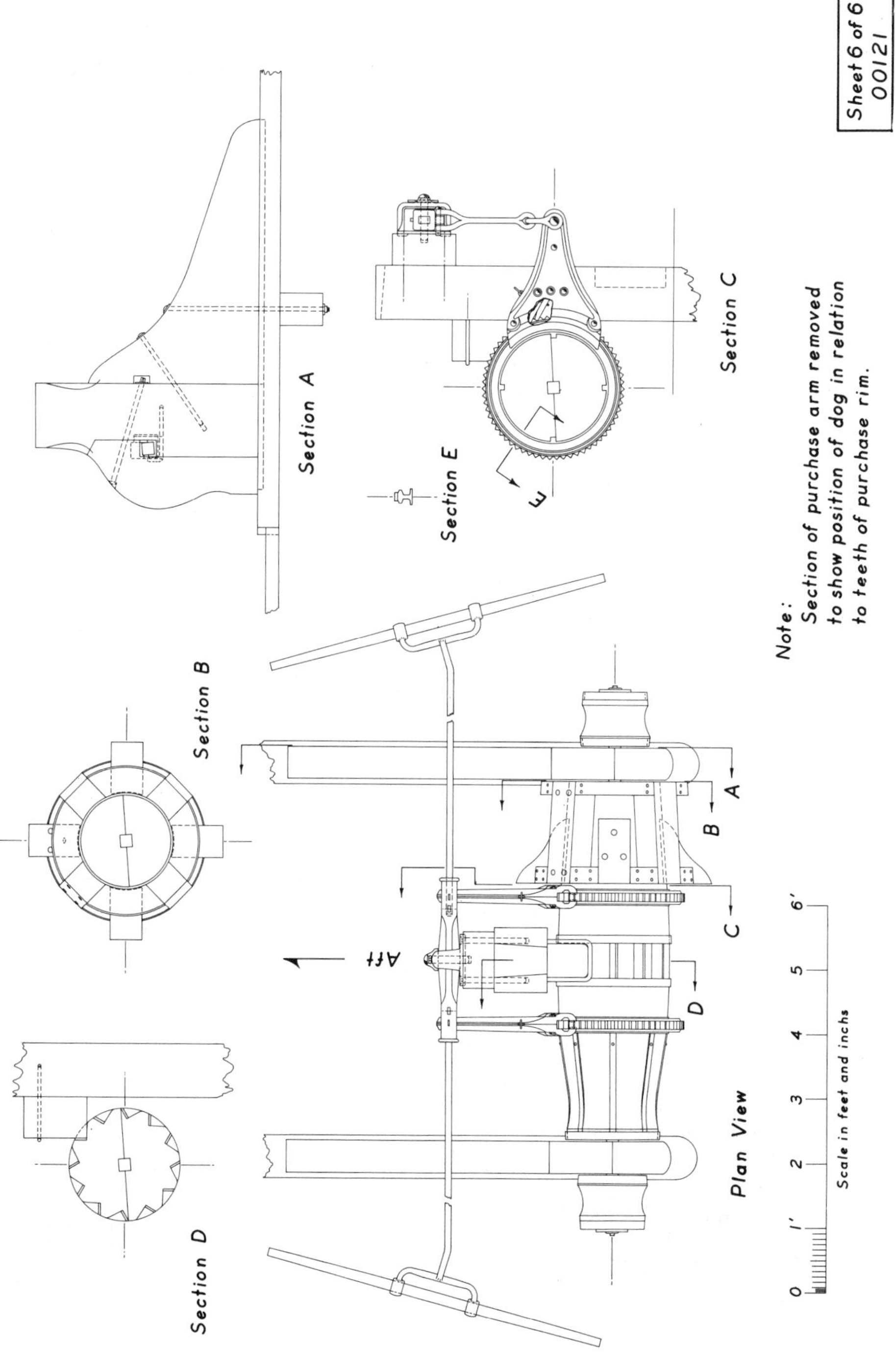

Sheet 6 of 6
00121
Section A
Section B
Section C
Section D
Section E
E
Plan View
Aft
A
B
C
D
Note:
Section of purchase arm removed
to show position of dog in relation
to teeth of purchase rim.
0
1'
2
3
4
5
6'
Scale in feet and inchs

WINDLASS, DETAIL

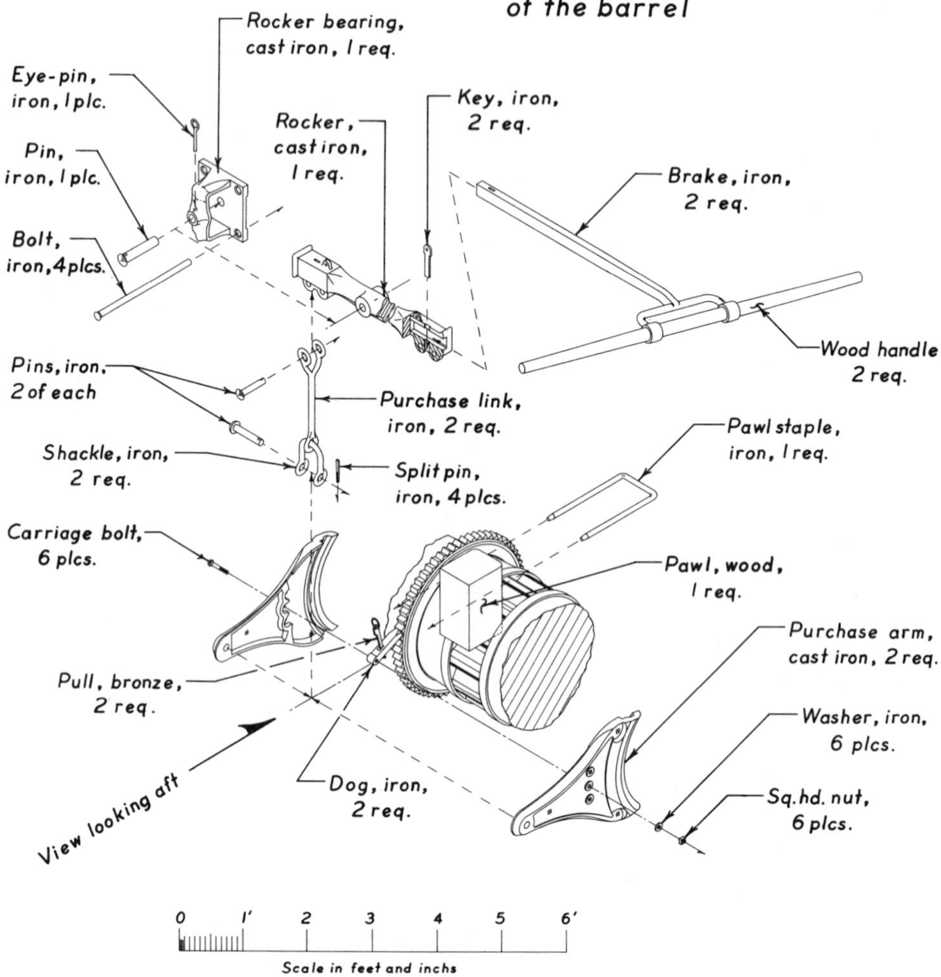
Detail parts of windlass assembly
used for rotating and braking
of the barrel
Rocker bearing,
cast iron, 1 req.
Eye-pin,
iron, 1 plc.
Pin,
iron, 1 plc.
Bolt,
iron, 4 plcs.
Rocker,
cast iron,
1 req.
Key, iron,
2 req.
Brake, iron,
2 req.
Wood handle,
2 req.
Pins, iron,
2 of each
Purchase link,
iron, 2 req.
Shackle, iron,
2 req.
Split pin,
iron, 4 plcs.
Pawl staple,
iron, 1 req.
Carriage bolt,
6 plcs.
Pawl, wood,
1 req.
Purchase arm,
cast iron, 2 req.
Pull, bronze,
2 req.
Washer, iron,
6 plcs.
Sq. hd. nut,
6 plcs.
Dog, iron,
2 req.
View looking aft
0 1' 2 3 4 5 6'
Scale in feet and inchs

Note:

1- Left hand purchase rim, link and two halves of left hand purchase arm shown, right side assemblied in the same manner.

2- Rocker is cut away in two areas to show shape of rocker and show slot into which brake is inserted.

Sheet 5 of 6
00121

WINDLASS, DETAIL

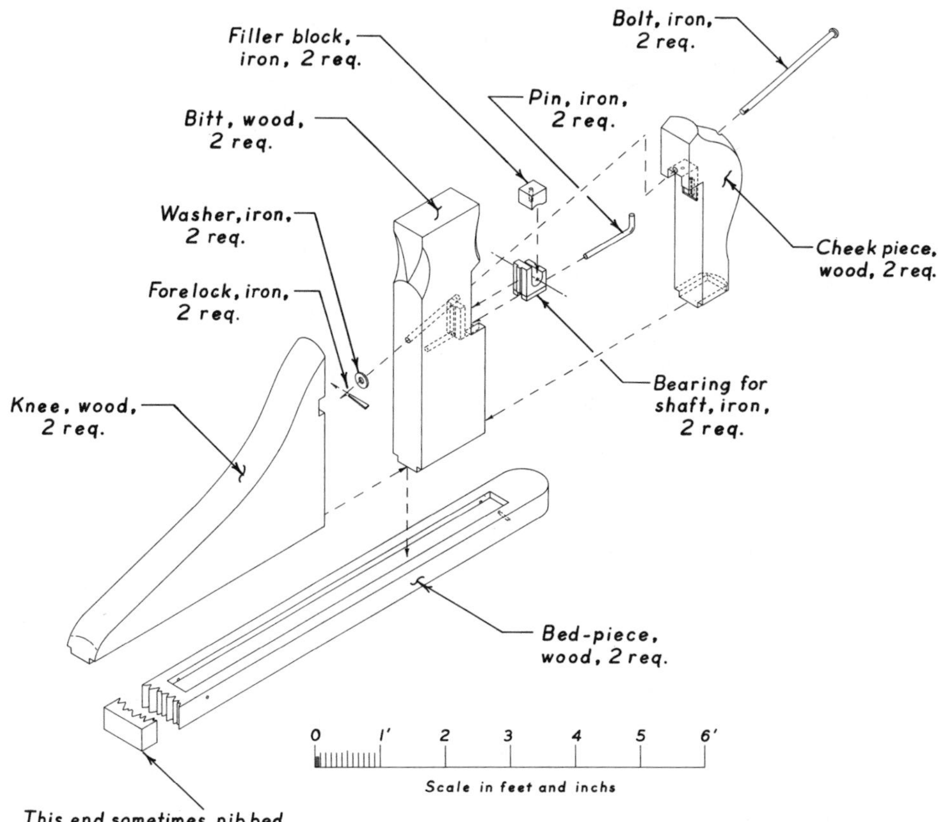
Structure which supports barrel assembly
Filler block, iron, 2 req.
Bolt, iron, 2 req.
Pin, iron, 2 req.
Bitt, wood, 2 req.
Washer, iron, 2 req.
Cheek piece, wood, 2 req.
Fore lock, iron, 2 req.
Knee, wood, 2 req.
Bearing for shaft, iron, 2 req.
Bed-piece, wood, 2 req.
0 1' 2 3 4 5 6'
Scale in feet and inchs
This end sometimes nib bed into waterways.
Sheet 4 of 6
00121

WINDLASS, DETAIL

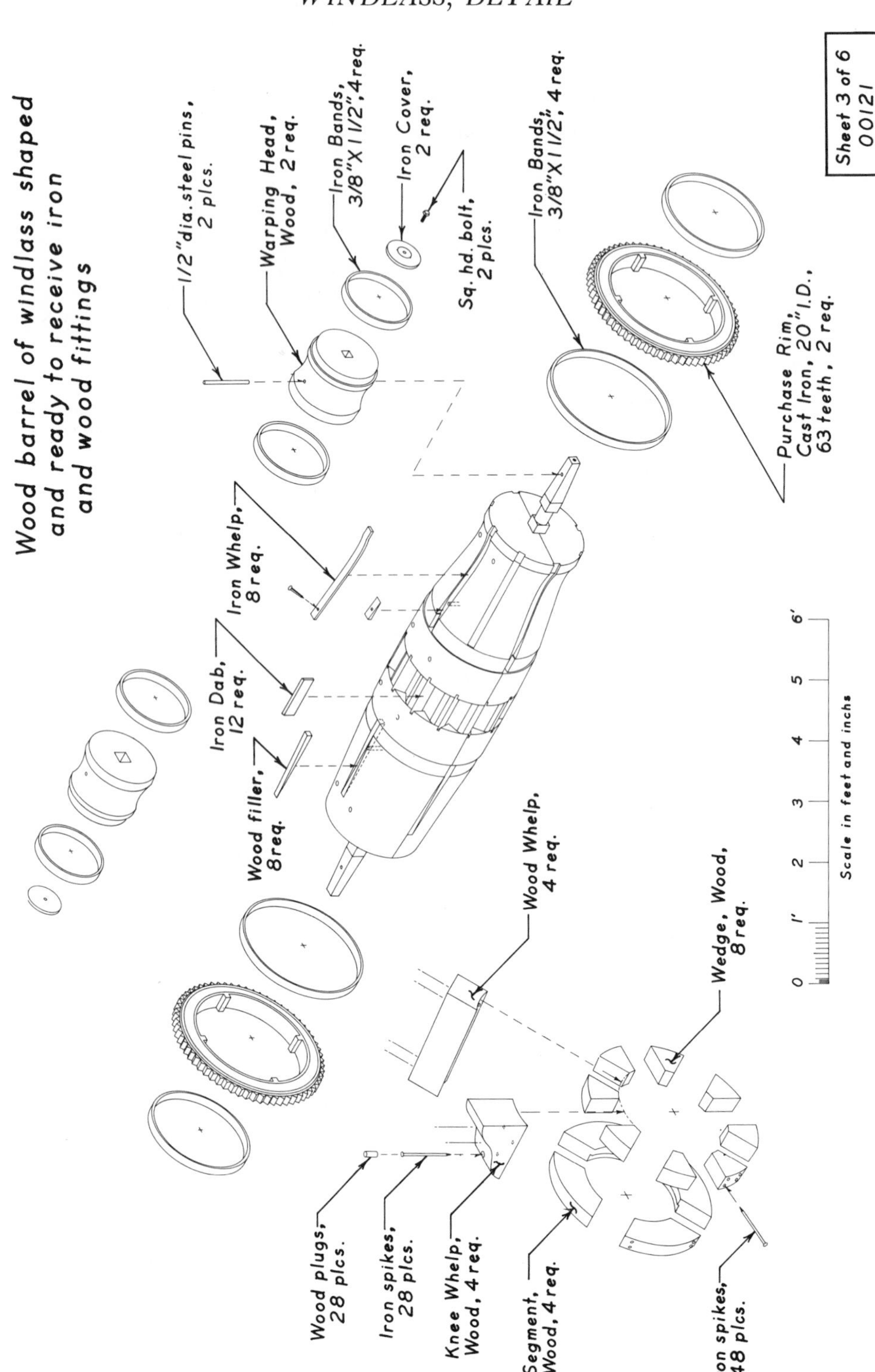
Wood barrel of windlass shaped and ready to receive iron and wood fittings
1/2"dia. steel pins, 2 plcs.
Warping Head, Wood, 2 req.
Iron Bands, 3/8"X 1 1/2", 4 req.
Iron Cover, 2 req.
Sq. hd. bolt, 2 plcs.
Iron Bands, 3/8"X 1 1/2", 4 req.
Sheet 3 of 6
00121
Purchase Rim, Cast Iron, 20" I.D., 63 teeth, 2 req.
Iron Whelp, 8 req.
Iron Dab, 12 req.
Wood filler, 8 req.
Wood Whelp, 4 req.
Wedge, Wood, 8 req.
0 1' 2 3 4 5 6'
Scale in feet and inchs
Wood plugs, 28 plcs.
Iron spikes, 28 plcs.
Knee Whelp, Wood, 4 req.
Segment, Wood, 4 req.
Iron spikes, 48 plcs.

WINDLASS, DETAIL

Detail parts of barrel, before assembly and turning operation

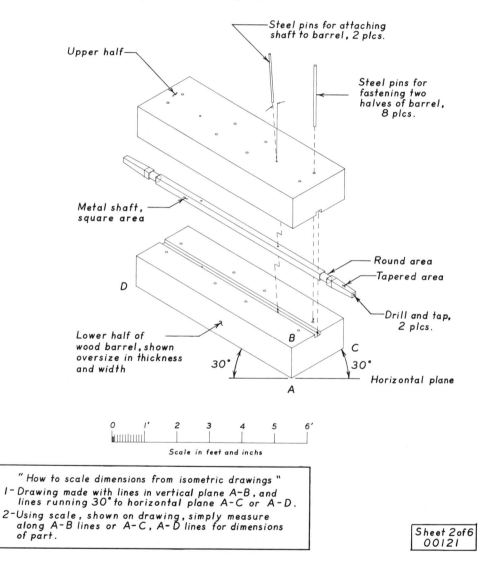

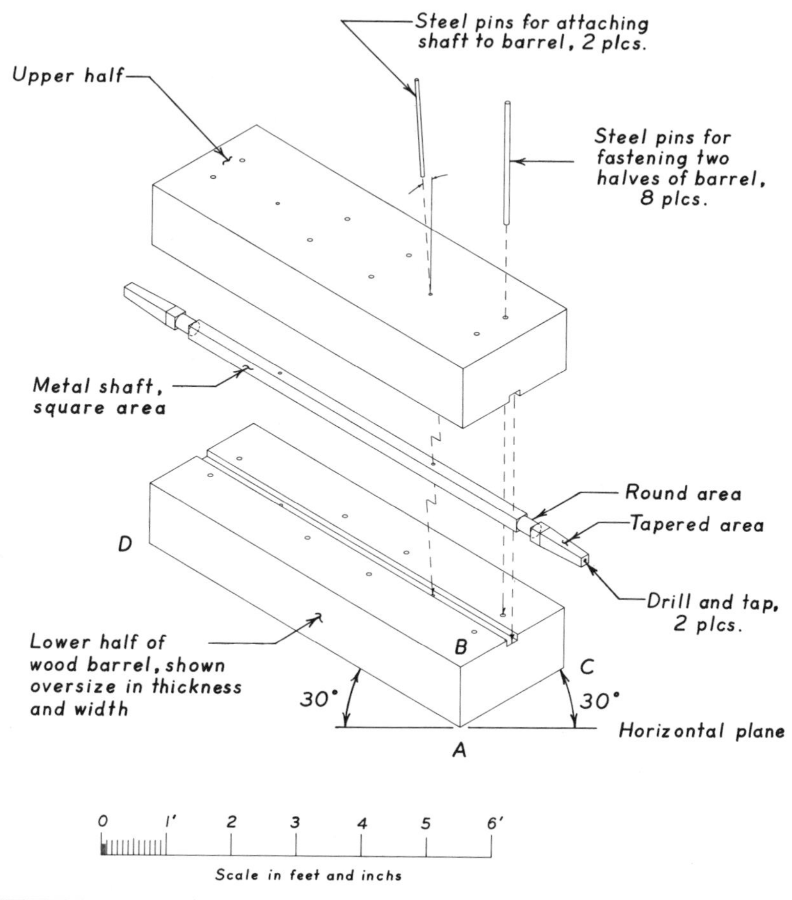
Steel pins for attaching shaft to barrel, 2 plcs.
Upper half
Steel pins for fastening two halves of barrel, 8 plcs.
Metal shaft, square area
Round area
Tapered area
D
Drill and tap, 2 plcs.
Lower half of wood barrel, shown oversize in thickness and width
B
C
30°
30°
Horizontal plane
A
0 1' 2 3 4 5 6'
Scale in feet and inchs

" How to scale dimensions from isometric drawings "

1- Drawing made with lines in vertical plane A-B, and lines running 30° to horizontal plane A-C or A-D.

2-Using scale, shown on drawing, simply measure along A-B lines or A-C, A-D lines for dimensions of part.

Sheet 2of6
00121

SPLIT BARREL WINDLASS

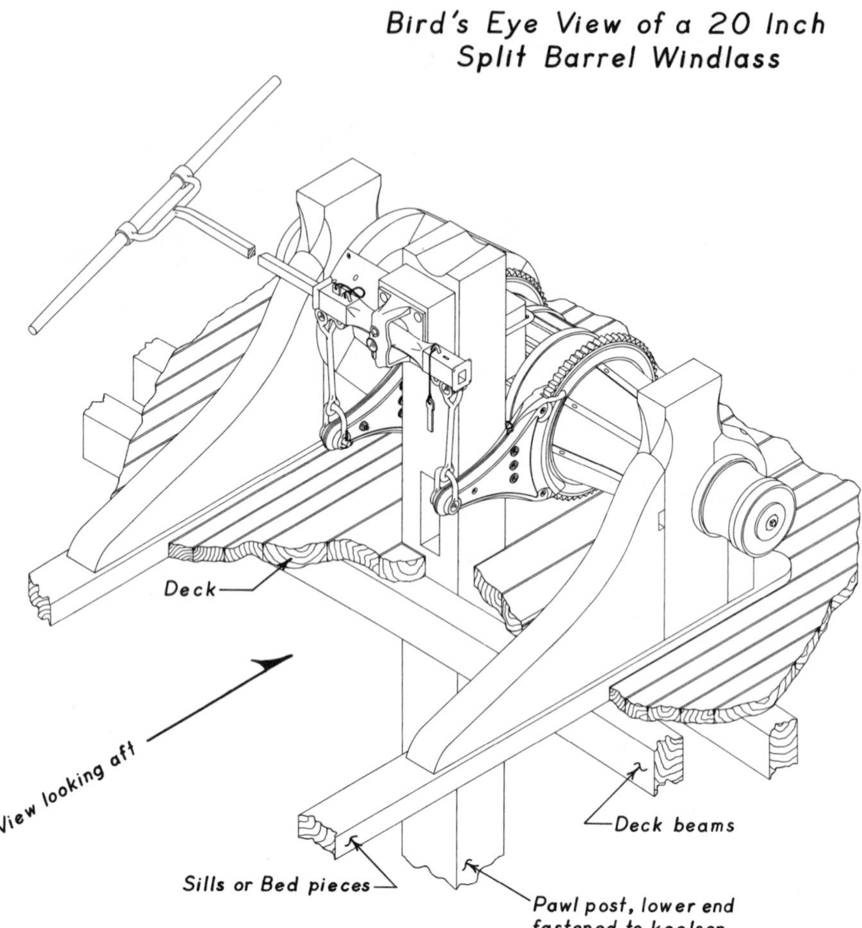
Bird's Eye View of a 20 Inch
Split Barrel Windlass
Deck
View looking aft
Deck beams
Sills or Bed pieces
Pawl post, lower end
fastened to keelson

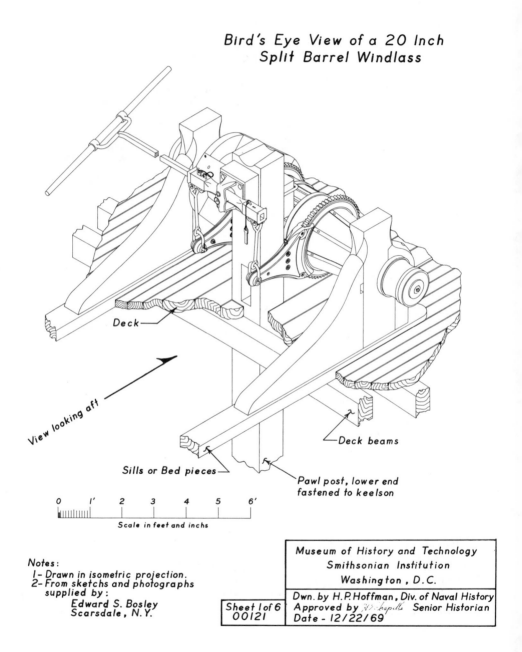

0 1' 2 3 4 5 6'

Scale in feet and inchs

Notes:
1- Drawn in isometric projection.
2- From sketchs and photographs supplied by:
Edward S. Bosley
Scarsdale, N.Y.

Museum of History and Technology
Smithsonian Institution
Washington, D.C.

Dwn. by H.P. Hoffman, Div. of Naval History
Approved by [illegible] Senior Historian
Date - 12/22/69

Sheet 1 of 6
00121

WINDLASSES
(SEE "SAMPSON, OR PAWL, POSTS")

The old log windlass was used on fishing schooners until the late 1840s. This style of windlass was operated by "handspikes" or heaving bars. The ends of these were placed in holes in the barrel, giving leverage to turn the drums; each heave with the handspike gave about a quarter turn to the drums. The longer the handspike, the greater the power, but in practice the length was limited by the need of shifting the handspike for each heave. In the older log windlasses, the barrel was 8-sided and had two sets of handspike holes around it, near the windlass bitts on each side. The barrel usually had an iron bar axle round in the wake of the windlass bitts. In order to give the men room to heave, this style of windlass was usually wide between the bitts, so was often placed abaft the foremasts in fishing schooners and in the Chebaccos. The log windlass was inexpensive and reliable, but very slow in working ground tackle. In the early 1800s the barrels were worked round; tapered toward the bitts, with warping heads outside the bitts. The pawl, preventing the barrel from turning back between heaves, was an oak clapper; its forward end hinged on the after face of the pawl post or, on Chebaccos, on the foremast. The clapper engaged teeth cut in the circumference of the barrel, at its midlength.

In the late 1840s, or thereabouts, new types of windlasses, having ratchet-acting purchases, were patented in England. These did not require the shipping and unshipping of the handspikes, or brakes, for each heave. This allowed rapid and continuous operation of brakes and barrel. Power was increased by the mechanical design of the ratchets in the purchases and by more effective locations of the brakes.

The obvious advantages of the pump-brake windlass led to its introduction into the United States, and by the early 1850s the wooden, or log, windlass, with pump-brake ironwork, was in use in New England fishing fleet. The ship carpenters made the barrel, pawl, windlass bitts, warping heads, cheeks and knees. Foundries in Gloucester and Newburyport furnished the rocker arm and its fittings, ring gears, bands, purchase castings, bearings and links. The retention of the wooden barrel, bitts, etc., was due to its low cost and only relatively small castings were required in the ironwork. This type of windlass remained almost unchanged for over 50 years.

The only patented addition made to the basic pump-brake windlass was the "Wonson patent windlass attachment," August 1890. This allowed the use of more brakes than the standard windlass permitted, and over 40 fishing schooners were fitted with the Wonson attachment. However, the introduction of powered hoisters, in 1915, made it obsolete.

The following dimensions were taken from windlasses of schooners, 85′ to 105′ tonnage length, or from other sources of a more general nature.

The barrels ranged in size, that is in maximum diameter, 20″, 18″, 16″, 14″, and 12″. Those under 18″ dia. were made of one large timber, turned to size, with the axle driven into the ends and pinned. The 18″ and 20″ barrel were made of two timbers, each grooved to take the square parts of the axle. The two timbers were treenailed together and turned. The barrels were made to fit the ironwork for the sizes listed above.

The axles were from 1¼″-3″ square depending on the dia. of the barrel, rounded in the wake of the bearings, 2½″-3″ wide, in the bitts in the 18″ and 20″ dia. barrels.

The tapers of the barrels were alike, port-and-starboard, in vessels built before about 1885, apparently, with deep whelps on the starboard side, usually. But in vessels built after this period the starboard side was larger in diameter with straight taper inside the whelps.

The maximum barrel diameter was at the hull ℄ extending 8″ to 12″ outboard on each side, to a width a little more than that of the pawl teeth. Sometimes the dia. at ℄ was 1″ to 1½″ greater over the pawl teeth than alongside. The teeth were 5″ to 7″ wide.

The profile of the barrel, as shaped after 1885, is shown in the accompanying drawings. Four large wooden whelps handled the big hemp (manila later) "Banks Cable."

Their outside diameter, just inside of the windlass bitts, was 24″ to 28″. At this place the diameter of the barrel was about 18″. The inboard diameter of the four wooden whelps increased the same as that of the barrel, that is, from 18″ to 20″. The intermediate knee-whelps increased to 36″ to keep the cable from over-running the purchase gearing. These diameters are for the 20″ diameter barrel windlass.

The port side of the barrel usually had eight iron strap (½″ x 1½″) whelps spiked to it. This part of the barrel was then fitted to handle chain. However, iron strap whelps were sometimes fitted on the starboard side and the chain worked from starboard, as in the racer "Mayflower." The minimum diameter of the 20″ barrel was about 16″, the outboard end diameter was 17″.

Outside of the windlass bitts were the warping heads projecting out 9″ to 12″ from the bitts, the head 13″ diameter inboard end, 11½″ at middle, and 12″ at outboard end.

The barrel was supported by bearings in the windlass bitts, P.&S. These consisted of a vertical timber 4″ to 6″ thick, 10″ to 14″ wide, standing 40″ to 44″ above the sills. On the foreside of the bitt was a large knee, 3′ to 4′ long on the sills, with its upright arm extending upward to within 8″ to 10″ short of the top of the bitt. On the after face of the bitt was the cheek piece with its heel tenoned into the sill. Knee and cheek were of the same thickness as the bitt.

The sills were thick deck plank, usually about 4″ thick and 8″ to 10″ wide, running from a few inches abaft the heel of the cheek to a few inches forward of the fore-end of the knee, or tapered down to deck thickness and then nibbed into the covering board or plank-sheer. The heels of cheek and bitt, and of the deck arm of the knee were tenoned into the sills, into which small scupper, or "weep holes," were bored sloping downward from the bottom of the tenon to top of deck.

The ℄ of the barrel was commonly 21″ above the sills; the range was 20″-23″ in the vessels measured, all having 18″-20″ windlasses. The length of the barrel, inside of the windlass bitts, was 4′-6″ to 5′-6″, depending upon its position abaft the stem.

Forward of the barrel of the windlass, on the hull ℄, was the pawl bitt. This was usually a heavy timber, 10″ x 14″, or 12″ x 15″, stepped on the keelson and well-blocked where it came above the deck beam. It stood a foot or a little more above the height of the windlass bitts. In many vessels, the head was cut to form a pair of timber-heads and the pawl bitt served as a boom crotch for the jumbo boom and as a bowsprit heel bitt. In knockabouts the pawl bitt was the after support of the forestay gallows, the rocker arm was on its forward face.

The pawl post cleared the forward side of the windlass barrel within 1½″-2″. On the afterside of the pawl post was a rectangular block, held loosely within an iron staple, riding on the pawl teeth cut into the barrel. The heel of the block engaged the pawl teeth, preventing the barrel from reversing. The block was of oak, 12″ to 15″ long and 5″ x 5″ to 6″ x 6″ square. The staple holding it was ½″-¾″ diameter iron.

The foreside of the pawl post was occupied by the rocker arm and its pivot casting. Brakes, set into the ends of the rocker arms, transmitted power and linkage from rocker activated the purchases which in turn revolved the barrel. In the drawing the rocker arm and pivot casting are mounted on a block fastened to the foreside of the pawl post. The use of this mounting indicates an oversize purchase had been used, or a small post. In knockabouts a heavy plank connected the pawl post with another post forward, to which the forestay was secured, the heavy plank supported the tack fittings abaft the forestay. The two posts and connecting plank formed the knockabouts "gallows."

The pump-brake shafts were inserted in holes in the ends of the rocker arms. The shaft of the brake was bent, as shown in sketch and windlass drawings, to bring the cross-handle parallel to the inside of the rail cap, or nearly so. Its length was determined by the space between handle and rail being sufficient to allow two men to work the brake. This was a little over 26″.

The edges of the timbers making up the windlass bitts were rounded off. Due to the massive strains they received, these windlasses were securely bolted to the deck framing, using through-bolts. These passed through deck beams at throat and toe of the windlass bitt knees, with one below the throat bolt through the intermediate beam. Other bolts in the deck arm of the knee set up under the deck blocking. The sills were bolted to the beams and blocking independent of the knees, bitts, and cheeks. The knees were bolted in the upright arm to the bitts with at least two bolts, one through knee and bitt, set up under the cheek.

The cheek was secured so that it could be unshipped to repair or maintain the bearings. Before about 1885 the cheeks not only stepped with a tenon into the sills, but a U-shaped strap was placed around the heel with its arms reaching forward to allow one of its bolts to pass through the knee a few inches above the sills. Two bolts in these straps went through the bitts and one through the cheek. A head bolt or cheek bolt went through the top of the cheeks and bitts, in a slightly over-bored hole, to set up in a recess in the head of the knees with a clench ring and wedge or split pin. One or two bolts were driven "blind," under the cheeks from the aftersides of the bitts into the knees.

After about 1885 the heel straps of the cheeks were discarded apparently, for they do not appear in any photographs yet seen. It is probable that these straps were employed for only a short time, probably in the 1870s in bankers.

WINDLASS BRAKE OR "HEAVER"

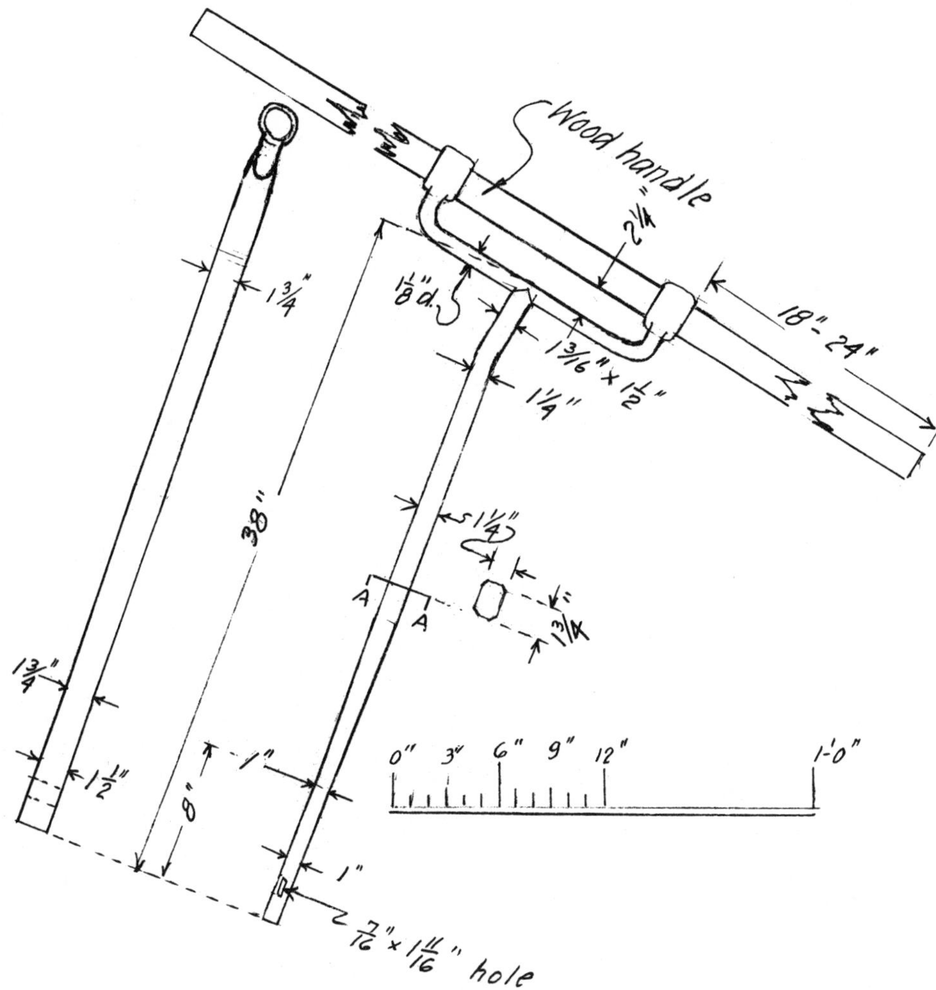
Wood handle
2¼"
18"-24"
1⅛" d.
1¾"
1 3/16" x 1½"
1¼"
38"
A
A
1¾"
1½"
8"
1"
1"
7/16" x 1 11/16" hole
0" 3" 6" 9" 12" 1'-0"

for 18"-20" dia. barrel

After two measured by
Ed. Bosley.

WINDLASS PUMP, BRAKE HANDLE

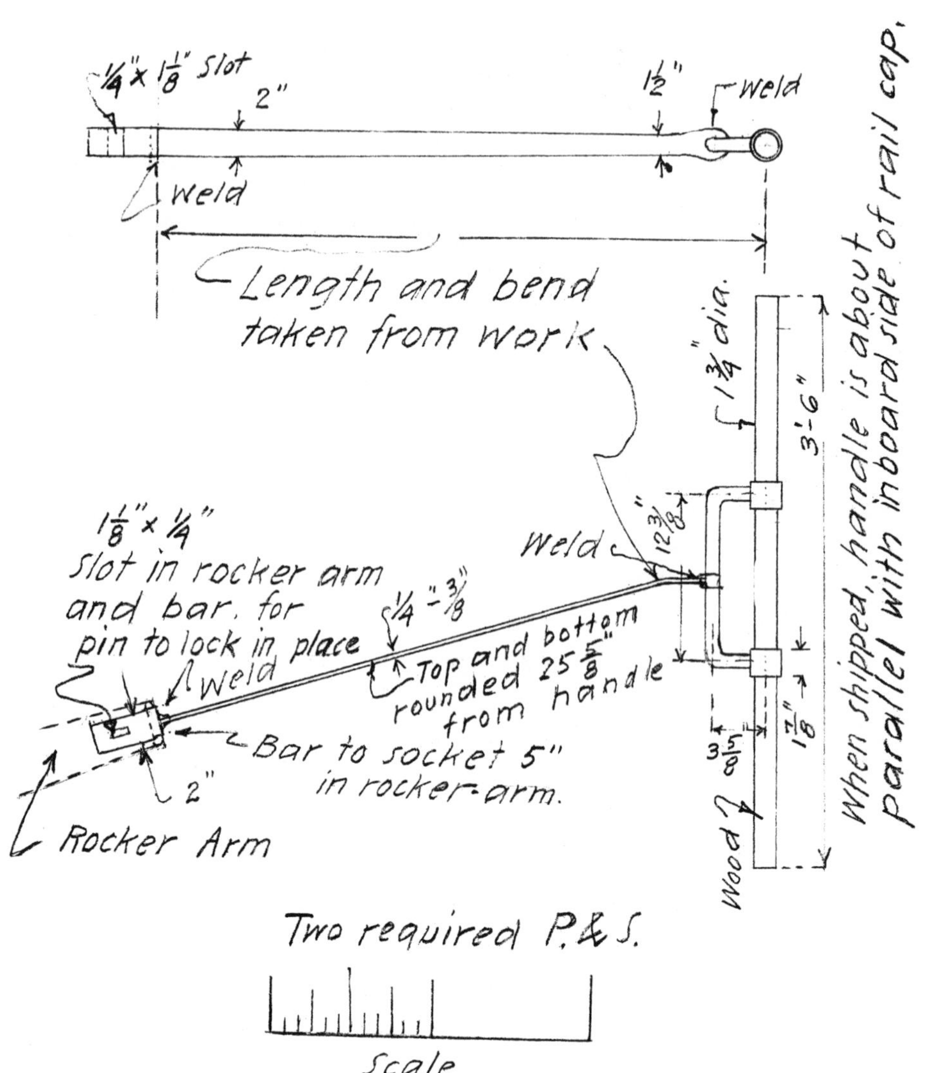
1/4" x 1 1/8" Slot
2"
1 1/2"
Weld
Weld
Length and bend taken from work
1 3/4" dia.
3'-6"
When shipped, handle is about parallel with inboard side of rail cap.
1 1/8" x 1/4" Slot in rocker arm and bar, for pin to lock in place
Weld
12 3/8"
1/4" - 3/8"
Top and bottom rounded 25 5/8" from handle
Weld
Bar to socket 5" in rocker-arm.
2"
3 5/8"
1 7/8"
Wood
Rocker Arm
Two required P. & S.
Scale.

WONSON'S PATENT WINDLASS ATTACHMENT
(PATENTED AUG. 26, 1890)

WONSON'S

Patent

Windlass

Attachment.

(PATENTED AUG. 26, 1890.)

TO BE USED ON ANY VESSEL CARRYING A HAND WINDLASS.

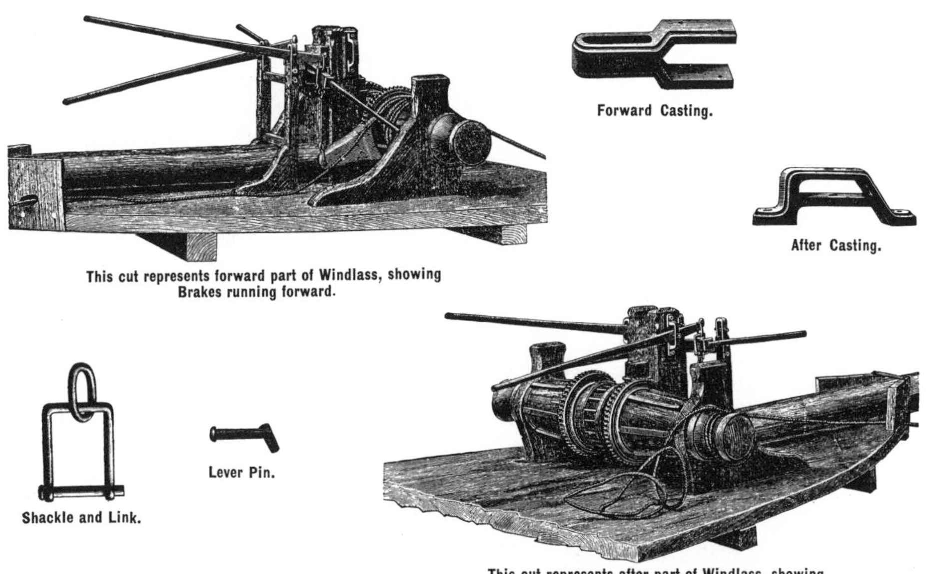

Forward Casting.

After Casting.

This cut represents forward part of Windlass, showing Brakes running forward.

Shackle and Link.

Lever Pin.

This cut represents after part of Windlass, showing Brakes running aft.

Brake or Lever.

Brakes are attached so as to be worked forward or aft of Windlass, or both, and do not interfere with the athwart-ship brakes.

This attachment more than doubles the power of the Windlass. It is very simple and easily applied.

Over one hundred vessels are already using this Windlass. Here are some of the names among the Fishing Fleet:

Nannie C. Bohlin
Lizzie Griffin
Gladiator
Parthia
Hazel Oneita
Thetis
Neried
Columbia
Orpheus
Mildred V. Lee
Henry L. Stanley
Talisman
Glorianna
Maggie E. McKenzie
Alice R. Lawson
Alton S. Marshall
Hustler
Oliver W. Holmes
Golden Hope
Commonwealth
Sea Fox
Eben Parsons
Lizzie Jones
Lucille
Lizzie M. Stanwood
Mayflower
Masconomo
Mary G. Powers
Gov. Russell
Marshall L. Adams
Maggie and May
Louisa J. Kenney
Joseph Rowe
Edith McInnis
Florence E. Stream
Hiram Lowell
E. A. Swift
Iceland
Madonna
Braganza

Index